THE RODALE WHOLE FOODS COOKBOOK

With More Than 1,000 Recipes for Choosing, Cooking & Preserving Natural Ingredients

Rodale books may be purchased for business or promotional use or for special sales. For information, please write to:
Special Markets Department, Rodale Inc., 733 Third Avenue, New York, NY 10017

Printed in the United States of America
Rodale Inc. makes every effort to use acid-free ♾, recycled paper ♲.

Recipe photos on front cover (*clockwise, left to right*): Eight-Grain Sprouted Wheat Bread (*page 557*); Israeli Couscous with Lime & Mint (*page 458*); and Roasted Root Vegetables with Thyme (*page 440*)

Recipe photos on back cover (*clockwise, left to right*): Broiled Shrimp, Ceviche-Style (*page 165*); Potato & Greens Frittata (*page 338*); and Pappardelle with Asparagus and Oyster Mushrooms (*page 361*)

Color photos by Kate Mathis
Interior design by Christopher Rhoads

Library of Congress Cataloging-in-Publication Data
The Rodale whole foods cookbook : with more than 1,000 recipes for choosing, cooking & preserving natural ingredients.
p. cm.
Includes index.
ISBN-13 978-1-60529-543-5 hardcover
ISBN-10 1-60529-543-4 hardcover
1. Cookery (Natural foods) I. Rodale (Firm) II. Title: Whole foods cookbook.
TX741.R624 2009
641.5'636—dc22 2009038552

Distributed to the trade by Macmillan
2 4 6 8 10 9 7 5 3 1 hardcover

We inspire and enable people to improve their lives and the world around them
For more of our products visit **rodalestore.com** or call 800-848-4735

Contents

Part 3: In the Kitchen

Introduction

The past three decades have been a period of remarkable change on nearly every front, but perhaps nowhere are these changes more evident than in the aisles of your local grocery store. Where condensed soups, frozen TV dinners, and boxed cake mixes once represented the height of culinary sophistication and convenience (What party was considered complete without onion dip made from dehydrated soup powder and full-fat sour cream?), you now find an inspiring array of organic vegetables and fruits; hormone-free poultry and meats; natural sweeteners; wholesome whole grains and flours; and much more. Our understanding of the role that nutrition and food play in preventing disease—and helping to keep our planet healthy—has grown by leaps and bounds, too.

Yet all this bounty and variety has given rise to confusion. Should white flour—and white rice and white sugar and just about any white food, period—be banished from our tables? What exactly is agave and can it be used in baked goods? And what, in heaven's name, does one do with millet?

This book is designed to answer all these questions and many, many more. It is a compendium of information and recipes created for people who want to prepare dishes that are not only delicious but also free from both artificial ingredients and products that have been more than minimally processed.

Our interest in natural foods stems from a basic Rodale tradition: Natural is better. There is no mystery in that. It is an incontrovertible truth that Nature knows more about the best composition of food and how it should taste than any manufacturer does.

A good cook chooses food in its freshest, least-tampered-with state—fresh fruits that are not sweetened, colored, or canned; a freshly caught fish, herbed and broiled, not ground up and pressed into flavorless, breaded fingers; a home-baked, whole-grain, firm-textured bread, not a bleached white, cotton experience. Of course, the natural product is miles ahead nutritionally, plus its marvelous flavor simply leaves any processed, packaged, and additive-laden counterpart in the dust.

Cooking with whole foods also enables the cook to know precisely what she and her family are eating. While processed foods are invariably packed with sodium, sugar in its many forms (including high-fructose corn syrup), and other chemical additives intended to prolong shelf life, natural whole foods, especially organic foods, are free of chemicals and full of wholesome nutrients.

While we all know that we should be including more of these healthful whole and natural foods in our diets, though, many of the books available on the topic fail to address the daily needs of a busy, contemporary family. These days it's commonplace for a vegan and an unrepentant carnivore to coexist under the same roof, or for a family of bread lovers to count a gluten-intolerant member among their number. And who has time to consult one book for inspiration on cooking whole grains, another on making good use of fresh produce, and yet another on preparing tofu and other soyfoods? Our intention was to create a basic, comprehensive book that would offer recipes for the broadest possible range of occasions with the broadest possible range of ingredients—a go-to resource whether you're making a batch of chili for the game, healthy treats to stuff in a lunch box, or a show-stopping dessert for a celebration dinner or bake sale—all in a healthier, more wholesome vein.

And if you are still consulting that battle-worn cookbook packed with traditional standbys presented to you by your mother (or perhaps even handed down from a grandparent) for the essential kitchen information it offers, you can finally relegate that spattered tome to the give-away pile. We've included all the handy guidelines and reference lists you need, from equivalents and substitutions to a foolproof guide to roasting meats.

Of course, helping people eat well has always been at the core of Rodale's mission. Our very first magazine, *Organic Gardening,* was devoted to helping home gardeners create bounteous, productive gardens without the use of chemical fertilizers or pesticides, and one of our most important culinary laboratories (and sounding boards) is the commissary at our own offices.

This is the kind of background and experience that lies at the core of this book. It is the key to our confidence in presenting the definitive natural foods cookbook.

Open this book to any section and you will also find the kind of extensive general reference material and instruction you require from any of the best all-purpose cookbooks. It tells you everything from how to carve a turkey and how big a roast it takes to serve eight, to how to rescue a curdled hollandaise sauce or make homemade bouillon cubes. Dozens of tables provide quick access to food basics and directions to help you master even the most complicated cooking skills—some with step-by-step illustrations! Cooks stumped for new ideas will delight in page after page of marvelous recipes for quick-to-make family meals, dinner parties, no-meat meals, brunches, and low-cost meals.

However, we believe the special value of this book is in the extraordinary information and cooking ideas it contains. Part 2: At the Market covers the gamut of certified organic whole foods from your produce to your proteins. Part 3: In the Kitchen shows you the exciting creations you'll be able to make with all the wonderful foods you'll be discovering.

The Breads chapter focuses on the baking properties and nutritional values of whole grains. It includes a list of suggested whole-grain combinations intended to increase the nutrient value of your loaves and to introduce your family to new flavors and textures in all sorts of breads.

Nuts and seeds contain superior food value, but more than that, they offer a largely unexplored versatility. Aside from the usual, our book shows cooks how to use nuts and seeds in interesting new ways as butters, meals, and milks.

Sprouts, whose value is universally recognized by knowledgeable cooks and nutritionists, rarely get serious attention anywhere these days. We believe, however, that they merit every cook's careful consideration so we devote a full section to sprouting and recipes that feature sprouts.

Sea vegetables, basic to the diets of many sophisticated cultures throughout the world, are a mystery to most Americans. However, the variety and taste appeal of these low-cost, mineral-rich foods are so impressive that we want to be sure you'll try them. You will learn the characteristics of various types, how to shop for them, and how to use them in cooking.

Desserts are the biggest challenge for the health-conscious cook. We present practical alternatives to such items as sugar and white flour, and we offer recipes that use nutritious whole-grain flours, natural sweeteners, nuts, yogurt, and fruits as ingredients in irresistible sweets.

Our Beverages section stresses wholesome fruit and vegetable juices as bases for delicious and refreshing drinks. It also presents the opportunity for you to augment your usual coffee and tea drinks to a wide selection of herb drinks that can soothe you or energize you, depending on your mood.

What's New?

The concept of whole, natural foods is hardly new, and those who were eating and cooking in the 1970s, when the first edition of this book was compiled, may encounter some nostalgic favorites in these pages. But tastes and fashions in food are constantly evolving, changing. As a nation we have developed more sophisticated palates and know much more about nutrition, ingredients, and ethnic cuisine—and want to learn more still. For that reason, nearly half of the recipes that comprised the first edition, published in 1972, have been replaced by entirely new dishes to reflect our growing appetites for ethnic foods, and the greater spectrum of produce and other foods available to us today.

The recipes here also reflect a return to simplicity of presentation and a straightforward approach to flavor. Gone are many of the elaborate molded salads and aspics that represented the height of sophistication three decades ago as well as fussy dishes involving numerous components—often served stuffed into yet another element. Classical French preparations (often with the traditional generous quantities of cheese, butter, and cream) have given way to lighter Italian and Mediterranean fare.

Also new to these pages are many ingredients considered esoteric or exotic until recently, among them grains like kamut, spelt, and quinoa; produce including Chioggia beets, Russian kale, and jicama; and essential flavorings and condiments like smoked paprika, balsamic vinegar, and chipotle peppers.

What remains unchanged is our commitment to bringing a balanced and forward-looking group of recipes that will please every member of the family while providing them with the widest possible variety of nutrients and flavors. The more than 1,000 recipes in this book prove that natural ingredients can be used to create every kind of dish from homey Roasted Heirloom Carrots to luscious Maple Semifreddo or Peanut Butter Cup Mousse. With this book you can please plain eaters with simple Corn Muffins or Apple Pie, or you can impress sophisticated diners with Miso-Egg Drop Soup or Apricot Soufflé.

These few examples can only hint at the fresh attitudes toward food and food preparation that have inspired this book. The resources of the Rodale Test Kitchen are devoted to the proposition that the purest, most nutritious food is also the best tasting. We believe that the information and the recipes in this book will convince any cook that this is true.

With pride and confidence, we invite you to use and enjoy it, always in good health.

PART 1

Before You Start

Eating for Your Health

Ask any nutritionist how to get all the important nutrients you need to stay healthy, and you will be told to eat a variety of foods. If you do not exclude any category and do not focus too heavily on any category, you will be fine.

That said, the typical American diet has lost its bearings over the years. Because of the fast pace of living that we all seem caught up in, getting variety in our diets has become a challenge. Fast food, takeout food, and convenience food have thrown our dietary balance out of whack.

Here's how to get the balance back:

- Choose whole foods over refined or processed foods whenever possible.
- Eat more whole grains. This is one of the biggest shortfalls in the American diet.
- Eat more vegetables, and eat a rainbow of colors, especially the more deeply colored vegetables. They are the highest in antioxidants and other phytochemicals. See "A Short Guide to Phytochemicals" (page 5).
- Choose good carbs over bad carbs. This means choosing complex carbohydrates—such as beans, grains, or potatoes—over simple carbohydrates, which are bascially sugars.
- Consume more fiber-rich foods, especially those high in heart-healthy soluble fiber, such as oats, apples, and beans.
- Choose good fats over bad fats. This means choosing unsaturated fats, especially monounsaturated, over saturated fats. See "Comparative Fats" (page 111).
- Try to get protein at every meal. It keeps your metabolism in good working order. The protein can be from animal or plant sources.
- Choose lean animal sources of protein, with the exception of fish because the fattier species are high in healthful omega-3 fatty acids. See "Omega-3s in Fish" (page 41) and "The Cholesterol in Shellfish" (page 47).

Eating Organic

In 1990, Congress passed the Organic Foods Production Act. The act required the United States Department of Agriculture (USDA) to develop national standards for organically produced agricultural products. The USDA's Agricultural Marketing Service established something called the National Organic Program (NOP) whose task was to develop the standards and to establish an organic certification program. The NOP came up with a definition for organic (below) and then came up with the requirements for food labels.

The official definition: To be deemed organic, an agricultural product must be grown without the use of most conventional pesticides, petroleum-based fertilizers, or sewage sludge–based fertilizers. In the case of animals, their feed must comply with the above; in addition the animals must be raised with no growth hormones or antibiotics. The regulations also prohibit genetic engineering, ionizing radiation, and sewage sludge in production and handling. There are also specific regulations about the use of synthetic substances.

The NOP has defined three label categories that can use the term organic. Only the first two are allowed to bear the official USDA Organic seal.

100 percent organic: a single ingredient, such as raw fruits and vegetables, produced according to organic regulations; or products with multiple ingredients, each of which must have been organically produced. If any processing aids are used, those too must conform to the definition of organic. Is allowed to bear the USDA Organic seal.

Organic: must contain by weight (excluding water and salt) at least 95 percent organically produced raw or processed agricultural product. Up to 5 percent of the ingredients may include nonorganic ingredients in minor amounts—such as spices, flavors, colorings, oils, vitamins, and minerals. Can bear the USDA Organic seal.

Made with organic ingredients: for labeling and market information purposes, agricultural products that are multi-ingredient products containing between 70 and 95 percent organic agricultural ingredients by weight or fluid volume (excluding water and salt). May *not* bear the organic seal.

For products with less than 70 percent organic ingredients (by weight or fluid volume, excluding water and salt), organic labeling is limited to the information panel only.

Read the Label

The main thrust of this book is to avoid as much processed food as possible, but the reality for most of us is that this can't happen 100 percent of the time. So the next best thing is to be label-savvy and understand what information you can glean from a product's packaging.

Serving size: Before you read the nutrition numbers on the label, be sure you check the serving size. Some packaging is misleading (although the government is cracking down on this).

Total fat: By law, a food product has to have more than 0.5 gram of fat per serving before the manufacturer has to list it. So if a product says there are a total of 4 servings in the package and each serving has 0 grams of fat, it's conceivable that a serving has .44 grams. If you ate all 4 servings, you'd be getting almost 2 grams of fat. This is one reason some manufacturers alter serving sizes.

Saturated fat: Check the saturated fat; ideally it should be no more than 33 percent of the total fat.

Trans fats: These should be nonexistent or as low as possible.

Vitamins and minerals: Food manufacturers are only required to list vitamin A, vitamin C, calcium, and iron percentages on the label's nutrition panel. The absence of other nutrients listed has nothing to do with whether or not they are in the product, though many manufacturers will add that information if their product is particularly high. Also note that the percentages are based on the Daily Value, which is an average of recommended intakes with no respect to gender or age. For example, the Daily Value for calcium is 900 milligrams. If you are a woman over the age of 51, your recommended intake is much higher than that—1,200 milligrams.

Ingredients list: The ingredients are listed in descending order of weight.

Allergen alerts: Any product that contains gluten, soy, peanuts, tree nuts, eggs, dairy, crustaceans, or sulfites must clearly state the fact; in addition, there must also be an alert if the product was produced in a facility with any of these allergens present.

A SHORT GUIDE TO PHYTOCHEMICALS

In the past 10 or 15 years, there has been a sea of change in the world of nutrition in the form of phytochemical research. Phytochemicals are compounds, found in plants, that are being studied for a whole host of health benefits, from cancer prevention to improved brain function. There is still much research to be done in order to determine exactly how these compounds can help us, as well as how much of a substance you would have to consume to get a health benefit. This field of study is in its infancy and changes often. This table highlights a tiny fraction of what is being researched (there are thousands and thousands of phytochemicals).

PHYTOCHEMICAL	WHAT IT IS/WHAT IT MAY DO	SOME GOOD SOURCES
ALLYL SULFIDES	Compounds being studied for anticancer potential	Garlic, onion family
ALPHA-LINOLENIC ACID (ALA)	An essential fatty acid (EFA) that the body converts to omega-3 fatty acids, which are being studied for their ability to suppress inflammatory compounds and improve cardiovascular health	Canola oil, flaxseed, walnuts, hemp seed, chia seed
ANTHOCYANINS	Red and blue pigments found in certain fruits and vegetables; being studied for anticancer potential	Berries, plums, pomegranates, red cabbage
ANTIOXIDANTS	A broad category of compounds that fight free radicals, which are cell-damaging rogue oxygen molecules	Lots of foods fall into this category. Some prominent examples include tea and fruits. (See "Antioxidants in Food," page 7.)
PHYTOCHEMICAL	WHAT IT IS/WHAT IT MAY DO	SOME GOOD SOURCES
BETA-CAROTENE	An orange food pigment, converted by the body into vitamin A; a powerful antioxidant	Carrots, sweet potatoes, dark leafy greens, winter squash
BETA-GLUCAN	A type of dietary soluble fiber that can lower blood cholesterol	Oatmeal, barley, shiitake mushrooms

A SHORT GUIDE TO PHYTOCHEMICALS—*CONTINUED*

PHYTOCHEMICAL	WHAT IT IS/WHAT IT MAY DO	SOME GOOD SOURCES
CAPSAICIN	The substance that gives chili peppers heat; an antioxidant that may also have antibacterial properties	All chili peppers; more in the hottest varieties (see "The Heat in Chilies," page 123).
EPIGALLOCATECHIN GALLATE (EGCG)	A flavonoid with powerful antioxidant attributes, found in tea	Green tea, white tea
FLAVONOIDS	A class of phytochemicals that are powerful antioxidants	Tea, fruits, wine
FRUCTOOLIGO-SACCHARIDES (FOS)	Indigestible carbohydrate compounds that encourage the growth of friendly bacteria in the intestinal tract; often referred to as prebiotics	Bananas, onion family
INDOLES	A class of phytochemicals being investigated for anticancer properties	Broccoli, Brussels sprouts, cabbage, turnips
ISOFLAVONES	A major class of phytoestrogens (see below)	Soybeans, soyfoods
ISOTHIOCYANATES	Phytochemicals large responsible for the pungent taste of cruciferous vegetables (cabbage family); being studied for anticancer properties	Broccoli, cabbage, mustard greens, watercress
LIGNANS	A type of phytoestrogen (see below)	Flax meal, beans, grains
LUTEIN AND ZEAXANTHIN	Bright yellow and orange food pigments linked to eye health	Corn, oranges, spinach, collard greens
LYCOPENE	A red food pigment with antioxidant power	Tomatoes, watermelon, red grapefruit
PHYTOESTROGENS	Plant compounds that mimic human estrogenic activity; being studied for its impact on estrogen-related cancers	Beans, flaxseed, soyfoods
PHYTOSTEROLS	Structurally similar to cholesterol; may protect against heart disease	Grains, nuts, seeds
PROBIOTICS	A group of beneficial bacteria that keep the human digestive system in good working order	Yogurt with active cultures
QUERCETIN	A potent flavonoid phytochemical with possible anti-inflammatory and anti-histaminic properties	Apples, red onions, tea, wine
RESVERATROL	A compound being investigated for its potential to improve cardiovascular health	Red and purple grape juice, red wine

Antioxidants in Food

Over a decade ago, a group of scientists developed a method of measuring the antioxidant activity of foods. Antioxidants are compounds that are known to eliminate free radicals, which are unstable oxygen molecules implicated in a wide range of health issues, from tumor formation to wrinkling of the skin. The method measures what the researchers call Oxygen Radical Absorbance Capacity (ORAC).

What follows is a list of 30 foods that scored well on the ORAC scale. It starts with the highest score and goes down. It includes the commonest foods and does not include foods you couldn't eat enough of to get any health benefit. For example, ground cloves and cinnamon are right at the top of the ORAC scale, but one doesn't consume enough of these spices for them to be a significant dietary source.

Açai berry

Cocoa powder, unsweetened

Baking chocolate, unsweetened

Pecans

Walnuts

Hazelnuts

Cranberries

Beans: kidney, pink, black

Pistachios

Black currants

Black plums

Lentils

Artichokes

Blueberries

Prunes

Soybeans

Blackberries

Garlic

Wine

Raspberries

Basil, fresh

Almonds

Red apples, with skin

Strawberries

Figs

Cherries

Peanuts

Broccoli rabe

Pears

Pomegranate juice

Kitchen Equipment

The tools for cooking and baking need not be elaborate. When possible, choose multi-purpose kitchen tools to save on space and money. This applies to electric appliances as well, which often represent a considerable investment.

Cookware and bakeware can be made of earthenware, glass, metal, or silicone. Each material has its own characteristics and particular responses to different kinds of heat used in the kitchen. See the guide below to help you make choices.

A GUIDE TO COOKWARE & BAKEWARE MATERIALS

TYPE OF MATERIAL	HEATING PROPERTIES	RESPONSE TO FOODS	USE AND CARE	SUITABLE FOR
ALUMINUM	Good, even heat conduction; cools quickly	Will discolor foods and affect taste of foods left in pan for more than 15 minutes. Acid foods will also discolor pan's surface.	Cool before washing in warm, soapy water and dry immediately. Undissolved salt may cause pitting, so add salt to hot liquid and stir in before adding the liquid to pot.	Soup pots, skillets, bakeware, roasting pans, measuring utensils, cooking utensils
CAST IRON	Good conductor of heat, but is slow to heat up and may be uneven, causing "hot spots"; good conductor of radiant (oven) heat; very slow to cool down, so not good for delicate dishes	May transfer some residual flavors and odors to foods and cause discoloration, especially acid foods.	Must be seasoned according to manufacturer's instructions to prevent rusting. Wash with water or in a light, soapy solution; scrub with a brush only if necessary. Never soak; always dry immediately.	Skillets, muffin tins, Dutch ovens, griddles, grill pans
COPPER	Excellent, uniform heat conduction; cools quickly	Reacts with all foods, creating a potentially poisonous substance, thus copper utensils must be lined with another metal, often tin. Exception: copper bowls used for beating egg whites	Wash lining with soapy water; polish copper with commercial copper cleaner or with mixture of flour, salt, and vinegar.	Pots, saucepans, baking pans, teapots, molds, mixing bowls
EARTHENWARE	Absorbs heat slowly, but well; retains heat for a long time	May retain tastes and odors and transfer them to foods unless utensil is glazed.	Cool before washing with warm water and abrasive scrubber. Soap alone may be used to clean glazed surfaces.	Casseroles, slow cooker inserts

A GUIDE TO COOKWARE & BAKEWARE MATERIALS—*CONTINUED*

TYPE OF MATERIAL	HEATING PROPERTIES	RESPONSE TO FOODS	USE AND CARE	SUITABLE FOR
ENAMELED CAST IRON	Absorbs heat very slowly, but retains for a long time; absorbs radiant (oven) heat particularly well	None	Cool before washing with warm, soapy water. Avoid use of harsh abrasives. Soak to loosen cooked-on food. Clean stained surface with baking soda.	Dutch ovens, baking pans, casseroles, bakeware, roasting pans
GLASS	Absorbs heat very slowly, but retains for a long time	May cook or bake foods faster on the outside unless temperature is adjusted.	Cool before washing in warm, soapy water with abrasive scrubber.	Baking dishes, casseroles, pie plates, loaf pans
NONSTICK FINISH	Depends on metal of vessel or utensil	None, unless it chips or peels	Season if manufacturer's instructions say to do so. Wash in hot, soapy water using soft sponge or dishcloth. Do not use sharp or rough-edged utensils on nonstick surfaces. Avoid high heat.	Most cookware, bakeware, cooking utensils
SILICONE (SYNTHETIC RUBBER)	Heats evenly and cools off quickly	Does not react to foods; does not hold odors; most foods will not stick to it	Pans are very flexible and need to be on a baking sheet to stabilize them. The pans can go straight into water for soaking even if still hot.	Bakeware, cooking utensils, rolling pins, nonstick baking pan liners
STAINLESS STEEL	Good heat conduction if combined with aluminum or copper.	May cause slight discoloring of highly acid foods.	Wash with warm, soapy water. Avoid use of harsh, abrasive cleaners. Soak briefly to remove burned-on food. Dry immediately after cleaning.	Skillets, stockpots, saucepans, baking pans, roasting pans

Knives

Experienced cooks believe a set of good, sharp knives is the cook's most indispensable tool. Good knives are expensive but well worth, it, for they perform many vital functions. With proper care knives will serve you well and last a long time.

When shopping for a set of knives, look for the best quality possible. Check to see if the manufacturer's name is engraved on the blade; this is usually a sign of good workmanship. Hold the knife in your hand. It should feel comfortable to you, and the blade should seem well anchored in the handle. Depending on what you will use the knife for, you should also note the weight, balance, flexibility, and sharpness of each knife in a set. Some of the things to observe are:

The type of material(s) used: Forged carbon steel knives, among the most expensive, are the choice of professional chefs. High-carbon steel is generally regarded as the most satisfactory material for knives because it takes a good, sharp edge most efficiently and keeps it for a long time. The knives require more care, however, than knives made of other materials, and acid foods will discolor it.

Stainless steel knives may be cheaper than carbon steel knives. They are harder than carbon steel and keep their sharpness longer, but they are more difficult to sharpen when they do become dull. However, stainless steel has the advantage of being rustproof, and will not affect the flavor and color of food as carbon steel will when it is not properly cared for. An intermediate choice for quality and budget purposes is stainless steel with a high percentage of carbon. This alloy combines some of the qualities of both carbon and steel. Knives of tempered stainless steel with a high carbon content are considered among the best.

The grind of the blade: Most professional knives are taper ground, or forged in one piece from bar steel with all parts of the knife shaped in a series of processes. The handle is added before the edge is ground. The blade is machine ground with a taper from back to edge and from handle to blade tip. Carbon and stainless steel knives may both be taper ground.

Hollow ground knives have broad, concave cutting surfaces. They are very good for slicing but are easily damaged. Most of the cheaper knives cut from thin strips of stainless steel are hollow ground.

The handle material: The handle should be made from a material that does not absorb moisture and that resists shrinking and warping. The best handles are made from close-grained hardwood, plastic-wood laminates, or polypropylene. Maple and walnut, rosewood, bone ivory, hard rubber, stainless steel, and aluminum may also be used for knife handles. Some knives, especially smaller knives, now have silicone-coated handles, which makes them nonslip.

The way the knife is put together: Examine the way the handle is secured to the knife. The tang, or the part of the blade that extends into the handle, may run the full length or part of the length of the handle, depending on the type of knife. The tang on good knives is forged from the same piece of metal as the blade, which lends strength to the knife. It should be securely fastened inside the handle, ideally with two or three good-sized rivets. Small nails, brads, or a metal collar are not sturdy enough and will not hold a knife together for very long.

The type of cutting edge: The cutting edges of knives vary in shape and thickness, depending on the blade's intended use. When choosing knives for the various cutting jobs in food preparation, consider the length, shape, and degree of flexibility of the entire blade as well as the type of cutting edge.

The following are the most commonly needed knives:

paring knife: a small, usually 2½- to 3-inch blade; gives leverage without unnecessary strain on the fingers; used for paring and trimming small and light vegetables

chef's knife: (sometimes called a French knife): blades can range from 6 to 14 inches long; the slight curve to the blade makes it good for rocking on a cutting board when mincing and chopping; the shorter blades, 6 to 8 inches, are the most multi-purpose and are often called utility knives; used to cut large vegetables and to slice, cube, and mince vegetables, nuts, and herbs; may also be used to trim meat, cut poultry, clean fish, or do anything for which a paring knife is too short

santoku knife: a Japanese-style chef's knife with a 6- to 8-inch straight-edged blade (as opposed to the curved blade edge of the French-style knife) whose Japanese name translates to three uses—slicing, dicing, and chopping; ground thinner than other chef's knives

serrated knives: fine-toothed knives with saw-like points cut into the blade edge; used to cut smooth, soft foods such as bread, tomatoes, grapefruits, and cucumbers. A serrated bread knife, which is most useful, should be fairly rigid and long to slice across large loaves. A grapefruit knife is small, with a curved, double-edged serrated blade, to cutaway sections of grapefruit halves.

carving knife: should be very sharp, slightly flexible, and long in order to cut through the meat fibers of large roasts and whole roasted birds; should have a long, thin point that curves in order to cut around bones

ham knife: long, rigid knife with a rounded tip and hollows ground out of the blade; used to cut very dense meat such as ham; the hollows, or scallops, create small air pockets between the blade and the material being sliced to make the slices fall away more easily

boning knife: used for removing bones from raw meat and poultry; should have a rigid, narrow, broad-backed blade with a sharp point

filleting knife: should be strong, thin-backed, and have a pointed, sharp, and flexible blade

butcher knife: a thick and heavy knife with a long, 5½- to 10-inch, firm blade for cutting, trimming, and finishing cuts of meat

cleaver: a strong and heavy knife used to cut through bone and to tenderize meat; also good for light chopping, mincing, dicing, scraping, and shredding of meats, fish, and vegetables

Other Cutting Utensils

apple corer: a circular, stainless steel blade surrounded by sharp "wheel spokes" that, when pressed down on an apple, cores and divides it into neat wedges; also can be a hand-held fluted blade with a pointed tip that takes out the apple core without cutting the apple into sections

cheese wire: a stainless steel wire and roller with a plastic handle, used to evenly slice hard and semihard cheeses as thin or thick as needed

cutting board: a block of wood, plastic, or silicone used to protect counters and tabletops as well as knife blades when chopping meats and vegetables or slicing bread and other foods

egg slicer: utensil of fine wires stretched across a slotted base that can slice peeled hard-cooked eggs into neat, uniform slices for garnishes or other decorative pieces

grater: a box with four variously perforated sides used to grate foods from fine to coarse, or a flat sheet with two types of surfaces and a slicing blade

peeler/parer: used to thinly peel or shave the skins of fresh vegetables; can be of various designs, but the most popular one has a fluted blade and a tip that can be used to core or to scoop out blemishes from vegetables

SHARPENING KNIVES

Sharpen knives with a handheld steel or a sharpening stone. To use a sharpening steel, draw the knife blade lightly down the steel at a shallow (20-degree) angle. Repeat, putting the knife first to the front of the steel, then to the back.

To use a sharpening stone, place the stone on a flat surface, with a damp cloth underneath to keep it secure. Support the stone with one hand and gently draw the knife blade across its length at a shallow angle. Do this several times. Then turn the blade over and repeat in the opposite direction. If the stone has both a coarse and a fine surface, run each side of the blade over the coarse surface first.

---

scissors: a good, sharp pair useful for cutting paper and jobs for which shears may be too awkward

shears: used to cut through tough materials such as small bones, poultry joints, shellfish, and raw meat; the cutting edges need not be as sharp as those of scissors, but their construction needs to be sturdy

zester: an instrument designed to remove the thin colored outer layer of citrus fruits; the classic zester has a curved blade containing five little holes that, when drawn firmly across the skin of a citrus fruit, removes the zest in little curls; the more modern zester resembles a woodworking tool and rasps off the zest in very fine shreds

Stovetop Cookware

double boiler: a 2- to 4-cup capacity is best

saucepans: having several sizes is useful, preferably 1-quart, 2-quart, and 3-quart, with covers

pots: pans with two short handles; 4-quart and 6-quart

stockpot: 8- to 10-quart pan with sides taller than its diameter

pressure cooker: an airtight pot that cuts cooking time by 50 to 70 percent; suitable for cooking stocks, soups, stews, beans, grains, and hard vegetables (such as potatoes or beets); also useful for canning and preserving

Dutch oven: heavy covered pan that can be used over direct heat and go in the oven; 6-quart or 8-quart

skillets: a 7-inch, 10-inch, and 12-inch skillet are useful

crêpe/omelet pan: a shallow pan with sloping sides (an omelet pan maybe slightly deeper than a crêpe pan)

griddle: large heavy plate that fits over two burners; good for cooking pancakes evenly and in quantity

wok: a bowl-shaped metal pan used in Chinese cooking for stir-frying; also available with a flat bottom and a wooden handle

steamer: three basic forms: a perforated basket insert that fits into a large pot, such as those sold for boiling pasta, a collapsible metal basket that fits inside different-shaped pots, and a multi-tiered bamboo steamer; the larger the steamer the better

Electrical Appliances

blender: good for blending liquids and for making sauces

hand blender: also called an immersible blender or stick blender; useful for pureeing foods right in the cooking pot

food processor: takes the tedium out of chopping, slicing, and shredding normally done by hand with a sharp knife; with attachments can also knead dough, puree, and beat batters, thus replacing the need for a blender or electric mixer

mini food processor: small version of a food processor; useful for chopping small amounts of ingredients

spice grinder/coffee grinder: good for making batches of homemade spice mixtures, such as curry powder, and grinding coffee beans

handheld mixer: useful for blending loose mixtures in any shape bowl and in saucepans; usually not strong enough for heavy mixing, as for stiff doughs

stand mixer: valuable to those who bake often; frees the cook to do other jobs as the batter is blending; generally has a stronger motor than a hand-held; can also knead dough

sandwich press/nonstick grill: a hinged grill with nonstick heat plates; good for making grilled sandwiches, such as panini, and for cooking with little fat

---

SHOPPING TIPS FOR POTS & PANS

Here's what you should look for when selecting pots and pans:

- Construction should be solid. Covers should fit snugly; look for covers with skirts (rims that fit inside the vessels).
- There should be no crevices at joints and seams where food might lodge, and no imperfections in the surface.
- Flat bottoms or concave bottoms designed to flatten on heating are best in cookware.
- Materials should be good conductors of heat (see "A Guide to Cookware & Bakeware Materials," page 8).
- The heavier the pot, the better it is for cooking. A thick iron pot retains heat better and diffuses it more economically than a lightweight one. Cheap, lightweight pots heat up more rapidly and unevenly, so food is more likely to burn and stick.
- No part of a pot or pan should be inaccessible to a mixing spoon.
- Handles and knobs (preferably heat resistant) should be sturdy with a comfortable grip that will keep your hand a safe distance from hot metal.
- Rivets are good fasteners for handles to pots; they should be flush to the surface. Screws are less secure. Spot welding, often used for spouts, is a good fastening method, as is brazing (the handle is bonded to the pot with copper or brass).

toaster oven: more useful than a regular toaster; especially good for grilling sandwiches, reheating foods, and for toasting nuts

microwave oven: useful for reheating and melting food; can be used to very quickly steam vegetables and fish; good for baking potatoes

rice cooker: not an essential tool, but an extremely useful one if you have room for it; cooks rice to perfection

slow cooker: an electric pot that cooks soups, stews, and similar dishes very slowly; especially helpful to working cooks who wish to leave meals to cook slowly throughout the day

food dehydrator: good for those who want to make dried foods

juice extractor: machine that separates juice from pulp and seeds in fruits and vegetables; good for making healthful drinks

Crushing & Grinding Utensils

food mill: a mechanical-type sieve with three different cutting disks to puree food from fine to coarse (often replaced today by a food processor)

garlic press: a utensil held like a pair of scissors and squeezed to force a crushed garlic clove through tiny holes in its head

citrus juicer: can range from large device with a presser arm to a reamer set over a cup to catch the juice to a handheld reamer for squeezing juice right into dishes; electric juicers also available

meat grinder: a hand-operated machine, usually of cast-iron framework and attached to a table by clamps, into which meat is dropped and then hand-cranked through a disk for the desired coarseness; also available as an attachment to some stand mixers

meat pounder: a hand-held utensil of various designs with which meat is pounded to flatten or tenderize it; comes with two sides, a flat one for pounding and a spiked one for tenderizing

mortar and pestle: a primitive but efficient instrument consisting of a smooth, regularly curved bowl (mortar), usually of marble or wood, and a compatibly shaped grinder (pestle) of the same material; very useful for pulverizing nuts and seeds, garlic, herbs, and whole spices

nut/shellfish cracker: a sturdy, steel utensil that should permit some control over pressure to crack nuts and shellfish shells without crushing their contents

pepper mill: a handheld wooden, metal, or plastic container with a grinding mechanism in its base for grinding whole peppercorns when freshly ground pepper is called for in a recipe

salt mill: similar to a pepper mill, used to freshly grind coarse salt

potato masher: a handheld utensil with either a coiled metal base or a flat, slotted one for mashing and pureeing cooked potatoes and other root vegetables directly in the cooking pan

ricer: a tool that resembles a giant garlic press; forces cooked foods such as chestnuts or potatoes through perforations to obtain dry, rice-like grains

Draining Utensils

colander: a bowl-shaped container with many small holes for draining pasta and vegetables

sieve/strainer: a mesh basket, usually with a handle, used for separating liquids from solids; some have a coarse mesh, some a fine mesh, and some a double layer of mesh for very fine straining

salad spinner: a round plastic container with an inner, rotating plastic basket that, when spun quickly, forces excess water from lettuce and other leafy vegetables into the outer container

Skimming, Lifting & Turning Utensils

skimmer or slotted spoon: large, metal, flat spoon with holes, used to lift food from boiling water or to skim grease or scum from soups and stocks

spatula: a flat wooden, metal, plastic, or silicone utensil for lifting and turning foods in a skillet, or for transferring hot foods from a pan to a plate; sometimes referred to as a pancake turner

tongs: a flexible, metal grabber for turning sautéing foods, serving spaghetti, and lifting vegetables and other foods out of hot water

Thermometers

candy thermometer: made of glass and stainless steel with a clip for attaching to the side of a pan; gradations up to 350°F; increases accuracy in determining the stages of sugar in candy making

dairy thermometer: a glass alcohol thermometer in a plastic case; used for checking temperatures when making yogurt and cheese

deep-frying thermometer: made of glass and stainless steel with a clip for attaching it to the side of the pan; gradations from 100° to 500°F; aids in determining the oil temperature for frying foods

freezer thermometer: made of glass and plastic; used to measure the coldness of a freezer

meat thermometer: made of stainless steel; used to check the internal temperatures of meats; two types—one stays in the meat while it roasts, the other is "instant-read" and is inserted in the meat only when the temperature is being checked

multipurpose thermometer: measures from 40° to 220°F; good for checking room temperatures when making yogurt or bread

oven thermometer: a glass mercury tube set in stainless steel; used to determine the accuracy of an oven's thermostat

Measuring Utensils

measuring cups, liquid: clear plastic or glass cups with graduated markings and pouring spouts

measuring cups, dry: handled cups that usually come in a nested set of four (1 cup, ½ cup, ⅓ cup, ¼ cup); ingredients are measured flush to the rim. There are also larger sets with odd sizes, including 2 cups, 1½ cups, ⅔ cup.

measuring spoons: a set made of plastic or metal spoons in four sizes—¼ teaspoon, ½ teaspoon, 1 teaspoon, and 1 tablespoon—for accurately measuring wet and dry ingredients

scale: used to measure by weight instead of volume; available in either digital, balance, or spring models

Mixing Utensils

bowls: various sizes for mixing; preferably made of glass or stainless steel

rotary beater (egg beater): a handheld utensil with two four-bladed beaters operated by a small hand turned crank; useful for mixtures that may be too heavy for a wire whisk

spatula, rubber or silicone: a flexible paddle attached to a wooden or plastic handle for scraping batter and dough mixtures from mixing bowls and remaining condiments from jars

wire whisks: handheld metal utensils with looped, springy wires ideal for stirring sauces and beating egg whites; come in various sizes

wooden spoons: useful for mixing, stirring where a metal spoon is undesirable

Basic Bakeware

Baking pan sizes vary; standard sizes are listed below.

angel food (tube): 10-inch

baking sheet: 14 × 10-inch, with or without rim

bundt pan: 12-cup

cake pans, round: 8-inch, 9-inch

cake pans, square: 8-inch, 9-inch

cake pans, rectangular: 9 × 13-inch, 7 × 11-inch

jelly-roll pan: 15½ × 10½ × 1-inch

loaf pans: 8½ × 4½-inch, 9 × 5-inch, 6 × 3½-inch (mini)

muffin/cupcake pan: contains six or twelve 2½ × 1¼-inch cups

pie plates: 8-inch, 9-inch, or 10-inch; also deep-dish

springform pan: 8-inch, 9-inch, 10-inch

Special Bakeware

ramekins: small, often round or oval, ovenproof dishes made of earthenware or porcelain and used as molds or individual serving dishes

quiche pan: a porcelain pie plate with straight sides and fluted edges

soufflé dish: a round, deep, straight-sided, ovenproof dish

tart pan: a two-piece pan with fluted sides and a removable bottom

brioche pan: a fluted metal mold for baking brioche

popover pan: like a muffin pan, but with very deep cups

Basic Ovenware

Most baking pans (see Basic Bakeware, left) do double-duty for savory dishes and baked goods.

There are some pans, though, that are specific to savory dishes:

gratin dish: a shallow ceramic or enameled metal baking dish designed to go under the broiler

lasagna pan/dish: deep-sided baking pan about 9 × 13 inches

roasting pan: deep-sided pan, with or without cover, for roasting large cuts of meat; comes in multiple sizes, with the average being about 14 × 17 inches; often comes with a rack

dutch oven: heavy deep-sided pot, with a cover, that can be used over direct heat and in the oven; useful for dishes that start cooking on the stovetop and end up in the oven for a final baking or roasting

casseroles: deep, covered dishes in a range of sizes, from 1½ quarts to 8 quarts; can be glass, ceramic, or enameled metal; only metal casseroles (which are really Dutch ovens) can be used over direct heat.

terrine: a straight-sided clay, porcelain, or cast-iron pot with a lid; for making pâtés or terrines

Baking & Oven Utensils

baster: a syringe-like plastic or metal tube with a flexible bulbous end, for drawing up the juices of cooking meat or fowl for basting

cake rack (also called wire rack): a wire grate used to allow air to circulate freely around cooling cakes, breads, and other baked goods

cookie cutters: variously shaped metal cutters for shaping rolled cookie dough quickly

pastry bag: a canvas or nylon bag that is cone shaped with a plain tip and decorative pastry tips for piping whipped cream and icing; also comes with larger tips for piping doughs and fillings

pastry blender: a utensil consisting of five or six steel cutters (wires or blades) fastened in an arc on both ends to a wooden handle; used for quickly cutting fat into flour in pastry making

pastry brush: a brush resembling a small house-painting brush; used to apply washes of beaten egg, milk, or syrup to dough or pastries before or after baking

roasting rack: a metal, grate-like stand used to keep roasting meat or poultry raised above the fat or juices dripping from it in a roasting pan

rolling pin: a wooden, marble, or silicone cylinder for rolling out dough; American-style pins have handles, French pins do not

sifter: a utensil similar to a sieve but deeper and with an oscillating mechanism for sifting flour for cakes and other baked goods or for dredging

trussing needle: a large sewing needle for sewing up poultry or stuffed meats; comes in various lengths

trussing skewers: long, needle-like, steel pins used to hold meat and poultry firmly in shape during cooking

MEASURING, EQUIVALENTS & SUBSTITUTIONS

Accurate measuring of ingredients often makes the difference between success and failure when you're following a recipe. Most people don't realize that there is a significant different between the method and tools used to measure liquids versus those tools used to measure dry ingredients.

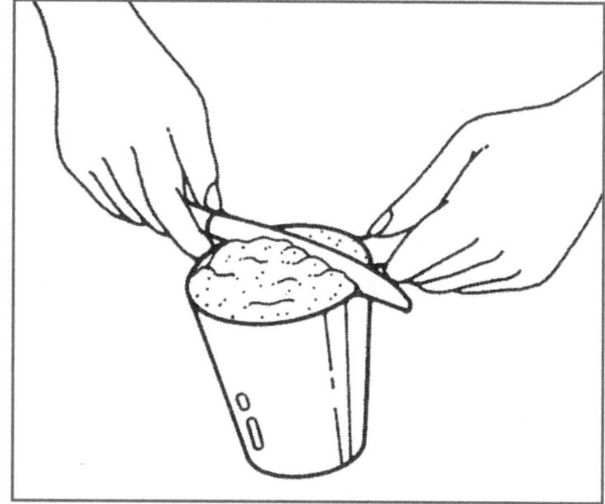

To measure liquid ingredients: Place a liquid measuring cup on a level surface. Fill the cup slowly to the desired level; then, without lifting the cup, check the amount at eye level. When measuring sticky ingredients such as syrup, honey, or molasses, oil the cup lightly before adding the ingredient so the amount measured will come out of the cup easily; use a spatula to get every last drop. For liquid amounts under $^1/_4$ cup, use tablespoons.

To measure dry ingredients (such as flour or sugar): Either whisk the ingredient to break up lumps (or, for some recipes, sift the flour). Spoon the ingredient lightly into a dry measuring cup until it is overflowing, then level off the excess with the flat edge of a knife. Do not tap the cup, shake down the contents, or otherwise pack the ingredients unless the recipe instructs you to.

The Tools

liquid measuring cups: generally made of clear glass or plastic with visible markings for every 1/4 and 1/3 cup. They can be as small as 1 cup or as large as 8 cups. The containers are marked so that the last marking is far enough below the rim that when it contains the full amount of liquid you can still pick it up without spilling. The cup should have a handle and a pouring spout.

dry measuring cups: usually come in a set of four cups that nestle one inside the other; made of metal or plastic. The cups range in size from 1/4 cup to 1 cup, and each measures flush to the rim. This feature enables you to level the ingredients with the flat edge of a knife.

measuring spoons: come in sets, with spoons ranging in size from 1/4 teaspoon to 1 tablespoon. Some sets also include 1/8 teaspoon and 1/2 tablespoon. Like dry measuring cups, you are meant to level off dry ingredients flush with the edges of the spoon.

Equivalents

Cooks are constantly being called upon to make decisions and to improvise. If a recipe calls for 2 cups of honey, the cook must decide if a jar marked "8 fluid ounces" will fill the requirement. If a recipe calls for 750 milliliters of wine, what is that in cups? Will 1 pound of cabbage yield 3 cups shredded cabbage? Some of these answers come with experience, but the handy tables that follow will quickly resolve most doubts.

EQUIVALENT VOLUME MEASURES

Pinch or dash	=	less than 1/8 teaspoon
3 teaspoons	=	1 tablespoon
2 tablespoons	=	1 fluid ounce
1 jigger	=	1 1/2 fluid ounces
4 tablespoons	=	1/4 cup or 2 fluid ounces
5 tablespoons + 1 teaspoon	=	1/3 cup
8 tablespoons	=	1/2 cup or 4 fluid ounces
10 tablespoons + 2 teaspoons	=	2/3 cup
12 tablespoons	=	3/4 cup
16 tablespoons	=	1 cup or 8 fluid ounces
1 cup	=	1/2 pint
2 cups	=	1 pint or 16 fluid ounces
4 cups	=	1 quart or 32 fluid ounces
4 quarts	=	1 gallon
8 quarts	=	1 peck
4 pecks	=	1 bushel

NOTE: All measures are level.

METRIC EQUIVALENTS FOR WEIGHTS AND VOLUME

WEIGHT
1 gram = 0.035 ounce
5 grams = approximately 1 teaspoon
28.35 grams = 1 ounce
50 grams = 1¾ ounces
100 grams = 3½ ounces
227 grams = 8 ounces
1,000 grams (1 kilogram) = 2 pounds + 3¼ ounces
VOLUME
1 deciliter = 6 tablespoons + 2 teaspoons
¼ liter = 1 cup + 2¼ teaspoons
½ liter = 1 pint + 4½ teaspoons
1 liter = 1 quart + scant ¼ cup
4 liters = 1 gallon + 1 scant cup
10 liters = approximately 2½ gallons + 2½ cups

EQUIVALENT AMOUNTS OF COMMON INGREDIENTS

INGREDIENT		AMOUNT	EQUALS	EQUIVALENT AMOUNT
ALMONDS	Unshelled	1 pound	=	1¼ cups nutmeats
	Shelled	1 pound	=	4–4½ cups nutmeats
APPLES		1 pound	=	3 cups raw, sliced
		1 pound	=	1⅔ cups cooked, chopped
		1 pound	=	1 cup pureed
APRICOTS, DRIED		1 pound	=	3 cups
BANANAS		1 pound (3–4 medium)	=	1 cup mashed
BRAZIL NUTS	Unshelled	1 pound	=	1½ cups nutmeats
	Shelled	1 pound	=	3 cups nutmeats
BREAD		1 slice	=	½ cup soft crumbs
BUTTER	Stick	1 stick	=	8 tablespoons
		1 stick	=	½ cup
		1 stick	=	4 ounces
	Whipped	1 pound	=	3 cups

EQUIVALENT AMOUNTS OF COMMON INGREDIENTS—*CONTINUED*

INGREDIENT		AMOUNT	EQUALS	EQUIVALENT AMOUNT
CABBAGE		1 pound	=	4½ cups shredded
CARROTS		1 pound	=	3 cups shredded
CHEESE	Blue	4 ounces	=	1 cup crumbled
	Cheddar	8 ounces	=	2 cups shredded
	Cream	3 ounces	=	6 tablespoons
	Parmesan	2 ounces	=	⅓ cup grated
COCONUT, FLAKED		7 ounces	=	2⅔ cups
COTTAGE CHEESE		½ pound	=	1 cup
CREAM, HEAVY		1 cup	=	2 cups whipped
GELATIN		¼-ounce envelope	=	2½ teaspoons
LEMON		1 medium	=	1–2 teaspoons grated zest
		1 medium	=	3 tablespoons juice
LIME		1 large	=	1 teaspoon grated zest
		1 large	=	2 tablespoons juice
MUSHROOMS		½ pound	=	3 cups sliced
ONION		1 medium	=	½ cup minced
ORANGE		1 medium	=	2 tablespoons grated zest
		1 medium	=	⅓ cup juice
PASTA		1 pound	=	8 cups cooked
PEANUTS	Unshelled	1 pound	=	2 cups nutmeats
	Shelled	1 pound	=	4–4½ cups nutmeats
PECANS	Unshelled	1 pound	=	2¼ cups nutmeats
	Shelled	1 pound	=	4–4½ cups nutmeats
PEPPER, BELL		1 large	=	1 cup diced
POTATOES		1 pound	=	1¾ cups mashed
RAISINS		1 pound	=	2¾ cups
SPINACH		1 pound	=	1½ cup cooked
WALNUTS	Unshelled	1 pound	=	1¾ cup nutmeats
	Shelled	1 pound	=	4–4½ cups nutmeats
YEAST	Active dry	¼-ounce envelope	=	2½ teaspoons
	Cake	0.6-ounce cake	=	1 package active dry

Substitutions

Of course, a wise cook plans ahead before starting to prepare a dish, but even the best cooks sometimes turn to the cupboard for a vital ingredient and find it bare. If there is no time to run to the store, substitutions are often possible. Oil can replace butter in many recipes; raisins may be used in place of prunes, and so forth. Here are some simple substitutes that might save you in a pinch.

EMERGENCY SUBSTITUTIONS

IF YOU DON'T HAVE...		AMOUNT	USE ...
ALLSPICE		1 teaspoon	3/4 teaspoon cinnamon plus a generous pinch each of cloves and nutmeg
ARROWROOT		2 teaspoons	1 tablespoon cornstarch or 4 teaspoons flour
BAKING POWDER		1 teaspoon	1/4 teaspoon baking soda plus 1/2 teaspoon cream of tartar
BALSAMIC VINEGAR		1/4 cup	1/4 cup red wine vinegar plus 1/2 teaspoon honey
BUTTER, MELTED		1/2 cup (1 stick)	1/2 cup vegetable oil
BUTTERMILK		1 cup	1 tablespoon vinegar or lemon juice plus enough milk to measure 1 cup; let stand 5 minutes
CAYENNE PEPPER		1/8 teaspoon	3 or 4 drops hot pepper sauce
CHINESE FIVE-SPICE POWDER		...	see recipe page 226
CHOCOLATE	Semisweet	1 ounce	1 ounce unsweetened chocolate plus 1 tablespoon sugar plus 1 tablespoon vegetable shortening
	Unsweetened	1 ounce	3 tablespoons unsweetened cocoa powder plus 1 tablespoon vegetable oil
CORNSTARCH		1 tablespoon	2 tablespoons flour
CRAB BOIL		...	see recipe page 266
CRACKER CRUMBS		3/4 cup	1 cup bread crumbs
CREAM	Heavy	1 cup	3/4 cup milk plus 1/3 cup butter
	Light	1 cup	3/4 cup plus 2 tablespoons milk plus 3 tablespoons butter; or 1/2 cup heavy cream plus 1/2 cup milk
	Half-and-half	1 cup	3/4 cup plus 2 tablespoons milk plus 2 tablespoons butter; or 1/2 cup light cream plus 1/2 cup milk
	Sour	1 cup	1 cup Greek yogurt or whole-milk regular yogurt

EMERGENCY SUBSTITUTIONS—*CONTINUED*

IF YOU DON'T HAVE...		AMOUNT	USE ...
CRÈME FRAÎCHE		...	see recipe page 487; or use Greek yogurt
FLOUR (AS A THICKENER)		1 tablespoon	1½ teaspoons cornstarch or arrowroot; or 1 tablespoon instant tapioca
FLOUR, CAKE		1 cup	1 cup all-purpose flour minus 2 tablespoons
GINGER, FRESH, GRATED		1 tablespoon	¼ teaspoon ground ginger
HERBES DE PROVENCE		...	see recipe page 437
HONEY		1 cup	1¼ cups granulated sugar plus ¼ cup liquid
ITALIAN HERB SEASONING		...	see recipe page 407
LEMON JUICE		1 teaspoon	½ teaspoon vinegar
MAYONNAISE		½ cup	½ cup Greek yogurt or sour cream blended with 1 teaspoon Dijon mustard
MILK, WHOLE		1 cup	⅓ cup nonfat dry milk plus 1 cup water plus 2 teaspoons butter
MUSTARD, PREPARED		1 tablespoon	1 teaspoon dry mustard plus ⅛ teaspoon salt
PICKLING SPICE		...	see recipe page 661
POULTRY SEASONING		...	see recipe page 255
PRUNES, PITTED, CHOPPED		½ cup	½ cup raisins
PUMPKIN PIE SPICE		...	see recipe page 541
RICOTTA		1 cup	1 cup pureed low-fat cottage cheese
SAFFRON		⅛ teaspoon	½ teaspoon turmeric
SUGAR, CONFECTIONERS'		1 cup	1 cup granulated sugar plus 1 tablespoon cornstarch processed in a food processor
TAPIOCA (AS A THICKENER)		1 tablespoon	½ tablespoon flour
TOMATO JUICE		1 cup	½ cup tomato sauce plus ½ cup water
TOMATO SAUCE		2 cups	¾ cup tomato paste plus 1 cup water
YOGURT	In baking	1 cup	1 cup sour cream or buttermilk
	Greek	1 cup	1 cup reduced-fat sour cream

PART 2

At the Market

Meats

Americans have had a long-standing reputation for being meat eaters. But concern about fat intake and more specifically, saturated fat, coupled with meat's relatively high cost, got people to cut back, or even eliminate meat from their diets entirely. While cutting back is not a bad idea, meat remains an excellent source of high-quality protein. And, if you make smart choices and eat meat in moderation, you can keep within your budget and enjoy a healthy diet.

Buying Meats

Shop for meat the way you would for produce, grains, or any other product. Pick a market that has a high turnover and where you know you'll be getting the freshest product. Specialty meat markets, farmer's markets, co-ops, and some supermarkets have butchers on hand. By asking questions, you can learn a great deal about the right cut to buy for your specific purpose.

If you shop where the meat is prepackaged, carefully examine the package and label. See-through trays that permit you to inspect both sides of the meat are ideal. The label should provide the name of the type of meat, the cut (chuck, round, shank, loin), the specific retail name of the cut (steak, rib roast, chop), the price per pound, and the sell-by date.

Other Label Claims

Organic/certified organic: To put "Organic" or "Certified Organic" on a label, farmers must receive certification from a third-party certifier approved by the USDA through its National Organic Program (NOP). To qualify, the animals must be fed a diet of 100 percent organic feed, with no antibiotics, no growth hormones, and no animal by-products. The animals must be raised free of (most) fertilizers, genetic engineering, radiation, sewage sludge, and artificial ingredients. The animals must also have access to the outdoors (though this is often overlooked or very liberally interpreted); see "Certified humane," below.

Raised without antibiotics: There is no third-party certification for this claim.

No Chemicals added: A meaningless claim, unsupported by government oversight and not even officially defined.

No additives: The government defines additive as something that provides a "technical effect" in food (e.g., coloring, flavoring, or preservatives). There is no third-party certification, and because the terms of the label are vague, an animal might have been fed hormones but the producer could still apply this label.

Grass fed: Cattle fed on grass produce meat with higher levels of omega-3s and lower levels of saturated fat (though it's not clear just how much grass in the diet produces this effect). The USDA has established a standard for grass-fed labeling that states only cattle that have a diet solely from grass and hay and no grain or grain products can be labeled grass-fed.

Certified humane/free farmed: These are

trademarked stamps from third-party companies, each with its own very strict set of standards and verifications. Both require the animals to be raised in an environment that includes, among other things, proper protection from weather, adequate space to move around, and care by "humane-trained" handlers. These label terms do not imply anything about organic feed, hormones, or antibiotics.

Natural: Legally this means that the product contains nothing artificial. It has nothing to do with the animal's diet, hormones, antibiotics, or living conditions.

Something to keep in mind while shopping for meat is that the shape of the bone is usually a good guide to the tenderness of the piece (see illustration below).

When choosing fresh meats, look for these qualities:

Beef: A uniform, bright, cherry-red color is characteristic of good beef. Lean meat is firm with a fine texture and little marbling (distribution of fat particles throughout the lean), while fattier cuts are well marbled. Red, porous bones also indicate good-quality beef. The fat should be white.

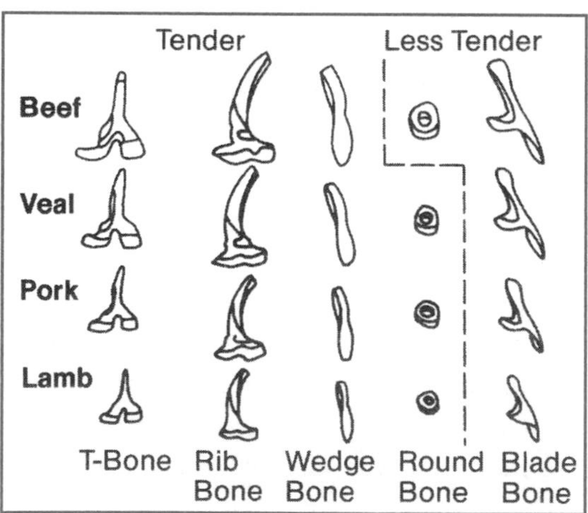

Lamb: Young lamb should be pink to light red in color, firm, and fine textured with slender, porous bones. The meat of older lamb is light to deep red, and the bones are drier than that of younger lamb. The external fat on both should be firm.

Pork, fresh: Good-quality fresh pork has a high proportion of lean to fat and bone. The lean is firm, fine textured, and grayish pink to light red in color. Leaner cuts, such as pork tenderloin and center-cut loin, have exterior fat but little interior fat; fattier cuts such as pork shoulder are well marbled.

Pork, cured: A deep pink color is typical of the meat of cured pork. Sodium nitrate and sodium nitrite are commonly used in curing pork (as well as beef). While several decades ago there was great concern about these curing agents causing cancer, today the National Academy of Sciences, the American Cancer Society, and the National Research Council agree there is no cancer risk associated with the consumption of cured meats. The Food and Drug Administration and the United States Department of Agriculture (USDA) agree, providing the amount is at regulated levels. In fact, the cured meat industry is using these preservatives in less than the amounts allowed by the government. That said, there are now many more nitrate- and nitrite-free choices available.

Veal: The meat of very young veal is pale pink to grayish pink; that of somewhat older veal is slightly red. All veal should have a smooth texture with practically no marbling.

Buying Ground Meat

Although ground beef is the most common and popular of the ground meats, lamb, veal, and pork are also available in ground form. Often a combination of ground pork, veal, and beef will be sold as "meat loaf mix." As you buy ground meats, notice whether the meat is liberally specked with white. Fatty ground meats show a great deal of white throughout, causing the overall color to be light pink. By comparison, the white is less noticeable in lean ground meats, so they look fairly dark and red. Many markets will mark the fat or lean percentage on the label, often choosing the lean percentage because it's more impressive (i.e., 93 percent lean, rather than 7 percent fat).

Here's what ground beef labels mean, by law:

- **Ground hamburger:** any cut of beef (though generally from less-tender cuts) and can have fat added, but not more than 30 percent fat by weight
- **Ground beef:** any cut of beef but cannot have any *added* fat and must have no more than 30 percent fat by weight
- **Lean ground beef:** must have no more than 22 percent fat
- **Extra-lean ground beef:** has no more than 15 percent fat; often as low as 7 percent fat (93 percent lean)

Buying Variety Meats

Variety meats include the liver, heart, kidneys, tongue, brains, sweetbreads (thymus gland), and tripe (stomach lining). Consumed regularly in other parts of the world, these meats have never been very popular in this country. Although they are usually economically priced and rich in nutrients, there are other concerns to be aware of. For example, the function of the liver is to filter out toxins in the body, so if you are buying liver from an animal that hasn't been raised organically, you may be consuming unwanted substances. And certain organs are fairly high in cholesterol—sweetbreads, for example, have 250 milligrams of cholesterol in a 3-ounce serving. By comparison a 3-ounce portion of sirloin steak has 57 milligrams. We've narrowed the field here to the cuts we think most people might try.

Beef or calf's liver: Beef liver will be a deep red-brown color. Calf's liver, the more popular of the two, is pale and grayish pink in color. Calf's liver tends to be sweeter than beef liver. Both will be sold in slices. If the skin is still on, remove it with your fingers.

Tongue: Tongue is firm, with a rough skin covering. Beef and veal tongue are available pickled, corned, smoked, and fresh. Pork and lamb tongue are often sold cooked and ready to serve, but can also be found fresh.

Tripe: Plain (or smooth), tripe is the tissue lining of the first stomach of beef or veal; honeycomb tripe comes from the second stomach. Tripe is available fresh, pickled, and canned. Although fresh tripe is actually partially cooked when sold, it must still be cooked for a couple more hours before it is edible.

Oxtail: Weighing under 2 pounds, fresh oxtail has a rosy appearance and is more often than not sold already cut into pieces. It is often sold frozen.

Buying Sausage

Sausage varieties can be divided into two broad categories: 1) uncooked, which includes fresh, cured, smoked, and air-dried sausage, and 2) fully cooked and ready to serve, which only needs to be heated if it's for a hot dish.

Commercially made sausage is seldom merely fresh meat and seasonings stuffed into natural animal casings (pork, lamb, or beef intestines). It can also contain fillers, additives to retard spoilage, and preservatives. Be a smart consumer, check the label, and choose the packages with the least amount of ingredients beyond the meat and seasonings.

As with other meats, choose the freshest sausage that you can. Quality deteriorates in all sausage during storage, even if it has been smoked and dried. Look at the links or patties. The fat (tasty sausage is about one-third fat) should be evenly distributed throughout, and the links should be unbroken and lightly packed. Broken or overstuffed sausage will split during cooking. Check the label to see whether the sausage is fully cooked or if it must be cooked before serving. Examine the exposed surfaces and avoid those that are slimy or have any liquid present.

For the freshest sausage, try making it yourself (see page 32).

Inspection & Grading

Before and after slaughter, all meat must be federally inspected for wholesomeness. (Some states have their own equivalent inspection for meat sold within the state.) Those meats passing the inspection have a round, purple mark to indicate that the meat came from a healthy animal and that it was processed under sanitary conditions. The stamp is put only on carcasses and major cuts, so it will rarely appear on small retail cuts. If the stamp does appear on a piece of meat, don't bother trimming off the blue marking—it is harmless, as it is made with a food-grade dye.

For a fee, the USDA offers grading of beef, lamb, and veal as an optional service to packers. The grade marking, a shield-shaped stamp, is a guide to quality—tenderness, juiciness, marbling, and flavor—in meat. U.S Prime has the most marbling and is the most tender, but rarely makes it to the market; rather most of it is sold to restaurants (and some high-end butchers). U.S. Choice is the most widely available, with less marbling than Prime. U.S. Select is the leanest and least tender of the three.

Spending Wisely

When selecting from the many cuts of meat available, always try to figure the cost per serving. A cut with a high price per pound and with little waste is often more economical than one that is less expensive but has lots of waste. Of course, the actual number of servings in a pound depends on individual appetites.

Storing & Thawing Meat

All fresh and cooked meats are perishable. Store fresh meats, loosely covered with waxed paper or foil, in the coldest part of your refrigerator. While some fresh meat will keep for 5 to 7 days, most are best if used within 1 to 3 days. (See "Home Storage of Meat," opposite.) Cover cooked meats and meat dishes and keep them in the refrigerator for no more than 4 days. Always store gravy, stuffing, and meat in separate containers. For longer storage, freeze fresh and cooked meats as well as meat dishes, gravies, and stuffings (see "Freezing Meats," page 627, and "Freezing Prepared Foods," page 628).

To maintain safety and high quality, thaw fresh and cooked meats, still wrapped, in the refrigerator. For a quicker method you can immerse a package of raw meat in its watertight wrapper in cold water. Change the water every 30 minutes. Thaw until pliable. Meat that is cold enough to retain ice crystals may be safely refrozen, but quality will suffer.

If, at any time, the meat has an off-odor, a slimy surface, or mold, throw it away.

HOME STORAGE OF MEAT

MEAT		KEEPS IN THE REFRIGERATOR (DAYS)	KEEPS IN THE FREEZER (MONTHS)
BEEF, VEAL	Ground	1-2	3-4
	Pieces for stew	1-2	3-4
	Chops, cutlets	3-5	6-9
	Roasts	3-5	6-9
	Steaks	3-5	6-12
	Tenderloin, tournedos	3-5	3-4
LAMB	Ground	1-2	3-4
	Pieces for stew	1-2	3-4
	Chops, steaks	3-5	6-9
	Roasts, leg	3-5	6-9
PORK	Ground	1-2	3-4
	Pieces for stew	1-2	3-4
	Chops	3-5	6-9
	Roast, tenderloin	3-5	4-8
	Sausages	1-3	1-2
	Ribs	1-3	1-2

MAKING FRESH SAUSAGE

Making your own seasoned sausage is fun and easy. And you know the ingredients are natural, fresh, and wholesome. Basically, fresh, homemade sausage contains meat, fat, and seasonings. Vegetables, grains, and dry milk solids may be added to increase nutrients as well as to change texture and flavor.

While pork is most commonly used to make sausage, beef and poultry are also good. Fat is a necessary ingredient; it adds flavor, binds the meat and the seasonings, and lubricates the casings. As a rule, one part fat to two parts meat makes a moist, juicy sausage. Pork fat is the most common type used.

Sausage Making Equipment

The only equipment needed for making sausage is a meat grinder, a sharp knife, and, if you are making links, a funnel or a stuffing attachment for the meat grinder. For links you will also need to make your own cloth casings or purchase animal casings.

Sausage Casings

Casings made from pork, lamb, or beef intestines, as well as those made from cheesecloth or muslin, help sausages retain their shape during cooking. Pork or lamb casings are a good size for small sausages and beef casings work well for larger sausages.

Animal casings can be purchased fresh or packed in salt. They are available from some butchers or meat wholesalers.

For most recipes, you'll need about 4 feet of 1-inch-diameter pork or lamb casings for every 3 pounds of sausage; 1 foot of 1½-inch-diameter pork or lamb casings for each pound of sausage; or 2 feet of 3- to 4-inch-diameter beef casings for every 5 pounds of sausage. Buy more than you think you'll need, as casings tear easily.

Preparing animal casings for use: If originally packed in salt, first soak them in lukewarm water for about 30 minutes, changing the water two or three times. Rinse under running water; then open and run cold water through the inside several times. Remove the inner membrane. Fill casings and tie off lengths with string. Store unused casings, packed in salt, in a sealed plastic bag in the refrigerator or freezer. They will keep this way indefinitely.

Making a cloth casing: Cut cheesecloth or muslin into a long, narrow rectangle (15 x 6 inches). Dip the cloth into cold water; then wring out excess water and spread the cloth on a flat surface. Spoon sausage meat lengthwise down the center of the rectangle and fold the cloth over the meat. Roll to form a long, regular shape. Use string to tie the ends shut.

How to Make Sausage

Grind meat and fat in a meat grinder or finely chop with a knife. Blend the meat mixture and seasonings together in a bowl. Next, shape patties and loaves by hand, or fill casings using a funnel and the long handle of a wooden spoon, or the stuffing nozzle on the meat grinder. Do not overfill since overly plump casings tend to burst during filling or cooking. Break air bubbles with a pin; then twist or tie sausage to desired lengths.

Fresh sausage may be stored in the refrigerator up to 3 days. For longer storage, freeze—but it is best not to keep longer than 6 weeks. The high fat content in sausage encourages rancidity.

Poultry

We have come a long way from the days when a "chicken in every pot" was a promise of prosperity and the Sunday roast chicken was a luxury. Today chicken (and to a lesser extent turkey) can probably be found on the American dinner table a couple of times a week. Its mild, meaty flavor has universal appeal and is a kid's favorite, yet gourmet cooks are delighted with the way it takes to complex seasonings. And, no small bonus, it is economically priced and relatively low in calories and fat.

Buying Poultry

Except for poultry purchased directly from small farms, all fresh and frozen whole poultry on the market is ready-to-cook (dressed and plucked) and usually comes with the giblets and neck packed in the body cavity. Fresh birds are commonly sold whole, or in halves, quarters, or parts, but frozen birds are generally available only whole. In addition, many individual parts are available skinned, or skinned and boned.

When you purchase fresh, chilled poultry, look for these signs of quality:

- There should be no odor and a minimum of coarse pinfeathers.
- The skin should be soft and tear easily; and it should be smooth, cream colored, and moist but not wet.
- If you are buying a whole bird (or just breasts), the breasts should look plump and meaty.

Frozen poultry has slightly less flavor than fresh, but the texture is usually good. Since many frozen birds such as turkeys are prebasted with butter, fat, or stock, read the label to know what you are buying. Some frozen birds also have built-in thermometers that will pop up when the internal temperature reaches the well-done point.

When buying frozen poultry, check the following items:

- The wrap should form a complete seal. Broken wraps usually mean freezer burn, resulting in dry, unpalatable flesh.
- The flesh should be solidly frozen with no discoloration.
- There should be no evidence of pink ice around the meat, and there should be no blocks of frozen juices at the bottom of the package. These are indications that the bird has thawed and been refrozen. With repeated thawing and freezing, quality suffers—the flesh becomes stringy and tasteless.

When deciding how much fresh or frozen poultry to buy, remember that with whole birds or cuts that have the bone in and skin on, up to half the weight can be lost in waste—fat, skin, bones. Use the following as general guides for whole birds: For a whole bird under 12 pounds, figure on 1 pound per person. So, a 6-pound roaster chicken, for example, should yield enough meat to serve 6 people. Over 12 pounds, figure on 3/4 pound per person; over 20 pounds, 1/2 pound per person. For boneless poultry, buy 1/3 to 1/2 pound per person. For bone-in poultry, buy 1/2 to 3/4 pound per person, depending on the cut: the lower amount for meaty cuts like breast and the higher amount for bony cuts like drumsticks.

Reading the Label

Inspected: All poultry with a United States Department of Agriculture (USDA) inspection mark (circle) has been inspected for wholesomeness by the federal government or by an equivalent state inspection program. The mark indicates that the poultry came from a healthy flock, was processed under rigid sanitary conditions, contains no harmful chemicals, is properly packaged, and is labeled truthfully and informatively.

Organic/certified organic: To put "Organic" or "Certified Organic" on a label, farmers must receive certification from a third-party certifier approved by the USDA through its National Organic Program (NOP). To qualify, the animals must be fed a diet of 100 percent organic feed, with no animal by-products, no growth hormones, and no antibiotics. The animals must be raised free of (most) fertilizers, genetic engineering, radiation, sewage sludge, and artificial ingredients. The animals must also have access to the outdoors (though this is often overlooked or very liberally interpreted); see "Certified humane," right.

Raised without antibiotics: There is no third-party certification for this claim.

No chemicals added: A meaningless claim, unsupported by government oversight and not even officially defined.

No additives: The government defines addi-

CUTTING UP A WHOLE BIRD

You can usually save money by cutting up your own poultry. Chicken, duck, pheasant, guinea fowl, game hen, and squab are easily cut at home, but large turkeys and geese are rather cumbersome.

Halving: To halve a whole bird, place it breast-side down on a cutting board and use poultry shears or a sharp knife to cut along each side of the backbone. Remove the bone and reserve it for the stockpot. Cut the breast cartilage, flesh, and skin; then pull the halves apart and remove the keel bone.

Quartering: For chicken, pheasant, and guinea fowl quarters, halve the birds, and cut diagonally along the bottom rib. (Game hens and squabs are too small to quarter.)

Disjointing: To cut up, or disjoint, poultry, place the bird breast-side up on a cutting board and, using a sharp knife, cut the skin between the thighs and the body. Grasp one leg of the bird in each hand and lift the bird from the board. As you lift, bend the legs back until the bones break at the hip joints. Next, turn the bird to one side and completely remove the leg and thigh by cutting from the tail toward the shoulder and cutting through the joint near the bird's back. Repeat on the other side. To separate thighs and legs (drumsticks), locate the knee joint by bending the thigh and leg together, then cut through the joint. With the bird on its back, remove the wings by cutting inside the wing over the joint. It is easiest to cut from the top down. Finally, separate the breast from the back by placing the bird on its back and cutting through the joints on either side of the rib cage. The breasts, wings, legs, and thighs are now ready for cooking. If you prefer breast halves, split the breast by cutting the wishbone at the V.

DEBONING POULTRY BREASTS

Although boneless breasts are readily available, you can save some money by deboning chicken breasts yourself. Breasts are easily deboned if you use a boning knife with a sharp, flexible blade that lets you feel the bones as you work.

Place the breast with skin-side down on your cutting board, and cut the white gristle at the neck end of the keel bone (A). Bend the breast back, and press flat to expose the bone (B). With your finger, loosen the bone and lift it out. On one side of the breast, insert the knife tip under the long rib bone (C), then slide the knife under the bone to cut the meat free. Continue to cut the flesh free of the ribs until you can lift the rib cage out. Repeat on the other side. Remove the wishbone and white tendons.

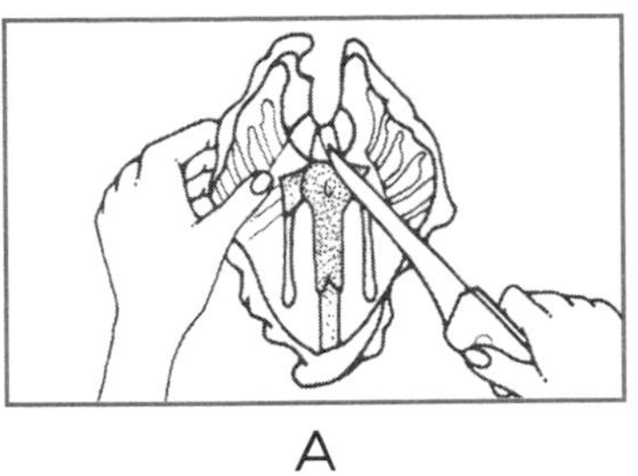

A

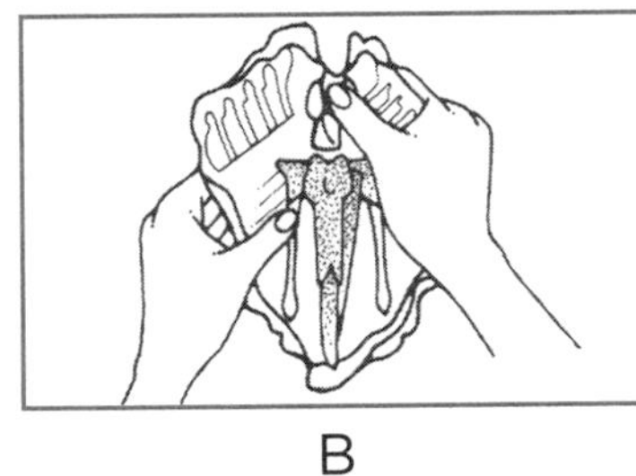

B

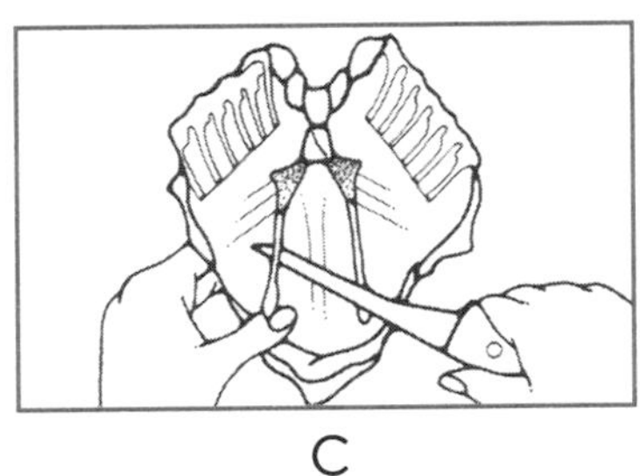

C

---

tive as something that provides a "technical effect" in food (e.g., coloring, flavoring, or preservatives). There is no third-party certification, and because the terms of the label are vague, an animal might have been fed hormones but the producer could still apply this label.

Free range (or cage free): NOP regulations allow producers to use this if the animal has the "option" of being outside (there has to be an open door from the indoors to the outdoors) even if only for a minute or two. It is not necessarily a meaningful designation and does *not* mean that the bird is organic. There is no third-party certification for this label claim.

Certified humane or free-farmed: These are trademarked stamps from third-party companies, each with its own very strict set of standards and verifications. Both require the animals to be raised in an environment that includes, among other things, proper protection from weather, adequate space to move around, and care by "humane-trained" handlers. However, this does not imply anything about organic feed, hormones, or antibiotics.

Natural: Legally this means that the product contains nothing artificial. It has nothing to do with the animal's diet, hormones, antibiotics, or living conditions.

Storing Poultry

Chilled, uncooked poultry is highly perishable and will keep best if the store wrap (which clings tightly and encourages spoilage) is removed and the bird is loosely rewrapped in waxed paper, placed on a plate, then refrigerated. (You can

COMMON MARKET FORMS OF POULTRY

POULTRY		DESCRIPTION
CHICKEN	Broiler-fryer	Young, all-purpose bird; $2\frac{1}{2}$ to 5 pounds; available ready-to-cook in whole, halves, quarters, or parts; good broiled, fried, braised, roasted, poached
	Capon	Meaty, tender, juicy, castrated male; 8–10 pounds; available whole; superb roasted
	Roaster	Large, plump, young bird (12 weeks old); 4–7 pounds; available whole or halves; excellent roasted
	Cornish hen	Crossbreed of Plymouth Rock chicken and Cornish gamecock; small, tender, meaty; available whole, fresh and frozen; 1–2 pounds; ideal roasted but also tasty braised, broiled, or fried
DUCK	Pekin	Most widely available duck breed, 8 weeks or younger; 3–6 pounds; available fresh and frozen, whole and breasts
	Moulard	Large meaty duck breed; 6–10 pounds; most available as breasts; best pan-grilled or pan-fried
GOOSE (GOSLING)		Fatty, all dark meat; best roasted when 4–12 pounds; good braised when over 14 pounds and older than 6 months; most available frozen
GUINEA FOWL		Dry, delicately gamey bird; hen preferable; 2–4 pounds; ready-to-cook available at gourmet butchers; most are frozen; good roasted, braised, poached
PHEASANT (FARM-RAISED)		Plump, dry bird; 2–4 pounds; most marketed frozen; ready-to-cook occasionally available at gourmet butchers; usually roasted or braised
QUAIL		Mild flavored game bird; all white meat, extremely lean; under 5 ounces; usually sold frozen
SQUAB		Young, domesticated pigeon; weighs less than 1 pound; usually marketed frozen but sometimes available fresh; ideal roasted but also good braised
TURKEY	Fryer-roaster	Small, tender hen or tom (16 weeks old) with smooth skin and flexible breastbone; 4–9 pounds; excellent broiled, roasted, grilled
	Young	Hen or tom (5–7 months old) with tender meat and skin; weight varies with age but usually 7–15 pounds; best roasted, grilled
	Yearling	Mature hen or tom (just over 1 year old); fairly tender; weight varies with age and breed but may be 20–30 pounds; usually roasted or braised
	Parts	Breast (bone-in and boneless); whole and halves; drumsticks; wings, cutlets; tenderloins

eliminate the rewrapping step if the poultry has been prepackaged in a heavy transparent wrap specially designed for storage both in the meat case and at home.) When storing a whole bird, always remove the giblets and store separately. Never stuff the bird before storing. Use raw, refrigerated poultry within 2 days of purchase.

To store cooked poultry, cool it quickly, wrap it loosely, and place it in the coldest part of the refrigerator. Cutting the meat from the carcass before storing will conserve space. The bones can then be used to make a stock.

If leftover cooked poultry has been stuffed, remove the stuffing and store it separately. Any gravy or broth should also be stored separately in a tightly closed container. You should use the stuffing and broth or gravy within 2 days, but you can keep the poultry itself up to 4 days.

For longer storage, both raw and cooked poultry can be frozen. But never stuff a bird before freezing. For top-quality poultry, store no longer than the maximum length of time (see "Freezer Storage Time for Poultry," page 628).

Thawing Poultry

As a rule, thawed poultry cooks more evenly and retains better texture than frozen poultry.

THAWING POULTRY

POULTRY	WEIGHT (POUNDS)	TIME IN REFRIGERATOR	TIME IN COLD WATER
CHICKEN			
Whole	3-4	12-16 hours	1-2 hours
	over 4	1-1½ days	4-6 hours
Pieces	¼-¾ each	3-9 hours	1 hour
Duck	3-6	1-1½ days	4-6 hours
Goose	6-12	1-2 days	4-6 hours
Guinea fowl	2-4	12-16 hours	1-2 hours
Pheasant	2-4	12-16 hours	1-2 hours
Quail	¼-½	3-6 hours	1 hour
Squab	under 1	6-12 hours	1 hour
TURKEY			
Whole	4-12	1-2 days	4-6 hours
	12-20	2-3 days	6-8 hours
	20-24	3-4 days	8-12 hours
Halves, breast	5-11	1-2 days	4-6 hours
Boneless roast	3-10	12-18 hours	1-3 hours
Pieces	1-3	3-9 hours	1 hour

Poultry, whether whole or cut in parts, is easily thawed in one of three ways. Whichever method you choose, thawing will be quicker for a whole bird if the package of giblets and neck has been removed from the body cavity before freezing. Of course, parts that are wrapped in small packages thaw the quickest.

Refrigerator: Thawing in the refrigerator is the slowest but safest way, since the outside surfaces remain cool during the entire thawing time. Keep the bird in its original wrap or cover it lightly with waxed paper if unwrapped. Place poultry on a tray for easy handling and to catch any drippings. Thaw until the flesh is pliable and the giblets can be taken from the body cavity. Allow 1 to 4 days for thawing (see "Thawing Poultry" chart, page 37).

Cold water: The fastest way to thaw poultry is in cold water. (Hot water is not recommended because it warms the outer surfaces too much while the interior is still frozen.) Keep the bird sealed in the original wrap or in another watertight plastic bag, and submerge it in cold (not warm or hot) water. Change the water often, and thaw until the meat is pliable and the giblets can be removed. You may also partially thaw poultry in the refrigerator and complete the thawing in cold water.

Room temperature: If your refrigerator is crowded with other foods, poultry can be thawed at room temperature, although the other methods are safer. Wrap the bird in a double paper bag or in several layers of newspaper. Keep tightly closed and place on a large tray to catch any drippings that escape the wrappings. Allow 1 hour per pound for thawing. Thaw until pliable, and remove the giblets. Cook immediately. If it becomes necessary to wait several hours before cooking, refrigerate the thawed poultry.

Fish

Fish in the marketplace include both saltwater and freshwater fish. Both types are classified according to their fat content: Less than 2 percent fat in the edible flesh is considered a lean fish; 2 to 6 percent, moderately fatty; and over 6 percent, fatty. However, the fat in fish is mostly polyunsaturated (i.e., healthy) and doctors recommend eating fish twice a week to maintain a healthy diet. All fish are an excellent source of protein, and fatty fish—such as salmon, mackerel, tuna, and sardines—have the added bonus of being chock-a-block with heart-healthy omega-3 fatty acids (see "Omega-3s in Fish," page 41). Sadly, because of overfishing and pollution, good choices in the marketplace can be limited (see "Fish to Eat, Fish to Avoid," below).

Buying Fish

The type of fish you'll find in your market depends on where you live. However, many types of fish are caught, iced down, and quickly shipped to markets all over the country and are quite fresh. Here's what to look for when buying fish:

Fresh fish: When choosing fresh fish at the market, whether whole or filleted, it should smell of the sea; briny and fresh—never fishy. Its flesh should be firm and if whole, its eyes should be bright, clear, and bulging, its gills reddish pink, and its scales tight. Fillets should be shiny, without any cracks or browning.

Frozen fish: Frozen fish may be purchased whole or dressed, as steaks, fillets, or chunks. Frozen fish should have little or no odor, and be wrapped in moistureproof and vaporproof material. When buying frozen fish, choose packages

---

FISH TO EAT, FISH TO AVOID

Nearly all fish and shellfish contain traces of mercury, but some contain a lot more than others. The risks depend upon the amount and type of fish consumed and the health of the consumer. The Environmental Protection Agency (EPA) advises pregnant women or women who may become pregnant, nursing mothers, and small children to avoid or limit their intake of certain fish.

The Monterey Bay Aquarium keeps a fish watch to inform consumers about which fish should or should not be eaten or limited. Their lists include not only fish that should be avoided for health reasons because of their mercury content, but also fish that should be avoided because they've been overfished. It is up to the individual consumer to make a choice about sustainability and what they should and should not be consuming. Check out the Seafood Watch (www.montereybayaquarium.org/cr/seafoodwatch.aspx) for up-to-date information.

CALCIUM IN CANNED FISH

Most canned salmon and sardines contain both the skin and bones; they're pressure-cooked so the bones become soft and edible, making these canned fish a rich source of calcium and magnesium, in addition to omega-3s.

---

that feel solid, which will tell you that the fish hasn't been thawed and refrozen.

Canned fish: Canned fish can be an acceptable alternative to fresh fish. Tuna, salmon, sardines, and mackerel are the most commonly consumed canned fish in this country.

There are actually several species of fish that may be labeled tuna. Only the albacore species may be labeled white meat. Light meat tuna refers to all other species. Tuna comes packed in three different styles: fancy or solid pack, chunk style, and flaked or grated style. All represent good-quality tuna. Bonito is also a variety of fish (related to the tuna species) that is commonly canned. It usually costs less than fish labeled tuna and has a similar taste.

When purchasing tuna or any other canned fish, check the label to see whether it is packed in water or oil. Water-packed tuna has fewer calories, but some people find it has less flavor than oil-packed—specifically olive oil–packed. However, water-packed tuna actually has more omega-3s than oil-packed. This is because some of the natural fat from the fish leaches into the oil it is packed in, and when you toss the oil, you toss some of the omega-3s. Since water and oil don't mix, with water-packed tuna the oil from the fish doesn't leach into the water.

As with tuna, there are several species of salmon that are canned. Pink salmon is light in color and flavor. The deep-colored, red-fleshed sockeye salmon is usually more expensive, fattier, and more flavorful.

Salmon and tuna are also packed in pouches, both plain and seasoned.

Storing Fish

Ideally fish should be eaten the day it is caught or purchased. However, with proper care, and if it was very fresh when purchased, fish can be kept for a day or two. Rinse fish, place in a shallow pan, and top with waxed paper. Place a bag of ice on top of the paper to keep the fish cold and place in the coldest spot of the refrigerator.

If you do not intend to cook fish within this time, it should be frozen at once. If wrapped properly, most fish can be frozen for up to 3 months. Before freezing fresh fish, clean it well and cut it to the desired form and recipe-size portions. Wrap the whole fish or the cut portions individually in freezer paper or heavy-duty foil. Freezing fish as wet as possible helps prolong its storage life. Be sure to squeeze all air out of the package and tape it securely. Label the package with the type of fish, how it is cut, and the date.

Whole lean fish may be preserved by using ice-glazing, a process which prevents dehydration and thus increases storage life. Dip the fish in ice cold water, then wrap it while wet and freeze until an ice crust forms. Unwrap and repeat once more.

OMEGA-3S IN FISH

The chart below is a list of the fish that contain the highest amounts of heart-healthy omega-3 fatty acids, from highest to lowest. Be aware that some fish may contain higher concentrations of mercury (see "Fish to Eat, Fish to Avoid," page 39). Although there is no government guideline on how much omega-3s to get in a day, the American Heart Association recommends two servings of fatty fish a week for the general population, and 1 gram of omega-3s daily (from fish and other sources) daily for anyone with diagnosed heart disease.

FISH (3 OUNCES COOKED)	OMEGA-3S (G)	TOTAL FAT (G)
MACKEREL, BOSTON	2.2	15
SALMON, WILD	1.6	11
HERRING	1.4	9.9
TUNA, CANNED, WHITE (WATER-PACKED)	1.3	2.5
SARDINES, CANNED	1.2	9.7
SALMON, CANNED	1.1	6.2
BLUEFISH	1.0	4.6
HALIBUT	0.8	2.5
SMELT	0.8	2.6
STRIPED BASS	0.7	2.5
TROUT	0.5	6.1
TUNA, YELLOWFIN	0.3	2.5
CATFISH	0.2	6.8
FLOUNDER	0.2	1.3
HADDOCK	0.2	0.8
TUNA, CANNED, LIGHT (WATER-PACKED)	0.2	0.7
COD	0.1	0.7

PREPARING FISH YOURSELF

You can purchase fish cut in just about any style desired (see "Market Forms of Fresh Fish," page 44). However, if you catch your own fish or just prefer to buy it whole, you will find it surprisingly simple to prepare the fish yourself.

With a little practice, anyone can learn to clean and fillet a whole fish. Turning out fillets with a maximum amount of flesh may be awkward at first, but you will soon discover the most comfortable way to do the job. Here are some tips for making things easier:

- Have the proper tools at hand: a fish scaler (a rigid, sharp knife blade held at an angle may also be used); a very sharp boning knife, especially important for filleting; strong scissors, helpful for cutting away the gills and fins; a strong cleaver or a saw, essential for cutting through the spine if the fish is large enough to make into fish steaks.
- Put several layers of newspaper on the cutting surface to catch the scales. Remove the top layers of the newspaper after scaling each side of the fish.
- If the fish is extremely slippery, hold the tail with a cloth, a pair of rough finished kitchen gloves, or a large-pronged serving fork when scaling and cutting.

Cleaning a Whole Fish

The following steps are necessary to prepare any freshly caught whole fish for cooking:

1. Remove the scales. Hold the fish firmly by the tail and, with a scaler or sharp knife, remove the scales using a brushing motion from the tail end toward the head.
2. Eviscerate the fish. (This preliminary step is often done by fishermen when the fish is caught so that it can be washed as it is gutted.) Cut the belly from the level of the gills down to the anal opening. Inside the belly look for the roe in the form of two long sacs, and cut them away carefully. Wash and reserve if desired.
3. Remove the gills. Hold them firmly in your hand and cut around the membrane with a knife, then with scissors cut them off where they join the body.
4. Remove the fins. Fins may be cut from the fish with large scissors or a sharp knife. If using a knife, make a V-shaped incision around the fin and lift it out.

Left to right: Scaling a fish; holding the fish in position with a fork; opening the belly to remove the innards; cutting out the gills; cutting of the fins.

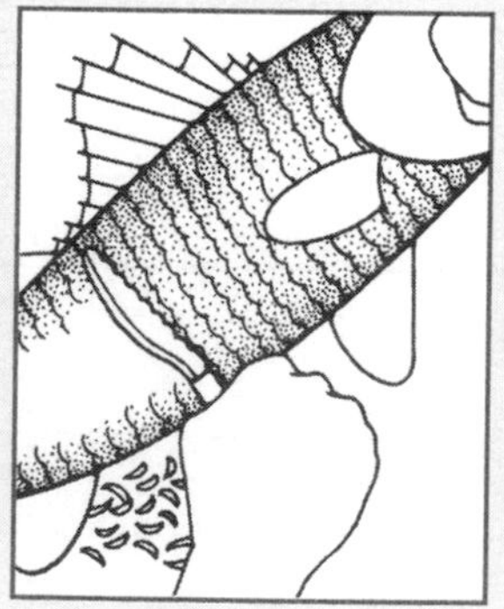

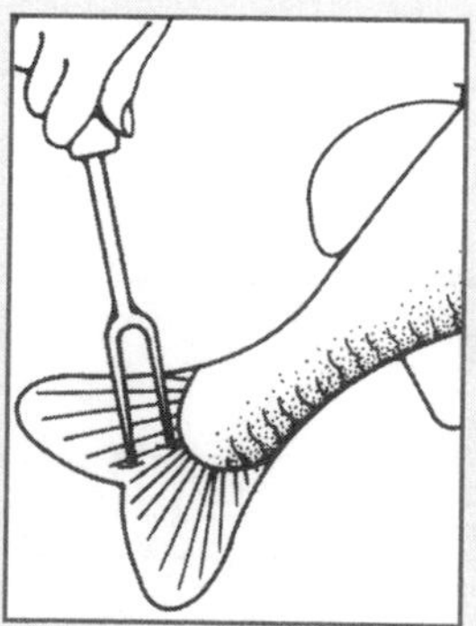

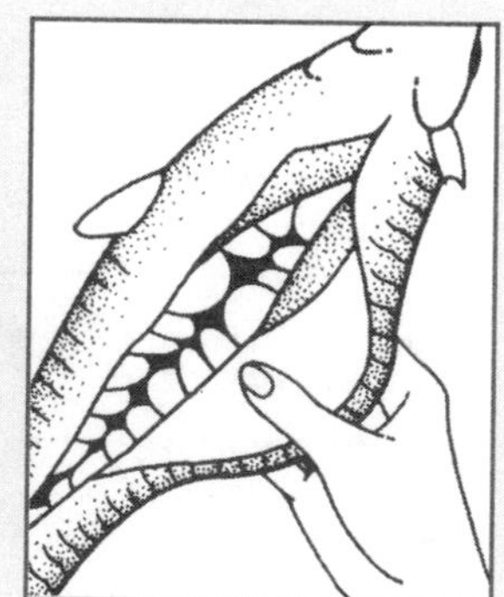

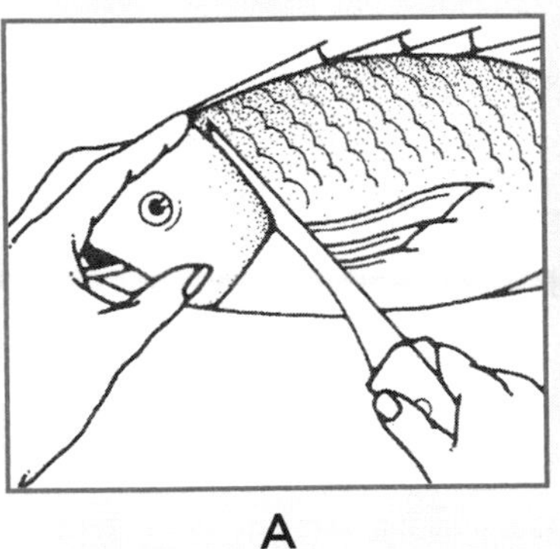

A

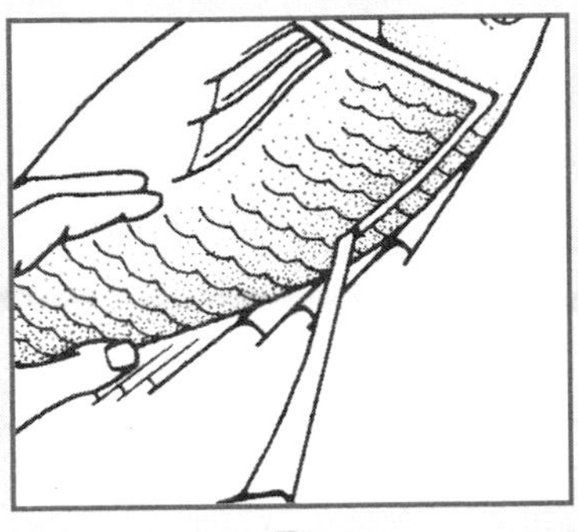

B

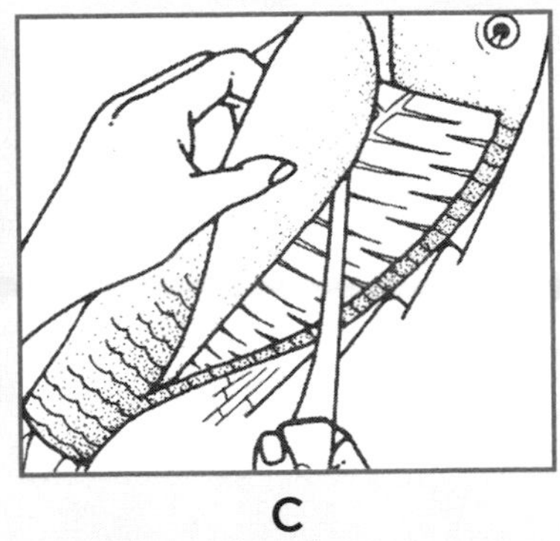

C

5. Wash the fish thoroughly under running water, making sure all blood spots and entrails are removed. Wipe the fish dry with paper towels.

At this point you have a whole dressed fish ready to be cooked. If you do not intend to cook the fish right away, wrap it in foil or plastic wrap and refrigerate or freeze immediately (see "Storing Fish," page 40).

Making Fish Fillets

1. Make an incision behind the gills (A). Lay the fish on its side and cut from the top of the fish diagonally down to the belly.
2. Make a cut from the head down to the tail, holding the fish's backbone toward you, with the fish still on its side (B). The cut should be about 1 inch deep—you should feel the backbone with the knife.
3. Slice the flesh from the center bone, following the plane of the backbone, but not breaking the structure. With your free hand pull back the flesh as you slice (C). Do not cut fillet off at the tail end; leave the tail attached.
4. Turn the fish over and repeat step 3 on the other side.
5. Cut both fillets away at the tail. Reserve the carcass for fish soups or Fish Stock (page 173).
6. Skin the fillet by moving a large knife blade in a sawing motion between the skin and flesh. Work with the blade at a slight angle to the skin and press it firmly against the skin. The fillet should be clean looking. Cook or store immediately.

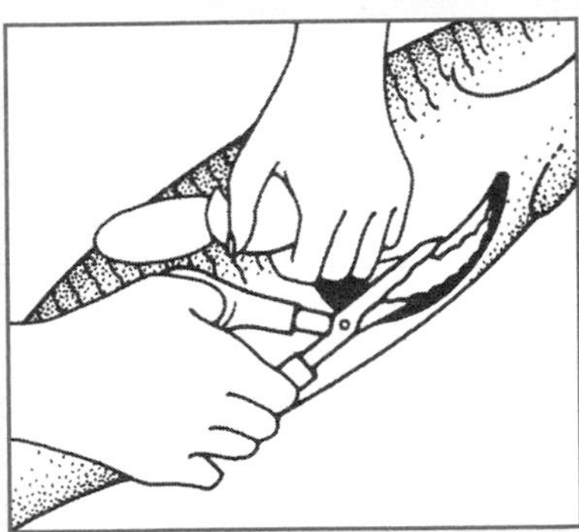

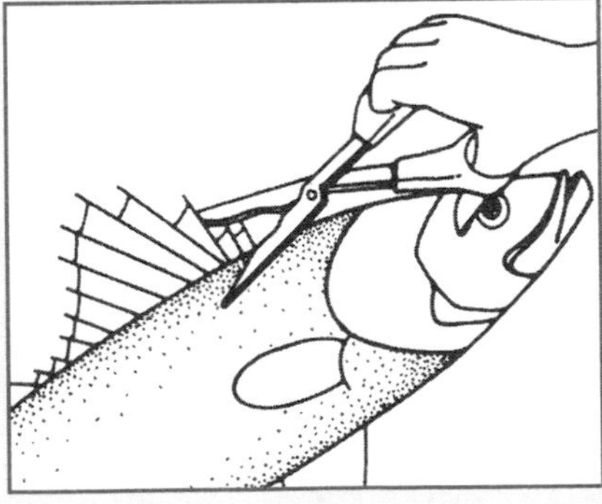

MARKET FORMS OF FRESH FISH

MARKET FORM	DESCRIPTION	AMOUNT TO ALLOW PER SERVING (POUNDS)	COMMON COOKING METHODS
WHOLE OR ROUND FISH	Fish exactly as it comes from the water	$\frac{3}{4}$–1	Steam, poach, bake (stuffed or unstuffed)
WHOLE DRESSED FISH	Fish that has been gutted, scaled, with fins removed	$\frac{3}{4}$–1	Steam, poach, bake (stuffed or unstuffed)
DRAWN FISH	Fish that has been gutted only	$\frac{3}{4}$–1	Steam, bake (stuffed or unstuffed)
PAN-DRESSED FISH	Usually small fish, gutted, with head, tail, fins removed	$\frac{1}{2}$–$\frac{3}{4}$	Bake (stuffed or unstuffed); if small, pan-fry or oven-fry
STEAKS	Crosscut sections of the dressed fish (generally larger sizes of firm-fleshed ones such as halibut, salmon, cod, swordfish)	$\frac{1}{3}$–$\frac{1}{2}$	Bake, broil, steam
FILLETS	Sides of the fish cut lengthwise away from backbone; may be skinned or unskinned, but are always boned	$\frac{1}{4}$–$\frac{1}{3}$	Pan-fry, oven-fry, deep-fry, bake, broil
BUTTERFLIED FILLETS	The two sides of the fish cut away from the backbone and held together by the belly skin of the fish	$\frac{1}{3}$–$\frac{1}{2}$	Pan-fry, oven-fry, bake, broil
CHUNKS	Cross sections of fish after it has been dressed; portions of the backbone left in	$\frac{1}{2}$–$\frac{3}{4}$	Bake, broil, steam, poach
STICKS	Uniform pieces of fish, cut lengthwise or crosswise from fillets or steaks	$\frac{1}{4}$–$\frac{1}{3}$	Pan-fry, oven-fry, deep-fry, bake, broil

Shellfish

Shellfish, invertebrates covered by some type of outer shell, are divided into two groups—crustaceans and mollusks. Crustaceans have crustlike shells with segmented bodies. They include crabs, lobsters, and shrimp. Mollusks have soft structures partially or totally enclosed in a hard shell.

One type of mollusk is the bivalve (an animal that lives inside a hinged shell), a group that includes clams, oysters, scallops, mussels, and abalones. To be certain that the bivalves you purchase are safe, buy from reliable dealers who know and can control their sources. If you are harvesting your own, make sure the water is safe and free of pollutants—check with the local fish and game authorities. While mollusks are often eaten raw, it can be chancy, so it is safer to cook them before serving. High temperatures destroy most of the life-threatening organisms they harbor.

Another class of mollusks are the cephalopods, which includes squid and octopus.

Crustaceans and cephalopods are found in deeper waters that are less likely to be polluted than shallow waters. Further, they do not tend to retain pollutants in the high concentrations that bivalves do.

Crabs

You can buy whole hard-shell crabs either alive or fully cooked. When buying live crabs, they must be kept alive until cooked (for safety), so make sure they are kicking when you purchase them. Fortunately it's become easier and easier to find these live crustaceans. They will keep for a day or two in the refrigerator. Do not keep them in water. Instead leave them in a paper bag in the cold fridge. Crab claws are generally not pegged (held shut with wooden pegs or rubber band) as lobster claws are, so be wary when you pick them up as they can pinch.

Soft-shell crabs should only be bought live. They too should be refrigerated (not in water). No need to put them in a paper bag, though, because they can't escape.

Fresh, packed crabmeat is available in most areas frozen or canned, usually fully cooked. As with all seafood, it should have a fresh, sweet smell. Crabmeat comes in several styles: lump, backfin, or flaked. Lump meat, the large white chunks of body meat, is considered the finest. Backfin meat comes in smaller chunks than lump meat and may be used the same way in most recipes. Flaked meat comes from various parts of the crab. It is less expensive than lump and backfin meat and may be mixed with them in recipes. One pound of lump, backfin, or flaked meat will serve 4 to 6, depending on the recipe.

Fresh crabmeat is sometimes sold canned, having first been pasteurized. The meat will remain fresh as long as the can is not opened. Once opened, keep it refrigerated and use within a day or two. Pasteurized cooked crab may be frozen, but its taste won't be as sweet and its texture may be spongy. When using crabmeat, be sure to pick it over to remove small bits of shell and cartilage.

Lobster

Fresh lobsters are available in many markets, where they can be found swimming in tanks. In this country the most popular variety is the Maine lobster with its delicious claw meat. But there are other equally delectable varieties. The spiny lobster is found in Europe and off the coast of Florida. This is the variety sold here as rock lobster tail. The langoustine or *scampo* (as it is called in Italy) is also available here but is less popular than Maine and spiny lobsters. It is found exclusively in European waters.

When buying live lobsters, make sure they are fairly active. Store live lobsters in a paper bag or in the bag they came in (*not* in a sealed plastic bag) in the refrigerator until you are ready to cook them. If buying cooked lobster, use within a day.

Lobster meat is also available in the form of frozen, uncooked tails (rock lobster). Cooked lobster meat is available fresh, frozen, or canned.

Edible meat usually equals about one-fourth of the lobster's weight, so a 2-pound lobster will yield about ½ pound of meat. A large or jumbo one will often supply enough meat for 1 to 2 servings, depending on how it is prepared.

Lobster is graded according to weight: 1 pounders are called chickens; 1¼ pounders are called quarters; 1½-pound lobsters are called halves; 2 pounders are selects, and 2½ pounders are jumbos. There are some that grow as big as 20 pounds (or more).

If you are looking for a good deal, ask if the market carries culls; these are lobsters that are missing one claw.

Shrimp

Probably the most popular shellfish around, shrimp are available in several forms: fresh either with their shells on or peeled and deveined; and frozen, shell-on or peeled and deveined. Fresh, uncooked shrimp should be firm in the shell, not soft and mushy. Frozen shrimp work very well in recipes; in fact the shrimp you buy "fresh" in a seafood market or the seafood department of a supermarket is actually thawed frozen shrimp, since shrimp are usually frozen right after they are caught.

The number of shrimp in a pound will vary with size, from tiny (up to 160 per pound) to colossal (under 8 per pound).

Clams

Hard-shell clams include butter clams, quahogs (also called cherrystones or littlenecks), Pacific butter clams (smaller than the eastern variety), razor clams, and Pismo clams. Soft-shell clams, also known as steamers or longnecks, are also available.

Clams can be found year-round and are generally sold by the dozen. When shucked, they are sold by the pint or the quart. Clams sold in the shell should be alive when bought. Hard-shell clams will be tightly closed. If slightly open, they should close tightly when tapped. Soft-shell clams may be partially open because of the long siphon or neck extending from inside their shells.

When buying shucked clams, look for plump ones with a fresh, clear surface, packed in their liquor. Store all fresh clams, shucked or unshucked, in the refrigerator until you are ready to prepare them. Shucked clams should be used within a day, while clams in the shell can keep for a few days. You can freeze shucked clams, in well-sealed containers, cooked or uncooked, for up to 3 months. If uncooked, cover them in their liquor first. If cooked, add some stock or other liquid before freezing.

Oysters

The varieties of these flavorful mollusks are innumerable. Almost 90 percent of the American oyster catch comes from the Atlantic. The rest comes from the Pacific or the Gulf of Mexico off the Louisiana coast. Pacific oysters are creamy with a slight mineral taste, while Atlantic oysters tend to be brinier.

Oysters are best in flavor from September through April, when they are not spawning. They may be marketed alive in the shell, sold by the dozen, or shucked and sold by the pint or quart. Shucked oysters may also be found packed in jars, frozen, or canned.

When buying oysters in the shell, make sure they are alive—the shells will be tightly closed. Shucked oysters should be plump and sold in clear, clean, fresh-smelling liquor that is free of sand. This tasty liquor adds flavor to soups and sauces.

Shucked oysters should be eaten within a day

THE CHOLESTEROL IN SHELLFISH

Shellfish have gotten a bad rap over the years for their cholesterol content. While it's true that some shellfish have a higher cholesterol content than low-fat finfish, they are very low in saturated fat. And it is saturated fats (and trans fats) that are the real culprits in high levels of blood cholesterol. If the food you are eating is high in cholesterol but low in saturated fats, its impact on your cholesterol levels is insignificant.

The chart below lists the cholesterol counts in shellfish as well as saturated fats and omega-3 fatty acids (since shellfish do actually provide some of these heart-healthy fats). The chart is organized by omega-3s, from high to low. To put the numbers in the chart into perspective, a 3-ounce piece of broiled sirloin has 65 milligrams of cholesterol and 2.5 grams of saturated fat; a 3-ounce portion of cooked chicken breast has 72 milligrams of cholesterol and 0.9 gram of saturated fat.

SHELLFISH (3 OUNCES COOKED)	OMEGA-3S (G)	SATURATED FAT (G)	CHOLESTEROL (MG)
SCALLOPS	0.8	0.6	34
MUSSELS	0.7	0.7	48
SQUID	0.5	0.9	239
CRAB	0.4	0.2	85
OYSTERS	0.4	0.6	32
SHRIMP	0.3	0.3	166
OCTOPUS	0.3	0.4	82
CLAMS	0.3	0.2	57
CRAYFISH	0.2	0.2	117
LOBSTER	0.1	0.1	61

as they spoil quickly. Oysters in the shell can be stored in the refrigerator for a day or two. Oysters may be stored in the freezer in the same way as shucked clams.

Scallops

Scallops, with their buttery texture and delicately sweet flavor, need little embellishment. There are two kinds of scallops sold in this country, both available fresh or frozen. The tiny cream-colored bay scallops come from shallow waters. The larger white sea scallops are dredged from deep waters. Diver scallops are sea scallops that are collected by divers, who pick only the largest.

Scallops should be fresh, sweet smelling, and plump. They should have a moist appearance but should be sold without any liquid. To appreciate their delicate flavor, you should eat them soon after they are caught. Purchase fresh, and keep for no longer than 24 hours after purchasing. Scallops may be stored in the freezer in the same manner as shucked clams.

Mussels

The most popular mussels are blue mussels and green-lipped mussels. The blue mussels are found all over the world, but mostly along the Pacific and Atlantic coasts. Green-lipped mussels come from New Zealand. Mussels can be found both wild and farmed, but chances are the mussels you are getting at your local seafood market are farmed. Mussels should be tightly closed and their shells should not be cracked. Once purchased, they should be stored in the refrigerator and used within a day.

Octopus & Squid

You can find both squid and octopus in fish markets, either frozen or thawed. While you can get fresh squid and octopus from farmer's markets, what you find in the seafood store has usually been frozen and thawed. Once purchased, they should be refrigerated and used within a day; or you can freeze them for use later.

EGGS

Eggs are surely the most useful and adaptable of all foods. They are the core of such comforting dishes as custard and scrambled eggs. They provide the loft in impressive soufflés and the leavening power in many baked goods. With bread crumbs they become a coating for fish or poultry. They keep oil and vinegar from separating in mayonnaise. They bind hearty meat loaves together and can be spun out into feathery meringues.

Along with the marvelous versatility that cooks love, a shape that artists adore, and an economy that penny-pinchers crave, eggs are also low in calories and loaded with nutrients. They are, however, high in cholesterol, though not as high as once thought. (See "The Cholesterol in Eggs," page 50.)

Buying Fresh Eggs

Most supermarkets carry eggs in several sizes, grades, and colors. What kind to buy depends on how you plan to use them. If you're scrambling, frying, or poaching the eggs by themselves, you can certainly substitute one size for another. However, if you are baking, using the size called for in the recipe is very important.

Egg sizes, established by the United States Department of Agriculture (USDA) in the 1930s, are based not on the measurement of the eggs but on the weight of a dozen (see "Market Sizes of Eggs," page 51). To get the most egg for your money, buy the larger size when the price difference between two sizes is less than 10 percent.

Although most recipes (including all of those in this book) call for large eggs—which is the size most readily available in markets—don't let that keep you from buying other sizes if they represent a savings.

Do not pay extra for eggs with a particular shell color. The color of the shell simply depends on the breed that laid the eggs. The quality and nutritive value of brown eggs and of white ones are virtually identical.

When you shop for eggs, check the grade stamped on the carton. Grading gives you a general idea about the quality of the egg in the box. The depth of the yolk, thickness of the white, size of the air sack, and position of the yolk all determine whether the egg is graded AA, A, B, or C. Grades AA and A eggs, with high firm yolks, thick whites, and obvious ropelike strands (chalazae) anchoring the yolks, are the ones found most frequently in markets. Grades B and C, which have flat, watery whites, usually go to commercial bakeries and food producers. Since Grade A eggs can drop to Grade B eggs if they are stored improperly or kept too long, always buy fresh eggs that have been kept under refrigeration.

Although eggs are inspected by the producers for cracks or other defects, you may occasionally come across one that is cracked. A good trick before you buy a carton of eggs is to make sure that all the eggs move freely in their little compartments. Just give them a little push to see if they move. Any egg that doesn't move may be "glued" in position by egg white leaking from a crack. If you happen to crack any eggs in transport, just cook them right away.

THE CHOLESTEROL IN EGGS

One large egg contains 212 milligrams of cholesterol. The recommended daily limit for cholesterol intake is 300 milligrams for people with normal LDL (bad) cholesterol levels. The American Heart Association takes a conservative approach and recommends that if you eat an egg a day, you restrict other dietary sources of cholesterol, particularly if you are at any risk for heart disease. Note that, in spite of claims to the contrary, eggs from free-range or organic eggs have no less cholesterol than any other type of egg.

Once home, you can check the freshness of the eggs you bought by putting them in water. If the eggs sink, they are fresh. If they float upright with the large end on top, they are not the freshest. If they rise to the surface, return them to the store or throw them out.

Label Claims

Organic/certified organic: To put "Organic" or "Certified Organic" on a label, farmers must receive certification from a third-party certifier approved by the USDA through its National Organic Program (NOP). To qualify, the hens must be fed a diet of 100 percent organic feed, with no animal by-products or antibiotics. The animals must be raised free of (most) fertilizers, genetic engineering, radiation, sewage sludge, and artificial ingredients. The animals must also have access to the outdoors (though this is often overlooked or very liberally interpreted); see "Certified humane," below. The organic classification also requires that hens not be fed growth hormones, but no commercial laying hen rations ever contain hormones. So even eggs without the organic label will not have growth hormones in them.

Raised without antibiotics: There is no third-party certification for this claim. You just have to trust the producer.

Cage free: This refers to eggs laid by hens at indoor floor operations, sometimes called free-roaming hens. The hens may roam in a building, room, or open area, usually in a barn or poultry house, and have unlimited access to food and water. NOP regulations allow producers to use this if the animal has the "option" of being outside even if only for a minute or two. It is not necessarily a meaningful designation and does *not* mean the hen is organic. There is no third-party certification.

Free range: Eggs produced by hens raised outdoors or that have access to the outdoors, as weather allows. In addition to consuming a diet of grains, these hens may forage for wild plants and insects and are sometimes called pasture-fed hens. The USDA has a definition for "free-range," but there is no third-party certification. It also does not mean that the animals have been treated humanely.

Natural: Legally this means that the product contains nothing artificial. It has nothing to do with the animal's diet or living conditions.

Certified humane: This is a trademarked stamp from a third-party company (Humane Farm Animal Care) with its own very strict set of standards and verifications. They require the animals to be raised in an environment that includes, among other things, proper protection from weather, adequate space to move around, and care by "humane-trained" handlers. It does not imply anything about organic feed or antibiotics.

Omega-3-enhanced: Regular eggs contain a small amount of healthful omega-3 fatty acids, on average about 30 milligrams per egg. Omega-3-enhanced eggs provide more, from 100 to over 600 milligrams per egg.

Pasteurized: Pasteurized eggs have been exposed to heat in order to destroy potential bacteria. The heat process may diminish some of the egg's heat-sensitive vitamins, such as the B vitamins riboflavin, thiamin, and folate. Using pasteurized shell eggs is an option for safely preparing recipes calling for raw or undercooked eggs. If you use unpasteurized eggs in a recipe that requires beaten egg white, you may need to beat them up to four times longer for foam formation.

Vegetarian: Eggs produced by hens fed rations containing only vegetable foods.

Egg Products

Substitutes for fresh eggs, defined by the USDA as "egg products," fall into two main categories: liquid and dried. (There are also some frozen egg products.) Dried eggs have been around since the late nineteenth century. Liquid egg products began to be available in the early 1970s in response to concerns about cholesterol. The products in both of these categories are required by law to be pasteurized.

Dried whole eggs: Used primarily by commercial bakers and institutions, some cooks like to keep dried eggs on hand for an emergency. As a general guide, 8 ounces dried eggs is the equivalent of 16 large whole eggs. Store dried eggs in a tightly covered container so that they do not absorb odors or take on moisture, which makes them lumpy and hard to mix. If kept in the refrigerator, they should stay good for about a year.

Dried egg whites: This product has become especially useful to cooks who are concerned about *Salmonella* (see "Egg Safety," page 324), but want to make recipes that call for uncooked beaten egg whites (certain mousses, for example). It is of particular interest to bakers who like to decorate with the classic royal icing, a combination of confectioners' sugar and raw egg white. A 3-ounce container of dried egg whites is the equivalent of about 20 eggs.

Liquid whole-egg substitute: These are made from egg whites that have been flavored and colored to resemble whole beaten eggs. They are cholesterol- and fat-free, and are fortified with vitamins. Some brands are also enhanced with omega-3 fatty acids.

Liquid egg whites: Just egg whites.

MARKET SIZES OF EGGS

EGG SIZE	APPROXIMATE WEIGHT OF 1 DOZEN (OUNCES)
Jumbo	30
Extra large	27
Large	24
Medium	21
Small	18
Peewee	15

Storing Eggs

Whole eggs: Store eggs with the large end of the shell up (to keep the yolks centered in their shells) in a covered container in the refrigerator. Since the shells are porous, eggs tend to absorb odors, so keep them away from strong-smelling foods such as onions and garlic. For best quality, use fresh eggs within a week. You can keep shelled beaten eggs in the freezer for 4 months. To prevent the eggs from becoming grainy, for every 4 large eggs, add 1 teaspoon sugar or honey, or 1⁄8 teaspoon salt before freezing in a tightly covered container. Be sure to label whether you used sugar or salt.

Yolks: Cover with cold water and store in the refrigerator in a tightly covered container. Use within 2 days. Pour off the water before using. To store yolks in the freezer, add 1 1⁄2 teaspoons sugar or honey, or 1⁄8 teaspoon salt for every 4 yolks before freezing in a tightly covered container. Be sure to label whether you used sugar or salt. Use within 4 months.

Whites: Refrigerate extra whites in a tightly covered container. Ideally, the whites should be used within 2 days. To freeze, put the whites in an ice cube tray (one white per compartment) or freeze in bulk in a sealed container. Whites will keep this way for 6 months.

Dairy Products

Milk & Milk Products

Among foods, milk has a unique distinction. In itself it can provide the entire diet for young mammals. Naturally, the composition of each animal's milk is especially suited to the best nourishment of its species, but all the milks are interchangeable as a satisfying food or beverage. Cow's milk and its products—cream, yogurt, cheese—are the most popular dairy foods in the United States, with goat's milk products ranking second.

Milk lends its distinctive flavor and pleasing, smooth texture to a range wide enough to include hot chocolate drinks that warm body and soul on chilly mornings and ice cream desserts that take the heat out of a hot summer's night. The taste of milk products runs the gamut from tangy fermented yogurt to rich fresh cheese.

An excellent buy in terms of nutrition, milk is just about the most concentrated food source of calcium known. It is also an excellent source of B vitamins and protein. In addition, almost all milk sold commercially in this country is fortified with vitamins A and D.

Types of Milk

Organic: The United States Department of Agriculture (USDA) organic seal indicates that the milk has come from cows fed and raised without the use of pesticides, synthetic fertilizers, antibiotics, and hormones.

Whole milk: contains 3.25% milk fat by weight, which translates to about 50 percent of its calories from fat

Reduced-fat milk (2%): about 35 percent of its calories from fat

Low-fat milk (1%, light): about 23 percent of its calories from fat

Fat-free milk (skim, nonfat): under 0.5% milk fat by weight and just 5 percent of its calories from milk fat

Lactose-free/lactose-reduced milk: treated with the enzyme lactase to make milk that can be consumed by those with lactose intolerance.

Dried Milk

Powdered milk comes in full-fat and nonfat versions, as well as buttermilk. You can cook with it in either its reconstituted or its dried form. For the fullest flavor of reconstituted milk, mix with water at least 2 hours before using, and refrigerate. If you are substituting reconstituted nonfat milk for fresh whole milk and want to retain richness, add 2 teaspoons of butter for each cup of reconstituted milk.

Adding nonfat dry milk to baked goods will boost their protein levels. Add when you add the other dry ingredients. For each cup of flour, replace up to ¼ cup of the flour with powdered milk. The added milk will contribute to nicely browned crusts. And you can add nonfat dried milk to liquid fat-free milk to give it a calcium boost.

Cultured Milks

For centuries European and Asian peoples have enjoyed the zing of cultured milks, including yogurt, kefir, piima, skyr, and buttermilk. The live cultures in these fermented milks are purported to have special healthful properties, such as establishing a balance of beneficial bacteria in the intestines. Because fermentation results in a small, tender curd, and because lactose is transformed into lactic acid, many people who have problems with fresh milk are able to digest cultured milks easily. Cultured milks give sauces and soups a luscious smoothness. And, when used in breads, cakes, and biscuits, the acid in cultured milks interacts with the protein in flour to all but guarantee a tender crumb.

Buttermilk: Traditional buttermilk, thick and mildly acidic with flecks of butter, was originally the liquid residue of butter making. Today it is a cultured (soured) milk made from either low-fat or fat-free milk. Confusingly, buttermilk labeled "low-fat" actually has more fat than regular buttermilk, which is made with fat-free milk. Baked goods made with buttermilk have an exceptionally tender crumb and pleasing brown crust.

Yogurt: Yogurt, a tangy, custard-like fermented milk, has long been a popular dietary staple in the Middle East and Russia. Though America was introduced to yogurt in the 1930s, it was not until the 1960s that it gained real acceptance. Yogurt comes in whole-milk, 1%, and fat-free versions (see "Calories, Fat & Calcium in Dairy Products," opposite page).

Greek yogurt: This creamy yogurt is regular yogurt that has been drained to remove much of the water. The resulting product is extremely dense and about the consistency of thick sour cream. It comes in whole-milk, 5%, 2%, 1%, and 0% versions (see "Calories, Fat & Calcium in Dairy Products," opposite page). It makes a great substitute for sour cream: Cup for cup, full-fat Greek yogurt has fewer calories and less fat than the same amount of *reduced-fat* sour cream.

Kefir: Popular in the Middle East, Eastern Europe, and Russia, kefir is one of the oldest-known fermented milks, yet it is a rarity in the United States. In many ways kefir resembles yogurt, but its flavor is somewhat milder and sweeter.

Piima: In the Scandinavian countries, piima is a favored cultured milk. It is milder tasting than either yogurt or kefir.

Skyr: From Iceland, skyr is technically a soft cheese but it closely resembles Greek yogurt. It is made from pasteurized nonfat milk and is

CALORIES, FAT & CALCIUM IN DAIRY PRODUCTS

DAIRY PRODUCT	SERVING	CALORIES	FAT (G)	CALCIUM (MG)
MILK, WHOLE	1 cup	150	8.2	290
MILK, 2%	1 cup	121	4.7	298
MILK, 1%	1 cup	102	2.6	300
MILK, FAT-FREE	1 cup	86	0.4	301
BUTTERMILK	1 cup	99	2.2	284
CREAM, HEAVY	1 tablespoon	51	5.5	9
CREAM, LIGHT	1 tablespoon	29	2.9	10
HALF-AND-HALF	1 tablespoon	20	1.7	15
YOGURT, WHOLE-MILK	1 cup	149	8	296
YOGURT, LOW-FAT	1 cup	154	4	448
YOGURT, FAT-FREE	1 cup	137	0	488
YOGURT, GREEK, WHOLE-MILK	½ cup	150	12	100
YOGURT, GREEK, 5%	½ cup	120	6.8	102
YOGURT, GREEK, 2%	½ cup	75	2.3	110
YOGURT, GREEK, 0%	½ cup	60	0	125
SOUR CREAM, FULL-FAT	2 tablespoons	46	4.7	26
SOUR CREAM, REDUCED-FAT	2 tablespoons	40	3.6	31
SOUR CREAM, LIGHT (LOW-FAT)	2 tablespoons	40	2.5	36
SOUR CREAM, FAT-FREE	2 tablespoons	22	0	38
CREAM CHEESE, FULL-FAT	2 tablespoons	99	9.9	28
CREAM CHEESE, REDUCED-FAT (NEUFCHÂTEL)	2 tablespoons	72	6.5	33
CREAM CHEESE, LOW-FAT (LIGHT)	2 tablespoons	60	4.6	44
CREAM CHEESE, FAT-FREE	2 tablespoons	29	0.3	98
COTTAGE CHEESE, CREAMED	½ cup	110	4.8	93
COTTAGE CHEESE, 2%	½ cup	97	2.8	103
COTTAGE CHEESE, 1%	½ cup	81	1.2	69
COTTAGE CHEESE, NONFAT	½ cup	81	0.3	97
RICOTTA CHEESE, WHOLE-MILK	½ cup	216	16	257
RICOTTA CHEESE, PART-SKIM	½ cup	171	9.8	337

coagulated with rennet, as cheese would be. It is then strained through a fine-mesh fabric, which gives it a yogurt-like consistency. It is somewhat tarter than yogurt.

Nondairy Milks

There are many people who have eliminated milk (and other dairy products) from their diets, including those following a vegan regime, those with lactose intolerance, and those who find that milk gives them respiratory congestion. Luckily, there are numerous nondairy alternatives available. Manufacturers often enrich the nondairy milks with vitamin D and calcium, the key bone-building nutrients found in dairy milk. The amounts differ with the brand, so be sure to check the label.

Almond milk: This beverage is made by soaking crushed almonds in water, then pressing them to extract the nut "milk." Almonds are a good source of vitamin E and also have a bit of calcium. Check the labels to see if other nutrients have been added.

Rice milk: Made from brown rice and often other ingredients to give it thickness. Check the label for additives and nutrients.

Soymilk: See "Soyfoods," page 84.

Coconut milk: Made by steeping shredded coconut meat in water, then pressing it to get out the milk. The first pressing is very high in fat and is often labeled coconut cream. It is not suitable for drinking. Subsequent pressings yield coconut milk that is lower in fat. However, it is not really sold as a substitute for dairy milk and does not have nutrients added.

Hemp milk: High in proteins and essential fatty acids, with some calcium. Check the label for nutrients added.

Homemade nut or seed milk: Any nut or seed can be made into a milk-like beverage. See "Making Nut or Seed Meal, Milk & Butter," page 94. Though the resulting milk will be nutritious and tasty, it won't have the nutrients necessary to bone health.

Storing Milk

Store milk in the refrigerator. Do not freeze milk unless necessary—it may separate and develop an off-flavor. Store milk in opaque containers to protect it from bright light, which causes a loss of B vitamins. Keeping the containers tightly closed will prevent absorption of flavors from other foods in the refrigerator.

Always return milk to the refrigerator immediately after pouring. Exposure to temperatures above 40°F for even a few minutes quickly reduces milk's shelf life. Never return a small portion of unused milk to the original container. Store it separately.

Cooking with Milk

Milk is exceptionally sensitive to heat. When warmed, it coats the bottom of the pan with a type of gel that can easily scorch and leave the milk with a light brownish color and unpleasant, burnt taste. You can avoid scorching milk by heating it over very low heat for a short time. Better yet, heat milk in a double boiler or in a heavy-bottomed saucepan.

Even the most carefully warmed milk usually evaporates a little to form a "skin" on the top. Frequent stirring helps prevent its appearance on delicate white sauces, thick cream soups, and creamy puddings. (Constant stirring keeps those mixtures from lumping, too.) Cover puddings and cream pies with waxed paper as they cool to eliminate this skin that spoils the appearance and texture of silky, rich, chilled desserts.

Curdling often occurs in casseroles and soups made with milk. To avoid this, use a low temperature and wait until just before serving to blend tomatoes, lemon juice, or other acidic foods into dishes that contain milk. Slowly add the acid foods to the milk, rather than the reverse order. You will find that evaporated milk, which is thick and rich, is more stable than homogenized milk when heated and mixed with vegetables and fruits. Salted, cured foods such as ham added to scalloped potatoes can also cause curdling.

SCALDING MILK

Scalding milk was originally used to kill bacteria in unpasteurized milk. Since this is not a problem for most people, the only reasons for scalding will be specific to a recipe. For example, some recipes call for scalding to improve texture or to hasten fermentation.

To scald milk, first rinse a saucepan with cold water to lessen sticking. Then, heat the milk over very low direct heat, or in the top of a double boiler, until tiny bubbles form around the edge of the pan. Do not let the milk boil up. Cool the milk slightly before adding it to other ingredients.

Cooking with Buttermilk

You can use buttermilk in place of sweet milk in baked goods, but you must remember to adjust the recipe to accommodate the acidity of the buttermilk. Add ½ teaspoon of baking soda (which is alkaline) for each cup of buttermilk. Conversely, if a recipe calls for buttermilk and you only have sweet milk, you can sour the milk with a little lemon juice or white vinegar. Place 1 or 2 teaspoons of the acid in a glass measuring cup, and pour milk to come up to the level of the amount called for in the recipe. Let the milk sit at room temperature for about 5 minutes to curdle.

Cooking with Yogurt

Cooking with yogurt can be somewhat tricky. Always heat it over low heat. And to reduce the chance of it separating or curdling, do not add it to hot foods until shortly before they are finished cooking. If lengthy cooking should be required, stabilize the yogurt by stirring in 1 tablespoon of flour, cornstarch, or arrowroot for every 1 quart of yogurt. The thickener will help bind the yogurt's proteins and whey together.

HOMEMADE DAIRY PRODUCTS

The cultures for each of these products are available online or in natural foods stores.

Yogurt

It takes only two ingredients to make yogurt: milk and a starter. Just about any milk—cow, goat, sheep, water buffalo, and even soybean—will produce a tasty yogurt, though the texture and flavor will vary with each. Whole cow's milk (the one most commonly used in the United States) makes a smooth, custardlike, tart yogurt; fat-free milk makes a fairly thin one; and a combination of half milk and half light cream yields a rich, thick, sweet product. Adding ⅓ cup of powdered nonfat milk to 1 quart of fat-free milk will produce a firmer, more nutritious yogurt.

The starter can be a packet of freeze-dried culture (bacteria) that is available in natural foods stores, or yogurt from a previous homemade batch (or commercial yogurt). Though the freeze-dried culture is the most reliable, a reserved tablespoon or two of yogurt will give excellent results most of the time. The specific bacteria that turn milk into yogurt are *Lactobacillus bulgaricus* and *Streptococcus thermophilus*.

If you use a commercial yogurt as a starter, be absolutely certain it contains a live culture. Today, many commercial yogurts have been pasteurized to increase their shelf life, but, unfortunately, the heat treatment inactivates the bacteria. Freshness of the yogurt is also important: Old cultures tend to be weak. Select a yogurt without added gelatins, flavors, or sweeteners. The extras interfere with the growth of the bacteria.

The equipment needed for making yogurt is relatively simple. Use an enameled, stainless steel, or glass vessel for heating the milk, since none of those materials will taint the taste. A glass bowl or jar works best for the incubation period.

To make yogurt, slowly heat 1 quart of milk until it just reaches the boiling point. Do not let it actually boil and foam. (Pasteurize the milk if it is raw. Bacteria in raw milk will interfere with the yogurt culture.) Cool the milk to between 105° and 110°F. At that temperature a drop of milk on your wrist should feel lukewarm, and you should be able to keep your little finger in the milk for a slow count of ten. Stir in one packet of freeze-dried culture, or 1 or 2 tablespoons of yogurt from a previous batch. Incubate the mixture—do not jiggle it during incubation—in a covered container at 105° to 110°F for 5 to 10 hours. (See "Heat Sources for Incubating Yogurt," opposite.) The longer the incubation, the tarter the yogurt.

Chill the thickened yogurt in a covered container at 40°F for at least 12 hours before serving. Yogurt will stay fresh for 4 to 5 days, though it will taste tarter on the fifth day than on the first. If a watery, yellowish liquid (whey) accumulates on the top, drain it off if you like a thick consistency, or stir it in if you prefer a thin one.

Flavorings should be added to yogurt right before serving. If you want to retain a thick yogurt consistency, gently fold instead of stirring. Pureed fruits, homemade preserves, honey, maple syrup vanilla, and cinnamon combine deliciously with yogurt for light desserts and snacks.

Heat Sources for Incubating Yogurt

Insulated picnic cooler: Place filled jars in the cooler and surround them with warm water (105° to 110°F). If possible, the water should be up to the midpoint of the jars. However, too much water will make the cooler unwieldy. Check the temperature every hour and add or subtract water as needed.

Oven: An electric oven set on very low heat will do the job. So will a gas oven with only a pilot light. In both cases use a thermometer, and set the jars in a pot of water to be sure the temperature remains constant.

Warming tray: A thermostatically controlled tray used for keeping food warm works well. A thermometer and a jar of water will help you find the right temperature setting.

Thermos: This is a good method if you are making only 1 quart of yogurt. Pour the inoculated milk into a prewarmed, wide-mouthed thermos, cap it, and let it sit undisturbed.

Electric yogurt maker: Pour the heated, inoculated milk into the jars that come with the unit and follow the manufacturer's directions.

Buttermilk

You can make 1 quart of cultured buttermilk at home by simply adding a packet of freeze-dried culture or ½ cup of buttermilk to fresh fat-free milk. Let the mixture ferment at room temperature for 16 to 18 hours. Store it in the refrigerator as you would fresh milk.

Kefir

To make kefir, scald milk, then let it cool to room temperature. Add the culture and put the mixture in containers to incubate at room temperature for 12 to 24 hours. Successive batches of kefir can be made with small amounts of kefir set aside from each previous batch.

Piima

As for yogurt and kefir, once you have made piima from a freeze-dried culture, you can go on indefinitely, making new batches with a few spoonfuls from a previous batch. To make piima, simply stir the culture into milk at room temperature (about 70°F). Use only milk—piima bacteria grow best when they have no competition. Let the mixture incubate for 8 to 24 hours. The piima will ferment more slowly in a cool room (one below 70°F).

Cheese

Hundreds of types of cheese with individual flavors and textures are made all over the world, and they adapt readily to countless uses, from simple main dishes to salad dressings to creamy rich desserts, not to mention being savored on their own.

Though no two types of cheese are alike, all cheese makers start the cheese-making process in the same way. First, they add a culture (bacteria) or rennet (an enzyme from the lining of a calf's stomach) to coagulate (curdle) the protein in milk. Then they cut or break up the resulting solid (curd) and drain off the liquid (whey). After a brief draining, soft, fresh cheeses such as cottage cheese are ready for eating. Firmer cheeses require additional steps such as pressing and ripening (curing).

The unique flavor and texture of each cheese depend on many factors including: 1) the amount of whey drained and pressed from the curd, 2) the seasonings used, 3) the type of bacteria added during curing, and 4) the ripening conditions—temperature, humidity, and length of time.

Though cheese finds a very welcome place on our tables, its fat content can be a bit of a concern. Likewise, people who are limiting their intake of sodium should avoid certain cheeses. To begin with, milk has a naturally high amount of sodium, and in the cheesemaking process, liberal quantities of salt are often added during curing to flavor, to inhibit unwanted mold growth, and to draw out excess moisture.

Buying Cheese

Specialty shops and well-stocked supermarkets carry a large assortment of imported and domestic cheeses. For top-notch cheese, shop in a market where the turnover is high, select only wrapped cheese kept in chilled cases, and read labels carefully to check contents. Some cheese, however, will also contain ingredients that are not always listed on the label:

Bleaching agents: Benzoyl peroxide is sometimes used to bleach the milk in blue cheese, provolone, Parmesan, and Romano.

Water-binding agents: A gum or gelatin is often used in cream cheese and spreads to help bind moisture to the curd.

Preservatives: Sorbic acid, potassium sorbate, or sodium sorbate is often added to cheese sold in slices to inhibit mold growth.

Determine freshness, too, by sampling cheese whenever possible. In specialty stores where cheese is cut from large wheels and blocks, customers are usually permitted to sample the cheese. Take advantage of the opportunity to be sure the cheese you are considering is of peak quality.

Storing Cheese

Since hard cheese is fairly low in moisture, it stores well for several months. Soft, fresh cheese, on the other hand, has a high moisture content and keeps for only 3 to 5 days.

Before you store cheese in the refrigerator, the

general rule is to wrap it snugly in foil or plastic wrap to keep it from drying out and from picking up unwanted moisture. Blue cheese should be loosely wrapped or placed in a covered container because it keeps best when surrounded by a small amount of air. Always store a strong cheese like Limburger in a tightly closed container; otherwise, the contents of your refrigerator will pick up Limburger's distinctive aroma.

For extended keeping you can seal the cut surfaces of cheese with hot paraffin. An alternative is freezing, but the texture of any cheese that has been frozen tends to be crumbly and either mealy or pebbly. The cheeses most successfully frozen are brick, cheddar, Edam, Gouda, mozzarella, Muenster, Port du Salut, and provolone. Freeze the cheese in 1-inch-thick pieces for no longer than 6 months, and use frozen cheese quickly after thawing.

If cheese becomes hard and dry during storage, all is not lost. Simply grate the cheese and use as a topping for pasta, vegetables, and soups. If mold grows on cheese you are keeping, however, it maybe a matter for concern, since some molds contain dangerous aflatoxins. To be on the safe side, discard any cheese that grows moldy spots.

A GUIDE TO CHEESE

This country now makes just about every type of cheese there is. Sometimes the cheeses are made in the style of a European classic (such as Camembert or Cheddar), and sometimes it's a cheese unique to this country (Maytag blue). And cheese stores are filled with more and more interesting imported cheeses every day. This makes it impossible to do a comprehensive cheese chart. Instead, this chart is organized to give you a sense of the category of cheeses. This way, if you've tasted Cheddar, then chances are you'll have a good idea what another one in the same category will taste like.

As a general guideline to the categories in the chart: unripened cheeses are used primarily for cooking; the soft cheeses are used primarily for serving on their own; the semi-soft, firm, and blue cheeses are used for both cooking and serving; and the hard, grating cheeses are used just for cooking.

CHEESE NAME		DESCRIPTION
UNRIPENED (FRESH)	Boursin	Mild, delicate; like whipped cream cheese; from France
	Cottage cheese	White to creamy white; soft, moist, delicate curds; mild, slightly acidic
	Cream cheese	Smooth, buttery; white; mild, delicate, slightly acidic
	Goat cheese, fresh	White; creamy, mild
	Mozzarella	Slightly firm, plastic; creamy white; delicate; melts easily
	Neufchâtel	Smooth, creamy; white; mild
	Ricotta	Soft, loose, fine-grained curds, moist or dry; white; bland, sweet

A GUIDE TO CHEESE—*CONTINUED*

CHEESE NAME		DESCRIPTION
SOFT	Brie	Creamy yellow interior; brown, edible exterior; mild to pungent
	Brillat-Savarin	Rich, buttery, triple-crème; from France
	Camembert	Soft, almost runny when fully ripe; thin edible crust; creamy yellow interior; mild to pungent
	Chaource	Soft, creamy; thin edible crust; similar to Brie; from France
	Explorateur	Triple-crème cheese; very rich; from France
	Feta	Creamy, smooth; white; tangy, pleasantly salty
	Livarot	Creamy yellow; light orange edible crust; extremely robust; from France
	Robiola	Tan-colored, buttery; mildly pungent; from Italy
	Saint André	Very creamy; triple-crème cheese; similar to Brillat-Savarin; from France
SEMI-SOFT	Bel Paese	Creamy; mild, sweet flavor; creamy yellow interior; gray brown surface; sometimes covered with yellow wax; from Italy
	Brick cheese	Creamy yellow to orange interior; brick shaped; mild to moderately sharp
	Caciocavallo	Firm to hard; light interior; tan surface; flavor similar to provolone; from Italy
	Gouda	Smooth; creamy yellow; usually with red wax coating; mellow, nutlike, sometimes slightly acidic; from Holland
	Havarti	Smooth, creamy; white paraffin coating, deep yellow rind, or rindless; ivory to light yellow interior; mild to tangy; from Denmark
SEMI-SOFT	Limburger	Smooth; creamy white to yellow; highly pungent; from Germany
	Monterey Jack, young	Smooth; creamy white; mild
	Muenster	Smooth; white interior; yellowish tan surface; mellow
	Port du Salut	Smooth, buttery; creamy yellow interior; russet surface; mild to robust; from France
	Provolone	Compact; light, creamy interior; brown or golden yellow surface; mild to sharp
FIRM	Edam	Rubbery; creamy yellow with red wax coating; mellow, nutlike; from Holland
	Fontina	White; mild; good melting cheese
	Gjetost	Very firm; golden; salty caramel flavor; from Norway
	Goat cheese, aged	Crumbly; mold-covered exterior; pungently goat-y
	Manchego, young	White; nutty; tastes like a young Parmesan; from Spain
FIRM (CHEDDAR-STYLE)	Colby	Somewhat open texture; light yellow to orange; mild to mellow
	Caerphilly	Crumbly; white; from Wales
	Cheddar	Fine-grained; white to medium yellow-orange; mild to sharp
	Cheshire	Tan, mild-flavored; from England

A GUIDE TO CHEESE—*CONTINUED*

CHEESE NAME		DESCRIPTION
FIRM (SWISS-STYLE)	Emmentaler	Large holes; mild, nutty flavor; from Switzerland
	Gruyère	Smooth, tiny holed; light yellow; nutlike, salty; melts easily
	Jarlsberg	Irregular holes (eyes); light yellow; forms tears when cut; taste similar to Emmentaler or Gruyère; from Norway
HARD (GRATING)	Asiago	Hard, granular; tiny holes; light yellow; piquant, sharp in aged cheese
	Mimolette	Bright orange; similar to Parmesan; from France
	Monterey Jack, aged	Mild, pleasant grating cheese
	Parmesan	Granular; yellowish white; sharp, distinctive flavor
	Romano	Granular; yellowish white interior; greenish black surface; sharp, piquant
	Sapsago	Light green (clover-like herb added); sharp, pungent; from Switzerland
BLUE	Cabrales	Crumbly; peppered with blue; pungent; from Spain
	Gorgonzola	Creamy white interior, streaked with blue-green mold; light tan exterior; tangy, spicy, rich; from Italy
	Maytag Blue	Crumbly; green-blue veins; pungent
	Roquefort	White, marbled with blue-green mold; sharp, peppery; from France
	Stilton	White interior streaked with blue-green mold; spicy; from England

---

Making Cheese at Home

Tasty soft cheese is easy to make at home. Hard cheese, on the other hand, requires quite a bit of equipment and time. It takes approximately 10 pounds (or about 5 quarts) of milk to make 1 pound of cheese. You also need these seven items:

- earthenware crock, glass baking dish, or stainless steel or enameled pot
- dairy thermometer
- long-handled spoon (preferably made from glass, wood, stainless steel, or enamel)
- spatula or wide knife
- large pan or shallow pot that is larger than your crock
- cheesecloth
- colander

All equipment must be scrupulously clean. Unwanted bacteria will interfere with the curdling process and produce off-flavors and strange textures. Wash the equipment with soapy water and rinse it thoroughly with very hot water.

For more detailed instructions for making your own soft cheese, see "Basic Steps for Making Soft Cheese," on page 64.

To give you a taste of cheesemaking, try "Homemade Cottage Cheese," page 66. It's the perfect cheese for beginners.

BASIC STEPS FOR MAKING SOFT CHEESE

Salt is added to most cheeses after the curds have formed and the whey has been drained off. The amount needed is really a matter of taste, and you can make any of these cheeses with no salt at all if you'd prefer. As a very rough guideline, use a generous ¼ teaspoon for every quart of milk. It's better to undersalt than oversalt, especially for cheeses that get pressed.

STEPS	COTTAGE CHEESE	FARMER CHEESE	SOFT WHITE CHEESE	MOZZARELLA
START WITH BASIC INGREDIENTS	Skim or whole milk	Skim or whole milk	Skim or whole milk	Skim or whole milk
ADD CULTURE	¼ cup yogurt or ½ cup buttermilk per gallon	Same as for cottage cheese	½ cup buttermilk per gallon	½ cup buttermilk per gallon
WARM	Warm to room temperature.	Same as for cottage cheese	Warm to 92–94°F.	Warm to 90°F.
ADD RENNET (¼ TABLET PER GALLON)	Add rennet for milky, large-curd cheese.	Same as for cottage cheese	Add rennet.	Add only ½ rennet solution.
CURD FORMS	Cut curd after 12–36 hours at 72°–85°F.	Same as for cottage cheese	Cut curd after 30 minutes.	Cut curd after 20–30 minutes.
HEAT	Stir 30–45 minutes at 95°–120°F.	Same as for cottage cheese	Stir 30 minutes at 92–94°F.	Stir 15 minutes at 90°F.
DRAIN	Strain through cheesecloth-lined colander; then hang; rinse.	Same as for cottage cheese (becomes pot cheese at this step)	Pour off whey.	Pour off and reserve whey.
PRESS		Wrap in several layers of cheesecloth, press with 1- or 2-pound weight.	Pack into weighted press 2–4 hours.	Pack curds, cut into 3 x 3-inch blocks.
COOL				Bathe in cool water 15 minutes.
REFRIGERATE				Tie in cheesecloth; refrigerate in whey 1–3 days.
REHEAT				Bring curd to room temperature; heat whey to 180°F.
KNEAD				Knead curds in whey until smooth and plastic.
SHAPE				Form small balls; cool quickly in cold water.

*Traditional ricotta is made from whey. It was originally produced in Italy and is still commonly found in many European countries.

**New World ricotta is made from a combination of milk and whey. This type is generally more popular in the United States.

	CREAM CHEESE	NEUFCHÂTEL	MYSOST	TRADITIONAL RICOTTA*	NEW WORLD RICOTTA**
	Whole milk and cream	Whole milk and cream	Whey and ¼ cup cream per quart	Whey (2½ gallons yield 1 pound)	Skim or whole milk plus ¼ cup whey powder per quart
	½ cup buttermilk per gallon				
	Warm to 60–65°F.	Warm to 86°F.	Simmer until thick cream forms.	Heat until cream rises; add 1 cup milk per gallon At 200°F.	Warm to room temperature.
	Add rennet.	Add only ½ rennet solution.		Add 6 tablespoons vinegar per gallon.	Add 2 tablespoons buttermilk or lemon juice or vinegar per quart.
	Custard forms after 12 hours; do not cut.	Custard forms after 18–24 hours; do not cut.		Remove from heat; dip out curds.	Leave undisturbed 24 hours.
			Continue to cook to apple butter consistency.		Heat very slowly to 200°F.
	Strain through cheesecloth-lined colander; then hang overnight.	Pack into molds; drain 12–24 hours.		Strain through cheesecloth-lined colander.	Dip out curds; drain through cheesecloth.
					Knead 10 minutes at room temperature.
					Pack into molds to harden.

HOMEMADE COTTAGE CHEESE

This is the cheese for beginners to try. The time element is a consideration, but it is not "work" time, and it does not require the cook's presence as the mixture sets. Only a minimum of skill is required. After the first batch, most cooks will feel confident about the procedure. This cheese can be made in 16 to 36 hours.

1 gallon fat-free or whole milk
¼ cup yogurt or ½ cup cultured buttermilk

Pour the milk into a very clean, large, stainless steel or enameled pot. Set the pot on a rack inside a larger pot. Fill the outside pot with hot water. Warm on the stove over low heat until the milk reaches 85°F.

Turn off the heat. Stir the yogurt or buttermilk into the milk with a wire whisk. Cover with a towel. Incubate the milk without disturbing it, at a temperature of 72° to 85°F until the milk becomes firm and yogurt-like; this will take between 12 and 36 hours. Temperature may fluctuate during this time but milk may not be jiggled. It's ready when the curd pulls away from the side of the pot and a clear liquid is visible around the edges of pot.

It is now time to separate the whey, a clear liquid, from the curds, which are white and made of coagulated proteins. With a long thin stainless steel knife, cut the curd into squares while still in the pot. Next, hold the knife at a 45-degree angle and slice diagonally through the lines that are already made. These cuts will allow whey to seep out of curds and will facilitate even heating in the next step.

Place fresh hot water in the outside pot, and heat the curds over low heat until they reach 90°F, checking the temperature near the edge of the pot. At no time allow the water in the outside pot to get hotter than 170°F. Slowly stir the curds from the outside edges into the center and bring the curd from the bottom to the top, using a rubber spatula or a large metal spoon. The curds are still soft at this point and easily broken. Continue to raise the temperature of the curds to 120°F, stirring gently every 10 minutes. Do not rush this process: The time needed to raise the temperature to 120°F from room temperature should be regulated to take about 45 minutes.

Hold the curds at 120°F until they feel firm, 10 to 20 minutes longer. When the curds show resistance to being squeezed and feel slightly springy but still a long way from being rubbery, they are ready to drain. The whey will be very clear with a golden tinge. Rinse a cheesecloth and line a colander with it. Gently ladle the curds into the colander. Pour the whey through the curds. Rinse gently with cool water. If water drains too slowly, shift the curds about in the cheesecloth. Rinse again to finish cooling the curds. Tie the ends of the cheesecloth together and hang to drain for another 30 minutes.

At this point, you should add a small amount of salt to the drained curds. Start with 1 teaspoon and mix well. Taste the cheese and add more if you'd like. Or for a very low sodium cheese, do not add any salt at all. Refrigerate. **Makes 4 cups**

VEGETABLES

Vegetables are the edible parts of plants—roots, bulbs, stems, blossoms, seeds, and fruits. Custom and starch content usually dictate when we call something a vegetable. For example, tomatoes, peppers, and eggplant are all technically fruits, but they are served as—and called—vegetables. Peas are actually seeds, but they are prepared and served as a vegetable as well.

When you plan vegetables for a menu, consider your choice in the context of the whole meal. You want flavors, colors, shapes, and textures to balance and enhance the other dishes, not compete with them. Never plan several purees, all white foods, or all highly spiced foods for a single meal. Instead, dramatize monochromatic grain dishes, for example, by serving them with slices of juicy red tomatoes or deep-orange glazed carrots.

Buying Vegetables

Fresh: For top-quality, tasty vegetables at the best price, buy them fresh and in season when the supply is plentiful. If you can, buy directly from a farm producing its own vegetables or a farmer's market. If that is not convenient, shop in a market where the turnover is high. Always buy vegetables as close to the time you plan to eat them as you can, since some (peas and corn, for example) become starchy quickly and others (such as salad greens) wilt rapidly. Look for vegetables that are without defects and are of moderate size. Oversized or undersized ones are rarely a bargain. Fresh vegetables should have a bright color and should be ripe yet feel firm. Seek out organic vegetables to avoid chemical residues that are difficult, or impossible, to remove (see "Removing Waxes & Pesticides," page 68). Even better, grow your own if time and space permit.

Frozen: Select packages of frozen vegetables from a freezer case where the temperature registers 0°F or below. Look to see that the package is clean and firm. Dirty or soggy packages indicate mishandling. Shake the package. The food within should rattle around if the package has remained completely frozen while in storage. If it does not, the food has probably thawed and become refrozen as a solid block. Taste, texture, color, and nutrients suffer each time vegetables thaw and refreeze.

Canned: Canned vegetables should be your last choice, because their texture is not as firm as frozen (or certainly fresh) and they often have added salt. Look for no-salt-added versions for fresher flavor. Never buy rusted, dented, or bulging cans; the contents are suspect and could have dangerous levels of bacteria or toxins.

The quality of canned vegetables is often indicated by these grades:

- **USDA Organic:** Vegetables that are grown according to the United States Department of Agriculture requirement for organic may bear this seal. For more information see "Eating Organic" (page 3).

- **Fancy or U.S. Grade A:** The best-looking vegetables available. This grade may appear on labels.
- **Extra Standard or U.S. Grade B:** Not as nice looking as Grade A. Vegetables with this grade are often unmarked.
- **Standard or U.S. Grade C:** Overmature vegetables that lack uniform shape. This grade is rarely indicated on the label, probably because manufacturers prefer no label to one showing the contents as only standard. (Since nutrients are the same for all three grades, Standard is often a good buy for use in stews and purees.)

Dried: Many dried vegetables are only available as ingredients in instant soups and other processed foods. The significant exceptions to this are legumes (see "Dried Beans, Peas & Lentils," page 81), sun-dried tomatoes (also sold marinated in oil), and dried mushrooms. There are also several companies that make dried vegetables as snacks, and of course camping stores sell just about any type of dried vegetable you can think of. Look for dried vegetables that do not have preservatives added, and in the case of dried mushrooms, look for packages with large pieces rather than small, broken bits.

Storing Vegetables

Keeping vegetables in top condition at home is easy if you follow a few basic rules. Never wash fresh vegetables before storing them, since moisture encourages rot. To maintain crispness, refrigerate most fresh vegetables in the crisper bin or in plastic bags to maintain proper humidity. Store hard-rind winter squashes, sweet potatoes, white potatoes, and dry onions in a cool (45° to 50°F), dry, dark area instead of in the refrigerator. (Don't put onions and potatoes together in a container because onions will pick up moisture from the potatoes and spoil quickly as a result.)

Frozen vegetables should be kept solidly frozen and canned ones stored in a cool, dry area. Use tightly covered containers or plastic bags for dried vegetables and put them in a cool, dry place. Always refrigerate leftover vegetables in covered containers and use them within 2 days.

REMOVING WAXES & PESTICIDES

Waxes: Some vegetables, such as rutabagas and cucumbers, often feel waxy because producers have applied a coating to prevent shriveling from moisture loss. Although these wax coatings have been approved for consumption, you may find them unappealing and feel concern about eating them. The best and most certain way to remove the coatings is to peel off the outer layer of the vegetable.

Pesticides: Although in theory vegetables sprayed with pesticides are harmless when applied correctly, there is absolutely no way for consumers to monitor this for themselves. The best bet is to buy organic produce (although there are unscrupulous growers in this area as well). If in doubt, you can remove some of the surface pesticide residue by scrubbing the produce thoroughly under running water. There is no way, however, to get rid of pesticides that have been absorbed into the flesh beneath the skin of the vegetable or absorbed through a vegetable's root system.

A GUIDE TO VEGETABLES

In this day and age, you can get almost any vegetable you want any time of the year. There are only a very few vegetables that are still available only in season, and they are on the esoteric side: Ramps, fiddlehead ferns, fresh fava beans, and green chickpeas are examples. All other vegetables are available either from other parts of the world (like South America) where growing seasons are the reverse of ours; from states like Florida, Texas, and California that enjoy very long growing seasons; or from hothouse gardens. The fact still remains, however, that the best way to buy vegetables—for price, flavor, and environmental awareness—is locally grown, and during the vegetable's natural peak season.

VEGETABLE		PEAK SEASON	LOOK FOR	STORAGE
ARTICHOKES		April–May	Plump heavy globe; tight fleshy leaves of uniform green color	Refrigerate in plastic bags; will keep 3–4 days.
ASPARAGUS		April–June	Firm, smooth, round spears; closed compact tips; rich green color	Wrap stems in moist toweling. Refrigerate in plastic bags or in covered container; will keep 2–3 days.
BEANS	Fava	June–August	Well filled, tightly closed, long green pods. If sold shelled, beans should be plump and tight-skinned.	Refrigerate in pods; will keep 2–5 days.
	Lima	April–August	Well filled, clean, shiny green pods. The beans within should be grass-green; lighter colored beans will be starchy.	Refrigerate in pods; will keep 2–5 days.
	Snap: green and wax	May–October	Crisp, long, slender pods; velvety feel; seeds less than half grown; should snap when broken. Green beans: bright green. Wax beans: pale yellow.	Refrigerate in plastic bags; will keep 2–5 days.
BEETS: RED, GOLDEN, AND CHIOGGIA		June–October	Smooth, firm, round root with slender tap. Red: rich, deep-red. Golden: brownish red. Chioggia: reddish orange on the outside and striped red and white on the inside.	Cut off tops 2 inches above root; refrigerate in plastic bags; will keep 1–2 weeks.
BOK CHOY		Year-round	Firm, white stems; crisp, dark green leaves	Refrigerate in plastic bags; will keep 3–5 days.

A GUIDE TO VEGETABLES—*CONTINUED*

VEGETABLE		PEAK SEASON	LOOK FOR	STORAGE
BROCCOLI		October–May	Small, closed buds with no trace of yellow; moderate size; firm yet tender stems and branches; dark almost purplish green head	Refrigerate in plastic bags; will keep 3–5 days.
BROCCOLI RABE, BROCCOLINI		October–May	Firm, crisp stems; deep green and crisp leaves	Refrigerate in plastic bags; will keep 3–5 days.
BRUSSELS SPROUTS		October–November	Hard heads with tight-fitting leaves; bright green color	Refrigerate in plastic bags; will keep 2–4 days.
CABBAGE	White (green) and red	Year-round	Hard, tight-leaved, compact head; heavy for size; greenish white or purple-red	Refrigerate in plastic bags; will keep 1–2 weeks.
	Savoy	Year-round	Crumpled leaves; dark green color	Refrigerate in plastic bags; will keep 1–2 weeks.
	Napa	June–November	Elongated, fleshy, white ribs with frilly pale green leaves in a tight head	Refrigerate in plastic bags; will keep 1–2 weeks.
CARROTS		Year-round	Crisp, smooth, tapering roots; yellow to orange red color	Cut off tops; discard. Refrigerate in plastic bags; will keep at least 1–2 weeks.
CAULIFLOWER		September–January	Firm, clean head with compact florets; white to creamy white color; tender green leaves	Refrigerate in plastic bags; will keep 3–5 days.
CELERY		Year-round	Rigid, crisp, tightly packed stalks with good heart formation; glossy surface	Refrigerate in plastic bags; will keep at least 1 week.
CELERY ROOT (CELERIAC)		August–May	Four inches across or less; rough, brownish skin; crisp	Refrigerate in plastic bags; will keep 1 week.
CORN		May–September	Moist, green husks; bright, plump, yellow or white kernels	Refrigerate in husks; will keep 1–2 days. Best when used within 1–2 hours after harvest.
CUCUMBERS		May–July	Tender, dark green skins; crisp and firm; slender	Refrigerate in plastic bags; will keep 3–5 days.
EGGPLANT		August–September	Firm, heavy body; 4–6 inches in diameter; small blossom end scar; rich purple color; shiny, tight, smooth skin	Store in cool place or in refrigerator; put in plastic bag to retain moisture; will keep 2–4 days.

A GUIDE TO VEGETABLES—*CONTINUED*

VEGETABLE		PEAK SEASON	LOOK FOR	STORAGE
FENNEL		October-January	Compact, greenish white bulb; crisp green stalks with green feathery fronds	Refrigerate in perforated plastic bags; will keep 5-7 days.
GARLIC		Year-round	Plump, very firm cloves in a tightly packed head	Keep at room temperature in a well-ventilated spot away from direct sunlight. Will keep for at least 1 month.
GREENS	Cooking: amaranth, beet greens, collards, kale, mustard greens, and turnip greens	Varies	Crisp, tender leaves; bright green color typical of variety; fine veins and stems	Refrigerate in perforated plastic bags; will keep 3-5 days.
	Salad (also see "Popular Salad Greens," page 371)	Year-round	If possible, buy unpackaged greens.	Refrigerate (washed or unwashed) in plastic bags with paper towels to absorb moisture; will keep 2-4 days.
JERUSALEM ARTICHOKE (SUNCHOKE)		October-March	Firm unscarred tuber; tender beige to brown skin	Refrigerate in perforated plastic bags; will keep 2 days.
JICAMA		Year-round	Hard, unblemished root, heavy for its size	Store in a cool, dark place; will keep 1 month.
KOHLRABI (CABBAGE TURNIP)		June-July	Firm, crisp bulbs 2-3 inches in diameter; crisp green tops; light green bulb	Refrigerate. Green tops will keep 2-3 days. Bulbs will keep 1-2 weeks in plastic bags.
LEEKS		May-August	Unwilted, dark-green leaves; firm white bulbs with roots attached	Refrigerate in plastic bags; will keep 3-4 days.
MUSHROOMS	Button and cremini	Year-round	Small to medium, clean, creamy white or light brown caps; pink or light tan gills, if showing; caps closed around stem	Refrigerate in a closed paper bag; will keep 1 week.
	Portobello	Year-round	Firm, smooth tops; fresh gills with no slime	Refrigerate in a closed paper bag; will keep 1 week.
	Shiitake	Year-round	Dry, unblemished caps; fresh looking gills	Refrigerate in a closed paper bag; will keep 1 week.
OKRA		May-October	White or bright green color; pods tender enough to bend under light pressure and less than $4\frac{1}{2}$ inches long	Store in a cool, damp place or refrigerate in perforated plastic bags; will keep 3-4 days.

A GUIDE TO VEGETABLES—*CONTINUED*

VEGETABLE		PEAK SEASON	LOOK FOR	STORAGE
ONIONS	Dry: Bermuda, red, Spanish, white, and yellow	Year-round	Clean, hard, well-shaped globes with dry, papery skins	Store in net bags in a cool, dry, dark place; will keep at least 1 month.
	Sweet	Late spring-early summer	Smooth and firm; no soft spots	Store in a cool, dark place; will keep 2 weeks.
PARSNIPS		October-March	White; smooth, firm, clean, tapered root of small to medium size	Refrigerate in plastic bags; will keep 2 weeks.
PEAS	Edible pod: Sugar snaps, snow peas	May-September	Crisp, slender, bright green pods with immature peas	Refrigerate in plastic bags; will keep 1-2 days. Best when used quickly after harvesting.
	Green	February-July	Crisp, bright green pods filled but not bulging with peas	Refrigerate, uncovered, in pods; will keep 2-4 days. Best when used quickly after harvesting.
PEPPERS	Bell	June-September	Glossy, medium to dark green or red color; relatively heavy; firm walls and sides	Refrigerate in plastic bags; will keep 3-5 days.
	Chili*	June-October	Smooth skin; no soft spots	Refrigerate in plastic bags; will keep 4-7 days.
POTATOES: RUSSET (BAKING) AND BOILING (RED, WHITE, YUKON GOLD)		Year-round	Well-shaped, firm, with no green discoloration under skin	Store in a cool, dry, well-ventilated, dark place; will keep 2 months. Use before they sprout.
RADISHES: BLACK, RED, WHITE (ICICLE), AND DAIKON		April-June	Firm, smooth roots with good color	Refrigerate in plastic bags; will keep 2 weeks.
RUTABAGA (SWEDISH TURNIP)		October-December	Medium size; smooth; heavy for size; thick, yellow to buff skin; few leaf scars	Store in a cool, dry place; will keep several weeks.
SALSIFY (OYSTER PLANT)		October-November	Firm, tapered roots with black or white skin	Refrigerate in plastic bags; will keep 2-3 weeks.

* For information on using chili peppers, see Chilies, page 122.

A GUIDE TO VEGETABLES—*CONTINUED*

VEGETABLE		PEAK SEASON	LOOK FOR	STORAGE
SCALLIONS (GREEN ONIONS)		Year-round	Crisp, bright-green tops; white, tender bulbs with roots attached	Refrigerate in plastic bags; will keep 3–4 days.
SPINACH		April–November	Dark-green, smooth leaves with no slime spots	Refrigerate in perforated plastic bags; will keep 2–4 days.
SQUASHES	Summer: pattypan, yellow, and zucchini	April–August	Firm, glossy, tender skin; fairly heavy for size. Pattypan: 4 inches or less in diameter. Others: slender, 6–8 inches long.	Refrigerate in plastic bags; will keep 3–5 days.
	Winter: acorn, buttercup, butternut, chayote, hubbard, kabocha, pumpkin, and spaghetti	October–February	Hard rind (chayote with soft rind is exception); heavy for size. Acorn, buttercup: dark green rind. Butternut: beige rind. Chayote: pale green rind. Hubbard: bumpy, blue-gray rind. Kabocha: dark green mottled with gray-green. Pumpkin: warm orange rind. Spaghetti: yellow rind.	Store in cool, dry place; will keep several months.
SWEET POTATOES: YELLOW-FLESHED AND ORANGE-FLESHED (YAMS)		September–December	Smooth, well-shaped, firm tubers; medium size	Store in a cool, dry place; will keep 1–2 days.
SWISS CHARD: RUBY, WHITE, YELLOW, AND BRIGHT LIGHTS (MULTI-COLORED)		June–November	Blemish-free leaves, with brightly colored veins and crisp ribs; ruby-red to yellow to white	Refrigerate wrapped in paper towels in a plastic bag; will keep 3–5 days.
TOMATILLOS		July–October	Shiny green fruit with papery husk firmly attached	Store in a paper bag in the refrigerator; will keep 1 month.
TOMATOES		May–September	Firm, plump bodies with uniform red, yellow, or orange color; small blossom end scar; shape varies with type	Keep unripe tomatoes at room temperature but not in sun. Refrigerate when ripe; will keep 1 week.
TURNIPS		October–March	Small to medium size, 2–3 inches in diameter; round shape with flat top; uniformly tender white skin with purple tinge; heavy for size; few leaf scars or roots	Refrigerate in plastic bags; will keep at least 1 week.

GROWING YOUR OWN SPROUTS

There is a lot of controversy swirling around the safety of sprouted vegetables in the marketplace. Commercial sprouts seem to be especially vulnerable to foodborne pathogens, either through growers using polluted water or through mishandling in the food delivery system. This is a shame, because sprouts are not only a refreshing and crisp addition to salads and sandwiches, but they are a significant source of nutrients. So, it makes perfect sense to learn how to make them at home. It doesn't take a lot of skill, just time. The key, however, is in locating a reliable source of organic seeds to sprout.

Growing sprouts in your kitchen is almost like growing vegetables in your yard, but without all the work. They are vegetables that can be grown and harvested at any time of the year and added to your diet in many novel ways. Most sprouts require no cooking, and those that do are ready after only a few minutes of stir-frying. You can add them to soups, breads, and main dishes, or eat them as is in salads or on sandwiches. Once you learn how simple it is to unlock the tremendous store of good nutrients that lie dormant in every seed (nuts, grains, and legumes are all seeds), you can enjoy fresh produce in every season.

Home-grown sprouts develop rapidly and are among the most economical foods available. Just 1 cup of mung beans will yield about 4 cups of sprouts in 3 to 5 days. Three tablespoons of alfalfa seeds will give you 4 cups of sprouts.

Sprouts actually are seeds that have begun to germinate. Soaking the seed activates the life forces packed away for its growth. Feeding itself on the starch surrounding its embryo, the seed can grow for several days without acquiring nutrients from soil, increasing its own protein and vitamin value in the process. Sprouting generates significant increases in beta-carotene and vitamins B, C, and E, as well as amino acids.

What to Sprout

Not all seeds and beans yield edible or palatable sprouts. Potato sprouts are considered poisonous. The sprouts of fava beans and lima beans require so much cooking to deactivate a potentially toxic substance that they become mushy and unpleasant by the time they are safe to eat. Many spice and herb seeds—coriander and pepper, for example—will sprout well, but the sprouts are unpalatable. However, seeds, grains, and legumes that can be successfully sprouted still present an impressive choice (see "A Guide to Sprouting Seeds," page 76). Mung beans and alfalfa are the most popular, perhaps because they are the easiest to sprout. Wheat sprouts are nutty and sweet; radish sprouts have a crisp, tangy taste. Rye sprouts taste a lot like wild rice. And broccoli sprouts are absolute powerhouses of substances with possible anticancer benefits.

How to Sprout

Sprouting is very simple, even for beginners. All you need are seeds, a jar, a piece of cheesecloth, a rubber band, and clean water. Just about any container will work, but avoid those made of wood or metal, because wood absorbs moisture and may grow mold or mildew and some metals may give sprouts an off-taste.

Many natural foods stores stock seeds and sprouting equipment as well. You may also want to check online sources if you intend to keep a variety of seeds sprouting. Buy only organic seeds. As you measure the seeds, wash them thoroughly, removing any chaff or broken or cracked seeds.

1. To begin the sprouting process, soak the seeds in a 1-quart jar filled with warm water (70° to 80°F) at a ratio of 1 part

seeds to 4 parts water. Seeds should be soaked for 8 to 12 hours, with small seeds taking a little less time and beans a little longer. Put the soaking seeds in a dark, warm place.

2. Drain the soaked seeds and rinse in a strainer or colander; return to the jar. Stretch a piece of cheesecloth over the top of the jar and secure it in place with a rubber band. Return the jar of seeds to the same dark, warm place as before, resting it on its side, slightly tilted toward the mouth end so excess moisture will drain through the cheesecloth.

3. Sprouts should be rinsed at least twice a day, but they will thrive even better with more rinsings. The rinsing feeds them with water and washes away the by-products of growth that encourage spoilage. No need to remove the cheesecloth; just fill the jar with water, swish around briskly, then drain thoroughly. Any water left in the jar can cause mold.

Harvesting

The sprouts can be harvested in 1 to 6 days, depending on the type of seed. Some seeds, especially grains and beans, are ready to be used within 24 hours, or as soon as a sprout appears. Others may take up to 6 days. Timing is important. Sprouts left too long will grow roots, lose their flavor, and become bitter. Vitamins and minerals are also diminished in sprouts that are allowed to become too old. As a rule, sprouts should go no longer than 5 or 6 days.

Sprouts may benefit from a few hours of direct sunlight before harvesting. It enables the sprouts to produce additional chlorophyll, thus increasing their nutritional value and coloring them a pleasant green.

Sprouting Combinations

Once you discover how easily sprouts grow, you may want to experiment with combinations of sprouts. Alfalfa and mung beans grow quite well together in the same jar, the alfalfa growing in the large spaces between the mung bean sprouts. Try sprouting a mixture of sunflower, alfalfa, lentil, fenugreek, and mung bean. It is also a good idea to have at least three jars of sprouts growing at once—a bean, a grain, and a small seed—because their protein patterns complement each other when they are used in the same meal.

Storage

Sprouts are best when used as soon as they are harvested. If you choose to store sprouts, place them loosely in a covered plastic or glass container, with a folded paper towel in the bottom of the container to absorb any remaining moisture. Do not use plastic bags, as tender shoots are easily crushed or broken in nonrigid containers and the sprouts will quickly spoil. Store them in the coldest part of the refrigerator for no more than 2 or 3 days. Some sprouts continue to grow even under refrigeration.

Leftover Sprouts

If you find that you are growing sprouts faster than you can consume them and they are accumulating, freezing them is not the answer—the shoots become soggy and limp when thawed. However, an oversupply of sprouts can be dried quickly in a warm oven (about 250°F for 45 minutes) without losing many nutrients. Then you can process the dried sprouts into powder in a food processor and store the powder in airtight jars. Use it as a nutritional supplement to regular flour in baking. Sprouted dried beans—chickpeas or soybeans—can be chopped or ground and used to replace nuts in recipes.

A GUIDE TO SPROUTING SEEDS

SEED	RINSES (PER DAY)	LENGTH OF SPROUTS AT HARVEST	SPROUT TIME (DAYS)	APPROXIMATE YIELD (SEEDS= SPROUTS)	COMMENTS
ALFALFA	2	1-2 inches	3-5	3 tablespoons = 4 cups	Easy to sprout. Pleasant, light taste.
ALMOND	2-3	¼ inch	3-5	1 cup = 1½ cups	Similar to unsprouted nuts; crunchy, nutty flavor
AMARANTH	3	¼ inch	2-3	3 tablespoons = 1 cup	Mild taste
ANISE	6	1 inch	2	3 tablespoons = 1 cup	Strong, anise flavor; good if used sparingly
BARLEY	2-3	Sprout is length of seed.	3-4	½ cup = 1 cup	Chewy texture, pleasant taste, not sweet; toasting enhances flavor
BEANS (ALL KINDS EXCEPT THOSE LISTED INDIVIDUALLY)	3-4	1 inch	3-5	1 cup = 4 cups	For tender sprouts, limit germination time to 3 days.
BUCKWHEAT	1	¼-½ inch	2-3	1 cup = 3 cups	Easy to sprout. Buy raw, hulled groats for sprouting.
CHIA	1	¼ inch	1-4	2 tablespoons = 3-4 cups	Hard to sprout. Tend to become gelatinous when wet. Sprinkle rather than rinse. Strong flavor.
CHICKPEA	4	½ inch	3	1 cup = 3 cups	Best lightly cooked
CORN	2-3	½ inch	2-3	1 cup = 2 cups	Sweet corn taste, with chewy texture. Difficult to find untreated kernels for sprouting.
CRESS	2	1-1½ inches	3-5	1 tablespoon = 1½ cups	Gelatinous seed; strong, peppery taste
FENUGREEK	1-2	1-3 inches	3-5	¼ cup = 1 cup	Spicy taste, good in curry dishes; bitter if sprouted too long
FLAX	2-3	1-2 inches	4	2 tablespoons = 1½-2 cups	Tend to become gelatinous when wet. Sprinkle rather than rinse. Mild flavor.
LENTIL	2-4	¼-1 inch	3	1 cup = 6 cups	Chewy bean texture; can be eaten raw or steamed lightly

A GUIDE TO SPROUTING SEEDS—*CONTINUED*

SEED	RINSES (PER DAY)	LENGTH OF SPROUTS AT HARVEST	SPROUT TIME (DAYS)	APPROXIMATE YIELD (SEEDS= SPROUTS)	COMMENTS
MILLET	2-3	¼ inch	3-4	1 cup = 2 cups	Similar to barley sprouts
MUNG BEAN	3-4	1½-2 inches	3-5	1 cup = 4-5 cups	Easy to sprout. Popular in oriental dishes. Sprouts begin to lose crispness after 4 days of storage.
MUSTARD	2	1-1½ inches	3-4	2 tablespoons = 3 cups	Spicy, tangy taste, reminiscent of fresh English mustard
OAT	1	Sprout is length of seed.	3-4	1 cup = 2 cups	Only unhulled oats will sprout. Water sparingly; too much water makes sprouts sour.
PEA	2-3	Sprout is length of seed.	3	1½ cups = 2 cups	Taste like fresh peas; best when steamed lightly
PUMPKIN	2-3	¼ inch	3	1 cup = 2 cups	Hulled seeds make best sprouts. Light toasting improves flavor
RADISH	2	⅛-2 inches	2-6	1 tablespoon = 1 cup	Taste like the vegetable
RICE	2-3	Sprout is length of seed.	3-4	1 cup = 2½ cups	Similar to other sprouted grains. Only whole grain brown rice will sprout.
RYE	2-3	Sprout is length of seed.	3-4	1 cup = 3½ cups	Easy to sprout. Very sweet taste, with crunchy texture.
SESAME	4	Sprout is length of seed.	3-4	1 cup = 3½ cups	Only unhulled seeds will sprout. Delicious flavor when young; sprouts over 1/16 inch turn bitter.
SOYBEAN	4-6	1-2 inches	4-6	1 cup = 4-5 cups	Need frequent, thorough rinses. Should be cooked before eating for optimum protein availability.
SUNFLOWER	2	Sprout is no longer than seed	1-3	½ cup = 1½ cups	Good snacks, especially if lightly roasted; bitter if grown too long.
TRITICALE	2-3	Sprout is length of seed.	2-3	1 cup = 2 cups	Similar to wheat sprouts
WHEAT	2-3	Sprout is length of seed.	2-4	1 cup = 3½-4 cups	Easy to sprout. Very sweet taste.

Sea Vegetables

The cultures of Asia have long honored sea vegetables as a source of delicious, readily available nourishment. Cooks there commonly use them to enfold rice or fish, flavor soup, or accompany other vegetables. But sea vegetables are not confined to the cuisines of China and Japan. They appear in the native diets of regions throughout the world where they are easily harvested right from the ocean. The beautiful purple seaweed Porphyra (also called nori, laver, or amanori) grows as abundantly off the rocky European shores as it does off the Japanese coast. The Welsh make a bread out of seaweed, and the English, Irish, and French all make use of its gelatinous quality for cooking.

The nutritional contents of seaweed, including a small amount of protein, enhances its value as a food source. Although sea vegetables have some vitamins, in varying proportions, thier greatest nutritional attribute is their minerals. They usually contain iodine in abundance and have traces of many other minerals, including the interdependent elements calcium, phosphorus, and magnesium.

Popular Types of Sea Vegetables

The bulk of the edible sea vegetables sold commercially in the United States comes from Japan. They are packaged in dried form and sold under Japanese names—nori, kombu, hijiki, wakame, arame. Once you have some experience with the different sea vegetables, their broad differences in taste will soon become apparent. Though the flavors vary considerably, you can successfully substitute one type of seaweed for another in most recipes.

Nori: Grows at the water's edge as a long, thin leaf and tastes like briny corn when fresh. Dried sheets of nori are used in making sushi.

Kombu: Like nori, used as a wrapping for other foods—rice, tofu, vegetables, meat, and seafood. Kombu has a briny, mushroom-like flavor.

Hijiki: A feathery seaweed with a mild, almost beany flavor that blends well with sharper-tasting foods; often served alone with a sprinkling of vinegar or lemon juice

Wakame: Somewhat akin to leafy land vegetables; makes a tasty cold salad. Its nutritional goodness includes a good dose of calcium.

Arame: Closely related to wakame and often used in the same way

Dulse: The most prolific of edible American seaweeds, its thin fronds resemble a waving hand. When freshened (reconstituted from the dried state by soaking in water), it is often used as one would use spinach.

Kelp: Flourishes on the Pacific coast and is the seaweed most revered by nutritionists—due largely to its abundant stores of calcium and iodine. Its high sodium content, however, warrants its use in moderation. Granular kelp can improve the nutritional value of soups, sauces, and spreads, as well as thickening and flavoring. Kelp powder is most often used as an alternative

NUTRIENTS IN SOME COMMON SEA VEGETABLES

SEA VEGETABLE DRIED (3½ OUNCES)	ARAME	DULSE	HIJIKI	KELP	KOMBU	NORI (LAVER)	WAKAME
CALORIES	235	—	173	—	219	235	276
PROTEIN (G)	6.0	20	4.5	—	5.6	22.2	12.7
FAT (G)	0.1	3.2	0.8	1.1	1.0	1.1	1.5
CALCIUM (MG)	1,170	296	1,400	1,093	955	434	1,300
PHOSPHORUS (MG)	150	267	56	240	199	350	260
IRON (MG)	12	150	29	—	11.2	28.3	—
SODIUM (MG)	—	2,100	—	3,007	2,500	1,294	1,100
POTASSIUM (MG)	—	8,060	—	5,273	—	3,503	—
RIBOFLAVIN (B_2) (MG)	0.20	0.50	0.02	—	0.26	1.34	0.02

to table salt. If you decide to use it in this way, use about half as much kelp as you would table salt.

Sea Gelatin

Agar and Irish moss are two sea vegetables famed for their jelling qualities. The use of agar as a jelly in Japan dates back to the 16th century. Kanten, agar, and agar-agar are names used interchangeably for this natural gelatin.

Irish moss, or sea moss, yields the extract carrageenan, named after the Irish town Carragheen. Irish moss is used interchangeably with agar, but unlike agar, it will not gel and retain its firmness without refrigeration. Like the other sea vegetables, agar and Irish moss add nutrition to food as well as bulk that appeases the appetite, yet they contain fewer calories than does animal gelatin.

A GUIDE TO SEA VEGETABLES

SEA VEGETABLE	PRIMARY SOURCES	APPEARANCE (DRIED FORM)	PREPARATION	MOST COMMON USES
ARAME	Southern coastal regions of Japan	Charcoal black, wavy fronds	Soak in water 3–5 minutes.	Curries, salads, sauces, soups, tomato dishes
DULSE	Atlantic and Pacific coastal waters	Thin, glove-shaped fronds	Soak in water 5–7 minutes.	Relishes, salad dressings, salads, sandwiches; grain, meat, vegetable casseroles
HIJIKI	Rocky, low waters of northern and southern coasts of Japan	Short, thin, curling strands; blackish color	Soak in water 12–15 minutes.	Garnishes; salads, soups, stews, stuffings, wok-cooked vegetables
KELP	Pacific coast from Mexico to Canada	Powdered, granular, or tablet form	Use as is.	Seasoning for grain casseroles, salads, sauces, soups, spreads, meats, vegetables
KOMBU	Pacific coastal waters	Strands or wide, flat sheets	Soak in warm water 7–10 minutes.	Condiment for fish, meat, poultry, rice dishes; stuffed with cheese, grains, vegetables; toasted
NORI (LAVER)	Rocky coastal waters of southernmost islands of Japan and both coasts of United States	Ruffled, fan-shaped, thin, parchment-like sheets	Use as is, or crisp dried sheets by holding over stove burner for a few seconds or by placing in a 250°F oven for 2–3 minutes.	Cold salads; cooked with meat, rice; layered casseroles; wrapping for sushi
WAKAME	Waters near southernmost islands of Japan	Olive green to brownish strands	Soak in water 2–3 minutes.	Bean stews, leafy salads, meats, miso, soup stock, rice, vegetable dishes

Dried Beans, Peas & Lentils

In spite of their centuries-old reputation as poor man's food, the stunning variety of textures and flavors among beans, peas, and lentils ensures that everybody will have a few favorites. And for vegetarians, legumes (which is the category these vegetables fall into) are a vital staple. Legumes also star in dishes favored by those anxious to limit their meat intake for health reasons.

By themselves, legumes have most of meat's protein values, but not all—a lack easily remedied by serving them with grains or dairy foods. And although they are high in carbohydrates, their value as a protein source offsets the concern; in addition, a 4-ounce serving of cooked beans contains only 135 calories and just a minuscule amount of fat. In fact, they are an ideal food for weight control because their complex carbohydrates are very satisfying and make you feel full longer.

Add low cost to the many other attractions of legumes. They provide more protein for the money than do many other foods. Easily grown, dried, and stored, beans, peas, and lentils are a versatile resource that provides new opportunities to stretch a tight budget, enhance the family's nutrition, and break away from monotonous menus. Their popularity is well deserved.

Legumes dominate the cuisine of many cultures that consider meat a luxury. The result is a legacy of imaginative savory dishes—Mexican *frijoles refritos*, Italian *pasta e fagioli*, and Indian *dal*, to name a few.

The legume family is a colorful and varied clan that can add depth and zest to both main courses and side dishes. Crunchy, nutlike chickpeas (garbanzos), meaty kidney beans, peppery French lentils, and grainy split peas—they and their cousins all promise eating pleasure. And they are most accommodating, mixing well as a part of or as an accompaniment to many dishes.

Buying Beans

American supermarket shelves only hint at the variety of legumes that are commonly available in other countries. Split peas, lentils, and several of the more common varieties of beans are usually displayed in our markets. However, if an Indian or Hispanic community is nearby, demand requires that the choice be more varied.

If you cannot find the type of bean you want where you usually shop, check out ethnic groceries or other specialty sources—gourmet stores, food co-ops, natural foods stores, and online stores.

Whether buying the 1-pound bags of supermarket beans or loose beans in bulk, check the color and the size. Beans, peas, and lentils should have a fairly clear uniform color. A faded look suggests too-long storage. The size of the beans in the package should be uniform; mixed sizes will result in uneven cooking. Look for any visible defects. Cracked or shriveled seed coats,

BEAN FLOUR

Any type of bean, pea, or lentil can be ground into a flour. Many cuisines use these flours as a thickener in dishes, or to make bread or a side dish (similar to polenta). You can also cook up a bean flour with seasonings to make an almost instant bean dip, or use it to give a nutrition boost to baked goods (for every cup of regular flour called for in a recipe, omit 2 to 3 tablespoons and substitute with 2 to 3 tablespoons of bean flour). In most natural foods stores you'll find chickpea flour, fava bean flour, and chickpea-fava blend. In specialty stores, you'll find almost any bean flour you can think of. Making your own is easy, though, if you have a powerful food processor or are willing to grind small batches in a spice grinder.

---

foreign material, and pinholes caused by insects are signs of low quality.

Storing Beans

Store uncooked dried beans in tightly covered glass jars. In a cool dry place, they will keep for months. Adding a couple of bay leaves to each container discourages insects and other unwanted creatures.

Mini-Guide to Dried Beans

There are so many beans available these days, especially with the renewed interest in heirloom varieties, that this is just a short list of some of the more popular types:

Adzuki beans: Small, dark red beans with a thin white line along the ridge; in addition to savory side dishes, this little bean is used to make Asian red bean ice cream

Anasazi and appaloosa beans: Heirloom varieties shaped like kidney beans with red and cream splotches

Black beans (turtle beans): Small matte black beans with an earthy flavor; higher in antioxidants than other beans because of the dark pigments in their skin

Canary beans: Similar in size to cannellini, with less of a kidney shape and a more yellow color

Cannellini (white kidney beans): Mild and smooth-textured; also called *fagioli* in Italian and *haricots blancs* in French

Cranberry beans: Similar in shape to red kidney beans but streaked white and cranberry red; often available fresh

Fava beans: Large brown beans available whole, or skinned and split; also available fresh in season

Flageolets: Small white or greenish-white kidney beans famous for their role in the French dish cassoulet

Great Northern: Large white beans commonly used to make baked beans

Greek elephant beans (gigantes): Very large, flat white beans; extremely meaty tasting

Lima beans: Flat creamy white to greenish-white beans; also available fresh or frozen

Mung beans: Very small matte green beans most often used for sprouting, but cooked as well; they need no presoaking before cooking

Navy beans: Small white beans; used in commercial pork and beans

Pinto or pink beans: Pale pink, with streaks; common in Southwestern and Mexican dishes

Red beans: Small and dark red, these are the beans used in the classic Louisiana dish red beans and rice

Red kidney beans: Firm, meaty, red-skinned beans; the most common bean used in American chilis

Soybeans: These enormously important beans get a separate discussion; see page 84.

Mini-Guide to Dried Peas & Lentils

Whether a legume is called a pea or a bean is simply a matter of usage, though what we call peas all tend to be spherical. Lentils, on the other hand, are in a class of legume defined by their botanical attributes.

Beluga lentils: Tiny black lentils named for their resemblance to fish roe

Black-eyed peas: Small, cream-colored peas with a black spot (the eye) on one side; famous in the Southern New Year's dish Hoppin' John; also available fresh and frozen

Chickpeas (garbanzos): Very meaty tasting; used extensively in many cuisines, notably Indian and Italian; available fresh in the spring

French (du Puy) lentils: Small black-green lentils with a peppery flavor

Green lentils: The common supermarket lentil; the name is confusing because the lentils are actually brown in color

Green split peas: Green peas that have been skinned, dried, and halved

Green whole peas: Dried but left whole and unskinned; take longer to cook than split peas but have more fiber

Pardina lentils: Small gray-brown lentils that hold their shape when cooked

Pigeon peas (gunga peas): Yellowish-gray and the size of a green pea; used extensively in Caribbean dishes

Red lentils: Small and salmon-colored; most often sold skinned and split, making them very fast-cooking

Yellow split peas: A yellow variety of peas; skinned, dried, and halved

Soyfoods

Entire books have been devoted exclusively to the soybean and its many derivatives. Soybeans and soyfoods (soybean products) are a familiar part of the culinary scene in Asian cultures and have been for many centuries. Today, they have a much wider appeal. The following list of soy products commonly used today suggests the scope of the soybean world. Most of these products can be found in natural foods stores, co-ops, and many supermarkets. Some, such as tofu and soymilk, can be made right in your kitchen (page 86).

Soybeans

These round tan or black beans have the distinction of being the only vegetable that is a source of complete protein, for which reason they are a staple of many cuisines. Dried soybeans can be purchased year-round and are prepared for eating in the same way as other dried beans (see "A Guide to Cooking Dried Beans, Peas & Lentils," page 443). Fresh green soybeans, called edamame, are available in the freezer department of most supermarkets where they can be found either in the pod or shelled.

Tofu

Tofu is one of the most versatile soyfoods. Because its own flavor is on the bland side, it blends readily with strong-flavored foods and with any kind of seasoning. Tofu may even be whipped in the blender to make a base for mayonnaise, dips, and salad dressings. It can also be used in sweet dishes, such as cheesecake and other desserts. Refridgerate the tofu in water to cover, and in a tightly covered container.

Firm tofu: This is the Chinese-style of tofu and is best for use in recipes where you would like the tofu to keep its shape.

Extra-firm tofu: More water has been squeezed out of this, and it's quite sturdy.

Soft tofu: Soft tofu, preferred in Japanese cuisine, may be specified for use in recipes where its high water content and soft texture make it easily blended or creamed.

Silken tofu: This is Japanese tofu that has been strained to be extra smooth; it comes in varying degrees of firmness.

Light tofu: Any of the tofus can generally also be found in a reduced-fat version.

Soymilk

This milk, prepared from soybeans, can be a substitute for cow's milk in many recipes or it can be used as a beverage on its own. Those who have allergies to other milks find soymilk a particularly valuable resource. Many commercial soymilks are thickened with natural thickeners (like seaweed) to give the milk some heft.

You can buy it in any supermarket in a number of forms: flavored (and sweetened), plain, light (reduced-fat), organic, enriched (with calcium and vitamins), or with added omega-3s.

Soymilk is also used to make a number of dairy-product alternatives, including yogurt, cream cheese, and cheese.

Miso

A mixture of soybeans, grain (either rice or barley), salt, water, and a starter, miso is a fermented seasoning that takes 2 months to 3 years to make. It has the consistency of peanut butter and is used as a condiment, soup starter, or spread. It comes in a range of colors—white (shiro), red (aka), and brown (hatcho). The darker colored misos are the most aged and have the most pungency. Misos should be refrigerated after opening.

Soy Sauce

Brewed from soybeans, this rich-flavored seasoning adds a meatlike taste to many dishes. There are numerous styles of soy sauce, including tamari, Chinese dark, and Chinese light. All are relatively high in sodium and are best added to foods in small amounts. Lower-sodium soy sauce has relatively less sodium, but should still be used sparingly. Most soy sauces include wheat in their formulations, but tamari (meaning "liquid drip") is a Japanese fermented soy sauce that does not. Note, however, that most soy sauces labeled tamari in this country are actually Chinese-style soy sauces and *do* have wheat: Be sure to read the label if wheat concerns you.

TSP & Meat Analogs

Protein extracted from soybeans is used to make a whole host of meat substitutes. Many of them are flavored to taste just like their meat counterpart (hot dogs, for example); be sure to read the labels to see if you have any objection to the flavorings that have been added.

TSP (TVP): Texturized soy protein (also called texturized vegetable protein) is made from defatted soy flour. When reconstituted, it resembles cooked ground meat. It's a great source of fat-free protein and can be used in many of the same situations in which you would use ground meat.

Soy crumbles: This is TSP that has been commercially flavored and reconstituted so you just need to break open the package and add it to your dish. As with any flavored soy product, check the label to see what is in it.

Other Soyfoods

Soy flakes: Whole soybeans are toasted for about 30 seconds, then flaked in a roller mill to make this product. The flakes have all the qualities of whole soybeans with the advantage of being easier and faster to cook.

Soy flour: See "Flours," page 104.

Soy grits: These are coarsely ground soybeans. (Sometimes the oil is removed for even quicker cooking.) They differ from soy flakes in that they are neither cooked nor treated with heat, but simply mechanically ground. Grits can be cooked with rice pilaf or added to any grain dish. They also add a nutritional boost to baked foods.

Tempeh: This Indonesian soyfood is made by inoculating cooked soybeans with a special culture and then incubating them for 24 hours. The result is a fragrant, firm, white cake with a chewy texture and mild, meaty flavor. Tempeh can be fried, baked, broiled, or simmered. It works well as a burger, or in tempura, soups, and casseroles.

Okara: This by-product of making soymilk and/or tofu is a granular mixture with a bland flavor and coarse texture, but it has some protein and a significant amount of fiber. Add it to ground meat dishes as an extender. Okara should be heated thoroughly before being used, to eliminate the beany flavor.

HOMEMADE TOFU

This recipe will yield enough soymilk to make 1 pound of tofu—fine for a first try, but time-consuming considering the modest-size brick you get for your effort. After you have made it once, if you like the results, double or triple the recipe. It all depends on how much tofu you eat.

1 cup dried soybeans

2¼ teaspoons Epsom salt, dissolved in 1 cup water

Soak the soybeans overnight in water to cover by at least 2 inches. Drain the beans. In a food processor, puree 1 cup soaked beans and 1½ cups water. Transfer the puree to a large heavy-bottomed pot. Repeat with the remaining soaked beans.

Add 4½ cups of water to the pot. Bring to a slow rolling boil, stirring frequently to minimize sticking. After it has reached the boiling point (when foam suddenly rises, threatening to overflow), reduce the temperature and simmer for 15 minutes.

Line a colander with cheesecloth and set in a large bowl. Ladle the mixture into the colander. Pull the cheesecloth up and over the residue (called okara) to form a bag and squeeze to get out as much soymilk as possible. Lift the cheesecloth bag out of the colander, place it in a separate container full of cold water, and swirl it through the water. Return the cheesecloth bag to the colander and again squeeze out more soymilk. Open the cheesecloth, pour 2 cups of water through the okara, again squeezing and pressing to get more soymilk into the bowl.

Pour the soymilk into a 4-quart saucepan. Bring to a boil and remove from the heat. Add ⅓ cup of the Epsom salt solution, stirring well. Wait for the milk to settle, then sprinkle another ⅓ cup of the solution over it and stir gently. Cover and let stand for 7 to 8 minutes. Gently sprinkle the remaining solution over the milk, cover, and again let the soymilk stand, this time for about 4 minutes. Gently stir just the top 2 or 3 inches of the mixture as the curdled soymilk gathers together into soft curds. The yellow, clear liquid left between the curds is the whey.

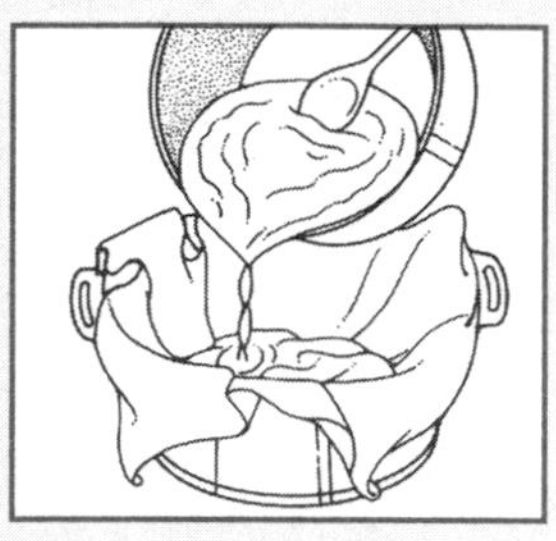

Line a colander or tofu forming box (sold in some natural foods stores) with a quadrupled layer of cheesecloth. Place the colander or forming box over a large bowl or pan, and gently ladle the curds and whey into the cheesecloth. The whey will slowly drain out. (Save this whey, as it is a good soup or sauce stock, high in protein and B vitamins.)

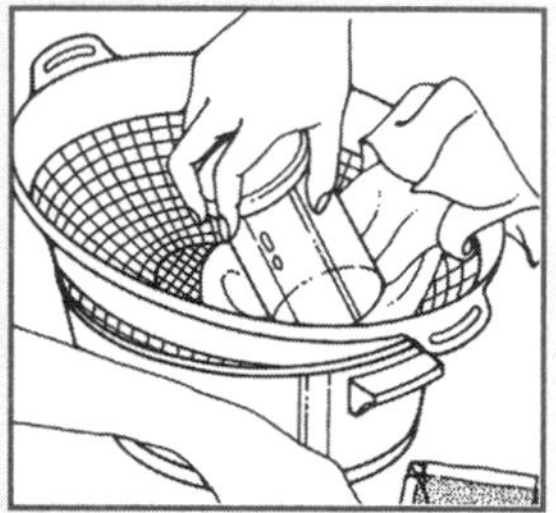

Fold the cloth over the top of the drained curds and place a flat object weighing 3 to 5 pounds (such as a water-filled jar) on top of the wrapped curds. Try to distribute the weight as evenly as possible over the draining curds. Whey will continue to drip out under the pressure, allowing the curds to solidify into a block of tofu. The more whey that is allowed to drain out, the firmer your tofu will be. Depending on how much weight you use, a usable block of tofu will form in 1½ to 2 hours. When the tofu has cooled well, unwrap it. Tofu may be covered with water in a well-sealed container and stored in the refrigerator for a week, or slightly longer if you change the water occasionally. **Makes about 1 pound**

FRUITS

Fruit is nature's fast food: Grab a piece of fresh fruit and eat it while you're on your way somewhere; keep a stash of dried fruit at your desk for snacks; slice fresh fruit to have on top of cereal or stirred into yogurt; or put it into a blender or a juicer to make a naturally sweet drink.

And that's just the beginning: Fruit pairs beautifully with savory dishes, from chicken to shrimp, grains to vegetables, ham to lamb. And if you dress fruit up just a little more, you have a vast array of breads, pastries, cakes, cookies, pies, and dozens of other desserts . . . not to mention preserves, jams, and jellies (see "Jams & Jellies," page 649). It's hard to imagine a well-stocked kitchen without fruit in some form.

The bonus with fruits—and it's no small bonus—is that many of them contain substantial amounts of heart-healthy fiber as well as some of the most powerful antioxidants found in any food (see "Antioxidants in Food," page 7). So, here you have a food that tastes delicious *and* is good for you? Not bad.

Buying Fruit

Fresh: Fruit that is at the peak of its local growing season (see "Choosing & Storing Fresh Fruit," page 89) boasts the highest quality and often the most reasonable price. Look for firm, plump fruit with bright, full colors and no dark, soft, bruised areas or other signs of aging or decay. A fruit that feels heavy for its size is often the juiciest. But be wary of oversize specimens; they can be fibrous and pithy. Look for fruit that is just ripe. Refrigerated, ripe fruit will keep for several days, whereas unripe fruit may never ripen and, of course, overripe fruit spoils rapidly. Since ripe fruit does deteriorate quickly, buy only the quantity you can use within a few days.

Purchase fresh fruit directly from the grower whenever you can. A pick-your-own operation is the best buy, where you can select the choicest fruit and pick it yourself. What could be fresher? Otherwise, shop in a market that has a fast turnover of fresh produce that is displayed in chilled cases, or at least not in direct sunlight.

Frozen: Frozen fruit has most of the flavor and all of the nutrients of fresh fruit but usually lacks optimum texture. However, it is a great option for making baked fruit desserts or sauces off-season. Be sure to buy unsweetened fruit. Choose packages whose pieces of fruit rattle around inside. If the pieces are not loose, they have probably thawed and refrozen into a solid block. Each time thawing and refreezing take place, ice crystals form, breaking down some of the fruit's cell walls. Eventually, the fruits take on the texture of a watery puree.

Canned: Always read the label of canned fruit, which will tell you whether the fruit is packed in natural juice or in a sugar syrup; whether the fruit is whole or has been cut into halves, slices, or odd-shaped pieces; and whether the fruit is Grade A (U.S. Fancy), Grade B (U.S. Choice), or Grade C (U.S. Standard).

Grades are based on color, texture, flavor, shape, and freedom from defects. Since the nutritional values of all grades are the same, you may want to use Grades B or C, which are lower in price than Grade A, for making cobblers and other dishes in which flavor is more important than appearance.

Dried: There are several advantages to using dried fruit. You can store it in any cool, dry place, taking up little space, and it travels well to picnics and lunches. Pick up a package of fruit and squeeze it gently; quality dried fruit is pliable. Dried fruit available in natural foods stores is usually slightly darker in color since it contains none of the preservatives used to keep the fruit's color bright.

Storing Fruit

Fresh: Unripe fruit ripens nicely at room temperature and out of direct sunlight. If you are in a hurry, put it in a paper bag to ripen. Twist the top of the bag to lock in the air. If you have a banana or an apple handy, put that in the bag too. The ethylene gases naturally given off by the ripe fruit will help the unripe fruit ripen. Check the progress every 24 hours.

Once ripe, fruit should be stored in the refrigerator. You can wash and dry them either before or after chilling. (Berries, strawberries, and cherries are the exception; they should always be stored unwashed.) Avoid crowding the pieces, and put them in the crisper section or in plastic bags. There, most fruit will remain plump and firm for 2 to 5 days. For longer storage, fruit should be frozen, canned, or dried (see "Preserving," page 621).

Frozen: Store frozen fruit at 0°F or lower, a temperature at which it will retain high quality for 8 to 12 months. Never refreeze a fruit once it has thawed; the fruit's firm texture will surely deteriorate.

Canned: Stored in a cool, dry place, homemade or store-bought canned fruit will maintain its quality for as long as a year. If you keep them longer than that (or keep them in a warm place), quality will suffer even though the contents will still be safe to eat.

After opening a can of fruit, you can leave the remaining portion in the open can if you cover and refrigerate it. Stored that way, however, some fruits acquire an unpleasant, if harmless, metallic taste. Instead, remove from the can and store in a jar or dish. Use within 3 days.

Dried: In hot, humid weather, refrigerate dried fruits. The rest of the year, they keep well at room temperature in a tightly covered container.

CHOOSING & STORING FRESH FRUIT

Fruit bought in season will be cheaper and better tasting, however it's a little difficult these days to pinpoint exactly when a fruit's peak season is. Some fruits—such as strawberries—grow in all parts of the country and can truly be said to have a local growing season. But for most parts of the country, a vast majority of fruit in the market is imported from somewhere else (there are no locally grown bananas in Michigan, for example). In addition, much of the fruit grown in tropical and subtropical regions is available in our markets year-round. Therefore, the "peak seasons" listed below merely represent times of the year when certain fruits are more abundant, and therefore less expensive. There are a few exceptions though: Cranberries, apricots, cherries, and pomegranates still have a relatively small, seasonal window of availability.

FRUIT		QUANTITY FOR 4 SERVINGS	PEAK SEASON	LOOK FOR	STORAGE
APPLES		4 medium	September-May	Firm; unblemished skin; bright color for variety	Refrigerate in perforated plastic bags; will keep 2 weeks.
APRICOTS		12 medium	June-July	Plump, juicy looking; smooth skin; bright golden orange color; yield to gentle pressure	Ripen at room temperature. Refrigerate when ripe; will keep 3-5 days.
AVOCADOS, HASS		2	Year-round	Pebbly, purple black skin; feel slightly soft	Ripen at room temperature. Refrigerate when ripe; will keep 3-5 days.
BANANAS		4 medium	Year-round	Unblemished skin with or without brown speckles; yellow color	Ripen at room temperature. Refrigerate when ripe (skin will blacken); will keep 2-3 days.
BERRIES	Blackberries	2 cups (1 pint)	June-August	Plump; bright color for variety	Refrigerate, unwashed and uncovered; will keep 1-2 days.
	Blueberries	2 cups (1 pint)	May-August	Well-rounded shape; firm; dry; bright, purple blue color with slightly frosted appearance	Refrigerate, unwashed and uncovered; will keep 1-2 days.
	Cranberries	2 cups	October-December	Firm; plump; high luster. (Good berries will bounce like rubber balls.)	Refrigerate, unwashed and uncovered; will keep 1-2 days.
	Raspberries	2 cups	June-August	Plump; bright color for variety	Refrigerate, unwashed and uncovered; will keep 1-2 days.
	Strawberries	4 cups (1 quart)	April-September	Firm; dry; clear red color with bright green caps	Refrigerate, unwashed and uncovered; will keep 1-2 days.

CHOOSING & STORING FRESH FRUIT—*CONTINUED*

FRUIT	QUANTITY FOR 4 SERVINGS	PEAK SEASON	LOOK FOR	STORAGE
CHERRIES: SOUR AND SWEET	1 pound	June–July	Firm; stems attached; good color for variety	Refrigerate, unwashed and uncovered; will keep 1–2 days.
CURRANTS, FRESH	2 cups	Midsummer	Firm; plump; bright red, almost translucent color	Refrigerate, unwashed and uncovered; will keep 1–2 days.
DATES	12 medium	Year-round	Shiny skin; gold brown color	Refrigerate, tightly wrapped; will keep several months.
FIGS	4 medium	Midsummer	Slightly firm; light yellow, reddish brown, or black color	Ripen in refrigerator; will keep 1–2 days.
GRAPEFRUITS	2 medium	Year-round	Heavy for size; well-rounded shape; smooth, thin skin	Refrigerate; will keep 1–2 weeks.
GRAPES	1–1½ pounds	Year-round	Plump; firmly attached to green, pliable stems; good color for variety	Refrigerate; will keep 4–6 days.
GUAVAS	1 pound	May–October	Depending on variety: pear or fig shape, red or yellow color	Ripen at room temperature. Refrigerate when ripe; will keep 2–3 days.
KIWIFRUIT: GREEN AND GOLDEN	4 medium	Year-round (green) June–September (golden)	Firm; fuzzy, brown skin	Ripen at room temperature. Refrigerate when ripe; will keep 3–6 weeks.
KUMQUATS	10–12 medium	November–February	Heavy for size: firm; bright, orange yellow color	Refrigerate; will keep several days.
LEMONS	2 medium	Year-round	Heavy for size; firm; glossy thin skin; light yellow color	Refrigerate; will keep 2 weeks.
LIMES	2 medium	Year-round	Heavy for size; firm; glossy thin skin; bright green color	Refrigerate; will keep 2 weeks.
MANGOES: TOMMY ATKINS AND ATAULFO (CHAMPAGNE)	2 Tommy Atkins or 4 Ataulfo	May–August	Tommy Atkins: deep green color with tinges of yellow and red. Ataulfo: deep yellow, kidney bean–shaped. Both yield to gentle pressure.	Ripen at room temperature. Refrigerate when ripe; will keep 2–3 days.

CHOOSING & STORING FRESH FRUIT—*CONTINUED*

FRUIT		QUANTITY FOR 4 SERVINGS	PEAK SEASON	LOOK FOR	STORAGE
MELONS	Muskmelons:, cantalopes, casaba, crenshaw, honeydew, persian	1-2 medium	May-October	Heavy for size; pleasant, fruity aroma; color varies with variety; yield to slight pressure at blossom end	Ripen at room temperature. Refrigerate when ripe, tightly wrapped; will keep 2-3 days.
	Watermelon	¼ large	May-September	Smooth, velvety skin; creamy, not white or pale green, underside; firm, juicy flesh with good red or cream color; shiny, brown or black seeds	Refrigerate. Once cut, wrap exposed surface; will keep 1 week.
NECTARINES		4 medium	May-October	Firm; plump; smooth skin; reddish yellow color; slight softening along seam edge	Ripen at room temperature. Refrigerate when ripe; will keep 3-5 days.
ORANGES	Blood	4 medium	December-March	Heavy for size; firm; bright skin, with a dark red blush	Refrigerate; will keep 2 weeks
	Sweet or juice	4 medium	Year-round	Heavy for size; firm; bright, smooth skin	Refrigerate; will keep 2 weeks.
	Mandarin: clementine, tangelo, tangerine	4 medium	November-March	Heavy for size; firm; loose skin. Tangerines: glossy skin	Refrigerate; will keep 1-2 weeks.
PAPAYAS		1 large or 2 small	Year-round	Green (unripe) to bright orange or yellow (ripe) color; yield to gentle pressure	Ripen at room temperature. Refrigerate when ripe; will keep 3-4 days.
PEACHES		4 medium	May-October	Firm; plump; slightly fuzzy skin; white to yellow color with red blush; yield to gentle pressure	Ripen at room temperature. Refrigerate when ripe; will keep 3-4 days.
PEARS		4 medium	Fall-winter	Firm but starting to soften; plump; color varies with variety	Ripen at room temperature. Refrigerate when ripe; will keep 3-5 days.
PERSIMMONS: HACHIYA AND FUYU		4 medium	October-December	Hachiya: heart-shaped fruit; green stem caps. Fuyu: squat, tomato-shaped. Both types are a deep orange color.	Hachiya: Must be completely soft and ripe to be edible; ripen in a bag. Fuyu: Can be eaten when firm-ripe. Refrigerate when ripe; will keep 1-2 days.

CHOOSING & STORING FRESH FRUIT—*CONTINUED*

FRUIT	QUANTITY FOR 4 SERVINGS	PEAK SEASON	LOOK FOR	STORAGE
PINEAPPLES	1 large	Year-round	Large; heavy; sweet aroma; depending on variety, green or golden yellow color; fresh, deep green crown leaves; nearly all eyes at base are yellow. Avoid pineapples with soft or discolored spots, watery or dark eyes, or brown leaves.	Refrigerate; will keep 1–2 days.
PLUMS	4 medium or 8 small	June–September	Plump; good color for variety; yield to gentle pressure	Refrigerate; will keep 3–5 days.
POMEGRANATES	4 medium	January–August	Heavy for size; thin skin; purple red color	Refrigerate; will keep 1 week.
RHUBARB	1 pound	February–May	Crisp, reddish green stalks	Refrigerate; will keep 3–5 days.

Nuts & Seeds

Both seeds and nuts (which are also seeds in a sense) contain all the ingredients necessary to nourish and sustain a new plant. In fact, they hold even more nutrients, and in greater concentrations, than the plants they come from. The only caution when it comes to these nutritious foods is their high fat and calorie content. The fat in nuts and seeds is very healthful unsaturated fats to be sure, but they are extremely energy dense, and just a small handful packs in quite a few calories.

Buying Nuts

Nuts are in season in autumn and early winter, so that is the time to find the best-quality in-the-shell nuts. But you can usually buy several common types of nuts in supermarkets throughout the year. Specialty shops and natural foods stores are likely to have a good supply of the more unusual kinds. Buy nuts in stores that seem to sell a lot of them. That means quick turnover and less chance that the stock has become stale or rancid. Nuts tend to spoil quickly because of the oils they contain.

Whole nuts can be purchased either shelled or unshelled with the exception of cashews and macadamia nuts, which are only sold shelled. Roughly speaking, 1 pound of unshelled nuts will yield about ½ pound of shelled nuts. Shelled nuts are sold raw or roasted and blanched (skins removed) or natural (skins on).

Shelled nutmeats should be plump and fairly uniform in color and size, and they should look firm, not limp or rubbery. Dark or shriveled kernels suggest staleness and poor quality.

Buying Seeds

Sunflower seeds and pumpkin seeds can be purchased hulled or unhulled, raw or roasted, and unsalted or salted. Hulled pumpkin seeds are often sold under the name pepitas.

Sesame seeds come hulled and unhulled; the hulled seeds are a pearly white, and unhulled ones are a matte tan.

Poppy seeds can be bought in bulk in gourmet food shops and some ethnic markets, or in smaller jars in the spice aisle of supermarkets. White poppy seeds are available in Indian markets.

Chia seeds, known mostly in this country for the novelty of sprouting them on terra-cotta figurines, are actually very high in healthful fatty acids and soluble fiber.

Flaxseeds are available in whole seed form, both dark brown and golden, and also as a ground meal. The seeds are also pressed for oil, which is generally sold not for cooking but as a dietary supplement. The oil goes rancid very quickly and needs to be stored in the refrigerator.

Hemp seeds are available whole, as a ground meal, as flour, and as a milk (and yogurt). The seeds are pressed for oil, which is highly unsaturated and turns rancid quickly (like flaxseed oil). It must be kept refrigerated.

Storing Nuts & Seeds

The chemical changes that lead to rancidity in nuts begin almost as soon as the outside hull is

MAKING NUT OR SEED MEAL, MILK & BUTTER

Nut or seed meal makes exceptionally nutritious bread or porridge, or it can be used in sauces, piecrusts, cakes, and tortes. To make a nut or seed meal, grind the nuts or seeds, ¼ cup at a time, with either a small nut grinder or a mini food processor. Grinding in small batches produces a nut meal that is dry, not oily. To use the meal in breads, replace 2 or 3 tablespoons of wheat flour with nut meal for every 1 cup of flour. The texture of the bread will be changed only slightly.

Nuts and seed milk is as nutritious and good tasting as whole nuts. Nut milk, which incidentally is as perishable as cow's milk, can be used as a quick energy drink or for sauces and soups. To make nut or seed milk, lightly roast and grind any nuts or seeds. While grinding, gradually add water (whole or reconstituted dry milk can also be used) until a desired consistency is reached. (When using sesame seeds, strain the blended mixture.) One-quarter cup of nuts or seeds will yield 1 cup of milk. Sweeten it with sugar, honey, or molasses, and add a few drops of vanilla extract if you like.

Nut or seed butter is made by grinding the nuts or seeds with a little bit of oil.

Place the 1 cup roasted peanuts, cashews, almonds, sunflower seeds, pumpkin seeds, or hemp seeds and 4 teaspoons vegetable oil in a food processor or large mini food processor. Pulse to combine, then process on high speed, scraping down the sides of the container as necessary. Blend until smooth. Store tightly covered in a cool place. **Yields 1 cup**

---

removed. Pine nuts are especially susceptible to spoilage because they contain unstable resinous oils. Most shelled nuts will keep at least 4 months in the refrigerator, a good place to store them. (Nutmeats, packed airtight, also freeze well for up to a year.) Unshelled nuts will keep longer—about 1 year—in a cool, dry place and even longer under refrigeration.

Seeds, too, will go rancid if not refrigerated. This is especially true of flaxseeds and hemp seeds whose oils are particularly vulnerable to rancidity.

Preparing Nuts & Seeds

Blanching Nuts

The process that exposes the creamy white nutmeat by removing the thick skin that clings to the kernel is called blanching. Although this skin contains nutrients, some cooks remove it simply for the sake of appearance; others to better savor the nut's own delicate flavor.

To blanch shelled almonds: Cover with boiling water and let stand for 1 to 2 minutes. Drain, rinse under cold water, and slide the skins off with your fingers. Spread the blanched nuts on paper towels to dry.

To blanch shelled chestnuts: Place in a pot of boiling water and let boil for 3 minutes. Remove a few at a time and let cool; then peel with a paring knife. If they don't peel easily, boil for another minute or two.

To blanch hazelnuts by roasting: Spread shelled nuts in a single layer in a shallow baking pan. Bake at 300°F for 10 to 15 minutes, or until heated

A GUIDE TO NUTS & SEEDS

NUT OR SEED	APPEARANCE	CHARACTERISTICS
ALMONDS	Oval-shaped, woody shells; smooth, white nutmeat; reddish brown skin	Sweet or bitter varieties. Bitter almonds yield extract only. Sweet almonds yield high-protein flour and oil.
BRAZIL NUTS	Dark brown, very hard, rippled shells resembling orange segments; large, beige nutmeat; thick woody skin	Taste best in winter; rich and creamy flesh
CASHEWS	Wrinkled, crescent-shaped, eggshell-colored nutmeat	Available shelled only; sweet-tasting with a high fat content
CHESTNUTS	Mound-shaped; mahogany-colored skin	Grow inside hard, outer husks; contain much less oil than other nuts
HAZELNUTS (FILBERTS)	Hard, reddish brown shells; long or squat, roundish oval nutmeat	When ground, contain enough oil and mealiness to replace flour and fat in cookies and cakes
HICKORY NUTS (BUTTERNUTS)	Similar to walnuts and pecans	Similar to black walnut; sweet; rich in oil
MACADAMIA NUTS	Light beige; large, uneven, sphere-shaped nutmeat	Available shelled only; sweet and buttery; often roasted in coconut oil
PEANUTS	Soft, papery shells; two bean-shaped nutmeats	Technically not a nut, but a member of legume family; rich in cooking oil
PECANS	Semihard shells; squat, irregular, curly halves (nutmeats)	Sweet, pulpy texture; can be interchanged with walnuts
PINENUTS (PIGNOLI)	White; long, thin, pellet-shaped nutmeat	Come from pinecones and have sweet, taste; very expensive
PISTACHIOS	Hard off-white shell; naturally split at one end; pale green nutmeat; thin reddish skin	Mild flavor; noted especially for its color
WALNUTS — Eastern black	Resemble English walnuts, but not as plump and with a dark skin covering white nutmeat	Shells are very hard and difficult to crack; stronger tasting than English walnuts.
WALNUTS — English	Hard shells; squat, irregular, curly halves (nutmeats)	Mild and sweet tasting; rich in cooking oil; called green walnuts when fresh; sometimes pickled
CHIA SEEDS	Small egg-shaped, mottled gray-black	Nutty flavor; very high in ALA (fatty acid that is a pre-cursor to omega-3s); also high in fiber
FLAXSEEDS	Small, very shiny, pointed ovals; dark brown or golden	Nutty flavor; high in ALA (pre-cursor to omega-3s); high in fiber; sold whole, pressed into oil, ground into meal
HEMP SEEDS	Round; brown to beige; the size of peppercorns	High in protein and essential fatty acids; sold whole, pressed into oil, ground into meal, made into "milk"
POPPY SEEDS	Tiny, bluish black spheres (sometimes available white)	Pleasantly nutty when baked
PUMPKIN SEEDS	Long, flat, dark green seeds with white outer shells	Shelled, unshelled, raw, roasted, salted, unsalted; pressed into oil
SESAME SEEDS	Unhulled: small, tan ovals; hulled: white	Hulled, unhulled, raw; pressed into oil
SUNFLOWER SEEDS	Grayish oval seeds in soft black and white seed coats	Shelled, unshelled, raw, roasted, salted, unsalted; pressed into oil

MAKING SESAME SEED OR SUNFLOWER SEED YOGURT

Yogurt made from sesame or sunflower seeds is delicious as a salad dressing or as a dip for raw or cooked vegetables. To make the yogurt, soak ½ cup hulled, raw seeds for a full 24 hours. Drain the seeds and grind them in a mini food processor or blender; add ½ cup water and process the mixture at high speed for 20 seconds. Gradually add another ½ cup water and process for about 2 minutes. The consistency should be that of heavy cream. Pour the mixture into a yogurt maker, if you have one, or into a glass container (closed but not airtight), and let it stand for 8 to 24 hours at 70° to 80°F.

When it is ready, the yogurt will have a slightly tart flavor. Sunflower-seed yogurt will have a grayish color and the top sometimes turns very dark—unappetizing, but not harmful. Eat it or scrape it off. The yogurt will keep, refrigerated, for a week.

---

through, stirring occasionally to prevent burning. Place them in a kitchen towel and rub vigorously to get the skins off (they will not all come off).

Chopping Nuts

Chopped nuts make an attractive garnish as well as a delectable ingredient in many dishes. They can be chopped in a nut chopper, or you can chop them on a board or on a clean dish towel on a flat surface. Some cooks prefer a wooden bowl with a rounded chopper for this. You may also use a food processor, but you have to take care not to process the nuts into a paste.

Opening a Coconut

Technically a nut, but significantly different from other foods called nuts, the coconut is the fruit of a tropical palm. The nut contains thick, edible meat and a potable clear liquid called "milk."

To open a coconut, pierce two of its three "eyes" with an ice pick or large nail, and drain the milk from the coconut. Refrigerate and enjoy as a refreshing drink. To remove the shell easily, bake the drained coconut at 350°F for 20 to 30 minutes, or put it in the freezer for 1 hour. Place the coconut on a firm surface and give the shell a quick, sharp blow with a hammer; it should break cleanly in two. Separate the meat from the shell with a sharp knife. The

Piercing the "eyes" of a coconut

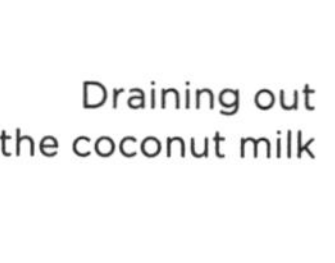

Draining out the coconut milk

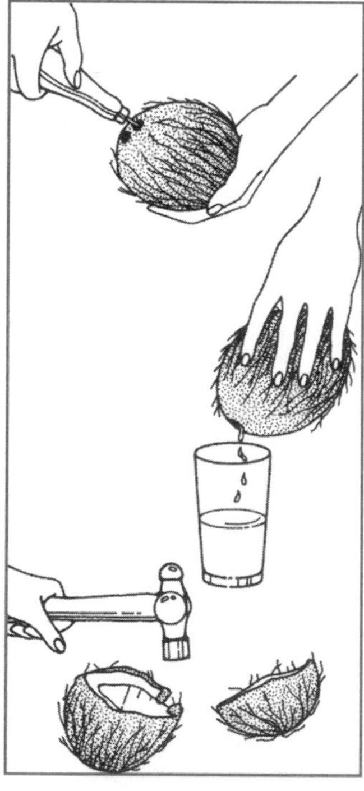

dark brown skin that clings tightly to the white meat can be peeled off with a vegetable peeler, if desired.

Store fresh coconut in the refrigerator. Whole, unshelled coconuts retain their quality for as long as a month in the refrigerator.

Roasting or Toasting Nuts & Seeds

Slight roasting or toasting of nuts and seeds heightens their rich flavor. You have to tend them carefully, however, because they can go very quickly from nicely browned to burned and bitter. There are three main methods:

Stove-top: In an ungreased heavy skillet, toast the nuts or seeds over medium heat, stirring regularly, for 10 to 15 minutes. Once they have taken on the color you want, scrape onto a heatproof plate to stop the cooking.

Oven: Spread the nuts or seeds in a shallow pan or on a baking sheet and slide into a 350°F oven. Roast, stirring occasionally, until fragrant and lightly browned, 5 to 10 minutes. Scrape onto a heatproof plate to stop the cooking.

Toaster oven: This is a good energy-saving method for seeds and small amounts of nuts. Roast at 350°F for 3 to 5 minutes. This goes more quickly than a conventional oven because it's such an enclosed space.

Roasting Chestnuts

Although technically classed as a tree nut, like almonds and walnuts, chestnuts do not have the same high fat content and need to be treated differently. To roast chestnuts, slash an X through the shells on the flat sides of the nuts. Place them, cut-side up, on baking sheets and roast at 400°F until tender, about 20 minutes. Insert a fork to test them for tenderness. When cool enough to handle, peel off the shells.

MAKING COCONUT MILK OR CREAM

The sweet liquid found inside a fresh coconut is called the "milk," though it is anything but milky and is more technically called coconut water. The ingredient called coconut milk is made from the coconut oils pressed from the coconut flesh. It's the core ingredient in Thai curries and adds richness to many Asian and Polynesian dishes. Coconut milk is available in cans and is sold in thin and thick (sometimes called coconut cream) forms; it is also sold in a lower-fat version. Neither of these should be confused with the canned sweetened cream of coconut used to make piña coladas. Here's how to make your own coconut milk or cream:

To make coconut milk or cream: Either coarsely chop or grate fresh coconut meat. In a food processor, process no more than $\frac{1}{2}$ cup coconut with $\frac{1}{4}$ cup of hot water at a time. Press the mixture in a strainer to extract the liquid. This first pressing, which is very rich, is generally referred to as coconut cream. If you continue to press the coconut, adding more water as you do, you will have a thinner liquid called coconut milk. To do this, return the puree to the food processor. For each $\frac{1}{2}$ cup of puree, add another $\frac{1}{2}$ cup of water, and blend again. Strain and measure.

Grains & Rice

Whole grains present a limitless source of low-cost, nutrition-rich eating pleasure. When you replace some of the meat on the menu with grains, you serve less fat (particularly less saturated fat) more fiber and trace minerals.

To bring whole grains into your own diet, you might take inspiration from some world-famous dishes—the oatmeal porridge of Scotland, the polenta (cornmeal) of Italy, the kasha (buckwheat) of Russia, the quinoa of Peru, and the couscous (wheat) of north Africa, to name a few. You will find that grains work well as a fundamental base for all other foods. Serving just a little milk and fruit or vegetable with any of the staple grains will give you a dish that provides both variety and sustenance. Adding a dairy product to any grain raises the grain's protein value. Grains are best when processed in the simplest way, with the germ and the bran intact.

In addition to the most common forms listed below, many grains are also available as pressed flakes (like rolled oats), grits, and flours (see "Flours," page 104).

Amaranth

Amaranth, a significant crop in scattered areas of the world, is still little known to American cooks except in some packaged multi-grain breakfast cereals. The seeds of the plant are rich in high-quality protein (higher than any other grain). Boiled in water and then chilled, amaranth seeds can be used to replace cornstarch as a thickening agent. The leaves of the plant are also used as a vegetable.

Barley

Barley is most often associated in American minds with beer brewing, but its best use is in the kitchen in soups, salads, and casseroles, or as a side dish in place of rice or noodles.

Hulled (whole-grain) barley: This is the least processed form of barley; it has only the inedible outer husk removed. It must be soaked overnight before cooking.

Scotch barley (pot barley): This form of barley is somewhat more processed than hulled barley but still has the germ intact (unlike Pearled barley, below).

Pearled barley: The outer husk, bran, and germ have been removed by abrasion. This is the most readily available form of barley.

Black barley: Also known as purple barley, these purple-mahogany grains have their bran layer intact.

Buckwheat

Botanically speaking, buckwheat is a fruit (related to the rhubarb plant), but its three-cornered seed is treated as a grain. The nutty, appealing flavor of buckwheat receives the most serious attention in Russian cuisine—in kasha or blini—and American cooks may also be familiar with Japanese soba noodles, which are made with buckwheat flour. Buckwheat groats that are roasted are sold as kasha , which comes whole or crushed into fine, medium, or coarse granulations.

Corn

Whole kernel dried corn: Dried hominy and small yellow corn (chicos) are reconstituted and cooked; used especially in Southwestern cuisine.

Hominy and hominy grits: Hominy is the Algonquin name for large corn kernels that have been hulled and degermed. Hominy grits are dried hominy, ground to a meal to give uniform granular particles. The corn germ and bran are almost completely absent in both of these products.

Cornmeal: This meal (which is coarser than flour) is ground from white, yellow, or blue corn kernels. White cornmeal, when cooked, has a slightly rougher texture than yellow or blue, but there is so little difference in flavor that they are virtually interchangeable in recipes. Most cooks use the color specified in a recipe only to get the texture intended. Whichever you choose, try to buy stone-ground cornmeal. Bolted and degermed cornmeal have had much of the germ-bearing hull removed with sieves, thus losing large portions of the nutrients present in whole cornmeal. Whole meal is more perishable, but better all around.

Kamut

This ancient grain is a relative of modern-day wheat. It's available in many of the same whole grain and processed forms as wheat.

Millet

Millet has a texture and taste somewhere between egg-rich pasta and cornmeal. It swells tremendously when cooked, and makes a delicious breakfast cereal when topped with fruit and maple syrup. It is the major staple grain in Africa.

Oats

Oats are the only grain that emerge from processing still clinging to their nutrients. Only the fibrous hull, which has little nutritional value, is removed in milling, leaving the groat, which contains the bulk of the bran, endosperm, and germ.

Steel-cut oats: Made by cutting the groats into pieces with steel rollers.

Rolled oats: The most familiar form, these are made by flattening the groats into flakes, a process that cracks the kernel and makes the nutrients in it more available to the digestive system. At the same time it permits the oats to absorb liquid faster, and so reduces cooking time.

Quick-cooking oats: These are rolled oats that have been cut into smaller pieces for even quicker cooking.

Oat bran: The bran of processed oats is sold separately and can be added to baked goods or sprinkled over cereal or eaten by itself as a hot cereal. It's a very good source of fiber.

Quinoa

This ancient grain has long been prized by the people of the Andes in South America. It has an exceptionally high amount of an important amino acid called lysine, which is critical to the synthesis of protein. This makes the grain an extremely important source of plant protein. Quinoa is about the size of millet and comes in white (the commonest), pale-yellow, reddish-brown, and black. You can also find quinoa flakes and flour.

A QUICK GUIDE TO GRAINS

GRAIN	APPEARANCE	COMMON USES	SUBSTITUTES
AMARANTH	Seeds about the size of millet, ranging in color from purple-black to buff yellow	Toasted seeds can be milled into flour or boiled in fruit juice as cereal, also popped like corn or used as thickening agent.	Millet, sorghum
BARLEY	Short, stubby kernels with a hard, outer shell. Pearled barley (outer layer removed) is white translucent.	Flavors and thickens soups, stews. Flakes or whole grains make chewy breakfast cereal. Sprouts are used to make malt.	Brown rice, wheat, farro
BUCKWHEAT GROATS	Groat contained inside dark-brown, 3-cornered seeds that resemble beechnuts	Used most often as flour in pancakes, blini, biscuits, muffins. Whole groats are used for hot cereal and kasha.	Oats, bulgur
CORN	Dried corn comes in all the colors that fresh corn comes in: white, yellow, purple/blue. Sold whole, ground coarse grits, or fine cornmeal.	Whole corn is used in stews. Grits are used as a side dish. Cornmeal is used in sweet puddings and in polenta and quick breads.	Amaranth, millet
FARRO	Similar to wheat berries	Similar to wheat berries	Spelt, kamut, wheat, triticale
KAMUT	Similar to wheat berries	Similar to wheat berries	Wheat, spelt, triticale
MILLET	Tiny, round, yellow; resembles seeds more than grains	Boiled like rice for breakfast and main dishes; thickens and flavors soups, stews. (Often sold as bird seed.)	Amaranth, corn grits, sorghum
OATS	Long, light brown. Grain is seldom seen in its whole form. Rolled oats are flat tan flakes with brownish flecks. Cut oats are chunky pieces of oat groats.	Thickens and enriches soups; stretches meat dishes; used in stuffings, pilafs, breads, cakes, pancakes, dry breakfast cereals	Buckwheat groats, brown rice
QUINOA	Small, round pale-yellow, reddish-brown, or black; the size of millet	Used in pilafs, salads, and baked goods	Millet
RICE	Comes in short-, medium-, and long-grain forms. Brown rice is pale brown because it has the bran layer intact; white rice does not.	Boiled as basic food; served alone or with meat, vegetables, in casseroles, soups, stews, stuffings, puddings, pilaf	Barley, wheat
RICE, WILD	Long, dark, almost black kernels, slightly longer and thinner than long-grain rice	Used in stuffings, in breads, as a side dish for fish or poultry	Long-grain brown rice
RYE BERRIES	Long, dark-brown kernels longer and thinner than wheat berries	Boiled and mixed with other grains, legumes, vegetables as a side dish; added to soup and stews; ground to make flour	Triticale, wheat

A QUICK GUIDE TO GRAINS—*CONTINUED*

GRAIN	APPEARANCE	COMMON USES	SUBSTITUTES
SORGHUM	Roundish seeds (slightly smaller than peppercorns); brown with mixed yellow and red coloration	Boiled seeds can be eaten whole, like boiled rice; ground into meal for cereal, or milled into flour.	Amaranth, millet
SPELT	Similar to wheat berries	Similar to wheat berries	Wheat, kamut, triticale
TRITICALE	Gray-brown, oval-shaped kernels. Larger than wheat berries and plumper than rye berries	Cooked whole or cracked to make breakfast cereal; milled to make flour	Rye, wheat, spelt, kamut
WHEAT	Whole berries are short, rounded kernels of varying shades of brown. Also comes coarsely cracked, and cracked and par-boiled (bulgur).	Boiled and served as a hot side dish or grain salad; added to meat loaf or burger mixtures	Rye, triticale, spelt, kamut, farro

Rice

In the United States, white rice—which has been milled to have its husk, bran, and most of the germ removed—must, by law, have many of the stripped nutrients put back. This makes it, ironically, a better source of some B vitamins than brown rice. But brown rice has more fiber and vitamin E (from the germ). Most of the different rices on the market today come in both white and brown forms.

Rice comes in three basic lengths: short-grain, medium-grain, and long-grain. Generally speaking, the shorter the grain, the more starch the rice will have, making short-grain rice useful for certain dishes like sushi or risotto.

Here's a short list of rice and rice products:

Arborio rice: A starchy short-grain rice used to make the Italian dish risotto

Aromatic rices: An umbrella term for rices with exceptional toasty, nutty flavor. Some aromatics include basmati, jasmine, Kalijira, popcorn rice, and pecan rice.

Bhutanese red rice: Very short grains with red husks

Bomba rice: A short-grain rice used in Spanish dishes, especially paella

Forbidden rice: A black-hulled, short-grain rice

Rice bran: The nutty-tasting outer bran layer that is a by-product of processed rice. Add to baked goods or cereals and use in much the same way as wheat bran. It has gained some attention for its possible role in reducing cholesterol.

Rice grits: Coarsely cracked brown rice that adds taste and chewy texture to soups, stews, and casseroles. Use grits cup for cup to replace whole rice, following the same cooking directions.

Sticky rice (sushi rice): A very starchy, sticky rice used to make sushi; available in short- and long-grain

Parboiled or converted rice: falls midway between brown rice and white rice in terms of nutrition. This rice is steamed before being dried, and then polished to make it white. The steaming forces 70 percent or more of the B vitamins and some minerals in the bran and germ into the rice kernel.

Rice, Wild

Wild rice is not a grain but the seed of an aquatic grass related to the rice family. Its unique flavor is akin to that of grains, however, and it is used in much the same way. As its name implies, it is a wild crop, growing in northern Minnesota, Wisconsin lake country, and southern Canada. The system of harvesting, carefully controlled by law and custom, makes it rare and, consequently, expensive. To get a taste of it without breaking the bank, try it in a brown rice and wild rice blend. They work well together because they take about the same amount of time to cook.

Rye

Rye flour is the most common form of this grain. It is most popular in Scandinavian countries where people eat a lot of *knäckebröd,* a rye crisp bread baked from unsifted whole rye flour. Rye grain is quite hardy and can be used much the same as whole wheat or triticale grain. Whole rye grains, called rye berries, will cook faster if allowed to soak for several hours (see "Tips for Cooking Grains," page 446).

Sorghum

Sorghum, also known as milo, is another grain that has a much better image in other parts of the world than it does in the United States. Here it is used mainly by industry as a sweetener in the form of syrup boiled down from the sap of sweet sorghum stalks. In Africa and parts of India, sorghum is a major cereal grain; the Chinese and Japanese savor it boiled, as they would rice.

Triticale

Triticale is a crossbreed of wheat and rye. Its name derives from *triticum* and *secale,* the Latin words for wheat and rye. The hybrid grain successfully combines the best in flavor, nutrition, and cooking possibilities of wheat and rye.

Wheat

Wheat berries: The whole wheat grain. Wheat berries can also be heated and pressed flat and sold as wheat flakes, which resemble oatmeal in appearance and can be used similarly.

Bulgur: Cracked wheat that has been hulled and parboiled. The parboiling conserves most of the nutrients by leaching them from the outer layer to the center of the grain.

Cracked wheat: Whole wheat grain cracked between rollers

Farro: The name given in Italy to one of several types of whole grain wheat (including spelt; see below) prepared as a side dish or salad, or added to soups. It is often sold in semipearled form, which makes it faster to cook.

Farina: A wheat product prepared by grinding and sifting the wheat grain to a granular form. It has the bran and most of the germ removed. Enriched farina has some of the B vitamins and minerals returned.

Spelt: A species of wheat with slightly lower amounts of gluten than regular wheat

Storing Grains

Unhulled grain with its germ still intact has a higher oil content than refined grain, so it must be protected against rancidity by proper storage. Stored in a cool, dry place, most grains will keep for about a year. Because they are especially quick to spoil, buckwheat groats and oatmeal should be refrigerated or stored in the freezer. If that is not possible, try to use them within a month. Bulgur stores very well because it has been parcooked, giving it a good resistance to rancidity.

Since insects thrive on grain, use tightly closed containers to protect your supply against infestation.

WHEAT GERM & BRAN

The bran and the germ are typically milled off grains of wheat when making white flour. The germ is removed because its fat content makes it subject to rancidity and can reduce the shelf life of flour. The bran is removed more for aesthetic reasons than any other. It's the bran (which is the grain's brown husk) that gives whole wheat flour its characteristic color and "wheat-y" flavor.

Bran is a concentrated source of B vitamins and minerals, but fiber is its greatest asset. Now that the role of fiber in the prevention of many modern-day diseases has been defined and upheld by medical research, bran is finding its way into more diets as a supplement. It can be found in most natural foods stores and is easy to add to all types of dishes—sprinkle it on top of breakfast cereals; include it in the mix for homemade bread, muffins, and cookies; or add a few tablespoons to casseroles and meat loaves. Toast the bran for a nice nutty flavor.

Wheat germ, the tiny embryo of the grain, contains a nutritional powerhouse—the entire B complex (except B_{12}), plus vitamin E, protein, iron, and other minerals. Wheat germ can be eaten by itself as a cereal (cold or hot), added to a smoothie, or sprinkled on ice cream. It can also be added to pancakes and any baked goods. Wheat germ also makes a superb coating mix for fish or chicken.

Because the germ is perishable, it should be stored tightly sealed and refrigerated. Toasting is the best way to preserve wheat germ, though it reduces the nutrient content slightly. Toasted germ will keep from 2 to 6 months if refrigerated or stored in the freezer. Of course, if it smells rancid or tastes bitter, discard it. Frozen wheat germ can be used directly from the freezer.

Flours

Buy stone-ground flours whenever possible because less heat is involved in the milling process. That means fewer nutrients are destroyed. Most stone-ground flours are milled by stone rollers propelled by water power.

Because whole-grain flours, with their germ and bran intact, spoil easily, they should be kept in the refrigerator (or the freezer, if you have space) and used within 3 months. Just be sure to bring the flour back to room temperature before using.

Wheat Flours

White flour: Flour ground from the endosperm of the wheat kernel, with the bran and germ removed. Different flours have different levels of gluten (the protein in wheat) depending on the "hardness" of the type of wheat used to make it. All-purpose flour has a medium amount of gluten and makes it suitable for breads, pastries, cakes, and general use. Cake flour is the "softest" flour with a low gluten content, producing very tender cakes, muffins, and quick breads. Bread flour is at the other end of the spectrum, with the most protein, which provides good structure for yeast-risen breads. Pastry flour falls between all-purpose and cake flours. It produces delicate pastries and has enough structure to stand up well to yeast-rising.

Unbleached flour: Freshly ground wheat flour has a yellowish tinge, which lightens as the flour ages. Many manufacturers are impatient and use bleach. Unbleached flours are allowed to age naturally, which in the process also strengthens the flour's gluten.

Gluten flour: White flour mixed with concentrated wheat protein. Adding gluten flour to bread dough gives it greater structure—add 2 tablespoons per 1 cup flour in whole grain bread. Increase kneading time to activate the extra gluten.

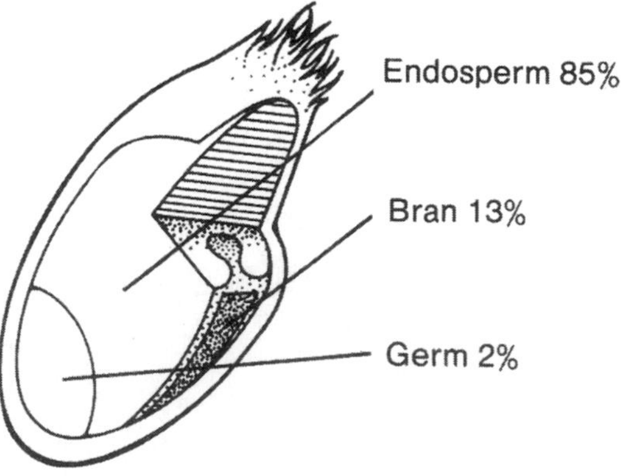

Whole wheat flour: Flour made from all three parts of the wheat kernel—bran, germ, and endosperm; also available as whole wheat pastry flour, which is lower in gluten and produces more tender baked goods. Whole wheat flour made from hard wheat (higher in gluten) is sometimes sold as graham flour.

White whole wheat flour: Whole-grain flour made from white wheat grains referred to as albino wheat. The flour is as nutritious as regular whole wheat flour. It produces bread that is slightly more refined than traditional whole wheat flour.

Nonwheat Flours

Only wheat flours have enough gluten to make a high-rising bread or delicate pastry, but other flours can contribute great flavor, texture, and important nutrients to baked goods. For some advice on how to use them in baking, see "Using Nonwheat Flours in Bread Making," (page 551).

Amaranth flour: Made from the peppery-tasting seeds of the amaranth plant; high in fiber and an amino acid called lysine. It has no gluten.

Buckwheat flour: A common ingredient in pancakes and Japanese soba noodles. Comes in light and dark varieties.

Bean flours: Any dried bean can be ground into a flour. The best-known are chickpea flour (used in Indian and Italian cooking), fava bean flour (often used in conjunction with chickpea flour in gluten-free baking mixtures and sometimes labeled garfava flour for garbanzo and fava), and lentil flour (used in Indian cooking to make pappadum).See "Bean Flour," (page 82) for more suggestions.

Barley flour: Mildly flavored flour with a small amount of gluten, though not enough to be used on its own to make bread

Masa harina: A special corn flour popular throughout Mexico and Latin America that is used to make tortillas and tamales. This very finely ground cornmeal comes from corn kernels that have first been soaked in a lime solution to make them easier to hull. The lime gives corn tortillas their characteristic nutty-sweet flavor.

Nut flours: Finely ground nuts; made from nut solids after the kernels have been pressed for oil. They add rich flavor to baked goods or to breading.

Quinoa flour: Made from quinoa, an ancient grain from South America. The flour is made from either milled or unmilled quinoa. Milled quinoa flour produces a lighter texture, while unmilled makes for a coarser crumb. High in both protein and fiber. Not good on its own for bread making.

Rice flour: Comes in both white and brown varieties

Rye flour: Comes in light, medium, and dark varieties. Light rye flour is usually "bolted," which means that the bran and germ have been sifted out. Dark rye is "unbolted," and thus has more fiber and a much more pronounced rye flavor. Rye has a little bit of gluten, but not enough to be used on its own to make bread.

Soy flour: Flour made of ground soybeans with a high protein (35 percent) and high fat (20 percent) content. To add significant protein to any baked goods, substitute 2 tablespoons in every cup of wheat flour. Because products containing soy flour brown more quickly, baking time or temperature may need to be reduced slightly.

Spelt flour: Made from a grain related to wheat, but lower in gluten than regular wheat flour

Teff flour: A nutty-flavored flour made from an ancient grain; used in Ethiopia to make a pancake-like bread called *injera.*

Triticale flour: Made from a wheat-rye hybrid and has more gluten than a lot of nonwheat flours. It still needs to be combined with wheat flour for the right texture in baked goods.

GRINDING YOUR OWN GRAINS

Freshly milled grain is superior in taste to store-bought whole-grain flour, and you can grind just the amount of grain you need for each recipe. Finally, it permits a wider choice of flours to use in baking. Some grains, such as sorghum, amaranth, and millet, are not always available in flour form, so you may have to grind your own if you want to enjoy them.

Mills

Three types of grain mills are available—large electrical units, small hand units, and units that attach to appliances such as stand mixers. If you are considering the purchase of a grain mill, check your stand mixer first to see if there is a grain mill attachment available for it. The motors on heavy-duty mixers have sufficient power to grind grains.

Electric mills are available with either stone or steel burr plates for grinding. Stone mills grind the flour finer, produce less heat at finer settings, and wear better. Steel-plate mills do not grind the flour as finely, but they can be cleaned easily and can be used for grinding foods other than grain—coffee beans, spices, nuts, beans, and peas, for example. Since stone grinders are not washable, only dry grain can be used in them.

Whether you choose an electric mill or a hand mill, be sure all the working parts are accessible for cleaning. Particles of grain left in the machinery turn rancid and affect the taste of the next batch of whole grain you grind. These bits also attract insects.

Choosing the Fineness of the Grind

A fine flour is best for making fine-textured sandwich breads that are to be sliced thin and have to hold together. Bread made with coarse flour has more flavor and rises well but tends to fall apart easily. Coarse flour works particularly well in pancake recipes.

A fine grind exposes more surface area, and that allows for better assimilation of the grain's vitamins and minerals. But when the bran is ground too finely, its value as a fiber food is diminished. Try for a mix of textures and uses for your home-ground grains.

Pasta & Noodles

The history of pasta in the West is as colorful and varied as its numerous shapes and sizes and the many sauces that flavor it. The most popular legend has it traveling from China to Italy with Marco Polo. However, drawings of pasta cookware in Etruscan caves show that pasta existed in Italy long before that famed voyage. Another theory holds that pasta was actually introduced to Italy by Arabs who had easy access to Venice during the Middle Ages. At that time both the Arabs and the Indians were already eating noodles, calling them the Persian and Indian words for "thread." Italians eventually called their version spaghetti—from the word *spago*, or string.

In the Western world, Italian versions may dominate the pasta scene, but Asian cuisine has created a unique variety of noodles—Chinese cellophane noodles and rice noodles and Japanese soba noodles, to name but a few.

Traditionally, commercial pasta has been made from semolina, the starchy endosperm of hard durum wheat. This golden grain gives store-bought pasta its yellow color and an exceptionally high amount of gluten, which produces a hard-textured pasta that stands up well to cooking and to sauces.

While at one time this was the only pasta available, today a host of whole-grain wheat pastas are available. When whole wheat pasta was first introduced, it was not well received. Although higher in fiber than its white flour counterparts, the complaints ranged from it having a dry mealy texture to having a somewhat raw taste. Today there are countless brands of whole wheat pasta (as well as multigrain pasta), and its taste and texture have vastly improved. Some people even find they prefer it to semolina pasta. Note that taste and texture vary from brand to brand, and shape to shape, so it's smart to try a couple and see which brand you prefer.

Even though pastas made from refined flour are "enriched" with B vitamins to put back some of the nutrients removed in the refining process, they are still lacking in fiber: A typical serving of regular pasta (2 ounces dry) has about 2 grams of fiber; the same size serving of whole wheat pasta has 6 grams.

When shopping for pasta, it may help you to know that federal food-labeling regulations permit products labeled "macaroni" to be prepared from just flour and water. However, those labeled "noodles" must contain eggs in some form (fresh, dried, or frozen). The exception to this is Asian pasta (see page 108), which can be labeled noodle.

Nonwheat Pastas

In addition to the wheat pastas, there is a whole range of nonwheat pastas, perfect for people who are gluten intolerant. Note that pastas made from farro, kamut, or spelt all contain some gluten, because these grains are actually relatives of wheat. Of the nonwheat pastas available, those made with soy flour, beans, and lentils are the highest in protein. You can also get pasta made from brown rice, corn, corn-rice blend, quinoa, rye, and jerusalem artichoke flour.

Asian Noodles

Noodles play an important role in Asian cuisines, which have a long history of making pasta with starches other than wheat, including arrowroot, cornstarch, potato starch, and tapioca starch.

Buckwheat pasta: Noodles made from buckwheat flour or a combination of buckwheat and wheat flour are known as *qiao mian* in Chinese, soba in Japanese, and *naeng myun* in Korean.

Cellophane noodles: Made from sweet potato starch or mung bean starch and water. Also known as glass noodles, slippery noodles, bean thread, or bean vermicelli.

Chinese wheat noodles: These come in a variety of shapes, colors, and thickness and are sold both fresh and dried. Similar to Western-style pasta, they're eaten in lo mein and chow mein.

Egg noodles: Known as *dan mian* or *don mein* in Chinese. They are sold fresh, either cut as noodles, or in sheets ready to be made into wontons and egg rolls.

Harusame: Japanese vermicelli; they are thin, translucent, and made from sweet

---

PASTA SHAPES

Most people are familiar with all the classic pasta shapes—spaghetti, elbows, wagon wheels, bow ties—but there is an astonishing array of shapes available, with the choices growing almost daily. Here's a quick compendium of the some of the more unusual shapes you can buy in the supermarket:

Bucatini: Long, hollow strands; like a thick spaghetti with a hole running down the center. Its name comes from *buco*, the Italian word for hole.

Campanelle: A frilly-edged pasta rolled into a cone shape; its name means *little bells.*

Cavatappi: Short lengths of tubular pasta in a corkscrew shape.

Cavatelli: Thick discs of dough rolled into a not-quite-closed cylinder; its name comes from the Italian verb meaning "to hollow."

Creste di gallo: Like large elbow macaroni but with a ruffle running down the outer curve; its name means *rooster's crest.*

Fiori: Like wagon-wheel pasta but with flower petals surrounding the central hub instead of spokes.

Foglie d'ulivo: Flat, leaf shapes; the name means *olive leaf.*

Gemelli: A thick strand of pasta doubled over and twisted together into a short length; its name means *twins.*

Gnochetti: A dried pasta made to look like the fresh dumplings called *gnocchi.*

Lumache: A hollow pasta shape that looks like a snail shell; its name means *snail.*

Orecchiette: A flat disc that is domed in the center; its name means *little ear.*

Perciatelli: This is like bucatini (left), but is thicker; its name comes from the word for *pierced.*

Radiatore: Small, tight ruffles; named for their resemblance to old-fashioned radiators.

Strozzapreti: A short rectangle of dough rolled up tight; it means *priest chokers* in Italian, although it is not known how it got this name.

Trofie: Short lengths of thick, tightly twisted strands

potato, potato, rice, or mung bean starch.

Pancit luglug: Philippine noodles made from cornstarch.

Ramen: Japanese noodles generally sold in packages of instant soup. The noodles are precooked by steaming, making them perfect for quick cooking.

Rice noodles: Made from rice flour and known by many names: *sha he fen, sa ho fun, gan he fen, gon ho fun* in Chinese. In Vietnamese: *banh pho, bun,* and *banh hoi*. Dried, they come coiled in bags and are either very thin noodles or spaghetti-like threads. Thinner, they're sold as rice vermicelli; the thicker strands are called rice sticks. They are also sold fresh in wide strips that are cut into wide ribbons or used as dumpling-like wrappers.

Rice papers or wrappers: Sold dry in round, square, or triangular shapes, these translucent sheets need a brief soaking in cold water before being wrapped around different fillings.

Seaweed noodles: Chinese noodles made from seaweed, they are similar to bean threads.

Shirataki: Japanese noodles, also known as *ito konnayaku*, made from a type of yam called devil's tongue. They can be found canned or fresh.

Somen: Japanese wheat noodle generally served cold. Another type of Japanese somen has egg yolks and is called *tamago somen*.

Tofu noodles: Also known as soybean curd noodles and called *gan si*. They can be found fresh, dried, or frozen.

Udon: Japanese wheat noodles sold fresh or dried; they are thick and chewy.

MAKING HANDMADE RAVIOLI

Make "Fresh Whole Wheat Egg Pasta" (page 348). Also make about 4 cups of filling for 5 dozen ravioli.

Divide the dough into four pieces. Let dough rest for several minutes, then knead each piece into a ball. Work with one ball at a time, keeping the rest covered with an inverted bowl.

With a pasta machine, follow the manufacturer's directions to create a sheet of dough ¹⁄₁₆ inch thick. Make a second sheet of dough.

Spoon tablespoons of the filling mixture 2 inches apart onto one sheet (A). Cover with the second sheet of dough.

Gently press down the spaces between the lumps of filling (B). Cut out squares with a knife or a pasta crimper (C). (If using a knife, crimp edges closed with a fork.)

Ravioli can be prepared up to 6 hours ahead of time; freeze for longer storage. To freeze: Arrange ravioli in single layers on towel-lined, cornmeal dusted baking sheets, and freeze. When frozen solid, transfer to plastic freezer bags, in portions if you like, or shallow airtight containers. They will keep for several months in the freezer. They can be cooked straight from frozen.

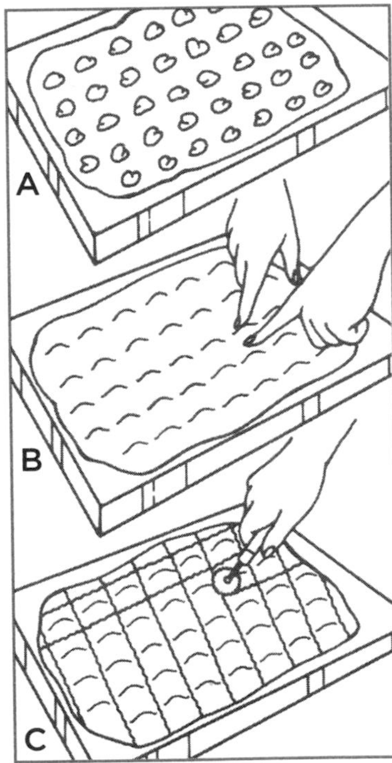

Fats & Oils

Fat not only is key to sustaining life—our bodies require fat as an energy source—but also it is extremely important to the cooking process and to the flavor of dishes. There are, however, differences in the health risks and benefits associated with each type of fat. Here are some quick guidelines for the sensible use of fat in your cooking:

- When possible, choose liquid oils over solid fats (like butter or shortening). Solid fats are higher in either saturated fats or trans fats, which are the types of fat that have been implicated in a whole host of diseases. Oils, on the other hand, are mostly healthful unsaturated fats (with the exception of some tropical oils).
- In baking, although solid fats often produce the best results, experiment with substituting oil for some of the solid fat.
- Butter adds remarkable flavor to dishes. However, instead of using all butter in sautéing, use a combination of butter and oil. Or use all oil and then add just a very little bit of butter at the end of cooking, for flavor.
- Avoid margarines and butter blends or spreads that have trans fats.
- When choosing oils, choose those higher in monounsaturated fats and/or lower in saturated fats. See "Comparative Fats," opposite.

TRANS FATTY ACIDS

To make vegetable oils solid at room temperature, thus making them more shelf stable, food manufacturers partially hydrogenate (add hydrogen molecules to) them. The process converts unsaturated fats to more saturated fats, creating something called trans fatty acids, or trans fats. Studies have shown that trans fats increase blood cholesterol levels and are even more unhealthful than saturated fats. For this reason, the United States Food and Drug Administration has mandated that trans fats be listed on food labels.

Vegetable Oils

Other than the choices you might make for health reasons, there are other factors involved in your choice of cooking or salad oil. (For more information on the flavor differences among oils, see "Salad Oils" on page 372.)

Unrefined oils: Most oils are refined by means of chemicals and high heat to remove solids, color, flavor, and aroma and to prolong shelf life. Unrefined oils have a much stronger flavor, a deeper color, and may darken even more at high cooking temperatures.

Expeller-pressed oils: These oils are pressed simply by crushing nuts or seeds. The only heat involved comes from the friction naturally produced in the pressing process.

Cold-pressed oils: These are expeller-pressed oils that are produced in a heat-controlled environment. The cold-press process is used for

COMPARATIVE FATS

Every type of fat, from lard to canola oil, is a blend of (primarily) three types of fats: monounsaturated, polyunsaturated, and saturated. The list below is organized by percentages of fat type, starting with those lowest in saturated fat—the least healthy type of fat. Margarines are not listed because with the huge difference among brands, you're better off reading the label to determine the breakdown.

	PERCENT SATURATED FAT	PERCENT MONOUNSATURATED FAT	PERCENT POLYUNSATURATED FAT
HAZELNUT OIL	7	78	10
CANOLA OIL	7	59	30
ALMOND OIL	8	70	17
WALNUT OIL	9	23	63
SAFFLOWER OIL	9	12	75
SUNFLOWER OIL	10	84	4
AVOCADO OIL	10	71	13
FLAXSEED OIL	10	17	69
CORN OIL	13	24	59
OLIVE OIL	14	74	8
PISTACHIO OIL	14	49	33
SESAME OIL	15	40	41
SOYBEAN OIL	15	11	45
PEANUT OIL	17	46	32
SOLID VEGETABLE SHORTENING	23	64	7
LARD	40	42	14
BUTTER	62	29	4

delicate oils that are particularly heat sensitive. However, because there are no regulations on the definition of cold-pressed, the use of this term on the label is not a guarantee that the oil is either expeller-pressed or unrefined.

Toasted or roasted oils: Certain seed oils (such as sesame or pumpkin seed) and some nut oils are roasted before the oil is pressed out. These oils have very deep flavor and are best used in small amounts.

Vegetable oils: Many supermarket oils are simply sold as vegetable oil. They can be from a single source (such as soybeans or sunflower seeds) or they can be a blend of oils. To choose an oil that is high in healthful unsaturated fats, check the label, which should have the total fat broken down by saturated, monounsaturated, polyunsaturated, and trans fats. An oil that is high in unsaturated oils is one that is no more than 7 percent saturated fat. To determine the percentage, note the grams of saturated fat and divide by the total grams of fat. Keep in mind that the result will be a ballpark figure, since the gram amounts on the label are rounded-off numbers.

Nut oils: Nut oils can come both roasted and cold-pressed. The cold-pressed oils are most commonly found in health food stores; roasted oils tend to be found in high-end supermarkets and gourmet shops. The exception to this is peanut oil, which is readily available in supermarkets.

Storing Oils

As a general rule, oils that are higher in unsaturated fats (see "Comparative Fats," page 111) go rancid more quickly than those with more saturated fats. Those oils are best stored in the refrigerator. Some clouding under refrigeration is normal.

Herbs, Spices & Chilies

Herbs & Spices

For centuries, clever cooks have used small amounts of fresh herbs and fragrant spices to add new tastes to familiar dishes or to heighten the good flavors already present. Using these seasonings is neither tricky nor mysterious, but a cook's effective use of them does involve a certain amount of experience. There are many classic pairings—cumin and oregano in Mexican food, basil and mint in Thai dishes—and you can't go wrong if you stay with the tried and true. But as you develop your own sense of what herbs and spices taste like, you should get creative. Just be aware that in seasoning, keeping it simple is probably the best advice, especially when it comes to combining herbs and spices. Many work well together and some can even be substituted for each other, but sometimes the combinations will yield unexpectedly unpleasant results.

Because individual tastes differ so much, it is difficult to give precise directions for seasoning with herbs and spices. Enhancement to one person may be ruination to another, so it is best to find your way to the ideal measurement by starting with small amounts to avoid overseasoning.

Buying Herbs & Spices

When buying fresh herbs, the rule is the same as for any fresh leafy vegetable: The leaves should be fresh looking and not wilted. Some fresh herbs come with their roots still on (basil and cilantro), which helps them keep longer. For dried herbs and spices, buy in bulk only if you use the seasoning regularly because dried seasonings lose their potency over time. Buy in small quantities to be sure that you aren't wasting your money.

Storing Herbs & Spices

Fresh herbs are more flavorful than dried herbs. These days you can get fresh herbs year-round, although as with all vegetables, they will be cheaper and more abundant during your local growing season. Parsley, dill, basil, and mint, however, have become such staples that their off-season prices are decent.

Fresh herbs should be stored in the refrigerator with the same care you would give other leafy green vegetables. Wash fresh herbs gently and pat them dry with paper towels or dry them in a salad spinner. Be sure they are as dry as possible before refrigerating them since moisture invites mold growth. Then wrap in paper toweling to absorb excess moisture and place loosely in a plastic bag. They will keep this way for 3 to 4 days.

If you find you have an overabundance of fresh herbs and want to store them for longer than a few days, snip the leaves from their stems with scissors (after you have rinsed and dried them). Place the leaves—chopped or whole—in plastic sandwich bags and store in the freezer. They will retain most of their fresh flavor this way and can be used directly from the freezer for cooking. For more information, see "Freezing Herbs," page 627.

Dried herbs and spices should be stored in a cool spot away from direct sunlight.

Preparing Fresh Herbs

There are several basic ways to prepare fresh herbs, depending on the herb type.

Large leaves: Basil and mint are examples of herbs where (generally) just the leaves are used. Pull the leaves off the stem and chop, or tightly roll up the leaves cigar fashion and cut crosswise into shreds.

Feathery herbs: Dill, chives, and fennel are best "snipped" with a pair of kitchen scissors because they are too thin to effectively chop with a knife.

Stemmed herbs: Some herbs have flavorful enough stems that you can chop them right along with the leaves (cilantro, parsley), but many herbs have stems that are too tough and/or not very flavorful. For those herbs—such as thyme, rosemary, and oregano—pull the leaves off the stems before chopping.

Preparing Spices

Sometimes you want to add whole spices to certain dishes (cinnamon stick in a mulled cider, for example) and sometimes you want to have the ground form (ground cinnamon in a muffin). If you have both whole and ground forms available, then you have the choice.

Spices that have been freshly crushed, ground, or grated will have a fresher flavor than the preground. An electric spice grinder is very handy for grinding whole spices. A small spice grater for whole nutmeg is also useful, and comes in handy for grating fresh ginger as well. For crushing herbs and spices and blending them into other ingredients, a mortar and pestle is very efficient.

If you use a blender to grind spices and herbs try this method: A pint canning jar with a standard-size mouth will fit perfectly into many blender bases. Just put the spices in the jar, place the blade, rubber, and screw bottom of the blender container onto the jar as you would a lid. Turn the jar upside down, place in the blender base, and proceed with grinding.

When to Add Herbs & Spices to Dishes

The rule of thumb is that you add spices early on in the dish so they can develop flavor. For example, meats and poultry are often rubbed with spices before cooking, and in Indian cuisine spices are heated in the cooking oil (or butter) before the other ingredients go in.

Similarly, dried herbs should be added to soups, stews, and sauces toward the beginning of cooking so they can infuse the liquid with flavor. But fresh herbs should be added toward the very end so they do not lose pungency. For very long-cooking soups, stews, or sauces, wait until the last 30 minutes to add any seasonings because the prolonged cooking will dissipate rather than concentrate the flavors.

POPULAR HERB & SPICE BLENDS

A number of herb and spice blends are classic and nice to have around premixed for convenience. Traditional mixtures such as curry powder might have 6 to 20 different ingredients. Versions of these blends are commonly available commercially, but these may not offer the exact balance of flavors you desire. It might be more satisfying to make your own at home where you can control the degree of fire. As with any seasoning, you should freely vary the amounts of each herb or spice to suit your own taste. Use the same precautions to store these blends as you would all herbs and spices.

BLEND	USUAL INGREDIENTS
CHILI POWDER	Allspice, chili peppers, cloves, cumin, garlic, onion, oregano
CHINESE FIVE-SPICE POWDER	Cinnamon, cloves, fennel, pepper, star anise
CRAB BOIL	Bay leaf, ginger, mustard seeds, pepper
CREOLE SEASONING	Cayenne pepper, black pepper, thyme, oregano, garlic, salt
CURRY POWDER	Allspice, cardamom, cumin, pepper, cinnamon, coriander, cumin, fennel seeds, fenugreek, ginger, mace, turmeric
GARAM MASALA	Pepper, cloves, cardamom, star anise, coriander, bay leaves, mace, fenugreek
HERBES DE PROVENCE	Thyme, chervil, rosemary, savory, lavender, marjoram, tarragon, oregano, bay leaves
ITALIAN SEASONING	Basil, marjoram, oregano, sage, rosemary, thyme, savory
JERK SEASONING	Cayenne, thyme, allspice, turmeric, pepper, salt
OLD BAY SEASONING	Celery seed, cardamom, mustard seed, bay leaves, nutmeg, cloves, ginger, paprika
PICKLING SPICE	Allspice, bay leaves, cinnamon, cloves, coriander, ginger root, mustard, pepper (sometimes anise, dill)
POULTRY SEASONING	Marjoram, pepper, sage, savory, thyme (sometimes rosemary)
PUMPKIN PIE SPICE	Cinnamon, ginger, mace, nutmeg

A GUIDE TO HERBS & SPICES

HERB/SPICE		APPEARANCE & FLAVOR	DRIED FORMS AVAILABLE	READILY GROWN AT HOME?	SUBSTITUTION
ALLSPICE		Reddish brown berry; pungent flavor similar to a blend of cinnamon, nutmeg, cloves	Whole seeds; ground	No	Cinnamon, cloves, nutmeg
ANISE SEEDS		Small, grayish brown, oval-shaped seed; tastes of licorice	Whole seeds; ground	No	Fennel
BASIL		Bright, green leaves when fresh; brownish olive when dried; sweetly pungent; comes in a variety of types, including opal and lemon	Crushed leaves	Yes	Marjoram, oregano, thyme
BAY LEAF		Long, green leaves; woody, menthol flavor (bitter if used too freely)	Whole leaves; ground	Yes	Mint
CAPERS		Small, olive greenish pods; sharp, pungent, briny flavor	Packed in salt or vinegar	No	Pickled green peppers
CARAWAY		Small, brown, crescent-shaped seed; common flavoring for rye bread	Whole seeds	Yes	Anise seeds
CARDAMOM		Small, brown or greenish-beige pod containing small black seeds; gingery-lemon, aromatic flavor	Whole pods; ground	No	Coriander, ginger
CAYENNE		Ground red chili pepper; quite hot	Ground	Yes	Hot paprika, chipotle powder
CELERY SEEDS		Small, light brown seeds; celery taste; not from the plant of the same name, but a different plant in the parsley family	Whole seeds; ground	No	Finely chopped celery leaves
CHERVIL		Delicate, feathery leaves; light licorice/parsley taste	Whole leaves; ground	Yes	Tarragon
CHILIES (SEE ALSO CAYENNE)	Ancho	Large dried chili, usually from the poblano pepper; mild to moderate heat	Whole pods; ground	N/A	Cayenne; chipotle
	Chipotle	Jalapeño pepper that's been smoked; quite hot with a smoky flavor	Whole pods; ground; packed in adobo sauce	N/A	Ancho chili; cayenne
CHIVE		Thin, green, tubular leaves; delicate onion flavor	Freeze-dried minced	Yes	Scallions
CILANTRO		Short stemmed with thin, round, slightly fringed leaves; looks like pale parsley; pungent smell and taste	Available dried, but not very flavorful	Yes	Italian parsley

A GUIDE TO HERBS & SPICES—*CONTINUED*

HERB/SPICE		APPEARANCE & FLAVOR	DRIED FORMS AVAILABLE	READILY GROWN AT HOME?	SUBSTITUTION
CINNAMON		Reddish brown, rolled-up quill-like sticks; sweet, mildly hot; true cinnamon is from the bark of *Cinnamomum zeylanicum.*	Sticks; ground	No	Allspice, nutmeg
CLOVES		Dried, unopened buds of a tropical evergreen; strong, sweet, and pungent	Whole buds; ground	No	Allspice, ginger
CORIANDER		Dried, ripe berries of cilantro plant; almost round with straight and wavy ridges; flavor of lemon peel and sage	Whole seeds, ground	Yes	Cardamom, ginger
CUMIN		Long, thin seed, yellow brown in color; dry earthy taste	Whole seeds; ground	No	Turmeric
DILL	Seeds	Small tan, flattish seeds; the flavor commonly associated with dill pickles	Whole seeds	Yes	Caraway
	Weed	Feathery leaves of dill plant	Available dried, but is less pungent than fresh	Yes	Basil
FENNEL SEEDS		Long, greenish seeds; licorice flavor	Whole seeds; ground	Yes	Anise seeds, tarragon
FENUGREEK		Smooth, red brown, unevenly shaped seeds; the sweetish flavor that most people identify with curry	Whole seeds; ground	No	Anise, caraway, fennel seeds
GINGER		Gnarl-shaped, light brown root; sweet, piquant, peppery	Ground; crystallized; preserved	No	Cardamom, coriander
JUNIPER BERRIES		Hard round, dark-brown seeds; a resinous, pine-y taste; used to flavor gin and marinades for game	Whole seeds	No	Allspice, black pepper
MACE		Lacy, fibrous covering around the nutmeg shell; tastes like nutmeg but milder	Whole blades; ground	No	Nutmeg
MARJORAM		Gray-green leaves; musky, slight oregano bouquet	Whole leaves; crushed	Yes	Oregano
MINT		Dark emerald leaves; warm menthol flavor	Whole leaves; crushed	Yes	Basil, bay leaf
MUSTARD		Tiny, white, yellow, or brown seeds; sharp, tangy biting	Whole seeds; ground	Yes	Prepared mustard

A GUIDE TO HERBS & SPICES—*CONTINUED*

HERB/SPICE		APPEARANCE & FLAVOR	DRIED FORMS AVAILABLE	READILY GROWN AT HOME?	SUBSTITUTION
NUTMEG		Very hard, brown, ovular seed pods; spicy, mellow, nutty	Whole pods; ground	No	Cinnamon, mace
OREGANO		Grayish green leaves; strong, aromatic, slightly menthol	Whole leaves; crushed	Yes	Basil, marjoram, thyme
PAPRIKA	Sweet or hot	Slightly piquant peppers ripened to bright red and dried; comes in sweet (mild) and hot forms	Ground	No	Ancho powder, cayenne
	Smoked	Bright red powder made from the same type of pepper as sweet paprika, but smoked before drying; deeply flavored and smoky	Ground	N/A	Sweet paprika; chipolte
PARSLEY		Curly small or flat green leaves (Italian parsley); herbal, sweet flavor	Available as dried flakes but not very flavorful	Yes	Basil
PEPPER	Black	Round, black, shriveled berries; hot, biting, pungent taste	Whole pepper-corns; ground	No	Cayenne pepper, red pepper
	Szech-uan	Rough, reddish brown shell and black seed; warm, peppery flavor	Whole pods	No	White pepper
	White	Small ivory berry; milder than black pepper; from the same plant as black pepper but with the black hull removed	Whole peppercorns	No	Black pepper
PEPPERS, CHILI (SEE CHILIES)					
PEPPERCORNS, GREEN		Small green berries; mildly pungent; the unripe fruit of the pepper plant	Whole, water-packed or brined	No	Capers
PEPPER FLAKES, RED		Dried cayenne peppers; quite spicy	Crushed flakes	N/A	Ground cayenne
ROSEMARY		Gray green, curved, pine needle leaves; sweet, minty taste (perfumy if overused)	Whole leaves; ground	Yes	Mint, sage
SAFFRON		Delicate, orange yellow filaments; pleasantly bitter	Whole threads; ground	No	Turmeric (for color only)
SAGE		Silver-tipped, gray green leaves; strong, astringent, slightly bitter flavor	Whole leaves; ground; rubbed	Yes	Rosemary, savory
SAVORY		Dried, brownish green leaves; aromatic, piquant	Whole leaves; ground	Yes	Sage

A GUIDE TO HERBS & SPICES—*CONTINUED*

HERB/SPICE	APPEARANCE & FLAVOR	DRIED FORMS AVAILABLE	READILY GROWN AT HOME?	SUBSTITUTION
STAR ANISE	Star-shaped dark-brown pods with 5 to 8 points, each containing a shiny brown seed; tastes of licorice	Whole pods	No	Anise seeds, fennel seeds, tarragon
TARRAGON	Long, thin, green leaves; sweet, slight licorice taste	Whole leaves; ground	Yes	Chervil, fennel
THYME	Gray green, curly leaves; warm, slightly lemony	Whole leaves; ground	Yes	Basil, marjoram, oregano
TURMERIC	Yellow orange root; similar to ginger root in shape; musky, slightly bitter	Ground	No	Cumin
VANILLA BEAN	Very dark, long, slender seed pods; sweet, pleasantly perfumy flavor	Whole beans	No	Vanilla extract

Guide to Specialty Herbs

Here's a quick guide to a number of interesting herbs that you won't find in supermarkets. To use any of these herbs fresh, you will probably have to grow them yourself (see "Growing Herbs at Home," page 120), but for the dried form, there are numerous online sources for just about any dried herb you can think of.

Borage: This plant produces beautiful blue flowers. It must be used fresh immediately or washed and frozen in plastic bags since its flavor diminishes quickly. Its light, refreshing flavor (reminiscent of cucumber) is most welcome in fish dishes, soups, and salad dressings. You may also cook it as you would other greens.

Burnet: A perennial herb, burnet contributes a hint of cucumber to fresh salads; its leaves may also be floated in iced beverages.

Chamomile: This fragrant herb is most often used in herbal teas; a small amount may also be added to meat stocks for a light, lemony flavor.

Costmary: Its leaves may be steeped to make a tea with a light mint flavor. Costmary is also good in soups, sauces, green salads, chicken, and fish dishes.

Horehound: This plant's curly leaves are most often made into an extract used to flavor candy.

Hyssop: The minty leaves of hyssop may be used in vegetable or fruit salads. Its flowers are also used for a tisane.

Lemon balm: This herb has fragrant leaves and is most often used in tisanes. The leaves may also be used to garnish fruit punches.

Lemon verbena: This sweet, lemon-flavored herb is best used in teas, but may also be used to garnish fruit salads and desserts.

GROWING HERBS AT HOME

Starting an herb garden indoors is very easy. Any window that gets bright sun for at least 6 hours of the day will serve well as a growing area. Here are just a few rules.

- Herbs started indoors for later transplanting out in the garden are best started from seed no earlier than March; otherwise they will not grow into strong, healthy plants.
- Seed each variety in a separate container to allow for the varying length of time each needs to germinate. Some herbs, for example, germinate within 48 hours, while others might take 3 weeks or longer.
- Choose a container that will make it possible to plant the seeds in rows rather than having to scatter them over the whole surface area. The rows should be at least 1 inch apart and about ¼ inch deep, the growing medium itself 1 inch below the rim of the container.
- After the seeds have been thinly sown in the row or rows, water them with a fine mist of water and cover the container with two sheets of newspaper. Place the container in a warm area—preferably 70°F or a little warmer—just until the seeds germinate. Then keep the growing seedlings at 60° to 65°F to keep them from shooting up too rapidly. From then on the seeds need misting with water only enough to keep the soil constantly moist but not soggy.
- Once the seedlings develop their first seed leaves, usually in 7 to 10 days, transplant into pots, one to a pot, or into flats with a minimum spacing of 1¼ inches. The seedlings should have a single root. Set the plant itself into the soil deeper than it grew in the seed flat. The soil into which these little plants are set may be regular potting soil or at least a richer medium than that of the seed flat.
- After 4 weeks the plants will be ready for transplanting into 3-inch pots and from there, after another 3 to 4 weeks, the plants may be planted outside any time depending on variety and weather.
- Clip the sprigs or leaves as you need them. The plants will grow more if they are trimmed often, so use herbs whenever possible. Cut with scissors, always snipping from the top of the plant.

Extending the Season

After the outdoor growing season, repot the herbs and bring them indoors. These general rules will help ensure success with an indoor windowsill herb garden:

- Use a potting mix of equal parts of peat moss, perlite, and good potting soil.
- Keep the herbs in a sunny window where they will get at least 6 hours of sun a day. Protect them from drafts in extremely cold weather.
- Arrange the pots on a tray containing pebbles and a small amount of water to keep the humidity level constant around the plants, and water the plants often enough to keep the soil moist but not soggy.
- Fertilize about every 2 weeks with deodorized fish emulsion.
- Clip sprigs and leaves from tops regularly to encourage new growth.

Lovage: The flavor of lovage is so close to that of celery that its leaves and stalks are often substituted for it. A tea may be made from lovage leaves. The seeds may be used in cakes and cookies, or pickled like capers.

Sweet cicely: Its sweet-smelling leaves and green seeds may be added to salads or vegetables. The dried seeds may be used to flavor cakes and confections.

Woodruff: The Germans celebrate the advent of spring with *Maibowle,* a wine punch flavored with this sweet woodland herb. Fresh woodruff leaves may also be floated in other cold punches.

HOMEMADE HERB VINEGARS

Fresh herbs soaked in vinegar result in sweet, aromatic infusions. You may use a sprig of any fresh herb—or combine several—with vinegar and allow the herbs to exude their delicate flavors. Herb vinegars can be used in salad dressings, and to marinate meat, fish, and cooked vegetables. Store herb vinegars at room temperature. If a vinegar becomes too strong after standing, dilute with the same type of vinegar from which it was made.

Using the chart below, choose a vinegar, an herb (or a combination), and an optional extra. Place the herb (and extra, if using) in a 1-pint jar. Pour in the vinegar. Let sit for at least 1 week (unless you're using a chili pepper, in which case check it after 1 or 2 days to be sure it's not getting overpowering).

VINEGAR (2 CUPS)	HERBS (1 SPRIG)	OPTIONAL EXTRA
White wine	Tarragon	1 clove garlic, halved
Red wine	Chervil	2 strips orange zest
Sherry wine	Dill	¼ small jalapeño pepper
Champagne	Mint	¼ teaspoon black peppercorns
Cider	Thyme	3 coin-sized slices fresh ginger
Rice	Rosemary	2 strips lemon zest

Chilies

The classification of the chili as a fruit belies its truly volatile nature. It is the chili's characteristic bite and zing (thanks to a chemical called capsaicin) that people either relish or avoid with equal passion.

Chilies have varying degrees of heat (see "The Heat in Chilies," opposite), so people who would otherwise abstain can savor some chili dishes without the risk of a fire-eating experience. Although climate, soil, and similar variables dictate the pungency of all types of chilies, you can look to appearance as a clue to the degree of heat. Contrary to what one might expect, size and shape—not color—are most telling. Very generally speaking, the smaller the chili is, the hotter it is. This is not true across the board, however, so always take a tiny (really tiny) taste of a fresh chili before you consider putting it in a dish.

Color does, however, indicate ripeness and, in some cases, spiciness. Red chilies, despite their flamboyant "hot" color, may be milder than green chilies. That is because red chilies are riper and their sweetness masks some of the heat. The pale green chilies are the most immature and they are milder than the riper dark green ones. Dark green chilies that are just streaked with light red are generally seething with spiciness and fire.

Buying & Storing Chilies

The fresh chilies most commonly found in supermarkets (outside the Southwest) are jalapeños and serranos. Farmer's markets and markets in Asian and Latin communities will carry a much broader range of fresh chilies. Dried whole chilies, available in cellophane packages, can be found year-round (though they may be less prevalent in the eastern part of the country). You can usually also find jarred pickled or brined chilies in most supermarkets.

When buying fresh, look for firm, smooth, blemish-free chilies. Avoid any that look mushy or have begun to shrivel. Dried chilies should be dark red (almost maroon) and have long uniform pods. Avoid any gnarled or withered ones that display signs of mold or decay from improper drying.

Dried powdered chilies are also available in many supermarkets. In addition to the ubiquitous cayenne pepper, also known as ground red pepper, there are also other chili-specific powders (not to be confused with "chili powder," which is a spice blend sometimes labeled "chili seasoning"). The mostly commonly found powdered chilies are ancho, pasilla, and chipotle.

Refrigerate fresh chilies wrapped in absorbent paper for up to 4 days. Store dried chilies in your kitchen cabinet for up to 6 months.

Preparing Fresh Chilies

When handling fresh chilies, it is a good idea to protect your hands from the irritating effects of capsaicin by wearing gloves.

Many recipes call for chilies to have their seeds and ribs (the spongy material to which the seeds are attached) removed because this is where much of the chili's heat is located. For a hotter dish, leave the ribs and seeds in.

If the recipe calls for peeling the chilies, here's how: Preheat the broiler. Rinse the chilies under cold water and slit them at the stem with a knife tip. Spread them on a baking sheet. Broil as close to the heat as possible until the skin parches and blisters, about 10 minutes. Remove the chilies from the baking sheet, place in a bowl, and cover with a cool, damp towel. Allow to stand for about 10 minutes and then peel.

Preparing Dried Chilies

When using dried chilies, rinse them first to remove any dust that may have accumulated in storage. As with fresh chilies, you would be wise to use gloves to protect your hands from the capsaicin, which is not in any way diminished by the drying process. In fact, the volatile and fiery oils are more concentrated in the dried chilies. You can add chopped dried chilies directly to soups, stews, or moist meat mixtures or any dish that will cook for at least 30 minutes—long enough for the chilies to rehydrate. You can also rehydrate dried chilies before adding them to a dish by chopping them and placing them in a bowl with enough water to cover. Drain and use after 1 hour.

THE HEAT IN CHILIES

In the early 1900s, a pharmacist named Wilbur Scoville developed an index for the "heat" in chili peppers. The heat is measured in Scoville Units, with each unit representing 15 parts per million of capsaicin, which is the substance that makes chilies fiery. Pure capsaicin has 16 million Scoville Units. On the other end of the spectrum is bell peppers with 0 Scoville Units. Some of the peppers in the chart below have a range, because you can find milder and hotter versions of the same pepper depending on growing conditions.

CHILI PEPPER	SCOVILLE UNITS
Cherry	100-500
New Mexico	500-1,000
Ancho	1,000-1,500
Poblano	1,000-1,500
Pasilla	2,000-2,500
Jalapeño	2,500-5,000
Chipotle	10,000
Serrano	10,000-20,000
Cayenne	30,000-50,000
Thai	50,000-75,000
Scotch bonnet	100,000-350,000
Habanero	200,000-300,000

Sweeteners

All sugars are pretty much the same. They are simple carbohydrates used by the body as a source of quick energy. Of the sugars that we add to foods (as opposed to sugars found naturally in whole foods, such as fruits), there are very few differences as far as your health goes. The calories and metabolic influences of honey and white sugar, for example, are nearly identical. However, there are other reasons to choose one type of sweetener over another.

Flavor: Some sweeteners (brown sugar, maple syrup, molasses) bring more than just sweetness to a recipe; they also add an interesting depth of flavor.

Nutrients: Sugars that are closer to their natural states (unpasteurized honey, molasses) tend to have more minerals, though the quantities are so small that you would have to consume a huge amount of the sweetener to make any difference. Recent studies also suggest that honey may have some antioxidant compounds.

Calories: Since liquid sweeteners tend to be perceived as sweeter, you may use smaller amounts and improve your calorie count, though the differences are small.

Blood sugar levels: A sweetener made from the agave plant is metabolized more slowly by the body, making it a better choice for anyone concerned with blood sugar levels.

In baked goods, the nature of the sweetener—liquid versus granulated—influences texture and crispness. For example, cookies made with honey will be moist and soft (honey has an ability to retain water); the same cookie made with granulated sugar will come out crisper. We have developed recipes with this in mind. If you substitute one type of sugar for another in the recipes in this book, you will not get the same results.

In non-baked goods, it's easier to swap out sweeteners, keeping in mind that most (but not all) liquid sweeteners are much sweeter than the granulated; taste as you go.

Granulated Sweeteners

White sugar: Refined from sugar cane (more common) or sugar beets. Look for organic, unbleached varieties. Confectioners' sugar, or powdered sugar, is made by processing white sugar to a very fine powder with cornstarch added to prevent clumping.

Brown sugar: White sugar mixed with molasses to give it its characteristic flavor and color. Comes in light brown and dark brown. Nutritional differences between this and white sugar are negligible.

Raw sugar: The first batch of crystals separated from cane syrup in the refining process; it is steam-cleaned but not bleached white. (Truly raw sugar is banned from sale in this country because it contains many impurities.) This caramel-colored sugar comes in a variety of flavors including demerara, dark muscovado, and turbinado. It is nutritionally equal to white sugar.

Evaporated cane juice: Made from organic

sugar cane with minimal processing and no chemical additives; the flavor is similar to light brown sugar. Sold under the trade name Sucanat.

Maple sugar: Evaporated maple syrup; tastes sweeter than sugar but has fewer calories. It is not a practical substitute, however, because of its cost.

Liquid Sweeteners

Honey: A sweet liquid made by bees from flower nectar. The color and flavor vary with the nectar's source and run from very mild (orange blossom, clover) to dark and deep (buckwheat). Honey contains small quantities of minerals such as potassium, calcium, and phosphorus, but should not be considered as an important dietary source for any of these. All honey, even raw honey, is heated to some extent during processing. However, some honey found in supermarkets is heated for unnecessarily long periods and at high temperatures, simply to keep it clear for a long shelf life.

Maple syrup: The boiled-down sap of maple trees; sweeter than white sugar but not quite as sweet as honey. Grade A maple syrup is the commonest grade available, but Grade B, sometimes labeled amber, has a much deeper maple flavor.

Molasses: A by-product of sugar refining; contains trace amounts of minerals. Light molasses comes from the first stage of the refining process; dark molasses comes from the second stage; blackstrap comes from the third stage and is the darkest and most bitter of the three. Unsulfured molasses is more delicately flavored than sulfured molasses; whether or not sulphur is used in the processing depends on whether or not the sugar cane was sun-ripened (no sulphur) or harvested green.

Sorghum syrup: Boiled down juice from the sorghum plant (a cereal grass). It is sometimes called sorghum molasses and tastes like light molasses.

Barley malt: Made from roasted sprouted barley cooked down to make a thick syrup that tastes similar to molasses. It is only half as sweet as white sugar.

Corn syrup: Made by converting the starches in corn to sugar. Comes in light and dark.

Rice syrup: Made from a combination of malted barley (see Barley malt above) and cooked brown rice; sometimes sold as brown rice syrup. Chai teas are often sweetened with rice syrup.

Agave nectar (agave syrup): Made from the core of the agave cactus. It resembles honey, ranging from pale to dark amber, but dissolves more easily in liquids. Like most liquid sweeteners, agave is sweeter than white sugar. Agave is metabolized by the body so slowly that this is the sweetener of choice for those with diabetes.

PART 3

In the Kitchen

Beverages

An invitation to stop by for a drink is an invitation to relax and spend time chatting with a friend. Whatever you choose to serve will be welcome—a comforting cup of hot herb tea on a cold afternoon, a high-protein smoothie to replenish after a workout at the gym, a tall glass of icy homemade lemonade on a lazy summer day.

Aside from their social value, beverages play an important role in maintaining good health. To be at your best, you should drink eight to ten glasses of fluids a day. And that need increases when you are exposed to hot weather, very active, or sick.

Fruit Juice

Sweet or tangy, pulpy or clear, fresh fruit juice is a treat any time of day. At breakfast, plain juice starts the day right. Or whipped with milk or yogurt, it makes a great grab-and-go lunch. And it's a lovely basis for a warming hot drink mulled with spices.

Most fruit juice is rich in nutrients, so you can also think of it as a delicious way to get your vitamins. For example, citrus juices are rich in vitamin C, pomegranate juice is a rich source of antioxidants, and grape juice has plentiful amounts of the cardio-protective phytochemical resveratrol.

Whenever possible, serve freshly processed fruit juice (see "Making Fruit Juice," page 130). It is sweeter and more delicately flavored than frozen or canned juice. This is particularly true of citrus juice.

As far as sweetening goes, juices from apples, apricots, melons, grapes, peaches, sweet cherries, pears, pineapples, and some berries are sweet enough as they are. Sometimes, a bit of grated zest and a squeeze of citrus juice (orange, lemon, or lime) will give juice a nice tart edge and also help preserve a fresh color. Juices from sour cherries, cranberries, currants, plums, pomegranates, and rhubarb need sweetener to relieve the puckery effect.

Blends of two or more juices, herb teas, and other liquids often have intriguing flavors. But be careful in planning combinations because some mixtures, such as orange juice added to a red juice, can result in a murky brown or gray color; pineapple juice added to a red juice can turn the blend blue.

Vegetable Juice

Tomato juice is still the favorite vegetable juice, but carrot, spinach, cabbage, celery, and cucumber juices are definitely not to be overlooked. Spike any of these with bell pepper, parsley, watercress, or even garlic to add more flavor and food value.

For a drink with heft, use a food processor and serve the drink unstrained. Or if you have a juicer, you can get rid of some of the pulp. Note, however, that the yields of juiced vegetables are smaller than you might expect: For example, 1 pound of

MAKING FRUIT JUICE

To extract the juice from fruits, you can either use an electric juicer that will force the juice out mechanically, or you can use one of these alternate methods:

Clear juice: In a heavy nonaluminum pot, simmer fruit, tightly covered, in a very small amount of water (or in its own juice). When the fruit is tender, press it through two layers of cheesecloth or through a fine-mesh sieve or a food mill. Straining through cheesecloth will give you the clearest juice. Save the pulp for making preserves (see "Jams & Jellies," page 649).

Thick juice: For a pulpier juice that is somewhat diluted in flavor, simply process peeled and chopped fresh fruit with a small amount of liquid in a food processor. One cup of cubed fruit blended with ¼ cup water (or apple juice) will yield about ¾ cup juice.

---

carrots yields only 1 cup of juice, and 1 pound of spinach yields only half a small glass.

Vegetable juices will keep fresh for several days if refrigerated in a covered container. Freeze them for longer storage.

Milk & Yogurt Drinks

Dairy-based drinks, from frothy smoothies to hot mugs of cocoa, consistently have an irresistible rich, sweet taste. The bonus is that because of the calcium (and vitamin D), milk is also very good for bone health.

Fat gives milk and yogurt its smooth texture, but it adds calories, so choose a fat level you're comfortable with: Start with full-fat or 2% and trade down to 1% if that still tastes good to you.

Nothing could be simpler than whipping up fruit with yogurt or cold milk. A blender works best, making a foamy, thoroughly mixed drink in a matter of seconds. When combining milk and an acid fruit puree or juice, gradually pour the fruit into the milk rather than vice versa. Slowly adding the acid source lessens the chance that the milk will curdle.

For hot drinks, warm milk cautiously over low heat or in the top of a double boiler. (Milk scorches very easily.) To prevent a skin from forming on hot milk, stir frequently with a wire whisk. Heat milk only until you see steam rising from the pan. Never boil milk; it will have a "cooked" taste.

Chocolate Drinks

The health benefits of chocolate are now well known, especially for dark chocolate, which has high levels of antioxidant phytochemicals. But unfortunately, there were generations of health-conscious people who avoided chocolate because of its (very small) caffeine content and because of an alkaloid substance called theobromine (also found in tea). The amount of theobromine in chocolate, however, is not dangerous to humans, and in fact some studies even suggest it can actually lower blood pressure. However, it is toxic to dogs and cats.

This newer understanding of chocolate's health benefits has prompted an explosion of interest, with all manner of single-origin chocolates (made from cocoa beans grown in a specific location) now available. There are two basic forms of chocolate used for making drinks—cocoa powder and drinking chocolate. Both are combined with a sweetener and hot milk to make a drink.

Cocoa powder: Unsweetened cocoa is made by finely grinding cacao beans and removing about 90 percent of the fat content (cocoa butter). It comes in regular, dark, and extra-dark. Take care when using extra-dark in a recipe that calls for regular cocoa, because it may need a little more sweetener. There are also Dutch-process cocoas, which have been treated with alkaline compounds to make the cocoa less acidic. Dutch-process cocoa tends to be darker in color and milder in flavor than regular cocoa.

Drinking chocolate: Drinking chocolates resemble cocoa powder, but have more of the cocoa butter left in them. They make an exceptionally rich cup of hot chocolate.

Tea

The Chinese were the first to brew leaves from the *Camellia sinensis* plant, making the piping hot cups of clear, slightly astringent beverage we call tea. Gradually its use spread to the Middle East, to Europe, and then to America, courtesy of the English colonists.

The four basic categories of tea—white, green, oolong (red), black—all come from the same tea plant, but represent different amounts of fermentation. Within the categories of black and oolong teas there are numerous varieties, based largely on where the tea was grown.

White tea: The leaves for white tea are picked from the tea plant before they fully open. They are dried but not in any other way processed. It produces a very mild brew.

Green tea: Leaves for green tea are from fully opened leaves, and are dried right after picking, with no fermentation. They produce a greenish yellow beverage of distinctive flavor.

Oolong (red) tea: Leaves for oolong tea are partially fermented, then dried. The brewed tea has a subtle flavor and bouquet and a light, brownish green color.

Black tea: Black tea leaves are allowed to ferment before they are dried and make a hearty brew with a rich, full, amber color.

You will also find that some teas are labeled pekoe and orange pekoe. These terms refer to the size of the tea leaves, not to variety or flavor.

THE HEALTH BENEFITS OF TEA

Numerous studies have confirmed that tea has significant health benefits because of its phytochemical content, specifically a category of antioxidant compounds called flavonoids (also found in citrus, wine, and chocolate).

All types of tea, from white to black, appear to confer health benefits, although each type has a different phytochemical profile. White and green teas are high in flavonoids called catechins. In red and black teas, the fermentation process appears to convert some of the flavonoids to a substance called theaflavin, which is also being studied for its health benefits. Drinking any kind of tea (from the tea plant) seems to be a win-win choice for health.

ROOIBOS TEA

Rooibos, or red bush, tea is made from the leaves of a bush in the legume family. It tastes like a mild tea (from the tea plant) but has no astringent tannins or caffeine. The leaves are processed in much the same way as regular tea (see "Tea," page 131), which is what makes the leaves (and the brewed tea) red. There are also "green" rooibos teas. Rooibos is being studied for its potentially healthful antioxidant compounds.

Tea, like coffee, has no calories if served without milk or honey. Like coffee, too, it contains caffeine. The caffeine in a cup of tea is usually less than that in a cup of coffee, and white and green teas have even less caffeine than black tea.

Herbal Tea

Supermarkets and natural foods stores carry an amazing array of herbal teas. You can find just about any kind of herbal you could possibly imagine. However, it would also be fun to make your own from either dried herbs that you purchase or those you grow yourself (see "Growing Herbs at Home," page 120). You can make the teas from the fresh herbs or dry them for later use (see "Drying Herbs," page 655). Be sure that you research the potential side effects before you start drinking tea made with an herb you are unfamiliar with. Just because it's "natural" and an herb does not mean it is safe.

You can prepare herb teas by decoction or by infusion.

To decoct an herb: Boil 1 ounce of the herb's roots, bark, or seeds in 3 cups of fresh water for 30 minutes, uncovered; strain. This will give you about 2 cups of concentrated herb tea. It can be diluted to the desired strength by adding fresh boiling water or ice cubes.

To infuse an herb: Bring fresh water to a rapid boil and remove from the heat. For every 5 to 6 fluid ounces of water (standard teacup size), add ¼ to ½ teaspoon of the dried leaves or flowers and steep for 3 to 10 minutes. (If the herb is fresh or very mild, use ½ to 1 tablespoon of leaves or flowers.) Keep the pot or teapot covered to retain heat. Strain out the herb as soon as the tea has reached the desired strength. A well-prepared cup of herb tea is crystal clear.

Coffee

Throughout the world, coffee-serving customs differ almost as much as do people and their cultures. In the United States, being the true melting pot nation, we have embraced many different styles of coffee, from inky espresso to sweet Vietnamese coffee to milky caffe latte.

For home-brewing, the range of coffees avail-

FAIR TRADE

Many coffee beans, teas, and chocolates are now certified as Fair Trade products. This means that the producers of these products in third-world countries are guaranteed a fair price for their goods. The idea behind Fair Trade is to help marginalized workers move toward economic stability, which in turn promotes sustainability.

able is remarkable. You can buy single-origin coffees (those grown in a very specific place, like Ethiopia or Sumatra); you can buy beans classed according to the altitude at which they were grown, or beans that are classified by their size; you can buy beans by the depth of their roast (e.g., light, dark, espresso); and you can buy proprietary blends. Blends are mixtures of coffee beans that are intended to produce a certain style of coffee. It's much like buying wine that blends two types of grapes together. Generally speaking, unless you know a lot about single-origin coffees, you may be better off buying a blend from a producer or roaster you trust.

COFFEE SUBSTITUTES

Although the jury is still out on the health benefits of caffeine—many studies say that caffeine is a powerful antioxidant, others suggest it can be detrimental to your health—there are still plenty of people who avoid caffeine because they don't like the effect it has on them. For those who like the comforting toasted flavor of coffee but don't want the caffeine, toasted nuts or grains make nice alternatives. Try the recipe for Mugi Cha (page 135), which is made from toasted barley, or the Toasted Sesame Seed Tea (page 134).

HOT GINGERED CIDER WITH LADY APPLES

This cider may be prepared up to 6 hours before serving. The longer the mixture steeps, the more the clove and ginger flavor will be enhanced. Remove the clove-pierced apples to reheat.

16 whole cloves, or more to taste

8 lady apples, or other small apples

2 quarts fresh apple cider

1 piece fresh ginger (3 inches), peeled and roughly chopped

Push 2 cloves into each apple.

In a Dutch oven or soup pot, combine the cider, ginger, and apples, and bring to a boil over high heat. Reduce to a simmer and cook, partially covered, until heated through, 10 to 15 minutes.

Strain the ginger from the cider and serve hot with a clove-pierced apple in each mug.

MAKES 10 SERVINGS

HOMEMADE COCOA MIX

This mix makes enough for 6 mugs of hot cocoa, but the recipe is easily multiplied to make more. To make one cup of cocoa, spoon a generous 3 tablespoons of the mix into a mug and moisten with 1 tablespoon cold water. Stir in 1 cup boiling water until thick and smooth.

⅓ cup unsweetened cocoa powder, sifted

1 envelope (3.2 ounces) nonfat dry milk

3 tablespoons sugar

1 teaspoon cinnamon

¼ teaspoon ground cloves

¼ teaspoon ground allspice

¼ teaspoon salt

- 1/8 teaspoon nutmeg
- 3 ounces mini chocolate chips

In a large bowl, whisk together the cocoa powder, nonfat dry milk, sugar, cinnamon, cloves, allspice, salt, and nutmeg. Stir in the chocolate chips.

MAKES 6 SERVINGS

ORANGE-GINSENG TEA

Garnish each cup of tea with a lemon slice. For a special touch, pierce the rind of each lemon slice with 1 or 2 whole cloves.

- 1 teaspoon dried mint
- 1/4 teaspoon powdered ginseng root
- 1 cup boiling water
- 1 cup orange juice

In a small teapot, combine the mint and ginseng. Add the boiling water and steep for 5 minutes. Add the orange juice and mix well.

MAKES 2 SERVINGS

SPICED FRESH-MINT TEA

This could also be made with dried mint (about 1 tablespoon), though the flavors won't be quite as strong.

- 1/4 cup water
- 2 tablespoons turbinado or light brown sugar
- 2 tablespoons chopped fresh mint
- 1/8 teaspoon ground allspice
- 2 cups boiling water
- 1/2 cup orange juice
- 1/4 cup lemon juice

In a small saucepan, combine the 1/4 cup water and sugar and bring to a boil. Cook at a high simmer for 5 minutes.

Off the heat, stir in the mint and allspice and set aside to steep for 10 minutes. Strain the syrup and refrigerate until needed.

When ready to make the tea, in a teapot, combine the syrup, boiling water, orange juice, and lemon juice. Serve hot or chilled.

MAKES 3 TO 4 SERVINGS

TOASTED SESAME SEED TEA

An unusual drink with a rich, toasty flavor.

- 1/4 cup sesame seeds
- 2 cups boiling water

In a small heavy skillet, toast the sesame seeds over low heat, stirring often, until dark golden brown, 15 to 20 minutes. Scrape out of the pan onto a plate to cool.

In a spice grinder or coffee mill, grind the seeds very briefly. Place the ground seeds in a drip-style coffee maker and pour the boiling water over them. Serve hot.

MAKES 2 SERVINGS

FRESH GINGER-CITRUS TEA

Perfect for when you've got a cold, or your stomach is a little queasy.

- 4 cups water
- 1/2 cup thinly sliced fresh ginger
- 4 strips (2 x 1/2 inch) lemon zest
- 4 strips (2 x 1/2 inch) orange zest

In a small saucepan, combine all the ingredients and bring to a boil over high heat. Reduce to a gentle simmer, partially cover, and cook until the tea is spicy and flavorful, about 15 minutes.

Drink hot, or cool to room temperature and chill.

MAKES 4 SERVINGS

MUGI CHA

In Korea, mugi cha (roasted barley tea) is traditionally served warm, while the equivalent drink in Japan is served chilled. The choice is yours. In addition, it is usually served without sweetener, but that's up to you as well. The flavor is toasty and soothing. Look for roasted barley in specialty shops, either loose or in large tea bags.

- 3 tablespoons roasted barley
- 2 quarts water

In a medium saucepan, bring the barley and water to a boil over high heat. Reduce to a simmer, cover, and simmer for 15 minutes. Remove from the heat and let steep for 5 minutes. Strain and serve.

MAKES 8 SERVINGS

CHAI

Make up a big batch of the tea, without adding the milk, and keep it in the refrigerator for either chilled chai or to gently heat with milk and honey. While black tea, such as Assam or Darjeeling, is typical in a chai mixture, feel free to experiment with other types.

- 3 cups water
- 2 cinnamon sticks (2 inches each), split lengthwise
- 2 teaspoons cardamom seeds
- 8 whole cloves
- 5 peppercorns
- 3 allspice berries
- 2 strips (2 x ½ inch) orange zest
- 2-inch piece fresh ginger, thinly sliced (no need to peel)
- 1 tablespoon Assam or Darjeeling tea leaves
- 1 cup milk
- 2 tablespoons plus 2 teaspoons honey

In a small saucepan, combine the water, cinnamon, cardamom, cloves, peppercorns, allspice, orange zest, and ginger. Bring to a boil over high heat. Reduce to a simmer, cover and simmer 10 minutes. Remove from the heat, stir in the tea, cover, and steep 2 minutes. Strain into a teapot.

In a small saucepan, heat the milk until small bubbles appear around the edges. Stir the milk and honey into the teapot and serve.

MAKES 4 SERVINGS

MEXICAN COFFEE

Traditionally brewed with a darkly roasted bean similar to Viennese roast, cafe de olla ("coffee from the pot") is an aromatic and spicy Mexican favorite. To warm coffee mugs, fill them with hot tap water and let stand for a few minutes.

- 3 tablespoons coarsely ground French roast or other dark-roast coffee
- 2 tablespoons muscovado or dark brown sugar
- 2 cinnamon sticks (2 inches each), broken in half
- 2 whole cloves
- 2 cups water

In a small saucepan, combine all the ingredients. Bring to a boil, stirring over high heat. Reduce the heat to medium-low, cover, and simmer 10 minutes. Strain into warmed coffee mugs and serve hot.

MAKES 2 SERVINGS

ICED GREEN TEA WITH GINGER

Cooling the water for 5 minutes after it has boiled will bring the temperature down to about 170°F. This prevents the leaves from getting scorched, which would make a bitter tasting tea. Once you've used the tea leaves, don't discard them; they are good for at least another pot of tea, if not two.

¼ cup thinly sliced fresh ginger (no need to peel)

4½ cups water

4 teaspoons green tea leaves

In a small saucepan, bring the ginger and water to a boil over high heat. Remove from the heat, transfer to a teapot, and let stand 5 minutes.

Add the green tea to the pot and let steep for 2 minutes. Strain and refrigerate until chilled. Serve over ice.

MAKES 4 SERVINGS

ICED HIBISCUS TEA

Hibiscus flowers have a whole host of health benefits (including possibly lowering blood pressure)—but they make a great tea, too.

5 cups water

3 tablespoons dried hibiscus flowers

5 allspice berries

2 whole cloves

½ cup orange juice

¼ cup agave nectar

In a small saucepan, combine 1½ cups of the water, the hibiscus flowers, allspice berries, and cloves, and bring to a boil.

Remove from the heat and stir in the orange juice, agave nectar, and remaining 3½ cups water. Refrigerate overnight.

Strain and serve over ice.

MAKES 4 TO 6 SERVINGS

WHITE TEA WITH VANILLA

White tea is more delicate and less grassy tasting than green tea. Here its flavor is heightened by the addition of a vanilla bean. Don't toss the vanilla bean after using, simply rinse it and let it dry. You can use it again for tea, custards, or even to lend a mild vanilla aroma to the sugar in your canister.

2 cups water

2 white tea bags

1 vanilla bean, split lengthwise

Honey (optional)

In a small pot, bring the water to a boil. Remove from the heat and let stand 1 minute. Place the tea bags and the vanilla bean in a teapot, pour the water over, and let steep 5 minutes. Strain and serve hot or chilled, with a little honey if desired.

MAKES 2 SERVINGS

ORANGE ROOIBOS

The slightly sweet herbal tea rooibos is complemented by the floral notes of Earl Grey tea, which is flavored with an orangelike citrus fruit called bergamot. Orange zest, cloves, and allspice further enhance the flavor.

2 cups water

1 rooibos tea bag

1 Earl Grey tea bag

3 whole cloves, lightly crushed

2 allspice berries, lightly crushed

3 strips (2 x ½ inch) orange zest

In a small saucepan, bring the water to a boil. Add the rooibos and Earl Grey tea bags, the cloves, allspice, and orange zest, cover, and remove from the heat. Let steep 5 minutes then strain through a sieve. Serve hot or chilled.

MAKES 2 SERVINGS

CHERRY LIMEADE

To make this even better (and not dilute its flavor), freeze some cherry juice in ice cube trays and use the cherry ice cubes in your drink.

- 2 cups unsweetened cherry juice
- 2 tablespoons lime juice
- 4 teaspoons agave nectar
- ½ cup sparkling water
- 4 ice cubes

In a large measuring cup, combine the cherry juice, lime juice, agave nectar, and sparkling water. Place the ice cubes in 2 tall glasses and pour the mixture over.

MAKES 2 SERVINGS

POMEGRANATE-CUCUMBER COOLER

This combination is remarkably refreshing. The cucumbers give up their flavor to the juice, while the mint (or basil) adds a surprising herbal touch.

- 4 cups pomegranate juice
- 2 kirby cucumbers, peeled and thinly sliced
- ¼ cup fresh mint or basil leaves, torn

In a pitcher, combine the pomegranate juice, cucumbers, and mint. Refrigerate at least 4 hours or up to overnight. Serve as is, or over ice.

MAKES 4 SERVINGS

ORANGE-ALMOND COOLER

Be sure to use blanched slivered almonds instead of sliced almonds here unless you don't mind specks of almond skin in your drink.

- ½ cup slivered almonds
- 4 cups water
- 4 cups orange juice
- ¼ cup brown rice syrup

In a blender, process the almonds with ½ cup of the water until pasty. Add another ½ cup water and process again. Add the remaining 3 cups water, the orange juice, and rice syrup, and blend until as smooth as possible. Strain and chill before serving.

MAKES 8 SERVINGS

APRICOT-WATERMELON WHIZ

Some apricot nectars can be very sweet, which is why you may not want any honey in this drink.

- 4 cups diced watermelon, seeds removed
- 1 cup apricot nectar
- ¼ cup lime juice
- 2 to 3 tablespoons honey (optional)
- Lime slices, for garnish

In a blender, liquefy the watermelon. Add the apricot nectar and lime juice and blend again. Taste and add honey if desired. Serve in tall glasses garnished with lime slices.

MAKES 6 SERVINGS

GINGER-PEACH FROTH

This could easily be made with 3 cups of frozen sliced peaches since they're going to be pureed anyway. In fact, if you puree them while still frozen, you'll have a frosty peach milk shake.

- 4 large peaches
- 4 cups milk

- 2 tablespoons dark honey
- ½ teaspoon ground ginger

Bring a large saucepan of water to a rolling boil. Dip the peaches in the boiling water for 30 to 45 seconds (longer for less-ripe peaches) to loosen the skins. Run under cold water to stop the cooking. Pull off the peels.

Cut up the peaches and place in a blender with the milk, honey, and ginger and blend to a froth. Serve at once in stemmed goblets.

MAKES 6 SERVINGS

PEACH CRUSH

Welcome your guests with a glass of this adult slushie. If using sparkling wine, add about 1 tablespoon of your favorite sweetener when you puree the peaches.

- 2 cups diced frozen peaches
- 2 cups crushed ice
- ¼ cup loosely packed basil leaves, preferably opal basil, plus sprigs for garnish
- 1 bottle (750ml) sparkling apple cider or sparkling white wine, chilled

In a blender, combine the peaches, ice, and basil and puree until smooth. Pour the puree into chilled glasses until half full. Add the sparkling cider. Serve each glass garnished with a basil sprig.

MAKES 8 SERVINGS

KEFIR-BANANA FROTH

The slightly acidic edge of kefir, a cultured milk drink similar in flavor to mild yogurt, makes it an excellent companion for the citrus in this recipe. The sweet banana and vanilla smooth it all out.

- 1 banana, cut into chunks
- 2 cups plain kefir
- Grated zest of 1 orange
- 1 cup fresh orange juice
- 3 tablespoons honey
- 1 tablespoon lime juice
- 2 teaspoons vanilla extract
- 6 ice cubes

In a blender, combine all the ingredients and puree until thick and smooth.

MAKES 2 TO 4 SERVINGS

MANGO-SOY SMOOTHIE

If you can find Ataulfo mangoes (sometimes called champagne mangoes), use them here, because they are less fibrous. Use two of them since they're smaller than other mangoes.

- 1 container (6 ounces) plain soy yogurt
- 1 mango, cut into large chunks (about 1 cup)
- ½ cup orange juice
- ½ teaspoon ground ginger
- ½ teaspoon ground cardamom
- 5 ice cubes

In a blender, combine all the ingredients and puree until thick and smooth.

MAKES 2 SERVINGS

SUNFLOWER BREAKFAST SHAKE

If you prefer, use 2 slices of juice-packed canned pineapple instead of the fresh.

- 1 slice fresh pineapple, 2 inches thick, cut into chunks

- 1 cup plain soymilk
- ¼ cup sunflower seeds
- 1 tablespoon golden raisins

In a blender, combine all the ingredients and puree until smooth. Chill to serve.

MAKES 1 SERVING

DATE SHAKE

This would actually be tasty with just a hint of almond extract in it. Just a drop or two will do, because it tends to be quite strong.

- 4 blanched almonds, coarsely chopped
- 1 cup plain low-fat yogurt
- 1 cup milk
- 12 pitted dates, halved
- 4 ice cubes

In a spice grinder or mini food processor, grind the almonds to a fine meal.

In a blender, combine the almond meal, yogurt, milk, dates, and ice cubes, and process until smooth and thick.

MAKES 2 SERVINGS

HORCHATA

A traditional Mexican rice drink, this can be made with just rice, or rice and almonds, as here. Serve well chilled over ice.

- ½ cup long-grain white rice
- ¾ cup almonds
- 5½ cups water
- 1½ teaspoons grated lime zest
- 1 teaspoon cinnamon
- ⅓ cup agave nectar or sugar

In a blender, pulverize the rice until smooth. Add the almonds and pulse several times until the almonds are coarsely ground. In a bowl, combine the rice-almond mixture, 2½ cups of the water, the lime zest, and cinnamon, and stir to combine. Refrigerate for at least 6 hours.

Working in batches, transfer the mixture to a blender and puree. Set a fine-mesh sieve over a bowl and pour all of the batches of the puree into it, pressing to extract as much liquid as possible.

Return the rice-almond solids to the blender, add 1½ cups water, and process again. Strain this liquid into the bowl, pressing on the solids. Puree the solids a third time with another 1½ cups water. Strain, pressing the solids.

GINGER-SPICE BOUQUET

Here is an unusual way to flavor punches or brewed tea that does not involve the usual suspects (cinnamon and cloves). This bouquet is enough for 2½ to 3 quarts of punch or tea.

- 1 thick slice (½ inch) peeled fresh ginger
- 1 whole star anise pod
- 1 teaspoon dried lemon or orange zest

Crush the ginger with the back of a spoon. Place the ginger, star anise, and citrus zest in a stainless steel tea ball, or combine them in a piece of cheesecloth and tie closed with a string.

Add to punch before chilling or to hot water when steeping tea. When desired flavor has been extracted, discard the spices.

Discard the solids. Stir the agave nectar into the rice-almond milk and chill well.

MAKES 8 SERVINGS

BROWN RICE HORCHATA: Use brown rice instead of white, and dark honey instead of agave nectar.

EMERALD ISLE

The watercress and parsley produce a lovely green-flecked drink.

- 6 cups pineapple juice
- 10 leaves lettuce, chopped
- ⅓ cup chopped celery leaves
- ⅓ cup chopped parsley
- ⅓ cup watercress

In a blender, process all the ingredients until liquefied. Chill before serving.

MAKES 6 SERVINGS

ONION-APPLE BRACER

There is a phytochemical (called quercetin) found in apples and onions that is very good for your respiratory system, making this a great drink to have if you think you're coming down with a cold.

- ½ cup chopped peeled apple
- ¼ cup chopped sweet onion
- 1 rib celery, coarsely chopped
- 1 thin slice lime
- 1 cup water

In a blender, combine all the ingredients and process to a smooth puree.

MAKES 2 SERVINGS

TOMATO KICK

If you want to kick this drink up even further, go for either more jalapeño sauce, or dose it with a more powerful hot sauce.

- 3 cups tomato juice
- 2 teaspoons green hot pepper (jalapeño) sauce
- 1 sprig parsley
- 1 scallion
- 1 rib celery, with leaves
- 1 tablespoon lemon juice
- ½ teaspoon drained horseradish, or to taste (optional)

In a blender, combine the tomato juice, hot pepper sauce, parsley, scallion, celery, and lemon juice. Process until smooth. Taste and add horseradish if desired.

MAKES 4 SERVINGS

SPICY HOLIDAY PUNCH

When fresh cranberries are in season, buy a couple of extra bags and throw them in the freezer. That way you can make this tasty punch any time you want.

CRANBERRY SYRUP

- 2 cups fresh or frozen cranberries
- 2 cups water
- 2 tablespoons honey

PUNCH

- 1 cup water
- ¼ cup honey
- 3 sticks (2 inches each) cinnamon
- 1 teaspoon whole cloves
- 1½ cups pineapple juice

- **½ cup lemon juice (2 to 3 lemons)**
- **4 cups sparkling water**
- **Pineapple slices and lemon slices pierced with whole cloves, for garnish (optional)**

To make the cranberry syrup: In a medium saucepan, combine the cranberries and water, bring to a low boil, and cook until the berries pop, about 5 minutes.

Set a sieve over a bowl and pour the mixture into the sieve, pressing with the back of a spoon to extract all the juice. Discard the pulp. (You should have about 2 cups juice.)

Return the juice to the saucepan, add the honey, and simmer for 10 minutes. Do not let boil and do not overcook or the cranberry syrup will jell. Store in the refrigerator.

To make the punch: In a medium saucepan, combine the water, honey, cinnamon, and cloves. Bring to a boil and continue to boil gently for 5 minutes. Discard the cinnamon and cloves. Transfer to a large bowl and let cool.

Add the cranberry syrup, pineapple juice, and lemon juice to the honey mixture and chill until serving time.

Just before serving, pour the punch over ice in a punch bowl and add the sparkling water. If desired, garnish with pineapple and lemon slices.

MAKES 2 QUARTS

RHUBARB-HONEY PUNCH

The red pigments in rhubarb are from healthful phytochemicals called antrocyanins.

RHUBARB JUICE

- **5 cups chopped rhubarb**
- **5 cups water**
- **⅔ cup sugar or honey**

PUNCH

- **⅓ cup honey**
- **½ cup orange juice**
- **⅓ cup lemon juice**
- **4 cups sparkling water**

To make the rhubarb juice: In a large saucepan, combine the rhubarb, water, and sugar. Cook over medium heat until the rhubarb is soft, about 12 minutes. Set a fine-mesh sieve over a bowl and pour in the rhubarb mixture. Discard the pulp.

To make the punch: In a large saucepan, combine the rhubarb juice and honey. Bring the mixture to a low boil and cook for 5 minutes. Let cool to room temperature.

Add the orange juice and lemon juice and chill thoroughly.

Just before serving, pour the punch over ice in a punch bowl and stir in the sparkling water.

MAKES 3 QUARTS

RASPBERRY-LEMON PUNCH

Frozen unsweetened raspberries would be a fine substitute in this punch.

- **4 cups raspberries**
- **2 cups warm water**
- **½ cup mild honey**
- **½ cup lemon juice (2 to 3 lemons)**
- **8 cups very cold sparkling water**
- **Lemon slices**

In a medium saucepan, combine the raspberries and 1 cup warm water. Bring to a boil and simmer for 10 minutes. Transfer to a blender and puree. Set a fine-mesh sieve over a bowl and press through to remove the seeds.

Pour the remaining 1 cup warm water into a large bowl and stir in the honey until dissolved. Add the raspberry puree and lemon juice. Pour the punch over ice in a punch bowl and stir in the sparkling water. Garnish with lemon slices.

MAKES 3 QUARTS

BATIDA

A batida is basically a Hispanic milk shake. For any of the combinations listed below, put all the ingredients in a blender and process until thick and smooth. These suggestions make one batida each but can be easily doubled or tripled.

- 1 cup sliced peaches (frozen or fresh), ¼ cup coconut milk, 1 tablespoon agave nectar, ¼ teaspoon ground ginger, 3 ice cubes
- 1 cup frozen strawberries, ⅓ cup milk, 1 tablespoon honey, pinch of allspice, 3 ice cubes
- 1 cup orange juice, ¼ cup coconut milk, 1 tablespoon agave nectar, 3 ice cubes
- 2 tablespoons peanut butter, ½ cup coconut milk, 1 tablespoon honey, 3 ice cubes

Appetizers

Just about any savory dish that can be eaten as "finger food" or in small quantities can be served as an appetizer. Any light dish—a soup, salad, or pâté for instance—served as a first course at sit-down meals is considered an appetizer. In this section we are primarily concerned with finger foods. No matter how they are served, appetizers are a wonderful way for the creative cook to set the stage for the meal to come.

Here are some general guidelines when planning and presenting appetizers:

- Don't offer too many appetizers, or appetizers that are too rich, since this would satisfy rather than stimulate appetites.
- If the meal is heavy and rich, keep the appetizers light and simple.
- If the meal is light and simple, have a single appetizer that is on the rich side.
- Avoid any flavors or ingredients planned for the main course.
- Simple touches lift an appetizer out of the ordinary: fresh fruit and vegetable garnishes, sprigs of fresh herbs, mixtures piped in professional swirls with a pastry bag.
- Serve a spread or dip in several small bowls of varying shapes, colors, and materials, instead of one large one.

The Cheese Board

A simple and popular appetizer course is the cheese board (see the Cheese Board chart on page 144 for some guidelines). Serve only four types of cheese, and plan on only 1 ounce of each type of cheese per person. So for a party of six people, that would be four 6-ounce chunks of cheese, or 1½ pounds total. Cut back to three cheeses if the meal to follow is rich.

With the cheese, serve plain breads and crackers—no seasoned or salted ones. Seasonings tend either to fight with or mask the flavor of the cheese.

Do not cut the cheese ahead of time. Precutting, which exposes many surfaces to the air, causes the cheese to dry out.

Serve aged cheeses at room temperature to enjoy their full flavors and creamy textures. Allow 20 to 60 minutes for a cheese to warm up, and only warm the amount of cheese needed. Continual rewarming ages cheese. While the cheese is warming, keep it covered to prevent the surfaces from drying out. Fresh cheeses are tastiest when chilled. Leave them in the refrigerator until just before ready to serve.

CHILI-LIME TORTILLA CHIPS

Since there are so many different flavors of flour tortillas available these days, experiment with a couple of them. It would be fun, too, to use some in different colors to make your chips more playful. How about spinach (green), tomato (red), and curry (yellow)?

6 tablespoons lime juice (2 to 3 limes)

1 tablespoon chili powder

1½ teaspoons ground coriander

4 multi-grain flour tortillas (6 inches)

Preheat the oven to 400°F. In a small bowl, combine the lime juice, chili powder, and coriander. Brush the spiced lime juice mixture on the tortillas and cut each into 6 wedges. Bake until crisp, about 10 minutes.

MAKES 24 CHIPS

HERBED PITA CHIPS

Change up the herbs, or try a flavored pita bread, like onion.

2 whole wheat pita breads (6 inches)

3 tablespoons extra-virgin olive oil

1½ teaspoons oregano

¼ teaspoon salt

Preheat the oven to 400°F. Stack the pitas and cut into 8 wedges (16 total). Separate the wedges horizontally to make 32 wedges.

CHEESE BOARD

An interesting cheese board can be either different versions of one type of cheese or a mixture of several different types. Unless you know your guest's tastes very well, you're probably better off with mixing and matching the different types. Use the chart below as a guide, and choose one cheese from each category. The cheeses listed are merely representational of what you could put on your cheese board because the options, both domestic and imported, are staggering.

UNRIPENED	BLUE	SEMI-SOFT	FIRM
Montrachet (French goat cheese)	Cabrales (Spanish)	Port du Salut	Manchego
Boursin	Roquefort (French)	Gouda	Parrano
String cheese	Gorgonzola (Italian)	Oka	Cheshire
Mozzarella	Stilton (English)	Saint Paulin	Jarlsberg
American goat cheese	American blue cheese	Taleggio	American Cheddar

Another category of cheese, called soft-ripened, has some of the most delicious cheeses available. But because they tend to be very high in fat (which is what makes them great tasting, of course), they are a little harder to fit into an appetizer course. However, if you reduce the total amount of cheese you put out, then by all means consider one of these: Brie, Camembert, Brillat-Savarin, Saint André, Robiola, Chaource, or any other double-crème or triple-crème cheese.

Place on a baking sheet and toss with the oil, oregano, and salt.

Bake for 7 minutes, then turn the chips over and bake 3 to 4 minutes, or until crisp. Cool on a rack.

MAKES 32 CHIPS

PARMESAN CHEESE TOASTS

These make great appetizers, but would also be a great accompaniment to soup.

- 1 whole wheat baguette (about 15 inches)
- ¼ cup olive oil
- ½ teaspoon Italian herb seasoning, store-bought or homemade (page 407)
- 1 cup grated Parmesan cheese

Preheat the oven to 350°F. Cut the baguette on a slight diagonal into slices about ½ inch thick.

In a small bowl, combine the oil and Italian seasoning. Brush both sides of the bread slices with the oil mixture. Place on a baking sheet and bake 7 minutes.

Turn the slices over and sprinkle the Parmesan on top. Bake for 5 minutes, or until the edges are crisp and the cheese has melted and is lightly browned.

MAKES 30 TOASTS

LEMON & HERB-MARINATED OLIVES

The olives can be marinated up to 1 week in advance. Store in a tightly covered container in the refrigerator before using. Be sure to bring them to room temperature before serving.

- 1 lemon
- ⅓ cup extra-virgin olive oil
- 3 cloves garlic, thinly sliced
- 1 teaspoon fennel seeds, crushed
- ½ teaspoon red pepper flakes
- 2 large sprigs fresh thyme
- 2 cups kalamata or other brine-cured black olives

Using a citrus zester or Microplane grater, zest the lemon into a medium bowl. Cut the lemon in half. Add the juice from one half to the zest (save

---

SALSAS

Salsas make simple appetizers. Serve them with chips, crudités, or whole-grain toasts.

Roasted Tomatillo Salsa (page 607)
Fresh Tomato-Chipotle Salsa (page 608)
Roasted Vegetable Salsa (page 608)
Autumn Pear Salsa (page 609)
Tomato & Lime Salsa (page 608)
Mango-Jicama Salsa (page 609)
Nectarine Salsa (page 609)

the remaining half for another use). Add the oil and garlic, and whisk to combine.

Add the fennel seeds, red pepper flakes, and thyme sprigs to the bowl. Add the olives and toss. Cover and let marinate at room temperature for at least 1 hour.

MAKES 2 CUPS

LEMON-OLIVE TAPENADE

You can prepare this delicious olive puree up to a week in advance—its flavors only improve. Serve with crackers or use as a sandwich spread.

1 cup pitted brine-cured black olives, such as Niçoise or kalamata

1 medium shallot, quartered

1 large clove garlic

4 anchovy fillets

2 tablespoons capers

1 tablespoon finely grated lemon zest

2 tablespoons lemon juice

⅛ teaspoon pepper

¼ cup extra-virgin olive oil

2 tablespoons chopped flat-leaf parsley

In a food processor, combine the olives, shallot, garlic, anchovies, capers, lemon zest, lemon juice, and pepper, and process until it forms a smooth paste. With the processor running, slowly pour in the oil. Transfer to a medium bowl and fold in the parsley. Refrigerate in a sealed container for up to 10 days.

MAKES 1¼ CUPS

OLIVADE

You can use this savory spread on bread or as a dip for crudités. Fromage blanc is a moist, fresh cheese. If you have difficulty finding it, substitute part-skim ricotta.

8 ounces fromage blanc

2 tablespoons minced red onion

1 tablespoon capers, chopped

½ cup finely chopped pitted kalamata or other brine-cured black olives

¼ cup extra-virgin olive oil, plus more for drizzling

1 tablespoon snipped chives

Coarse salt and pepper

Chopped parsley, for garnish

Put the cheese in a medium bowl and blend in the onion and capers. Fold in the olives, oil, and chives. Season to taste with salt and pepper. Serve right away or refrigerate, but bring back to room temperature to serve. Sprinkle with parsley and drizzle with a little extra oil before serving

MAKES 1½ CUPS

PEAR TOMATO BRUSCHETTA

You can use grape tomatoes or cherry tomatoes in place of the pear tomatoes.

24 slices (½-inch-thick) multi-grain Italian bread (12 ounces total)

2 tablespoons olive oil

3 cloves garlic, halved

1¼ pounds red and yellow pear tomatoes, coarsely chopped

⅓ cup chopped cilantro, basil, or parsley

1 teaspoon honey

3/4 teaspoon salt

1/2 teaspoon grated lemon zest

1/4 teaspoon pepper

Preheat the oven to 400°F. Brush the bread with 1 tablespoon of the oil. Place on a baking sheet and bake for 7 minutes, or until golden brown and crisp. Rub the toasted bread very lightly with one of the cut garlic cloves.

In a small pan of boiling water, cook the remaining 2 cloves garlic for 3 minutes to blanch. Finely chop.

In a medium bowl, combine the chopped garlic, tomatoes, cilantro, honey, salt, lemon zest, pepper, and remaining 1 tablespoon oil. Spoon on top of the toasted garlic bread.

MAKES 24 BRUSCHETTA

BLACK KALE BRUSCHETTA

These simple toasts make a great appetizer or a side dish for a hearty bean soup. If desired, top with a little grated Parmesan cheese.

1 1/2 pounds black kale (or other kale), long stems removed

2 tablespoons extra-virgin olive oil, plus more for brushing

Large pinch of red pepper flakes

5 cloves garlic, 3 thinly sliced and 2 whole

Coarse salt and black pepper

1/2 loaf crusty whole wheat Italian bread, cut into eight 1/2-inch-thick slices

Slice the kale leaves in half crosswise. In a large, deep skillet or wok, heat the 2 tablespoons oil over medium heat. Add the red pepper flakes and sliced garlic. Cook, stirring, about 30 seconds (do not brown).

Add the kale, in batches if necessary, and cook until just tender (but not completely limp). Remove from the heat and season to taste with salt and black pepper. Cover and keep warm.

Toast or grill the bread until slightly crusty. Lightly brush with olive oil. Cut the whole garlic cloves in half and lightly rub over the toasts. Top the toasts with the cooked kale.

MAKES 8 BRUSCHETTA

BROCCOLI RABE BRUSCHETTA

Broccoli rabe has a slight bitterness that some people are not fond of, but you could make this with milder broccolini if you'd like.

3 tablespoons extra-virgin olive oil, plus more for brushing

5 cloves garlic, 4 coarsely chopped, 1 halved

Pinch of red pepper flakes

2 bunches broccoli rabe, tough ends trimmed (1 1/2 pounds)

Coarse salt and black pepper

1/4 cup water

4 large slices olive or rosemary bread

2 tablespoons sun-dried tomato pesto

1/3 cup shredded provolone cheese

In a large nonstick skillet, heat 2 tablespoons of the oil over medium heat. Add half the chopped garlic, the pepper flakes, and broccoli rabe, stirring to coat. Season with salt and black pepper to taste. Add the water, cover, and steam for 5 minutes, stirring occasionally.

Add the remaining 1 tablespoon oil and chopped garlic, and cook until the rabe is tender, 3 to 5 minutes. Remove from the heat.

Preheat the broiler. Toast the bread, and, while still hot, lightly brush one side with oil and rub lightly with a cut garlic half. (Leave the broiler on.)

Spread the tomato pesto on the toasts. Top with the broccoli rabe, pressing down to make it stick. Top each slice with 1 generous tablespoon cheese and broil until the cheese melts, 1 to 2 minutes. Serve warm or at room temperature.

MAKES 4 BRUSCHETTA

RADISH SANDWICHES WITH CRESS BUTTER

This is one of the easiest and tastiest ways to enjoy fresh spring radishes. You can find Easter Egg radishes in pretty pink, purple, and white hues at the market in April and May, but any small, thin-skinned variety is fine.

- **¼ cup (½ stick) butter, at room temperature**
- **½ cup goat cheese, at room temperature**
- **1 cup loosely packed watercress sprigs, tough stems discarded**
- **¼ teaspoon coarse salt, plus more for sprinkling**
- **8 slices whole wheat baguette**
- **8 large Easter Egg or other radishes, thinly sliced**

In a food processor, combine the butter, goat cheese, watercress, and salt. Pulse until blended into a paste. Spread the bread slices with the cress butter. Top with radish slices and sprinkle very lightly with salt.

MAKES 8 OPEN-FACE SANDWICHES

CELERY ROOT PANCAKES WITH CRÈME FRAÎCHE

Little appetizer pancakes are often served with crème fraîche and caviar, but for a cheaper alternative, our version uses olive paste (tapenade) instead.

- **2 medium celery roots**
- **2 ½ teaspoons coarse salt**
- **1 cup unbleached all-purpose flour**
- **¼ cup whole wheat flour**
- **½ teaspoon baking powder**
- **2 large eggs, beaten**
- **½ cup plus 2 tablespoons milk**
- **¼ cup (½ stick) butter, melted and cooled**
- **3 tablespoons extra-virgin olive oil**
- **1 cup crème fraîche, store-bought or homemade (page 487) or sour cream**
- **½ cup Lemon-Olive Tapenade (page 146)**
- **2 tablespoons snipped chives**

Peel and trim the celery roots. Shred in a food processor or on a box grater. Place in a large bowl and sprinkle with 1½ teaspoons of the salt. Let stand for 20 minutes. Squeeze out the excess water until dry and fluffy.

In a large bowl, stir together the all-purpose and whole wheat flours, remaining 1 teaspoon salt, and the baking powder.

In a small bowl, whisk together the eggs, milk, and melted butter. Gradually add the egg mixture to the flour mixture, and whisk until creamy and smooth. Fold in the celery root until well blended to form a batter. Let the batter rest in the bowl for 20 minutes.

Preheat the oven to 400°F. Place a baking sheet on the center rack.

Brush a large nonstick skillet with some of the olive oil and place over medium heat. Add 1 rounded tablespoon of batter to the pan to form a thin 2-inch pancake. Fill the pan with pancakes but do not crowd. Cook until golden on one side, about 4 minutes. Turn and cook for 3 minutes. Transfer the pancakes to the oven to continue cooking until tender, about 4 minutes. Repeat the process until all the batter is used.

Remove the cooked pancakes from the oven and cover with a tea towel to keep warm. To serve, place a dollop of crème fraîche and then a spoonful of tapenade on top of each pancake. Sprinkle with the chopped chives.

MAKES 12 SERVINGS

CHUNKY GUACAMOLE

Serve with store-bought baked chips or homemade Chili-Lime Tortilla Chips (page 144).

2 Hass avocados

½ teaspoon salt

¾ cup grape tomatoes, chopped

⅓ cup minced red onion

⅓ cup minced cilantro

2 tablespoons lime juice

1 teaspoon green hot pepper (jalapeño) sauce

Halve the avocados and scoop the flesh into a large bowl. Add the salt and mash with a fork or potato masher. Mash in the tomatoes, onion, cilantro, lime juice, and pepper sauce.

MAKES 3 CUPS

ROMESCO DIP

Based on a traditional sauce from Spain that is used for topping grilled vegetables, this dip goes perfectly with a variety of vegetables, or try it with Herbed Pita Chips (page 144).

1 red bell pepper, cut lengthwise into flat panels

2 tablespoons olive oil

1 large clove garlic, smashed and peeled

1 ounce Italian or French bread, torn

10 whole almonds

1 tablespoon tomato paste

2 tablespoons orange juice

2 tablespoons 2% Greek yogurt

¼ teaspoon salt

Preheat the broiler. Broil the pepper pieces, skin side up, 4 inches from the heat for 12 minutes, or until the skin is charred. Turn the pepper pieces over on the broiler pan to cool. Peel.

In a small skillet, heat the oil over low heat. Add the garlic, bread, and almonds, and cook until the bread is golden brown, about 3 minutes.

Transfer to a food processor and add the roasted pepper and tomato paste and puree until not quite smooth. Add the orange juice, yogurt, and salt, and pulse until combined.

MAKES 1 CUP

CREAMY SPINACH DIP

Reduced-fat cream cheese is labeled by most food companies as "⅓ Less Fat." It will often also bear the label Neufchâtel somewhere on the packaging. Whatever you call it, it's a good choice for creamy dips because it's softer than full-fat cream cheese.

1 tablespoon olive oil

1 clove garlic, smashed and peeled

⅛ teaspoon red pepper flakes

1 package (10 ounces) frozen chopped spinach, thawed and squeezed dry

4 ounces reduced-fat cream cheese (Neufchâtel)

¼ cup grated Parmesan cheese

¼ teaspoon salt

In a small skillet, heat the oil over low heat. Add the garlic and pepper flakes, and cook until the garlic is fragrant and golden, about 3 minutes.

Transfer to a food processor, add the spinach and cream cheese, and pulse until well combined. Add the Parmesan and salt, and pulse again. Refrigerate until ready to use.

MAKES 1½ CUPS

EDAMAME DIP

Edamame (green soybeans) can be found in the freezer section of many supermarkets. They're a great source of protein (8 grams per ½ cup), so keep them on hand for this dip or for of Spiced Edamame (page 162).

1 cup frozen shelled edamame

⅔ cup packed fresh basil leaves

¼ cup olive oil

1½ teaspoons grated lemon zest

3 tablespoons lemon juice

¼ teaspoon salt

In a small pot of boiling water, cook the edamame until tender, about 4 minutes. Drain.

Transfer to a food processor along with the basil, oil, lemon zest, lemon juice, and salt, and puree until smooth.

MAKES 1 CUP

LEMON-CARROT HUMMUS

Carrot adds a subtle sweetness to this lighter rendition of the classic chickpea dip. Dark sesame oil, sometimes called toasted sesame, lends a sesame flavor with a lighter touch than traditional tahini.

1 carrot, thinly sliced

3 cloves garlic

1¾ cups cooked chickpeas

3 tablespoons dark sesame oil

3 tablespoons lemon juice

3 tablespoons plain low-fat yogurt

¼ teaspoon salt

In a small saucepan, combine the carrot and garlic with water to cover. Cook over medium heat until tender, about 10 minutes. Reserving the cooking liquid, drain and transfer the solids to a food processor. Add 2 tablespoons of the reserved cooking liquid.

Add the chickpeas, sesame oil, lemon juice, yogurt, and salt, and process until smooth.

MAKES 1⅔ CUPS

ROASTED-PEPPER HUMMUS

Serve the hummus with vegetable dippers or wedges of mini whole wheat pita breads. If you're in a rush, you can use a 15.5-ounce can of chickpeas (rinsed and drained) and jarred roasted red peppers.

1¾ cups cooked chickpeas

½ cup Roasted Red Peppers (page 660)

⅓ cup tahini

3 large cloves garlic, smashed and peeled

3 tablespoons lemon juice

3 tablespoons extra-virgin olive oil

1 teaspoon ground cumin

- 1 teaspoon salt
- ⅛ teaspoon black pepper
- Pinch of cayenne pepper

In a food processor, combine the chickpeas, roasted peppers, tahini, garlic, lemon juice, oil, cumin, salt, black pepper, and cayenne, and process until smooth and creamy. Season with additional salt and black pepper, if desired.

MAKES 2 CUPS

PINTO BEAN DIP

Red or white kidney beans would work nicely here, as would other mild, meaty beans like cranberry.

- 2 cups dried pinto beans
- 2 slices bacon, cut crosswise into ¼-inch slices
- 3 large cloves garlic
- 4 teaspoons chili powder
- 2 teaspoons ground cumin
- 1 teaspoon salt
- 2 large tomatoes, coarsely chopped
- 1 small pickled jalapeño pepper, halved
- 1 small Vidalia or other sweet onion, finely minced

In a medium saucepan, combine the beans with water to cover. Bring to a boil and cook for 3 minutes. Remove from the heat, cover, and set aside for 1 hour. Drain the beans.

In the same saucepan (wiped dry), cook the bacon over medium-high heat until it has rendered most of its fat. Add the drained beans, garlic, chili powder, cumin, and salt. Add water to cover by 2 inches and bring to a boil. Partially cover and cook at a low boil until the beans are tender, or 40 minutes to 1 hour.

Reserving the cooking liquid, drain the beans and transfer to a food processor. Add the tomatoes and jalapeño, and process to a smooth puree. Use some of the cooking liquid, if necessary, to get the dip to the right consistency. Taste and adjust the seasoning.

Stir in the onion and transfer to a serving bowl.

MAKES 3 CUPS

CASHEW DIP

The natural sweetness of the cashews works nicely in this sweet and sour dip. Serve with fresh vegetables.

- ½ cup raw cashews
- 4 teaspoons vegetable oil
- 1 tablespoon Major Grey's chutney
- 1 tablespoon rice vinegar
- 1 tablespoon sliced fresh ginger
- 2 scallions, thinly sliced
- 1 teaspoon mild curry powder
- ½ teaspoon salt
- ⅛ teaspoon cayenne pepper
- 2 tablespoons water

In a food processor, combine the cashews, oil, chutney, vinegar, ginger, scallions, curry powder, salt, cayenne, and water, and puree until not quite smooth, with a little texture.

MAKES ⅔ CUP

VEGAN ONION DIP

For a mild Indian twist, add about ¼ teaspoon curry powder and substitute cilantro for the parsley.

- 1 cup soft silken tofu (8 ounces)
- 1 tablespoon avocado oil or extra-light olive oil
- 1 small onion, coarsely chopped

3 cloves garlic, smashed and peeled

1 tablespoon white wine vinegar

1 tablespoon chopped parsley

¾ teaspoon salt

¼ teaspoon pepper

In a coffee filter or a sieve lined with cheesecloth or paper towels, drain the tofu for 5 to 10 minutes to remove excess water.

Meanwhile, in a medium skillet, heat the oil over medium heat. Add the onion and cook, stirring, until golden, 8 to 10 minutes. Add the garlic and cook, stirring, until the garlic just begins to brown, about 3 minutes. Remove from the heat.

Place the sautéed onions and garlic in a mini food processor and process until almost smooth. Add the drained tofu and process until smooth. Add the vinegar, parsley, salt, and pepper, and process briefly to blend.

MAKES ¾ CUP

CARAMELIZED ONION DIP

Nonfat Greek yogurt makes a lovely creamy backdrop to the flavors of fresh dill and caramelized onion.

1 tablespoon olive oil

1 large onion, finely chopped

¼ cup water

1 container (7 ounces) 0% Greek yogurt (generous ¾ cup)

¼ cup snipped fresh dill

¼ teaspoon salt

¼ teaspoon pepper

In a large skillet, heat the oil over low heat. Add the chopped onion and water, cover, and cook, stirring occasionally, until the onion is soft, about 15 minutes. Uncover and cook, stirring occasionally, until the onion is golden brown, about 10 minutes.

Transfer to a bowl and let cool to room temperature. Stir in the yogurt, dill, salt, and pepper. Chill until ready to serve.

MAKES 1⅓ CUPS

YOGURT CHEESE WITH THREE FLAVORS

For the sun-dried tomato cheese, if your sun-dried tomatoes are very dry, soak them in hot water until softened before using.

1 container (17.6 ounces) Greek yogurt

Place a coffee filter or paper towel–lined sieve over a bowl and spoon in the yogurt. Cover, and let drain overnight. Discard the whey.

Stir one of the three following flavors into the cheese.

ROASTED GARLIC: Preheat the oven to 400°F. Wrap 1 unpeeled garlic head in foil, place on a baking sheet, and bake for 45 minutes or until the package gives to gentle pressure. Remove from the oven. When cool enough to handle, cut off the stalk end of the garlic bulb and squeeze the garlic pulp into a bowl. Mash with a fork. Whisk into the drained yogurt and season with salt to taste.

SUN-DRIED TOMATO & ROSEMARY CHEESE: Fold ⅓ cup soft sun-dried tomatoes, finely chopped, and 1½ teaspoon minced fresh rosemary into the drained yogurt.

BLACK PEPPER & FENNEL CHEESE: Fold 2 teaspoons coarsely ground pepper and 1½ fennel seeds into the drained yogurt. Season with salt to taste.

MAKES 1½ CUPS

Clockwise from top right:
Romesco Dip • *page 149*
Edamame Dip • *page 150*
Chili-Lime Tortilla Chips • *page 144*
Lemon-Carrot Hummus • *page 150*
Iced Hibiscus Tea • *page 136*

Thai Summer Rolls • *page 158*

Broiled Shrimp, Ceviche-Style • *page 165*

Laquered Chicken Sate with Zucchini Salad • *page 164*

Classic Cheese Fondue • *page 155*

Lentil-Escarole Soup with Sausage ● *page 187* and Sage Focaccia ● *page 562*

Corn & Red Potato Chowder with Bacon • *page 191*

Golden Beet & Fennel Salad with Beet Vinaigrette • *page 389*

TOASTED WALNUT-CHEDDAR SPREAD

If you don't have a toaster oven, toast the walnuts in a small heavy skillet over medium heat.

½ cup walnuts

1 pound sharp Cheddar cheese, finely shredded

1½ cups plain low-fat yogurt

2 teaspoons Dijon mustard

In a toaster oven at 350°F, toast the walnuts until lightly toasted, 3 to 5 minutes. When cool enough to handle, finely chop.

In a small bowl, combine the walnuts, Cheddar, yogurt, and mustard. Chill thoroughly before serving.

MAKES 3 CUPS

SALMON MOUSSE

Salmon mousse is great spread on whole-grain crackers, of course, but try it on mini rice cakes.

1 envelope unflavored gelatin

½ cup cold water

1 can (14.75 ounces) pink salmon, drained, skin removed

¾ cup Greek yogurt or reduced-fat sour cream

⅔ cup plain low-fat yogurt

2 tablespoons drained prepared horseradish

2 tablespoons grated onion

2 ½ teaspoons grated lemon zest

1 tablespoon lemon juice

¾ teaspoon salt

⅓ cup snipped chives

In a heatproof glass measuring cup, sprinkle the gelatin over the cold water. Let stand 5 minutes to soften. Set the measuring cup in a small saucepan of simmering water and heat until the gelatin has melted, about 2 minutes. Set aside to cool slightly.

In a food processor, pulse the salmon until smooth. Add the yogurts, horseradish, onion, lemon zest, lemon juice, and salt, and pulse until the mixture is blended. Add the gelatin mixture and chives, and pulse until combined.

Transfer to a 4-cup bowl or decorative mold, cover, and refrigerate for at least 3 hours for the mousse to set. If you like, unmold onto a platter to serve.

MAKES 8 SERVINGS

GRUYÈRE CANAPÉS

The French word canapé actually means "couch" (as in sofa), so the appetizer of the same name always has a little toast, or "couch," with a topping on it.

6 slices whole-grain bread, toasted

¾ cup thick Béchamel Sauce (page 598)

½ cup shredded Gruyère cheese

¼ cup grated Parmesan cheese

Cayenne pepper

Preheat the oven to 375°F.

Cut each piece of toast into 4 squares or triangles.

In a small bowl, stir together the Béchamel and Gruyère, and spread thickly on the toast pieces. Sprinkle the Parmesan and a dash of cayenne over each canapé.

Place on an ungreased baking sheet and bake for 10 minutes, or until the tops are golden brown.

MAKES 24 CANAPÉS

DOUBLE-BAKED SWEET POTATO SKINS

This is the type of recipe that can be easily doubled or tripled if you are feeding a crowd. Pure chili powders made from a single type of chili pepper (like chipotle or ancho) are available in most supermarkets. If you can't find one, simply substitute a chili powder blend.

- **3 sweet potatoes (8 ounces each), well scrubbed**
- **1 tablespoon olive oil**
- **½ cup crumbled feta cheese (2 ounces)**
- **½ teaspoon chipotle or other chili powder**
- **Lime wedges, for serving**

Preheat the oven to 425°F. Place the sweet potatoes on a foil-lined baking sheet and bake for 1 hour, or until fork-tender but not mushy. Reduce the oven temperature to 400°F.

When the sweet potatoes are cool enough to handle, halve lengthwise and scoop out most of the flesh, leaving a ¼-inch shell. Then halve them lengthwise again.

Drizzle olive oil over the flesh side of the potatoes. Bake, flesh-side down, for 20 minutes.

Turn flesh-side up and sprinkle with the feta and chipotle powder. Bake for 5 minutes, or until the skins are crisp and the cheese has melted. Serve with lime wedges.

MAKES 12 WEDGES

SPICY QUESADILLAS WITH HONEY MUSTARD

This is extra spicy because it uses both pickled jalapeños as well as pepper Jack cheese. To temper this a bit, you could cut back on the jalapeños or go to plain Monterey Jack cheese.

- **⅓ cup chopped cilantro**
- **3 tablespoons honey mustard**
- **2 teaspoons lemon juice**
- **2 pickled jalapeño peppers, minced**
- **8 whole-grain flour tortillas (7 inches)**
- **⅓ cup shredded pepper Jack cheese**

NUTTY TREATS

Bowls of plain nuts make good appetizers, but you can also up the ante with one of these recipes:

Seeded Almond Mix (page 614)
Curried Cashew Mix (page 614)
Pepper Nuts (page 615)
Mexican Mix (page 615)
Maple Pepitas (page 615)
Spicy Roasted Chickpeas (page 615)

1 green bell pepper, cut into thin slivers

1 red bell pepper, cut into thin slivers

Preheat the oven to 425°F.

In a small bowl, combine the cilantro, honey mustard, lemon juice, and jalapeños.

Arrange 4 of the tortillas on a baking sheet and brush evenly with the mustard mixture. Sprinkle the cheese and bell peppers on top of each tortilla, leaving a ¼-inch border. Top with the remaining tortillas.

Bake for 10 minutes or until crispy. Cut each quesadilla into 6 wedges.

MAKES 24 WEDGES

MANCHEGO CORNMEAL GEMS

Smoked paprika, once a fairly esoteric spice, is now available in many supermarkets from national brand-name spice companies.

- ½ cup yellow cornmeal
- ½ cup flour
- 2 teaspoons baking powder
- 3 tablespoons butter
- ½ cup diced Manchego cheese
- ¼ cup frozen corn kernels, thawed
- 1 tablespoon chopped red bell pepper
- 1 tablespoon chopped scallion
- ¼ cup plus 2 tablespoons buttermilk
- 1 large egg
- Pinch of smoked paprika

Preheat the oven to 400°F. Heavily grease a baking sheet.

In a small bowl, combine the cornmeal, flour, and baking powder, and blend well. With a pastry blender or two knives scissor fashion, cut the butter into the cornmeal mixture until the mixture resembles coarse crumbs.

Toss the Manchego, corn, chopped pepper, and scallion in the flour mixture until coated and well distributed.

In a separate bowl, mix together the buttermilk, egg, and paprika until blended. Quickly stir into the flour mixture. Drop the batter by rounded tablespoons onto the baking sheet, placing several inches apart. Bake for 15 to 20 minutes, or until browned.

MAKES 4 SERVINGS

CLASSIC CHEESE FONDUE

The traditional dunk of choice for cheese fondue is bread cubes, but try it with vegetables or fruits: apple wedges, pear wedges, bell pepper strips, broccoli florets.

- 2 cups shredded Gruyère cheese (8 ounces)
- 2 cups shredded Emmentaler cheese (8 ounces)
- 1 tablespoon cornstarch
- 1 clove garlic, halved
- 1 cup dry white wine
- 3 ounces cream cheese, cut into chunks

In a medium bowl, toss the Gruyère and Emmentaler with the cornstarch until coated.

Rub the garlic halves all around the inside of the top of a double boiler, then discard.

Add the wine to the double boiler and place over simmering water. Gradually add the cheese and cornstarch mixture, stirring until the cheeses are melted. Swirl the cream cheese into the mixture. Remove from the heat. Keep warm in a fondue pot or other container that can sit over a food warmer.

MAKES 4 TO 6 SERVINGS

GARLIC-MARINATED MUSHROOMS TOPPED WITH AVOCADO

Keep a container in your freezer that you can use for vegetable trimmings, like the mushroom stems below. You can throw in carrot peelings, onion skins, asparagus trimmings, tomato cores. Then when the container is full, use the trimmings to perk up a chicken broth, or use them as the basis for a homemade vegetable broth.

1 pound mushrooms

½ cup olive oil

¼ cup white wine vinegar

12 sprigs parsley, minced

3 cloves garlic, minced

¼ teaspoon pepper

2 Hass avocados

2 tablespoons lemon juice

¼ teaspoon salt

1 bunch watercress

Lemon wedges, for garnish

Stem the mushrooms. In a large bowl, combine the oil, vinegar, parsley, garlic, and pepper, and mix well. Add the mushroom caps and turn to coat well. Cover and refrigerate overnight.

Halve the avocados and scoop the flesh into a medium bowl. With a fork or potato masher, mash the avocados with the lemon juice and salt. Taste for seasoning and add more lemon juice or salt if needed.

Remove the mushroom caps from the marinade. (Don't discard the marinade; it will make a perfectly nice salad dressing.) Fill each cap with avocado puree.

Line a serving platter with the watercress and top with the mushrooms. Garnish with the lemon wedges.

MAKES 6 TO 8 SERVINGS

ROASTED RED PEPPER ROLLS

You can make the roasted pepper strips well in advance. This will also give them more time to take on some pickle-y flavor from the vinegar.

2 large red bell peppers, cut lengthwise into flat panels

2 tablespoons balsamic vinegar

3 tablespoons olive oil

1 tablespoon butter

½ pound mushrooms, minced

1 large clove garlic

1 tablespoon Worcestershire sauce

2 tablespoons cream cheese, at room temperature

Preheat the broiler. Broil the pepper pieces, skin side up, 4 inches from the heat for 12 minutes, or until the skin is charred. Remove from the broiler, turn the pieces skin-side down and let cool for 10 minutes. Peel, cut lengthwise into 2 or 3 strips each, and place in a shallow bowl. Sprinkle with the vinegar and set aside.

In a medium skillet, heat the oil and butter over medium-high heat. Add the mushrooms, garlic, and Worcestershire sauce, and cook, stirring constantly with a wooden spoon, until the mushroom liquid has evaporated and the mixture is very dry. Remove from the heat and let cool.

In a small bowl, stir the cream cheese until softened. Stir in the mushroom mixture. Spread each peeled pepper strip with a thin layer of mushroom paste and roll, jelly-roll fashion. Secure with toothpicks. Serve at room temperature.

MAKES 16 TO 24 PIECES

YELLOW PEPPER ROLLS WITH GOAT CHEESE: Use yellow bell peppers instead of red, and soft goat cheese instead of cream cheese.

GRILLED EGGPLANT & MOZZARELLA ROLLS

An elegant summer appetizer, this simple dish is easy to make ahead and pull out of the fridge to broil at the last minute.

- 2 small eggplants (½ pound each)
- Coarse salt
- 8 ounces shredded mozzarella cheese
- 4 ounces soft goat cheese, at room temperature
- 2 tablespoons snipped chives
- Pepper
- 1 cup extra-virgin olive oil, plus more for brushing
- 25 large fresh basil leaves plus ½ cup loosely packed, coarsely chopped basil

Cut the eggplants lengthwise into ½-inch-thick slices. Sprinkle the slices on both sides with salt, and let them drain in a colander for 15 minutes to release excess moisture. Rinse the eggplant slices and pat dry with paper towels.

Preheat the grill or broiler to medium.

In a bowl, stir together the mozzarella, goat cheese, 1 tablespoon of the chives, and salt to taste. Set aside.

Brush both sides of the eggplant slices lightly with oil. Grill or broil the eggplant for 3 to 4 minutes, or until golden and seared. Season with salt and pepper, turn over, brush with more oil, and grill or broil for 3 to 4 minutes longer, or until the eggplant just begins to soften. Remove and let sit 10 minutes. (Leave the broiler on; or if you used a grill, preheat the broiler now.)

Transfer the eggplant to a work surface. Arrange whole basil leaves in a slightly overlapping pattern across one slice of eggplant. Place a heaping tablespoon of the cheese mixture at the narrow end of the slice. Roll up cigar fashion and secure with a toothpick. Repeat with the remaining basil, filling, and eggplant slices.

EASY CANAPÉS

The easiest canapé of all is a cracker topped with cream cheese, soft goat cheese, or a slice of mild cheese, then crowned with a dab of sweet-tart relish or chutney. Try one of these:

- Apricot Chutney (page 610)
- Corn Relish (page 611)
- Fresh Cranberry Relish (page 611)
- Stone-Fruit Chutney (page 610)
- Cucumber Relish (page 612)
- Sweet Onion-Cauliflower Relish (page 612)
- Cranberry-Cherry Chutney (page 610)
- Spicy Cranberry-Pineapple Relish (page 611)
- Roasted Onion Relish (page 612)

Arrange the rolls, seam-side down, in a lightly oiled 9 x 13-inch glass baking dish. Broil 4 to 6 inches from the heat for 3 to 5 minutes, or until the cheese is just melted and bubbling.

In a blender or food processor, combine the chopped basil, remaining 1 tablespoon chives, and 1 cup oil. Season with salt to taste. Transfer the cooked eggplant rolls to a platter or serving plates, and drizzle with the basil oil.

MAKES 16 SERVINGS

EGGS STUFFED WITH TOFU GUACAMOLE

For an even smoother mixture, puree the tofu-egg yolk mixture in a mini food processor, but leave the avocado with some texture.

½ cup (4 ounces) soft silken tofu

12 hard-cooked large eggs, halved lengthwise and yolks removed

3 scallions, finely chopped

1 teaspoon salt

Dash of hot pepper sauce

1 Hass avocado

Lemon juice

Paprika, for garnish

In a small bowl, combine the tofu, egg yolks, scallions, salt, and hot sauce, and mash with a fork.

Halve the avocado and scoop the flesh into a small bowl. With a fork or potato masher, mash the avocado with lemon juice to taste. Add the egg-yolk mixture and stir until thoroughly blended.

Mound the mixture into the egg white halves. Garnish with a sprinkling of paprika.

MAKES 24 PIECES

GREEK STUFFED EGGS

If you have easy access to fresh oregano and mint, use them here in place of dried: about ½ teaspoon of each.

6 hard-cooked large eggs, halved lengthwise and yolks removed

2 tablespoons butter

⅔ cup minced mushrooms

2 shallots, minced

¼ teaspoon oregano

¼ teaspoon mint

¼ teaspoon pepper

½ cup crumbled feta cheese

Pass the egg yolks through a sieve into a small bowl.

In a medium skillet, melt the butter. Add the mushrooms and shallots, and cook until tender. Stir in the oregano and mint. Cool slightly, then stir into the sieved egg yolks. Add the pepper and feta and stir to blend well.

Mound the mixture into the egg white halves. Serve the eggs chilled or at room temperature.

MAKES 12 PIECES

THAI SUMMER ROLLS

Spring roll wrappers, made from rice flour, have an extremely delicate texture. They can be a little hard to work with at first, but you'll soon get the hang of it.

PEANUT SAUCE

¼ cup peanut butter

¼ cup cilantro leaves

2 tablespoons water

4 teaspoons honey

- 1 tablespoon rice vinegar
- 1 tablespoon soy sauce
- 1 clove garlic, smashed and peeled
- ⅛ teaspoon cayenne pepper

SUMMER ROLLS

- 2 ounces thin rice or cellophane noodles
- 1 small red bell pepper, slivered
- 1 medium carrot, cut into thin matchsticks
- ⅓ cup fresh basil leaves, torn into bite-size pieces
- ¼ cup cilantro leaves
- 1 tablespoon rice vinegar
- 2 teaspoons Dijon mustard
- 2 teaspoons dark sesame oil
- 8 round spring roll wrappers (6 inches)

To make the peanut sauce: In a food processor, combine the peanut butter, cilantro, water, honey, vinegar, soy sauce, garlic, and cayenne. Process until smooth. Set aside.

To make the rolls: Cook the noodles according to package directions. Drain, rinse under cold water, and drain again. Transfer to a medium bowl. Add the bell pepper, carrot, basil, cilantro, vinegar, mustard, and sesame oil, and toss to combine.

One at a time, submerge the spring roll wrappers in tepid water until tender, about 30 seconds. Lay flat on a clean kitchen cloth. Lay a mound of noodle mixture down the center, leaving a 1-inch border all around. Fold 2 sides in over the mound then roll up from the bottom. Repeat with the remaining wrappers. Serve the rolls with the peanut sauce.

MAKES 8 SUMMER ROLLS

POT STICKERS WITH SESAME GINGER SAUCE

If you are looking to add more whole grains to your diet, you might want to make Whole Wheat Wonton Wrappers (page 160).

- 1 pound lean ground pork, lamb, or beef
- 1 cup finely chopped bok choy
- 1 small onion, minced
- 2 teaspoons minced fresh ginger
- 1 teaspoon minced garlic
- 2 tablespoons soy sauce
- 1 tablespoon lemon juice
- 36 wonton wrappers
- Oil, for frying
- Sesame Ginger Sauce (page 160)

In a large bowl, combine the ground meat, bok choy, onion, ginger, garlic, soy sauce, and lemon juice, and blend well.

Place a tablespoon of the filling in the center of each wonton wrapper. Moisten the edges and bring all the sides up into the center and pinch the edges of the wrapper together, pinching firmly together to seal.

In large pot, bring 4 quarts of water to a rapid boil in a large pot. Add a few of the dumplings, one at a time. When they rise to the surface, they are cooked. With a slotted spoon, transfer the dumplings to a tray covered with paper towels to drain. Repeat with the remaining dumplings.

In a large skillet or wok, heat a thin skin of oil. Add the dumplings in batches and cook until lightly browned on the bottom. Serve with the Sesame Ginger Sauce.

MAKES 36 POT STICKERS

SESAME GINGER SAUCE

This is good as a dipping sauce but can also be poured over poached or baked fish.

2 tablespoons dark sesame oil

2 tablespoons grated fresh ginger

1 tablespoon soy sauce

1 tablespoon lemon juice

1 tablespoon water

½ cup chopped scallions

In a small saucepan, combine the sesame oil, ginger, soy sauce, lemon juice, water, and scallions. Bring to a boil. Serve hot.

MAKES ½ CUP

MALFATTI DUMPLINGS

Freshly grated Parmesan cheese will make all the difference in this recipe.

2 packages (10 ounces each) frozen leaf spinach, thawed and squeezed very dry

3 cups part-skim ricotta cheese

3 large eggs, beaten

2¾ cups grated Parmesan cheese

¼ cup flour

1 slice firm-textured whole-grain sandwich bread, finely crumbled (½ cup)

⅛ teaspoon nutmeg

⅛ teaspoon pepper

Butter

Finely mince the spinach. In a large bowl, stir together the spinach, ricotta, eggs, 2¼ cups of the Parmesan, the flour, bread crumbs, nutmeg, and pepper. Mix thoroughly. With floured hands, use 1 tablespoon of the mixture to form a little oval about 1½ inches long and ½ inch wide. Repeat until all the dumplings are formed.

In a large pot, bring 4 quarts of water to a rapid boil. Reduce the heat and add a few of the dumplings, one at a time. When they rise to the surface, they are cooked. With a slotted spoon, transfer to a warm serving platter. Repeat with the remaining dumplings.

WHOLE WHEAT WONTON WRAPPERS

1½ cups whole wheat flour

2¼ cups unbleached all-purpose flour

1 cup cold water

2 large eggs

Cornstarch (optional)

In a large bowl, combine the flours. In a separate bowl, beat the water and eggs together. Make a well in the center of the flour mixture, and pour the egg mixture into it.

Mix together until a soft ball of dough is formed. Knead on a floured surface until the dough is satiny and smooth, 5 to 10 minutes. Divide into 4 or more portions.

On a floured surface, roll out each portion of dough 1/16 inch thick. Cut the dough into 3-inch squares.

If making ahead for use later, dust each piece with cornstarch, stack, and wrap tightly in plastic wrap. Freeze or refrigerate. Return to room temperature before using.

When a layer of dumplings covers the bottom of the platter, dot with butter and some of the remaining Parmesan. Keep warm in the oven. Repeat the layers. Serve hot on warm plates.

MAKES 8 SERVINGS

PHYLLO TARTLETS WITH SMOKED SALMON

This recipe can be easily doubled or tripled for a large crowd. If you prefer, you can prepare the cream cheese mixture by simply pulsing it in a food processor.

- 1 package (15) mini whole wheat phyllo shells
- 3 ounces cream cheese, at room temperature
- 1½ teaspoons grated lemon zest
- 2 teaspoons lemon juice
- ¼ teaspoon pepper
- 1 ounce smoked salmon, finely chopped
- 2 teaspoons nonpareil capers, rinsed
- 1 tablespoon snipped chives, for garnish

Preheat the oven to 350°F. Place the phyllo shells on a baking sheet and bake for 3 to 5 minutes, or until crisp. Cool to room temperature.

With a fork, mash the cream cheese with the lemon zest, lemon juice, and pepper. Fold in the smoked salmon and capers. Spoon into the shells and top with the chives.

MAKES 15 TARTLETS

SALMON & SMOKED GOAT CHEESE TURNOVERS

If you can't find smoked goat cheese, use regular goat cheese and smoked Gouda. To make the bread crumbs, finely chop the half slice of bread with a knife or pulse in a mini food processor.

- Multi-Grain Pie Dough (Double Crust), page 531
- 2 cans (6 ounces each) salmon, drained and flaked
- ¼ cup whole-grain bread crumbs (½ slice)
- ¼ cup minced green bell pepper
- 1 tablespoon minced onion
- ⅛ teaspoon black pepper
- ½ cup soft smoked goat cheese (4 ounces)
- ½ cup shredded Gouda cheese (4 ounces)
- 1 large egg, beaten

On a floured surface, roll out the pastry about ⅛ inch thick and cut into about fourteen 4-inch squares.

In a medium bowl, combine the salmon, bread crumbs, bell pepper, onion, and black pepper. In a small bowl, blend the goat cheese and Gouda.

Preheat the oven to 400°F.

Place about 1 tablespoon of the salmon mixture in the center of each pastry square. Top with 1 tablespoon of the cheese mixture. Fold the pastry squares in half to form triangles, sealing the edges with beaten egg. Make a small slit in the top of each turnover and brush with egg.

Place on a baking sheet and bake for 15 minutes, or until golden.

MAKES 14 TURNOVERS

SNAPPY SNAP PEAS

For an easy variation, spread ½ teaspoon filling on unpeeled cucumber slices.

- 18 large sugar snap peas
- 4 ounces mild goat cheese
- 2 teaspoons tomato paste
- ½ teaspoon ancho chili powder or hot paprika

Split the sugar snaps along one side, taking care to leave the pod attached on the other side.

In a small bowl, beat together the goat cheese, tomato paste, and chili powder until fluffy. Taste and add more chili powder to taste (note that it will get hotter as it stands).

Spoon or pipe a heaping teaspoon of cheese filling into each pea pod. Serve chilled.

MAKES 18 PIECES

SPICED EDAMAME

Edamame are green soybeans, available in the freezer compartment of most supermarkets. They are sold both shelled and in the pod. Make sure you get the type still in the pod. Once steamed and tossed with a salt-spice mixture, they are served in the pod. Each diner bites a pod to release the rich-tasting beans within.

- **2 teaspoons coarse sea salt**
- **3/4 teaspoon Szechwan peppercorns or 1/2 teaspoon ancho chili powder, Chinese five-spice powder, or dried lavender**
- **1 bag (1 pound) frozen edamame in the pod**

In a small skillet, combine the sea salt and your choice of seasoning. Toast over low heat until fragrant. Set aside.

In a steamer, cook the edamame for 4 or 5 minutes. Remove from the steamer, transfer to a bowl, and toss with the salt-spice mixture while the edamame are still hot.

MAKES 6 SERVINGS

CHERRY TOMATOES WITH WATERMELON

This surprisingly delicious combination can be served chilled or at room temperature. Serve the tomatoes with bread sticks wrapped in thin slices of prosciutto.

- **1/2 pint yellow cherry tomatoes**
- **1/2 pint red cherry or grape tomatoes**
- **1 small seedless watermelon (red or yellow)**
- **1/2 teaspoon coriander seeds**
- **1/4 teaspoon white peppercorns**
- **Coarse salt**
- **1 tablespoon extra-virgin olive oil**
- **1 tablespoon slivered fresh mint leaves**

Cut half of the tomatoes in half and place in a large bowl along with the remaining whole tomatoes.

Cut the watermelon into cubes (or use a melon baller) and add to the bowl. (You should have about 4 cups melon.)

With a mortar and pestle, crush the coriander, peppercorns, and a large pinch of salt until coarsely ground (or place in a kitchen towel and pound with a mallet). Sprinkle the mixture over the tomatoes and melon.

Add the oil and mint, and gently toss to coat.

MAKES 6 SERVINGS

CITRUS-POACHED PEARS WITH RADICCHIO & PROSCIUTTO

This dish falls more into the category of first course for a sit-down dinner: It's definitely not finger food.

- **1 bottle (750ml) good-quality dry white wine**
- **1 cup sugar**
- **1/2 teaspoon saffron threads (optional)**
- **Zest and juice of 1 orange**
- **Zest and juice of 1 lemon**
- **4 medium pears, peeled, bottoms trimmed so they stand upright**

- **16 thin slices prosciutto (¼ pound)**
- **½ head radicchio, leaves separated**
- **⅓ cup extra-virgin olive oil**
- **Salt and pepper**

In a nonaluminum saucepan, combine the wine, sugar, saffron (if using), orange zest and juice, and lemon zest and juice. Bring to a simmer over medium heat. Add the pears upright, cover, and poach gently until cooked but not mushy, 30 to 40 minutes. Remove the pears and set aside.

Strain the liquid and return it to the saucepan. Over medium-high heat, reduce the liquid to syrup consistency, about 20 minutes, stirring occasionally. Remove from the heat and taste for seasonings.

Arrange four prosciutto slices and several large radicchio leaves on each plate. Place a pear in the center of each plate. Drizzle the radicchio with olive oil and some of the reduced syrup. Season with salt and pepper.

MAKES 4 SERVINGS

SPINACH-TOFU PUFFS

These balls may be prepared in advance and then frozen (unbaked). When ready to use, thaw for 10 to 15 minutes and then bake as directed.

- **1 package (10 ounces) frozen spinach, thawed and squeezed dry**
- **1½ cups whole-grain cracker crumbs or dried bread crumbs**
- **1 pound firm tofu, mashed**
- **½ cup finely chopped Vidalia onion**
- **3 large eggs, lightly beaten**
- **⅓ cup butter, melted**
- **¼ cup grated Parmesan cheese**
- **1 teaspoon minced garlic**
- **½ teaspoon salt**
- **½ teaspoon pepper**
- **¼ teaspoon thyme**

Preheat the oven to 325°F. Grease a baking sheet.

In a large bowl, combine the spinach, cracker crumbs, tofu, onion, eggs, butter, Parmesan, garlic, salt, pepper, and thyme, and mix well. Shape into 1-inch balls and place on the baking sheet. Bake for 15 to 20 minutes, until puffed and cooked through.

MAKES 6 TO 8 SERVINGS

CHIPOTLE-TURKEY MEATBALLS

You can find cans of chipotle peppers (smoked jalapeños) in adobo sauce in Latin American markets and in the ethnic aisle of most supermarkets. Once you've opened a can, transfer the chipotles, in their sauce, to a container and refrigerate or freeze.

- **1¼ pounds 93% lean ground turkey**
- **4 scallions, thinly sliced**
- **½ cup crumbled feta cheese**
- **⅓ cup panko bread crumbs**
- **1 large egg**
- **1½ teaspoons ground coriander**
- **1 teaspoon ground cumin**
- **1 teaspoon oregano, crumbled**
- **1 teaspoon salt**
- **¼ cup flour**
- **2 tablespoons olive oil**
- **1 cup chicken broth store-bought or handmade (page 172)**
- **2 tablespoons tomato paste**
- **1 tablespoon chopped chipotle in adobo sauce**

In a large bowl, combine the turkey, scallions, feta, panko crumbs, egg, coriander, cumin, oregano, and salt, and mix gently to combine. Shape into 20 golf-ball-size meatballs.

Dredge the meatballs in the flour, shaking off the excess. In a large skillet, heat the oil over medium heat. Add the meatballs, working in batches if necessary, and cook until browned all over, about 5 minutes. Transfer to a plate.

Pour off any fat remaining in the skillet, add the broth, tomato paste, and chipotle, and bring to a boil. Boil for 2 minutes to reduce slightly.

Return the meatballs to the pan and reduce to a simmer. Cover and cook until the meatballs are tender and cooked through, about 10 minutes. Serve the meatballs with the sauce.

MAKES 20 MEATBALLS

LACQUERED CHICKEN SATE WITH ZUCCHINI SALAD

Use a thick teriyaki sauce or Korean barbecue sauce. Thinly sliced young zucchini is so sweet, it needs no cooking. Soak the wooden skewers in water for at least 30 minutes before threading the chicken.

¼ cup teriyaki sauce

1¼ pounds skinless, boneless chicken breasts, cut lengthwise into thin strips

4 zucchini (1½ pounds total)

1 tablespoon lemon juice

1 teaspoon dark sesame oil

Sea salt and pepper

2 teaspoons sesame seeds, lightly toasted

Place the teriyaki sauce in a large glass dish or bowl. Add the chicken and toss to coat. Cover tightly and refrigerate for at least 20 minutes, or overnight if desired.

Trim off the ends of the zucchini. With a swivel-head vegetable peeler or large knife, slice the zucchini lengthwise as thinly as possible. Toss with the lemon juice and sesame oil. Season to taste with salt and pepper. Arrange on a platter.

Preheat the grill to medium-high. Thread the chicken onto wooden skewers. Grill, covered, for 3 minutes per side, until the chicken is seared and just cooked through. Transfer to the platter with the zucchini, sprinkle with the sesame seeds, and serve hot.

MAKES 6 SERVINGS

CREAMED CORN WITH SPICY SHRIMP

Pureeing corn kernels creates the "cream" in this dish without using a lot of butter or cream. We've called for frozen, but in season use fresh: You'll need 10 ears.

24 ounces frozen white corn kernels, thawed

3 tablespoons butter

⅓ cup finely chopped onion

Coarse salt and pepper

1½ tablespoons canola oil

1 teaspoon red pepper flakes

4 cloves garlic, sliced

1 pound shrimp, peeled and deveined, tails left on

1 tablespoon lemon juice

½ cup plus 1 tablespoon coarsely chopped fresh basil

Place half the corn in a food processor or blender with ⅓ cup of water. Process until pureed. Set aside.

In a large, deep skillet, melt 2 tablespoons of the butter over medium heat. Add the onion, cover, and cook until soft, about 8 minutes. Add the unprocessed corn kernels and ½ cup of water. Cook, uncovered, stirring occasionally, until the corn is almost tender, 6 to 8 minutes. Stir in the pureed corn, and salt and pepper to taste. Cook, stirring, until hot and bubbling, about 3 minutes.

In a large skillet or wok, heat the oil over medium-high heat until hot but not smoking. Add the pepper flakes and garlic, and stir-fry for 1 minute (don't burn the garlic). Add the shrimp and stir-fry until opaque throughout, about 2 minutes.

Remove from the heat and toss with the lemon juice and ½ cup of the basil. Stir the remaining 1 tablespoon butter and 1 tablespoon basil into the corn. Serve the shrimp on a bed of the corn puree.

MAKES 6 SERVINGS

COCONUT FRIED SHRIMP

Leave the tails on the shrimp so they are easier to pick up with your fingers.

- ½ cup mayonnaise
- 2 tablespoons honey mustard
- ½ cup cornstarch
- 1 cup unsweetened shredded coconut
- 2 large egg whites
- ¼ teaspoon salt
- 16 large shrimp (1 pound), peeled and deveined, tails left on
- Vegetable oil, for deep-frying
- Lemon and/or lime wedges, for serving

In a small bowl, mix together the mayonnaise and honey mustard. Refrigerate until serving time.

Measure ¼ cup of the cornstarch into a shallow bowl or pie plate. Place the coconut in another shallow bowl or pie plate.

In a small bowl, beat together the remaining ¼ cup cornstarch, egg whites, and salt to make a smooth batter.

Dredge the shrimp in the dry cornstarch, shaking and tapping off the excess. Holding by their tails, dip the shrimp, one at a time, in the egg-white batter and then in the coconut to coat evenly. Place in a single layer on a baking sheet.

In a deep-fryer or small Dutch oven, heat at least 2 inches of oil to 300°F. Add the shrimp, 4 at a time, and cook until golden brown and opaque throughout, 3 to 4 minutes. Drain on paper towels.

Serve with lemon or lime wedges and the honey-mustard sauce.

MAKES 16 PIECES

BROILED SHRIMP, CEVICHE-STYLE

A nice variation on this is to use pineapple juice instead of orange juice. Just be aware that the pineapple juice may turn the shrimp mushy if you make the dish more than about 2 hours in advance.

- 1½ teaspoons ground cumin
- ¾ teaspoon salt
- 1½ pounds medium shrimp, peeled and deveined
- 2 teaspoons grated orange zest
- 2 cups orange juice
- 2 tablespoons lime juice
- ¼ teaspoon cayenne pepper
- 1 orange or yellow bell pepper, cut into thin strips
- ½ cup chopped cilantro
- ¼ cup diced red onion
- 1 Hass avocado, cut into ½-inch chunks
- 3 tablespoons hulled pumpkin seeds (pepitas), toasted

MAKING CHICKEN DRUMETTES

Take a chicken wing and cut off and discard the wing tip. Then separate the remaining wing at the "elbow" joint. The smaller half will have 2 bones, the larger only 1. Start with the larger one, scraping the meat away from the bone and toward one end. Turn the meat inside out to form a miniature drumstick. Repeat with the piece with 2 bones in it and when you've exposed the bones, twist off and discard the smaller of the two bones.

In a small ungreased skillet, heat the cumin over medium heat until fragrant and toasty smelling, about 2 minutes.

In a large bowl, combine 1 teaspoon of the cumin and ¼ teaspoon of the salt. Add the shrimp, tossing to coat.

In a separate bowl, combine the orange zest, orange juice, lime juice, remaining ½ teaspoon cumin, remaining ½ teaspoon salt, and the cayenne, stirring to combine. Stir in the bell pepper, cilantro, and onion.

Preheat the broiler. Place the shrimp on a broiler pan and broil 6 inches from the heat for 3 minutes, or until opaque throughout. Turn them once halfway through. Transfer the shrimp to bowl with the orange mixture, and toss. Serve at room temperature or chilled, topped with the avocado and pumpkin seeds.

MAKES 6 SERVINGS

JERK CHICKEN DRUMETTES

When handling any type of chili peppers, especially ones as incendiary as Scotch bonnets, it is important that you wear gloves and wash your hands immediately after using. This dish is extremely flavorful and spicy.

¼ cup lime juice

3 tablespoons vegetable oil

2 tablespoons soy sauce

2 tablespoons distilled white vinegar

4 scallions, sliced

2 cloves garlic, smashed and peeled

1 small to medium Scotch bonnet chili pepper, ribs and seeds removed

1½ teaspoons sugar

2 teaspoons ground allspice

1¾ teaspoons thyme

¾ teaspoon black pepper

½ teaspoon grated nutmeg

½ teaspoon ground cinnamon

2 pounds drumettes (about 16), store-bought or homemade (above)

In a blender, combine the lime juice, oil, soy sauce, vinegar, scallions, garlic, Scotch bonnet chili, sugar, allspice, thyme, black pepper, nutmeg, and cinnamon, and puree until smooth.

Transfer the mixture to a large bowl. Add the chicken and turn to coat. Refrigerate for at least 1 hour or up to overnight.

Preheat the oven to 450°F. Lift the chicken from the marinade and place on a foil-lined baking sheet. Bake until richly brown and cooked through, about 30 minutes.

MAKES 16 PIECES

CRISPY CHICKEN DRUMETTES

You can buy already prepared drumettes, or you can make them yourself. See "Making Chicken Drumettes" (opposite).

- 1 cup buttermilk
- 3 tablespoons extra-virgin olive oil
- 2 cloves garlic, minced
- ½ teaspoon coarse salt
- 4 teaspoons black pepper
- 3 pounds chicken drumettes (about 24), store-bought or homemade (opposite)
- 3 cups corn flakes, preferably organic
- ½ cup grated Parmesan cheese
- 4 teaspoons cayenne pepper
- ¼ cup (½ stick) butter, melted

In a large, shallow dish, stir together the buttermilk, oil, garlic, salt, and black pepper. Add the chicken and turn to coat. Cover tightly and refrigerate for 4 hours, or overnight.

Arrange a rack on top of a large baking sheet. Place the corn flakes in a blender and grind to make fine crumbs. In a large bowl, combine the crumbs, Parmesan, and cayenne.

Remove the chicken from the marinade and allow the excess to drip off. Dredge each piece in the crumb mixture and transfer to the rack. Let rest 15 minutes. (The chicken may be prepared to this point earlier in the day and refrigerated until ready to cook.)

Preheat the oven to 425°F. Arrange the chicken in a single layer on a lightly greased baking sheet. Drizzle generously with the butter and bake for 35 to 40 minutes, or until crisp, golden, and cooked through. Serve hot or at room temperature.

MAKES 24 PIECES

ANTIPASTO PLATE

Do as the Italians do, and put out a plate with a variety of complementary textures and flavors. Good possibilities include thinly sliced meats, mild cheese, olives, and a selection of pickled things. Try one of these recipes to add to your antipasto:

- Sweet-Hot Carrot Chips (page 660)
- Roasted Red Peppers (page 660)
- Marinated Roasted Red Peppers (page 660)
- Pickled Green Peppers (page 660)
- Spicy Pickled Peppers (page 660)
- Pickled Butter Bean Medley (page 661)
- Red-Pickled Eggs (page 661)
- Bread & Butter Pickles (page 662)
- Pickled Carrot & Mango Sticks (page 661)

Soups

Almost everyone seems to find comfort in a steaming bowl of soup. In the olden days, a kettle of soup slowly simmering over the hearth meant daily sustenance in lean times. And for many of us, a hot bowl of soup was part of the cure our mothers or grandmothers offered when we were feeling poorly. So it's no wonder soup has the power to make people feel good.

In addition to its restorative properties, soup is also a way to stretch food, so every peasant culture has developed a host of possibilities. And the bonus for the cook is that soup-making is an extremely forgiving art form. Any well-chosen combination of ingredients, simmered in a liquid until the flavors are absorbed into it, becomes a good-tasting soup.

Stocks & Broths

At the base of all good soups is a stock, either one that is made ahead and saved for use in soups, or one that gets made in the process of simmering the soup ingredients together. Making homemade stocks to have on hand does require some time—but little work, as a rule. Stocks can be made of meat, poultry, fish, or vegetables. Although in classic cooking this flavorful liquid is usually called a stock, it is also known by its more familiar name, broth—especially in store-bought brands.

A stock or broth is made by gently simmering flavor-rich ingredients. The gentle simmer cannot be overemphasized—small bubbles should barely ripple on the surface of the liquid. A rolling boil will encourage an overabundance of scum to collect on the surface. In meat stocks, the scum comes from albumin, a protein secretion from the meat bones. Nutritionists point out that the unattractive scum is rich in protein, and worth retaining with the stock. However, skimming with a slotted spoon or large spatula is a traditional procedure during the first half hour of simmering, when the scum appears.

A meat- or poultry-based stock can be made a day ahead and refrigerated overnight. This actually makes it easier to degrease the stock, because the fat will have collected on the surface and solidified. However, if you intend to keep the stock refrigerated for several days, the fat on top will help to preserve it, so do not remove the fat until the day the stock is to be used.

Although long, slow cooking is a cardinal requirement for meat stocks, fish and vegetable stocks may require as little as 30 to 60 minutes of cooking.

Stock Ingredients

Bones provide the natural gelatinous quality for most stocks. Any cooked or uncooked bones with some meat remaining make good soup bones, but you can get equally good results from bare bones coupled with an inexpensive piece of stew meat. When possible, have a butcher chop large bones into smaller pieces—about 2 inches long—to expose the interior goodness and to fit into the pot more easily. Lamb and hambones in the stockpot produce a dominating flavor, so unless a meat stock recipe specifically calls for such bones, use them sparingly.

EQUIPMENT FOR MAKING SOUPS & STOCKS

The equipment needed for making stocks and soups is so basic to all types of cooking that you probably have all the items in your kitchen already. Check this list if you want to be sure you have everything necessary for the various steps involved in making soups and stocks:

- Large heavy pot (4- to 6-quart capacity, preferably stainless steel or enameled)
- Slotted spoon, large spatula, or stock skimmer
- Large sieve
- Gravy separator
- Cheesecloth or loosely woven dish towel (for straining)
- Ladle
- Storage containers with tightly fitting lids

Carrots, onions, leeks, and celery are the most common aromatics added to the stockpot. Beware of vegetables such as asparagus, broccoli, cabbage, and turnips, whose strong flavors may be too overbearing if used in large quantities. It is not necessary to peel vegetables, but they should be well scrubbed and any blemishes or bad spots should be removed. Cut vegetables into large pieces; small pieces tend to turn to mush and disintegrate, thus clouding the stock.

Fresh spices and herbs—such as parsley, thyme, and bay leaves—may be used to further season the stock. When herbs are dried, the flavor intensifies, so use about one-third the amount you would use if the herbs were fresh. To ensure easy retrieval, gather the spices and herbs into a bundle (bouquet garni): If using whole large leaves or fresh sprigs, fasten them all together with a string tied to a stalk of celery or a leek leaf. Smaller fragments, such as seeds, crumbled herbs, and ground spices, should be tied into a piece of cheesecloth and anchored down beneath a soup bone.

When you have placed the necessary ingredients in the stockpot, add water until it covers everything by about 1½ inches. Always use cold water, because it drains the flavorful juices from the ingredients, whereas hot water tends to sear the ingredients, sealing in the juices. Hot water may be added during cooking if the liquid in the stockpot gets too low. The amount of liquid suggested in a recipe is only an approximation; if you find that too much water has been used, it can always be reduced through longer cooking. It is essential to keep the ingredients in the pot covered by water at all times.

Types of Stock

Brown Stock

Some stocks (such as "White Stock," page 170) are made by adding the meat or poultry to the stockpot as is , and then slowly simmering the liquid. Brown stocks, on the other hand, are made from meat or poultry and vegetables that have been browned first. This caramelizes the natural sugars in the ingredients and adds a depth of flavor and color to the stock.

The meat and bones are usually roasted in a hot oven (425°F) for 1 hour, or until nicely colored. Turn the bones occasionally to promote even cooking. During the final 30 minutes of roasting, carrots and unpeeled onions are added. Leaving the skins on the onions adds sweetness and helps color to the stock. Transfer the roasted bones, meat, and vegetables to the stockpot.

The next step is to degrease and deglaze the roasting pan. To do this, spoon any fat out of the roasting pan (use a syringe if necessary), leaving behind any juices. Add a little cold water and scrape the brown caramelized particles from the pan's bottom with a wooden spoon. Pour all this into the stockpot and carry on with the recipe.

White Stock

A white stock is made from veal or poultry meat and bones that have not been browned. It may be the base for a delicate soup or sauce, as its paleness works well with the pure white of dairy products. Onion skins, often added to brown stocks, are not used in a white stock. Vegetables are added to the stock only after the bones and water have come to a boil and the stock has been skimmed.

Poultry Stock

Poultry stock is economical and easy to make. Collect leftover poultry bones and carcasses (raw or cooked), hack them into small pieces, and freeze them until you are ready to make the stock. Place the frozen bones in the pot; they will defrost as you bring the water to a rolling boil. Drain and rinse the bones and the pot, getting rid of surface scum. Then cover bones, vegetables, and seasonings with fresh cold water and simmer for 3 to 4 hours.

Chicken stock may be made from virtually all parts of the chicken—wing tips, carcasses, gizzards, hearts, backs, and necks—except the liver. Never use liver for chicken stock; it gives off an unpleasant flavor and darkens the liquid. Chicken feet are rich in the natural gelatin that gives body to the stock. (If your butcher doesn't stock them, poultry farms, Chinese markets, and Jewish neighborhood shops are good sources for chicken feet.) Blanch them in boiling water for 5 minutes and peel or rub off the yellow skin before adding to the stockpot.

Vegetable Stock

A vegetable stock may be made with any combination of fresh vegetables or leftover vegetable trimmings. Unlike meat and poultry stocks, vegetable stocks seldom require skimming, and the cooking time is much shorter—30 minutes to 1 hour. You need only remember a few basic precepts: Strong vegetables yield strong stock, so use only a touch of them to strengthen the stock. Starchy vegetables such as corn, peas, and potatoes tend to cloud the stock, so it is best to use them in small quantities. Parsnips and carrots sweeten the liquid. If you want to intensify the stock's flavor, sauté the vegetables lightly in a little oil before adding them.

Fish Stock

Fish stock is easy and quick to make. Everything may be put into the pot and simmered for 1 hour, then strained and reduced. Longer cooking would yield a bitter, disagreeable taste. A good fish stock can be made from parts of the fish that are usually discarded. Fish heads, carcasses, trimmings of lean white fish—all can be used. Do not use fatty or oily fish such as salmon, mackerel, or herring, for they flavor the stock too strongly. A fish stock will not be as clear as one made from meat or vegetables, and will be much less gelatinous than meat stock.

Straining & Reducing Stock

When all the ingredients in the stockpot have yielded their goodness and flavors to the cooking liquid, it is time to strain the stock to separate liquid from solids.

To strain the stock, line a large sieve or colander with a dampened cheesecloth and place it over a clean bowl or pan. Ladle the stock into the sieve, then wash out the pot used to cook the stock. The strained stock may be returned to the pot for further reducing, if desired. The solid ingredients should be discarded.

Reducing the stock concentrates its body and flavor into a smaller volume, as with a glace de viande, or meat glaze. To reduce stock, boil it vigorously, uncovered, until the volume is decreased by one-third to one-half. Skim, if necessary.

To discourage unwelcome bacteria from growing in the warm liquid, the strained and reduced stock should be cooled, uncovered, as quickly as possible. This is done before refrigerating the stock. To cool quickly, place the pot in a larger basin or bowl, or a stoppered sink, surround it with ice and water, and stir the stock until it is completely cool.

HOMEMADE BOUILLON CUBES

When meat or poultry stock is strained and reduced until very thick and syrupy, it becomes a highly concentrated essence that, like commercial bouillon cubes, can be reconstituted, or used in small quantities to flavor soups and stews. Homemade bouillon cubes have much better flavor and a lot less sodium than commercial products. Two quarts of stock will yield 8 bouillon cubes.

Place 2 quarts of any meat or poultry stock in a medium saucepan. Bring the stock to a boil and cook, uncovered, over medium heat for about 1 hour, or until it is reduced by half. Strain through a fine sieve into a smaller pan and continue to cook until this is reduced by half, about 30 minutes or longer.

Strain once more into an even smaller pan, and turn the heat down to very low. Continue to cook for about 20 minutes.

At this point it is absolutely essential to maintain the stock at a low temperature and to keep a close watch on the pan so that the reduced stock does not stick to the bottom or burn. It will become thick and syrupy with bubbles on the surface. When the stock will lightly coat a metal spoon, transfer it to a heatproof bowl and let stand to cool a bit.

To store it, pour the lukewarm glaze into ice cube trays and freeze. When completely frozen, pop them out of the ice cube tray and store in an airtight freezer container. Later on to reconstitute them, mix 1 cube with 1 cup of water for regular strength broth, or use ½ cup water for a rich broth. You can also throw whole cubes directly into soups or stews.

Storing Stock

The cooled stock, stored in covered containers, should be refrigerated at once. It will keep in the refrigerator for about a week. If you wish to keep stock on hand longer, freeze it in small covered containers or in ice cube trays. The frozen cubes can be unmolded and stored in sealed plastic bags, then used as needed, without having to thaw a large quantity of stock. Label and date the stock you freeze. It will keep for up to a year. Before using any stock that has been frozen, bring it to a full rolling boil to kill any harmful bacteria.

Soups should be stored with the same precautions used for stocks. Soups made with cream, milk, or eggs should not be kept refrigerated for longer than 2 days. All soups may be frozen, but those made with cream, milk, or eggs tend to separate when thawed. As with stock, reheat soup to the boiling point before serving.

BEEF STOCK/BROTH

This is a hearty beef stock that starts with browning the meat to caramelize the meat juices.

- 4 pounds meaty beef bones, preferably sawed into small pieces
- 3 unpeeled onions, quartered
- 2 carrots, cut into large pieces
- 5 quarts cold water
- 1 pound shin beef, trimmed of fat and cut into chunks
- 5 sprigs parsley
- 2 sprigs fresh thyme
- 1 leek, cut into large pieces
- 1 rib celery, cut into large pieces
- 2 teaspoons peppercorns

Preheat the oven to 425°F.

Spread the bones in a shallow 12 × 18-inch roasting pan. Roast until browned, about 1 hour. Turn occasionally to promote even browning. During the last 30 minutes of roasting, add the onions and carrots.

Transfer the bones and vegetables to an 8-quart soup pot. Add 2 cups of the water to the pan drippings in the roasting pan and stir, scraping up the browned bits. Add the deglazed pan drippings into a gravy separator. Pour the degreased liquid to the soup pot.

Add the shin beef, parsley, thyme, leek, celery, peppercorns, and the remaining 4½ quarts cold water. Bring to a boil, reduce the heat, and simmer very gently, covered or partially covered, for 6 hours. Skim off any surface scum that accumulates during the first 30 minutes of simmering.

Strain the stock through a fine sieve. Cool quickly and refrigerate. When chilled, remove the surface fat.

MAKES 2 QUARTS

RICH BEEF STOCK: After straining and degreasing, simmer the stock uncovered until reduced by one-third to one-half.

POULTRY STOCK/BROTH

Buy drumsticks and thighs, bone-in, for this. They will give you the richest flavor. Wings have a very high fat-to-flesh ratio, and you can use them, but you'll have more fat to skim off.

- 4 pounds chicken or turkey parts, preferably all dark meat
- 4 quarts cold water
- 1 large unpeeled onion, stuck with 2 cloves and halved
- 1 carrot, thickly sliced
- 1 rib celery, thickly sliced

IMPROMPTU POULTRY STOCK

Any time you roast a chicken or turkey, save the carcass to make stock. Place the carcass in a large, heavy-bottomed soup pot or stockpot. Add water to cover. If you have any pan drippings, deglaze the roasting pan with some water and add that to the pot, too. Throw in vegetables like onions, celery, and carrots if you have them around. Add some garlic if you'd like. Bring to a boil, reduce the heat, and simmer for 3 hours. Strain the stock, cool quickly, and refrigerate.

- 2 bay leaves
- 6 sprigs parsley
- 10 peppercorns

In an 8-quart soup pot, combine the poultry parts and water. Bring to a boil, reduce the heat, and skim off any scum that rises to the surface.

Add the onion, carrot, celery, bay leaves, parsley, and peppercorns, and simmer very gently, uncovered, for 3½ hours.

Strain the stock through a fine sieve. Cool quickly and refrigerate. When cold, remove the surface fat.

MAKES 2½ QUARTS

RICH POULTRY STOCK: After straining and degreasing, simmer the stock uncovered until reduced by one-third to one-half.

VEGETABLE STOCK/BROTH

For an earthier stock, add some mushrooms. This is also a good way to use mushroom trimmings, like stems. Just keep a bag of them in the freezer and throw them into the pot when you're making stock.

- 5 large unpeeled onions, halved
- 10 carrots, halved
- 8 large plum tomatoes, quartered
- 5 ribs celery, halved
- 1 bunch parsley
- 1 large clove garlic, minced
- 4 quarts cold water

In a 6- to 8-quart soup pot, combine the onions, carrots, tomatoes, celery, parsley, garlic, and water. Bring to a boil, reduce to a simmer, cover, and cook for 1 hour.

Let sit for 30 minutes, and then strain the broth through a large sieve. Cool the stock, then refrigerate or freeze it.

MAKES 4 QUARTS

RICH VEGETABLE STOCK: After straining, simmer the stock uncovered until reduced by one-third to one-half.

FISH STOCK

Do not use strongly flavored or fatty fish such as salmon, mackerel, herring, or bluefish for this.

- 2 pounds fish heads, backs, and bones
- 6 cups cold water
- Juice of 1 large lemon
- 2 large unpeeled onions, quartered
- 3 ribs celery, quartered
- 3 carrots, quartered
- 1 bay leaf
- 10 peppercorns

- 3 sprigs parsley
- 1 sprig fresh thyme

In a 5-quart soup pot, combine the fish parts, water, lemon juice, onions, celery, carrots, bay leaf, peppercorns, parsley, and thyme. Bring to a boil, reduce to a simmer, and cook, uncovered, for 1 hour. Skim any scum that rises to the surface.

Line a sieve with a triple layer of dampened cheesecloth. Strain the broth through the cheesecloth. Cool the stock and refrigerate or freeze until needed.

MAKES 1½ QUARTS

RICH FISH STOCK: After straining, simmer the stock uncovered until reduced by one-third to one-half.

GARLIC STOCK

Garlic stock is a savory liquid that may be used as a base for vegetable, poultry, or meat soups. Lengthy cooking subdues the garlic's pungency without diminishing its distinct flavor.

- 4 quarts cold water
- 24 unpeeled cloves garlic, smashed
- 4 carrots, halved
- 4 ribs celery, halved
- 2 large unpeeled onions, quartered
- 2 turnips, peeled and quartered (optional)
- 2 sprigs parsley
- 2 teaspoons salt

In a 6- to 8-quart soup pot, combine the water, garlic, carrots, celery, onions, turnips (if using), parsley, and salt. Bring to a boil. Reduce to a simmer, cover, and cook for 1 hour.

Strain the stock through a large sieve. Cool, then refrigerate or freeze.

MAKES 3 QUARTS

RICH GARLIC STOCK: After straining, simmer the stock uncovered until reduced by one-third to one-half.

EGG DROP SOUP

This is an extremely simple soup to make. If you're watching cholesterol, make this with just 1 whole egg and 2 egg whites beaten together.

- 4 cups chicken broth, store-bought or homemade (page 172)
- 4 teaspoons soy sauce
- 2 large eggs, well beaten
- 2 tablespoons rice vinegar
- 1 teaspoon dark sesame oil
- 2 tablespoons finely sliced scallions

In a small saucepan, combine the broth and soy sauce and bring to a boil. Remove from the heat and pour the egg very slowly in a thin stream into the hot soup. When the egg has coagulated, stir slowly. Add the vinegar and oil. Serve sprinkled with the scallions.

MAKES 4 SERVINGS

MISO-EGG DROP SOUP: Make the soup with vegetable broth, store-bought or homemade (page 173), instead of chicken broth. Blend 1 tablespoon shiro miso in 1 teaspoon water and stir into the broth before adding the egg.

AVGOLEMONO

Avgolemono is a Greek lemon-flavored chicken broth made with eggs and rice.

- 6 cups Rich Poultry Stock (page 172)
- ½ cup brown rice
- 1 large egg
- 2 large egg yolks

¼ cup lemon juice

2 tablespoons snipped fresh dill, plus small sprigs for garnish

Salt and pepper

In a medium heavy-bottomed saucepan, bring the stock to a boil. Add the rice, reduce to a simmer, cover, and cook until tender, 30 to 35 minutes.

In a medium bowl, whisk together the whole egg and egg yolks until light and frothy. Slowly beat in the lemon juice.

Beating constantly, whisk 1 cup of hot stock into the egg mixture. Then gradually return the mixture to the hot stock, stirring constantly. Bring almost to the boiling point, but do not boil or the soup will curdle.

Stir in the snipped dill. Season with salt and pepper to taste. Remove from the heat and serve hot, garnished with dill sprigs.

MAKES 4 TO 6 SERVINGS

LEMONY TURKEY & BARLEY SOUP

Roast turkey gets a second life in this rich, creamy, Greek-inspired soup. Instead of cinnamon, you can use a pinch of saffron.

4 cups turkey or chicken broth, store-bought or homemade (page 172)

Zest strips from 1 large lemon

3-inch piece of cinnamon stick

1 bay leaf

2 large eggs

2 large egg yolks

2 tablespoons lemon juice

¼ teaspoon cayenne pepper

2 cups finely shredded roast turkey

1½ cups cooked barley

Coarse salt and black pepper

½ cup cooked broccoli florets, finely chopped

2 tablespoons minced fresh basil or flat-leaf parsley

In a large heavy soup pot, combine the broth, zest strips, cinnamon, and bay leaf. Bring to a boil, cover, and cook for 5 minutes, Discard the zest, cinnamon, and bay leaf.

In a medium bowl, whisk together the whole eggs, egg yolks, lemon juice, and cayenne.

Remove the pot from the heat and slowly pour ½ cup of the hot broth into the egg mixture, whisking constantly. Continuing to whisk, slowly pour the egg mixture back into the broth in the pot.

EGG RAIN

The simplest soup of all is a consommé, which is just clear broth. To notch the soup up a bit, you can add an "egg rain," which adds substance and richer taste to the clear broth. To make egg rain: For every 1 quart of broth, mix 2 eggs with 1 tablespoon of flour. Beat the batter until very smooth, then drizzle the mixture through a wide, perforated spoon into simmering broth. Continue to cook for 4 to 5 minutes.

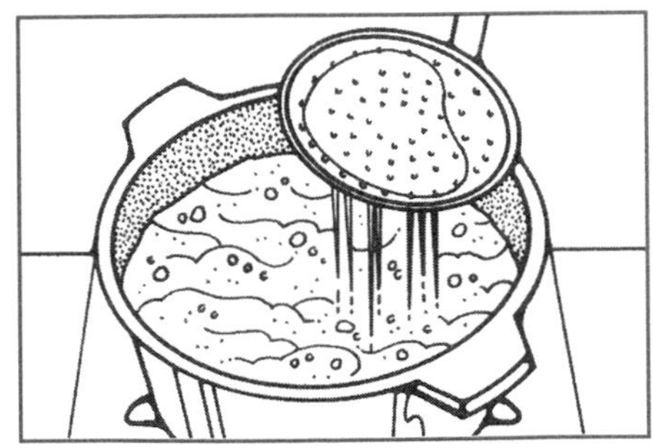

Cook, still whisking constantly, over low heat until thickened slightly, about 5 minutes. (Do not allow the broth to boil, or the eggs will scramble.)

Stir in the turkey and barley and cook, stirring constantly, until heated through. Season with salt and black pepper to taste. Serve in bowls sprinkled with broccoli and basil.

MAKES 4 SERVINGS

ZESTY TOMATO-RICE SOUP WITH FRESH HERBS

The surprise of orange zest and nutmeg turns this simple soup into a gourmet treat. It is best made when fresh tomatoes are at their peak.

- 1 tablespoon butter
- 1 tablespoon olive oil
- 1 large onion, finely chopped
- 2½ pounds tomatoes (7 to 8 medium), peeled and quartered
- 4 cups chicken broth, store-bought or homemade (page 172)
- 3 tablespoons minced fresh basil
- 4 sprigs fresh thyme, tied together with string
- 1 bay leaf
- 1 long strip orange zest
- 1 cup cooked brown rice
- ¼ cup light cream or half-and-half
- Salt
- 2 teaspoons sugar (optional)
- Pinch of nutmeg

In a large heavy-bottomed saucepan, heat the butter and oil over medium heat. Add the onion and sauté until wilted but not browned.

Stir in the tomatoes and broth, and bring to a boil. Add 1 tablespoon of the basil, the thyme, bay leaf, and orange zest. Reduce to a simmer, cover, and cook for 20 minutes.

Remove the thyme, bay leaf, and orange zest. Puree the soup in a food processor or blender and return to the pot. Add the cooked rice and simmer for 10 minutes.

Add the cream. Taste for seasoning, and add salt to taste and sugar if desired.

Serve sprinkled with the remaining 2 tablespoons basil and the nutmeg.

MAKES 6 SERVINGS

LEEK, FENNEL & YOGURT SOUP

Silky-smooth, yogurt-based soups are common throughout the eastern Mediterranean. Be careful not to boil the soup or the yogurt will curdle and separate.

- 4 medium leeks, dark green leaves trimmed
- 1 tablespoon olive oil
- 3 tablespoons butter
- 2 cups diced fennel
- 1½ teaspoons mint
- 4 cups vegetable broth, store-bought or homemade (page 173)
- 1 large egg
- 2 tablespoons flour
- 3 cups plain whole-milk yogurt, well stirred
- Coarse salt and pepper

Halve the leeks lengthwise and then slice crosswise into ½-inch pieces. (You should have 4 to 5 cups.) Place in a colander and rinse under cold running water to remove any grit.

In a deep, heavy-bottomed soup pot, heat the oil and 1 tablespoon of the butter. When the butter starts to foam, add the leeks and fennel, stirring to coat. Cover tightly and cook over medium-low heat, stirring occasionally, until very soft, 8 to 10 minutes (the leeks should just start to brown).

Stir in the mint and cook for 1 minute. Add the broth and bring to a boil. Reduce to a simmer and cook for 10 minutes.

In a medium bowl, whisk the egg and flour together until blended with no lumps. Whisk in a large spoonful of yogurt. Add the remaining yogurt. Slowly add a ladleful of hot broth, stirring until smooth.

Add the yogurt mixture to the pot, stirring in a little at a time. Bring the soup to just below the boiling point, stirring occasionally. Remove from the heat as soon as it begins to steam, about 10 minutes; do not boil. Season to taste with salt and pepper.

While the soup cools slightly, in a small saucepan, melt the remaining 2 tablespoons butter and then heat until it begins to turn a nutty brown color (but not too dark), about 5 minutes.

Ladle the soup into warm bowls and spoon on a little of the browned butter.

MAKES 6 SERVINGS

ROASTED BUTTERNUT, GARLIC & SAGE SOUP

You can make this up to 2 days ahead. Reheat gently before serving.

- 5 pounds (2 medium) butternut squash
- 2 medium onions, quartered
- ½ head garlic, separated into cloves (do not peel)
- 2 tablespoons olive oil
- 2 teaspoons ground cumin
- 2 teaspoons coarse salt
- ½ teaspoon pepper
- 1 small bunch fresh sage (about 6 stems)
- 6 cups chicken broth, store-bought or homemade (page 172)
- 2 teaspoons red wine vinegar or lemon juice
- Maple Pepitas (page 615)

Position a rack in the middle of the oven and preheat to 425°F. Peel the squash, cut in half, and remove and discard the seeds. Cut each half into 2 pieces.

Place the squash, onions, and garlic in a single layer in a large roasting pan. (Use 2 roasting pans or a large baking sheet, if necessary.) Drizzle the vegetables with the oil, using your hands to coat each piece well. Sprinkle the cumin over the squash and sprinkle all the vegetables with the salt and pepper. Scatter three-fourths of the sage in the pan. Roast for 30 minutes, turning the vegetables occasionally to avoid sticking. Continue to roast until the squash is tender, about 30 minutes more. Remove from the oven and let cool.

Transfer the onions to a food processor. Squeeze the garlic out of their skins into the processor. Add the squash and any liquid remaining in the roasting pan (discard the sage). Process until pureed.

Transfer the puree to a soup pot and stir in the broth. Bring the soup to a simmer over high heat. Reduce the heat and let simmer until heated through. Stir in the vinegar. Add more salt and pepper to taste.

Serve hot, sprinkled with Maple Pepitas and garnished with a couple of sage leaves.

MAKES 10 SERVINGS

CREAMY ROASTED SQUASH SOUP: Stir ½ cup light cream into the soup at the very end.

WINTER SQUASH & WILD MUSHROOM SOUP

Choose wild mushrooms—chanterelles, black trumpet, hen-of-the-woods, shiitake, oyster, or cremini—that are moist to the touch, with no shriveled dried edges, bruises, or spots.

- 8 cups vegetable broth, store-bought or homemade (page 173)
- ½ ounce dried porcini or morel mushrooms
- 1 cup diced butternut squash
- 1 bay leaf

3 tablespoons olive oil

1 cup sliced red onion

1 pound assorted fresh wild mushrooms, tough stems removed and cleaned and sliced

1 cup orzo or ditalini pasta

Coarse salt and pepper

¼ cup chopped flat-leaf parsley

⅓ cup grated Parmesan cheese

In a large soup pot, heat the broth. Place the mushrooms in a small heatproof bowl and add 1 cup of the hot broth. Let stand for 20 minutes or until softened. Reserving the soaking liquid, scoop out the mushrooms. Rinse the mushrooms and dice. Strain the soaking liquid through a coffee filter or a paper towel–lined sieve. Add the soaking liquid to the broth.

Add the squash and bay leaf to the broth. Bring to a boil then reduce to a simmer.

Meanwhile, in a large skillet, heat the oil over medium heat. Add the onion and cook until soft, 5 to 8 minutes. Add the dried and fresh mushrooms and cook until soft and lightly browned, about 10 minutes, adding a little broth if they become too dry. Transfer to the pot of broth.

Add the pasta to the broth and cook until the pasta is done and the squash is tender, 5 to 8 minutes. Discard the bay leaf. Season to taste with salt and pepper. Stir in the parsley. Serve the soup topped with the Parmesan.

MAKES 6 SERVINGS

TOMATO, LEEK & ONION SOUP

To wash the leeks, slice them and place in a large bowl of water. Swish the leeks around. The leeks will float and the sand that is lodged in them will fall to the bottom of the bowl. Repeat more than once if the leeks are still sandy. Spin dry in a salad spinner before sautéing them.

¼ cup olive oil

2 medium red onions, diced

2 leeks, thinly sliced

3 cloves garlic, minced

3 cups chicken broth, store-bought or homemade (page 172)

1 can (14.5 ounces) diced tomatoes

2 tablespoons chopped parsley, plus more for garnish

1 teaspoon minced fresh tarragon or ½ teaspoon dried

1 bay leaf

Salt

In a large skillet, heat the oil over medium heat. Add the onions, leeks, and garlic, and cook until just beginning to brown.

In a 2-quart saucepan, combine the sautéed vegetables with the broth, tomatoes, parsley, tarragon, and bay leaf. Cover and simmer for 20 minutes to meld the flavors. Discard the bay leaf.

Season with salt if needed. Serve garnished with chopped parsley.

MAKES 4 TO 6 SERVINGS

SPINACH & WILD RICE SOUP WITH PUMPKIN SEED PESTO

The variation on pesto in this soup gets its richness from pumpkin seeds and is dairy-free, because no cheese is involved.

6¼ cups water

1 cup wild rice

1 large onion, finely chopped

1 large carrot, halved lengthwise and thinly sliced crosswise

¼ cup dried porcini mushrooms, coarsely broken up and rinsed

3 cloves garlic, minced

1 ½ teaspoons salt

¼ teaspoon thyme

⅛ teaspoon nutmeg

2 packages (10 ounces each) frozen chopped spinach

¼ cup hulled pumpkin seeds (pepitas)

½ cup packed fresh basil leaves

2 tablespoons lemon juice

In a Dutch oven, combine 6 cups of the water, the wild rice, onion, carrot, porcini, garlic, salt, thyme, and nutmeg, and bring to a boil over high heat. Reduce to a simmer, cover, and cook for 40 minutes.

Add the spinach and cook until the wild rice is tender and the spinach is heated through, about 10 minutes.

Meanwhile, in a small heavy skillet, heat the pumpkin seeds until they begin to pop, about 2 minutes. Transfer to a food processor or blender and add the basil, lemon juice, and remaining ¼ cup water. Puree until smooth. Pour the pesto into a small bowl and set aside.

Spoon 1 cup of the wild rice soup into the processor (no need to clean the bowl) and process until smooth. Stir the pureed soup and pesto into the soup remaining in the Dutch oven.

MAKES 4 SERVINGS

COLLARD-WILD RICE SOUP WITH PISTOU: Use frozen collards instead of spinach and cook for 5 minutes longer. Use smoked paprika instead of thyme. Omit the pumpkin seed pesto and use ¾ cup of Pistou (page 601) instead.

ITALIAN CHARD SOUP

If you make this soup in tomato season, use beefsteak tomatoes instead of plum tomatoes.

1 tablespoon olive oil

1 small onion, coarsely chopped

2 cloves garlic, minced

3 tablespoons minced flat-leaf parsley

2 tablespoons minced fresh basil

3 cups chicken broth, store-bought or homemade (page 172)

½ pound plum tomatoes, finely chopped

½ pound Swiss chard, coarsely chopped

Juice of 1 lemon

½ teaspoon pepper

Salt

Grated Parmesan cheese, for serving

In a 3-quart saucepan, heat the oil over medium heat. Add the onion and garlic, and cook until softened. Add the parsley and basil, and cook for 2 minutes.

Add the broth and tomatoes, and bring to a low boil. Add the Swiss chard and simmer, covered, for 15 minutes.

Stir in the lemon juice and pepper. Taste and add salt if desired. Pass Parmesan at the table for sprinkling on the soup.

MAKES 4 SERVINGS

BORSCHT

This traditional Russian beef soup improves with overnight aging. It can be served hot or cold.

4 medium beets, peeled and shredded

4 cups beef broth, store-bought or homemade (page 172)

½ medium head cabbage, shredded (½ pound)

¼ cup cider or red wine vinegar

2 tablespoons honey

½ cup tomato puree

Salt and pepper

Greek yogurt or reduced-fat sour cream, for serving

In a large soup pot, combine the beets and broth. Cover and cook over medium heat until the beets are tender, 20 to 25 minutes.

Add the cabbage, vinegar, and honey. Cover and cook until the cabbage begins to soften, 7 to 10 minutes.

Stir in the tomato puree and cook for 15 minutes to soften the cabbage completely and blend the flavors. Season with salt and pepper to taste.

Serve the soup with dollops of yogurt on top.

MAKES 4 TO 6 SERVINGS

VEGAN BORSCHT: Use garlic stock (page 174) or vegetable broth, store-bought or homemade (page 173) instead of beef broth. Use 1 tablespoon brown sugar (or more to taste) instead of honey. Serve with a dollop of plain soy yogurt.

SOUPE AU PISTOU

This hearty French vegetable soup is named after the pungent pesto-like sauce that is added to provide undeniable character.

- 1 cup dried navy beans, soaked overnight, drained
- 8 cups water
- 1 large onion, thinly sliced
- 1 clove garlic, minced
- 1 large leek, thinly sliced
- 3 medium carrots, sliced
- 3 large red potatoes, cubed
- 2 teaspoons coarse salt
- 1 bouquet garni (page 185) with a 2-inch piece orange zest added to it
- 1 cup whole wheat elbow macaroni
- 1½ cups cut green beans (1-inch pieces)
- 2 small zucchini, sliced
- 1 medium pattypan squash, cubed
- Pistou (page 601)

Place the beans in a large heavy-bottomed soup pot. Add the water and bring to a boil. Add the onion, garlic, leek, carrots, potatoes, salt, and bouquet garni. Reduce to a simmer, cover, and cook until the beans are soft but not mushy, about 45 minutes.

Add the macaroni to the pot and cook for 5 minutes. Add the green beans, zucchini, and pattypan squash, and cook until the pasta is tender, about 12 minutes. Discard the bouquet garni. If the soup is too thick, add about 1 cup hot water.

When ready to serve, place the pistou in a small serving bowl so that each diner can stir a portion into his/her soup before eating.

MAKES 8 TO 10 SERVINGS

ASIAN SOUP WITH RICE NOODLES

A good stock and just a few ingredients will give you a rich, flavorful dinner in a bowl. If you don't have homemade stock on hand, the addition of ginger, scallions, and garlic will boost the flavor of store-bought broth. Either way, dinner will be ready in a flash.

- 6 cups chicken broth, store-bought or homemade (page 172)
- 8 ounces shiitake mushrooms, stems discarded, caps thinly sliced
- ¼ cup minced fresh ginger
- 4 scallions, thinly sliced
- 4 teaspoons soy sauce
- 3 cloves garlic, thinly sliced
- 4 ounces thin rice noodles, broken in half
- 14 to 16 ounces firm tofu, cut into 1-inch chunks
- 1 large bunch watercress, tough stems trimmed
- 1 tablespoon dark sesame oil
- 4 teaspoons rice vinegar

In a large saucepan, combine the broth, mushrooms, ginger, scallions, soy sauce, and garlic, and bring to a boil over medium heat. Add the noodles and cook until almost tender, 3 to 5 minutes.

Add the tofu and watercress, and cook until the watercress is tender, about 2 minutes. Stir in the sesame oil and vinegar.

MAKES 4 SERVINGS

RED LENTIL & RICE SOUP

This mildly spiced soup is brightened with fresh ginger. To add more heat, drizzle the finished soup with Asian chili oil instead of olive oil.

- 2 tablespoons extra-virgin olive oil, plus more for drizzling
- 1 medium onion, chopped
- 2 cloves garlic, chopped
- 2 medium carrots, chopped
- 1 tablespoon finely minced fresh ginger
- 2 teaspoons ground cumin
- 5 cups water
- 2 cups vegetable broth, store-bought or homemade (page 173)
- 1½ cups red lentils
- 1½ cups cooked brown rice
- 1 cup chopped cherry tomatoes
- Coarse salt and pepper

In a large, heavy saucepan, heat the oil over medium heat. Add the onion and cook until soft, about 5 minutes. Add the garlic, carrots, ginger, and cumin, and cook for 2 minutes. Add the water, broth, and lentils. Bring to a boil. Reduce the heat to a simmer and cook until the lentils are just tender, about 20 minutes.

Add the rice and tomatoes, and simmer for 5 minutes. Remove about one-fourth of the soup (about 2 cups) and puree in a blender. Return to the pot and stir. Season to taste with salt and pepper. Drizzle with a little olive oil before serving.

MAKES 6 SERVINGS

RUSSIAN BARLEY SOUP

For a richer soup, use Greek yogurt (1% or 2%) instead of regular yogurt.

- 3 cups chicken broth, store-bought or homemade (page 172)
- ½ cup pearled barley
- ½ teaspoon ground coriander
- ½ teaspoon mint
- ¼ teaspoon salt
- 1 tablespoon butter
- 1 small onion, minced
- 1 tablespoon flour
- 2 large eggs, beaten
- 1 cup plain low-fat yogurt
- 2 tablespoons lemon juice
- 2 tablespoons snipped fresh dill

In a medium saucepan, combine the broth, barley, coriander, mint, and salt. Bring to a boil over medium heat and reduce to a simmer. Cover and cook until the barley is tender, about 45 minutes.

Meanwhile, in a small skillet, heat the butter over medium heat. Add the onion and cook until softened. Add the onion to the cooked barley.

In a small bowl, blend the flour and eggs, then carefully stir in the yogurt. Stir a little hot broth into the egg-yogurt mixture to warm it, then stir the warmed mixture into the soup. Stir in the lemon juice and dill and heat very gently. Do not let boil or the soup will "break."

MAKES 4 TO 6 SERVINGS

EIGHT-VEGETABLE SOUP WITH BLACK BARLEY

Cold-pressed sesame oil, available in most natural foods stores, has a very subtle nutty flavor.

- 3 tablespoons cold-pressed sesame or peanut oil
- 2 medium Vidalia onions, chopped
- 4 carrots, chopped
- 3 ribs celery with leaves, chopped
- 1 large russet (baking) potato, chopped
- 2 small zucchini, chopped
- ½ pound (2 cups) sliced green beans
- 7 cups chicken broth, store-bought or homemade (page 172)
- 2 medium tomatoes, chopped
- 1 bay leaf
- 1 teaspoon salt
- ¼ teaspoon pepper
- 8 leaves ruby Swiss chard, finely shredded
- 1 cup cooked black or regular barley
- ¼ teaspoon nutmeg

In a large soup pot, heat the oil over medium-high heat. Add the onions and cook until translucent.

Add the carrots, celery, potato, zucchini, and beans. Stir in the broth and tomatoes and bring to a boil. Reduce the heat and add the bay leaf, salt, and pepper. Cover and simmer for 45 minutes.

Let the soup cool. Discard the bay leaf. Puree the soup in a food processor or through a food mill. Return to the same pot and stir in the shredded Swiss chard, barley, and nutmeg.

Adjust the seasoning, if desired. Simmer for 5 minutes, or until heated through.

MAKES 12 SERVINGS

BLACK BEAN SOUP

This is a very basic black bean soup that lends itself to all manner of variations (right).

- 1 cup dried black beans, soaked overnight, drained
- 3 tablespoons vegetable oil
- 1 medium onion, chopped
- 1 green bell pepper, chopped
- 1 rib celery, chopped
- 1 carrot, chopped
- 2 cloves garlic, chopped
- 2 cups chicken broth, store-bought or homemade (page 172)
- Lemon juice
- Salt and pepper
- Snipped chives, for garnish

Place the beans in a 4-quart heavy-bottomed saucepan and add fresh water to cover. Cover the pan and simmer until the beans are almost tender, about 1 hour 30 minutes. Drain. Return the beans to the pan.

Meanwhile, in a large skillet, heat the oil. Add the onion, bell pepper, celery, carrot, and garlic, and cook until almost tender. Add to the beans along with the broth. Cover, and simmer until the beans are very tender, 45 to 60 minutes. Remove from the heat and cool slightly.

Transfer the soup to a food processor and puree (or puree right in the pan with a hand blender). Return the puree to the pan and stir in lemon juice, salt, and pepper to taste. Heat over low heat until hot. Serve garnished with chives.

MAKES 6 TO 8 SERVINGS

SPICY GARLIC BLACK BEAN SOUP: Use home-made garlic stock (page 173) instead of chicken broth and add 2 teaspoons chopped chipotle pepper (in adobo) when you puree the soup. Garnish with chopped cilantro instead of chives.

THAI BLACK BEAN SOUP: Cook the beans and vegetables in a combination of coconut milk and chicken broth. Season with lime juice instead of lemon juice, and garnish with chopped fresh mint.

FRENCH BLACK BEAN SOUP: Use a leek instead of the onion, and add 1 teaspoon tarragon to the beans while they cook.

CHINESE BLACK BEAN SOUP: Add a couple of pieces of star anise to the beans while they cook. Add 1 teaspoon of dark sesame oil when sautéing the vegetables. Season with Chinese black vinegar instead of lemon juice.

WHITE BEAN SOUP WITH KALE & BACON

If you have a hand blender, use it to thicken the soup right in the pot.

- 3 slices bacon, finely chopped
- 1 tablespoon olive oil
- 1 medium onion, finely chopped
- 4 cloves garlic, minced
- 4 cups chicken broth, store-bought or homemade (page 172)
- 4 cups cooked cannellini beans
- 1 small sprig fresh rosemary
- 1 sprig fresh sage
- 3 cups finely chopped kale
- Salt and pepper

In a heavy-bottomed soup pot, cook the bacon over medium heat until the fat has rendered and the bacon is crisp, 10 to 12 minutes.

Add the olive oil, increase the heat to medium-high and add the onion and garlic. Cook until the onion is softened and translucent, 5 to 7 minutes. Add the broth, beans, rosemary, and sage, and bring to a boil. Reduce the heat to medium-low and simmer for 15 minutes.

Remove and discard the herbs. Transfer half of the solids to a food processor or blender and process until smooth. Add back to the soup pot and stir to combine. Bring the soup back to a quick boil, remove from the heat, and add the kale. Season to taste with salt and pepper.

MAKES 6 SERVINGS

SPLIT PEA SOUP

For a change-up, use a smoked turkey leg instead of smoked ham hocks.

- 2 cups green split peas
- 1 pound smoked ham hocks
- ¼ teaspoon pepper
- 10 cups cold water
- 2 tablespoons vegetable oil
- 2 cups finely diced carrots
- 1 cup diced celery
- ½ cup chopped onion

In a 4-quart heavy-bottomed soup pot, combine the split peas, ham hocks, pepper, and water. Bring to a boil over medium heat. Reduce the heat, cover, and let simmer while sautéing the vegetables.

In a skillet, heat the oil over medium-high heat. Add the carrots, celery, and onion, and cook until softened. Add to the soup and cook until the split peas are very tender, about 1 hour 30 minutes.

Remove the ham hocks and cut the meat from them. Return the meat to the soup.

MAKES 6 TO 8 SERVINGS

CURRIED YELLOW SPLIT PEA SOUP: Use yellow split peas instead of green. Sprinkle the vegetables with 1 teaspoon curry powder when sautéing them.

GARLICKY SPLIT PEA SOUP: Make the soup with homemade Garlic Stock (page 174) and garnish with Homemade Garlic Croutons (page 382).

CHUNKY LAMB SOUP: Use lamb instead of beef and add cooked white beans instead of corn kernels. Increase the garlic to 3 cloves. Omit the oregano and use crumbled rosemary instead.

CHUNKY BEEF SOUP WITH FRESH HERBS

This is a perfect recipe to make in the summer when you have access to local tomatoes and fresh herbs.

- 4 cups beef broth, store-bought or homemade (page 172)
- 1 cup diced peeled tomatoes
- ½ cup diced onion
- ½ cup diced celery
- ½ cup diced carrot
- 1 clove garlic, minced
- 1 tablespoon minced parsley, plus more for garnish
- 1 teaspoon minced fresh oregano
- 1 teaspoon minced fresh thyme
- 1 bay leaf
- 1 cup diced cooked beef
- ½ cup sliced green beans (1-inch lengths)
- ½ cup corn kernels, fresh or frozen
- Salt and pepper

In a large saucepan, combine the broth, tomatoes, onion, celery, carrot, garlic, parsley, oregano, thyme, and bay leaf. Cover and bring to a boil over medium heat. Reduce the heat to a simmer and cook for 30 minutes.

Add the beef, green beans, and corn. Cover and continue to simmer for 20 minutes, or until the beans are tender. Discard the bay leaf.

Season with salt and pepper to taste. Serve garnished with parsley.

MAKES 4 SERVINGS

CHUNKY SUMMER VEGETABLE SOUP WITH CHICKEN

This is a good use for leftover chicken, but you can also make the soup from scratch. Just poach or microwave ½ to ¾ pound skinless, boneless breasts or thighs.

- 4 cups chicken broth, store-bought or homemade (page 172)
- 1 cup diced peeled tomatoes
- ½ cup diced onion
- ½ cup diced celery
- ¼ cup diced red bell pepper
- 2 cups diced yellow summer squash
- 1 cup frozen green peas
- 1½ cups diced cooked chicken
- 2 tablespoons minced fresh basil, plus more for garnish
- Salt and pepper

In a large saucepan, combine the broth, tomatoes, onion, celery, and bell pepper. Cover and bring to a boil over medium heat. Reduce to a simmer and cook for 30 minutes.

Add the squash and peas. Cover and simmer for 15 minutes. Add the chicken and basil, and simmer just until heated through. Season to taste with salt and pepper. Garnish with minced basil before serving.

MAKES 6 SERVINGS

CHUNKY SUMMER VEGETABLE SOUP WITH TOFU: Use Vegetable Stock (page 173) and 1½ cups cubed drained tofu (see "Draining Tofu," page 311) in place of the chicken.

THAI COCONUT CHICKEN SOUP

Make sure to get coconut milk, not cream of coconut for this delicately flavored soup. Fish sauce is available in many supermarkets and Asian grocery stores. If you can't find it, substitute an equal amount of soy sauce plus 2 anchovy fillets.

- 1 cup hot water
- ½ cup stemmed dried shiitake mushrooms
- 1 cup chicken broth, store-bought or homemade (page 172)
- 1 cup unsweetened coconut milk
- 1 tablespoon minced fresh ginger
- 1 tablespoon minced fresh lemongrass
- 2 strips (2 x ½ inch) lime zest
- ¾ pound skinless, boneless chicken breasts, cut crosswise into thin strips
- 3 tablespoons fish sauce
- 1 tablespoon muscovado or dark brown sugar
- ¼ cup lime juice (about 2 limes)
- ½ cup cilantro leaves

In a small heatproof bowl, combine the hot water and shiitakes. Let stand for 20 minutes, or until the mushrooms have softened. Reserving the soaking liquid, scoop out the mushrooms and thinly slice. Strain the soaking liquid through a coffee filter or a paper towel–lined sieve.

In a medium saucepan, combine the mushrooms, mushroom soaking liquid, broth, coconut milk, ginger, lemongrass, and lime zest. Bring to a boil over medium heat, then reduce to a simmer and cook 5 minutes to blend the flavors.

Add the chicken, fish sauce, and brown sugar, and cook until the chicken is just cooked through, about 1 minute. Stir in the lime juice and cilantro leaves.

MAKES 4 SERVINGS

SANCOCHO

A beloved Latin American stew, sancocho can include a variety of ingredients—chicken, seafood, and vegetables. Coconut milk makes this version rich and creamy.

- 1 medium sweet potato
- 6 cups chicken broth, store-bought or homemade (page 172)
- 2 skinless, bone-in chicken thighs
- 2 tablespoons vegetable oil
- 2 large shallots, thinly sliced
- 1 serrano chili pepper, seeded and thinly sliced
- 1 cup corn kernels, fresh or frozen
- 1 ripe plantain, halved and sliced

BOUQUET GARNI

The bouquet garni is a traditional combination of herbs that is added to soups, stews, and sauces to enhance their flavor.

- 1 bay leaf
- 2 sprigs parsley
- 1 sprig fresh thyme

Tie the herbs together with a string and place in a piece of cheesecloth and tie it closed, or place in a metal tea ball. For even more flavor, tie the herbs between 2 stalks of celery.

1 can (14 ounces) unsweetened coconut milk

2 plum tomatoes, seeded and sliced lengthwise

Coarse salt

½ cup cubed avocado

3 tablespoons chopped cilantro

Lime wedges, for serving

Prick the sweet potato a few times and microwave on high 3 minutes, until partially cooked. When cool enough to handle, peel and cut into ½-inch pieces. Set aside.

Meanwhile, in a large soup pot, bring the broth to a boil. Add the chicken and simmer until just cooked through, 15 to 20 minutes. Transfer the chicken to a cutting board, and when cool enough to handle, dice. Discard the bones. Set the chicken aside.

In a small saucepan, heat the oil. Add the shallots and chili pepper and cook until soft, about 3 minutes. Transfer to the soup along with the sweet potato, corn, and plantain. Cook until the plantain is soft, about 10 minutes. Stir in the chicken, coconut milk, and tomatoes. Season to taste with salt. Simmer for 5 minutes to heat through.

Serve the soup topped with the avocado and cilantro, and with lime wedges for squeezing.

MAKES 6 SERVINGS

CHUNKY TURKEY SOUP WITH WINTER VEGETABLES

For a more pronounced turnip flavor (if you're a fan), use white turnips instead of rutabaga.

4 cups turkey or chicken broth, store-bought or homemade (page 172)

1 cup dry white wine or apple juice

2 cloves garlic, minced

1 teaspoon thyme

½ teaspoon rosemary

1 cup diced butternut squash

½ cup diced rutabaga

½ cup diced celery

½ cup diced onion

1½ cups small broccoli florets

1 cup diced cooked turkey

Salt and pepper

Shredded Gruyère cheese, for serving (optional)

In a large saucepan, combine the broth, wine, garlic, thyme, and rosemary. Bring to a boil over medium-high heat and boil for 5 minutes.

Add the butternut squash, rutabaga, celery, and onion. Cover and return to a boil. Reduce to a simmer and cook for 30 minutes.

Add the broccoli and simmer until all the vegetables are tender, 10 to 15 minutes.

Stir in the turkey and cook to heat through. Season with salt and pepper to taste. Serve with Gruyère (if desired).

MAKES 4 SERVINGS

ROASTED TOMATO-BASIL SOUP WITH MEATBALLS

Plum tomatoes have a high pulp-to-seed ratio, making them ideal for roasting.

1 red onion, thickly sliced

1½ pounds plum tomatoes, halved lengthwise

2 red bell peppers, halved lengthwise and seeded

6 ounces lean ground turkey

¼ cup plain dried bread crumbs, preferably whole wheat

¼ cup low-fat (1%) milk

- $\frac{1}{8}$ teaspoon black pepper
- 6 tablespoons chopped fresh basil
- 2 cups chicken broth, store-bought or homemade (page 172)
- 1 tablespoon balsamic vinegar
- 1 clove garlic, minced
- 2 teaspoons paprika
- $\frac{1}{2}$ teaspoon salt

Preheat the broiler. Place the onion slices, tomatoes, and bell peppers, cut-sides down, on a broiler pan. Broil 4 inches from the heat for 12 minutes, or until the pepper and tomato skins are blackened. When cool enough to handle, peel the tomatoes and peppers.

Meanwhile, in a medium bowl, combine the turkey, bread crumbs, milk, black pepper, and 2 tablespoons of the basil, stirring to thoroughly blend. Shape the turkey mixture into $\frac{3}{4}$-inch balls, using about 1 rounded teaspoon per ball.

Transfer the broiled vegetables to a food processor or blender, and puree until smooth, about 1 minute. Pour the vegetable puree into a large saucepan along with the broth, vinegar, garlic, paprika, and salt. Bring to a simmer and cook for 3 minutes to blend the flavors.

Drop the meatballs into the soup, and simmer until cooked through, about 5 minutes. Stir in the remaining 4 tablespoons basil.

MAKES 4 SERVINGS

LENTIL-ESCAROLE SOUP WITH SAUSAGE

Escarole, a much overlooked soup green, matches beautifully with Italian pork sausage.

- $\frac{3}{4}$ pound Italian pork sausage, cut into bite-size chunks
- 1 cup chopped leeks
- 1 cup lentils
- 1 teaspoon basil
- Salt
- 2 cups chicken broth, store-bought or homemade (page 172)
- 2 cups chopped escarole
- 1 tablespoon lemon juice
- Pepper

In a large heavy-bottomed soup pot, brown the sausage. Add the leeks and cook for 3 minutes.

Add the lentils, basil, $\frac{1}{2}$ teaspoon of salt, and the broth. Cover and simmer until the lentils are almost tender, about 30 minutes.

Add the escarole and cook for 10 minutes. Just before serving, add the lemon juice and season to taste with pepper and more salt.

MAKES 4 TO 6 SERVINGS

POTATO, CHORIZO & WINTER GREENS SOUP

This classic Portuguese soup, caldo verde, is usually made with kale, but you can substitute any winter green. To cut the leaves into slivers, remove the stems, stack the leaves, roll them up like a cigar, and then thinly slice. Serve with Corn Bread (page 569).

- 4 tablespoons extra-virgin olive oil
- 2 medium leeks, chopped
- 5 large (2 pounds) russet (baking) potatoes, peeled and thinly sliced
- 1 large clove garlic, minced
- 6 cups chicken broth, store-bought or homemade (page 172)
- 2 cups water
- 6 ounces hard-cured chorizo, pepperoni, or other dry sausage, diced
- 1 pound mustard greens or kale, stemmed and thinly sliced
- Coarse salt and pepper

In a large saucepan, heat 3 tablespoons of the oil over medium heat. Add the leeks, cover, and sweat until soft, about 10 minutes.

Uncover, add the potatoes, and cook until they begin to brown, about 10 minutes. Add the garlic and cook for 1 minute.

Add the broth and water, and bring to a boil. Reduce to a simmer, cover, and cook until the potatoes are soft, about 20 minutes. Remove from the heat. Slightly mash the potato until thick, but leave some texture.

Meanwhile, in a large skillet, heat the remaining 1 tablespoon oil over medium heat. Add the chorizo and cook until light brown.

Add the chorizo to the soup along with the greens. Return to a simmer and cook until the greens are just tender (they should still be bright green), about 5 minutes. Season to taste with salt and pepper.

MAKES 6 SERVINGS

SPICY SALMON & RICE NOODLE SOUP

This Malaysian soup, called laksa, gets its heat from red curry paste, available in most supermarkets and Asian shops. If you're not ready to spring for wild salmon, you can use any firm-fleshed fish, such as halibut, mahi-mahi, or striped bass.

1 package (6 to 7 ounces) rice stick noodles

1 tablespoon canola oil

1 shallot, thinly sliced

4 teaspoons finely grated fresh ginger

1 tablespoon red curry paste

1 can (14 ounces) unsweetened coconut milk, well stirred

4 cups vegetable broth, store-bought or homemade (page 173)

¼ cup fish sauce

Juice of 1½ limes

¾ pound skinless wild salmon fillet, thawed if frozen, cut into 12 pieces

4 ounces snow peas

Minced cilantro, for garnish

Lime wedges, for serving

Bring a large pot of water to a boil. Add the noodles and cook for 5 minutes, or just until tender. Drain and rinse in a colander under cold running water. Cover with a damp paper towel and let continue to drain.

In a large, heavy-bottomed pot, heat the oil over medium heat. Add the shallot and stir-fry until soft, about 2 minutes. Carefully add the ginger and curry paste (it will sputter). Stir-fry for 1 minute. Gradually add the coconut milk and broth, and bring to a boil. Reduce the heat to medium and simmer for 10 minutes.

Add the fish sauce, lime juice, and salmon. Stir gently. Cover partially and simmer until the fish is cooked through, 5 to 6 minutes. Add the snow peas and remove from the heat. Rinse the noodles briefly with hot water. Drain.

To serve, place the noodles in deep soup bowls and immediately ladle the soup on top. Garnish with cilantro and serve with lime wedges.

MAKES 4 SERVINGS

CREAM OF ASPARAGUS SOUP

Peeling away the tough skin from the asparagus will make a more delicate soup.

3 cups water

1 pound asparagus

¼ cup finely chopped onion

¼ cup finely chopped celery

1 clove garlic, minced

- 1 tablespoon butter
- 1 tablespoon olive oil
- 2 tablespoons flour
- 1 cup half-and-half or milk
- 1 tablespoon lemon juice
- Salt

In a medium saucepan, bring the water to a boil. Cut 2 inches off the tip ends of the asparagus spears (reserve the remainder) and add to the boiling water. Cook until tender, about 3 minutes. With a slotted spoon, remove the tips from the pan, cut into ½-inch pieces, and set aside. (Do not discard the cooking water.)

Trim the woody ends from the remainder of the spears and pare the tough outer peel, if desired. Cut into small pieces and place in the same cooking water along with the onion, celery, and garlic. Cover and bring to a boil. Reduce to a simmer and cook for 30 minutes.

Puree the mixture in a food processor or through a food mill. Set the puree aside.

In a 3-quart saucepan, heat the butter and oil. Stir in the flour and cook for a few minutes, but do not brown.

Gradually stir in the half-and-half, whisking constantly until smooth. Cook over medium heat until thickened, about 5 minutes.

Add the asparagus puree and lemon juice, stirring constantly. Heat through, but do not boil. Add salt to taste.

Serve garnished with the reserved asparagus tips.

MAKES 4 TO 6 SERVINGS

CREAMY ASPARAGUS-CHEESE SOUP: Before adding the asparagus puree, add ½ cup freshly grated Parmesan cheese to the thickened white sauce, and stir until the cheese is melted and the sauce is smooth.

ZESTY CREAM OF ASPARAGUS SOUP: Add 1 teaspoon each Dijon mustard and horseradish to the thickened white sauce.

CREAM OF CAULIFLOWER SOUP

For a vegan soup, use olive oil instead of butter, vegetable broth instead of chicken broth, and almond milk instead of half-and-half.

- 2 tablespoons butter
- 1 small onion, chopped
- 1 cup chicken broth, store-bought or homemade (page 172)
- 2 large russet (baking) potatoes, diced
- Salt
- 1 small head cauliflower (1 pound), broken into florets
- ½ cup boiling water
- ½ teaspoon white pepper
- ¼ teaspoon ground coriander
- ⅛ teaspoon nutmeg
- 2 cups half-and-half or milk
- Chopped watercress, for garnish

In a large saucepan, melt the butter over medium heat. Add the onion and cook until softened. Add the broth, potatoes, and ½ teaspoon salt. Cover and cook until the potatoes are tender, 7 to 10 minutes.

Transfer the mixture to a blender or food processor and puree. Return the puree to the saucepan.

Meanwhile, in another saucepan, combine the cauliflower and boiling water, and cook until barely tender, about 7 minutes. (Do not drain.) With a slotted spoon, remove 1 cup florets and set aside. Puree the remaining cauliflower with its cooking water and add to the potato puree.

Cut the reserved florets into very small pieces (½-inch lengths) and set aside.

Add the pepper, coriander, and nutmeg to the soup and simmer for 3 minutes. Stir in the half-and-half, then add the reserved florets. Heat through but do not boil. Taste for seasoning and add more salt and pepper if desired.

Serve garnished with chopped watercress.

MAKES 4 TO 6 SERVINGS

THAI-STYLE CREAM OF CAULIFLOWER SOUP: Use coconut milk instead of half-and-half. Omit the nutmeg and increase the coriander to ½ teaspoon. Garnish with shredded fresh basil and/or mint.

CREAM OF BROCCOLI SOUP: Use 1 pound broccoli instead of cauliflower: Peel and dice the stems and cut the tops into small florets. Use cumin instead of coriander. Omit the nutmeg. Use black pepper instead of white pepper. Garnish with diced red bell pepper instead of watercress.

CREAM OF TWO-MUSHROOM SOUP

Porcini have an incredible depth of flavor, so it's worth spending a little money to use them in this recipe. You might be able to find dried cèpes or dried Polish mushrooms, both of which are related to the porcini, but are cheaper.

- ¼ cup dried porcini mushrooms
- 2½ cups boiling water
- 2 tablespoons olive oil
- ¼ cup finely chopped shallots
- 1 clove garlic, minced
- ½ pound cremini mushrooms, finely chopped
- 1 teaspoon tarragon
- 1 teaspoon white pepper
- ½ teaspoon salt
- 1 tablespoon flour
- 1 cup half-and-half or milk
- Snipped chives, for garnish

In a small heatproof bowl, combine the dried porcini and boiling water. Let sit until softened, about 20 minutes. Reserving the soaking liquid, lift out the porcini and set aside. Strain the soaking liquid through a coffee filter or a paper towel–lined sieve into a 2-cup measure. If necessary, add water to come to 2 cups.

In a 2-quart saucepan, heat the oil over medium heat. Add the shallots and garlic and cook until softened. Add the cremini mushrooms, tarragon, white pepper, and salt, and cook until the mushrooms soften and lose their liquid.

Sprinkle the flour over the mixture and continue cooking for several minutes. Gradually add the mushroom soaking liquid, stirring constantly. Bring to a boil, then reduce to a simmer, cover, and cook for 15 minutes.

Transfer the mixture to a food processor and add the porcini mushrooms. Puree and return to the saucepan. Stir in the half-and-half and heat thoroughly, but do not boil.

Serve garnished with chives.

MAKES 4 SERVINGS

SUNSHINE SOUP

Onion, celery, herbs, and tomatoes are combined with broth in the bottom of a steamer. This helps flavor the squash and potato as they steam and at the same time creates a flavorful soup base.

- 2 cups chicken broth, store-bought or homemade (page 172)
- 1 cup chopped tomatoes
- 1 medium onion, sliced
- ½ rib celery, chopped
- 1 sprig fresh thyme or ½ teaspoon dried
- 1 sprig fresh savory or ½ teaspoon dried
- 4 cups cubed peeled acorn, pumpkin, butternut, or hubbard squash

1 medium russet (baking) potato, cubed
1 cup reduced-fat (2%) milk
2 tablespoons peanut butter
Salt

In the bottom of a vegetable steamer, combine the broth, tomatoes, onion, celery, thyme, and savory. Place the squash and potato in the steamer basket or insert. Cover, bring to a boil, and steam until the squash is very tender, 15 to 20 minutes.

Transfer the squash and potato to a food processor and process to a smooth puree. Transfer the puree to a saucepan.

Strain the broth from the bottom of the steamer into the saucepan and discard the solids. Stir the soup well, bring to a simmer, and cook until slightly thickened, 5 to 10 minutes.

Stir enough of the milk into the peanut butter to get a smooth sauce the consistency of heavy cream. Stir the remaining milk into the soup and heat through but do not boil. Season with salt to taste.

Just before serving, swirl the peanut butter mixture into the soup.

MAKES 4 TO 6 SERVINGS

CORN & RED POTATO CHOWDER WITH BACON

Feel free to use turkey bacon, but since it won't render as much fat as regular bacon you'll need to brown it in about 2 tablespoons vegetable oil.

6 cups chicken broth, store-bought or homemade (page 172)
5 medium ears corn, kernels removed (about 4 cups) and cobs reserved
1½ pounds red potatoes, diced (about 4 cups)
4 slices bacon, finely chopped
1 medium sweet onion, diced
¼ cup (½ stick) butter, cut into 4 pieces
¼ cup white whole wheat flour*
4 cups milk
1 medium red bell pepper, diced
¼ cup fresh basil leaves, finely chopped
Salt and pepper

**milled from white wheat grains*

In a large saucepan, combine the broth, corn cobs, and potatoes. Cover and bring to a boil over high heat. Reduce the heat to medium-low and simmer until the potatoes are tender, about 10 minutes.

Meanwhile, in a large heavy-bottomed soup pot, cook the bacon until crisp, 10 to 12 minutes.

Add the onion, and cook until beginning to soften and brown at the edges, about 5 minutes. Add the corn kernels and cook until deep yellow and soft, about 5 minutes.

Add the butter. When melted, add the flour and cook, stirring constantly, until evenly distributed and just beginning to brown, about 2 minutes.

When the potatoes are cooked, discard the corn cobs. Add the potatoes and broth to the pot with the corn. Add the milk and bring to a boil over medium heat. Reduce the heat to medium-low, and simmer until thickened, about 2 minutes.

Add the bell pepper and basil, and stir to combine. Season with salt and pepper to taste.

MAKES 6 SERVINGS

LIMA BEAN CHOWDER

Baby lima beans would make this creamy chowder more delicate.

2 tablespoons olive oil
1 tablespoon butter
1 cup chopped onions

1 cup chopped celery

5 cups frozen lima beans, thawed

1 can (14.5 ounces) diced tomatoes with jalapeños

2 cups corn kernels, fresh or frozen

¼ teaspoon salt

3 cups reduced-fat (2%) milk

¾ cup shredded Monterey Jack cheese (3 ounces)

In a large heavy-bottomed soup pot, heat the oil and butter over medium heat. Add the onions and celery, and cook for 5 minutes.

Stir in 4 cups of the lima beans, the tomatoes, corn, and salt, and simmer for 10 minutes.

In a mini food processor, puree the remaining 1 cup lima beans with ½ cup of the milk. Add the lima bean puree and remaining 2 ½ cups milk to the soup and simmer until heated through. (Do not boil.)

Serve the cheese on the side for sprinkling on the hot soup.

MAKES 10 TO 12 SERVINGS

BROCCOLINI CHOWDER

Broccolini is a skinny cousin of broccoli. You can also make this soup with regular broccoli, though you should peel the tough part of the lower stem.

1¼ pounds broccolini, coarsely chopped

½ pound unpeeled Yukon Gold potatoes, diced

1 small onion, chopped

1½ cups water

2 cups reduced-fat (2%) milk

¼ cup flour

1 teaspoon tarragon

½ teaspoon salt

¼ teaspoon black pepper

¼ cup shredded white Cheddar cheese

½ cup minced red bell pepper for serving

In a large saucepan, combine the broccolini, potatoes, onion, and water. Cover and bring to a boil over high heat. Reduce to a simmer, cover, and cook until the broccolini and potatoes are tender, about 5 minutes.

In a small bowl, whisk the milk into the flour. Add the milk mixture to the pan along with the tarragon, salt, and black pepper. Stirring constantly, cook until the mixture comes to a boil and is thickened, about 7 minutes.

Serve the soup topped with the cheese and bell pepper.

MAKES 4 SERVINGS

MANHATTAN FISH CHOWDER

By definition, Manhattan chowder includes tomatoes.

2 teaspoons olive oil

3 slices bacon, cut into ½-inch pieces

1 small onion, finely chopped

2 carrots, halved lengthwise and thinly sliced crosswise

2 cups Fish Stock (page 173) or bottled clam juice

¾ pound red or white potatoes, cut into ½-inch chunks

1 can (14.5 ounces) diced tomatoes

¼ teaspoon thyme

¼ teaspoon hot pepper sauce

¼ teaspoon Worcestershire sauce

1 pound firm-fleshed white fish fillets, cut into 1-inch chunks

In a large saucepan, heat the oil over medium heat. Add the bacon and cook, stirring occasionally, until crisp, about 5 minutes.

Add the onion and carrots, and cook, stirring occasionally, until the carrots are tender, about 7 minutes.

Stir in the stock and bring to a boil. Add the potatoes and cook 5 minutes.

Stir in the tomatoes, thyme, hot sauce, and Worcestershire, and bring to a boil. Reduce to a simmer, add the fish, cover, and cook just until the fish is cooked through, about 7 minutes.

MAKES 4 SERVINGS

CHILLED CARROT SOUP

The natural sweetness of carrots and apples is combined to make a wonderful chilled soup.

- 3 cups cold water
- 2 cups apple juice
- 1 pound carrots, thinly sliced (2½ cups)
- ½ cup diced onion
- ½ cup short-grain brown rice
- 1 clove garlic, minced
- ½ teaspoon salt
- 1 tablespoon lemon juice
- Greek yogurt, for serving
- Minced fresh herbs (parsley, dill, chives, or chervil), for garnish

In a 3-quart saucepan, combine the water, apple juice, carrots, onion, rice, garlic, and salt. Cover and bring to a boil. Reduce to a simmer and cook until rice is tender, about 45 minutes.

Puree the mixture in a blender or food processor. Place the puree in a bowl and stir in the lemon juice. Cover and chill.

Serve with dollops of Greek yogurt sprinkled with fresh herbs.

MAKES 4 TO 6 SERVINGS

RICH CARROT SOUP: Before serving, stir in 1 cup light cream.

ZESTY CARROT SOUP: Stir in 1 teaspoon each horseradish and Dijon mustard during cooking.

ORANGE-CARROT SOUP: Omit the garlic. Use orange juice instead of apple juice. Omit the lemon juice. Stir in ½ teaspoon ground ginger before chilling.

CHILLED MINTED PEA SOUP

If it's fresh pea season, use them instead of frozen. Cook them for 20 minutes, or until tender.

- 3 cups frozen green peas
- 2 cups water
- 1½ cups shredded lettuce
- ½ cup sliced scallions
- 3 tablespoons minced fresh mint, plus more for garnish
- ¼ teaspoon salt
- ⅓ cup Greek yogurt or reduced-fat sour cream

In a 3-quart saucepan, combine the peas, water, lettuce, scallions, mint, and salt. Cover and bring to a boil. Reduce to a simmer and cook until the peas are heated through, about 10 minutes.

Puree the soup in a food processor or through a food mill. Place the puree in a covered container and refrigerate until chilled.

Just before serving, stir in the yogurt and blend thoroughly. Serve garnished with mint.

MAKES 4 TO 6 SERVINGS

CHERRY TOMATO–FENNEL SOUP

Chilling the soup for an hour before serving—or stowing it in your picnic basket—intensifies the flavors.

4 cups cherry tomatoes, halved
2 tablespoons minced fennel fronds
1 small clove garlic, minced
2 teaspoons extra-virgin olive oil
2 small kirby cucumbers, finely diced
4 cups finely diced fennel
Coarse salt and black pepper
Pinch of cayenne pepper
Lemon wedges, for serving

In a blender or food processor, combine the tomatoes, fennel fronds, garlic, and oil, and pulse until just pureed.

Transfer to a bowl. Fold in the cucumbers and diced fennel. Season to taste with salt, black pepper, and cayenne. Serve with lemon wedges for squeezing into the soup.

MAKES 6 SERVINGS

BREAD SOUPS

Many European soup recipes include thick slices of stale bread or toast. In addition to being a great way to use up stale bread, it also adds a splendid thickness to soups. French onion soup, with its rounds of coarse bread drenched in onion broth, is probably the best known. Other soups, such as bouillabaisse, are served by ladling the broth over a slice of bread in the bottom of a soup bowl. Sturdy coarse-textured peasant-type bread is the best for such soups; finer-grained breads fall apart.

MEATS

Generally speaking, meat requires very little preparation before cooking and will stay wholesome (and safe) if handled as little as possible and kept well chilled in the refrigerator until cooking time. When you are ready to use it, trim away excess fat and other waste, and wipe the meat with a clean, damp cloth. (To prevent illness and cross contamination, after handling raw meat use hot, soapy water to wash your hands, the utensils, and the work surfaces thoroughly.)

Flavoring Meat before Cooking

There are two basic ways of imparting flavor to meat before cooking: rubs and marinades.

Dry rubs: A mixture of spices and/or herbs, coarse salt, and a little sugar, a dry rub can be rubbed into a thick or thin cut of meat that will either be roasted, broiled, or grilled. The rub, along with a little oil, is rubbed into all sides of the meat, which then sits in the refrigerator anywhere from 10 minutes to 24 hours.

Marinades: Marinating gives flavor to meat and tenderizes it at the same time. Marinades, unlike rubs, are wet and usually contain oil, an acid ingredient (vinegar, wine, juice—even buttermilk) for tenderizing, and salt and seasonings for flavor. Use marinades on less-tender cuts of meat (like flank steak and London broil). In general, marinating is more important in cuts that are going to be cooked with dry heat, such as roasting, broiling, and grilling. But some larger cuts of meat that require long, slow, moist cooking can also benefit from a marinade and are often cooked right in the marinade.

Steaks, kebabs, and other small or flat cuts are more successfully tenderized with a marinade than are larger cuts since the marinade can easily penetrate the meat from all sides.

To marinate, soak the meat for 3 to 24 hours in enough of the marinade to cover the meat. For thicker pieces, you can use less marinade; just make sure it covers the bottom of the meat, then turn the meat occasionally so that it coats all of it.

Meat marinated for 24 hours will pick up more flavor and be more tender than meat soaked for 3 or 4 hours. However, avoid marinating very small cubes of meat or extremely thin cuts for more than 3 hours. Lengthier marinating might actually begin to "cook" the meat and make it mealy. You can marinate meat for up to 1 hour at room temperature, but it must be refrigerated if marinating longer.

You can use the marinade to baste the meat as it cooks, but don't use it during the last 5 minutes because if the marinade contains any bacteria, 5 minutes of cooking isn't long enough to kill them. For the same reasons, you should never serve a marinade that's had a basting brush dipped in and out of it unless you first boil the marinade for 5 minutes.

Guidelines for Cooking & Serving Meat

Now that you've got that perfect cut of meat, what should you do with it? How it's cooked, at what temperature, and for how long will all affect its taste, appearance, and tenderness.

Select a method of cooking that suits the cut. Some large cuts (leg of lamb, beef tenderloin, pork loin roast) do well with dry-heat methods such as roasting or grilling. Less-tender large cuts (chuck roast, breast of lamb, pork shoulder) benefit from moist cooking such as braising and stewing. The table, opposite page, lists the various commercial cuts, matching them to their best cooking methods (based on their tenderness and size).

Rare, Medium, or Well Done

When cooking beef or lamb, individual taste is the only important consideration guiding the degree to which the meat is cooked. Rare beef or lamb has a brown exterior and deep red, juicy interior. Cooked to medium, it is light pink inside and slightly less juicy. Well done, it's dark on the outside, light brown throughout, and considerably dry.

While veal is almost never cooked rare, it can be cooked medium-rare to well done.

Pork should be cooked until it's cooked through but still juicy, with some pink. Trichinosis is killed at 137°F, well below our recommended cooking temperature of 155°F (note that the United States Department of Agriculture [USDA] is more conservative and suggests 160°F). Cured pork (ham) labeled "cook before eating" must be cooked to 165°F. Cured pork marked "fully cooked" may be heated or eaten as it is.

BASIC MARINADE FOR MEAT

A typical marinade that nicely flavors and tenderizes beef, lamb, or pork starts with a simple vinaigrette dressing such as this. It may be varied according to taste and to the ingredients you have on hand in the kitchen. This recipe makes ¾ cup marinade, enough for 1 to 1½ pounds of meat. Double or triple the recipe if needed for larger cuts of meat. Cider vinegar, red or white wine vinegar, and herb vinegar are equally good and impart subtle differences in flavor. If you use an herb vinegar, omit the herbs called for in the recipe.

½ cup olive oil
¼ cup vinegar, lemon juice, or wine
2 garlic cloves, crushed
1 tablespoon chopped mixed fresh herbs or 2 teaspoons dried

In a small bowl, combine the oil, vinegar, garlic, and herbs. Place the meat in a shallow nonmetal container. Pour the marinade over the meat. Set aside to marinate, turning occasionally if necessary.

Barbecue-Style Marinade: Add 1 tablespoon sweet ingredient (tomato-based chili sauce, ketchup, or honey) and 1 tablespoon salty ingredient (Worcestershire sauce, soy sauce, or mustard). Use 1 teaspoon ground ginger and ⅛ to ¼ teaspoon cayenne pepper instead of the herbs.

Spicy Marinade: Add 1 teaspoon chipotle chili powder to either the plain marinade or the barbecue version.

MATCHING THE CUT TO THE METHOD

Choosing the right method for cooking different cuts of meat will determine whether the final dish is tender and moist, or tough and dry. Some cuts lend themselves to dry heat (roasting, broiling, grilling, panfrying) while others need long slow cooking with some liquid (braising, stewing) in order to be tender.

MEAT	CUTS FOR DRY HEAT	CUTS FOR MOIST HEAT
BEEF	Roasts, tenderloin, prime rib, round, steaks, flank steak	Brisket, pieces for stew, short ribs, rump roast, chuck roast, shank
LAMB	Leg, roast, chops	Pieces for stew, shoulder, shank
PORK	Loin roast, chops, cutlets, ham	Shoulder, hock, shank, pieces for stew
VEAL	Loin roast, rib roast, chops, cutlets	Breast, shoulder, shank, rump roast, pieces for stew shank

Testing for Doneness

There are four quick, easy ways to test how well cooked your meat is. One test is usually enough to determine doneness, but occasionally it is helpful to use two or more methods.

Internal temperature: Checking the internal temperature with a meat thermometer is the most accurate means of knowing when the meat is done. There are two basic types of meat thermometers. One style is inserted in the meat and left there while the meat cooks. This style of thermometer should be checked 20 to 30 minutes before you expect the meat to be done. An instant-read thermometer, which is not ovenproof, is inserted in the meat when it's on a pulled-out oven rack. For both styles, the sensor should be placed in the thickest part of the meat, avoiding bone. When the needle registers 5°F below the desired temperature, remove the meat from the heat and allow it to rest. During this period, the internal temperature will rise to the correct degree and the juices will recede into the meat.

Fork-tenderness: This method is best for testing braised, simmered, or stewed meats. Insert a slender, two-pronged fork into the meat toward the end of the suggested cooking time. When the meat is cooked to tenderness, the fork will slide in easily.

Tenderness to touch: A touch test, popular in restaurant kitchens, is to prod the meat with your finger. If the meat feels soft, it is rare; if hard, it is well done. The feel of medium meat is in between.

Color of meat and juices: Usually, this is the best way to test small cuts that are broiled or panfried. With a sharp knife, make a very small slit near the bone (if there is no bone, cut into the middle or thickest part). Check the color of the meat and its juice. Rare meat is dark red with red juice; medium meat is pink in the middle with light pink juice; and well-done meat is grayish brown throughout with clear to slightly yellow juice.

WHY THE COOKING TIME OF MEAT VARIES

The time it takes to cook meat will be longer or shorter depending on the following factors:

Temperature: Was the meat just out of the refrigerator or at room temperature at the start of cooking?

Size of the roast: A small roast requires less time to cook than a large one.

Thickness of the cut: A thick cut takes longer to cook than a thin one of the same weight.

Fat cover: A roast with an outside layer of fat takes longer to cook than one with little or no fat cover.

Amount of bone: Boneless and rolled roasts need more cooking time per pound than cuts with bone.

Extent of aging: Aged meat cooks slightly faster than meat that has not been aged.

Pan Juice & Gravy

The drippings left in the pan after roasting, panbroiling, or panfrying meat can be deglazed and served as is with the meat, or used as the base for flavorful gravy.

To make pan juice: First, skim off any fat. Then, add a little water or stock, place the pan over medium heat, and use a wooden spoon to scrape the brown particles from the bottom and sides of the pan, mixing them into the liquid. Cook for a few minutes to reduce the juice if the flavor is too diluted, and serve over the meat.

To make pan gravy: See the directions on page 596, "Gravy for Meat and Poultry."

Meat Cooking Methods

Roasting

Roasting, which cooks meat by dry air, is ideal for cooking medium to large tender roasts such as beef ribs, pork loin, and leg of lamb.

To roast: First, make sure your oven is working properly. To insure that your oven is at the right temperature, it's a good idea to invest in an oven thermometer with numbers that are easy to read.

Take the meat out of the refrigerator and let it sit at room temperature for 15 to 20 minutes while the oven preheats. Do not allow it to stand at room temperature much longer than that to discourage any growth of bacteria.

Place meat, fat-side up, on a wire rack set in a large shallow roasting pan. By putting the fat-side on top, the melting fat bastes the meat during roasting. The shallow pan and the rack allow air to circulate around the entire piece of meat. The rack also keeps the meat away from any drippings. Rib roasts can be roasted without a rack since the bones act as a natural rack.

There are several schools of thought on roasting temperatures, from very low to very high. We prefer to take a more moderate route. In general, a roast cooked at 375°F will be moist throughout, while developing a crust on the outside. In some instances, however, a recipe will call for starting at a high temperature, then reducing to a lower temperature and adding liquid to the pan.

Cook meat without interruption until it is done. Never partially cook meat and then finish the cooking at another time. Partial cooking allows bacteria to build up and can make meat unsafe to eat.

A roast may be cooked until it is rare, medium, or well done, depending on personal preference and on the type of meat (some cuts, like round, are much better when cooked rare or medium-rare). The amount of time needed for roasting depends on several factors (see "Why the Cooking Time of Meat Varies," opposite page). Therefore, although some cooks follow a prescribed formula of minutes per pound to cook a roast, more accurate and consistent results can be achieved by using the roasting table (page 200) to find the approximate cooking time needed for your cut of meat. Also, inserting a meat thermometer into the roast is the safest way to determine when the meat is cooked to your liking.

Plan to finish roasting 20 to 30 minutes before serving time so that the meat can rest. During that time, the meat will continue to cook somewhat. Meat that has been allowed to rest retains juice when carved and cuts more easily.

CARVING MEAT

Once your roast or steak has been cooked, carving it will be easy if you follow these basic steps:

1. Determine the direction of the grain in the meat and the position of the bone, if any.
2. Anchor the meat firmly with a curved, two-pronged fork. Because juices escape each time the fork pierces the meat, place the fork so that you don't have to move it too often.
3. Use a sharp carving knife and, for most roasts, slice across the grain. Steaks that are very tender may be cut with the grain; brisket of beef and flank steaks should be sliced at a 30- to 45-degree angle to get large serving pieces. Use a gentle sawing motion as you slice, and do not change the angle of the knife once you have started cutting. Some people find an electric knife particularly useful for getting thin, even slices.

Broiling

Broiling cooks meat by dry, direct heat. This method is nicely suited to cuts that are at least 3/4 to 1 inch thick. Steaks, chops, and ground beef or lamb are particularly well suited to broiling.

Thinner cuts, such as cutlets, will overcook before they get any color and are therefore best suited to panfrying.

To broil: Score the fat (if there is any) every 2 inches around the edge of the meat to prevent curling. Lightly oil the broiler pan and place the meat on top. Cook the meat 4 to 6 inches from the heat in the preheated broiler. To avoid excessive browning, place thick pieces, which take longer to cook, farther from the heat.

Turn the meat over halfway through, unless otherwise stated in the recipe. (See "Cooking Times for Meat: Broiling & Grilling," page 203, for cooking times.) To preserve tasty juices, use tongs for turning instead of a fork.

Grilling

In spite of some concerns about the health aspects of grilling (see "Grilling & Health," page 202), grilling remains one of the most popular ways of cooking meat, from hamburgers to large cuts of meat. It is a distinctly American way of cooking, and we have turned it into an art form, with grills that range from modest little charcoal-fueled hibachis to giant stainless-steel contraptions that are like full-fledged kitchens.

To grill: On any grill, regardless of size, it's

good to find the hot spots and the less hot spots, because when cooking, you should start large pieces of meat over direct high heat, then move to cooler indirect heat to continue cooking. Do not turn things over (especially steaks, chops, and burgers) until they have formed a crust on the bottom, or they will stick. And don't be tempted to press down on burgers as they cook—you will be pressing out the juices, making for a dry burger.

You can also get some of the effects of grilling by using a stovetop grill pan. These heavy cast-iron pans with ridged bottoms require little oil, making them a good low-fat alternative to pan-broiling meat (below). They leave characteristic grill marks on the meat, but no grilled flavor.

PAN-BROILING

Pan-broiling, which cooks meat over moderately dry heat, is excellent for cooking tender beefsteaks, ham steaks, and lamb chops as well as

---

COOKING TIMES FOR MEAT: ROASTING

There are many theories on how meat should be roasted. There's the low and slow theory (cooked at 300°F), the very hot theory (500°F), and the start-high, then go-slow method. We've chosen a middle ground. Meat roasted at 375°F will develop a crust on the outside and remain juicy inside.

The times given below will produce meat cooked to 135°F for medium-rare. For meat cooked less or more, adjust times accordingly. Keep in mind, meat temperatures will rise about 5°F while sitting. An instant-read thermometer is a good and inexpensive investment.

CUT OF MEAT	APPROXIMATE COOKING TIME PER POUND AT 375°F (MINUTES)
Beef, rib roast	15–18
Beef, tenderloin	12–15
Beef, sirloin, tri-tip	12–15
Beef, bottom round	17–18
Beef, eye round	20–22
Beef, rump roast	15–17
Lamb, leg, bone-in	17–18
Lamb, leg, boneless	15–17
Lamb, rib roast "rack"	10–12
Lamb, crown roast	25–30
Pork, loin, bone-in	25–30
Pork, loin, boneless	17–18
Pork, rib roast	25–30
Pork, tenderloin	15–16
Veal, rib roast	18–20

ground meat patties. Cuts less than $^3/_4$ inch thick are best suited to pan-broiling.

To pan-broil: Season the meat. Score the edge of the meat every 2 inches to prevent curling. If the meat is very lean, add a little oil to the skillet. Preheat the skillet to medium. Add the meat and cook, turning with tongs once a crust has formed on the bottom. Remove drippings as they accumulate; otherwise, moist heat will actually cook the meat. Watch carefully and adjust the heat accordingly.

Panfrying

Panfrying, sometimes called sautéing, is a tasty, quick way to cook tender steaks, chops, and patties that are less than 1 inch thick. Because panfried meat is cooked uncovered, in a small amount of fat, it has a nicely browned, crisp crust.

To panfry: Score the edges of the meat to prevent curling. For an extra crisp exterior, coat the meat with whole-grain flour, cornmeal, or fine dried bread crumbs. (We're especially fond of panko, Japanese-style bread crumbs that are very light and crunchy. You can also mix regular bread crumbs with crushed dried herbs for added flavor.) Dip the meat first in flour, then in lightly beaten egg, and then in crumbs. Chill breaded meat for several minutes to set the coating.

Heat some oil in a large skillet. When it is hot but not smoking, add the meat and panfry until golden brown and crisp—timing will vary depending on thickness. Remove it with a pair of tongs, let drain on paper towels, and serve with either a simple lemon wedge or a piquant sauce.

Braising

Braising cooks meat very slowly with moist heat. It is ideal for cooking the less-tender beef, lamb, and pork roasts as well as chops and steaks.

To braise: Heat a small amount of oil in a heavy skillet over medium heat. Use only enough oil to keep the meat from sticking to the pan. For a rich brown color, lightly flour the meat first, shaking off any excess. Brown the meat all over in the hot oil. Add liquid to come about 1 inch up the side of the meat. Bring it to a boil and reduce to a simmer. Cover the pan with a tight-fitting lid, and simmer slowly on the stovetop or in a 325° to 350°F oven. If the liquid cooks away, add more as needed. But avoid using too much—it dilutes the rich flavor of braised meat. Using broth, wine, or vegetable juices instead of water as the cooking medium enhances the taste.

Simmering

Simmering, sometimes called poaching, cooks meat with moisture and is ideal for cooking large cuts of less-tender meats—brisket of beef, veal shanks, boneless pork shoulder butt, and boneless, rolled breast of lamb.

To simmer: Brown the meat in a small amount of fat in a Dutch oven or large, heavy saucepan. Pour in enough water or broth to cover the meat, then add your favorite seasonings—perhaps a bay leaf, a few whole peppercorns, a celery stalk, a carrot, and a small, whole onion. Cover with a tight-fitting lid and cook slowly over low heat or in a 325°F oven. Do not boil.

Cold simmered meat has more flavor and juice if it is chilled quickly in the broth it was cooked in, rather than draining the broth from the meat before chilling.

Stewing

As a moist-heat method of cooking, stewing is ideal for tenderizing cuts of beef, lamb, pork, and veal that have been cut into either 1-inch cubes or thin strips. Shoulder, shin, and neck are all excellent cuts for stew.

GRILLING & HEALTH

Grilling has been a subject of concern for a while, as there are two potential carcinogens that may be found in grilled meats. The first, polycyclic aromatic hydrocarbons (PAHs), are found in the smoke that billows up as the fat from the meat drips onto the coals or the gas burner. The second, heterocyclic amines (HCAs), have more to do with the temperature the meat has been cooked to than the method of cooking. Meat cooked to well done—whether roasted, grilled, fried, or broiled—has HCAs.

There are a couple of ways of reducing these potential carcinogens. Don't cook fatty cuts on the grill, or precook them to get rid of some of the fat. Don't cook those cuts over direct heat, where the fat will drip down onto the heat source; or if you do, place a piece of aluminum foil between the meat and the heat source. These methods can eliminate the PAHs almost entirely.

Marinating meat even for just a little while seems to reduce HCAs by about 90 percent. And to further avoid HCAs, don't cook meat until it is well done or charred.

To stew: Trim excess fat from meat cubes and dredge the cubes in flour. In a Dutch oven or heavy saucepan, brown the cubes in some oil. Drain off any excess fat, and cover the meat with liquid—water, broth, wine, vegetable juice. Add seasonings, such as garlic and onions, then cover the pot with a tight-fitting lid. Cook the meat slowly—either on top of the stove or in a 325° to 350°F oven. If necessary, add more liquid.

Cooking Sausage

There are two types of sausages: fresh and fully cooked. Fully cooked sausages only need heating and can be either simmered, broiled, or panfried. Fresh sausage needs to be fully cooked.

To simmer: Place links or patties in a cold skillet with 2 to 4 tablespoons of water. (If cooking links, prick the casings.) Cover the pan with a tight-fitting lid and simmer the sausage until thoroughly cooked, 20 to 30 minutes, depending on size. You can then broil the sausages if desired.

To broil: Brush simmered sausage with oil and place on a lightly oiled broiler pan. Broil until evenly browned (5 to 8 minutes), turning often with tongs.

To panfry: In a heavy skillet, brown sausages in 1 to 2 tablespoons of oil. Or, start the sausages (be sure to prick the casings) in ¼ inch of water, and cook until the sausages have given up some of their fat. When the water evaporates, cook the sausages in the fat in the pan until they have an even color.

To bake: Spread links or patties in a single layer in a shallow roasting pan. (Prick sausage links with a fork in several places.) Cover with foil, and bake at 350°F for 10 to 15 minutes, depending on size. Uncover and continue to bake for 10 to 15 minutes, until lightly browned and thoroughly cooked. During baking, turn the sausages often with tongs and remove any excess drippings as they accumulate.

COOKING TIMES FOR MEAT: BROILING & GRILLING

Cooking times below are based on broiling or grilling 4 to 6 inches from the heat source. Broilers and grills vary in heat intensity, so as a rule of thumb, check the meat a few minutes before the time indicated to avoid overcooking.

MEAT	CUT	THICKNESS (INCHES)	APPROXIMATE COOKING TIME FOR RARE (MINUTES)	APPROXIMATE COOKING TIME FOR MEDIUM (MINUTES)	APPROXIMATE COOKING TIME FOR WELL DONE (MINUTES)
BEEF	Ground, burger	1	6	10	14
	Steaks: club, porterhouse, rib, sirloin, T-bone. Filet mignon	1	6	8	12–15
	Steak, flank	1	8	10	14
	Chuck, with bone	1	8	10	15
	Chuck, boneless	1	7	9	14
	Cubes for kebabs	1	6–8	8–9	12
LAMB	Ground, burger	1	6	10	14
	Chops, loin, rib, shoulder	1	7–8	9–10	12
	Boneless leg, butterflied	4	30	40	55
	Cubes for kebabs	1	6–7	8–9	12
PORK	Chops	1	...	9–10	12
	Cubes for kebabs	1	...	8–9	12
VEAL	Chops	1	...	9	12
	Cubes for kebabs	1	...	8–9	12

USING A SLOW COOKER OR PRESSURE COOKER

Slow cookers and pressure cookers both cook meat by moist heat and are ideal for the busy person who has little time to spend in the kitchen. Because slow cookers are regulated by a thermostat, they can be left untended to cook meat gently for several hours. Temperatures are kept low, so the cooked meat is tender, flavorful, and juicy. Pressure cookers, on the other hand, cook meat in just minutes, using 10 to 15 pounds of pressure. To use either appliance to best advantage, follow the manufacturer's instructions.

STEAK AU POIVRE

To get the most pungency out of pepper, use freshly cracked peppercorns. To crack peppercorns, place in a sturdy plastic bag and whack with a mallet or small heavy skillet.

2 teaspoons coarsely cracked black pepper

½ teaspoon salt

1 well-trimmed beef sirloin (1 pound), cut into 4 steaks

2 tablespoons olive oil

3 bell peppers, mixed colors, cut into 2 x ¼-inch strips

¼ cup brandy

1 cup chicken broth, store-bought or homemade (page 172)

¼ cup milk

½ teaspoon thyme

1 teaspoon cornstarch blended with 1 tablespoon water

On a plate, combine the cracked pepper and ¼ teaspoon of the salt. Coat both sides of the steaks with the pepper mixture.

In a medium skillet, heat the oil over medium-high heat. Add the steaks and cook 2 to 3 minutes per side for medium-rare. Transfer to a plate.

Add the bell peppers to the skillet, reduce the heat to medium, and cook, stirring frequently, until crisp-tender, about 4 minutes. Remove the pan from the heat, add the brandy, and return to the heat. Cook until the brandy has almost evaporated, about 1 minute. Add the broth and cook until reduced by one-third, about 4 minutes.

Add the milk, thyme, and remaining ¼ teaspoon salt, and bring to a boil. Stir in the cornstarch mixture and cook, stirring, until slightly thickened, about 1 minute. Return the steaks to the pan and gently cook until heated through, about 2 minutes.

MAKES 4 SERVINGS

GRILLED SPICE-RUBBED FLANK STEAK

Flank steak has a tendency to get dry when cooked much beyond medium-rare, but if you keep an eye on it and cook just to medium-rare, it will be tender and juicy.

1 tablespoon plus 2 teaspoons turbinado or light brown sugar

2 teaspoons oregano

2 teaspoons chili powder

1½ teaspoons coarse salt

1½ teaspoons smoked paprika

1½ teaspoons cumin

¾ teaspoon cinnamon

¼ teaspoon cayenne pepper

1 flank steak (1½ to 2 pounds)

In a bowl or jar, combine the brown sugar, oregano, chili powder, salt, paprika, cumin, cinnamon, and cayenne. Rub the mixture all over the steak. Cover the steak and refrigerate for at least 2 hours or up to overnight.

Preheat the grill to high. Lightly oil the grill grates. Grill the steak 4 inches from the heat for 3 to 4 minutes per side for medium-rare. Remove from the heat, cover with foil, and let stand 10 minutes. Slice the steak thinly across the grain and at an angle diagonal to the cutting board.

MAKES 6 SERVINGS

BROILED STEAK WITH ORANGE-CHIPOTLE MARINADE

The real trick to perfect flank steak is in the slicing. Hold a knife at a 30- to 45-degree angle to the cutting board and cut the steak across the grain on the diagonal. This shortens up the meat fibers and makes the meat more tender.

2 pounds flank steak

Orange-Chipotle Marinade (page 607)

Place the flank steak in a shallow bowl, pour the marinade over it, and toss to coat. Cover and refrigerate for at least 1 hour or up to overnight.

Preheat the broiler. Broil the steak 4 to 6 inches from the heat, without turning, for 10 minutes. Brush with any remaining marinade and broil another 5 minutes, or until medium-rare. Place on a carving board and let rest for 15 minutes. Slice the steak thinly across the grain and at an angle diagonal to the cutting board.

MAKES 8 SERVINGS

BROILED SIRLOIN WITH PAPAYA CHUTNEY

If you can't find papayas, make the chutney with 1 pound nectarines instead.

2 papayas (1½ pounds total), peeled, seeded, and cut into ½-inch chunks

1 orange or red bell pepper, diced

1 small red onion, finely diced

¼ cup lime juice (about 2 limes)

2 tablespoons apricot all-fruit spread

¾ teaspoon salt

½ teaspoon maple sugar

½ teaspoon oregano

¼ teaspoon black pepper

4 well-trimmed sirloin steaks (6 ounces each)

In a large bowl, combine the papayas, bell pepper, onion, lime juice, fruit spread, and ¼ teaspoon of the salt. Cover and refrigerate the chutney until serving time.

Preheat the broiler.

In a small bowl, combine the remaining ½ teaspoon salt, the maple sugar, oregano, and black pepper. Rub the mixture into the steaks.

Broil the steaks 6 inches from the heat for 3 minutes per side for medium-rare. Thinly slice each steak on the diagonal and serve with the chutney.

MAKES 4 SERVINGS

FLATIRON STEAK WITH BALSAMIC-MUSTARD SAUCE

A flatiron steak is a rectangular piece of meat cut from the shoulder. Sirloin steak is a good substitute.

1 tablespoon vegetable oil

4 flatiron steaks (6 to 8 ounces each)

- ¼ teaspoon salt
- ¼ teaspoon pepper
- ¼ cup balsamic vinegar
- ¾ cup chicken broth, store-bought or homemade (page 172)
- 1 teaspoon Dijon mustard
- 1 tablespoon butter

In a large skillet, heat the oil over medium-high heat. Season the steaks with the salt and pepper. Add the steaks to the pan and cook about 3 minutes per side for medium-rare. Remove from the skillet, cover with foil, and keep warm while you make the sauce.

Add the vinegar to the skillet, and cook for about 30 seconds, scraping up any browned bits that cling to the bottom of the pan. Add the broth and mustard, and cook until slightly thickened, about 3 minutes.

Add the butter and swirl the pan until the butter has melted. Serve the steak with the sauce spooned on top.

MAKES 4 SERVINGS

CIDER CHUCK ROAST WITH SWEET POTATOES

Overnight marinating gives this tender roast an interesting flavor.

- 1 boneless chuck roast (3 pounds)
- 2 cups apple cider, or more as needed
- 1 tablespoon peppercorns
- 1 tablespoon whole cloves
- 1 tablespoon celery seeds
- 1 tablespoon allspice berries
- 1 tablespoon mustard seeds
- 3 bay leaves
- 1 tablespoon vegetable oil
- 1 large onion, chopped
- ½ teaspoon salt
- 2 pounds sweet potatoes, cut into ½-inch chunks
- 1 pound green beans, cut into 2-inch lengths

Place the meat in a glass or ceramic bowl, and add enough cider to completely cover it. Add the peppercorns, cloves, celery seeds, allspice, mustard, and bay leaves. Cover and marinate overnight in the refrigerator, turning the meat over once.

Lift the meat out of the marinade and scrape off all the seeds. Strain the marinade and reserve. Pat the meat dry with paper towels.

In a Dutch oven or a large heavy-bottomed pot, heat the oil over medium heat. Add the roast to the pan and brown on all sides, adding the onion and salt halfway through. Pour in enough of the reserved marinade to come 1 inch up the sides of the meat. Cover and bring to a boil over high heat. Reduce to a simmer and cook, turning the roast occasionally, for 3 hours, or until the meat is tender. Check the liquid level from time to time, adding more marinade if needed.

Add the sweet potatoes and green beans to the pan, cover, and simmer until the vegetables are tender, 15 to 20 minutes. Skim any fat from the pan juices before serving.

MAKES 8 SERVINGS

BRAISED BEEF SHORT RIBS

The stems and roots of many herbs are often discarded, but actually have quite a bit of flavor. In this recipe, parsley stems are used to add significant parsley flavor to the broth.

- 12 beef short ribs (4½ to 5 pounds)
- Salt and pepper
- 4 tablespoons vegetable oil
- 1 bottle (750ml) full-bodied red wine

- 2 large carrots, coarsely chopped
- 2 medium onions, coarsely chopped
- 3 ribs celery, coarsely chopped
- 6 cloves garlic, coarsely chopped or smashed
- 1 bunch parsley stems plus 2 tablespoons finely chopped parsley
- 3 sprigs fresh thyme
- 4 cups chicken broth, store-bought or homemade (page 172)

Generously season the short ribs with salt and pepper. In a large skillet, heat 2 tablespoons of the oil over medium-high heat. In batches, sear the ribs on all sides until browned, about 5 minutes per side. Set the ribs aside.

Drain the fat from the skillet and return to the heat. Pour in the wine and bring to a boil, stirring to scrape up any browned bits that cling to the pan. Remove from the heat. Set aside.

In a large heavy-bottomed stockpot, heat the remaining 2 tablespoons oil over medium-high heat. Add the carrots, onions, celery, and garlic, and cook until the vegetables are browned at the edges and beginning to soften, 8 to 10 minutes.

Add the parsley stems, thyme, and broth, and bring to a boil. Add the short ribs and wine, and return to a boil. Reduce the heat to low and simmer, covered, until the meat is very tender, about 2½ hours. Transfer the ribs to a plate.

Strain the cooking liquid into a medium pot, discarding the solids. Bring the liquid to a boil over high heat. Reduce the heat to low, and simmer until reduced to about 2½ cups, about 40 minutes. Remove from the heat and let sit 10 minutes so that the fat rises to the top. Skim off and discard most of the fat.

Add the short ribs to the pot and bring to a boil. Add the chopped parsley, and season with salt and pepper to taste.

MAKES 6 SERVINGS

GRILLED SPICE-RUBBED BEEF RIBS

This is an ideal dish for a barbecue or tailgate picnic, because you cook the ribs part way and then finish them on the grill at the barbecue. After you've baked the ribs for 3 hours, let them come to room temperature and refrigerate until you're ready to set out. You'll finish them when you get to the picnic spot (or backyard).

- ¼ cup packed turbinado or light brown sugar
- ¼ cup coarse salt
- 1 tablespoon chili powder
- 1 tablespoon ground cumin
- 1 teaspoon black pepper
- ½ teaspoon cayenne pepper
- 3 full racks beef ribs (8 pounds total)
- 1 cup lager beer

Preheat the oven to 300°F.

In a small bowl, combine the brown sugar, salt, chili powder, cumin, black pepper, and cayenne. Rub the mixture all over the ribs.

Pour the beer into a large roasting pan. Add the ribs and cover tightly with foil. Bake for 3 hours, or until the ribs are very tender.

Preheat the grill to medium. Grill the ribs for 15 to 20 minutes, turning once, or until crisped and heated through.

MAKES 6 SERVINGS

WINE-BRAISED BRISKET

Be prepared to cook the brisket at least one day in advance of serving; it benefits from cooling in the cooking liquid and absorbing the most flavor. Refrigerating the meat overnight also allows the fat to rise and solidify on the surface of the sauce, making it easier to remove before reheating the meat and pureeing the sauce.

- 3 tablespoons olive oil
- 1 beef brisket (flat end, 5½ to 6 pounds)

4 large onions, sliced

1 head garlic (8 to 10 cloves), finely chopped

2 tablespoons tomato paste

1 bottle (750ml) dry red wine

1 can (14.5 ounces) diced tomatoes

1 teaspoon thyme

1 sprig fresh rosemary

2 bay leaves

1 tablespoon salt

1 teaspoon pepper

Preheat the oven to 300°F.

Heat a 12-inch skillet over medium-high heat. Add 2 tablespoons of the oil to the pan, and sear the brisket until browned on both sides, about 5 minutes per side. Transfer the brisket to a large Dutch oven. Set aside.

Add the remaining 1 tablespoon oil to the pan and stir in the onions. Cook, stirring occasionally, until softened and golden brown, about 5 minutes. Stir in the garlic and tomato paste, and cook for 1 minute. Measure out ½ cup of wine and set aside. Add the remaining wine, tomatoes, thyme, rosemary, bay leaves, salt, and pepper to the pan. Bring to a boil, scraping up any browned bits from the bottom of the pan. Pour the wine and vegetable mixture over the brisket.

Cover and bake for 3½ to 4 hours, or until the brisket is fork-tender. Let cool to room temperature, then cover and refrigerate overnight.

Preheat the oven to 300°F. Remove any fat that has solidified on the surface of the brisket. Reheat the brisket in the oven, covered, for at least 30 minutes, or until warmed through and bubbling gently.

To serve, remove the brisket from the cooking juices, and slice across the grain into ½-inch-thick slices. Discard the bay leaves and rosemary stem. With a hand blender, puree the vegetables and juices to form a thick, smooth sauce. (Or if you don't have a hand blender, transfer the pan juices and solids to a blender and puree, then return the sauce to the Dutch oven.)

Place the Dutch oven over medium-high heat and bring the sauce to a boil. Stir in the reserved ½ cup wine and continue boiling, stirring occasionally, for 1 or 2 minutes to cook off some of the alcohol. Remove the sauce from the heat and serve with the sliced brisket.

MAKES 10 SERVINGS

THAI BEEF SALAD

You don't have to seek out an Asian market to make this wonderfully crisp and flavorful salad—all the ingredients are available at larger supermarkets. Serve in smaller portions for a first course.

DRESSING

2 tablespoons lime juice

1 tablespoon fish sauce or lower-sodium soy sauce

2 teaspoons sugar

1 teaspoon minced Thai or red serrano chili pepper

SALAD

1 boneless beef strip steak (10 ounces), 1½ inches thick

Coarse salt and pepper

1 cup thinly sliced radishes

1 small red onion, thinly sliced, rinsed and drained

1 medium kirby cucumber, unpeeled, thinly sliced

¼ cup fresh mint leaves, coarsely chopped

10 large fresh basil leaves, slivered

- 4 cups slivered romaine lettuce hearts (small inner leaves can be left whole), about 2 hearts

To make the dressing: In a large bowl, whisk together the lime juice, fish sauce, sugar, and chili pepper. Measure out 1 tablespoon and set aside.

To make the salad: Season the steak generously on both sides with salt and pepper. Grill on a grill or in a lightly oiled stovetop grill pan over medium-high heat, 4 to 5 minutes per side (steak is best rare to medium and still pink in the center). Set aside and keep warm.

To the bowl with the dressing, add the radishes, onion, cucumber, mint, basil and lettuce, and toss. Arrange on a large platter. Thinly slice the steak across the grain and toss with the reserved 1 tablespoon dressing. Arrange on top of the salad.

MAKES 4 SERVINGS

CITRUS-GRILLED BEEF SALAD

Serve with thick slices of whole-grain sourdough peasant bread.

- 3 tablespoons frozen orange juice concentrate
- 2 tablespoons lime juice
- 3/4 teaspoon salt
- 3/4 teaspoon hot pepper sauce
- 1/2 teaspoon ground cumin
- 1 trimmed top round of beef (10 ounces)
- 1 red onion, cut into thick rounds
- 2 red bell peppers, cut lengthwise into flat panels
- 1 green bell pepper, cut lengthwise into flat panels
- 1 large tomato, cut into wedges
- 1 tablespoon olive oil

In a medium bowl, combine the orange juice concentrate, lime juice, 1/4 teaspoon of the salt, the hot sauce, and cumin. Add the beef and onion, turning to coat. Set aside to marinate for 30 minutes at room temperature.

Preheat the grill to medium. Oil a grill grate (and grill topper, if possible). Reserving the marinade, place the meat on the grate, cover, and grill for 3 minutes. Place the onion and bell peppers (skin-sides down) on the grill topper, re-cover, and grill, turning and basting the beef and onion with some of the reserved marinade, for 7 minutes, or until the beef is medium-rare, the peppers are charred, and the onion is crisp-tender.

Let the beef stand for 10 minutes before thinly slicing. When cool enough to handle, peel the peppers and cut into 1/2-inch-wide strips.

In a medium bowl, toss together the beef, peppers, onion, tomato wedges, oil, and remaining 1/2 teaspoon salt.

MAKES 4 SERVINGS

STIR-FRIED BEEF WITH LEMONGRASS

To get the most flavor out of lemongrass, pound it before cutting it up. This releases the aromatic oils.

- 2 tablespoons finely chopped fresh lemongrass
- 2 tablespoons olive oil
- 2 cloves garlic, minced
- 2 teaspoons fish sauce
- 1 teaspoon ground allspice
- 1/2 teaspoon cornstarch
- 1/4 teaspoon sugar
- 1 flank steak (1 1/2 pounds)
- 2 scallions, minced
- 2 tablespoons coarsely chopped dry-roasted peanuts for serving

In a shallow bowl, combine the lemongrass, 1 tablespoon of the oil, the garlic, fish sauce, allspice, cornstarch, and sugar.

Halve the flank steak lengthwise (following the grain). Cut each half crosswise into 1/4-inch-wide slices. Pound the slices lightly. Add to the lemongrass mixture and toss to coat.

In a wok or large skillet, heat the remaining 1 tablespoon oil over medium-high heat. Add the beef and stir-fry until just cooked, 2 to 3 minutes. Stir in the scallions.

Serve sprinkled with the peanuts.

MAKES 4 SERVINGS

KOREAN-STYLE STIR-FRIED BEEF

For easier slicing, place the beef in the freezer for 30 minutes before slicing. Serve the stir-fry with barley.

- 3 tablespoons lower-sodium soy sauce
- 1 tablespoon honey
- 2 teaspoons dark sesame oil
- 3 cloves garlic, minced
- 1 tablespoon minced fresh ginger
- 1 teaspoon red pepper flakes
- 1/2 teaspoon black pepper
- 1/2 teaspoon salt
- 3/4 pound beef sirloin, cut into matchsticks
- 2 teaspoons olive oil
- 1 large onion, halved and thinly sliced
- 2 carrots, cut into 2-inch-long matchsticks
- 1 zucchini, cut into 2-inch-long matchsticks
- 3/4 cup beef broth, store-bought or homemade (page 172)
- 1 teaspoon cornstarch

In medium bowl, combine the soy sauce, honey, sesame oil, garlic, ginger, red pepper flakes, black pepper, and salt. Add the beef and toss to coat. Cover and marinate at room temperature for 30 minutes (or refrigerate for up to 8 hours).

In large nonstick skillet, heat the olive oil over medium heat. Add the onion and cook, stirring frequently, until just softened and lightly browned, about 3 minutes. Add the carrots and zucchini, and cook until the carrots are crisp-tender, about 2 minutes.

Lift the beef from the marinade, reserving the marinade. Add the beef to the pan and cook, stirring, until no longer pink, about 1 minute.

In a small bowl, combine the broth, cornstarch, and reserved marinade. Pour into the pan and cook until lightly thickened, about 1 minute.

MAKES 4 SERVINGS

THAI BEEF WITH UDON

Marinating the beef at room temperature for about 20 minutes works just as well as a couple of hours in the fridge. This Thai-inspired dish is medium spicy. If you want it hotter, add more curry paste, but only a teaspoon at a time.

- 1 pound trimmed sirloin steak, cut into 1/2-inch-thick strips
- 2 tablespoons vegetable oil
- 2 teaspoons Thai red curry paste
- 3/4 teaspoon coarse salt
- 1/4 teaspoon pepper
- 1 package (7 ounces) udon noodles
- 2 large shallots, thinly sliced
- 1 can (14 ounces) unsweetened coconut milk, well stirred
- 1/2 teaspoon sugar
- 1 cup loosely packed fresh basil leaves
- Lime wedges, for serving

Place the steak, 1 tablespoon of the oil, the curry paste, salt, and pepper in a medium bowl, and toss to coat. Cover and marinate for at least 20 minutes at room temperature (or in the refrigerator for up to 8 hours).

Meanwhile, in a large pot of boiling salted water, cook the udon according to the package directions. Drain and rinse briefly with warm water. Set aside.

In a wok or 12-inch skillet, heat the remaining 1 tablespoon oil over medium-high heat. Add the shallots and stir-fry until golden brown, 3 to 4 minutes. Add the steak and stir-fry until browned all over, 2 to 3 minutes.

Reduce the heat to medium and stir in the coconut milk and sugar. Bring to a simmer and cook until slightly thickened, about 2 minutes. Stir in the noodles and basil, and simmer 30 seconds. Serve in deep bowls with lime wedges.

MAKES 4 SERVINGS

STEWED BEEF WITH GUINNESS

When browning the meat, do not stir—this inhibits proper caramelization. Allow the pieces to sit and cook undisturbed. When they start cooking they will stick to the pan, but when they are properly browned they will start to release easily from the pan and be easier to turn. You can make the stew 1 or 2 days in advance of serving—in fact, it will taste better! Reheat in a 300°F oven until very hot.

3 pounds trimmed beef chuck, cut into 2-inch chunks

Salt and pepper

¼ cup white whole wheat* or unbleached all-purpose flour

4 tablespoons canola oil or other vegetable oil

2 large onions, diced

1 bottle (12 ounces) Guinness stout

1 cup beef broth, store-bought or homemade (page 172)

3 cloves garlic, minced

1 heaping tablespoon tomato paste

2 teaspoons turbinado or light brown sugar

1 teaspoon thyme

1 bay leaf

½ pound carrots, cut into 3-inch pieces

**milled from white wheat grains*

Preheat the oven to 300°F.

Season the beef with salt and pepper. Dredge the beef cubes in the flour, shaking off the excess.

In a large stockpot or Dutch oven, heat 1 tablespoon of the oil over medium-high heat. Add one-third of the beef cubes and brown well on all sides. Do not stir the beef as it cooks. Transfer the beef to clean bowl. Repeat for two more batches with 2 tablespoons of the remaining oil and the beef cubes, transferring the beef to the bowl when browned.

Add the remaining 1 tablespoon oil to the pan and reduce the heat to medium. Add the onions and cook, scraping up any browned bits from the bottom of the pan, until the onions are translucent and just beginning to brown around the edges, about 5 minutes.

Add the stout, broth, garlic, tomato paste, sugar, thyme, and bay leaf. Increase the heat to medium-high and bring to a boil. Cook for 1 minute, then remove the pan from the heat and add the reserved beef and the carrots. Season the mixture with salt and pepper to taste. Cover the pan and bake for 2½ to 3 hours, or until the beef is fork-tender. Discard the bay leaf.

MAKES 8 SERVINGS

BEEF & PUMPKIN STEW

Be sure to pick small sugar pumpkins, not jack-o'-lantern pumpkins, for this mildly spiced dish. For an interesting change, swap in kabocha squash, a sweet and starchy winter squash. Serve the stew over couscous, barley, or brown rice.

2 tablespoons vegetable oil

1½ pounds trimmed beef chuck, cut into 1-inch chunks

1 large onion, coarsely chopped

1 rib celery, thinly sliced

1 green bell pepper, diced

¾ teaspoon salt

½ teaspoon ground ginger

¼ teaspoon nutmeg

¼ teaspoon cardamom

¼ teaspoon black pepper

1½ cups water

2 pounds fresh pumpkin, peeled and cut into 3-inch chunks

2 tablespoons lemon juice

1 tablespoon cornstarch blended with ¼ cup water

In a Dutch oven, heat the oil over medium heat. Add the beef, working in batches if necessary, and cook until browned all over. Using a slotted spoon, transfer the beef to a bowl.

Add the onion, celery, and bell pepper to the pan and cook, stirring occasionally, until the onion is tender, about 7 minutes.

Stir in the salt, ginger, nutmeg, cardamom, and black pepper. Return the beef to the pan. Add the water and bring to a boil. Reduce to a simmer, cover, and cook 45 minutes.

Stir in the pumpkin and lemon juice. Cover and simmer until the meat and pumpkin are tender, about 30 minutes.

Stir in the cornstarch mixture and cook, stirring constantly, until the sauce bubbles and thickens, about 3 minutes.

MAKES 4 SERVINGS

BEEF & CHICKPEAS OVER BULGUR

The spices used in this dish are very similar to the Indian spice blend called garam masala. If you happen to have some on hand, use 2 teaspoons of garam masala and omit the cumin, coriander, and cloves.

2 tablespoons vegetable oil

2 pounds trimmed beef chuck, cut into 1-inch chunks

3 medium onions, quartered

3 carrots, cut into 1-inch chunks

2 cloves garlic, minced

1 teaspoon ground ginger

¾ teaspoon ground cumin

¾ teaspoon ground coriander

½ teaspoon salt

⅛ teaspoon ground cloves

2 cups medium-grain bulgur

Boiling water

2 cups cooked chickpeas

2 small zucchini, halved and thinly sliced

¼ cup chopped cilantro

In a large Dutch oven, heat the oil over medium heat. Working in batches, add the beef and cook until browned all over, about 5 minutes per batch. Once all the beef is browned, return to the pan.

Add the onions, carrots, garlic, ginger, cumin, coriander, salt, cloves, and enough water to just cover the beef. Bring to a boil over high heat. Reduce to a simmer, cover, and cook, stirring occasionally, for about 1 hour 30 minutes, or until the beef is tender.

Meanwhile, place the bulgur in a bowl and add enough boiling water to cover it by 2 inches. Cover the bowl and let stand at room temperature for 20 minutes. Stir in the chickpeas and zucchini, cover, and let stand until the water has been absorbed and the bulgur is tender, about 10 minutes longer.

Stir the cilantro into the bulgur. Serve the beef over the bulgur.

MAKES 6 SERVINGS

CHILI CON CARNE

If you're pressed for time, you can use 3 cups canned beans, rinsed and drained, instead of dried beans. Skip the first step, and use 2 cups beef or chicken broth in place of the bean cooking liquid.

- 8 ounces dried small red beans, soaked overnight, drained
- 1 tablespoon olive oil
- ½ pound trimmed beef chuck, cut into ½-inch chunks
- 1 large onion, finely chopped
- 2 red bell peppers, cut into 1-inch pieces
- 3 cloves garlic, minced
- 4 teaspoons ground cumin
- 1 tablespoon unsweetened cocoa powder
- 2 teaspoons oregano
- 1½ teaspoons ancho chili powder
- 1½ teaspoons salt
- 1 can (28 ounces) whole peeled tomatoes in juice
- 1 pound sweet potatoes, peeled and cut into 1-inch chunks

In a medium saucepan, combine the beans and water to cover by 2 inches. Bring to a boil and reduce to a simmer. Partially cover, and cook until the beans are tender, 45 minutes to 1 hour. Reserving the liquid, drain the beans.

In a lare saucepan or Dutch oven, heat the oil over medium heat. Add the beef and cook until browned, about 5 minutes. With a slotted spoon, transfer the beef to a plate.

Add the onion, bell peppers, and garlic to the pan and cook, stirring frequently, until the vegetables are tender, about 15 minutes.

Stir in the cumin, cocoa powder, oregano, ancho powder, and salt, and cook for 1 minute. Add the tomatoes and their juice, the beef, and 2 cups of the bean cooking liquid (add water if you don't have 2 cups) and bring to a boil. Reduce to a simmer, cover, and cook for 45 minutes.

Stir in the sweet potatoes and beans, and cook until the beef and sweet potatoes are tender, 45 minutes to 1 hour.

MAKES 4 SERVINGS

COTTAGE PIE

A close relative of a shepherd's pie (which is made with lamb), a cottage pie is made with ground beef.

- 2 tablespoons olive oil
- 1 medium onion, chopped
- 2 cloves garlic, minced
- 1 pound lean ground beef
- 1½ teaspoons basil
- ¾ teaspoon salt
- 1 pound russet (baking) potatoes, peeled and thinly sliced
- 1 cup shredded cheddar cheese (4 ounces)
- ½ pound green beans, halved crosswise
- 1 cup diced canned tomatoes

Preheat the oven to 350°F.

In a large skillet, heat 1 tablespoon of the oil over medium heat. Add the onion and garlic, and cook, stirring occasionally, until the onion is tender, about 7 minutes. Add the beef, basil, and ½ teaspoon of the salt, and cook, stirring occasionally until the beef is no longer pink, about 5 minutes.

Meanwhile, in a medium pot of boiling water, cook the potatoes until tender, about 15 minutes. Drain well. Return the potatoes to the same pot, add the remaining 1 tablespoon oil, ¼ teaspoon salt, and the cheese, and mash with a potato masher until the cheese has melted.

In a steamer, cook the green beans until crisp-tender, about 4 minutes (timing will vary depending on the size of the beans).

Stir the green beans and tomatoes into the meat mixture, then transfer to a 9-inch pie plate or 1½-quart baking dish.

Top the beef mixture with the potatoes, making decorative peaks with a fork. Bake for 15 to 20 minutes, or until the potatoes are piping hot and the meat is bubbling.

MAKES 4 SERVINGS

STUFFED ESCAROLE

This is a somewhat simpler alternative to stuffed cabbage; escarole leaves are easier to separate than cabbage leaves and require no blanching.

SAUCE

- ¼ cup olive oil
- 1 medium onion, chopped
- 2 ribs celery, thinly sliced
- 2 cloves garlic, minced
- 2 cans (14.5 ounces each) diced tomatoes
- 1 carrot, grated
- ½ cup turkey or chicken broth, store-bought or homemade (page 172)
- ½ cup golden raisins
- 2 tablespoons cider vinegar
- ½ teaspoon salt
- ½ teaspoon pepper

STUFFING & ESCAROLE

- 1 pound lean ground beef
- 2 cups cooked brown rice
- 1 medium onion, chopped
- ¼ cup chopped parsley
- ½ teaspoon salt
- ¼ teaspoon pepper
- 2 heads escarole (large outer leaves only)

To make the sauce: In a large skillet, heat the oil over medium heat. Add the onion, celery, and garlic, and cook until the onion is tender, about 7 minutes. Add the tomatoes, carrot, broth, raisins, vinegar, salt, and pepper. Simmer uncovered, stirring occasionally, for 30 minutes.

Preheat the oven to 350°F. Oil a 9 × 13-inch baking dish.

To make the stuffing: In a large bowl, mix together the beef, rice, onion, parsley, salt, and pepper.

Cut out the tough core of the escarole leaves with a V-shaped notch. Place a rounded tablespoon of stuffing at the large end of each leaf. Fold the sides over the stuffing and roll up. Repeat until all the stuffing has been used. Place the rolls, seam-side down, in the baking dish, in 1 or 2 layers as needed.

Pour the sauce over the rolls. Cover with foil and bake for 45 minutes, or until the escarole is tender and the stuffing is piping hot.

MAKES 6 SERVINGS

SPICY MEXICAN BEEF BURGERS

Top the burgers with Roasted Onion Relish (page 612) or one of the other suggested Hamburger Toppings (right).

- 1 pound well-trimmed beef sirloin, cut into chunks

- 1/4 cup flaxseeds
- 2 pickled jalapeño peppers, minced
- 1 teaspoon ground cumin
- 1/2 teaspoon salt
- 1/2 cup corn kernels
- 1/3 cup chopped cilantro
- 1/4 cup oil-packed sun-dried tomatoes, drained and coarsely chopped

In a food processor, grind the beef until finely chopped. In a mini food processor, spice grinder, or coffee grinder, grind the flaxseeds until finely ground.

In a medium bowl, combine the beef, ground flaxseeds, jalapeño peppers, cumin, and salt until well mixed. In a small bowl, combine the corn, cilantro, and sun-dried tomatoes.

Shape the beef mixture into 4 patties. Make a well in the center of each patty and stuff with the corn mixture. Shape the meat around the filling.

Preheat the broiler. Broil the burgers 6 inches from the heat, for 4 minutes per side for medium.

MAKES 4 SERVINGS

WALNUT & HERB-STUFFED MEAT LOAF

The combination of walnuts and basil gives this meat loaf filling a flavor reminiscent of pesto.

STUFFING

- 1 cup finely chopped walnuts
- 1 cup soft whole-grain bread crumbs (2 slices)
- 1/4 cup chopped fresh basil
- 1 large shallot, minced
- 1/2 teaspoon rubbed sage
- 1/2 teaspoon thyme
- 1/2 teaspoon pepper
- 1/4 teaspoon salt

MEAT LOAF

- 1 pound lean ground beef
- 1 pound ground pork
- 1 large shallot, minced
- 2 large eggs
- 1/2 teaspoon salt
- 3/4 cup tomato sauce

HAMBURGER TOPPINGS

In addition to the usual suspects for topping hamburgers, try one these sauces:

Blue Cheese Sauce: In a small bowl, beat 1 cup low-fat cottage cheese with 1 tablespoon lemon juice and 1/8 teaspoon pepper. Beat in 3 tablespoons crumbled blue cheese. Refrigerate until ready to serve.

Onion Sauce: Cut 1 medium sweet onion into slices, then separate into rings (you should have about 2 cups). In a medium saucepan, heat 2 teaspoons vegetable oil over medium heat. Add the onion rings and cook until just tender, 3 to 5 minutes. Stir in 1/4 cup ketchup, 1 tablespoon lemon juice, and 1 tablespoon spicy brown mustard. Reduce to a simmer, cover, and cook for 5 to 7 minutes. Cool and refrigerate until ready to serve.

Rosy Sauce Louis: Combine 1/2 cup mayonnaise, 2 tablespoons snipped chives, 1 tablespoon tomato paste, 2 teaspoons lemon juice, and 1 teaspoon drained horseradish. Refrigerate until ready to use.

Preheat the oven to 350°F.

To make the stuffing: In a medium bowl, combine the walnuts, bread crumbs, basil, shallot, sage, thyme, pepper, and salt. Moisten with just enough water so that the stuffing holds its shape when pressed between your fingers.

To make the meat loaf: In a large bowl, mix together the beef, pork, shallot, eggs, salt, and ¼ cup of the tomato sauce.

On a large piece of waxed paper, pat the meat mixture into a 12 x 15-inch rectangle. Pat the stuffing into a layer on top, leaving a 1-inch border all around.

With a long side facing you, lift the waxed paper and roll the meat over the stuffing. Pinch the seam and ends closed, and pat together any breaks in the meat. Lift the waxed paper to transfer the roll to a roasting pan, placing it seam-side down. Pour the remaining ½ cup tomato sauce over all. Bake for 40 to 45 minutes, until cooked through and the juices run clear when the loaf is pierced. Let rest for 10 minutes before slicing.

MAKES 6 TO 8 SERVINGS

PECAN-STUFFED LAMB LOAF: In the stuffing, use pecans instead of walnuts. Use parsley instead of basil, and rosemary instead of sage. In the meat mixture, substitute lamb for the beef.

FREEFORM MEAT LOAF

Oats and wheat germ take the place of bread crumbs in this freeform loaf.

- **2 tablespoons vegetable oil**
- **1 medium onion, finely chopped**
- **2 pounds ground chuck**
- **½ cup old-fashioned rolled oats**
- **⅓ cup wheat germ**
- **2 large eggs**
- **½ cup tomato juice**
- **¼ cup sour cream or Greek yogurt**
- **2 tablespoons chopped parsley**
- **1 teaspoon salt**
- **¾ teaspoon herbes de Provence**
- **½ teaspoon pepper**

Preheat the oven to 350°F. Lightly oil a rimmed baking sheet.

In a large skillet, heat the oil over medium heat. Add the onion and cook, stirring occasionally, until tender, about 7 minutes. Transfer to a large bowl and let cool to room temperature.

Add the beef, oats, wheat germ, eggs, tomato juice, sour cream, parsley, salt, herbes de Provence, and pepper. Mix thoroughly.

Transfer the mixture to the baking sheet with your hands, shape into a log about 5 × 9 inches. Bake for 1 hour 15 minutes, or until set, golden brown, and cooked through. Let rest for 10 minutes before slicing and serving.

MAKES 6 TO 8 SERVINGS

VITELLO MILANESE

This classic dish is a contrast in flavors, textures, and temperatures. The hot, crisp veal is topped with a cool citrusy, and slightly peppery salad: perfect. Panko bread crumbs are light in texture and crunchy. Look for them alongside other bread crumbs in the bread aisle of the supermarket.

SALAD

- **3 tablespoons olive oil**
- **2 tablespoons lemon juice**
- **¼ teaspoon salt**
- **1 bunch arugula**
- **1 large tomato, cut into 12 wedges**

VEAL

- ¼ cup flour
- Salt
- 1 large egg
- 1 tablespoon water
- 1 cup panko bread crumbs, preferably whole wheat
- ½ cup grated Parmesan cheese
- 1 pound veal cutlets (about 8)
- ⅓ cup olive oil

To make the salad: In a large bowl, whisk together the oil, lemon juice, and salt until well combined. Top with the arugula and tomato, but don't toss.

To make the veal: Place the flour in a shallow bowl. Season lightly with salt. In another shallow bowl, lightly beat the egg with the water. In a third bowl, combine the panko and Parmesan.

Dredge the veal first in the flour, shaking off the excess. Then dip in the egg, letting the excess drip off. Finally dredge in the bread crumb mixture, pressing to adhere.

In a large nonstick skillet, heat 2 tablespoons of the oil over medium heat. Working in batches, and adding more oil as necessary, sauté the veal until golden brown and cooked through, about 1 minute per side.

Toss the arugula and tomato with the dressing. Serve the veal topped with the salad.

MAKES 4 SERVINGS

OSSO BUCO

This Italian classic is delicious served with a side dish of farro: Try Farro & Shiitakes (page 459).

- 2½ pounds veal shank, cut into 4 or 5 pieces
- ¼ cup flour
- 3 tablespoons olive oil
- 1 large onion, finely chopped
- 1 carrot, halved lengthwise and thinly sliced crosswise
- 3 cloves garlic, thinly sliced
- 1 cup dry white wine
- 1 cup canned tomatoes with juice, chopped
- ½ teaspoon salt
- ¼ teaspoon pepper
- 1 sprig fresh rosemary or ½ teaspoon dried
- 1 sprig fresh mint or small sprig fresh basil
- 2 strips (3 x ½ inch) orange zest

Preheat the oven to 350°F.

Dredge the veal in the flour, shaking off the excess. In a Dutch oven, heat the oil over medium heat. Add the veal and cook until golden brown, about 4 minutes per side. Transfer the veal to a plate.

Add the onion, carrot, and garlic to the pan, and cook over medium heat, stirring frequently, until the vegetables are tender, about 10 minutes.

Add the wine, tomatoes, salt, pepper, rosemary, mint, and orange zest, and bring to a boil.

Return the veal to the pan, cover, and bake for about 1 hour 15 minutes, or until the veal is very tender.

Remove the veal from the pan. Skim off any fat from the surface of the sauce. Serve the veal with the sauce and vegetables spooned over the top.

MAKES 4 SERVINGS

GARLIC-MARINATED ROASTED FRESH HAM

Fresh ham is the cut of pork that ordinarily is cured or smoked and sold as ham. Note that the ham needs to marinate for 2 days before you cook it, so plan accordingly. Serve with Fresh Plum Sauce (page 218).

12 cloves garlic

1 tablespoon coarse salt

2 teaspoons fennel seed

2 teaspoons oregano

½ teaspoon peppercorns

1¼ cups water

Half fresh ham, bone-in (10 pounds)

1½ cups orange juice

3 tablespoons lemon juice

In a mini food processor, combine the garlic, salt, fennel, oregano, and peppercorns, and pulse until coarsely chopped. Add ¼ cup of the water and process until smooth.

With a sharp knife, make cross hatches in the skin of the ham, cutting to, but not into, the flesh. Rub the garlic mixture all over the ham, including into the cuts. Cover and refrigerate for 1 day.

Pour the orange juice and lemon juice over the ham. Cover and refrigerate, turning the ham once or twice, for 1 day.

Preheat the oven to 425°F.

Reserving the marinade, place the ham on a rack in a roasting pan and roast for 45 minutes. Remove the ham from the rack and set it in the pan.

Pour the reserved marinade over the ham. Reduce the oven temperature to 325°F, and bake the ham for 2 hours 15 minutes to 2 hours 30 minutes, or until a thermometer registers 150°F. Baste every 30 minutes. Add the remaining 1 cup of water after 2 hours.

Let the ham rest for 20 minutes before slicing. Skim off the fat from the pan and serve the ham with the pan juices.

MAKES 10 TO 12 SERVINGS

OVEN-BARBECUED PORK SHOULDER

Maple syrup adds an interesting note to a homemade barbecue sauce that's slathered on pork shoulder.

1 bone-in pork shoulder roast (4 to 4½ pounds)

1 can (14.5 ounces) crushed tomatoes

2 carrots, finely chopped

FRESH PLUM SAUCE

The deep fruity flavors of this sauce are a particularly nice match for pork loin or fresh ham. This makes 2 cups.

½ cup full-bodied red wine

1 tablespoon cornstarch

1 cup chicken broth, store-bought or homemade (page 172)

1 teaspoon cinnamon

½ teaspoon salt

Pinch of nutmeg

10 Italian prune plums, coarsely chopped

In a screw-top jar, combine the wine and cornstarch, and shake well. In a small saucepan, heat the broth, cinnamon, salt, and nutmeg. Whisking constantly, add the wine mixture and simmer until the sauce has thickened. Add the plums and cook to heat through.

2 cloves garlic, minced

⅓ cup tomato paste

⅓ cup water

⅓ cup cider vinegar

¼ cup maple syrup or dark agave nectar

1 tablespoon Worcestershire sauce

1 teaspoon dry mustard

1 teaspoon oregano

1 teaspoon paprika

½ teaspoon salt

½ teaspoon pepper

½ teaspoon hot pepper sauce

Preheat the oven to 375°F. Place the pork on a rack in a small roasting pan. Roast, uncovered, for 1 hour.

Meanwhile, in a large skillet, combine the tomatoes, carrots, garlic, tomato paste, water, vinegar, maple syrup, Worcestershire, dry mustard, oregano, paprika, salt, pepper, and hot sauce. Bring to a boil, reduce to a simmer, and cook until the carrot has softened and the flavors have combined, about 20 minutes. If the sauce becomes too thick, add a little water.

After the pork has cooked for 1 hour, spoon off the accumulated fat from the pot and discard. Pour the sauce over and under the pork. Reduce the oven temperature to 325°F, and continue to cook, basting several times, for 1 hour 15 minutes, or until tender when pierced with a knife.

MAKES 8 SERVINGS

HERB-RUBBED PORK LOIN ROAST

Ask your butcher to hinge the roast for you. What that means is to cut around the rib bones, without removing them. That way you can season both the surface and the underside of the pork. Meat cooked on the bone tends to be juicier and more flavorful.

4 bay leaves, crumbled

1 teaspoon coarse salt

¾ teaspoon rosemary, crumbled

½ teaspoon rubbed sage

½ teaspoon pepper

¼ teaspoon lavender, crumbled (optional)

1 bone-in pork loin (3¼ pounds), preferably end cut

⅔ cup dry white wine or apple juice

In a small bowl, combine the bay leaves, salt, rosemary, sage, pepper, and lavender (if using). Rub the spice mixture all over the pork, both on the surface and on the side closest to the bone. Let stand at least 1 hour at room temperature or, for best flavor, refrigerate overnight.

Let the pork come to room temperature.

Preheat the oven to 425°F.

Place the pork in a roasting pan, and roast for 25 minutes, or until beginning to brown.

Add the wine to the pan and tent with foil. Reduce the oven temperature to 350°F, and roast until the pork is cooked through but still juicy, about 30 minutes.

Let stand for 10 minutes before slicing.

MAKES 6 TO 8 SERVINGS

MUSTARD-HONEY ROAST PORK

If you have a good honey mustard, use about ½ cup of it in place of the honey and mustard called for here.

1 teaspoon salt

½ teaspoon rosemary, crumbled

2 cloves garlic, minced

1 trimmed boneless center-cut pork loin (2½ pounds)

¼ honey

3 tablespoons Dijon mustard

2 teaspoons lemon juice

Preheat the oven to 425°F. Rub the salt, rosemary, and garlic into the pork. Place the roast in a small roasting pan, and roast for 20 minutes.

Meanwhile, in a small bowl, combine the honey, mustard, and lemon juice. Brush half of the mixture over the top of the roast. Return the pork to the oven and roast, basting twice with the honey-mustard mixture, for 15 minutes, or until the pork is cooked through but still juicy and nicely glazed.

Let stand for 10 minutes before slicing.

MAKES 6 SERVINGS

GRILLED GARLIC-STUDDED PORK LOIN

Brining the pork loin overnight keeps the meat juicy and flavorful.

8 cups water

⅓ cup packed turbinado or light brown sugar

⅓ cup coarse salt

6 cloves garlic, peeled

1 tablespoon peppercorns

3 bay leaves

½ teaspoon red pepper flakes

½ teaspoon thyme

1 trimmed boneless pork loin (3½ pounds)

2 tablespoons olive oil

In a Dutch oven or large soup pot, combine the water, brown sugar, and salt. Heat over high heat, stirring until the sugar and salt are dissolved. Remove from the heat and stir in 4 cloves of the garlic, the peppercorns, bay leaves, red pepper flakes, and thyme. Let cool to room temperature and then add the pork loin. Cover and refrigerate overnight.

The next day, preheat the grill to medium. You want to maintain a steady temperature of 400°F to 450°F. Bank the coals or turn off one burner on a gas grill if necessary to regulate the heat. Oil the grill grates.

Remove the pork from the brine. Discard the brine and pat the meat dry. Cut the remaining 2 cloves garlic into thin slivers. Cut slits all over the pork with a sharp knife, and insert one or two garlic slivers into each cut. Rub the meat with the oil.

Place the pork on the grill. Cover and grill for 20 minutes, or until well browned on the underside. Turn, and grill for 20 minutes longer. Turn again and grill, covered, for 10 to 20 minutes longer to brown all sides, regulating the heat as best you can, until the pork is cooked through but still juicy. Remove the pork from the grill, and let stand for at least 10 minutes before thinly slicing.

MAKES 8 SERVINGS

BROILED TENDERLOIN WITH ROMESCO SAUCE

Romesco sauce is a roasted red pepper puree with garlic, ground almonds, and cayenne that can be prepared well in advance. It goes nicely with broiled or grilled poultry as well as pork.

2 red bell peppers, cut lengthwise into flat panels

3 cloves garlic, smashed and peeled

3 tablespoons orange juice

2 tablespoons tomato paste

1 tablespoon natural (unblanched) almonds

⅛ teaspoon cayenne pepper

1 teaspoon paprika

¾ teaspoon oregano

½ teaspoon sage

¼ teaspoon salt

¼ teaspoon sugar

1 pork tenderloin (1 pound)

Preheat the broiler. Broil the bell pepper pieces, skin-side up, 4 inches from the heat for 12 minutes, or until the skin is charred. Leave the broiler on. When the peppers are cool enough to handle, peel them.

Meanwhile, in a small saucepan of boiling water, blanch the garlic for 2 minutes. Drain.

Transfer the bell peppers and garlic to a food processor along with the orange juice, tomato paste, almonds, and cayenne. Process until well combined and smooth. Set the romesco sauce aside.

In a small bowl, stir together the paprika, oregano, sage, salt, and sugar. Rub the spice mixture into the pork. Broil 4 to 6 inches from the heat for 10 minutes, or until browned and cooked through but still juicy.

Let rest for 10 minutes. Then slice and serve with the sauce on the side.

MAKES 4 SERVINGS

APRICOT-GLAZED PORK TENDERLOIN

If you shop in a supermarket, you may only be able to get two pork tenderloins packaged together. Your options are to a) go to the butcher department and see if they'll sell you just one; b) freeze one of the tenderloins for later; or c) bake up a double batch of this recipe and have leftovers.

1 pork tenderloin (1 pound)

1½ teaspoons herbes de Provence

½ teaspoon salt

1 tablespoon vegetable oil

⅓ cup apricot all-fruit spread

2 teaspoons balsamic vinegar

2 teaspoons Dijon mustard

Preheat the oven to 400°F. Place the pork tenderloin in a shallow roasting pan or on a foil-lined rimmed baking sheet.

In a small bowl, combine the herbes de Provence and salt. Rub the mixture all over the pork. Rub with the oil. Roast for 15 minutes or until lightly browned.

Meanwhile, in a small bowl, stir together the fruit spread, vinegar, and mustard.

Brush half the apricot mixture over the pork. Roast for 5 minutes. Brush with the remaining mixture and roast for 5 to 10 minutes longer, or until the pork is cooked through but still juicy.

Let stand for 10 minutes before slicing.

MAKES 4 SERVINGS

CRANBERRY-BRAISED TENDERLOIN

Serve the pork with roasted new potatoes and Green Beans with Walnuts (page 412).

¼ cup sugar

1 teaspoon rosemary, crumbled

¾ teaspoon salt

½ teaspoon pepper

½ teaspoon ground ginger

1 pork tenderloin (1 pound), halved crosswise

2 tablespoons olive oil

12 cloves garlic, peeled

8 scallions, cut into 2-inch lengths

4 carrots, cut into matchsticks

1 bag (12 ounces) fresh or frozen cranberries

⅔ cup orange juice

3 tablespoons honey

1 bay leaf

Preheat the oven to 350°F. In a large bowl, stir together the sugar, rosemary, salt, pepper, and ginger. Add the pork and turn to coat with the spice mixture.

In a Dutch oven, heat the oil over medium-high heat. Lift the pork from the spice mixture and add to the pan along with the garlic. Cook the pork for 2 minutes per side, or until it is richly browned. Transfer the pork to a plate.

Add the scallions and carrots to the pan, and cook until the carrots begin to color or about 3 minutes. Stir the cranberries, orange juice, honey, and bay leaf into the pan, and bring to a boil.

Return the pork to the pan, reduce to a simmer, cover, and transfer to the oven. Bake for 30 minutes, or until the pork is cooked through but still juicy.

Lift the pork from the pan and let sit for 10 minutes before slicing. Discard the bay leaf. Serve the pork with vegetables and sauce on top.

MAKES 4 SERVINGS

GRILLED PORK TENDERLOIN & VIDALIAS

Serve the grilled pork with your favorite store-bought barbecue sauce, or try one of these: Spicy Mango BBQ Sauce (page 605), Healthy Barbecue Sauce (page 604), or Apple-Wasabi Barbecue Sauce (page 605).

- 2 pork tenderloins (1½ to 2 pounds total)
- 2 tablespoons turbinado or light brown sugar
- 1 tablespoon paprika
- 1 teaspoon ground cumin
- 1 teaspoon salt
- ½ teaspoon garlic powder
- 1 large Vidalia onion, cut into 6 wedges
- Olive oil or peanut oil, for brushing

With a sharp knife, cut the tenderloins lengthwise, cutting about two-thirds of the way through the meat. Open the tenderloins so they lie flat, like an open book.

In a small bowl, combine the brown sugar, paprika, cumin, salt, and garlic powder. Spread this rub evenly over the pork, coating both sides.

Brush the pork and the onion wedges lightly with oil, and place in a covered container or a large ziplock plastic bag. Refrigerate for at least 1 hour or overnight.

Remove the pork from the refrigerator and let stand at room temperature for 30 minutes before grilling.

Preheat the grill to medium-high. Grill the pork and onion wedges, turning once halfway through cooking, for 20 to 25 minutes, until the pork is cooked through but still juicy and the onion wedges are tender. Let the pork stand for 10 minutes, then cut into ¼-inch-thick slices. Serve with the onion.

MAKES 6 SERVINGS

BAKED SPARERIBS WITH SPICY MANGO BARBECUE SAUCE

To make the ribs ahead of time, bake for 3 hours, until tender. Let cool to room temperature, then refrigerate in the foil until about 1 hour before serving time. Slice the racks into individual ribs and reheat in a 350°F oven. Remove from the oven to brush with the BBQ sauce and at the same time increase the oven temperature to 500°F. Proceed with the recipe as directed.

- 2 racks pork spareribs (2½ to 3 pounds each)
- ¼ cup packed muscovado or dark brown sugar
- 3 tablespoons coarse salt
- 1 tablespoon chili powder

1 tablespoon paprika

1 teaspoon pepper

Spicy Mango BBQ Sauce (page 605)

Line two rimmed baking sheets with foil, allowing the foil to hang well over the sides. Place a rack of ribs on each baking sheet.

In a small bowl, combine the brown sugar, salt, chili powder, paprika, and pepper. Rub both sides of the rib racks with the brown sugar mixture, and let sit at room temperature for 1 hour. Fold the foil around the ribs to completely enclose.

Preheat the oven to 325°F.

Bake the ribs for 3 hours, or until the meat is very tender and the ribs are almost falling apart. Let sit, still wrapped in foil, until cool enough to handle, 30 to 40 minutes. Cut the racks into individual ribs.

Preheat the oven to 500°F.

Reserving ½ cup of the barbecue sauce, brush the ribs liberally all over with the remaining sauce and place on a clean, foil-lined baking sheet. Bake the ribs, turning occasionally, for 10 minutes, or until hot, crusty and caramelized. Serve hot with the reserved sauce.

MAKES 6 SERVINGS

POMEGRANATE-GLAZED PORK CHOPS

Pomegranate juice and ketchup combine to make a simple glaze for broiled pork. Try one of the pomegranate-fruit juice blends, such as cherry or mango, for an easy variation on the theme. If your market does not have boneless loin chops, buy a pork loin roast and cut it into four 6-ounce slices.

1½ cups pomegranate juice

2 tablespoons ketchup

1 tablespoon balsamic vinegar

¼ teaspoon pepper

⅛ teaspoon salt

4 boneless pork loin chops (6 ounces each)

In a large saucepan, combine the pomegranate juice, ketchup, vinegar, pepper, and salt. Bring to a boil and cook until reduced to ¾ cup, about 15 minutes. Measure out ¼ cup and set aside.

Preheat the broiler. Brush the pork with half of the barbecue sauce, and broil 6 inches from the heat for 4 minutes. Turn the pork over, brush with the remaining sauce, and broil for 4 minutes, or until the pork is cooked through but still juicy.

Serve with the reserved sauce on the side.

MAKES 4 SERVINGS

PORK CUTLETS WITH SAGE & WINE

Although the lemon wedges that are served with the cutlets may seem like an optional garnish, they are actually an important flavor component of the dish. The acidity of the lemon complements the richness of the pork and the sauce.

2 pork tenderloins (1 pound each)

¾ teaspoon salt

½ teaspoon pepper

24 fresh sage leaves

½ cup white whole wheat* or unbleached all-purpose flour

Olive oil

3 tablespoons butter, 2 tablespoons cut into small pieces

1 large shallot, minced

3/4 cup dry white wine

Lemon wedges, for serving

**milled from white wheat grains*

Cut each pork tenderloin crosswise in 6 pieces. Place each piece between 2 pieces of plastic wrap, and pound to 1/8-inch thickness with a meat mallet.

Sprinkle the salt and pepper over both sides of the cutlets. One at a time, place a cutlet on a cutting board. Arrange 2 sage leaves spaced apart on the cutlet and pound in lightly but firmly with the meat mallet. Put the flour in a pie plate and lightly coat each cutlet with flour.

Preheat the oven to 250°F.

In a large, heavy skillet, heat 2 tablespoons oil over medium-high heat. Working in batches, add a single layer of cutlets, leaf-side down, to the pan and cook, turning once, until cooked through but still juicy, 3 to 4 minutes. Transfer to an ovenproof platter, cover loosely with foil, and place in the oven to keep warm. Repeat with the remaining cutlets, adding more oil to the pan if necessary and reducing the heat if the pan gets too hot.

Pour off any pan drippings. Add 1 tablespoon of the butter to the skillet and melt over medium heat. Add the shallot and cook, stirring, until tender, about 1 minute. Add the wine, increase the heat to high and bring to a boil, stirring to scrape up any browned bits in the pan. Boil until reduced by two-thirds, about 2 minutes.

Gradually whisk in the 2 tablespoons cut-up butter, whisking until all has been added and the sauce is lightly thickened. Pour in any accumulated pork juices from the platter.

Season the sauce to taste. Spoon the sauce over the cutlets and serve warm with lemon wedges.

MAKES 6 SERVINGS

PEACH-ROASTED PORK & QUINOA SALAD

Quinoa has a slightly soapy-tasting coating that should be rinsed off before cooking.

1/4 cup peach all-fruit spread

2 tablespoons Dijon mustard

1 teaspoon grated lemon zest

2 tablespoons lemon juice

1 teaspoon chili powder

1 pork tenderloin (1 pound)

3/4 teaspoon salt

2 cups water

1 cup quinoa, rinsed and drained

1/4 cup orange juice

1 tablespoon olive oil

2 nectarines, cut into 1/2-inch chunks

8 cups watercress, large stems removed

Preheat the oven to 400°F. In a large bowl, whisk together the fruit spread, mustard, lemon zest, lemon juice, and 1/2 teaspoon of the chili powder. Measure out 3 tablespoons of the peach-mustard mixture to use as a barbecue sauce for the pork. Set the remaining mixture aside to use to make the dressing later.

Place the pork in a small roasting pan. Rub the pork with the remaining 1/2 teaspoon chili powder and 1/4 teaspoon of the salt. Roast for 15 minutes. Brush the 3 tablespoons of barbecue sauce over the pork, and continue roasting for 10 minutes, or until cooked through but still juicy. When cool enough to handle, thinly slice.

Meanwhile, in a large saucepan, bring the water to a boil. Add the quinoa and the remaining 1/2 teaspoon salt, and return to a boil. Reduce to a simmer, cover, and cook the quinoa is until tender, about 12 minutes. Drain.

In a large bowl, whisk together the reserved peach-mustard mixture, orange juice, and oil to make the dressing. Add the drained quinoa and the nectarines, tossing to combine.

Serve the quinoa salad on a bed of watercress topped with the sliced pork.

MAKES 4 SERVINGS

BARBECUED PORK, SLAW & POTATO SALAD

This is a good make-ahead salad. Serve it at room temperature or chilled.

- 2 cans (8 ounces each) no-salt-added tomato sauce
- ½ cup distilled white vinegar
- 3 tablespoons packed muscovado or dark brown sugar
- 1¾ teaspoons salt
- ½ teaspoon black pepper
- 2 pork tenderloins (1 pound each)
- 2 teaspoons paprika
- 1 teaspoon cumin
- 1½ pounds sweet potatoes, peeled and cut into ½-inch chunks
- 2 large red bell peppers, slivered
- 1½ cups frozen corn kernels, thawed
- 6 cups shredded cabbage

Preheat the oven to 400°F.

In a large bowl, combine the tomato sauce, 2 tablespoons of the vinegar, the brown sugar, salt, and black pepper. Remove ¼ cup of the mixture to use as a baste for the pork, and set the large bowl aside.

Rub the pork with the paprika and cumin, place in a small roasting pan, and roast for 10 minutes. Brush with the reserved tomato baste, and roast for 20 to 25 minutes longer, or until cooked through but still juicy. Let cool to room temperature, then thinly slice and cut into bite-size pieces.

Meanwhile, in a vegetable steamer, cook the sweet potatoes until firm-tender, 8 to 12 minutes. Add the bell peppers for the last 1 or 2 minutes. Transfer to the bowl with the remaining tomato sauce mixture, along with the pork and corn.

Add the remaining 6 tablespoons vinegar and the cabbage to the bowl, and toss to combine.

MAKES 8 SERVINGS

INDIAN-SPICED BONELESS PORK CHOPS

Garam masala is an Indian blend of both sweet and savory spices. Here it forms the base of an aromatic rub. Great on pork, the rub would also be good on chicken.

- 2 teaspoons garam masala
- 1 teaspoon sugar
- ½ teaspoon salt
- ½ teaspoon cinnamon
- 4 boneless pork loin chops (5 ounces each), ½- to ¾- inch thick
- 4 teaspoons vegetable oil

Preheat the broiler.

In a small bowl, combine the garam masala, sugar, salt, and cinnamon. Rub the mixture all over the chops, then rub with the oil.

Broil 4 inches from the heat for 3 minutes per side, or until the pork is just cooked through but still juicy.

MAKES 4 SERVINGS

FIVE-SPICE MARINATED PORK CHOPS

If you happen to have tomato paste but no tomato sauce on hand, you can use it here. Just use 1 tablespoon of tomato paste thinned with 3 tablespoons of water.

¼ cup tomato sauce

¼ cup honey

½ teaspoon Chinese five-spice powder, store-bought or homemade (below)

2 teaspoons soy sauce

1 clove garlic, minced

6 pork loin chops (6 ounces each), ½ inch thick

In a small bowl, whisk together the tomato sauce, honey, five-spice powder, soy sauce, and garlic.

Place the pork chops in a shallow container and pour the marinade on top. Cover and marinate in the refrigerator for at least 1 hour.

Preheat the broiler. Place the chops on a foil-lined broiler pan and cook 6 inches from the heat for about 4 minutes per side, or until cooked through but still juicy.

MAKES 6 SERVINGS

PORK GOULASH

For an interesting, slightly smoky flavor, substitute a Spanish smoked paprika for the Hungarian. Be sure you are using a sweet, not a hot, paprika or the dish will be too spicy.

2 tablespoons vegetable oil

3 pounds boneless pork shoulder, cut into 1-inch chunks

1 large onion, coarsely chopped

1 red bell pepper, cut into ½-inch pieces

1 yellow bell pepper, cut into ½-inch pieces

½ cup water

2 tablespoons sweet Hungarian paprika

1½ teaspoons caraway seeds

¾ teaspoon salt

¼ teaspoon cayenne pepper

1 can (28 ounces) whole tomatoes in juice

2 tablespoons red wine vinegar

Greek yogurt or reduced-fat sour cream (optional)

Snipped fresh dill (optional)

Preheat the oven to 350°F.

CHINESE FIVE-SPICE POWDER

Add 1 tablespoon (or to taste) to meat dishes made to serve 6.

1 star anise pod, broken unto pieces

2 teaspoons fennel seeds

2 teaspoons peppercorns

2 teaspoons whole cloves

2-inch piece of cinnamon stick, broken

In a spice mill or coffee grinder, grind all the spices to a fine powder. Store in an airtight container.

In a 5-quart Dutch oven, heat 1 tablespoon of the oil over medium heat. Working in batches, sauté the pork until browned, about 2 minutes per side. With a slotted spoon, transfer the pork to a bowl.

Add the remaining 1 tablespoon oil, the onion, and bell peppers to the pan, and toss to coat. Add the water, cover, and cook, stirring occasionally, until the vegetables are tender, about 15 minutes.

Stir in the paprika, caraway seeds, salt, and cayenne. Add the tomatoes (and their juice), squeezing them with your hands as you add them to break them up. Add the pork (and any juices in the bowl) and bring to a boil. Cover and transfer to the oven.

Bake, stirring once or twice, for 1 hour 45 minutes, or until the pork is tender. Skim off any fat that has risen to the surface. Stir in the vinegar and serve. If desired, serve with yogurt and dill.

MAKES 6 SERVINGS

NEW MEXICO GREEN CHILI

Though in Texas the meat of choice for a Texas-style chili is beef, in New Mexico chili is made with pork.

- **2 tablespoons olive oil**
- **1 pound pork tenderloin, cut into 1-inch chunks**
- **2 tablespoons flour**
- **6 scallions, thinly sliced**
- **3 cloves garlic, minced**
- **1 large green bell pepper, cut into ½-inch pieces**
- **1 large pickled jalapeño pepper, finely chopped**
- **1½ cups packed chopped cilantro**
- **¾ teaspoon salt**
- **½ teaspoon ground coriander**
- **1¼ cups water**
- **1½ cups frozen peas, thawed**
- **2 tablespoons lime juice**
- **1 red bell pepper, diced, for serving**

Preheat the oven to 350°F. In a Dutch oven, heat the oil over medium heat. Dredge the pork in the flour, shaking off the excess. Add the pork to the pan and cook until golden brown, about 4 minutes. With a slotted spoon, transfer the pork to a plate.

Add the scallions and garlic to the pan, and cook until the scallions are tender, about 1 minute. Add the green bell pepper and jalapeño, and cook until the bell pepper is crisp-tender, about 4 minutes. Stir in ¾ cup of the cilantro, the salt, ground coriander, and water, and bring to a boil.

Return the pork to the pan and cover. Place in the oven and bake for 25 minutes, or until the pork is tender.

Stir in the peas, lime juice, and remaining ¾ cup cilantro. Re-cover and let stand for 3 minutes. Serve topped with diced red bell pepper.

MAKES 4 SERVINGS

PORK ENCHILADAS WITH FETA

If you live anywhere with access to Mexican ingredients, use queso blanco instead of feta cheese.

- **1 tablespoon plus 2 teaspoons vegetable oil**
- **4 scallions, thinly sliced**
- **3 cloves garlic, minced**
- **1 large pickled jalapeño pepper, minced**
- **⅔ cup chopped cilantro**
- **1 tablespoon lemon juice**
- **⅔ cup reduced-fat (2%) milk**
- **1 tablespoon flour**

- **¾ pound boneless center-cut pork loin chops, cut into 2 x ¼-inch strips**
- **½ teaspoon salt**
- **1 large tomato, coarsely chopped**
- **½ cup frozen corn kernels, thawed**
- **8 spinach whole wheat tortillas (6 inches)**
- **⅓ cup crumbled feta cheese**

In a large skillet, heat 1 tablespoon of the oil over medium heat. Add the scallions, garlic, and jalapeño, and cook until the scallions and garlic are tender, about 2 minutes. Transfer the mixture to a food processor. Add ⅓ cup of the cilantro and the lemon juice, and process until smooth. Add the milk and flour, and process until well combined. Set aside.

Preheat the oven to 350°F.

In the same skillet, heat the remaining 2 teaspoons oil over medium heat. Add the pork, sprinkle with the salt, and cook until just cooked through, about 3 minutes. Remove the pan from the heat and stir in the tomato, corn, and remaining ⅓ cup cilantro. Spoon the pork mixture down the center of each tortilla and roll up.

Spoon ¼ cup of the sauce into a 7 × 11-inch baking dish. Place the enchiladas, seam-side down, in the dish, and spoon the remaining sauce on top. Cover with foil and bake for 15 minutes. Uncover, sprinkle the feta on top, and return to the oven for 5 minutes, or until the cheese is just melted.

MAKES 4 SERVINGS

LEG OF LAMB WITH HERB-NUT STUFFING

Parsley, mint, and lemon juice are the perfect foil for the richness of lamb.

- **2 tablespoons olive oil**
- **4 scallions, thinly sliced**
- **2 cloves garlic, minced**
- **1 package (10 ounces) frozen chopped spinach, thawed and squeezed dry**
- **¼ cup chopped parsley**
- **¼ cup chopped fresh mint**
- **½ cup pine nuts**
- **½ cup soft whole-grain bread crumbs (1 slice)**
- **1 large egg**
- **2 teaspoons finely grated lemon zest**
- **½ teaspoon salt**
- **1 leg of lamb (7 to 9 pounds), boned and butterflied**
- **¼ cup lemon juice**
- **½ teaspoon pepper**

In a small skillet, heat 1 tablespoon of the oil over low heat. Add the scallions and garlic, and cook until tender, about 2 minutes. Transfer to a large bowl.

Add the spinach, parsley, mint, pine nuts, bread crumbs, egg, lemon zest, and salt to the bowl and blend well.

Place the lamb on a work surface, boned-side up. Sprinkle with the lemon juice and pepper. Spoon the nut-herb stuffing over the lamb and spread evenly. Roll the meat up and secure with skewers to keep the meat in place while you tie it. Tie the lamb roll several times with string to make a compact oblong roast. Remove the skewers. Rub the outside of the roast with the remaining 1 tablespoon oil, and place on a rack set in a roasting pan. Set aside to marinate at room temperature for 1 hour.

Preheat the oven to 325°F.

Roast the lamb, uncovered, for 12 minutes per pound for medium-rare or 20 minutes per pound for well done. Baste often with pan juices during roasting. Let the roast rest for 10 minutes before slicing. Serve with the pan juices.

MAKES 8 SERVINGS

RACK OF LAMB WITH ROASTED POMEGRANATE JUS

This is a special occasion dish for two. Have your butcher trim the lamb and french the bones by scraping away the fat.

Olive oil

1½ cups pomegranate seeds (from 1 large fruit), plus more for garnish

1 small sprig fresh rosemary

2 tablespoons plus ¼ cup dry red wine

1 tablespoon peppercorns

1 tablespoon coriander seeds

Coarse salt

One 8-bone rack of lamb (2 pounds), trimmed and frenched

½ cup chicken broth, store-bought or homemade (page 172)

Preheat the oven to 425°F. Lightly coat a 12-inch ovenproof skillet with oil. Mound 1¼ cups of the pomegranate seeds in the center of the skillet, along with the rosemary and 2 tablespoons of the wine.

In a spice mill or coffee grinder, coarsely grind the peppercorns, coriander, and 1 teaspoon of salt. Brush the lamb with 2 teaspoons of oil and rub with the spice mixture. Cover the bones with foil and place the rack, fat-side down, on top of the seeds. Roast for 20 to 25 minutes, or until a thermometer reads 130°F for medium rare or 140°F for medium. Remove the meat and let rest 5 minutes.

Place the skillet over medium-high heat. Add the remaining ¼ cup wine and the broth. Simmer 5 minutes. Discard the rosemary. Transfer the contents to a blender with the remaining ¼ cup uncooked pomegranate seeds, and puree. Strain the sauce through a fine-mesh sieve, pushing the seeds with a wooden spoon. Season with salt to taste. Slice the rack into chops. Serve with spoonfuls of sauce. Garnish with the pomegranate seeds.

MAKES 2 SERVINGS

GRILLED LAMB & POTATO BROCHETTES

Serve these tender bites of lamb and potato on their skewers.

½ cup extra-virgin olive oil

8 sprigs fresh thyme, lightly pounded

8 sprigs fresh rosemary, lightly pounded

12 cloves garlic, smashed and peeled

2½ pounds leg of lamb, trimmed and cut into 1½-inch chunks

16 baby Yukon Gold potatoes

Coarse salt and pepper

In a glass dish, combine the oil, herb sprigs, and garlic. Add the lamb and toss to coat. Cover and refrigerate overnight, or for up to 2 days.

Place the potatoes in a pot of salted cold water and bring to a boil. Reduce to a simmer and cook until just tender, 12 to 15 minutes. Drain and refrigerate overnight so that the potato starches bind.

Preheat the grill or broiler to medium-high.

On eight 12-inch skewers, thread 3 lamb cubes alternately with 2 potatoes. Season lightly with salt and pepper. Grill or broil for 7 minutes on each side for medium/medium-rare. Let rest for 5 minutes before serving.

MAKES 8 SERVINGS

HERB-MARINATED LAMB CHOPS

Double-rib chops are like mini lamb racks and easy to cook to medium-rare. If you can only get single loin chops, buy 16 of them.

- 8 sprigs fresh thyme, lightly pounded
- 8 large sprigs fresh rosemary, lightly pounded
- 8 large cloves garlic, smashed and peeled
- 3 tablespoons extra-virgin olive oil
- 2 teaspoons crushed peppercorns
- 8 double-cut rib lamb chops
- Sea salt
- Lemon-Olive Tapenade (page 146)

In a large glass baking dish, combine the thyme, rosemary, garlic, oil, and peppercorns. Add the lamb chops and toss to coat. Cover and marinate in the refrigerator at least 1 hour 30 minutes or overnight. Remove the chops from refrigerator 30 minutes before cooking.

Preheat the oven to 400°F. Scrape the marinade off the chops and sprinkle lightly with salt.

Heat a 12-inch ovenproof skillet over medium-high heat. Sear the chops on both sides, about 3 minutes each. (Cook in batches, transferring the chops to a warm plate.) Arrange the chops in the skillet on their edges, fat-side down, with the bones facing up. Transfer the skillet to the oven and roast for 5 to 8 minutes, until a meat thermometer registers about 130°F for medium-rare.

Transfer the chops to a cutting board and cover loosely with foil. Let rest for 8 minutes. Slice the chops between the bones and serve with dollops of tapenade.

MAKES 8 SERVINGS

LAMB SHANKS & CHICKPEAS

Meaty chickpeas are a traditional match for lamb.

- 2 tablespoons olive oil
- 4 small, meaty lamb shanks (12 ounces each)
- 1 medium onion, finely chopped
- 2 carrots, halved lengthwise and thinly sliced crosswise
- 3 cloves garlic, minced
- 2 cups water
- 2 tablespoons tomato paste
- 3 strips (2 × ½ inch) orange zest
- 1 teaspoon ground coriander
- ½ teaspoon oregano
- ½ teaspoon salt
- ¼ teaspoon pepper
- 2 cups cooked chickpeas

Preheat the oven to 350°F.

In a Dutch oven or large ovenproof skillet, heat the oil over medium heat. Add the lamb shanks and cook, turning, until browned, about 5 minutes. With tongs, transfer to a bowl.

Add the onion, carrots, and garlic to the pan and cook until the carrots are crisp-tender, about 5 minutes.

Stir in the water, tomato paste, orange zest, coriander, oregano, salt, and pepper, and bring to a boil. Return the lamb shanks to the pan, cover and bake for 1 hour.

Add the chickpeas and bake about 1 hour longer, until the meat is tender.

MAKES 4 SERVINGS

MOROCCAN-STYLE LAMB STEW

Serve the stew over whole wheat couscous, barley, or brown rice.

- 2 tablespoons vegetable oil
- 1½ pounds boneless lamb shoulder, cut into 1-inch chunks

2 large onions, chopped

1 clove garlic, minced

1 can (14.5 ounces) crushed tomatoes

1 cup chicken broth, store-bought or homemade (page 172)

½ cup golden raisins

¾ teaspoon ground coriander

½ teaspoon ground cumin

½ teaspoon ground ginger

½ teaspoon salt

¼ teaspoon pepper

¼ teaspoon cinnamon

½ cup chopped cilantro

½ cup natural (unblanched) almonds, coarsely chopped, for serving

In a Dutch oven or large skillet, heat the oil over medium heat. Add the lamb, working in batches if necessary, and cook until browned. With a slotted spoon, transfer the lamb to a bowl.

Add the onions and garlic to the pan and cook, stirring occasionally, until the onions are tender, about 7 minutes.

Return the lamb to the pan, along with the tomatoes, broth, raisins, coriander, cumin, ginger, salt, pepper, and cinnamon, and bring to a boil. Reduce to a simmer, cover, and cook until the lamb is tender, about 1 hour 30 minutes.

Stir in the cilantro. Serve sprinkled with the almonds.

MAKES 4 SERVINGS

FARMER'S SUPPER SAUSAGE

Because potatoes don't freeze well, these sausages are best eaten fresh.

3 large red potatoes

1 tablespoon vegetable oil

1 large onion, finely chopped

1 green bell pepper, finely chopped

1 tart apple, peeled and finely chopped

1¾ pounds ground beef chuck

¼ pound ground pork shoulder

¼ cup finely crumbled soft whole-grain bread crumbs (½ slice)

¼ cup half-and-half

¾ teaspoon salt

½ teaspoon thyme

½ teaspoon sage

¼ teaspoon pepper

In a medium saucepan of boiling water, cook the potatoes until just tender enough to be pierced with a paring knife. When cool enough to handle, peel and cut into small dice.

Meanwhile, in a large skillet, heat the oil over medium heat. Add the onion, bell pepper, and apple, and cook, stirring occasionally, until tender, but not browned, 7 to 10 minutes. Transfer to a large bowl and cool to room temperature.

Add the potatoes, beef, pork, bread crumbs, half-and-half, salt, thyme, sage, and pepper to the vegetables. With dampened hands, gently blend the ingredients. Mix thoroughly, being careful not to crush the potatoes.

Shape into patties 1 inch thick and 2½ inches across. Cover loosely with waxed paper and refrigerate overnight.

Preheat the broiler. Broil the patties 4 to 6 inches from the heat for 4 minutes per side, or until cooked through.

MAKES 8 PATTIES

OVEN-BRAISED OXTAILS

While a pile of mashed potatoes might seem like the perfect accompaniment to this dish, try some bulgur wheat for a change.

3 tablespoons vegetable oil

4 pounds meaty oxtails, trimmed

2 large onions, chopped

2 ribs celery, thinly sliced

2 carrots, coarsely chopped

2 cloves garlic, minced

2 cans (28 ounces each) diced tomatoes

1½ teaspoons basil

½ teaspoon marjoram

½ teaspoon salt

¼ teaspoon pepper

½ teaspoon grated lemon zest

3 tablespoons lemon juice

Preheat the oven to 350°F.

In a large Dutch oven, heat the oil over medium heat. Add the oxtails, working in batches if necessary, and cook until browned, about 5 minutes per batch. With a slotted spoon, transfer the oxtails to a bowl.

Drain off all but 1 tablespoon fat from the pan. Add the onions, celery, carrots, and garlic, and cook until soft but not brown. Add the oxtails, tomatoes, basil, marjoram, salt, pepper, lemon zest, and just enough water to cover. Cover and bake for 2 hours to 2 hours 15 minutes, or until the meat is very tender.

With a slotted spoon, transfer the oxtails to a serving platter. Skim off and discard the fat from the pan juices. Stir in the lemon juice and spoon the juices over the oxtails.

MAKES 4 SERVINGS

HOMEMADE FRESH CHORIZO

Chorizo is a spicy fresh sausage from Mexico. (There is also a hard-cured sausage of the same name from Spain.) If you'd prefer, you can skip the casings and use the sausage mixture to form patties, or add the mixture directly to a pasta sauce.

1 pound ground beef chuck

1 pound ground pork

2 cloves garlic, minced

2 tablespoons red wine

2 tablespoons sweet smoked paprika

1 teaspoon oregano

1 teaspoon ground cumin

¾ teaspoon salt

½ teaspoon cinnamon

¼ teaspoon red pepper flakes

2 to 3 feet pork casings

In a large bowl, combine the beef, pork, and garlic. Add the wine, paprika, oregano, cumin, salt, cinnamon, and red pepper flakes. Using dampened hands, mix thoroughly.

Fill the casings and tie off in 2-inch links. Cover and refrigerate for 2 days. Then cook as desired, or wrap well and freeze.

MAKES 6 SAUSAGES

POULTRY

Because most poultry on the market is ready-to-cook—it has been drawn, plucked, and cleaned—it requires very little preparation before cooking. After preparation, just be sure to always clean the countertop and all utensils thoroughly and scrub the cutting board to reduce the risk of cross-contamination by *Salmonella* bacteria.

Whole birds: Simply remove the giblets and excess fat from the body cavity, then rinse the outside with cold water. Also rinse the body cavity thoroughly under cold running water to remove any blood that may have accumulated. Pat dry.

Poultry parts: Cut-up poultry needs only rinsing and drying unless you do your own cutting and deboning (see "Cutting Up a Whole Bird," page 34, and "Deboning Poultry Breasts," page 35). Keep in mind that the skin is where all the fat is, so it's good to learn how to cook skinless cuts. There are times when cooking poultry with skin on (like roasting) keeps the meat moist, but you always have the option of taking the skin off before eating.

STUFFING POULTRY

Well-seasoned stuffing, or dressing, makes a delightful accompaniment for poultry. The most basic stuffing consists of bread cubes or crumbs, onions, and herbs. Modifications are endless: You can substitute rice, bulgur, potatoes, corn bread, or chestnuts for the bread. Add nuts, chopped fresh fruit, dried fruits, celery, peppers, mushrooms, oysters, sausage, or giblets. Since the stuffing will absorb the fat from the bird, for healthier stuffing, a good option is to stuff a small amount in the bird and then bake the remaining stuffing separately in a baking dish.

Allow ½ to 1 cup of stuffing—¾ cup is a good average—for each pound of poultry (8 to 9 cups for a 12-pound bird). Spoon the stuffing lightly into the body and neck cavities. Avoid packing the stuffing tightly for several reasons: 1) The stuffing will expand during cooking, 2) densely packed stuffing may not cook thoroughly, and 3) it tends to acquire an unpleasant, rubbery texture. Extra stuffing can always be wrapped in foil or packed in a baking dish and baked separately.

After stuffing, truss the bird to keep the stuffing in place (see Trussing Poultry, below) and roast immediately. Never stuff poultry ahead of time. The warm dressing and dark, damp interior of the bird provide a perfect growing medium for microorganisms that, in large numbers, can cause serious food poisoning. Of course, the safest way to cook stuffing is to bake it separately.

TRUSSING POULTRY

Whether stuffed or not, poultry cooks more evenly, stays moister, and retains a better shape for carving if it is trussed (tied) before roasting—or braising or stewing for that matter.

To truss: Pull the skin flaps over the body and neck cavities and either sew the skin in place with a trussing needle and twine or use skewers. Tie the legs together, then fold the wings back and under the bird and tie them close to the body.

During the last 30 minutes of roasting, untie the legs to permit browning of the inside of the legs.

Marinating Poultry

Marinades lend delightful, intricate flavors to poultry parts and halves. The principal ingredient in any marinade is an acid: citrus juice, vinegar, wine, yogurt, or buttermilk. Oil is often added, but its function is not to marinate but to keep the poultry moist during broiling and grilling. Marinate for 3 to 24 hours—a long soak in the marinade imparts the most flavor. After marinating, reserve the marinade to use as a baste, but don't baste during the last 5 minutes of cooking because if the marinade contains any bacteria, you'll need at least 5 minutes of cooking to kill them. For the same reasons you should never serve a marinade that's had a basting brush dipping in and out of it unless you first boil the marinade for 5 minutes.

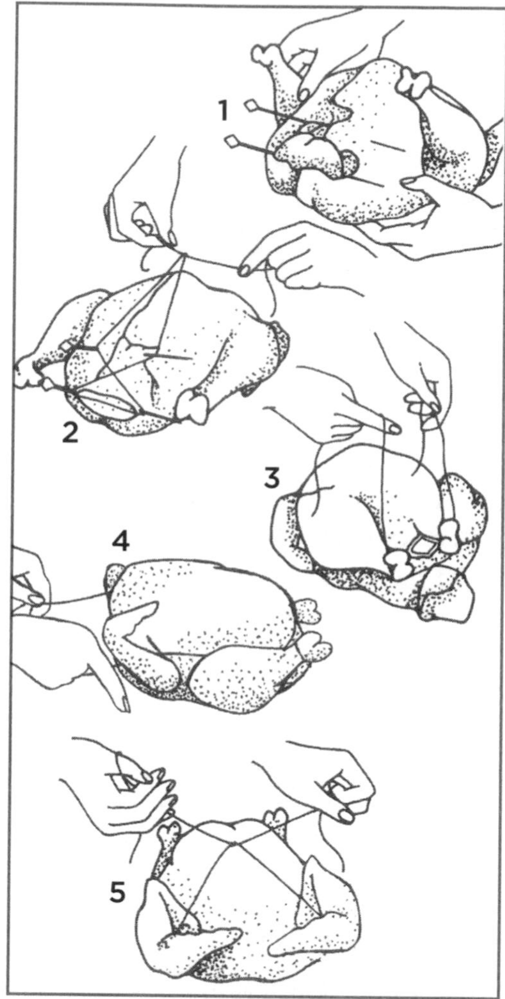

Trussing Poultry: Pull up the skin at the neck cavity and pin in place with several skewers, making sure the stuffing (if there is some) is well covered. With the bird breast-side up, pull up the skin flap at the tail cavity and pin in place with several skewers (1). With kitchen string, lace up the skewers (2) as though you were lacing ice skates and tie off. With a long piece of kitchen string (about 30 inches for a chicken), tie the drumsticks together (3), pass the string to the back of the bird between the body and the wings (4). Loop around the wings to catch them in the twine and then pull tight to bring the wings close to the body (5). Tie off.

Testing for Doneness

For maximum flavor, as well as safety, always cook poultry until cooked through. There are several methods of checking for doneness, with the internal temperature being the most accurate.

The wiggle test: If you're cooking a whole bird, the leg should move up and down easily (the hip joint may even break).

Fork-tenderness: Insert a fork into the breast or thick part of the thigh. When done, the fork slides in easily.

Color of juices: Pierce the thickest part of the thigh with a skewer or the tip of a sharp knife. The juices will be clear (not pink) if the meat is done.

Internal temperature: Insert an instant-read thermometer into the middle of a thigh, the thickest part of a breast, or into the center of a stuffed bird (taking care not to touch bone). The thermometer should register from 160° to 165°F in the breast, 170° to 175°F in the thigh, or 160° to 165°F in the stuffing of a stuffed bird. Stop the cooking 5°F before the correct temperature, because the temperature will rise the final 5 degrees from retained heat once removed from the oven.

Poultry Cooking Methods

Roasting

Roasting is one of the simplest and homiest ways to cook poultry. Place a whole bird, breast-side up, on a rack in a shallow pan and place in the oven. (Prick the skin of a duck or a goose with a fork to let the fatty juices run out.) Baste, if desired, every 30 to 45 minutes. If a whole bird starts to brown too quickly, place a loose tent of foil over it. Let roasted poultry rest for 15 to 30 minutes before serving. The muscle fibers will relax and the juices will settle into the bird, making the flesh juicier and the bird easier to carve.

Broiling & Grilling

Halves, quarters, and pieces of chicken and turkey work well with broiling. Leave the skin on to keep the skin moist, even if you remove it before eating. With any piece of poultry, start it skin-side down on a lightly oiled broiler rack. Let it cook for half of the cooking time, then turn skin-side up for the second part of the cooking. Skinless duck breast can be broiled, but broiling skin-on duck is not recommended because of the good possibility of a grease fire.

Grilling is one of the most popular ways of cooking poultry, although cooking skin-on duck is not recommended because of the amount of fat and significant danger of flare-ups. Grilling works in much the same way as broiling, except the heat source comes from below instead of above. There are various schools of thought on whether poultry should be started skin-side up or down on the grill; it's best to follow the individual recipe. However, if a baste or sauce is involved, the last part of the cooking is always skin-side up so the poultry can get a final coating of the baste or sauce. Follow the same safety procedures for cooking poultry on the grill as you would for meat (see "Grilling & Health," page 202).

Braising & Stewing

Long, slow cooking in a little liquid (braising) or a lot of liquid (stewing) is best with dark meat, because it holds up better. White meat can be substituted in recipes that call for dark meat, but the cooking times should be shortened.

You can also cook a whole bird in a large pot of water, then take the meat off the bone for use in salads. The by-product of cooking a whole bird this way is a tasty stock. Place a whole bird in enough water to cover and season with onions, celery, and your favorite herbs. Tightly cover the pot and bring the water to a boil. Reduce the heat and simmer the bird until tender. When cool enough to handle, pull the meat off the bones and discard the fat. If you want to make a richer broth, return the bones to the pot with any pieces of the chicken you are unlikely to eat (wings, backs) and continue simmering to get more flavor into the stock.

Poaching & Steaming

Individual skinless cuts can be successfully cooked in a skillet of seasoned boiling water or in a steamer. This is a good way to cook chicken for use in sandwiches or salads. To poach, place the poultry in a skillet with enough water to just barely cover. Add seasonings if desired (onions, celery, herbs, pepper, garlic, or citrus zest). Cover tightly, bring to a boil, and cook just until the meat is still quite pink (timing will vary with the cut, but start checking 10 minutes after the poaching liquid comes to a boil). Remove from the heat and let cool in the poaching liquid (where it will continue cooking). To steam, cook the poultry in a steamer for 20 to 45 minutes, depending on the size and cut.

Frying

Both panfrying and stir-frying are tasty methods of preparing poultry. Stir-frying cooks small pieces of poultry very quickly in a small amount of very hot oil. Panfrying can be in $\frac{1}{8}$ to $\frac{1}{4}$ inch of oil (shallow-frying) or a lot of oil (deep-frying). Shallow-frying is the more healthful choice. You can panfry with the skin on, although skinless is certainly better for your health.

Coating the chicken pieces before frying with one of the following options helps keep the flesh moist and juicy.

ROASTING TIMES FOR POULTRY

Poultry can be roasted at low temperatures (325° to 350°F) or high (400°F). When properly cooked and ready to eat, the breast meat should register 160° to 165°F on a meat thermometer. The thigh needs to cook to 170° to 175°F. and stuffing needs to be 160° to 165°F. Stuffed birds will take 10 to 20 minutes longer than unstuffed birds. Note that duck starts at a very low temperature in order to slowly render the significant amount of fat from under the skin. Once the fat has been poured out of the roasting pan, the oven temperature is increased.

POULTRY		WEIGHT (POUNDS)	OVEN TEMPERATURE (°F)	APPROXIMATE ROASTING TIME
CHICKEN, WHOLE	Broiler/fryer	3-5	400	1 hour
	Stuffer/roaster	6-8	400	1 hour 25 minutes
CAPON		8-10	400	1 hour 40 minutes
CORNISH HEN		1-2	400	30-40 minutes
DUCK, WHOLE		5-7	250/350	3 hours 45 minutes
GOOSE		10-12	325	3 hours
TURKEY	Whole	8-12	350	2 hours 45 minutes
		12-14	350	3 hours 30 minutes
		14-18	350	3 hours 45 minutes
		20-24	325	5 hours
	Breast, bone-in, whole	5-7	325	2 hours 15 minutes
	Breast, bone-in, half	3-5	325	1 hour 15 minutes

Seasoned flour: In a paper bag, mix ½ cup flour, 1 teaspoon paprika, ½ teaspoon salt, and ⅛ teaspoon pepper. Shake one or two pieces of poultry in the bag at once. Repeat until all pieces are coated.

Breading: In a shallow bowl, whisk together 1 large egg and 3 tablespoons milk or water. Dredge the poultry pieces in flour, then dip into the egg mixture, and finally roll in fine, dried bread crumbs, Japanese panko bread crumbs, rolled oats, or wheat germ.

Batter: In a medium bowl, whisk together 1 cup flour, ¾ cup milk, 1 large egg, and 1 teaspoon salt. Dip the poultry pieces into the batter and drain.

Carving Whole Birds

Poultry carves most easily and retains maximum juice when allowed to rest for 15 to 30 minutes. Because slices of poultry lose heat quickly and tend to dry out, carve only what is needed. Cut fresh slices for seconds.

For nice even slices, patiently carve the meat using a sharp carving knife and a fork with two long tines (designed for the purpose of carving). With the bird breast-side up, follow these steps:

- Remove the leg by pulling it away from the body and cutting through the skin, meat, and joint close to the body. Separate the drumstick and thigh by cutting through the knee joint.
- Remove the wing by cutting through the joint and as close to the body as possible.
- Make a horizontal cut (parallel to the cutting board) in the bottom of the breast, cutting all the way in to the rib cage. Then carve the breast meat by slicing in thin, vertical slices from the top down to the horizontal cut.

ROSEMARY-LEMON ROAST CHICKEN

If you've got the time, season the chicken with the rosemary and salt a day ahead, cover, and refrigerate. This will help the skin get even crisper. If not, no problem—the chicken will still emerge from the oven with crisp skin and a juicy interior.

1½ teaspoons rosemary, crumbled

1½ teaspoons salt

1 chicken (3½ pounds)

1 lemon, pricked all over with a fork

In a small bowl, combine the rosemary and salt. With your fingers, carefully loosen the skin from the breast and thighs of the chicken, leaving the skin intact. Rub the salt mixture under the skin and in the inner cavity of the chicken. If time allows, cover and refrigerate overnight.

Preheat the oven to 450°F. Tuck the wing tips of the chicken under. Pat the chicken dry and place the lemon inside the cavity. Tie the drumsticks together. Place the chicken in a shallow, heavy roasting pan and roast, without turning, for 45 minutes, or until a thermometer registers 175°F when inserted in the thigh.

Remove from the oven and tent loosely with foil to keep warm. Let stand 15 minutes. Remove the lemon before carving.

MAKES 4 SERVINGS

GARLIC ROAST CHICKEN WITH PECAN-RICE STUFFING

If you don't have a v-shaped rack, just roast the chicken breast-side up for the whole time. The pecan-rice dressing is cooked separately so you can control the amount of fat. If you roast the stuffing in the bird, fat from the chicken skin would drip into the dressing.

- 6 cloves garlic, minced
- ¾ teaspoon salt
- 6 ounces mushrooms, thinly sliced
- 2 cups carrot juice
- 1 cup brown basmati rice
- ¼ cup pecans
- 3 shallots, finely chopped
- ¼ cup chopped fresh basil
- 1 teaspoon olive oil
- 1 chicken (3 pounds)
- 1 clementine, pricked all over with a fork

In a medium ovenproof saucepan, combine half of the garlic, ¼ teaspoon of the salt, the mushrooms, and carrot juice. Bring to a boil and stir in the rice. Cook until almost tender, about 40 minutes.

Preheat the oven to 375°F. Toast the pecans on a baking sheet in the oven until crisp, about 5 minutes. (Leave the oven on.) When the pecans are cool enough to handle, coarsely chop. Set aside.

In a small bowl, combine the shallots, basil, oil, and remaining garlic and ½ teaspoon salt.

With your fingers, carefully loosen the skin from the breast of the chicken, leaving the skin intact. Spread the shallot-basil mixture under the skin. Place the clementine in the cavity of the chicken. Truss the chicken by tying together the legs with string.

Place the chicken, breast-side down, in a v-shaped rack in a small roasting pan, and roast for 30 minutes.

Turn the chicken breast-side up and continue to roast, basting occasionally with the pan juices, for 30 minutes, or until a thermometer registers 175°F when inserted in the thigh. When turning the chicken, also cover the saucepan of rice dressing, place in the oven with the chicken, and cook until heated through.

Stir the pecans into the rice dressing and serve with the chicken.

MAKES 4 SERVINGS

SPLIT CHICKEN

You can buy chicken halves, or if you'd rather do it yourself, use a pair of poultry shears to cut out the backbone of a whole bird. You can leave the chicken connected at the breastbone if you have a pan large enough to hold it. If not, cut the chicken apart at the breastbone, too.

- 2 tablespoons olive oil
- 4 cloves garlic, minced
- 2 teaspoons marjoram
- ¾ teaspoon salt
- 1 chicken (3½ pounds), split in two
- 1 lemon, thinly sliced and seeds removed

Preheat the oven to 425°F.

In a small bowl, stir together 1 tablespoon of the oil, the garlic, marjoram, and ½ teaspoon of the salt.

With your fingers, gently loosen the skin from the chicken, leaving the skin intact, and rub the marjoram mixture under the skin. Place the lemon slices under the skin.

In a very large ovenproof skillet, heat the remaining 1 tablespoon oil over medium heat. Add the chicken and cook, skin-side down, until golden brown and lightly crisped, 5 to 7 minutes. Turn the chicken over and sprinkle with the remaining ¼ teaspoon of salt. Cover just the chicken (but not the whole skillet) with foil and place a heavy ovenproof skillet on top. Place in the oven and roast until the chicken is cooked through, about 30 minutes. Transfer the chicken to a cutting board.

Pour the pan juices into a bowl or gravy separator and remove the fat. Serve each person one-quarter of a chicken with the degreased pan juices spooned over.

MAKES 4 SERVINGS

POT-ROASTED CHICKEN

This one-pot meal will make mouths water as its aroma fills the house. Leave the root ends of the onions mostly intact to keep them from falling apart.

1 chicken (4 pounds), cut into quarters
Salt and pepper
2 tablespoons extra-virgin olive oil
12 small white boiling onions, peeled
4 carrots, cut into 2-inch pieces
4 ribs celery, cut into 2-inch pieces
8 small Yukon Gold potatoes, cut in half
2 cups dry white wine
6 or 7 sprigs fresh thyme
6 sprigs flat-leaf parsley
1 large bay leaf, preferably fresh

Preheat the oven to 400°F. Season the chicken well with salt and pepper.

In a large Dutch oven, heat the oil over high heat. Add the chicken and brown well on all sides. Remove from the pan.

Add the onions, carrots, celery, and potatoes. Season with salt and pepper. Add the wine, bring to a simmer, and reduce by half, about 5 minutes.

Add the chicken, thyme, parsley, and bay leaf. Fill the pot with cold water almost to the top of the chicken and cover. Bring to a boil.

Transfer to the oven and bake for 45 minutes. Uncover and bake 30 minutes longer, or until the chicken is cooked through. Correct the seasoning and discard the bay leaf.

MAKES 6 SERVINGS

CHICKEN WITH PRUNES & WALNUTS

If you'd rather not have the chicken skin, cook the chicken for the first 15 minutes with the skin. Then, before you cook the chicken with the prunes and walnuts, remove the skin.

2 tablespoons vegetable oil
2½ pounds bone-in chicken parts, with skin
1 tablespoon flour
½ cup water
12 pitted prunes
½ cup chopped walnuts
½ teaspoon coarse salt
¼ teaspoon pepper
½ cup Greek yogurt or reduced-fat sour cream

In a large heavy skillet with a tight-fitting lid, heat the oil until shimmering. Add the chicken, skin-side down, and cook over medium-high heat until the skin is well browned, about 10 minutes. Turn over and cook for 5 more minutes. Remove from the heat. Transfer the chicken to a plate.

Sprinkle the flour into the skillet and mix well with a wire whisk. Whisk in the water. Place the skillet back on the heat and stir until the mixture comes to a boil.

Return the chicken to the skillet. Add the prunes, walnuts, salt, and pepper. Cover and cook over low heat until the chicken is cooked through, about 35 minutes.

Remove the chicken from the skillet and cover to keep warm. Stir the yogurt into the skillet and heat over very low heat until nice and hot. Spoon the hot sauce over the chicken.

MAKES 4 SERVINGS

CURRIED CASHEW CHICKEN: Use cashews instead of walnuts. Add 1 teaspoon curry powder along with the flour. Garnish the finished dish with minced cilantro.

OVEN-BAKED CRISPY MUSTARD CHICKEN

To cut a whole chicken into 8 serving pieces, separate it into drumsticks, thighs, and breasts. Cut each breast in half. Save the wings and backs for making stock. If you can't find Italian-flavored panko bread crumbs, use regular (unflavored) panko crumbs with a big pinch of Italian seasoning.

3 tablespoons olive oil

2 large egg whites

¼ cup coarse-grained mustard

½ teaspoon salt

½ teaspoon pepper

1 chicken (4 pounds), cut into 8 serving pieces, skin removed

2 cups Italian-flavored panko bread crumbs

Preheat the oven to 425°F. Using 1 tablespoon of the oil, coat a rimmed baking sheet.

In a large bowl, whisk the egg whites until foamy. Whisk in the mustard, salt, and pepper. Add the chicken and turn to coat well. Put the bread crumbs in a pie plate.

One piece at a time, lift the chicken from the mustard mixture and roll in the crumbs, pressing them so they adhere. Place the chicken on the oiled baking sheet. Drizzle the chicken with the remaining 2 tablespoons oil.

Bake the chicken for 30 minutes, or until crispy, browned, and cooked through.

MAKES 4 SERVINGS

BARBECUE-BAKED DRUMSTICKS

If you're not a fan of drumsticks, make this with 3 pounds of bone-in skinless breasts. Bake for 45 minutes to 1 hour.

1 medium onion, quartered

2 cloves garlic

1 cup ketchup

1 cup balsamic vinegar

½ cup honey

¼ cup lemon juice (1 to 2 lemons)

2 teaspoons dry mustard

1½ teaspoons thyme

1 teaspoon salt

½ teaspoon cayenne pepper

4 sprigs parsley

4 pounds chicken drumsticks, skin removed

Preheat the oven to 325°F. Lightly oil a large baking pan.

In a blender or food processor, combine the onion, garlic, ketchup, vinegar, honey, lemon juice, mustard, thyme, salt, cayenne, and parsley, and process to a smooth puree.

Arrange the chicken in the pan. Pour the sauce over the chicken, turning to coat. Bake, uncovered, basting frequently, for 1 hour, or until the chicken is cooked through.

MAKES 6 TO 8 SERVINGS

CHICKEN BREASTS WITH PINE NUTS & TANGERINES

Pine nuts can be a little pricey, so if you prefer, make this dish with slivered almonds.

4 skinless, boneless chicken breast halves (5 ounces each)

2 tablespoons butter

1 tablespoon vegetable oil

1 large clove garlic, minced

½ cup pine nuts

6 tablespoons orange juice

- **2 scallions (green tops only), chopped**
- **1 tangerine, peeled and separated into segments**

Place the chicken breasts between 2 pieces of waxed paper and pound with the flat side of a meat pounder or a small heavy skillet to even them out.

In a large skillet, heat the butter and oil over medium-high heat. Add the chicken breasts and cook until they just begin to brown slightly, about 2 minutes per side. Transfer to a plate.

Add the garlic and pine nuts to the skillet and cook until the pine nuts just begin to brown.

Remove from the heat, but while it is still hot, add 3 tablespoons of the orange juice. Stir it around the bottom of the skillet, scraping up all the browned bits. Add the scallion greens.

Return the chicken to the skillet and spoon the pine nut mixture on top of chicken. Add the remaining 3 tablespoons orange juice. Cover the skillet and cook over low heat for about 5 minutes. Add the tangerine segments and cook for 3 minutes, or until the chicken is cooked through.

Serve the chicken topped with the tangerines and pine nut sauce.

MAKES 4 SERVINGS

YOGURT-MARINATED CHICKEN

The acid in the yogurt helps to tenderize the chicken.

- **¾ cup plain low-fat yogurt**
- **½ teaspoon grated lemon zest**
- **¼ teaspoon nutmeg**
- **4 skinless, boneless chicken breast halves (5 ounces each)**
- **¼ cup soft whole-grain bread crumbs (½ slice)**
- **½ teaspoon basil**
- **¼ teaspoon sage**

In a shallow dish, combine the yogurt, lemon zest, and nutmeg. Add the chicken and turn to coat evenly with the marinade. Cover and refrigerate for at least 4 hours.

Preheat the oven to 475°F. Lightly oil a 9 × 9-inch baking pan.

In a shallow bowl or pie plate, combine the bread crumbs, basil, and sage. One piece at a time, lift the chicken from the marinade and press the chicken into the crumbs, coating each side lightly. Arrange the chicken in a single layer in the baking pan. Bake, uncovered, for 10 to 12 minutes on each side, or until golden, crisp, and cooked through.

MAKES 4 SERVINGS

GRILLED JERK CHICKEN

Allspice is an extremely versatile spice that lives up to its name. It has hints of cinnamon, clove, and nutmeg, all rolled into one spice.

- **¼ cup white wine vinegar**
- **1 tablespoon minced fresh ginger**
- **4 cloves garlic, minced**
- **1 large pickled jalapeño pepper, minced**
- **1½ tablespoons turbinado or light brown sugar**
- **1½ tablespoons vegetable oil**
- **1 tablespoon allspice**
- **1¼ teaspoons black pepper**
- **¾ teaspoon salt**
- **4 skinless, boneless chicken breast halves (5 ounces each)**

In a large bowl, combine the vinegar, ginger, garlic, jalapeño, brown sugar, oil, allspice, black pepper, and salt. Add the chicken and turn to coat on all sides. Cover and refrigerate for 1 hour. (Don't leave the chicken longer than 1 hour or it will start to get mushy.)

Preheat the grill to medium.

Lift the chicken from the marinade and place the chicken on the grill. Grill 4 to 6 inches from the heat, turning once, for 10 to 15 minutes, or until cooked through.

MAKES 4 SERVINGS

GRILLED CHICKEN WITH PARSLEY PESTO

The chicken is rubbed with a wet marinade of soy, honey, garlic, and a collection of "warm" spices (ginger, cinnamon, red pepper flakes) before grilling.

- 3 tablespoons lower-sodium soy sauce
- 2 tablespoons honey
- 2 cloves garlic, minced
- ½ teaspoon ground ginger
- ¼ teaspoon cinnamon
- ¼ teaspoon red pepper flakes
- 4 skinless, boneless chicken breast halves (6 ounces each)
- 1 cup parsley leaves
- ⅓ cup chicken broth, store-bought or homemade (page 172)
- 1 slice (1 ounce) multi-grain sandwich bread, torn into small pieces

In a small bowl, stir together 2 tablespoons of the soy sauce, 1 tablespoon of the honey, the garlic, ¼ teaspoon of the ginger, the cinnamon, and red pepper flakes. Rub the mixture onto the chicken breasts and set aside.

Preheat the broiler or prepare the grill. Broil or grill the chicken 6 inches from the heat, turning once, for 10 to 15 minutes, or until cooked through.

Meanwhile, in a food processor or blender, combine the parsley, broth, bread, and remaining 1 tablespoon soy sauce, 1 tablespoon honey, and ¼ teaspoon ginger. Process until smooth.

Serve the chicken with the pesto spooned on top.

MAKES 4 SERVINGS

ROASTED FETA-STUFFED CHICKEN BREASTS

Make sure you buy feta in a block, not crumbled. It is much easier—and less messy—to stuff the chicken with a slice of cheese than the smaller crumbles.

- 4 ounces grated Parmesan cheese (about 1 cup)
- 4 teaspoons grill seasoning of your choice
- 4 ounces feta cheese, in a single block
- 4 large skinless, boneless chicken breast halves (8 ounces each)
- Salt and pepper
- 2 tablespoons lemon juice
- 1 tablespoon olive oil
- Fresh herb sprigs, for garnish (optional)

Preheat the oven to 400°F. Oil a 9 × 13-inch baking dish.

In a shallow bowl or pie pan, stir together the Parmesan and grill seasoning. Set aside. Cut the block of feta into 4 slices.

Place a chicken breast on a cutting board. Using a sharp paring knife, cut a horizontal pocket into the fat side of the breast, starting ½ inch down from the wide end of the breast and stopping ½ inch short of the narrow tip. Repeat for the remaining chicken breasts.

Place 1 slice of feta into each pocket, pressing it in firmly. Season each chicken breast lightly with salt and pepper. Dredge the stuffed chicken breasts in the seasoned Parmesan, making sure to coat the chicken thoroughly. Place the coated breasts in the baking dish.

In a small bowl, whisk together the lemon juice and olive oil. Drizzle evenly over the chicken breasts. Bake for 1 hour, basting with the cooking juices every 15 minutes, or until the chicken is cooked though and has a golden brown, crisped crust. Serve hot.

MAKES 4 SERVINGS

CHICKEN CUTLETS WITH LEMON

Chicken cutlets are sometimes labeled thin-cut chicken breasts. Just be sure to get pieces that are under 4 ounces each. If you can only find chicken breast halves, then buy the smallest ones you can find and use a meat pounder or a small heavy skillet to pound them to an even thickness of just under ½ inch.

- **1 large egg**
- **Pinch of cayenne pepper**
- **2 chicken cutlets (3½ ounces each)**
- **½ cup whole wheat panko bread crumbs**
- **1 tablespoon vegetable oil**
- **1 tablespoon butter**
- **Juice of 1 lemon**
- **2 tablespoons chopped parsley**
- **2 lemon wedges for serving**

In a shallow bowl, beat the egg with the cayenne. Dip the chicken cutlets into the egg, then coat with the panko crumbs.

In a large skillet, heat the oil and butter until foamy. Add the chicken and cook, turning once, or until cooked through, about 6 minutes.

Transfer the chicken to a serving platter. Pour the lemon juice into the skillet and cook over high heat for about 1 minute, stirring constantly. Add the parsley. Pour the sauce over the chicken, and serve with lemon wedges.

MAKES 2 SERVINGS

CHICKEN ARRABBIATA WITH ARTICHOKES

The Italian word arrabbiata *means enraged or angry, a reference to the spicy heat of this pepper-laced sauce.*

- **1 cup dried shiitake mushrooms**
- **1½ cups boiling water**
- **2 tablespoons olive oil**
- **2¼ pounds skinless, bone-in chicken thighs**
- **2 tablespoons flour**
- **1 medium onion, finely chopped**
- **6 cloves garlic, sliced**
- **1 tablespoon rosemary, crumbled**
- **¾ teaspoon red pepper flakes**
- **1½ cups canned crushed tomatoes**
- **1 package (9 ounces) frozen artichoke hearts**
- **½ teaspoon salt**

In a small heatproof bowl, combine the dried mushrooms and boiling water, and let stand for 20 minutes, or until softened. Reserving the soaking liquid, scoop out the dried mushrooms. Discard any stems from the mushrooms, and thinly slice the caps. Strain the soaking liquid through a coffee filter or a paper towel–lined sieve.

In a large skillet, heat 1 tablespoon of the oil over medium heat. Dredge the chicken in the flour, shaking off the excess. Add the chicken to the pan and cook until golden brown, about 3 minutes per side. Transfer the chicken to a plate.

Add the remaining 1 tablespoon oil, the onion, and garlic to the pan and cook for 3 minutes. Add the mushrooms, rosemary, and red pepper flakes, and cook for 1 minute. Add the reserved mushroom soaking liquid, and bring to a boil. Boil until slightly reduced, about 2 minutes.

Stir in the tomatoes, artichokes, and salt, and return to a boil. Return the chicken to the pan, reduce to a simmer, cover, and cook until the chicken is cooked through, about 30 minutes.

MAKES 4 SERVINGS

WINE-BRAISED CHICKEN

You can also use a large gravy separator to degrease the broth.

- 6 whole chicken legs (8 to 10 ounces each)
- Salt and pepper
- 6 tablespoons vegetable oil
- 1 bottle (750ml) full-bodied red wine
- 3 medium carrots, coarsely chopped
- 2 medium onions, coarsely chopped
- 4 ribs celery, coarsely chopped
- 4 cloves garlic, smashed and peeled
- 3 cups chicken broth, store-bought or homemade (page 172)
- 3 sprigs fresh thyme
- 1 bunch parsley stems plus 4 tablespoons finely chopped parsley
- 1 pound whole-grain egg noodles
- 8 tablespoons (1 stick) butter
- 10 ounces pearl onions
- 10 ounces small button mushrooms, halved
- ¼ cup white whole wheat flour* or unbleached all-purpose flour

**milled from white wheat grains*

Season the chicken liberally with salt and pepper. In a large skillet, heat 2 tablespoons of the oil over medium-high heat. Working in batches, add the chicken and cook until golden brown, 2 to 3 minutes per side. Transfer to plate and set aside.

Add the wine to the skillet and cook, scraping the pan to loosen any browned bits, until the wine is reduced by half, about 10 minutes.

Meanwhile, in a heavy-bottomed soup pot, heat 2 tablespoons of the oil over medium-high heat. Add the carrots, onions, celery, and garlic, and cook until softened and beginning to brown, 6 to 8 minutes.

Add the chicken to the pot along with the reduced wine, chicken broth, thyme, and parsley stems, and bring to a boil. Reduce the heat to low, cover, and cook until the chicken is tender and cooked through, about 40 minutes. Transfer the chicken to a plate. When cool enough to handle, remove and discard the skin.

Strain the cooking liquid into a medium bowl and discard the solids (but keep the pot, you'll need it again). Let the broth sit, undisturbed, so that the fat rises to the top. Using a ladle, remove and discard most of the fat that has risen to the top of the broth (it's okay if some remains).

In a large pot of boiling salted water, cook the noodles according to package directions. Drain and toss with 2 tablespoons of the butter and 2 tablespoons of the chopped parsley.

Meanwhile, in a large skillet, heat the remaining 2 tablespoons oil over medium-high heat. Add the pearl onions and cook until just beginning to brown, about 5 minutes. Add 2 tablespoons of the butter and, when melted, add the mushrooms. Cook until the mushrooms and onions are browned and cooked through, 10 to 12 minutes. Season with salt and pepper to taste. Sprinkle with the remaining 2 tablespoons parsley.

In the original pot, melt the remaining 4 tablespoons butter over medium-high heat. Add the flour and cook, stirring constantly, until browned, 1 to 2 minutes. Add the degreased broth and bring to a boil. Add the chicken and the mushroom-onion mixture and return to a boil. Season with salt and pepper to taste. Serve the chicken and vegetables over the noodles.

MAKES 6 SERVINGS

SPICY CHICKEN EMPANADAS

In Spanish, empanada means wrapped in bread or dough. These savory turnovers are filled with a spicy chicken and cheese filling.

- 2 cups whole wheat flour
- 1 cup unbleached all-purpose flour
- ½ teaspoon salt
- 1 cup (2 sticks) cold butter, cut into 1-inch pieces
- ½ cup cold water
- 2 tablespoons vegetable oil
- 4 cloves garlic, minced
- 1 medium onion, finely chopped
- 1 teaspoon ground cumin
- ½ teaspoon chili powder
- 1 fresh jalapeño pepper, finely chopped
- 2 cups chicken broth, store-bought or homemade (page 172)
- 2 pounds skinless, boneless chicken thighs
- Salt and black pepper
- 2 cups shredded pepper Jack cheese or other spicy cheese (8 ounces)
- 1 large egg, lightly beaten

With an electric mixer, blend the flours and salt. Add the butter and mix until the mixture resembles coarse sand, about 1 minute. Add the water and mix until just combined and the dough comes together, less than a minute. Shape the dough into a disk, wrap in plastic wrap, and refrigerate while you prepare the filling.

In a large skillet, heat the oil over medium-high heat. Add the garlic and cook until aromatic and just beginning to brown, about 1 minute. Add the onion and cook until golden brown and soft, 3 to 5 minutes. Add the cumin, chili powder, and jalapeño, and cook until fragrant, about 1 minute. Add the broth and stir to combine. Add the chicken and press to submerge. Bring to a boil over high heat, cover, reduce the heat to low, and simmer until the chicken is cooked through, about 30 minutes.

Uncover and cook until all the liquid is absorbed, about 30 minutes. As it cooks, use a spoon to gently break up the chicken. Season with salt and black pepper to taste. Transfer to a cutting board and roughly chop the chicken.

Preheat the oven to 375°F. Lightly oil two baking sheets.

On a lightly floured surface, roll out the dough to an ⅛-inch thickness. Using a 6-inch cutter or the bottom of a coffee can, cut out 18 rounds (you may need to re-roll the scraps to get 18).

Place a scant 2 tablespoons filling in the center of each round and top with a scant 2 tablespoons cheese. Moisten the edges of the dough with water and fold over the filling, pressing with your fingertips to seal. With a fork, crimp the edges of the empanada.

Arrange the empanadas on the baking sheets and brush with the egg. Bake for 15 minutes, or until golden brown. Serve hot.

MAKES 6 SERVINGS

POMEGRANATE-GLAZED CHICKEN

If desired, you can marinate the chicken for a while in the sauce before baking. Make the sauce, let it cool, and pour over the chicken. Refrigerate for up to 4 hours. Remove from the refrigerator 15 minutes before baking.

- 2 pounds chicken wings and/or drumsticks
- 2 teaspoons vegetable oil

2 cloves garlic, minced

1 cup pomegranate juice

2 tablespoons honey

1 tablespoon soy sauce

1 teaspoon hot pepper sauce

Preheat the oven to 375°F. Arrange the chicken in a large glass baking dish.

In a small, heavy saucepan, heat the oil over medium heat. Add the garlic and cook for a few seconds, until fragrant. Add the pomegranate juice, honey, soy sauce, and hot sauce. Increase the heat to medium-high and cook, stirring occasionally, until the sauce is slightly syrupy, about 5 minutes. Pour the sauce over the chicken.

Bake the chicken, basting once or twice with the pan juices, for 40 to 45 minutes, until cooked through.

MAKES 6 SERVINGS

OVEN-BAKED CHICKEN TENDERS

Chicken tenders are the pieces of chicken breast that are just behind the breast bone. Most boneless chicken breasts have had them removed, and they are sold separately as tenders.

½ cup toasted wheat germ

⅓ cup old-fashioned rolled oats

3 tablespoons flax meal

2 tablespoons sesame seeds

2 teaspoons vegetable oil

¼ cup flour

1 large egg

1 tablespoon water

1½ pounds chicken tenders

Salt (optional)

Preheat the oven to 350°F. Generously oil a rimmed baking sheet.

In a food processor, pulse the wheat germ, oats, flax meal, sesame seeds, and oil until coarsely ground. Transfer to a shallow bowl. Place the flour in a shallow bowl. In another shallow bowl, lightly beat the egg with the water.

Dredge the chicken in the flour, shaking off the excess. Then dip in the egg, allowing excess to drip off. Next dredge the chicken in the oat mixture, pressing to adhere.

Place the chicken on the baking sheet. Bake for 15 minutes, without turning, until the chicken is crisp and cooked through. If desired, sprinkle with salt before serving.

MAKES 4 SERVINGS

GINGER CHICKEN WITH ALMONDS

Mango chutney adds a slight sweetness to this gingery Indian-flavored stir-fry. A Microplane zester is terrific for finely grating ginger—just peel the root first.

5 teaspoons canola oil

2 teaspoons white wine vinegar

2 teaspoons ground coriander

1 teaspoon grated fresh ginger plus ¼ cup slivered fresh ginger

½ teaspoon coarse salt

¼ teaspoon pepper

1¼ pounds skinless, boneless chicken breasts, cut across the grain into ½-inch slices

4 large or 6 small scallions

½ cup mango chutney, large pieces chopped

¼ cup chicken broth, store-bought or homemade (page 172), or water

1 teaspoon minced garlic

¼ cup sliced almonds, toasted

In a medium bowl, combine 2 teaspoons of the oil, the vinegar, coriander, grated ginger, salt, and pepper. Add the chicken and toss to coat. Cover and marinate at room temperature for at least 15 minutes (or overnight in the refrigerator).

Thinly slice the white parts of the scallions. Sliver the green parts; set aside. In a small bowl, stir together the chutney, broth, and garlic.

In a wok or 12-inch skillet, heat the remaining 3 teaspoons oil over medium-high heat. Add the slivered ginger and scallion whites and stir-fry for 30 seconds. Add the chicken and stir-fry until cooked through, 4 to 6 minutes. Add the scallion greens and chutney mixture and cook, stirring, for 2 minutes. Serve sprinkled with the almonds.

MAKES 6 SERVINGS

MU SHU CHICKEN

Traditional mu shu (or moo shoo) dishes are served with Mandarin pancakes. Here whole wheat flour tortillas take over the job.

- ½ ounce dried porcini mushrooms
- ¾ cup chicken broth, store-bought or homemade (page 172)
- ½ pound skinless, boneless chicken breasts, cut crosswise into ½-inch strips
- 1½ teaspoons lower-sodium soy sauce
- 1 teaspoon sugar
- 4 teaspoons olive oil
- 1 fresh jalapeño pepper, minced
- 4 teaspoons grated fresh ginger
- 3 large carrots, cut into long matchsticks
- 3 cups small broccoli florets
- 1 large red bell pepper, cut into thin strips
- 1 large egg
- 1 large egg white
- ½ cup diagonally sliced scallions
- 8 whole wheat flour tortillas (8 inches), heated
- 2 tablespoons plus 2 teaspoons hoisin sauce

In a small saucepan, combine the mushrooms and broth. Bring to a boil over high heat. Remove from the heat, cover, and let stand until softened, about 5 minutes. Reserving the soaking liquid, lift out the mushrooms. Strain the soaking liquid through a coffee filter or paper towel–lined sieve. Pour the broth into a medium skillet. Chop the mushrooms and set aside.

Place the broth over medium heat and bring to a boil. Stir in the chicken and simmer, turning frequently, until cooked through, 3 to 5 minutes.

With a slotted spoon, transfer the chicken to a plate and drizzle with ¾ teaspoon of the soy sauce and sprinkle with the sugar. Cover to keep moist. Over high heat, reduce the broth in the skillet by half and set aside.

In a large skillet, heat the oil over high heat. Stir in the jalapeño and ginger, and stir-fry until fragrant, 20 to 30 seconds. Add the carrots, broccoli, bell pepper, and remaining ¾ teaspoon soy sauce, and stir-fry until the vegetables begin to soften, about 2 minutes. Add a little water if the pan is getting dry.

Add the reduced broth, chopped mushrooms, and chicken, and bring to a simmer. Reduce the heat to low, cover, and simmer for 5 minutes.

Meanwhile, in a small bowl, beat the whole egg and egg white together until frothy. Increase the heat under the skillet with the chicken-vegetable mixture to medium-high. Pour in the eggs and scramble just until set, 1 to 2 minutes. Remove from the heat and sprinkle with the scallions.

To serve, spread each tortilla with 1 teaspoon of hoisin sauce, add the chicken-vegetable mixture, and roll up.

MAKES 4 SERVINGS

CHICKEN CHILI & BEANS

As with any good chili, this can be made ahead and reheated.

¼ cup flour
1 tablespoon chili powder
½ teaspoon oregano
½ teaspoon cumin
2 pounds skinless, boneless chicken thighs, cut into ½-inch chunks
8 teaspoons olive oil
8 scallions, thinly sliced
6 cloves garlic, finely chopped
2 carrots, thinly sliced
1 red bell pepper, cut into ½-inch squares
1 green bell pepper, cut into ½-inch squares
⅓ cup water
2 ½ teaspoons muscovado or dark brown sugar
1 ½ teaspoons unsweetened cocoa powder
1 teaspoon salt
½ teaspoon black pepper
2 cups chicken broth, store-bought or homemade (page 172)
3 ½ cups cooked red kidney beans

On a sheet of waxed paper, combine the flour, chili powder, oregano, and cumin. Dredge the chicken in the flour mixture, shaking off and reserving the excess.

In a Dutch oven, heat 4 teaspoons of the oil over medium heat. Add half the chicken and cook until golden brown, about 4 minutes. Transfer the chicken to a plate. Repeating with the remaining 4 teaspoons oil and chicken.

Add the scallions and garlic to the pan and cook, stirring frequently, until tender, about 2 minutes. Add the carrots, bell peppers, and water. Cover and cook, stirring occasionally, until the carrots are tender, about 5 minutes.

Add the reserved flour mixture, the brown sugar, cocoa, salt, and black pepper, stirring to coat. Add the broth and bring to a boil over medium heat. Return the chicken to the pan, and stir in the beans. Reduce to a simmer, cover, and cook until the chicken is cooked through and the dish is full-flavored, about 15 minutes.

MAKES 8 SERVINGS

CHICKEN HARIRA

This Moroccan-inspired chicken stew is rich with North African spices.

2 teaspoons olive oil
3 carrots, thinly sliced
1 red bell pepper, diced
2⅓ cups chicken broth, store-bought or homemade (page 172)
2 yellow summer squash, quartered lengthwise and thinly sliced
3 cups water
½ cup dry white wine
1 tablespoon chopped fresh ginger
2 teaspoons ground cumin
2 teaspoons paprika
1 teaspoon ground coriander
½ teaspoon thyme
¼ teaspoon turmeric
¾ pound skinless, boneless chicken thighs, cut into ½-inch cubes
2 cups cooked chickpeas
⅓ cup whole wheat couscous
3 tablespoons chopped cilantro or fresh basil
2 tablespoons lime juice
Hot pepper sauce, for serving

In a large saucepan, heat the oil over medium heat. Add the carrots and bell pepper, stirring to coat. Add 1/3 cup of the broth, cover, and cook over low heat until the carrots are softened, about 4 minutes. Add the squash and cook until crisp-tender, about 3 minutes.

Add the remaining 2 cups broth, the water, wine, ginger, cumin, paprika, coriander, thyme, and turmeric, and bring to a simmer over medium heat.

Stir in the chicken and chickpeas, and cook just until the chicken is cooked through, about 4 minutes. Stir in the couscous, cilantro, and lime juice. Remove from the heat, cover, and let stand for 5 minutes, or until the couscous is tender. Serve with hot sauce.

MAKES 4 SERVINGS

CHILIED CHICKEN & CORN

This dish is fairly mildly spiced. If you like hot food, add 1 small diced pickled jalapeño to the cornmeal mixture.

- 1 tablespoon vegetable oil
- 1 teaspoon butter
- 1 large onion, chopped
- 1 green bell pepper, chopped
- 1 large clove garlic, chopped
- 2 cups tomato sauce
- 3 teaspoons chili powder
- 2 cups water
- 1/2 cup yellow cornmeal
- 1/2 teaspoon salt
- 1 cup shredded pepper Jack cheese
- 1 cup corn kernels, fresh or frozen
- 2 cups diced cooked chicken

Preheat the oven to 350°F.

In a large skillet, heat the oil and butter over medium heat. Add the onion, bell pepper, and garlic, and cook until the onion is translucent. Add the tomato sauce and 2 teaspoons of the chili powder, and simmer for 15 minutes.

Meanwhile, in a small bowl, stir 1/2 cup of the water into the cornmeal. In a small saucepan, bring the remaining 1 1/2 cups water and 1 teaspoon chili powder, and the salt to a boil. Stir in the cornmeal mixture and simmer for 10 minutes. Stir in 1/2 cup of the cheese.

Stir 1/4 cup of the cheese, the corn, and chicken into the tomato sauce and transfer to a 1 1/2-quart baking dish.

Spread the cornmeal mixture over the chicken. Sprinkle with the remaining 1/4 cup cheese. Bake, uncovered, for 30 minutes, or until bubbling hot.

MAKES 4 SERVINGS

CHILIED TURKEY & PEAS: Use green peas instead of corn, and turkey instead of chicken. Change the green bell pepper to a red.

CHICKEN BURGERS WITH CRANBERRY MUSTARD

For a leaner burger, use all breast meat, or a combination of thigh and breast.

- 1 pound skinless, boneless chicken thighs, cut into small pieces
- 1/3 cup finely chopped scallions
- 1/4 cup plain low-fat yogurt
- 1/4 cup plain dried bread crumbs
- 4 teaspoons Dijon mustard
- 1/2 teaspoon rosemary, crumbled
- 1/2 teaspoon salt
- 4 teaspoons olive oil
- 2 tablespoons water
- 1 cup whole-berry cranberry sauce

In a food processor, process the chicken until finely ground. Transfer to a medium bowl and add the scallions, yogurt, bread crumbs, 2 teaspoons of the mustard, the rosemary, and salt, and mix gently to just blend. Shape the chicken mixture into 4 patties.

In a large skillet, heat the oil over medium heat. Add the patties and cook until browned, about 2 minutes per side. Add the water, cover, and cook until the burgers are cooked through, about 10 minutes.

In a small bowl, combine the remaining 2 teaspoons mustard and the cranberry sauce. Serve the sauce with the burgers.

MAKES 4 SERVINGS

CHICKEN, PECAN & RICE SALAD

Celery leaves have an intense celery flavor, but if you buy celery hearts, with no leaves, go to the center of the bunch and find the pale green ribs in the center, and use those instead.

- **¼ cup plain low-fat yogurt**
- **¼ cup mayonnaise**
- **2 teaspoons grated orange zest**
- **2 tablespoons orange juice**
- **¼ teaspoon salt**
- **¼ teaspoon pepper**
- **1 cup cooked brown basmati rice**
- **½ cup pecans, toasted and coarsely chopped**
- **6 scallions, chopped**
- **1 rib celery with leaves, minced**
- **2 cups cubed cooked chicken**

In a large bowl, whisk together the yogurt, mayonnaise, orange zest, orange juice, salt, and pepper. Add the rice, pecans, scallions, and celery, and toss well. Add the chicken and toss. Taste and adjust the seasonings.

MAKES 4 TO 6 SERVINGS

TURKEY, WALNUT & RICE SALAD: Use cooked turkey instead of chicken and toasted walnuts instead of pecans. Add a couple of drops of hot pepper sauce.

GINGERED CHICKEN SALAD

This salad would work very nicely with cooked turkey or pork.

- **2-inch piece fresh ginger**
- **2 tablespoons oil**
- **1 tablespoon rice vinegar**
- **1 teaspoon spicy brown mustard**
- **1 teaspoon honey or agave nectar**
- **½ teaspoon salt**
- **2½ cups shredded cooked chicken**
- **1 yellow bell pepper, cut into thin strips**
- **½ small jicama (5 ounces), peeled and cut into matchsticks**
- **2 scallions, thinly sliced**
- **1 rib celery, thinly sliced on the diagonal**
- **⅓ cup roasted cashews, coarsely chopped, for serving**

Using the smallest holes of a box grater, grate the ginger. Working over a strainer, squeeze the ginger with your hands into a large bowl (you should get about 2 teaspoons juice).

Add the oil, vinegar, mustard, honey, and salt, and whisk to combine.

Add the chicken, bell pepper, jicama, scallions, and celery, and toss to combine.

Serve topped with the cashews.

MAKES 4 SERVINGS

ROASTED SWEET POTATO & CHICKEN SALAD

Use any small, peppery green for this vitamin-packed salad—watercress, arugula, and even curly endive sliced into 1-inch pieces work well. The potatoes and chicken should still be warm when you toss the salad so the greens wilt slightly.

- 3 medium sweet potatoes (2 pounds)
- $2\frac{1}{2}$ tablespoons olive oil
- 2 teaspoons chipotle chili powder
- Coarse salt
- Grated zest of 1 lemon
- 1 tablespoon lemon juice
- 1 tablespoon honey
- 2 teaspoons Dijon mustard
- 2 pounds skinless, boneless chicken breasts
- Pepper

DRESSING & GREENS

- 5 tablespoons extra-virgin olive oil
- 2 tablespoons white wine vinegar
- $1\frac{1}{2}$ tablespoons lemon juice
- 1 clove garlic, minced
- Pinch of chipotle chili powder
- 6 cups baby arugula

Preheat the oven to 400°F. Arrange the oven racks in the lower and upper thirds of the oven (the chicken and sweet potatoes roast at the same time). Lightly oil a glass baking dish.

Halve the unpeeled sweet potatoes crosswise, then cut each half into 5 or 6 wedges. Put the potatoes on a rimmed baking sheet and toss with 2 tablespoons of the oil, the chipotle powder, and 1 teaspoon of salt. Roast the potatoes on the lower oven rack, turning halfway through, for 20 to 25 minutes, or until golden brown and tender.

Meanwhile, in a medium bowl, combine the remaining $\frac{1}{2}$ tablespoon oil, the lemon zest, lemon juice, honey, and mustard. Add the chicken and toss to coat. Place the chicken in the baking dish and sprinkle with salt and pepper. Place on the top oven rack and roast along with the potatoes for 20 to 25 minutes, until cooked through.

When the chicken is cool enough to handle, thinly slice and return to the pan with the baking juices.

To make the dressing: In a large salad bowl, whisk together the oil, vinegar, lemon juice, garlic, and chipotle powder. Add half the dressing to the chicken and toss.

Combine the chicken, sweet potatoes, and arugula in the salad bowl with the dressing and toss.

MAKES 4 SERVINGS

TEA-SMOKED CHICKEN SALAD WITH FENNEL & WATERCRESS

Cooking the chicken over loose tea and rice imparts wonderful flavor to otherwise bland breast meat. The watercress sauce is also good with fish or even steak.

- $1\frac{1}{2}$ tablespoons dark sesame oil
- 4 teaspoons turbinado or light brown sugar
- 1 pound skinless, boneless chicken breasts
- 4 Earl Grey tea bags
- 1 tablespoon uncooked white rice
- Coarse salt
- 2 bunches watercress or baby arugula
- $\frac{2}{3}$ cup Greek yogurt or sour cream
- 2 tablespoons lemon juice
- 1 tablespoon snipped chives, plus more for garnish
- Pepper
- 1 small bulb fennel, thinly sliced
- 2 tablespoons extra-virgin olive oil

In a small bowl, combine the sesame oil and 2 teaspoons of the brown sugar. Rub the chicken with the mixture and marinate for 20 minutes at room temperature (or refrigerate overnight).

Preheat the oven to 400°F. Line a large roasting pan with heavy-duty foil.

Empty the tea from the bags onto the bottom of the roasting pan. Add the remaining 2 teaspoons sugar and the rice. Place a roasting rack on top of the foil. Place the pan over medium heat. When the mixture begins to smoke, remove from the heat. Place the chicken on the rack and, with oven mitts, cover tightly with a sheet of foil. Transfer the pan to the oven and roast for 30 to 35 minutes, until the chicken is cooked through. Let the chicken stand in the pan, covered, for 5 minutes, then transfer to a cutting board and let cool to barely warm. (The chicken can be prepared to this point and refrigerated until ready to serve.) Thinly slice the chicken on the diagonal and sprinkle with salt to taste.

Meanwhile, in a blender or food processor, puree 1 bunch of the watercress with the yogurt, 1 tablespoon of the lemon juice, the chives, and a pinch each of salt and pepper. Set aside.

Trim the thick stems from the remaining watercress and place with the fennel in a large salad bowl.

Stir together the oil, remaining 1 tablespoon lemon juice, and ½ teaspoon of salt. Add the dressing to the salad greens and toss.

Serve the chicken on a bed of greens, topped with dollops of the watercress sauce, a few grinds from a pepper mill, and chives.

MAKES 4 SERVINGS

GRILLED CHICKEN SALAD WITH ORANGE SESAME DRESSING

If you like pungent greens (arugula, mizuna), replace half of the shredded romaine with them.

1 pound skinless, boneless chicken breasts

2 tablespoons lower-sodium soy sauce

2 cloves garlic, minced

1 pound asparagus, cut on the diagonal into 2-inch pieces

¼ cup orange juice

2 tablespoons minced cilantro

1 tablespoon dark sesame oil

2 teaspoons balsamic vinegar

2 teaspoons Dijon mustard

¼ teaspoon hot pepper sauce

6 cups shredded romaine lettuce

2 red bell peppers, cut into thin strips

1 tablespoon sesame seeds (optional)

Preheat the broiler or prepare the grill. Combine the chicken, soy sauce, and garlic in a ziplock bag. Push out all the air, seal, and marinate in the refrigerator for 20 minutes. Remove the chicken from the bag, and broil or grill 6 inches from the heat, turning once, for 8 to 10 minutes, until the chicken is just cooked through. Set the chicken aside to cool slightly.

Meanwhile, in a vegetable steamer, cook the asparagus until crisp-tender, about 6 minutes. Set aside to cool slightly.

In a small bowl, whisk together the orange juice, cilantro, sesame oil, vinegar, mustard, and hot sauce.

Place the lettuce in a medium bowl and toss with 2 tablespoons of the dressing.

Tear the chicken into shreds and place in a large bowl. Add the asparagus, bell peppers, and remaining dressing, tossing to coat. To serve, make a bed of the lettuce mixture and top with the chicken mixture. Sprinkle with sesame seeds, if using.

MAKES 4 SERVINGS

GRILLED BUFFALO CHICKEN SANDWICHES

The spicy, salty flavors of Buffalo chicken are pretty seductive. Here you find them in a sandwich made with grilled chicken and a creamy blue cheese–dressed salad, all stuffed into whole wheat pitas.

- 1 small red bell pepper, cut lengthwise into flat panels
- 1 teaspoon Worcestershire sauce
- ⅓ cup plain low-fat yogurt
- 2 tablespoons sour cream
- 2 tablespoons mayonnaise
- 2 ounces blue cheese, crumbled
- 1 rib celery, diced
- 1 carrot, diced
- 1 scallion, thinly sliced
- 1 teaspoon thyme
- ¼ teaspoon salt
- ¼ teaspoon cayenne pepper
- 1 pound skinless, boneless chicken breasts
- 2 tablespoons lime juice
- 4 whole wheat pita breads (7 inches)
- 2 cups shredded romaine lettuce

Preheat the broiler. Broil the pepper pieces, skin-side up, 4 inches from the heat for 10 to 12 minutes, or until the skin is charred. When cool enough to handle, peel and coarsely chop. Transfer to a bowl, sprinkle with the Worcestershire sauce, and toss to coat.

In a medium bowl, combine the yogurt, sour cream, mayonnaise, and blue cheese. Stir in the celery, carrot, scallion, and roasted pepper mixture. Cover and refrigerate until serving time.

In a small bowl, combine the thyme, salt, and cayenne. Rub the mixture onto the chicken breasts, sprinkle the lime juice over, and set aside to marinate while the grill preheats.

Preheat the grill to medium. Oil the grate. Grill the chicken, covered, turning once, for 8 minutes or until cooked through.

Slice the pita breads open along one edge. Place the pitas on the grill for 1 minute to lightly toast them.

Cut the chicken into thin diagonal slices. Dividing evenly, spoon half of the blue cheese mixture into the pitas, top with the chicken and the lettuce, and spoon the remaining blue cheese mixture on top.

MAKES 4 SERVINGS

TAJ MAHAL WRAPS

Nonfat yogurt is used to marinate the chicken here because it has a higher acid content than other yogurts and does a better job at marinating.

TANDOORI CHICKEN

- 1 pound skinless, boneless chicken breasts
- 2 tablespoons lemon juice
- Salt
- ½ cup plain nonfat yogurt
- 1 tablespoon grated fresh ginger
- 1 clove garlic
- ¼ teaspoon ground cumin
- ¼ teaspoon ground coriander
- ⅛ teaspoon cayenne pepper
- ⅛ teaspoon turmeric

CURRIED CHICKPEAS

- 1 tablespoon olive oil
- ½ cup chopped onion
- 2 cups cooked chickpeas
- ¼ cup vegetable broth, store-bought or homemade (page 173)
- 1½ teaspoons curry powder
- ½ teaspoon ground cumin

WRAPS

- 4 flour tortillas (10 inches)
- Fresh Tomato-Ginger Chutney (page 611)
- ½ cup golden raisins
- ¼ cup minced cilantro

To make the tandoori chicken: Arrange the chicken breasts in a single layer in a glass baking dish. Sprinkle with the lemon juice and season with salt. In a small bowl, combine the yogurt, ginger, garlic, cumin, coriander, cayenne, and turmeric. Pour the yogurt marinade over the chicken and turn to coat. Cover and refrigerate for 3 to 8 hours.

Preheat the broiler or grill to medium-high. Remove the chicken from the marinade (do not wipe clean). Grill or broil the chicken 4 to 6 inches from the heat for about 5 minutes per side, or until just cooked through. When cool enough to handle, cut on the diagonal into thin slices.

Meanwhile, to make the curried chickpeas: In a large skillet, heat the oil over medium-low heat. Add the onion and cook until soft. Add the chickpeas, broth, curry powder, and cumin, and simmer until the liquid reduces.

To make the wraps: On each tortilla, place one-fourth of the chicken, ½ cup chickpeas, ¼ cup tomato-ginger chutney, 2 tablespoons raisins, and 1 tablespoon cilantro. Roll up tucking the edges in as you go. Cut in half on a diagonal to serve.

MAKES 4 SERVINGS

BASIC ROAST TURKEY

Stuff the turkey with Multi-Grain Bread Stuffing (page 261).

- 1 turkey (12 to 14 pounds)
- ½ cup (1 stick) butter, at room temperature
- 2 shallots, finely chopped
- 2 teaspoons poultry seasoning, store-bought or homemade (opposite)
- Salt and pepper
- 3 cups water

Preheat the oven to 350°F. Remove the neck, giblets, and liver from the turkey cavity and set aside.

In a small bowl, combine the butter, shallots, and poultry seasoning. Using your fingers, carefully lift the turkey skin, without tearing, and rub half the butter mixture under the skin of the breast and thighs. Season the turkey inside and out with salt and pepper. Tuck the wing tips under and tie the legs together.

Place the turkey on a rack in a roasting pan and rub the remaining butter mixture over the turkey. Scatter the neck and giblets around the turkey in the bottom of the pan (discard the liver). Pour the water into the bottom of the pan. Cover the breast tightly with foil.

Roast for 2 hours, lifting the foil and basting frequently after 1 hour.

Uncover the breast and roast, basting frequently, for 1 to 1 hour 30 minutes longer, or until the juices at the joint between thigh and drumstick run clear and the turkey is golden brown. If the turkey is stuffed, the stuffing needs to measure 165°F on an instant-read thermometer.

Loosely tent the turkey with foil and let stand for 30 minutes before carving.

MAKES 10 TO 12 SERVINGS

SWEET & TANGY TURKEY

Honey, mustard, and lemon are the perfectly seductive balance of sweet, savory, and tart in the marinade for this broiled turkey breast.

- ⅓ cup lemon juice
- ⅓ cup honey

2 tablespoons brown mustard

1 bone-in turkey breast (5½ pounds)

In a measuring cup, whisk together the lemon juice, honey, and mustard.

Cut the turkey breast in half. Remove the breast meat, with skin on, in one piece, from each half. (Also remove the small chunks of turkey on the underside.) Place the breast halves and chunks of turkey in a bowl and pour the marinade over them. Let stand at room temperature for 1 hour.

Preheat the broiler.

Pour the marinade off the turkey into a small saucepan and simmer over medium heat for 5 minutes. Set aside.

Place the turkey skin-side down on a broiler pan and broil 6 inches from the heat for 10 minutes. Turn over and cook for 5 more minutes. Lower the pan a notch and broil for 5 minutes longer, or until the turkey is cooked through. If not done, turn over and cook for 5 more minutes. (It does not matter if the skin burns.)

Rewarm the marinade. Remove any burned skin from the turkey. Slice the turkey across the grain into thin slices. Serve with the marinade for spooning over it.

MAKES 4 TO 6 SERVINGS

TURKEY CUTLETS WITH ASPARAGUS & CHEESE

Turkey breast cutlets tend to be fairly thick, so to speed up the cooking time, pound them slightly to make them thinner.

½ pound asparagus, cut on the diagonal into thin slices

2 turkey breast cutlets (8 ounces each)

2 plum tomatoes, seeded and chopped

Salt and pepper

1 cup shredded part-skim mozzarella (4 ounces)

Preheat the oven to 400°F. Lightly oil a baking sheet.

In a steamer, cook the asparagus until crisp-tender.

With the flat side of a meat pounder or a small, heavy skillet, pound the cutlets until ¼ inch thick. Cut each in half and place on the baking sheet.

Cover each piece of turkey with asparagus and tomatoes. Season lightly with salt and pepper. Cover the vegetables with the mozzarella and sprinkle with more pepper.

Bake for 10 to 15 minutes, or until the turkey is cooked through and the cheese has melted.

MAKES 4 SERVINGS

CHILIED TURKEY WITH SMOKED MOZZARELLA: Add 1 teaspoon chili powder when seasoning the turkey and use smoked mozzarella.

HOMEMADE POULTRY SEASONING

Sprinkle this classic seasoning mixture on poultry before cooking, or add to stuffings, soups, stews, or casseroles.

4 teaspoons marjoram

4 teaspoons onion powder

2 teaspoons thyme

2 teaspoons sage

2 teaspoons savory

1 teaspoon celery seeds

1 teaspoon white pepper

Combine all the ingredients in a blender or spice grinder and grind to a powder. Store in an airtight container.

TURKEY AU POIVRE WITH CREAMY PEA PUREE

Two different kinds of heat are in this dish: black and white pepper on the turkey and fresh chili pepper in the sweet pea puree.

¾ cup chicken broth, store-bought or homemade (page 172)

2 cups frozen peas, thawed

4 scallions, 2 cut into large pieces, 2 thinly sliced

1 fresh jalapeño pepper

1 tablespoon Dijon mustard

½ teaspoon salt

1¼ teaspoons black pepper

¾ teaspoon white pepper

6 thin-cut turkey cutlets (scaloppini), 1 pound, halved crosswise

4 tablespoons flour

2 tablespoons olive oil

¼ cup brandy

3 tablespoons sour cream

In a food processor, combine the peas, broth, large pieces of scallion, jalapeño, mustard, and ¼ teaspoon of the salt, and process until smooth. Set aside.

Press the black pepper and white pepper into the turkey cutlets, and sprinkle with the remaining ¼ teaspoon salt. Dredge the cutlets in 2 tablespoons of the flour, shaking off the excess.

In a large skillet, heat the oil over medium heat. Add the turkey, in batches if necessary, and cook until lightly browned and just cooked through, about 1 minute per side. Transfer the cutlets to a plate.

Remove the pan from the heat, add the brandy, and return to the heat. Cook, scraping up any browned bits that cling to the pan, until the brandy has almost evaporated, about 1 minute. Add the pea puree, reduce the heat to low, and bring to a boil.

In a small bowl, combine the sour cream and remaining 2 tablespoons flour. Whisk into the skillet and cook, stirring, until thick and smooth, about 2 minutes. Return the turkey to the pan and cook just until heated through, about 1 minute. Serve sprinkled with the thinly sliced scallions.

MAKES 4 SERVINGS

GRILLED TURKEY SAUSAGE WITH BALSAMIC PEPPERS & ONIONS

Feel free to use any kind of precooked sausage (even pork or chicken) and any kind of bread for this dish. Spicy sausages pair well with the vinegary peppers, but steer clear of heavily flavored specialty sausages that may overpower the relish. The same holds true for the bread: Simple sub rolls or even a French baguette work best, since there's nothing competing with the flavor of the sausage and peppers.

6 large precooked turkey sausages (3 pounds)

2 red bell peppers, cut lengthwise into flat panels

1 green bell pepper, cut lengthwise into flat panels

1 medium red onion, cut lengthwise into 8 wedges

2 tablespoons balsamic vinegar

Salt and black pepper

6 sub rolls or small baguettes, halved

Preheat the grill to medium-high.

Grill the sausages, peppers, and onion 4 to 6 inches from the heat, until the sausages are heated through and the peppers and onion are slightly charred and soft, about 15 minutes.

Transfer the peppers and onions to a cutting board and chop. Transfer to a medium bowl and toss with the balsamic vinegar. Season to taste with salt and pepper.

Just before serving, place the sub rolls on the grill to toast lightly. Serve the sausages on the toasted rolls with the onions and peppers alongside.

MAKES 6 SERVINGS

CHIPOTLE TURKEY BURGERS

Spicy burgers moistened with red onion are pleasantly flecked with chipotles. Pepper Jack cheese and pickled jalapeños add different varieties of heat, which are offset by the cooling cucumbers and yogurt.

- 1 pound ground turkey
- 1/4 cup minced red onion plus 4 thin slices red onion
- 2 to 3 tablespoons minced chipotle peppers in adobo
- Coarse salt and black pepper
- 1 tablespoon extra-virgin olive oil
- 4 ounces sliced pepper Jack cheese
- 1 small kirby cucumber, very thinly sliced
- 4 soft whole wheat buns, split
- 1/4 cup plain Greek yogurt
- 2 pickled jalapeño peppers, seeded and sliced into strips
- 1 avocado, thinly sliced

In a bowl, combine the turkey, minced onion, and chipotles. Shape into 4 patties, each 3/4 inch thick. Season with salt and pepper to taste.

Preheat the grill to medium-high. Brush the burgers with the oil, and grill 4 to 6 inches from the heat for 5 minutes. Flip the burgers and top with the cheese. Grill for 5 more minutes, or until the burgers are cooked through.

To assemble the burgers, pile one-fourth of the cucumbers on each bottom bun. Add a burger, followed by a tablespoon of yogurt, one-fourth of the jalapeño peppers, a few avocado slices, and a red onion slice.

MAKES 4 SERVINGS

GINGER MEATBALL STIR-FRY

These flavorful meatballs can be prepared up to 1 day ahead and chilled until ready to cook. Covered, the rice should stay warm for 45 minutes, so don't worry if it is done before the rest of the meal.

- 4 scallions, dark green parts separated
- 1 1/4 pounds ground turkey or chicken
- 1 tablespoon lime juice
- 2 teaspoons grated fresh ginger
- 1 teaspoon coarse salt
- 1/4 teaspoon pepper
- 1 cup jasmine rice
- 1 3/4 cups water
- 3 tablespoons canola oil
- 4 large cloves garlic, thinly sliced
- 12 ounces shiitake mushrooms, stems discarded, caps torn in half
- 2 teaspoons cornstarch
- 1 tablespoon rice wine or dry sherry
- 3/4 cup chicken broth, store-bought or homemade (page 172)
- 3 tablespoons hoisin sauce
- 1 pound baby bok choy

Mince the white and light green parts of the scallions. Cut the dark green parts into 2-inch-long pieces, and then cut lengthwise into slivers; set aside.

In a medium bowl, combine the minced scallions, turkey, lime juice, ginger, 1/2 teaspoon of the salt, and the pepper. Blend with your hands until just combined (if you overwork the meat, the meatballs will be tough). Wet the palms of your hands and form the mixture into 1-inch balls.

In a 2-quart saucepan with a lid, combine the rice, water, and remaining ½ teaspoon salt. Bring to a boil, stir the rice once, and reduce the heat to low. Cover tightly and cook for 10 minutes. Remove from the heat, but keep covered. Let stand for 5 minutes, so the rice can steam. Keep covered until ready to serve.

In a large wok or nonstick skillet, heat 2 teaspoons of the oil. Add half of the meatballs and brown on all sides, about 5 minutes. Transfer to a paper towel–lined platter. Repeat with 2 teaspoons oil and the remaining meatballs.

Wipe out the skillet and place over medium-high heat. Add the remaining 5 teaspoons oil. When hot, add the garlic and stir-fry for 30 seconds. Stir in the mushrooms and stir-fry until soft and tender, 2 to 4 minutes (if the mushrooms are dry, add 1 to 2 tablespoons water).

In a small bowl, stir together the cornstarch and rice wine until smooth, then add the broth and hoisin sauce. Return the meatballs to the skillet, add the bok choy, and stir-fry for 2 minutes. Stir in the cornstarch mixture. Bring to a boil and cook until the sauce has thickened, 2 to 3 minutes (if it gets too thick, add additional broth). Remove from the heat and stir in the slivered scallion greens.

Fluff the rice with a fork. Serve the rice topped with the stir-fry.

MAKES 4 SERVINGS

TURKEY HASH

The traditional way to serve hash is with a poached egg on top. Poach the eggs separately while you cook the hash.

3 ounces pancetta, coarsely chopped

1 tablespoon vegetable oil

1 medium onion, minced

½ red bell pepper, minced

2 cups diced cooked turkey

2 cups diced cooked potatoes

¼ cup minced sun-dried tomatoes

1 tablespoon minced parsley

⅛ teaspoon black pepper

Pinch of coarse salt

½ teaspoon poultry seasoning, store-bought or homemade (page 255)

In a large heavy skillet, cook the pancetta in the oil over medium heat until crisp, about 4 minutes.

Add the onion and bell pepper, and cook until the onion is pale golden.

Add the turkey, potatoes, sun-dried tomatoes, parsley, black pepper, and salt. Press down with a wide spatula and cook, uncovered, without stirring, for about 10 minutes, or until a brown crust forms on the bottom. Turn the hash and brown the other side for about 10 minutes.

MAKES 4 SERVINGS

TURKEY CHILI

Serve the chili by itself or over brown rice or barley.

3 cups dried kidney beans, soaked overnight, drained

3 large cloves garlic, 1 left whole, 2 chopped

1 bay leaf

2 tablespoons olive oil

2 large onions, chopped

1¼ pounds ground turkey

1 tablespoon chili powder

2 teaspoons ground cumin

1 teaspoon salt

½ teaspoon red pepper flakes

4 cups tomato sauce

¼ cup tomato paste

1½ cups shredded sharp Cheddar cheese (6 ounces)

6 scallions, thinly sliced

Place the beans in a large saucepan and add water to cover by 2 inches. Add the whole garlic and the bay leaf and bring to a boil over high heat. Reduce to a simmer, partially cover, and cook until soft, 2 to 3 hours. Drain and discard the garlic and bay leaf.

In a large pot, heat the oil over medium heat. Add the onions and chopped garlic, and cook until translucent. Add the turkey, breaking it up with a spoon, and cook until it turns white. Sprinkle with the chili powder, cumin, salt, and red pepper flakes, and stir to combine.

Add the drained beans, tomato sauce, and tomato paste. Simmer for 1 hour or more, adding water if necessary, until the flavors are deepened.

Serve the chili topped with the Cheddar and sliced scallions.

MAKES 4 TO 6 SERVINGS

TURKEY CUBANO SANDWICH

The only equipment needed to make a nicely compressed and crisped panini-style sandwich is a heavy skillet plus something to weight down the sandwiches, like a foil-wrapped brick or a few cans. Feel free to use a panini press if you have one, but adjust the cooking time according to the manufacturer's instructions.

4 whole wheat hero rolls (6 inches long), split almost to the edge

2 tablespoons yellow mustard

6 slices ham (6 ounces)

¾ pound roasted turkey breast, cut into ¼-inch-thick slices

4 ounces sliced Swiss cheese

2 sour dill pickles, sliced lengthwise into 12 slices

2 teaspoons olive oil

Spread both sides of the rolls with mustard. On the bottom half of each roll, dividing evenly, layer the ham, turkey, cheese, and pickles. Fold the rolls to close. Brush the outsides of the sandwiches with the oil.

Heat a large, heavy skillet over medium-low heat. Put the sandwiches in the skillet. (Work in two batches if all the sandwiches don't comfortably fit.) Weight them down with a foil-wrapped brick or a few cans. Cook until the bread becomes crisp and golden, about 3 minutes. Flip the sandwiches, replace the weight, and cook until the cheese is melted and the other ingredients are hot, another 3 minutes. Cut the sandwiches in half to serve.

MAKES 4 SERVINGS

GRILLED DUCK BREAST

What most people don't know is that once you take the skin off duck breast, the meat is actually leaner than chicken.

2 teaspoons turmeric

¾ teaspoon sugar

½ teaspoon ground ginger

¼ teaspoon salt

4 skinless, boneless duck breast halves (5 ounces each)

1 tablespoon olive oil

In a small bowl, stir together the turmeric, sugar, ginger, and salt. Rub the mixture into both sides of the duck breasts.

Brush a grill pan or skillet with the oil. Add the duck and cook for 3 minutes per side for medium-rare. To serve, cut the duck across the grain on the diagonal into thin slices.

MAKES 4 SERVINGS

GAME HENS WITH TARRAGON & MUSHROOMS

Serve the hens on a bed of brown rice–wild rice mix.

- **½ cup (1 stick) butter, at room temperature**
- **¼ cup minced shallots or onion**
- **¼ cup minced parsley**
- **6 teaspoons minced fresh tarragon or 2 teaspoons dried**
- **2 tablespoons lemon juice**
- **Pepper**
- **3 Cornish hens (1½ to 1¾ pounds each)**
- **2 tablespoons olive oil**
- **¾ pound mushrooms, thickly sliced**

Preheat the oven to 400°F.

In a small bowl, blend ¼ cup of the butter, the shallots, parsley, 4 teaspoons of the fresh tarragon (or 1 teaspoon of the dried), the lemon juice, and pepper to taste. With your fingers, carefully loosen the skin from the breast of the hens, leaving the skin intact. Dividing evenly, stuff the butter mixture between the skin and breast, spreading it out as much as possible.

In a Dutch oven, heat the oil over medium-high heat. Add the mushrooms and cook until softened, 2 to 3 minutes. Remove the mushrooms and set aside.

Add the remaining ¼ cup butter to the pan and put it in the oven. When the butter had melted, put in the hens, breast-side down, and brush the backs with the melted butter. Roast for 10 minutes. Turn the birds over, brush with the butter, and roast for 10 more minutes.

Reduce the temperature to 350°F. Return the mushrooms to the pan and sprinkle the remaining 2 teaspoons fresh (or 1 teaspoon dried) tarragon over all. Cover and roast for 35 minutes longer, or until the hens are cooked through.

Serve the hens (halved if desired) with the mushrooms and pan juices spooned over them.

MAKES 3 TO 6 SERVINGS

BULGUR, APPLE & ALMOND STUFFING

This is enough stuffing for a large turkey breast or two roaster chickens. Or you can bake it by itself in a shallow baking pan, covered with foil, for 30 minutes at 350°F, just until heated through.

- **5 tablespoons butter**
- **1 cup chopped onions**
- **1 cup chopped celery**
- **1 large clove garlic, minced**
- **4 cups water or chicken broth, store-bought or homemade (page 172)**
- **1 cup bulgur**
- **2 cups diced apples**
- **½ cup almonds**
- **½ teaspoon nutmeg**
- **¼ teaspoon ground allspice**
- **¼ teaspoon salt**
- **¼ teaspoon pepper**

In a medium saucepan, melt the butter. Add the onions, celery, and garlic, and cook until softened. Add the water and stir in the bulgur. Bring to a boil and reduce to a simmer. Cover and cook for 25 minutes.

Add the apples, almonds, nutmeg, allspice, salt, and pepper, and mix well.

MAKES 4½ CUPS

MULTI-GRAIN BREAD STUFFING

Use to stuff a 12-pound turkey, or bake separately in a buttered baking dish at 325°F until lightly browned, 45 to 60 minutes.

- **3 tablespoons olive oil**
- **1 tablespoon butter**
- **1 cup chopped red onion**
- **1 cup chopped fennel bulb or celery**
- **1 clove garlic, minced**
- **4 cups multi-grain bread cubes (about 8 slices)**
- **½ cup toasted wheat germ**
- **2 large eggs, beaten**
- **1 teaspoon fennel seeds, crushed**
- **½ teaspoon salt**
- **¼ teaspoon pepper**
- **1 to 2 cups chicken broth, store-bought or homemade (page 172), or milk**

In a large skillet, heat the oil and butter. Add the onion, fennel bulb, and garlic, and cook until the onion is translucent. Transfer to a large bowl and stir in the bread cubes. Add the wheat germ, eggs, fennel seeds, salt, and pepper, and toss. Stir in enough broth to moisten the mixture.

MAKES 8 CUPS

CORN BREAD & EDAMAME STUFFING

If you have a favorite corn bread recipe use it instead; or use a good store-bought corn bread. Whichever you choose, cut the corn bread up and let it dry out for an hour or so before you make the stuffing.

- **5 cups crumbled stale Corn Bread (page 569)**
- **⅓ to ½ cup milk**
- **2 tablespoons vegetable oil**
- **2 tablespoons sesame seeds**
- **2 medium onions, finely chopped**
- **1 rib celery, finely chopped**
- **1 cup shelled edamame**
- **2 tablespoons minced parsley**
- **2 teaspoons poultry seasoning, store-bought or homemade (page 255)**
- **½ teaspoon salt**
- **¼ teaspoon pepper**
- **2 large eggs, beaten**

In a large bowl, combine the corn bread and enough milk to moisten it without becoming mushy.

In a skillet, heat the oil over medium heat. Add the sesame seeds and stir for about 30 seconds. Add the onions and celery, and cook until the celery softens.

Stir in the edamame, parsley, poultry seasoning, salt, and pepper, and cook for 1 minute longer. Add the mixture to the corn bread along with the eggs, and stir well.

MAKES 4 CUPS

PRUNE & POPPY SEED STUFFING

This makes enough to stuff a turkey breast or a large roasting chicken.

- **½ cup dry red wine**
- **1 cup pitted prunes**
- **¼ cup (½ stick) butter**
- **1 cup chopped onion**
- **1 cup chopped celery**
- **3 cups multi-grain bread cubes (6 slices)**

½ cup poppy seeds

Water

1 large egg, beaten

In a small saucepan, bring the wine to a low simmer. Remove from the heat and add the prunes. Let cool to room temperature.

Meanwhile, in a large skillet, melt the butter. Add the onion and celery, and cook until translucent.

In a large bowl, combine the vegetables and bread cubes. Stir in the prunes (and their soaking liquid) and the poppy seeds. If the bread isn't evenly moistened, sprinkle with a little bit of water and toss again. Stir in the beaten egg.

MAKES 6 CUPS

CORN BREAD & PEPITA STUFFING

This makes enough stuffing for a large turkey breast or two roaster chickens. Or you can bake the stuffing by itself in a buttered shallow baking pan, covered with foil, for 20 to 30 minutes at 350°F, just until heated through.

4½ cups crumbled stale Corn Bread (page 569)

1 cup hulled pumpkin seeds (pepitas)

1 apple, chopped

2 tablespoons olive oil

2 tablespoons butter

1½ large onions, chopped

½ green bell pepper, chopped

½ cup unsweetened applesauce

¼ cup water

1 large egg, beaten

In a large bowl, combine the corn bread, pumpkin seeds, and apple.

In a large skillet, heat the oil and butter over medium heat. Add the onions and bell pepper, and cook until softened. Stir in the applesauce and water. Add the mixture to the corn bread and blend.

Blend in the egg.

MAKES 5½ CUPS

Fish & Shellfish

Fish

In general, fish is best when cooked quickly and simply. The method you choose depends on the size of the fish, the cut (whole, steaks, or fillets), and the fat content. A quick-cooking method such as sautéing works well for fillets, while thicker cuts, such as steaks, need longer cooking and may be best roasted, broiled, or grilled. To prevent them from drying out, very lean fish (like halibut) either needs to be quickly cooked, or cooked with a moist-heat method such as steaming or poaching. Fatty fish, such as salmon, tuna, mackerel, and bluefish, are less likely to dry out and take particularly well to baking, roasting, broiling, and grilling.

Fish Cooking Methods

Broiling & Grilling

Fatty fish takes well to broiling and grilling. Chunks of fish on skewers, whole fish that are butterflied so they lie flat, and fatty fillets and steaks all are good cooked by these methods. Fish to be broiled or grilled should range in thickness from to 3⁄4 to 1 inch; if thicker, the flesh will dry out before being fully cooked. (Baking is a more effective method for thicker fish.) Cook the fish 4 to 6 inches from the heat. Under the broiler or on the grill, a thicker piece of fish can be cooked on one side, gently turned, and brushed with a baste or barbecue sauce. Fish less than 1⁄2 inch thick should not be grilled. And under the broiler they are too fragile to turn, so cook on only one side. Baste the top with oil or sauce to keep it from drying out.

Baking & Roasting

If you're stuffing whole fish, baking is the way to go. But smaller fillets and steaks can also be baked. Place the fish in an oiled baking dish, and bake in a preheated oven (anywhere from 350° to 400°F, depending on the size and cut of the fish). Allow more time for fish that is stuffed, and test often to see whether it is done.

Frying

Frying or sautéing is a quick cooking method that works best for small fillets, small whole fish, and thin steaks.

THE 10-MINUTE RULE

To calculate the approximate cooking time for all fish and for all cooking methods, measure the thickest portion of the fish, and allow 10 minutes per inch of thickness.

BATTER FOR FRIED FISH

This basic recipe makes enough batter to coat about 1½ pounds of fish.

- **½ cup whole wheat flour**
- **½ cup yellow cornmeal**
- **½ teaspoon baking powder**
- **½ teaspoon salt**
- **½ cup sparkling water**

In a shallow bowl or baking dish, combine the flour, cornmeal, baking powder, and salt. Dip fillets into the mixture, coating evenly on both sides. Set aside.

When ready to add the fish to a skillet of hot oil, stir the sparkling water into the remaining flour mixture, stirring just enough to blend. Dip and coat each piece of fish with the batter and place in the hot oil.

Panfrying: Panfried fish is first lightly breaded, or dredged in flour or cornstarch. Then it's cooked in a skillet with a small amount of oil over medium heat. Thin fillets work best here and take about 2 minutes per side, until they are golden brown and cooked through.

Oven-frying: Oven-fried fish is lightly breaded, then placed in a well-oiled baking dish in a 450° to 500°F oven. This method works especially well for thicker cuts of fish. The fish does not have to be turned over. Check it after 5 minutes as it cooks quickly.

Deep-frying: Fish cooks so quickly that deep-frying is an acceptable option, if you don't mind using the amount of oil required. The key to successful deep-frying is the temperature of the oil. Use an oil that withstands high temperatures, such as safflower oil. The oil needs to be very hot (370°F), but not smoking. To be sure the oil is hot enough, it's best to use a deep-frying thermometer, although there is a quick, though less accurate, visual test: The oil is hot enough if, when you drop in a bit of flour, it sizzles. Deep-fried fish is first dipped in a batter (left) and then cooked until crisp and golden brown. If frying more than a couple of pieces of fish, work in batches. Don't overcrowd the pan as the temperature will drop too low and the fish will absorb the oil rather than becoming crisp. Use only fresh vegetable oil for deep-frying, and drain the fish on absorbent paper.

POACHING

Whole dressed fish, sides of fish, and fillets can all be poached in a variety of ways. Whole fish can be wrapped in a double layer of moistened cheesecloth and submerged in an aromatic broth such as a Court Bouillon (right) or Fish Stock (page 173). This can be done in a fish poacher or a roasting pan that can fit across two burners. The broth should be boiling when the fish is first added, then turned down to a simmer and covered. When done, allow the fish to cool and drain before removing the cheesecloth. The poaching liquid can be strained, frozen, and reused for poaching or as a base for soups or sauces. Fillets and steaks can be poached in a skillet and do not need to be wrapped in cheesecloth.

STEAMING

Fish can be steamed in a regular steamer (set on a plate), in a fish poacher, or even in the oven set on a rack in a covered roasting pan. Steam the fish

COURT BOUILLON

Court bouillon, which translates loosely as "quick broth," is a good way to add flavor to poached fish. This makes about 2 quarts.

6 cups cold water
1½ cups dry white wine or water
2 carrots, quartered
4 shallots or 1 onion, chopped
2 small leeks or 4 scallions, chopped
2 sprigs tarragon or ½ teaspoon dried
2 sprigs thyme or ¼ teaspoon dried
2 bay leaves
4 sprigs parsley
10 peppercorns
Juice of 2 lemons

In a stockpot, combine the water, wine, carrots, shallots, leeks, tarragon, thyme, bay leaves, parsley, and peppercorns. Bring to a boil, reduce to a simmer, cover, and cook for 30 minutes. Strain the broth through a large sieve and stir in the lemon juice. Use right away or refrigerate.

---

above either simmering water or a flavored broth. Cooking time will vary with the fish, so test often to avoid overcooking.

Testing for Doneness

Fish is fully cooked as soon as its translucent flesh becomes opaque but is still moist. If you pull at the flesh with a fork, it should just barely pull apart in big, fat flakes. If it easily flakes and the flakes look dry, then the fish is overcooked. The fish should also be easily pierced with the tip of a paring knife; gently prod its thickest section (near the center backbone if whole). Test fish often during cooking, beginning about halfway through its recommended cooking time.

Shellfish

Crabs

Both hard-shell crabs (such as blue or Dungeness) and soft-shell crabs should be live when purchased and cooked while still alive, as they deteriorate rapidly once dead.

Hard-shell crabs: Whole hard-shell crabs need no preparation. They should be shallow-steamed in a large pot with just a couple of inches of water. Bring the water to a boil and add the crabs one at a time using tongs. Cover and cook until their shells are bright red, 8 to 10 minutes (more for larger crabs). The water may be seasoned with "crab boil" seasoning (right) or with any desired combination of herbs and spices.

Soft-shell crabs: To prepare soft-shell crabs for cooking, first make sure they are still alive. Then find the apron or carapace that folds under the rear of the body. With a sharp knife, cut it off. Turn the crab and cut off the face at the point just behind the back of the eyes. Lift each point of the crab at the sides and, using your finger, scrape away and discard the soft porous gills underneath the shell. All of the remaining parts are edible.

Soft-shell crabs are best dredged in flour or cornstarch and briefly shallow-fried in hot oil until crisp, 2 to 3 minutes per side. Be sure to blot them dry before adding to the hot oil. Once you've added them, stand back as they have a tendency to sputter.

Lobster

Lobster cooks quickly. The most popular and easiest cooking methods are boiling and steaming. The classic way to enjoy whole cooked lobster meat is with a simple dipping sauce of melted butter and lemon juice. Its delicately sweet taste really needs little else to enhance it. You can also use the methods below to cook lobster to use in salads, omelets, and quiches:

Boiling: Bring a pot of salted water to a rapid

CRAB BOIL

To use a crab boil: For every 6 cups of water needed, add 1 tablespoon crab boil and simmer for 15 minutes before cooking crab or shrimp according to recipe directions.

- 8 bay leaves, crumbled
- 2 teaspoons peppercorns
- 2 teaspoons mustard seeds
- 2 teaspoons ground ginger
- 2 teaspoons dill seeds
- 2 teaspoons allspice berries
- 1 teaspoon red pepper flakes
- 1 teaspoon whole cloves
- 1 teaspoon sweet paprika (optional)

Mix all ingredients together until well blended. Store in an airtight container.

REMOVING MEAT FROM COOKED HARD-SHELL CRABS

This is best done by hand. Begin by removing the claws from the body and setting aside. Remove the apron or carapace on the bottom side of the crab, taking with it the top shell. Remove and discard the inedible, spongy white gills, and the sand bags and intestines. Break the body in half and extract the white meat from the segmented sections. Crack the claws with a nutcracker or lobster cracker to remove the meat. A 6-ounce crab will yield about 1 to 2 ounces of meat. If not eating the crabmeat right away, refrigerate for up to 2 days or freeze for up to 1 month. Never freeze whole crabs either cooked or uncooked.

---

boil, making sure there's enough water to cover the lobster when it is plunged in. Slip the live lobster into the boiling water, head first, cover, and return to a boil. Turn the heat down to a simmer and start timing: Cook 8 minutes for a 1¼-pound lobster and add 2 minutes cooking time for each additional pound.

Steaming: To steam lobster, place a steaming rack in a pot large enough to hold the lobster. Fill with water to just below the rack. Cover and bring to a boil. Then place the lobster on the rack and cover tightly. Calculate cooking time as for boiling.

Broiling & grilling: Don't broil or grill whole lobster; it's easy to overcook. Store-bought lobster tails, however, can be cooked under the broiler or on the grill. Be sure to brush with a little oil or butter so they don't dry out.

Shrimp

Shrimp can be boiled, steamed, sautéed, broiled, or grilled. They cook in almost no time, so they're easily overcooked. Cooked shrimp should be juicy, but firm in texture. They should be cooked just to the point where their flesh is no longer translucent.

In preparing shrimp for cooking, sometimes the shell is left on to keep the flesh from drying out, but more often it has its shell and dark vein (which runs along the outer curve) removed. There are three ways to do this. The simplest but most time-consuming way is to use your fingers to pull the shell off; then with a knife, cut along

---

REMOVING MEAT FROM COOKED LOBSTER

To remove the meat, begin by twisting the claws off. Then, cut through the entire length of the lobster's underside from head to tail, and break apart. Remove the intestinal vein and the stomach. The exposed tail meat can be easily extracted. Take off the legs; break them to expose the meat and suck it out. Finally, crack the claws with a nutcracker and remove the meat with your fingers.

Tomalley and Coral: The tomalley, or liver, is the green substance you will find when you open a cooked lobster. It is edible and delicious. In cooked female lobsters you will also find the bright red roe, or coral; it is also edible and good tasting. Both the tomalley and the coral may be used to flavor and color sauces.

BUTTERFLYING SHRIMP

Butterflying shrimp adds a decorative touch and is useful for shrimp that are to be stuffed. You can butterfly shrimp shelled or unshelled, but be sure to use shrimp that are large. Insert the tip of a sharp knife at the top part of the rounded side of the shrimp, and cut through the outer shell, cutting down toward the tail. Gently pull off the outer shell, but do not remove the tail and do not cut through the shrimp. Force the two sides of the shrimp outward at the cut so that it will lie flat. The shrimp can then be covered with a bread crumb stuffing, drizzled with some oil, and baked or broiled.

---

the back of the shrimp to expose the vein and pull it out with the tip of the knife. Or, use a pair of kitchen scissors to cut along the back of the shell and with the tip of the scissors push out the vein at the same time. The fastest way requires a specialized tool called a shrimp deveiner, which pushes under the shell and forces the shell to split off and pushes the vein out in one efficient motion. It's a worthwhile investment if you cook a lot of shrimp.

Boiling: Fill a pot with enough water to cover the shrimp, and bring to a boil. You may season the water with any seafood seasonings. Add the shrimp to the boiling water and cook, uncovered, until their color turns rosy and they are opaque throughout, 3 to 5 minutes (timing will vary with the size of the shrimp). Drain immediately.

Boil-steaming: In a pot with a tight-fitting lid, cover medium shrimp with water. Bring to a boil uncovered. Pour off the water from the shrimp and cover the pot tightly. Remove from the heat and leave the shrimp covered for 10 minutes to cook in the residual heat.

Steaming: In a steamer, steam shrimp in the shell or peeled and deveined, in a single layer, until opaque throughout, 2 to 3 minutes (timing will vary with size).

Broiling: Place peeled and deveined shrimp, rubbed with oil, on a broiler pan, and broil 4 to 6 inches from the heat, without turning, until opaque throughout, 2 to 3 minutes.

Grilling: Thread peeled and deveined shrimp onto pairs of skewers side by side, or special double-prong skewers designed for this purpose (this stops them from spinning around when you turn the skewers). Brush with oil and grill for 2 to 3 minutes, turning the skewers once, until opaque throughout.

Sautéing: Depending on the number of shrimp, heat oil in a medium or large skillet until hot. Add peeled and deveined shrimp, season with salt, and cook, tossing occasionally until opaque throughout, 3 to 5 minutes. Serve on their own, or with a sauce or a wedge of lemon.

Clams

Clams in the shell may be very sandy, so it is best to soak them a short while in cold water, then scrub and rinse them well before cooking. Discard any clams that float or have broken shells. Four quarts of clams in the shell will reduce to about a pint when shucked. Allow 7 to 8 medium-size clams per person for a recipe, or less if combined with other ingredients.

Although hard-shell clams are often eaten raw on the half shell, we recommend thoroughly cooking them (and all shellfish) to kill any dangerous organisms. Clams lend themselves to many easy ways of cooking. Large hard-shell clams, more strongly flavored than the soft-shell varieties, are a good choice for chowders. Small hard-shell clams are usually cooked in their shells and the meat taken out after; medium-size clams can be either cooked in the shell or shucked and then cooked. Soft-shell clams are almost always cooked in the shell.

To shuck hard-shell clams, soak them first in ice cold water for 5 to 10 minutes until they open slightly. Gently remove one at a time and quickly insert a short, rigid clam knife to pry it open. Open clams over a bowl so that you can catch the flavorful clam liquor to add to the dish you are cooking or to fish soups or sauces.

Steaming: Steaming in the shell is one of the easiest ways to prepare clams. To steam clams, place them in a steamer in a covered pot with an inch or two of water. Add 1 to 2 tablespoons of minced fresh herbs such as oregano, thyme, and parsley, if desired. Simmer over medium heat for 8 to 10 minutes, or until the shells have opened. Discard any that do not open. If you do not have a steamer large enough to hold the clams, place them directly in the water and cook for the same amount of time.

Frying: To panfry clams, pat shucked clams dry, then sauté in oil until golden brown, turning once or twice, 3 to 5 minutes. You can also bread them before frying by dipping them in beaten egg and then in seasoned bread crumbs. Clams can also be deep-fried, either simply coated in seasoned bread crumbs or coated in a batter (see "Batter for Fried Fish," page 264). Cook for about 2 minutes in oil heated to 375°F.

Baking: Cover clams on the half-shell with bread crumbs, garlic, and olive oil or butter. Bake at 450°F for 8 to 10 minutes.

Oysters

When opening fresh oysters in the shell, work over a strainer set above a bowl to catch the liquor. Use a sturdy oyster-shucking knife. Hold the oyster shell deep down in the palm of one gloved hand (be sure it's a heavy-duty glove). Insert the point of the knife into the hinge area of the two shells. Twist the knife until the hinge breaks. Slide the knife around the whole rim, cutting through the hinge muscle attached to one shell. When finished shucking the oysters, strain the liquor through a double thickness of cheesecloth. If the oysters are not to be cooked immediately, refrigerate them packed in their liquor in a sealed container.

Oysters can be cooked in much the same way as clams (left). Allow 6 to 8 oysters per person, a dozen if small.

Mussels

Fresh mussels in the shell should be cleaned well with a scrub brush. They have a "beard," the strong threadlike strands that the mussel uses to attach itself to rocks and pilings. It runs into the shell between the two halves near the hinge. It should be pulled out by hand. Discard any mussels that are open and do not close back up when tapped, or those whose shells slide easily across each other. Allow 12 mussels per serving—about half that if they are to be combined with other ingredients in a recipe.

To cook mussels: Place cleaned mussels in a deep pot with a shallow amount of water, wine, or sauce, and bring to a boil. Cover and cook the mussels until they open, shaking the pot occasionally. Timing will vary depending on how crowded the pot is. Be sure to discard any that do not open.

ASIAN-STYLE STEAMED FISH

If you have a steamer large enough to hold two fish, steam them on top of the stove. Otherwise, this simple oven method works very well. Fermented black beans can be found in the Asian section of your supermarket; they lend a smoky, salty flavor to the dish.

2 whole sea bass (1½ pounds each), gutted, gills removed, scaled

3 tablespoons slivered fresh ginger

2 tablespoons fermented black beans

2 tablespoons mirin, rice wine, or sherry

2 tablespoons soy sauce

1 teaspoon sugar

2 scallions, thinly sliced

2 tablespoons dark sesame oil

Preheat the oven to 450°F.

With a sharp knife, make 3 crosswise slashes on both sides of each fish. In a small bowl, combine the ginger, fermented black beans, mirin, soy sauce, and sugar.

Bring a large pot of water to a boil. Set a rack in a roasting pan and place an ovenproof plate, large enough to hold the fish in a single layer, on top of the rack. Place the fish on the plate and spoon the ginger mixture over.

Pour water to come just below the rack in the roasting pan, and cover the entire pan with foil. Place in the oven and bake/steam for about 20 minutes, or until the fish is just cooked through (the eyes will whiten and you will be able to pierce the fish with a knife).

Remove the plate with the fish, and scatter the scallions over the top of the fish. In a small skillet, heat the oil over medium heat. Drizzle the hot oil over the scallions and fish.

MAKES 4 SERVINGS

SPICED OVEN-ROASTED TILAPIA

Sweet-salty Asian flavors work well with a meaty fish like tilapia.

1 whole tilapia (3 to 4 pounds)

4 whole cloves

½ teaspoon fennel seeds

3 star anise pods

2 tablespoons turbinado or light brown sugar

2 wide strips orange zest, slivered

2 tablespoons dry sherry

1 tablespoon tamari or soy sauce

1 teaspoon honey

3 scallions, cut into 2-inch lengths

Salt and pepper

Clean the fish well and trim off the fins. Pat dry. Poke the skin all over with the tines of a fork.

In a spice grinder or coffee mill, or using a mortar and pestle, lightly grind the cloves, fennel seeds, and star anise. Combine with the brown sugar and orange zest.

Rub the mixture onto the fish. Lightly oil a large rimmed baking sheet and place the fish on top. Cover and refrigerate for 1 hour to let the flavors penetrate fish.

Preheat the oven to 500°F.

In a small bowl, blend the sherry, tamari, and honey. Brush the fish on both sides with the sherry mixture. Reserve the rest for basting.

Fill the cavity of the fish with the scallions. Roast for about 25 minutes, basting as necessary, until the flesh just flakes when tested with a fork.

Discard the scallions. Transfer the fish to a platter with any juices, and season with salt and pepper to taste.

MAKES 4 TO 6 SERVINGS

OVEN-FRIED TARRAGON FISH

Panko—crispy, flaky bread crumbs originally from Japan—are now being made by many companies in the United States and are widely available.

- 1 large egg
- 1 tablespoon water
- 1 cup whole wheat panko bread crumbs
- 1 scallion, minced
- 1 teaspoon tarragon
- ¼ teaspoon salt
- ¼ teaspoon pepper
- 4 flounder or other flatfish fillets (6 ounces each)
- 2 tablespoons olive oil
- 1 tablespoon butter, melted
- Lemon wedges, for serving

Preheat the oven to 500°F. Lightly oil a baking dish large enough to hold the fish in a single layer.

In a shallow bowl, beat the egg with the water. In another shallow bowl, mix together the panko crumbs, scallion, tarragon, salt, and pepper.

Dip the fish in the egg and then coat with the crumb mixture, patting it on to adhere. Arrange the fish in the baking dish.

Drizzle the oil and butter over the fish. Bake on the upper rack of the oven for 5 to 8 minutes, depending on the thickness of the fish, or until the fish just flakes when tested with a fork and the crust is golden brown. Serve with lemon wedges.

MAKES 4 SERVINGS

BAKED COD STEAK & POTATOES

If you've got cooked potatoes left over from another dinner, by all means use them here or, if you prefer, simply serve the fish over pasta.

- 1½ pounds white potatoes
- 2 tablespoons olive oil
- 1 small onion, finely chopped
- 2 cloves garlic, minced
- 1 can (14.5 ounces) diced tomatoes
- 2 tablespoons chopped parsley
- 2 tablespoons champagne vinegar
- ½ teaspoon thyme
- ½ teaspoon salt
- ¼ teaspoon pepper
- 1½ pounds codfish fillets

In a medium saucepan of boiling salted water, cook the potatoes until tender. Drain and thickly slice.

Preheat the oven to 400°F.

In a medium saucepan, heat the oil over medium heat. Add the onion and garlic, and cook until the onion is tender, about 7 minutes. Add the tomatoes, parsley, vinegar, thyme, salt, and pepper. Bring to a boil and cook for 5 minutes.

Place one-third of the sauce in the bottom of a 7 × 11-inch baking dish. Arrange the fish in a single layer over the sauce with the potato slices around and between the fillets. Top with the remaining sauce. Bake for 20 minutes, or until the fish just flakes when tested with a fork.

MAKES 4 SERVINGS

MEDITERRANEAN BAKED FISH

These packets can be assembled early in the day, refrigerated, and then baked at dinner time.

- 6 tablespoons butter, at room temperature
- 2 tablespoons lemon juice
- 2 tablespoons olive oil
- ¼ teaspoon salt
- 6 white fish fillets (6 to 8 ounces each)
- 6 slices red onion
- 6 thick slices tomato
- 6 green bell pepper rings
- 6 thin slices lemon
- 6 small sprigs fresh rosemary

Preheat the oven to 375°F.

Cut 6 large pieces of heavy-duty foil. Rub the bottom half of the pieces with 3 tablespoons of the butter, leaving a 1-inch border all around. Place a fillet on the buttered half of a piece of foil.

In a small bowl, stir together the lemon juice, oil, and salt. Spoon 2 teaspoons of the the lemon mixture over the fish. Top with a slice of onion, tomato, bell pepper, lemon, and sprig of rosemary. Dot with the remaining 1½ teaspoons butter. Repeat for 6 packets.

To make a packet, fold the top of the foil over the fish and fold the edges over to seal. Place the packets on a rimmed baking sheet and bake for 10 to 15 minutes. Open one of the packets after 10 minutes and test the fish with a fork. If the fish flakes and is not translucent, it is done.

MAKES 6 SERVINGS

ORANGE-THYME BAKED FISH: Use thin slices of orange instead of lemon and thyme instead of rosemary.

ALMOND-COATED FISH WITH MUSTARD

Mayonnaise and mustard not only give the fish flavor, but also keep it moist as it bakes.

- 1½ pounds tilapia fillets
- ½ teaspoon salt
- ¼ teaspoon pepper
- 2 tablespoons Dijon mustard
- 2 tablespoons mayonnaise
- 2 teaspoons lemon juice
- 2 tablespoons butter
- 1 cup finely crumbled soft whole-grain bread crumbs (2 slices)
- ½ cup almonds, coarsely ground

Preheat the oven to 425°F. Lightly oil a rimmed baking sheet.

Place the fish on the baking sheet and sprinkle with the salt and pepper.

In a small bowl, stir together the mustard, mayonnaise, and lemon juice. Spread the mixture over the top of the fish fillets.

In a small skillet, melt the butter over medium heat. Add the bread crumbs and almonds, and toss to combine. Spread the crumb mixture over the fish.

Bake for 10 to 15 minutes, or until the top is golden brown and the flesh just flakes when tested with a fork.

MAKES 4 SERVINGS

CASHEW-COATED TILAPIA: Use cashews instead of almonds, and add ¼ teaspoon curry powder to the mustard mixture.

BAKED MACKEREL WITH CHICKPEAS

Either Boston or Spanish mackerel would be good here, but Boston is a little less oily so may need a few minutes less cooking time.

- 2 tablespoons olive oil
- 1½ pounds mackerel fillets
- 2 cloves garlic, thinly sliced
- ½ teaspoon red pepper flakes
- 1 can (14.5 ounces) crushed tomatoes
- ¾ teaspoon ground cumin
- ¾ teaspoon chili powder
- ½ teaspoon oregano
- ½ teaspoon salt
- 1 cup cooked chickpeas

Preheat the oven to 425°F. Grease a shallow baking pan with 1 tablespoon of the oil, and place the fish in the pan.

In a large skillet, heat the remaining 1 tablespoon oil over low heat. Add the garlic and pepper flakes, and cook until the garlic starts to turn golden about 2 minutes.

Add the tomatoes, cumin, chili powder, oregano, and salt, and simmer for 5 minutes. Stir in the chickpeas.

Pour the sauce over and around the fish. Bake for 15 to 20 minutes, or until the fish just flakes when tested with a fork.

MAKES 4 SERVINGS

LIME-BAKED SEA BASS

Simple, yet flavorful—sometimes less is more. Feel free to substitute grouper or even mackerel.

- 2 pounds black sea bass fillets
- 2 tablespoons Dijon mustard
- 2 tablespoons lime juice
- 1 tablespoon olive oil
- 1 teaspoon tarragon
- 1 lime, sliced

Preheat the oven to 350°F. Lightly grease a baking dish big enough to hold the fish in a single layer.

In a small bowl, combine the mustard, lime juice, oil, and tarragon. Brush on both sides of the fish.

Arrange the fish in the dish and place the lime slices on top of the fish. Bake for 15 minutes, or until the fish just flakes when tested with a fork.

MAKES 4 SERVINGS

MAHI-MAHI WITH COCONUT & PINEAPPLE SALSA

Mahi-mahi is a rich, meaty fish. The crisp bread crumb-coconut coating is complemented by the pineapple salsa.

- 1 large egg
- 1 tablespoon water
- 1 cup plain dried whole wheat bread crumbs

ELIMINATING FISHY ODORS

To help remove the odor of fish from utensils, plates, dishcloths, and cookware, soak them briefly in a solution of 1½ teaspoons baking soda and 1 quart water. To remove the smell from your hands, rub them with lemon juice before washing.

- ⅓ cup unsweetened shredded coconut
- 1½ pounds mahi-mahi steaks, cut into 16 chunks
- ½ teaspoon salt
- ¼ teaspoon pepper
- 3 tablespoons olive oil
- 1 can (15 ounces) juice-packed pineapple chunks, drained
- ¼ cup minced red bell pepper
- 2 scallions, thinly sliced
- 1 tablespoon honey
- 2 teaspoons lime juice

Preheat the oven to 375°F.

In a shallow bowl, beat the egg with the water. In another shallow bowl, combine the bread crumbs and coconut.

Sprinkle the fish with the salt and pepper. Dip in the egg mixture and then in the bread crumb mixture until well coated. Pat to adhere.

Place the fish on a baking sheet and drizzle with the oil. Bake for 15 minutes, or until the crumbs are crisp and the fish chunks can be easily pierced with the tip of a knife.

Meanwhile, in a medium bowl, combine the pineapple, bell pepper, scallions, honey, and lime juice. Serve the fish with the salsa on the side.

MAKES 4 SERVINGS

MARINATED BROILED CODFISH

Cod and scrod are closely related; scrod is younger and generally not quite as thick as cod. Either would work in this preparation, as would grouper or tilapia.

- ½ cup wine vinegar
- 2 tablespoons olive oil
- 4 garlic cloves, minced
- 1 teaspoon thyme
- 2 pounds thick codfish fillets

In a baking dish, whisk together the vinegar, oil, garlic, and thyme. Add the fillets, turning to coat. Cover and marinate in the refrigerator for 1 hour.

Preheat the broiler.

Lift the cod from the marinade and place on a broiler pan. Broil 4 inches from the heat, basting once with the marinade, for 7 minutes, or until the fish just flakes when tested with a fork.

MAKES 4 SERVINGS

DEVILED GROUPER

The chili sauce used here is tomato based; look for it alongside the ketchup in the condiment aisle.

- ⅓ cup tomato juice
- 2 tablespoons lemon juice
- 2 tablespoons soy sauce
- 1 tablespoon Worcestershire sauce
- ½ teaspoon dry mustard
- ½ teaspoon salt
- 4 grouper fillets (8 ounces each)
- ⅓ cup tomato-based chili sauce
- 1 teaspoon drained horseradish
- 1 teaspoon Dijon mustard

In a large glass baking dish, whisk together the tomato juice, lemon juice, soy sauce, Worcestershire, mustard, and salt. Place the fish in the dish, turning to coat. Cover and marinate in the refrigerator for 2 to 4 hours, turning the fish twice.

Preheat the broiler. Lift the fish from the marinade. Place on the broiler pan and broil 4 inches from the heat for 5 to 7 minutes, or until the fish just flakes when tested with a fork.

Meanwhile, in a small bowl, combine the chili sauce, horseradish, and mustard. Serve on top of the fish.

MAKES 4 SERVINGS

ASIAN MAHI-MAHI

Look for dark (often called roasted or toasted) sesame oil in the Asian section of the supermarket. Once opened, store it in the refrigerator.

- **¼ cup soy sauce**
- **1 tablespoon cornstarch**
- **¼ cup water**
- **2 tablespoons rice vinegar**
- **1 tablespoon honey**
- **2 teaspoons dark sesame oil**
- **6 thin slices fresh ginger**
- **3 cloves garlic, minced**
- **4 mahi-mahi steaks (1½ pounds), 1 inch thick**

In a shallow glass dish, whisk the soy sauce into the cornstarch, whisk in the water, vinegar, cornstarch, honey, sesame oil, ginger, and garlic. Add the fish, turning to coat. Cover and marinate in the refrigerator for at least 6 hours or up to overnight.

Preheat the broiler. Lift the fish from the marinade and place on the broiler pan. Broil 4 inches from the heat for about 5 minutes per side, or until the fish just flakes when tested with a fork.

MAKES 4 SERVINGS

GRILLED FRESH SARDINES

Fresh sardines are highly perishable, so cook them the day you buy them. It's best to buy them whole and either have your fishmonger clean them for you or clean them yourself. Not only are they delicious, they're also high in omega-3s, making them a healthy choice. While we've made a sauce to go with them, they're also perfect with just a squeeze of fresh lemon.

- **1 small red bell pepper**
- **⅓ cup olive oil**
- **3 tablespoons red wine vinegar**
- **⅓ cup finely chopped red onion**
- **⅓ cup finely chopped celery**
- **⅓ cup finely chopped parsley**
- **Salt and black pepper**
- **12 fresh sardines, scaled, gutted, and rinsed**

EASY SAUCES TO SERVE WITH FISH

Any of these sauces would go beautifully with simply grilled or broiled fish.

Dill-Radish Sauce: In a small bowl, stir together 1 cup plain low-fat yogurt, ¼ cup mayonnaise, ¼ cup minced radishes, 1 tablespoon snipped fresh dill, and salt and pepper to taste.

Zesty Cucumber Sauce: In a small bowl, stir together ½ cup mayonnaise, ½ cup coarsely shredded peeled cucumber, 1 teaspoon grated lemon zest, 2 teaspoons lemon juice, 2 teaspoons minced cilantro, and a large pinch of cayenne pepper.

Tomato-Yogurt Sauce: In a small bowl, stir together 1 cup Greek yogurt, 2 diced plum tomatoes, 2 teaspoons ketchup, 1 teaspoon grated orange zest, ¼ teaspoon salt, and ¼ teaspoon pepper.

Red Pepper Puree: Puree Roasted Red Peppers (page 660) with 2 tablespoons sour cream.

Preheat the grill to high. Place the bell pepper on the grill and turn until the skin is charred on all sides. Set aside in a covered bowl. When cool enough to handle, peel and finely chop.

In a medium bowl, whisk together the oil and vinegar. Stir in the bell pepper, onion, celery, and parsley. Add salt and black pepper to taste.

Oil the grill grates. Sprinkle the sardines with salt and pepper. Grill until the fish just flakes when tested with a fork, about 3 minutes per side.

Serve with the sauce on the side.

MAKES 4 SERVINGS

SPICY GRILLED BLUEFISH

If you live in a part of the country where getting really fresh bluefish is a problem, make this with another firm-textured fresh fish, such as tilapia or cod.

¼ cup tomato-based chili sauce

2 tablespoons drained horseradish

2 teaspoons spicy brown mustard

2 teaspoons grated lemon zest

2 tablespoons lemon juice

¼ teaspoon pepper

4 bluefish fillets (4 ounces each)

In a shallow nonaluminum pan, combine the chili sauce, horseradish, mustard, lemon zest, lemon juice, and pepper. Add the fish, turning to coat. Set aside to marinate while you preheat the grill.

Preheat the grill. Lightly oil a grill grate.

Grill the bluefish covered, turning the fish once and basting with the marinade, for 10 to 15 minutes, or until the fish just flakes when tested with a fork.

MAKES 4 SERVINGS

BASS LATINO

If you really like spicy dishes, consider leaving the seeds in one or two of the peppers.

2 pounds striped bass or other firm-fleshed white fish fillets, cut into 4 chunks

½ teaspoon salt

¼ teaspoon pepper

½ cup flour

2 tablespoons plus ¼ cup olive oil

3 large onions, halved and thinly sliced

4 small fresh chili peppers, seeded and sliced into strips

½ teaspoon oregano

½ cup cider vinegar

Season the fish with the salt and pepper. Dredge in the flour, shaking off the excess.

In a large skillet, heat 2 tablespoons of the oil over medium heat. Add the fish and cook until the fish is golden brown and just flakes when tested with a fork, 3 to 4 minutes per side. Remove and keep warm.

Add the remaining ¼ cup oil to the skillet. Add the onions and chilies, and cook until the onions are tender. Add the oregano and cook 2 minutes longer. Add the vinegar, bring to a boil, and remove from the heat.

Serve the fish topped with the onion mixture.

MAKES 4 SERVINGS

SEARED HALIBUT WITH MÂCHE & ROASTED BEETS

You can substitute fillets of wild salmon, Pacific sole, hake, or striped bass for the halibut.

1 pound (3 to 4 medium) beets, scrubbed and quartered

- 5 tablespoons extra-virgin olive oil, plus more for drizzling
- Coarse salt and pepper
- 6 cups mâche or watercress (6 ounces)
- 2 cups diced peeled English (seedless) cucumber
- ⅓ cup plain whole-milk yogurt
- 1 tablespoon minced fresh tarragon or dill
- 4 skin-on halibut fillets (6 ounces each), 1 inch thick
- 2 tablespoons white balsamic or rice wine vinegar
- 2 tablespoons small capers

Preheat the oven to 425°F. Line an ovenproof skillet with foil. Place the beets on the foil, drizzle with a little olive oil, and sprinkle with some salt and pepper. Seal with more foil and roast for 35 to 40 minutes, until tender. When cool enough to handle, peel and slice.

Arrange the mâche on 4 plates. Top with the beets. Set aside. Toss the cucumber with the yogurt, half the tarragon, and a pinch of salt. Set aside.

Season the halibut with salt and pepper. Divide 3 tablespoons of the oil between 2 medium skillets, and place over medium-high heat until the oil is hot but not smoking. Place the fish in the pans skin-side up, reduce the heat to medium, and sear for 5 minutes. Turn and cook until the fish just flakes when tested with a fork, about 5 minutes longer. Transfer to a plate lined with paper towels, then transfer to the serving plates with the beets.

Drain the oil from 1 skillet and place over medium heat. Add the remaining 2 tablespoons oil, the remaining ½ tablespoon tarragon, the vinegar, capers, and a pinch of salt and pepper. Cook, stirring, for 30 seconds to heat up. Drizzle the warm vinaigrette over the fish, beets, and greens. Divide the cucumber salad among the plates and serve immediately.

MAKES 4 SERVINGS

HALIBUT WITH LEMON-CAPER SAUCE

Halibut is now available from Alaska almost year-round. If you can't find it, try Atlantic cod or sole instead.

- 1½ pounds halibut fillets
- Sea salt and pepper
- ½ cup flour
- 4 to 5 tablespoons extra-virgin olive oil
- ¼ cup nonpareil capers, rinsed and drained
- 2 tablespoons chopped shallots
- 1 teaspoon finely grated lemon zest
- 3 tablespoons lemon juice
- ¼ cup (½ cup) butter, cut into pieces
- 1 tablespoon chopped flat-leaf parsley

Season the halibut well on both sides with salt and pepper. Place the flour in a shallow bowl or pie plate.

In a 12-inch nonstick skillet, heat 2 tablespoons of the oil over medium-high heat. Dip half of the fish in the flour and place in the hot skillet. Cook, turning once, until the fish just flakes when tested with a fork and the edges are golden brown, 2 to 3 minutes. Transfer to a warm platter. Add another 1 tablespoon of oil to the skillet, if necessary, and repeat with the remaining fish.

After the fish is cooked, add the remaining 2 tablespoons oil, the capers, and shallots to the skillet. Cook until the shallots are golden, about 1 minute. Add the lemon zest and juice and bring to a boil. Simmer for 1 minute. Add ¼ teaspoon salt and a pinch of pepper. Remove from the heat and swirl in the butter and parsley. Spoon the sauce over the fish and serve.

MAKES 6 SERVINGS

CORNMEAL-FRIED CATFISH

When buying catfish, look for American farm-raised catfish. Unlike the river catfish of old, farmed catfish is sweet and mild.

2 pounds catfish fillets, thawed if frozen

3/4 teaspoon salt

1 teaspoon black pepper

1/4 teaspoon cayenne pepper

2 large eggs

1 1/2 cups cornmeal, preferably stone-ground

Canola oil, for shallow-frying

Cilantro-Lime Tartar Sauce (page 602)

Line a baking sheet with waxed paper. If the fillets are long, cut each piece in half crosswise. Lay the fillets on the waxed paper.

In a cup, mix the salt, black pepper, and cayenne. Sprinkle evenly over the catfish.

In a pie plate or shallow bowl, beat the eggs. Put the cornmeal in another pie plate or bowl.

One at a time, dip a piece of catfish into the eggs, letting the excess drip off. Coat the fish with the cornmeal, pressing it into the surface. Place the coated fish back on the waxed paper. Repeat with the remaining fish.

Preheat the oven to 250°F. Line another baking sheet with a double layer of paper towels.

In a large heavy skillet, warm 1/2 inch of oil over medium-high heat until hot but not smoking. (Test the heat by dropping in a piece of fish and seeing if it sizzles.) Add 3 or 4 pieces of fish and fry until golden on the underside, 3 to 5 minutes, depending on the thickness. Turn and fry until the fish is golden brown and just flakes when tested with a fork, 2 to 3 minutes longer. Drain on the paper towels, then transfer to an ovenproof platter and keep warm in the oven.

Repeat with the remaining fish, adding more oil to the skillet if necessary. Serve hot with the tartar sauce.

MAKES 6 SERVINGS

CARIBBEAN GROUPER

The combination of curry powder and coconut milk give this dish its Caribbean flavor. Make sure you buy coconut milk and not sweetened coconut cream. Once opened, transfer any remaining coconut milk to an ice cube tray and freeze.

1 1/2 cups orange juice

1/2 cup Fish Stock (page 173) or bottled clam juice

2 tablespoons lemon juice

2 tablespoons tomato paste

2 teaspoons curry powder

1 teaspoon ground ginger

1/2 teaspoon salt

1/2 teaspoon pepper

1 1/2 pounds sweet potatoes, swell scrubbed and thickly sliced

2 pounds grouper fillets, cut into large chunks

1/3 cup unsweetened coconut milk

1 large banana, sliced, for serving

1/4 cup almonds, toasted, for serving

In a large Dutch oven, bring the orange juice, fish stock, lemon juice, tomato paste, curry powder, ginger, salt, and pepper to a boil over high heat. Add the sweet potatoes and reduce to a simmer. Cover and cook until the sweet potatoes are barely fork-tender, about 15 minutes.

Push the sweet potatoes to the side of the pan and add the grouper and coconut milk. Cover and simmer until the fish just flakes when tested with a fork, 6 to 10 minutes.

Transfer the fish and sweet potatoes to a platter

and spoon some of the sauce over all. Garnish with the banana slices and toasted almonds. Serve the remaining sauce in a gravy boat.

MAKES 4 SERVINGS

FISH TACOS

While this recipe calls for cod, feel free to use whatever firm-fleshed white fish you like. You can make the cabbage and yogurt cream several hours ahead; just refrigerate until you're ready to use them.

- 2 teaspoons ground coriander
- 3/4 teaspoon paprika
- 1/2 teaspoon ground cumin
- 1/2 teaspoon salt
- 2 tablespoons plus 2 teaspoons lime juice
- 2 tablespoons vegetable oil
- 1 1/4 pounds cod fillets, 1 inch thick
- 8 ounces red cabbage, shredded
- 1/3 cup 0% Greek yogurt
- 3 tablespoons mayonnaise
- 1/4 cup chopped cilantro
- 2 teaspoons finely chopped fresh jalapeño pepper
- 8 flour tortillas (8 inches)

Preheat the oven to 425°F.

In a medium bowl, whisk together 1 teaspoon of the coriander, the paprika, cumin, and 1/4 teaspoon of the salt. Whisk in 2 tablespoons of the lime juice and oil.

Place the cod on a rimmed baking sheet and spoon 2 tablespoons of the lime mixture on top. Bake for 10 minutes, or until the fish just flakes when tested with a fork. Transfer to a bowl along with any of the pan juices.

Meanwhile, add the cabbage to the lime mixture remaining in the bowl and toss well.

In a separate bowl, whisk together the yogurt, mayonnaise, cilantro, jalapeño, and the remaining 2 teaspoons lime juice, 1 teaspoon coriander, and 1/4 teaspoon salt.

Using a pair of tongs, hold a tortilla over a burner and cook until lightly browned, about 10 seconds per side. Repeat with the remaining tortillas.

Let each person assemble his or her own tacos, spooning the fish, cabbage mixture, and yogurt mixture onto the tortillas.

MAKES 4 SERVINGS

COD CAKES

Instead of using eggs to bind the cod, this recipe uses mayonnaise. If you like, double or triple the recipe and freeze the uncooked extras to have on hand for a super-quick supper. There's no need to thaw before cooking.

- 2 tablespoons olive oil
- 1 small onion, minced
- 2 cups flaked cooked cod
- 1/3 cup soft whole-grain bread crumbs
- 1/4 cup chopped parsley
- 3 tablespoons mayonnaise
- 1 teaspoon smoked paprika
- 1/4 teaspoon salt
- Lemon wedges, for serving

In a medium skillet, heat 1 tablespoon of the oil over medium heat. Add the onion and cook, stirring occasionally, until golden brown, about 15 minutes.

Transfer the onion to a bowl and add the cod, bread crumbs, parsley, mayonnaise, paprika, and salt. Form into 4 patties. Cover and chill for 1 hour.

In a large skillet, heat the remaining 1 tablespoon oil over medium heat. Add the cod cakes and cook until golden brown and cooked through, about 4 minutes per side. Serve with lemon wedges.

MAKES 4 SERVINGS

SALT COD SALAD

Start a couple of days before you plan on serving this dish as the salt cod needs to soak. When shopping for salt cod, look for the thick, meaty, center-cut pieces.

- **1 pound thick-cut salt cod, cut into 4 pieces**
- **½ pound Yukon Gold potatoes**
- **2 tablespoons plus ¼ cup olive oil**
- **2 tablespoons red wine vinegar**
- **¼ teaspoon red pepper flakes**
- **¾ pound plum tomatoes, cut into ½-inch chunks**
- **⅓ cup kalamata olives, pitted**

Place the salt cod in a bowl of cold water to cover. Refrigerate, changing the water twice a day, for 3 days.

Place the potatoes in a medium saucepan of cold water. Bring to a boil over high heat. Reduce the heat to medium, and cook until the potatoes can be easily pierced with a knife, about 20 minutes. Drain. When the potatoes are cool enough to handle, slice them ½ inch thick.

Meanwhile, drain and pat dry the salt cod. In a large skillet, heat 2 tablespoons of the oil over medium heat. Add the salt cod, and cook until it is golden brown and can be easily pierced with a knife, about 5 minutes per side. Transfer to a plate. When cool enough to handle, shred the salt cod with a fork.

In a large bowl, whisk together the remaining ¼ cup oil, the vinegar, and red pepper flakes. Add the tomatoes and olives.

Add the potatoes and salt cod to the bowl and toss. Refrigerate until chilled.

MAKES 4 SERVINGS

SMOKED TROUT SALAD

Yuzu is a citrus fruit that has a flavor something like a Meyer lemon in that it is both sweet and tart. Yuzu juice is available in Japanese markets. If you can't find it, substitute more lemon juice and add a touch of sugar. Golden beets are luscious and slightly less earthy tasting than red beets.

- **¾ pound golden beets**
- **2 tablespoons olive oil**
- **3½ teaspoons lemon juice**
- **2 teaspoons yuzu juice**
- **½ teaspoon salt**
- **1 bunch watercress, thick stems trimmed**
- **2 endives, halved lengthwise and thinly sliced crosswise**
- **2 Asian pears, cut into ½-inch-thick wedges**
- **1 smoked trout (8 ounces), skin and bones removed**

Preheat the oven to 400°F. Rinse the beets, but do not peel. Wrap in foil and place on a baking sheet. Roast for 1 hour 15 minutes, or until the package yields to gentle pressure. When cool enough to handle, slip off the skins and cut the beets into thin wedges.

In a large bowl, whisk together the oil, lemon juice, yuzu juice, and salt. Add the watercress, endives, and Asian pear, and toss to coat.

Serve the beets and smoked trout on a bed of the salad.

MAKES 4 SERVINGS

Pappardelle with Asparagus & Oyster Mushrooms • *page 361*

High-Protein Vegetarian Chili ● *page 313*

Potato & Greens Fittata • *page 338*

Chipotle Turkey Burgers ● *page 257*

Chicken Breasts with Pine Nuts & Tangerines • *page 240*

Broiled Sirloin with Papaya Chutney • *page 205* and Nasturtium Salad • *page 378*

Pork Enchiladas with Feta ● *page 227*

Maple-Marinated Grilled Salmon • *page 282*

SPICY BAKED SALMON

Because salmon has such a rich, meaty flavor, it can stand up well to assertive flavors, like jalapeño and lime juice.

- **4 teaspoons olive oil**
- **1 small onion, finely chopped**
- **2 cloves garlic, minced**
- **1 teaspoon chili powder**
- **1 can (14.5 ounces) spicy diced tomatoes**
- **1 small pickled jalapeño pepper, minced**
- **¼ cup pitted green olives, coarsely chopped**
- **¼ teaspoon oregano**
- **¼ teaspoon thyme**
- **⅛ teaspoon cinnamon**
- **⅛ teaspoon salt**
- **¼ cup water**
- **4 salmon steaks (8 ounces each)**
- **2 tablespoons lime juice**

In a large skillet, heat the oil over medium heat. Add the onion and garlic, and cook until soft, about 5 minutes. Add the chili powder, stirring to coat.

Add the tomatoes, jalapeño, olives, oregano, thyme, cinnamon, salt, and water, and bring to a boil. Reduce to a simmer, cover, and cook for 30 minutes, or until the sauce is richly flavored.

Preheat the oven to 350°F.

Sprinkle the salmon with the lime juice and place in a 9 × 13-inch baking dish. Spoon ¾ cup of the sauce over the fish. Bake for 15 to 20 minutes, or until the salmon just flakes when tested with a fork. Reheat the remaining sauce and spoon over the fish before serving.

MAKES 4 SERVINGS

BROILED SALMON WITH MANGO-AVOCADO CHUTNEY

Salmon is rich in omega-3 fatty acids, a polyunsaturated fat known to help manage cholesterol levels. The mango-avocado mixture is what in Indian cuisine would be called a fresh chutney.

- **2½ teaspoons paprika**
- **2 teaspoons ground coriander**
- **¾ teaspoon salt**
- **4 skinless salmon fillets (6 ounces each)**
- **1 large mango, cut into ½-inch chunks (about 1½ cups)**
- **1 Hass avocado, cut into ½-inch chunks**
- **⅓ cup chopped cilantro**
- **2 tablespoons lemon juice**
- **2 teaspoons olive oil**
- **1 teaspoon curry powder**
- **6 cups frisée lettuce, torn into bite-size pieces, for serving**

Preheat the broiler. In a large bowl, stir together the paprika, coriander, and salt. Measure out 2 teaspoons of the mixture and sprinkle it over the salmon, rubbing it into the fish. Place the salmon, skinned-side down, on the broiler pan.

Broil the salmon 6 inches from the heat without turning for 5 minutes, or until the fish just flakes when tested with a fork.

Meanwhile, to the spice mixture remaining in the bowl, add the mango, avocado, cilantro, lemon juice, oil, and curry powder. Toss to combine.

Serve the salmon and chutney on a bed of frisée lettuce.

MAKES 4 SERVINGS

GRAPEFRUIT-BROILED SALMON

The tart, fresh flavor of grapefruit is a good match for the rich flavor of salmon.

- 3 tablespoons ruby grapefruit juice
- 2 teaspoons olive oil
- 1 teaspoon Dijon mustard
- ¼ teaspoon oregano
- ¼ teaspoon pepper
- 4 salmon fillets with skin (6 ounces each)

Preheat the broiler.

In a small bowl, blend the grapefruit juice, oil, mustard, oregano, and pepper.

Place the salmon, skin-side down, on the broiler pan. Brush with the grapefruit mixture. Broil 6 inches from the heat for 8 minutes, or until the fish just flakes when tested with a fork.

MAKES 4 SERVINGS

MAPLE-MARINATED GRILLED SALMON

Grade B maple syrup has a much deeper flavor than regular maple syrup.

- ⅓ cup maple syrup, preferably Grade B
- ¼ cup soy sauce
- 1 teaspoon cracked black pepper
- 2 cloves garlic, minced
- 1 large salmon fillet, with skin (2½ to 3 pounds)
- Cherry, apple, or alder wood chips
- Olive oil, for brushing
- Salt

In a small bowl, combine the maple syrup, soy sauce, pepper, and garlic. Place the salmon in a shallow glass or ceramic dish or in a gallon-size resealable plastic bag. (If using a bag, you may need to curl up the fillet or cut it in half.) Pour the marinade evenly over the salmon, cover the dish or seal the bag, and marinate in the refrigerator for up to 1 hour.

Meanwhile, soak the wood chips in cold water for at least 30 minutes.

If using a charcoal grill, prepare it for indirect heating: Pile the coals on each side of the grill, with a foil pan filled with about ¼ inch of water in the middle. If using a gas grill, heat it to medium heat. When the grill is ready, if using a charcoal grill, scatter the wet wood chips over the coals. If using a gas grill, wrap them loosely in foil, punch several holes in the foil, and place them over the heating element.

Remove the salmon from the marinade. Brush the salmon lightly with oil. If using a charcoal grill, place the salmon, skin-side down, in the center of the grill, over the water dish. It should not be directly over the charcoal. If using a gas grill, place the salmon on the grate so it is not directly over the burners. Cover the grill and cook the salmon for 35 to 45 minutes, or until the fish flakes easily but is still moist in the center. Season with salt to taste. Cut into serving sizes.

MAKES 6 SERVINGS

FRESH SALMON BURGERS

Occasionally a fish monger will have ends from the salmon (thin fillets) and may sell them at a discount. They would be perfect in this recipe since the salmon is getting chopped. Serve the burgers as they are, or place on whole-grain rolls and top with thick slices of tomato and slathers of additional mayo. For other mayo options, see "Mayo Variations," (page 603).

- **1½ pounds skinless salmon fillets, cut into chunks**
- **4 scallions, thinly sliced**
- **2 tablespoons mayonnaise**
- **1 tablespoon capers, finely chopped**
- **1 teaspoon grated lemon zest**
- **1 tablespoon lemon juice**
- **1 tablespoon vegetable oil**

In a food processor, pulse the salmon until finely chopped. Transfer to a bowl, add the scallions, mayonnaise, capers, lemon zest, and juice, and mix to combine. Shape into 4 patties. Place on a plate, cover, and refrigerate at least 30 minutes.

In a large skillet, heat the oil over medium heat. Add the patties and cook until just opaque throughout, about 4 minutes per side.

MAKES 4 SERVINGS

SALMON SALAD WITH ROASTED BEETS

Golden beets are beautiful paired with the pink-fleshed salmon, but red beets work well in this recipe too.

- **2 pounds beets**
- **⅓ cup natural (unblanched) almonds**
- **8 ounces whole wheat penne or ziti**
- **1 cup plain low-fat yogurt**
- **¼ cup lemon juice**
- **3 tablespoons balsamic vinegar**
- **1 tablespoon mayonnaise**
- **¼ teaspoon salt**
- **1 can (15 ounces) sockeye salmon, drained**
- **3 scallions, thinly sliced**

Preheat the oven to 400°F. Wrap the beets in foil, place on a baking sheet, and bake for 1 hour or until tender. While the oven is on, place the almonds on another baking sheet and roast for 5 to 7 minutes, until toasted. When cool enough to handle, coarsely chop.

Meanwhile, in a large pot of boiling water, cook the pasta according to the package directions. Drain.

Unwrap the cooked beets, and when they're cool enough to handle, peel and cut into ½-inch chunks.

In a large bowl, stir together the yogurt, lemon juice, vinegar, mayonnaise, and salt. Add the almonds, pasta, beets, salmon, and scallions, and toss to combine.

MAKES 4 SERVINGS

GRAVLAX-STYLE SALMON SALAD

If you don't want to use pumpernickel, feel free to substitute a multi-grain bread.

- **1 pound salmon fillets**
- **½ teaspoon salt**
- **2 teaspoons plus 3 tablespoons olive oil**
- **2 slices pumpernickel bread, cut into ½-inch cubes (2 cups)**
- **1 tablespoon coarse-grained mustard**
- **1 tablespoon balsamic vinegar**
- **2 teaspoons honey**
- **¼ cup snipped fresh dill**
- **3 kirby cucumbers, thinly sliced (2 cups)**
- **1 cup grape tomatoes, halved**
- **2 scallions, thinly sliced**

Preheat the oven to 450°F.

Place the salmon on a rimmed baking sheet, sprinkle with ¼ teaspoon of the salt, and drizzle with 2 teaspoons of the oil. Bake the salmon for 10 minutes, or until it just flakes when tested with a fork. At the same time, place the bread on another baking sheet, toss with 1 tablespoon of the oil, and bake for 5 minutes, or until lightly toasted.

Meanwhile, in a large bowl, whisk together the mustard, vinegar, honey, remaining 2 tablespoons oil, and remaining ¼ teaspoon salt. Stir in the dill. Add the cucumbers, tomatoes, scallions, and bread cubes.

Flake the fish, add to the bowl, and toss all to combine.

MAKES 4 SERVINGS

GRILLED FISH & WHITE BEAN SALAD

This is a perfect way to use up leftover grilled fish. Fish that has been cooked with almost any kind of seasoning—even teriyaki sauce—will be great here. Serve the salad on a bed of greens.

2 tablespoons extra-virgin olive oil

2 tablespoons lemon juice

1 teaspoon grated lemon zest

Coarse salt and pepper

1½ cups skinless grilled salmon or tuna pieces, broken into large chunks

2 cups cooked white beans

1 cup cooked green beans

1 cup grape tomatoes, halved

⅓ cup thinly sliced red onion

1½ teaspoons thinly shredded fresh sage or minced rosemary leaves

In a large bowl, whisk together the oil, lemon juice and zest, and pinch of salt and pepper.

Measure out 1 tablespoon of the dressing and toss with the salmon in a medium bowl.

To the remaining dressing in the large bowl, add the white beans, green beans, tomatoes, onion, and sage, and toss well.

Divide the vegetable mixture among 4 plates and top with the salmon. Serve at room temperature or chilled.

MAKES 4 SERVINGS

TUNA STEAK AU POIVRE

Add a little crushed coriander seed to the peppercorns for a citrus-y and slightly nutty touch.

3 tablespoons mixed black, pink, and white peppercorns

4 yellowfin tuna steaks (8 ounces each), 1 inch thick

Coarse salt

2 tablespoons vegetable oil

1 shallot, finely chopped

¼ cup brandy

½ cup heavy cream

Coarsely crush the peppercorns in a mortar and pestle or use the bottom of a heavy skillet. Spread the crushed peppercorns on a large plate. Season the tuna steaks on both sides with salt. Working with one steak at a time, lay a tuna steak onto the peppercorns and press one side down to adhere. Transfer the steaks to a plate, peppercorn-side up.

In large skillet, heat the oil over high heat. Arrange the steaks in the skillet peppercorn-side down and cook until well browned, about 3 minutes. Flip the steaks and continue cooking until slightly pink in the center, about 1 minute more. With a metal spatula, transfer the steaks to a plate and tent with foil to keep warm.

Return the skillet to the heat and add the shallot. Cook, stirring occasionally, until lightly browned, 1 to 2 minutes. Remove the skillet from the heat and add the brandy. Return to the heat and cook, stirring occasionally, until slightly reduced, about 30 seconds. Stir in the cream and cook, stirring occasionally, until the sauce is thick enough to coat the back of a spoon. Serve about 2 tablespoons of sauce with each steak.

MAKES 4 SERVINGS

SPICY GRILLED FRESH TUNA

For a change of pace, substitute cilantro or mint for the basil.

- 3 tablespoons minced fresh basil
- 2 cloves garlic, slivered
- ½ teaspoon salt
- 4 tuna steaks (6 ounces each), 1 inch thick
- 2 tablespoons ketchup
- 1 tablespoon green hot pepper (jalapeño) sauce

Preheat the grill or broiler.

In a small bowl, combine the basil, garlic, and salt. With a small, sharp knife, make several horizontal slits into the sides of each tuna steak. Insert the garlic-basil mixture into the slits.

In a small bowl, stir together the ketchup and hot pepper sauce. Rub each tuna steak all over with the mixture.

If grilling, oil the grates. Grill or broil the tuna steaks 6 inches from the heat for 3 minutes per side, or until the tuna is just slightly pink in the center.

MAKES 4 SERVINGS

CHICKPEA & TUNA SALAD

The tuna is not drained here, because the oil becomes part of the dressing for the salad.

- 1 small red onion, halved and thinly sliced
- 2 cloves garlic, smashed and peeled
- 3 tablespoons olive oil
- 1 can (6 to 7 ounces) tuna packed in olive oil (don't drain)
- 2 cups cooked chickpeas
- ¼ cup chopped parsley
- 1 teaspoon grated lemon zest
- 3 tablespoons lemon juice
- 1½ tablespoons white wine vinegar
- ¼ teaspoon pepper

In a medium bowl, combine the onion, garlic, and oil. Marinate for 1 hour at room temperature. Discard the garlic.

Add the tuna (and its oil), chickpeas, parsley, lemon zest, lemon juice, vinegar, and pepper.

MAKES 4 SERVINGS

BLACK BEAN & TUNA SALAD: Substitute black beans for the chickpeas and cilantro for the parsley.

NIÇOISE SALAD WRAP

A fresh tuna sandwich made with all of the components of a Niçoise salad: green beans, hard-cooked eggs, olives, tomatoes, and a vinaigrette.

- ¾ pound yellowfin tuna steaks
- 1 pound green beans
- 1 tablespoon lemon juice
- 1½ teaspoons white wine vinegar
- ½ teaspoon Dijon mustard
- 3 tablespoons olive oil
- 1 teaspoon tarragon
- ½ teaspoon coarse salt
- ½ teaspoon pepper
- 4 cups field greens
- 4 multi-grain sandwich wraps
- 16 cherry tomatoes, halved
- 2 hard-cooked eggs, sliced
- 16 pitted kalamata olives

Preheat the grill or broiler. Grill or broil the tuna 6 inches from the heat for 3 minutes per side, or until just slightly pink in the center. Allow to cool, and then flake.

In a steamer, cook the green beans until crisp-tender, 5 to 8 minutes. Cut into 1-inch pieces.

In a small bowl, combine the lemon juice, vinegar, and mustard. Slowly whisk in the olive oil until emulsified. Season with the tarragon, salt, and pepper.

For each sandwich, place salad greens across the lower half of a wrap. Top with green beans, tomatoes, egg, olives, and flaked tuna. Drizzle with 1 tablespoon of the dressing. Roll up burrito-style and cut on a diagonal to serve.

MAKES 4 SERVINGS

TUNA BURGERS

With their slightly Asian feel, these burgers would be great with a side of Thai Coleslaw with Napa Cabbage (page 381).

- 1½ pounds skinless tuna steaks, cut into chunks
- 2 tablespoons hoisin sauce
- 2 tablespoons Dijon mustard
- 2 tablespoons mayonnaise
- 1 tablespoon grated fresh ginger
- Salt (optional)
- 2 tablespoons vegetable oil

In a food processor, pulse the tuna until the consistency of ground beef. Transfer to a bowl and stir in the hoisin, mustard, mayonnaise, and ginger. Season with salt, if desired. Shape into 4 patties about 4 inches in diameter. Place on a plate, cover, and refrigerate for at least 30 minutes for the patties to firm up.

In a large skillet, heat the oil over medium heat. Add the patties and cook until browned, about 2 minutes per side for medium-rare (or longer if you prefer).

MAKES 4 SERVINGS

SEAFOOD GUMBO

If you have access to a good fishmonger, ask for 6 small to medium "gumbo crabs" and ask to have them cracked into quarters. If using whole crabs instead of crabmeat, cook for 30 minutes, adding the shrimp and oysters during the final 10 minutes of cooking time. Serve the gumbo over freshly cooked rice.

- 3 tablespoons vegetable oil
- 1 medium onion, chopped
- ½ cup chopped celery
- 1½ pounds okra, chopped
- 2 cups chopped plum tomatoes
- 3 bay leaves
- 2 tablespoons chopped parsley
- 2 tablespoons lemon juice
- ¾ teaspoon salt
- ½ teaspoon pepper
- ½ teaspoon cayenne pepper
- 6 cups water
- 1½ pounds lump crabmeat, picked over to remove any cartilage
- 1 pound medium shrimp, peeled and deveined
- 1 dozen small oysters, shucked

In a Dutch oven, heat the oil over medium heat. Add the onion and celery, and cook until the onion is tender, about 7 minutes. Add the okra, cover, and cook for 10 minutes, stirring frequently. If the okra begins to stick to the bottom of the pan, add a little water.

Add the tomatoes, bay leaves, parsley, lemon juice, salt, pepper, and cayenne. Cover and cook, stirring occasionally, until lightly thickened, about 20 minutes.

Add the 6 cups water and bring to a boil. Reduce to a simmer, cover, and cook for 1 hour.

Stir in the crab, shrimp, and oysters, and cook until the seafood is just cooked through, 10 to 15 minutes. Discard the bay leaves. Adjust the seasoning for desired hotness.

MAKES 8 TO 10 SERVINGS

SAUTÉED CLAMS OVER HERBED RICE

Look for clams that are on the smaller side, not chowder clams, which are not as tender as littlenecks.

- **6 cups water**
- **6 dozen littleneck clams, well scrubbed**
- **4 tablespoons olive oil**
- **1 medium onion, chopped**
- **1½ cups brown rice**
- **2 tablespoons lemon juice**
- **¾ teaspoon Italian herb seasoning, store-bought or homemade (page 407)**
- **¼ teaspoon cayenne pepper**
- **2 cloves garlic, minced**
- **¼ cup chopped parsley**

In a large pot, bring 3 cups of the water to a boil. Add the clams, cover, and steam until the clams open, 5 to 10 minutes (some may open before others, so take them out as they open). Discard any clams that don't open. Remove the clams from their shells, and set aside. Strain the broth through a double layer of cheesecloth set in a sieve, and reserve.

In a large saucepan, heat 1 tablespoon of the oil over medium heat. Add the onion and cook, stirring occasionally, until tender, about 7 minutes.

Add the remaining 3 cups water and bring to a boil. Add the rice, 1 tablespoon of the lemon juice, the Italian seasoning, and the cayenne. When the mixture returns to a boil, reduce to a simmer, cover, and cook until the rice is tender and no liquid remains, about 45 minutes.

In a large skillet, heat the remaining 3 tablespoons oil over medium heat. Add the clams and garlic, and cook until the garlic is tender, about 2 minutes. Add ¾ cup of the reserved broth, the remaining 1 tablespoon lemon juice, and the parsley. Serve the clam mixture spooned over the rice.

MAKES 4 SERVINGS

CHINESE-STYLE CRAB WITH MUSHROOMS & SNOW PEAS

This sauce would be perfect over a bowl of hot rice noodles. Serve with a drizzle of dark sesame oil.

- **3 tablespoons peanut oil**
- **¾ pound mushrooms, thinly sliced**
- **¼ pound snow peas, strings removed**
- **2 cloves garlic, thinly sliced**
- **4 thin slices fresh ginger**
- **½ teaspoon salt**
- **¾ pound king crabmeat, picked over to remove any cartilage**
- **1 cup chicken broth, store-bought or homemade (page 172)**
- **3 drops hot pepper sauce**
- **1 tablespoon cornstarch blended with ½ cup cold water**
- **2 scallions, minced**

In a large skillet, heat the oil over medium heat. Add the mushrooms, snow peas, garlic, ginger, and salt, and cook until the mushrooms have softened and the snow peas are bright green, about 3 minutes.

Add the crab, and cook for 1 minute. Add the broth and hot sauce, and bring to a boil. Stir in the cornstarch mixture and cook, stirring, until the sauce thickens, about 1 minute. Serve sprinkled with scallions.

MAKES 4 SERVINGS

SOUTHERN CRAB CAKES

In the South, crab cakes are on the spicy side and you will see that that is all to the good.

- **2 tablespoons butter**
- **½ red bell pepper, minced**
- **½ green bell pepper, minced**
- **3 scallions, minced**
- **¾ cup soft whole-grain bread crumbs (1½ slices)**
- **2 teaspoons Dijon mustard**
- **½ teaspoon Worcestershire sauce**
- **4 drops hot pepper sauce**
- **2 large eggs**
- **2 pounds lump crabmeat, picked over to remove any cartilage**
- **¾ cup plain dried whole wheat bread crumbs**
- **Vegetable oil, for frying**
- **Lemon wedges, for serving**

In a large skillet, melt the butter over low heat. Add the red and green bell peppers and the scallions, and cook until the peppers are soft, about 5 minutes. Transfer to a bowl and stir in the soft bread crumbs. Stir in the mustard, Worcestershire, hot sauce, and 1 of the eggs, until well combined. Gently fold in the crabmeat.

With wet hands, form the mixture into 12 balls, then flatten slightly with the palm of your hand. Chill for 15 minutes.

In a shallow bowl, beat the remaining egg. Place the dried bread crumbs in another bowl. Gently dip the cakes on both sides in the egg, then in the bread crumbs, patting to adhere. Chill again for 30 minutes.

Preheat the oven to 300°F.

In a large deep skillet, heat about ½ inch of oil until hot but not smoking. Fry a few crab cakes at a time, turning gently with a spatula, until browned on both sides. Drain on paper towels, and transfer to a baking sheet to keep warm in the oven. Serve with lemon wedges.

MAKES 12 CRAB CAKES

CRAB SALAD

This would be equally good as a sandwich on a whole-grain roll. Serve with coleslaw on the side.

- **⅓ cup mayonnaise**
- **2 teaspoons Dijon mustard**
- **1 teaspoon grated lemon zest**
- **2 teaspoons lemon juice**
- **½ teaspoon salt**
- **¼ teaspoon pepper**
- **4 scallions, thinly sliced**
- **1 rib celery, thinly sliced**
- **2 tablespoons chopped parsley**
- **2 cups lump crabmeat, picked over to remove any cartilage**
- **Salad greens, for serving**
- **Lemon wedges, for serving**

In a medium bowl, combine the mayonnaise, mustard, lemon zest, lemon juice, salt, and pepper. Stir in the scallions, celery, and parsley. Fold in the crab. Chill for at least 1 hour.

Serve on a bed of greens with lemon wedges on the side.

MAKES 4 SERVINGS

MARINATED CRAB

A recipe that takes care of itself while you do other things: Just mix the ingredients, allow 2 to 3 hours for the magic to work, and serve as a luncheon or buffet centerpiece, or as a summer supper dish.

- 2/3 cup olive oil
- 2 cloves garlic, minced
- 1½ teaspoons grated lemon zest
- 3 tablespoons lemon juice
- 1 tablespoon minced parsley
- 1 rib celery, minced
- 1 teaspoon oregano
- ½ teaspoon salt
- ⅛ teaspoon cayenne pepper
- 2 pounds crabmeat, picked over to remove any cartilage
- Salad greens for serving

In a medium bowl, combine the oil, garlic, lemon zest, and lemon juice. Add the parsley, celery, oregano, salt, and cayenne, and stir until all the seasonings are well blended. Stir in the crab, cover, and marinate in the refrigerator for 2 to 3 hours.

Serve the crab and marinade on a bed of spicy greens such as mizuna.

MAKES 4 TO 6 SERVINGS

SOFT-SHELL CRAB WITH GARLIC-GINGER MAYONNAISE

When you're picking out soft-shell crabs, they should be on the smallish side and moving a little to show they are still alive. As they get larger, their skin becomes harder. Feel free to omit the mayonnaise mixture, and simply serve the crab with lemon wedges.

- ⅓ cup mayonnaise
- 1 tablespoon lemon juice
- 1 teaspoon minced garlic
- 1 teaspoon ground ginger
- 6 soft-shell crabs
- ¾ cup flour
- ½ teaspoon salt
- ¼ teaspoon cayenne pepper
- ¼ cup vegetable oil
- Lemon wedges, for serving

In a small bowl, stir together the mayonnaise, lemon juice, garlic, and ginger.

Prepare the soft-shell crabs (see page 266).

In a shallow bowl, combine the flour, salt, and cayenne.

In a large skillet, heat the oil over medium-high heat. Dredge the crabs in the flour mixture, shaking off the excess. Cook in the hot oil until golden brown and lightly crisped, about 3 minutes per side.

Transfer the crabs to paper towels to drain. Serve the crabs with the mayonnaise and lemon wedges.

MAKES 3 SERVINGS

GARLIC LOBSTER WITH SAUTÉED VEGETABLES

This restaurant-style dish is easy to prepare at home and perfect for company. Serve over piping hot whole wheat linguine, brown rice, or barley.

- 2 tablespoons soy sauce
- 1 tablespoon sherry or dry white wine
- 1½ teaspoons rice vinegar
- 1 small slice fresh ginger
- 2 tablespoons peanut oil
- ½ cup diced carrots
- 1 cup sliced mushrooms

- 2 cups shredded napa cabbage
- 1 cup chopped bok choy
- 2½ tablespoons minced garlic
- 2 tablespoons chopped scallions
- ½ cup frozen peas, thawed
- 1 cup chicken broth, store-bought or homemade (page 172)
- 1 pound cooked lobster meat, diced
- 1 tablespoon cornstarch

In a small bowl, combine 1 tablespoon of the soy sauce, the sherry, vinegar, and ginger. Set the seasoning mixture aside.

In a large skillet or wok, heat the oil over medium heat. Add the carrots and mushrooms, and cook until the carrots are tender and the mushrooms begin to wilt, about 5 minutes.

Add the cabbage, bok choy, garlic, and scallions, and cook for 1 minute. Stir in the peas, ½ cup of the broth, the lobster, and the seasoning mixture, and bring to a boil.

Meanwhile, in a small bowl, combine the cornstarch, the remaining ½ cup broth, and the remaining 1 tablespoon soy sauce.

As soon as the vegetables and broth come to a boil, add the cornstarch mixture. Cook, stirring constantly, until the sauce is lightly thickened, about 1 minute.

MAKES 4 SERVINGS

LOBSTER SALAD WITH AVOCADO & MANGO

This would also make a great sandwich: Lightly mash the avocado and spread it on 4 or 6 slices of bread; top with the lobster salad. Omit the mango.

- ⅓ cup mayonnaise
- 3 tablespoons chopped cilantro
- 2 tablespoons lime juice
- 1 cup cooked lobster meat, diced
- Salad greens
- 1 Hass avocado, sliced
- 1 mango, sliced
- Lime wedges, for serving

In a medium bowl, stir together the mayonnaise, cilantro, and lime juice. Stir in the lobster.

Spoon the lobster salad onto a bed of greens. Arrange the avocado and mango around the lobster. Serve with lime wedges.

MAKES 2 TO 3 SERVINGS

MUSSELS IN CARROT JUICE

Mussels attach themselves to objects underwater by means of strong fibrous strands called byssus, or beard. To clean mussels, you need to pull the beard out from between the shells.

- 1½ cups carrot juice
- 3 scallions, thinly sliced
- 3 cloves garlic, minced
- 1 tablespoon minced fresh ginger
- ½ teaspoon salt
- ¼ teaspoon cayenne pepper
- 4 pounds mussels, well scrubbed and debearded
- 8 slices whole wheat baguette, for serving
- 2 tablespoons olive oil
- 2 teaspoons lemon juice

In a Dutch oven or large saucepan, bring the carrot juice, scallions, garlic, ginger, salt, and cayenne to a boil over high heat. Add the mussels, cover, and cook until the mussels have opened, 5 to 7 minutes. Discard any that have not opened.

Meanwhile, preheat the broiler. Brush both sides of

the bread with the oil. Broil 4 inches from the heat for 30 seconds per side, or until golden brown.

With a large slotted spoon, scoop out the mussels and divide among 4 serving bowls. Stir the lemon juice into the broth, and spoon it over the mussels. Serve the toasted bread alongside.

MAKES 4 SERVINGS

MUSSELS WITH WHITE WINE & SHALLOTS

This would work equally well with littleneck clams: Use 3 to 4 dozen clams in place of the mussels, and omit the salt. Follow the same procedure, but clams may take a little longer to cook.

- **2 tablespoons olive oil**
- **4 shallots, minced (about 1 cup)**
- **3 cloves garlic, minced**
- **1 cup dry white wine**
- **½ teaspoon salt**
- **4 pounds mussels, well scrubbed and debearded**
- **¼ cup chopped parsley**

In a Dutch oven or large saucepan, heat the oil over low heat. Add the shallots and garlic, and cook, stirring occasionally, until the shallots are tender, about 5 minutes.

Add the wine and salt, increase the heat to high, and bring to a boil. Add the mussels, cover the pan, and cook until the mussels have opened, 5 to 7 minutes. Discard any that do not open.

Spoon the mussels into 4 serving bowls. Add the parsley to the broth and spoon over the mussels.

MAKES 4 SERVINGS

OYSTER STEW

Oysters cook in a very gently simmering combination of milk and light cream. Serve with oyster crackers.

- **5 tablespoons butter**
- **2 tablespoons finely chopped onion**
- **1 dozen small oysters, shucked, liquor reserved**
- **1 cup milk**
- **1 cup light cream**
- **⅛ teaspoon pepper**

In a small skillet, melt 2 tablespoons of the butter over low heat. Add the onion and cook until soft, about 5 minutes.

In a double boiler or in a large saucepan, melt the remaining 3 tablespoons butter over very low heat. Stir in the onion, oysters and their liquor, milk, cream, and pepper, and cook until the oysters are opaque and have started to curl around the edges, about 10 minutes. If cooking in a saucepan, make sure the stew does not boil.

MAKES 4 SERVINGS

SAUTÉED BAY SCALLOPS

Cornstarch makes a lighter coating than flour for tender, sweet scallops.

- **1½ pounds small bay scallops**
- **½ cup cornstarch**
- **½ teaspoon salt**
- **3 tablespoons vegetable oil**
- **3 tablespoons butter**
- **¼ cup chopped parsley**
- **3 tablespoons lemon juice**

Dry the scallops well and dust lightly with the cornstarch. Sprinkle with the salt.

In a large skillet, heat the oil and butter over medium heat until the butter has melted. Add the scallops, working in batches if necessary to prevent crowding, and cook until the scallops are just opaque, 2 to 3 minutes.

Sprinkle with parsley and lemon juice.

MAKES 4 SERVINGS

HOT & SPICY SCALLOPS

If your scallops are not particularly thick, or if you use bay scallops, there's no need to cut them in half before cooking.

- 3 tablespoons peanut oil
- 1 large carrot, thinly sliced
- 2 cups thinly sliced mushrooms
- 5 thin slices fresh ginger, slivered
- 1½ teaspoons red pepper flakes
- 2 tablespoons chopped garlic
- 2 cups Fish Stock (page 173) or bottled clam juice
- 1 cup frozen peas
- 3 tablespoons soy sauce
- 1 tablespoon rice vinegar
- 6 scallions, cut lengthwise into quarters
- 2 pounds sea scallops, halved horizontally
- 2 tablespoons cornstarch blended with 2 tablespoons water

In a wok or large skillet, heat the oil over medium heat. Add the carrot, mushrooms, ginger, and pepper flakes, and cook until the carrot is crisp-tender, about 5 minutes. Add the garlic and cook, stirring frequently, for another 2 minutes.

Add the stock, peas, soy sauce, vinegar, and scallions. Bring the liquid to a slow boil and add the scallops. Cover and cook until the scallops are just opaque, about 2 minutes. Do not overcook.

Stir the cornstarch mixture into the wok and cook, stirring, until thickened. Adjust the seasonings for a spicier flavor if desired.

MAKES 4 TO 6 SERVINGS

GRILLED SCALLOPS WITH NOODLE SALAD

To make it easier to turn them on the grill, thread two wooden skewers horizontally through the scallops.

- 4 tablespoons lower-sodium soy sauce
- 2 teaspoons grated lime zest
- 1 pound sea scallops
- 8 ounces whole wheat linguine
- ¼ cup lime juice (2 to 3 limes)
- 3 tablespoons honey
- 1 tablespoon dark sesame oil
- ½ teaspoon anchovy paste
- ¼ teaspoon hot pepper sauce
- 1½ cups diced mango
- 1 cup shredded savoy cabbage
- 2 carrots, shredded
- 2 cloves garlic, minced
- ¼ cup chopped cilantro
- 2 tablespoons chopped fresh basil
- ½ teaspoon dried mint

Soak wooden skewers in a pan of cold water for 15 minutes.

In a medium bowl, combine 1 tablespoon of the soy sauce, 1 teaspoon of the lime zest, and the scallops. Set aside to marinate at room temperature while you make the noodle salad.

In a large pot of boiling salted water, cook the pasta according to the package directions. Drain well and rinse under cold water.

Meanwhile, in a large bowl, combine the remaining 3 tablespoons soy sauce, remaining 1 teaspoon lime zest, the lime juice, honey, sesame oil, anchovy paste, and hot sauce. Add the mango, cabbage, carrots, garlic, cilantro, basil, and mint, tossing to coat. Add the drained pasta, tossing gently to combine.

Preheat the grill to medium. Oil the grill grate. Thread the scallops onto skewers and grill, covered, turning once, until just opaque, 9 to 11 minutes. Watch carefully.

Serve the scallops on a bed of the noodle salad. Drizzle any dressing remaining in the salad bowl over the scallops.

MAKES 4 SERVINGS

MARINATED SHRIMP STIR-FRY

For a change of pace, swap in scallops or chunks of chicken or pork for the shrimp.

MARINATED SHRIMP

- 2 tablespoons rice vinegar
- 2 teaspoons soy sauce
- 2 teaspoons cornstarch
- 2 teaspoons ketchup
- 2 tablespoons water
- 1 pound medium shrimp, peeled and deveined

SAUCE

- ½ cup chicken broth, store-bought or homemade (page 172)
- 2 teaspoons cornstarch
- 2 teaspoons soy sauce
- 2 teaspoons honey

STIR-FRY

- 4 tablespoons safflower or peanut oil
- 4 cloves garlic, minced
- 1-inch piece fresh ginger, peeled and minced
- 6 shiitake mushrooms, stems discarded, caps thinly sliced
- 1 head napa cabbage, quartered lengthwise and thickly sliced crosswise
- 4 scallions, white and green parts separated and thinly sliced

To make the marinated shrimp: In a medium bowl, mix together the vinegar, soy sauce, cornstarch, ketchup, and water. Add the shrimp, turning to coat. Cover and marinate in the refrigerate for 2 to 3 hours. Reserving the marinade, drain the shrimp.

To make the sauce: In a small bowl, mix together the broth, cornstarch, soy sauce, and honey. Stir in the reserved shrimp marinade.

To make the stir-fry: In a wok or large skillet, heat 1 tablespoon of the oil over medium-high heat. When a small piece of scallion dropped in the oil dances around, the oil is ready.

Add half the shrimp, and stir-fry until opaque throughout. Transfer to a bowl. Repeat with the remaining shrimp.

Add the remaining 3 tablespoons oil to the wok and heat over medium heat. Add the garlic and ginger, and cook for 1 minute. Add the mushrooms, cabbage, and scallion whites. Add the sauce and cook, stirring constantly, until thickened. Return the shrimp to the wok and cook until warmed, about 1 minute.

Serve garnished with the scallion greens.

MAKES 4 SERVINGS

ITALIAN-STYLE BROILED GARLIC SHRIMP

If you like, you can leave the tails on the shrimp for a nice presentation. Serve as they are, or toss with hot cooked pasta.

- 3 tablespoons butter, melted
- 2 tablespoons olive oil
- 2 tablespoons lemon juice
- 1 large clove garlic, minced
- ½ teaspoon salt
- ¼ teaspoon pepper
- 2 pounds large shrimp, peeled and deveined
- 2 tablespoons minced parsley, for serving

Preheat the broiler. Line a broiler pan with foil.

In a large bowl, combine the butter, oil, lemon juice, garlic, salt, and pepper. Add the shrimp and stir until well coated.

Remove the shrimp from the butter mixture and arrange in a single layer on the broiler pan. Pour the butter mixture remaining in the bowl over all. Broil for 2 minutes. Turn with tongs and broil for 2 to 3 minutes longer, or until the shrimp are opaque throughout. Transfer, with the cooking juices, to a serving platter and sprinkle with the parsley.

MAKES 4 TO 6 SERVINGS

SIZZLING CHIPOTLE & GARLIC SHRIMP

This dish is prepared in two batches, because if you overcrowd the pan the shrimp will steam and not sauté. Assemble half of the shrimp-topped tortillas before going back and making the second batch.

- 6 tablespoons butter
- 4 large cloves garlic, minced
- 2 pounds large shrimp, peeled and deveined
- 1 teaspoon coarse salt
- 2 large chipotle peppers in adobo sauce, finely minced
- 2 tablespoons lime juice
- 4 tablespoons golden tequila
- Black pepper
- ½ cup chopped cilantro, plus sprigs for garnish
- 12 corn tortillas
- ½ head green cabbage, finely shredded
- Lime wedges, for serving

Heat a 12-inch skillet over medium-high heat. Melt 2 tablespoons of the butter in the skillet and add half of the minced garlic. When the garlic starts to sizzle, add half of the shrimp and sprinkle with ½ teaspoon of the salt. Cook, stirring occasionally, until the shrimp starts to curl up and turn pink, about 1½ minutes.

Add half the chipotles to the pan and toss to coat the shrimp. Increase the heat to high, and stir in 1 tablespoon of the lime juice and 2 tablespoons of the tequila. Bring to a boil and cook, stirring and flipping the shrimp until the shrimp are opaque throughout, 1 to 1½ minutes. Stir in 1 tablespoon butter to form a light sauce. Remove from the heat, season with a little black pepper, and toss with ¼ cup of the cilantro.

Heat 6 corn tortillas in a cast-iron or on a flat griddle over medium-high heat until they are warm and pliable and the scent of toasted corn fills the air. Fill each tortilla with a little shredded cabbage, about 4 shrimp, and a little of the pan sauce. Garnish with cilantro sprigs and serve with lime wedges.

Repeat with the remaining shrimp and the rest of the sauce ingredients.

MAKES 6 SERVINGS

CAJUN-STYLE GRILLED SHRIMP

If you have a high tolerance for spice heat, add hot pepper sauce to the corn mixture.

- 1¾ teaspoons light brown sugar
- 1½ teaspoons oregano
- ¾ teaspoon thyme
- ¾ teaspoon salt
- ½ teaspoon black pepper
- ¼ teaspoon cayenne pepper
- 1½ pounds large shrimp, peeled and deveined
- 2 teaspoons vegetable oil
- ⅓ cup ketchup
- 2 tablespoons plus 2 teaspoons red wine vinegar
- ½ teaspoon ground ginger
- 2 cups frozen corn kernels, thawed
- 2 scallions, thinly sliced

In a medium bowl, combine 1 teaspoon of the brown sugar, the oregano, thyme, salt, black pepper, and cayenne. Add the shrimp and oil, tossing to coat. Cover and refrigerate for 30 minutes.

Meanwhile, combine the ketchup, vinegar, remaining ¾ teaspoon brown sugar, and the ginger. Stir in the corn and scallions.

Preheat the broiler. Broil the shrimp 6 inches from the heat, turning once, for 4 minutes, or until opaque throughout. Toss the hot shrimp with the corn mixture.

MAKES 4 SERVINGS

THAI SHRIMP GREEN CURRY

The flavor of this dish is dependent on the quality of the curry paste (a heady mixture of lemongrass, chilies, kaffir lime leaves, and shrimp paste), so try to find an authentic brand such as Mae Ploy or Maesri, both of which are available in most Asian markets and online.

- 2 tablespoons vegetable oil
- 6 tablespoons Thai green curry paste
- 1 medium carrot, thinly sliced on the diagonal
- 1 small Japanese eggplant, halved lengthwise and thinly sliced on the diagonal
- 1 red bell pepper, cut into 1-inch pieces
- ½ medium zucchini, thinly sliced on the diagonal
- 6 ounces green beans, cut into 1-inch pieces
- 2 cans (13.5 ounces each) unsweetened coconut milk
- 1 cup cold water
- 3 tablespoons fish sauce
- 2 tablespoons lime juice
- 2 tablespoons muscovado or dark brown sugar
- 1½ pounds medium shrimp, peeled and deveined
- 3 scallions, thinly sliced on the diagonal
- ½ cup chopped cilantro

In a large pot, heat the oil over medium-high heat. Add the curry paste and cook, stirring constantly, until fragrant, 1 to 2 minutes. Add the carrot, eggplant, bell pepper, zucchini, and green beans, and cook, stirring occasionally, until somewhat soft, about 3 minutes.

Add the coconut milk, water, fish sauce, lime juice, and brown sugar, and bring to a boil over high heat. Reduce the heat to medium and simmer, stirring occasionally, until the vegetables are crisp-tender, about 8 minutes.

Add the shrimp and scallions, and cook, stirring occasionally, until the shrimp are opaque throughout, about 3 minutes. Stir in the cilantro.

MAKES 6 SERVINGS

ASIAN CALAMARI SALAD

The herbal combination of fresh basil, cilantro, and mint is especially refreshing in this squid salad. If you like, toss with some noodles for a cold noodle salad.

½ cup olive oil

⅓ cup lime juice (about 3 limes)

1 clove garlic, finely chopped

½ teaspoon salt

¼ teaspoon pepper

4 pounds baby squid, cleaned, bodies cut into ½-inch-wide rings, tentacles left whole

1 small yellow bell pepper, diced

¼ cup chopped fresh basil

3 tablespoons chopped cilantro

3 tablespoons chopped fresh mint

In a large bowl, whisk together the oil, lime juice, garlic, salt, and pepper.

In a steamer, cook the squid until tender, about 4 minutes. Transfer the squid to the bowl with the dressing.

Add the bell pepper, basil, cilantro, and mint, and toss to combine. Refrigerate for at least 2 hours or up to overnight.

MAKES 6 SERVINGS

Meatless Main Courses

There is indisputable evidence that eating a diet rich in fruits, vegetables, and grains is good for your health. Any health-conscious person has certainly made an effort to add those foods to their dietary choices; some have chosen to forego animal foods all together. But it doesn't need to be all or nothing. You can adopt any vegetarian diet (below) to improve your health—as long as the meat or poultry you leave out is replaced by vegetables and grains.

The recipes in this chapter include dairy and eggs, but no meat, poultry, or fish. A handful of them are vegan (see "Vegan Main Courses," page 306, for the list of recipes).

Types of Vegetarians

Vegan: Excludes all animal-derived foods, including meat, poultry, fish, dairy, eggs, honey, and any food that processed with animal products

Lacto vegetarian: Excludes meat, poultry, fish, and eggs, but includes dairy

Ovo vegetarian: Excludes meat, poultry, fish, and dairy, but includes eggs.

Lacto-ovo vegetarian: Excludes meat, poultry, and fish, but includes dairy and eggs

Pesco vegetarian: Excludes meat and poultry, but includes dairy, eggs, and fish

Flexitarian: Includes dairy, eggs, fish, and poultry, and only occasional meat

What about Protein?

The body needs protein to repair itself. Protein provides the building blocks (amino acids) necessary to keep bodily tissues healthy. The dietary recommendation for protein intake is 50 to 65 grams per day (the actual amount depends largely on body weight). This is definitely not a problem for those who eat meat (the most efficient source of protein), but it can be a problem for those who eat no meat. Luckily, plant foods also supply protein. Substituting plant protein for some of the meat in your diet immediately translates into reduced consumption of saturated fat and a higher intake of valuable dietary fiber. The best plant sources of protein are legumes, nuts, seeds, and many grains. See "Protein in Various Plant Sources," page 298.

Complementary Protein

Most plant sources of protein are deficient in certain "essential" amino acids that are required for sustaining human life. However, if you combine certain plant foods at the same meal, or even in the same day, they can supplement one another's missing amino acids. This concept seems to have been instinctive to many cultures where meat has played a small or nonexistent role in the diet. Consider the traditional black beans and rice of South America, corn tortillas and pinto beans of Mexico, polenta (cornmeal and cheese) of Italy, as well as pasta (wheat) dishes that include beans or cheese.

Soyfoods

Soyfoods are especially important in meatless diets because they are among the best concentrated sources of plant protein. For all the different forms of soyfoods, see page 84.

PROTEIN IN VARIOUS PLANT SOURCES

FOOD	SERVING SIZE	PROTEIN (G)
TEMPEH	4 ounces	24
SOYBEANS, COOKED	1 cup	22
LENTILS, COOKED	1 cup	18
EDAMAME, SHELLED	¾ cup	17
BLACK BEANS, COOKED,	1 cup	15
CHICKPEAS, COOKED	1 cup	15
KIDNEY BEANS, COOKED	1 cup	15
TVP, DRY	½ cup	15
LIMA BEANS, BABY, COOKED	1 cup	12
TOFU, FIRM	4 ounces	9.2
PEANUT BUTTER	2 tablespoons	8.1
WHEATBERRIES, COOKED	¾ cup	8.1
GREEN PEAS, COOKED	1 cup	7.5
PASTA, WHOLE-WHEAT, COOKED	1 cup	7.5
QUINOA, COOKED	1⅓ cups	7.4
PUMPKIN SEEDS, HULLED	1 ounce	7
SOYMILK	1 cup	6.7
FLAXSEED	¼ cup	6.7
PEANUTS	1 ounce	6.7
SUNFLOWER SEEDS	1 ounce	6.5
BULGUR WHEAT, COOKED	1 cup	5.6
TOFU, SOFT SILKEN	4 ounces	5.4
BARLEY, PEARLED, COOKED	1 cup	5
RICE, BROWN, COOKED	1 cup	5

WARM FRENCH LENTIL SALAD WITH GOAT CHEESE

The flavors of this salad are best when it is served warm, but you could also make it well ahead and serve at room temperature.

- 2 cups water
- 1 cup French (du Puy) lentils
- 1 teaspoon oregano
- ½ teaspoon salt
- ¼ teaspoon pepper
- 2 large carrots, diced
- 1 pint grape tomatoes, halved
- ½ cup chopped sweet onion, such as Vidalia
- ¼ cup chopped cilantro
- 3 tablespoons olive oil
- 2 tablespoons white wine vinegar
- 1 tablespoon lemon juice
- 1 tablespoon Dijon mustard
- 6 cups baby spinach leaves
- 1 cup crumbled mild goat cheese (4 ounces)

In a medium saucepan, bring the water to a boil over medium-high heat. Add the lentils, oregano, salt, and pepper. Reduce the heat to low, cover, and simmer for 15 minutes.

Add the carrots and cook until the lentils are just tender, about 10 minutes. Drain in a colander.

Meanwhile, in a large bowl, combine the tomatoes, onion, cilantro, oil, vinegar, lemon juice, and mustard.

Add the drained lentils to the tomato mixture. Serve the salad warm on a bed of baby spinach sprinkled with the goat cheese.

MAKES 4 SERVINGS

BLACK & WHITE BEAN SALAD WITH ORZO

If you're cooking your own beans for this, do not be tempted to cook the two together, because the black beans will turn the white beans gray. Serve the salad on a bed of lettuce or watercress.

- 8 ounces whole wheat orzo
- 1 teaspoon plus ½ cup olive oil
- ¼ cup white wine vinegar
- ½ teaspoon oregano
- ¼ teaspoon salt
- ⅛ teaspoon pepper
- 1 small clove garlic, smashed and peeled
- 1 cup cooked cannellini beans
- 1 cup cooked black beans
- 4 hard-cooked eggs, chopped
- 1 small Vidalia onion, minced
- 4 medium tomatoes, chopped
- 1 cup shredded part-skim mozzarella cheese (4 ounces)

In a large pot of boiling water, cook the pasta according to the package directions. Drain, toss with 1 teaspoon of the oil, and chill.

In a screw-top jar, combine the remaining ½ cup oil, the vinegar, oregano, salt, pepper, and garlic. Shake well and set aside to develop flavor.

In a large bowl, combine the chilled pasta, beans, eggs, onion, tomatoes, and mozzarella.

Pour the dressing over the salad (taking care to hold back the garlic) and toss to coat.

MAKES 4 SERVINGS

BLACK & TAN SALAD: Use chickpeas instead of cannellini and smoked mozzarella instead of regular. Add 1 teaspoon dark sesame oil to the dressing.

GREEK SALAD WITH CANNELLINI

The basic Greek salad of vinaigrette-dressed greens with red onion and tangy feta cheese gets a protein boost with the addition of white beans.

DRESSING

- 3 tablespoons extra-virgin olive oil
- 2 tablespoons red wine vinegar
- 1 tablespoon lemon juice
- 1 small clove garlic, minced
- 1 teaspoon minced fresh oregano or ½ teaspoon dried
- ½ teaspoon salt
- ½ teaspoon pepper

SALAD

- 4 cups mixed field greens
- 2 cups cooked cannellini beans
- 5 plum tomatoes, cut lengthwise into eighths
- 2 cucumbers, halved lengthwise, seeded, and cut into chunks
- ½ cup thinly sliced red onion
- ½ cup crumbled feta cheese (2 ounces)
- 12 pitted kalamata or other brine-cured black olives, quartered
- Lemon wedges, for serving

To make the dressing: In a salad bowl, whisk together the oil, vinegar, lemon juice, garlic, oregano, salt, and pepper.

To make the salad: Add the greens, cannellini, tomatoes, cucumbers, onion, feta, and olives to the dressing, and toss to mix. Serve with the lemon wedges.

MAKES 4 SERVINGS

COUSCOUS, PEPPER & CHICKPEA SALAD

Whole wheat couscous has a somewhat heartier flavor than regular. It can usually be found alongside regular couscous in the grains aisle of your supermarket. Using a fork to fluff the grains prevents the couscous from packing down and becoming lumpy.

- 2 cups water
- 1½ cups whole wheat couscous
- 1 carrot, quartered lengthwise and thinly sliced crosswise
- ¾ teaspoon salt
- ¼ teaspoon pepper
- ¼ cup olive oil
- ⅓ cup lemon juice (about 2 lemons)
- 1¾ cups cooked chickpeas
- Marinated Roasted Red Peppers (page 660), cut into 1-inch pieces
- 1 cup fresh mint leaves, torn
- 4 ounces mild goat or feta cheese, crumbled

In a small saucepan, bring the water to a boil. Add the couscous, carrot, salt, and pepper, and remove from the heat. Cover and let stand for 5 minutes, until the water has been absorbed.

With a fork, gently stir in the oil and lemon juice. Add the chickpeas and fluff with the fork. Let cool to room temperature.

With a fork, fold in the roasted peppers, mint, and goat cheese. Serve at room temperature or chilled.

MAKES 4 TO 6 SERVINGS

BARLEY SALAD WITH SHIITAKES & FETA

If you can't get fresh tarragon, just add 2 teaspoons dried tarragon to the mushrooms when you cook them.

- 6½ cups water
- 2 cups pearled barley
- 2 teaspoons grated lemon zest
- ¾ teaspoon salt
- 3 cloves garlic, minced
- 1 tablespoon plus ¼ cup lemon juice (about 2 lemons)
- ½ pound shiitake mushrooms, stems discarded, caps thinly sliced
- ½ pound button mushrooms, thinly sliced
- 3 tablespoons olive oil
- ½ teaspoon pepper
- 8 scallions, thinly sliced
- 2 tablespoons chopped fresh tarragon
- 1¼ cups crumbled feta cheese (5 ounces)

In a medium saucepan, bring 6 cups of the water to a boil over medium heat. Add the barley, lemon zest, and ¼ teaspoon of the salt. Reduce to a simmer, cover, and cook until the barley is tender, 30 to 40 minutes. Drain. Set aside.

Meanwhile, in a large skillet, combine the remaining ½ cup water, the garlic, and 1 tablespoon of the lemon juice. Bring to a boil over medium heat. Simmer for 1 minute until the garlic is fragrant.

Add the shiitake and button mushrooms, cover, and cook until just tender, about 5 minutes.

In a large bowl, combine the remaining ¼ cup lemon juice, remaining ½ teaspoon salt, the oil, and pepper. Add the barley, mushrooms (and their cooking liquid, if any), scallions, and tarragon.

Sprinkle the feta on top and toss well. Serve warm, at room temperature, or chilled.

MAKES 4 SERVINGS

INDONESIAN VEGETABLE SALAD

To seed a cucumber, cut it in half lengthwise and use the tip of a spoon to scrape out the seeds.

- 1 pound red potatoes, cut into ½-inch cubes
- ¾ pound shelled edamame
- ¼ cup lower-sodium soy sauce
- ¼ cup water
- 3 tablespoons lime juice (1 to 2 limes)
- 3 tablespoons peanut butter
- 2 teaspoons muscovado or dark brown sugar
- 2 cloves garlic, peeled
- ¼ teaspoon red pepper flakes
- 16 soft lettuce leaves, such as Boston or Bibb
- 2 cups bean sprouts
- 2 tomatoes, cut into 8 wedges each
- 1 cucumber, peeled, halved lengthwise, seeded, and thinly sliced
- 2 cups fresh or juice-packed canned pineapple chunks

In a large pot of boiling salted water, cook the potatoes until tender, about 7 minutes. With a slotted spoon, transfer the potatoes to a bowl. Add the edamame to the boiling water and cook until tender, about 4 minutes. Drain and add to the potatoes.

Meanwhile, make the peanut sauce: In a mini food processor, combine the soy sauce, water, lime juice, peanut butter, brown sugar, garlic, and red pepper flakes, and process to a smooth puree.

Line 4 plates with the lettuce leaves. Top with the bean sprouts, tomatoes, cucumber, and pineapple. Spoon the potatoes and edamame on top, and drizzle the peanut sauce over all.

MAKES 4 SERVINGS

MUSHROOM & SPINACH SALAD WITH ROASTED GARLIC-TOFU DRESSING

The protein in this salad comes from the tofu dressing.

- 1 head garlic (3½ ounces)
- 1 pound silken tofu
- 1½ teaspoons grated lemon zest
- ¼ cup lemon juice
- 1 tablespoon dark sesame oil
- ¾ teaspoon salt
- 1 tablespoon olive oil
- ½ pound shiitake mushrooms, stems discarded, caps thinly sliced
- ½ pound button mushrooms, thinly sliced
- 1 pound spinach leaves, torn into bite size pieces (16 cups)
- 3 cups halved cherry tomatoes

Preheat the oven to 400°F. Wrap the garlic in foil, place on a baking sheet, and bake for 45 minutes, or until the foil package feels soft to the touch. When cool enough to handle, unwrap, cut off the top of the bulb, and squeeze the garlic pulp into a blender or food processor. Add the tofu, lemon zest, lemon juice, sesame oil, and salt, and process until smooth.

In a large nonstick skillet, heat the olive oil over medium heat. Add the shiitake and button mushrooms, and cook, stirring frequently, until the mushrooms are tender, about 5 minutes.

Pour the dressing into a large serving bowl. Add the mushroom mixture, spinach, and tomatoes, and toss well to coat.

MAKES 4 SERVINGS

INDIVIDUAL CREMINI-ZUCCHINI PIZZAS

You can serve these thin and crispy single-portion pizzas hot or at room temperature. They're also fun to make with kids.

- Yellow cornmeal, for sprinkling
- 1 tablespoon olive oil, plus more for drizzling
- 10 ounces cremini mushrooms, thinly sliced
- Multi-Grain Pizza Dough (page 561)
- 1 medium zucchini, thinly sliced on the diagonal
- 1½ cups thinly sliced sweet onions, such as Vidalia or Texas Sweet
- 2½ teaspoons minced fresh thyme
- Coarse salt and pepper
- ½ cup shredded Gruyère cheese

Preheat the oven to 475°F. Sprinkle 2 ungreased baking sheets with cornmeal.

In a large nonstick skillet, heat the oil over medium-high heat. Add the mushrooms and cook until golden brown, 5 to 8 minutes.

Divide the pizza dough into four equal portions. On a well floured surface, pat into 7- to 8-inch rounds, about ¼ to ½ inch thick. Transfer to the baking sheets. Arrange the mushrooms on the dough. Top with the zucchini and onions. Sprinkle with the thyme and drizzle generously with oil. Season lightly with salt and pepper.

Bake the pizzas for 12 minutes, or until golden brown around the edges. Remove from the oven and top with the Gruyère. Return to the oven for 2 minutes, just until the cheese melts.

MAKES 4 SERVINGS

GRILLED VEGETABLE & MOZZARELLA SANDWICHES

The spiciness of these sandwiches depends on the type of barbecue sauce you use.

- 3 tablespoons water
- 1 tablespoon cider vinegar
- 2 teaspoons olive oil
- 1 teaspoon turbinado or light brown sugar
- 1 summer squash (8 ounces), cut lengthwise into ¼-inch-thick slices
- 1 large red onion, thickly sliced
- 1 red bell pepper, cut lengthwise into flat panels
- 1 loaf whole-grain Italian bread (8 ounces), halved lengthwise
- ½ cup bottled barbecue sauce
- 4 ounces part-skim mozzarella cheese, thinly sliced

Preheat a grill to medium. Lightly oil the grill grate.

In a large bowl, whisk together the water, vinegar, oil, and brown sugar. Add the squash and onion, and toss gently to coat.

Place the bell pepper, skin-side down, on the grill grate. Add the yellow squash and red onion.

Grill the squash and onion for 10 minutes, turning them occasionally, until crisp-tender. Grill the pepper for 10 minutes without turning, until the skin is charred. Transfer the vegetables to a plate. When cool enough to handle, peel the pepper and cut into thick strips.

Grill the bread, cut-side down, for 30 seconds, or until lightly toasted. Brush the toasted surfaces of the bread with the barbecue sauce.

Top the bread with the mozzarella and vegetables. Close up the sandwich and return to the grill. Cover and grill for 30 seconds, or until the cheese has melted. Cut crosswise into 4 sandwiches.

MAKES 4 SERVINGS

PITAS STUFFED WITH TOMATO & GORGONZOLA SALAD

Rinsing the red onion slices reduces some of the bitterness. Be sure to drain them well.

- 2 tablespoons extra-virgin olive oil
- 1 tablespoon red wine vinegar
- 1 teaspoon Dijon mustard
- ½ teaspoon sugar
- ½ teaspoon coarse salt
- ¼ teaspoon pepper
- 8 cups mesclun greens
- ½ cup thinly sliced red onion, rinsed and drained
- ½ cup thinly sliced celery heart
- 1 cup cherry tomatoes, halved
- 4 ounces gorgonzola cheese, crumbled
- 4 whole wheat pita breads (7 inches), halved

In a small bowl, whisk together the oil, vinegar, mustard, sugar, salt, and pepper. Lightly toss with the salad greens. Add the onion, celery, tomatoes, and gorgonzola, and toss well. Stuff the pita halves with the salad.

MAKES 4 SERVINGS

FENNEL & PEAR TOMATO PITAS: Use fresh fennel instead of celery, and yellow pear tomatoes instead of cherry tomatoes. Change the vinegar to white wine vinegar.

HOT & SOUR TOFU SANDWICHES

Tofu is a blank canvas for pungent flavors. Here, it is flavored with a hot and sour marinade, sautéed, and then served in pita bread along with a carrot and red pepper slaw.

- 2 tablespoons soy sauce
- 2 tablespoons balsamic vinegar
- 1 tablespoon minced garlic
- 1 tablespoon soy mayonnaise
- 1 tablespoon turbinado or light brown sugar
- ¼ teaspoon red pepper flakes
- 1 pound firm tofu, cut into 8 triangles
- 3 large carrots, shredded
- 1 large red bell pepper, slivered
- 1¼ cups chopped watercress
- 2 teaspoons dark sesame oil
- 4 whole wheat pita breads (7 inches)

In a measuring cup, combine the soy sauce, vinegar, and garlic. Pour out half of the mixture into a medium bowl and whisk in the soy mayonnaise.

To the mixture remaining in the cup, add the brown sugar and pepper flakes to make the marinade. Place the tofu in a shallow container, drizzle with the marinade, and turn to coat. Cover and marinate for at least 20 minutes or up to several hours.

To the mayo mixture, add the carrots, bell pepper, and 1 cup of the watercress, and toss to combine. Refrigerate until ready to serve.

In a large nonstick skillet, heat the sesame oil over medium heat. Reserving the marinade, add the tofu to the skillet and sauté until crisp and golden brown, about 3 minutes per side. Add the reserved marinade to the pan and cook until syrupy, about 2 minutes.

Slit the pitas open on the side. Spoon the carrot mixture in, then top with the tofu. Top with the remaining watercress and any pan juices.

MAKES 4 SERVINGS

MOCK PEKING DUCK

Seitan (wheat gluten) is used in many Chinese dishes as a meat substitute. Here it stands in for duck. Serve the seitan the way you would Peking Duck: wrapped in flatbread (small flour tortillas would work), along with shredded scallions and a little extra hoisin sauce brushed on the bread.

- 2 teaspoons dark sesame oil
- 2 teaspoons hoisin sauce
- 2 teaspoons maple syrup or brown rice syrup
- 1 teaspoon soy sauce
- 1 teaspoon rice vinegar
- ½ teaspoon Chinese five-spice powder, store-bought or homemade (page 226)
- 1 package (8 ounces) seitan, cut into bite-size strips

In a bowl, whisk together the sesame oil, hoisin, maple syrup, soy sauce, vinegar, and five-spice powder. Add the seitan and toss to coat. Cover and marinate for at least 1 hour at room temperature or overnight in the refrigerator.

Preheat the broiler. Lift the seitan from the marinade and place on a foil-lined broiler pan. Broil 4 to 6 inches from the heat until heated through and glazed but not crisp.

MAKES 4 SERVINGS

CRANBERRY BEAN BURRITOS

Why go for the expected pinto bean in a burrito? Cranberry beans—or any bean with the same mild, meaty taste—are delicious here.

- 2 cups tomato sauce
- 2 teaspoons hot pepper sauce
- 1 teaspoon cumin
- 6 whole wheat tortillas (burrito size)
- 2 tablespoons vegetable oil

- 2/3 cup chopped onion
- 2 cups cooked cranberry beans, mashed
- 3/4 cup chopped cherry tomatoes
- 1 cup shredded Cheddar cheese (4 ounces)
- 1/2 cup shredded lettuce
- 1 Hass avocado, coarsely chopped

In a small saucepan, combine the tomato sauce, hot sauce, and cumin. Warm over low heat.

Preheat the oven to 350°F. Place the tortillas in a large covered baking dish, and place in the oven to warm while you prepare the filling.

In a large skillet, heat the oil over medium heat. Add the onion and cook until tender but not brown. Add the beans and 1/4 cup of the tomato sauce mixture. Cook, stirring and mashing to blend well, until heated through.

Remove the tortillas from the oven (leave the oven on). Spoon about 1/3 cup of the bean mixture onto the center of each tortilla. Top with the tomatoes, Cheddar, lettuce, and avocado. Fold the bottom edge (nearest you) of each tortilla up and over the filling, then fold in the two sides (envelope fashion) and fold the top edge down.

Arrange the burritos, seam-side down, on an ungreased baking sheet. Bake for 15 minutes, or until just heated through. Serve with the remaining tomato sauce on the side.

MAKES 6 SERVINGS

CARIBBEAN BEAN BURRITOS: Increase the hot sauce to 1 tablespoon. Omit the cumin and add 1/2 teaspoon allspice. Use pigeon peas instead of cranberry beans. Omit the cherry tomatoes and add 1 mango, chopped.

GRILLED THREE-BEAN BURRITOS

If you have barbecue guests who don't eat meat, this is the perfect dish.

- 2 teaspoons olive oil
- 1 red bell pepper, cut into thin strips
- 2 cloves garlic, minced
- 4 scallions, sliced
- 1 tablespoon chili powder
- 1 teaspoon ground cumin
- 1 small pickled jalapeño pepper, minced
- 1 3/4 cups cooked red kidney beans
- 1 can (14.5 ounces) diced tomatoes, drained
- 1 3/4 cups cooked black beans
- 1 cup cooked green beans, halved lengthwise
- 4 whole wheat spinach tortillas (8 inches)
- 1/2 cup shredded Cheddar cheese (2 ounces)

In large skillet, heat the oil over medium heat. Add the bell pepper and cook until softened, about 5 minutes. Stir in the garlic, scallions, chili powder, and cumin. Cook for 2 minutes to soften the scallions and blend the flavors.

Add the jalapeño, kidney beans, and tomatoes. Cook for 3 minutes, mashing about half of the beans to thicken. Add the black beans and green beans, stirring to combine.

Preheat the grill to medium. Tear off four 24-inch lengths of heavy-duty foil, fold each in half to form a 12 × 18-inch rectangle, and lightly oil.

Place a tortilla in the center of each rectangle. Spoon the bean mixture into the center of each tortilla, spreading it into a rectangle. Top with the Cheddar. Fold the tortilla over the filling and roll up. Seal the packets and grill for 12 minutes, or until warmed through.

MAKES 4 SERVINGS

THREE SISTERS FAJITAS

In Native American agriculture, there were three crops—the three sisters—that were planted together: corn, beans, and squash. Each plant played an important role. The corn provided a stalk for the beans to climb up; the beans added nitrogen to the soil; and the squash spread over the ground and kept weeds from invading.

- 1 tablespoon olive oil
- 4 scallions, thinly sliced
- 3 cloves garlic, finely chopped
- 2 zucchini, halved lengthwise and thinly sliced
- 1 large poblano or green bell pepper, cut into thin strips
- 1¾ cups cooked pinto beans
- 2 tomatoes, seeded and coarsely chopped
- 1½ cups fresh or frozen corn kernels
- 2 tablespoons lime juice
- ½ small chipotle chili pepper in adobo, minced
- 8 whole wheat tortillas (8 inches)
- ½ cup shredded Monterey Jack cheese (2 ounces)

In large skillet, heat the oil over medium heat. Add the scallions and garlic, and cook for 1 minute, or until fragrant. Add the zucchini and poblano pepper, and cook until the pepper is crisp-tender, about 2 minutes.

Add the beans, tomatoes, corn, lime juice, and chipotle pepper, and cook for 3 minutes, stirring frequently, to heat through.

Meanwhile, preheat the oven to 400°F. Wrap the tortillas in foil and heat for 3 to 5 minutes, just until warmed.

Place 2 tortillas on each of 4 plates. Spoon the vegetables onto the tortillas, sprinkle with the cheese, and roll up.

MAKES 4 SERVINGS

VEGAN MAIN COURSES

Many of the recipes in this chapter can be adapted for a vegan diet by changing butter to oil or leaving out cheese toppings, but here are some recipes in the book that need no tinkering:

THREE-VEGETABLE BURGERS

If you count the scallions and garlic, these burgers are actually made with five vegetables, not three. Cook the whole carrots and potato in a vegetable steamer or the microwave.

- 2 teaspoons butter
- 2 scallions, minced
- 1 clove garlic, minced
- 2 cups cooked green split peas
- 1 medium white potato, cooked until firm-tender, then grated
- 2 carrots, cooked until crisp-tender, then grated
- 2 large eggs, beaten
- 1 cup finely crumbled soft whole-grain bread crumbs (2 slices)
- 1 teaspoon salt
- Pinch of cayenne pepper
- About 4 tablespoons olive oil

In a small skillet, heat the butter over medium heat. Add the scallions and garlic, and sauté until tender.

In a large bowl, mash the split peas lightly with a fork. Add the scallion mixture, potato, carrots, eggs, ½ cup of the bread crumbs, the salt, and cayenne. Shape into 6 or 8 patties, then dredge in the remaining ½ cup bread crumbs.

In a large skillet, heat 2 tablespoons of the oil over medium heat. Add half the patties and cook, adding more oil if needed, until lightly browned, about 3 minutes per side. Repeat with another 2 tablespoons oil and the remaining patties.

MAKES 6 TO 8 SERVINGS

GOLDEN BURGERS: Use yellow split peas instead of green and a sweet potato instead of a white potato. Add ½ teaspoon curry powder.

TEMPEH BURGERS

Instead of the tomato, try the burgers with Marinated Roasted Peppers (page 660). This is a good strategy in the winter when it's hard to find flavorful, locally grown tomatoes.

- 2 large eggs, beaten
- 8 ounces tempeh, crumbled
- ½ cup chopped grape tomatoes
- ½ cup finely crumbled soft whole-grain bread crumbs (1 slice)
- ¼ cup minced sweet onion
- 1 tablespoon olive oil
- 4 or 6 whole-grain burger buns
- 1 clove garlic, halved
- 2 teaspoons mayonnaise
- Lettuce and tomato

In a large bowl, combine the eggs, tempeh, tomatoes, bread crumbs, and onion, and mix well. Form into 4 or 6 patties.

In a large skillet, heat the oil over medium heat. Add the patties and cook until golden brown, about 3 minutes per side.

Meanwhile, split the buns and toast them. Rub the toasted sides lightly with the cut garlic clove. Spread with the mayonnaise.

Top the buns with lettuce, tomato, and burgers.

MAKES 4 OR 6 SERVINGS

TOFU CHEESEBURGERS

Drain the tofu well in a strainer lined with cheesecloth before you start. If you're a fan of soy cheese, use it in place of the provolone.

- 2 large eggs, beaten
- 1½ cups soft tofu (12 ounces)

½ cup minced red onion

2 tablespoons grated Parmesan cheese

1 clove garlic, minced

1½ teaspoons Italian seasoning, store-bought or homemade (page 407)

¼ teaspoon pepper

1½ cups cooked brown rice

½ cup finely crumbled soft whole-grain bread crumbs (1 slice)

2 teaspoons olive oil

4 or 6 slices provolone cheese

4 or 6 whole-grain sandwich-size English muffins, toasted

4 or 6 slices beefsteak tomato

In a large bowl, combine the eggs and tofu, using a fork to mash them together. Add the onion, Parmesan, garlic, Italian seasoning, and pepper. Mix well, then stir in the rice and bread crumbs. (If the mixture is too loose, add some more bread crumbs.) Form into 4 or 6 patties.

In a large skillet, heat the oil over medium heat. Add the patties and cook until golden brown on both sides. Turn off the heat. Top the burgers with the provolone, and cover the skillet so the cheese will melt.

Serve on the toasted muffins with the tomato.

MAKES 4 OR 6 SERVINGS

BULGUR & BEAN CHEESEBURGERS

For extra chewiness, seek out coarse bulgur instead of the more common medium granulation.

2 cups boiling water

½ cup bulgur

3½ cups cooked pinto beans

2 tablespoons lime juice

1½ teaspoons ground coriander

½ teaspoon cayenne pepper

1 red bell pepper, finely chopped

1 yellow bell pepper, finely chopped

4 scallions, thinly sliced

¼ cup ketchup

2 tablespoons olive oil

¼ cup flour

¾ cup shredded Monterey Jack cheese (3 ounces)

4 whole-grain hamburger buns, split and toasted

Boston lettuce

In a medium bowl, combine the boiling water and bulgur, and set aside to soften for 30 minutes. Drain.

In a large bowl, combine the beans with the drained bulgur. With a potato masher, mash the beans and bulgur until almost smooth with some lumps remaining. Add the lime juice, coriander, and cayenne, stirring to combine. Add ½ cup of the red bell pepper, ½ cup of the yellow bell pepper, and ¼ cup of the scallions. Shape into 4 patties, 4 inches in diameter.

In a small bowl, combine the ketchup with the remaining bell peppers and scallions. Set aside.

In a large skillet, heat the oil over medium heat. Dredge the patties in the flour, shaking off the excess. Cook the patties until crisp on the outside and heated through, about 4 minutes per side. Sprinkle the cheese on top, cover, and cook until the cheese is melted, about 1 minute.

Serve the cheeseburgers on the buns with the ketchup mixture and lettuce.

MAKES 4 SERVINGS

DOUBLE PORTOBELLO BURGERS

These giant mushroom caps cook nicely under the broiler, but can just as easily be cooked on an outdoor grill during the cookout season.

- **8 portobello mushrooms (3 ounces each), stems discarded**
- **1/3 cup extra-virgin olive oil**
- **3 tablespoons balsamic vinegar**
- **2 cloves garlic, finely minced**
- **2 teaspoons fresh thyme leaves, chopped**
- **1/2 teaspoon coarse salt**
- **4 soft multi-grain rolls**
- **4 ounces soft goat cheese, crumbled**
- **1 teaspoon truffle oil (optional)**
- **4 slices sweet onion, such as Vidalia or Maui**
- **8 arugula leaves**

With a small spoon, scrape the black gills out of the mushroom caps.

In a small bowl, stir together the oil, vinegar, garlic, thyme, and salt. Brush on both sides of the mushroom caps, and let the mixture seep in for 20 minutes.

Preheat the broiler. Lightly oil a baking sheet.

Arrange the mushrooms in one layer, gill-side up, on the baking sheet. Broil 6 inches from the heat for 6 minutes, or until somewhat soft. Flip and continue cooking until the mushrooms are hot and tender, about 6 minutes more.

To assemble each burger, place a mushroom, gill-side up, on a bottom bun. Top with goat cheese and drizzle with 1/4 teaspoon truffle oil (if using). Add a second mushroom, gill-side down, an onion slice, two arugula leaves, and the top bun.

MAKES 4 SERVINGS

VEGETARIAN SLOPPY JOES

Serve the mixture over split and toasted whole-grain rolls or English muffins.

- **1/4 cup olive oil**
- **1 cup chopped onions**
- **1 cup chopped red or green bell pepper**
- **3 cups cooked black beans**
- **1 cup tomato sauce**
- **2 tablespoons red wine vinegar**
- **1 teaspoon maple syrup**
- **1/4 teaspoon cumin**
- **1/4 teaspoon smoked paprika**
- **1/4 teaspoon salt**

In a large skillet, heat the oil over medium heat. Add the onions and pepper, and sauté until the vegetables are softened.

Add the beans, tomato sauce, vinegar, maple syrup, cumin, paprika, and salt. Simmer for 15 minutes to blend the flavors.

MAKES 4 TO 6 SERVINGS

BROWN-RICE DOSAS WITH ONION-POTATO FILLING

The rice and lentils used in this Indian pancake-like bread are soaked overnight and then pureed and left to ferment for another 24 hours to enhance flavor and lightness.

DOSAS

- **1 cup short-grain brown rice**
- **3 1/2 cups water**
- **1/2 cup lentils**

1 tablespoon butter, melted

1/8 teaspoon cayenne pepper

Pinch of baking soda

FILLING

2 tablespoons butter

1/2 teaspoon mustard seeds

1 medium onion, chopped

1 large tomato, coarsely chopped

3/4 pound white or red potatoes, cooked and diced

1/4 teaspoon cayenne pepper

1/4 teaspoon turmeric

1/8 teaspoon black pepper

1 tablespoon minced cilantro

Yogurt, for topping

To make the dosas: Place the rice in a bowl with 2 cups of the water, and soak overnight. In a separate bowl, soak the lentils in the remaining 1½ cups water overnight.

Reserving the soaking water, drain the rice and lentils. Keep them separate, but combine the soaking waters.

In a food processor, puree the rice with ¼ cup of the reserved soaking water. Transfer the puree to a bowl. Repeat the process with lentils and ¼ cup soaking water and add to the rice puree. Stir to combine, cover, and set aside in a warm place for 24 hours to ferment.

To make the filling (the next day), before completing the dosas: In a medium skillet, melt the butter. Add the mustard seeds and cook, stirring, for 1 minute. Add the onion and sauté for 5 minutes.

Add the tomato and cook for 2 minutes. Add the potatoes, cayenne, turmeric, and black pepper. Stir and cook until the liquid has been absorbed and the mixture is dry. Stir in the cilantro. Keep warm while cooking the dosas.

When ready to prepare the dosas, preheat the oven to warm.

Add just enough water to the fermented dosa mixture to make a batter the consistency of heavy cream. Stir in the 1 tablespoon melted butter, ⅛teaspoon cayenne, and baking soda.

Heat a 9-inch skillet over medium-high heat. When hot, add ½ cup of the batter, turning the pan quickly to distribute the batter into a thin layer about 6 inches in diameter. Cook until the surface is dry and small bubbles form on the top, then invert onto a sheet of waxed paper. Place another piece of waxed paper on top and invert again. Peel the surface piece of waxed paper off and invert uncooked side of bread back into the pan to cook for 1 to 2 minutes more. Slide the bread carefully out of the pan and keep in a warm oven. Repeat with the remaining batter.

To serve, place several spoonfuls of the onion-potato filling in the middle of each dosa and top with a spoonful of yogurt. Fold 2 edges over the filling, then gently fold up, as you would for a stuffed crêpe.

MAKES 4 SERVINGS

VEGAN DOSAS: Use olive oil instead of butter and soy yogurt for the topping.

ROASTED HOISIN TOFU

Serve with brown rice as a meatless main course alongside a lightly dressed salad of napa cabbage or cucumbers. Or let come to room temperature, refrigerate, and then cut into cubes to use in a salad, soup, stew, or stir-fry.

2 packages (15 ounces each) extra-firm tofu

1/4 cup hoisin sauce

2 tablespoons rice wine vinegar

- **1 tablespoon dark sesame oil**
- **1 teaspoon Asian chili garlic sauce**

Drain the tofu for 30 minutes (see "Draining Tofu," below).

Preheat the oven to 375°F.

In a small bowl, stir together the hoisin, vinegar, sesame oil, and chili garlic sauce. Pat the tofu pieces dry and brush them all over with the hoisin mixture. Roast for 45 to 50 minutes, flipping occasionally, until browned and hot.

MAKES 4 SERVINGS

ROASTED MISO-GINGER TOFU

Use the roasted tofu in salads, cut up and added to stir-fries, or by itself as a meatless main course.

- **2 packages (15 ounces each) extra-firm tofu**
- **3 tablespoons miso paste**
- **1 tablespoon vegetable oil**
- **2 scallions, white and 2 inches of greens, thinly sliced**
- **1 tablespoon grated fresh ginger**
- **1 clove garlic, finely minced**

Drain the tofu for 30 minutes (see "Draining Tofu," below).

Preheat the oven to 375°F.

In a small bowl, stir together the miso, oil, scallions, ginger, and garlic. Pat the tofu pieces dry and brush them all over with the miso mixture. Roast for 45 to 50 minutes, flipping occasionally, until browned and hot.

MAKES 4 SERVINGS

ROASTED LEMON-HERB TOFU

Serve hot as a meatless main course, or cool to room temperature and refrigerate until needed. Cut into cubes and add to stir-fries, salads, soups, or stews.

- **2 packages (15 ounces each) extra-firm tofu**
- **2 tablespoons lemon juice**
- **1 tablespoon extra-virgin olive oil**
- **1 clove garlic, finely minced**
- **2 tablespoons loosely packed fresh basil leaves, chopped**
- **2 teaspoons fresh oregano leaves, chopped**
- **1 teaspoon fresh rosemary leaves, chopped**
- **1 teaspoon coarse salt**

DRAINING TOFU

Draining excess water out of tofu makes it much sturdier for adding to stir-fries and soups. It also makes the tofu more receptive to absorbing flavorful marinades.

Cut a block of tofu horizontally in half. Then cut each piece crosswise in half to make rectangles roughly $3\frac{1}{4} \times 2\frac{1}{4}$ inches. Arrange the tofu pieces in an even layer on a baking sheet. Prop the baking sheet up at one end by at least an inch (more if possible) and have the other end overhang the sink. Cover with 2 thicknesses of paper towel and top with another baking sheet or a cutting board. Weight down with a heavy skillet or a few cans. Let the tofu drain into the sink for at least 30 minutes.

Drain the tofu for 30 minutes (see "Draining Tofu," page 311).

Preheat the oven to 375°F.

In a small bowl, stir together the lemon juice, oil, garlic, basil, oregano, rosemary, and salt. Pat the tofu pieces dry and brush them all over with the herb mixture. Roast for 45 to 50 minutes, flipping occasionally, until browned and hot.

MAKES 4 SERVINGS

CRISPY MARINATED TOFU CUTLETS

Serve hot with rice and steamed vegetables, or serve cold as an appetizer.

- 1 pound firm tofu
- ¼ cup rice vinegar
- ¼ cup lower-sodium soy sauce
- 4 tablespoons water
- 1 tablespoon chopped cilantro
- 2 cloves garlic, minced
- 2 teaspoons minced fresh ginger
- 1 teaspoon pepper
- 1 large egg
- Whole wheat panko bread crumbs
- Sunflower oil, for frying

Drain the tofu for 30 minutes (see "Draining Tofu," page 311).

Cut the tofu into slices about 2 inches square.

In a shallow container, combine the vinegar, soy sauce, 2 tablespoons of the water, the cilantro, garlic, ginger, and pepper. Add the tofu and turn to coat. Let sit for 1 hour to absorb the marinade, turning once or twice.

In a shallow bowl, beat the egg with the remaining 2 tablespoons water. Place the panko crumbs in another shallow bowl.

In a large heavy skillet, heat about ¼ inch oil until hot but not smoking. Dip the tofu first in the beaten egg and then in the crumbs, pressing the crumbs on. Add the tofu to the pan and cook until golden brown on both sides, adding more oil if needed. Drain on paper towels.

MAKES 4 SERVINGS

LATTICE-TOPPED SPINACH & FETA PIE

To make a quick lattice top, see "Easy Lattice Top" (page 528).

CRUST

- 1 cup whole wheat pastry flour
- ⅓ cup unbleached all-purpose flour
- ¼ cup cold milk
- 2 tablespoons olive oil
- ½ teaspoon salt

FILLING

- 2 pounds baby spinach leaves
- ⅓ cup olive oil
- 2 bunches scallions, chopped
- 2 tablespoons minced fresh dill
- 2 cups crumbled feta cheese (8 ounces)
- Pepper

Preheat the oven to 350°F.

To make the crust: In a bowl, mix together the flours, milk, oil, and salt. Roll the dough between 2 sheets of lightly floured waxed paper to fit an 8-inch pie plate. Trim the edges and make a fluted rim. Reserve the trimmings for the lattice top. Prick the crust generously with a fork and bake for 7 minutes. Set aside. (Leave the oven on.)

Meanwhile, to make the filling: In a steamer, cook the spinach until just wilted. Squeeze dry and chop.

In a medium skillet, heat the oil over medium heat. Add the scallions and cook until softened. Add the spinach, dill, and feta. Stir to mix. Season with pepper to taste.

Spoon the filling into the baked pie crust. Roll out the pastry trimmings, cut lattice strips, and use to top the pie. Bake for 20 to 25 minutes, until the crust is browned.

MAKES 4 TO 6 SERVINGS

HIGH-PROTEIN VEGETARIAN CHILI

Black soybeans and TVP give this vegetarian chili its protein boost. Look for them in natural foods stores.

- 1 cup dried shiitake mushrooms
- 2½ cups warm water
- 2 tablespoons olive oil
- 1 large onion, finely chopped
- 1 large carrot, quartered lengthwise and thinly sliced crosswise
- 3 cloves garlic, slivered
- 1 tablespoon minced fresh ginger
- 3 cups cooked black soybeans
- 1¾ pounds butternut or kabocha squash, peeled and cut into 1-inch chunks (4½ cups)
- 1 can (28 ounces) crushed tomatoes
- 1½ cups (3 ounces) texturized vegetable protein (TVP)
- 2 teaspoons ancho chili powder
- 1 teaspoon salt

In a medium bowl, soak the mushrooms in the warm water. Let stand until the mushrooms are rehydrated and tender, about 30 minutes. Using your fingers, scoop the mushrooms out of the liquid. Strain the liquid through a fine-mesh sieve and set aside. Disgard the stems and thinly slice the mushrooms.

In a 5-quart Dutch oven or large saucepan, heat the oil over medium heat. Add the onion, carrot, garlic, and ginger, and cook, stirring frequently, until the onion is tender, about 12 minutes

Add the mushrooms and their soaking liquid, the beans, squash, tomatoes, TVP, ancho chili powder, and salt, and bring to a boil. Reduce to a simmer, cover, and cook until the squash is tender, about 30 minutes.

MAKES 8 SERVINGS

THAI-STYLE TOFU & VEGETABLE STEW

If you have the time, drain the tofu (page 311) to firm it up before adding to the stew. Serve the stew over freshly cooked brown jasmine or basmati rice.

- 1 tablespoon olive oil
- 4 scallions, thinly sliced
- 2 tablespoons minced fresh ginger
- 1 pound cremini mushrooms, thickly sliced
- 1 can (14.5 ounces) no-salt-added diced tomatoes
- 1 tablespoon lime juice
- 1 teaspoon turbinado or light brown sugar
- ½ teaspoon salt
- 1½ cups frozen peas
- ⅓ cup chopped fresh mint
- ⅓ cup chopped fresh basil
- 8 ounces extra-firm tofu, cut into 1-inch cubes

In a large skillet, heat the oil over medium heat. Add the scallions and ginger, and cook, stirring frequently, until the scallions are softened, about 2 minutes.

Add the mushrooms and cook, stirring occasionally, until the mushrooms are almost tender, about 4 minutes.

Stir in the tomatoes, lime juice, brown sugar, and salt, and bring to a boil. Add the peas, mint, and basil, and simmer gently for 3 minutes to blend the flavors.

Stir in the tofu and simmer just until the tofu is warmed through, about 3 minutes.

MAKES 4 SERVINGS

VEGAN BARLEY STEW

Quick-cooking barley has all the nutrients of pearled barley; it's just been rolled and steamed so that it cooks in 15 minutes instead of 45. If you prefer the texture of pearl barley, cook it separately in a pot of boiling water for about 30 minutes. Drain the barley and measure out the cooking water. Use 3⅓ cups of it (or add to it if you don't have that much) for the stew.

- 1 tablespoon olive oil
- 4 skinny carrots, cut on the diagonal into 1-inch lengths
- ½ pound small white turnips, peeled and cut into 8 wedges each
- ½ pound red potatoes, cut into ½-inch cubes
- ⅓ cup quick-cooking barley
- ¾ teaspoon salt
- ½ teaspoon thyme
- ¼ teaspoon pepper
- 3⅓ cups water
- 1 pound green beans, cut into 1-inch lengths

In a large saucepan, heat the oil over medium heat. Add the carrots and turnips, and cook, stirring frequently, until lightly browned, about 5 minutes.

Add the potatoes, barley, salt, thyme, and pepper, stirring to coat. Add the water and bring to a boil. Reduce to a simmer, cover, and cook until the vegetables and barley are tender, about 10 minutes.

Stir the green beans into the pan, cover, and cook until they are tender, about 7 minutes.

MAKES 4 SERVINGS

SUNSHINE BARLEY STEW: Use rutabaga (yellow turnip) instead of white turnips, Yukon Gold potatoes instead of red potatoes, and yellow wax beans instead of green beans.

STUFFED BEEFSTEAK TOMATOES

When choosing beefsteak tomatoes for this recipe, avoid any that have deformations at the blossom end. The deformation, called catfacing, is harmless, but it can extend into the tomato, making it hard to hollow out for stuffing.

- 2 teaspoons olive oil
- 1 small onion, minced
- ⅔ cup brown rice
- ⅔ cup vegetable broth, store-bought or homemade (page 173)

MAIN-COURSE EGG DISHES

- 1 tablespoon lemon juice
- 1/4 teaspoon pepper
- 4 beefsteak tomatoes
- 1/4 cup minced parsley
- 1/2 cup shredded sharp Cheddar cheese
- 1/4 cup coarsely chopped walnuts or pecans

In a medium skillet, heat the oil over medium heat. Add the onion and cook until golden. Stir in the rice, broth, lemon juice, and pepper. Bring to a boil, cover, and cook until the rice is tender and the broth has been absorbed, about 45 minutes.

Meanwhile, with a small, sharp knife, cut out the middles of the tomatoes, leaving 1/2-inch shell all around. Coarsely chop the tomato flesh.

Remove the rice from the heat, fluff with a fork, and stir in the chopped tomatoes, the parsley, and 1/4 cup of the Cheddar. Stir well to distribute the cheese.

Preheat the broiler. Stuff the tomatoes with the rice mixture. Top with the nuts and remaining 1/4 cup Cheddar. Broil until the cheese is melted and bubbling. Serve hot.

MAKES 4 SERVINGS

BEAN-STUFFED PEPPERS WITH MANCHEGO

Manchego is a Cheddar-style cheese from Spain. A substitute here would be a very young Parmesan.

- 1 large red bell pepper, halved lengthwise and seeded
- 1 large green bell pepper, halved lengthwise and seeded
- 1 tablespoon olive oil
- 1 large red onion, finely chopped
- 5 cloves garlic, minced
- 2 cups cooked canary beans or cannellini beans
- 2 tablespoons tomato paste
- 2 teaspoons sesame seeds
- 1 1/2 teaspoons unsweetened cocoa powder
- 1/2 teaspoon oregano
- 1/2 teaspoon cinnamon
- 1/2 teaspoon salt
- 1 1/2 cups canned crushed tomatoes
- 1/3 cup raisins
- 1/3 cup water
- 4 ounces Manchego cheese, shredded

In a steamer, cook the pepper halves, cut-sides down, until crisp-tender, about 10 minutes.

Meanwhile, in a medium skillet, heat the oil over low heat. Add the onion and garlic, and cook until the onion is golden brown, about 5 minutes.

To make the filling, measure out 1/4 cup of the onion mixture and transfer to a bowl. Add the beans and tomato paste, and mash with a potato masher or a spoon. Set aside.

To make the sauce, add the sesame seeds, cocoa powder, oregano, cinnamon, and salt to the onion mixture remaining in the skillet. Cook for 1 minute. Stir in the crushed tomatoes and raisins, and bring to a boil. Reduce to a simmer, cover, and cook for 5 minutes to blend the flavors. Transfer to a food processor or blender, and puree.

Return the sauce to the skillet, stir in the water, and add the steamed peppers, cut-side up. Spoon the filling into the peppers, cover, and cook until the filling is heated through, about 5 minutes. Spoon a little of the sauce over the bean mixture and sprinkle the Manchego on top. Cover and cook for 2 minutes to melt the cheese.

To serve, spoon some of the sauce onto each plate, and top with a pepper half and a little more sauce.

MAKES 4 SERVINGS

BAKED PEPPERS STUFFED WITH FAVAS & BULGUR

Cooking with fresh fava beans is a labor of love since they need to be shelled twice: once to remove them from the pod, and then again to remove their tough skins. If you prefer, make this with fresh baby lima beans.

- 1 cup bulgur
- 2 cups boiling water
- 2 cups cooked fresh fava beans, mashed slightly
- 1 can (28 ounces) no-salt-added diced tomatoes, drained
- 1 medium onion, chopped
- ½ cup chopped almonds
- ¼ cup plus 2 tablespoons olive oil
- 2 tablespoons lemon juice
- 1 teaspoon minced garlic
- 8 small green bell peppers, halved lengthwise

In a medium heatproof bowl, combine the bulgur and water, and let stand for 20 minutes.

Preheat the oven to 350°F. Oil a 9 × 13-inch baking dish.

Drain the bulgur thoroughly, pressing out the moisture, and return to the bowl. Stir in the beans, tomatoes, onion, almonds, ¼ cup of the oil, the lemon juice, and garlic.

Spoon the mixture into the pepper halves and place in the baking dish. Drizzle the remaining 2 tablespoons oil over the tops. Bake until the peppers are tender, about 40 minutes.

MAKES 4 SERVINGS

BAKED ZUCCHINI "CUSTARD"

A traditional custard is made with dairy milk. This "custard" is made with silken tofu instead.

- 1½ pounds small zucchini (4 or 5)
- 2 tablespoons butter
- ¾ cup chopped onion
- ½ cup chopped red bell pepper
- 1 teaspoon hot paprika
- ½ teaspoon salt
- 10 ounces soft silken tofu
- 2 large eggs, beaten

MEATLESS PASTA MAINS

1 cup shredded sharp Cheddar cheese (4 ounces)

Preheat the oven to 350°F. Grease a 1-quart baking dish.

In a steamer, cook the whole zucchini until firm-tender, 3 to 5 minutes. When cool enough to handle, cut into ⅓-inch dice.

In a large skillet, melt the butter over medium-high heat. Add the onion and bell pepper, and cook until golden. Remove from the heat and stir in the zucchini, paprika, and salt.

In a blender, combine the tofu and eggs, and blend to a smooth puree. Transfer to a medium bowl and stir in the vegetable mixture, along with ¾ cup of the Cheddar. Spoon the mixture into the baking dish and top with the remaining ¼ cup Cheddar. Bake for 30 minutes, until the custard is set.

MAKES 4 TO 6 SERVINGS

RICOTTA-TOPPED EGGPLANT CASSEROLE

The casserole base can be assembled a day ahead and the ricotta topping added just before baking.

CASSEROLE BASE

- **1 large eggplant (1 pound), peeled and cut into ½-inch slices**
- **5 tablespoons olive oil**
- **1 large red onion, finely chopped**
- **3 large cloves garlic, minced**
- **4 large tomatoes, chopped**
- **1 teaspoon turbinado or light brown sugar**
- **1 teaspoon oregano**
- **1 teaspoon salt**
- **¼ teaspoon black pepper**
- **1 cup frozen peas**
- **2 cups cooked brown basmati rice**
- **½ cup coarsely chopped walnuts**

RICOTTA TOPPING

- **2 tablespoons butter**
- **2 tablespoons flour**
- **1½ cups low-fat (1%) milk**
- **1 cup part-skim ricotta cheese**
- **¼ teaspoon salt**
- **¼ teaspoon white pepper**
- **⅛ teaspoon nutmeg**
- **2 large eggs, beaten**
- **¼ cup grated Parmesan cheese**

To make the casserole base: Preheat the oven to 400°F. Lightly oil a 9 × 13-inch baking pan.

Place the eggplant slices in the pan and drizzle 3 tablespoons of the oil over them. Bake on the lowest rack in the oven for 15 minutes. (If making the casserole base the day before, turn off the oven; otherwise leave it on.)

Meanwhile, in a large skillet, heat the remaining 2 tablespoons oil over medium heat. Add the onion and garlic, and stir-fry until the onion has wilted. Add the tomatoes, brown sugar, oregano, salt, and black pepper, and cook for 1 minute. Remove from the heat and stir in the peas.

Spread the rice in a layer over the eggplant slices and evenly spoon the tomato mixture on top. Sprinkle with the walnuts. (If making ahead, cover and refrigerate. When ready to proceed the next day, let the casserole base come to room temperature, and preheat the oven to 350°F, while you make the topping.)

To make the ricotta topping: In a 1-quart saucepan, melt the butter over low heat and then stir in the flour. Whisking constantly, gradually add the milk and cook until the sauce is slightly thickened, about 10 minutes. Remove from the heat and whisk in the ricotta cheese, salt, white pepper, and nutmeg. Add the eggs, whisking well. Whisk in the Parmesan.

Pour the ricotta topping over the casserole base and bake for 45 minutes, or until the topping is puffed and lightly browned in spots and the filling is piping hot.

Let stand for 15 minutes before cutting into squares to serve.

MAKES 6 TO 8 SERVINGS

BAKED SPINACH-STUFFED CRÊPES

This would make an elegant brunch dish, or an intriguing first course (serving 8).

- Whole Wheat Crêpes (page 589)
- 2 packages (10 ounces each) frozen chopped spinach, thawed and squeezed very dry
- 3/4 cup low-fat cottage cheese
- 3 large eggs, beaten
- 1/3 cup shredded sharp Cheddar cheese
- 1/4 teaspoon salt
- 1/8 teaspoon nutmeg
- 3 tablespoons butter, melted
- 1/4 cup grated Romano cheese

Make the crêpe batter 2 hours before you are ready to assemble this dish. Then cook the crêpes.

Preheat the oven to 350°F. Butter a shallow baking dish large enough to hold 8 rolled-up crêpes in a single layer.

In a medium bowl, mix together the spinach, cottage cheese, eggs, Cheddar, salt, and nutmeg.

Place about 1/2 cup of the mixture onto each crêpe, roll up, and arrange in the baking dish. Brush with the butter and sprinkle with the Romano. Bake for 20 minutes, or until heated through.

MAKES 4 SERVINGS

SPINACH & PANEER

Paneer is an Indian fresh cheese made by curdling whole milk with lemon juice. Though extremely simple to make, it does take 2 1/2 hours, so plan accordingly.

- 6 cups milk
- 3 tablespoons lemon juice
- 1 cup brown basmati rice
- 1 teaspoon salt
- 2 tablespoons olive oil
- 2 cloves garlic, minced
- 1 tablespoon chopped fresh ginger
- 1 1/2 teaspoons cumin
- 1 1/2 teaspoons coriander
- 1 teaspoon turmeric
- 3 packages (10 ounces each) frozen chopped spinach, thawed and squeezed dry
- 1 1/2 cups water
- 1/4 cup no-salt-added tomato paste
- 1 cup cooked chickpeas

In a medium, heavy-bottomed saucepan, bring the milk to a boil over medium heat. Remove from the heat, stir in the lemon juice, and let stand until the curds and whey separate, about 15 minutes. Strain through a cheesecloth-lined colander. Discard the strained liquid.

Tie the ends of the cheesecloth and squeeze to remove as much water as possible. Hang the cheese to drain for 1 hour 30 minutes.

Once the cheese has drained, place it, still in the cheesecloth, on a plate and place a heavy frying pan on top. Weight down for 30 minutes. Remove the weight, unwrap the paneer, and cut into 1-inch chunks.

Meanwhile, in a large saucepan, cook the brown rice according to package directions, using 1/2 teaspoon of the salt.

In a large skillet, heat 1 tablespoon of the oil over medium heat. Add the paneer cubes and cook until golden brown all over, about 5 minutes per side. With a slotted spoon, transfer the paneer to a bowl.

Add the remaining 1 tablespoon oil to the pan. Add the garlic and ginger, and cook, stirring frequently, until the garlic is tender, about 2 minutes. Stir in the cumin, coriander, and turmeric, and cook for 10 seconds.

Stir in the spinach, water, tomato paste, and remaining ½ teaspoon salt, and cook, stirring frequently, until the spinach is tender and hot, about 5 minutes. Stir in the chickpeas and paneer, and cook, stirring gently once or twice, until the chickpeas are heated through. Serve over the rice.

MAKES 4 SERVINGS

CARROT RISOTTO WITH CHICKPEAS

Comforting risotto is transformed into a filling main dish with the addition of chickpeas, carrots, and green beans. The brown rice is cooked in carrot juice for a golden hue and a heaping amount of beta-carotene.

- 1 tablespoon olive oil
- 1 clove garlic, minced
- 1¼ cups short-grain brown rice
- 1½ cups carrot juice
- 1 cup water
- ½ teaspoon salt
- 2 carrots, finely chopped
- 6 ounces green beans, cut into 1-inch lengths
- 1 cup cooked chickpeas
- 3 scallions, thinly sliced
- ¾ cup grated Parmesan cheese (2½ ounces)

In a medium saucepan, heat the oil over medium heat. Add the garlic and cook until fragrant, about 1 minute. Stir in the rice.

Add the carrot juice, water, and salt, and bring to a boil. Reduce the heat to low, cover, and simmer for 25 minutes.

Stir in the carrots, green beans, chickpeas, and scallions, and cook until the rice is tender and the liquid is absorbed, about 20 minutes.

Stir in the Parmesan. Serve hot.

MAKES 4 SERVINGS

BLUE-CHEESE POLENTA WITH MUSHROOM SAUCE

Try this polenta with Maytag blue cheese, a world-class cheese from Iowa that has been produced on the Maytag family farm since 1941.

- 1 tablespoon olive oil
- 3 cloves garlic, minced
- 10 ounces cremini mushrooms, thinly sliced
- 2¾ cups water
- 1 cup tomato sauce
- ¼ teaspoon crumbled rosemary
- ⅛ teaspoon red pepper flakes
- ¾ teaspoon salt
- 1 cup yellow cornmeal
- ½ cup crumbled blue cheese (2 ounces)

In a large skillet, heat the oil over medium heat. Add the garlic and cook until fragrant, about 1 minute. Add the mushrooms and ¼ cup of the water, and bring to a boil. Reduce to a simmer, cover, and cook until the mushrooms are softened, about 3 minutes.

Add the tomato sauce, rosemary, red pepper flakes, and ¼ teaspoon of the salt. Cook until the sauce is slightly reduced and the flavors are blended, about 5 minutes. Set aside.

In a medium bowl, combine the cornmeal and 1 cup of the water. In a medium saucepan, bring the remaining 1½ cups water to a boil over medium heat. Add the remaining ½ teaspoon salt and reduce to a gentle simmer. Stirring constantly, gradually add the cornmeal mixture. Cook until the mixture is thick and leaves the side of the pan, about 7 minutes. Add the blue cheese and stir until melted.

Gently reheat the mushroom sauce over low heat. Serve the polenta topped with the sauce.

MAKES 4 SERVINGS

BAKED SPELT WITH NUTS

The combination of whole grains, nuts, cheese, and eggs provides ample protein in this meatless main course. Serve with a crisp green salad.

- 1 tablespoon vegetable oil
- 1 tablespoon butter
- 1 large onion, chopped
- 3 large ribs celery with leaves, chopped
- 1 cup cooked spelt berries
- 1 cup whole-milk ricotta cheese
- 2 large eggs, beaten
- ½ cup chopped cashews
- ½ cup chopped walnuts
- ½ cup sunflower seeds
- 3 tablespoons chopped parsley
- 1 tablespoon minced fresh thyme or 1 ½ teaspoons dried
- 1 teaspoon salt
- ¼ cup wheat germ
- ¼ cup sesame seeds

Preheat the oven to 350°F. Oil a 2-quart baking dish.

In a large skillet, heat the oil and butter over medium heat. Add the onion and cook until wilted. Add the celery, cover, and cook for 5 minutes.

In a mixing bowl, combine the spelt, ricotta, eggs, cashews, walnuts, sunflower seeds, parsley, thyme, and salt. Add the onion mixture and mix thoroughly.

Sprinkle half of the wheat germ on the bottom and up the sides of the baking dish, then spoon in the spelt-nut mixture. Sprinkle the remaining wheat germ and the sesame seeds on top. Bake for 1 hour, or until the eggs are cooked through and the top is lightly browned.

MAKES 6 TO 8 SERVINGS

FARRO WITH PEPITAS & CRANBERRIES: Use farro instead of spelt. Omit the cashews and sunflower seeds, and add ½ cup hulled pumpkin seeds and ½ cup dried cranberries. Use 1 teaspoon ground cumin in place of the thyme.

MUSHROOM & CARAMELIZED ONION PANINI

Low heat is essential in producing caramelized onions. Both the mushrooms and onions can be prepared a day ahead and refrigerated.

- 3 tablespoons canola oil, plus extra for brushing
- 2 large onions (1¼ pounds total), thinly sliced
- ½ teaspoon coarse salt
- 3 portobello mushrooms
- 6 ounces shiitake mushrooms, stems discarded, caps thinly sliced

2 teaspoons fresh oregano leaves, chopped

4 whole wheat hero rolls (6 inches)

2 teaspoons red wine vinegar

6 ounces sliced Gruyère cheese

Warm a medium, heavy skillet over low heat. Add 2 tablespoons of the oil and the onions, and sprinkle with ¼ teaspoon of the salt. Cook over low heat, stirring now and then, until the onions are very soft and deep golden brown, about 1 hour. Set aside.

Meanwhile, with a small spoon, scrape the gills from the portobellos. Discard the stems and cut the caps into ½-inch slices.

In a large skillet, heat the remaining 1 tablespoon oil. Add the portobellos, shiitakes, oregano, and remaining ¼ teaspoon salt. Cook without stirring until the mushrooms soften and start to release liquid, about 3 minutes. Continue to cook, stirring, until the mushrooms are soft and juicy, about 4 minutes.

Open the rolls and drizzle the vinegar on the bottom halves. Top with the mushrooms, Gruyére, and onions. Close the top halves of the rolls. Brush the outsides of the rolls with a little oil.

Heat a large, heavy skillet over medium-low heat. Put the sandwiches in the skillet. (Work in two batches if all the sandwiches don't comfortably fit at the same time.) Weight them down with a foil-wrapped brick or a few cans. Cook until the bread becomes crisp and golden, about 3 minutes. Flip the sandwiches, replace the weight, and cook until the cheese is melted and the other ingredients are hot, about 3 minutes. Cut the sandwiches in half to serve.

MAKES 4 SERVINGS

VEGAN CASSOULET

Traditionally, the French baked bean dish called cassoulet is loaded with meats of all sorts. But the density and flavors of baked tofu manage to provide a good vegan substitute. If you don't want to make your own baked tofu, find a good commercial brand with a smoky flavor (wipe off any extra seasoning before using).

¼ cup sunflower oil

1 medium onion, chopped

5 cloves garlic, minced

2 teaspoons thyme

1 bay leaf

½ teaspoon salt

¼ teaspoon pepper

4 cups cooked flageolets or navy beans

Roasted Lemon-Herb Tofu (page 311)

1 cup vegetable broth, store-bought or homemade (page 173)

2 tablespoons chopped parsley

½ cup whole wheat panko bread crumbs

Preheat the oven to 300°F.

In a large skillet, heat the oil over medium heat. Add the onion and garlic, and cook until soft. Add the thyme, bay leaf, salt, and pepper, and cook for 3 minutes longer. Stir in the beans, tofu, and broth.

Transfer the mixture to a 1-quart baking dish. Sprinkle the top with the parsley and ¼ cup of the panko crumbs. Bake for 45 minutes.

Remove from the oven, stir the contents down gently, and sprinkle with the remaining panko. Bake for 30 minutes, or until the topping is crisp. Discard the bay leaf.

MAKES 6 SERVINGS

MEATLESS MOUSSAKA

In many baked eggplant dishes, the slices of eggplant are first panfried before combining with other ingredients. Because the vegetable is such a sponge, you can end up with more oil than you want. By tossing the eggplant with a small amount of light vinaigrette and then baking, you can control the amount of oil the eggplant absorbs.

2 tablespoons plus 2 teaspoons olive oil

2 tablespoons red wine vinegar

2 small eggplants (8 ounces each), cut lengthwise into ¼-inch slices

8 ounces whole wheat orzo

1 large onion, coarsely chopped

5 cloves garlic, minced

2 tablespoons flour

1½ cups reduced-fat (2%) milk

3 ounces whole-milk mozzarella cheese, shredded (about ¾ cup)

½ teaspoon oregano

½ teaspoon rosemary

½ teaspoon salt

¼ teaspoon pepper

1 cup tomato sauce

Preheat the oven to 425°F. Oil a 9 × 9-inch baking dish.

In a large bowl, combine 2 tablespoons of the oil and the vinegar. Add the eggplant slices, tossing to coat. Arrange the eggplant slices in a single layer on two baking sheets and bake for 15 minutes, or until soft. (Leave the oven on.)

Meanwhile, in a large pot of boiling water, cook the orzo according to the package directions. Drain well and set aside.

In a large saucepan, heat the remaining 2 teaspoons oil over medium heat. Add the onion and garlic, and cook, stirring frequently, until the onion is softened, about 7 minutes. Add the flour and cook, stirring constantly, until lightly golden, about 4 minutes. Gradually whisk in the milk and cook, whisking frequently, until the mixture is slightly thickened, about 4 minutes.

Remove from the heat and stir in the orzo, all but 2 tablespoons of the mozzarella, the oregano, rosemary, salt, and pepper.

Place half of the eggplant slices in the bottom and up one side of the baking dish, letting the eggplant hang over by 2 inches. Repeat on the opposite side of the dish. Spoon the orzo mixture over the eggplant, fold the overhanging eggplant ends over the mixture, and pour the tomato sauce on top. Bake for 20 minutes, or until the moussaka is piping hot. Sprinkle the remaining 2 tablespoons mozzarella on top and bake for 2 minutes longer, or until the cheese is melted.

MAKES 4 SERVINGS

Eggs & Cheese

Eggs

Eggs and cheese belong in the same chapter for a variety of reasons: They are both considered dairy (at least as far as supermarket departments are concerned); they are both good sources of sustainable protein; and they are absolutely delicious when put together in dishes, which they frequently are. Dishes that highlight these delicious foods can range from the very simple (scrambled eggs, grilled cheese) to the elegant (cheese soufflés) to hearty family fare (cheese enchiladas, stratas).

Cooking Eggs

No matter how much you are tempted to do so, never hurry the cooking of an egg. Always cook it at low to moderate heat; high temperatures set the protein in the white and the yolk much too rapidly. As the protein sets, it shrinks, and the egg—scrambled, baked, hard-cooked, poached, or fried—becomes tough and rubbery. If the egg is part of a sauce when the shrinking takes place, it won't hold any liquid, and the mixture will curdle, showing small, tough lumps of egg.

You can avoid overheating eggs in sauces, puddings, and soft custards by using a double boiler, and by tempering the eggs (see "Tempering Eggs," page 465). For sauces and puddings, cook the starch first—it needs extra time to thicken and get rid of its raw taste—then add the eggs.

Hard- & Soft-Cooked Eggs

Some cooks call them hard- and soft-"boiled" eggs, while to others they are "coddled," but the names all mean the same thing. The term "boiled eggs" is a misnomer, since eggs should never be boiled, and "coddled" eggs are simply eggs that were started in boiling water instead of cold water. Whatever you call them, they are useful in dozens of ways. Sliced hard-cooked eggs make an attractive garnish; chopped ones make a tasty salad; stuffed ones, quick hors d'oeuvres; and whole ones, great lunch-bag filler. In a pinch you can even substitute a soft-cooked egg for a poached one.

Prepare hard- and soft-cooked eggs in one of these three ways:

Method one: Place cold eggs in a saucepan or pot and cover with cold water. Since both the eggs and the water are cold, there is no need to worry about the shells cracking. Bring the water just to a boil, then reduce the heat to simmer. For soft-cooked eggs, simmer for 3 to 5 minutes, depending on how firm you want the whites. For hard-cooked eggs, simmer for 10 to 15 minutes.

Method two: This is a variation on the above method in which you start the cold eggs in cold water. After bringing the water to a boil, remove the pan from the heat and let the eggs sit in the

EGG SAFETY

Eggs can carry a strain of bacteria called *Salmonella*. Even though the rate of contamination is low (about 1 in 20,000 eggs), it's best to take precautions when making dishes with raw or barely cooked eggs. Buy eggs that are as fresh as possible, and keep them very well refrigerated. If an egg is carrying *Salmonella*, the bacteria will multiply to potentially dangerous levels if the conditions (time and temperature) are right. But never serve raw or undercooked eggs, no matter how fresh, to very young children, pregnant women, the elderly, or anyone whose immune system is impaired. If you seek out pasteurized eggs, you can completely sidestep the problem.

---

hot water for the same times as given above. This method produces a slightly moister egg yolk.

Method three (coddled eggs): Reduce the chances of cracking the shells by piercing the large ends of the shells with a pin or an egg piercer to release trapped air and also by letting the eggs warm to room temperature before cooking (it takes about 45 minutes). Bring a pot of water to a boil and, with a large spoon or wire basket, carefully lower the eggs into the water. Cover the pan and remove it from the heat. Let soft-cooked eggs stand for 4 to 5 minutes, hard-cooked ones for 10 to 15 minutes.

Serve soft-cooked eggs while they are hot; hard-cooked ones should be plunged into cold water immediately to stop the cooking. If a hard-cooked egg is not cooled rapidly (or if it is cooked in boiling water), the white sticks to the shell, and the iron in the yolk combines with the sulfur in the white to form an unattractive green ring on the outer edge of the yolk. A dry, mealy yolk shows that the hard-cooked egg was cooked just right. If the yolk is waxy, the egg was undercooked. A soft-cooked egg properly done will have a moist, tender white and a runny yolk.

Peel a hard-cooked egg by first tapping it on a hard surface to crack the shell. Then roll it between your hands until you loosen the shell. Starting at the large end, remove the shell and the thin membrane under it. If the shell is stubborn—an egg 3 or 4 days old is usually easier to peel than a fresher one—try holding it under cold running water as you peel.

Crack the shell of a soft-cooked egg by tapping it around the middle with a knife handle. Carefully remove the shell from the small end. Next, use a spoon to scoop the egg from the large end.

Store hard-cooked eggs in the refrigerator for use within a few days. If you forget which eggs are cooked and which are raw, spin them on the counter. Cooked eggs spin evenly and quickly; raw ones wobble. (Some cooks simply pencil "HC" on hard-cooked ones before refrigerating.)

Poached Eggs

Poached eggs have much to recommend them—delicate flavor, no added fat, silken texture, few calories, and quick preparation. They are a little tricky for beginners, so it is a good idea to make them once or twice for yourself before preparing them for a crowd.

Always use the freshest eggs available. They

will poach into compact, tidy spheres with the whites piled high around the yolks; older ones will not. To help shape those spheres perfectly and prevent streamers of white from forming, some cooks use poaching rings (which mold the eggs into neat rounds) or an egg poacher (which actually steams instead of poaches the eggs). But neither is really necessary if you follow this simple method:

Fill a shallow pan with just enough boiling water (or milk or broth) to cover the egg or the eggs. Break one egg, still cold from the refrigerator, into a saucer or small sauce dish. Create a little whirlpool in the simmering water with a wooden spoon, place the edge of the dish at the side of the whirlpool, and gently slip the egg into it. It is not necessary to add salt, vinegar, or lemon juice to hasten the setting of the whites, as many cookbooks suggest. In fact, acids and salt make the surface of the egg shrivel and pucker. Let the water return to a gentle simmer (boiling water leaves poached eggs with tough whites and a misshapen appearance). Either cover the pan and let the eggs stand until they are done, 3 to 5 minutes, or gently spoon the hot water over the eggs occasionally for 2 to 3 minutes.

When the eggs are done, use a slotted spoon to remove them from the water. They should have opaque, tender, jellylike whites and runny yolks covered by thin veils of white. Drain them and serve at once. If you must delay serving, cool the eggs instantly in cold water. You can store poached eggs for up to 24 hours in refrigerated ice water. When ready to serve, immerse them in hot water for 1 minute.

Baked & Shirred Eggs

Baking is one of the easiest ways to prepare tender, tasty eggs. Even an inexperienced cook will have no trouble achieving first-class results by following these simple directions:

Break eggs into lightly buttered individual ramekins, custard cups, or muffin tins. Cover each container with a circle of parchment paper and place the containers in a pan of hot water. Both of those steps help distribute heat evenly during cooking and ensure moist, tender eggs. To lock in moisture without covering the containers, top each egg with a dab of butter or a dollop of cheese sauce or cream. Bake the eggs at a moderate temperature (325°F) for 5 to 15 minutes, until the whites are a milky color and the yolks are soft but not runny. Remove the still-soft eggs from the oven and water bath right away, because the containers will hold enough heat to continue the cooking for several seconds.

Shirred eggs are a cross between baked eggs and fried eggs, and they are also very easy to make. First, cook the eggs in a lightly buttered ovenproof skillet on the stove over medium heat until the whites just start to set; then, transfer the pan to the oven and bake for about 5 minutes, until the whites are set and the yolks are partially cooked but still runny in the center.

Fried Eggs

The perfect fried egg—tender white, pliant yolk, greaseless—is within the grasp of every cook. The secret is a simple one: Replace most of the frying fat with water. Here is the method:

Lightly grease a heavy skillet with ¼ to ½ teaspoon oil or butter—just enough to prevent the eggs from sticking. Place over low heat until a few drops of water sprinkled in the pan bounce. Carefully break the eggs, one at a time, into a saucer or custard cup, then slide the egg into the skillet. As each egg is added to the pan, be certain to allow enough room between the eggs to keep them separate; otherwise, you will have to cut the whites apart when you turn the eggs or serve them. Add

1 tablespoon of water to the pan for each egg. Cover with a tight-fitting lid and steam-fry the eggs, 2 to 3 minutes until the whites are set and slightly thick, and the yolks are covered by a thin veil of white. While the eggs are cooking, you can baste them once or twice with the water if you like your eggs sunny-side up. If you prefer them "over easy," use a spatula to lift them carefully, so that the yolk will not be broken, and turn them over for the last few seconds of cooking.

Scrambled Eggs

Mention scrambled eggs and most people think of breakfast, but add minced cheese, vegetables, or cooked meat to those light-yellow, softly textured eggs, and you have a welcome main dish for a light lunch or supper.

Although most recipes call for adding water, cream, or milk, the only ingredient that is really necessary for scrambled eggs is eggs! If you like, you can add a tablespoon of liquid for each egg you are cooking (1 to 2 eggs per person) but don't use more. Too much added liquid will turn tender, fluffy scrambled eggs into watery, lumpy ones.

The size of the pan and how evenly it distributes heat also influence volume and texture. If the pan is too large, the scrambled egg mixture spreads out too thin and cooks too quickly; in a pan that is too small, the mixture is too thick (more than an inch deep), and, inevitably, the bottom cooks too quickly. An 8-inch pan is ideal for cooking 4 scrambled eggs. But if you want extra-creamy, soft scrambled eggs, a double boiler is the perfect utensil. It solves the heat problem nicely, since the simmering water maintains an even temperature.

You can mix eggs in three different ways to get scrambled eggs just the way you like them. With a fork or wire whisk, blend them thoroughly if you like eggs that are solid, delicate yellow; blend only lightly if you prefer flecks of white and yellow; or beat whites separately if you want maximum lightness and volume, then fold in the beaten yolks. (Adding an extra white also helps.)

After blending the eggs and any optional liquid or seasonings, heat a lightly buttered pan over low heat. Add the eggs and, as they begin to set, stir only enough to keep them from sticking to the pan and to let the uncooked portion flow to the bottom. Constant stirring makes dry, crumbly scrambled eggs. Add any desired vegetables, cheese, or meat—usually ¼ to ⅓ cup is a good amount for 4 eggs—a minute before the eggs are done. When they are puffy and hold their shape but are still moist and slightly undercooked, in 2 to 3 minutes, take them off the heat. The eggs will continue to cook for a few seconds after they are removed from the heat, so they will be done by the time you serve them.

Plain Omelets

The classic plain omelet, very delicately browned on the outside and creamy yellow on the inside, is versatile enough to be served at any meal. With a little knowledge and some practice, you can have one ready to eat in just minutes.

A plain omelet has three basic ingredients: eggs, a liquid, and butter. Two or three eggs will make a small omelet that serves one person. Eggs allowed to warm to room temperature before cooking make an omelet with the best volume. Most recipes call for 1 tablespoon of water or milk for each egg used (fruit or vegetable juice can be substituted). Water makes a tender omelet; milk makes one that is firmer.

A simple way to enhance the flavor of the eggs in a plain omelet is to blend a small amount—about

$^1/_4$ teaspoon—of an herb or spice into the eggs before cooking. Chives, oregano, basil, tarragon, dillweed, parsley, marjoram, white pepper, and thyme, alone or in a combination, complement eggs.

The quality and type of pan you use has a lot to do with the success of your omelet. The pan should be heavy enough for even cooking, but light enough to manipulate easily. Omelet pans range from 6 to 10 inches in diameter and have 2-inch sloping sides. A 6- or 7-inch pan, which nicely cooks a two-egg omelet, is best for home use. Larger omelets are more difficult to handle and require close monitoring or they will cook unevenly. In any case, a two-egg omelet cooks so rapidly you can make another in a jiffy.

Omelet pans can be either nonstick or steel. Before using a steel omelet pan for the first time, it needs to be seasoned. Pouring $^1/_2$ inch of oil into it, then warm it over low heat for 20 minutes. Drain off the excess oil and wipe the pan dry.

Because the actual mixing and cooking of an omelet is quick, it is wise to assemble the ingredients before you break the eggs. You may also want to heat fillings (except cheese) before adding them. Use a light touch with a wire whisk or fork to beat the eggs and the liquid only until there are no visible lumps of white or yellow, 20 to 30 seconds. Overbeating makes a tough omelet.

Add a pat of butter to a moderately hot pan over medium-high heat. (Omelets are an exception to the rule that says eggs should be cooked at low temperatures.) When the butter stops foaming but before it starts to brown, pour in the egg mixture no more than $^1/_4$ inch deep. As the eggs cook, use a fork or a spatula to draw the edges of the eggs toward the center of the pan. At the same time, tilt the pan to let the uncooked portion flow underneath. Continue until the top of the omelet is moist but no longer runny, 15 to 30 seconds. If you are adding a filling—$^1/_3$ to $^1/_2$ cup is plenty—spread it on half of the omelet. Remove the finished omelet from the heat and fold it in half as you slide it onto a warm plate.

After making an omelet in a steel pan, do not wash the pan; simply wipe it with a paper towel. If you do decide to wash it, reseason before cooking again.

Fluffy Omelets

The steps in cooking a tender, fluffy omelet are simple. First, you beat the yolks and whites separately. Then partially cook the omelet as you would a plain omelet, but then transfer to the oven to finish cooking.

To begin, preheat the oven to 350°F and heat an ovenproof skillet over medium-high heat. Then, to shape the framework of the omelet, you need to beat the egg whites and yolks separately. Beat the yolks with a whisk to a thick, yellow foam, and the whites to airy peaks. Add butter to the hot skillet. After beating, immediately fold the yolks into the whites (see "Folding Beaten Egg Whites," page 328). Now you must work swiftly. Delaying a minute or two before cooking gives the liquid in the eggs time to seep from the mixture and then collect on the bottom of the pan. Pour the egg mixture immediately into the skillet in which butter is bubbly but not browned. Cook until the bottom is set but the top is still moist, 3 to 5 minutes, then switch the omelet to the oven. After the omelet is in the oven for a few minutes and looks puffy, touch the surface lightly: It will spring back when done and will look slightly dry on the surface.

As soon as you remove the omelet from the oven, fold it in half, slip it onto a warm plate, and serve at once.

FOLDING BEATEN EGG WHITES

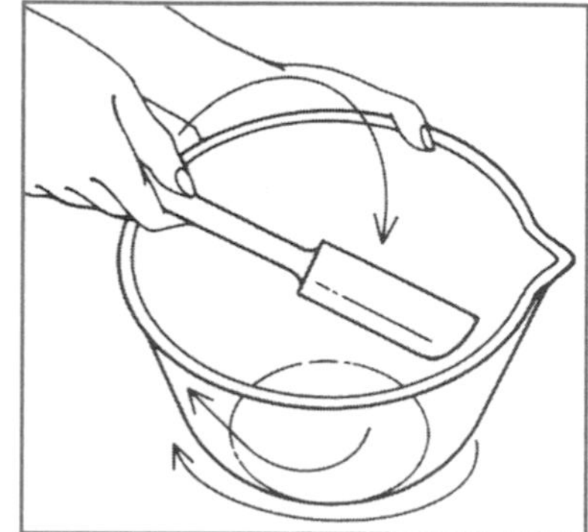

When the success of a recipe depends on keeping beaten egg whites light and airy, beaten egg yolks—and sauces or other ingredients—are folded into the whites. To fold, carefully spoon the yolks over the whites. With a spatula, gently spread the yolks; then lift the whites from the bottom and gently turn them over the yolks. Repeat until there are no streaks of white or yellow. When there is a significant amount of sauce or other mixture to be combined with beaten egg whites, about one-third of the whites are stirred into the mixture first, to lighten it. Then the lightened mixture is folded into the whites as described above.

Frittatas

In making a frittata, the famous Italian omelet, you mix the filling with the eggs and cook the whole thing at once. Sizes can vary considerably, from small frittatas for 2 to 3 people (about 3 eggs) to larger versions with 8 or more eggs. A good rule of thumb is 1 to 1½ eggs per serving, and about 1 cup cooked chopped vegetables, meat, poultry, or flaked fish for every 3 eggs. Cook the frittata in a skillet on the stovetop, the way you would a plain omelet, but when the bottom is set, you can either lightly brown the top under a hot broiler for 1 to 2 minutes, or bake it in the oven until the top is puffed and browned. Serve the frittata cut into wedges.

Soufflés

Light, high, feathery, yet creamy—a soufflé is actually a version of the fluffy omelet made with a sauce that contains the egg yolks. It is baked in a deep dish that permits it to rise as its top bakes into a crusty dome. Like omelets, soufflés make elegant main courses (as well as grand desserts).

Soufflés puff to impressive heights when air bubbles trapped in the beaten egg whites expand during baking. The degree of expansion depends on the way you handle the egg whites and sauce, and how you bake the soufflé. For maximum volume and lightness, use 3 egg whites for every 2 yolks. First, prepare the sauce. Then, beat the whites until they form a thick, glossy foam with peaks that have slightly rounded tips. Be careful not to overbeat, or your delicate foam is likely to disintegrate into small, dry curds. Immediately after beating, gently fold the sauce, which has been lightened (thinned) with a small portion of the beaten whites, into the whites. Do this quickly or the whites will deflate.

As soon as the sauce base is thoroughly folded into the beaten whites, gently pour the soufflé mixture into a prepared baking dish. For the classic high soufflé, use a standard porcelain soufflé dish that holds 6 cups or less. When the traditional appearance is of no concern, any deep, straight-sided baking dish will serve. Stay away from dishes with sloping sides unless you are prepared to deal with a soufflé that slumps.

Prepare the soufflé dish by buttering the bottom only, or by buttering the entire inside and then lightly sprinkling flour over it. (If you are making a cheese soufflé, sprinkle with grated Parmesan cheese as a tasty substitute for the flour.) The soufflé clings to the flour granules as it rises in the dish. After baking, the same granules keep the crust from sticking to the dish.

After filling the dish, rush the soufflé to a preheated oven. Center the soufflé on a rack 6 inches from the bottom of the oven and bake for 40 to 50 minutes. Do not open the oven to check on the soufflé's progress. A cool draft can cause instant collapse!

Most Americans like dry soufflés, considered "done" when a knife inserted in the center comes out clean. The European preference is for slightly underbaked, unstable soufflés, with the sauce still runny in the center.

When the soufflé is done as you like it, hurry your steaming soufflé to the table while it is still high, and divide it so that each serving has some of the crust. In an emergency, you can hold a soufflé in the oven for up to 10 minutes after the baking is done, but be sure to turn off the heat, and do not open the oven door.

Separating Egg Whites from Egg Yolks

Some recipes require only the white or the yolk of an egg; some call for adding the white and the yolk at different times. The technique for separating eggs is easily mastered.

Use a knife blade to crack the shell of a cold egg in the middle, or tap the middle of the egg against the edge of a bowl. While holding the egg over an empty cup or small bowl, gently pull the shell into two pieces with your thumbs. Very carefully pass the yolk from one half of the shell to the other, letting the white drop into the cup or bowl. Place the yolk in its own separate container. If a fragment of shell falls into the white, pick it out with a piece of the shell, paper toweling, or a teaspoon. If the yolk breaks and runs into the white, set that egg aside, since even a tiny speck of yolk will ruin the white for beating. (Use the egg to make scrambled eggs or a plain omelet.) Pour the separated white into a large bowl. Repeat until you have the number of whites or yolks needed.

Beating Egg Whites & Yolks

Under the right conditions egg whites, properly beaten, can inflate to six times their original volume. To get the kind of expansion necessary for creating light, airy dishes, several things are critical: temperature, humidity, bowl, beaters, and ingredients.

Egg whites beat best when the humidity is low and when they have been held at room temperature for 45 minutes. Add a pinch of cream of tartar or a little salt to help stabilize the whites. Place the whites in a bowl made of glass, stainless steel, ceramic, or copper. Some cooks prefer a copper one because the slight acidity of copper seems to make a fuller, longer lasting foam. Never use an aluminum bowl (it turns the whites gray) or a plastic one (it may prevent foaming). Select a bowl that has a rounded bottom so that the beaters pick up all the whites. The bowl and beaters must be absolutely clean. Even the slightest speck of fat (including egg yolk, which contains fat) can seriously hinder the beating process.

You can use either a wire whisk, a hand-held rotary beater, or an electric mixer to beat egg whites. Gourmet cooks prefer balloon wire whisks, which do not cut the foam the way a rotary beater does. If you are in a hurry, you may decide

DRESSING UP A SOUFFLÉ

Will your soufflé wear a 2-inch cap or a high hat? These are two methods of giving a soufflé an impressive, professional look.

Cap: For a small cap, fill the dish almost to the top, and level the mixture with a spatula. With your thumb, make a groove around the edge of the soufflé mixture. This will allow the center portion of the soufflé to rise higher than the sides, making it look as though it's wearing a cap.

High hat: For the impressive high hat, choose a soufflé dish that is 1 to 2 cups smaller than what the recipe calls for. Cut off a piece of waxed paper long enough to go around the soufflé dish with some overlap. Fold the waxed paper in half lengthwise and brush one side of the collar with oil or melted butter. Position the collar around the outside of the dish, buttered-side in, extending it 3 inches above the rim. Secure it with string or paper clips.

---

to use an electric mixer. Start the mixer at low speed until the whites are foamy; then increase to medium speed. Be wary of overbeating when using an electric mixer.

Beat the whites until they are glossy and moist, not dry. If they become dry, they have been overbeaten; they will lack volume and elasticity. Fortunately, you can rescue overbeaten whites by adding 1 to 2 tablespoons of cold water and beating again, briskly and briefly.

Underbeaten whites create as many problems for the cook as do their overbeaten counterparts. They leak water and added ingredients, and they do not hold their shape. Well-beaten whites should stand in either soft or stiff peaks. Follow the recipe for directions concerning the degree of stiffness desired.

Beaten egg yolks are not nearly as fragile as whites are. They can be beaten successfully in any bowl, at any time, with any type of beater. Yolks might be lightly beaten just to blend several together. With more beating they become thick and lemon colored. With still more beating, yolks become thick enough to form a thin, flat ribbon that doubles back on itself when dropped from the beater (see below).

Cheese

Cooking with Cheese

Cooked cheeses add body and flavor to all types of dishes, but there are certain rules for ensuring smooth, creamy results.

Always cook cheese over warm, not high, heat and keep the cooking time minimal. At high temperatures, or during prolonged cooking, the protein in cheese separates from the fat and the cheese becomes a stringy, rubbery mass floating in an oily liquid.

When using cheese in sauces and fondues, shred, grate, crumble, or dice it. Cheese in small pieces blends readily and melts faster. Add cheese to a liquid or a sauce that is already hot and, if possible, cook the mixture over boiling water in a double boiler. Remove it from the heat as soon as the cheese and the liquid (or the sauce) are smoothly blended.

To broil cheese, place it 4 to 5 inches below the heat. It will melt in 1 to 3 minutes, so keep a close watch. Broiled cheese is delightful on an open-faced sandwich of meat, tomatoes, poultry, or fish.

When baking cheese dishes, keep the oven temperature low to moderate—about 325° to 350°F is fine. Bake cheese custards in a larger pan filled with water to prevent them from overcooking. And to help keep cheese toppings from toughening or hardening during baking, cover them with fine bread crumbs, or wait to add the cheese until just a minute or two before removing the food from the oven. Sometimes cheese can be sprinkled over a dish once it's out of the oven if there's enough residual heat to melt it.

FAT CONTENT IN COOKING CHEESES

Generally speaking, the higher the fat content the more readily a cheese will melt. Here is a list of common cooking cheeses and the amount of fat they have per ounce, ranking from the most to the least.

CHEESE (1 OUNCE)	TOTAL FAT (G)
CHEDDAR	9.4
GRUYÈRE	9.2
COLBY	9.1
FONTINA	8.8
ROQUEFORT	8.7
MONTEREY JACK	8.6
MUENSTER	8.5
GOUDA	7.8
PROVOLONE	7.6
ROMANO	7.6
PARMESAN	7.3
MOZZARELLA, WHOLE-MILK	6.3
FETA	6.0
GOAT CHEESE, SOFT	6.0
MOZZARELLA, PART-SKIM	4.5

Grating & Shredding Cheeses

Grated and shredded cheeses make nice garnishes on casseroles and blend readily into sauces. Shred, grate, or crumble 4 ounces (¼ pound) of cheese for every cup of cheese called for in a recipe. The very hard cheeses are excellent for fine grating and the softer ones work best when shredded. Trying to grate a soft cheese too finely will only result in a clogged grater. For easiest grating and shredding, use cheeses that are very cold.

OLD-FASHIONED DEVILED EGGS

To efficiently fill the egg whites, transfer the yolk mixture to a resealable plastic bag and press the filling down towards one corner. Cut off about ½ inch of the corner of the bag to fashion a piping bag. Carefully pipe the filling evenly into the egg whites.

- 12 large eggs
- ½ cup mayonnaise
- 2 tablespoons grated sweet onion
- 1 teaspoon dry mustard
- ½ teaspoon salt
- ¼ teaspoon black pepper
- Pinch of cayenne pepper
- Paprika, for garnish
- Minced parsley, for garnish

Place the eggs in a large saucepan with cold water to cover. Bring just to a boil, reduce the heat, and simmer for 15 minutes. Cool under cold running water. Refrigerate to cool completely.

When cool, peel the eggs, then cut in half. Remove the yolks and transfer to a small bowl.

Add the mayonnaise to the yolks and use a fork to mash until creamy. Stir in the onion, mustard, salt, black pepper, and cayenne. Taste for seasoning, and add more salt and pepper, if desired.

Spoon the yolk mixture evenly into the egg white halves. Sprinkle lightly with paprika and parsley. Place the deviled eggs on a serving platter, cover, and refrigerate until ready to serve.

MAKES 24 DEVILED EGGS

FOUR-PEPPER DEVILED EGGS: Add 1 teaspoon minced pickled jalapeño pepper and 2 tablespoons finely minced red bell pepper to the yolk mixture. Use chipotle chili powder instead of cayenne. Use minced scallion greens instead of onion.

BETTER-FOR-YOU EGG SALAD

Soft silken tofu stands in for mayonnaise in this more healthful version of egg salad.

- 4 large eggs
- 8 ounces soft silken tofu
- 4 teaspoons brown mustard
- ½ teaspoon salt
- ⅛ teaspoon hot pepper sauce
- ⅓ cup minced onion
- ¼ cup chopped parsley

In a medium saucepan, place the eggs with cold water to cover by several inches. Bring to a boil over high heat. Remove from the heat, cover, and let stand 12 minutes. Run the eggs under cold water until chilled. Peel, halve, and transfer to a large bowl.

Add the tofu, mustard, salt, and hot sauce, and mash with a potato masher until some small chunks remain. Fold in the onion and parsley. Cover and chill until serving time.

MAKES 4 SERVINGS

BACON & POACHED EGGS ON MIXED GREENS

This warm and pleasing classic bistro dish is best when made with farm-fresh organic eggs.

8 thick-cut bacon slices, halved crosswise

About 1/4 cup extra-virgin olive oil

6 ounces frisée (curly endive), about 7 cups

2 small heads Bibb lettuce, leaves separated

2 tablespoons finely chopped shallot

2 tablespoons red wine vinegar

1 teaspoon Dijon mustard

Coarse salt and pepper

4 large eggs, poached (see page 324)

Preheat the oven to 350°F. Arrange the bacon on a rimmed baking sheet. Bake for 25 to 30 minutes, until crisp. Transfer to a large plate lined with paper towels. Pour the drippings into a measuring cup. Add enough olive oil to make 1/3 cup.

Tear the frisée into bite-size pieces and arrange on 4 plates with the Bibb leaves. Divide the bacon pieces among the plates.

In a small skillet, heat the oil-bacon fat mixture over medium-high heat. Add the shallot and cook, stirring, until soft, 1 to 2 minutes. Whisk in the vinegar and mustard, and simmer for 1 minute. Add a large pinch of salt and some pepper. Set aside and keep warm.

Place the warm poached eggs on top of the salad greens. Immediately drizzle with the warm dressing. Sprinkle with salt and pepper to taste.

MAKES 4 SERVINGS

HUEVOS RANCHEROS

Fine for breakfast, of course, this classic Mexican egg dish also works well as a low-cost main course for lunch or dinner. Serve with guacamole and a big green salad.

3 tablespoons vegetable oil

4 corn tortillas

1/2 cup chopped onion

2 cloves garlic, minced

1 1/2 cups tomato sauce

1 can (4.5 ounces) chopped mild green chilies

1/2 teaspoon ground cumin

4 large eggs

3/4 cup shredded sharp Cheddar cheese (3 ounces)

In a medium skillet, heat 2 tablespoons of the oil over medium-high heat. Add the tortillas, one at a time, and cook, turning once, to heat through. Drain on paper towels and keep warm.

Add the onion and garlic to the skillet, and cook until softened. Add the tomato sauce, chilies, and cumin. Bring to a boil over high heat. Reduce to a simmer and cook for 15 minutes.

Preheat the broiler.

In a small skillet, using a scant teaspoon of oil for each, fry one egg at a time, sunny-side up. Place one egg on each tortilla, then on ovenproof serving plates. Top each egg with sauce and sprinkle with Cheddar. Place under the broiler until the cheese melts.

MAKES 4 SERVINGS

HERBED SCRAMBLED EGGS

As with many pan-cooked egg dishes, it's best to prepare this in a smaller pan; you can make multiple batches if you're feeding more than two people. This way you can cook the eggs quickly, and they'll stay moist.

1 tablespoon butter or oil

3 large eggs

3 tablespoons milk or water (optional)

1 tablespoon minced fresh herbs (parsley, basil, tarragon, or thyme)

¼ teaspoon salt

In a medium skillet, melt the butter over low heat.

Beat the eggs lightly with the milk (if using). Beat in the herbs and salt. Pour the eggs into the skillet. Cook, occasionally stirring with a wooden spoon, until the entire mixture is softly set and moist. Remove from the heat and serve hot.

MAKES 2 SERVINGS

ITALIAN SCRAMBLE: For the herbs, use a combination of 1 tablespoon minced parsley and ½ teaspoon oregano. Add 2 tablespoons minced sun-dried tomatoes.

CILANTRO-SCALLION SCRAMBLE: Use 1 tablespoon minced cilantro and 2 tablespoons minced scallions for the herbs.

CURRIED SCRAMBLE: Use cilantro for the herbs and add ½ teaspoon curry powder.

TEX-MEX EGGS & CHEESE

A satisfying one-dish meal for the cook on a budget. Serve with crusty whole-grain peasant bread.

2 tablespoons vegetable oil

1 green bell pepper, diced

1 medium onion, diced

4 medium tomatoes, seeded and diced

1 cup fresh or frozen corn kernels

2 tablespoons diced fresh jalapeño pepper

½ teaspoon salt

8 large eggs, beaten

8 slices Monterey Jack cheese

In a large skillet, heat the oil. Add the pepper, onion, tomatoes, corn, jalapeños, and salt. Cook until the vegetables are tender.

Add the eggs and cook over medium heat, stirring occasionally, until the eggs are set but not dry. Top with slices of cheese, cover, and let cook for 1 to 2 minutes, until the cheese is melted.

MAKES 4 SERVINGS

BASIC OMELET

The classic way to add flavor to omelets is to top it with other ingredients. See some suggestions in "Filled Omelets" (page 336).

4 large eggs

3 tablespoons milk

Pinch of salt

Pinch of white pepper

½ tablespoon butter

Beat the eggs until fluffy. Beat in the milk, salt, and pepper.

In an omelet pan, heat the butter over medium heat.

Pour the egg mixture into the pan. When the underside is set, lift the omelet slightly with a fork or a spatula to let the uncooked portion flow underneath.

As soon as the mixture is set, fold the omelet in half and serve hot.

MAKES 2 SERVINGS

FLUFFY OMELET

It's one extra step to beat egg whites for an omelet, but the results are rewarding.

3 large eggs, separated, plus 1 large egg white

1 tablespoon milk or water

Pinch of salt

1 teaspoon butter

Preheat the oven to 375°F.

In a small bowl, lightly beat the egg yolks, milk, and salt together. In a medium bowl, with a wire whisk, beat the 4 egg whites until they are glossy and form soft peaks.

In 7- or 8-inch ovenproof omelet pan, melt the butter over medium-high heat.

Fold the egg yolk mixture lightly into the whites. When the butter is bubbling, gently pour the egg mixture the pan. Cook until the bottom is set but the top is still moist, about 5 minutes.

Transfer the pan to the oven, and bake until the omelet is puffy and firm to the touch, about 11 minutes. Remove from the oven and fold in half. Slide onto a warm plate and serve hot.

MAKES 2 SERVINGS

GARDEN OMELET

In the summer use fresh baby peas if you can find them. Blanch them for about 30 seconds in boiling water.

- 1 tablespoon vegetable oil
- ¼ cup chopped scallions
- ½ cup shredded lettuce
- 1 cup frozen peas, thawed
- 6 large eggs
- ¼ cup cold water
- ½ teaspoon dried mint
- 2 teaspoons butter

In a small skillet, heat the oil over medium heat. Add the scallions and cook until softened. Stir in the lettuce and peas, and remove from the heat.

In a medium bowl, beat the eggs until light and fluffy. Stir in the water and mint.

In 10-inch omelet pan, melt the butter until bubbling. Pour the egg mixture into the pan. When the underside is set, lift the omelet slightly with a fork or a spatula to let the uncooked portion flow underneath. Spread the pea mixture over half the omelet. Fold the other half over the filling and slide out of the pan. Serve hot.

MAKES 4 TO 6 SERVINGS

BACON & AVOCADO OMELETS

Omelets are usually made in two-serving amounts. You can prep all the filling ingredients together, but the eggs need to be beaten separately for each omelet you make.

- 3 Hass avocados
- Lime juice
- ⅔ cup reduced-fat sour cream
- ½ cup shredded Monterey Jack cheese
- ¼ cup chopped cilantro
- 20 large eggs
- Oil, for the pan
- 10 slices bacon, cooked, drained, and crumbled
- Sea salt and pepper

Peel and slice the avocados. Sprinkle with lime juice as you work, to keep them from discoloring.

In a bowl, stir together the sour cream, cheese, and cilantro.

In a small bowl, beat 2 eggs until frothy. Lightly oil an omelet pan and heat over medium heat. Pour the egg mixture into the pan. When the underside is set, lift the omelet slightly with a fork or a spatula to let the uncooked portion flow underneath.

Spread 1 tablespoon of the sour cream mixture over one side of the omelet. Top with bacon bits and about 3 slices of avocado. Fold the other half over the omelet to cover the filling and slide out of the pan. Season with salt and pepper to taste.

Repeat the procedure with the remaining eggs and filling.

MAKES 10 SERVINGS

PASTA FRITTATA

A frittata is a grand way to use leftovers, including those times when you miscalculate and cook too much pasta.

8 ounces whole wheat vermicelli or spaghettini, broken in half

2 teaspoons plus 2 tablespoons olive oil

4 large eggs

½ cup coarsely shredded carrots

⅓ cup grated Parmesan or Romano cheese

¼ cup minced flat-leaf parsley

¼ teaspoon salt

¼ teaspoon pepper

In a large pot of boiling salted water, cook the pasta according to the package directions. Drain and toss with 2 teaspoons of the oil.

Preheat the broiler.

In a 10-inch broilerproof skillet, heat the remaining 2 tablespoons oil over medium-high heat. Add the pasta, flatten it evenly across the pan with a spatula, and cook until the bottom is crisp and brown, 10 to 15 minutes.

In a medium bowl, beat the eggs well. Stir in the carrots, Parmesan, parsley, salt, and pepper. (The mixture will be somewhat thick.) Pour over the pasta.

Broil for several minutes, or until the frittata is puffy and browned. Cut into wedges to serve.

MAKES 6 SERVINGS

BROWN RICE FRITTATA: Use 4 cups cooked brown rice instead of the pasta. Add ¼ cup slivered sun-dried tomatoes to the egg mixture.

CREMINI FRITTATA WITH PROSCIUTTO & FONTINA

Be sure to ask for the prosciutto in one unsliced slab so you can cut it into dices.

2 tablespoons butter

2 tablespoons olive oil

1 slice (¼-inch-thick) prosciutto, cut into ¼-inch dice

12 cremini mushrooms, sliced ¼ inch thick

FILLED OMELETS

For a filled omelet, make the Basic Omelet (page 334) and spread any of the following fillings on one side of the omelet before folding.

- ¾ cup diced cooked chicken, turkey, salmon, or shrimp
- ½ cup shredded Manchego, goat Gouda, or Gruyère cheese
- ½ cup cubed sautéed apple or pear
- ½ cup chopped cooked asparagus, green beans, or broccoli
- ½ cup minced, seeded tomato and half an avocado, diced
- ¼ cup crumbled cooked bacon (or minced smoked ham) and ¼ cup green peas

Pepper

8 large eggs

½ cup shredded Italian fontina cheese

Preheat the oven to 450°F.

In a large ovenproof skillet, melt the butter with the oil over medium-high heat. Add the prosciutto and cook, stirring, until the fat is rendered, 2 to 3 minutes.

Add the mushrooms, season lightly with pepper, and cook, stirring often, until the mushrooms are softened, about 6 minutes. Remove with a slotted spoon and drain on paper towels.

In a large bowl, whisk the eggs. Pour into the skillet, reduce the heat to medium-low, and cook until slightly set, 2 to 3 minutes. Scatter the prosciutto and mushrooms over the eggs and continue cooking, lifting up the bottom and allowing the uncooked eggs to run underneath, until set, 1 to 2 minutes.

Put the skillet in the oven and bake for 5 to 6 minutes, until slightly puffy. Sprinkle with the fontina and bake until the cheese melts, about 3 minutes.

Cut into wedges to serve.

MAKES 4 TO 6 SERVINGS

SPINACH & FETA FRITTATA

Triple-washed baby spinach leaves are a real boon to the cook, but if you can't get them, just buy about 1¼ pounds large spinach and discard the tough stems. Slice the spinach leaves crosswise into thin shreds, then wash in a bowl of water, swishing to dislodge any sand. Dry in a salad spinner.

3 tablespoons olive oil

¼ cup chopped onion

2 cloves garlic, minced

1 pound baby spinach leaves

4 large eggs

4 large egg whites

¼ cup very finely crumbled soft whole-grain bread crumbs (½ slice)

2 tablespoons slivered fresh basil

2 teaspoons grated lemon zest

½ teaspoon pepper

1 cup crumbled feta cheese (4 ounces)

In a large skillet, heat 1 tablespoon of the oil over medium heat. Add the onion and garlic, and cook for 5 minutes.

Add the spinach and stir until wilted. Remove from the pan and keep warm.

In a medium bowl, beat together the whole eggs and egg whites. Beat in the bread crumbs, basil, lemon zest, and pepper.

In the same skillet, heat the remaining 2 tablespoons oil over medium heat. Stir the spinach mixture and the feta into the egg mixture, then pour into the skillet. Reduce the heat and cook until the top of the frittata is set.

Cut into wedges to serve.

MAKES 4 TO 6 SERVINGS

TOMATO & WHITE BEAN FRITTATA

This frittata is made with fewer whole eggs and more egg whites to reduce the amount of cholesterol. With all the seasonings in the dish you won't even notice.

4 teaspoons olive oil

1 cup thinly sliced onion

3 large eggs

6 large egg whites

1 tablespoon milk

- ½ teaspoon pepper
- ½ teaspoon oregano
- ¼ teaspoon basil
- ¼ teaspoon salt
- ¼ cup cooked white beans
- 2 large plum tomatoes, thinly sliced
- 3 ounces smoked mozzarella cheese, shredded

In a 10-inch skillet, heat the oil over medium heat. Add the onion, and cook until softened and just beginning to brown, about 5 minutes.

Meanwhile, in a medium bowl, beat the whole eggs and egg whites with the milk, pepper, oregano, basil, and salt. Stir in the beans.

Pour the egg-bean mixture into the skillet and lay the tomatoes on top. Cook the frittata until nearly firm, lifting the edges to let the uncooked egg run underneath, about 7 minutes.

Sprinkle the mozzarella evenly over the frittata, cover, and cook until the cheese is just melted and the frittata is completely set, 1 to 2 minutes.

Cut into wedges to serve.

MAKES 4 SERVINGS

POTATO & GREENS FRITTATA

You can use sliced Canadian bacon for a lower-fat version of this hearty egg dish.

- 1½ tablespoons olive oil
- 2 large sweet onions, thickly sliced
- 1 teaspoon coarse salt
- ¼ teaspoon pepper
- 2 teaspoons balsamic vinegar
- 1¼ cups cubed (½ inch) cooked potatoes
- ¾ cup cooked greens, such as mustard or kale, chopped
- 2 slices bacon, cooked and crumbled (optional)
- 8 large eggs, beaten

Preheat the oven to 350°F.

In a 10-inch ovenproof skillet, heat the oil over medium heat. Add the onion slices, ½ teaspoon of the salt, and ⅛ teaspoon of the pepper. Cook, turning with tongs, until well browned, about 10 minutes. Sprinkle with the vinegar and cook 1 minute longer.

Add the potatoes, greens, bacon (if using), and remaining ½ teaspoon salt and ⅛ teaspoon pepper. Pour the eggs over the vegetables and stir to blend. Cook over medium heat until the mixture begins to set, about 3 minutes.

Place the skillet in the oven and bake for 15 minutes, or until set. Let stand 5 minutes, then invert onto a platter. Cut into wedges to serve.

MAKES 6 SERVINGS

POTATO TORTILLA

A tortilla is a Spanish egg cake, similar to a frittata.

- 5 teaspoons olive oil
- 1 cup diced cooked potatoes
- ¼ cup chopped onion
- ½ teaspoon salt
- Pinch of smoked paprika (optional)
- 6 large eggs
- ¼ cup half-and-half or milk
- ½ cup shredded Manchego or white Cheddar cheese
- ⅓ cup diced green bell pepper
- ¼ teaspoon thyme

In a 10-inch cast-iron skillet, heat the oil over medium-high heat. Add the potatoes, onion, salt, and paprika (if using). Cook and stir until the potatoes are golden brown.

In a medium bowl, beat the eggs and then beat in the half-and-half. Stir in the Manchego, bell pepper, and thyme. Pour over the potatoes and onion. Sprinkle with the paprika (if using). Cook over low heat until the eggs are set.

MAKES 4 SERVINGS

HAM & CHEDDAR BAKED EGGS

A wonderful breakfast indulgence for a cold winter morning. Serve with toasted slices of coarse whole-grain peasant bread.

- **½ cup (1 stick) butter**
- **½ cup flour**
- **2½ cups fat-free milk**
- **1½ cups shredded Cheddar cheese (6 ounces)**
- **5 ounces ham, diced**
- **2 tablespoons chopped flat-leaf parsley**
- **Sea salt and pepper**
- **6 large eggs**

Preheat the oven to 375°F.

In a saucepan, melt the butter over medium heat. Add the flour and cook, stirring, for 1 minute. Whisking constantly, gradually add the milk. Cook, whisking, until it thickens and boils. Remove from the heat and stir in the Cheddar, ham, parsley, and salt and pepper to taste.

Spread the sauce over the bottom of a shallow baking dish. Make six indentations in the sauce with the back of a large spoon. Break an egg into each indentation.

Bake for 10 minutes, or until the eggs are done.

MAKES 6 SERVINGS

ASPARAGUS TIMBALES

You can also make this in a 1½-quart mold, but you'll need to bake it for up to 45 minutes.

- **4 large eggs**
- **1½ cups light cream, warmed**
- **1 tablespoon minced parsley**
- **½ teaspoon salt**
- **¼ teaspoon white pepper**
- **⅓ cup shredded sharp Cheddar cheese**
- **2 cups chopped steamed asparagus**

Preheat the oven to 325°F. Lightly butter four 6-ounce ramekins.

In a medium bowl, lightly beat the eggs. Whisking constantly, add the warm (not hot) cream. Whisk in the parsley, salt, and white pepper.

Place the ramekins on a rack set in a roasting pan. Fill with the egg mixture. Sprinkle the tops with the Cheddar and asparagus, and push down into the egg mixture.

Place the roasting pan on a pulled-out oven rack and add 1 inch of water to the pan. Cover all with a loose-fitting lid or a piece of parchment paper. Bake for 20 to 30 minutes, or until a knife inserted in the centers of the timbales comes out clean.

MAKES 4 SERVINGS

TEX-MEX TIMBALES: Substitute 2 cups chopped cooked bell peppers for the asparagus. Add ½ teaspoon oregano and 1 teaspoon minced pickled jalapeño to the egg mixture.

TIMBALES NEPTUNE: Add 1 cup flaked cooked salmon and reduce the asparagus to 1 cup. Use shredded mozzarella instead of Cheddar.

WATERCRESS-MUSHROOM TIMBALES: Use 1½ cups sliced sautéed mushrooms instead of the asparagus. Add ½ cup chopped watercress. Use feta instead of Cheddar.

SCALLION QUICHE

The crust can also be made in a food processor.

CRUST

- 1 cup whole wheat flour
- 1 cup cornmeal
- ½ teaspoon salt
- ¾ cup (1½ sticks) cold butter, cut up
- 1 teaspoon lemon juice
- 3 tablespoons ice water

FILLING

- 1 tablespoon butter
- 1 cup sliced scallions
- 6 ounces Gruyère cheese, shredded
- 3 large eggs
- 1½ cups milk or half-and-half
- ¼ teaspoon nutmeg
- ¼ teaspoon salt

To make the crust: In a large bowl, whisk together the flour, cornmeal, and salt. With a pastry blender or two knives used scissor fashion, cut in the butter until the mixture resembles coarse crumbs. Add the lemon juice and water, and mix until the dough can be formed into a ball (add more water if necessary). Flatten the dough into a disk, wrap, and refrigerate for 30 minutes.

Preheat the oven to 450°F.

On a lightly floured work surface, roll the dough out to a 12-inch round. Fit the dough into a 9-inch pie pan, pressing it into the bottom and up the sides without stretching the dough. Using kitchen scissors, trim the edge, leaving a 1-inch overhang. Fold the overhang under and flute with your fingers (see "Make a Decorative Edge on a Pie," page 530), or crimp with a fork.

Prick the dough all over with a fork. Bake for 5 minutes. (Leave the oven on.)

Meanwhile, assemble the filling: In a medium skillet, melt the butter over medium heat. Add the scallions and cook until tender, 2 to 3 minutes.

Place the partially baked crust on a rimmed baking sheet. Sprinkle the scallions and Gruyère over the bottom of the crust.

In a medium bowl, whisk together the eggs, milk, nutmeg, and salt. Pour the egg mixture over the scallions and cheese. Bake for 15 minutes. Reduce the oven temperature to 350°F and bake 10 to 15 minutes longer, until the top is golden brown and the filling is just set. Place on a wire rack and let stand 20 minutes before cutting.

MAKES 6 SERVINGS

CREMINI MUSHROOM QUICHE

Take this quiche in a different direction and use fresh shiitake mushrooms.

- Multi-Grain Pie Dough (Single Crust), page 531
- 2 teaspoons olive oil
- 4 ounces cremini mushrooms, thinly sliced
- 3 large eggs
- 2 cups milk or light cream
- 1 tablespoon snipped chives
- ¼ teaspoon salt
- ¼ teaspoon pepper
- 1 large egg white
- ½ cup grated Parmesan cheese

Preheat the oven to 375°F.

On a lightly floured work surface, roll the dough out to a 12-inch round. Fit the dough into a 9-inch pie plate, pressing it into the bottom and up the side without stretching the dough. With kitchen scissors, trim the edge, leaving a 1-inch overhang.

Fold the overhang under and flute with your fingers (see "Making a Decorative Edge on a Pie," page 530) or crimp with a fork.

In a large skillet, heat the oil over medium heat. Add the mushrooms, and cook until they are tender and no liquid remains in the pan. Let cool to room temperature.

In a large bowl, whisk together the whole eggs, milk, chives, salt, and pepper. Lightly beat the egg white and brush over the pie shell. Sprinkle with the Parmesan. Scatter the mushrooms over the cheese.

Gently pour the egg mixture over the cheese and mushrooms. Place on a rimmed baking sheet and bake for 35 to 40 minutes, until the top is golden brown and the filling is set. Place on a wire rack and let stand 20 minutes before cutting.

MAKES 6 SERVINGS

CHICKEN-SWISS CHEESE QUICHE: Substitute ¼ pound shredded cooked chicken and ½ cup shredded Swiss cheese for the Parmesan and mushrooms.

GREEN VEGETABLE QUICHE: Substitute 1 cup lightly steamed and well dried chopped spinach, kale, or Swiss chard and 1 tablespoon grated onions for the mushrooms.

ONION-CHEDDAR QUICHE: Substitute 1 cup sautéed sliced onions and 1 cup shredded Cheddar cheese for the Parmesan and mushrooms.

MEXICAN STRATA

Make sure the peppers you use for roasting have thick walls, or they will roast too quickly and be difficult to peel.

- 2 green bell peppers, cut lengthwise into flat panels
- 2 tablespoons butter, at room temperature
- 12 slices whole-grain sandwich bread
- 1 package (10 ounces) frozen corn kernels, thawed
- 2 cups shredded pepper Jack cheese (8 ounces)
- 4 large eggs
- 4 cups reduced-fat (2%) milk
- 1 teaspoon salt
- ½ teaspoon oregano
- ½ teaspoon cumin

Preheat the broiler. Broil the peppers, skin-side up, 4 inches from the heat for 12 minutes, or until the skin is well charred. Remove from the broiler and turn the pepper pieces skin-side down to cool. When cool, peel and cut into strips.

Grease a 9 × 13-inch baking dish.

Butter one side of each slice of bread and cut the slices in half. Arrange half of the slices, butter-side up, on the bottom of the baking dish. Cover with half of the corn and half of the pepper strips. Sprinkle with half of the cheese. Repeat the layer, using the remaining bread, corn, pepper strips, and cheese.

In a medium bowl, beat the eggs. Beat in the milk, salt, oregano, and cumin. Pour the mixture over the layers in the baking dish. Allow to stand for 30 minutes.

Preheat the oven to 350°F.

Bake the strata for 40 minutes, or until puffed and set. Serve piping hot.

MAKES 6 SERVINGS

GREEK-STYLE STRATA

What makes this strata Greek is the use of feta cheese and the combination of mint and lemon zest. And instead of the sandwich bread used in most stratas, the bread here is pita, a Greek word that means pie, cake, or bread.

3 whole wheat pita breads, cut into sixths
1 cup low-fat (1%) cottage cheese
1 cup low-fat (1%) milk
2 tablespoons flour
3 large eggs
2 large egg whites
3 ounces feta cheese, crumbled
4 scallions, thinly sliced
½ cup frozen peas
½ cup snipped fresh dill
¼ cup chopped fresh mint
1 teaspoon grated lemon zest
⅛ teaspoon salt
¼ teaspoon pepper
1 tomato, thinly sliced

Preheat the oven to 350°F. Toast the pitas on a baking sheet in the oven until lightly crisp, about 5 minutes.

Meanwhile, in a food processor, combine the cottage cheese, milk , and flour, and process until smooth, about 1 minute. Transfer to a medium bowl, and stir in the whole eggs, egg whites, feta, scallions, peas, dill, mint, lemon zest, salt, and pepper.

Place the pitas in an 11 × 7-inch glass baking dish and pour the egg mixture over. Let stand at room temperature for 10 minutes.

Arrange the tomato slices over the top. Bake for 35 minutes, or until the custard is just set.

MAKES 4 SERVINGS

SPINACH & GOAT CHEESE STRATA

Although stratas generally call for whole eggs, this version has been slimmed down a bit through the use of some egg whites in place of a whole egg and 1% instead of whole milk.

8 slices whole-grain sandwich bread
5 teaspoons olive oil
3 tablespoons minced scallions
2 cloves garlic, minced
2 packages (10 ounces each) frozen chopped spinach, thawed and squeezed dry
1 teaspoon sugar
¼ teaspoon salt
⅛ teaspoon nutmeg
⅛ teaspoon pepper
3 large eggs
2 large egg whites
½ cup low-fat (1%) milk
4 ounces soft goat cheese, crumbled

Generously oil a 7 × 11-inch baking dish. Lay half the bread slices in the dish and set aside.

In large skillet, heat the oil over medium heat. Add the scallions and garlic, and cook, stirring frequently, until the scallions have softened, about 2 minutes.

Stir in the spinach, sprinkle with the sugar, salt, nutmeg, and pepper, and continue cooking until the spinach has softened and is heated through, about 4 minutes. Remove from the heat. Spoon half of the spinach mixture over the bread in the baking dish.

In a medium bowl, whisk together the whole eggs, egg whites, and milk. Pour half of this mixture over the spinach layer. Sprinkle with half the cheese. Top with the remaining bread, spinach, egg mixture, and cheese. Let sit for 30 minutes.

Preheat the oven to 350°F. Bake the strata for 30 minutes, or until golden, puffed and set. Let stand for 10 minutes before serving.

MAKES 4 SERVINGS

MANCHEGO SOUFFLÉ WITH SCALLIONS

Manchego cheese, from Spain, has a rich, nutty flavor, like a cross between a mild Cheddar and a Gruyère. If you can't find it, use a mixture of Cheddar and Gruyère.

- **3½ tablespoons butter**
- **¼ cup white whole wheat flour***
- **1½ cups milk, scalded**
- **6 large eggs, separated**
- **⅔ cup minced scallions**
- **1 tablespoon Dijon mustard**
- **Pinch of coarse salt**
- **Pinch of cayenne pepper**
- **1 cup shredded Manchego cheese (4 ounces)**

**milled from white wheat grains*

Preheat the oven to 325°F. Butter the bottom and sides of a 2-quart soufflé dish, and dust with flour.

In a medium saucepan, melt the 3½ tablespoons-butter over medium heat. Add the flour and blend until smooth. Add the hot milk and stir briskly until smooth. Bring almost to a boil. Remove from the heat and cool slightly.

In a bowl, beat the egg yolks vigorously. Stir in the scallions, mustard, salt, and cayenne. Stir into the sauce.

In a separate bowl, beat the egg whites until stiff peaks form. Fold the egg whites alternating with the Manchego into the sauce until the mixture is smooth and light.

Pour into the soufflé dish. Bake for 50 to 55 minutes, or until set. Serve immediately.

MAKES 4 TO 6 SERVINGS

ASPARAGUS & GOAT CHEESE SOUFFLÉ

You can lighten a soufflé by using more egg whites than egg yolks, as done here.

- **¾ pound asparagus, cut into ½-inch pieces**
- **¾ cup cooked cannellini beans**
- **⅓ cup low-fat (1%) milk**
- **3 tablespoons flour**
- **6 tablespoons soft goat cheese**
- **3 large eggs, separated, plus 3 large egg whites**
- **½ teaspoon tarragon**
- **½ teaspoon salt**
- **¼ teaspoon white pepper**
- **⅛ teaspoon cream of tartar**

Preheat the oven to 375°F. Lightly grease an 8-cup soufflé dish.

In a steamer, cook the asparagus until barely tender, about 2 minutes. Drain on paper towels.

Mash the beans with a potato masher to a coarse-textured puree.

In a large saucepan, whisk the milk into the flour, whisking until no lumps remain. Bring to a boil and cook, whisking frequently, until the mixture is slightly thickened, about 4 minutes.

Remove from the heat, and stir in the mashed beans and goat cheese. Whisk in the 3 egg yolks, tarragon, ¼ teaspoon of the salt, and the white pepper, until well combined.

In a large bowl, with an electric mixer, beat the 6 egg whites, the remaining ¼ teaspoon salt, and the cream of tartar, until stiff, but not dry, peaks form. Stir about 1 cup of the egg whites into the goat cheese-bean mixture, then gently fold in the remaining whites. Gently fold in the asparagus.

Spoon the mixture into the soufflé dish. Bake for 30 minutes, or until the soufflé is golden brown, puffed, and just set. Serve immediately.

MAKES 4 SERVINGS

CHEESE ENCHILADAS

Carrots are the surprise ingredient in the spicy sauce for these enchiladas. They add natural sweetness and beta-carotene.

- 2 teaspoons olive oil
- 3 large carrots, diced
- ⅓ cup water
- 1 can (14.5 ounces) crushed tomatoes
- 1 large onion, quartered
- 2 chipotle peppers in adobo
- ½ teaspoon salt
- 2 cups cooked cannellini beans
- 12 corn tortillas
- 10 ounces Monterey Jack cheese, shredded
- 1 can (4.5 ounces) chopped mild green chilies

In a large skillet, heat the oil over medium heat. Add the carrots and water, and cook, stirring frequently, until tender, about 5 minutes.

In a food processor or blender, combine the carrots and any liquid in the skillet with the tomatoes, onion, chipotles, and salt. Process to a puree. Return the puree to the skillet, and cook over medium heat, stirring occasionally, for 10 minutes, to thicken the sauce and blend the flavors.

Preheat the oven to 350°F. With a potato masher or the back of a spoon, mash the beans. Spoon ½ cup of the sauce into the bottom of a 7 × 11-inch glass baking dish.

Dip both sides of each tortilla briefly in the sauce. Spread the beans down the middle of each tortilla. Sprinkle half the cheese and all of the green chilies over the beans. Roll the tortillas up.

Place the filled tortillas, seam-sides down, in the baking dish. Spoon the remaining sauce over the tortillas. Sprinkle the remaining cheese on top.

Cover and bake for 25 minutes, or until piping hot and bubbling.

MAKES 6 SERVINGS

GRILLED CHEESE & QUINCE

You can make these deluxe grilled cheese sandwiches using quince (or even strawberry) jam or poached quince.

- 6 tablespoons butter, at room temperature
- 16 thick (¼-inch) slices brioche or good-quality peasant bread
- 16 thin slices Cheddar-style cheese
- 16 dabs quince paste (membrillo) or quince jam

Butter each slice of bread on one side. Place 8 slices buttered-side down. Top each with 1 slice of cheese, 2 dabs of paste or jam, and another slice of cheese, then with a second slice of buttered bread, buttered-side up. (Sandwiches may be prepared in advance up to this point, wrapped tightly, and stored in the refrigerator until ready to cook.)

Heat a large skillet over medium heat until hot. Place the sandwiches in the skillet and toast on one side until golden. Turn over and press lightly with a spatula. Lower the heat if the bread browns too quickly. When the cheese has melted and the second side is golden, remove from the pan. Slice on the diagonal and serve hot.

MAKES 8 SERVINGS

CAPRESE WRAP

Use bottled roasted red peppers for this, or roast your own (see Roasted Red Peppers, page 660).

- **4 cups baby spinach**
- **8 slices (¼ inch) tomato**
- **1 cup roasted red peppers, cut into strips**
- **6 ounces fresh mozzarella, cut into 4 slices**
- **4 tablespoons chopped fresh basil**
- **4 whole wheat spinach wraps (12 inches)**
- **¼ cup Red Wine Vinaigrette (page 375)**

Layer 1 cup spinach, 2 slices tomato, ¼ cup roasted pepper strips, 1 slice mozzarella, and 1 tablespoon basil on each wrap. Roll up tightly and tuck in the ends. Cut the sandwich on the diagonal. Serve the vinaigrette on the side for drizzling into the open ends of the sandwich.

MAKES 4 SERVINGS

Pasta & Noodles

Traditional Western (as opposed to Asian) pasta is made almost exclusively of wheat, usually a high-gluten wheat called semolina. The pasta can be made with eggs, in which case it is often sold fresh, or it can be made without eggs, in which case it is usually sold dried.

Cooking Pasta

Cook pasta, uncovered, in a large pot of boiling salted water, using at least 4 quarts of water for every pound of pasta. Use a pot large enough to hold the water and pasta without boiling over. When you add the pasta, and stir so that it is submerged in the boiling water. Read the label and cook the pasta for the time indicated on the package (cooking times can vary with the size, shape, and gluten content of the individual pasta). The package will usually give a time range, so start checking when you hit the first time in the range.

Pasta should be cooked until it is al dente ("to the tooth" in Italian), which means firm, with a slight bite, but never crunchy or starchy. If you bite into a piece of pasta and you can see a thin starch line, it hasn't cooked long enough. Fresh pasta cooks somewhat faster than dried. If you're cooking homemade fresh pasta and have no label to go by, the rule of thumb is that you add the pasta to the boiling water, and the minute the water comes back to the boil, the pasta should be done. Check the pasta a little before that to be certain, especially if you've made the pasta with a soft (low-gluten) wheat, because it will cook more quickly.

If the pasta is not being served right away, do what lots of restaurants do: Toss the drained and rinsed pasta with some oil and refrigerate. At serving time, the pasta can be briefly cooked in hot sauce or run under hot water to reheat. Leftover cooked pasta will keep in the refrigerator for 3 days. If already sauced, it can be reheated on top of the stove, or covered and warmed in the oven.

Soup Pastas

There are numerous small pasta shapes—including alphabets, tubettini, and some as small as peppercorns (*acini di pepe*)—that are cooked right in a broth instead of being cooked separately in a large pot of water. These are called soup pastas (*pastine* in Italian). The smallest shapes are best in clear broths. Slightly larger shapes like ditalini or tubetti hold up well in chunkier soups like minestrone.

Stuffed Pastas & Dumplings

There are a host of stuffed Italian pastas, including ravioli, agnolotti, and tortellini. Ravioli are generally sold fresh and refrigerated (or you can make your own; see "Fresh Cheese Ravioli," page 363). Tortellini are sold both fresh and dried (shelf-stable). Be sure when following a recipe with a stuffed pasta that you know if fresh or dried is being called for, because there is a significant difference in weight. There are also non-Italian stuffed pastas such as pierogies, kreplach, wontons, and pot stickers.

There are several types of fresh dumplings, usually made with a wheat-based dough but sometimes made with potatoes. German spaetzle, small pasta/dumplings, are traditionally served with stews or meat dishes. Gnocchi, a type of Italian dumpling, comes in several varieties. Those made with mashed potato are potato gnocchi; those made with semolina, milk, and cheese are *gnocchi alla Romana*. There are also gnocchi made with pumpkin and some with sweet potato. *Gnudi*, a type of gnocchi, are made with ricotta cheese and spinach. With the exception of the *gnocchi alla Romana* (which are baked), they are all boiled.

The Sauce

Match the pasta sauce to the pasta shape. Sturdy shapes like penne and ziti can take hearty sauces. Any pasta shape with a lot of nooks, crannies, ruffles, and ridges—fusilli, radiatore, fiori, ruote—is good for sauces that have bits and pieces (the curls catch the bits). Strand pastas (spaghetti, linguine) are good with smooth sauces that cling to the strands. Very thin strands (capellini, spaghettini, vermicelli) need light delicate sauces (think butter and some grated Parmesan), or they will be weighed down and get gummy. Some sauces are lightly tossed with hot pasta before serving, while others are traditionally poured on top of the pasta and tossed at the table. Cream sauces should always be mixed with pasta until each strand is well coated. Serve extra sauce in a pitcher to be added by the diners as desired.

Asian Noodles

Asian noodles are made with a variety of different starches: wheat flour (with and without egg), rice flour, mung bean flour, sweet potato starch, and buckwheat. As a result, their cooking methods are quite different.

Wheat noodles: Thick or thin, these noodles can be found dried, fresh, and even precooked. Thicker noodles are dressed with hearty sauces or added to soups. Thinner noodles are great for stir-fries.

Egg noodles: These noodles come wide, flat, thick, thin, fresh, dried, and sometimes precooked. They are cooked in the same way as their Western counterparts.

Soba noodles: Soba are made from buckwheat and wheat flour and are popular in Japanese cuisine. They're chewy in texture and nutty tasting and are available fresh, dried, or frozen; they're boiled briefly before being tossed with simple earthy sauces. Mushrooms are a good match, as is a simple toss of soy sauce and dark sesame oil. They are often served chilled.

Rice noodles: Noodles made from rice flour can be found in many different forms and thicknesses. Some need as little as 30 seconds to cook. Depending upon their shape, they can be used in soups, stir-fries (see Rice Stick Noodles with Pork, page 367), and salads. Their texture is chewy, creamy, slippery, and springy. Fresh rice noodles are boiled to cook them; the dried noodles are soaked in cold water to make them pliable and then added to soups to cook, or briefly boiled in water before being stir-fried. Flat broad noodles are often served rolled up and stuffed (like a lasagna roll) and served in a light sauce. Or they can be cut in wide strips and tossed in sauce.

Cellophane noodles: Also called glass noodles, these thin, translucent noodles are made from different starches depending on where they're from. Korean cellophane noodles are made with sweet potato starch; the Chinese versions are made from mung bean starch. They are both fairly mild and flavorless, making them perfect for absorbing thin, highly seasoned sauces. Sweet potato noodles need no soaking before cooking, while Chinese cellophane noodles need a soak in cold water before using. Both need a brief boiling, but sweet potato cellophane noodles need a little more time. Great in salads, they're also used for stuffing spring rolls and in soups.

Asian dumplings: Squares of dough used to wrap up fillings can be made of wheat-and-egg dough or a rice-flour dough. The rice paper wrappers come dried and do not need any cooking; they only need to be soaked in water to make them pliable enough to wrap. These are used for making stuffed rolls called summer rolls or salad rolls (for a good recipe, try Thai Summer Rolls, page 158). The Chinese-style wrappers, made of wheat dough, come in two sizes: small for wontons (stuffed dumplings) and larger for making egg rolls or spring rolls. Wontons are stuffed and boiled (and then sometimes pan-fried to make pot stickers); and egg rolls and spring rolls are both stuffed and then deep-fried. Although you can buy Chinese wonton wrappers in supermarkets, you might consider making your own whole wheat version (see "Whole Wheat Wonton Wrappers," page 160).

FRESH WHOLE WHEAT EGG PASTA

This makes enough pasta for 4 main-course servings. A quick way to cut the pasta into noodles is to gently roll up a strip of dough and cut through the roll into whatever width noodle you want.

1¾ cups whole wheat flour

½ teaspoon coarse salt

2 large eggs

1 tablespoon water

1 teaspoon oil

In a food processor, pulse the flour and salt together to blend. With the machine on, add the eggs, one at a time. Then add the water and oil. Process until the dough forms a ball. Transfer to a work surface and knead just long enough to come together to form a smooth ball. Cover with plastic wrap and let stand at room temperature for 30 minutes.

Cut the dough into two pieces. Run through a pasta machine (following the manufacturer's instructions) until you have a long sheet of pasta about 1⁄16 inch thick. Cut the pasta into whatever shapes you want.

MAKES 1 POUND

FRESH WHOLE WHEAT SPINACH PASTA

Making your own fresh whole wheat spinach pasta is satisfying, and the product is reliably fresh and nutritious. This recipe yields enough pasta for 8 to 10 main-course portions.

1 pound fresh spinach

2 cups whole wheat flour

1 cup unbleached all-purpose flour

- **3 extra-large eggs**
- **1 tablespoon olive oil**

In a steamer, cook the spinach until tender. Drain well, making sure the spinach is as dry as possible. Puree in a blender or food processor and set aside until cool.

Place the flours in a large bowl and make a well in the center. Drop the spinach, eggs, and oil into the well. Gently blend together with the flour, gradually bringing in more flour as you mix. Incorporate as much flour as is necessary to make a cohesive ball of dough.

Cut the dough into two pieces. Run through a pasta machine (following the manufacturer's instructions) until you have a long sheet of pasta that is about $^1/_{16}$ inch thick and evenly colored. Cut the pasta into whatever shapes you want.

MAKES 2 POUNDS

WHOLE WHEAT GNOCCHI

Gnocchi are small Italian potato dumplings with a soft, noodlelike texture. Serve them tossed with a little olive oil and grated Parmesan, or try any of the sauces in this chapter.

- **1 russet (baking) potato (8 ounces)**
- **1 tablespoon olive oil**
- **1 tablespoon butter**
- **1 small onion, finely chopped**
- **1 large egg yolk**
- **$^1/_3$ cup grated Parmesan cheese**
- **$^1/_4$ cup part-skim ricotta cheese**
- **1 cup whole wheat pastry flour**

Prick the potato in several places and microwave on high for 5 minutes, or until cooked through. Let sit for 1 minute, then while it is still hot, slice the potato lengthwise to let steam escape. When cool enough to handle, peel the potato and cut into largish chunks.

In a small skillet, heat the oil and butter over medium heat. Add the onion and cook until tender. Set aside to cool slightly.

While the potato is still warm, rice or sieve it into a medium bowl. Stir in the onion, egg yolk, Parmesan, and ricotta. Mix in $^3/_4$ cup of the flour. On a floured surface, knead into a soft smooth dough, using up to $^1/_4$ cup flour to prevent sticking. Avoid overkneading—the dough should be soft.

Shape the dough into long finger-thick ropes and cut crosswise into $^1/_2$-inch pieces. Shape by using a lightly floured fork: Holding the fork on the work surface with the tines facing away from you, use a finger to press a piece of dough against the front of the tines while pulling your finger across the dough to roll it toward the fork handle. The dough will roll into a shell shape with an indentation. Let the gnocchi fall onto a plate. Repeat until all the pieces are formed.

In a large pot, bring 4 quarts of water to a boil. Cook 2 dozen gnocchi at a time. Drop them into the water and boil for 15 seconds after the dough rises to the surface. Test the first few; they should be slightly chewy, with no raw taste. If overcooked, they become waterlogged. Remove them with a slotted spoon and drain in a sieve. Serve hot.

MAKES 4 SERVINGS

GREEN GNOCCHI

These spinach gnocchi are formed into simple ovals.

- **1 russet (baking) potato (8 ounces)**
- **1 tablespoon olive oil**
- **1 tablespoon butter**
- **2 tablespoons minced onion**
- **5 cups finely chopped spinach leaves**

1¼ cups whole wheat flour

1 large egg yolk

3 tablespoons farmer's cheese

½ teaspoon salt

Prick the potato in several places, and microwave on high for 5 minutes, or until cooked through. Let sit for 1 minute, then while it is still hot, slice the potato lengthwise to let steam escape. When cool enough to handle, peel the potato and cut into largish chunks.

In a large saucepan, heat the oil and butter over medium-high heat. Add the onion and cook for 3 minutes. Add the spinach and cook, stirring occasionally, until the liquid evaporates. The mixture must be quite dry. Cool quickly by transferring to a bowl set in cold water.

Place 1 cup of the flour in a shallow medium bowl. Make a well in the center. Rice or sieve the potatoes into the well. Top with the cooled greens and mix lightly with a fork.

Add the egg yolk, farmer's cheese, and salt, and stir until the dough is smooth enough to knead. Knead lightly for 3 to 5 minutes, using as little of the remaining flour as possible. Do not overwork the dough—the dough should be soft and smooth.

Shape the dough into ropes ¾ inch thick and 12 inches long. Pinch off a small piece from the roll and quickly shape into a marble-size oval between the palms of your hands. Repeat until all the gnocchi are formed.

In a large pot, bring 4 quarts of water to a boil. Cook 2 dozen gnocchi at a time. As they float to surface of the water, keep them from touching. Cook for 3 to 4 minutes after the water returns to a boil. Test the first few; they should be slightly chewy, with no raw taste. If overcooked, they become waterlogged. Remove them with a slotted spoon and drain in a sieve. Serve hot.

MAKES 4 TO 6 SERVINGS

CABBAGE-SPINACH GNOCCHI: Use 2½ cups chopped spinach and 2½ cups finely sliced cabbage.

SPAETZLE

A spaetzle maker is a metal plate or bowl with large holes in it (similar to a colander, only with bigger holes), through which spaetzle dough is pushed to form little noodles. Many spaetzle makers are designed to hook over the rim of the cooking pot so you have both hands free to push the dough through the holes into the boiling water.

1½ cups unbleached all-purpose flour

1 cup white whole wheat flour*

1½ teaspoons salt

¼ teaspoon nutmeg

½ cup milk

½ cup cold water

1 large egg

2 tablespoons butter, melted

Chopped parsley, for garnish (optional)

**milled from white wheat grains*

In a large bowl, combine the flours, salt, and nutmeg. Make a well in the center.

In a small bowl, whisk together the milk, water, and egg. Pour the milk mixture into the well in the flour mixture. Gradually whisk the flour into the liquid to form a smooth, thick dough. Let the dough rest for about 10 minutes.

Meanwhile, bring a large pot of salted water to a boil over high heat. Reduce the heat to a simmer.

Using a large, flat metal spoon, press the spaetzle dough through the large holes of a colander (not a sieve) or a spaetzle-maker into the simmering water to form little odd-shaped dumplings. Do not overcrowd the pot. Cook until the dumplings rise to the surface, 3 to 4 minutes.

With a slotted spoon, transfer the spaetzle to a large bowl, toss with the melted butter, and sprinkle with chopped parsley, if desired. Serve immediately.

MAKES 6 SERVINGS

OLIO E AGLIO

The name of this simple and classic Italian pasta sauce means simply "oil and garlic." Parmesan and pepper may be sprinkled on top or passed at the table.

- **½ cup olive oil**
- **5 cloves garlic, smashed and peeled**
- **1 small dried hot chili pepper**
- **½ teaspoon salt**
- **1 tablespoon minced parsley**

In a small saucepan, heat the oil over low heat. Add the garlic and chili pepper, and cook until the garlic is lightly browned. Remove from the heat. With a slotted spoon, remove and discard the garlic and chili. Let the oil cool for a few minutes before tossing with pasta (or it will make the pasta gummy).

To serve, toss 1 pound hot pasta with the garlic oil. Add the salt and parsley, and toss again.

MAKES ½ CUP (FOR 1 POUND PASTA)

OIL, GARLIC & ROSEMARY SAUCE: Add 2 sprigs rosemary to the hot oil along with the garlic and chili.

PESTO

This flavorful and very aromatic sauce is best when you have fresh basil straight out of the garden and freshly grated Parmesan cheese. A little goes far—about 2 tablespoons per serving. Covered and refrigerated, it keeps well up to 1 week.

- **1½ cups fresh basil leaves**
- **½ cup pine nuts**
- **3 cloves garlic, quartered**
- **½ cup freshly grated Parmesan cheese**
- **¾ cup olive oil**

TRIFOLATI SAUCE

Simple garlic and oil sauce becomes Trifolati Sauce when you add vegetables to it. Follow the recipe for Olio e Aglio (above) through the first step. Then add ½ cup chicken stock and any one of the following vegetables:

- 3 cups thinly sliced broccoli florets
- 3 cups shredded fresh spinach
- 2 cups thinly sliced mushrooms
- 2 cups coarsely shredded carrots
- 1 cup pureed cooked artichoke hearts thinned with 2 tablespoons light cream

Cover the pan and simmer for 2 to 4 minutes. Remove the pan from the heat. Let the sauce cool for a few minutes before tossing with hot pasta (or it will make the pasta gummy).

In a food processor, pulse the basil, pine nuts, and garlic together. Pulse in the Parmesan. Then slowly add the oil and process until smooth.

MAKES 2 CUPS

PARSLEY PESTO: Substitute parsley for some or all of the basil.

PECAN PESTO: Use ½ cup coarsely chopped pecans instead of pine nuts.

REDUCED-FAT PESTO: Reduce the olive oil to ½ cup and add ¼ cup water.

MARINARA SAUCE

The best canned tomatoes for making pasta sauce are the meaty San Marzanos.

- 3 tablespoons olive oil
- 2 small onions, chopped
- 2 small carrots, minced
- 1 large clove garlic, minced
- 1 can (28 ounces) San Marzano tomatoes
- 1 small bay leaf
- ¼ teaspoon thyme
- ¼ teaspoon salt
- ¼ teaspoon black pepper
- 1 teaspoon grated lemon zest
- ⅛ teaspoon red pepper flakes

In a large skillet, heat 2 tablespoons of the oil over medium heat. Add the onions, carrots, and garlic, and cook until softened, about 5 minutes.

Add the tomatoes, bay leaf, thyme, salt, and black pepper. Cook over low heat, uncovered and stirring often, for 15 to 20 minutes.

Puree the mixture in a food mill or pass through a strainer. Discard any skins or seeds. Stir in the remaining 1 tablespoon oil, the lemon zest, and red pepper flakes. Taste and adjust the seasonings.

MAKES 3 CUPS (FOR 1 POUND PASTA)

RED & GREEN TOMATO SAUCE WITH YELLOW PEPPERS

If you have a garden, or a friend who does, try this colorful sauce of both green and ripe tomatoes. Use with medium-size, tubular pasta or other shapes best suited to holding sauce.

- ½ cup olive oil
- 3 cloves garlic, smashed and peeled
- 2 large onions, thinly sliced
- 4 medium green tomatoes, sliced
- 3 yellow bell peppers, cut into ½-inch strips
- 5 large ripe tomatoes, peeled and cubed
- ½ teaspoon salt
- ¼ teaspoon red pepper flakes
- ¼ teaspoon rosemary
- Pinch of oregano
- 2 tablespoons minced parsley
- ¼ teaspoon black pepper

In a large heavy skillet , heat the oil over medium heat. Add the garlic and cook until it begins to brown. Immediately remove the garlic from the skillet and discard.

Add the onions to the hot oil and cook, stirring, for 8 minutes.

Add the green tomatoes and yellow peppers, and cook for 5 minutes. Stir in the ripe tomatoes, salt, red pepper flakes, rosemary, and oregano, and cook for another 5 minutes. Stir in the parsley and black pepper. Taste and adjust the seasonings.

MAKES 3½ CUPS (FOR 1 POUND PASTA)

RED CLAM SAUCE

Vongole (clams) and pasta are a popular combination in Italian cuisine. Serve this tasty tomato-based sauce over spaghetti.

- 2 cups water
- 2 dozen cherrystone clams, well scrubbed
- 3 tablespoons olive oil
- 1 small onion, chopped
- 1 clove garlic, minced
- 3 cups canned whole tomatoes, drained and chopped
- 2 tablespoons minced parsley
- ½ teaspoon oregano
- ¼ teaspoon salt
- ⅛ teaspoon pepper
- ¼ cup tomato paste

Place the water in a large steamer or pot and steam the clams until they open. Discard any that do not open. Drain, reserving ½ cup of the clam juice. Strain the clam juice through a double layer of cheesecloth set in a large sieve. Reserve both the clams and juice.

In a large skillet, heat the oil over medium heat. Add the onion and garlic , and cook until the onion is translucent. Add the reserved clam juice, tomatoes, parsley, oregano, salt, and pepper, and simmer for 5 minutes. Stir in the tomato paste and simmer for 5 minutes longer.

Meanwhile, remove the clams from the shells and chop them.

Add the clams to the sauce and cook until heated through.

MAKES 4 CUPS (FOR 1 POUND PASTA)

WHITE CLAM SAUCE

The reward in added flavor is well worth any extra effort it takes to get fresh clams for this classic sauce. Serve with linguine.

- 8 tablespoons olive oil
- 2 dozen cherrystone clams, well scrubbed
- 1 clove garlic, quartered
- 2 tablespoons chopped parsley
- 1 tablespoon chopped fresh basil or 1 teaspoon dried
- ½ teaspoon salt
- ⅛ teaspoon black pepper
- ¼ teaspoon red pepper flakes (optional)

In a large skillet, heat 2 tablespoons of the oil. Add the clams and cook over medium heat, pushing them around with a wooden spoon, until all have opened. Remove the clams and set aside. (Discard any clams that do not open.) Strain the oil and juice through a double layer of cheesecloth set in a large sieve and reserve. When cool enough to handle, remove the clams from the shells and chop them.

In the same skillet, heat the remaining 6 tablespoons oil over medium heat. Add the strained clam juice, chopped clams, garlic, parsley, basil, salt, black pepper, and red pepper flakes (if using). Simmer for 15 minutes. Discard the garlic.

MAKES 2¼ CUPS (FOR 1 POUND PASTA)

RICOTTA-PISTACHIO SAUCE

If you can only find salted pistachios, use them here and omit the salt in the recipe, then taste after pureeing and see if you still want to add salt.

- ½ cup part-skim ricotta cheese
- ⅓ cup unsalted shelled pistachios
- ¼ cup olive oil
- ¼ cup light cream
- ¼ cup chopped flat-leaf parsley
- 1 small clove garlic, minced
- ¼ teaspoon salt
- Pinch of nutmeg

In a blender or food processor, combine the

ricotta, pistachios, oil, cream, parsley, garlic, salt, and nutmeg. Process until smooth.

MAKES 1¼ CUPS (FOR 1 POUND PASTA)

CREAMY CILANTRO-CASHEW SAUCE: Use cilantro instead of parsley, pecans instead of pistachios, and cayenne instead of nutmeg.

TOASTED WALNUT CREAM SAUCE

A quick, uncooked sauce, this works best with cavatelli or any other small pasta that holds sauce well.

- 1½ cups walnuts, toasted
- 2 tablespoons chopped parsley
- 1 tablespoon chopped fresh marjoram or ½ teaspoon dried
- 1 clove garlic, quartered
- 3 tablespoons olive oil
- 1 cup part-skim ricotta cheese
- ½ cup milk
- ¼ teaspoon salt
- ⅛ teaspoon cayenne pepper

In a blender or food processor, chop together the nuts, parsley, marjoram, and garlic. Add the oil and blend until incorporated. Add the ricotta, milk, salt, and cayenne, and process again until smooth. (Thin with additional milk if the sauce is too thick.) Taste and adjust the seasonings.

MAKES 2½ CUPS (FOR 1 POUND PASTA)

TOASTED ALMOND CREAM SAUCE: Use almonds instead of walnuts. Substitute basil for the marjoram, and black pepper for the cayenne.

SPAGHETTI BOLOGNESE

One of the distinguishing features of a true ragú Bolognese is the milk that is stirred into the meaty tomato sauce.

- ¼ ounce dried porcini mushrooms
- ¾ cup boiling water
- 3 slices bacon, coarsely chopped
- 3 tablespoons water
- 1 onion, finely chopped
- 1 carrot, finely chopped
- 1 rib celery, finely chopped
- ½ pound lean ground beef
- 1 can (6 ounces) no-salt-added tomato paste
- ½ cup dry red wine
- ½ teaspoon salt
- ½ teaspoon pepper
- 1¼ cups milk
- 1 pound whole wheat spaghetti

In a small heatproof bowl, combine the dried porcini and the boiling water, and let stand for 10 minutes or until softened. Reserving the soaking liquid, scoop out the mushrooms, rinse, and finely chop. Strain the soaking liquid through a coffee filter or a paper towel–lined sieve and set aside.

In a large skillet, combine the bacon and water over low heat. Cook for 4 minutes, or until the bacon has rendered its fat but is not crisp. Add the onion, carrot, and celery, and cook for 5 minutes or until the onion is soft.

Crumble in the beef and add the reserved mushroom soaking liquid, chopped mushrooms, tomato paste, wine, salt, and pepper. Bring to a boil, reduce to a simmer, and cook for 5 minutes, or until the liquid has almost evaporated.

Add half of the milk and cook until it has been absorbed. Add the remaining milk and simmer until the sauce is thick and richly flavored, 12 minutes.

Meanwhile, in a large pot of boiling salted water, cook the pasta according to package directions. Drain and toss with the sauce.

MAKES 4 SERVINGS

FUSILLI WITH PORK-TOMATO SAUCE

The secret to using roast pork as a leftover? Don't overcook it the first time around, and just warm it the second. That way, it remains moist.

- 2 tablespoons olive oil
- 1½ cups finely chopped red onions
- 1 tablespoon minced fresh ginger
- 1 clove garlic, minced
- Large pinch of red pepper flakes (optional)
- 1 can (35 ounces) whole tomatoes, chopped, juices reserved
- 1 cup cooked pork, cut into ½-inch cubes
- 12 ounces long fusilli, whole wheat or fiber-added
- ½ cup freshly grated Parmesan cheese, plus more for serving
- 1 tablespoon chopped cilantro, for serving

In a medium saucepan, heat the oil over medium heat. Add the onions, ginger, garlic, and red pepper flakes (if using), and cook, stirring, until softened, 5 minutes.

Stir in the tomatoes and half of their reserved juices. Simmer, stirring occasionally, until the tomatoes soften and the sauce thickens slightly (add more juice as needed), about 15 minutes.

Stir in the pork and simmer for 1 minute.

Meanwhile, in a large pot of boiling salted water, cook the pasta according to the package directions. Drain and transfer to a large serving bowl. Toss with the Parmesan, then with the sauce. Garnish with cilantro. Pass extra Parmesan at the table.

MAKES 4 SERVINGS

SPAGHETTINI WITH FISH & LEMON-TOMATO SAUCE

Use any firm-fleshed white fish in this recipe.

- 1 pound whole wheat spaghettini
- ¼ cup olive oil
- ¼ cup finely chopped shallots
- ½ cup Fish Stock (page 173) or bottled clam juice
- 1 cup chopped tomatoes
- ½ teaspoon minced fresh thyme or ¼ teaspoon dried
- 1 pound halibut, cut into 1-inch cubes
- 1 teaspoon grated lemon zest
- 2 tablespoons lemon juice
- ¼ cup minced parsley

In a large pot of boiling salted water, cook the pasta according to the package directions. Drain.

Meanwhile, in a large saucepan, heat the oil over medium-high heat. Add the shallots and cook, stirring, until softened. Add the stock and cook for 1 minute. Stir in the tomatoes and thyme and cook for 2 minutes to break the tomatoes down a bit.

Add the fish cubes and cook until just opaque, 6 to 8 minutes. Stir in the lemon zest, lemon juice, and parsley.

Toss with the hot pasta.

MAKES 4 TO 6 SERVINGS

SPAGHETTINI WITH SALMON & ORANGE-TOMATO SAUCE: Use chicken broth instead of fish stock. Use salmon instead of halibut, and sprinkle lightly with salt and pepper before adding to the pan. Omit the lemon zest and juice, and use 2 teaspoons grated orange zest and 3 tablespoons orange juice.

LINGUINE WITH COD, FRESH TOMATOES & PARSLEY

Because the rest of the dish is fairly mild, be sure that the fresh tomatoes you are using are very flavorful. If not, use 2½ cups chopped canned whole tomatoes or drained diced tomatoes.

- 1 pound whole wheat linguine
- ¼ cup olive oil
- 1 teaspoon minced garlic
- 1 pound cod, cut into small chunks
- Salt
- 1 teaspoon minced fresh oregano or ½ teaspoon dried
- 2 tomatoes, peeled, seeded, and chopped
- ⅓ cup chopped flat-leaf parsley
- ¼ teaspoon black pepper
- ⅛ teaspoon red pepper flakes
- Grated Parmesan cheese, for serving

In a large pot of boiling salted water, cook the pasta according to the package directions. Drain.

Meanwhile, in a 10-inch skillet, heat the oil over medium-high heat. Add the garlic and cook for 1 minute.

Add the fish, season lightly with salt, and cook over medium heat until just opaque throughout. Sprinkle with the oregano and stir well.

Remove from the heat and stir in the tomatoes, parsley, black pepper, and red pepper flakes. Toss with the spaghetti. Serve with Parmesan for sprinkling.

MAKES 4 TO 6 SERVINGS

SPINACH LINGUINE WITH SARDINES & FENNEL

If you are not a fan of sardines—though they are a superb source of omega-3 fatty acids—use tuna instead. Use 1½ cans (6 ounces each) tuna, well-drained and separated into flakes.

- 1 tablespoon olive oil
- 2 cloves garlic, sliced
- 1 bulb fennel, thinly sliced (2½ cups)
- 1 red bell pepper, cut into ½-inch pieces
- 1 can (28 ounces) no-salt-added crushed tomatoes
- ¼ cup golden raisins
- ½ teaspoon salt
- ½ teaspoon fennel seeds
- 3 cans (3¾ ounces each) sardines, drained
- 12 ounces whole wheat spinach linguine
- ¼ cup orange juice

In a large skillet, heat the oil over medium heat. Add the garlic and cook for 1 minute, until tender. Stir in the sliced fennel and bell pepper, and cook, stirring frequently, until the vegetables are crisp-tender, about 10 minutes.

Stir in the tomatoes, raisins, salt, and fennel seeds, and bring to a boil. Reduce to a simmer and cook until the sauce is lightly thickened, about 10 minutes. Gently stir in the sardines and cook for 5 minutes.

Meanwhile, in a large pot of boiling salted water, cook the pasta according to the package directions. Drain. Combine the pasta and sauce in a large bowl. Add the orange juice and toss well to coat.

MAKES 4 SERVINGS

SESAME NOODLES

You can serve the noodles slightly warm or at room temperature. If you make it ahead and chill it, let it come to room temperature to serve.

- 8 ounces whole wheat spaghetti
- ¼ cup peanut butter
- ¼ cup cider vinegar
- 2 tablespoons soy sauce
- 2 tablespoons dark sesame oil
- 1 clove garlic
- ¾ teaspoon ground ginger
- 3 scallions, thinly sliced
- 1 tablespoon sesame seeds, toasted

In a large pot of boiling salted water, cook the pasta according to the package directions. Drain and rinse under cold water. Drain well and transfer to a bowl.

In a food processor, combine the peanut butter, vinegar, soy sauce, sesame oil, garlic, and ginger, and process until smooth. Add to the spaghetti along with the scallions and toss to coat.

At serving time, sprinkle with the sesame seeds.

MAKES 4 SERVINGS

PENNE WITH FENNEL & SAUSAGE SAUCE

Flavored with just a touch of sausage, this quick sauce is chunky with vegetables.

- 1 pound whole wheat penne
- 1 tablespoon olive oil
- ¼ pound sweet Italian pork sausage, casings removed
- 1 medium onion, chopped
- 2 small dried chili peppers
- 2 bulbs fennel, thinly sliced
- 1 red bell pepper, slivered
- 3 medium tomatoes, peeled and diced
- 1 teaspoon chopped fresh oregano or ½ teaspoon dried
- ½ teaspoon salt
- ¼ teaspoon pepper
- Grated Parmesan cheese, for serving

In a large pot of boiling salted water, cook the pasta according to the package directions. Drain.

Meanwhile, in a large heavy skillet, heat the oil over medium heat. Crumble in the sausage and cook for 5 minutes, stirring often. Add the onion and chili peppers. Cook and stir for 2 minutes.

Add the fennel, bell pepper, tomatoes, oregano, salt, and pepper. Bring to a boil over high heat. Reduce to a simmer and cook, uncovered, for 10 to 12 minutes. Taste and adjust the seasonings.

Discard the chili peppers. Toss the sauce with the pasta and serve with Parmesan for sprinkling.

MAKES 4 TO 6 SERVINGS

PENNE RIGATE WITH EDAMAME & MUSHROOMS

Rigate means ridged in Italian. Certain tubular pastas, like penne, have ridges so that sauce will stick better.

- 2 tablespoons olive oil
- 2 cups sliced cremini mushrooms
- 2 large cloves garlic, minced
- 2 cups frozen shelled edamame, thawed
- 1 can (14.5 ounces) diced tomatoes
- 2 tablespoons wine vinegar

- 1 tablespoon basil
- ½ teaspoon oregano
- Pinch of tarragon
- 1 pound whole wheat penne rigate
- ¼ cup grated Romano cheese, plus more for serving

In a large saucepan, heat the oil over medium-high heat. Add the mushrooms and garlic, and cook for 2 minutes.

Add the edamame, tomatoes, vinegar, basil, oregano, and tarragon. Cover and simmer for 10 minutes. Uncover and simmer 10 minutes to thicken slightly.

Meanwhile, in a large pot of boiling salted water, cook the pasta according to the package directions. Drain.

Stir the Romano into the sauce and toss with the hot pasta. Serve extra Romano for sprinkling.

MAKES 4 TO 6 SERVINGS

ZITI WITH SUGAR SNAP PEAS & HAM

If the sugar snap peas you get are on the large side, be sure that you pull the string from both sides of the pea. The bigger the peas get, the tougher the string is.

- 12 ounces whole wheat ziti
- 1 pound sugar snap peas, strings removed
- ¾ cup chicken broth, store-bought or homemade (page 172)
- ⅓ cup snipped fresh dill
- 3 scallions, thinly sliced
- 3 tablespoons Greek yogurt or reduced-fat sour cream
- 1 tablespoon butter
- 1 teaspoon grated lemon zest
- 2 tablespoons lemon juice
- ½ teaspoon salt
- ¼ pound Black Forest ham, finely diced

In a large pot of boiling salted water, cook the pasta according to the package directions. Add the sugar snaps for the last 1 minute of cooking. Drain.

Meanwhile, in a large bowl, combine the broth, dill, scallions, yogurt, butter, lemon zest, lemon juice, and salt.

Add the hot pasta and sugar snaps to the sauce, tossing well. Add the ham and toss again.

MAKES 4 SERVINGS

RIGATONI WITH SUN-DRIED TOMATO PESTO

Be sure to use dry-packed, not oil-packed, sun-dried tomatoes.

- ½ cup sun-dried tomatoes
- 1 cup boiling water
- 1 tablespoon olive oil
- 1 onion, halved and thinly sliced
- 2 red bell peppers, thinly sliced
- 2 cloves garlic, thinly sliced
- ½ cup chicken broth, store-bought or homemade (page 172), or water
- 1 tablespoon balsamic vinegar
- ½ teaspoon salt
- 12 ounces whole wheat rigatoni
- 2 cups small broccoli florets
- ⅓ cup slivered kalamata or other brine-cured black olives

In a small bowl, combine the sun-dried tomatoes and boiling water and let stand until the tomatoes have softened, about 20 minutes. Reserving the soaking liquid, drain the tomatoes.

Meanwhile, in a large skillet, heat the oil over medium heat. Add the onion and cook, stirring occasionally, until golden brown, about 8 minutes.

Add the bell peppers and garlic, stirring to combine. Add the broth and cook, stirring occasionally, until the peppers are softened, about 7 minutes. Transfer the mixture to a food processor along with the sun-dried tomatoes, the reserved soaking liquid, the vinegar, and salt, and process until smooth, about 1 minute. Transfer the sauce to a large bowl.

Meanwhile, in a large pot of boiling salted water, cook the pasta according to the package directions. Add the broccoli to the pot for the last 2 minutes of cooking. Drain well.

Add the pasta and the broccoli to the sauce, tossing to combine. Add the olives and toss again.

MAKES 4 SERVINGS

SUMMER MARKET PASTA

Small to medium eggplants work best for this recipe. Search for variegated or Japanese varieties with tender skins. If you use white eggplants, peel them first.

- 2 pounds small to medium eggplants
- 4 tablespoons extra-virgin olive oil, plus more for brushing
- Coarse salt and pepper
- 1 onion, diced
- 1 red bell pepper, diced
- 1 medium yellow summer squash, diced
- 2 cloves garlic, minced
- 1 large tomato, seeded and diced
- 3 tablespoons water
- 2 tablespoons minced flat-leaf parsley
- 1 pound whole wheat radiatore
- 2-ounce chunk of Parmesan cheese, for serving

Preheat the broiler.

Trim the ends of the eggplants and slice lengthwise into ½-inch-thick pieces. Brush lightly with some oil and sprinkle with salt and pepper. Place in a single layer on a baking sheet (you may need two) and broil 4 to 6 inches from the heat, turning once, about 10 minutes per side, until tender. Transfer to a cutting board. When cool enough to handle, cut into bite-size pieces.

Meanwhile, in a large saucepan, heat 3 tablespoons of the oil over medium heat. Add the onion, bell pepper, squash, and garlic, and cook until the vegetables are soft, about 10 minutes.

Add the eggplant, tomato, and water, and cook until the vegetables are nicely stewed and soft, about 5 minutes. Remove from the heat and stir in the remaining 1 tablespoon oil, the parsley, and salt and pepper to taste.

Meanwhile, in a large pot of boiling salted water, cook the pasta according to the package directions. Drain.

Add the pasta to the vegetables and toss. Serve with Parmesan shavings on top (use a vegetable peeler).

MAKES 4 TO 6 SERVINGS

GEMELLI ALLA CAPRESE

Gemelli, which means twins in Italian, is pasta made of two small lengths of dough twisted together.

- 4 large tomatoes, seeded and sliced into thin strips
- 1 small yellow bell pepper, slivered
- 4 cloves garlic, minced
- ⅓ cup shredded fresh basil leaves
- ⅓ cup extra-virgin olive oil
- 1 tablespoon rice vinegar
- ¾ teaspoon coarse salt
- ¼ teaspoon black pepper
- 1 pound whole wheat gemelli or other pasta twists

- ½ pound part-skim mozzarella cheese, shredded

In a large bowl, combine the tomatoes, bell pepper, garlic, basil, oil, vinegar, salt, and pepper. Let stand at room temperature for at least 1 hour.

In a large pot of boiling salted water, cook the pasta according to the package directions. Drain, add the mozzarella, and toss until the cheese begins to melt slightly. Add the marinated tomato mixture and toss again. Serve slightly warm.

MAKES 4 TO 6 SERVINGS

ORECCHIETTE WITH ROASTED BUTTERNUT, FRIED SAGE & BACON

Winter squash and sage are a classic Italian pairing.

- 1 small butternut squash, peeled and cut into ½-inch cubes
- 1 small onion, chopped
- 6 tablespoons extra-virgin olive oil
- 1 teaspoon brown sugar
- Salt and pepper
- 1 pound orecchiette
- 12 large fresh sage leaves
- 4 slices bacon, cut into ½-inch pieces
- ½ cup freshly grated Parmesan cheese

Preheat the oven to 400°F. Toss the squash with the onion and 2 tablespoons of the oil. Sprinkle with the brown sugar, and salt and pepper to taste. Roast on a baking sheet for 30 to 40 minutes, until tender and caramelized.

In a large pot of boiling salted water, cook the pasta according to the package directions. Reserving ¼ cup of the cooking liquid, drain the pasta and return it to the pot.

Meanwhile, in a large skillet, heat the remaining 4 tablespoons oil over medium heat. Add the sage leaves, 6 at a time, and cook until the oil stops sizzling and the edges are crisp. Drain on a paper towel. Pour out the sage-flavored olive oil (and save for another use).

Add the bacon to the skillet and cook over medium heat until golden and almost crisp. With a slotted spoon, transfer the bacon to paper towels and drain.

Add the roasted butternut and bacon to the pasta, and toss to coat. Season lightly with salt and pepper. Add the reserved pasta cooking water and the Parmesan, and toss well. Serve garnished with the sage leaves.

MAKES 6 SERVINGS

FIORI WITH BROCCOLI RABE

Fiori, which means flowers, is a beautiful pasta shape, but it may be difficult to find a whole-grain version. If you prefer, choose another ruffled or twisty shape, like radiatore or wagon wheels.

- ½ cup sun-dried tomatoes
- 1 large bunch broccoli rabe (1¼ pounds), cut into 1-inch lengths
- 8 ounces whole-grain fiori pasta
- 1 tablespoon olive oil
- 4 cloves garlic, minced
- 1 teaspoon red pepper flakes
- 2 tablespoons tomato paste
- ¾ teaspoon salt
- ¼ teaspoon black pepper
- ⅓ cup golden raisins
- ⅓ cup grated Parmesan cheese

To a large pot of boiling water, add the sun-dried tomatoes and cook for 5 minutes, or until softened.

With a slotted spoon, remove the sun-dried tomatoes. When cool enough to handle, coarsely chop.

Add the broccoli rabe to the boiling water and cook until crisp-tender, about 4 minutes. With a slotted spoon, transfer the broccoli rabe to a colander and drain.

Add the pasta to the boiling water and cook according to package directions. Reserving 1½ cups of the cooking water, drain and transfer to a large serving bowl.

In a large skillet, heat the oil over low heat. Add the garlic and red pepper flakes, and sauté for 3 minutes. Add the sun-dried tomatoes, broccoli rabe, tomato paste, salt, black pepper, and the reserved cooking water. Cook, stirring, until the broccoli rabe is heated through and tender, about 4 minutes. Add to the hot pasta along with the raisins and Parmesan, and toss well to combine.

MAKES 4 SERVINGS

ORZO WITH MEATBALLS

In this dish, the proportion of sauce to pasta is somewhat inverted. The sauce and meatballs are really the stars here, and the orzo plays a supporting role.

- ½ pound lean ground beef
- ½ (10-ounce) package frozen chopped spinach, thawed and squeezed dry
- 2 large egg whites
- ⅓ cup plain dried bread crumbs, preferably whole wheat
- 2 tablespoons grated Parmesan cheese
- 1½ teaspoons dried basil
- ½ teaspoon black pepper
- 1 tablespoon olive oil
- 2 large red bell peppers, slivered
- 4 cloves garlic, minced
- ¼ cup water
- 1 can (28 ounces) crushed tomatoes
- 8 ounces orzo

Preheat the oven to 400°F. Lightly oil a rimmed baking sheet.

In a food processor, combine the beef, spinach, egg whites, bread crumbs, Parmesan, ¾ teaspoon of the basil, and ¼ teaspoon of the black pepper, and pulse until blended. Shape into 20 meatballs.

Place the meatballs on the baking sheet and bake, turning once, for 12 to 15 minutes, or until no longer pink in the center.

Meanwhile, in a Dutch oven, heat the oil over high heat. Add the bell peppers and garlic, and cook for 1 minute. Reduce the heat to medium, add the water, the remaining ¾ teaspoon basil, and the remaining ¼ teaspoon black pepper, and cook until the peppers are tender, about 5 minutes.

Stir the tomatoes into the pot and bring to a boil. Add the meatballs, reduce the heat to medium-low, and simmer, stirring frequently, for 10 minutes, to blend the flavors.

Meanwhile, in a medium pot of boiling water, cook the pasta according to the package directions. Drain and transfer to a serving bowl. Spoon the meatballs and sauce over the pasta, and serve hot.

MAKES 4 SERVINGS

PAPPARDELLE WITH ASPARAGUS & OYSTER MUSHROOMS

Pappardelle is a broad, ribbonlike pasta. If you can't find it, use fettuccine. If your market carries fresh morels, buy a few and add them to the dish with the oyster mushrooms.

- 8 ounces pappardelle
- 2 tablespoons extra-virgin olive oil

- 3/4 pound oyster mushrooms
- 1/4 pound spring onions, baby leeks, or very large scallions, sliced
- 1 pound thin asparagus, cut into 2-inch pieces
- 1/4 cup dry white wine
- 1/2 cup vegetable broth, store-bought or homemade (page 173)
- 1/4 cup (1/2 stick) unsalted butter
- Sea salt and freshly ground pepper
- 1 tablespoon chopped chervil (optional)

In a large pot of boiling salted water, cook the pasta according to the package directions. Drain and transfer to a large bowl.

Meanwhile, in a 12-inch skillet, heat the oil over medium-high heat. Add the mushrooms and cook, stirring, until lightly browned, about 5 minutes. Add the onions and cook, until softened, 1 to 2 minutes. Add the asparagus and cook 2 minutes.

Add the wine and simmer until the liquid has evaporated, 1 to 2 minutes. Add the broth and bring to a boil. Add the butter and toss until melted into the vegetables. Season to taste with salt and pepper.

Mix the sauce and chervil (if using) into the pasta. Season with salt and pepper.

MAKES 6 SERVINGS

PUMPKIN TORTELLINI GIARDINIERA

The filling for commercial pumpkin tortellini is usually pumpkin puree, Parmesan, and crushed amaretti (sweet almond cookies).

- 12 ounces refrigerated or frozen pumpkin tortellini
- 2 tablespoons olive oil
- 2 cloves garlic, minced
- 2 carrots, diced
- 1 1/4 pounds plum tomatoes (about 5), coarsely chopped
- 3 1/2 cups broccoli florets
- 1/2 cup vegetable broth, store-bought or homemade (page 173), or water
- 1 1/2 cups frozen peas
- 3 tablespoons chopped fresh basil
- 3/4 teaspoon salt
- 1/4 teaspoon pepper

In a large pot of boiling salted water, cook the tortellini according to the package directions. Drain and return to the pot.

Meanwhile, in a large skillet, heat the oil over medium heat. Add the garlic and cook, stirring frequently, until fragrant, about 30 seconds. Stir in the carrots and cook, stirring frequently, until softened, about 5 minutes.

Add the tomatoes, broccoli, and broth, and cook until the broccoli is tender and the sauce is slightly thickened, about 4 minutes. Stir in the peas, basil, salt, and pepper, and cook until the peas are heated through, about 2 minutes.

Add the vegetables to the tortellini and toss.

MAKES 4 SERVINGS

RAVIOLI WITH SWEET PEPPER SAUCE

The bell pepper sauce can be prepared almost entirely in advance, making for a quick and easy main course.

- 5 teaspoons olive oil
- 3 large red bell peppers, thinly sliced
- 1 large red onion, halved and thinly sliced
- 3 cloves garlic, minced
- 1 cup water
- 2 tablespoons tomato paste

½ teaspoon rubbed sage

½ teaspoon turbinado or light brown sugar

¼ teaspoon salt

1¼ pounds whole wheat chicken ravioli

In a large skillet, heat the oil over low heat. Add the bell peppers, onion, and garlic, and cook until very soft, about 15 minutes.

Stir in the water, tomato paste, sage, brown sugar, and salt. Cover and cook until the peppers and onion are meltingly tender, about 20 minutes.

Transfer the bell pepper mixture to a food processor and process to a smooth puree. Return the puree to the skillet.

Meanwhile, cook the ravioli in a large pot of boiling salted water, until they float to the surface or according to the package directions. Reserving ½ cup of the cooking water, drain the ravioli.

Stir the reserved pasta cooking water into the pepper puree and bring to a simmer. Add the drained ravioli and cook until heated through, about 1 minute. Serve hot.

MAKES 4 SERVINGS

FRESH CHEESE RAVIOLI

The ravioli are formed individually here, but you could also do them in batches (see "Making Handmade Ravioli," page 109). Serve the ravioli with your favorite sauce.

15 ounces part-skim ricotta cheese

2 large eggs

⅓ cup grated Parmesan cheese

¼ cup chopped parsley or basil

1 tablespoon chopped fresh thyme, oregano, or a combination

½ teaspoon pepper

Fresh Whole Wheat Egg Pasta (page 348), prepared through cutting the dough into 2 pieces

1 tablespoon vegetable oil

In a large bowl, combine the ricotta, eggs, Parmesan, parsley, thyme, and pepper, and stir to blend well.

Divide each piece of dough into 2 pieces. (Keep the dough not being worked covered until ready for use.) Pass 1 piece of dough through a pasta machine to form a rectangle about 1/16 inch thick. Cut into 4 × 2-inch strips.

Place a rounded teaspoon of filling at one end of one strip, leaving room to seal the edges. Wet the edges with a bit of water, fold the dough in half lengthwise over the filling, and pinch together. Crimp or press to seal well. Repeat with the remaining dough and filling.

To a large pot of boiling salted water, add the oil. Add about half the ravioli at a time and cook, uncovered, until tender, about 8 minutes. Remove with a slotted spoon and let drain.

MAKES 4 TO 6 SERVINGS

CHEESY BAKED ROTINI WITH ARTICHOKES & CAULIFLOWER

This baked pasta would be lovely made with Roasted Cauliflower (page 418). Use 1 cup and skip the sautéing step for the cauliflower, and just heat the artichokes in the skillet.

2 cups whole wheat rotini pasta

3 tablespoons butter

2 tablespoons flour

2 cups milk

⅓ cup shredded sharp Cheddar cheese

¼ cup grated Parmesan cheese

2 tablespoons olive oil

- **1 cup small cauliflower florets**
- **Salt and pepper**
- **1 package (9 ounces) frozen artichoke hearts, thawed and coarsely chopped**

Preheat the oven to 350°F. Lightly grease a 2-quart baking dish.

In a large pot of boiling salted water, cook the pasta according to the package directions. Drain.

Meanwhile, in a large saucepan, melt the butter. Stir in the flour to make a paste. Slowly stir in the milk and bring to a boil. Stirring constantly, cook until lightly thickened, about 3 minutes. Add the Cheddar and Parmesan, and stir just until melted. Remove the sauce from the heat.

In a large skillet, heat the oil over medium-high heat. Add the cauliflower. Season lightly with salt and pepper. Cook, stirring, until the cauliflower takes on some color. Add the artichoke hearts and cook just to heat through.

Add the pasta and vegetables to the cheese sauce, and toss lightly. Transfer to the baking dish. Bake for 20 minutes or until hot and bubbling.

MAKES 4 SERVINGS

CHICKEN-MUSHROOM MANICOTTI

The stuffed manicotti may be assembled ahead. Cover and refrigerate, and increase the baking time to 1 hour.

SAUCE

- **¼ cup olive oil**
- **1 cup sliced mushrooms**
- **1 small onion, chopped**
- **1 clove garlic, minced**
- **1 can (28 ounces) diced tomatoes**
- **2 teaspoons oregano**
- **1 teaspoon basil**
- **¼ teaspoon salt**
- **1 can (6 ounces) tomato paste**

FILLING

- **2 tablespoons butter**
- **1 large onion, chopped**
- **½ cup chopped mushrooms**
- **1 clove garlic, minced**
- **1 pound ground chicken or turkey**
- **1 cup plain Greek yogurt or reduced-fat sour cream**
- **½ teaspoon salt**
- **¼ teaspoon pepper**
- **12 whole wheat manicotti shells, cooked**

To make the sauce: In a large skillet, heat the oil over medium heat. Add the mushrooms, onion, and garlic, and cook until the onion is translucent. Add the tomatoes, oregano, basil, and salt. Stir in the tomato paste. Bring to a boil over high heat, reduce to a simmer, and cook until the tomatoes collapse into the sauce, about 15 minutes.

Preheat the oven to 350°F.

To make the filling: In another large skillet, melt the butter over medium heat. Add the onion, mushrooms, and garlic, and cook until the onion is translucent and the mushroom liquid has evaporated. Add the chicken, breaking it up with a spoon, and sauté until cooked throughout.

With a slotted spoon, transfer the chicken and vegetables to a bowl and let cool to room temperature. Stir in the yogurt, salt, and pepper.

Spread a thin layer of the sauce over the bottom of a 9 × 13-inch baking pan. Stuff the manicotti and arrange them in a single layer in the pan. Pour the remaining sauce over them. Bake for 40 minutes, or until the sauce is bubbling and the manicotti are heated through.

MAKES 4 TO 6 SERVINGS

MANICOTTI STUFFED WITH ALMOND-CHICKPEA PUREE

Try using smoked almonds here—they would add a nice flavor to the filling.

- 2 red bell peppers, cut lengthwise into flat panels
- 2 cups cooked chickpeas
- 4 cloves garlic, peeled
- 3 tablespoons roasted almonds
- 1 tablespoon tomato paste
- 1½ teaspoons cumin
- ¼ teaspoon salt
- ¼ teaspoon black pepper
- 8 whole wheat manicotti shells (5 ounces)
- 1 can (14.5 ounces) spicy diced tomatoes
- 1 can (8 ounces) no-salt-added tomato sauce
- ¼ teaspoon cinnamon
- ¾ cup shredded part-skim mozzarella cheese (3 ounces)
- ¼ cup crumbled feta cheese

Preheat the broiler. Broil the pepper pieces 6 inches from the heat, skin-side up, for 12 minutes, or until the skin is charred. Remove from the broiler, turn the pepper pieces upside down on the pan, and set aside to cool. Peel the peppers and place in a food processor.

Add the chickpeas, garlic, almonds, tomato paste, cumin, salt, and black pepper, and process until almost smooth but with some texture.

In a large pot of boiling water, cook the manicotti according to the package directions. Drain well.

Preheat the oven to 425°F.

In a medium bowl, combine the diced tomatoes, tomato sauce, and cinnamon. Spread about ½ cup of the sauce over the bottom of a 9 × 9-inch glass baking dish.

Fill the cooked manicotti shells with the chickpea mixture. Transfer the filled shells to the baking dish and spoon the remaining tomato sauce on top. Cover and bake for 20 minutes, or until the manicotti are piping hot.

Meanwhile, toss the mozzarella and feta together to distribute them evenly. Uncover the manicotti, sprinkle with the cheese mixture, and bake for about 4 minutes to melt the cheese.

MAKES 4 SERVINGS

MUSHROOM & TOFU LASAGNA

If you have time, drain the tofu (see "Draining Tofu," page 311) before mixing in the Parmesan and seasonings.

- 1 pound whole wheat lasagna noodles
- 2 tablespoons olive oil
- 1 pound cremini mushrooms, thinly sliced
- 10 ounces firm tofu
- ¼ cup grated Parmesan cheese
- 2 cloves garlic, minced
- ¼ teaspoon pepper
- ¼ cup chopped parsley
- 2½ cups tomato sauce
- 2 cups shredded whole-milk mozzarella cheese (8 ounces)

In a large pot of boiling salted water, cook the lasagna noodles according to the package directions. Drain and rinse with cool water to stop the cooking. Separate and drain on paper towels.

In a large skillet, heat the oil over medium heat. Add the mushrooms and cook until softened. Set aside to cool slightly.

In a medium bowl, mash the tofu with a fork. Stir in the Parmesan, garlic, and pepper.

Preheat the oven to 350°F. Oil as 9 × 12-inch baking pan.

Line the bottom of the baking pan with a layer of noodles. (Save the noodles that are in the best shape for the top layer.) Dot with half of the tofu mixture, then top with half of the mushrooms, half of the parsley, about ½ cup sauce, and one-third of the mozzarella.

Repeat this layering once. Top with a final layer of noodles, sprinkle with the remaining mozzarella, and top with the remaining tomato sauce. Bake for 45 minutes, or until nicely browned. Let the lasagna sit for at least 10 minutes before slicing.

MAKES 6 TO 8 SERVINGS

SPINACH LASAGNA

If you want to make this with fresh spinach, you'll need a little over 2 pounds. Discard the large stems and steam the whole spinach leaves until tender, 3 to 4 minutes. Turn the spinach as it steams so that it cooks evenly. When slightly cool, coarsely chop and then squeeze dry.

- 6 whole wheat lasagna noodles (5½ ounces)
- 5 teaspoons olive oil
- 1 large onion, finely chopped
- 3 cloves garlic, minced
- 10 ounces mushrooms, thinly sliced
- 2 packages (10 ounces each) frozen chopped spinach, thawed and squeezed dry
- 1½ teaspoons grated lemon zest
- 1½ teaspoons salt
- ½ teaspoon pepper
- 1½ cups part-skim ricotta cheese
- ½ cup low-fat (1%) cottage cheese
- ½ cup grated Parmesan cheese
- 1 can (8 ounces) tomato sauce
- ¼ cup tomato paste
- 1 large egg
- 2 large egg whites

In a large pot of boiling water, cook the lasagna noodles according to the package directions. Drain and rinse with cool water to stop the cooking. Separate and drain on paper towels.

Preheat the oven to 350°F. Lightly oil a 7 × 11-inch glass baking dish.

In a large skillet, heat the oil over medium heat. Add the onion and garlic, and cook until soft, about 5 minutes. Add the mushrooms and cook until they begin to give up their liquid, about 4 minutes.

Add the spinach and cook, stirring, until no liquid remains. Transfer to a medium bowl and add the lemon zest, ¾ teaspoon of the salt, and ¼ teaspoon of the pepper. Toss well.

In a food processor, combine the ricotta, cottage cheese, ¼ cup of the Parmesan, the tomato sauce, tomato paste, whole egg, egg whites, the remaining ¾ teaspoon salt, and the remaining ¼ teaspoon pepper, and process to a smooth puree.

Line the bottom of the baking dish with 2 of the lasagna noodles. Spoon half of the spinach mixture and then one-third of the cheese mixture over the noodles. Repeat one time. Top with the remaining noodles and the remaining cheese mixture. Sprinkle the remaining ¼ cup Parmesan on top.

Bake for 30 minutes, or until hot. Let the lasagna sit for at least 10 minutes before slicing.

MAKES 4 SERVINGS

PASTITSIO

When you make the cheese sauce, be sure the milk is very cold. Adding cold liquid to a butter-flour roux makes a smoother sauce.

CHEESE SAUCE

- ½ cup (1 stick) butter
- ½ cup unbleached all-purpose flour

- ½ cup white whole wheat flour*
- 4 cups cold milk
- 1 teaspoon salt
- ¼ teaspoon white pepper
- ⅛ teaspoon nutmeg
- 2 large eggs
- ½ cup grated Pecorino-Romano cheese

FILLING AND PASTA

- 3 tablespoons butter
- 1 small onion, diced
- 1 pound ground beef
- ½ cup dry red wine
- 1 cup tomato sauce
- ¼ teaspoon oregano
- ⅛ teaspoon cinnamon
- Salt and black pepper
- 2 tablespoons plain dried bread crumbs
- 1 pound whole wheat rigatoni pasta
- 1 cup grated Asiago cheese
- ½ cup grated Pecorino-Romano cheese

**milled from white wheat grains*

To make the cheese sauce: In a medium saucepan, melt the butter. Stir in the flours to form a smooth paste. Add the milk, salt, white pepper, and nutmeg, and cook over medium heat, stirring constantly, until the sauce thickens, about 5 minutes. Let come to a boil and cook, stirring constantly, for 1 minute. Reduce to a simmer and cook, stirring occasionally, for 2 minutes. Remove from the heat, and whisk in the eggs and Pecorino. Set aside.

To make the filling: In a 12-inch skillet, melt 2 tablespoons of the butter over medium heat. Add the onion and cook, stirring occasionally, until translucent and just beginning to turn brown, about 5 minutes. Crumble the beef into the pan and cook until browned, about 10 minutes.

Drain the excess fat from the pan and add the wine. Bring to a boil and cook, stirring, until the wine is fully incorporated into the beef, about 3 minutes. Stir in the tomato sauce, oregano, and cinnamon, and season with salt and black pepper to taste. Simmer for 2 minutes.

Preheat the oven to 350°F. On the stovetop or in the microwave, melt the remaining 1 tablespoon butter. Use the melted butter to coat a 9 × 13-inch baking dish. Sprinkle the bottom of the pan with the bread crumbs.

Cook the pasta in a large pot of salted boiling water according to the package directions. Drain the pasta and mix with 1 cup of the cheese sauce.

Spread half of the pasta in the baking dish. Top with all of the tomato-meat sauce and sprinkle with the Asiago. Top with the remaining pasta. Cover with the remaining cheese sauce and sprinkle with the Pecorino.

Bake on the middle oven rack of the for 30 to 40 minutes, until the topping is golden brown and the pasta is hot and bubbling.

MAKES 8 SERVINGS

RICE STICK NOODLES WITH PORK

Do all your prep first, and have everything ready and waiting to go when you heat up the wok. Your reward will be in the speed of the cooking.

- 6 dried shiitake mushrooms
- Boiling water
- 1 pound rice stick noodles, ½ inch wide
- 1 teaspoon dark sesame oil
- 1 tablespoon peanut oil
- 2 cloves garlic, minced
- 5 thin slices fresh ginger, minced

- 1 pound boneless pork loin chops, trimmed and cut into thin strips
- 1 tablespoon soy sauce
- Pinch of pepper
- ¼ pound snow peas
- 4 scallions, cut on the diagonal into 1½-inch pieces
- 3 cups slivered napa cabbage
- 1¼ cups chicken broth, store-bought or homemade (page 173)
- 1 teaspoon cornstarch blended with 3 tablespoons water

In a small heatproof bowl, cover the mushrooms with the boiling water and let stand until softened, about 40 minutes. Drain. Discard the stems, thinly slice the caps and set aside.

Place the rice stick noodles in a bowl and add enough cold water to cover. Soak until pliable, about 30 minutes. Drain. In a large pot of boiling water, cook the noodles until tender but not sticky, 1 to 2 minutes. Drain well and place in a bowl. Toss with the sesame oil and set aside.

Heat a wok or a large skillet. Add the peanut oil. When the oil is hot but not smoking, add the garlic and ginger, and stir-fry until golden. Add the pork strips, soy sauce, and pepper, and stir-fry until the pork loses its pink color, about 3 minutes. With a slotted spoon, transfer the pork to a plate.

Add the shiitakes, snow peas, scallions, and cabbage to the wok, and stir-fry for 2 minutes. Add half of the broth and continue cooking until hot. Add the cooked noodles, pork (and any accumulated juices), and the remaining broth.

Push the vegetables and meat to one side and slowly pour the cornstarch mixture into the bottom of the wok, blending it thoroughly with the pan juices. When the sauce begins to thicken, push the vegetables and meat into the sauce and stir to blend. Serve hot.

MAKES 6 SERVINGS

PAD THAI

If you have the time, drain the tofu (see "Draining Tofu," page 311) to firm it up. This is especially important if you can't find extra-firm tofu.

- 8 ounces rice noodles, ¼-inch wide
- 1 large egg
- 1 large egg white
- 6 teaspoons extra-light olive oil
- 3 tablespoons lower-sodium soy sauce
- 2 tablespoons lemon juice
- 1½ teaspoons turbinado or light brown sugar
- 1 teaspoon anchovy paste
- 2 tablespoons minced garlic
- 4 large shrimp, peeled, deveined, and coarsely chopped
- 4 ounces extra-firm tofu, cut into ¼-inch cubes
- 2 scallions, thinly sliced
- 1 cup mung bean sprouts
- ¼ cup chopped cilantro
- ¼ cup chopped dry-roasted peanuts

Place the rice noodles in a bowl and add enough cold water to cover. Soak until pliable, about 30 minutes. Drain. Meanwhile, bring a large pot of water to a boil.

Cook the soaked noodles in the boiling water until just tender to the bite, about 1 minute. Drain. Set aside.

In a small bowl, beat the whole egg and egg white until frothy. In a large skillet, heat 2 teaspoons of the oil over medium-high heat. Add the beaten eggs to the skillet and spread out to form a large pancake. Cook until just set, about 45 seconds. Turn the pancake over and cook until just set on the second side, about 10 seconds. Transfer to a cutting board to cool. Cut into ¼-inch-wide strips. Set aside.

In a small bowl, combine the soy sauce, lemon juice, brown sugar, and anchovy paste, and stir until the anchovy paste is dissolved.

Add 2 teaspoons of the oil and the garlic to the skillet, and cook until fragrant, about 30 seconds. Add the shrimp, tofu, and scallions, and cook until the shrimp is opaque, 1 to 2 minutes.

Add the remaining 2 teaspoons oil, the drained noodles, egg strips, and bean sprouts, and then swirl in the soy sauce mixture. Gently toss to combine. Serve sprinkled with the cilantro and peanuts.

MAKES 4 SERVINGS

SOBA PANCAKE WITH SCALLIONS & GINGER

Serve this crisp and flavorful soba-noodle pancake with stir-fries as a nice change-up to rice.

8 ounces soba noodles

¼ cup minced scallions

2 tablespoons soy sauce

1 teaspoon dark sesame oil

1 teaspoon grated fresh ginger

3 or 4 drops hot pepper oil

2 tablespoons peanut oil

Preheat the oven to 500°F.

In a medium pot of boiling salted water, cook the noodles according to the package directions. Drain and place in a bowl.

Add the scallions, soy sauce, sesame oil, ginger, and hot pepper oil. Stir to coat the noodles.

In a 10-inch cast-iron (or other ovenproof) skillet, heat the peanut oil over medium heat. Add the noodle mixture, pressing down and spreading evenly across the bottom of the pan.

Place the skillet on the lowest oven rack. Bake for 20 to 25 minutes, or until the pancake is crisp and dark golden. Slide the pancake out and cut into wedges. Serve hot.

MAKES 6 SERVINGS

Salads

Whether at the beginning of a meal to get the appetite going, as a side dish with heavier dishes, or after the main course to cleanse the palate, salads should be refreshing. While there aren't really any hard and fast rules for putting together a salad, there are a few important things to keep in mind:

- Tired vegetables may be suitable for a soup or stew, but salads call for the freshest of ingredients.
- Let what's in season be your guide.
- Try to balance textures, colors, and flavors. An assertive green such as arugula makes a great salad on its own, but if you use too much in combination with a soft, mild, buttery lettuce such as Bibb, it takes over.

Preparing Greens

There are differing opinions about the best time for washing salad greens. Some like to wash greens as soon as they are brought in from the garden or the store. Others like to wash them right before use. Either method is fine, so long as you thoroughly dry the greens after rinsing.

Salad spinners are great tools for washing and drying greens. Remove and discard any damaged leaves. Fill the spinner with cold water, add the leaves and swish them around. Lift them out with your hands, leaving any grit behind. Repeat several times until the water is clear. Spin the greens to dry them thoroughly. If not using right away, place in a resealable plastic bag or a container with a paper towel to absorb moisture.

To clean head lettuce, first rap the core sharply on a work surface to loosen it, then remove it; or, cut out the core with the point of a sharp knife. (If you plan to store lettuce for several days, though, leave the core intact.) Next hold the head under cold running water. The force of the water will separate the leaves and flush out dirt. Drain and pat dry.

Heads of cabbage with their compact, tight leaves are more difficult to wash. First, discard the outermost tough leaves. Slice through the core to cut the cabbage into quarters, then rinse and pat dry.

Once washed, greens are easy to prepare for eating. Break away coarse stems, and tear large leaves into bite-size pieces. With a sharp chef's knife, coarsely shred cabbage. As a rule, 1 to 2 cups of greens will serve one person.

Salads based on greens should be well chilled. Prepare these salads shortly before serving so that the weight of other ingredients does not crush the greens. To keep greens crisp, add dressings (and juicy tomato wedges and cucumber slices) at the last possible minute. With salads destined for picnics, keep the greens crisp by carrying them undressed in a plastic bag. When ready to serve, pour the dressing into the bag and gently shake it until all the greens are coated.

POPULAR SALAD GREENS

Most supermarkets carry a wide variety of interesting salad greens these days. The following chart lists some of the more popular salad components, including some you may find only in farmer's markets.

SALAD GREEN	DESCRIPTION
ARUGULA	Small oak-shaped leaves, on long stems; peppery flavor that is more pronounced in older, larger leaves
BASIL	Dark green, sweet; mild mint or licorice flavor
BELGIAN ENDIVE	Bullet shaped, white or red (white is more common), bittersweet taste
CABBAGE (GREEN, RED, SAVOY)	Round compact head; color depends on variety; coarse leaves (ruffled on savoy); distinctive flavor
CHICORY (CURLY ENDIVE)	Frilly, sprawling heads; coarse leaves with dark-green edges, white center; bitter flavor
CILANTRO	Similar to flat-leaf parsley in looks but leaves are paler and more delicate; aromatic, herbal, sprightly
DANDELION	Small, dark leaves; slightly bitter flavor; best when young
ESCAROLE	Grows in loose heads, broad wavy leaves; mildly bittersweet
FRISÉE (YOUNG CHICORY)	Pale green frilly leaves; mildly bitter taste
GARDEN CRESS	Small leaves; spicy hot flavor
LAMB'S-QUARTERS	Small, dark, spoon-shaped leaves in loose clusters; biting, radish-like flavor
LETTUCE, BIBB	Small head; pale to medium green; tender leaves; delicate, mellow flavor
LETTUCE, BOSTON (BUTTERHEAD)	Loose head; deep green, large, soft leaves; delicate flavor
LETTUCE, ICEBERG	Large head; crisp leaves; little flavor
LETTUCE, LOOSE-LEAF	Curly, loose, coarse leaves; mild flavor
LETTUCE, RED-LEAF	Red-tinged, large, loose leaves; tender texture; delicate flavor
LETTUCE, ROMAINE	Medium green; large, long, crisp leaves; mild flavor
MÂCHE	Spoon shaped leaves, velvety; delicate and mild tasting
MESCLUN	A mixture of young salad greens that often includes leaf lettuce and radicchio
MIZUNA	Crisp, green, feathery leaves; mild bite
NAPA CABBAGE	Long, tight head; pale green; mild flavor
NASTURTIUM	Many-colored flowers that are often used in salads, along with their leaves, slightly scalloped in shape; peppery in flavor
PARSLEY (CURLY, FLAT-LEAF)	Dark green; small flat or frilly leaves; distinctive flavor
PURSLANE	Thick, green leaves (like a succulent) that are fleshy and slightly crunchy
RADICCHIO	Pale red to dark-reddish purple, comes in both round and bullet-shaped heads; spicy, peppery flavor
SORREL	Bright green; crisp, tongue-shaped leaves; sour flavor
SPINACH	Dark green; tender leaves; mild but distinctive musky flavor
TATSOI	Large bunches with spoon shaped leaves, resembles a giant flower; mild, sweet flavor
WATERCRESS	Dark green; dime-size, glossy leaves; spicy, peppery flavor

Matching the Dressing to the Greens

Whether you're dressing a bowl of a single green or putting together a mixed-greens salad, it's important to keep a several things in mind:

- Pair greens with dressings that will complement, not overpower, them. Strong, assertive greens such as arugula, frisée, and radicchio will hold up to highly flavored dressings such as those with garlic or shallots, which would overshadow a mild, green like Bibb lettuce.
- Consider mixing and matching something mild with something peppery. Or add a surprise element like basil or cilantro leaves.

SALAD OILS

Salad oils vary in both flavor and intensity. While some oils, like extra-virgin olive, are good on their own, other very strong flavored oils, like nut oils, do best when combined with another, milder oil. In some instances, a dressing can be made with a combination of olive oil, a little nut oil, and a splash of a neutral oil such as safflower, sunflower, or canola.

OIL	FLAVOR
ALMOND	Mild, light
AVOCADO	Rich and nutty, mild avocado taste
CANOLA	Neutral
CANOLA-OLIVE BLEND	Mild flavored
CORN	Mild, tastes faintly of corn
GRAPESEED	Neutral
HAZELNUT, COLD-PRESSED	Mildly nutty
HAZELNUT, ROASTED	Rich, nutty
MACADAMIA	Mild
OLIVE, EXTRA-LIGHT	Mild, almost imperceptible olive taste
OLIVE, EXTRA-VIRGIN	Rich, slightly peppery
OLIVE, VIRGIN	Medium olive taste
PEANUT, COLD-PRESSED	Mild, nutty
PEANUT, ROASTED	Rich, nutty
PECAN, COLD-PRESSED	Mild, nutty
PECAN, ROASTED	Rich, nutty
PISTACHIO	Rich, nutty
PUMPKIN SEED	Deep, rich, nutty flavor
SAFFLOWER	Neutral
SESAME, COLD-PRESSED	Mild, light
SESAME, DARK (TOASTED)	Rich sesame taste
SOY	Neutral
SOY-OLIVE BLEND	Mild
SUNFLOWER SEED	Mild

- Peppery greens such as arugula, nasturtium leaves, and watercress, as well as bitter greens like chicory or radicchio, take well to dressings with a hint of sweetness.
- Texture is as important as flavor in greens. For instance, sturdy greens like romaine and iceberg can take thick creamy dressings without wilting, while soft lettuces like Bibb or Boston work better with light buttermilk dressings and vinaigrettes.

Oil & Vinegar

Most salad dressings are fundamentally a combination of oil and vinegar, even when they have other creamy ingredients—such as buttermilk, sour cream, or mayonnaise—added to them. So part of choosing the right dressing for a salad is also about choosing the right oil and vinegar, and knowing what flavors they will contribute.

Dressing the Salad

The best time to dress a salad depends on what's in the salad. Add vinaigrettes to crisp vegetables, greens, and fresh fruits just before serving to prevent wilting. Keep the salad ingredients well chilled until serving time, but bring vinaigrette dressings to room temperature.

Mayonnaise-based or other creamy dressings for meat, poultry, potato, fish, pasta, and cabbage salads can be added 1 to 2 hours ahead of serving because these salads improve by marinating. And for any cooked meats that are to be added to tossed salads, be sure to marinate them in a vinaigrette

VINEGARS

Vinegars can be used in salad dressings, as part of a marinade, splashed into a stew or sauce at the end to give it a little acidity, or even drizzled over fruit. The list of vinegars could go on and on, as you can pretty much turn anything into vinegar. Below are some of the most common and readily available.

VINEGAR	SOURCE	CHARACTERISTIC
BALSAMIC, AGED (TRADIZIONALE)	Concentrated grape juice, aged 12 years or more	Thick, syrupy, sweet
BALSAMIC, RED	Concentrated grape juice	Sweet, tart
BALSAMIC, WHITE	White grape must and wine vinegar	Mildly sweet and tart
CIDER	Apple cider	Mild, slightly sweet
INFUSED, HERB AND FRUIT	Wine vinegar with fruit or herbs infused	Tastes of the fruit (like raspberries) or the herb
MALT	Malted barley or sour unhopped beer	Assertive
RICE	Glutinous rice	Mild, slightly sweet
WHITE OR DISTILLED	Diluted distilled alcohol	Sharp flavor
WINE, CHAMPAGNE	Champagne	Slightly fruity
WINE, PORT	Port wine	Like a fruity red wine vinegar
WINE, RED	Red wine	Robust and acidic
WINE, SHERRY	Sherry	Nutty
WINE, WHITE	White wine	Mildly acidic

SALAD BOWLS

In selecting a bowl for preparing salads, consider the size of the bowl as well as its composition. A salad bowl should be roomy enough to toss and dress the ingredients. Glass or ceramic bowls are easy to clean. Wood is attractive, but hard to clean and over time may taste a little like rancid oil.

---

for an hour or so before tossing them with the greens (using more of the same vinaigrette for the rest of the salad).

Avoid overdressing salads because the delicate flavors of other ingredients are easily masked. Generally speaking, 3 to 4 tablespoons of dressing are ample for 1 quart of prepared greens. One-quarter to ½ cup mayonnaise readily coats 3 to 4 cups of potatoes or coleslaw. Use a dressing that is thin enough to blend easily with the salad but not so thin that it won't coat.

Trickle or spoon the dressing over the salad and gently toss until all ingredients glisten with a light coating. Or make the dressing right in the bowl, add the salad ingredients and toss. For salads dressed at the last minute, you can toss the salad with the dressing before serving, or pass the salad and dressing separately so each person can apply his own. If for convenience you'd prefer to have the dressing and greens already in the salad bowl ready to be tossed, place the dressing in the bottom of the bowl and cover with several sturdy greens first to protect the more tender greens from the moisture. Toss the salad at serving time.

BASIL-GARLIC OIL

This adds a lovely summery taste to salads.

1½ cups basil leaves and tender stems, well washed

2 cups olive oil

2 tablespoons minced garlic

In a medium pot of boiling water, blanch the basil for 15 seconds. Drain and transfer to paper towels to dry well.

Transfer the blanched basil to a food processor. Add 2 tablespoons of the oil and puree. Transfer to a container with a lid, add the garlic and the remaining oil, and stir to combine. Cover and refrigerate for 1 day.

Strain through a fine-mesh sieve, pressing on the basil to extract as much oil as possible. Pour into a jar or a container with a lid.

MAKES 2 CUPS

SPICY RASPBERRY VINEGAR

This would make a great addition to any fruit salad dressing that calls for vinegar.

2 cups raspberries

1 tablespoon turbinado or brown sugar

3 cups distilled white vinegar

½ teaspoon red pepper flakes

In a medium bowl, crush the raspberries with the sugar. Transfer to a large jar and add the vinegar and red pepper flakes. Let stand for 24 hours. Strain and transfer the vinegar to a clean bottle.

MAKES 3 CUPS

RED WINE VINAIGRETTE

A good all-purpose dressing.

9½ tablespoons red wine vinegar
1 clove garlic, minced
⅛ teaspoon salt
⅛ teaspoon pepper
1¼ cups extra-virgin olive oil

In a medium bowl, combine the vinegar, garlic, salt, and pepper. Slowly whisk in the olive oil.

MAKES SCANT 2 CUPS

BALSAMIC VINAIGRETTE: Use white or red balsamic vinegar.

SHERRY VINAIGRETTE

Good on sturdy greens with some character, like frisée or escarole.

3 tablespoons sherry wine vinegar
1 teaspoon finely minced shallot
½ teaspoon Dijon mustard
½ teaspoon coarse salt
Pinch of pepper
⅔ cup extra-virgin olive oil

In small bowl, whisk together the vinegar, shallot, mustard, salt, and pepper. Whisking constantly, slowly drizzle in the oil.

MAKES SCANT 1 CUP

WHITE WINE–GARLIC VINAIGRETTE: Use white wine vinegar instead of sherry vinegar, and minced garlic instead of shallot.

LEMON-DIJON VINAIGRETTE

Lovely on soft-leaved lettuces like buttercrunch or Bibb.

2 tablespoons lemon juice
1 tablespoon white wine vinegar
2 teaspoons Dijon mustard
¼ teaspoon coarse salt
¼ teaspoon pepper
6 tablespoons extra-virgin olive oil

In a small bowl, whisk together the lemon juice, vinegar, mustard, salt, and pepper. Slowly whisk in the oil.

MAKES GENEROUS ½ CUP

FRESH HERB VINAIGRETTE

Good on mixed field greens.

⅓ cup extra-virgin olive oil
¼ cup balsamic or red wine vinegar
½ teaspoon Dijon mustard
¼ teaspoon salt
1 tablespoon minced fresh herbs: chives, tarragon, rosemary, parsley, or a combination

In a medium screw-top jar, combine the oil, vinegar, mustard, and salt. Cover and shake until well combined. Add the herbs and shake again.

MAKES ⅔ CUP

HERB-CHEESE VINAIGRETTE

Use on crisp greens like romaine.

- 1½ cups vegetable oil
- ½ cup white wine vinegar
- ⅓ cup grated Parmesan cheese
- 2 cloves garlic, smashed and peeled
- ½ teaspoon basil
- ½ teaspoon oregano
- Pepper

In a quart-size screw-top jar, combine the oil, vinegar, Parmesan, garlic, basil, oregano, and pepper to taste. Cover and shake well. Refrigerate overnight to develop the flavors.

MAKES 2 CUPS

SPICY MISO DRESSING

Good on noodles, rice, grains, and sturdy greens.

- 2 tablespoons wasabi powder
- 2 tablespoons water
- 2 tablespoons shiro miso paste
- ¼ cup lime juice (about 2 limes)
- 1 tablespoon dark sesame oil
- 1 tablespoon honey
- ½ teaspoon salt
- ½ teaspoon ground ginger

In a large bowl, stir together the wasabi powder and water to form a paste. Stir in the miso.

Whisk in the lime juice, sesame oil, honey, salt, and ginger until smooth.

MAKES ½ CUP

FRESH GINGER-TAHINI DRESSING

In addition being good on to cold noodles, this would make an interesting coleslaw dressing.

- ¼ cup tahini (sesame butter)
- 1 tablespoon soy sauce
- 3 tablespoons water
- 2 tablespoons lemon juice
- 1 teaspoon grated fresh ginger

KEEPING GARLIC TAME IN SALADS

Garlic adds a delightful assertive snap to salad. Too much, though, overpowers all other ingredients. Here are four easy ways to make the garlic flavor subtle:

- Drop peeled garlic into boiling water for a minute then drain and finely chop. The blanching will remove the bite of the garlic, but not its flavor.
- Before adding the greens, rub the bowl with a cut garlic clove.
- Place 2 or 3 crushed cloves in the bottom of the salad bowl, add the dressing, and allow the flavors to mellow for 10 minutes. Remove the cloves before adding the salad greens.
- Slice garlic into the salad oil, then warm it briefly over low heat. Cool the garlic in the oil, then remove. You now have mild garlic oil.

1 clove garlic, minced

In a small bowl, blend the tahini and soy sauce until smooth. Beat in the water and lemon juice, 1 tablespoon at a time, until creamy. Blend in the ginger and garlic.

MAKES 1 CUP

TOASTED SESAME SEED DRESSING

Good in rice or noodle salads.

½ cup vegetable oil
1 tablespoon sesame seeds
1 clove garlic, smashed and peeled
2 tablespoons cider vinegar
2 teaspoons soy sauce

In a small saucepan, combine the oil, sesame seeds, and garlic. Cook over medium heat until the seeds and garlic have become a toasted color, about 2 minutes. Do not overbrown.

Remove from the heat and set aside to cool to room temperature. Discard the garlic.

Place the cooled oil and seeds in a screwtop jar. Add the vinegar and soy sauce, cover, and shake to blend.

MAKES ¾ CUP

SPICED YOGURT-LIME DRESSING

This would be delicious on a mixture of mixed berries, either as a side salad or dessert.

1 cup Greek yogurt
1 teaspoon grated lime zest
1 tablespoon lime juice
¼ teaspoon grated fresh ginger
¼ teaspoon ground mace

In a small bowl, combine the yogurt, lime zest, lime juice, ginger, and mace.

MAKES 1 CUP

STEAKHOUSE DRESSING

A hearty dressing for crisp lettuces.

3 tablespoons plus 2 teaspoons olive oil
2 tablespoons plus 1 teaspoon cider vinegar
2 tablespoons tomato paste
2 teaspoons honey
1 teaspoon paprika
½ teaspoon Worcestershire sauce
¼ teaspoon salt

In a small screw-top jar, combine the oil, vinegar, tomato paste, honey, paprika, Worcestershire, and salt. Cover and shake well to combine.

MAKES GENEROUS ½ CUP

BLUE CHEESE DRESSING

Good with fresh garden tomatoes and green salads.

1¼ cups reduced-fat sour cream or Greek yogurt
¾ cup mayonnaise
4 ounces blue cheese, coarsely crumbled
Milk, if needed

In a small bowl, whisk together the sour cream, mayonnaise, and blue cheese. Refrigerate, covered, for the flavors to blend. Just before serving, whisk in some milk, if necessary, to loosen the dressing.

MAKES 2½ CUPS

BABY ARUGULA SALAD WITH SHAVED PARMESAN

Baby arugula has all the flavors of the grown-up version, but is a little less pungent.

- 1½ tablespoons extra-virgin olive oil
- 1 tablespoon lemon juice
- 1 small clove garlic, minced
- 1 bag (5 ounces) baby arugula
- Salt and pepper
- 1 ounce Parmesan cheese, shaved into thin strips

In a large bowl, whisk together the oil, lemon juice, and garlic. Add the arugula and toss gently to combine. Season with salt and pepper to taste.

Divide the salad among plates and sprinkle with the Parmesan shavings.

MAKES 6 SERVINGS

SPRING LETTUCES WITH STRAWBERRIES & FETA

Look for small organic strawberries from the farmer's market; they have a lovely strong scent and a tart flavor.

- 12 cups assorted lettuce greens
- 1 cup herb sprigs, such as chives, chervil, or mint
- About 3 tablespoons Sherry Vinaigrette (page 375)
- 1 cup crumbled goat or sheep's milk feta cheese (4 ounces)
- ½ cup sliced small strawberries

Place the greens and herbs in a large bowl. Add the vinaigrette and gently toss to coat. Taste and add additional vinaigrette, if desired. Top with the feta and berries.

MAKES 8 SERVINGS

WATERMELON & GOAT CHEESE SALAD: Use small cubes of seeded watermelon instead of the strawberries, and mild goat cheese instead of the feta. Pair them with young mint sprigs.

NASTURTIUM SALAD

The yuzu is a member of the citrus family. It looks like a very small and somewhat lumpy grapefruit. It is not eaten as a fruit, but its juice—which is very tart and aromatic—is used the way lemon juice would be. In fact, if you can't find yuzu juice (look in Asian markets), use lemon juice in this recipe.

- 1 tablespoon olive oil
- 2 teaspoons yuzu juice
- ¼ teaspoon salt
- 1 sweet apple (such as Pink Lady, Barber, or Fuji), quartered and thinly sliced crosswise

---

FLOWERS FOR SALADS

Edible flowers—which include honeysuckle, nasturtiums, carnations, violets, and roses—are delicious and beautiful in salads. If you grow your own flowers, and therefore know they haven't been sprayed, pick them when they are at their peak. The petals are the most flavorful part; just rinse before using. Otherwise, only buy edible flowers from producers who have grown them specifically to be eaten. Never eat flowers from a flower shop. Some flowers, such as honeysuckle and carnations, are sweet; while others, such as nasturtiums, have pungent and peppery flavors.

2 cups nasturtium flowers and green leaves

1 cup arugula

In a medium bowl, whisk together the oil, yuzu, and salt. Add the apple and toss. Add the nasturtium flowers and leaves and the arugula, and toss again.

MAKES 4 SERVINGS

CAESAR SALAD

Our take on the classic, with a quick and easy dressing. To make this into a main dish, simply add grilled chicken, sautéed or grilled shrimp, or for a vegetarian alternative, cooked beans.

4 ounces whole-grain bread, cut into ³⁄₄-inch cubes

2 tablespoons olive oil

¹⁄₄ teaspoon salt

¹⁄₄ teaspoon pepper

1 clove garlic

2 anchovy fillets, mashed

2 tablespoons mayonnaise

2 tablespoons lemon juice

¹⁄₄ cup grated Parmesan cheese

1 head romaine lettuce (1 pound), halved lengthwise and thickly sliced crosswise

Preheat the oven to 450°F. In a medium bowl, toss the bread cubes with the oil, salt, and pepper. Transfer to a baking sheet. Bake, tossing once, for 7 to 10 minutes, until the bread is lightly browned. Transfer the croutons to a plate to stop the cooking.

In a small pan of boiling water, blanch the garlic for 1 minute. Drain and finely chop. Transfer to a large bowl along with the anchovies. Whisk in the mayonnaise, lemon juice, and Parmesan. Add the romaine and croutons, and toss well.

MAKES 4 SERVINGS

TOFU CAESAR: Top the salad with Roasted Lemon-Herb Tofu (page 311).

GINGER-DRESSED HIJIKI SALAD

The dressing is served on the side of this interesting salad. Drizzle 1 or 2 tablespoons over each portion.

¹⁄₂ cup crumbled dried hijiki

2 cups apple juice

¹⁄₄ cup rice vinegar

2 tablespoons soy sauce

1 head Boston lettuce, torn into bite-size pieces

¹⁄₂ bunch watercress

1 small daikon radish, cut into matchsticks

Fresh Ginger-Tahini Dressing (page 376)

In a small bowl, soak the hijiki in the apple juice for 20 minutes. With a slotted spoon, transfer the hijiki to a small saucepan. Allow the soaking liq-

---

MAKING GINGER JUICE

Ginger juice is a great addition to salad dressings. Although you can buy bottled ginger juice, it's extremely easy to make. Grate fresh ginger on a ginger grater, the smallest holes on a box grater, or a Microplane citrus zester. Scrape the juices and pulp into a small strainer set over a bowl. Press with a spoon to extract juice. Then pick up the pulp with your fingers and squeeze to get as much additional juice as you can.

uid to settle, then gently pour 1 cup juice over the seaweed; discard the gritty residue.

Add the vinegar and soy sauce to the pan, and bring to a simmer. Cover and simmer for 15 minutes. Drain and cool.

In a large salad bowl, mix the lettuce, watercress, and radish. Chop the hijiki coarsely a few times and sprinkle over the greens. Serve with the dressing.

MAKES 4 TO 6 SERVINGS

JAPANESE SPINACH SALAD WITH CARROT-GINGER DRESSING

This will remind you of a salad from a Japanese restaurant—redolent of sesame, sweet from the carrots, and with a hit of spice from the ginger. Any dressing you don't use can be refrigerated for up to 3 days. If you like, garnish the salad with toasted sesame seeds. Once opened, store sesame oil in the fridge to extend its shelf life.

- 2 carrots (6 ounces total), thinly sliced
- 1 clove garlic, peeled
- 1 piece (2 inches) fresh ginger, peeled and thinly sliced
- ¼ teaspoon salt
- Water
- 3 tablespoons vegetable oil
- 1 tablespoon dark sesame oil
- 1 pound spinach, stems discarded, leaves washed and well dried

In a small skillet, combine the carrots, garlic, ginger, salt, and 1 cup water. Bring to a boil, reduce to a simmer, and cook until the carrots are tender, about 10 minutes. Transfer the mixture to a blender.

Add the vegetable oil, sesame oil, and 1 tablespoon water, and puree until smooth. Add another tablespoon of water if the dressing is too thick. Refrigerate until ready to use.

Place the spinach in a large bowl. Add enough dressing to just coat the leaves and toss well. Pass extra dressing at the table.

MAKES 4 SERVINGS

SPINACH-MUSHROOM SALAD WITH HONEY-MUSTARD DRESSING

If you don't mind spending the money, this would be a good place to experiment with one of the wild mushrooms you can get in the market.

DRESSING

- 2 tablespoons champagne or white wine vinegar
- 1 tablespoon honey
- ¼ cup vegetable oil
- 1 teaspoon Dijon mustard
- Pepper

SALAD

- 1 tablespoon vegetable oil
- 1 pound mushrooms, sliced
- 1 small onion, chopped
- 1 tablespoon lemon juice
- ¼ teaspoon salt
- ⅛ teaspoon pepper
- 1 pound baby spinach leaves
- 3 hard-cooked eggs, sliced or coarsely grated
- ½ cup garlic croutons, store-bought or homemade (see page 382)

To make the dressing: In a small saucepan, heat the vinegar and honey over low heat, stirring, until the honey is dissolved.

Transfer to a screw-top jar. Add the oil, mustard, and pepper to taste. Cover and shake well.

To make the salad: In a medium skillet, heat the oil over high heat. Add the mushrooms and brown quickly, stirring often. Add the onion during the last 30 seconds of cooking. (Do not overcook.) Transfer the mixture to a bowl. Sprinkle with the lemon juice, salt, and pepper, toss lightly, and set aside to cool.

In a large salad bowl, combine the cooled mushrooms and the spinach. Add the dressing and toss. Top with the eggs and croutons.

MAKES 6 SERVINGS

HEARTS OF CELERY SALAD

Celery hearts have the tougher outer ribs removed and are often sold with the top segments (where the celery rib branches out and has leaves) cut off.

- 3 celery hearts
- 2 plum tomatoes, cut into thin wedges
- ⅓ cup olive oil
- 2 tablespoons lemon juice
- 3 tablespoons chopped flat-leaf parsley
- 1 tablespoon minced fresh basil
- ¼ teaspoon salt

If there are still any dark-green ribs attached to the celery hearts, remove them. Halve each celery heart lengthwise. Cut off the root and cut out the hard core. Cut into crosswise 1½-inch pieces and place in a salad bowl. Add the tomato wedges.

In a small bowl, whisk together the oil, lemon juice, parsley, basil, and salt. Pour over the celery and tomatoes. Mix well.

MAKES 6 SERVINGS

CELERY-FENNEL SALAD: Substitute a fennel bulb for one of the celery hearts.

HERBED COLESLAW

Fresh herbs lift a coleslaw way out of the ordinary.

- 2 cups shredded cabbage
- 1 cup diced celery
- 1 carrot, shredded
- 2 sprigs fresh dill, chopped
- 2 tablespoons shredded fresh basil
- ¼ teaspoon salt
- 3 tablespoons mayonnaise
- 2 tablespoons white wine vinegar
- 1 teaspoon poppy seeds (optional)
- Pepper

In a large bowl, combine the cabbage, celery, carrot, dill, and basil. Sprinkle with the salt and toss well. In a small bowl, combine the mayonnaise, vinegar, poppy seeds (if using), and pepper to taste. Add to the vegetables and toss again. Chill for at least 1 hour before serving to allow the flavors to blend.

MAKES 4 SERVINGS

THAI COLESLAW WITH NAPA CABBAGE

If you don't have fish sauce, use reduced-sodium soy sauce instead. Start with just 1 tablespoon and taste before adding more.

- 2 tablespoons fish sauce
- 2 tablespoons rice vinegar
- 1 tablespoon vegetable oil
- ¾ teaspoon sugar

¼ cup packed fresh basil leaves, chopped

¼ cup packed cilantro, chopped

½ head napa cabbage (12 ounces), sliced crosswise into thin shreds

1 red or yellow bell pepper, cut into thin matchsticks

1 carrot, cut into thin matchsticks

In a large bowl, whisk together the fish sauce, vinegar, oil, and sugar. Add the basil and cilantro, and toss to combine.

Add the cabbage, bell pepper, and carrot, and toss well. Refrigerate for 30 minutes before serving for the flavors to combine.

MAKES 4 TO 6 SERVINGS

DILLED CUCUMBER SALAD

To seed a cucumber, halve it lengthwise and use a small teaspoon to scrape out the seeds.

1 medium cucumber, halved, seeded, and thinly sliced

1 tablespoon snipped fresh dill

¼ teaspoon sugar

⅛ teaspoon salt

⅛ teaspoon pepper

1 medium sweet onion, very thinly sliced

2 tablespoons vegetable oil

2 tablespoons cider vinegar

Place the cucumber slices in a shallow bowl and lightly sprinkle with the dill, sugar, salt, and pepper.

Separate the onion slices into rings and add to the cucumbers. Add the oil and toss until each slice is coated. Add the vinegar and toss again. Chill for 1 hour. Lightly toss with a fork before serving.

MAKES 4 SERVINGS

CUCUMBER RAITA

Kirby cucumbers are small unwaxed cucumbers usually used for pickling. Serve this mildly spiced Indian "salad" alongside a curry, or as a topper for burgers or broiled fish.

3 kirby cucumbers (1 pound), halved and seeded

1 container (6 ounces) plain low-fat yogurt

1 teaspoon ground cumin

1 teaspoon garam masala

¼ cup chopped cilantro

1 tablespoon lemon juice

¼ teaspoon salt

Grate the cucumbers on the large holes of a box grater. Squeeze dry, transfer to a medium bowl, and stir in the yogurt.

In a small skillet, toast the cumin and garam masala over low heat, stirring, until fragrant, about 1 minute. Stir the spices into the cucumber mixture along with the cilantro, lemon juice, and salt. Refrigerate at least 1 hour for the flavors to blend.

MAKES 4 SERVINGS

HOMEMADE GARLIC CROUTONS

Here's a quick and easy way to make whole-grain garlic croutons: Brush firm-textured whole-grain sandwich bread very lightly with olive oil. Toast in the oven or toaster oven. Rub the toast with the cut side of a halved garlic clove. Cut into cubes.

SWEET ONION SALAD WITH AVOCADO & GARLIC DRESSING

This dressing also makes a tangy dip for vegetables or chips.

- 2 medium Vidalia or other sweet onions, sliced into thick rounds
- 2 small heads red leaf lettuce (½ pound), torn into pieces
- 1 cup thinly sliced kirby cucumber
- 2 Hass avocados
- ⅓ cup loosely packed fresh basil leaves
- ¼ cup plain low-fat yogurt or buttermilk
- 3 tablespoons white wine vinegar
- 2 tablespoons lemon juice
- 1½ teaspoons minced garlic
- ⅓ cup grapeseed or olive oil
- Coarse salt and pepper

In a large bowl of cold water, soak the onion slices for 10 minutes. Drain.

Arrange the onions, lettuce, and cucumber in a bowl.

Halve the avocados and scoop the flesh into a food processor. Add the basil, yogurt, vinegar, lemon juice and garlic, and process until combined.

With the machine running, slowly add the oil through the feed tube and process until smooth. The dressing should be pourable, but if it's too thin, add another tablespoon of yogurt. Season to taste with salt and pepper.

Spoon the dressing over the salad.

MAKES 6 SERVINGS

FRESH CREMINI SALAD

Throw the mushrooms stems into a bag and freeze for making vegetable stock.

- 1 pound cremini mushrooms
- ¼ cup plus 1 tablespoon olive oil
- 2 tablespoons red wine vinegar
- ¼ cup chopped parsley
- 1½ tablespoons chopped fresh tarragon or 1 teaspoon dried
- ⅛ teaspoon salt
- ⅛ teaspoon pepper
- Watercress, for serving

Remove the stems from the mushrooms and reserve for another use. Thickly slice the caps and place in a large bowl. Add the oil, vinegar, parsley, tarragon, salt, and pepper. Toss well, then cover and chill for 1 hour to blend the flavors.

Serve the salad on a bed of watercress.

MAKES 6 SERVINGS

MUSHROOM & DILL SALAD: Substitute 1½ tablespoons snipped fresh dill for the tarragon.

GRILLED MUSHROOMS, ASPARAGUS & LEAF LETTUCE WITH GOAT CHEESE

Use fresh goat cheese or indulge in an aged goat cheese—but only 1 or 2 small slices per person, since the flavor is quite strong.

- ¼ cup hoisin sauce
- 2 tablespoons balsamic vinegar
- 2 cloves garlic, minced
- Coarse salt and pepper
- 8 medium portobello mushrooms, stems discarded, gills removed

- 1 bunch thin asparagus (1 pound)
- 8 cups mixed leaf or baby lettuces, such as mesclun
- 1 cup mixed fresh herb leaves such as flat-leaf parsley, chervil, and dill
- 1 cup cherry tomatoes, halved
- ¼ cup Red Wine Vinaigrette (page 375)
- 8 ounces goat cheese, cut into slices

In a large resealable plastic bag, shake together the hoisin sauce, vinegar, garlic, and a pinch of salt and pepper. Add the mushrooms, seal, and shake to coat. Marinate for 20 minutes (or longer in the refrigerator).

Preheat the grill to medium-high or preheat the broiler. Remove the mushrooms from the marinade and grill or broil 6 inches from the heat for 6 to 7 minutes on each side until tender. Transfer to a cutting board and let cool.

Meanwhile, in a vegetable steamer, cook the asparagus until just tender, 4 to 5 minutes. Immediately plunge into a large bowl of ice water to stop the cooking. Drain and dry on paper towels.

In a large bowl, toss the lettuce, herbs, and tomatoes with the vinaigrette. Serve the lettuce mixture topped with asparagus and slices of cheese. Slice the mushrooms and arrange on top of the salads.

MAKES 6 TO 8 SERVINGS

EGGPLANT, OLIVE & GRAPE TOMATO SALAD

Serve this substantial salad, a spin on the Italian eggplant dish called caponata, alongside chicken or fish. Look for firm eggplants without any soft spots or bruising.

- 2 medium eggplants (2 pounds total), unpeeled and cut into 1-inch chunks
- 3 tablespoons red wine vinegar
- 3 tablespoons olive oil
- 1 tablespoon honey
- ¾ teaspoon salt
- 2 ribs celery, halved lengthwise and thinly sliced crosswise
- 2 cups grape tomatoes, halved
- ⅓ cup olives (Sicilian, kalamata, or a combination), pitted and coarsely chopped
- ⅓ cup golden raisins
- ½ cup packed fresh basil or mint leaves, coarsely chopped

In a steamer, steam the eggplant until tender, about 7 minutes.

In a large bowl, whisk together the vinegar, oil, honey, and salt. Add the eggplant, celery, tomatoes, olives, raisins, and basil, and stir gently to combine. Refrigerate for at least 4 hours to blend the flavors.

MAKES 4 TO 6 SERVINGS

TOMATO "STEAK" SALAD

Mingle assorted heirloom and beefsteak tomatoes for maximum visual impact. Opal basil has deep purple leaves; if it's not available, substitute regular basil or Thai basil.

VINAIGRETTE

- 2 tablespoons sherry wine vinegar
- 1 clove garlic, minced or squeezed through a garlic press
- ½ teaspoon sugar
- ½ teaspoon coarse salt
- ⅛ teaspoon pepper
- 3 tablespoons extra-virgin olive oil

SALAD

- 2 ears fresh corn, kernels cut from ears
- 4 large heirloom tomatoes (or 4 pounds of smaller heirlooms, mixed varieties)

1 pound fresh mozzarella, cut into 12 slices

1 cup thinly sliced red onion, rinsed and drained

¼ cup slivered opal basil

3 tablespoons snipped fresh chives

To make the vinaigrette: In a small bowl, whisk together the vinegar, garlic, sugar, salt, and pepper. Gradually whisk in the oil.

To make the salad: In a steamer, cook the corn kernels, just until slightly tender, about 2 minutes. Let cool to warm. Cut each tomato crosswise into 4 thick slices.

Assemble the salads on four plates: Place a tomato slice on each plate and drizzle with a little vinaigrette. Top with a slice of mozzarella and a slice of onion. Sprinkle with corn, basil, and chives. Continue layering the ingredients, finishing with a tomato slice and the remaining vinaigrette. Let marinate for at least 15 minutes at room temperature before serving.

MAKES 4 SERVINGS

GREEN BEANS VINAIGRETTE

A cool side dish or an easy take-along dish for a picnic.

1 cup vegetable oil

⅓ cup red wine vinegar

1 small red bell pepper, very finely minced

1 tablespoon snipped fresh chives

¼ teaspoon salt

1 pound green beans

In a quart-size screw-top jar, combine the oil, vinegar, bell pepper, chives, and salt. Cover and shake well.

Place the beans in a large bowl and pour the dressing over them. Cover and refrigerate for at least 3 hours, stirring occasionally. Drain to serve.

MAKES 4 SERVINGS

FRESH FENNEL & BEAN SALAD

You can use all green beans in this make-ahead salad if you can't find wax beans.

½ pound green beans

½ pound yellow wax beans

2 tablespoons extra-virgin olive oil

1 tablespoon red wine vinegar

1 clove garlic, minced

2 cups thinly sliced fennel bulb

1 small red onion, thinly sliced

2 teaspoons snipped fresh dill

Coarse salt and pepper

In a steamer, cook the green and yellow beans until crisp-tender, about 5 minutes. Rinse in a

---

SLIVERED BASIL

Thinly slivered basil leaves are sometimes referred to as a chiffonade (the term also applies to other finely slivered green herbs). Here's how to make a chiffonade:

Stack about 8 basil leaves on top of one another. Roll up the leaves lengthwise into a tight cylinder, like a cigar. Cut the cylinder crosswise into very thin slices.

colander under cold running water to stop the cooking. Drain.

In a large bowl, whisk together the oil, vinegar, and garlic. Add the beans, fennel, onion, and dill. Toss and season with salt and pepper to taste.

Cover and chill for at least 1 hour (or up to 6 hours) to blend the flavors. Serve the salad chilled or at room temperature.

MAKES 6 SERVINGS

WARM TOMATO, OLIVE & ARUGULA SALAD

Make a hearty main course of this side salad by adding crumbled feta or shaved Parmesan. Steam the beans in the microwave or on the stove while you prep the other ingredients.

3 tablespoons balsamic vinegar

6 cups baby arugula

1 tablespoon olive oil

1 medium red onion, sliced into thin rings

10 kalamata olives, pitted

6 plum tomatoes, seeded and cut into wedges

½ pound green beans, steamed until tender

¾ teaspoon fresh thyme leaves

Coarse salt and pepper

In a small saucepan, simmer the balsamic vinegar over medium-high heat until reduced by half. Set aside. Place the arugula on a large platter and set aside.

In a large skillet, heat the oil over medium-high heat. Add the onion and olives, and stir-fry until the onions are soft, about 4 minutes.

Add the tomatoes, beans, and thyme, and cook, stirring, just until hot (the tomatoes should remain firm), about 2 minutes. Remove from the heat and season with salt and pepper to taste.

Top the arugula with the cooked vegetables and drizzle with the reduced balsamic.

MAKES 4 SERVINGS

DUTCH VEGETABLE SALAD

Anything called Dutch usually implies a certain frugality in cooking—like this salad, designed for leftover cooked vegetables. If you're starting from scratch, quickly microwave a medium to large beet (8 to 10 ounces) and about 1 pound red potatoes.

2 cups diced cooked red potatoes

1 cup diced cooked beets

1 cup frozen peas, thawed

2 tart apples, diced

3 tablespoons vegetable oil

3 tablespoons cider vinegar

Coarse salt and pepper

Lettuce, for serving

3 slices bacon, cooked until crisp, drained, and crumbled

In a large bowl, combine the potatoes, beets, peas, apples, oil, and vinegar. Toss gently to mix. Refrigerate for at least 1 hour to blend the flavors. Season with salt and pepper to taste.

Serve the vegetables on a bed of lettuce, and sprinkle with the bacon.

MAKES 4 TO 6 SERVINGS

PEAS & CHEESE SALAD

Here's a variation on the classic American picnic standby, but with a little Tex-Mex makeover.

½ cup mayonnaise

2 teaspoons minced chipotle pepper in adobo

- **8 cups shredded romaine lettuce**
- **¼ cup thinly sliced scallions**
- **¼ cup minced cilantro**
- **1 package (10 ounces) frozen peas, thawed**
- **6 ounces Monterey Jack cheese, shredded**

In a small bowl, blend the mayonnaise and chipotle together. Refrigerate.

In a large bowl, make a layer of the lettuce. Top with the scallions, then the cilantro and peas. Top everything with the cheese. Cover and refrigerate until serving time.

Add the dressing and toss everything to coat well.

MAKES 4 TO 6 SERVINGS

CELERY ROOT SALAD

Celery root is the star and retains its crunch in this sweet and tangy salad.

- **⅔ cup cider vinegar**
- **3 tablespoons sugar**
- **2 teaspoons mustard seeds**
- **½ teaspoon cumin seeds**
- **⅛ teaspoon ground allspice**
- **Pinch of cayenne pepper**
- **1 pound celery root, peeled, thinly sliced, and cut into julienne strips (4 to 5 cups)**
- **2 cups small cauliflower florets**
- **1 cup slivered red bell pepper**
- **1 cup green beans, halved crosswise**
- **¼ teaspoon salt**

In a large skillet, combine the vinegar, sugar, mustard seeds, cumin, allspice, and cayenne, and bring to a boil over medium heat.

Add the celery root, cauliflower, bell pepper, and green beans, and cook, stirring occasionally, until the celery root is tender, about 15 minutes. Add the salt and stir to combine. Let cool to room temperature, then refrigerate. Serve chilled.

MAKES 4 SERVINGS

MOROCCAN CARROT SALAD

Cutting the carrots into ribbons with a vegetable peeler adds a refined look and pleasant texture. If you are short on time, however, just use the same amount of coarsely shredded carrots.

- **4 large carrots (1 pound), peeled**
- **1 cup raisins**
- **1 cup loosely packed cilantro leaves**
- **3 tablespoons extra-virgin olive oil**
- **Zest and juice of 1 small lemon**
- **1 teaspoon ground cumin**
- **1 teaspoon sweet paprika**
- **1 clove garlic, finely minced**
- **⅛ teaspoon cayenne pepper (optional)**
- **Coarse salt**

Shave the carrots into long, thin ribbons using a vegetable peeler and transfer to a medium bowl.

Add the raisins, cilantro, oil, lemon zest and juice, cumin, paprika, garlic, and cayenne (if using), and toss well. Season with salt to taste.

Refrigerate for at least 30 minutes or several hours to let the flavors meld.

MAKES 4 SERVINGS

SPICED CAULIFLOWER & ONION SALAD

Prepare this salad a day ahead to allow the flavors to blend well, but serve it at room temperature to bring out the spices.

- 1 head cauliflower (2½ pounds), separated into small florets
- 2 teaspoons sesame seeds
- ¾ teaspoon mustard seeds
- ½ teaspoon cumin seeds
- ¼ teaspoon coriander seeds
- 4 cardamom pods
- 6 tablespoons butter
- 1 pound onions, thinly sliced
- 1½ cups plain low-fat yogurt
- ¼ teaspoon pepper
- 2 tablespoons minced cilantro or parsley, for garnish (optional)

In a steamer, cook the cauliflower until crisp-tender, 5 to 6 minutes. Rinse under cold water, drain, and set aside.

In a small heavy skillet, combine the sesame, mustard, cumin, and coriander seeds. Break open the cardamom pods and add the seeds. Heat the spices over medium heat until the mustard seeds start to "dance." Transfer to a spice or coffee grinder, mini food processor, or mortar and pestle, and pulverize until fine. Set aside.

In a large skillet, melt the butter over low heat. Stir in the onions, cover, and cook, stirring frequently, until softened, about 10 minutes.

Uncover, increase the heat to high, and continue to stir and cook until the onions are lightly browned, 10 to 12 minutes.

Add the ground spices and cook for 1 to 2 minutes, stirring constantly. Add the cauliflower and cook, stirring, for 1 to 2 minutes. Remove from the heat. Stir in the yogurt and pepper, blend well, and refrigerate overnight. If you like, garnish with cilantro before serving.

MAKES 6 SERVINGS

SPRING BEET SALAD

A quartet of red-tinged vegetables looks beautiful against a backdrop of dark-green watercress.

SALAD

- 3 small beets, peeled and quartered
- Olive oil, for coating
- 1 small head radicchio, torn into bite-size pieces
- 1 small head red leaf lettuce, torn into bite-size pieces
- 3 scallions, chopped
- 6 small radishes, thinly sliced
- 1 bunch watercress, tough stems discarded

DRESSING

- 2 tablespoons lemon juice
- 2 teaspoons drained horseradish
- 1 teaspoon Dijon mustard
- ¼ cup extra-virgin olive oil
- Sea salt and cracked pepper

Preheat the oven to 425°F.

In a medium bowl, toss the beets with a small amount of olive oil, just enough to lightly coat. Place on a baking sheet and roast for 40 minutes, or until fork-tender. Set aside to cool to room temperature.

In a large salad bowl, combine the radicchio, lettuce, scallions, radishes, and watercress.

To make the dressing: In a food processor or blender, combine the lemon juice, horseradish, and mustard. With the machine running, slowly add the olive oil. Add salt and pepper to taste.

Toss the salad greens with all but 1 tablespoon of the dressing. Toss the beets with the remaining dressing.

Serve the beets on a bed of the greens.

MAKES 6 SERVINGS

BEET, APPLE & WALNUT SALAD

Wearing gloves while peeling and shredding beets will keep the juice from staining your hands. For a more decorative presentation, the walnuts can be sprinkled on top of the finished salad instead of stirred in.

3 tablespoons cider vinegar

1 tablespoon Dijon mustard

½ teaspoon coarse salt

½ teaspoon pepper

⅓ cup extra-virgin olive oil

1 large raw beet (1 pound), peeled and coarsely shredded

1 large Granny Smith apple (8 ounces), peeled and coarsely shredded

¾ cup walnuts, toasted and coarsely chopped

½ cup loosely packed parsley leaves, slivered

In a large bowl, whisk together the vinegar, mustard, salt, and pepper. Add the oil in a slow, steady stream while whisking until smooth.

Add the beet, apple, walnuts, and parsley, and toss to combine. Let sit at least 30 minutes to let the flavors blend.

MAKES 4 SERVINGS

GOLDEN BEET & FENNEL SALAD WITH BEET VINAIGRETTE

Once upon a time, the only beets you could get were the classic ruby-red variety. These days you can get golden beets and even white-and-red striped beets.

4 tablespoons extra-virgin olive oil, plus more for drizzling

2 dozen golden baby beets, trimmed but unpeeled

2 small fennel bulbs, stalks discarded, fronds reserved with fronds, cored

Coarse salt and pepper

1 tablespoon balsamic vinegar

1 teaspoon honey

1 teaspoon minced garlic

6 ounces fresh farmer's cheese, crumbled

Preheat the oven to 400°F.

Drizzle a small amount of oil over the beets and toss well to coat. Wrap in foil, leaving a small tent above them to allow for steam. Place on a baking sheet and bake for 25 minutes, or until the beets are cooked but still firm enough to slice. When cool enough to handle, peel and thinly slice the beets with a vegetable slicer, such as a Japanese mandoline, or a sharp knife. Chop 1 tablespoon of the beets and reserve.

Meanwhile, slice the fennel bulbs paper thin with a vegetable slicer or a sharp knife. Chop 1 tablespoon of the fennel fronds and transfer to a medium bowl. Add 1 tablespoon of the oil and a pinch of salt to the fronds. Set aside.

In a blender or food processor, combine the reserved chopped beets, remaining 3 tablespoons oil, the vinegar, honey, and garlic. Puree until smooth. Season with salt and pepper to taste.

To serve, arrange the sliced fennel on 6 plates. Top with the farmer's cheese and the sliced beets. Drizzle with the vinaigrette.

MAKES 6 SERVINGS

ROASTED ROOT VEGETABLE SALAD

Roasting brings out the natural sugars in vegetables.

6 baby carrots, cut into matchsticks
6 small red potatoes, halved
3 parsnips, cut into matchsticks
4 shallots, halved
1 tablespoon olive oil
3 cups arugula
Lemon-Dijon Vinaigrette (page 375)
Salt and pepper
½ cup crumbled feta cheese

Preheat the oven to 425°F.

In a large bowl, combine the carrots, potatoes, parsnips, and shallots. Drizzle with the oil and toss well to coat. Transfer to a rimmed baking sheet and roast for 30 minutes, or until tender. Let cool to room temperature.

In a salad bowl, toss the arugula and root vegetables with the dressing. Season with salt and pepper to taste. Serve sprinkled with the feta.

MAKES 4 SERVINGS

FINGERLING POTATO SALAD WITH CIDER-CARAWAY DRESSING

This light version of German potato salad is alot less sweet than the traditional rendition. Caraway and celery seeds lend subtle flavor, while chives and parsley add a fresh touch. You can make this salad day ahead. If you can't find fingerling potatoes, just use very small round potatoes.

4 pounds red fingerling potatoes, well scrubbed
¾ cup apple cider vinegar
⅓ cup extra-virgin olive oil
3 tablespoons turbinado or light brown sugar
2 teaspoons coarse salt
1 teaspoon caraway seeds
1 teaspoon celery seeds
½ teaspoon black pepper
¼ teaspoon red pepper flakes
3 ribs celery, chopped
3 scallions, chopped
⅓ cup coarsely chopped flat-leaf parsley
3 tablespoons snipped chives

In a large pot of boiling salted water, cook the potatoes until just tender, about 30 minutes. Drain and let cool. When cool enough to handle, cut on the diagonal into ½-inch-thick slices. Transfer to a large bowl.

Meanwhile, in a small saucepan, whisk together the vinegar, oil, brown sugar, salt, caraway seeds, celery seeds, black pepper, and red pepper flakes. Stir over medium heat until the sugar dissolves. Pour the hot dressing over the warm sliced potatoes and toss gently.

When the potatoes are barely warm, stir in the celery, scallions, parsley, and chives. Season to taste with additional salt and pepper, if necessary. Serve at room temperature or chilled.

MAKES 6 SERVINGS

YUKON GOLD & YELLOW BEAN SALAD

Fingerling or banana potatoes would be great in this salad.

8 medium Yukon Gold potatoes
2½ pounds yellow wax beans
2 teaspoons malt vinegar
1 tablespoon chopped fresh basil
4 scallions, chopped
½ teaspoon salt

- 1/4 teaspoon pepper
- About 1/2 cup extra-virgin olive oil

In a large pot of boiling salted water, cook the potatoes until fork-tender, 30 to 40 minutes. Drain. When cool enough to handle, cut into bite-size pieces and transfer to a bowl.

Meanwhile, in a steamer, cook the beans until crisp-tender, 5 to 10 minutes. When cool enough to handle, cut into bite-size pieces. Add to the potatoes.

While the vegetables are still warm, sprinkle with the vinegar, basil, scallions, salt, and pepper, and toss well. Add enough oil to lightly coat and toss again. Let sit for 1 hour before serving.

MAKES 8 SERVINGS

BLUE POTATO & FRENCH BEAN SALAD WITH GRILLED TOMATO DRESSING

Blue potatoes can be hard to come by, so just use any small thin-skinned boiling potatoes. This tomato dressing is also great on grilled fish or tossed with cold noodles.

- 1 pound small blue potatoes, scrubbed
- 1 pound thin French green beans (haricots verts), or small regular string beans, halved lengthwise
- 6 plum tomatoes, halved lengthwise
- Coarse salt and pepper
- 1/3 cup extra-virgin olive oil
- 2 tablespoons minced shallot
- 1 tablespoon red wine vinegar
- 1 teaspoon Dijon mustard
- 1/4 cup chopped flat-leaf parsley

In a large pot of boiling salted water, cook the potatoes until fork-tender, 15 to 20 minutes. Drain. When cool enough to handle, cut into 1/2-inch-thick pieces and transfer to a bowl.

In a steamer, cook the beans until just barely tender and still bright green, about 4 minutes. Rinse under cold water to stop the cooking. Add to the potatoes.

Meanwhile, preheat a grill to medium-high. Grill the tomatoes until lightly charred, about 3 minutes on each side. When cool enough to handle, discard the skins, if desired. Season the tomatoes with salt and pepper to taste. Scrape the seeds from 1 tomato half into a blender and add the oil, shallot, vinegar, and mustard. Blend until smooth. Season to taste with salt and pepper.

Add the dressing to the potatoes and beans, and toss well. Just before serving, stir in the tomatoes and parsley. Season to taste with salt and pepper.

MAKES 6 SERVINGS

GOLDEN ASPARAGUS & POTATO SALAD

Carrot juice gives this salad a rich golden color.

- 1/2 cup carrot juice
- 2 tablespoons red wine vinegar
- 4 teaspoons Dijon mustard
- 4 teaspoons extra-virgin olive oil
- 1 teaspoon tarragon
- 3/4 teaspoon salt
- 1/4 teaspoon pepper
- 1 pound Yukon Gold potatoes, cut into 1-inch batons
- 3/4 pound mushrooms, thinly sliced
- 2 pounds asparagus, cut on the diagonal into 1-inch lengths

In a large bowl, whisk together the carrot juice, vinegar, mustard, oil, tarragon, salt, and pepper.

In a steamer, cook the potatoes until tender, about 10 minutes. Transfer the potatoes to the bowl with the dressing.

Add the mushrooms and toss to coat with the dressing. Let stand until most of the liquid has been absorbed, about 20 minutes.

Meanwhile, add the asparagus to the steamer and cook until crisp-tender, about 4 minutes. Let the asparagus cool to room temperature before adding to the salad bowl.

Add the asparagus and toss well to combine. Serve at room temperature or chilled.

MAKES 4 SERVINGS

NEW POTATO & SNAP PEA SALAD

Small boiling potatoes are commonly called new potatoes, although technically a new potato is one that is freshly dug out of the ground. It's unlikely you'll find a true new potato in a supermarket, but farmer's markets are a good bet.

DRESSING

- ¼ cup extra-virgin olive oil
- 2 tablespoons white wine vinegar
- 1 tablespoon grated lemon zest
- 1 tablespoon lemon juice
- ½ teaspoon oregano
- Sea salt and cracked black pepper

SALAD

- 1 pound small red new potatoes
- 8 ounces mushrooms, sliced
- ½ pound sugar snap peas
- ¼ pound Black Forest ham, cut into matchsticks
- ½ green bell pepper, sliced into thin strips
- ½ rib celery, chopped
- 1 tablespoon snipped fresh chives
- 1 small head green leaf lettuce, separated into leaves

To make the dressing: In a food processor, combine the oil, vinegar, lemon zest and juice, oregano, and salt and pepper to taste.

To make the salad: In a large pot of boiling salted water, cook the potatoes until fork-tender, about 15 minutes. Drain. When cool enough to handle, cut them in half.

In a large bowl, combine the mushrooms, peas, and 1 tablespoon of the dressing. Add the potatoes, ham, bell pepper, celery, and chives. Add the remaining dressing and toss well.

Serve the salad on a bed of the lettuce leaves.

MAKES 6 SERVINGS

ARUGULA & SWEET POTATO SALAD WITH PANCETTA

Toast the almonds in a 350°F toaster oven for 3 to 5 minutes. Watch carefully as they can burn easily.

DRESSING

- ¼ cup canola oil
- 3 tablespoons apple cider vinegar
- 1 teaspoon Dijon mustard
- 1 teaspoon turbinado or light brown sugar
- ½ teaspoon cinnamon
- ½ teaspoon red pepper flakes

SALAD

- 2 cups bite-size pieces peeled sweet potato
- 2 tablespoons apple cider or unsweetened apple juice

- 1 tablespoon canola oil
- Salt and pepper
- ¼ pound pancetta
- 5 cups arugula
- ½ cup slivered almonds, toasted

To make the dressing: In a food processor or blender, combine the oil, vinegar, mustard, brown sugar, cinnamon, and red pepper flakes, and process until emulsified.

To make the salad: Preheat the oven to 425°F. In a medium bowl, toss the sweet potatoes with the apple cider, oil, and salt and pepper to taste. Place on a baking sheet and roast for 10 to 15 minutes, or until tender but not overly soft. Set aside to cool slightly.

Meanwhile, in a large skillet, cook the pancetta until crisp. Drain and crumble.

In a large salad bowl, combine the roasted sweet potatoes, pancetta, arugula, and almonds. Drizzle with the dressing and lightly toss.

MAKES 4 SERVINGS

CHILLED BLACK-EYED PEA SALAD

You can buy frozen black-eyed peas in 16-ounce packages, which is just what you need for this salad.

- ½ cup shredded yellow summer squash
- ¼ teaspoon salt
- 2 cups cooked black-eyed peas
- 1 cup seeded and chopped tomatoes
- 1 cup shredded carrots
- 1 small onion, minced
- 6 tablespoons sunflower oil
- 2 tablespoons almond oil or sunflower oil
- ¼ cup cider vinegar
- 1 teaspoon maple syrup or light agave nectar
- ¼ teaspoon hot pepper sauce

Place the summer squash in a colander, sprinkle with the salt, and toss well. Let drain while you prep the other vegetables.

In a large bowl, combine the black-eyed peas, tomatoes, carrots, and onion.

In a screw-top jar, combine the sunflower oil, almond oil, vinegar, maple syrup, and hot sauce. Cover and shake well.

Squeeze excess moisture out of the squash and add to the salad bowl. Add the dressing and toss to coat. Refrigerate the salad until well chilled.

MAKES 4 SERVINGS

BLACK-EYED PEA SALAD WITH BACON: Cook 3 of slices bacon until crisp. Drain and crumble. Serve the salad topped with the crumbled bacon.

FAVA BEAN SALAD WITH PECORINO

An Italian favorite, favas take time to clean, but their nutty flavor is your reward. If you can't find favas, try shelled edamame (green soybeans), available in the freezer section of the supermarket. You'll need 1 cup.

- 2 pounds unshelled fresh fava beans
- 1 tablespoon lemon juice
- 1 tablespoon minced shallot
- 2 tablespoons extra-virgin olive oil
- Sea salt and pepper
- 1 head escarole (½ pound), torn into pieces
- 2 teaspoons chopped fresh mint
- 2 teaspoons chopped flat-leaf parsley
- 4 ounces Pecorino-Romano cheese

Shuck the fava beans. In a pot of boiling salted

water, cook the favas for 2 minutes to blanch. Drain. When cool enough to handle, peel the favas.

In a small bowl, whisk together the lemon juice and shallot. Slowly whisk in the olive oil. Season to taste with salt and pepper.

In a large salad bowl, toss the beans together with the escarole, mint, parsley, and dressing. Season to taste with salt and pepper. Shave Pecorino-Romano over the salad and serve.

MAKES 6 SERVINGS

FRENCH LENTIL SALAD

Small dark-green French lentils have a sturdy texture and a slightly peppery flavor. They are a nice counterpoint to the rich-tasting, but slightly blander edamame. The smokiness of the bacon and the sweetness of the sun-dried tomatoes contribute to the well-rounded flavor of this dish.

- 2 teaspoons vegetable oil
- 4 slices bacon (4 ounces), cut into ½-inch-wide strips
- 3 tablespoons cider vinegar
- ½ teaspoon salt
- 1 cup French (de Puy) lentils
- 1 cup shelled edamame
- ⅓ cup sun-dried tomatoes, slivered

In a large skillet, heat the oil over medium heat. Add the bacon and cook until crisp, about 5 minutes. With a slotted spoon, transfer the bacon to paper towels to drain. Set aside.

Measure out 2 tablespoons of the bacon fat and place in a large bowl. Whisk in the vinegar and salt. Set aside.

Meanwhile, in a large pot of boiling water, cook the lentils for 15 minutes. Add the edamame and sun-dried tomatoes, and cook until the edamame are tender, about 2 minutes.

Drain well and transfer to the bowl with the bacon dressing. Add the bacon, toss well, and let sit at least 1 hour. Serve at room temperature or chilled.

MAKES 4 TO 6 SERVINGS

BELUGA LENTIL TABBOULEH

Beluga lentils are lovely small black lentils that resemble caviar when cooked.

- 1½ cups cooked beluga lentils
- 1½ cups cooked bulgur
- 2 tablespoons vegetable oil
- 2 tablespoons rice vinegar
- ½ cup chopped fresh mint or parsley
- ½ cup minced sweet onion
- 1 teaspoon minced garlic
- 1 teaspoon oregano
- Coarse salt and cracked pepper

In a large bowl, combine the lentils and bulgur.

In a small bowl, whisk together the oil, vinegar, mint, onion, garlic, and oregano until well blended. Pour over the lentils and bulgur, and toss gently until well coated with dressing. Season with salt and pepper to taste. Chill for at least 1 hour to blend the flavors.

MAKES 4 TO 6 SERVINGS

BROWN RICE SALAD WITH RADISHES & SNOW PEAS

To blanch the snow peas, immerse them in a large pot of boiling water for about 30 seconds, or until they turn bright green.

- 2 cups cooked brown rice
- ¾ cup finely chopped celery with leaves

¼ pound snow peas, blanched

1 cucumber, diced

8 large red radishes, thinly sliced

1 small red bell pepper, finely chopped

4 scallions, chopped

⅓ cup minced parsley

2 tablespoons rice vinegar

2 tablespoons lemon juice

1 tablespoon soy sauce

½ teaspoon paprika

¼ teaspoon pepper

⅓ cup canola oil

In a large bowl, combine the rice, celery, snow peas, cucumber, radishes, bell pepper, scallions, and parsley.

In a small bowl, combine the vinegar, lemon juice, soy sauce, paprika, and pepper. Slowly whisk in the oil until well blended. Pour the dressing over the rice and vegetables, and toss to combine. Cover and chill for 2 hours before serving.

MAKES 6 SERVINGS

SUSHI SALAD

This salad takes many of the ingredients and flavors in sushi and turns them into a satisfying salad. To "shred" carrot with a vegetable peeler, use it to peel off many little lengths of carrot—not big long strips—that are similar to shredded carrot.

1½ cups sushi rice

1¾ cups water

½ cup rice vinegar

3 tablespoons sugar

2 teaspoons wasabi powder

1 teaspoon salt

½ pound carrots, cut into shreds with a vegetable peeler

½ cup pickled ginger, coarsely chopped

5 scallions, thinly sliced

1 tablespoon dark sesame oil

1 Hass avocado, diced

Rinse the rice in cold water 3 times. Place in a medium saucepan with the water. Let stand for 30 minutes. Then bring to a boil, reduce to a simmer, cover, and cook until rice is tender and the water has been absorbed, about 20 minutes. Transfer to a bowl and fluff with a fork.

In a large bowl, whisk together the vinegar and sugar until the sugar has dissolved. Whisk in the wasabi powder and salt.

Add the hot rice and carrots to the bowl, and fluff with a fork to combine. When the rice is cool, add the ginger, scallions, and sesame oil, and toss to combine. Add the avocado and gently toss. Serve at room temperature or chilled.

MAKES 4 TO 6 SERVINGS

SPELT SALAD WITH APPLES & PINE NUTS

While many recipes call for soaking kamut or spelt overnight, we've found that it cooks up just fine without soaking.

4 cups boiling water

1¼ cups spelt or kamut

1 teaspoon salt

2 large Fuji, Gala, or Braeburn apples, cut into ½-inch chunks

⅓ cup dried currants

¼ cup pine nuts, toasted

2 tablespoons olive oil

2 tablespoons cider vinegar

¼ teaspoon pepper

In a large saucepan, combine the boiling water, spelt, and salt. Bring to a boil and reduce to a simmer. Cover and cook until the water has been absorbed, about 1 hour 30 minutes.

Stir in the apples, currants, pine nuts, oil, vinegar, and pepper, and toss well. Serve at room temperature or chilled.

MAKES 6 SERVINGS

SPELT SALAD WITH PISTACHIOS & PEARS: Use lemon juice instead of vinegar, red Bartlett pears instead of apples, golden raisins instead of currants, and pistachios instead of pine nuts.

LAYERED MILLET SALAD

The longer this layered millet and beet salad sits, the redder it will become. It will keep, refriderated, for 3 to 4 days.

- **½ cup red wine vinegar**
- **¼ cup water**
- **2 tablespoons safflower oil**
- **2 teaspoons soy sauce**
- **2 teaspoons pickling spices, store-bought or homemade (page 661)**
- **¼ teaspoon dark sesame oil**
- **2 cups cooked millet**
- **1½ cups shredded carrots**
- **2 medium beets, shredded**
- **1 large green bell pepper, diced**
- **2 tablespoons snipped chives**

In a small saucepan, combine the vinegar, water, safflower oil, soy sauce, pickling spices, and sesame oil. Bring to a boil over high heat. Reduce to a simmer and cook for 5 minutes. Set aside to cool to room temperature.

In a clear glass bowl with deep sides, make layers in this order: millet, carrots, beets, and bell pepper. Pour the dressing through a strainer over the salad. Sprinkle with the chives. Cover and refrigerate for several hours or overnight.

Bring the salad to the table untossed, and just before serving, toss the ingredients together.

MAKES 6 SERVINGS

PASTA SALAD CAPRESE

Wait until tomatoes are at their ripest for this pasta salad. Fresh mozzarella has a creamier, softer consistency than regular, but if you can't find it, go ahead and use regular.

- **8 ounces whole wheat penne**
- **⅓ cup olive oil**
- **3 cloves garlic, slivered**
- **1 tablespoon red wine vinegar**
- **½ teaspoon salt**
- **1 pound tomatoes, cut into 1-inch chunks**
- **6 ounces fresh mozzarella cheese, cut into ½-inch chunks**
- **⅔ cup packed fresh basil leaves, torn**

In a pot of boiling salted water, cook the pasta according to the package instructions. Drain, rinse under cold water, and drain again.

Meanwhile, in a small skillet, heat the oil and garlic over low heat, and cook until the garlic is soft but not browned, about 5 minutes. Immediately transfer the oil and garlic to a large bowl.

Whisk in the vinegar and salt. Add the penne, tomatoes, and mozzarella, and toss well. Refrigerate for at least 1 hour. Just before serving, add the basil.

MAKES 4 SERVINGS

SOBA SALAD

Toast the sesame seeds in a small ungreased skillet over medium-low heat until they are fragrant. Have a plate at the ready so you can scrape the seeds out as soon as they are toasted, or they will keep cooking from the residual heat in the pan.

- 12 ounces dried soba noodles
- 3 tablespoons lower-sodium soy sauce
- 3 tablespoons white wine vinegar
- 1 tablespoon dark sesame oil
- 1½ teaspoons Dijon mustard
- 3 tablespoons water
- 2 carrots, shredded
- 1 red bell pepper, slivered
- 2 teaspoons olive oil
- 4 scallions, thinly sliced
- 1 tablespoon minced fresh ginger
- 2 cloves garlic, minced
- 2 teaspoons toasted sesame seeds

In a large pot of boiling salted water, cook the soba according to the package directions. Drain and rinse under cold water. Drain well.

In a large bowl, combine the soy sauce, vinegar, sesame oil, mustard, and water. Add the soba, carrots, and bell pepper, and toss well.

In a small skillet, heat the oil over medium heat. Add the scallions, ginger, and garlic, and cook until the scallions are softened. Add to the noodle mixture and toss well.

Serve the salad at room temperature, sprinkled with the toasted sesame seeds.

MAKES 4 TO 6 SERVINGS

WHOLE-GRAIN PANZANELLA

Originally started as a way to use up stale bread, panzanella (Italian bread salad) has come into its own. By all means, if you've got stale bread, use it here. Feel free to add bell pepper, capers, or even some cheese to the recipe.

- 3 cups cubed (½-inch) crusty whole-grain bread
- ⅓ cup olive oil
- 3 tablespoons white balsamic vinegar
- Salt
- 1 pound red tomatoes, cut into 1-inch chunks
- ½ pound yellow tomatoes, cut into 1-inch chunks
- 1 small English (seedless) cucumber, quartered lengthwise and thinly sliced crosswise
- 1 small red onion, halved and thinly sliced
- ¾ cup packed fresh basil leaves, torn
- ¼ cup Gaeta olives, halved and pitted

Preheat the oven to 250°F. Place the bread on a baking sheet and bake until dried out, but not brown, 10 to 15 minutes.

In a large bowl, whisk together the oil and vinegar. Season with salt to taste.

Add the tomatoes, cucumber, onion, basil,and olives, and toss well. About 30 minutes before serving, add the bread cubes and toss to coat. Serve at room temperature.

MAKES 4 SERVINGS

APPLE & CELERY SALAD WITH GOAT CHEESE

Technically the jewel-like "seeds" of the pomegranate are called arils. The seeds themselves are the small white crunchy centers inside the ruby-colored flesh.

½ head celery, including leaves, cut into matchsticks

1 Granny Smith apple, thinly sliced

1 endive, separated into leaves

½ cup chopped flat-leaf parsley

⅓ cup lemon juice (about 2 lemons)

⅓ cup walnut oil

Salt and pepper

4 ounces mild goat cheese, cut into small chunks

½ cup pomegranate seeds

In a large bowl, combine the celery, apple, endive, and parsley.

In a small bowl, whisk together the lemon juice, oil, and salt and pepper to taste.

Add enough dressing to the salad to just coat (or add more to taste). Serve sprinkled with the goat cheese and pomegranate seeds.

MAKES 4 SERVINGS

APPLE-JICAMA SLAW

Jicama is a large, thin-skinned tuber that is used in a lot of Hispanic dishes.

1 medium jicama, peeled and cut into very thin matchsticks (about 3 cups)

3 crisp red apples, cut into very thin matchsticks (about 3 cups)

1 small red onion, very thinly sliced

1 small fresh jalapeño pepper, finely chopped

¼ cup finely chopped cilantro

2 tablespoons vegetable oil

2 tablespoons orange juice

1 tablespoon lime juice

1 tablespoon honey

Salt and black pepper

In a large bowl, combine the jicama, apples, onion, jalapeño, and cilantro.

In a separate bowl, whisk together the oil, orange juice, lime juice, and honey. Add the dressing to the vegetables and toss to evenly coat. Season with salt and black pepper to taste. Refrigerate for at least 1 hour before serving.

MAKES 6 SERVINGS

PEAR, ARUGULA & RADICCHIO SALAD

Sweet, bitter, salty, and toasty flavors are in harmony in this autumnal salad.

3 cups arugula

1 small head radicchio, torn into bite-size pieces

2 Bosc pears, thinly sliced

½ cup pecans, toasted

½ cup dried cranberries

¼ cup Red Wine Vinaigrette (page 375)

½ cup gorgonzola, crumbled (2 ounces)

In a large bowl, combine the arugula, radicchio, pears, pecans, and cranberries. Add the vinaigrette and toss to coat.

Serve the salad topped with the gorgonzola.

MAKES 4 SERVINGS

GINGER-MARINATED PEAR SALAD

Toast the walnuts in a dry skillet over medium heat or in a toaster oven at 350°F. It will only take a couple of minutes, so watch carefully.

2 firm-ripe large Bartlett pears

1-inch piece of fresh ginger, sliced

¼ cup olive oil

3 tablespoons red wine vinegar

6 cups (3 ounces) mixed salad greens

¼ cup walnuts, toasted and chopped

SNIPPING HERBS

Certain skinny or feathery herbs—dill, fennel, chives—are more easily "minced" with a pair of kitchen scissors than a knife. This is what our recipes mean when they called for a certain amount of "snipped" herb.

Halve and core the pears and cut lengthwise into slices. Place in a glass or ceramic dish with the ginger. Whisk together the oil and vinegar, and drizzle the dressing over the pears and ginger. Toss to coat. Refrigerate.

Just before serving, place the greens in a salad bowl. Add the pears, ginger, and dressing, and toss to coat. Add the walnuts and toss again.

MAKES 4 SERVINGS

ROASTED SPICED PEAR & BLUE CHEESE SALAD

Pears and blue cheese are natural partners. The crisp sweetness of the fruit is the perfect counterpoint to the creamy saltiness of the cheese.

- 3 firm-ripe red-skinned pears (such as Comice or Anjou), quartered
- 2 teaspoons plus 1 tablespoon honey
- 2 teaspoons plus 1 tablespoon extra-virgin olive oil
- ½ teaspoon ground coriander
- Salt and pepper
- 1 teaspoon lemon juice
- 5 ounces baby lettuce mix
- 4 ounces blue cheese, crumbled

Preheat the oven to 400°F.

In a large bowl, combine the pears with 2 teaspoons of the honey, 2 teaspoons of the oil, the coriander, and salt and pepper to taste. Toss to evenly coat. Arrange the pears in an even layer on a baking sheet. Roast for 8 to 10 minutes, or until golden brown.

In a medium bowl, combine the remaining 1 tablespoon honey, remaining 1 tablespoon oil, and the lemon juice. Add the lettuce and toss gently to coat. Season with salt and pepper to taste.

Divide the lettuce among 6 salad plates. Top each with 2 pieces of pear and sprinkle evenly with the blue cheese. Serve immediately.

MAKES 6 SERVINGS

PERSIMMON, CANDIED ALMOND & GOAT CHEESE SALAD

To turn this into the perfect finger food for parties, leave the endive leaves whole and spoon some of the salad mixture into them.

VINAIGRETTE

- ½ cup extra-virgin olive oil
- ¼ cup champagne vinegar
- 1 small shallot, finely minced
- Coarse salt and pepper

SALAD

- ½ cup natural (unblanched) almonds
- ¼ teaspoon extra-virgin olive oil
- 2 tablespoons sugar
- ¼ teaspoon coarse salt
- Pepper
- ¾ pound escarole, cut into thin strips
- ¾ pound endive, thinly sliced
- 8 ounces mild goat cheese
- 4 ounces dried persimmons or apricots, thinly sliced

To make the vinaigrette: In a small bowl, whisk together the oil, vinegar, and shallot. Season to taste with salt and pepper.

To make the salad: In a medium skillet, toss the almonds with the oil and cook over medium heat until they begin to pop. Sprinkle with the sugar and stir. Add the salt and a few grinds of pepper. Remove from the heat and continue tossing the nuts until the sugar hardens. Set aside to cool, then coarsely chop.

Toss the escarole in a large bowl with ¼ cup of the vinaigrette. Add the almonds, endive, goat cheese, and persimmons, and toss again. Add more vinaigrette to taste.

MAKES 6 SERVINGS

ORANGE, FENNEL & WATERCRESS SALAD

To prep the fennel, cut off the stalks (they're too fibrous to eat) and halve the bulb. Thinly slice the fennel halves crosswise. If the fennel came with feathery fronds, mince some and add to the salad.

4 large navel oranges

1 tablespoon white wine vinegar

2 teaspoons honey mustard

⅛ teaspoon pepper

⅓ cup extra-virgin olive oil

2 small bulbs fennel, thinly sliced

⅓ cup raisins

1 bunch watercress, tough stems trimmed

With a sharp paring knife, remove the peel and the outer membrane of the oranges. Holding one over a strainer set in a large bowl, cut between the membranes to release the segments into the strainer. Squeeze the juice from the membranes into the bowl. Repeat. Set the orange sections aside.

To the orange juice in the bowl, whisk in the vinegar, honey mustard, and pepper. Slowly whisk in the oil.

Add the fennel and raisins. Cover and marinate for 30 minutes.

Add the oranges and watercress to the bowl and toss to coat.

MAKES 4 TO 6 SERVINGS

BLOOD ORANGE-TOMATO ASPIC

Blood orange juice has a special depth of flavor and a good amount of antioxidant pigments called anthocyanins.

2 cups blood orange juice

2 cups tomato juice

1 tablespoon white wine vinegar

Juice of 1 lemon

2 teaspoons honey

Pinch of cayenne pepper

2 envelopes unflavored gelatin

Watercress, for serving

In a 2-quart saucepan, combine the orange juice, tomato juice, vinegar, lemon juice, honey, and cayenne. Sprinkle the gelatin over the mixture and set aside for 5 minutes, until the gelatin has softened.

Bring the mixture to a simmer over medium-high heat, stirring constantly, until the gelatin has completely dissolved.

Pour the mixture into a 6-cup mold and refrigerate for several hours, until firm. To serve, unmold onto a serving plate lined with watercress.

MAKES 4 TO 6 SERVINGS

Vegetables

Good preparation techniques can make the difference between great-looking vegetables and those that are simply passable. Wash vegetables thoroughly, but never soak them. (Exceptions are sandy spinach and cauliflower, broccoli, and cabbage that can have bugs. Soak those vegetables only long enough to remove the unwanted extras.) While washing, inspect the vegetables for damaged spots, and remove them before cooking. Damaged parts tend to discolor during cooking and often impart off-flavors. Pare hard-skinned vegetables such as rutabagas and winter squash. Others—potatoes, carrots, parsnips, young beets, and immature turnips—need only scrubbing. Leave skins intact, since they are a source of fiber and valuable nutrients.

Cook vegetables whole when possible, since cut-up vegetables with many exposed surfaces more lose nutrients to the cooking water. Young, tender, succulent vegetables can always be cooked whole. But to reduce cooking times and avoid uneven cooking of roots, tubers, and large vegetables with tough, woody portions, cut them into quarters or 1-inch pieces. Since exposure to light and air begins the destruction of nutrients, cut just before you are ready to cook. (Never soak cut potatoes to stop them from darkening; you will lose water-soluble vitamin C. Besides, the color change is reversed during cooking.) To lessen bruising, use a sharp knife to cut firm vegetables, but simply tear sensitive greens.

Cooking Vegetables

Vegetables are delightful when served raw and crunchy or cooked in any one of several basic ways. You can add variety by dressing up plain cooked vegetables with freshly snipped herbs, grated cheese, or toasted bread crumbs, and by mixing several vegetables together.

Steaming: This is an excellent way to cook vegetables and yet retain nutrients, shape, and distinctive flavor. There is a whole host of steaming options, from multi-tiered electric steamers, to bamboo steamer trays, to perforated inserts sold with pasta-cooking pots, to the simplest of all, the collapsible steamer that will fit in almost any pot. Steam the vegetables (in a single layer, if possible, for the most efficient steaming) over an inch of boiling water. Tightly cover and keep the water at a boil. If the water starts to evaporate, add more water, but be sure the water you add is very hot. If you add cold water, it slows the steaming and will increase the cooking time. The best method is to keep a tea kettle of almost boiling water on standby. The vegetables are done when they are still brightly colored and just fork-tender. Be sure to take them out of the steamer, or they will continue cooking.

Boiling: This is not the best option for cut-up

vegetables because there is too much nutrient loss, but it's fine for whole, unpeeled vegetables. After the vegetable is cooked, you can cut it up for serving. Certain vegetables are also very briefly boiled to blanch them (set their color) or to loosen the skins—to peel a tomato, for example. And starchy vegetables that are being cooked for mashing (i.e., potatoes or parsnips) are often boiled in small pieces to speed the cooking time and to keep them moist for the mashing process.

Pressure-cooking: If properly timed, vegetables cooked in a pressure cooker retain about the same nutritional value and textures of steamed vegetables. However, even though any vegetable can be cooked in a pressure cooker, it's best reserved for sturdy, longer-cooking vegetables such as potatoes. Tender vegetables such as asparagus can quite easily become overcooked. Always follow the manufacturer's directions for filling the pan, regulating the pressure, and venting the steam. When done, reduce the pressure and cool the cooker according to manufacturer's directions or as directed in an individual recipe.

Baking: Baking brings out a full, pleasant flavor in vegetables, especially in those with thick skins and enough moisture that they cook from the inside. As they bake, steam forms inside their jackets and cooks the flesh. Good candidates are potatoes, winter squash, sweet potatoes, and eggplant. Most vegetables are baked at about 350°F.

Roasting: At a higher temperature than baking—375° to 475°F—roasting brings out the natural sugars in vegetables. The method works for almost any vegetable, though those with a relatively sturdy structure—potatoes, sweet potatoes, asparagus, squash, corn, turnips, carrots, green beans, cauliflower, broccoli—hold up better. Very wet vegetables—eggplant, summer squash, tomatoes, greens—can be cooked at roasting temperatures, but they will collapse. The vegetables are cut up and tossed with the merest amount of oil to keep them from drying out. Sometimes herbs are a nice addition.

Grilling: As with roasting, vegetables to be grilled need to be lightly coated in oil to keep them moist and prevent them from sticking to the grill. The time it takes to grill vegetables depends entirely on the type of grill being used (gas, electric, or charcoal; covered or not covered), so it's up to the individual grill cook to figure out when a vegetable is done, but you can use the roasting times in the "A Guide to Simple Vegetable Preparation" (opposite) as a guide.

Stir-frying: This method of preparing vegetables originated in China where fuel supplies were scant, so cooking foods rapidly was particularly desirable. Cut vegetables into small pieces or thin slices, or shred them so they'll cook quickly. Heat a small amount of oil in a large, heavy skillet or wok over medium-high heat. The pan is ready for cooking when water droplets dance when sprinkled in. The hot oil will seal in fresh vegetable flavor and juices and keep the vegetables from sticking to the pan. Add the vegetables and cook, tossing them quickly and constantly, until they are crisp-tender. If you are cooking a mixture of vegetables, add the extra-firm vegetables first and cook briefly, then add the tender, quick-cooking ones. If you prefer vegetables slightly softer than crisp-tender, finish the cooking by covering the pan. For some extra-firm vegetables, add 1 to 2 tablespoons of water before covering the pan.

A GUIDE TO SIMPLE VEGETABLE PREPARATION

The best ways to prepare vegetables as side dishes are the simplest: steaming, baking, and roasting. Other simple methods include microwaving and pressure-cooking, which are basically steaming, but in an appliance. Those cooking times are not included here since the instructions from the manufacturer are more reliable.

For steaming times: The cooking times start from when the water is at a full boil. The ranges cover smaller to larger sizes of vegetable. (All times will be longer at high altitudes.)

For baking times: The times are for whole vegetables in their skins. The ranges cover smaller to larger sizes.

For roasting times: These are based on cut-up vegetables (tossed with a little oil) in a single layer in a roasting pan.

VEGETABLE	QUANTITY FOR 4 SERVINGS	PREP	STEAM (MINUTES)	BAKE AT 350°-375°F (MINUTES)	ROAST AT 425°-450°F (MINUTES)
ARTICHOKES	4 large or 8 small	Remove loose leaves; cut off top third. Cut off all but 1 inch of stem.	30-45	...	...
ASPARAGUS	1 pound	Break off woody stem where it easily snaps.	10-20	...	10-15
BEANS, FAVA	2 pounds unshelled	Remove beans from pods. If serving raw or lightly cooked, peel beans first; if cooking; peel afterward.	10-15	...	...
BEANS, SHELL (LIMA, CRANBERRY)	2½ pounds unshelled or 1 pound shelled	Shell by snapping or cutting pod open and squeezing out beans.	15-25	...	...
BEANS, SNAP (GREEN, WAX)	1 pound	Snap off stem ends.	5-10	...	10-15
BEETS	1½ pounds	Scrub with a vegetable brush. Leave 1-2 inches of stems on. Slip off skins after cooking.	40-75	40-60	35-40
BOK CHOY	1½ pounds	Leave baby bok choy whole. Separate larger heads from stalks. Cut off tough ends.	10-20	...	...
BROCCOLI	1½-2 pounds	Remove tough outer leaves and ends of stalks. Peel stalks if they're very tough.	5-15	...	10-15
BROCCOLI RABE	1½-2 pounds	Trim tough ends; pull off lower leaves	5-15	...	15-20
BROCCOLINI	1½-2 pounds	Trim tough ends; pull off lower leaves	5-15	...	15-20

A GUIDE TO SIMPLE VEGETABLE PREPARATION—*CONTINUED*

VEGETABLE	QUANTITY FOR 4 SERVINGS	PREP	STEAM (MINUTES)	BAKE AT 350°–375°F (MINUTES)	ROAST AT 425°–450°F (MINUTES)
BRUSSELS SPROUTS	1 ½ pounds	Remove insects by soaking in cold water for 10 minutes. Cut off stem ends and peel away any discolored leaves.	10–20	...	35–40
CABBAGE	1 pound	Discard outer leaves. Halve or quarter and cut out hard core.	9–12	...	15
CABBAGE, NAPA	1 pound	Pull off any wilted leaves; remove core.	10–20	...	...
CARROTS	1–2 pounds	Scrub with a vegetable brush. Peel thinly if desired. Trim ends.	15–40	30–60	25–35
CAULIFLOWER	3–3½ pounds	Remove leaves and hard core.	5–25	...	45–60
CORN	8 ears	Remove silk and husks. Or remove silk only and soak in water to moisten husks.	10–15	...	20
EGGPLANT	1½ pounds	Peel if skin is tough. Prick in several places if baking whole.	15–20	25–30	...
FENNEL	2 bulbs	Discard woody stalks. Save feathery fronds to use as an herb (and garnish). Halve or quarter bulb and cut out hard core.	25–30	...	20–25
GREENS, COOKING, STURDY (KALE, COLLARDS)	1½–2 pounds	Rinse thoroughly. Remove thick stems if desired.	20–25	...	...
GREENS, COOKING, TENDER (BEET GREENS, MUSTARD GREENS, TURNIP GREENS)	1½–2 pounds	Rinse thoroughly. Remove thick stems, if desired.	5–10	...	...
JERUSALEM ARTICHOKES	1 pound	Scrub with a vegetable brush. Peel thinly if desired.	35	30–60	25–45
KOHLRABI	6–8 bulbs	Peel. Save greens for salads.	30–35	...	30–45
LEEKS	4 large	Cut off root ends. If using in pieces, cut up and rinse thoroughly. If using whole, split the leek up to where the leaves turn green and wash out the soil caught between the leaves.	10–20	...	30–35

A GUIDE TO SIMPLE VEGETABLE PREPARATION—*CONTINUED*

VEGETABLE	QUANTITY FOR 4 SERVINGS	PREP	STEAM (MINUTES)	BAKE AT 350°–375°F (MINUTES)	ROAST AT 425°–450°F (MINUTES)
MUSHROOMS, BUTTON, AND CREMINI	1 pound	Wipe clean with a soft brush or damp cloth. Trim off ends of stems.	15	...	30
MUSHROOMS, PORTOBELLO	1½ pounds	Wipe clean with a soft brush or damp cloth. Trim off ends of stems. Scoop out the black gills.	...	20–35	15–25
MUSHROOMS, SHIITAKE	1 pound	Wipe clean with a soft brush or damp cloth. Discard stems.	10	...	20
OKRA	1 pound	Cut off stems.	20	...	5–10 (roasted whole)
ONIONS	1½ pounds	Peel and cut off root ends.	...	50–60	20–25
PARSNIPS	1 pound	Scrub with a vegetable brush. Peel thinly if desired. Trim ends.	35–40	35–40	40
PEAS, EDIBLE POD (SNOW PEAS, SUGAR SNAPS)	1 pound	Snap off blossom ends. On sugar snaps, pull off string that runs down one side; on older peas, pull off strings from both sides.	5–10	...	10
PEAS, GREEN	2–3 pounds unshelled or 1 pound shelled	Split open pods and pop peas out.	10–20	...	10
PEPPERS, BELL	4 peppers	If cutting up, remove stem, seeds, and ribs.	...	25–30	20–25
POTATOES, BAKING	4 medium	Scrub with a vegetable brush and remove any eyes (sprouts). If baking whole, prick in several places to let steam escape.	...	45–60	20–30
POTATOES, WAXY	1½ pounds	Rinse. Cook unpeeled.	20–45	30–50	20–30
PUMPKIN	2–3 pounds	Halve and remove stringy pulp and seeds (save seeds for roasting).	25–30	60	30–40

A GUIDE TO SIMPLE VEGETABLE PREPARATION—*CONTINUED*

VEGETABLE	QUANTITY FOR 4 SERVINGS	PREP	STEAM (MINUTES)	BAKE AT 350°-375°F (MINUTES)	ROAST AT 425°-450°F (MINUTES)
RUTABAGA (SWEDES, YELLOW TURNIPS)	1-2 pounds	Peel if waxed.	35-40	...	45-50
SALSIFY (OYSTER PLANT)	1-1½ pounds	Cut off tops. Peel thinly if desired. To slow browning, drop in cold water that contains a small amount of lemon juice or vinegar.	10	35-40	40
SPINACH	1½-2 pounds	Rinse thoroughly. Remove thick stems, if desired.	3-5	...	...
SQUASH, SPAGHETTI	3-4 pounds	Halve and seed. Add a little water to the baking pan, cover with foil, and steam-bake cut-sides down.	...	60	...
SQUASH, SUMMER	2-3 pounds	Cut off stems and blossom ends.	15-20	30-60	15-20
SQUASH, WINTER	2-3 pounds	Peel, halve, and remove stringy pulp and seeds (save seeds for roasting).	25-30	60	30-40
SWEET POTATOES	1-2 pounds	Scrub well. Peel if cutting up.	...	30-50	20-25
SWISS CHARD	1½-2 pounds	Rinse thoroughly. Trim off any split or bruised ends from the ribs.	5-10	...	...
TOMATOES	1-2 pounds	Wash; cut out stem and hard core. Peel if recipe calls for it (blanch first in boiling water for 30 to 60 seconds to loosen skin).	10	15-30	...
TURNIPS	1-2 pounds	Cut off roots and greens (save greens); scrub and peel thinly (if desired).	15-25	...	15-20

VEGETABLE COOKING TIPS

- Cooking times should always be minimal. Lengthy cooking of any vegetable works against maintaining flavor, nutrients, and color. Strong-tasting vegetables—brussels sprouts, broccoli, cauliflower, and turnips—become stronger when overcooked because they release sulfur compounds.
- Do not use baking soda to heighten the color of green vegetables. Baking soda destroys vitamin C and B vitamins; it also imparts a bitter taste and leaves vegetables mushy.
- On the other hand, a tablespoon of vinegar or lemon juice added to red cabbage or red beets will help them stay red. If you forget to put the acid in during cooking, add some later. The color change in red vegetables, unlike that of green vegetables, is reversible.
- Top vegetables with acidic sauces (such as tomato sauce) only after the cooking is complete because acids slow the cooking process.

HERB-STUFFED ARTICHOKES

Artichoke season runs from March through May.

8 large globe artichokes

1½ cups soft whole-grain bread crumbs (3 slices)

½ cup grated Parmesan cheese

2 tablespoons olive oil

4 teaspoons Italian herb seasoning, store-bought or homemade (right)

2 cloves garlic, minced

½ teaspoon salt

Cut off the artichoke stems and trim ½ inch from the tops of the artichoke leaves.

In a large bowl, mix together the bread crumbs, Parmesan, oil, Italian herb seasoning, garlic, and salt. Holding each artichoke over the bowl, stuff the breading into the spaces between the leaves.

Place the artichokes on a rack above boiling water in a large pot. Cover and steam over medium heat, for 30 to 45 minutes, or until the leaves pull away easily.

MAKES 6 TO 8 SERVINGS

BABY ARTICHOKE STEW

Serve this gorgeous green dish alongside grilled lamb chops or chicken.

1 lemon, halved

12 baby artichokes

Coarse salt

2 tablespoons butter

1 tablespoon extra-virgin olive oil

4 baby Vidalia onions (or 1 large), very coarsely chopped

1 pound thin to medium asparagus, cut on the diagonal into 3-inch pieces, steamed until tender

½ pound sugar snap peas, steamed until tender

ITALIAN HERB SEASONING

2 teaspoons basil

2 teaspoons oregano

2 teaspoons rosemary

½ teaspoon sage

½ teaspoon thyme

3 tablespoons water

¼ cup chopped fresh herbs, such as parsley, chervil, and mint

Bring a large pot of water to a boil.

Squeeze 1 lemon half into a large bowl of cold water. Trim off the stem and top quarter of each artichoke. Using a sharp paring knife, peel off the outer green leaves until you reach the pale inner leaves. Cut the artichokes in half lengthwise. Place in the lemon water as you finish.

Squeeze the remaining lemon half into the boiling water and add a pinch of salt. Add the artichokes and cook until just tender, about 10 minutes. Drain in a colander and dry on paper towels.

In a large skillet, heat 1 tablespoon of the butter and the oil over medium heat. Add the onions and cook, stirring, until softened, 3 to 5 minutes.

Add the artichokes and cook 2 minutes. Add the asparagus, sugar snaps, water, and salt to taste. Simmer, stirring, until the vegetables are just cooked through, about 5 minutes. Add the herbs and cook for 1 minute. Stir in the remaining 1 tablespoon butter. Serve hot.

MAKES 6 SERVINGS

ROASTED BABY ARTICHOKES

Baby artichokes aren't really "babies" at all, just pint-size fully mature artichokes that grow on the bottom of the main stem.

1 lemon half

24 baby artichokes (2 pounds)

4 large shallots

2 tablespoons extra-virgin olive oil

Sea salt and pepper

1 cup chicken broth, store-bought or homemade (page 172)

2 teaspoons fresh thyme leaves

Preheat the oven to 400°F.

Squeeze the lemon half into a large bowl of cold water. Trim off the stem and top quarter of each artichoke. Using a sharp paring knife, peel off the outer green leaves until you reach the pale inner leaves. Cut the artichokes in half lengthwise. Place in the lemon water as you finish.

Peel the shallots and cut lengthwise into ¼-inch slices.

In a 12-inch ovenproof skillet, heat the oil over medium-high heat. Add the artichokes and cook, stirring, for 2 minutes. Add the shallots and cook until the artichokes are golden on the edges, about 2 minutes. Season to taste with salt and pepper. Add the broth and thyme, and bring to a boil.

Transfer the skillet to the oven. Roast, turning once or twice, until the artichokes are just tender, 20 to 25 minutes. (Check halfway through. Add a little water if the broth has evaporated.) Season with salt and pepper and serve hot.

MAKES 6 SERVINGS

STEAMING GREENS

Most greens are so tender, and require so little time to soften up under heat, that they are "steamed" by cooking them in just the water that clings to the leaves after you wash them. Cook them well covered, and stir once or twice to move the uncooked greens to the bottom. Most are done in a matter of minutes. Sturdier greens, such as kale, or the stems of some greens,such as chard, need longer cooking.

ASPARAGUS-TOMATO SAUTÉ

You can use small, sweet grape tomatoes instead of cherry tomatoes in this quick side dish.

- 1 tablespoon olive oil
- 1 medium onion, chopped
- 1 pound asparagus, cut into 1-inch pieces
- ¼ teaspoon salt
- ⅛ teaspoon pepper
- 2 cups chopped cherry tomatoes
- 2 tablespoons chopped fresh basil

In a large skillet, heat the oil over medium heat. Add the onion and cook until soft. Stir in the asparagus, salt, and pepper, and cook for 1 minute.

Add the tomatoes, partially cover, and cook until the asparagus is crisp-tender, 3 to 5 minutes. Stir in the basil and serve hot.

MAKES 4 SERVINGS

ASPARAGUS & YELLOW TOMATOES: Use yellow pear tomatoes instead of cherry tomatoes. Season with 2 teaspoons minced fresh tarragon instead of basil.

STIR-FRIED ASPARAGUS WITH SESAME SEEDS

Cornstarch gives low-fat sauces the "mouth feel" of a high-fat sauce.

- ⅓ cup water
- 1 teaspoon cornstarch
- 4 teaspoons olive oil
- ½ cup minced scallions
- 2 teaspoons minced fresh ginger
- 1 teaspoon minced garlic
- 2½ pounds asparagus, cut into 2-inch pieces (5½ cups)
- 1 tablespoon sesame seeds, for serving
- 2 teaspoons, dark sesame oil
- ¼ teaspoon salt

In a small bowl, blend together the water and cornstarch.

In a large skillet, heat the olive oil over medium-high heat. Add the scallions, ginger, and garlic, and stir-fry until fragrant, about 30 seconds.

Add the asparagus and stir-fry until the asparagus turns bright green, about 1 minute.

Add the cornstarch mixture and bring to a simmer. Cook, stirring, until the sauce has thickened slightly. Cover and steam over medium-high heat until the asparagus is crisp-tender, 2 to 3 minutes.

Meanwhile, in a small skillet, stir the sesame seeds over medium heat until toasted, 2 to 4 minutes. Transfer to a plate.

Add the sesame oil to the asparagus and stir-fry for 30 seconds. Remove from the heat, sprinkle with the salt, and toss to combine. Serve the asparagus sprinkled with the toasted sesame seeds.

MAKES 6 SERVINGS

HOT & SPICY BUTTER BEANS

Butter bean is another name for lima bean because its texture is considered creamy and buttery.

- 3 pounds unshelled fresh lima beans
- 2 tablespoons vegetable oil
- 1 large onion, chopped
- 2 cloves garlic, finely chopped
- 1 medium tomato, chopped
- 1 small fresh jalapeño pepper, sliced
- 1 teaspoon ground coriander
- ½ teaspoon turmeric

½ teaspoon smoked or sweet paprika

½ teaspoon salt

In a steamer, cook the beans in their pods until tender, about 15 minutes. When cool enough to handle, shell the beans.

In a medium skillet, heat the oil over medium heat. Add the onion and garlic, and cook for 3 minutes.

Stir in the lima beans, tomato, jalapeño, coriander, turmeric, paprika, and salt. Cover and cook for 5 minutes over medium heat to blend the flavors.

MAKES 8 SERVINGS

TARRAGON CORN & LIMAS

Fresh baby limas are a wonderful treat in season but not always easy to find. If they're not available, make this with thawed frozen baby limas instead.

- 2 tablespoons olive oil
- 1 bunch scallions, sliced
- 1 cup fresh baby lima beans
- 1 cup corn kernels, fresh or frozen
- ½ cup water
- ½ teaspoon salt
- ½ teaspoon pepper
- ¼ teaspoon tarragon
- 3 tablespoons reduced-fat sour cream

In a large skillet, heat the oil over medium heat. Add the scallions and cook until wilted.

Add the beans, corn, water, salt, pepper, and tarragon, and cook, covered, until the beans are tender, about 10 minutes.

Off the heat, stir in the sour cream.

MAKES 4 SERVINGS

SUCCOTASH

This dish is a colorful bed for fish or great on its own. Use any type of tomato.

- 3 cups fresh baby lima beans
- 3 tablespoons butter
- 1 medium red onion, chopped
- 2 cups fresh corn kernels (3 to 4 ears)
- 1 cup seeded and chopped tomatoes
- 2 tablespoons chopped flat-leaf parsley
- Coarse salt and pepper

In a saucepan, bring ¾ cup salted water to boil. Add the beans and cook until not quite tender, about 5 minutes. Drain and rinse under cold running water.

In a large skillet, melt the butter over medium heat until the foam subsides. Add the onion and cook, stirring, until softened, about 2 minutes.

Add the corn and cook for 5 minutes. Add the beans and cook for 3 minutes. Stir in the tomatoes and parsley, and simmer for 1 minute. Season to taste with salt and pepper.

MAKES 6 SERVINGS

FRESH FAVAS WITH SHAVED PARMESAN

To ensure you are getting the sweetest fava beans and the most for your dollar, choose pods that are not too large. Each pound of beans in the pod will yield about ¾ cup shelled. If you'd like, blanch the favas (once you've removed them from their pods) in boiling water for 1 to 2 minutes; this will make it easier to remove the tough skin.

- 2 pounds unshelled fresh fava beans
- 1 tablespoon olive oil
- ¼ teaspoon salt
- ⅛ teaspoon pepper
- 1 cup shaved Parmesan cheese, for serving

Remove the favas from their pods, then remove the tough outer skins.

In a medium pot of boiling water, cook the favas for 1 minute. Drain. Transfer to a bowl and add the oil, salt, and pepper. Serve with shaved Parmesan on top.

MAKES 4 SERVINGS

SIMMERED ROMA & CRANBERRY BEANS

Roma, or pole, beans look like string beans but have thicker pods and are more flavorful. Tender cranberry beans have a beautiful red-speckled skin that turns a rosy brown when cooked. Serve this hearty dish with bread to soak up the broth.

- 1½ pounds unshelled fresh cranberry beans
- 1½ pounds Roma or other green pole beans, strings removed
- 3 tablespoons extra-virgin olive oil, plus more for drizzling
- 1 large onion, diced
- 2 cloves garlic, minced
- 2 teaspoons minced fresh oregano
- Coarse salt and freshly ground pepper

Shell the cranberry beans and place them in a large deep saucepan or Dutch oven. Cover with cold water by 1 inch. Bring to a boil, reduce to a simmer, and cook until just tender, 20 to 25 minutes. Remove from the heat and let cool slightly. Reserving 1 cup of the cooking liquid, drain the beans.

Meanwhile, in a large pot of boiling salted water, cook the Roma beans until tender but still bright green, 12 to 15 minutes. Drain.

In a large saucepan, heat 2 tablespoons of the oil over medium heat. Add the onion and garlic, and cook, stirring occasionally, until the onion is soft, about 8 minutes.

Add the cranberry beans, Roma beans, and oregano, and cook for 3 minutes. Add the reserved bean cooking liquid and remaining 1 tablespoon oil, and bring to a simmer. Season to taste with salt and pepper. Drizzle with additional oil before serving in bowls.

MAKES 8 SERVINGS

HERBED GREEN BEANS WITH SUNFLOWER SEEDS

You can toast raw sunflower seeds in a small ungreased skillet, or buy already roasted sunflower seeds.

- 1 pound green beans, cut into 1-inch pieces
- 2 tablespoons chopped parsley
- 1 tablespoon snipped chives
- 1½ teaspoons Italian herb seasoning, store-bought or homemade (page 407)
- 2 tablespoons vegetable oil
- 1 small onion, chopped
- 1 clove garlic, minced
- ½ cup sunflower seeds, toasted
- Salt and pepper

In a steamer, cook the beans until crisp-tender, about 5 minutes.

Meanwhile, in a small bowl, combine the parsley, chives, and Italian seasoning.

In a large skillet, heat the oil over medium heat. Add the onion and garlic, and cook until softened. Stir in the herb mixture and sunflower seeds.

Add the cooked beans and season lightly with salt and pepper. Toss to combine and serve hot.

MAKES 4 TO 6 SERVINGS

YELLOW BEANS & PEPITAS: Use yellow wax beans instead of green beans, cilantro instead of parsley, and hulled pumpkin seeds (pepitas) instead of sunflower seeds.

GREEN BEANS WITH WALNUTS

If you don't have walnut oil, use peanut oil or another tablespoon of olive oil.

- 1 pound green beans, cut into 1-inch pieces
- ½ medium sweet onion, minced
- 1 small clove garlic, minced
- 2 tablespoons olive oil
- 1 tablespoon walnut oil
- 1 tablespoon white wine vinegar
- Salt and pepper
- ¼ cup walnuts, toasted and minced, for serving

In a steamer, cook the beans until crisp-tender, about 5 minutes.

Transfer the hot beans to a serving bowl. Add the onion, garlic, olive oil, walnut oil, and vinegar. Season to taste with salt and pepper.

Serve topped with the toasted walnuts.

MAKES 4 TO 6 SERVINGS

ROASTED BEANS & MUSHROOMS

Green beans barely need any trimming these days. Years ago, they were called string beans because they had tough strings that had to be pulled off, but this characteristic has been bred out of them.

- 1½ pounds green beans
- 10 ounces small button mushrooms, quartered
- 2 tablespoons olive oil
- 1 teaspoon chopped fresh thyme leaves
- 4 cloves garlic, minced
- Salt and pepper

Preheat the oven to 450°F.

In a large bowl, combine the beans, mushrooms, oil, thyme, and garlic, and toss to evenly coat. Season with salt and pepper to taste, and toss again.

Arrange in an even layer on two rimmed baking sheets. Roast for 25 minutes, or until golden brown and tender.

MAKES 6 SERVINGS

SAUTÉED BEET GREENS

In addition to being a great side dish, this makes a delicious pasta sauce: Cook 8 ounces of fusilli or penne, drain, and toss with the hot beet greens. Add a sprinkling of grated Parmesan cheese if you like.

- ⅓ cup golden raisins
- ½ cup boiling water
- 2 tablespoons olive oil
- 3 cloves garlic, peeled
- 8 cups shredded beet greens (from about 3 bunches beets)
- 1 teaspoon finely slivered orange zest
- ½ teaspoon salt
- 3 tablespoons chopped green olives
- 2 tablespoons tomato paste

In a small heatproof bowl, soak the raisins in the boiling water for 10 minutes to soften.

Meanwhile, in a large skillet, heat the oil over low heat. Add the whole cloves of garlic and cook, turning the garlic as it colors, until soft, 5 to 7 minutes. Remove the garlic and mash it with the flat side of a chef's knife. Set aside.

Add the beet greens, orange zest, and salt to the pan and cook, stirring frequently, until the greens are wilted, about 3 minutes.

Add the olives, tomato paste, the raisins and their soaking liquid, and the mashed garlic to the pan and cook until the greens are tender, about 5 minutes.

MAKES 4 SERVINGS

LEMON BROCCOLI

Just a small amount of butter is used for flavor in the lemon sauce for the broccoli, but vegans can simply use an additional 1 tablespoon olive oil instead.

- 1 pound broccoli, divided into florets and stalks
- 4 teaspoons olive oil
- 1 large red onion, diced
- 5 cloves garlic, minced
- 1 tablespoon butter
- 2 teaspoons grated lemon zest
- 1 tablespoon lemon juice
- ½ teaspoon salt
- ¼ teaspoon pepper

Peel the broccoli stalks and cut crosswise into ½-inch pieces. In a steamer, cook the broccoli stems and florets until crisp-tender, 3 to 5 minutes.

In a large skillet, heat the oil over medium-high heat. Add the onion and garlic, and cook until the onion begins to brown, 3 to 5 minutes.

Remove the skillet from the heat and stir in the butter, lemon zest, lemon juice, salt, and pepper. Stir to melt the butter.

Add the broccoli to the skillet and toss to coat with the sauce. Serve warm or at room temperature.

MAKES 4 SERVINGS

ORANGE BROCCOLI: Substitute orange juice and zest for the lemon.

BROCCOLINI WITH ORANGE-GINGER SAUCE

A cross between Chinese kai lan and broccoli, the stalks of this deep-green vegetable have a mild broccoli-like flavor and loose heads that absorb sauce nicely.

- 1 pound broccolini, tough ends trimmed
- ½ teaspoon cornstarch
- ½ cup orange juice
- 1 tablespoon dark sesame oil
- 2 scallions, thinly sliced on the diagonal
- 3 cloves garlic, thinly sliced
- 1-inch piece of fresh ginger, peeled and cut into thin matchsticks
- ½ teaspoon salt

Bring a large pot of salted water to a boil over high heat. Plunge half of the broccolini into the water and cook until dark green and pliant, about 5 minutes. Remove from the water with a skimmer or tongs, drain well, and place on a serving plate. Repeat with the remaining broccolini.

In a small bowl, stir together the cornstarch and orange juice until smooth.

Meanwhile, in a large skillet, heat the sesame oil over medium heat. Add the scallions, garlic, ginger, and salt, and cook, stirring, until the garlic is golden brown, 2 to 3 minutes. Stir in the orange juice mixture and bring to a boil. Cook, stirring constantly, until lightly thickened, 1 to 2 minutes. Spoon the sauce over the broccolini.

MAKES 4 SERVINGS

BROCCOLI RABE WITH DRIED TOMATOES AND RAISINS

Broccoli rabe is slightly bitter (a sign that the vegetable is very high in certain healthful compounds) and not to everyone's taste. This recipe uses the sweetness of raisins and dried tomatoes to counter some of the bitterness, but it could also be made with broccolini, which is milder in taste but shaped a lot like broccoli rabe.

- **¼ cup plump sun-dried tomatoes**
- **2 tablespoons raisins**
- **½ cup hot water**
- **2 tablespoons olive oil**
- **2 cloves garlic, slivered**
- **2 anchovies, mashed**
- **¼ teaspoon red pepper flakes**
- **1 bunch broccoli rabe (1 pound), tough ends trimmed, bunch sliced ½ inch thick**
- **¼ teaspoon salt**

In a small bowl, combine the sun-dried tomatoes, raisins, and hot water, and set aside to plump while you cook the broccoli rabe.

In a large skillet, heat the oil over low heat. Add the garlic, anchovies, and red pepper flakes, and cook until the garlic is fragrant and the anchovies have melted, 3 to 4 minutes.

Add the broccoli rabe and stir to coat. Cover and cook until the broccoli rabe begins to wilt, about 4 minutes. Add the sun-dried tomatoes and raisins, their soaking liquid, and the salt. Cook uncovered until the liquid has evaporated and the broccoli rabe is tender, about 7 minutes.

MAKES 4 SERVINGS

BRUSSELS SPROUTS IN WALNUT-BUTTER SAUCE

To speed the cooking of the brussels sprouts, cut a small X in the stem end of each.

- **2 containers (10 ounces each) brussels sprouts**
- **¼ cup (½ stick) butter**
- **1 cup coarsely chopped walnuts**

In a steamer, cook the brussels sprouts until tender, about 10 minutes.

Meanwhile, in a heavy cast-iron skillet, combine the butter and walnuts, and cook over medium-high heat until the butter foams and turns deep tan and the nuts are toasted.

Place the brussels sprouts in a serving dish, and pour the butter evenly over the sprouts.

MAKES 4 TO 6 SERVINGS

STIR-FRIED BRUSSELS SPROUTS

Quartering brussels sprouts makes them cook faster when stir-frying.

- **1 tablespoon olive oil**
- **2 containers (10 ounces each) brussels sprouts, quartered**
- **1 carrot, cut into thin matchsticks**
- **2 cloves garlic, minced**
- **¼ teaspoon salt**
- **1¼ cups plus 2 tablespoons water**
- **2 tablespoons lower-sodium soy sauce**
- **¾ teaspoon cornstarch**
- **¾ teaspoon ground ginger**

In a large skillet, heat the oil over medium heat. Add the brussels sprouts and carrot, and cook, stirring frequently, until crisp-tender, about 7 minutes. Add the garlic and cook for 2 minutes.

Add the salt and 1¼ cups water, and bring to a boil. Reduce to a simmer, cover, and cook until the sprouts are tender, about 7 minutes.

In a small bowl, whisk together the soy sauce, cornstarch, ginger, and remaining 2 tablespoons of water. Add to the pan, bring to a boil, and cook until the sauce is slightly thickened, about 1 minute.

MAKES 4 SERVINGS

BRUSSELS SPROUTS & CHESTNUTS WITH BACON

If you can find them, jarred chestnuts are a much easier alternative to roasting your own, though of course, home-roasted ones taste much better. To roast your own, carefully score an X into each chestnut and arrange on a baking sheet, X side up. Roast at 425°F for 15 to 20 minutes, or until the X on each shell begins to open up and curl back. Cool completely before shelling.

- 4 slices bacon, finely chopped
- 2 pounds brussels sprouts, halved (if they're especially large, quarter them)
- 1 cup chicken broth, store-bought or homemade (page 172)
- 1 cup chopped cooked chestnuts
- 2 tablespoons butter
- Salt and pepper

In a large skillet, cook the bacon over medium heat until crisp, 10 to 12 minutes. Leaving the rendered fat in the pan, transfer the bacon to paper towels to drain.

Add the brussels sprouts to the pan and cook, stirring, for 1 minute. Add the broth, cover, and cook until the brussels sprouts are tender, 8 to 10 minutes. Uncover, increase the heat to medium-high, and cook until all the liquid has evaporated, 3 to 5 minutes.

Add the chestnuts and butter, and toss to combine. Add the bacon and toss. Season to taste with salt and pepper.

MAKES 6 SERVINGS

ROASTED BRUSSELS SPROUTS

Roasting brings out the natural sweetness in these miniature heads of cabbage.

- 2 pounds brussels sprouts
- 1/4 cup olive oil
- 1 teaspoon salt
- 1/2 teaspoon pepper

Preheat the oven to 400°F.

In a large bowl, toss the brussels sprouts with the oil, salt, and pepper. Spread out on a baking sheet in a single layer. Roast, stirring halfway through, for 30 to 40 minutes, until crisp and browned.

MAKES 6 SERVINGS

NAPA CABBAGE ROLL

This strudel-like roll is a tempting side dish.

- 2 tablespoons butter
- 2 tablespoons olive oil
- 1 medium head napa cabbage, finely chopped
- 2 cups soft whole-grain bread crumbs (4 slices)
- 1 cup finely chopped walnuts
- 1 cup golden raisins
- 1 teaspoon cinnamon
- Sour Cream Pie Dough (page 532)

In a large skillet, melt the butter in the oil. Add the cabbage and cook, stirring occasionally, until it turns light brown. With a slotted spoon, transfer the cabbage to a medium bowl. When cool, stir in the bread crumbs, walnuts, raisins, and cinnamon. Set aside.

Preheat the oven to 375°F.

Roll out the dough to a 14 × 16-inch rectangle, about ⅛ inch thick. Spread the cooled cabbage filling evenly over the pastry, leaving a 1-inch border all around. With a long edge toward you, roll the pastry up carefully.

Place seam-side down on a rimmed baking sheet. Bake for 30 minutes, or until the pastry is golden brown.

MAKES 8 TO 10 SERVINGS

STIR-FRIED BOK CHOY

If you can get baby bok choy, use it here. Cut it lengthwise into ½-inch slices.

- 3 tablespoons water
- 1 tablespoon olive oil
- 1 carrot, cut into matchsticks
- 2 tablespoons slivered fresh ginger
- 1 pound bok choy, cut into ½-inch-wide slices
- 3 tablespoons orange juice concentrate
- 1 tablespoon turbinado or light brown sugar
- 1 tablespoon lower-sodium soy sauce
- ½ teaspoon salt
- ½ cup frozen peas, thawed
- 1 teaspoon cornstarch blended with 1 tablespoon water

In a large skillet, heat the water and oil over medium heat. Add the carrot and ginger, and cook, stirring frequently, until the carrot is crisp-tender, about 3 minutes.

Add the bok choy, orange juice concentrate, brown sugar, soy sauce, and salt. Cover and cook until the bok choy begins to wilt, about 3 minutes.

Uncover and cook, stirring frequently, until the bok choy is crisp-tender, about 2 minutes. Stir in the peas and the cornstarch mixture, and cook, stirring constantly, until the vegetables are nicely coated, about 1 minute.

MAKES 4 SERVINGS

SNAPPY SAVOY CABBAGE

Crinkly-leaved savoy cabbage has a milder flavor and more delicate texture than green cabbage.

- 1 small head savoy cabbage, shredded
- 3 tablespoons butter, melted
- 1 teaspoon lemon juice
- 1 teaspoon drained horseradish
- 1 teaspoon sugar
- Salt and pepper

In a steamer, cook the cabbage until crisp-tender, about 5 minutes. Transfer to a serving dish.

In a small bowl, combine the butter, lemon juice, horseradish, and sugar. Add to the cabbage and toss. Season with salt and pepper to taste, and toss again.

MAKES 6 TO 8 SERVINGS

SWEET & SOUR CABBAGE

Pull out the food processor to prep the cabbage: Cut it into 2-inch chunks, and then pulse on and off in the food processor until finely chopped.

- 1 small head red or green cabbage, finely chopped
- 1 cup water
- 2 tablespoons butter
- ½ teaspoon salt
- ¼ teaspoon pepper
- 2 tart apples, sliced
- 2 tablespoons cider vinegar

- 1 tablespoon honey
- 1/2 teaspoon caraway seeds
- 1 tablespoon cornstarch blended with 1/4 cup cold water

In a large saucepan, combine the cabbage, water, butter, salt, and pepper. Cook, covered, until the cabbage is crisp-tender, about 10 minutes.

Add the apples and cook until soft, 3 to 5 minutes.

Stir in the vinegar, honey, and caraway seeds. Pour in the cornstarch mixture, stirring gently over low heat until the sauce bubbles and thickens. Simmer for 1 minute.

MAKES 6 SERVINGS

BAKED CARROTS & APPLES

For a prettier presentation, cut the carrots on the diagonal to produce oval slices.

- 3 cups thinly sliced carrots
- 4 apples, thinly sliced
- Salt and pepper
- 2 tablespoons flour
- 4 tablespoons honey
- 1/4 cup (1/2 stick) butter
- 3/4 cup orange juice

Preheat the oven to 350°F.

In a steamer, cook the carrots until beginning to get tender, about 10 minutes.

Put half the apples in a shallow 1-quart baking dish and cover with half of the carrots. Season lightly with salt and pepper. Sprinkle with 1 tablespoon of the flour. Drizzle with 2 tablespoons of the honey and dot with 2 tablespoons of the butter. Repeat the layers.

Pour the orange juice over everything. Bake for 40 to 45 minutes, until the carrots are tender and the mixture is bubbling. Serve hot.

MAKES 6 SERVINGS

GLAZED CARROTS WITH INDIAN SPICES

This recipe is based on a French treatment of carrots called carottes Vichy, *in which the carrots are cooked with a splash of Vichy mineral water and butter.*

- 1 pound carrots, sliced 1/4 inch thick
- 1 cup water
- 1 tablespoon butter
- 2 teaspoons agave nectar or mild honey
- 1/2 teaspoon garam masala
- 1/4 teaspoon cardamom
- 1/4 teaspoon salt

In a large skillet, combine the carrots, water, butter, agave nectar, garam masala, cardamom, and salt. Bring to a boil over high heat, and cook until the carrots are tender and glazed and the liquid has evaporated, 10 to 12 minutes. Add a little more water if the carrots aren't cooked by the time the water has evaporated.

MAKES 4 SERVINGS

CARROTS & ZUCCHINI WITH CILANTRO

Cut the zucchini and carrots into approximately the same size matchstick strips, 2 to 3 inches long.

- 1 pound carrots, cut into matchsticks
- 3 medium zucchini, cut into matchsticks
- 3 tablespoons butter, melted

½ cup chopped cilantro or parsley

½ teaspoon salt

¼ teaspoon pepper

In a steamer, cook the carrots until crisp-tender, about 15 minutes. Add the zucchini for the last 5 minutes. (Or if your steamer isn't big enough, steam them separately.)

Transfer the vegetables to a large bowl and toss with the butter, cilantro, salt, and pepper.

MAKES 6 TO 8 SERVINGS

ROASTED HEIRLOOM CARROTS WITH HERB SALT

If you can't find heirloom carrots, just use regular carrots, but try to find slender ones.

2 pounds small heirloom carrots, mixed varieties

1½ tablespoons olive oil

2 teaspoons Herb Salt (page 420)

Preheat the oven to 425°F.

Trim the ends and all but ½ inch of the carrot stems. Scrub or peel the carrots. Place on a large baking sheet. Drizzle with the oil and sprinkle with the herb salt. Toss and spread the carrots evenly. Roast for 20 to 25 minutes, turning twice, until just tender and slightly browned. Serve hot or at room temperature.

MAKES 8 SERVINGS

THYME-ROASTED CARROTS

Baby carrots aren't actually immature carrots. They are short pieces of a variety of carrot that is very slender and straight-sided.

1 pound baby carrots

1 tablespoon olive oil

½ teaspoon sugar

¼ teaspoon thyme

¼ teaspoon coarse salt

Preheat the oven to 425°F. Lightly oil a rimmed baking sheet.

Arrange the carrots on the baking sheet. Drizzle with the oil and sprinkle with the sugar, thyme, and salt. Toss to mix.

Roast the carrots, stirring 3 or 4 times, for 30 minutes, or until tender and lightly browned.

MAKES 4 SERVINGS

ROASTED CAULIFLOWER

Once you've tried roasting cauliflower, you'll never go back. Roasting brings out the natural sweetness of the vegetable while giving it lightly crisped edges. If the garlic has gotten soft, serve it, in its skin, allowing each diner to squeeze out some of the soft, mellow garlic to enjoy along with the cauliflower.

1 large head cauliflower (3 pounds), broken into large florets

⅓ cup olive oil

4 cloves garlic, unpeeled

1 sprig fresh rosemary or ½ teaspoon dried

Salt

Preheat the oven to 400°F.

In a large roasting pan, toss the cauliflower with the oil, garlic, and rosemary. Roast, tossing occasionally, for 1 hour, or until tender and lightly browned.

Season with salt to taste and serve warm or at room temperature.

MAKES 4 TO 6 SERVINGS

NEW ENGLAND CORN PUDDING

If you can get fresh white corn, or one of the multicolored (white and yellow) corns, use it here.

- 1⅓ cups reduced-fat (2%) milk
- 3 tablespoons flour
- 3 tablespoons butter, melted and cooled slightly
- 2 large eggs
- 1 teaspoon sugar
- ¼ teaspoon white pepper
- 2 cups fresh corn kernels (4 to 5 ears)
- Pinch of nutmeg

Preheat the oven to 325°F. Butter a 1½-quart baking dish.

In a blender, combine the milk, flour, butter, eggs, sugar, and white pepper, and mix well. Pour into the baking dish. Stir in the corn and sprinkle with the nutmeg.

Place the baking dish in a roasting pan. Set the roasting pan on a pulled-out oven rack, and pour hot water into the roasting pan to come one-third the way up the sides of the baking dish. Bake for 45 minutes, or until a knife inserted in the center comes out clean.

MAKES 4 TO 6 SERVINGS

SAUTÉED CORN WITH SOUR CREAM

To get the most out of a fresh ear of corn, use the sharp side of a knife to slice off the kernels, then use the dull back side to push the corn germ out of the cobs.

- 4 teaspoons butter
- ¼ cup chopped red bell pepper
- 2 tablespoons chopped sweet onion
- 2 cups fresh corn kernels (4 to 6 ears)
- Pinch of cayenne pepper
- Salt
- ¾ cup sour cream

In a medium skillet, melt the butter over medium heat. Add the bell pepper and onion, and cook until softened, about 5 minutes.

Stir in the corn and cayenne, and cook until crisp-tender, about 5 minutes.

Season lightly with salt. Stir in the sour cream.

MAKES 4 SERVINGS

HOMINY WITH CILANTRO & QUESO FRESCO

Hominy, which is hulled and dried corn kernels, can be found dried or already cooked. Cans of cooked hominy are usually found alongside canned beans in the supermarket. Queso fresco is a mild, crumbly fresh cheese with a slightly tangy flavor; if you can't find it, substitute a mild feta.

- 2 cans (16 ounces each) white hominy, rinsed and drained
- ½ cup water
- 1 tablespoon olive oil
- ⅓ cup chopped cilantro
- 3 tablespoons finely minced red onion
- 1 tablespoon lime juice
- 2 ounces queso fresco, crumbled
- ¼ teaspoon chili powder

In a medium saucepan, combine the hominy, water, and oil, and cook over medium-high heat, stirring occasionally, until heated through, about 5 minutes. Remove from the heat and stir in the cilantro, onion, and lime juice.

Transfer to a serving dish, top with the crumbled queso fresco, and sprinkle with the chili powder.

MAKES 4 SERVINGS

GRILLED LEMON-TARRAGON CORN

Soaking the unhusked corn in water for an hour or so keeps the husk from burning on the grill. Just peel back the husks and remove the silk, close the husks back up, and soak. When ready to grill, proceed with brushing the tarragon oil over the corn.

3 tablespoons lemon juice

1 tablespoon extra-light olive oil

1 teaspoon tarragon

4 ears of corn, unhusked

Salt

Preheat the grill to medium. In a small bowl, combine the lemon juice, oil, and tarragon. Set aside.

Peel back the husks from the corn ears and remove the corn silk, leaving the husk attached. Rinse the corn under cold running water to dampen the husks. Brush the lemon-tarragon mixture over the corn kernels, then pull the husks back over the corn and tie with kitchen string (be sure the kitchen string is dampened, too).

Cook the corn in a covered grill, turning as the husks blacken, for 20 minutes, or until piping hot. To serve, remove the string and husks and sprinkle lightly with salt.

MAKES 4 EARS OF CORN

BASIL-LIME CORN: Use lime juice instead of lemon juice and basil instead of tarragon.

GRILLED EGGPLANT PARMIGIANA

This works well on a stovetop grill pan, but you could also grill the eggplant on an outdoor grill.

2 medium eggplants, cut lengthwise into ½-inch slices

Olive oil

1 teaspoon minced garlic

1 can (28 ounces) peeled whole tomatoes, drained

¼ cup tomato paste

2 tablespoons minced fresh basil or 1 teaspoon dried

2 tablespoons minced parsley

¼ teaspoon pepper

½ cup grated Parmesan cheese

8 ounces part-skim mozzarella cheese, sliced

Preheat a grill pan. Brush both sides of the eggplant slices with a little oil. Grill the eggplant

---

HERB SALT

Herb salt is easy to make and adds subtle flavoring to vegetables, fish, and chicken. Keep the leftovers in a jar in the refrigerator and use a pinch at a time to season food at the table.

2 tablespoons kosher or coarse sea salt

2 teaspoons fresh thyme or marjoram leaves

¼ teaspoon fennel seeds

¼ teaspoon peppercorns

Place 1 tablespoon of the salt, the thyme, fennel seeds, and peppercorns in a blender, spice mill, or coffee grinder. Pulse until finely ground. Transfer to a small bowl or glass jar. Stir in the remaining 1 tablespoon salt.

until tender and nicely browned on both sides, 8 to 10 minutes.

Meanwhile, in a medium skillet, heat 1 tablespoon of oil over medium heat. Add the garlic and cook for 2 minutes. Add the tomatoes, tomato paste, basil, parsley, and pepper, and simmer, stirring occasionally, for 20 minutes.

Preheat the oven to 350°F.

Layer the eggplant, sauce, and Parmesan in an 8 × 11-inch baking pan, beginning and ending with the sauce and Parmesan. Arrange the mozzarella slices on top. Bake for 35 minutes, or until browned and bubbling.

MAKES 6 TO 8 SERVINGS

ROASTED EGGPLANT

Putting slices of fresh garlic into the roasting eggplant is a great way to add flavor from the inside out.

- 1 large eggplant
- 5 cloves garlic, cut in half
- Pepper
- 3 tablespoons olive oil
- Wine vinegar

Preheat the oven to 375°F. Oil a baking dish large enough to hold the eggplant.

Cut 5 lengthwise slits in the eggplant. Place 2 halves of garlic in each "pocket" of eggplant. Sprinkle pepper in the pockets.

Place the eggplant in the baking dish and brush with 1 tablespoon of the oil. Bake for 50 minutes, or until fork tender. Cool.

Remove the skin and garlic and place the eggplant in a serving dish. Sprinkle with the remaining 2 tablespoons oil. Season with vinegar to taste.

MAKES 6 SERVINGS

SESAME EGGPLANT: Replace 2 teaspoons of the olive oil with dark sesame oil. Sprinkle the eggplant with a little soy sauce along with the vinegar at the end.

RATATOUILLE

Ratatouille can also be served cold as a condiment alongside meat or poultry.

- 2 tablespoons olive oil
- 1 large onion, halved and thinly sliced
- 2 cloves garlic, minced
- 1 small eggplant, cubed
- 2 medium green bell peppers, coarsely chopped
- 4 large tomatoes, coarsely chopped
- 3 zucchini, cut into ½-inch slices
- 2 tablespoons chopped parsley
- 1 teaspoon basil
- ½ teaspoon oregano
- ½ teaspoon thyme
- Salt

In a large saucepan, heat the oil over medium heat. Add the onion and garlic, and cook until soft, about 7 minutes.

Add the eggplant and stir until coated with the oil. Add the bell peppers and stir in well. Cover the pan and cook for 10 minutes, stirring occasionally to avoid sticking.

Add the tomatoes, zucchini, parsley, basil, oregano, and thyme, and mix well. Cover and cook over low heat until the eggplant is tender, but not mushy, 15 to 20 minutes. Season with salt to taste. Serve hot.

MAKES 4 SERVINGS

ROASTED FENNEL

Fennel is very good when roasted, but it can dry out as it cooks, which is why it is enclosed in a foil packet.

2 bulbs fennel (1 pound each), stalks discarded

2 tablespoons olive oil

1 tablespoon balsamic vinegar

¾ cup grated Parmesan cheese

Preheat the oven to 400°F.

Stand the fennel on end and cut vertically into ½-inch-thick slices.

In a bowl, toss the fennel with the oil and vinegar. Lay a sheet of foil on a baking sheet and top with the fennel in a single layer. Drizzle any liquid remaining in the bowl over the fennel. Top with another sheet of foil and crimp the edges together to seal. Bake until the fennel is tender, 20 to 25 minutes.

Remove the top layer of foil and sprinkle the Parmesan over the fennel. Bake for 3 to 5 minutes longer, until the cheese has melted.

MAKES 4 SERVINGS

GRILLED SCALLIONS, FENNEL & PEPPERS

If you don't have a grill pan or grill topper, you can use a double thickness of heavy-duty foil pierced with holes to keep the vegetables from falling through the grate.

5 large scallions, roots and top half of the dark green part trimmed

2 red bell peppers, cut lengthwise into ½-inch-wide strips

1 large bulb fennel, stalks discarded, bulb cut lengthwise into ½-inch-thick slices

1 tablespoon olive oil

8 large cherry tomatoes, halved

1 to 2 tablespoons balsamic vinegar

Salt and black pepper

Preheat the grill to medium.

Arrange the scallions, bell peppers, and fennel on a grill topper. Brush lightly with the oil.

Grill for 7 to 8 minutes, or until the vegetables are just beginning to char. Scatter the cherry tomato halves over the vegetables and continue grilling for 3 to 4 minutes, or until the tomatoes are softened and the fennel and peppers are crisp-tender.

Transfer the vegetables to a large serving plate and sprinkle lightly with 1 tablespoon of the vinegar. Season lightly with salt and black pepper. Taste for seasoning and add another tablespoon of vinegar if desired.

MAKES 4 SERVINGS

ROASTED JERUSALEM ARTICHOKES

Funny, but Jerusalem artichokes, aren't from Jerusalem, and they're not artichokes. They are small tubers that resemble gnarly potatoes. Also called sunchokes, they have a nutty taste when cooked.

1 pound Jerusalem artichokes, well scrubbed

2 tablespoons olive oil

1 sprig fresh thyme or ½ teaspoon dried

2 bay leaves

Salt

Preheat the oven to 400°F.

In a large roasting pan, toss the Jerusalem artichokes with the oil, thyme, and bay leaves. Roast for 45 minutes, tossing occasionally, until golden brown and tender. Discard the bay leaves. Season with salt to taste. Serve hot.

MAKES 4 SERVINGS

SAUTÉED JICAMA

Jicama is crisp and sweet; it resembles a potato in appearance. When shopping for jicama, choose medium-size bulbs (less than 2 fists together), without any bruising. Here it is cut into matchsticks and sautéed, which makes it both sweet and buttery. It also lends itself to being eaten raw and can stand in for water chestnuts in stir-fries, soups, and salads.

- 2 tablespoons olive oil
- 1 pound jicama, peeled, halved, and cut into thick matchsticks
- 1 carrot, cut into thick matchsticks
- 1 clove garlic, thinly sliced
- ⅓ cup water
- Salt

In a large skillet, heat the oil over medium heat. Add the jicama, carrot, and garlic, and cook, tossing frequently, until the jicama is golden brown around the edges, about 7 minutes.

Add the water and cook until the jicama and carrot are crisp-tender and the water has evaporated, 3 to 5 minutes. Season with salt to taste.

MAKES 4 SERVINGS

SAUTÉED RUSSIAN KALE WITH BACON

Russian kale has flatter leaves than regular kale, and the stems and veins are reddish or purple.

- 1 pound Russian kale, tough stems removed
- 3 slices bacon, cut crosswise into ¼-inch pieces
- 1 large red onion, finely chopped
- 4 cloves garlic, minced
- ¼ teaspoon red pepper flakes
- 1 cup water
- ½ teaspoon salt
- ¼ teaspoon black pepper

In a large steamer, cook the kale (in batches if necessary) until wilted, about 3 minutes. Set the kale aside.

In a large skillet, cook the bacon over medium heat until crisp. With a slotted spoon, transfer the bacon to paper towels.

Add the onion and garlic to the pan, and cook until the onion is soft, about 7 minutes. Stir in the red pepper flakes.

Add the kale, bacon, water, salt, and black pepper. Cook until the kale is tender, about 4 minutes.

MAKES 4 SERVINGS

BRAISED COLLARDS & CORN

Sturdy collard greens soften and mellow when cooked slowly with the meaty, salty flavors of ham.

- 4 teaspoons olive oil
- 6 scallions, thinly sliced
- 2 cloves garlic, finely chopped
- 10 cups firmly packed collard greens, torn into bite-size pieces, or 2 packages (10 ounces each) frozen collard greens
- ¼ pound smoked ham or turkey, cut into ¼-inch dice
- ½ cup chicken broth, store-bought or homemade (page 172)
- ½ teaspoon pepper
- ½ teaspoon oregano
- ¼ teaspoon salt
- 1½ cups frozen corn kernels
- 4 teaspoons balsamic or red wine vinegar, plus more for the table

In a large skillet, heat the oil over medium heat. Add the scallions and garlic, and cook until the scallions are soft, about 3 minutes.

Add the greens, stirring to coat. Add half of the ham, the broth, pepper, oregano, and salt, and cook, partially covered, until the greens are wilted and very tender, about 30 minutes.

Stir in the corn and remaining ham, and cook just until heated through. Stir in the vinegar and serve the greens with their cooking liquid. Pass additional vinegar at the table.

MAKES 4 SERVINGS

MUSTARD GREENS WITH DILL & LEMON

Wonderfully pungent, mustard greens are a favorite in Chinese cuisine, which is probably why they taste so good with soy sauce.

- 2 tablespoons olive oil
- 1 medium onion
- 1 pound fresh mustard greens, chopped, or 2 packages (10 ounces each) frozen mustard greens, thawed and chopped
- ¼ cup lemon juice
- 2 tablespoons lower-sodium soy sauce
- 1 tablespoon snipped fresh dill
- Pepper

In a large skillet, heat the oil over medium heat. Add the onion and cook until softened.

Add the mustard greens and stir to mix. Reduce to a simmer, cover, and gently steam for 15 minutes.

Add the lemon juice, soy sauce, dill, and pepper to taste, and steam 10 minutes until the greens are tender, about 1 minute.

MAKES 4 TO 6 SERVINGS

WARM LEEKS WITH LEMON-MUSTARD DRESSING

Leeks are the sophisticated member of the onion family. Their flavor is mild, with a slight earthiness. Make sure to clean them well, as they can be quite gritty.

- 1 bunch leeks (3 to 4), dark green tops discarded
- 1 tablespoon lemon juice
- 1 tablespoon olive oil
- ½ teaspoon Dijon mustard
- ¼ teaspoon salt

Cut the leeks in half lengthwise, then cut into 2-inch lengths. Place in a large bowl of cool water and swish them around. Let them sit a minute, then using your hands, scoop the leeks out, without agitating the water (the grit will sink to the bottom of the bowl). Repeat 2 or 3 times, until the water is clear.

Bring a large skillet of salted water to a simmer. Add the leeks and cook until just tender, 7 to 10 minutes. Timing will vary depending upon the thickness of the leeks. Drain well.

Meanwhile, in a large bowl, whisk together the lemon juice, oil, mustard, and salt.

Add the drained, but still warm, leeks to the dressing and toss to combine. Serve at room temperature.

MAKES 4 SERVINGS

SAVORY LEEK & SOURDOUGH BREAD PUDDING

Combining the ingredients in the baking dish and refrigerating for 6 hours makes a lighter, fluffier bread pudding because it gives the bread time to soak up all the custard before baking.

- 3 tablespoons butter
- 1 cup thinly sliced leeks (white and pale green parts only), well washed
- 4 large eggs
- 2 cups half-and-half
- ½ teaspoon salt
- ¼ teaspoon pepper
- 8 ounces whole wheat sourdough bread, crust removed, cut into small cubes
- 1 ½ cups shredded Fontina cheese (6 ounces)
- ⅓ cup grated Parmesan cheese

Butter an 8-inch round or square baking dish. Set aside.

In a medium skillet, melt 2 tablespoons of the butter over medium-high heat. Add the leeks and cook, stirring occasionally, until limp and tender and just beginning to brown slightly, 3 to 4 minutes. Remove from the heat.

In a large bowl, whisk together the eggs, half-and-half, salt, and pepper until smooth. Stir in the cooked leeks and bread cubes. Allow the bread to absorb the egg mixture for a few minutes.

Spoon one-third of the bread mixture into the baking dish and sprinkle with half of the Fontina. Top with another one-third of the bread mixture and the remaining Fontina. Top with the remaining bread mixture and sprinkle with the Parmesan. Dot with the remaining 1 tablespoon butter. Cover the bread pudding with plastic wrap and refrigerate for at least 6 hours, or overnight.

Remove the pudding from the refrigerator and preheat the oven to 350°F. Bake uncovered on the middle rack of the oven for 1 hour, or until the pudding is puffed and golden brown and a skewer inserted into the middle comes out clean.

Let the pudding cool slightly before serving. Serve warm.

MAKES 6 SERVINGS

GLAZED KOHLRABI

Sometimes referred to as turnip cabbage, kohlrabi has a mildly sweet cabbage flavor. This simple preparation highlights its sweetness.

- 3 medium kohlrabi (1 pound) peeled, halved lengthwise, and sliced ¼ inch thick
- 2 tablespoons butter
- 2 teaspoons sugar
- ¼ teaspoon salt
- ⅛ teaspoon nutmeg
- ½ cup water

In a large skillet, combine the kohlrabi, butter, sugar, salt, nutmeg, and water. Bring to a boil over high heat. Reduce the heat to medium and cook, uncovered, tossing occasionally, until the kohlrabi is tender and glazed and no water remains, about 15 minutes.

MAKES 4 SERVINGS

MARINATED MUSHROOMS WITH CORIANDER

The mushrooms need to marinate overnight, so plan accordingly.

- 4 tablespoons olive oil
- ½ Spanish onion, chopped
- 4 teaspoons ground coriander
- 2 cups dry white wine
- 1 bouquet garni (page 185)
- 2 pounds white button mushrooms, stems discarded
- 1 cup dried currants or raisins
- 3 tablespoons lemon juice
- 1½ tablespoons coriander seeds
- 10 large plum tomatoes, seeded and pureed
- 1 tablespoon tomato paste

Salt and pepper

½ pound chanterelles or other wild mushrooms (or more button mushrooms), stems discarded

1 tablespoon snipped chives, for garnish

In a saucepan, heat 3 tablespoons of the olive oil over medium heat. Add the onion and ground coriander, and cook until the onion softens, about 5 minutes.

Add the wine and bouquet garni, and bring to a boil. Add the button mushrooms, currants, lemon juice, and coriander seeds. Stir. Return to a boil, cover, and simmer until the mushrooms are tender, 5 to 10 minutes. Reserving the liquid, drain the mushrooms. Discard the bouquet garni.

Return the reserved cooking liquid to the pan. Add the tomatoes and tomato paste, and cook until fairly thick, about 15 minutes.

Add the cooked mushroom mixture and salt and pepper to taste to the tomato mixture, and cook until heated through. Cover and marinate in the refrigerator overnight.

Before serving, reheat the marinated mushrooms. In a separate saucepan, heat the remaining 1 tablespoon oil. Add the chanterelles and cook until tender. Add the marinated mushrooms to the chanterelles and toss. Serve garnished with chives.

MAKES 4 SERVINGS

LEMON-GRILLED PORTOBELLOS

Removing the gills from the portobellos reduces the amount of gritty black liquid the mushrooms exude as they cook. Just use a teaspoon to scrape the gills out of the caps.

3 tablespoons extra-virgin olive oil

1 tablespoon lemon juice

1 clove garlic, minced

¼ teaspoon honey

¼ teaspoon salt

⅛ teaspoon pepper

6 large (3- to 4-inch) portobello mushrooms, gills removed if desired

2 tablespoons chopped flat-leaf parsley

½ teaspoon grated lemon zest

In a small screw-top jar, combine the oil, lemon juice, garlic, honey, salt, and pepper. Cover and shake to mix well.

Place the mushrooms on a rimmed baking sheet. Pour the dressing over both sides of the mushrooms and rub it in. Let stand for 10 to 15 minutes.

Meanwhile, preheat the grill to medium-high. In a small bowl, blend the parsley and lemon zest.

Grill the mushrooms rounded-side up for 5 to 6 minutes, until they start to become tender. Turn and grill 3 to 5 minutes longer, until the mushrooms are tender in the center. Served hot, sprinkled with the parsley mixture.

MAKES 6 SERVINGS

OKRA WITH TOMATOES, GINGER & BASIL

The ginger in this vibrant dish will convert even the biggest okra skeptic. Cooking small okra pods whole keeps them from becoming viscous and mushy.

2 tablespoons vegetable oil

2 cloves garlic, chopped

1 tablespoon chopped fresh ginger

1 shallot, chopped

¼ teaspoon red pepper flakes

1 pound small fresh okra, untrimmed

1½ cups yellow grape tomatoes, halved
½ cup loosely packed fresh basil leaves
Coarse salt and black pepper

In a heavy skillet, combine the oil, garlic, ginger, shallot, and pepper flakes, and cook over medium heat, stirring, for 1 minute.

Add the okra and cook, covered, until just tender, about 10 minutes.

Add the tomatoes and cook for 1 minute. Remove from the heat and stir in the basil. Season to taste with salt and black pepper.

MAKES 6 SERVINGS

PEARL ONIONS AGRODOLCE

Agrodolce is the Italian word for sweet and sour, and it's a common way to cook onions.

1 tablespoon olive oil
1 pound frozen pearl onions, thawed
2 tablespoons turbinado or light brown sugar
½ teaspoon salt
½ cup chicken broth, store-bought or homemade (page 172)
⅓ cup red wine vinegar
1 tablespoon butter
2 tablespoons chopped parsley
2 tablespoons chopped fresh mint

In a large skillet, heat the oil over medium heat. Add the pearl onions and cook, shaking the pan, until nicely coated, about 2 minutes.

Sprinkle the brown sugar and salt over the onions, and continue cooking and shaking the pan until the sugar is melted and bubbly, about 3 minutes.

Add the broth and vinegar, reduce to a simmer, and cook until the sauce is slightly syrupy and the onions are tender, about 4 minutes. Remove from the heat and stir in the butter, parsley, and mint.

MAKES 4 SERVINGS

PARSNIPS À L'ORANGE

The mild sweetness of parsnips is enhanced by a honey-orange glaze.

1 pound parsnips, peeled and cut into chunks
2 teaspoons grated orange zest
¾ cup orange juice
2 tablespoons butter
1 tablespoon honey
½ teaspoon salt
Pinch of cinnamon

In a medium saucepan, combine the parsnips, orange zest, orange juice, butter, honey, salt, and cinnamon. Cover tightly and cook over medium heat until the parsnips are tender, about 15 minutes. If there is still liquid in the pan, uncover and stir until the parsnips are glazed and the liquid has evaporated.

MAKES 4 TO 6 SERVINGS

CREAMY PARSNIP PUREE

Slightly sweet, starchy parsnips make a heavenly mash when enriched with butter and cream. If you want to make a slightly lower-fat version, use whole milk instead of cream and cut the butter to 2 tablespoons.

2 pounds parsnips, peeled and cut into 2-inch chunks
¼ cup (½ stick) butter

½ cup light cream

Salt and pepper

In a medium saucepan, combine the parsnips with cold water to cover. Bring to a boil over high heat. Reduce the heat to low and simmer until the parsnips are tender, 10 to 15 minutes. Drain and transfer to the bowl of an electric mixer.

Meanwhile, in a small saucepan, combine the butter and cream, and cook over medium heat until the butter is melted, 1 to 2 minutes.

Add the cream mixture to the parsnips and mix on medium speed until the mixture is smooth, about 1 minute. Season with salt and pepper to taste.

MAKES 6 SERVINGS

BRAISED PEAS WITH CROUTONS

To wash the leeks, trim the root ends, cut off the green tops, and chop. Place in a large bowl of cold water and swish around. The leeks will float and the grit will fall to the bottom of the bowl. Scoop out the leeks and repeat the rinsing process until the water in the bowl is clear. To dry the leeks well for sautéing, spin them in a salad spinner.

2 tablespoons olive oil

2 leeks (white parts only) or 1 medium onion, chopped

2 cups shredded iceberg lettuce

2 pounds shelled fresh peas or 2 packages (10 ounces each) frozen peas

2 tablespoons water

1 tablespoon minced fresh mint or 1 teaspoon dried

1 tablespoon minced fresh basil or 1 teaspoon dried

½ teaspoon salt

¼ teaspoon pepper

2 tablespoons butter

1 cup soft multi-grain bread cubes (2 slices)

In a medium skillet, heat the oil over medium heat. Add the leeks and cook until soft.

Add the lettuce, peas, and water. (If using frozen peas, omit the water.) Cover and simmer until the peas are tender, 10 to 15 minutes (5 minutes for frozen). Stir in the mint, basil, salt, and pepper, and simmer for 1 minute.

Meanwhile, in a medium skillet, melt the butter over medium heat. Add the bread cubes and sauté until toasted and golden, about 5 minutes.

Serve the peas topped with the croutons.

MAKES 6 SERVINGS

THAI-STYLE SUGAR SNAPS

Mint and basil are common companions in Thai cooking, but you could easily make this with all basil if you prefer.

1½ pounds sugar snap peas, strings removed

¼ cup chopped fresh mint

¼ cup chopped fresh basil

1 tablespoon olive oil

1 tablespoon lime juice

¾ teaspoon salt

In a steamer, cook the sugar snaps until crisp-tender, 5 to 10 minutes (depending on their size and age).

Transfer the hot sugar snaps to a large bowl and add the mint, basil, oil, lime juice, and salt. Toss to combine.

MAKES 4 SERVINGS

SUGAR SNAPS, RADISHES & EDAMAME WITH LEMON BUTTER

Edamame, or young soybeans, are available in large supermarkets. When fresh green peas are in season in the spring, use them instead.

1 pound sugar snap peas, strings removed

1 cup shelled frozen edamame or fresh green peas

4 teaspoons extra-virgin olive oil

2 tablespoons minced shallot

1 bunch radishes, thinly sliced

1 tablespoon butter

2 teaspoons finely grated lemon zest

Salt and pepper

In a large pot of boiling salted water, cook the sugar snaps and edamame or peas for 5 minutes. Drain under cold running water.

In a large skillet, heat the oil over medium heat. Add the shallot and cook until soft, 2 to 3 minutes.

Add the radishes and cook until just tender, 2 to 3 minutes.

Add the snap peas and edamame, and cook to heat through. Add the butter, zest, and salt and pepper to taste. Cook, stirring, until the butter melts.

MAKES 6 SERVINGS

MIXED SWEET PEPPER & ONION RAGOUT

This versatile ragout of vegetables can be served as a side dish. Or double the recipe and sprinkle it with crumbled goat cheese for a satisfying meatless main course.

2 tablespoons olive oil

1 pound onions, cut lengthwise into ½-inch-thick wedges

3 large bell peppers (mixed colors), cut lengthwise into ½-inch-wide strips

1 cup dry red wine

¼ cup dark or golden raisins

1 teaspoon brown sugar

½ teaspoon salt

Pepper

Dash of red wine vinegar

In a Dutch oven, heat the oil over medium heat. Add the onions and cook until translucent, about 5 minutes.

Stir in the bell peppers, wine, raisins, and brown sugar, and bring to a boil over high heat. Reduce the heat to low and cook, uncovered, until the mixture is soft and the wine is reduced to a syrup-like consistency, 45 minutes to 1 hour.

Remove the pan from the heat. Season with the salt, and pepper to taste, and a dash of vinegar.

MAKES 4 SERVINGS

ROASTED NEW POTATOES WITH PARMESAN

Taking off a thin strip of the potato peel is just for looks, so you can skip it if you'd like.

1½ pounds small red potatoes

1 tablespoon extra-virgin olive oil

3 cloves garlic, peeled and halved

¾ teaspoon rosemary

½ teaspoon sage

1½ teaspoons grated lemon zest

½ teaspoon salt

¼ cup grated Parmesan cheese

Preheat the oven to 400°F.

With a vegetable peeler, peel a thin band around the circumference of each potato. In a large pot of boiling water, cook the potatoes for 5 minutes. Drain.

Meanwhile, in a large roasting pan, combine the oil, garlic, rosemary, and sage. Roast until the garlic and herbs are fragrant and the oil is hot, about 4 minutes.

Stir in the potatoes, lemon zest, and salt, and roast for 20 minutes, turning occasionally, for 20 minutes, or until the potatoes are crisp, golden, and tender. Sprinkle the Parmesan over the potatoes and roast for 2 minutes longer, or just until the cheese is melted and golden brown.

MAKES 4 SERVINGS

HERB-ROASTED POTATO WEDGES

Roasted potato wedges are a great alternative to deep-fried steak fries.

6 large russet (baking) potatoes, quartered

6 medium onions, quartered

⅓ cup vegetable oil

2 teaspoons Italian herb seasoning, store-bought or homemade (page 407)

1 teaspoon salt

½ teaspoon pepper

Preheat the oven to 375°F.

Place the potatoes and onions in a shallow roasting pan. Drizzle with the oil and sprinkle with the Italian herb seasoning, salt, and pepper. Stir the vegetables to coat with the oil and seasonings. Roast for 1 hour, turning occasionally to keep the vegetables from sticking to the bottom of the pan, until fork-tender.

MAKES 6 SERVINGS

GARLIC MASHED POTATOES

The best way to mash potatoes is the old-fashioned way, with a potato masher. It produces the most delicate results.

6 medium russet (baking) potatoes, peeled and quartered

6 large cloves garlic, peeled

3 tablespoons butter

1 teaspoon salt

¼ teaspoon pepper

1 cup warm milk

In a 6-quart saucepan, combine the potatoes, garlic, and enough water to cover. Bring to a boil over high heat, reduce to a simmer, and cook until the potatoes are very tender, 20 to 25 minutes. Drain and transfer to a bowl.

With a potato masher, coarsely mash the potatoes and garlic. Mash in the butter, salt, and pepper. Gradually mash in the warm milk until the potatoes are light and fluffy.

MAKES 6 TO 8 SERVINGS

SMASHED NEW POTATOES WITH SCALLIONS

Try this versatile recipe with baby Yukon Gold potatoes or thin-skinned California long whites. You could also add a cheesy touch with a sprinkling of grated Parmesan, shredded Cheddar, or crumbled feta or mild goat cheese.

1½ pounds small red potatoes, cut into 1-inch chunks

1 large clove garlic, thinly sliced

Salt

2 tablespoons butter

4 scallions, thinly sliced

Pinch of pepper

In a large saucepan, combine the potatoes, garlic, water to barely cover, and a pinch of salt. Cover and bring to a boil over high heat. Reduce the heat to a simmer and cook, partially covered, until the potatoes are fork-tender, 10 to 12 minutes.

Reserving the cooking liquid, drain the potatoes and return to the saucepan. Cook, stirring, over medium heat to dry the potatoes (they'll start to look floury). Measure out and reserve ¾ cup of the cooking liquid, and discard the remainder.

Off the heat, mash the potatoes to a chunky texture in the saucepan with a potato masher. Cover and keep warm.

In a small skillet, melt the butter over medium heat. Add the scallions and cook, stirring often, until wilted, about 2 minutes. Stir the scallions into the potatoes. Add enough of the reserved cooking liquid to moisten the potatoes and beat with a wooden spoon until well mixed, adding more cooking liquid if needed. Stir in ⅛ teaspoon salt and the pepper.

MAKES 8 SERVINGS

YUKON GOLD POTATOES & SPINACH

Just a small amount of bacon (and bacon fat) contributes big flavor to this potato side dish.

- 1 slice bacon
- 1 tablespoon olive oil
- 1½ pounds Yukon Gold potatoes, peeled, halved lengthwise, and thinly sliced crosswise
- 2 cloves garlic, minced
- 4 cups baby spinach leaves
- 1 tablespoon red wine vinegar
- Salt and pepper

In a large skillet, cook the bacon over medium heat until crisp. Drain the bacon on paper towels.

Add the olive oil to the bacon drippings in the pan and heat briefly. Add the potato slices and cook over medium heat, turning once, until the potatoes are tender, 10 to 15 minutes.

Add the garlic and spinach, a handful at a time, and cook just until the spinach is wilted, 2 to 3 minutes.

Crumble the bacon and add it to the pan. Stir in the vinegar. Season with salt and pepper to taste.

MAKES 4 SERVINGS

MASHED RUTABAGA & CARROTS

Rutabaga, a member of the turnip family, is sometimes referred to as yellow turnip, Swedish turnip, or just swede.

- 1¾ pounds rutabaga, peeled, quartered, and thinly sliced
- 1 russet (baking) potato, peeled and thinly sliced
- ½ pound carrots, thinly sliced
- 5 cloves garlic, peeled
- 1 bay leaf
- ¾ teaspoon salt
- ½ teaspoon thyme
- ¼ teaspoon pepper
- 4 cups water
- 1 tablespoon olive oil
- ¼ cup grated Parmesan cheese

In a large saucepan, combine the rutabaga, potato, carrots, garlic, bay leaf, ¼ teaspoon of the salt, the thyme, pepper, and water. Bring to a boil over medium heat and reduce to a simmer. Cover and cook until tender, about 30 minutes. Reserving ½ cup of the cooking liquid, drain the vegetables. Discard the bay leaf.

With a potato masher, mash the vegetables along with the reserved cooking liquid and the oil. Stir in the Parmesan and the remaining ½ teaspoon salt.

MAKES 4 SERVINGS

SAUTÉED SPINACH & PINE NUTS

Pine nuts are a bit of a luxury—you could easily make this with slivered almonds instead.

- 3 tablespoons olive oil
- 2 large cloves garlic, smashed and peeled
- ½ teaspoon red pepper flakes
- ¼ cup pine nuts
- 2 tablespoons sesame seeds
- 1 pound baby spinach leaves
- 2 tablespoons water
- ¼ teaspoon salt
- Lemon wedges, for serving

In a large, deep skillet or Dutch oven, heat the oil over medium heat. Add the garlic and red pepper flakes, and cook until the garlic is golden.

Discard the garlic. Add the pine nuts and sesame seeds to the oil and cook, stirring constantly, until lightly toasted, 1 to 2 minutes. Add the spinach, water, and salt. Cover and cook over high heat, tossing with a fork once or twice, just until wilted and tender, 4 to 5 minutes. Serve hot with lemon wedges.

MAKES 4 SERVINGS

VEGAN "CREAMED" SPINACH

Suavely rich without a whisper of butter or cream.

- 1 cup soft silken tofu
- 2 packages (10 ounces each) frozen whole-leaf spinach
- ½ cup water
- 1 teaspoon salt
- ½ teaspoon pepper
- ⅛ teaspoon nutmeg
- 1 cup plain soy milk

Line a colander with several thicknesses of paper towel. Add the tofu and set aside for 10 minutes to drain off excess liquid.

In medium saucepan, combine the spinach and water. Bring to a boil over high heat. Reduce the heat to medium-low, cover, and cook until just tender, 7 to 10 minutes.

Drain the spinach in a colander. Using the back of large spoon, press against the spinach to remove as much water as possible. (You should be able to remove at least ½ cup.)

Place the drained spinach in a food processor and process until almost smooth. Add the drained tofu, salt, pepper, and nutmeg, and process until smooth.

Add the soy milk and process until just combined. Serve hot (reheat if necessary).

MAKES 4 SERVINGS

BAKED ACORN SQUASH

Try this with golden acorn squash, or a combination of golden and regular green acorn squash.

- 3 medium acorn squashes
- ¼ cup (½ stick) butter
- ⅓ cup maple syrup
- ⅓ cup apple cider
- ½ teaspoon cinnamon
- ½ teaspoon ground ginger
- Salt and pepper
- ½ cup hulled pumpkin seeds (pepitas), toasted and coarsely chopped, for serving

Preheat the oven to 375°F.

Cut the squashes in half lengthwise and scoop out the seeds. Arrange the squashes, cut-side down, in an 11 × 15-inch shallow baking pan and add ¼ inch of hot water to the pan. Bake for 30 minutes.

Meanwhile, in a small saucepan, melt the butter.

Stir in the maple syrup, cider, cinnamon, and ginger. Bring to a boil over high heat, reduce to a simmer, and cook for 4 to 5 minutes.

Remove the squashes from the oven. Pour out the liquid from the baking pan and turn the squashes cut-side up. Sprinkle the squashes lightly with salt and pepper. Brush the butter mixture over the cut sides of the squash and then pour the rest into the cavities. Bake, basting occasionally with sauce, for 20 minutes, or until the squash is completely tender and the cut sides are nicely browned.

Served sprinkled with the pepitas.

MAKES 6 SERVINGS

APRICOT BAKED SQUASH: Use apricot nectar instead of apple cider and brown rice syrup instead of maple syrup.

ROASTED SQUASH & SHIITAKES

Kabodra squash or pumpkin would be great here. Look for them in pumpkin season in early Fall.

- 1/3 cup sun-dried tomatoes
- Boiling water
- 3 tablespoons olive oil
- 6 cloves garlic, sliced
- 6 cups cubed (1 inch) butternut squash
- 1/2 pound fresh shiitake mushrooms, stems discarded, caps thickly sliced
- 2 large Braeburn or other juicy red apples, unpeeled, cut into 1-inch chunks
- 1 teaspoon rosemary, crumbled
- 1/2 teaspoon salt
- 1/4 cup grated Parmesan cheese

In a small heatproof bowl, cover the sun-dried tomatoes with boiling water and let sit for 20 minutes to soften. Reserving the liquid, drain and sliver the tomatoes.

Preheat the oven to 400°F.

In a large roasting pan, combine the oil and garlic. Heat for 3 minutes in the oven. Add the sun-dried tomatoes and their soaking liquid, the squash, mushrooms, apples, rosemary, and salt, and toss to combine.

Roast for 30 minutes, tossing the vegetables every 10 minutes, until they are tender. Sprinkle the Parmesan on top and roast 5 minutes longer.

MAKES 4 SERVINGS

CIDER-ROASTED WINTER SQUASH

For easier peeling and cutting, prick the squash in several places with a knife, microwave on high power for 4 to 5 minutes, until the squash begins to steam a bit. Let sit until cool enough to handle, then cut and peel.

- 1 butternut squash (2 1/2 pounds)
- 3/4 cup apple cider
- 2 tablespoons butter, cut into bits
- 2 tablespoons turbinado or light brown sugar
- Salt and pepper

Preheat the oven to 375°F.

Halve the squash, cut it into 2- to 3-inch chunks, and peel. Butter a baking pan large enough to hold the cut squash in a single layer.

Place the squash in the pan. Pour the cider over the squash, then sprinkle with the butter and brown sugar.

Roast for 35 to 45 minutes, stirring once or twice, until the squash is tender.

MAKES 4 SERVINGS

LEMON-PEAR WINTER SQUASH: Use pear nectar instead of apple cider and add 1 tablespoon lemon juice.

SPAGHETTI SQUASH SPECIAL

This unusual squash, which pulls apart into strands when cooked, is baked alla Parmigiana—with mozzarella, tomato sauce, and Parmesan.

1 large spaghetti squash

1 pound part-skim mozzarella cheese, sliced

1 to 1½ cups tomato sauce

½ cup grated Parmesan cheese

Place the squash, whole, in a large pot and add water to cover. Bring to a boil, then reduce to a simmer, cover, and cook until the skin is easily pierced, about 30 minutes. Remove from the pot and allow to cool.

Preheat the oven to 350°F. Butter a 1½ to 2-quart baking dish.

When the squash is cool enough to handle, halve lengthwise and scoop out the seeds. With a fork, scrape the pulp from the shell and pull apart into spaghetti-like strands.

Arrange the squash, mozzarella, and tomato sauce in layers in the baking dish and sprinkle with the Parmesan. Bake for 30 minutes, or until the cheese has melted and the filling is piping hot.

MAKES 4 SERVINGS

PANKO-COATED SUMMER SQUASH

No need to stand at the stove frying; these strips of yellow squash are baked in a coating of crispy, crunchy panko crumbs.

½ cup unbleached all-purpose flour

1 large egg

1 tablespoon water

1¼ cups panko bread crumbs

½ teaspoon salt

½ teaspoon tarragon

4 teaspoons oil

1 pound summer squash, cut lengthwise ¼ -inch-thick slices

Preheat the oven to 400°F. Line a baking sheet with parchment paper.

Place the flour in a shallow bowl. In another shallow bowl, lightly beat the egg with the water until combined.

In a third, shallow bowl, combine the panko crumbs, salt, and tarragon. With a fork, stir in the oil until the panko is coated.

Dredge the squash slices in the flour, shaking off the excess. Next, dip them in the egg mixture , allowing the excess to drip off. Then dip in the panko mixture, pressing to help it adhere. Place on the parchment-lined baking sheet. Bake for 25 minutes, turning once, until the crust is crisp and golden and the squash is tender.

MAKES 4 SERVINGS

STUFFED SUMMER SQUASH

Serve these ricotta-stuffed squash halves as a side dish or as a first course at a dinner party.

6 small summer squash

1 tablespoon butter

1 tablespoon olive oil

1 cup finely diced onion

2 teaspoons minced garlic

2 large squash blossoms, slivered (optional)

1 cup whole-milk ricotta cheese

6 tablespoons grated Parmesan cheese

- 3 tablespoons plain dried whole wheat bread crumbs
- 1 large egg, beaten
- 2 tablespoons minced fresh marjoram or basil
- ½ teaspoon salt
- ⅛ teaspoon pepper

Preheat the oven to 375°F. Butter a 9 × 13-inch baking dish.

Halve the squashes lengthwise. Scrape out the seeds. Slice a little off the bottoms so they will rest flat, cut-side up.

In a skillet, heat the butter and oil over medium heat. Add the onion and garlic, and cook until soft. Add the squash blossoms (if using) and cook for 1 minute. Transfer to a bowl and let cool slightly.

Add the ricotta, 4 tablespoons of the Parmesan, 2 tablespoons of the bread crumbs, the egg, marjoram, salt, and pepper to the sautéed onion, and stir until blended. Spoon into the squash shells. Sprinkle the remaining 2 tablespoons Parmesan and the bread crumbs over the tops. Bake for 25 minutes, or until the squashes are tender. Broil for 3 minutes, or until the tops are golden.

MAKES 6 SERVINGS

SAVORY SWEET POTATO PIE

Sweet potatoes and cheddar are surprisingly suited to one another in this savory side dish pie.

- 6 medium sweet potatoes
- Multi-Grain Pie Dough (Single Crust), page 531
- 2 large eggs, beaten
- ½ cup milk
- 1 cup shredded sharp Cheddar cheese (4 ounces)
- 1 tablespoon flour
- ½ teaspoon salt
- ⅛ teaspoon ground ginger
- Pepper

In a 6-quart saucepan, combine the sweet potatoes with water to cover. Bring to a boil over high heat and reduce to a simmer. Cover and cook until fork-tender, 20 to 30 minutes. Drain. When cool enough to handle, peel the sweet potatoes and place in a large bowl.

Meanwhile, on a lightly floured surface, roll the dough out to a 12-inch round. Fit the dough into a 9-inch pie plate, pressing it into the bottom and up the side, without stretching the dough. With kitchen scissors, trim the edge, turn under and flute with your fingers (see "Making a Decorative Edge on a Pie," page 530) or crimp with a fork.

Preheat the oven to 375°F.

Mash the sweet potatoes, then add the eggs and milk, and mix well. In a small bowl, toss the Cheddar with the flour. Stir the cheese into the sweet potatoes. Season with the salt, ginger, and pepper to taste.

Scrape the sweet potato mixture into the pie shell. Bake for 45 to 50 minutes, or until a knife inserted in the center comes out clean.

MAKES 6 TO 8 SERVINGS

CURRIED SWEET POTATO PIE: Add ¼ teaspoon cayenne pepper to the pie dough and 1 teaspoon curry powder to the mashed sweet potatoes.

JAMAICAN SWEET POTATOES

These skillet-cooked sweet potatoes are sweet, tart, and spicy—earmarks of Caribbean cooking.

- 5 small sweet potatoes
- 3 tablespoons butter

- 3/4 teaspoon curry powder
- 2/3 cup coarsely chopped pecans
- 1/4 cup chopped onion
- 1/4 teaspoon grated lime zest
- 1 tablespoon lime juice
- 1/2 cup apple cider

In a medium saucepan, combine the sweet potatoes with water to just cover. Bring to a boil over high heat, reduce to a simmer, cover, and cook until just tender, about 30 minutes. Drain and let cool slightly.

Meanwhile, in a large skillet, heat 1 tablespoon of the butter and the curry powder over medium heat. Add the nuts and cook toasted, about 6 minutes. With a slotted spoon, transfer the nuts to a bowl. Set aside.

Add the remaining 2 tablespoons butter to the skillet and melt. Add the onion and cook until soft. Stir in the lime zest, lime juice, and cider.

When the sweet potatoes are cool enough to handle, peel, halve lengthwise, and cut into 1/2-inch slices.

Add the sweet potatoes to the skillet with the onion mixture. Cover and cook over low heat for 5 minutes. Stir in the pecans.

MAKES 6 SERVINGS

BAKED SWEET POTATOES & APPLES

Here's a healthy take on classic candied sweet potatoes, with most of the sweetness coming from the sweet potatoes, apples, raisins, and pineapple juice. A mere 1 tablespoon of sugar is added to the mix.

- 4 medium sweet potatoes, peeled and sliced
- 4 small tart apples, sliced
- 1/2 cup raisins
- Salt
- 1/4 cup pineapple juice
- 3 tablespoons butter, melted
- 1 tablespoon brown sugar

Preheat the oven to 350°F. Butter a 2-quart baking dish.

Arrange the sweet potatoes, apples, and raisins in alternate layers in the dish, seasoning lightly with salt as you layer.

In a small bowl, stir together the pineapple juice, butter, and brown sugar. Pour over the sweet potatoes and apples. Cover and bake for 30 minutes, or until the sweet potatoes are cooked through.

MAKES 6 TO 8 SERVINGS

ROSEMARY SWEET POTATO WEDGES

Skip the home fries and try these sweet potato wedges instead. Baked in the oven, they are packed with beta-carotene and are lower in fat than a fried potato—but still have a satisfyingly crisp skin.

- 2 tablespoons butter
- 2 tablespoons olive oil
- 1 tablespoon chopped fresh rosemary or 2 teaspoons dried
- 3 medium sweet potatoes
- 1 teaspoon salt
- 1/4 teaspoon pepper

Preheat the oven to 450°F.

In a small saucepan, melt the butter with the oil over medium heat. Stir in the rosemary.

Cut the sweet potatoes lengthwise into 1 1/2-inch-thick wedges and place in a large bowl. Season with the salt and pepper, and drizzle with the rosemary mixture. Toss gently.

Arrange the wedges on a large baking sheet in a single layer so they don't touch. Bake in the upper third of the oven for 20 minutes, turning once, or until softened and lightly browned. Season again with salt and pepper, and carefully remove from the sheet (the wedges are relatively fragile after cooking).

MAKES 4 SERVINGS

HOOSIER FRIED GREEN TOMATOES

Just for fun, try making this with blue cornmeal.

- **1 cup cornmeal**
- **1½ teaspoons pepper**
- **1 teaspoon salt**
- **6 large green tomatoes, cut into ½-inch slices**
- **6 tablespoons butter**
- **½ cup heavy cream**
- **1 tablespoon minced fresh basil (optional)**

In a shallow bowl, combine the cornmeal, pepper, and salt. Dip the tomato slices into the cornmeal mixture.

In a large heavy skillet, melt the butter over medium heat. When hot, add the tomato slices, in batches if necessary. Reduce the heat to medium-low and cook slowly until browned on one side. Turn carefully and cook until the inside is tender and the second side is browned. Transfer to a warm serving dish.

Add the cream to the pan drippings and stir. Cook, stirring constantly, until slightly thickened. Pour over the tomatoes. Sprinkle with basil, if desired.

MAKES 4 TO 6 SERVINGS

OVEN-ROASTED TOMATOES

In the dead of winter, when tomatoes aren't at their best, this method of cooking brings out their sweetness.

- **10 plum tomatoes (2 pounds), halved lengthwise**
- **2 tablespoons olive oil**
- **1 teaspoon herbes de Provence, store-bought or homemade (below)**
- **½ teaspoon salt**

Preheat the oven to 325°F. Line a rimmed baking sheet with foil.

In a large bowl, toss the tomatoes with the oil, herbs, and salt. Place the tomatoes, cut-side up, on the baking sheet. Bake for 2 ½ hours, or until the tomatoes have collapsed on themselves and are tender. Serve warm, at room temperature, or chilled.

MAKES 20 TOMATO HALVES

HERBES DE PROVENCE

- **1 teaspoon thyme**
- **1 teaspoon rosemary**
- **1 teaspoon marjoram**
- **1 teaspoon savory**
- **½ teaspoon oregano**
- **½ teaspoon lavender**
- **½ teaspoon tarragon**
- **½ teaspoon chervil**
- **2 bay leaves, crumbled**

SPICED TURNIPS & APPLES

Turnips, though pungent, definitely have their sweet side, which comes out in this gently spiced sauté.

- 2 tablespoons butter
- 1 tablespoon vegetable oil
- ½ teaspoon black or yellow mustard seeds
- ½ teaspoon cinnamon
- ¼ teaspoon pepper
- 3 medium white turnips, peeled and diced
- ½ teaspoon salt
- 2 apples, peeled and diced

In a large skillet, heat the butter, oil, mustard seeds, cinnamon, and pepper over medium-low heat. Add the turnips, sprinkle with the salt, and toss to coat. Increase the heat to medium and cook, stirring, until the turnips take on some color.

Add the apples and cook for 2 minutes. Cover and steam for 5 minutes. Uncover and cook until the turnips are tender, 3 to 5 minutes.

MAKES 6 SERVINGS

SPICED RUTABAGA & PEARS: Use 1 pound rutabaga instead of the white turnips and Bosc pears instead of the apples. Add 2 teaspoons lemon juice when you cook the pears.

ZUCCHINI PANCAKES

Sprinkling the zucchini with a little salt before cooking helps get rid of the some of the moisture in the vegetable.

- 2 cups coarsely grated zucchini
- Salt
- 2 large eggs, beaten
- 1 cup shredded Jarlsberg cheese (4 ounces)
- ½ medium onion, grated
- ½ cup whole wheat flour
- 1 teaspoon grated lemon zest
- ¼ teaspoon curry powder
- ¼ teaspoon pepper
- Oil, for the griddle

Place the zucchini in a colander and sprinkle very lightly with salt. Toss to distribute. Place the colander in a bowl or the sink to drain for about 30 minutes.

Squeeze the zucchini dry and place in a bowl. Add the eggs, Jarlsberg, onion, flour, lemon zest, curry powder, and pepper, and blend well.

Preheat a griddle and brush lightly with oil.

Spoon the batter by about ⅓ cupfuls onto the griddle and cook until the cakes are browned on both sides, 5 to 10 minutes.

MAKES 10 PANCAKES

SPICY ZUCCHINI PANCAKES: Use pepper Jack cheese instead of Jarlsberg. Use orange zest instead of lemon zest.

GRILLED VEGETABLES WITH GINGER-LIME MARINADE

Not only is this marinade great for vegetables, it is also perfect for shrimp or scallops (it makes enough to coat about 2 pounds). If you can't find bottled ginger juice, make your own (see "Making Ginger Juice," page 379). You'll need to squeeze about ⅓ cup of grated fresh ginger to get 2 tablespoons of juice.

- 1 teaspoon grated lime zest
- 3 tablespoons lime juice
- 2 tablespoons bottled ginger juice
- 4 teaspoons olive oil

- 2 teaspoons maple sugar or turbinado sugar
- ½ teaspoon salt
- 1 zucchini (8 ounces), cut into ½-inch chunks
- 1 yellow squash (8 ounces), cut into ½-inch chunks
- 1 large red bell pepper, cut into 2-inch pieces
- 1 large red onion, halved and cut into 1-inch wedges

In a large bowl, whisk together the lime zest, lime juice, ginger juice, oil, sugar, and salt.

Add the zucchini, yellow squash, bell pepper, and onion, and toss gently to coat with the marinade. Let stand for 30 minutes at room temperature.

Preheat the grill to medium. On eight 10-inch skewers, alternately thread the zucchini, yellow squash, pepper, and onion. Grill the vegetables for 10 minutes, turning as they color until they are tender, about 10 minutes. Use any remaining marinade as a baste.

MAKES 4 SERVINGS

ROASTED ROOT VEGETABLES WITH THYME

Chioggia beets, also called candy-stripe beets, are striped magenta and white.

- 2 medium Chioggia beets, peeled
- 2 medium unpeeled white turnips
- 2 medium unpeeled Yukon Gold potatoes
- 2 medium carrots, peeled
- 2 medium parsnips, peeled
- 2 small yellow onions
- ¼ cup extra-virgin olive oil
- 3 teaspoons minced fresh thyme leaves, stems reserved
- 4 cloves garlic, smashed and peeled
- Salt and pepper

Cut the beets, turnips, and potatoes into 6 wedges each. Halve the carrots and parsnips lengthwise and then crosswise. Cut the onions into quarters.

Preheat the oven to 400°F.

In a small skillet, combine the oil, thyme stems, and garlic. Simmer over low heat for 5 minutes. Remove from the heat. Discard the thyme and garlic.

In a large bowl, toss the beets with 1 teaspoon of the oil mixture, 1 teaspoon of the thyme leaves, and salt and pepper to taste. Transfer to a large baking pan and arrange in an even layer. Roast for 15 minutes.

Meanwhile, use the same bowl to combine the turnips, potatoes, carrots, parsnips, onions, 2 tablespoons of the oil mixture, the remaining 2 teaspoons thyme, and salt and pepper to taste. Add the vegetables to the pan with the beets in an even layer and stir to combine. Continue to roast for 30 minutes, turning the vegetables once, until tender.

Transfer the vegetables to a serving platter. Drizzle with another 2 teaspoons of the oil mixture (you will have some left over) and season with salt and pepper to taste. Serve warm.

MAKES 6 SERVINGS

ROASTED MEDITERRANEAN VEGETABLES

If you've never tasted mellow roasted garlic before, you're in for a treat.

- **¾ pound carrots, cut into 3-inch pieces**
- **1 large red bell pepper, cut into ½-inch-wide pieces**
- **1 large yellow bell pepper, cut into ½-inch-wide pieces**
- **1 red onion, cut into eighths**
- **1 head garlic, divided into unpeeled cloves**
- **2 sprigs fresh rosemary**
- **2 sprigs fresh thyme**
- **5 tablespoons olive oil**
- **Salt and black pepper**
- **2 small zucchini, cut into 1-inch rounds**
- **2 small Japanese eggplant, unpeeled, cut into 1-inch chunks**

Preheat the oven to 400°F.

On a rimmed baking sheet, toss the carrots, bell peppers, onion, garlic, rosemary, and thyme with 3 tablespoons of the oil. Sprinkle lightly with salt and pepper. Roast for 15 minutes.

Meanwhile, in a small bowl, toss the zucchini and eggplant with the remaining 2 tablespoons oil and sprinkle with salt and pepper.

Add the zucchini and eggplant to the roasting pan and toss. Continue roasting for 20 to 25 minutes, until the vegetables are tender.

Squeeze the roasted garlic from their skins onto the vegetables and toss well to distribute.

MAKES 6 SERVINGS

Stir-Fried Bok Choy • *page 416*

Sugar Snaps, Radishes & Edamame with Lemon Butter • *page 429*

Panko-Coated Summer Squash (top) • *page 434*
Roasted Lemon-Herb Tofu (bottom) • *page 311*

Brussels Sprouts & Chestnuts with Bacon • *page 415*

Roasted Root Vegetables with Thyme • *page 440*

Cheddar & Prosciutto Biscuits with Rosemary (far left) ● *page* 578
Eight Grain Sprouted Wheat Bread (rear) ● *page* 557
Rye Quick Bread (right) ● *page* 571

Israeli Couscous with Lime & Mint (rear) • *page 458*
Orange-Pistachio Bulgur (front) • *page 457*

Beans, Grains & Rice

Dried Beans, Peas & Lentils

The proper preparation of dried beans is neither mysterious nor complicated. Though beans do require time to cook, they need little attention during the process. In fact, beans should not even be stirred very often as they cook, since too much disturbance will break their skins.

Before cooking, sort through the beans and remove any little stones or other debris and rinse well.

Preparing Dried Beans

Beans are a dried food so they must be rehydrated. A simple, no-fuss presoaking method is used for all legumes, except for split peas and lentils, which need no presoaking. Soaking begins the process of increasing the volume of the dried beans, which cooking then completes.

Overnight soak: Soak the beans in cold water that is three to four times their volume for 6 to 8 hours, or overnight. If you choose to soak the beans overnight, they should be refrigerated; otherwise, they might start to ferment. Before proceeding with cooking, remove any beans that float. (Beans that float indicate premature harvesting. The bean will "shrink" within its seed coat, and may become moldy or contain trapped dirt.)

Quick soak: An alternate method is to combine the beans and water to cover by 2 inches in a saucepan. Bring to a boil and cook the beans for 2 minutes, then remove from the heat and let the beans sit for 1 hour or more. Boiling ruptures the hard shells of the beans so the beans swell. Then they cook the same as they would after an overnight soak.

Bean Cooking Methods

Basic Method

After soaking beans, either cook them in the original soaking water or add fresh water. (Soybeans are an exception; the soaking water becomes bitter, so it must be drained and replaced.) Either way, make sure the beans are covered by at least 1 inch of water, then cover the pot and simmer over low heat.

If you must stir the beans to ensure even cooking, do so as little as possible, and use a wooden spoon to avoid breaking the beans' skins. Otherwise, no stirring is necessary.

Refer to the "A Guide for Cooking Dried Beans, Peas & Lentils" (opposite) for approximate cooking times. But note that the cooking times are subject to several variables—where the beans were grown, their age, the altitude of the cooking place, and the hardness of the water in which they are cooked—so it is difficult to be exact about it. Generally speaking, most beans will cook in 1½ to 2½ hours, with lentils and peas requiring less time, and chickpeas and soybeans requiring more. The times given in this chapter should therefore be regarded as approximate. Taste the beans after an appropriate amount of time has passed. When ready, they should be firm but tender, and not mealy. A simple test is to spoon out a few beans and blow on them; if the skins burst, the beans are sufficiently cooked.

Beans cook most efficiently by themselves: Sweeteners, fats, salt, and acids such as tomato or vinegar all harden the bean's skin and lengthen cooking time. If you're using them, if possible add them after the beans are tender. Do not add baking soda to the water to hasten the cooking process—it tends to destroy the B vitamins and can have an adverse effect on the taste of the beans.

Pressure-Cooker Method

Pressure-cooking greatly reduces the time it takes to cook beans. Soak the beans, using either the overnight or the quick-soak method, and place in the cooker with the water. The new generation of pressure cookers has multiple safeguards against the danger of explosion, but most manufacturers still advise filling the cooker only to a certain level to avoid possible clogging of the vent pipe by foam. Check the documentation that came with your cooker. (In addition, 1 tablespoon of vegetable oil added to the pot will prevent the contents from foaming up.) Follow the manufacturer's directions for sealing the cooker and bringing it to the desired pressure. Start to monitor the cooking time as soon as the pressure is reached.

Cook the beans as directed by the manufacturer. At the end of the cooking (or any time before that, if you want to check the contents), reduce the interior pressure by removing the cooker from the heat and letting it stand for about 5 minutes, until the pressure drops. The skins are less likely to break if the pressure is allowed to rise and fall gradually.

THE GAS PROBLEM

If the flatulence that sometimes follows eating dried beans concerns you, try this: Soak the dried beans in water for at least 3 hours. Throw away the soaking water and cook the beans in fresh water for at least 30 minutes. Discard the cooking water, add fresh water, and continue cooking until the beans are done. This process does lose some nutrients, but it rids the beans of some of their oligosaccharides, the culprits in the gas problem.

Preparing Dried Peas & Lentils

As for beans, sort through the peas or lentils for any small stones or debris, and rinse well. Lentils and split peas do not require any presoaking. Dried black-eyed peas can be cooked without soaking, though it won't hurt to give them a presoak. Whole dried peas, chickpeas, and pigeon peas, however, do benefit from presoaking. Refer to the table on the opposite page for amounts of water and cooking times.

A GUIDE TO COOKING DRIED BEANS, PEAS & LENTILS

The cooking times are for beans that have been presoaked (except lentils and split peas, which need no presoaking). Use the water amounts as general guidelines, but to be safe, make sure the beans are covered by 1 to 2 inches of water.

1 CUP DRIED BEANS	WATER (CUPS)	APPROXIMATE COOKING TIME	COOKED YIELD (CUPS)
ADZUKI	4	45-50 minutes	2½
ANASAZI	4	1½ hours	2½
APPALOOSA	4	1½ hours	2½
BLACK (TURTLE)	4	45-60 minutes	2½
CANARY	4	1½ hours	2½
CANNELLINI	4	1½ hours	2½
CHICKPEAS (GARBANZOS)	4	2 hours	3¼
CRANBERRY	4	1½ hours	2½
FAVA	4	45-60 minutes	2½
FLAGEOLETS	4	45-60 minutes	2¾
GREEK ELEPHANT	4	45 minutes	2½
KIDNEY	3	1½ hours	2½
LENTILS, GREEN OR BROWN	4	30 minutes	2¾
LENTILS, RED	3	20 minutes	2½
LENTILS, SMALL (BELUGA, PARDINA, FRENCH)	3	25 minutes	2½
LIMA	4	45-60 minutes	2½
LIMA, BABY	4	45-50 minutes	2½
MUNG	4	1½ hours	2½
PEAS, BLACK-EYED	4	1 hour	2½
PEAS, SPLIT (GREEN OR YELLOW)	3	35-40 minutes	2¼
PEAS, WHOLE	4	1 hour	2½
PEAS, PIGEON	4	1 hour	2½
PINTO	3	1½ hours	2
RED	4	45-60 minutes	2½
SOYBEANS	5	3 hours	2¾
WHITE (GREAT NORTHERN, MARROW, NAVY, PEA)	4	45-60 minutes	2½-3

USING CANNED BEANS

Although home-cooked beans are vastly preferable from the point of view of both texture and sodium levels, there are many brands of canned beans that are just fine. Use this chart as a rough guide to help you figure out how many cans of beans you need for the cooked beans called for in the recipes. Actual yields will vary with the brands, so read the label. Always be sure to drain the beans and rinse under cold running water to reduce sodium levels.

CAN SIZE	YIELD (DRAINED)
10.5 ounces	1¼ cups
15-16 ounces	1¾ cups
19 ounces	2 cups
29 ounces	3½ cups
40 ounces	4½ cups

Storing Cooked Beans, Peas & Lentils

Since preparing dried beans or peas is a lengthy procedure, cook what you want now and for some future meals all at once. Beans and peas freeze well and keep for as long as 5 months. Freeze the extra in several separate containers that you can thaw as needed. Remember to date the containers. Most peas and beans keep their shape and texture nicely, though lentils and split peas tend to become mushy.

Or freeze peas or beans in a way that will let you add small amounts to soups or salads, for example, use this method of freezing: Spread room-temperature cooked beans or peas in one layer on a rimmed baking sheet. Place the sheet in the freezer and leave until they are frozen solid. Scrape the frozen beans or peas into an airtight freezer container.

Grains

Grains are easy to prepare; they need only be cooked in liquid until swollen and tender. The same basic cooking method works with all the cereal grains. Just remember that they do expand in cooking. Millet and barley grow to three or four times their original volume, while other grains more than double—even triple—in volume. Plan to serve ½ cup of cooked grains per person for breakfast or as a side dish, and 1 cup of cooked grains for main-dish servings.

Grain Cooking Methods

Basic Method

Refer to the "A Guide to Cooking Grains" (page 447) to find the appropriate amount of cooking liquid and length of cooking time. Note that the cooking times in the chart start from when the grain is added to the boiling liquid.

1. Rinse the raw grain in cold water and drain well. This helps remove both grit and excess starch and starts the swelling process as well.

2. Bring the cooking liquid to a boil in a pot large enough to accommodate the increase in volume after cooking. Water, stock (meat, poultry, or vegetable), milk (dairy or soy), or juice (especially for breakfast cereals) may be used. The more flavorful the cooking liquid, the more flavorful the cooked grain will be.

3. Add the grain to the boil, and stir once.

4. Allow the liquid to return to a boil, then reduce the heat to the lowest possible setting. Cover and let the grain simmer slowly, until it is soft and the cooking liquid has been absorbed. This will take anywhere from 15 minutes for bulgur to 2 hours for wheat berries and the harder grains.

5. To determine if the grain is cooked, use the taste test: Well-cooked grain will be chewy but not pasty, tough, or hard. If not quite done, add a little more liquid, cover, and continue cooking.

Other Cooking Methods

For the time and attention required, the basic cooking method is the most efficient. However, there may be times when one of the following cooking methods better suits your needs:

Thermos method: All grains may be cooked by the thermos method. Place 1 cup of grain in a 1-quart thermos (preferably wide-mouthed) and add boiling water almost to the top, leaving a 1-inch headspace between the water and the stopper of the thermos. Using a long wooden spoon handle, stir the grain to distribute the water evenly. Close the thermos and let it stand for 8 to 12 hours. (For brown rice, add only 1½ cups of boiling water and let stand for only 8 hours.)

Pilaf method: Cooking time for the pilaf method is about the same as for the basic method. Brown rice, bulgur, barley, millet, and wild rice are especially good when cooked this way. Sauté the

TIPS FOR COOKING GRAINS

- Cook grain in a large, heavy-bottomed pan to avoid possible scorching.
- Too much stirring makes the grain gummy, so stir only as suggested—and use a fork.
- To attain distinct, separate cooked grains, add 1 tablespoon of vegetable oil or butter to the cooking water.
- For a creamier grain for porridge or pudding, do not heat the cooking liquid initially; instead, first combine it with the uncooked grain, then bring the mixture to a boil, cover, and cook.
- Cooked grain can be held in a covered pot off the heat until needed. It will hold its heat for quite a while.
- To enhance the flavor and shorten the cooking time, toast grain in a dry, medium-hot iron skillet, stirring constantly, until it has a pleasant fragrance and takes on a darker color. This also makes it easier to "crack" the grain by briefly grinding it in an electric blender. The cracked grain will cook move quickly.
- You may shorten the cooking time of hard grains such as wheat, rye, and triticale by bringing them to a boil in the required amount of water, letting them boil for 10 minutes, then soaking them for 8 to 12 hours in this same water. After soaking they may be cooked in the same water for 15 to 20 minutes and will be tender enough to eat.

---

grain, usually mixed with minced onion, in oil, and then add stock or water—approximately twice as much liquid as grain. Cook the grain, covered, over medium-low heat until the liquid has been absorbed and the grain is tender.

Egg method: Buckwheat is traditionally prepared by this method, which involves stirring a raw egg into the dry grain before adding stock or water and cooking until tender. This replaces the need for sautéing the buckwheat in oil and is done to keep the grains separate throughout the cooking process.

Oven method: Grains can bake in the oven to bring out their subtle nut flavor. If you are already using the oven to bake something else, you may consider this method so as to conserve energy. At 400°F, the grain will cook about the same length of time in the oven as with the basic stovetop method. Before putting it in the oven, sauté 1 cup grain in 1 tablespoon oil in an Dutch oven or flameproof baking dish for about 1 minute. Add the correct amount of water, then cover and bake until the grain is tender and all the water has been absorbed.

A GUIDE TO COOKING GRAINS

Grains that have their bran layers intact—whole-grain barley, wheat, rye, triticale, kamut, and spelt—should be soaked overnight to shorten their cooking time. If you don't soak, the cooking time will be longer by an hour or more. Also, most grains benefit from a standing time of about 10 minutes, with the pot cover still on, after they've been cooked.

1 CUP DRY GRAIN	WATER (CUPS)	APPROXIMATE COOKING TIME	COOKED YIELD (CUPS)
AMARANTH	3	20-25 minutes	2½
BARLEY, PEARLED	3	55 minutes	3
BUCKWHEAT GROATS	2	15 minutes	2½
CORNMEAL	4	25 minutes	3
FARRO, UNHULLED	3	2 hours	3⅔
FARRO, SEMIPEARLED	3	30 minutes	3
KAMUT	3	2 hours	2⅔
MILLET	3	45 minutes	3½
OATS, ROLLED	3	15 minutes	3½
OATS, STEEL-CUT	3	30-40 minutes	3½
QUINOA	2	12-15 minutes	3½
RICE, BLACK	2	30 minutes	3
RICE, BROWN	2	35-45 minutes	3
RICE, RED	2	20 minutes	3
RICE, WHITE	2	20 minutes	3
RICE, WILD	3	1 hour	4
RYE BERRIES	4	1 hour	2⅔
SORGHUM	3	45 minutes	3½
SPELT	3	2 hours	2⅔
TRITICALE	4	1 hour	2½
WHEAT, BERRIES	3	2 hours	2⅔
WHEAT, BULGUR	2	15-20 minutes	2½
WHEAT, CRACKED	2	25 minutes	2⅓

PARMESAN-CRUSTED ADZUKI BEAN PATTIES

There's nothing like the satisfying flavor of a crispy cheese crust, a nice counterpoint to the soft potato-bean patty mixture.

- 5 small russet (baking) potatoes
- 1 large egg
- 2 tablespoons butter
- ½ teaspoon salt
- ¼ teaspoon pepper
- 1 cup dried adzuki beans, soaked overnight, drained
- 3 tablespoons chopped parsley
- 1 cup grated Parmesan cheese
- ¼ cup vegetable oil

In a large pot of boiling salted water, cook the potatoes until tender. Remove with a slotted spoon. When cool enough to handle, peel the potatoes and transfer to a large bowl. Add the egg, butter, salt, and pepper, and mash together.

Meanwhile, add the beans to the pot of boiling water and cook, covered, until the beans are tender, 45 to 50 minutes. Drain.

Stir the beans and parsley into the potatoes and shape into 12 patties. Dredge the patties in the Parmesan, pressing the cheese onto all sides of the patties.

In a large skillet, heat the oil over medium-high heat. Add the patties and cook until golden brown, about 3 minutes per side.

MAKES 12 PATTIES

MUNG-BEAN PATTIES: Use dried mung beans instead of adzuki beans. Reduce the butter to 1½ tablespoons and add 1 teaspoon dark sesame oil to the mashed potatoes. Substitute minced scallions for the parsley.

ITALIAN BAKED BEANS

The next time you buy a hunk of Parmesan cheese, save the rind for this Italian-inspired bean dish. The rind will keep for several months in the freezer. If you don't have a rind, you can use grated Parmesan.

- 1 tablespoon olive oil
- 3 ounces pancetta or bacon, coarsely chopped
- 3 cloves garlic, slivered
- 4 cups cooked cannellini beans
- 1½ cups water
- ½ cup chopped fresh basil
- ½ cup tomato paste
- ¾ teaspoon salt
- 1 Parmesan cheese rind or ½ cup grated Parmesan

Preheat the oven to 325°F.

In a small Dutch oven or heavy ovenproof saucepan with a lid, heat the oil over medium heat. Add the pancetta and garlic, and cook until the pancetta is crisp and the garlic is tender, about 5 minutes.

Stir in the beans, water, basil, tomato paste, and salt. Tuck the cheese rind into the beans. Bring the mixture to a boil. Cover and transfer to the oven. Bake for 1 hour. Uncover and bake for 30 minutes, or until most of the liquid has been absorbed.

MAKES 6 SERVINGS

BAKED KIDNEY BEANS & SMOKED PORK

If you can't find smoked pork chops, use 4 ounces of bacon, diced, and ½ pound smoked turkey, cut into cubes. Add the bacon to the casserole when you start to cook the beans, and add the turkey when you would have added the pork.

- 1¼ cups dried kidney beans, soaked overnight, drained
- 1 medium onion, chopped
- 1 green bell pepper, chopped
- 2 tablespoons molasses
- ¾ teaspoon salt
- ½ teaspoon dry mustard
- ½ teaspoon chili powder
- Boiling water
- 2 smoked pork chops, cut into ½-inch pieces

Preheat the oven to 350°F.

In a 2-quart baking dish, combine the beans, onion, bell pepper, molasses, salt, mustard, chili powder and enough boiling water to just cover the beans.

Partially cover and bake for 1 hour 30 minutes. Stir in the pork and bake 30 minutes to 1 hour, or until the beans are tender. Add more boiling water if the beans seem too dry, but do not add so much as to make them soupy.

MAKES 4 SERVINGS

MEXICAN PINTO BEANS

If you like spicy food, you might want to upgrade from the jalapeño by using a pepper with a little more kick, like a serrano.

- 2 tablespoons peanut oil
- 1½ cups sliced red onions
- 1 fresh jalapeño pepper, minced
- 2 large cloves garlic, minced
- 1 large green bell pepper, cut into strips
- 2 teaspoons chili powder
- ½ teaspoon ground cumin
- ½ teaspoon salt
- 2 cups chopped plum tomatoes
- 2 cups cooked pinto beans
- 2 cups vegetable broth, store-bought or homemade (page 173), or water
- Chopped cilantro, for garnish (optional)

In a large skillet with a tight-fitting lid, heat the oil over medium heat. Add the onions, jalapeño, and garlic, and cook, stirring frequently, for 3 minutes.

Add the bell pepper, chili powder, cumin, and salt, and cook for 1 minute. Add the tomatoes, beans, and vegetable broth. Bring to a boil, stirring occasionally. Reduce to a simmer, cover, and cook for 30 minutes, to blend flavors.

Serve garnished with cilantro (if desired).

MAKES 4 TO 6 SERVINGS

NEW ENGLAND BAKED BEANS

The traditional baked bean recipe. If you can't find fatback, use 3 or 4 strips of bacon, cut in half, instead.

- 2 cups dried navy beans, soaked overnight, drained
- 2 medium onions, peeled
- 8 whole cloves
- 2 ounces fatback, cut into 2 pieces
- ¾ cup dark molasses
- 2 teaspoons dry mustard
- 1 teaspoon salt

In a medium pot, combine the beans with water to cover by 2 inches. Bring to a boil over high heat. Reduce the heat to a simmer and cook until the beans are tender, 45 minutes to 1 hour. Reserving the liquid, drain the beans.

Preheat the oven to 350°F.

Stud the onions with the cloves and place in a

4-quart deep baking dish or Dutch oven. Add the beans and fatback.

In a medium bowl, combine the reserved bean cooking liquid with the molasses, mustard, and salt. Add to the casserole. If there isn't enough liquid to come to 1 inch from the top of the dish, add water.

Cover and bake for 2 hours. Uncover and bake for 2 hours longer, or until the beans are cooked through but still moist. Add boiling water if necessary to keep the beans moist during baking.

MAKES 4 TO 6 SERVINGS

BOURBON BAKED BEANS

Kentucky bourbon and a touch of coffee make these baked beans extra special.

- 1 medium onion, minced
- 2 large cloves garlic, minced
- 1 cup ketchup
- ½ cup packed muscovado or dark brown sugar
- ½ cup chicken broth, store-bought or homemade (page 172)
- ¼ cup bourbon
- ¼ cup strong brewed coffee
- ¼ cup coarse-grained mustard
- 1 tablespoon Worcestershire sauce
- 1 teaspoon hot paprika
- 1 teaspoon coarse salt
- ½ teaspoon pepper
- 1 cup diced ham
- 14 cups cooked Great Northern beans
- 6 slices bacon

Preheat the oven to 350°F. Lightly oil a 9 × 13-inch glass or ceramic baking dish.

In a large bowl, mix together the onion, garlic, ketchup, brown sugar, broth, bourbon, coffee, mustard, Worcestershire, paprika, salt, and pepper. Fold in the ham and beans, and transfer to the baking dish.

Place the bacon strips across the top. Bake for 1 hour, or until the beans are thick and bubbling and the bacon is crisp. (If necessary, place the dish beneath the broiler to crisp the bacon.)

MAKES 12 SERVINGS

SAVORY BLACK BEANS

Either the chipotle or pasilla chili powder adds an interesting smoky heat to the beans without being too hot. If you prefer, you can substitute regular chili powder (chili seasoning) or simply leave it out.

- 1 generous cup (8 ounces) dried black beans, picked over and rinsed
- 6 cloves garlic, slivered
- 1 teaspoon oregano
- 1 tablespoon olive oil
- 1 large onion, finely chopped
- 1 red bell pepper, coarsely chopped
- 1 tablespoon tomato paste
- 1 teaspoon ground cumin
- ¾ teaspoon salt
- ½ teaspoon chipotle or pasilla chili powder
- 1 tablespoon red wine vinegar

Place the beans in a pot with cold water to cover by several inches. Bring to a boil and cook for 2 minutes. Remove from the heat, cover, and let stand 1 hour. Drain.

Return the beans to the pot with 3 cups of water, half the garlic, and ½ teaspoon of the oregano. Bring to a boil, reduce to a simmer, and cook, partially covered, until the beans are tender but not mushy, 45 minutes to 1 hour. (If the water is cooking off, add a little more.)

Meanwhile, in a medium skillet, heat the oil over medium heat. Add the remaining garlic, the onion, and bell pepper, and cook until the onion is tender, about 7 minutes. Stir in the tomato paste, cumin, salt, chili powder, and remaining ½ teaspoon oregano.

Transfer the mixture to the pot with the beans and bring to a boil. Reduce to a simmer, cover, and cook until the flavors have blended, about 20 minutes. Stir in the vinegar.

MAKES 4 TO 6 SERVINGS

RED BEANS & RICE

If you can't find small red beans, use red kidney beans.

- **3 slices thick-sliced bacon, cut into ¼-inch pieces**
- **1 large onion, chopped**
- **½ cup chopped red bell pepper**
- **1½ cups brown aromatic rice such as basmati or jasmine**
- **⅛ teaspoon salt**
- **3 cups boiling chicken broth, store-bought or homemade (page 172), or water (or a combination)**
- **1¾ cups cooked small red beans**

In a large heavy saucepan, cook the bacon over medium heat until just starting to get crisp, about 3 minutes. Transfer the bacon to paper towels to drain, leaving the drippings in the pan.

Add the onion and bell pepper to the saucepan and cook over medium heat, stirring often, until tender and starting to brown, about 5 minutes. Add the rice and salt. Cook and stir until the rice smells toasty, about 1 minute.

Add the boiling broth and return to a boil. Reduce the heat to very low, cover, and simmer until the rice is tender and the liquid has been absorbed, 35 to 45 minutes.

Remove from the heat. Fluff the rice with a fork and add the beans. Cover and let stand for at least 10 minutes. Sprinkle with the reserved bacon before serving.

MAKES 6 SERVINGS

SPICED CHICKPEAS WITH SPINACH

Torn pieces of bread thicken and add an earthy note to this deeply flavored side dish. To transform it into dinner, top each serving with a fried egg.

- **3 tablespoons extra-virgin olive oil**
- **4 cloves garlic, thinly sliced**
- **1 tablespoon plus 1 teaspoon sweet paprika**
- **2 teaspoons cumin seed**
- **¼ teaspoon coarse salt**
- **⅛ teaspoon pepper**
- **1 cup soft whole-grain bread crumbs (2 slices)**
- **2 cups cooked chickpeas**
- **¾ cup water**
- **1 tablespoon plus 2 teaspoons white wine vinegar**
- **5 ounces baby spinach leaves**

In a medium saucepan, heat the oil and garlic over medium heat. Cook, stirring, until the garlic is translucent and fragrant, about 30 seconds. Stir in the paprika, cumin, salt, and pepper. Add the bread crumbs and cook until the crumbs are toasted, about 2 minutes.

Add the chickpeas, water, and vinegar, and simmer for 3 minutes. Stir, breaking up the bread to help it dissolve into the sauce. Add the spinach and simmer, stirring occasionally, until wilted, about 2 minutes. Serve hot.

MAKES 4 SERVINGS

GREEK ELEPHANT BEANS

Elephant beans are available in specialty food stores or from any grocery in a neighborhood with a large Greek immigrant population. The beans are sometimes labeled gigantes.

- 8 ounces elephant beans, soaked overnight, drained
- 3 cloves garlic, smashed and peeled
- 1 teaspoon oregano
- 2 tablespoons olive oil
- ¼ teaspoon salt

In a large pot, combine the beans, garlic, oregano, and water to cover by 2 inches. Bring to a boil over high heat. Reduce to a simmer, partially cover, and cook until the beans are tender, about 45 minutes. Check periodically to make sure the beans are covered with water as they cook, adding more water if necessary.

Drain, add the oil and salt, and toss to combine. Serve warm or at room temperature.

MAKES 4 SERVINGS

QUICK HOPPIN' JOHN WITH PORCINI

Hoppin' John is a traditional New Year's Day dish, especially in the South. Eating the black-eyed pea dish on January 1 is meant to bring you luck for the rest of the year.

- ½ ounce dried porcini mushrooms (about ½ cup)
- 1 cup boiling water
- 1 cup white rice
- 1 teaspoon salt
- 1 tablespoon olive oil
- 1 large red onion, coarsely chopped
- 2 packages (10 ounces each) frozen black-eyed peas
- 1¼ cups water
- 2 tablespoons red wine vinegar
- ½ teaspoon pepper

In a small heatproof bowl, combine the mushrooms and the boiling water, and let stand for 20 minutes or until softened. Reserving the soaking liquid, scoop out the dried mushrooms and finely chop. Strain the soaking liquid through a coffee filter or a paper towel–lined sieve.

Meanwhile, in a medium saucepan, cook the rice according to the package directions, using ¼ teaspoon of the salt.

In a large saucepan, heat the oil over medium heat. Add the onion and cook, stirring frequently, until tender, about 7 minutes.

Add the reserved mushroom soaking liquid, the mushrooms, the remaining ¾ teaspoon salt, the black-eyed peas, and the water, and bring to a boil. Reduce to a simmer, cover, and cook until the peas are almost tender, about 10 minutes.

Uncover and cook until the peas are fully tender and the water has evaporated, about 5 minutes. Add the vinegar, pepper, and cooked rice, and stir well to combine.

MAKES 8 SERVINGS

INDIAN LENTILS

Lentil puree, usually served with rice, is a common side dish in Indian cuisine. On restaurant menus it is usually listed as dal, which is also the word for the hulled, split lentils and peas that are used to make the dish.

- 1 cup lentils
- 3 cups water

1 tablespoon vegetable oil
½ teaspoon turmeric
½ teaspoon ground cumin
1 clove garlic, minced
1 medium onion, sliced
1 plum tomato, quartered
¼ teaspoon cayenne pepper
¼ teaspoon salt

In a medium saucepan, combine the lentils and water. Bring to a boil over high heat. Reduce to a simmer, partially cover, and cook until the lentils are very tender, about 45 minutes.

Meanwhile, in a medium skillet, heat the oil over medium heat. Add the turmeric, cumin, and garlic, and cook until fragrant, about 30 seconds. Add the onion and cook until the onion has softened. Add the tomato, cayenne, and salt, and cook until the mixture is well blended.

Transfer the lentils and onion mixture to a food processor and puree until smooth.

MAKES 4 TO 6 SERVINGS

CHICKPEA CROQUETTES

A croquette is a mixture that is formed into small cakes or sausage shapes, coated in bread crumbs, and panfried. It comes from the French verb croquer, *to crunch.*

3 tablespoons olive oil
1 cup chopped onions
2 cloves garlic, minced
2 cups cooked chickpeas
2 large eggs, beaten
1 cup chopped cherry tomatoes
1 cup chopped walnuts
¼ cup lemon juice
2 cups soft whole-grain bread crumbs (4 slices)
2 teaspoons butter

Preheat the oven to warm.

In a small skillet, heat 1 tablespoon of the oil over medium heat. Add the onions and garlic, and cook until golden.

In a large bowl, combine the onion mixture, chickpeas, eggs, tomatoes, walnuts, lemon juice, and 1 cup of the bread crumbs. Mix well. Form into 8 to 10 croquettes and coat them with the remaining bread crumbs.

In a large skillet, heat 1 tablespoon of the oil with 1 teaspoon of the butter. Add half the croquettes and cook, turning, until golden brown all over. Keep warm in the oven. Repeat with the remaining 1 tablespoon oil, 1 teaspoon butter, and croquettes.

MAKES 4 TO 6 SERVINGS

WHITE BEAN & HAZELNUT CROQUETTES: Use cooked white beans instead of chickpeas and chopped toasted hazelnuts instead of walnuts.

HERBED BULGUR, AMARANTH & ALMOND PILAF

Delicate herbs, such as chervil, do not stand up well to heat, which dissipates their flavor. This is why they are almost always added at the end of the cooking.

2 tablespoons butter
1 large onion, chopped
1 carrot, halved lengthwise and thickly sliced
1 rib celery, finely chopped
2 cloves garlic, minced
¼ cup brown amaranth
½ cup bulgur
1¼ cups water
1 teaspoon sage
½ teaspoon salt
⅓ cup slivered almonds, toasted
¼ cup grated Parmesan cheese

- 2 tablespoons minced mixed fresh herbs (such chervil, dill, and parsley)

In a 1½- to 2-quart heavy-bottomed saucepan, melt 1 tablespoon of the butter over medium heat. Add the onion, carrot, and celery, and cook until the onion begins to soften, 1 to 2 minutes. Add the garlic and amaranth, and cook, stirring occasionally, for 5 minutes.

Add the remaining 1 tablespoon butter and the bulgur. Cook and stir until the bulgur becomes more golden. Stir in the water, sage, and salt. Cover and bring to a boil. Stir thoroughly, scraping the bottom of the pan, then cover again and reduce the heat to a slow simmer. Cook until the bulgur is tender and fluffy, about 30 minutes.

Just before serving, stir in the almonds, Parmesan, and herbs.

MAKES 4 SERVINGS

BULGUR & MILLET PILAF: Omit the celery and increase the carrots to 2. Substitute millet for the amaranth. Add ¼ teaspoon pepper.

BLACK BARLEY & RICE PILAF

Black barley cooks up with a lovely sheen and lends a dramatic flair to a simple grain side dish.

- 2 tablespoons olive oil
- 1 medium onion, chopped
- 2 cloves garlic, minced
- ½ cup black barley
- ½ cup brown rice
- 2½ cups chicken broth, store-bought or homemade (page 172)
- ½ teaspoon salt
- 1 small red bell pepper, diced
- 2 teaspoons lemon juice

In a medium saucepan, heat 1 tablespoon of the oil over medium heat. Add the onion, garlic, barley, and rice, and cook, stirring constantly, until the onion is translucent.

Add the broth and salt, and stir briefly with a fork. Bring to a boil over high heat, then reduce to a simmer, cover tightly, and cook until the liquid has been absorbed and the barley and rice are tender, about 1 hour.

Meanwhile, in a small skillet, heat the remaining 1 tablespoon oil over medium-high heat. Add the bell pepper and cook until softened. Stir in the lemon juice.

When the barley mixture is done, stir in the bell pepper.

MAKES 4 TO 6 SERVINGS

BARLEY & RICE PILAF WITH YELLOW TOMATOES: Omit the bell pepper and the 1 tablespoon oil used to sauté it. Omit the lemon juice. When the barley mixture is done, stir in 1 cup chopped yellow pear tomatoes.

BARLEY WITH PEAS, SHREDDED CARROTS & MINT

This side dish is quick to prepare and is especially good with chicken.

- 2 tablespoons vegetable oil
- 1 tablespoon butter
- 1 medium onion, finely chopped
- 3 cups cooked pearled barley
- 1 cup shredded carrots
- 1 package (10 ounces) frozen peas, partially thawed
- ½ cup Rich Poultry Stock (page 172)
- ¼ teaspoon salt
- ¼ teaspoon pepper

2 tablespoons minced fresh mint or 1 teaspoon dried

In a large skillet, heat the oil and butter over medium heat. Add the onion and cook until lighted browned.

Stir in the barley and cook for 5 minutes. Add the carrots, peas, stock, salt, and pepper. Cover and cook for 5 minutes. Stir in the mint.

MAKES 6 SERVINGS

BARLEY WITH FENNEL & CORN: Decrease the oil to 1 tablespoon and increase the butter to 2 tablespoons. Use 1 cup diced fresh fennel instead of the carrots and 1 package (10 ounces) frozen corn kernels instead of the peas. Instead of the mint, use 1 teaspoon minced fresh tarragon or ½ teaspoon dried.

KASHA WITH FRESH SHIITAKE MUSHROOMS

Kasha is an excellent alternative to potatoes or rice as part of a meal. It goes especially well with beef brisket and gravy.

- 1 large egg, beaten
- 1½ cups roasted buckwheat groats (kasha)
- 3 to 4 cups boiling water
- 2 tablespoons vegetable oil
- 1 medium onion, diced
- 1 cup thinly sliced shiitake mushroom caps
- 1 tablespoon lower-sodium soy sauce

In a medium bowl, stir the egg and buckwheat together.

Heat a large heavy skillet and add the buckwheat mixture. Stir constantly over medium heat until the groats are dry and toasty. Gradually add 3 cups boiling water while stirring. Cover the pan, reduce the heat, and cook until the grains fluff up and are tender, about 15 minutes. If it begins to dry out, add more boiling water, a little at a time.

Meanwhile, in a medium skillet, heat the oil over medium heat. Add the onion and cook until beginning to soften. Add the shiitakes and soy sauce, and cook until the onion and mushrooms are soft. Stir them into the buckwheat.

MAKES 6 SERVINGS

BUCKWHEAT & RED LENTIL PILAF

The toasty flavor of buckwheat and the hearty flavor of red lentils make this pilaf an especially satisfying side dish. The combined nuts and dried fruit are common ingredients in pilafs.

- ¼ cup walnut halves
- 2 teaspoons olive oil
- 4 cloves garlic, minced
- 1 cup roasted buckwheat groats (kasha)
- ½ cup red lentils
- 2 cups boiling water
- 1 cup carrot juice
- ¾ teaspoon ground coriander
- ¾ teaspoon salt
- ½ teaspoon pepper
- ½ cup raisins
- 1 Granny Smith apple, peeled and diced
- 2 teaspoons walnut oil or olive oil

Toast the walnuts in a 350°F toaster oven or small ungreased skillet over medium heat until crisp and fragrant, 5 to 7 minutes. When cool enough to handle, coarsely chop.

In a large skillet, heat the olive oil over medium heat. Add the garlic and cook until softened, about 1 minute. Stir in the buckwheat groats and lentils, and cook until the buckwheat is well coated, about 3 minutes.

Add the boiling water, carrot juice, coriander, salt, and pepper, and bring to a boil. Reduce to a simmer, cover, and cook until the buckwheat is tender, about 15 minutes. Stir in the toasted walnuts, raisins, apple, and walnut oil.

MAKES 6 SERVINGS

WHITE CORN SPOON BREAD

A cross between corn bread and pudding, spoon bread is moist and sweet. To cut corn kernels from the cob, hold it upright on a cutting board. With a sharp knife, slice downward to remove the kernels. Use the back of the knife to scrape the milk from the cob.

- ½ cup white cornmeal
- 2 tablespoons sugar
- 1 teaspoon baking soda
- ½ teaspoon coarse salt
- 1½ cups buttermilk
- ½ cup light cream
- 4 large eggs
- 3 tablespoons butter, melted
- 3 cups fresh white corn kernels (4 to 6 ears)

Preheat the oven to 350°F. Butter a 9-inch cast-iron skillet or a 7 × 11-inch baking dish.

In a large bowl, whisk together the cornmeal, sugar, baking soda, and salt. In a blender or food processor, pulse together the buttermilk, cream, eggs, and melted butter until smooth. Add the corn and pulse a few more times (the mixture should be lumpy with visible kernels).

Whisk the buttermilk mixture into the cornmeal mixture. Pour into the skillet. Bake for 35 to 40 minutes, until the edges are golden brown but the center is still slightly jiggly. Transfer to a rack to cool. Serve warm or at room temperature.

MAKES 8 SERVINGS

POLENTA CHEESE SQUARES

Polenta appears at dinner tables in many regions of Italy in place of pasta; and like pasta, can be served with a variety of sauces.

- 5 cups water
- ½ teaspoon salt
- 1½ cups yellow cornmeal
- ½ cup shredded sharp cheddar cheese
- ½ cup grated Parmesan cheese

In a large heavy saucepan, bring the water and salt to a boil. Stirring constantly, slowly pour in the cornmeal and stir until the mixture is thick and free from lumps. Cook over low heat, stirring occasionally, until the polenta leaves the sides of the pan, 20 to 30 minutes. Stir in the cheddar.

Lightly oil an 8 x 8-inch baking pan. Scrape the polenta into the pan and let cool to room temperature. Refrigerate for 3 to 4 hours, until stiff enough to cut.

Preheat the oven to 400°F. Oil a 9 × 13-inch baking dish.

Cut the polenta into 16 squares. Arrange in the baking dish and sprinkle with the Parmesan. Bake for 15 minutes, or until the Parmesan has browned.

MAKES 6 TO 8 SERVINGS

BULGUR PILAF WITH SHALLOT BUTTER & PARSLEY

Shallots taste like an onion that flirted with garlic, a nice blend of both flavors.

- 2½ tablespoons butter
- 6 shallots, finely chopped
- 1½ cups coarse bulgur
- 3 cups chicken broth, store-bought or homemade (page 172)
- ¾ teaspoon salt
- ½ cup minced parsley
- ¼ teaspoon pepper

In a large skillet, melt the butter over medium heat. Add the shallots and cook until wilted. Stir in the bulgur, broth, and salt, and bring to a boil. Remove from the heat, cover, and let stand for 45 minutes.

Before serving, toss with 2 forks and warm over low heat for 5 to 10 minutes. Stir in the parsley and pepper.

MAKES 6 SERVINGS

ORANGE-PISTACHIO BULGUR

Orange and pistachio are not only natural flavor companions, but they also bring some good color to this bulgur side dish.

- 1 orange
- 2 tablespoons vegetable oil
- 2 tablespoons butter
- 1 cup coarsely shredded carrots
- ½ cup chopped onion
- ½ cup chopped celery
- 1 cup bulgur
- 2 tablespoons chopped flat-leaf parsley
- ¼ teaspoon ground fennel
- 2 cups carrot juice
- ¾ cup unsalted pistachios, toasted and chopped, for serving

Grate the zest from the orange, for serving and reserve. Peel the orange, separate into segments, and coarsely chop. Set aside.

Preheat the oven to 325°F.

In a large skillet, heat the oil and butter over medium-high heat. Add the carrots, onion, and celery, and cook until the onion begins to brown. Add the bulgur and continue cooking and stirring until the bulgur is lightly browned. Stir in the orange zest, parsley, and fennel. Transfer to a 5-cup baking dish.

Add the carrot juice to the skillet and stir over low heat to deglaze any browned bits. Pour over the bulgur. Cover and bake for 40 to 45 minutes, until all the liquid has been absorbed. Stir once or twice during baking.

Serve warm or at room temperature, sprinkled with the chopped oranges and pistachios.

MAKES 6 SERVINGS

CLEMENTINE-PECAN BULGUR: Use 2 clementines in place of the orange. Grate the zest from both of them. Use pecans instead of pistachios.

LEMON-TARRAGON BULGUR WITH CAULIFLOWER

Be sure the cauliflower florets are quite small or they will be way out of proportion to the rest of the dish.

- 3 cups small cauliflower florets
- 1 tablespoon olive oil
- 2 tablespoons butter
- 1½ cups coarse bulgur
- 2½ cups chicken broth, store-bought or homemade (page 172)
- ½ cup minced scallions
- 1 carrot, shredded
- 1 tablespoon grated lemon zest
- Juice of ½ lemon

- **1 tablespoon minced fresh tarragon or ½ teaspoon dried**
- **¼ teaspoon pepper**

In a steamer, cook the cauliflower until just crisp-tender, about 8 minutes.

In a large skillet, heat the oil and 1 tablespoon of the butter over medium heat. Add the bulgur and cook, stirring occasionally, until lightly browned.

Pour the broth over the bulgur and bring to a boil. Reduce to a simmer, cover, and cook until the broth has been absorbed, about 15 minutes.

Meanwhile, in another large skillet, melt the remaining 1 tablespoon butter. Add the scallions and cook, stirring, for 1 minute. Add the steamed caulifower, the carrot, lemon zest, lemon juice, tarragon, and pepper, and toss to combine. Cook for 1 minute.

Add the cauliflower mixture to the bulgur, and fluff with 2 forks.

MAKES 6 SERVINGS

ISRAELI COUSCOUS WITH LIME & MINT

Pearl-like Israeli couscous is larger than regular couscous and has a chewier texture. Unlike its super-simple relative, Israeli couscous does require cooking, rather than simple steeping in hot liquid.

- **1 tablespoon olive oil**
- **3 cloves garlic, thinly sliced**
- **1 teaspoon minced fresh jalapeño pepper**
- **1¼ cups Israeli couscous, preferably whole wheat**
- **2½ cups boiling water**
- **1½ teaspoons grated lime zest**
- **¾ teaspoon salt**
- **¼ cup chopped fresh mint**
- **¼ cup snipped chives**

In a medium saucepan, heat the oil over medium heat. Add the garlic and jalapeño, and cook until the garlic is tender, about 1 minute. Add the couscous and stir to coat.

Add the boiling water, lime zest, and salt. Bring to a boil, reduce to a simmer, cover, and cook until the couscous is tender and the liquid has been absorbed, about 12 minutes.

Using a fork, stir in the mint and chives, and fluff the couscous.

MAKES 4 SERVINGS

FARRO & CORN CASSEROLE

Farro adds a great chewiness to this baked succotash.

- **2 cups frozen corn kernels, thawed**
- **1 can (14.5 ounces) spicy diced tomatoes**
- **1 cup chopped red onion**
- **½ cup cooked lima beans**
- **2 cloves garlic, minced**
- **½ teaspoon oregano**
- **¼ cup tomato paste**
- **½ cup chicken broth, store-bought or homemade (page 172)**
- **2½ cups cooked farro**
- **⅓ cup grated Parmesan cheese**

Preheat the oven to 350°F. Lightly grease a 2- to 3-quart baking dish.

In a large bowl, combine the corn, tomatoes, onion, lima beans, garlic, and oregano. In a small bowl, combine the tomato paste and broth.

Place half the farro on the bottom of the baking dish. Cover with the corn-tomato mixture. Drizzle with the tomato paste mixture. Cover with the remaining farro and sprinkle with the Parmesan. Bake, uncovered, for 30 minutes, or until the cheese is golden and the farro is piping hot.

MAKES 6 TO 8 SERVINGS

FARRO & SHIITAKES

The meaty flavor of shitakes is a nice match to the chewy farro. Together they make a delicious accompaniment to meat dishes.

- 1 tablespoon olive oil
- 1 small onion, finely chopped
- 3 cloves garlic, slivered
- 8 ounces shiitake mushrooms, stems discarded, caps thinly sliced
- 2³⁄₄ cups water
- 1 tablespoon tomato paste
- 1 cup semipearled farro
- ½ teaspoon rubbed sage
- ½ teaspoon salt
- ¼ teaspoon pepper

In a large saucepan, heat the oil over medium-low heat. Add the onion and garlic, and cook, stirring frequently, until the onion is golden brown, about 10 minutes.

Add the mushrooms and cook until they begin to color, about 3 minutes. Add ¼ cup of the water and cook, stirring occasionally, until the onion has wilted, about 5 minutes. Stir in the tomato paste until well coated.

Add the farro, the remaining 2½ cups water, the sage, salt, and pepper, and bring to a boil. Reduce to a simmer, cover, and cook until the farro is tender and the liquid has been absorbed, about 30 minutes.

MAKES 4 TO 6 SERVINGS

QUINOA WITH SUNFLOWER SEEDS & GOLDEN RAISINS

Rinsing quinoa gets rid of the green, raw, and slightly soapy taste the grain can have.

- ⅓ cup sun-dried tomatoes
- Boiling water
- 2 tablespoons olive oil
- 2 cups quinoa, rinsed and drained
- 4 cups water
- ½ teaspoon salt
- ½ teaspoon pepper
- 2 medium red onions, finely chopped
- 2 cloves garlic, minced
- ⅓ cup golden raisins
- ¼ cup grated Parmesan cheese
- 3 tablespoons salted dry-roasted sunflower seeds

In a small heatproof bowl, combine the sun-dried tomatoes and boiling water to cover. Let stand until softened, about 20 minutes. (Timing may vary depending upon the dryness of the tomatoes.) Drain and thinly slice. Set aside.

In a large skillet, heat 1 tablespoon of the oil over medium heat. Add the quinoa and cook, stirring constantly, until lightly golden, about 5 minutes. Add the 4 cups water, salt, and pepper, and bring to a boil. Reduce to a simmer, cover, and cook until the quinoa is tender, 12 to 15 minutes.

Meanwhile, in a medium skillet, heat the remaining 1 tablespoon oil over medium heat. Add the onions and garlic, and cook, stirring frequently, until the onions are lightly browned, about 5 minutes.

Transfer the quinoa to a large bowl. Stir in the sun-dried tomatoes, onions, raisins, Parmesan, and sunflower seeds. Toss with a fork to combine.

MAKES 4 SERVINGS

QUINOA WITH BUTTERNUT SQUASH & SAUSAGE

Cooking quinoa in a plentiful amount of boiling water, just like pasta, makes this small tasty grain into an everyday side dish. To make the dish vegetarian, simply use a vegetable-based meatless sausage and add an extra tablespoon of olive oil.

- **1 cup quinoa, rinsed and drained**
- **1 tablespoon extra-virgin olive oil**
- **4 ounces sweet Italian sausage, casings removed**
- **1½ cups cubed (½ inch) peeled butternut squash (8 ounces)**
- **½ teaspoon salt**
- **¼ teaspoon pepper**
- **1 large shallot, minced**
- **3 tablespoons chopped parsley**

In a medium pot of boiling salted water (at least 6 cups), cook the quinoa until tender and a white spiral germ appears around the grains, about 13 minutes. Drain well.

Meanwhile, in a large skillet, heat the oil over medium-high heat. Add the sausage and cook, breaking it into small pieces with a wooden spoon, until no longer pink, about 6 minutes. With a slotted spoon, transfer the sausage to a plate.

Add the squash to the pan, season with the salt and pepper, and cook, stirring occasionally, until softened, about 10 minutes.

Add the shallot and reserved sausage, and cook, stirring, until the shallot turns golden and the squash is soft and browned on one or two sides, about 5 minutes.

Gently stir the quinoa and parsley into the squash mixture, and cook until heated through. Serve hot or at room temperature.

MAKES 4 SERVINGS

FOUR-GRAIN PILAF

The earthy combination of these four grains with lentils yields a perfect side dish for roast chicken. Adding a little bit more oil at the end makes the pilaf especially satisfying.

- **3 tablespoons olive oil**
- **1 large onion, finely chopped**
- **⅓ cup pearled barley**
- **⅓ cup brown basmati rice**
- **⅓ cup buckwheat groats**
- **⅓ cup lentils**
- **¼ cup millet**
- **4 cups boiling water**
- **¾ teaspoon salt**
- **¼ teaspoon thyme**
- **⅛ teaspoon pepper**
- **½ cup chopped parsley**

In a large saucepan, heat 2 tablespoons of the oil over medium heat. Add the onion and cook, stirring frequently, until golden brown, 10 to 12 minutes.

Add the barley, rice, buckwheat, lentils, and millet, and stir until well coated. Add the boiling water and bring the mixture to a boil. Stir in the salt, thyme, and pepper. Reduce to a simmer, cover, and cook until the grains are almost tender and the water has been absorbed, about 30 minutes.

Remove from the heat and let stand 10 minutes so the grains will steam and continue cooking. Add the parsley and the remaining 1 tablespoon oil, and fluff with a fork.

MAKES 6 TO 8 SERVINGS

GREEN BASMATI RICE

This preparation works well with other aromatic rices such as jasmine, Kalijira, and pecan rice. If you have rice left over, turn it into a salad by adding oil and vinegar and additional vegetables of your liking.

- 1 tablespoon olive oil
- 2 scallions, thinly sliced
- ½ small green bell pepper, finely chopped
- 1 cup basmati rice
- 2 cups water
- ½ teaspoon salt
- ½ cup chopped cilantro

In a medium saucepan, heat the oil over medium heat. Add the scallions and bell pepper, and cook, stirring frequently, until the pepper is tender, about 3 minutes. Stir in the rice until well coated.

Add the water and salt, and bring to a boil. Reduce to a simmer, cover, and cook until the rice is tender and the water has been absorbed, about 15 minutes. Stir in the cilantro.

MAKES 4 SERVINGS

BASMATI RICE WITH RAISINS & ALMONDS

Turmeric adds a wonderful golden glow to the rice.

- 1 tablespoon vegetable oil
- 1 tablespoon butter
- 2-inch cinnamon stick
- 4 whole cloves
- 2 cups brown basmati rice
- 3¾ cups water
- 1 teaspoon turmeric
- ½ teaspoon salt
- ¼ teaspoon ground cardamom
- 1 cup raisins
- ½ cup slivered almonds, toasted

In a large heavy skillet, heat the oil and butter over low heat. Add the cinnamon and cloves, and stir to coat. Cook for about 5 minutes, taking care not to burn the spices.

Add the rice and stir to coat. Cook over low heat for 5 minutes. Add the water, turmeric, salt, and cardamom, and bring to a boil over high heat. Reduce to a simmer, cover, and cook until the rice is tender, 35 to 45 minutes. If there is any liquid remaining, drain it off.

Discard the cloves and cinnamon stick. Stir in the raisins and almonds.

MAKES 8 SERVINGS

SQUASH BLOSSOM SAFFRON RICE

You can usually find squash blossoms at farmer's markets and gourmet shops in the summer if you don't grow them yourself.

- 2 tablespoons olive oil
- ⅔ cup finely minced red onion
- 1½ cups jasmine rice or other aromatic long-grain rice
- Small pinch of saffron threads, crumbled
- 6 large squash blossoms, slivered
- 1½ cups chicken broth, store-bought or homemade (page 172)
- 1 cup water
- ¾ teaspoon coarse salt

In a medium saucepan, heat the oil over medium heat. Add the onion and cook, stirring, until just beginning to soften, about 1 minute. Add the rice and saffron, and stir to coat. Cook until the rice turns opaque, 1 to 2 minutes.

Add the slivered squash blossoms, broth, water, and salt. Bring to a boil over high heat. Reduce to a simmer, cover, and cook until the liquid is absorbed, about 15 minutes. Remove from the heat and let steam for 10 minutes. Fluff with a fork.

MAKES 6 SERVINGS

BROWN-RICE RISOTTO

Classic risotto from Milan is typically made with a short-grain rice called arborio, which is quite starchy and contributes a creaminess to the dish. To give the dish more fiber, we make it with short-grain brown rice instead. The results will still be delicious, just a little less creamy.

2 tablespoons butter

2 tablespoons olive oil

1 cup short-grain brown rice

1 cup sliced cremini mushrooms

1 cup chopped onions

1 clove garlic, minced

4 cups chicken broth, store-bought or homemade (page 172)

½ cup grated Parmesan cheese

In a 3-quart saucepan, heat the butter and oil. Add the rice and stir to coat. Add the mushrooms, onions, and garlic, and cook until the onions are golden.

Place the broth in a saucepan over medium-low heat.

Add 1 cup hot broth to the rice mixture and cook slowly, stirring occasionally, until the broth is almost absorbed. (Do not let the rice dry out.) Stir in 1 cup more broth and stir occasionally until absorbed. Continue adding broth, stirring occasionally until it is absorbed, and until all of it has been added and the rice is tender, about 1 hour. Remove from the heat and stir in the Parmesan.

MAKES 4 SERVINGS

SHIITAKE & SCALLION RISOTTO: Substitute 6 sliced scallions for half of the onions. Increase the garlic to 3 cloves. Use sliced fresh shiitake caps in place of the cremini.

ROASTED BEET RISOTTO

The key to great risotto is the right pot. Ideally, you should use a heavy-bottomed pan that is 3 to 4 inches deep—enameled cast iron and stainless steel both work well. Stirring risotto constantly will make the grains thick and gummy. Instead, stir the rice with a wooden spoon about every 2 minutes.

3 medium beets

2 teaspoons plus 1 tablespoon olive oil

Coarse salt and pepper

6 cups chicken broth, store-bought or homemade (page 172)

¾ cup finely chopped red onion

3 cloves garlic, minced

1½ cups arborio rice

½ cup dry red wine

1 tablespoon balsamic vinegar

2 tablespoons butter

½ cup grated Parmesan cheese

Preheat the oven to 425°F. Cut the beets into quarters and place on a large piece of heavy-duty foil. Toss with 2 teaspoons of the oil and sprinkle lightly with salt. Seal the foil around the beets to form a packet. Roast for 35 to 40 minutes, or until tender. When cool enough to handle, peel the beets, cut into medium dice, and set aside.

Place the broth in a saucepan over medium-low heat.

In a large, heavy-bottomed pan, heat the remaining 1 tablespoon oil over medium heat. Add the onion and cook until softened, about 2 minutes. Add the garlic and cook for 1 minute. Immediately add the rice and stir constantly until the grains become translucent, about 2 minutes.

Add the wine and balsamic vinegar, and stir until absorbed, about 1 minute. Stir in the chopped beets. Add the warm broth, 1 to 2 ladlefuls at a time, stirring well after each addition; when the liquid is absorbed but before the grains become dry, add more broth. Continue to cook over medium heat, stirring every 2 minutes. After 12 to 15 minutes of adding broth (you should have about one-fourth of it left), the rice will become increasingly thick and slow to absorb the liquid. Begin adding broth in smaller amounts. Start tasting for doneness: When ready, the rice should have a slightly firm bite in the center. After cooking 18 to 20 minutes, the final mixture will have a thick, creamy, yet still runny, consistency.

Remove from the heat and stir in the butter and Parmesan. Add salt and pepper to taste. Let rest 3 minutes. Stir once more and serve immediately.

MAKES 6 SERVINGS

WILD RICE & DILLED MUSHROOM PILAF

Wild rice is native to the northern reaches of the Midwest where there is also a sizable population of Scandinavian heritage. To honor this amalgam, this wild rice dish is flavored with dill.

2 tablespoons olive oil

3/4 cup minced Vidalia or other sweet onion

10 ounces cremini mushrooms, diced

1/4 cup snipped fresh dill

1/2 teaspoon salt

1/4 teaspoon pepper

2 teaspoons lemon juice

2 cups cooked wild rice

1/2 cup hot chicken broth, store-bought or homemade (page 172)

1 tablespoon butter

Preheat the oven to 450°F. Grease a 1½-quart baking dish.

In a large skillet, heat the oil over medium heat. Add the onion and cook until translucent. Add the mushrooms and cook for 5 minutes. Stir in the dill, salt, pepper, and lemon juice.

Stir the wild rice into the mushroom mixture and transfer to the baking dish. Pour the broth over the mixture and dot with the butter. Cover and bake for 15 minutes, or until hot and bubbling. Uncover and bake for 5 minutes.

MAKES 6 SERVINGS

Desserts

In addition to cakes, cookies, and pies, desserts comprise a huge range of sweet ways to end a meal, from elegant soufflés to humble fruit crisps. This chapter is filled with crisps, cobblers, fools, buckles, compotes, custards, mousses, sorbet—and that most American of desserts, ice cream.

Fruit Desserts

The most satisfying desserts are often the simplest. For example, unadorned fresh fruit served with cheese is a popular European way to end a meal. Fruit can also be simply poached, baked, sautéed, or broiled. And as a health bonus, any kind of cooking intensifies the natural sugar in fruits, lessening the need for added sweetener.

Simmering (poaching): Fruit can be simply poached in a lightly sweetened and flavored liquid. The poaching liquid can be water, juice, or wine, sweetened to taste or left as is. Seasonings such as fresh mint, grated orange or lemon zest, a stick of cinnamon, or whole cloves can be added. Bring the syrup mixture to a boil and add the fruit of your choice. Cover the pan and return a boil, then reduce the heat and simmer until the fruit is barely tender. Stir only enough to keep the fruit from sticking to the pan. Some recipes will have you cool the fruit in the poaching liquid (in which case the fruit should be slightly underdone before you turn off the heat); others will have you drain the fruit but save the poaching liquid for reducing as a syrup to be served over the fruit.

Sauce: A fruit sauce is an extraordinarily simple fruit dessert. Use it as an ice cream topping or as a drizzle over pound cake. Make fruit sauce by simmering chopped or whole small fruits in a small amount of water or juice until fully tender. Sweeteners should be added after rather than before simmering, because they make the fruit less able to absorb moisture and become fully tender. Larger fruits such as apples and peaches should be pureed in a food processor or put through a strainer or food mill. Berries and pitted cherries can be left intact for a chunky sauce or pureed for a smooth one. For a thin sauce, include the cooking liquid when you puree the fruit. Or, if the sauce is thinner than desired, cornstarch or arrowroot (which makes an especially translucent sauce) can be used to thicken it.

Baking: Baking is an attractive, simple way to prepare fresh apples, apricots, bananas, peaches, nectarines, pineapple, pears, and plums. Heat the oven to 400°F. Pit or core the fruit and arrange the pieces in a baking dish. Pour ½ to 1 cup water mixed with 2 teaspoons lemon juice and 2 tablespoons sweetener into the dish. Bake, uncovered, until the fruit is softened, 20 to 60 minutes.

Broiling: Place sliced fruits—apples, bananas, peaches, pears, or pineapple—on the broiler rack 4 to 6 inches from the heat. Broil on one side; then turn over and broil until warm and slightly browned. Watch closely; under the intense heat fruits can scorch in a matter of seconds.

Sautéing: Hot, bubbly, and lightly browned in sweet butter, sautéed fruits are a great dessert. Top with ice cream or a dollop of Greek yogurt. (They also make a tasty accompaniment to poul-

TEMPERING EGGS

Tempering is a way to prevent cold eggs from curdling when they are blended with a hot mixture. To temper eggs, add a couple of tablespoons of the hot mixture to the eggs to warm them up. This decreases the temperature difference between the two. Then slowly add the warmed eggs to the hot liquid, stirring constantly to evenly distribute the eggs.

---

try, meat, and fish.) Moderately thick slices of fruit work best. Sauté the fruit in melted butter until hot and just tender, 10 to 15 minutes. Sprinkle the slices with a sweetener and/or cinnamon, nutmeg, mace, or allspice.

Custards, Puddings & Soufflés

Many of the most delightful dishes—Bavarians, ice cream, custard pies, puddings—are based on creamy, satiny custards. Either soft or baked, true custards gain their tender firmness from eggs that are slowly cooked with milk, a sweetener, and a flavoring. No starchy thickener is ever used.

Soft custards (stirred custards): These sauces have the consistency of thick, heavy cream and can curdle without warning if you cook them over high heat or too long. Although you can rescue a curdled custard by beating it vigorously and then straining, the taste of most "saved" custards is slightly inferior. To prevent curdling, use a double boiler over simmering water and stir constantly to distribute the heat evenly. Cook until the sauce forms a thick coating on a spoon. Add fruits after cooking is complete, since acids also curdle a cooking custard. When it is done, quickly cool the custard over cold water and continue stirring to release trapped steam—the cause of a watery custard.

Baked custards: Baked custards are firm yet tender because they're cooked without stirring. Unlike soft custards they rarely curdle, but they often become weepy from too much heat. To avoid overcooking the outside before the center is set, bake the custards in a water bath (bain marie): Place filled custard cups in a larger pan, then add hot water to come halfway up the sides of the cups. When you think the custard is done, insert a knife halfway between the edge and the center of the custard. If the blade comes out clean, remove the custard from the oven and put it on a wire rack to cool. (There is so much heat in a custard that it will continue cooking; by the time it cools, the center will set.) If the center is firm when tested, cool the custard swiftly by setting the custard cups in an inch of cold water.

To unmold a baked custard, first let it cool for 10 to 15 minutes. Then run a knife around the inside edge of the mold. Hold an inverted dish over the mold, then turn both over, and lift away the mold.

Other puddings: In addition to custards, which are egg-thickened, there are pudding desserts that are thickened by other ingredients such as gelatin, flour, arrowroot, tapioca, and cornstarch. There are also puddings based on bread or whole grains such as rice, wheat, and cornmeal that need no added thickening agent. Like custards, puddings are often prepared slowly on the stovetop and stirred in order to prevent scorching and lumping. Certain puddings, such as rice pudding or bread pudding, are baked in the oven, and steamed puddings (see "Steamed Puddings," below) are steamed on the stovetop in a covered pan of boiling water.

Soufflés: The lightest of fancy desserts, soufflés have an airiness that is remarkable but fleeting. They are so delicate that they must be served almost immediately, or their fragile structure will begin to give way and collapse. The base of a soufflé may be made in advance and stored in the refrigerator in a well-covered container. When you are ready to bake the soufflé for serving, bring the mixture to room temperature before adding the beaten egg whites.

Frozen Desserts

Ice cream and other frozen delights are universal favorites. If you have the time, it is easy and fun to make them at home, either in an electric ice cream maker, an old-style hand-crank freezer (see "Old-Fashioned Hand-Cranked Ice Cream," opposite), or in a metal baking pan (see "Still-Freezing Desserts," page 494).

The freezing process is what dictates the consistency of the final product. Ice cream, sorbet, or sherbet, properly frozen and slowly churned, will be smooth and not grainy. During the freezing process the water in the mixture begins to form ice crystals. Stirring this mixture as it freezes is

---

STEAMED PUDDINGS

Steamed pudding, an age-old preparation, is still very popular during winter holidays. This dessert is most often very dense and filling, but it may be made light and delicate. The long cooking in humid heat keeps the pudding moist and allows the flavors to mellow and blend together.

There are two basic types of molds used to make steamed pudding:

- German-style molds are metal with tight-fitting lids. The mold often has a central tube for better heat distribution.
- Pudding basins are deep ceramic bowls with an exterior lip around which you tie a cloth, parchment, or foil cover to keep the steam in.

If you do not have a proper pudding mold, any heatproof bowl can be used. A coffee can also works fine.

Butter the inside of the mold or container lightly, and fill it only about two-thirds full to allow for rising and expansion. If using parchment paper or foil to cover the mold, butter the inside of that as well. Use a pot that is at least 4 inches larger than your pudding mold so you will have about 2 inches of space on each side.

Place a rack or steaming basket in the pot, and then place the mold on the rack. Pour boiling water into the pot until it comes halfway up the sides of the mold. Cover the pot and adjust the heat so that the water remains at the boiling point throughout the steaming period. Steam for the length of time suggested in the recipe.

OLD-FASHIONED HAND-CRANKED ICE CREAM

Even though electric ice cream machines abound, there's nothing like making hand-cranked ice cream on the back porch on a hot summer day. Here's how to make hand-churned ice cream.

Chill the ice-cream mixture an hour or two in the refrigerator (this reduces the processing time). Pour it into the freezer canister, filling it no more than two-thirds full to allow for expansion. Cover securely.

Fill the tub one-third full with crushed ice cubes, then layer more ice and rock salt (or regular household salt) to a level slightly above the level of the mixture in the canister.

Process (work the churn) until the ice cream is smooth and thick.

Remove the dasher (churning blade) from the canister and pack the ice cream down solidly with a wooden spoon.

The ice cream is now ready to be "hardened." This can be done by repacking the tub of the freezer, surrounding the canister with more ice and salt, and then covering the whole machine with burlap or newspapers. Or you can remove the container from the tub, cover it, and place it in the freezer to harden. Whatever system you use, the finished ice cream should be allowed to mellow and harden for 2 to 3 hours before serving.

---

what prevents those crystals from becoming too large and keeps the mixture pleasantly smooth. The stirring also aerates, therefore lightens, the mixture.

For some of the water- or milk-based frozen desserts, such as ices and granitas, a grainy texture is desirable. This means they can be made with the still-freeze method with only occasional blending to break down the ice crystals.

Here's a quick guide to the family of frozen desserts:

Frozen yogurt is a popular variation on ice milk or sherbet, in which most or all of the milk is replaced by yogurt, producing a tangy flavor. Frozen yogurts are most often flavored with fruits, but they readily accept the same flavorings as ice cream.

Frozen soy desserts are somewhat lighter than frozen dairy desserts. They can be made by using most of the same methods used in making other frozen desserts. For a richer dessert, some cream or milk may be substituted for the soymilk called for in a recipe. Conversely, in richer recipes soymilk can substitute for some of the milk or cream.

Gelato is rich Italian ice cream normally made with no eggs, though some recipes do call for a custard base.

Granitas are Italian ices with a snow-like texture.

Ice cream can be made two different ways—custard-based (or French) ice cream made with whole eggs or egg yolks, and plain, which is made with cream but no eggs.

Ice milk can be made from the same recipes as plain (no-egg) ice cream, substituting milk for the cream. Whole milk, 2%, 1%, or skim milk can be used. The texture and taste of the product will be different, but the result is quite satisfactory.

Ices contain neither eggs nor milk; they are made with pure fruit juice, perhaps some sweetener, and ice, all blended together, then frozen in an ice cream maker or baking pan. To attain the same smooth texture in the still-freeze method as in an ice cream freezer, the ice must be beaten well and often during the freezing process. Starting 1 hour after the mixture has been put into the freezer, when the ice is set around the sides but still mushy in the center, the beating should take place every half hour until the ice is frozen solid.

Semifreddo is an Italian dessert made with ice cream ingredients but not churned in an ice cream maker. It's placed in a freezer until frozen, and then allowed to soften up enough to serve. It's often made in the shape of a loaf and served in slices.

Sherbet is made from light fruit syrup and milk. It is fine-textured and often has gelatin or egg white added to make it smoother. The sherbets of yesteryear were often seasoned with liqueur or sweet wine.

Sorbet has the fine texture of a sherbet but is made with only thick fruit puree and a sweetener. It has no other thickeners and no milk.

HONEY-BAKED APPLES

The honey gets to shine in this dessert, so if you have a honey with an interesting flavor, this would be a good time to use it.

- **6 large apples**
- **3 tablespoons chopped walnuts**
- **3 tablespoons raisins**
- **1 cup water**
- **⅓ cup honey**
- **2-inch cinnamon stick**
- **1 tablespoon lemon juice**

Preheat the oven to 350°F.

With an apple corer, core the apples through the stem end, stopping ½ inch from the bottom. In a small bowl, combine the walnuts and raisins. Fill the apple cavities with the mixture and place in a baking dish.

In a small saucepan, combine the water, honey, and cinnamon. Place over medium heat and bring to a boil. Simmer for 5 minutes. Remove from the heat and stir in the lemon juice. Discard the cinnamon. Pour the syrup over the apples.

Bake, uncovered, basting occasionally, for 45 minutes, or until the apples are tender. Let cool to room temperature before serving.

MAKES 6 SERVINGS

APPLE-BLACKBERRY COBBLER

You can substitute almost any fruit—peaches, nectarines, raspberries—in this versatile cobbler. Serve it topped with sweetened Greek yogurt or ice cream.

- **½ cup (1 stick) butter**
- **4 cups sliced peeled Granny Smith apples**
- **1 pint blackberries**
- **1½ cups sugar**
- **1 cup milk**
- **¾ cup flour**

¼ cup flax meal

2 teaspoons baking powder

Pinch of salt

Preheat the oven to 375°F.

Place the butter in a 10-inch oval baking dish and put it in the oven to melt.

In a medium bowl, toss the apples and berries with ½ cup of the sugar.

Remove the dish from the oven and pour the melted butter into another medium bowl. Stir in the remaining 1 cup sugar, the milk, flour, flax meal, baking powder, and salt.

Pour the batter back into the baking dish. Place the fruit on top, but do not stir (the batter will rise as the cobbler bakes). Bake for 35 to 45 minutes, until the top of the crust is golden brown and the cobbler is thick and bubbling. (If necessary, run the cobbler under the broiler to brown the crust.) Serve warm.

MAKES 10 SERVINGS

BAKED BANANA DREAM

This hot banana dessert brings citrus and cinnamon into the picture for an appetizing contrast.

4 tablespoons butter

6 bananas, halved lengthwise

Grated zest of 2 oranges

½ cup orange juice

3 tablespoons lime juice

¼ cup honey

½ teaspoon cinnamon or ground ginger

1½ cups crème fraîche, store-bought or homemade (page 487)

Preheat the oven to 375°F. Place 2 tablespoons of the butter in a large shallow baking dish and put in the oven to melt the butter.

Take the baking dish out and turn the banana halves in the butter to coat well. Arrange in a single layer.

Sprinkle with the orange zest, orange juice, lime juice, honey, and cinnamon. Dot with the remaining 2 tablespoons butter. Bake for 15 minutes, or until bubbling hot.

Serve hot, topped with the crème fraîche.

MAKES 6 SERVINGS

BLACKBERRY FOOL

Blackberry seeds can be quite large, so don't skip the straining step.

2 cups blackberries

½ cup agave nectar

½ cup Greek yogurt

1 cup evaporated whole milk, very well chilled

In a food processor, puree the blackberries. Press the puree through a sieve into a bowl to remove the seeds. Stir in the agave nectar and yogurt.

In a medium bowl, whip the chilled evaporated whole milk until stiff peaks form. Fold the blackberry mixture into the whipped milk.

MAKES 4 SERVINGS

BLUEBERRY BUCKLE

A buckle, one of those old-fashioned baked desserts with colorful names like slump and grunt, is usually fruit baked in a cake-like batter with a crumb topping.

FILLING

¼ cup (½ stick) butter

¼ cup honey

1 large egg

1 cup whole wheat pastry flour

- 1/3 cup buttermilk or yogurt
- 1 teaspoon baking soda
- 2 cups fresh or frozen blueberries

TOPPING

- 1/3 cup whole wheat pastry flour
- 1/4 cup (1/2 stick) butter
- 2 tablespoons honey
- 1/2 teaspoon cinnamon
- 1/4 teaspoon salt

Preheat the oven to 350°F. Butter an 8 × 8-inch baking dish.

To make the filling: In a medium bowl, cream together the butter, honey, and egg. Add the flour, buttermilk, and baking soda. Mix well. Spread in the prepared baking dish and cover with the blueberries.

To make the topping: In a small bowl, combine the flour, butter, honey, cinnamon, and salt until the mixture resembles coarse crumbs.

Spread the topping over the blueberries. Bake for 40 minutes, or until the filling is set and the topping is nicely browned.

MAKES 6 TO 8 SERVINGS

CLAFOUTIS

Clafouti, a home-style dessert from the Limousin region of France, is easy to prepare. Traditionally, it is served at room temperature or cold. But it looks so tempting while still hot and puffy, we suggest serving it right from the oven.

- 1/2 cup plain dried whole wheat bread crumbs
- 1/2 teaspoon ground cardamom
- 3 cups sweet cherries, pitted
- 3 large eggs, beaten
- 1/4 cup plus 1 tablespoon whole wheat pastry flour
- 2 cups milk or light cream
- 1/4 cup light honey
- 1/4 teaspoon salt
- 1 cup crème fraîche, store-bought or homemade (page 487), or whipped cream, for serving

Preheat the oven to 375°F.

Butter 6 custard cups. Combine the bread crumbs and cardamom, and dust the inside of each cup with this mixture. Divide the cherries evenly among the cups and place on a rimmed baking sheet.

In a large bowl, combine the eggs and flour, and mix well. Add the milk and beat for 3 minutes. Add the honey and salt, and beat for 2 minutes.

Pour the batter into the custard cups. Bake for 30 minutes, or until the tops are lightly browned and puffy. Serve hot with crème fraîche.

MAKES 6 SERVINGS

APRICOT CLAFOUTIS: Use cinnamon instead of cardamom and sliced fresh apricots instead of cherries. Sprinkle the apricots with a total of 1 tablespoon sugar before topping with the batter.

CRANBERRY KISEL

Kisel is a light, tart fruit puree served chilled with sour cream or heavy cream. It has long been popular in northern Europe, where it is commonly prepared with lingonberries, cousin of the cranberry.

- 3 cups (12 ounces) fresh cranberries
- 2 cups water
- About 1/2 cup light honey
- 1 tablespoon cornstarch or arrowroot blended with 1 tablespoon water
- 1 cup Greek yogurt, for serving

In a 2-quart heavy-bottomed pot, combine the cranberries and water, and bring to a boil over high heat. Reduce to a simmer, and cook until the berries are tender and the skins break, 10 to 15 minutes.

Rub the mixture through a fine strainer or put through a food mill. Return the puree to the pot, stir in ½ cup of honey, and bring to a boil over high heat. Remove from the heat and taste for sweetness. Add more honey if desired.

Stir the cornstarch mixture into the puree. Return the mixture to medium heat and stir until it comes to a boil and thickens slightly. Remove from the heat and cool to room temperature.

Pour the cooled puree into a serving bowl or individual dessert glasses. Refrigerate until thoroughly chilled. Serve with a separate bowl of yogurt to use as a topping.

MAKES 6 SERVINGS

FIGS WITH RICOTTA & WILDFLOWER HONEY

Paired with a dollop of ricotta and a stream of honey, fresh figs make a heavenly dessert. Ricotta cheese is most flavorful served at room temperature.

- 12 large fresh figs
- 15 ounces whole-milk ricotta cheese, at room temperature
- 6 tablespoons wildflower honey

Quarter the figs and arrange on plates. Add 1 or 2 spoonfuls of ricotta to each fig and a generous drizzle of honey.

MAKES 6 SERVINGS

POMEGRANATE-POACHED FIGS

This sweet and warmly spiced dried fig compote is great served over scoops of frozen yogurt, or even served on its own as a snack.

- 16 whole dried figs
- 1 strip (3 x 1 inch) orange zest
- 1 whole star anise pod
- 4 green cardamom pods, lightly cracked
- 1 cup pomegranate juice
- ¼ cup maple syrup

In a small saucepan, combine the figs with the orange zest, star anise, and cardamom. Stir in the pomegranate juice and maple syrup. Bring to a boil over high heat. Reduce to a simmer, cover, and cook, stirring occasionally, until the figs are soft and plump, about 1 hour.

Remove and discard the orange zest, star anise, and cardamom pods, and let the figs cool to room temperature or chill in the refrigerator.

MAKES 4 SERVINGS

KIWI WITH YOGURT CREAM

Don't top the kiwi with the yogurt until the last minute, because an enzyme in kiwi (called actinidin*) will "eat" the protein in the yogurt.*

- ¼ cup plus 3 tablespoons sugar
- ¼ cup lime juice (about 2 limes)
- 8 kiwifruit, peeled and cut into ½-inch cubes
- ¾ cup Greek yogurt
- ½ teaspoon grated lime zest

In a medium bowl, combine ¼ cup of the sugar and the lime juice. Add the kiwi, tossing to combine. Cover and refrigerate until serving time.

In a small bowl, combine the remaining 3 tablespoons sugar, the yogurt, and zest. Serve the kiwi with its syrup, topped with the yogurt cream.

MAKES 4 SERVINGS

SPICED POACHED PEACHES

The peaches would also make a great addition to plain yogurt for breakfast. Or chop them up and serve as an accompaniment to roast pork.

6 large peaches

2 tablespoons lemon juice

3/4 cup light honey

3/4 cup water

6 whole cloves

Grated zest of 1 large orange

1 cup crème fraîche, store-bought or homemade (page 487)

In a large pot of boiling water, immerse the peaches for 30 to 45 seconds, then immediately plunge them into cold water. Slip off the skins.

Sprinkle the peeled peaches with the lemon juice to retard discoloration. In a heavy-bottomed pot large enough for all the peaches to fit in a single layer, combine the honey, water, cloves, and orange zest. Stir the mixture over medium heat until it comes to a boil. Reduce to a simmer and cook the syrup for 5 minutes.

Add the peaches, bathe them with syrup, and cover the pot. Simmer for about 10 minutes, turning them occasionally. (They should still seem raw after poaching because they will continue to soften in the hot syrup.) Remove the pot from the heat and allow to cool slightly. Refrigerate to chill thoroughly.

When chilled, drain the syrup from the peaches and remove the cloves. Halve the peaches and place, cut-sides down, in a chilled shallow serving bowl. Spoon the syrup around the peaches. Serve with crème fraîche.

MAKES 6 SERVINGS

PEACH CLOUD

A show-stopper dessert in about 40 minutes.

4 cups frozen sliced peaches, thawed

1 tablespoon lemon juice

2 tablespoons quick-cooking tapioca

1/4 cup toasted sliced almonds

5 large egg whites

2 tablespoons maple syrup

1/4 teaspoon cinnamon

Preheat the oven to 375°F. Butter a 9-inch pie plate.

Arrange the peaches in the pie plate. Sprinkle with the lemon juice, tapioca, and almonds. (Save a few almonds to decorate the top.) Cover with foil and bake, for 20 minutes, or until softened.

Meanwhile, with an electric mixer, beat the egg whites until stiff but not dry. Add the maple syrup and continue beating for a few minutes.

Remove the peaches from the oven and completely cover with the beaten egg whites, pulling the whites into peaks with a spatula. Sprinkle the cinnamon and a few almonds on top. Return to the oven and bake for 10 minutes, or until lightly browned.

MAKES 6 TO 8 SERVINGS

NECTARINE COBBLER

Peaches would be a great substitute here, though they need to be peeled (nectarines do not). Just blanch them for 30 seconds or so in a pot of boiling water to loosen their skins so you can peel them before slicing.

4 cups sliced nectarines

2 tablespoons honey

1 large egg, well beaten

1 tablespoon quick-cooking tapioca

1 cup white whole wheat flour*

1 teaspoon baking soda

⅓ cup buttermilk

1 tablespoon butter, at room temperature

1 cup English Custard Sauce (page 478)

**milled from white wheat grains*

Preheat the oven to 425°F. Butter a 9-inch-round baking dish.

In a medium bowl, combine the nectarines, honey, egg, and tapioca. Spread evenly over the bottom of the baking dish.

In another medium bowl, combine the flour, baking soda, buttermilk, and butter to make a dough. On a well-floured surface, roll the dough to a ½-inch thickness. Prick the dough with a fork and place loosely over the peaches. Bake for 20 to 30 minutes, until the filling is set and the topping is golden brown.

Serve warm, topped with the English Custard Sauce.

MAKES 6 SERVINGS

MAPLE-BAKED PEARS WITH ALMONDS

Nothing can beat the heady aroma of fruit baking with butter and maple syrup.

6 firm-ripe pears, cored and sliced

¼ cup maple syrup

1 teaspoon vanilla extract

½ cup slivered almonds

2 tablespoons butter

1 cup plain low-fat yogurt, for serving

Preheat the oven to 350°F. Butter a 9 × 9-inch baking dish.

Arrange the pears in attractive rows in the dish.

In a small bowl, blend the maple syrup and vanilla, and drizzle over the pears. Top with the almonds and dot with the butter. Bake for 10 to 15 minutes, basting frequently, until the pears are tender.

Serve hot or chilled, topped with the yogurt.

MAKES 6 SERVINGS

RASPBERRY-POACHED PEARS

Raspberry juice can usually be found as a frozen concentrate. If you can only find a raspberry blend (usually with apple juice), that will work fine here.

8 firm-ripe pears

1½ cups raspberry juice

2 tablespoons sugar

1 vanilla bean, 2 inches long, or 2 teaspoons vanilla extract

Fresh raspberries, for garnish

With an apple corer, core the pears from the stem end to within ½ inch of the bottom. Cut a thin slice from the bottom of each pear so it will stand upright.

In a saucepan large enough for all the pears to stand up on the bottom, heat the raspberry juice and sugar over low heat until the sugar dissolves. Cut the vanilla bean lengthwise, scrape the seeds into the syrup, and then add the pod (if using extract, add it later).

Stand the pears up in the syrup, cover the pan, and simmer, basting occasionally, until the pears are barely tender, 20 to 25 minutes. Do not overcook. Remove from the heat (if using vanilla extract, stir it in now). Let the pears cool slightly in the syrup.

To serve, cut the pears in half and place 2 halves in each of 8 individual fruit dishes. Garnish with raspberries.

MAKES 8 SERVINGS

POMEGRANATE-POACHED PEARS: Use pomegranate juice (or one of the pomegranate blends) instead of raspberry juice.

DRIED PLUM CRISP

Even though the California prune industry wanted to rechristen prunes as dried plums, it's been a losing battle since most people still refer to them as prunes. And in the marketplace, although many labels include both terms—dried plums and prunes—there are some brands that simply say prunes.

2 cups pitted prunes

2 cups unsweetened apple juice

½ cup quick-cooking oats

½ cup finely chopped walnuts

¼ teaspoon salt

¼ teaspoon ground allspice

6 tablespoons butter

In a medium bowl, soak the prunes in the apple juice until the juice is absorbed, several hours or overnight.

WHIPPED CREAM

There's nothing better on top of a fruit dessert than a dollop of lightly sweetened whipped cream. Here are some tips for making the perfect whipped cream:

- Use a bowl of appropriate size: It should be half full with liquid cream. The cream needs room to expand, but too much space results in prolonged whipping and poor volume. Whip large quantities (more than 2 cups) in two or more batches.
- Chill the bowl and beaters for 2 hours before whipping to get the best volume. When the temperature of the cream rises above 45°F, the butterfat tends to become oily, and it readily separates into butter and buttermilk.
- A hand rotary beater or an electric mixer does the best job of incorporating air into the cream whipping. If you use the electric mixer, watch the process carefully—it is easy to overdo and create butter instead of the intended fluff.
- Stop when you've reached the soft-peak stage: The foam will glisten and appear uniformly smooth. If the foam looks granular and watery, the cream is overwhipped and is about to become butter.
- If your cream threatens to turn into butter, beat in a little more cream (2 or more tablespoons) and continue to whip. The resulting foam will be smooth but stiff.

Change it up: Flavorings can be added to whipped cream, such as small amounts of vanilla extract (and any sweetener you use, such as sugar, honey, or maple syrup), lemon zest, orange juice, orange zest, cocoa powder, and espresso powder. Add flavorings near the end of the whipping; otherwise, they will raise the temperature of the cream and interfere with the whipping.

Preheat the oven to 350°F. Butter an 8 x 8-inch baking pan.

In a small bowl, blend the oats, walnuts, salt, and allspice. With your fingers, work in 4 tablespoons of the butter. Place half of the mixture in the prepared baking pan. Pour the prune mixture on top, sprinkle with the remaining oat mixture, and dot with the remaining 2 tablespoons butter.

Bake for 35 minutes, or until the topping is golden and crisp.

MAKES 6 TO 8 SERVINGS

RED PLUM CRISP: Use dried red plums instead of prunes (which are dried Italian prune plums). Soak the plums in cranberry juice (sweetened) instead of apple juice.

NECTARINE & PLUM COMPOTE

When toasting the almonds, be sure to immediately tip them out of the skillet once they're browned so they don't keep cooking.

- 1/4 cup orange all-fruit spread
- 2 tablespoons frozen orange juice concentrate
- 2 tablespoons water
- 1/8 teaspoon cinnamon
- 2 firm-ripe nectarines, cut into 3/4-inch-thick wedges
- 2 black plums, cut into thin wedges
- 1 tablespoon sliced almonds, for serving
- 2 tablespoons Greek yogurt or reduced-fat sour cream, for serving

In a medium saucepan, combine the fruit spread, orange juice concentrate, water, and cinnamon, and stir until syrupy. Fold in the nectarines and plums, and mix gently until well coated.

Place the pan over medium-high heat and bring to a simmer, stirring gently from time to time. Cover, reduce to a simmer, and cook, stirring gently several times, until the fruit is softened but not mushy, 5 to 8 minutes. Remove the pan from the heat and set aside, covered.

In a small skillet, toast the sliced almonds over medium-high heat, tossing frequently, until lightly browned.

To serve, spoon the nectarines and syrup into dessert dishes or goblets. Sprinkle with the toasted almonds and top with the yogurt.

MAKES 4 SERVINGS

GRILLED PLUM-BLACKBERRY SUNDAES

When you finish cooking supper on the grill, place pouches of sweetened blackberries and plums on the low coals to stew until you're ready for dessert. Add a scoop of vanilla ice cream and some cookie crumbs for the perfect end to a summer meal.

- 6 red or purple plums, pitted and sliced
- 1 pint blackberries
- 1 tablespoon butter
- 1 1/2 pints vanilla ice cream
- 1/2 cup gingersnap cookie crumbs, for serving

Cut two large sheets of heavy-duty aluminum foil. Place the plums in the center of one, and place the blackberries in the center of the other. Dot the fruit with the butter. Fold over and seal the edges, leaving a small tent above each to allow the fruit to steam.

Place the packets on a cool part of the grill and let warm about 30 minutes so that the berries cook slightly. Transfer the berries to a large bowl and lightly mash. Place scoops of ice cream in 6 bowls. Top with spoonfuls of berries and plums. Sprinkle with the gingersnap crumbs.

MAKES 6 SERVINGS

SUMMER PUDDING

The intense pink color and deep berry flavors in this pudding capture the essence of summer. It is best made when local berries are at their peak.

- **14 to 16 slices whole-grain sandwich bread, crusts trimmed**
- **4 cups raspberries**
- **2 cups blueberries**
- **4 cups strawberries, quartered**
- **¾ cup sugar**
- **¼ cup lime juice (about 2 limes)**
- **1 tablespoon finely grated orange zest**
- **1 teaspoon cinnamon**
- **½ cup water**

Preheat the oven to 350°F. Place the bread on a baking sheet and toast, flipping once halfway through, for 12 minutes, or until lightly toasted, but still pliant.

In a large saucepan, combine the berries, sugar, lime juice, orange zest, cinnamon, and water. Bring to a boil over high heat. Reduce to a simmer and cook, stirring, until juicy, about 6 minutes. With a measuring cup, scoop out ½ cup of the juice and reserve for serving. Transfer the remaining berries and juice to a medium bowl and set aside to cool.

Line a 4-inch-deep 2-quart bowl (8 inch diameter) with enough slices of bread to make a seamless lining, trimming the bread as needed to make it fit. Pour 3 cups of the berry mixture into the mold and cover with a layer of bread. Pour the remaining berry mixture on top and cover with another seamless layer of bread. Cover with plastic wrap. Place a small plate directly on top of the pudding and place a large can on top to weight it down. Refrigerate for at least 6 hours or overnight.

To serve, remove and discard the plastic wrap. Run a knife between the bread and the bowl. Invert the bowl over a serving plate and remove the bowl. Serve at once, with the reserved juice as a sauce.

MAKES 8 TO 10 SERVINGS

RHUBARB CRISP

The combination of tart rhubarb, sweet raspberry all-fruit spread, and dried cherries under a crispy topping is definitely a winner.

FILLING

- **2 pounds rhubarb, cut into 1-inch pieces (about 5 cups)**
- **½ cup raspberry all-fruit spread**
- **⅓ cup dried cherries**
- **¼ cup packed muscovado or dark brown sugar**
- **⅛ teaspoon ground allspice**

TOPPING

- **½ cup old-fashioned rolled oats**
- **¼ cup flour**
- **¼ cup (½ stick) cold butter, cut into pieces**
- **¼ cup packed muscovado or dark brown sugar**
- **¼ teaspoon salt**

Preheat the oven to 375°F.

To make the filling: In a large bowl, combine the rhubarb, all-fruit spread, cherries, brown sugar, and allspice. Spoon into a 9 × 9-inch baking dish.

To make the topping: In a food processor, combine the oats, flour, butter, brown sugar, and salt, and pulse until well combined but still somewhat clumpy.

Dot the top of the fruit with the oat mixture. Bake for 45 minutes, or until the topping is crisp and brown and the fruit is bubbling. Serve warm or at room temperature.

MAKES 6 SERVINGS

MAPLE CUSTARD

For a silkier and richer custard (but one higher in cholesterol, too), make this with 3 or 4 egg yolks instead of the 2 eggs.

- **2 cups milk**
- **2 large eggs**
- **¼ cup maple syrup, warmed**
- **1 teaspoon vanilla extract**
- **1 teaspoon grated lemon zest**

In a small saucepan, scald the milk and let cool slightly.

In the top of a double boiler, lightly beat the eggs and maple syrup together.

Stir about ¼ cup of the hot milk into the eggs to warm them. Stirring constantly, gradually add the remaining hot milk to the warmed eggs. Place over hot (not boiling) water and stir constantly until thick and smooth, about 7 minutes. Remove from the heat and let cool. Add the vanilla and lemon zest, then chill thoroughly.

MAKES 4 SERVINGS

HONEY CUPS

Here is a simple version of the classic French crème caramel. Instead of caramelizing granulated sugar to flavor a custard, this dessert uses the deep flavors of a dark honey.

- **2 tablespoons dark honey, such as buckwheat**
- **2 cups milk**
- **⅓ cup sugar**
- **2 large eggs**
- **2 large egg yolks**
- **1 teaspoon vanilla extract**

Preheat the oven to 325°F. Divide the honey among four 6-ounce custard cups.

In a small saucepan, combine the milk and sugar, and heat, stirring to dissolve the sugar, just until wisps of steam rise from the surface. Let cool slightly.

In a medium bowl, beat the whole eggs and egg yolks very lightly with a wire whisk. Stir about ¼ cup of the hot milk into the eggs to warm them. Stirring constantly, gradually add the remaining hot milk to the warmed eggs. Add the vanilla. (For a smoother, more elegant result, you should strain the custard at this point, but it's up to you.)

Place the cups in a baking pan. Very gently ladle the custard into the cups on top of the honey. Place the baking pan on a pulled-out oven rack and pour in hot water to reach halfway up the sides of the custard cups. Bake for 40 minutes, or until the centers of the custards are set.

Remove the custard cups from the water bath and let cool to room temperature. Refrigerate until well chilled, at least 4 hours. To unmold, loosen the edges with a knife and invert the custards onto individual plates.

MAKES 4 SERVINGS

BERRY TRIFLE

Though the English christened this dish trifle, it is anything but that—rich, flavorful, and fancy, it is a major attraction whenever it is served.

- **Maple Pound Cake (page 503)**
- **⅓ cup Raspberry Sauce (page 478)**
- **½ cup slivered almonds**

2 cups fresh berries (raspberries, strawberries, blueberries, or a mixture)

English Custard Sauce (right)

1 cup heavy cream, whipped

Select a glass serving bowl about 7 inches in diameter and 3 inches deep.

Cut enough ½-inch slices of cake to line the bottom of the dish and place them in the dish, trimming so there is even coverage. Cover with the raspberry sauce.

Cut the rest of the cake into cubes and scatter over the slices. Sprinkle ¼ cup of the almonds over the cubes.

Spread 1 cup of the fruit over the cake, then spoon all of the custard sauce over the fruit. Spread the whipped cream over the top. Decorate the whipped cream with the remaining 1 cup fruit and ¼ cup almonds.

MAKES 8 SERVINGS

RASPBERRY SAUCE

To thaw the raspberried, place them in a strainer set over the saucepan you will use to make the sauce.

2 packages (10 ounces each) frozen unsweetened raspberries, thawed

3 tablespoons honey

2 teaspoons cornstarch

3 tablespoons water

In a medium saucepan, combine the raspberries and honey. Stir over low heat until just below boiling.

In a small bowl, blend the cornstarch and water. Add to the berry-honey mixture and cook slowly until thick and smooth, 5 to 7 minutes. Strain the sauce through a coarse sieve.

MAKES 2 CUPS

ENGLISH CUSTARD SAUCE

Called crème anglaise *in French, this is a classic dessert sauce. Serve over bread puddings, steamed puddings, or cobblers.*

4 large egg yolks

⅓ cup light honey

2 teaspoons vanilla extract

1½ cups light cream

In a medium bowl, beat the egg yolks, honey, and vanilla until the mixture is light and thick.

In a medium saucepan, bring the light cream to a boil over medium-low heat. Whisking constantly, slowly pour the hot cream into the egg mixture. Return the egg mixture to the saucepan and stir over low heat until it thickens enough to coat the back of a spoon.

MAKES 2 CUPS

FLUFFY ENGLISH CUSTARD: Whip ½ cup heavy cream and fold it into the custard sauce.

TIRAMISÙ-STYLE TRIFLE

A tiramisù is an Italian dessert in which ladyfingers are soaked in brewed espresso and then layered with sweetened mascarpone, an extremely rich fresh cheese. We've taken the same ideas but substituted Greek yogurt and cream cheese for a much healthier (but still satisfyingly rich) dessert.

1 cup cold brewed espresso or other dark-roast coffee

2 tablespoons unsweetened cocoa powder

2 tablespoons plus ¼ cup agave nectar

1 container (7 ounces) 2% Greek yogurt

4 ounces reduced-fat cream cheese (Neufchâtel), at room temperature

½ cup heavy cream

- ½ teaspoon vanilla extract
- 1½ packages (3 ounces each) ladyfingers
- 1 ounce semisweet chocolate, grated, for serving

In a wide shallow bowl, gradually whisk the coffee into the cocoa until smooth. Whisk in 2 tablespoons of the agave nectar.

With an electric mixer, beat the remaining ¼ cup agave nectar, the yogurt, cream cheese, heavy cream, and vanilla, until light and fluffy.

Spread 3 tablespoons of the yogurt mixture in the bottom of a 6- to 8-cup glass serving bowl.

Split the ladyfingers in half horizontally. One at a time, lightly dip one-third of the ladyfingers in the coffee mixture and arrange in the bottom of the dish. Spread with one-third of the remaining yogurt mixture. Repeat twice, finishing with a layer of the yogurt mixture. Cover and refrigerate 8 hours or overnight.

At serving time, sprinkle the grated chocolate over the top.

MAKES 8 SERVINGS

COCONUT MOUNDS

You can use unsweetened or sweetened coconut for this, but be sure to use shredded coconut, not flaked.

- ½ cup brown rice
- 1¾ cups milk
- ⅓ cup honey
- 2 tablespoons cornstarch
- ½ cup chopped pecans
- 1 teaspoon vanilla extract
- 3 large eggs, separated
- ½ cup shredded coconut
- ¼ cup very finely ground pecans

Cook the brown rice according to the package directions. Set aside to cool.

Preheat the oven to 350°F. Butter 6 individual custard cups and place in a small roasting pan.

In a medium saucepan, combine the milk, honey, and cornstarch, and cook over low heat, stirring occasionally, until thickened. Remove from the heat and stir in the rice, chopped pecans, and vanilla.

In a small bowl, beat the egg yolks. Stirring constantly, gradually add the egg yolks to the milk mixture. Pour into the custard cups.

Place the roasting pan on a pulled-out oven rack and pour in hot water to come halfway up the sides of the cups. Bake for 30 minutes, or until firm. Cool slightly, then unmold onto a buttered baking sheet. (Leave the oven on.)

Meanwhile, in a small bowl, combine the coconut and ground pecans.

With an electric mixer, beat the egg whites until stiff but not dry. Spread over the tops and sides of the custards. Sprinkle the coconut-pecan mixture over the egg whites.

Return to the oven and bake for 5 minutes, or until the coconut is lightly browned.

MAKES 6 SERVINGS

INDIAN-SPICED COCONUT MOUNDS: Use brown basmati rice. Use cashews instead of pecans. Add ½ teaspoon ground cardamom to the custard.

BAKED BROWN RICE PUDDING

This homey, traditional treat is a welcome reminder of the good old days, a change of pace from complicated desserts.

- 3 large eggs, beaten
- ½ cup packed turbinado or light brown sugar

3 cups milk, scalded
1 cup cooked brown rice
½ cup golden raisins
½ teaspoon grated lemon zest
½ teaspoon vanilla extract
Nutmeg

Preheat the oven to 350°F. Butter 6 individual custard cups and place in a small roasting pan.

In a medium bowl, combine the eggs and brown sugar. Slowly add the milk, stirring constantly, until smooth. Stir in the rice, raisins, lemon zest, and vanilla.

Pour into the prepared cups and sprinkle nutmeg on top of each. Place the roasting pan on a pulled-out oven rack and pour in hot water to come half-way up the sides of the cups. Bake for 30 to 40 minutes, or until a knife inserted in center of a custard comes out clean.

MAKES 6 SERVINGS

INDIAN-STYLE RICE PUDDING

Thick, creamy, and oh so easy to make. If you like, add raisins or chopped dried apricots in addition to the chopped pistachios.

3 cups milk
⅓ cup brown basmati rice
¼ cup honey
1 teaspoon ground cardamom
½ teaspoon ground ginger
Pinch of salt
¼ cup sugar
¼ cup shelled pistachios, coarsely chopped

In a medium saucepan, bring the milk and rice to a boil over medium heat. Reduce the heat to low, stir in the honey, cardamom, ginger, and salt, and cook, stirring frequently, until the pudding is thick and creamy and the rice is very tender, about 1¼ hours.

Stir in the sugar and pistachios. Serve warm or chilled.

MAKES 4 SERVINGS

CRANBERRY-PECAN RICE PUDDING

Pecan rice is a type of aromatic rice with a distinctly nutty flavor. If you can't find it, basmati rice is a good substitute.

1 cup pecan rice
½ teaspoon salt
1 can (12 ounces) evaporated low-fat milk
⅓ cup packed turbinado or light brown sugar
1 teaspoon grated lemon zest
½ cup milk
½ teaspoon vanilla extract
¼ teaspoon cinnamon
½ cup dried cranberries or raisins
½ cup finely chopped pecans

In a medium saucepan, cook the rice according to the package directions, using the ½ teaspoon salt.

Stir in the evaporated milk, sugar, and lemon zest. Cover and cook for 10 minutes longer.

Uncover and cook, stirring frequently, until the rice is very creamy and most of the liquid has been absorbed, about 15 minutes.

Stir in the whole milk, vanilla, and cinnamon, and remove from the heat. Stir in the cranberries. Let cool to room temperature, then stir in the pecans. Refrigerate until chilled, about 2 hours.

MAKES 6 SERVINGS

OLD-FASHIONED RHUBARB TAPIOCA CREAM

To really gild the lily, serve this creamy dessert with cold English Custard Sauce (page 478).

RHUBARB PUREE

- 2 pounds rhubarb, cut into 1-inch pieces
- 3/4 cup light honey
- Grated zest of 1 lemon

TAPIOCA CREAM

- 2 cups milk
- 2 large eggs, beaten
- 1/4 cup light honey
- 3 tablespoons quick-cooking tapioca
- 1 teaspoon vanilla extract

CANDIED LEMON SHREDS

- 1 lemon
- 1/4 cup light honey
- 1/4 cup water

To make the rhubarb puree: In a deep heavy-bottomed pot, combine the rhubarb, honey, and lemon zest. Cover and cook for several minutes over low heat until the rhubarb is soft, stirring occasionally to prevent scorching. Puree the mixture in a blender or food processor. (You should have about 2 cups puree.) Chill thoroughly.

To make the tapioca cream: In a 1-quart heavy-bottomed pot, combine the milk, eggs, honey, and tapioca. Let the mixture stand for 5 minutes. Then cook over medium heat, stirring constantly, until the mixture comes to a boil, about 5 minutes.

Remove from the heat and cool to room temperature. Blend in the vanilla. Chill thoroughly.

To make the candied lemon shreds: Using a vegetable peeler, peel strips of zest from the lemon. With a very sharp paring knife, cut the zest on the diagonal into long hair-thin shreds. In a small saucepan, bring the honey and water to a boil. Add the lemon shreds and simmer for 5 minutes. Drain in a strainer and set aside.

Combine the rhubarb puree and tapioca cream and fold together until smooth. Transfer the mixture to a serving bowl and scatter the lemon shreds on top. Chill until serving time.

MAKES 4 TO 6 SERVINGS

MEXICAN CHOCOLATE TAPIOCA

A hint of cinnamon and vanilla extract give this its Mexican flair.

- 1 cup pearl tapioca
- 2 1/2 cups reduced-fat (2%) milk
- 1/8 teaspoon salt
- 1/4 cup packed muscovado or dark brown sugar
- 1/2 teaspoon cinnamon
- 1/2 teaspoon vanilla extract
- 1/8 teaspoon almond extract
- 1 large egg
- 1 large egg yolk
- 3 ounces bittersweet chocolate, chopped

Place the tapioca in a bowl and cover with cold water. Soak overnight in the refrigerator. Drain.

In a medium saucepan, combine the tapioca, 2 cups of the milk, and the salt. Bring to a simmer over medium-low heat and cook, stirring frequently, until thick, about 10 minutes.

Stir in the brown sugar, cinnamon, and vanilla and almond extracts, stirring until the sugar has melted, about 1 minute.

In a small bowl, whisk together the whole egg, egg yolk, and remaining 1/2 cup milk. Whisk the mixture into the pan. Cook over medium-low heat, whisking constantly, until the tapioca is thick, about 5 minutes. Remove from the heat and add the chocolate. Cover and let sit for 5 minutes. Uncover and stir the mixture to blend in the chocolate. Cool to room temperature, then refrigerate until ready to serve.

MAKES 6 TO 8 SERVINGS

CHOCOLATE TOFU PUDDING

A nice option for those who have eliminated dairy from their diets.

1/3 cup water

3 tablespoons unsweetened cocoa powder

2/3 cup mild honey

1 tablespoon mini chocolate chips

12 ounces soft silken tofu

1 tablespoon muscovado or dark brown sugar

1/2 teaspoon cinnamon

1/4 teaspoon almond extract

2 teaspoons toasted sliced almonds, for serving

In a small saucepan, stir the water into the cocoa powder. Stir in the honey and heat over very low heat until hot. Stir in the chocolate chips and stir until melted. Set the chocolate syrup aside to cool slightly.

In a food processor, combine the chocolate syrup, tofu, brown sugar, cinnamon, and almond extract. Puree until smooth.

Spoon into 4 dessert dishes and chill until serving time. To serve, scatter the nuts on top.

MAKES 4 SERVINGS

PEANUT BUTTER CUP MOUSSE

Who doesn't love chocolate and peanut butter together?

3 tablespoons cornstarch

1 1/2 cups milk

1/2 cup packed turbinado or light brown sugar

1 large egg

5 teaspoons creamy peanut butter

1/4 teaspoon salt

2 tablespoons chocolate or hazelnut liqueur

1/4 cup water

1/2 teaspoon unflavored gelatin

1/2 cup very cold half-and-half

3 tablespoons Greek yogurt

2 tablespoons honey

2 tablespoons chocolate chips, melted, for serving

1 tablespoon minced peanuts, for serving

In a small bowl, combine the cornstarch, 1/2 cup of the milk, and 1/4 cup of the brown sugar. In a small bowl, lightly beat the egg.

In a medium saucepan, combine the remaining 1 cup milk and 1/4 cup brown sugar, the peanut butter, and the salt. Bring to a boil over medium heat. Whisk the cornstarch mixture into the hot milk mixture and cook, whisking, until thickened, about 5 minutes.

Gradually whisk some of the hot milk mixture into the beaten egg, then whisk the warmed egg mixture back into the hot milk mixture and bring to a boil over medium heat. Reduce the heat to low and cook, whisking constantly, until the mixture is thickened, about 2 minutes. Remove from the heat and stir in the chocolate liqueur. Let cool to room temperature.

Meanwhile, place the water in a small heatproof bowl, sprinkle the gelatin over, and let stand until softened, about 4 minutes. Set the bowl over a small saucepan of simmering water and stir until the gelatin dissolves, about 3 minutes. Set aside to cool to room temperature.

With an electric mixer, beat the half-and-half and yogurt until foamy. Gradually add the honey and beat until thickened. Beat in the dissolved gelatin until well combined.

Fold the half-and-half mixture into the peanut butter mixture. Spoon the mousse into 4 serving bowls and chill until set, about 2 hours.

To serve, drizzle each serving with the melted chocolate and sprinkle with the peanuts.

MAKES 4 SERVINGS

BAKED AMARANTH PUDDING

A lemony, fragrant custard enhanced with the taste and texture of amaranth grains.

- 3 large eggs
- 1 cup milk
- ½ cup honey
- 2 cups cooked amaranth
- ½ cup raisins
- 1 teaspoon vanilla extract
- 1 teaspoon grated lemon zest
- 1 teaspoon lemon juice
- Boiling water

Preheat the oven to 350°F. Butter 8 individual custard cups and place in a large roasting pan.

In a large bowl, beat the eggs. Beat in the milk and honey. Stir in the amaranth, raisins, vanilla, lemon zest, and lemon juice.

Pour the mixture into the custard cups. Set the roasting pan on a pulled-out oven rack and pour in 1 inch of boiling water. Bake for 1 hour, or until the custards are firm and a knife inserted near the edge of a custard comes out clean. Remove from the water bath and let cool. Serve warm or chilled.

MAKES 8 SERVINGS

BAKED BARLEY-CHERRY CUSTARD

Barley makes a nice, chewy substitute for rice in a sweet, fruit-studded baked pudding.

- 4 cups milk
- ¼ cup pearled barley
- ¼ teaspoon salt
- 2 large eggs
- ¼ cup chopped dried cherries
- 2 tablespoons brown rice syrup or honey
- ½ teaspoon vanilla extract
- Cinnamon

In a large saucepan, combine the milk, barley, and salt. Cook over medium-low heat until the barley is tender, 45 to 55 minutes.

Preheat the oven to 350°F.

In a small bowl, beat the eggs. Add the cherries, rice syrup, and vanilla. Slowly stir the egg mixture into the barley and cook over very low heat for 5 minutes, stirring constantly.

Spoon the mixture into 4 to 6 individual custard cups and sprinkle lightly with cinnamon. Bake for 10 to 15 minutes, or until the custard is set. Cool, then refrigerate. Serve chilled.

MAKES 4 TO 6 SERVINGS

STEAMED CARDAMOM PUDDING

The exotic flavor and aroma of cardamom are seductive. Serve the pudding with hot Raspberry Sauce (page 478). To read more about steamed pudding molds, see "Steamed Puddings," page 466.

- 1/3 cup butter
- 1/3 cup white whole wheat flour*
- 1/2 teaspoon salt
- 1 1/4 cups milk, scalded
- 4 large eggs, separated
- 1/3 cup ground almonds, pistachios, or cashews
- 1/4 cup honey
- 1/2 teaspoon ground cardamom
- 1/8 teaspoon saffron (optional)

milled from white wheat grains

Butter a 2-quart steamed pudding mold. Select a pot wide enough and deep enough to hold the mold. Place a rack in the bottom of the pot.

In a 1-quart heavy-bottomed saucepan, melt the butter over medium heat. Stir in the flour and salt, and cook for several minutes, but do not brown. Pour in the milk and stir until well blended. Cook over low heat until very thick and smooth, stirring constantly. Remove from the heat and let the white sauce cool to lukewarm.

With an electric mixer, beat the egg whites until stiff but not dry.

In a separate large bowl, combine the egg yolks, nuts, honey, cardamom, and saffron (if using), and beat until frothy. Stir in the white sauce. Fold in the egg whites.

Pour the mixture into the pudding mold and cover tightly with a lid or 2 thicknesses of foil or parchment paper tied with string. Set the mold on the rack in the pot and pour boiling water into the pot until it reaches halfway up the sides of the mold. Cover the pot and set over low heat so the water boils gently, and cook for 2 hours, or until the pudding is firm and has pulled gently away from the sides of the mold. Add more water if necessary as the pudding cooks.

Let cool for 10 minutes. Unmold onto a serving plate.

MAKES 8 TO 10 SERVINGS

STEAMED FRUIT PUDDING

Serve with cold English Custard Sauce (page 478).

- 1 cup pineapple juice
- 1 large egg, beaten
- 1/4 cup dark honey
- 1/4 cup plain low-fat yogurt
- 3 tablespoons vegetable oil
- 1 cup chopped dates
- 1/2 cup chopped golden raisins
- 1/2 cup chopped nuts
- 1 teaspoon vanilla extract
- 1 1/2 cups whole wheat flour
- 1 teaspoon cinnamon
- 3/4 teaspoon baking soda
- 1/2 teaspoon salt
- 1/4 teaspoon nutmeg

Butter a 1-quart steamed pudding mold. Select a pot wide enough and deep enough to hold the mold. Place a rack in the bottom of the pot.

In a large bowl, combine the pineapple juice, egg, honey, yogurt, and oil. Stir in the dates, raisins, nuts, and vanilla. Mix well.

In a medium bowl, whisk together the flour, cinnamon, baking soda, salt, and nutmeg. Stir into the fruit mixture.

Pour the batter into the mold and cover tightly

with a lid or 2 thicknesses of foil or parchment paper tied with string. Set the mold on the rack in the pot and pour boiling water into the pot until it reaches halfway up the sides of the mold. Cover the pot and set over low heat so the water boils gently, and cook for 1 hour. Add more water if necessary as the pudding cooks.

Preheat the oven to 250°F.

Remove the mold from the steamer and transfer to the oven. Bake for 1 hour, or until the pudding is firm and cooked through.

Unmold the pudding onto a large serving plate.

MAKES 6 SERVINGS

HALVA

Rich as satin, this classic dessert is drenched in honey syrup in the style of the Middle East.

- **½ cup (1 stick) butter**
- **⅓ cup packed turbinado or light brown sugar**
- **2 large eggs**
- **1 cup farina (uncooked)**
- **½ cup finely chopped almonds**
- **½ teaspoon cinnamon**
- **¼ cup honey**
- **¼ cup water**

Preheat the oven to 350°F. Butter an 8 × 8-inch baking pan.

In a medium bowl, cream the butter and brown sugar. Beat in the eggs, one at a time. Gradually fold in the farina, almonds, and cinnamon. Pour into the pan and bake for 30 minutes. Let cool for 15 minutes.

In a small saucepan, simmer the honey and water for 10 minutes and pour over the halva. Cool and cut into squares or diamonds.

MAKES 16 SERVINGS

PUMPKIN CUSTARD PUDDING

Be careful not to buy canned pumpkin pie mix, which is sweetened and has spices added to it.

- **1 cup unsweetened pumpkin puree**
- **½ cup buttermilk**
- **½ cup orange juice**
- **¼ cup plus 1 tablespoon honey**
- **2 tablespoons butter**
- **½ teaspoon nutmeg**
- **2 tablespoons flour**
- **2 tablespoons water**
- **2 large eggs, separated**
- **⅛ teaspoon cream of tartar**
- **½ teaspoon grated orange zest**

Preheat the oven to 325°F. Butter a 1½-quart baking dish.

In a medium saucepan, combine the pumpkin puree, buttermilk, orange juice, ¼ cup of the honey, the butter, and nutmeg, and blend well. Bring to a boil.

In a small bowl, combine the flour and water, and stir into the pumpkin mixture. Simmer, stirring frequently, until thick and smooth, about 20 minutes. Remove from the heat.

With an electric mixer, beat the egg whites until foamy. Add the cream of tartar and continue beating. Gradually add the remaining 1 tablespoon honey and continue beating until stiff peaks form.

In another small bowl, lightly beat the egg yolks. Stir in a little of the hot pumpkin mixture to warm the yolks, then stir the yolks into the pumpkin mixture. Stir in the orange zest. Fold in the egg whites.

Pour the batter into the baking dish. Bake for 1 hour, or until firm. Serve warm.

MAKES 4 TO 6 SERVINGS

DATE NUT PUDDING

Serve with frozen yogurt or sherbet.

¼ cup (½ stick) butter

¼ cup packed muscovado or dark brown sugar

1 large egg

¾ cup plus 2 tablespoons whole wheat flour

½ teaspoon baking soda

⅛ teaspoon salt

⅓ cup buttermilk

1 cup coarsely chopped dates

1 cup chopped pecans or walnuts

Preheat the oven to 350°F. Butter an 8 × 8-inch baking pan.

In a medium bowl, cream the butter and brown sugar until light and fluffy. Add the egg and blend well.

In a small bowl, whisk together the flour, baking soda, and salt. Add portions of the flour mixture to the butter mixture, alternating with the buttermilk. Stir in the dates and pecans.

Scrape the batter into the pan. Bake for 30 minutes, or until the pudding is light brown and springs back when touched. Let cool slightly. Serve warm.

MAKES 8 SERVINGS

PRUNE PLUM & BREAD PUDDING

Italian prune plums are small oval plums with blue-purple skin and a light flesh. These are the plums that are dried to make prunes. Serve this delicious bread pudding with homemade crème fraîche (opposite).

6 tablespoons butter, at room temperature

2 tablespoons plus ½ cup light honey

10 slices whole-grain bread

½ cup water

2 strips (4 x ½ inch) orange zest

1½ pounds Italian prune plums (10 to 15), halved and pitted

2 large eggs

2 large egg yolks

1¼ cups milk

1 teaspoon vanilla extract

¼ teaspoon salt

Preheat the oven to 350°F. Butter a 5-cup shallow baking dish.

In a small bowl, blend the butter and 2 tablespoons of the honey together. Spread one side of each bread slice with the honey butter. Cut each slice into 4 squares and set aside.

In a deep heavy-bottomed pot, combine the remaining ½ cup honey, the water, and the orange zest. Stir over medium heat until the mixture comes to a boil, then reduce to a simmer and cook the syrup for 3 minutes.

Add the plums, cover, and simmer until the plums are tender but still firm, 5 to 8 minutes. (They should not become mushy or disintegrate.)

Arrange the bread butter-side down on the bottom of the baking dish. With a slotted spoon, transfer the plums to the bread. (Reserve the poaching syrup.) Cover the plums with the remaining squares of bread, butter-side up, in slightly overlapping rows. Transfer the baking dish to a roasting pan.

In a medium bowl, combine ¼ cup of the reserved poaching liquid, the whole eggs, egg yolks, milk, vanilla, and salt, and beat well.

Pour the custard mixture over the bread in the baking dish. Place the roasting pan on a pulled-out oven rack and add hot water to come halfway up the sides of the baking dish. Bake for 30 minutes, pressing down on the bread once or twice to keep it moist and in place.

Increase the oven temperature to 425°F and bake until the top browns. Serve warm or chilled.

MAKES 6 SERVINGS

CHOCOLATE & APRICOT BREAD PUDDING

Multi-grain sandwich bread gives body to this comforting dessert, but you can easily substitute brioche, sourdough, or even cinnamon raisin bread. It's fine to use reduced-fat 2% milk.

- 1 cup packed turbinado or light brown sugar
- 3 large eggs
- 4 large egg yolks
- 1 cup bittersweet or semisweet chocolate chips
- 4 cups milk
- 1 loaf (1 pound) stale multi-grain bread, crusts removed
- 1½ teaspoons vanilla extract
- 1 cup dried apricots (6 ounces), thinly sliced
- ⅓ cup sliced almonds

In a large metal bowl, whisk together the sugar, whole eggs, and egg yolks. Add ½ cup of the chocolate chips.

In a medium saucepan, bring the milk just to a boil over medium-high heat. Slowly stir the hot milk into the egg mixture, stirring vigorously until the chocolate is melted (it's okay if the mixture is not perfectly blended).

Cut the bread slices into 1½-inch squares (about 6 cups). Add the bread and vanilla to the milk mixture and stir to moisten the bread. Let sit for 30 minutes.

Preheat the oven to 325°F. Lightly oil a 9 × 9-inch baking pan and place in a large roasting pan.

Stir the remaining ½ cup chocolate chips and the apricots into the bread mixture. Spread evenly in the baking pan. Top with the almonds. Place the roasting pan on a pulled-out oven rack. Add boiling water to the roasting pan to come halfway up the sides of the baking pan. Bake for 1 hour 30 minutes, or until a knife inserted in the center comes out clean. Remove the baking pan from the water bath and let cool on a rack.

MAKES 10 SERVINGS

CHERRY BREAD PUDDING

If you can't get fresh tart cherries (they have a very short season), use sweet cherries and omit the sugar.

- 2 tablespoons butter
- 4 slices whole wheat bread
- 2 cups tart cherries, pitted
- 2 tablespoons sugar
- ⅓ cup honey

HOMEMADE CRÈME FRAÎCHE

A delicious alternative to sour cream and yogurt, crème fraîche is a thick, subtly tart fermented cream. Combine 2 tablespoons cultured buttermilk and 1 cup cream in a clean, warm jar with a screw top. Cover the jar tightly and set it in a warm place for 12 to 24 hours. When the mixture has set or is almost firm, transfer to the refrigerator to complete thickening. Crème fraîche will keep nicely in the refrigerator for up to 10 days.

- 3 large eggs
- 1 cup milk, scalded
- 1 teaspoon vanilla extract
- ¼ teaspoon salt
- ¼ teaspoon cinnamon
- ¼ teaspoon ground cloves
- Pinch of nutmeg
- English Custard Sauce (page 478)

Preheat the oven to 325°F. Butter an 8½ × 4½-inch loaf pan.

Lightly spread both sides of the bread slices with the butter. Place 2 slices of bread in the bottom of the loaf pan, trimming to fit if necessary. Cover with the cherries. Sprinkle with the sugar. Place the remaining 2 slices of bread on top.

In a medium bowl, gradually beat the honey into the eggs and continue beating until pale yellow, 2 to 3 minutes. Whisking constantly, slowly beat in the hot milk. Stir in the vanilla, salt, cinnamon, cloves, and nutmeg. Pour the custard over the bread and cherries. Let stand for 10 minutes to let the bread absorb the custard.

Cover with foil and bake for 30 minutes. Remove the foil and bake for 30 more minutes, or until the eggs are set and the top is nicely browned. Let cool slightly. Serve with the English Custard Sauce.

MAKES 6 TO 8 SERVINGS

FALLEN WALNUT SOUFFLÉ

A fallen soufflé is a dense, moist dessert, made extra rich here by the ground walnuts. Consider this recipe in the fall when nuts are plentiful in the market.

- 5 large eggs, separated
- ½ cup honey
- 1 cup white whole wheat flour*
- 1 cup walnuts, finely ground
- ¼ teaspoon salt
- ½ cup milk

**milled from white wheat grains*

Preheat the oven to 350°F. Butter the bottom and sides of a 1½- or 2-quart baking dish.

With an electric mixer, beat the egg whites until stiff but not dry. Set aside.

In a medium bowl, beat the egg yolks until frothy. Gradually beat in the honey, and beat until thick and lemon colored. Beat in the flour, nuts, and salt. Add the milk and blend well. Fold in the egg whites.

Pour the batter into the baking dish. Bake for 45 minutes, or until the edges are puffed and the center still looks a bit moist. Cool on a wire rack.

MAKES 4 TO 6 SERVINGS

HOMEMADE GREEK YOGURT

Greek yogurt is a thick, creamy yogurt that has had much of the whey drained from it so it is about double the thickness of regular yogurt. It is easy to make your own: Set a strainer over a bowl and line the strainer with dampened cheesecloth or paper towels. Spoon regular yogurt into the strainer and let drain in the refrigerator for 5 hours, or until reduced by half.

APRICOT SOUFFLÉ

Dried peaches or nectarines would also be great here. Cut them in half before measuring them, though, to approximate the same volume as apricots.

- **½ cup finely ground toasted almonds**
- **1 cup dried apricots**
- **1 tablespoon lemon juice**
- **1 tablespoon arrowroot**
- **½ teaspoon almond extract**
- **4 large eggs, separated**
- **⅓ cup plus 2 tablespoons honey**
- **¼ teaspoon cream of tartar**

Preheat the oven to 375°F.Butter the bottom and sides of a 1½-quart soufflé dish and dust with ¼ cup of the ground almonds.

In a small saucepan, combine the apricots and enough water to just cover. Bring to a boil. Reduce to a simmer and cook until they are very soft, about 20 minutes.

Drain the apricots, transfer to a blender or food processor, and puree. Blend in the remaining ¼ cup almonds, lemon juice, arrowroot, and almond extract.

In a medium bowl, beat the egg yolks until pale. Gradually add ⅓ cup of the honey and continue beating until light and fluffy. Beat in the apricot mixture.

In a separate bowl, beat the egg whites until foamy. Add the cream of tartar and continue beating. Gradually add the remaining 2 tablespoons honey and continue beating until stiff but not dry. Fold half of the egg whites into the apricot mixture to lighten it. Fold in the remaining egg whites just enough to combine.

Pour the batter into the soufflé dish. Bake for 25 to 30 minutes, until the soufflé is tall and puffed. Remove from the oven and serve immediately.

MAKES 4 TO 6 SERVINGS

CHOCOLATE SEMIFREDDO

If you like, fold in chunks of crisp cookies before turning the semifreddo into the loaf pan.

- **8 ounces bittersweet chocolate, chopped**
- **2 large eggs**
- **⅓ cup plus 1 tablespoon sugar**
- **1½ teaspoons vanilla extract**
- **Pinch of salt**
- **1⅓ cups heavy cream**

Line an 8 × 4-inch loaf pan with plastic wrap, leaving a 2-inch overhang all around.

Place the chocolate in a medium bowl set over, not in, a pan of simmering water. Do not stir, but when the chocolate looks about two-thirds melted, remove the bowl from the heat and stir until smooth. (The residual heat in the bowl does the rest of the job.)

Place the eggs and ⅓ cup of the sugar in a large bowl set over, not in, a pan of simmering water. Whisk until thick and the whisk leaves track marks in the mixture, about 5 minutes. Remove from the heat, whisk in the chocolate, vanilla, and salt, and let cool to room temperature.

With an electric mixer, beat the cream to soft peaks. Beat in the remaining 1 tablespoon sugar and beat to stiff peaks.

Fold about ½ cup of the whipped cream into the chocolate mixture to lighten it, then fold in the remaining whipped cream. Spoon into the loaf pan and fold the plastic wrap over to cover. Freeze for at least 6 hours.

To serve, uncover and invert the loaf onto a serving platter. Remove the plastic wrap and let the loaf stand at room temperature for 10 minutes before slicing.

MAKES 8 TO 10 SERVINGS

MAPLE SEMIFREDDO

Semifreddo means half-frozen, but it really implies a dessert made with the same ingredients as ice cream, but not churned in an ice cream machine.

4 large eggs

⅔ cup maple syrup

2 cups heavy cream, whipped

⅓ cup finely chopped walnuts, for serving

In the top of a double boiler, lightly beat the eggs, then gradually add the syrup. Set over hot water and cook, stirring with a wire whisk or wooden spoon, until thick and smooth, about 8 minutes. Remove from the heat and let cool.

Fold in the whipped cream. Spoon into individual soufflé dishes or parfait glasses. Freeze for several hours.

When ready to serve, top with the walnuts.

MAKES 6 TO 8 SERVINGS

MAPLE-RUM SEMIFREDDO: Add 1 tablespoon dark rum to the custard mixture.

HONEY-VANILLA ICE CREAM

Here's a basic, custard-based ice cream.

2 cups cold milk

⅓ cup honey

1 tablespoon cornstarch

2 large egg yolks, beaten

2 cups light cream

1 tablespoon vanilla extract

In a small bowl, combine ½ cup of the milk, the honey, and cornstarch. Stir until smooth.

In the top of a double boiler, scald the remaining 1½ cups milk. Stir in the cornstarch mixture very slowly. Cook over hot water for 8 minutes. Add the egg yolks and cook for 2 more minutes. The mixture should be thick and smooth. Remove from the heat and let cool.

Stir the cream and vanilla into the mixture. Pour into the canister of an ice cream maker. Freeze according to the manufacturer's instructions.

MAKES 3 PINTS

MELTING CHOCOLATE

Melting chocolate takes a little bit of finesse. Even the slightest bit of moisture that falls into a pot of melting chocolate will cause it to seize up and become unusable. There are several methods of melting chocolate that will make this less likely to happen:

Microwave method: Place the chocolate in a microwave safe bowl and microwave in 15-second increments, testing the chocolate each time to see if it has melted. Microwaved chocolate will hold its shape and not look melted, tempting some people to continue cooking it, which will burn the chocolate.

Double-boiler method: Melt the chocolate in the top of a double boiler. This is especially good if you're dealing with large quantities of chocolate, but somewhat inefficient if you only have an ounce or so to melt.

Bowl over hot water: With this method you can melt any quantity of chocolate and match the size of the bowl to your needs. Find a bowl that will rest on the top rim of a saucepan without falling into the pan. Bring an inch or so of water to a boil in the pan. Then turn off the heat, place the bowl over the just boiled water, and stir the chocolate until it melts.

PRUNE ICE CREAM: Add 1 cup pureed cooked prunes to the mixture before or after processing in the ice cream maker.

PUMPKIN ICE CREAM: Add 1 cup solid-pack pumpkin puree, sweetened with ⅓ cup honey and spiced with ½ teaspoon cinnamon, ⅛ teaspoon ground ginger, and ⅛ teaspoon ground cloves, to the mixture before processing.

PEACH ICE CREAM

Whipping the cream before combining it with the chopped peaches makes this eggless ice cream lighter than others.

- 4 cups sliced peeled peaches
- 3 tablespoons honey
- 1 tablespoon lemon juice
- ½ teaspoon unflavored gelatin
- 1 cup heavy cream, whipped

Place the peaches in a medium bowl. Add the honey and lemon juice, and toss well. Cover and set aside for 2 hours. Reserving the juices, drain the peaches and transfer to a food processor.

Place ¾ cup of the reserved juice in a small saucepan. Sprinkle with the gelatin and let sit for 5 minutes to soften. Stir over low heat until the gelatin is completely dissolved.

Add the gelatin mixture to the peaches and process until finely chopped. Transfer the peach mixture to a bowl and refrigerate until it begins to thicken. Fold in the whipped cream. Pour into the canister of an ice cream maker. Freeze according to the manufacturer's instructions.

MAKES 1 QUART

HONEY-LEMON ICE CREAM

Serve topped with Blueberry Sauce (below).

- ¾ cup light honey
- Grated zest of 3 lemons
- ½ cup lemon juice
- 6 large egg yolks
- 4 cups light cream

In a small saucepan, combine the honey, lemon zest, and lemon juice, and stir over low heat until blended.

In a large bowl, beat the egg yolks until light and thick. Continue beating while slowly adding the honey mixture. Beat until thick and thoroughly cooled. Stir in the cream. Pour into the canister of an ice cream maker. Freeze according to the manufacturer's instructions.

MAKES 1½ QUARTS

BLUEBERRY SAUCE

Fresh blueberry sauce makes a great ice cream topping, but you can also stir it into yogurt to make a dessert called a fool. To make a blueberry fool, lightly sweeten Greek yogurt with honey or maple syrup and swirl some of this blueberry sauce into it. Use about one part blueberry sauce to two parts yogurt.

- ¾ cup blueberry all-fruit spread
- 2 teaspoons lemon juice
- 3 cups blueberries

Rub the spread through a fine-mesh sieve into a 1-quart saucepan. Add the lemon juice and stir over low heat until it comes to a boil. Add the blueberries and continue to stir until the mixture is warm. (Do not cook too long; the berries should not fall apart.)

MAKES 3 CUPS

SOUR CREAM ICE CREAM WITH BERRIES & BASIL

This luxurious, slightly sour ice cream is adapted from a recipe from a gourmet diner in Greenwich Village in New York City. The fresh basil adds a peppery bite. You may substitute raspberries, blackberries, or strawberries for blueberries.

- 2 cups milk
- ½ cup granulated sugar
- 2 tablespoons brown rice syrup
- 2 cups sour cream
- 1 pint blueberries
- 2 tablespoons superfine sugar
- 1-inch piece of vanilla bean
- 2 teaspoons lemon juice
- 4 leaves fresh basil, slivered

In a medium saucepan, combine the milk, granulated sugar, and rice syrup. Stir over medium-low heat until the sugar has just dissolved, 2 to 3 minutes. Do not let the mixture scald or simmer. Remove from the heat, transfer to a bowl, and add the sour cream. Whisk until smooth.

Place the mixture in the freezer for about 10 minutes to quick-cool.

Pour the mixture into the canister of an ice cream maker. Freeze according to the manufacturer's instructions.

Meanwhile, in a medium bowl, gently crush three-fourths of the blueberries with the superfine sugar. Stir in the remaining whole berries. Slit open the vanilla bean and scrape the seeds into the mixture. Add the lemon juice and half the basil, and stir to mix. Let stand about 20 minutes, until the ice cream is ready.

To serve, spoon some of the berry mixture onto each dessert plate. Top with a scoop of ice cream and sprinkle with the remaining basil strips.

MAKES 12 SERVINGS

CHERRY BUTTERMILK SHERBET

You can make this any time of year because frozen cherries work just as well as fresh in this recipe. In fact, you can chop them while they're still frozen.

- 3 cups buttermilk
- 1 cup chopped sweet cherries
- ⅓ cup honey
- 3 tablespoons pineapple juice
- 1 teaspoon grated lemon zest

In a medium bowl, combine the buttermilk, cherries, honey, pineapple juice, and lemon zest, and mix well.

Pour the mixture into the canister of an ice cream maker. Freeze according to the manufacturer's instructions.

MAKES 1 QUART

PINEAPPLE-PECAN FROZEN YOGURT

When you drain the pineapple, be sure to save the juice to use to make the gelatin.

- 1 envelope unflavored gelatin
- ¼ cup pineapple juice
- 2 cups plain low-fat yogurt
- 1 cup juice-packed crushed pineapple, drained
- ¼ cup honey
- ¼ cup chopped toasted pecans

In a small saucepan, combine the gelatin and juice. Place over low heat and stir until the gelatin is completely dissolved, about 3 minutes.

In a medium bowl, whisk the yogurt until smooth. Stir in the crushed pineapple, honey, and nuts. Fold in the gelatin mixture, and whisk lightly until well blended.

Pour the mixture into the canister of an ice cream maker. Freeze according to the manufacturer's instructions.

MAKES 1½ PINTS

TANGERINE-BANANA ICE MILK

In a pinch, you could use canned mandarin oranges instead of tangerines.

- ⅓ cup brown rice syrup
- 2 teaspoons grated lemon zest
- 1 tablespoon lemon juice
- 2 cups milk
- ½ cup mashed banana
- ½ cup very finely chopped tangerines

In a small bowl, combine the rice syrup, lemon zest, and lemon juice. Mix well.

Pour the milk into a large bowl and slowly whisk in the lemon-syrup mixture. Stir in the banana and tangerines.

Pour the mixture into the canister of an ice cream maker. Freeze according to the manufacturer's instructions.

MAKES 1 QUART

BANANA-SOY ICE MILK

Flavored soymilks often have natural thickeners to give the beverage weight, which works well in this frozen dessert.

- 3½ cups vanilla soymilk
- 1½ cups very ripe banana slices
- ⅓ cup maple syrup

In a blender, process the soymilk, banana, and maple syrup until smooth.

Pour the mixture into the canister of an ice cream maker. Freeze according to the manufacturer's instructions.

MAKES 1 QUART

POMEGRANATE GRANITA

The more you break up a granita as it freezes, the finer the texture of the crystals. This granita is soft with medium-size crystals. Unlike the normal still-freezing method (see page 494), when you make a granita, you use a fork instead of a rotary beater to break up the ice crystals.

- ½ cup agave nectar
- 3 cups pomegranate juice
- 2 tablespoons fresh pomegranate arils (seeds), optional
- 6 mint leaves, for garnish

In a medium bowl, stir the agave nectar into the pomegranate juice until combined. Pour the mixture into a 9 × 13-inch glass or metal baking dish and freeze.

After an hour, use a fork to break up the mixture by raking across the surface to make fine-grained fragments. Repeat every 30 minutes until frozen, about 3 hours.

To serve, scrape up granita with a spoon and mound into dessert glasses. Top with the pomegranate arils if using, and a mint leaf.

MAKES 6 SERVINGS

FRESH MELON GRANITA

Instead of using a fork as in the traditional method of making dessert, this refreshing granita takes advantage of the power of a food processor. You can make this summer ice with cantaloupe, muskmelon, or watermelon. Look for a melon that is fragrant and feels heavy for its size. Adjust the amount of sugar in the recipe according to the sweetness of the fruit.

1 cup water

⅓ cup sugar

4 cups peeled, seeded ripe melon chunks

1 tablespoon lemon juice

In a small saucepan, heat the water and sugar over medium heat until the sugar dissolves. Let cool to lukewarm.

In a food processor, combine the cooled sugar mixture, melon, and lemon juice, and puree until smooth (makes about 4 cups). Transfer to a 9 × 3-inch glass or metal baking dish. Freeze for 1½ to 2 hours, stirring every 30 minutes, until frozen solid.

Break into chunks and puree in a food processor. Transfer to a plastic container and return to the freezer for 20 to 30 minutes, until the granita is firm. Serve in chilled dessert bowls or glasses.

MAKES 6 SERVINGS

STILL-FREEZING DESSERTS

Prepare any of these frozen dessert recipes as directed, but don't freeze in an ice cream maker. Instead, pour the mixture into one (or more, depending on the quantity in the recipe) 8- or 9-inch-square metal baking pans. Place in the freezer for about 1 hour, or until the mixture is mushy but not solid.

Transfer the mixture to a chilled bowl and beat rapidly with a chilled rotary beater until smooth. Work as quickly as possible to prevent melting.

Return the mixture to the pan(s) and return to the freezer. When it has frozen almost solid, remove and beat again until smooth.

Cover the pan(s) with plastic wrap to prevent ice crystals from forming on the top. Place in the freezer again to complete setting.

Cakes & Cookies

Cakes

Making cakes can seem daunting, but if you follow a few simple rules and have good ingredients and a few essential tools, it can be quite simple. First and foremost, always read a recipe through to the end before you begin. Making sure you have all the ingredients you need on hand, and allow yourself enough time.

The measurements are given as precisely as possible, so follow them for best results. Measure all ingredients carefully. Fancy equipment is not necessary, but measuring cups (both liquid and dry), measuring spoons, and mixing bowls are key. (For the proper way to measure dry and liquid ingredients, see "Measuring, Equivalents & Substitutions," page 18.)

Use only the best-quality and freshest ingredients when you make a cake. Generally speaking, ingredients should be brought to room temperature before mixing for best results. Eggs will have greater volume, and butter will cream faster and become fluffier. However, if eggs must be separated, it is easier to do so while they're still cold.

Always make sure you have the proper type and size pan required for the recipe. The wrong size pan can affect the cooking time and the texture of the cake. When the pan is too big, for example, the batter spreads out more than it should, so it bakes faster and doesn't rise well; when the pan is too small, the batter bakes more slowly, because it is too tightly confined, and will spill over the pan.

Most, if not all, recipes call for a preheated oven. Allow the oven 20 minutes to get up to the proper temperature. An oven thermometer, the type that is kept in the oven, is inexpensive and invaluable in judging whether your oven is set to the correct temperature.

Pay close attention to the mixing procedure called for in each cake recipe, such as *beating*, *blending*, and *creaming* (see Cake Mixing Terms, page 496). These steps are usually given in the order necessary for the most desirable results. Unless a recipe specifies otherwise, the batter is usually

CAKE MIXING TERMS

Beating: Mixing ingredients vigorously in a circular motion with a long wooden spoon, wire whisk, or electric mixer

Blending: Mixing two or more ingredients together until an even and consistent mixture is attained

Creaming: Beating butter, alone or with a second ingredient (often a sweetener), with an electric mixer until a pale, fluffy, creamy mixture is attained

Folding: Slow and careful manual mixing of ingredients in a folding motion with a spatula. It is often used to mix beaten egg whites with batter so that the individual texture of each is maintained in the mixture

---

beaten just long enough to blend the ingredients evenly. Overbeating will produce a dense-textured cake, and underbeating can cause the cake to be too coarse or to have large holes in it. In general, it should take no longer than 8 to 10 minutes to add all the ingredients and blend them. With a little experience you will be able to tell when the beaten batter is just right, by its texture and appearance.

Cake-Making Basics

Mixing the Batter

For most cake recipes the combined dry ingredients are portioned and added alternately with the liquid ingredients to the mixture of creamed butter or oil, sweetener, and egg. This is an efficient way to blend ingredients without overmixing, so the result is an even-textured cake.

First, soften room-temperature (about 70°F) butter by repeatedly working it against the side of a large bowl with the back of a wooden spoon or by beating it at low speed with an electric mixer until it is creamy. Next add the sweetener and beat with an electric mixer until light and well combined. The mixture should be smooth and a little thinner than the consistency of whipped cream.

The eggs are beaten in next, one at a time, until well combined and the mixture is thick, fluffy, and pale in color. At this point there is no need to worry about overbeating the batter, so beat it at high speed for several minutes to get the desired color and texture (usually specified in the recipe).

The flour and other dry ingredients are added to the batter next, alternating with the liquid ingredients. (It's best to whisk the dry ingredients together in another bowl beforehand, so that they are ready to be added.) Begin by gradually adding one-third of the flour mixture and beating it in at low speed. Add half the liquid, then another third of the flour mixture. Mix after each addition until just smooth. Complete the process with the second half of the liquid and the remaining flour mixture. Stop beating before you add each new ingredient and use a rubber spatula to scrape the sides of the bowl.

After the flour has been added, it is important to guard against hard or long beating of the batter because overbeating develops the flour's gluten, resulting in a very dense-textured cake. Blend just until the batter is smooth.

For a batter that incorporates beaten egg whites, the last step is to gently fold them into the batter by hand, using a rubber spatula, never with an electric mixer. Use a gentle folding motion and do not overfold.

Pans

Angel food cakes, and sometimes sponge cakes, are baked in ungreased tube pans with removable rims. The center tube provides support for these very light airy batters as they rise. If the pan has any traces of grease, clean it well and dry it, or the batter will not rise properly—it needs to cling to the sides of the pan.

Layer cakes are best baked in pans with straight sides. For butter and creamed cakes the bottom of the pan is usually buttered or oiled, then lightly dusted with flour. Medium-weight, shiny baking pans distribute heat evenly and give a light, nicely browned cake crust. Dark pans may cause cakes to brown too much or to burn. If using glass baking dishes, remember to lower the oven temperature by 25°F, but bake for the same amount of time.

Pour or spoon the batter into the pans, spreading it toward the sides and into the corners (for square pans). Leave the center slightly lower to guarantee a level, flat-topped cake. Fill the pans about two-thirds full with batter.

Baking

Cakes should be browned nicely and evenly and begin to pull away from the pan's sides when done. To test whether a cake is done, insert a toothpick into the center of the cake. Generally the toothpick should come out clean with no batter adhering to it, but occasionally the directions will say that a few moist crumbs should adhere. If unsure, gently press the top of the cake; it should be springy and show no fingerprints.

Removing Cakes from Pans

Most cakes should be removed from the pans soon after baking or they will become soggy and difficult to remove. Butter cakes should be allowed to cool in the pan for about 5 minutes after being removed from the oven. Cakes that are exceptionally rich (heavy, dense) should stay in the pan for 10 to 15 minutes. Use a knife or metal spatula to loosen the cake from the sides of the pan and carefully invert the cake onto a wire cooling rack. Invert again and allow the cake to cool top-side up on a rack.

Angel food and sponge cakes should be cooled thoroughly upside down in the pan before being removed. Once cool, loosen the edges of the cake and the center with a knife or metal spatula, and turn it out bottom-side up onto a cake plate.

Unless the recipe directs otherwise, allow cakes to cool completely before frosting or filling them.

CAKE TIPS

- At high altitudes, be especially careful not to overbeat egg whites and incorporate too much air into the batter. Raise the cake's baking temperature by 25°F.
- Lightly dust nuts, dried fruit, and lumpy ingredients with flour to keep them from sinking to the bottom of the batter. Fold them into the batter just before baking.
- If making cakes with white flour, enrich the flour according to the Cornell Formula (see page 000) for a more nutritious cake.

Frostings & Fillings

Some cakes are fine just as they are, without frostings or fillings. But frostings and fillings can add extra appeal to an ordinary cake, making it suit-

FROSTING REQUIREMENTS

NUMBER AND SIZE OF CAKE	AREA TO BE FROSTED	AMOUNT OF FROSTING NEEDED (CUPS)
One 8-inch round cake	Top and sides	¾
Two 8-inch round layers	Tops and sides	1½
One 9-inch round cake	Top and sides	1
Two 9-inch round layers	Tops and sides	2
One 9 x 5-inch loaf	Top and sides	1½
One 8-inch square cake	Top	¾
One 9 x 13-inch sheet cake	Top	2
12 cupcakes	Tops	1
10 x 15-inch jelly roll	Filling	2-2½

able for a special occasion. Frostings and fillings are simple to make and usually can be whipped up in the time it takes for the cake to cool.

Frostings are usually made with a high proportion of sweetener blended with rich ingredients such as butter, cream cheese, cream, or sour cream and flavored with cocoa, peanut butter, lemon or orange zests, or innumerable other natural flavorings.

Boiled icings are a traditional type of frosting based on a procedure for making what is known as Italian meringue—beating a hot syrup into beaten or unbeaten egg whites. These icings are very easily made with honey instead of sugar, usually with *unbeaten* egg whites. They will be soft, fluffy, and light but not quite as stiff as sugar frostings. All the ingredients, including the egg whites, may be put into the top of a double boiler and beaten with a wire whisk or a rotary beater while the mixture cooks. When it is ready, the frosting should be stiff enough to stand in peaks.

Use frostings as soon as they are made, or pack in a well-sealed container and refrigerate. Bring to room temperature before using.

Before applying frosting, make sure the cake is thoroughly cooled. Then lightly brush off any crumbs so the frosting will be smooth on the cake. Place the first cake layer top-side down on a plate. Arrange strips of waxed paper just under the edge of the bottom layer, all around the cake, allowing them to extend over the plate's edge so they catch any drips and keep the plate clean. (Wait until the frosting has set to remove the waxed paper.)

Cover the first layer with frosting or filling almost to the edge. Place the second layer top-side up on top of this. First frost the sides with frosting knife or metal spreader, working the frosting from the bottom to the top. The frosting should touch the waxed paper. Then scrape all the remaining frosting on top of the cake. With sweeping strokes, spread it out to the sides. Use a frosting knife or the back of a teaspoon to stroke decorative swirls or scrolls into the frosting.

Storing Cakes

Store cakes in covered containers away from other foods that might absorb moisture and dry the cake out or impart their flavor to the cake. Most cakes can be frozen unfrosted. Defrost, then fill or frost or both.

Cheesecakes

Cheesecakes, rich and delicate, are prepared from a sweetened mixture of fresh cheese, eggs, and flavorings. The cheese may be made from whole, low-fat, or skim milk. Cream cheese, ricotta, and cottage cheese are the most commonly used cheeses, their richness depending on their butterfat content. Cream, sour cream, or yogurt may be added to the cheese mixture for smoothness and to lighten the cake.

Eggs thicken and bind the other ingredients, giving its characteristic texture. They may be separated, the beaten egg whites folded in at the end to lighten the cake.

A small amount of flour or cornstarch may be used to stabilize cheesecake. Gelatin is used in unbaked cheesecakes, and must first be softened in cold liquid, then dissolved over hot water.

Any number of liquid sweeteners or sugar may be used to sweeten the cheesecake.

Springform pans are usually used for cheesecakes with crusts. This makes the cake easy to remove from the pan without breaking the cake.

Baking time and temperature depend on the creaminess of the finished cake. The creamier you want the cake to be, the shorter the time it should be baked. When the cake looks set and begins to pull away from the pan's edge but is still a bit wobbly in the center, it is done.

Cheesecakes are very delicate and have a tendency to crack, so they must be cooled slowly. A common practice is to allow the cake to remain in the turned off oven for 1½ to 2 hours while it slowly reaches room temperature. It should then be covered and refrigerated. It can also be frozen.

Cookies

You can make good-tasting sweets in the form of cookies and bars using all sorts of ingredients. Rolled oats, nonfat dry milk, wheat germ, yogurt, dried fruit, and nuts are just some of the nutritious extras that can be added. Cookies are perfect as desserts or snacks and travel well. There are four basic types of cookies:

Drop cookies are made from a fairly soft dough. You usually use one level teaspoon or tablespoon of dough for each cookie. If the dough doesn't drop easily from the spoon, push it off with your finger or another spoon. Allow plenty of space between cookies on the baking sheet because they spread as they bake.

Refrigerator cookies are popular because they are so easy to prepare. Also called icebox or slice-and-bake cookies, they are made from a log of dough that is chilled until firm enough to be thinly sliced. The dough is shaped into logs 1 to 2 inches in diameter, then wrapped in waxed paper or plastic wrap and refrigerated or frozen. When the dough is firm, unwrap it, thinly slice, and bake as directed.

Bar cookies are baked in a pan. Pour the batter into prepared buttered pans. For the right texture, make sure to use the pan size called for in the recipe. Once baked, these cookies can be cut into small bars or squares while still warm, then stored in the baking pan, covered, or transferred to airtight cookie tins when cooled.

Rolled cookies are the type in which the dough is rolled out on a lightly floured surface or on a pastry cloth and cut into shapes with cookie cutters. The dough can be made ahead and either refrigerated for up to 3 days, or frozen for up to 3 months. Bring the dough to room temperature before rolling with a lightly floured rolling pin.

Making cookies can be quick and easy. The ingredients may simply be stirred together, or creamed as for cakes, or mixed as for pastries. Honey and other liquid sweeteners produce softer batters and doughs than those made with sugar. It is up to the cook to decide on the texture of the cookies—thick and chewy, or thin and crispy. Whole wheat pastry flour yields a cookie dough that spreads out during baking to produce thin, delicate cookies. Regular whole wheat flour yields a firmer cookie that holds its shape while baking. The amount of flour used will also affect the texture of the cookie. You may find it necessary to add more flour to some recipes because of variations in the freshness and absorbency of flours.

Using butter as the shortening yields the most flavorful cookie, but where melted butter is called for, oil is an economical and healthful substitute, especially in recipes where strong flavorings such as cinnamon, cloves, or anise seeds are to be used.

In some cases a recipe will call for chilling the dough; this is to make it more manageable. Also, if you're working with a large amount of dough, you may want to refrigerate some of the dough while you work with a manageable portion. Some cookie doughs can be made several days in advance and chilled until ready for use (follow the recipe). You also may freeze cookie dough.

Baking Sheets

Cookies bake best on flat sheets made of heavy material. Cookies may also be baked on top of an overturned roasting pan if you do not have baking sheets. A recipe will generally direct you to grease, or grease and flour a baking sheet, or, for ease and simple cleanup, you may use parchment paper. Slide the whole sheet of parchment onto a wire rack to cool the cookies. Cool the baking sheet slightly before using it to bake a second batch. Parchment paper can be wiped clean with a paper towel and reused.

Place cookies of even sizes at least 1 inch apart on the sheet, although some recipes will specify more room between the cookies. Be sure there are at least 2 inches between the baking sheet edges and the oven walls so that heat can circulate freely. It is best to put just one baking sheet in the oven at a time, but this can take a long time if you are baking several batches. What you can do is rotate the baking sheets from top to bottom and front to back, midway through the baking time.

Baking Times

Baking times vary for different types of cookies, but all should be baked until the edges are just beginning to brown lightly. If the cookies do not seem to be browning around the edges, lift one with a spatula to check for browning underneath.

After cookies have been baked, use a large thin-bladed spatula to move them carefully to a wire rack to cool. In some cases, a recipe will instruct you to leave the cookies on the baking sheet for a minute or so before moving them to a rack. This is for cookies that need to firm up just a bit first. Bar cookies may be cut while still warm, but they should be left in the baking pan until cooled. Cookies are still fragile when warm, so handle them gently and never stack them on top of each other until completely cooled, or they will stick together.

COOKIE TIPS

- If a cookie recipe calls for nuts, use any kind. For a change of flavor and for added nutrition, try sunflower or pumpkin seeds, sesame seeds, or toasted wheat germ in addition to, or in place of, nuts.
- Freshen stale cookies by heating them in the oven for about 5 minutes at 325°F.
- Bar cookies and most drop cookies are firm and moist and suitable for travel. Very delicate, crisp, wafer cookies are fragile and do not travel well.

Storing Baked Cookies

Allow cookies to cool completely before storing them between layers of waxed paper in an airtight container. If you plan to keep the cookies for longer than a week, store them in the freezer. Do not store more than one kind of cookie in the same tin because flavors tend to mingle.

WHOLE WHEAT SPONGE CAKE

Fill these layers with Lemon Curd (page 526), whipped cream and berries, or a fruit filling. The top can simply be dusted with confectioners' sugar. This batter is quite versatile and can also be used to make ladyfingers (the variation at right).

6 large eggs, separated

1 tablespoon grated orange zest

½ cup orange juice

½ cup plus 2 tablespoons honey, warmed

1⅓ cups whole wheat pastry flour

¼ teaspoon salt

1 teaspoon cream of tartar

Preheat the oven to 325°F. Have three 8-inch round cake pans ready.

With an electric mixer, beat the egg yolks at high speed until thick and lemon colored, about 5 minutes. Beat in the orange zest and orange juice and beat 5 minutes more. Gradually beat in ½ cup of the honey, 1 tablespoon at a time, until the mixture is very thick and the batter flows back into the bowl in a thick ribbon when the beaters are lifted, 12 to 15 minutes. Do not underbeat—the lightness of this sponge cake depends on this beating process.

Evenly sprinkle the flour over the egg yolk mixture and gently fold it in. Set aside.

With an electric mixer, beat the egg whites and salt until foamy. Add the cream of tartar and beat until the mixture forms soft peaks. Gradually add the remaining 2 tablespoons honey and beat until the mixture is stiff but not dry. With a rubber spatula, gently fold the egg white mixture into the egg yolk mixture.

Pour the batter into the 3 unbuttered baking pans. Bake for 20 to 22 minutes, until the tops spring back when lightly touched and the cakes are beginning to pull away from the sides of the pans. Cool the cakes completely in the pans. Run a metal spatula around the edges of the pans and invert the cakes onto a rack. Fill and frost as desired.

MAKES 8 SERVINGS

LADY FINGERS: Prepare the batter as directed. Drop the batter by tablespoons onto the parchment to form fingers about ¾× 3 inches, spacing them 2 inches apart. Bake for 10 minutes, or until set and lightly golden. Cool on the pan fro 5 minutes, then remove from the paper, and place on a rack to cool completely. Makes 30 Ladyfingers.

LEMON ANGEL FOOD CAKE

Cake flour is milled from exceptionally soft wheat and makes a very light cake. Serve the cake with Raspberry Sauce (page 478).

12 large egg whites, at room temperature

1¼ teaspoons cream of tartar

½ teaspoon salt

1¼ cups sugar

3 tablespoons grated lemon zest

1 teaspoon vanilla extract

½ cup white whole wheat flour*

½ cup cake flour

**milled from white wheat grains*

Preheat the oven to 325°F. Have a 10-inch tube pan or angel food pan ready. If the pan does not have "legs" around the edge, have ready a bottle with a long neck that is narrow enough to fit in the center hole of the pan.

With an electric mixer, beat the egg whites, cream of tartar, and salt until foamy. Gradually beat in the sugar, 2 tablespoons at a time, until thick, soft peaks form. Beat in the lemon zest and vanilla.

Gently fold the flours into the egg white mixture, ¼ cup at a time, until incorporated. Spoon into the ungreased 10-inch angel food or tube pan. Bake for 50 minutes until the top springs back when lightly pressed.

Invert the cake pan either over the neck of a bottle or on the work surface if the pan has legs. Cool the cake completely before running a metal spatula around the edge and center, then inverting onto a cake platter.

MAKES 12 SERVINGS

ORANGE-ALMOND ANGEL FOOD: Substitute orange zest for the lemon zest and use ½ teaspoon almond extract instead of vanilla.

MAPLE POUND CAKE

Pound cake is rich and buttery on its own and needs no garnish, but if you like, serve with fresh berris.

- 1 cup (2 sticks) butter, at room temperature
- 1 cup maple syrup
- 4 large eggs
- 1 teaspoon vanilla extract
- 2 cups whole wheat pastry flour
- ½ teaspoon baking soda
- ¼ teaspoon salt
- ⅔ cup sour cream

Preheat the oven to 300°F. Butter and flour a 9 × 5-inch loaf pan.

With an electric mixer, beat the butter until light and fluffy. Add the maple syrup and beat to combine. Add the eggs one at a time, beating well after each addition. Beat in the vanilla.

In a separate bowl, whisk together the flour, baking soda, and salt. Alternately add portions of the flour mixture and the sour cream to the butter mixture, beginning and ending with the flour mixture.

Pour the batter into the pan. Bake for 1 hour 30 minutes, or until lightly browned and a toothpick inserted in the center of the cake comes out clean. Cool in the pan on a rack for 10 minutes, then run a spatula around the edges and invert the cake onto a rack. Turn upright and let cool completely on the rack.

MAKES 8 SERVINGS

LEMON POPPY SEED POUND CAKE

Using Meyer lemons will help make this pound cake moist. A cross between a lemon and an orange, a Meyer is sweeter and less acidic than a regular lemon.

- 2¼ cups flour
- 2 teaspoons baking powder
- ¾ teaspoon salt
- 1 cup (2 sticks) unsalted butter, at room temperature
- 1½ cups sugar
- 1 tablespoon grated lemon zest
- 3 large eggs, at room temperature
- ½ cup sour cream
- ¾ cup milk
- ½ cup poppy seeds (2 ounces)

Preheat the oven to 350°F. Butter and flour a 9 × 5-inch loaf pan.

In a medium bowl, stir together the flour, baking powder, and salt. Set aside.

In the bowl of a stand mixer fitted with a paddle attachment (or with an electric hand mixer), beat the butter, sugar, and zest on medium-high speed until light and fluffy, about 3 minutes. Beat in the eggs one at a time, until light and fluffy. Beat in the sour cream until just incorporated. Gradually add the flour mixture to the butter mixture in three parts, alternating with the milk, beginning and ending with the flour mixture. Fold in the poppy seeds by hand.

Spoon the batter into the pan and smooth the top. Bake for 55 to 60 minutes, or until a toothpick inserted in the center comes out clean. Let cool in the pan 10 minutes. Remove from the pan and transfer to a rack to cool completely. Wrap with plastic until ready to serve.

MAKES 12 SERVINGS

CHOCOLATE-SWEET POTATO CAKE

Sweet potatoes add moistness, natural sweetness, and a lot of beta-carotene.

- 3/4 pound sweet potatoes, peeled and thinly sliced
- 1 cup whole wheat flour
- 1 cup unbleached all-purpose flour
- 3/4 teaspoon baking soda
- 3/4 teaspoon cinnamon
- 1/4 teaspoon salt
- 3/4 cup granulated sugar
- 3/4 cup packed turbinado or light brown sugar
- 1/4 cup vegetable oil
- 2 large eggs
- 3 large egg whites
- 3 ounces unsweetened chocolate, melted
- 1 1/2 teaspoons vanilla extract
- 1/2 cup buttermilk
- 1 package (8 ounces) reduced-fat cream cheese (Neufchâtel)
- 1 package (8 ounces) full-fat cream cheese
- 1 cup confectioners' sugar
- 1/4 cup unsweetened cocoa powder
- 1/2 cup apricot all-fruit spread

In a steamer, cook the sweet potatoes until very tender, about 20 minutes. Transfer to a bowl and mash. Set aside.

Preheat the oven to 350°F. Lightly oil two 8-inch round cake pans.

In a medium bowl, stir together the flours, baking soda, cinnamon, and salt. Set aside

With an electric mixer, beat the granulated sugar, brown sugar, and oil until well combined. Beat in the whole eggs and egg whites one at a time, beating well after each addition. Beat in the mashed sweet potatoes, chocolate, and vanilla. Alternately fold in the flour mixture and the buttermilk, beginning and ending with the flour mixture.

Spoon the batter into the pans. Bake for 30 minutes, or until a toothpick inserted in the centers comes out clean. Cool 10 minutes in the pans on a rack, then turn out onto the rack to cool completely.

Meanwhile, with an electric mixer, cream the cream cheeses with the confectioners' sugar and cocoa.

Place one layer on a cake plate. Spread the top with the apricot fruit spread. Top with the second layer and frost the top and sides with the cream cheese frosting.

MAKES 16 SERVINGS

CAPPUCCINO PUDDING CAKE

The ingredients in this cake cause a layer of cake to rise to the top as it bakes, leaving a pudding layer below. When you serve the cake, invert it so that it has a natural "frosting."

- 3/4 cup packed muscovado or dark brown sugar
- 1/4 cup plus 2 tablespoons unsweetened cocoa powder
- 3/4 cup granulated sugar
- 1 teaspoon plus 2 tablespoons instant espresso powder
- 3/8 teaspoon salt
- 1 cup whole wheat flour

¼ cup nonfat dry milk

2 teaspoons baking powder

¼ teaspoon cinnamon

½ cup low-fat (1%) milk

¼ cup extra-light olive oil

1 teaspoon vanilla extract

1¾ cups very hot water

Preheat the oven to 350°F. In a small bowl, combine the brown sugar, ¼ cup of the cocoa powder, ¼ cup of the granulated sugar, 1 teaspoon of the espresso powder, and ⅛ teaspoon of the salt. Set the brown sugar mixture aside.

In a medium bowl, combine the flour, powdered milk, the remaining ½ cup granulated sugar, remaining 2 tablespoons cocoa, remaining 2 tablespoons espresso, remaining ¼ teaspoon salt, the baking powder, and the cinnamon.

In a 1-cup measure, combine the liquid milk, oil, and vanilla. Stir the milk mixture into the flour mixture until well combined.

Scrape the batter into an ungreased 9 × 9-inch baking pan and spread evenly. Sprinkle the reserved brown sugar mixture over the batter. Pour the hot water over. Bake for 40 minutes, or until the top is set and the mixture is bubbling.

Serve warm or room temperature.

MAKES 8 SERVINGS

MERINGUE NUT CAKE

Here the honey is warmed so that it can flow gently into the beaten egg whites. Fill the 3 layers with Lemon Curd (page 526) and decorate the top and sides with Stabilized Whipped Cream (page 524).

6 large egg whites

¼ teaspoon salt

½ teaspoon cream of tartar

½ cup honey, warmed

1 teaspoon vanilla extract

½ teaspoon almond extract

1½ cups blanched almonds or hazelnuts, lightly toasted

2 tablespoons cornstarch

Preheat the oven to 300°F. Butter and flour 2 large baking sheets. Using an 8-inch round cake pan as guide, make three circles on the two baking sheets.

With an electric mixer, beat the egg whites and salt on low speed until foamy. Add the cream of tartar, increase the speed to medium, and beat until soft peaks form. Gradually add the honey, 1 tablespoon at a time. Increase the speed to high and beat until the whites are stiff but not dry. Beat in the vanilla and almond extracts.

In a food processor, finely grind the nuts with the cornstarch. Sprinkle 4 or 5 tablespoons at a time over the egg whites and fold in.

Using a pastry bag with a plain tip or a spoon, spread the batter inside the circles on the baking sheets. Smooth the tops. Bake for 30 to 35 minutes, or until golden brown.

Set the baking sheets on racks until the meringues are cool enough to slide off the sheets.

MAKES 8 TO 10 SERVINGS

ORANGE WALNUT CAKE

Good enough on its own, all this needs to dress it up is a light dusting of confectioners' sugar.

2¾ cups whole wheat pastry flour

2 tablespoons grated orange zest

1 teaspoon baking soda

¼ teaspoon salt

1 cup (2 sticks) butter, at room temperature

1 cup honey

4 large eggs

½ cup orange juice

1 cup coarsely chopped walnuts, dusted with 2 tablespoons flour

Preheat the oven to 350°F. Butter and flour an 8-inch round springform or 10-inch tube pan.

In a large bowl, whisk together the flour, orange zest, baking soda, and salt.

With an electric mixer, beat the butter until light and fluffy. Gradually add the honey and continue beating at medium speed for 2 minutes. Beat in the eggs one at a time, beating well after each addition.

Slowly blend portions of the flour mixture into the butter mixture alternating with the orange juice. Fold in the walnuts.

Scrape the batter into the pan. Bake for 40 to 50 minutes, until a toothpick inserted into the center comes out clean. Let cool in the pan on a rack for 10 minutes. Then run a metal spatula around the edge of the pan (and the center if using a tube pan) and invert onto a rack to cool completely.

MAKES 10 TO 12 SERVINGS

WALNUT TORTE

This is a light and airy cake. Serve warm or cold with Blueberry Sauce (page 491).

4 large eggs, separated

¼ teaspoon salt

¼ cup plus 2 tablespoons honey

1 teaspoon vanilla extract

2 cups walnuts, finely ground

Preheat the oven to 350°F. Butter a 9 × 9-inch or 9-inch round baking pan.

With an electric mixer, beat the egg whites and salt until stiff but not dry.

With an electric mixer, beat the egg yolks until light and lemon colored. Beat in the honey and vanilla. Fold in the ground nuts. Gently fold in the egg whites.

Scrape the batter into the pan. Bake for 10 minutes. Reduce the oven temperature to 325°F and bake for 25 minutes, or until a toothpick inserted in the center comes out clean.

Cool in the pan for 10 minutes, then run a metal spatula around the edge of the pan and invert the cake onto a rack.

MAKES 6 SERVINGS

MAPLE-PECAN TORTE: Use pecans instead of walnuts, and maple syrup instead of honey.

SPICE CAKE WITH MUSCOVADO FROSTING

The secret ingredient in this cake is potatoes.

10 ounces russet (baking) potatoes, peeled and thinly sliced

2 cups whole wheat flour

1 teaspoon cinnamon

¾ teaspoon ground ginger

¾ teaspoon baking powder

½ teaspoon baking soda

¼ teaspoon salt

⅛ teaspoon allspice

⅓ cup cold-pressed sesame oil

1½ cups granulated sugar

1 large egg

2 large egg whites

8 ounces cream cheese, at room temperature

¼ cup packed muscovado or dark brown sugar

1 teaspoon vanilla extract

½ cup peach all-fruit spread

Preheat the oven to 350°F. Lightly oil a 9-inch springform pan. Line the bottom with a circle of waxed paper and oil the paper. Dust with flour, shaking off the excess.

In a large pot of boiling water, cook the potatoes for 12 minutes or until tender. Drain well. Mash with a potato masher.

On a sheet of waxed paper, combine the flour, cinnamon, ginger, baking powder, baking soda, salt, and allspice. With an electric mixer, beat the oil and granulated sugar until well blended. Add the whole egg and egg whites one at a time, beating well after each addition. Beat in the potatoes. Fold in the flour mixture.

Scrape the batter into the pan, smoothing the top. Bake for 45 minutes, or until a toothpick inserted in the center comes out just clean. Cool in the pan on a rack for 15 minutes. Invert onto the rack to cool completely.

With a long serrated knife, cut the cake into 2 horizontal layers. Place the bottom layer on a cake plate.

With an electric mixer, cream the cream cheese with the brown sugar and vanilla. In a small saucepan, melt the fruit spread over low heat. Spread the bottom layer with the fruit spread. Top with the second layer and spread the frosting over the top and sides of the cake.

MAKES 10 SERVINGS

BLACKBERRY JAM CAKE

Dusting the nuts and raisins with flour before adding them to the batter prevents them from sinking to the bottom of the cake. Serve the cake plain or fill or frost with Seven-Minute Frosting (page 524).

2⅓ cups whole wheat pastry flour

1 teaspoon baking soda

1 teaspoon allspice

1 teaspoon cinnamon

1 teaspoon nutmeg

1 teaspoon ground cloves

¼ teaspoon salt

½ cup (1 stick) butter, at room temperature

½ cup honey

3 large eggs

1 cup seedless blackberry jam

⅓ cup buttermilk

½ cup coarsely chopped walnuts, dusted with 1 tablespoon flour

½ cup raisins or chopped dates, dusted with 1 tablespoon flour

Preheat the oven to 350°F. Butter and flour two 8-inch round cake pans or one 7 × 11-inch baking pan.

In a large bowl, whisk together the flour, baking soda, allspice, cinnamon, nutmeg, cloves, and salt. Set aside.

With an electric mixer, beat the butter until light and fluffy. Gradually add the honey and continue beating at medium speed for 2 minutes. Beat in the eggs one at a time, beating well after each addition. Beat in the jam.

Gradually beat the flour mixture into the butter mixture just until blended. Quickly beat in the buttermilk. Fold in the nuts and fruit.

Scrape the batter into the pans. Bake for 30 to 35 minutes, until a toothpick inserted in the center comes out clean. Let cool in the pans on a rack for 10 minutes. Then run a metal spatula around the edge of the pans and invert the cakes onto the rack to cool completely.

MAKES 10 TO 12 SERVINGS

STRAWBERRY SHORTCAKES

Strawberry shortcake gets dolled up with the addition of toasted almond in the batter.

- 1 large egg
- 3 tablespoons honey
- 3 tablespoons milk
- 1 teaspoon vanilla extract
- 1 cup whole wheat pastry flour
- ½ cup flax meal
- 1½ teaspoons baking powder
- ¼ teaspoon salt
- ½ cup (1 stick) cold butter, cut up
- ½ cup almonds, toasted and coarsely chopped
- 1 cup heavy cream, whipped with 2 tablespoons honey
- 2 cups sliced strawberries

Preheat the oven to 425°F. Butter and flour a 9 × 9-inch baking pan.

In a medium bowl, whisk together the egg, honey, milk, and vanilla.

In a food processor, whisk together the flour, flaxmeal, baking powder, and salt. Add the butter and process until the mixture resembles coarse crumbs. Fold in the almonds. Add the egg-honey mixture and pulse briefly, just to combine. Do not overmix.

Scrape the dough into the pan, gently smoothing the top. Bake for 15 minutes, or until lightly browned and a toothpick inserted in the center comes out just clean. Cool slightly.

Cut into 8 serving pieces, then cut each piece in half horizontally. Spoon some whipped cream and all the berries on the bottom halves and top with more whipped cream. Replace the tops and serve immediately.

MAKES 8 SERVINGS

PEACH UPSIDE-DOWN CAKE

Choose firm-ripe peaches for this cake, or substitute nectarines or black plums.

- ¼ cup (½ stick) butter, melted
- ⅔ cup honey
- 1 teaspoon cinnamon
- ⅛ teaspoon nutmeg
- 2 cups sliced peeled peaches
- 1 cup white whole wheat flour*
- 1 teaspoon baking soda
- ¼ teaspoon salt
- ½ cup buttermilk
- ¼ cup vegetable oil
- 1 large egg
- 1 tablespoon grated lemon zest
- 1 teaspoon vanilla extract

**milled from white wheat grains*

Preheat the oven to 350°F. Butter the bottom and sides of an 8 x 8-inch baking pan. Pour the melted butter into the pan.

In a small bowl, stir together ⅓ cup of the honey, the cinnamon, and the nutmeg, and pour it over the butter, tilting the pan so that the honey and butter coat the bottom evenly.

Arrange the peaches over the butter mixture.

In a medium bowl, stir together the flour, baking soda, and salt.

In a separate bowl, whisk together the remaining ⅓ cup honey, the buttermilk, oil, egg, lemon zest, and vanilla. Add to the flour mixture and mix to combine.

Pour the batter over the peaches. Bake for 30 minutes, or until a toothpick inserted in the center comes out clean. Run a metal spatula around the edge of the pan and invert the cake onto a serving plate.

MAKES 6 TO 8 SERVINGS

PINEAPPLE UPSIDE-DOWN CAKE

The classic cake usually calls for maraschino cherries, but we use dried sweet cherries instead.

5 tablespoons butter

½ cup packed turbinado or light brown sugar

2 cans (8 ounces each) juice-packed pineapple rings, drained and juice reserved

8 dried cherries

1 cup whole wheat flour

1 cup cake flour

2½ teaspoons baking powder

½ teaspoon baking soda

¼ teaspoon salt

¼ cup Greek yogurt

1 cup granulated sugar

1 large egg

4 large egg whites

2 teaspoons vanilla extract

⅓ cup reduced-fat (2%) milk

Preheat the oven to 325°F. In a 10-inch ovenproof skillet, preferably cast iron, melt 1 tablespoon of the butter over low heat. Stir in the brown sugar and 2 tablespoons of the reserved pineapple juice. Cook until the sugar is dissolved and the mixture is smooth, about 1 minute. Remove from the heat.

Arrange the pineapple rings in a single layer on top of the brown sugar mixture. Place a dried cherry in the center of each pineapple ring. Set aside.

On a sheet of waxed paper, sift together the flours, baking powder, baking soda, and salt.

With an electric mixer, beat the remaining 4 tablespoons butter, the yogurt, and the granulated sugar until light and fluffy. Beat in the whole egg and egg whites one at a time, beating well after each addition. Beat in the vanilla. With a wooden spoon, alternately stir in portions of the flour mixture and the milk, beginning and ending with the flour mixture, until just combined.

Carefully spoon the batter over the pineapple slices. Bake for 50 to 55 minutes, or until a toothpick inserted in the center comes out clean. Cool the cake in the skillet on a rack for 5 minutes. Invert the cake onto a heatproof plate and serve.

MAKES 12 SERVINGS

GLAZED CARROT CAKE

If you'd rather frost the cake (instead of glazing it), invert the cake onto a cake platter after it has cooled and spread it with Basic Cream Cheese Frosting (page 525).

2 large eggs

¾ cup vegetable oil

½ cup agave nectar

¼ cup buttermilk

1½ cups grated carrots (½ pound)

½ cup chopped pistachios

1¼ cups whole wheat pastry flour

1 teaspoon baking soda

1½ teaspoons cinnamon

1 teaspoon ground ginger

½ teaspoon cardamom

¼ teaspoon salt

Apricot Glaze (page 523)

Preheat the oven to 300°F. Butter an 8 x 8-inch baking pan.

In a large bowl, beat the eggs until well combined. Add the oil, agave nectar, and buttermilk, and beat until well blended. Stir in the carrots and nuts.

In a separate bowl, stir together the flour, baking soda, cinnamon, ginger, cardamom, and salt. Fold into the carrot mixture and mix to combine.

Pour the batter into the pan. Bake for 45 minutes to

1 hour, until a toothpick inserted in the center comes out clean, but with some moist crumbs clinging to it. Cool for 10 minutes. Leave the cake in the pan and, with a small offset spatula, cover the top with the Apricot Glaze. Allow the cake to cool completely.

MAKES 8 SERVINGS

WARM APPLESAUCE CAKE WITH TIPSY RAISINS

The cake is lovely by itself, but you could also serve it with a scoop of ice cream or frozen yogurt. Or perhaps simply dust the top with some confectioners' sugar.

- 1 cup raisins
- 2 tablespoons dark Jamaican rum or orange or pineapple juice
- 2 cups flour
- 1½ teaspoons baking powder
- ½ teaspoon baking soda
- 2 teaspoons cinnamon
- ¾ teaspoon ground ginger
- ¾ teaspoon nutmeg
- ½ teaspoon salt
- ½ cup (1 stick) butter, melted and cooled slightly
- 2 large eggs, at room temperature
- 1 cup packed muscovado or dark brown sugar
- 1½ cups unsweetened applesauce
- ¾ cup coarsely chopped walnuts

Preheat the oven to 350°F. Grease an 8½ × 12-inch glass baking dish.

In a small bowl, soak the raisins in the rum (or juice) for 15 minutes.

In a large bowl, stir together the flour, baking powder, baking soda, cinnamon, ginger, nutmeg, and salt.

In a medium bowl, whisk together the butter, eggs, and brown sugar until smooth and lump-free. Stir in the raisins and rum, applesauce, and walnuts. Pour the applesauce mixture over the flour mixture and stir to mix.

Scrape into the prepared dish and smooth the top. Bake for 45 to 50 minutes, until a toothpick inserted in the center comes out clean. Transfer to a rack and cool slightly. Serve warm or at room temperature.

MAKES 9 SERVINGS

BANANA CRUNCH CUPCAKES

If you can't find oat flour, process rolled oats in a food processor until they are the consistency of flour.

- ½ cup old-fashioned rolled oats
- ⅓ cup date sugar
- 2 tablespoons butter, melted, plus ½ cup (1 stick) butter, at room temperature
- ½ teaspoon cinnamon
- ½ cup honey
- ¼ cup plain low-fat yogurt
- 3 large eggs
- 1 cup mashed bananas (from about 2 bananas)
- 1 teaspoon vanilla extract
- 1¼ cups oat flour
- ¾ cup flax meal
- 2 teaspoons baking soda
- ¼ teaspoon salt
- ½ cup chopped walnuts

Preheat the oven to 325°F. Line 18 muffin cups with paper or nonstick liners.

In a small bowl, mix together the oats, date sugar, melted butter, and cinnamon. Set aside.

In a large bowl, beat together the softened butter and honey. Beat in the yogurt, eggs, mashed bananas, and vanilla.

In a separate bowl, stir together the oat flour, flax meal, baking soda, and salt. Gradually stir the flour mixture into the butter mixture until combined. Fold in the nuts.

Spoon the batter into the muffin cups and sprinkle each with the date sugar mixture. Bake for 20 to 25 minutes, or until a toothpick inserted in the centers comes out clean. Cool in the pan for 5 minutes, then transfer the cupcakes to racks to cool completely.

MAKES 1½ DOZEN CUPCAKES

CHUNKY APPLE CUPCAKES

Reminiscent of an apple coffee cake, serve these as dessert or as part of a basket for breakfast.

- 1½ cups whole wheat flour
- ¾ cup unbleached all-purpose flour
- 2 teaspoons baking powder
- 1 teaspoon baking soda
- 1 teaspoon cinnamon
- ¼ teaspoon salt
- ½ cup (1 stick) butter, at room temperature
- ¼ cup vegetable oil
- ½ cup honey
- ½ cup sour cream
- 2 large eggs
- 1½ cups cubed peeled apples
- ½ cup chopped pecans

Preheat the oven to 325°F. Line 18 muffin cups with paper or nonstick liners.

In a large bowl, whisk together the flours, baking powder, baking soda, cinnamon, and salt.

With an electric mixer, beat the butter, oil, and honey until light and fluffy. Beat in the sour cream and eggs. Gradually blend with the flour mixture. Fold in the apples and nuts.

Spoon the batter into the muffin cups. Bake for 20 to 25 minutes, until a toothpick inserted in the center comes out clean. Cool for 5 minutes in the pan, then transfer to racks to cool completely.

MAKES 1½ DOZEN CUPCAKES

PINEAPPLE-CARROT CUPCAKES

Carrots and pineapple make the cupcakes moist and tender.

- 2¼ cups whole wheat flour
- 2 teaspoons baking soda
- 2 teaspoons baking powder
- 1½ teaspoons cinnamon
- ¼ teaspoon salt
- ½ cup vegetable oil
- 3 large eggs, beaten
- ¼ cup sour cream
- ¾ cup honey
- 1 teaspoon vanilla extract
- 3 carrots, grated on a box grater
- 1 cup angel flake coconut
- 1 cup canned juice-packed crushed pineapple

Preheat the oven to 350°F. Line 18 muffin cups with paper or nonstick liners.

In a large bowl, whisk together the flour, baking soda, baking powder, cinnamon, and salt. Stir in the oil, eggs, sour cream, honey, and vanilla, mixing after each addition. Beat by hand for 1 minute. Fold in the carrots, coconut, and pineapple.

Spoon the batter into the muffin cups. Bake for 25 minutes, or until a toothpick inserted into the centers comes out clean. Cool in the pan for 5 minutes, then transfer to racks to cool completely.

MAKES 1½ DOZEN CUPCAKES

GINGER-GLAZED CUPCAKES

Skip the ginger glaze if you want and frost the cupcakes with Basic Cream Cheese Frosting (page 525) or Honey-Orange Cream Cheese Frosting (page 525).

- 1 cup unbleached all-purpose flour
- ⅓ cup flax meal
- 4 teaspoons ground ginger
- 1 teaspoon baking soda
- ½ teaspoon cinnamon
- ¼ teaspoon salt
- ⅛ teaspoon allspice
- ½ cup packed muscovado or dark brown sugar
- ¼ cup brown rice syrup
- 3 tablespoons extra-light olive oil
- 2 large egg whites
- ½ cup buttermilk
- 3 tablespoons grated fresh ginger
- ½ cup confectioners' sugar

Preheat the oven to 350°F. Line 12 muffin cups with paper or nonstick liners.

On a sheet of waxed paper, combine the flour, flax meal, ground ginger, baking soda, cinnamon, salt, and allspice.

With an electric mixer, beat the brown sugar, rice syrup, and oil until well combined. Beat in the egg whites one at a time, until well incorporated and light in texture.

Alternately fold portions of the flour mixture and the buttermilk into the sugar mixture, beginning and ending with the flour mixture.

Spoon the batter into the muffin cups. Bake for 20 minutes, or until a toothpick inserted in the centers comes out clean. Cool in the pan on a rack.

Into a strainer set over a cup, squeeze the grated ginger with your fingers. Measure out 2 teaspoons of the ginger juice and transfer to a small bowl. Stir in the confectioners' sugar. Spread the tops of the cooled cupcakes with the ginger glaze.

MAKES 12 CUPCAKES

COCONUT CUPCAKES

Leave the cupcakes unfrosted, or go to town and top with Seven-Minute Frosting (page 524) and additional coconut, either toasted or plain.

- 1¾ cups whole wheat pastry flour
- 2 teaspoons baking powder
- 1 teaspoon baking soda
- ¼ teaspoon salt
- ½ cup honey
- ⅓ cup butter, at room temperature
- ¼ cup sour cream
- ¾ cup milk
- 3 large egg whites
- ½ teaspoon almond extract
- 3 cups angel flake coconut

Preheat the oven to 350°F. Line 12 muffin cups with paper or nonstick liners.

In a large bowl, whisk together the flour, baking powder, baking soda, and salt.

With an electric mixer, beat the honey, butter, and sour cream until well combined. Add the flour mixture and the milk, and beat on low for 2 minutes. Add the egg whites and almond extract, and beat 2 minutes more. Fold in the coconut.

Spoon the batter into the muffin cups. Bake for 20 to 25 minutes, until a toothpick inserted into the centers comes out clean. Cool for 5 minutes in the pan. Transfer to a rack to cool completely.

MAKES 12 CUPCAKES

LEMON CHEESECAKE

Not too sweet with a little bit of tang, this is the perfect make-ahead dessert. Once baked, it will keep for several days in the refrigerator. Serve with sliced strawberries.

- **½ cup plain dried whole wheat bread crumbs**
- **½ teaspoon cinnamon**
- **1½ cups low-fat (1%) cottage cheese**
- **¼ cup buttermilk**
- **6 tablespoons honey**
- **3 tablespoons flour**
- **½ teaspoon grated orange zest**
- **1½ teaspoons grated lemon zest**
- **Juice of 1 lemon**
- **1 tablespoon vanilla extract**
- **4 large eggs, separated**

Preheat the oven to 350°F. Butter the bottom and sides of a 9-inch springform pan. Combine the bread crumbs and cinnamon, and sprinkle the mixture into the pan, tilting the pan to lightly coat the sides. Press the crumbs into the bottom of the pan.

In a food processor, combine the cottage cheese, buttermilk, honey, flour, orange zest, lemon zest, lemon juice, and vanilla, and puree until smooth. Add the egg yolks and pulse to combine. Transfer to a large bowl.

With an electric mixer, beat the egg whites until stiff but not dry. Gently fold the egg whites into the cheese mixture.

Pour the batter into the pan. Bake for 40 minutes, or until puffed and set. Turn off the oven and open the door for 1 minute to reduce the heat. Close the door and let the cheesecake remain in the oven for 1 hour. Then refrigerate for several hours or overnight.

Remove the side from the pan to serve.

MAKES 8 TO 10 SERVINGS

CHOCOLATE MARBLE "CHEESE" CAKE

Instead of being made with just tofu, this cheesecake is also made with soy cream cheese.

- **19 ounces silken tofu**
- **10 graham crackers (5½ ounces)**
- **3 tablespoons extra-light olive oil**
- **1 pound tofu cream cheese**
- **3 tablespoons flour**
- **2 large eggs**
- **1 cup sugar**
- **1 teaspoon vanilla extract**
- **⅓ cup chocolate syrup**

Preheat the oven to 350°F. Line a colander with several thicknesses of paper towel. Place the tofu in the colander and set aside 5 to 10 minutes to drain the excess liquid.

In food processor, process the graham crackers to fine crumbs. Transfer the crumbs to a medium bowl. Stir in the oil until just combined. Place the mixture in a 9-inch springform pan and evenly press into the bottom and 1¼ inches up the sides.

Add the drained tofu to the food processor and process until smooth. Add the tofu cream cheese and process until smooth. Add the flour and process until smooth. Add the eggs, sugar, and vanilla, and process until well blended.

Transfer 1 cup of cheesecake mixture to a small bowl and stir in the chocolate syrup until well combined. Transfer the remaining mixture into the crust. Pour the chocolate mixture in a ring on top of batter and swirl in with a spoon.

Bake for 45 minutes. Turn off the oven and leave in the oven for 45 minutes undisturbed. Place on a cake rack in the refrigerator and chill overnight.

MAKES 10 WEDGES

FIG BARS

Our take on a childhood favorite.

FILLING

- 12 ounces dried figs, stems removed, coarsely chopped
- ⅓ cup honey
- 2 tablespoons honey
- 2 tablespoons orange juice
- 1 tablespoon lemon juice

DOUGH

- ½ cup (1 stick) butter, at room temperature
- ½ cup honey
- 1 large egg
- ½ teaspoon grated lemon zest
- 1 tablespoon lemon juice
- 3 cups whole wheat flour
- 1 teaspoon baking powder
- ½ teaspoon baking soda
- ¼ teaspoon salt

To make the filling: In a small saucepan, combine the figs, honey, water, orange juice, and lemon juice. Cook over low heat for 10 minutes, stirring occasionally. Remove from heat and set aside to cool.

Preheat the oven to 400°F. Oil a 9 x 13-inch baking pan.

To make the dough: With an electric mixer, cream the butter and honey together until light and fluffy. Add the egg and mix well. Stir in the lemon zest and lemon juice. Add the flour, baking powder, baking soda, and salt, mixing until combined. Divide the dough in half.

Press half of the dough into the baking pan. Spread the fig filling evenly over the dough. Roll out the remaining dough between two sheets of floured waxed paper into a 9 × 13-inch rectangle. Lay this dough over the filling, pressing down to seal.

Bake for 12 to 15 minutes, or until the dough springs back when pressed lightly with a finger. Cool and cut into 1 × 2-inch bars.

MAKES 4½ DOZEN BARS

APPLE-WALNUT BARS

Cakey bars that are a cross between apple crumb cake and blondies.

- 2 cups flour
- 2 cups packed turbinado or light brown sugar
- 2 cup (1 stick) plus 2 tablespoons unsalted butter, at room temperature
- 1 cup chopped walnuts
- 1 tablespoon cinnamon
- 1 teaspoon baking soda
- ½ teaspoon salt
- 1 cup sour cream
- 1 large egg
- 1 teaspoon vanilla extract
- 2 cups peeled, chopped tart apples, such as Granny Smith

Preheat the oven to 350°F. Oil a 9 × 13-inch baking pan.

With an electric mixer, combine the flour, brown sugar, and butter on low speed to make a crumbly dough. Stir in the nuts. Press 2 cups of this mixture evenly over the bottom of the pan.

To the remaining flour-sugar mixture, add the cinnamon, baking soda, and salt, and beat until incorporated. Beat in the sour cream, egg, and vanilla. Stir in the apples.

Spoon the batter over the crumb base. Bake for 25 to 35 minutes, or until the top is golden and a toothpick inserted in the center comes out clean. Let cool in the pan, then cut into bars.

MAKES 16 BARS

PEAR-ALMOND BARS: Use almonds instead of walnuts and pears instead of apples. Toss the pears with 1 teaspoon lemon juice. Use ½ teaspoon almond extract instead of vanilla.

CHERRY-PECAN BROWNIES

These brownies, though rich and decadent, are a little more healthy because the flaxseed and water combo takes the place of 2 large eggs. For an even tastier version, swap in walnut oil for the safflower oil.

- ½ cup (1 stick) butter
- ⅓ cup safflower oil
- 8 ounces bittersweet chocolate
- 2 heaping tablespoons flaxseeds
- ½ cup water
- 2 large eggs
- 1 cup granulated sugar
- 1 cup packed turbinado light brown sugar
- 2 teaspoons vanilla extract or bourbon
- ½ teaspoon salt
- 1 cup flour
- 1½ cups chopped pecans
- ¾ cup dried cherries, coarsely chopped

Preheat the oven to 350°F. Line a 9 × 13-inch baking pan with 2 sheets of foil crisscross. Oil the foil.

In a small ovenproof bowl, combine the butter, oil, and chocolate. Place it in the oven while it preheats, and let the butter and chocolate melt, about 10 minutes. Remove from the oven.

In a blender, pulse the flaxseeds until finely ground. Add the water and puree until smooth and thick.

In a large bowl, whisk the flaxseed mixture, eggs, sugars, vanilla, and salt. Stir in the melted chocolate mixture. Stir in the flour, and fold in the nuts and cherries.

Scrape the batter into the pan. Bake for 45 minutes, until the top is crackly and shiny, the sides begin to pull away from the foil, and a toothpick inserted into the center comes out with a few moist crumbs attached. Cool in the pan before cutting into 32 brownies.

MAKES 32 BROWNIES

SAUCEPAN MOCHA BROWNIES

These super simple brownies are unusually finely textured, with a hint of coffee in their deep chocolate flavor. A good quality chocolate, such as Ghirardelli, makes them even richer.

- 4 ounces unsweetened chocolate
- ½ tablespoon butter
- 1 cup sugar
- 2 teaspoons instant espresso powder
- 2 large eggs, beaten
- 4 cups milk
- 2 teaspoons dark rum or vanilla extract
- ½ cup flour
- ½ teaspoon baking powder
- ½ teaspoon salt

Preheat the oven to 350°F. Butter and flour an 8 × 8-inch baking pan.

Place the chocolate and butter in a medium, heavy-bottomed saucepan over very low heat and stir with a wooden spoon until melted. Remove from the heat and whisk in the sugar and espresso powder. When the mixture is nearly at room temperature, whisk in the eggs until blended. Stir in the milk and rum.

In a separate bowl, stir together the flour, baking powder, and salt. Add to the saucepan and whisk until just incorporated.

Scrape the batter into the baking pan with a spatula and smooth to the edges. Bake for 25 to 30 minutes, until a toothpick inserted in the center comes out clean. Cool completely in the pan on a rack. Cut into 9 squares. Wrap individually in waxed paper or place in a tightly sealed container.

MAKES 9 BROWNIES

BUTTERSCOTCH BLONDIES

Cousin to the brownie, blondies have no chocolate, but are chewy, and like their cousin, perfect for carrying along on a picnic.

- **2 large eggs**
- **2/3 cup honey**
- **2 tablespoons vegetable oil**
- **1 tablespoon molasses**
- **2 teaspoons vanilla extract**
- **2/3 cup whole wheat flour**
- **1/2 cup nonfat dry milk**
- **1/4 teaspoon salt**
- **1/3 cup finely ground raw peanuts**
- **1/2 cup chopped walnuts**

Preheat the oven to 350°F. Oil a 9 × 9-inch baking pan.

In a medium bowl, beat the eggs until light. Beat in the honey, oil, molasses, and vanilla until combined.

In a large bowl, whisk together the flour, dry milk, and salt, then whisk in the peanuts and walnuts. Make a well in the center of the flour mixture, add the honey, mixture and stir just until moistened.

Spread the batter evenly in the pan. Bake for 30 minutes or until the surface is firm to the touch. Cool in the pan before cutting into 16 bars.

MAKES 16 BLONDIES

GREEN TEA BISCOTTI WITH PISTACHIOS

Green tea, pulverized in a food processor, gives these biscotti an interesting, slightly herbal flavor. Lemon zest and lemon juice provide punch and the pistachios are just plain delicious. Store in a dry place for up to 2 weeks.

- **1 1/4 cups unbleached all-purpose flour**
- **1 cup whole wheat flour**
- **2 tablespoons cornstarch**
- **1/2 teaspoon baking powder**
- **1/2 teaspoon salt**
- **1/4 cup loose green tea**
- **1/2 cup (1 stick) butter, at room temperature**
- **1 cup packed turbinado or light brown sugar**
- **2 large eggs**
- **2 teaspoons grated lemon zest**
- **2 teaspoons lemon juice**
- **1 cup shelled pistachios**

Preheat the oven to 350°F. Line a large baking sheet with parchment paper or a nonstick liner.

In a large bowl, whisk together the flours, cornstarch, baking powder, and salt. In a food processor, grind the tea until finely ground. Stir the tea into the flour mixture.

With an electric mixer, cream the butter until smooth. Add the sugar and beat until light and fluffy. Beat in the eggs one at a time, beating well after each addition. Beat in the lemon zest and lemon juice.

Beat in the flour mixture until just combined. Fold in the nuts.

Place the dough on the baking sheet and, with dampened hands, shape into a log 15 inches long, 4 ½ inches wide, and ¾ inch high. Bake for 35 minutes, or until the top is firm and the edges are golden brown. (Leave the oven on.) Cool on the baking sheet on a rack for 15 minutes.

Using a serrated knife, slice the biscotti on the diagonal, ½ inch thick. Place on the baking sheet cut side down and bake for 20 minutes longer, or until crisp. Transfer to racks to cool completely.

MAKES 2½ DOZEN BISCOTTI

CHOCOLATE-ALMOND BISCOTTI

If you don't want to buy a bottle of coffee liqueur to make these biscotti, just use very strong brewed espresso instead.

3 cups plus 2 tablespoons flour
½ cup unsweetened cocoa powder
2¼ teaspoons baking powder
1 teaspoon salt
¾ cup (1½ sticks) butter
1¼ cups sugar
4 large eggs
2 tablespoons grated orange zest
2 tablespoons Kahlúa or other coffee liqueur
1 cup blanched almonds, coarsely chopped
1 cup semisweet mini chocolate chips

Preheat the oven to 325°F.

In a large bowl, whisk together the flour, cocoa, baking powder, and salt.

With an electric mixer, cream the butter and sugar until fluffy. Beat in the eggs one at a time, beating well after each addition. Beat in the orange zest and liqueur. At low speed, beat in the flour mixture until just combined. Stir in the almonds and chocolate chips.

Divide the dough into thirds. Roll each portion into a log 10 inches long and place on a baking sheet. Bake for 30 minutes. (Leave the oven on.) Cool on the baking sheet on a rack for 15 minutes.

Cut the logs on the diagonal into ½-inch slices. Place cut side down on two baking sheets and bake for 20 to 25 minutes longer, or until crisp. Transfer to racks to cool completely.

MAKES 4½ DOZEN BISCOTTI

WALNUT SHORTBREAD

Other nuts would work well in this shortbread. Try it with pecans, cashews, or almonds for the walnuts.

⅔ cup walnut halves, toasted
¾ cup unbleached all-purpose flour
½ cup whole wheat flour
½ cup confectioners' sugar
¼ teaspoon salt
¼ cup walnut oil
¼ cup extra-light olive oil
1½ teaspoons grated lemon zest
1 teaspoon vanilla extract

Preheat the oven to 325°F.

In a food processor, combine the walnuts and all-purpose flour, and process until the nuts are finely ground.

Transfer the flour-walnut mixture to a large bowl. Stir in the whole wheat flour, confectioners' sugar, and salt. Stir in the walnut oil, olive oil, lemon zest, and vanilla, until well combined.

Press the dough into the bottom of a 9-inch tart

pan with a removable bottom. With the tines of a fork, prick the bottom of the dough. With a sharp knife, score the dough into 16 wedges, cutting almost, but not quite through, to the bottom.

Bake for 30 minutes, or until crisp and lightly golden. Check after 20 minutes; if the shortbread is overbrowning, decrease the oven temperature to 300°F.

Remove from the oven and while still warm, cut the wedges through to the bottom. Cool in the pan on a rack.

MAKES 16 COOKIES

OATMEAL LACE COOKIES

These cookies are very thin, very rich, and delicate.

1 cup old-fashioned rolled oats

1 large egg

½ cup honey

¼ cup maple syrup

1 teaspoon vanilla extract

½ cup (1 stick) butter, melted

Preheat the oven to 350°F with racks in the upper and lower thirds. Line 2 baking sheets with parchment paper.

Place the oats in a blender and process for a few minutes, until they become a coarse flour.

In a medium bowl, combine the egg, honey, maple syrup, and vanilla. Beat until well combined. Add the butter and continue to beat until smooth. Stir in the oats.

Drop by teaspoons onto the baking sheets, about 3 inches apart. (They will spread while baking.) Bake for 12 minutes, until lightly golden around the edges, rotating the baking sheets from top to bottom and front to back halfway through. Using a thin-bladed metal spatula, transfer to racks to cool.

MAKES 4 DOZEN COOKIES

GINGER COOKIES

A touch of mustard powder gives these a special kick. The total number of cookies will depend on the size of the cookie cutters you choose.

⅓ cup butter, at room temperature

⅔ cup molasses

1 large egg

2½ cups white whole wheat flour*

1 teaspoon baking soda

2 teaspoons cinnamon

2 teaspoons ground ginger

¼ teaspoon dry mustard

¼ teaspoon salt

**milled from white wheat grains*

With an electric mixer, beat the butter and molasses until fluffy. Add the egg, beating until well combined.

In a medium bowl, stir together the flour, baking soda, cinnamon, ginger, mustard, and salt. Add to the liquid ingredients, beating just until combined. Refrigerate for several hours.

Preheat the oven to 375°F with racks in the upper and lower thirds. Line 2 baking sheets with parchment paper.

On a lightly floured work surface, roll the dough out to a ⅛-inch thickness. Cut the dough into shapes, using cookie cutters, and place on the baking sheets.

Bake for 5 minutes, or until the cookies are brown on the bottom and firm to the touch, rotating the baking sheets from top to bottom and front to back halfway through. Remove from the baking sheets and cool on racks.

MAKES 4 DOZEN COOKIES

NO-GRAIN COCONUT COOKIES

Perfect for those who are gluten-intolerant.

- 2 large eggs, beaten
- ½ cup honey
- 2 cups shredded coconut

Preheat the oven to 350°F with racks in the upper and lower thirds. Oil 2 baking sheets.

In a medium bowl, combine the eggs and honey. Stir in the coconut and mix well.

Drop by teaspoons, 1 inch apart, onto the baking sheets. Bake for 10 minutes, or until lightly browned and set, rotating the baking sheets from top to bottom and front to back halfway through. Remove from the baking sheets and cool on racks.

MAKES 3 DOZEN COOKIES

MAPLE BUTTER PECAN COOKIES

Choose a rich maple syrup—a grade B or medium amber—for these cookies.

- ½ cup (1 stick) butter
- ⅓ cup vegetable oil
- ½ cup maple syrup
- 2 teaspoons vanilla extract
- 2 to 2½ cups white whole wheat flour*
- ¼ teaspoon salt
- 1 cup chopped pecans
- 48 pecan halves

**milled from white wheat grains*

Preheat the oven to 325°F with racks in the upper and lower thirds.

With an electric mixer, beat the butter, oil, maple syrup, and vanilla, until smooth. Stir in the flour and salt. Add the chopped pecans and mix until combined.

Shape the dough into 1-inch balls and place 2 inches apart on 2 large baking sheets. Press a pecan half lightly into the center of each, flattening the cookies slightly. Bake for 15 to 20 minutes, until light brown and just set, rotating the baking sheets from top to bottom and front to back halfway through. Remove from the baking sheets and cool on racks.

MAKES 4 DOZEN COOKIES

PECAN-AMARANTH TASSIES

Amaranth seeds pop much like popcorn, but not as big or fluffy—and unlike popcorn, they won't fly out of the pan. To pop amaranth, heat a wok or heavy skillet (without oil) until very hot. Add 1 tablespoon amaranth and stir with a pastry brush to prevent burning. When all the seeds have popped, empty into a bowl and repeat with the remaining seeds.

PASTRY

- ¼ cup (½ stick) butter, at room temperature
- 4 ounces cream cheese
- 1 egg yolk
- 1 tablespoon sugar
- ⅔ cup whole wheat flour
- ⅓ cup amaranth flour
- ¼ teaspoon salt

FILLING

- 2 large eggs, beaten
- ⅓ cup honey
- 2 tablespoons molasses
- 2 tablespoons butter, melted
- 1 teaspoon vanilla extract
- ½ cup finely chopped pecans

2 tablespoons amaranth, popped

36 pecan halves

To make the pastry: With an electric mixer, beat the butter, cream cheese, egg yolk, and sugar until well combined. In a small bowl, combine the flours and salt. Beat the flour mixture into the butter mixture just until combined.

Divide the dough in half, place each half on a large sheet of waxed paper, and flatten to a ½-inch-thick square. Refrigerate at least 4 hours or overnight.

Preheat the oven to 350°F. Lightly butter 36 mini muffin cups.

Working with half of the dough at a time, turn out onto a floured surface and flour the top. Roll out to an ⅛-inch thickness and cut into 3-inch circles with a biscuit cutter. Ease each circle of dough into a cup of the tin, forming small pastry shells. The sides should be lightly scalloped. Refrigerate while you prepare the filling.

To make the filling: In a large bowl, combine the eggs, honey, molasses, butter, and vanilla. Add the chopped pecans and popped amaranth.

Fill the pastry shells almost to their tops with the filling. Decorate each with a pecan half. Bake for 15 minutes. Reduce the oven temperature to 250°F and bake for 10 minutes more, or until the filling is set.

Remove from the tins immediately and cool on racks.

MAKES 3 DOZEN COOKIES

DEMERARA-TOPPED PEANUT BUTTER COOKIES

Sprinkling the tops of these cookies with brown sugar crystals adds a nice crunch.

½ cup (1 stick) butter, at room temperature

1 cup packed turbinado or light brown sugar

1 large egg, beaten

½ cup natural crunchy peanut butter

1½ cups flour

1 teaspoon baking powder

½ teaspoon salt

⅓ cup coarse brown sugar crystals (such as demerara or florida crystals), for sprinkling

With an electric mixer, beat the butter and light brown sugar until creamy and light, about 3 minutes. Add the egg and beat until light. Gradually beat in the peanut butter until incorporated. Add half the flour, then the baking powder and salt. Beat on low speed until mixed. Add the remaining flour and beat just long enough to incorporate. Cover tightly and refrigerate the dough for 1 hour.

Preheat the oven to 350°F.

With a ¼-cup measuring cup, scoop up and level some dough. Roll in your palms to form a ball and place on an ungreased baking sheet. Repeat with the remaining dough, placing the balls about 2 inches apart. Using the back of a fork, press down on the balls in a crisscross pattern (dough should be ½ inch thick).

Sprinkle the tops with brown sugar crystals. Bake for 18 to 20 minutes, until the edges are lightly browned. Remove from the baking sheets and cool on a rack.

MAKES 12 LARGE COOKIES

APPLESAUCE YUMMIES

Chocolate chips, applesauce, and oats—sounds like the perfect cookie.

2 cups white whole wheat flour*

1 teaspoon baking powder

½ teaspoon baking soda

1 teaspoon cinnamon

¼ teaspoon salt

1½ cups old-fashioned rolled oats

- 1 cup unsweetened applesauce
- ½ cup honey
- ½ cup (1 stick) butter, at room temperature
- 1 large egg, beaten
- 1 teaspoon vanilla extract
- 1 cup dark chocolate chips

**milled from white wheat grains*

Preheat the oven to 375°F with racks in the upper and lower thirds. Line 2 baking sheets with parchment paper.

In a large bowl, stir together the flour, baking powder, baking soda, cinnamon, and salt.

In a medium bowl, stir together the oats and applesauce.

In another medium bowl, stir together the honey and butter, and mix in the egg. Combine the butter mixture with the oats and applesauce, and stir in the vanilla. Add to the flour mixture and fold in the chocolate chips.

Drop the dough by teaspoons, 2 inches apart, onto the baking sheets. Bake for 10 to 12 minutes, until the edges begin to brown, rotating the baking sheets from top to bottom and front to back halfway through. Remove from the baking sheets and cool on racks.

MAKES 4 DOZEN COOKIES

SPICY RAISIN DROP COOKIES

For even more spice, add about ¼ teaspoon black pepper to the dough along with the other spices.

- 3 cups whole wheat flour
- 1 teaspoon baking powder
- 1½ teaspoons cinnamon
- 1 teaspoon ground ginger
- ¼ teaspoon salt
- 1 cup (2 sticks) butter, at room temperature
- ¾ cup honey
- 1 large egg
- 1 teaspoon vanilla extract
- 2 cups raisins
- ½ cup chopped nuts

Preheat the oven to 375°F with racks in the upper and lower thirds. Oil 2 large baking sheets.

In a large bowl, whisk together the flour, baking powder, cinnamon, ginger, and salt.

With an electric mixer, beat together the butter, honey, egg, and vanilla. Mix the flour mixture into the butter mixture. Fold in the raisins and nuts.

Drop by teaspoons, 1 inch apart, onto the baking sheets. Bake for 10 to 12 minutes, until lightly browned, rotating the baking sheets from top to bottom and front to back halfway through. Remove from the baking sheets and cool on racks.

MAKES 2 DOZEN COOKIES

THANKSGIVING PUMPKIN COOKIES

You can easily swap in pureed butternut squash for the pumpkin.

- ½ cup honey
- ½ cup (1 stick) butter, at room temperature
- 1 cup unsweetened pumpkin puree
- 1 large egg, beaten
- 1 teaspoon vanilla extract
- 2 cups whole wheat pastry flour
- 2 teaspoons baking powder
- ½ teaspoon baking soda

- ¼ teaspoon salt
- 1 teaspoon allspice
- 1 teaspoon cinnamon
- 1 cup raisins
- 1 cup chopped nuts

Preheat the oven to 375°F with racks in the upper and lower thirds of the oven.

With an electric mixer, beat the honey and butter until light and fluffy. Add the pumpkin, egg, and vanilla, mixing until well combined.

In a large bowl, whisk together the flour, baking powder, baking soda, salt, allspice, and cinnamon. Gradually mix into the butter mixture. Fold in the raisins and nuts.

Drop by teaspoons, 2 inches apart, onto 2 large baking sheets and flatten with the back of a spoon. Bake until lightly browned, 8 to 10 minutes, rotating the baking sheets from top to bottom and front to back halfway through. Remove from the baking sheets and cool on racks.

MAKES 2 DOZEN COOKIES

CHOCOLATE CHIP COOKIES

A health makeover of classic tollhouse cookies, but with soy nuts instead of walnuts, and olive oil swapped in for some of the butter.

- 1 cup old-fashioned rolled oats
- 1½ cups flour
- 1 teaspoon baking soda
- ½ teaspoon salt
- ¼ cup (½ stick) butter, at room temperature
- 3 tablespoons extra-light olive oil
- ¾ cup granulated sugar
- ½ cup packed turbinado or light brown sugar
- 2 tablespoons low-fat (1%) milk
- 1 large egg
- 1 large egg white
- 1 teaspoon vanilla extract
- 1 cup unsalted roasted soy nuts (4 ounces)
- 1 cup mini chocolate chips

Preheat the oven to 375°F. Spread the oats on a baking sheet and toast for 10 minutes, or until golden brown. Leave the oven on. Lightly grease baking sheets.

Meanwhile, on a sheet of waxed paper, combine the flour, baking soda, and salt.

With an electric mixer, beat the butter, oil, granulated sugar, and brown sugar, until smooth. Beat in the milk, whole egg, egg white, and vanilla, until well combined. Fold in the toasted oats, flour mixture, soy nuts, and chocolate chips until well combined.

Drop by rounded teaspoons, 2 inches apart, onto the baking sheets. Bake for 10 minutes, or until the cookies are set and golden brown.

Remove from the baking sheets and cool on racks.

MAKES 5 DOZEN COOKIES

JUMBO GRANOLA COOKIES WITH CRANBERRIES

Store these chewy cookies at room temperature in an airtight container.

- 2 cups flour
- 1 teaspoon baking soda
- ½ teaspoon coarse salt
- 1 cup (2 sticks) butter, at room temperature
- 1 cup packed turbinado or light brown sugar
- ¾ cup granulated sugar
- 2 large eggs
- 1½ teaspoons vanilla extract

2 cups old-fashioned rolled oats

2 cups granola

2 cups dried cranberries or cherries

Preheat the oven to 375°F.

In a medium bowl, whisk together the flour, baking soda, and salt.

With an electric mixer, beat the butter and both sugars until light and fluffy. Beat in the eggs and vanilla until well combined. On low speed, beat in the flour mixture, just until blended. Stir in the oats, granola, and cranberries with a rubber spatula.

Place four ½-cup scoops of dough on an ungreased cookie sheet and shape into 4-inch rounds. Repeat with the remaining dough on 2 additional cookie sheets. In batches, bake for 20 to 25 minutes, until the cookies are golden brown, rotating the pan halfway through.

Let the cookies cool on the pans on a rack.

MAKES 12 LARGE COOKIES

MEXICAN CHOCOLATE COOKIES

This recipe makes 8 large cookies. For smaller cookies, drop the dough by well rounded tablespoons onto the prepared baking sheets, flatten them slightly, and bake for 10 minutes or until set.

1 cup flour

⅓ cup unsweetened cocoa powder

¾ teaspoon cinnamon

½ teaspoon baking powder

½ teaspoon baking soda

¼ teaspoon salt

⅓ cup reduced-fat sour cream

¼ cup extra-light olive oil

⅔ cup sugar

1 teaspoon vanilla extract

¼ cup mini chocolate chips

Preheat the oven to 350°F with the racks in the upper and lower thirds of the oven. Line 2 baking sheets with parchment paper.

In a medium bowl, whisk together the flour, cocoa powder, cinnamon, baking powder, baking soda, and salt.

In a large bowl, beat the sour cream and oil until well combined. Add the sugar and vanilla and beat until well combined. Fold in the flour mixture just until combined. Fold in the chocolate chips.

Place the dough by scant ⅓ cups, 3 inches apart, on the baking sheets for a total of 8 cookies. Flatten each to a 4-inch round. Bake for 20 minutes, until the cookies are just set, rotating the baking sheets from top to bottom and front to back halfway through. Remove from the baking sheets and cool on racks.

MAKES 8 LARGE COOKIES

APRICOT GLAZE

A nice complement to Glazed Carrot Cake (page 509), this glaze can also be used as a filling for cookies.

2 cups chopped apricots

⅓ cup honey

1 thin slice lemon with peel, chopped

In a medium saucepan, combine the apricots, honey, and lemon. Cook over low heat until the fruit is soft and juicy. Transfer to a blender and puree until smooth. Return the mixture to the saucepan and simmer, stirring frequently, until thickened, 5 to 8 minutes.

MAKES 1¾ CUPS

STABILIZED WHIPPED CREAM

With a little gelatin added to stabilize it, this whipped cream will hold up for several hours. Use it to frost a cake or fill shortcakes.

½ teaspoon unflavored gelatin
2 tablespoons cold water
1 cup heavy cream
2 tablespoons honey

In a heatproof glass measuring cup or bowl, sprinkle the gelatin over the cold water and let stand until softened, about 5 minutes. Place the cup in a pan of simmering water and heat until the gelatin has dissolved. Set aside briefly to cool to room temperature.

In a large bowl, beat the cream until it stands in soft peaks, gradually beating in the honey and gelatin.

MAKES 1 ½ CUPS

FLUFFY LEMON ICING

This is a soft icing, so when you use it to ice a cake it should be served the same day. Any longer, the icing might soak into the cake.

¼ cup honey
2 tablespoons lemon juice
⅛ teaspoon cream of tartar
1 large egg white
1 teaspoon grated lemon zest

In a double boiler over simmering water and with an electric mixer, beat together the honey, lemon juice, cream of tartar, and egg white. Beat for several minutes or until very thick. Increase the heat, bring the water to a boil, and beat until the mixture forms soft billowy peaks, 5 to 8 minutes. Remove from the heat and beat until thick enough to spread. Fold in the lemon zest.

MAKES 1 ½ CUPS

PEANUT BUTTER FROSTING OR FILLING

Use this as a frosting for cakes or cookies, or as a filling for sandwich cookies. For a thinner, creamier frosting, add more milk along with the cream cheese.

½ cup peanut butter
8 ounces cream cheese, at room temperature
⅓ cup honey
3 tablespoons milk

In a medium bowl, with an electric mixer, cream together all the ingredients.

MAKES 1¼ CUPS

SEVEN-MINUTE FROSTING

This versatile frosting is good on carrot cake, coconut cake, cupcakes, and other baked goods. Buckwheat honey has a deep, rich flavor.

3 large egg whites
⅔ cup buckwheat honey
1 teaspoon vanilla extract

In a double boiler, combine the egg whites and honey. With an electric mixer, beat at low speed while the water just comes to a boil. Continue to beat for 7 minutes, or until the mixture forms soft peaks.

Remove from the heat, add the vanilla, and continue beating until the frosting is stiff enough to hold its shape.

MAKES 3 CUPS

BASIC CREAM CHEESE FROSTING

Use on carrot cake, cupcakes, and as a filling for sandwich cookies.

8 ounces reduced-fat cream cheese (Neufchâtel)

2 tablespoons butter

⅓ cup agave nectar

½ teaspoon vanilla extract

With an electric mixer, beat the cream cheese and butter until smooth. Beat in the agave nectar and the vanilla, until well combined.

MAKES 1½ CUPS

HONEY-ORANGE CREAM CHEESE ICING

Use this icing to top an 8-inch round or 9-inch square cake. The perfect topping for carrot cake, it would also be good on a pan of brownies or blondies.

8 ounces cream cheese, at room temperature

⅓ cup honey

3 tablespoons orange juice concentrate

½ teaspoon vanilla extract

In a large bowl, with an electric mixer beat together the cream cheese, honey, orange juice concentrate, and vanilla, until light and fluffy, about 5 minutes.

MAKES 1 ½ CUPS

RASPBERRY FROSTING

You can use this to make cookie sandwiches with store-bought vanilla wafers or chocolate wafers, or as a frosting for a cake.

8 ounces cream cheese, at room temperature

½ cup seedless raspberry all-fruit spread

1 teaspoon vanilla extract

In a medium bowl, beat the cream cheese, fruit spread, and vanilla together. Refrigerate until the frosting reaches spreadable consistency.

MAKES 1½ CUPS

CREAMY VANILLA FILLING

Use as a layer cake filling or a filling for éclairs.

3 tablespoons cornstarch

1 cup milk

1 cup light cream

½ cup honey

4 large egg yolks, lightly beaten

1 teaspoon vanilla extract

Place the cornstarch in a medium, heavy-bottomed saucepan. Whisk in the milk until smooth. Whisk in the cream and honey until well combined. Bring the mixture to a boil over medium heat, stirring constantly, until thickened.

Mix a little of the hot mixture into the egg yolks to warm them. Add the egg yolk mixture to the saucepan. Cook, stirring constantly, until thick enough to coat the back of a spoon, about 2 minutes. Stir in the vanilla. Cool before using.

MAKES 2½ CUPS

LEMON CURD

Lemon curd is a popular English lemon butter that can be used in many ways: as a spread for toast at tea time, a filling for meringues, cakes, and sponge rolls.

½ cup (1 stick) butter

½ cup sugar

Grated zest of 1 lemon

½ cup lemon juice

3 large eggs, beaten

3 large egg yolks

In a double boiler, combine the butter, sugar, lemon zest, lemon juice, whole eggs, and egg yolks. Set over boiling water and cook, stirring constantly with a wooden spoon, until the mixture is thick and smooth with the consistency of thick honey, 15 to 20 minutes.

Remove from the heat and strain through a fine-mesh sieve set over a bowl. Cool to room temperature, then refrigerate.

MAKES 2¼ CUPS

Pies

The cardinal rule in making a good pastry crust is to have a light, cool hand and to handle the dough as quickly and as little as possible. Overworking the dough develops the gluten, which though desirable in bread making, will make a crust too tough. For this reason, when the shortening is added to the flour for the pie dough, it should be cold and added quickly and with minimal working of the dough: The cold shortening is "cut" into the flour with a pastry blender or two knives (scissor fashion) just until it has the texture of coarse crumbs. When you finally use your hands, handle the dough lightly, and the result will be a tender, flaky crust.

Piecrusts

Butter is the best choice of shortening for a tender, flavorful piecrust. Sometimes cheese—ricotta, cottage, or Cheddar—or sour cream or yogurt is added for an especially rich dough.

Ice water is added to the shortening-flour mixture to keep the shortening firm, resulting in less gluten development and a flakier crust. Always add water gradually in small quantities, and only add as much as is necessary to hold the dough together. When the dough has enough liquid, it should just form a ball and no longer stick to the sides of the bowl. Grab a piece of dough and pinch it between your fingers; if it comes together, it's ready.

Sweetener is added to some pastry doughs for crispness and better browning, but basic short-crust pie pastry is not sweetened, as a rule.

Sometimes eggs are added for richness and color. The whole egg may be used or, for extra richness, just the yolk. Egg pastry doughs are quite batter-like and elastic due to the egg protein.

Pie plates come in various sizes: The most common is 9 inches. Filled pie shells should never be baked in shiny plates, which reflect heat, or a soggy undercrust will result. For a tender browned undercrust, the best materials are glass, darkened tin, or enamelware.

Rolling a Piecrust

When all the ingredients come together, almost into a ball that is not too sticky or too stiff, the dough is ready for rolling. (If you are making a double-crust pie, divide the dough in half and flatten each half into a disk.) Chill the dough at least 30 minutes. Chilling the dough helps relax the gluten and makes it more manageable for rolling. Allow the dough to return to room temperature before rolling.

A pastry cloth and roller stocking are sometimes used to avoid using extra flour. Roll the dough from the center out, keeping it circular and rolling as little as possible. Roll the dough to about ⅛-inch thickness and wide enough to extend about 2 inches beyond the side of the pie plate when it is fitted in. Patch any tears carefully by pinching the dough together and rolling over the patch so it is unnoticeable.

When the dough has been rolled to the right size, you can ease it into the pie plate by flopping half of it over the rolling pin and gently lifting the other half with an outspread hand.

Arrange it gently (do not pull or stretch the

EASY LATTICE TOP

For an attractive lattice without the work of weaving, roll out the dough for the top crust into an oblong. Using a knife or pastry cutter, cut it into ½-inch-wide strips. Lay strips across the filling, parallel to each other, approximately 1 inch apart. Turn the pie slightly and, instead of laying the top strips perpendicular (at right angles) to the bottom layer of strips, lay them diagonally (on a slant). Lay a strip of pastry all around the rim of the plate, covering the ends of the other strips. Crimp this strip to make an attractive edge.

---

dough) and trim off the excess dough with a pair of kitchen scissors or running a knife around the edge of the plate. If making a single-crust pie, form a decorative fluted edge (see "Making a Decorative Edge on a Pie," page 530).

Double Crusts

When the bottom crust is in place and the filling has been added, roll out the top crust to extend 2 inches beyond the circumference of the pan. To position the top crust on the pie, you can fold the rolled-out dough in quarters, carefully place it on top of the filled bottom crust, and unfold. Trim the dough with a knife and gently press the top and bottom crusts together to seal them tightly. Crimp the edges with a fork or your fingers to reinforce the seal. This will keep the juices from seeping out during baking.

It is necessary to form vents in the top crust so that steam can escape; otherwise, the underside of the crust will become soggy. Pierce the top crust in several places with a knife or fork after it has been positioned over the filling, or cut three or four slits in the top crust. If you do not wish to cut slits in the crust, you can form a steam vent by inserting the wide end of a pastry tip in the middle of the top crust. Do so after the crust has been positioned and sealed. Be sure to remove the circle of dough that will be cut out by the pastry tip.

Pressed Piecrust

If you find you have great difficulty rolling a crust, you may prefer the never-fail pressed piecrusts. Instead of rolling the dough, you need only press it into the pie plate with your fingers, working it into the bottom and up the sides as evenly as possible. When the pressed crust is in place, use the bottom of a flat cup or glass to smooth the dough and set it firmly into the pie plate. A pressed crust will not be as thin or flaky as a rolled one.

Crumb pastries used for pressed piecrusts are very easy to make. They are not really pastries, but they are often used as shells for cream or cheesecake fillings. Crumb crusts can be made from finely crumbled cake or cookies. The crumbs are usually bound with melted butter or oil and are pressed into a pie plate. Dry cereal, shredded coconut, wheat germ, or ground nuts or seeds may also be added to the crumb mixture.

Glazing (or Egg Wash)

Top crusts may be glazed to enhance their appearance. The glaze gives an attractive color and luster to the crust. Piecrust glaze is usually made from egg yolk or egg white, mixed with milk or water. It should be applied lightly with a pastry brush just before the pie is baked.

Sometimes a bottom crust is glazed to help waterproof it against any moisture in the filling.

Pie Fillings

Some fillings are baked along with the crust; others are cooked separately, and then added to the baked pie shell (see "Blind Baking," below). Fruit fillings are usually baked in the crust.

The top crusts of fruit pies have a tendency to fall in the center because of excess moisture. For this reason the fruit mixture is usually thickened with flour or cornstarch. Generally 2 tablespoons of either flour or cornstarch per 2 cups of fresh, uncooked fruit is sufficient thickener. And sometimes fruit is tossed with instant tapioca. You may also sprinkle some dry cookie or cake crumbs on the bottom of the piecrust before adding the filling.

Custard fillings are most often baked with the crust. The mixture may also have fruits, nuts, or coconut. To prevent this type of pie from becoming soggy, cool it on a wire rack as soon as it comes out of the oven. Custard pies should not be stored for longer than 1 day; longer than that the filling will soften the crust.

Baking Pies

Baking time and temperature are as important as the correct plate size for pies, so make sure they are as accurate as possible by using an oven thermometer and kitchen timer.

Off center, toward the back of the oven is usually the best place to position a pie for even browning. If baking two pies at once, stagger them on two different racks but do not allow them to touch the oven walls.

If the crust seems to be browning too quickly, cover the crimped edges with foil. A done crust should be golden brown. A single crust will have browned, crisp edges, and the filling, if custard, should be well set.

Most pies should be cooled for several minutes on a wire rack before being cut. Some need to reach room temperature before being served and others must be chilled.

BLIND BAKING

When making a pie whose filling is already cooked, you need to bake the piecrust separately, with no filling in it. This is called *blind baking.*

To blind bake, prick the pastry with a fork in several places to let steam escape and prevent the dough from buckling. Line the crust with foil or parchment, leaving an overhang all around, and fill with dried beans or pie weights. Remove the foil and beans when the crust is partially baked as specified in the recipe. Reserve the beans to use over and over for more pies; set them aside in a special jar marked "pie beans" so you don't cook them by accident.

Sometimes crusts that are to be baked with their fillings are briefly blind baked. This is to set the dough and reduce its absorbency so the filling won't make it soggy. Follow the procedure as for regular blind baking but remove the foil and beans after the crust has baked for 10 minutes and is just set. The crust will continue to bake when it goes back in the oven with the filling.

MAKING A DECORATIVE EDGE ON A PIE

There are many ways to decorate the rim of a piecrust. Here are the two simplest:

To begin, fit the dough into the pie plate. For a single-crust pie, trim the overhang to 1 inch and turn the overhang under. For a double-crust pie, trim the overhang even with the lip of the pie plate, then add the filling. Fit the top crust over the filling, and trim the overhang to match the overhang of the bottom crust, so you have a double layer of crust sitting over the rim of the pie plate.

Fork crimping: Use the tines of a fork to press the two layers of dough together, making a decorative pattern (A). Or, if making a single-crust pie, simply use the fork to make a decorative edge in the folded-over overhang.

Fluting: With both hands, hold your thumb and forefinger like pincers and work on opposite sides of the crust edge (B).

Pinch the dough with one hand using the forefinger of the opposite hand to help form the crimp. This will produce a scalloped ridge.

Keep pinching all around the rim to seal the dough.

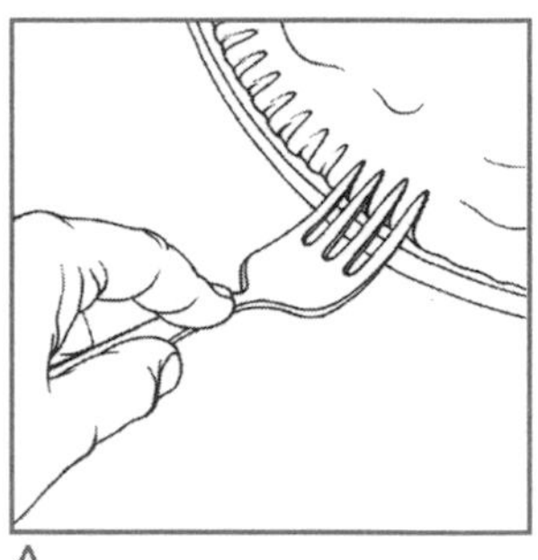

A

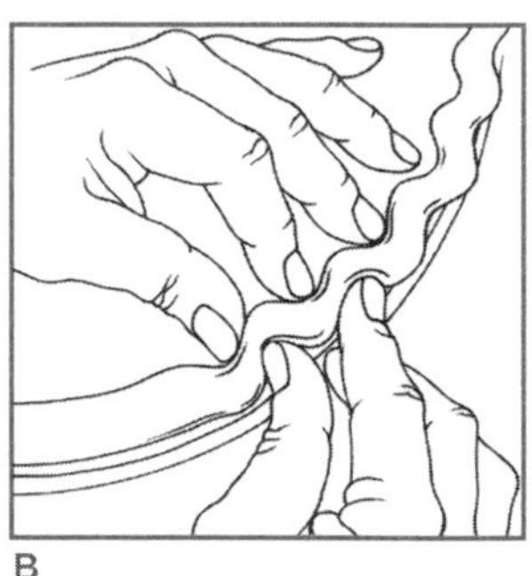

B

MULTI-GRAIN PIE DOUGH (SINGLE CRUST)

Whole wheat pastry flour has less gluten than regular whole wheat flour, making it a good choice for a tender crust. Flax meal adds a nuttiness to the dough, while toasted wheat germ lends rich flavor. Look for toasted wheat germ alongside regular wheat germ. The dough can be refrigerated for up to 3 days, or frozen for up to 3 months.

- 1¼ cups whole wheat pastry flour
- ¼ cup flax meal
- 2 tablespoons toasted wheat germ
- ¼ teaspoon salt
- 3 tablespoons cold butter, cut up
- 3 tablespoons canola oil
- 2 to 3 tablespoons ice water

In a large bowl, stir together the flour, flax meal, wheat germ, and salt. With a pastry blender or two knives scissor fashion, cut the butter and the oil into the flour mixture until it resembles coarse crumbs.

Gradually add the ice water, a tablespoon at a time, until you can gather the dough into a ball. Flatten into a disk and place on a sheet of floured waxed paper. Sprinkle a little more flour over it and top with another sheet of waxed paper. Refrigerate for at least 30 minutes before rolling out.

MAKES ONE 9-INCH CRUST

MULTI-GRAIN PIE DOUGH (DOUBLE CRUST)

The dough can be refrigerated for up to 3 days, or frozen for up to 3 months. To freeze, transfer (still wrapped in waxed paper) to a freezer container, and label and date.

- 2½ cups whole wheat pastry flour
- ½ cup flax meal
- ¼ cup toasted wheat germ
- ½ teaspoon salt
- 6 tablespoons cold butter, cut up
- 6 tablespoons canola oil
- 4 to 6 tablespoons ice water

In a large bowl, stir together the flour, flax meal, wheat germ, and salt. With a pastry blender or two knives scissor fashion, cut the butter and the oil into the flour mixture until it resembles coarse crumbs.

Gradually add the ice water, a tablespoon at a time, until you can gather the dough into a ball. Divide the dough in half and flatten each half into a disk. Place each disk on a sheet of floured waxed paper. Sprinkle a little more flour over each and top with two more sheets of waxed paper. Refrigerate for at least 30 minutes before rolling out.

MAKES TWO 9-INCH CRUSTS

BARLEY-OAT PIE DOUGH

If you can't find oat flour in your supermarket or health food store, simply make it yourself: Place rolled or quick-cooking oats in a food processor and process until finely ground. You'll need about 1⅓ cups of oats to make 1 cup of oat flour. Delicious for a fruit pie, or use in place of Multi-Grain Pie Dough (Single Crust).

- 1 cup barley flour
- 1 cup oat flour
- ¼ teaspoon salt
- ⅓ cup canola oil
- ¼ cup plus 2 tablespoons ice water

In a large bowl, stir together the barley flour, oat flour, and salt.

In a small bowl, combine the oil and ice water. With a fork, stir into the dry ingredients until a ball is formed.

On a lightly floured work surface, roll the dough out to a 12-inch round. Fit the dough into a 9-inch pie plate, pressing it into the bottom and up the sides without stretching the dough. Using kitchen scissors, even the edge, leaving a 1-inch overhang. Fold the overhang under and make a decorative edge (see "Making a Decorative Edge of a Pie," page 530). Refrigerate for 30 minutes before baking.

MAKES ONE 9-INCH CRUST

RICOTTA CHEESE PIE DOUGH

The combination of creamy ricotta and butter make for an especially rich and tender pie dough.

- **1¼ cups whole wheat pastry flour**
- **1 tablespoon sugar**
- **¼ teaspoon salt**
- **⅓ cup cold butter, cut up**
- **½ cup part-skim ricotta cheese**

In a large bowl, stir together the flour, sugar, and salt. With a pastry blender or two knives scissor fashion, cut in the butter and ricotta until the mixture just comes together. Flatten into a disk and wrap in waxed paper. Refrigerate at least 30 minutes.

To use, press into the bottom and up the sides of a 9-inch pie plate.

MAKES ONE 9-INCH CRUST

SOUR CREAM PIE DOUGH

For a slightly different flavor, substitute whole-milk Greek yogurt for the sour cream.

- **1¼ cups whole wheat pastry flour**
- **1 tablespoon sugar**
- **¼ teaspoon salt**
- **¼ cup (½ stick) cold butter, cut up**
- **¼ to ⅓ cup cold sour cream**

In a large bowl, stir together the flour, sugar, and salt. With a pastry blender or two knives scissor fashion, cut in the butter until the mixture resembles coarse crumbs. Stir in the sour cream, a little at a time, until the dough just comes together. Flatten into a disk and wrap in waxed paper. Refrigerate at least 30 minutes before rolling out.

MAKES ONE 9-INCH CRUST

CRUMB PIECRUST

Use your favorite cookie crumbs, such as graham crackers, shortbread, gingersnaps, or chocolate wafers, for this crust.

- **2 cups fine cookie crumbs**
- **3 tablespoons butter, melted**
- **3 tablespoons vegetable oil**
- **1 tablespoon honey**

In a medium bowl, combine the cookie crumbs, butter, oil, and honey, and mix thoroughly. (Reserve ½ cup of the crumb mixture for a topping, if desired.) Press the crumbs into the bottom and up the sides of a buttered 9-inch pie plate. Chill for 20 minutes.

To prebake: Preheat the oven to 325°F. Bake for 10 to 12 minutes, or until set. Cool on a rack.

MAKES ONE 9-INCH CRUST

CHERRY BAKEWELL PIE

This pie is based on a traditional English recipe where custard is baked on top of a fruit filling. While we've used the Multi-Grain Pie Dough here, the Ricotta Cheese Pie Dough (left) or the Sour Cream Pie Dough (left) would both work equally well.

Multi-Grain Pie Dough (Single Crust), page 531

1 cup cherry all-fruit spread

½ teaspoon grated lemon zest

1 tablespoon lemon juice

4 large eggs, separated

⅓ cup sugar

½ cup flour

⅓ cup chopped hazelnuts, toasted

½ cup heavy cream

On a lightly floured work surface, roll out the dough to a 12-inch round. Fit the dough into a 9-inch pie plate, pressing it into the bottom and up the sides without stretching the dough. Using kitchen scissors, even the edge, leaving a 1-inch overhang. Fold the overhang under and make a decorative edge (see page 530). Refrigerate for 30 minutes.

Preheat the oven to 425°F. Prick the bottom of the dough all over with a fork. Line with foil or parchment and weight down with dried beans or pie weights. Bake for 10 minutes. Remove the foil and weights. Cool the pie shell on a rack. Reduce the oven temperature to 350°F.

In a small bowl, combine the fruit spread, lemon zest, and lemon juice.

With an electric mixer, beat the egg yolks and sugar until thick and lemon colored. Fold in the flour and nuts.

In a separate bowl, beat the egg whites until stiff but not dry. Fold into the yolk mixture.

Spread the cherry mixture on the bottom of the pie shell. Spoon the egg mixture over the cherry mixture. Bake for 25 minutes, or until a toothpick inserted in the center of the pie comes out clean. Cool on a rack.

At serving time, whip the cream until it stands in soft peaks and mound in the center of the pie.

MAKES 6 SERVINGS

APPLE PIE

While many apples work well in an apple pie, some do not. Avoid McIntosh apples as they tend to break down quickly and turn to mush, and Granny Smiths, if used alone, are too dry. Some good choices are Cortland, Golden Delicious, Empire, Winesap, Braeburn, and Fuji.

Multi-Grain Pie Dough (Double Crust), page 531

7 cups sliced peeled apples

2 tablespoons honey

2 tablespoons sugar

1 tablespoon quick-cooking tapioca

1 tablespoon lemon juice

½ teaspoon vanilla extract

¾ teaspoon cinnamon

½ teaspoon ground ginger

⅛ teaspoon allspice

Preheat the oven to 400°F.

On a lightly floured work surface, roll out half the dough to a 12-inch round and fit into a 9-inch pie plate, pressing it into the bottom and up the sides of the plate.

In a large bowl, toss the apples with the honey, sugar, tapioca, lemon juice, vanilla, cinnamon, ginger, and allspice. Spoon the mixture into the pie shell.

On a lightly floured work surface, roll out the remaining dough to a 12- to 14-inch round and place over the filling. Press the top and bottom edges of the dough together to seal and, with a pair of kitchen scissors, trim the edges to make them neat. Using a fork, crimp the edges. With a paring knife, make several steam vents in the top. Place the pie plate on a rimmed baking sheet.

Bake for 15 minutes. Reduce the oven temperature to 350°F and bake for 30 minutes, or until the juices are bubbling and the crust is golden brown. Cool completely on a rack before slicing.

MAKES 8 SERVINGS

APPLE-PEACH PIE

A take on the traditional apple pie.

- Multi-Grain Pie Dough (Double Crust), page 531
- 3 cups thinly sliced peeled apples
- 3 cups thinly sliced peeled peaches
- ¼ cup honey
- 1 tablespoon lemon juice
- ¼ cup flour
- 1 teaspoon cinnamon
- ¼ teaspoon nutmeg
- 1 tablespoon butter, cut up

Preheat the oven to 400°F.

On a lightly floured work surface, roll out half the dough to a 12-inch round and fit into a 9-inch pie plate, pressing it into the bottom and up the sides of the plate.

In a large bowl, toss together the apples, peaches, honey, lemon juice, flour, cinnamon, and nutmeg. Spoon the mixture into the pie shell and dot with the butter.

On a lightly floured work surface, roll out the remaining dough to a 12- to 14-inch round and place over the filling. Press the top and bottom edges of the dough together to seal and with a pair of kitchen scissors, trim the edges to make them neat. Using a fork, crimp the edges. With a paring knife, make several steam vents in the top. Place the pie plate on a rimmed baking sheet.

Bake for 15 minutes. Reduce the oven temperature to 350°F and bake for 30 minutes, or until the juices are bubbling and the crust is golden brown. Cool completely on a rack before slicing.

MAKES 8 SERVINGS

THREE-BERRY PIE

A little bit of pepper added to the filling gives the berries an interesting flavor boost.

- Multi-Grain Pie Dough (Double Crust), page 531
- 4 cups mixed raspberries, blackberries, and sliced strawberries
- ¼ cup quick-cooking tapioca
- ⅓ cup honey
- ¾ teaspoon cinnamon
- ¼ teaspoon nutmeg
- ⅛ teaspoon pepper
- 2 tablespoons butter

Preheat the oven to 400°F.

On a lightly floured work surface, roll out half the dough to a 12-inch round and fit into a 9-inch pie plate, pressing it into the bottom and up the sides of the plate.

In a medium bowl, combine berries, tapioca, honey, cinnamon, nutmeg, and pepper. Spoon the mixture into the dough. Dot with the butter.

On a lightly floured work surface, roll out the remaining dough to a 12- to 14-inch round and place over the filling. Press the top and bottom edges of the dough together to seal and with a pair of kitchen scissors, trim the edges to make them neat. Using a fork, crimp the edges. With a paring knife, make several steam vents in the top. Place on a rimmed baking sheet.

Bake for 15 minutes. Reduce the oven temperature to 350°F and bake for 30 to 45 minutes, until the juices are bubbling and the crust is golden brown. Cool completely on a rack before slicing.

MAKES 8 SERVINGS

WINTER BLUEBERRY PIE

Individually frozen, plump blueberries are available year-round. You don't need to thaw the berries, but the pie will take longer to bake.

- **Multi-Grain Pie Dough (Double Crust), page 531**
- **½ cup plus 1 tablespoon granulated sugar**
- **¼ cup turbinado or light brown sugar**
- **¼ cup cornstarch**
- **¼ teaspoon nutmeg**
- **Pinch of allspice**
- **Pinch of cinnamon**
- **Pinch of salt**
- **5 cups frozen blueberries**
- **½ teaspoon grated lemon zest**
- **1 tablespoon lemon juice**
- **2 tablespoons butter, cut up**
- **Milk, for the crust**

On a lightly floured work surface, roll out half the dough to a 12-inch round and fit into a 9-inch pie plate, pressing it into the bottom and up the sides of the plate. Refrigerate for 30 minutes.

Preheat the oven to 375°F.

In a large bowl, stir together ½ cup of the granulated sugar, the brown sugar, cornstarch, nutmeg, allspice, cinnamon, and salt. Gently stir in the blueberries, lemon zest, and lemon juice. Pour the filling into the crust and dot with the butter.

On a lightly floured work surface, roll out the remaining dough to a 12- to 14-inch round and place over the filling. Press the top and bottom edges of the dough together to seal and with a pair of kitchen scissors, trim the edges to make them neat. Using a fork, crimp the edges. With a paring knife, make several steam vents in the top. Place on a rimmed baking sheet. Brush the crust lightly with milk and sprinkle with the remaining 1 tablespoon sugar.

Bake for 55 minutes to 1 hour 5 minutes, until the crust is browned and the filling is bubbling up out of the vents. If the edge of the crust starts to brown too quickly, cover with strips of foil.

MAKES 8 SERVINGS

STREUSEL-TOPPED GINGER PEACHY PIE

Crystallized ginger adds sparkle and a little bit of spicy heat to the filling. Look for it in the spice shelf of the supermarket, or buy it in bulk at natural foods or specialty stores.

- **Multi-Grain Pie Dough (Single Crust), page 531**
- **⅔ cup plus 2 tablespoons flour**
- **⅓ cup date sugar**
- **¼ teaspoon salt**
- **⅓ cup cold butter, cut up**
- **½ cup pecans, coarsely chopped**
- **4 cups thinly sliced peeled peaches**
- **¼ cup honey**
- **2 tablespoons finely chopped crystallized ginger**
- **1 tablespoon lemon juice**
- **½ teaspoon cardamom**

On a lightly floured work surface, roll out the dough to a 12-inch round. Fit the dough into a 9-inch pie plate, pressing it into the bottom and up the sides without stretching the dough. With kitchen scissors, trim the edge, turn under, and make a decorative edge (see "Making a Deorative Edge on a Pie," page 530). Refrigerate for 30 minutes.

Preheat the oven to 450°F.

In a medium bowl, stir together ⅔ cup of the flour, the date sugar, and salt. With a pastry blender or two knives scissor fashion, cut in the butter until the mixture resembles coarse crumbs. Stir in the pecans. Refrigerate while you prepare the filling.

In a medium bowl, combine the peaches with the remaining 2 tablespoons flour. Add the honey, crystallized ginger, lemon juice, and cardamom, and toss to combine. Spoon the mixture into the pie shell. Crumble the pecan mixture on the top.

Place the pie on a rimmed baking sheet. Bake for 10 minutes. Reduce the oven temperature to 350°F and bake for 20 to 25 minutes, until the topping is crisp and the juices in the pie are bubbling. Cool completely on a rack before serving.

MAKES 8 SERVINGS

PERFECT PLUM PIE

Quick-cooking tapioca takes the place of flour or cornstarch as a thickener.

- **3 pounds purple plums, halved, pitted, and thickly sliced**
- **⅓ cup packed muscovado or dark brown sugar**
- **3 tablespoons quick-cooking tapioca**
- **1 tablespoon lemon juice**
- **½ teaspoon allspice**
- **⅛ teaspoon ground cloves**
- **⅛ teaspoon salt**
- **Multi-Grain Pie Dough (Double Crust), page 531**
- **2 tablespoons butter, cut up**
- **1 cup heavy cream, whipped**

In a medium bowl, stir together the plums, brown sugar, tapioca, lemon juice, allspice, cloves, and salt. Let stand for 15 minutes, stirring occasionally (this will bring out some of the juices in the plums).

Preheat the oven to 425°F.

On a lightly floured work surface, roll out half the dough to a 12-inch round. Fit the dough into a 9-inch pie plate, pressing it into the bottom and up the sides without stretching the dough.

Spoon the filling into the dough and dot with the butter. On a lightly floured work surface, roll the remaining half of the dough out to a 12- to 14-inch round. Place the dough over the filling. Press the edges together to seal. With kitchen scissors, trim the edges, then crimp with a fork. With a paring knife, make several steam vents in the top crust.

Place the pie on a rimmed baking sheet. Bake for 15 minutes. Reduce the oven temperature to 350°F and bake for 20 to 25 minutes, until the juices are bubbling and the crust is golden brown. Let cool for 30 minutes on a rack before serving warm with dollops of whipped cream.

MAKES 8 SERVINGS

SPICED FIG PIE

Choose dried figs that are soft and supple. You can easily cut the figs into small pieces with a pair of scissors. Remove and discard the stems before cutting.

- **Multi-Grain Pie Dough (Single Crust), page 531**
- **3 tablespoons butter, at room temperature**
- **½ cup honey**
- **8 large eggs**
- **2 tablespoons lemon juice**
- **1 teaspoon cinnamon**
- **½ teaspoon nutmeg**
- **1½ cups chopped dried figs**
- **½ cup raisins**

2 tablespoons flour

½ cup chopped pistachios, walnuts, or almonds

On a lightly floured work surface, roll out the dough to a 12-inch round. Fit the dough into a 9-inch pie plate, pressing it into the bottom and up the sides without stretching the dough. Using kitchen scissors, even the edge, leaving a 1-inch overhang. Fold the overhang under and make a decorative edge (see "Making a Deorative Edge on a Pie," page 530). Refrigerate for 30 minutes.

Preheat the oven to 425°F. Prick the bottom of the dough all over with a fork. Line with foil or parchment and weight down with dried beans or pie weights. Bake for 10 minutes. Remove the foil and weights. Cool the pie shell on a rack. Reduce the oven temperature to 375°F.

With an electric mixer, beat the butter and honey until light and fluffy. Beat in the eggs, lemon juice, cinnamon, and nutmeg. In a small bowl, toss the figs and raisins with the flour until just coated. Stir into the batter along with the nuts.

Place the pie plate on a rimmed baking sheet and scrape the mixture into the pie shell. Bake for 40 minutes, or until the center is set. Cool on a rack before serving.

MAKES 8 SERVINGS

CHERRY-BERRY PIE

Fresh sour cherries have a very brief season, but cans and jars are around all the time. If you're lucky enough to get fresh ones, use them instead.

Multi-Grain Pie Dough (Double Crust), page 531

3 cups canned or jarred pitted sour cherries

1 cup blackberries

¼ cup honey

1 tablespoon butter

1 cup water

3 tablespoons cornstarch

3 large egg yolks, beaten

Preheat the oven to 450°F. On a lightly floured work surface, roll out half the dough to a 12-inch round. Fit the dough into a 9-inch pie plate, pressing it into the bottom and up the sides without stretching the dough.

In a medium saucepan, combine the cherries, blackberries, honey, butter, and ¾ cup of the water. Bring to a boil, reduce to a simmer, and cook, stirring frequently, until the fruit softens.

In a small bowl, whisk the remaining ¼ cup water into the cornstarch until smooth. Add to the saucepan and cook, stirring constantly until the mixture thickens, 1 to 2 minutes. Mix 2 tablespoons of the hot fruit mixture into the egg yolks to warm them, then mix the egg yolks into the saucepan and continue cooking, stirring constantly, for 2 more minutes. Spoon the filling into the pie shell.

On a lightly floured work surface, roll out the remaining dough to a 12- to 14-inch round and place over the filling. Press the top and bottom edges of the dough together to seal and, with a pair of kitchen scissors, trim the edges to make them neat. Using a fork, crimp the edges. Cut several steam vents in the top.

Place the pie plate on a rimmed baking sheet. Bake for 10 minutes. Reduce the oven temperature to 325°F and bake for 20 to 25 minutes, until just set. Cool on a rack before serving.

MAKES 8 SERVINGS

LEMON MERINGUE PIE

An irresistible American classic.

Sour Cream Pie Dough (page 532)
1⅓ cups sugar
⅓ cup cornstarch
1 teaspoon grated lemon zest
¼ teaspoon salt
1¾ cups water
2 large eggs, beaten
½ cup lemon juice (2 to 3 lemons)
2 teaspoons butter
3 large egg whites
¼ teaspoon cream of tartar

Preheat the oven to 375°F.

On a lightly floured work surface, roll out the dough to a 12-inch round. Fit the dough into a 9-inch pie plate, pressing it into the bottom and up the sides without stretching the dough. Using kitchen scissors, even the edge, leaving a 1-inch overhang. Fold the overhang under and make a decorative edge (see "Making a Deorative Edge on a Pie," page 530).

Prick the bottom of the dough all over with a fork. Line with foil or parchment and weight down with dried beans or pie weights. Bake for 15 minutes, or until just set. Remove the foil and weights, and bake for 10 minutes, or until golden brown. Leave the oven on. Let the pie shell cool slightly.

Meanwhile, in a medium saucepan, combine 1 cup of the sugar, the cornstarch, lemon zest, and salt. Add the water, stirring until smooth. Bring to a boil over medium heat, reduce to a simmer, and cook, stirring occasionally, until thickened, about 5 minutes. Remove from the heat.

In a medium bowl, combine the eggs, lemon juice, and butter. Stirring constantly, gradually add the sugar mixture. Pour into the pie shell. Bake for 10 minutes, or until the filling is just beginning to set.

While the filling is baking, with an electric mixer, beat the egg whites and cream of tartar until soft peaks form. Gradually beat in the remaining ⅓ cup sugar until the whites are stiff and shiny.

Pile the meringue lightly onto the pie, spreading it to the edges, taking care to make the meringue seal in the lemon filling completely. Bake the pie for 10 to 12 minutes, until the meringue is lightly browned and set. Refrigerate until chilled.

MAKES 8 SERVINGS

BUTTERMILK FRUIT PIE

If you have leftover cooked fruit, such as peaches, plums, or apricots, use them here and skip the cooking of the peaches.

Multi-Grain Pie Dough (Single Crust), page 531
½ cup (1 stick) plus 1 tablespoon butter, at room temperature
1½ cups sliced peeled peaches
1 cup honey
3 large eggs, separated
3 tablespoons cornstarch
1½ cups buttermilk
1 teaspoon grated lemon zest
1 tablespoon lemon juice
¼ teaspoon nutmeg

On a lightly floured work surface, roll out the dough to a 12-inch round. Fit the dough into a 9-inch pie plate, pressing it into the bottom and up the sides without stretching the dough. Using kitchen scissors, even the edge, leaving a 1-inch overhang. Fold the overhang under and make a decorative edge (see "Making a Deorative Edge on a Pie," page 530). Refrigerate for 30 minutes.

Preheat the oven to 350°F.

In a small skillet, heat 1 tablespoon of the butter over medium heat. Add the peaches and cook until soft and lightly browned, about 5 minutes.

In a large bowl, beat together the remaining ½ cup butter, the honey, egg yolks, and cornstarch, until combined. Beat in the buttermilk, lemon zest, and lemon juice. Fold in the peaches.

With an electric mixer, beat the egg whites until stiff but not dry. Gently fold the egg whites into the buttermilk mixture.

Place the pie plate on a rimmed baking sheet. Spoon the filling into the pie shell and sprinkle with the nutmeg. Bake for 20 minutes. Reduce the oven temperature to 300°F and bake for 15 to 20 minutes, until the filling is set. Cool on a rack before serving.

MAKES 8 SERVINGS

YOGURT-RAISIN PIE

Choose a whole-milk yogurt for this sweet and tangy pie.

- **Multi-Grain Pie Dough (Single Crust), page 531**
- **3 large eggs**
- **⅓ cup honey**
- **1½ cups plain whole-milk yogurt**
- **1½ cups raisins, chopped**
- **1½ tablespoons lemon juice**
- **¼ teaspoon nutmeg**

On a lightly floured work surface, roll out the dough to a 12-inch round. Fit the dough into a 9-inch pie plate, pressing it into the bottom and up the sides without stretching the dough. Using kitchen scissors, even the edge, leaving a 1-inch overhang. Fold the overhang under and make a decorative edge (see "Making a Deorative Edge on a Pie," page 530). Refrigerate for 30 minutes.

Preheat the oven to 450°F.

With an electric mixer, beat the eggs and honey until light and fluffy. Beat in the yogurt. Fold in the raisins, lemon juice, and nutmeg, and mix gently until combined.

Place the pie plate on a rimmed baking sheet. Pour the mixture into the pie shell. Bake for 10 minutes. Reduce the oven temperature to 350°F and bake for 35 minutes, or until set. Cool on a rack before serving.

MAKES 8 SERVINGS

MAPLE BLUEBERRY CUSTARD PIE

Our favorite maple syrup is grade B because of its robust flavor, but feel free to use whatever you have on hand.

- **Multi-Grain Pie Dough (Single Crust), page 531**
- **2 tablespoons plus ¼ cup maple syrup**
- **3 tablespoons cornstarch**
- **1 cup milk**
- **2 large eggs, beaten**
- **1 tablespoon butter**
- **1 teaspoon vanilla extract**
- **¼ cup water**
- **1½ cups blueberries**
- **1 teaspoon lemon juice**

On a lightly floured work surface, roll out the dough to a 12-inch round. Fit the dough into a 9-inch pie plate, pressing it into the bottom and up the sides without stretching the dough. Using kitchen scissors, even the edge, leaving a 1-inch overhang. Fold the overhang under and make a decorative edge (see "Making a Deorative Edge on a Pie," page 530). Refrigerate for 30 minutes.

Preheat the oven to 425°F. Prick the bottom of the

dough all over with a fork. Line with foil or parchment and weight down with dried beans or pie weights. Bake for 12 to 15 minutes, until the crust is golden brown and cooked through. Remove the foil and weights. Cool the pie shell on a rack.

In the top of a double boiler, whisk together 2 tablespoons of the maple syrup, 2 tablespoons of the cornstarch, and the milk. Add the eggs and whisk to combine. Place over simmering water and cook, stirring constantly, until the mixture is thick enough to coat the back of a spoon, about 5 minutes. Remove from the heat and immediately transfer to a bowl. Stir in the butter and vanilla. Cool and pour into the pie shell.

In a medium saucepan, combine the remaining ¼ cup maple syrup, the remaining 1 tablespoon cornstarch, and the water. Cook over medium heat, stirring constantly, until slightly thick, 1 to 2 minutes. Add the berries and lemon juice and cook, stirring constantly, for 5 minutes. Let cool.

Spread the berry mixture over the custard in the pie shell. Refrigerate and serve chilled.

MAKES 8 SERVINGS

ZUCCHINI CUSTARD PIE

In order for the custard in the pie to set and not be runny, it's important that the zucchini be squeezed very dry. The easiest way to do this is to place the gratded zucchini in a strainer and press on it until no more liquid remains.

Multi-Grain Pie Dough (Single Crust), page 531

4 medium zucchini (1½ pounds total)

1 cup milk

4 large egg yolks

¼ cup honey

½ teaspoon vanilla extract

½ teaspoon cinnamon

On a lightly floured work surface, roll the dough out to a 12-inch round. Fit the dough into a 9-inch pie plate, pressing it into the bottom and up the sides without stretching the dough. Using kitchen scissors, even the edge, leaving a 1-inch overhang. Fold the overhang under and make a decorative edge (see "Making a Deorative Edge on a Pie," page 530). Refrigerate for 30 minutes.

MERINGUE TOPPING FOR PIES

When topping a pie with meringue, gently pile the meringue whites on a hot filling. This will prevent the finished meringue from weeping and from sliding off the filling by spreading the whites so they cover the entire surface and touch the rim of the pie shell.

Use a light, quick hand to spread and swirl the whites in an attractive pattern. But avoid sweeping them into sharp peaks, which may burn before the rest of the meringue browns. If you dip the spatula into cool water occasionally, the whites will not stick to the spatula as you spread them.

Bake the meringue in a preheated 375°F oven until the background is a pleasing light brown and the peaks are slightly darker. When your meringue cools, you will know if it was underbaked (it weeps), or overbaked (the surface is tough and hard to cut).

Preheat the oven to 425°F. Prick the bottom of the dough all over with a fork. Line with foil or parchment and weight down with dried beans or pie weights. Bake for 10 minutes. Remove the foil and weights. Cool the pie shell on a rack. Reduce the oven temperature to 350°F.

Grate the zucchini and then squeeze out all the liquid.

In a 2-quart saucepan, whisk together the milk, egg yolks, honey, and vanilla. Cook over low heat, stirring constantly, until the mixture is thick enough to coat the back of a spoon. Remove from the heat. Stir in the zucchini and cinnamon.

Place the pie plate on a rimmed baking sheet. Pour the custard into the pie shell. Bake for 20 minutes, or until the custard is set. Cool on a rack, then refrigerate before serving.

MAKES 8 SERVINGS

SWEET POTATO-WALNUT PIE

While pumpkin pie is a Thanksgiving tradition, this nut-topped sweet potato pie could also become a holiday favorite.

- Multi-Grain Pie Dough (Single Crust), page 531
- 4 medium sweet potatoes (1½ pounds total), cooked, peeled, and cut up
- ⅔ cup plus 3 tablespoons honey
- 3 large eggs
- 1½ cups light cream or milk
- ½ teaspoon ground ginger
- ½ teaspoon cinnamon
- ½ teaspoon nutmeg
- 3 tablespoons butter
- ½ cup chopped walnuts
- Whipped cream (optional)

PUMPKIN PIE SPICE

- 1 tablespoon cinnamon
- 1½ teaspoons ground ginger
- ½ teaspoon nutmeg
- ½ teaspoon ground cloves
- ½ teaspoon allspice

On a lightly floured work surface, roll out the dough to a 12-inch round. Fit the dough into a 9-inch pie plate, pressing it into the bottom and up the sides without stretching the dough. Using kitchen scissors, even the edge, leaving a 1-inch overhang. Fold the overhang under and make a decorative edge (see "Making a Deorative Edge on a Pie," page 530). Refrigerate for 30 minutes.

Preheat the oven to 425°F.

In a food processor, puree the sweet potatoes, ⅔ cup of the honey, the eggs, cream, ginger, cinnamon, and nutmeg, until smooth and well combined.

Place the pie plate on a rimmed baking sheet. Pour the custard into the pie shell. Reduce the oven temperature to 350°F and bake the pie for 50 minutes, or until the center is barely firm. Cool on a rack.

In a small saucepan, melt the butter over medium heat. Add the remaining 3 tablespoons honey and bring to a boil. Remove from the heat and stir in the walnuts. Pour the mixture over the top of the pie. Just before serving, top with whipped cream, if desired.

MAKES 8 SERVINGS

CHICKPEA PIE

Chickpeas have a particularly nutty flavor and smooth texture that make them perfect for a pie filling.

Sour Cream Pie Dough (page 532)
3 cups cooked chickpeas
1 cup light cream or milk
¾ cup sugar
1 large egg
2 large egg whites
2 tablespoons brown rice syrup
1½ teaspoons vanilla extract
1 teaspoon cinnamon
¼ teaspoon salt
⅛ teaspoon nutmeg

On a lightly floured work surface, roll out the dough to a 13-inch round. Fit the dough into a 9-inch deep-dish pie plate, pressing it into the bottom and up the sides without stretching the dough. Using kitchen scissors, even the edge, leaving a 1-inch overhang. Fold the overhang under and make a decorative edge (see "Making a Deorative Edge on a Pie," page 530). Refrigerate for 30 minutes.

Preheat the oven to 425°F. Prick the bottom of the dough all over with a fork. Line with foil or parchment and weight down with dried beans or pie weights. Bake for 10 minutes. Remove the foil and weights. Cool the pie shell on a rack. Reduce the oven temperature to 350°F.

In a blender or food processor, combine the chickpeas, cream, sugar, whole egg, egg whites, rice syrup, vanilla, cinnamon, salt, and nutmeg, and process until smooth.

Place the pie plate on a rimmed baking sheet. Pour the chickpea mixture into the pie shell. Bake for 50 minutes, or until set. Serve warm or at room temperature.

MAKES 12 SERVINGS

PUMPKIN CHIFFON PIE

Make the Crumb Piecrust with half zweiback crumbs and half graham cracker crumbs.

Crumb Piecrust (page 532), unbaked
2 envelopes unflavored gelatin
½ cup water
6 ounces cream cheese
1 cup packed muscovado or dark brown sugar
1¼ teaspoons cinnamon
1 teaspoon vanilla extract
2 cups unsweetened pumpkin puree
2 tablespoons hazelnut liqueur (optional)
½ cup very cold heavy cream
¼ cup coarsely chopped pecans, toasted

Preheat the oven to 350°F. Bake the piecrust in the lower third of the oven for 8 to 10 minutes, or until the crust is just set. Transfer to a rack to cool.

Meanwhile, in a small heatproof bowl, sprinkle the gelatin over the water. Set the bowl over a small saucepan of simmering water and stir until the gelatin dissolves, about 3 minutes. Remove from the heat.

In a food processor, combine the cream cheese, brown sugar, cinnamon, and vanilla and process until creamy. Add the pumpkin and liqueur (if using) and process until smooth. Add the dissolved gelatin and process until combined. Transfer to a medium bowl and refrigerate until the mixture is just beginning to set and is the texture of raw egg whites, about 45 minutes.

With an electric mixer, beat the cream until very soft peaks form. With a rubber spatula, fold the whipped cream into the pumpkin mixture. Scrape the mixture into the pie shell and refrigerate until set, at least 1 hour 30 minutes. Sprinkle the pecans on top and serve.

MAKES 8 SERVINGS

CHOCOLATE-WALNUT PIE

Real whipped cream on the side or atop the pie is a must.

- **Multi-Grain Pie Dough (Single Crust), page 531**
- **2 cups walnuts**
- **3 ounces (3 squares) semisweet chocolate, cut into rough chunks**
- **1/4 cup (1/2 stick) butter, cut up**
- **3 large eggs, at room temperature**
- **2/3 cup packed muscovado or dark brown sugar**
- **3/4 cup brown rice syrup**
- **2 teaspoons vanilla extract**
- **1/4 teaspoon salt**

On a lightly floured work surface, roll the dough out to a 12-inch round. Fit the dough into a 9-inch pie plate, pressing it into the bottom and up the sides without stretching the dough. Using kitchen scissors, even the edge, leaving a 1-inch overhang. Fold the overhang under and make a decorative edge (see "Making a Deorative Edge on a Pie," page 530). Refrigerate for 30 minutes.

Preheat the oven to 350°F. Put the walnuts in a baking pan and bake, stirring often, until lightly toasted, about 15 minutes. Tip into a bowl and let cool. Break up with your fingers or coarsely chop.

In a medium microwaveable bowl, combine the chocolate and butter. Microwave on high for 45 seconds to 1 minute, until hot and starting to melt. Stir until the chocolate and butter are melted and creamy.

In a large bowl, whisk together the eggs and brown sugar until smooth. Whisk in the rice syrup, vanilla, and salt. Whisk in the chocolate mixture and stir in the walnuts.

Place the pie plate on a rimmed baking sheet. Pour the chocolate mixture into the pie shell. Bake for 50 to 60 minutes, until the pie is puffed at the edges, firm at the center, and the crust is lightly browned. Cool on a rack.

MAKES 10 SERVINGS

RICOTTA-PINEAPPLE PIE WITH A PECAN CRUST

Easy and delicious, this is the ideal pie for people who are intimidated by the thought of making pastry crusts. The filling is reminiscent of rice pudding.

- **1 1/2 cups plus 2 tablespoons finely ground pecans (7 to 8 ounces)**
- **2 tablespoons butter, cut into small pieces, at room temperature**
- **1 1/2 cups part-skim ricotta cheese**
- **3/4 cup cooked rice**
- **2 tablespoons frozen pineapple-orange juice concentrate**
- **1 can (8 ounces) juice-packed crushed pineapple, drained**
- **1 tablespoon honey**
- **1 teaspoon grated orange zest**
- **1 teaspoon vanilla extract**
- **1/8 teaspoon cinnamon**

Preheat the oven to 350°F.

In a small bowl, combine 1 1/2 cups of the pecans with the butter, mixing with your fingers until the nuts and butter are incorporated. Press the nut mixture into a 9-inch pie plate, covering the sides as well as the bottom of the plate (it will be a thin crust).

Bake for 10 minutes. Let cool.

In a large bowl, stir together the ricotta, rice, pineapple-orange juice concentrate, pineapple, honey, orange zest, and vanilla.

Spoon the filling into the cooled crust. Mix the remaining 2 tablespoons ground pecans with the cinnamon and sprinkle over the top of pie. Chill for 30 minutes before serving.

MAKES 6 SERVINGS

LEMON-BLUEBERRY TART

The toasted pecans in the crust add texture, flavor, and good-for-you fats.

CRUST

- ⅓ cup pecans
- 1 cup flour
- 2 tablespoons toasted wheat germ
- 2 tablespoons sugar
- ½ teaspoon salt
- 3 tablespoons pecan or hazelnut oil
- 1 tablespoon extra-light olive oil
- 2 tablespoons ice water

FILLING

- 1 teaspoon unflavored gelatin
- ¼ cup cold water
- 1½ teaspoons grated lemon zest
- ⅔ cup lemon juice
- 1 cup sugar
- ⅓ cup extra-light olive oil
- 2 large eggs
- 2 tablespoons sour cream
- 2 cups blueberries

To make the crust: Preheat the oven to 350°F. Place the pecans on a rimmed baking sheet and bake for 7 minutes, or until fragrant and lightly crisped. Set on a rack to cool. Increase the oven temperature to 400°F.

In a food processor, combine the pecans, flour, wheat germ, sugar, and salt. Process until the pecans are finely ground. Transfer to a large bowl.

In a small bowl, whisk together the pecan oil, olive oil, and ice water until well combined. Make a well in the center of the flour mixture, add the oil mixture, and stir with a fork until well combined. Shape the dough into a ½-inch-thick disk.

Roll the dough out between 2 sheets of lightly floured waxed paper into an 11-inch circle (⅛ inch thick). Transfer the dough to a 9-inch tart pan with a removable bottom and carefully fit the dough into the pan. Trim the edges even with the top of the tart pan. Prick the bottom all over with a fork.

Line the dough with foil or parchment and weight down with dried beans or pie weights. Bake for 15 minutes. Remove the foil and weights, and continue baking for 10 to 12 minutes, until the edge is golden brown and crisp. Set on a rack to cool completely.

Meanwhile, make the filling: In a small bowl, sprinkle the gelatin over the cold water. Let stand for 5 minutes to soften.

In a medium heavy-bottomed saucepan, whisk together the lemon zest, lemon juice, sugar, olive oil, and eggs, until well combined. Cook over low heat, whisking constantly, until the mixture is hot, about 3 minutes. Whisk in the softened gelatin and cook, whisking constantly, until the mixture is the consistency of thick honey, about 3 minutes. Transfer to a medium bowl and let cool to room temperature.

Fold the sour cream into the filling and spoon into the cooled tart shell. Chill until serving time. Just before serving, top with the blueberries.

MAKES 10 SERVINGS

RASPBERRY-TANGERINE TART

Tangerine juice can be hard to find, so orange juice is a good alternative.

- 1½ cups white whole wheat flour*
- ⅓ cup turbinado or light brown sugar
- 2 teaspoons grated tangerine or orange zest
- ½ teaspoon baking powder

½ teaspoon salt

¼ cup plus 3 tablespoons extra-light olive oil

8 tablespoons tangerine or orange juice

2 bags (12 ounces each) frozen raspberries

6 tablespoons mild honey

⅛ teaspoon nutmeg

3 tablespoons cornstarch

**milled from white wheat grains*

In a large bowl, stir together the flour, brown sugar, tangerine zest, baking powder, and salt. Stir in the oil and 2 tablespoons of the tangerine juice until the mixture comes together. Transfer to a lightly floured work surface and knead 10 times, until the dough forms a ball. Flatten into a disk, wrap in plastic wrap, and let sit for 30 minutes at room temperature.

Preheat the oven to 350°F. With your fingertips, gently press the dough onto the bottom and up the sides of a 9-inch tart pan with a removable bottom. Prick the bottom of the shell with a fork and line the pan with foil or parchment. Fill the foil with pie weights or dried beans. Bake the shell for 15 minutes. Remove the foil and weights and bake the shell for 10 minutes, or until golden brown. Cool on a rack.

Meanwhile, in a saucepan, combine the raspberries, honey, and nutmeg. Bring to a boil, reduce to a simmer, and cook for 5 minutes.

In a small bowl, stir together the remaining 6 tablespoons tangerine juice and the cornstarch. Stir the cornstarch mixture into the berries and cook for 2 minutes, or until the berry mixture is thick.

Cool the berry mixture to room temperature, then spoon into the baked shell. Chill for 1 hour before serving.

MAKES 8 SERVINGS

BREADS

There's something magical about bread baking. Imagine combining just a few simple ingredients, seeing them grow to double their original size, and then baking them into a perfect loaf.

The makings for a loaf of bread can be as elementary as flour, water, salt, and yeast—or they can become more elaborate, enriched with such ingredients as butter, milk, eggs, cheese, and yogurt. The bread can be a simple, traditionally shaped loaf, or it can be molded into small scalloped rounds, long rolled scrolls, or fancy braids. Some breads have flavored fillings. The world of bread making also encompasses quick breads, muffins, and flatbreads, none of which relies on yeast for rising—thus even simpler to make.

Things have changed tremendously in the world of bread. At one time, bread meant white bread. White bread, homemade or store-bought, is made with flour whose bran and germ have been removed. The starchy endosperm, or heart of the grain, that remains is milled into white flour. Although this flour is usually enriched with some of the nutrients it lost with the removal of the bran and germ, significant amounts of fiber are never recovered. Make your own bread, and you can pack it full of nutritious whole grains, starting with whole wheat flour. The result is a loaf packed full of fiber and nutrition with interesting flavor and texture.

Breads made with whole grains exclusively are denser and somewhat heavier than those made with refined flours, because the presence of the bran and wheat germ slightly inhibits the yeast's rising action. In many of the recipes in this book we've used white whole wheat flour, which is milled from hard white wheat for a more refined taste, but with the wholesomeness of whole wheat. In other recipes, we've used a combination of whole wheat flour and all-purpose flour to get a nutritious loaf that isn't too dense. These, in combination with other whole grains, make breads that are delicious, nutritious, and hearty without being too heavy.

Yeast Breads

Yeast is what makes bread rise and gives home-baked bread its wonderful flavor and aroma. These living, single-celled organisms convert starches from the flour into carbon dioxide and alcohol. The carbon dioxide inflates the dough, making it rise, and the alcohol bakes off, leaving flavor behind.

Components of Yeast Bread

YEAST

Store-bought yeast is available in a couple of forms: a compressed, moist cake, and a powder called active dry yeast. Active dry yeast comes in ¼-ounce envelopes, which hold 2¼ teaspoons yeast, and 4-ounce jars, which hold about ¾ cup. (There is also an instant, or rapid-rise, yeast that many bakers shun because the rising process can be so short that the dough doesn't have the time to develop good flavor.) The fresh cake should be compact and of an even, creamy-beige color. Compressed yeast and active dry yeast both have a use-by date on them. Store both in the refrigerator. The dry yeast and the cake yeast are equally suitable and interchangeable for bread making: 2½ teaspoons of active dry yeast is equivalent to 1 packed tablespoon of cake yeast.

Proofing the Yeast

The object of proofing yeast is to make sure that the yeast organisms are still alive and active. To proof yeast, it is dissolved in a warm liquid with a small amount of sweetener added to provide food for the organisms. The temperature of the liquid can range from 78° to 110°F. To test the liquid, sprinkle a few drops on the inside of your wrist. It should feel just warm but not hot. It is better to err on the cool side; liquid that is too hot will kill the yeast. Cooler liquid merely slows down the process.

An exception to this proofing method is with the mixer method of mixing the dough, which some bakers feel is quicker. In this case the yeast, which has been blended first with part of the dry ingredients, is proofed with liquid that is 120° to 130°F. The hotter liquid is tempered by the dry ingredients.

Allow the yeast to proof in a warm spot for 5 to 10 minutes. A frothy appearance indicates that it is working. If no bubbles appear after 5 minutes, discard the yeast and start over.

Enrichment

Bread lends itself to all kinds of embellishments that can vary its taste, texture, nutritional value, and even its keeping quality. Eggs, butter, and milk, for example, are commonly used and add some special qualities to the final product.

Eggs give bread a richer taste. Fats and oils flavor bread and enhance the gluten's elasticity by softening it, thereby producing a fuller risen loaf. But note that doughs that are high in fat usually require more yeast and may take longer to rise. A soft crust and moist interior result from small amounts of egg and butter. In addition, breads baked with eggs and butter or oil retain their moisture and stay fresh longer. Milk or beaten egg yolk brushed on top of the baking bread gives the crust a special crispness.

THE CORNELL FORMULA

Dr. Clive McCay of Cornell University came up with a formula for boosting the nutrients in bread recipes.

1 tablespoon nonfat dry milk solids
1 tablespoon soy flour
1 teaspoon wheat germ

Combine all ingredients in a measuring cup, and fill out the balance of the cup with unbleached white flour. Do this for each cup of flour called for in a recipe.

Liquid

The liquid used in bread can also influence its characteristics. Potato water—which is simply water in which potatoes have been boiled—adds its own sweet flavor and gives bread a rather delicate crumb. Plain water gives bread a dry, crunchy crust, while milk strengthens gluten and yields a smoother, moister crumb, which will keep longer. Milk also adds to the bread's nutritional value by boosting its protein and calcium content.

SPONGE DOUGHS

The sponge method of making bread produces a light, flavorful bread with a large crumb. To make a sponge dough, you proof the yeast in a large amount of liquid, and then mix it with just a portion of the flour. This sponge-like batter is allowed to rise for about an hour, then the remaining flour and ingredients are added. The dough rises one more time, before baking. Today most bread makers prefer the finer-grained breads that result from conventional dough mixing method.

Salt

Salt is an important ingredient in bread baking. It acts as a retarder for the yeast, allowing the bread to rise slowly so it can develop flavor and structure. However, do not allow the salt to come into direct contact with the yeast, as it will kill it and your bread will not rise. Instead, add the salt after you have added at least a cup or two of the flour. The recipes for the breads in this book all use table salt.

Sweetener

A yeast bread can be sweetened with molasses, honey, or any other liquid sweetener as well as granulated sugar. Sweeteners give bread a richer, darker color and act as a natural preservative. Too much sweetener, however, will inhibit the growth of yeast and cause the bread to burn.

Added Ingredients

Cheese, herbs, dried fruits, and chopped nuts can be used to add something unusual to a plain loaf of bread. When adding these ingredients, it is generally best to knead them in after the dough has risen once, so they will not hinder the yeast's leavening action. Cracked wheat, sesame seeds, or rolled oats baked on top of a loaf of bread contribute flavor and crunch as well as an appetizing appearance.

Procedure for Baking Yeast Bread

Mixing the Ingredients

Before you begin mixing the ingredients for a recipe, be sure to bring them all to room temperature. The order in which you mix them does not matter, but either add all the wet ingredients (including oil or butter) to the dry, or add all the dry to the wet. You can proof the yeast directly in the mixing bowl and then add the dry ingredients, which you have combined in another bowl. Mix all the ingredients with a long wooden spoon until you have incorporated them into a sticky mass that begins to resemble dough.

The amount of liquid absorbed by any type of flour depends on several variables, including weather and locale. On humid days the amount of liquid or flour may need to be altered slightly. Where and how the grain was grown, and its age, will also have an effect on a flour's absorbency. As you become more familiar with bread making, you will become more proficient at judging how to adjust the liquid for each recipe.

When possible, mix nonwheat flours with the other ingredients first, then incorporate the mixture gradually until the proper consistency is reached. You will have to knead the dough for a while before you know if enough flour has been incorporated.

Kneading the Dough

When all the ingredients have been mixed and moistened in the bowl, you may use your hands for kneading. Food processors and electric mixers with proper attachments can knead bread dough with speed and efficiency, but many bakers prefer to knead by hand.

Bear in mind as you knead the dough that the purpose is to distribute all the ingredients as uniformly as possible so that the yeast can raise the dough properly. Kneading also helps to develop the gluten that gives the bread structure and traps the bubbles of carbon dioxide produced as the yeast digests the starches in the dough.

Choose a hard, smooth surface and dust it with flour. To knead the dough, begin by pushing the dough away with the heels of your hands. Stretch and push the dough slowly with both hands, then fold it over itself, give it a one-quarter turn, and repeat the process. Do not be afraid to add flour as you knead, to keep the dough from sticking to your hands or the surface. However, whole grain bread doughs will be a little sticky and adding too much flour will cause them to dry out after baking.

Most dough should be kneaded for 8 to 10 minutes. Underkneading or overkneading can have adverse effects on the gluten development and consequently on your bread. Dough has been kneaded enough when it no longer sticks to your hands or to the work surface. It should be smooth and elastic, but manageable.

The Rising

When the dough has been thoroughly kneaded, roll it into a ball and place in a well-oiled bowl. Turn it over once to coat all sides of the dough with oil, which will keep a crust from forming as the dough rises. Cover the bowl with a damp cloth and place it in a warm, draft-free spot. Dough will rise well in a place where the temperature is 70° to 75°F. The warmer the spot, the faster the rise. For the best results in flavor and texture, dough should be allowed to rise slowly. You can hasten the rising if necessary, by exposing the dough to a temperature of 100°F. Rising can also be slowed down by putting the dough in a cool place or by refrigerating it. At any point the dough may be covered and refrigerated for up to a day. Before kneading and shaping refrigerated

---

BAKING WITH QUARRY TILES

Breads baked on quarry tiles have a special crustiness to them. The porous tiles absorb moisture from the baking loaves and give an added crispness to the bottom crusts. To keep the crust from setting too quickly, humidity must be present during the baking. This is supplied by a pan of hot water placed on the bottom shelf of an electric oven or the floor of a gas oven. During the baking, the interior of the oven should be sprayed periodically with water from an atomizer. (Take care not to spray the bulb of the oven light).

dough, allow it to warm to room temperature (about 2 hours.)

Dough must be allowed to rise at least once, and usually twice or more. Dough that has risen just once will produce a coarse-textured loaf with large holes. For the first rise, dough should rise until it doubles in bulk, generally between 1 hour and 1 hour 30 minutes. The timing will vary depending on the temperature of the room and the richness of the dough. A bread rich with eggs will take longer to rise than one that is leaner. (At high altitudes dough rises faster. No recipe adjustment is necessary, but do not allow dough to increase its volume more than is called for.)

Whenever you are in doubt about whether the dough has expanded to the proper volume, there is a foolproof test you can apply. Just poke two fingers into it. If the indentations remain, the dough is ready for you to punch down with your fist, reshape into a smooth ball, and allow to rise for a second time.

Punching down the dough lets carbon dioxide escape and mixes yeast cells more evenly throughout the dough, giving them access to fresh food and oxygen. The result is a more evenly grained bread and a lighter loaf. The second rising may be done after the loaves have been shaped and placed in the pans in which they will be baked. Be sure to allow room in the pan for the bread's expansion while baking. Individual recipes usually give instructions on how to prevent the baked bread from sticking. Generally, the pan or baking dish is oiled or buttered.

Baking Time & Temperature

You will find that the time and temperature for baking bread will vary with each recipe. A bread's actual baking time does not always coincide with the time specified in the recipe, and that can be due to altitude, ingredient freshness, or inconsistent oven temperature. It is wise to check the baking bread 15 to 20 minutes before the end of its stated baking time, to make sure it is not baking too fast. Often an oven is hotter in the back. If you find that yours is, rotate the pan 180 degrees midway through the baking. If the crust is browning too quickly, cover loosely with foil.

The bread is done when it pulls away from the sides of a pan (if baked in one), or when the top or bottom crust sounds hollow when tapped. If the bread isn't done in the time suggested, return it to the oven and test again after 10 minutes. Remove freshly baked bread from the pan and let cool on a wire rack, to allow the air to circulate so the crust remains crisp. Cool loaves completely before slicing so they won't crumble and their flavor will be fully developed.

Baking Bread with Nonwheat Flours

Experiment with combinations that appeal to you; try small amounts of cornmeal, rye, or buckwheat mixed with wheat flour, for example. Rye yields a moist, dense loaf; cornmeal adds a slightly dry, grainy texture. For greater detail on how nonwheat flours change the texture of bread, see "Using Nonwheat Flours in Bread Making" (opposite). Keep the pairings fairly simple so the flavor of each nonwheat flour retains its own identity in the final product.

Bear in mind, when combining nonwheat flours, that at least one-half to three-quarters of the flour for each recipe must be wheat if you are to get a well-risen loaf. Wheat flour alone contains the proper amount of gluten-forming protein needed to take advantage of the yeast's rising action. Rye and triticale flours contain only small amounts of gluten—too little to provide a good rise on their own. But experience and individual taste will be the best guide to what combinations work well for you.

Sourdough Bread

San Francisco is said to be the home of today's formula for sourdough bread. The misty atmosphere is perfect for making and keeping a sourdough starter. But bakers all over the country have learned to duplicate this primitive type of leavening, which gives bread a pleasantly sour

USING NONWHEAT FLOURS IN BREAD MAKING

For each cup of whole wheat flour in a bread recipe, replace the indicated amount with nonwheat flour.

FLOUR/MEAL	AMOUNT	CHARACTERISTICS OF BREAD
AMARANTH	2 tablespoons	Smooth, crisp crust; moist, fine crumb
BARLEY	¼ cup	Firm, chewy crust; cake-like crumb
BEAN	2 tablespoons	Light texture
BUCKWHEAT	¼ cup	Soft crust; moist, fine crumb
CHICKPEA	2 tablespoons	Light texture
CORNMEAL	¼ cup	Unpronounced crust; grainy, slightly dry crumb
FAVA BEAN	2 tablespoons	Light texture
FLAX MEAL	2 tablespoons	Rich, slightly gummy
GLUTEN	½ cup	Crisp, thin crust; fine-grained, crumbly interior
KAMUT	½ cup	Fine crumb
MILLET	¼ cup	Smooth, thin crust; moist, dense crumb
OAT	5 tablespoons	Firm crust; coarse, large crumb
POTATO	¼ cup	Soft, dry crust; fine, springy crumb
QUINOA	¼ cup	Light texture
RICE, BROWN	¼ cup	Soft crust; dry, fine crumb
RICE, WHITE	2 tablespoons	Slightly gummy
RYE	½ cup	Smooth, hard crust; moist, supple crumb
SORGHUM	2 tablespoons	Crisp crust; fine crumb
SOY	¼ cup	Spongy crust; moist, fine crumb
SPELT	¼ cup	Crusty crumb
TEFF	2 tablespoons	Tight crumb
TRITICALE	½ cup	Semi-firm crust; dense-grained crumb

taste. Use the Traditional Sourdough starter (opposite), or try the Handy Sourdough Starter (page 563), which uses commercial yeast to ensure a good bubbling batch. The Traditional Sourdough Starter relies on capturing so-called "wild" yeasts from the air and can be a little unreliable. If you start with commercial yeast, your starter is guaranteed. It all depends on how much of a purist you would like to be. Whichever type you make, sourdough starters should be replenished with equal amounts of flour and water after each use. Starter should be stored in the refrigerator, then taken out and brought to room temperature before being used.

For recipes that use sourdough starter as a leavener, try Sourdough English Muffins (page 563), Sourdough Pumpernickel Bread (page 564), and Sourdough Rye Bread (page 564).

Quick Breads

Sweetened, spiced, herbed, or filled, quick breads offer as many delicious variations as yeast breads, but they are simpler to make. They are leavened with baking powder or soda, or a combination, and require no proofing, kneading, or rising.

TIPS FOR A LIGHTER LOAF

Breads made with all whole wheat, or primarily whole wheat, flour tend to be denser than those made with refined wheat flour. Although the overall process of making bread with them differs very little, the dough may take longer to rise. This is especially true when nonwheat flours (with no gluten at all) are added to make breads even more nutritious. The taste and food value are certainly enhanced, but the additions do make for a slightly heavier bread. As you become more confident with bread making, you will discover there are tricks you can use to make a lighter bread.

- Add 1 teaspoon of baking powder or soda to the dry ingredients, to aid the yeast in raising the dough.
- Add gluten flour to help the rising process and increase the fluffiness of the bread. The protein in gluten flour gives the dough more elasticity.
- Add an acid such as lemon juice or vinegar. It helps soften the protein to increase the dough's elasticity. The result is a soft, light crumb and a higher risen loaf. Use 1 tablespoon of lemon juice or vinegar to every 2½ cups of flour. Don't add the acid ingredient until some of the flour has been mixed with the activated yeast, or the acid will interrupt the yeast fermentation.
- When eggs are called for in a bread recipe, try this formula for a lighter loaf: Separate the whites from the yolks. Beat the whites until stiff but not dry, and fold them into a small amount of the flour called for, before you add the rest of the flour and the other dry ingredients. Beat the yolks with oil or butter or, if no shortening is called for, any of the other liquid ingredients, then combine the two mixtures and proceed with the recipe directions.

Though quick breads lack the fine texture and keeping qualities of yeast breads, you can incorporate nonwheat flours into their recipes more easily, because they do not rely on gluten. You can also vary them in other ways: A cupful of chopped nuts adds new appeal to a plain banana bread, a pureed vegetable adds moisture and flavor when it replaces some of the liquid in a recipe, and yogurt instead of milk makes a heavier, moister product.

Leaveners

Baking powder and baking soda are the most commonly used leavenings for quick breads. In the presence of heat, moisture, and an acid, baking soda releases carbon dioxide, which causes the batter to expand. The acidic element can be buttermilk, sour milk, yogurt, cocoa powder, honey, or molasses. There has to be sufficient acid to activate the baking soda as well as neutralize its alkaline taste.

Baking powder is a combination of baking soda and cream of tartar, which is an acid. Double-acting baking powder leavens at two different stages. When liquid is added to the batter, the acid and baking soda react with one another and begin the leavening process. (Cornstarch in baking powder keeps the mixture dry enough so the soda and acid do not react in storage.) Then when the batter is placed in the oven, the baking powder is further activated by the heat.

Generally speaking, recipes with acidic ingredients specify baking soda; those with very little acid in the ingredients call for baking powder. A high proportion of acidic ingredients in a recipe may require additional alkalinity, and in such a case, both baking powder and baking soda may be called for.

The Batter

Quick breads have some obvious advantages over yeast breads, particularly in terms of time and convenience. Quick bread batters can be merely whisked together or mixed with a

TRADITIONAL SOURDOUGH STARTER

2 cups sweet acidophilus milk or low-fat (1%) milk

2 cups unbleached all-purpose or whole wheat flour

1 teaspoon honey

Place the milk in a small container, cover with cheesecloth, and leave at room temperature for 24 hours.

The next day, add the flour and honey, and stir well to blend. Cover the container with cheesecloth and put in a warm place.

After another 24 hours, captured yeast should begin to activate (though it could take a third day). When the starter becomes bubbly and begins to expand in size, it is ready for use.

STORING HOMEMADE BREAD

The best way to store freshly baked bread that is not meant to be eaten right away is to freeze it. Slice, then wrap in plastic wrap and foil and freeze. This will keep for up to 3 months. If freezing bread whole, wrap in plastic wrap or foil, and freeze. Allow a frozen loaf to thaw for 3 to 6 hours, or heat it in the foil (remove the plastic wrap) for 20 to 30 minutes at 400°F before serving.

HOMEMADE BAKING POWDER

Mix only as much baking powder as you need per recipe, since it may lose its potency in storage. If you need more than 1 teaspoon, double or triple this recipe and measure out what you need.

½ teaspoon cream of tartar
¼ teaspoon baking soda
¼ teaspoon cornstarch or arrowroot

---

wooden spoon or with an electric mixer. Dry ingredients can be mixed beforehand and set aside for a few hours or overnight. However, after the liquid is added to the batter, it should be baked immediately. The liquid activates the chemical reaction that will make the bread rise in the oven. If the batter is left too long, the rising power will dissipate.

If the batter is mixed by hand with a spoon, the dry ingredients should be blended together first, then the liquid ones added. With an electric mixer, the liquid ingredients are mixed first and the dry ingredients then added. Nuts, seeds, and dried fruits should be gently folded into the batter last.

The consistency of the batter will vary, depending on the type of quick bread, but it will always be thinner and moister than a yeast dough. If it is too stiff, add ¼ cup of a liquid to the batter. If too thin, add a little more flour and adjust the sweetener accordingly.

Baking Quick Breads

The baking times and temperatures for quick breads may vary with each recipe as they do with yeast breads. It is wise to test doneness about 15 minutes before the end of the specified baking time. A toothpick or a very thin knife inserted gently into the center of the bread should come out clean when it's done. Most quick breads can be briefly cooled, then served while they are still warm. When thoroughly cooled, they should be stored with the same care as yeast breads—securely wrapped in plastic wrap or foil.

Muffins, Biscuits & Popovers

Muffins, biscuits, and popovers are all basically quick breads, just in miniature form. Muffins and biscuits rely on baking powder or baking soda for leavening and require minimal mixing. In fact, too much mixing will cut down on the volume and make for a tough product. Popovers, though still technically quick breads because they cook quickly, owe their dramatic increase in volume not to baking powder or soda, but to the high proportion of liquid in the batter, the temperature at which they are baked, and the eggs in the batter. The high temperatures boil the liquid in the batter, creating steam. The steam pushes the batter up, and the egg protein in the batter hardens the walls of the popover to give it structure. Properly baked, a popover has crisp sides and top and a moist, eggy interior.

BRAN BREAD

After the loaves are baked and cooled, you can wrap one in foil and freeze for another time.

1 tablespoon active dry yeast

4 tablespoons honey

2¼ cups warm water (105° to 115°F)

About 5½ cups white whole wheat flour*

⅓ cup butter, melted, plus more for brushing

2 cups wheat or oat bran

1 teaspoon salt

**milled from white wheat grains*

In a large bowl, dissolve the yeast and 2 tablespoons of the honey in the warm water. Add 3 cups of the flour and stir well to combine. Set aside in a warm spot to proof (some bubbles appear on the surface), about 20 minutes.

Stir the butter and the remaining 2 tablespoons honey into the flour mixture. Stir in 2 more cups of the flour, ¾ cup of the bran, and the salt. The dough will be very soft and sticky. Scatter all but ¼ cup of the remaining bran onto a floured work surface.

Transfer the dough to the work surface, and knead in the bran and enough of the remaining ½ cup of flour so the dough is no longer sticky (don't be tempted to add more flour). Knead until the dough is smooth and elastic, about 10 minutes. Oil a large bowl, add the dough, and turn to coat. Cover and let rise in a warm place until doubled in bulk, 40 to 50 minutes.

Butter two 8½ × 4½-inch loaf pans.

Punch down the dough, turn out onto a floured surface, and lightly knead. Divide the dough in half, and shape each half into an 8-inch-long loaf. Place the loaves seam-side down in the pans.

Sprinkle the tops with the remaining ¼ cup bran. Cover and let rise again until doubled in bulk, 20 to 30 minutes. Do not let the bread rise too high.

Preheat the oven to 350°F.

Bake for 30 minutes. Brush the tops of the loaves with melted butter and return to the oven for 5 to 10 minutes, or until the loaves sound hollow when tapped. Remove from the pans and cool on racks.

MAKES 16 SERVINGS

WALNUT-ONION BRAN BREAD

If you like, cook the onion a day or two ahead and refrigerate it until you are ready to use it.

1 tablespoon active dry yeast

1¼ cups warm water (105° to 115°F)

1 cup warm milk

3 cups whole wheat flour

4 tablespoons molasses

½ cup (1 stick) butter

1 large onion, minced

2 teaspoons caraway seeds

2 cups wheat bran

1½ to 2 cups unbleached all-purpose flour

1½ teaspoons salt

1 cup rye flour

¾ cup chopped walnuts

Melted butter, for brushing

In a small bowl, sprinkle the yeast over ¼ cup of the warm water. In a large bowl, mix together the remaining 1 cup water, the milk, whole wheat flour, and 2 tablespoons of the molasses. After the yeast mixture foams, add it to flour mixture. Beat until the batter is completely smooth. Cover the bowl and let stand in a warm place for about 20 minutes, until bubbly and light.

In a small skillet, melt the butter over medium heat. Add the onion and cook, stirring occasionally until tender, about 7 minutes. Cool slightly.

Add to the yeast mixture, along with the caraway seeds, and the remaining 2 tablespoons molasses. Beat in ³⁄₄ cup of the bran, 1 cup of the all-purpose flour, and the salt.

Spread 1 cup of the remaining bran on a floured surface. With a rubber spatula, scrape one-third of the batter onto the bran. Knead the bran into the batter to form a rather stiff dough. Place in a small oiled bowl, and turn once to oil the top.

Knead the rye flour into the remaining dough on the floured surface. Knead in just enough of the remaining all-purpose flour to make the dough manageable. The dough will still be slightly sticky. Continue kneading until the dough is smooth. Work in the walnuts. Form the dough into a ball, place in a large oiled bowl, and turn once to oil the top.

Cover both bowls and let the two balls of dough rise in a warm place until doubled in bulk, 40 to 50 minutes.

Butter two 8½ × 4½-inch loaf pans.

Punch down both balls of dough, turn out onto a floured surface, and knead each again briefly. Divide the larger dough ball in half, shape each half into an 8-inch-long loaf, and set aside.

Sprinkle the floured surface with the remaining ¼ cup bran. Divide the smaller dough ball in half. Roll out the halves on the bran to form two 10-inch squares. Wrap the squares around the 8-inch loaves. Pinch the seams together. Place the loaves seam-side down in the pans. Cover and let rise again until doubled in bulk, about 30 minutes.

Preheat the oven to 350°F.

Bake for 30 minutes. Brush the tops of the loaves with melted butter and return to the oven for 5 to 10 minutes more, or until the loaves sound hollow when tapped. Remove from the pans and cool on racks.

MAKES 16 SERVINGS

HONEY-WHEAT LOAF

A nice bread to serve for breakfast or brunch.

1 tablespoon active dry yeast

2½ cups warm water (105° to 115°F)

¼ cup plus 2 tablespoons honey

3 tablespoons vegetable oil

3 cups whole wheat flour

3 cups unbleached all-purpose flour

¾ teaspoon salt

¾ cup raisins

¼ cup sunflower seeds, toasted

In a large bowl, sprinkle the yeast over the warm water. Add ¼ cup of the honey and let stand until the yeast is foamy, about 5 minutes. Stir in the oil.

Gradually add the flours and salt, until a stiff dough forms. Transfer to a floured work surface and knead in the raisins and sunflower seeds. Knead until smooth and elastic, 8 to 10 minutes.

Oil a large bowl, add the dough, and turn to coat. Cover and let rise in a warm place until doubled in bulk, about 1 hour.

Butter two 9 × 5-inch loaf pans.

Punch the dough down and form into 2 loaves. Place in the loaf pans, cover, and let rise again until doubled in bulk, 30 to 45 minutes.

Preheat the oven to 350°F.

Bake for 30 minutes, or until browned and the loaf sounds hollow when tapped. Brush with the remaining 2 tablespoons honey and return to the oven for 5 to 10 minutes to set the glaze. Cool on racks.

MAKES 16 SERVINGS

EIGHT-GRAIN SPROUTED WHEAT BREAD

Check out "Growing Your Own Sprouts" (page 74) for how to make sprouted wheat.

- 2 tablespoons active dry yeast
- 2½ cups warm water (105° to 115°F)
- 4 tablespoons molasses
- 1 large egg
- ¼ cup vegetable oil
- 2 tablespoons cider vinegar
- ¾ cup rye flour
- ½ cup amaranth flour
- ½ cup brown rice flour
- ½ cup soy flour
- ½ cup barley flour
- ¼ cup ground millet
- ½ cup old-fashioned rolled oats
- 1½ teaspoons salt
- 4 to 5 cups whole wheat flour
- 2 cups wheat sprouts, finely chopped

In a large bowl, sprinkle the yeast over the warm water. Stir in 1 tablespoon of the molasses and let stand until the yeast is foamy, about 5 minutes.

Stir in the remaining 3 tablespoons molasses, the egg, oil, vinegar, rye flour, amaranth flour, rice flour, soy flour, barley flour, millet, oats, salt, and 1 cup of the whole wheat flour. With an electric mixer, beat until smooth. Gradually beat in enough of the remaining whole wheat flour to make a stiff dough that can be kneaded.

Turn out onto a floured surface and knead until smooth and elastic, about 10 minutes, adding enough flour to keep the dough from sticking. Oil a large bowl, add the dough, and turn to coat. Cover and let rise in a warm place until doubled in bulk, 1 hour to 1 hour 30 minutes.

Butter two 9 × 5-inch loaf pans.

Turn out the dough onto a floured surface and knead in the wheat sprouts. Divide the dough in half and shape into 2 loaves. Place in the loaf pans. Cover and let rise again for 45 to 60 minutes. (They do not quite double.)

Preheat the oven to 350°F. Bake for 50 minutes, or until the loaves sound hollow when tapped. Remove from the pans and cool on a rack.

MAKES 16 SERVINGS

WHOLE WHEAT ANADAMA BREAD

This is the bread an anonymous "Anna" is said to have baked with such monotonous regularity that her husband was driven to violence. One night when it was served, he picked up a sack of cornmeal and hurled it at her, shouting, "Anna damn ya!" But she kept baking it, and her husband's unintentional christening has persisted through the centuries.

- 2½ cups water
- ½ cup molasses
- ¼ cup (½ stick) butter
- ½ cup cornmeal
- ⅓ cup nonfat dry milk
- 1 teaspoon salt
- 1 tablespoon active dry yeast
- 3 cups whole wheat flour
- About 1½ cups unbleached all-purpose flour

In a medium saucepan, bring the water, molasses, and butter to a boil over medium heat. Slowly stir in the cornmeal. Cook 2 minutes, stirring constantly. Add the dry milk and salt. Cool for 30 minutes.

In a large bowl, combine the yeast and 2 cups of the whole wheat flour.

With an electric mixer, gradually beat the cornmeal mixture into the flour mixture at low speed until just blended. Increase the speed to medium and beat 2 minutes. Beat in the remaining 1 cup whole wheat flour and enough of the all-purpose flour to make a thick batter. Continue beating 2 minutes, occasionally scraping the bowl. With a spoon, stir in enough additional flour to make a soft dough.

Turn out the dough onto a floured surface and knead until smooth and elastic. Shape the dough into a ball. Oil a large bowl, add the dough, and turn to coat. Cover and let rise in a warm place until doubled in bulk, about 1 hour.

Punch out the dough down and turn out onto a floured surface. Cover with a towel and let rest for 15 minutes.

Butter two 8½ × 4½-inch loaf pans.

Roll each piece of dough into a 12 × 8-inch rectangle. Starting at one short end, tightly roll the dough, jelly-roll fashion. Place seam-side down in the loaf pans. Cover and let rise again, for 40 minutes.

Preheat the oven to 375°F.

Bake the loaves for 40 minutes, or until browned and the loaves sound hollow when tapped. Remove from the pans and cool on racks.

MAKES 16 SERVINGS

WHOLE WHEAT WALNUT BREAD

Cocoa powder contributes to the color of this loaf, and buttermilk gives it a slight tang.

1 tablespoon active dry yeast

¼ cup warm water (105° to 115°F)

1 teaspoon plus 2 tablespoons honey

1 cup buttermilk, at room temperature

About 3 cups white whole wheat flour*

¼ cup wheat germ

2 tablespoons unsweetened cocoa powder

1 tablespoon vegetable oil

¼ teaspoon baking soda

1 teaspoon salt

1 cup coarsely chopped walnuts

**milled from white wheat grains*

In a large bowl, sprinkle the yeast over the warm water. Stir in 1 teaspoon of the honey and let stand until the yeast is foamy, about 5 minutes.

Add the remaining 2 tablespoons honey and the buttermilk. Stir in 1 cup of the flour, the wheat germ, cocoa powder, oil, baking soda, and salt, until smooth. Beat with a wooden spoon for 2 minutes. Stir in enough of the remaining flour to make a stiff dough.

BEAN PUREES

Bean purees can be used to boost the nutritional value of many baked goods. Puree cooked beans in a food processor, about 1 cup at a time, until a smooth consistency is reached. The puree can be used immediately or refrigerated for 3 to 6 days. It will thicken as it cools. Frozen, it keeps for up to 6 weeks.

To enrich baked goods, add 2 to 3 tablespoons of thick bean puree to yeast bread mixtures along with the liquid ingredients. For quick bread recipes, replace 1 tablespoon of each 1 cup of liquid with 1 tablespoon of bean puree. The resulting baked goods will be slightly denser and very moist.

Turn out onto a floured surface and knead until smooth and elastic, about 10 minutes, using only as much flour as needed to keep the dough from sticking. Oil a large bowl, add the dough, and turn to coat. Cover and let rise in a warm place until doubled in bulk, 1 hour to 1 hour 30 minutes.

Butter an 8½ × 4½-inch or 9 × 5-inch loaf pan.

Punch down the dough, turn out onto a floured surface, and knead a few times. Roll into a 15 x 9-inch rectangle. Sprinkle the nuts evenly over the dough. Roll up, jelly-roll fashion, from one short end. Pinch the ends together to seal and place seam-side down in the loaf pan. Cover and let rise again until doubled in bulk, about 1 hour.

Preheat the oven to 350°F.

Bake for 40 minutes, or until the loaf is golden and sounds hollow when tapped. Remove from the pan and cool on a rack.

MAKES 8 TO 10 SERVINGS

PANCETTA, CORN & WHEAT BREAD

You can go up or down on the amount of pepper here; it's entirely up to your taste.

- 1 pound pancetta or bacon, coarsely chopped
- ¾ teaspoon pepper
- 2 tablespoons active dry yeast
- 2¼ cups warm water
- ¼ cup molasses
- ¼ cup vegetable oil
- 1 large egg
- 1½ cups yellow cornmeal
- ¾ cup toasted wheat germ
- ½ cup soy flour
- ½ cup nonfat dry milk
- 1 teaspoon salt
- 2½ cups whole wheat flour
- 2½ to 3 cups unbleached all-purpose flour

In a large skillet, cook the pancetta over low heat until it has rendered its fat and is crisp, 10 to 15 minutes. Drain, reserving the pancetta and the fat separately. Toss the pancetta with the pepper and set aside.

In a large bowl, sprinkle the yeast over the warm water. Add the molasses and let stand until the yeast is foamy, about 5 minutes. Stir in the rendered fat from the pancetta, the oil, egg, cornmeal, wheat germ, soy flour, dry milk, and salt, until smooth. Gradually beat in the whole wheat flour. Cover the bowl and let rise in a warm place until almost doubled in bulk, about 30 minutes.

Stir in enough of the all-purpose flour to make a stiff dough. Turn out onto a floured surface. Knead until smooth and elastic, 8 to 10 minutes. Oil a large bowl, add the dough, and turn to coat. Cover and let rise in a warm place until doubled in bulk, about 1 hour.

Oil two 9 × 5-inch loaf pans.

Punch down the dough and turn out onto a floured surface. Knead in the pancetta. Divide the dough in half and shape each half into a loaf. Place in loaf pans. Cover and let rise again until doubled in bulk, about 30 minutes.

Preheat the oven to 375°F.

Bake for 35 to 40 minutes, until the loaves are golden and sound hollow when tapped. Remove from the pans and cool on racks.

MAKES 16 SERVINGS

GRANOLA BREAD

You can use store-bought granola, or make your own. Try one of these: Granola with Toasted Almonds & Cherries (page 582), Nantucket Granola (page 582), or Pecan Crunch Granola (page 583).

2 tablespoons active dry yeast

2 cups warm water (105° to 115°F)

1 cup milk, warmed

½ cup vegetable oil

¼ cup honey

4 cups whole wheat flour

1½ cups granola

2 tablespoons grated orange zest

4 cups unbleached all-purpose flour

1½ teaspoons salt

1 large egg beaten with 1 tablespoon milk

In a large bowl, combine the yeast, warm water, milk, oil, honey, and whole wheat flour. Stir in the granola, orange zest, all-purpose flour, and salt. Knead until smooth, 8 to 10 minutes. Oil a large bowl, add the dough, and turn to coat. Cover and let rise in a warm place until doubled in bulk, about 1 hour.

Punch down the dough, shape into a ball, cover, and let rise until doubled in bulk, about 1 hour.

Butter three 8½ × 4½-inch loaf pans.

Turn out the dough onto a floured surface and knead for 2 or 3 minutes, until smooth. Divide into 3 equal loaves and place in the loaf pans. Cover and let rise again until doubled in bulk, 45 to 60 minutes.

Preheat the oven to 350°F.

With a sharp knife, make several slashes in the tops of the loaves. Brush the egg mixture over the loaves. Bake for 45 to 50 minutes, until the loaves sound hollow when tapped. Remove from the pans and cool on racks.

MAKES 24 SERVINGS

WHOLE WHEAT PITA BREAD

While they bake, pita breads puff up, forming a pocket. In order for them to do this, they have to bake for the first 5 minutes in the hottest part of the oven (if using a gas oven, place the baking sheet directly on the oven floor).

1 tablespoon active dry yeast

1¼ cups warm water (105° to 115°F)

1 tablespoon vegetable oil

3 to 3½ cups whole wheat flour

1 teaspoon salt

In a large bowl, sprinkle the yeast over the warm water. Add the oil and 2 cups of the flour. Beat until the dough is smooth. Add 1 cup flour and the salt as you knead the dough in the bowl. Transfer the dough to a floured surface, and knead in some additional flour until the dough is firm. Oil a large bowl, add the dough, and turn to coat. Cover and let rise in a warm place until doubled in bulk, about 1 hour.

Punch down the dough and divide into 12 equal pieces. Form into balls. Cover with waxed paper or a towel to prevent them from drying out, and let rest for 20 minutes (this relaxes the dough, making it easier to roll out without springing back).

Preheat the oven to 500°F. Lightly oil 2 baking sheets.

Roll out the balls until they are ¼ inch thick and 4 inches in diameter. (If rolled to a larger diameter, the rounds may not puff all the way to the edges.) Place the rounds on the baking sheets.

Place one baking sheet on the lowest rack or the floor of the oven and bake for 5 minutes. Do not open the oven during this first baking. After 5 minutes, open the oven, place the baking sheet on a higher rack, and bake the rounds for 3 to 5 minutes longer, until the pockets have puffed up and are beginning to brown.

Repeat with the remaining baking sheet to bake the second batch.

MAKES 12 SERVINGS

MULTI-GRAIN PIZZA DOUGH

This is enough dough for 2 large or 4 small pizzas. Simply make the dough and follow your favorite recipe. The dough can be made and frozen up to 3 months.

1½ cups warm water (105° to 115°F)

1 tablespoon honey

2 tablespoons active dry yeast

¼ cup olive oil

2½ to 3 cups unbleached all-purpose flour

2 cups whole wheat flour

½ cup flax meal

1 teaspoon salt

In a large bowl, combine the warm water, honey, and yeast and let stand until the yeast is foamy, about 5 minutes.

Add the oil, 2 ½ cups of the all-purpose flour, the whole wheat flour, flax meal, and salt, and stir to make a firm dough.

Turn out the dough onto a floured surface and knead until smooth and elastic, adding more all-purpose flour as needed. Oil a large bowl, add the dough, and turn to coat. Cover and let rise in a warm place until doubled in bulk, about 1 hour.

Punch down the dough and knead briefly. Cover and let rise until doubled in bulk, 30 to 45 minutes.

MAKES ENOUGH DOUGH FOR 2 LARGE OR 4 SMALL PIZZAS

LEMON-ROSEMARY FOCACCIA

The first rising of a little bit of flour with the yeast and water gives the focaccia lots of flavor. Hints of lemon (from the zest) and rosemary give it some zip. Eat it on its own, or try it as sandwich bread.

1 envelope (¼ ounce) active dry yeast

1⅔ cups warm water (105° to 115°F)

2 cups whole wheat flour

1½ cups unbleached all-purpose flour

¾ cup olive oil

2 teaspoons salt

2 teaspoons grated lemon zest

1 teaspoon crumbled rosemary

Coarse salt

In a small bowl, sprinkle the yeast over the warm water and let stand until the yeast is foamy. Stir in 1 cup of the whole wheat flour, cover, and let stand until bubbly and doubled in bulk, about 1 hour.

Stir in the remaining 1 cup whole wheat flour, the all-purpose flour, ¼ cup of the oil, the salt, lemon zest, and rosemary until well combined. Turn out the dough onto a lightly floured surface and knead for 3 minutes, just until the dough comes together. Lightly flour a large bowl and place the dough in it. Cover and let stand at room temperature until doubled in bulk, about 1 hour.

Return the dough to the floured work surface and flatten it with your hands. Fold one side over onto another, both from the sides and the top and bottom. Return to the bowl, seam side down and cover. Let rise until doubled in bulk, about 45 minutes.

Preheat the oven to 450°F. Pour ¼ cup of the remaining olive oil into a 10½ × 15½-inch jelly-roll pan. Place the dough in the pan and turn it over so that both sides are coated in oil. Cover with plastic wrap and let the dough rest for 15 minutes. Leaving the plastic wrap in place, push the dough out to fit the pan. Uncover.

With your fingers make impressions all over without poking through the dough. Sprinkle with the remaining ¼ cup oil and coarse salt to taste.

Bake for 25 minutes, rotating the pan halfway through, until crisp and brown. Serve warm or at room temperature.

MAKES 8 SERVINGS

SAGE FOCACCIA

This makes exceptionally good sandwich bread.

- 2 cups whole wheat flour
- 2 tablespoons sage
- 1 tablespoon active dry yeast
- 1¼ cups hot water
- 4 tablespoons olive oil
- About 1½ cups unbleached all-purpose flour
- 2 teaspoons salt
- Coarse salt and pepper

Place 1 cup of the whole wheat flour, the sage, and the yeast in a large bowl. Gradually add the hot water and beat well with a wooden spoon for 2 minutes. Beat in 1 tablespoon of the oil, the remaining 1 cup whole wheat flour, and enough of the all-purpose flour to make a soft dough. Beat in the salt.

Turn out onto a floured surface and knead until smooth and elastic, about 10 minutes, using only as much remaining flour as needed to keep the dough from sticking. Oil a large bowl, add the dough, and turn to coat. Cover and let rise in a warm place until doubled in bulk, about 1 hour.

Lightly oil a baking sheet.

Punch the dough down and turn out onto a floured surface. Knead a few times and roll out to a ½-inch thickness. Place on the baking sheet. Using your fingertips, make a series of indentations in the dough. Drizzle with the remaining 3 tablespoons of oil and sprinkle with coarse salt and pepper to taste. Let rise again until doubled in bulk, about 20 minutes.

Preheat the oven to 400°F.

Bake for 25 to 30 minutes, until golden. Cool on a rack.

MAKES 8 SERVINGS

MAPLE-OATMEAL BATTER BREAD

Batter breads don't usually rise more than once, but here a second rise gives the bread a nice, light texture.

- 1¼ cups milk
- 1¼ cups old-fashioned rolled oats
- ¼ cup (½ stick) butter
- 1 tablespoon active dry yeast
- ¼ cup warm water (105° to 115°F)
- 4 tablespoons maple syrup
- 1 large egg
- ¼ cup toasted wheat germ
- 1 teaspoon salt
- ½ teaspoon cinnamon
- 1½ cups whole wheat flour
- ½ cup dried currants or raisins
- ½ cup dried apple, chopped
- 1 cup unbleached all-purpose flour
- ¼ cup sunflower seeds

In a medium saucepan, bring the milk to a boil over medium heat. Stir in 1 cup of the oats and the butter, and let cool to lukewarm.

In a large bowl, sprinkle the yeast over the warm water. Stir in 1 tablespoon of the maple syrup. Let stand until the yeast is foamy, about 5 minutes.

Stir in the oat mixture, the remaining 3 tablespoons maple syrup, the egg, wheat germ, salt, cinnamon, and 1 cup of the whole wheat flour. Beat with an electric mixer at medium speed for 3 minutes. Stir in the currants or raisins and apple. With a wooden spoon, gradually beat in the remaining whole wheat flour and the all-purpose flour until the batter is smooth. Scrape down the sides of the bowl, cover, and let rise in a warm place until doubled in bulk, about 45 minutes.

Butter a 1½-quart soufflé or baking dish, and sprinkle with the remaining ¼ cup oats.

Stir down the batter. Scrape into the soufflé dish, smooth the top, and sprinkle with the sunflower seeds. Cover and let rise again until doubled in bulk, 30 to 45 minutes.

Preheat the oven to 350°F.

Bake until the bread is golden brown and sounds hollow when tapped, about 40 minutes. Cool for a few minutes on a rack. Remove from the baking dish and serve warm.

MAKES 8 TO 10 SERVINGS

SOURDOUGH ENGLISH MUFFINS

When you make these muffins, in addition to making the sourdough starter two days before, be sure to plan on the milk-flour-starter mixture sitting overnight.

3 cups warm milk (105° to 115°F)

1 cup Handy Sourdough Starter (below)

8 cups whole wheat flour

1 tablespoon active dry yeast

½ cup warm water (105° to 115°F)

1 tablespoon honey

¼ cup plus 2 tablespoons vegetable oil

1½ teaspoons salt

¼ cup white cornmeal

In a large bowl, combine the milk and the sourdough starter. Gradually stir in 4 cups of the flour until thoroughly mixed. Cover loosely and leave in a warm place overnight (a turned off oven is a good spot).

Next morning, in a large bowl, sprinkle the yeast over the warm water. Add the honey, ¼ cup of the oil, and the remaining 4 cups flour. Set aside to proof until bubbly.

Stir down the starter mixture and add to the yeast mixture. Stir in the salt.

Turn out the dough onto a floured surface and knead until smooth and elastic, 10 to 12 minutes. Sprinkle a floured surface with the cornmeal and

---

HANDY SOURDOUGH STARTER

All sourdough starters should be replenished with equal amounts of flour and water after each use. Starter should be stored in the refrigerator, then taken out and brought to room temperature before being used.

1 tablespoon active dry yeast

2 cups warm water (105° to 115°F)

2 cups whole wheat flour

Combine all the ingredients in a glass or pottery (not metal) container. Cover with cheesecloth and let stand at room temperature for 48 hours, stirring down several times. A layer of bubbles and a fermented smell indicate the starter is ready for use. Stir down before using.

roll out the dough to a 3/8- to 1/2-inch thickness. Cut out rounds with a large round cookie or biscuit cutter and place on a baking sheet. Loosely cover and let rise in a warm place until doubled in bulk.

Heat a large iron skillet over medium-low heat. Add the remaining 2 tablespoons oil and cook the muffins until browned and puffed, about 5 minutes per side. Be careful, because they burn easily.

MAKES 2 DOZEN MUFFINS

SOURDOUGH PUMPERNICKEL BREAD

The sourdough starter for this bread will have to sit overnight with the liquid and flour before you continue with the recipe. If you can't find cracked rye, make your own by coarsely grinding rye berries in a blender. Leftover sponge can be stored in the refrigerator and "fed" flour periodically to keep it going.

- 1/2 cup yellow cornmeal
- 1 cup cracked wheat
- 2 cups cracked rye
- 3 1/2 cups boiling water
- 1 cup Handy Sourdough Starter (page 563)
- 1 1/2 cups warm water (105° to 115°F)
- 1/2 cup molasses
- 2 teaspoons active dry yeast
- 3 cups whole wheat flour
- 2 3/4 cups rye flour
- 1 1/2 teaspoons salt

In a large bowl, combine the cornmeal, cracked wheat, and cracked rye. Pour the boiling water over all, stirring briskly to avoid lumping. Cool to lukewarm and then add the sourdough starter, stirring until the dough is smooth. This is the sponge. Cover and leave overnight in a warm place (a turned off oven is a good spot).

Next morning, remove 1 cup of the sponge and combine it with 1 cup of the warm water. Cover and refrigerate for future use.

In a small bowl, combine the remaining 1/2 cup warm water and 1 tablespoon of the molasses. Dissolve the yeast in this mixture. Let stand until the yeast is foamy, about 5 minutes.

Add the yeast mixture and the remaining 7 tablespoons molasses to the remaining sponge. Then add the flours and the salt.

On a floured surface, knead the dough until no longer sticky. Oil a large bowl, add the dough, and turn to coat. Cover and let rise in a warm place for 2 hours 30 minutes.

Butter 1 large casserole or 2 small ones.

Punch down the dough and form into 1 large loaf or 2 smaller loaves. Place in a casserole. Cover and let rise again for 1 hour.

Preheat the oven to 200°F.

Cover the casseroles tightly with foil and/or a lid. Place on the lowest shelf of the oven along with an open pan of water (to humidify the oven). Bake the bread for 3 to 4 hours, until a toothpick inserted in the center comes out clean. Remove from the casseroles and cool before slicing.

MAKES 16 SERVINGS

SOURDOUGH RYE BREAD

Plan to let the starter-liquid-flour mixture sit overnight before going on with the rest of this recipe.

- 1 cup Handy Sourdough Starter (page 563)
- 1 1/2 cups water
- 4 cups rye flour
- 1/2 cup warm water (105° to 115°F)
- 1 tablespoon molasses
- 1 tablespoon active dry yeast

2 tablespoons vegetable oil

4 cups brown rice flour

1½ teaspoons salt

⅓ cup oat flour

In a large bowl, combine the sourdough starter, water, and 2 cups of the rye flour. Cover and set in a warm place overnight (a turned off oven is a good place).

Next morning, in a small bowl, combine the warm water, molasses, and yeast. Let stand until the yeast is foamy, about 5 minutes.

Stir down the sourdough mixture, add the yeast mixture, oil, and rice flour. With a wooden spoon, mix in the salt and as much of the remaining rye flour as possible.

Turn out the dough onto a well floured surface. Add the oat flour and knead the dough briefly to incorporate all the flour. Oil a large bowl, add the dough, and turn to coat. Cover and let rise again in a warm place until doubled in bulk, about 1 hour.

Oil a large baking sheet.

Shape the dough into 2 round loaves and place on the baking sheet. Cover loosely and let rise until almost doubled in bulk, 45 to 60 minutes.

Preheat the oven to 375°F. Bake for 35 minutes, until the loaves sound hollow when tapped. Cool on racks.

MAKES 16 TO 20 SERVINGS

RAISIN RYE ROLLS

The potato starter needs a minimum of 24 hours (2 to 3 days is even better) to develop flavor before it can be mixed with the other ingredients to make the dough.

1 tablespoon active dry yeast

1¼ cups warm water (105° to 115°F)

⅓ cup molasses

1 cup Potato Starter (below)

½ cup wheat bran

¼ cup unsweetened cocoa powder

3 tablespoons vegetable oil

1 tablespoon caraway seeds

POTATO STARTER

Use this starter for Raisin Rye Rolls (above). The starter should be stored in the refrigerator, then taken out and brought to room temperature before being used. After each use, replenish the starter by adding equal amounts of flour and warm water.

1 large potato (about 10 ounces), peeled and cut into chunks

1 tablespoon active dry yeast

2 cups whole wheat flour or rye flour, or 1 cup of each

In a small saucepan, combine the potato with enough cold water to cover. Bring to a boil and cook until tender. Reserving the cooking water, drain the potato and mash with a potato masher or fork. Measure the cooking water and if necessary add more water to equal 2 cups.

In a large bowl, dissolve the yeast in the reserved lukewarm potato water. Stir in the mashed potato and flour to make a smooth dough. Cover tightly and let stand at room temperature for at least 24 hours, preferably for 2 to 3 days for a fully developed flavor. Stir down once a day.

- 1 tablespoon grated orange zest
- 1 teaspoon salt
- 2½ cups rye flour
- 2 to 2½ cups whole wheat flour
- 1 cup raisins
- Cornmeal, for the pans
- 1 large egg white, lightly beaten
- Sesame seeds (optional)

In a large bowl, sprinkle the yeast over the warm water. Stir in 1 tablespoon of the molasses and let stand until the yeast is foamy, about 5 minutes.

Stir in the remaining molasses, the potato starter, bran, cocoa powder, oil, caraway seeds, and orange zest. Gradually stir in the salt, rye flour and enough whole wheat flour to make a soft dough.

Turn out the dough onto a floured surface and knead until smooth and elastic, 8 to 10 minutes, using only enough remaining flour to keep the dough from sticking. The dough will be slightly tacky. Oil a large bowl, add the dough, and turn to coat. Cover with a towel and let rise in a warm place until doubled in bulk, about 45 minutes.

Turn out the dough onto a floured surface, punch down, and knead a few times. Knead in the raisins. Invert a bowl over the dough and let rest for 10 minutes.

Lightly oil a baking sheet and sprinkle with the cornmeal.

Divide the dough into 18 equal pieces and shape into smooth balls. Place 2 to 3 inches apart on the baking sheet. Lightly cover and let rise again until doubled in bulk, 30 to 45 minutes.

Preheat the oven to 375°F. Brush the rolls with the egg white and sprinkle with sesame seeds (if using). Bake for 20 minutes, or until the rolls sound hollow when tapped. Cool on a rack.

MAKES 18 ROLLS

MULTI-GRAIN BAGELS

These are water bagels, meaning they get a brief boiling in water before baking.

- 1 medium potato, peeled and thickly sliced
- 1 tablespoon active dry yeast
- 3 teaspoons honey
- 3 cups whole wheat flour
- ½ cup flax meal
- ¾ cup oat bran
- 1½ teaspoons salt
- 2 large eggs, 1 whole, 1 separated
- 3 tablespoons vegetable oil
- 2 tablespoons molasses or malt syrup

In a medium saucepan, combine the potato and 3 cups cold water. Bring to a boil and cook until tender, about 15 minutes. Reserving the cooking water, drain the potato. Save the potato for another use.

Let the potato water cool to lukewarm. Place ½ cup of the potato water in a small bowl. Stir in the yeast and 1 teaspoon of the honey, and let stand until the yeast is foamy, about 5 minutes.

In a large bowl, whisk together the flour, the flax meal, ½ cup of the bran, and the salt. Stir in the yeast mixture, and add ½ cup of the potato water, the remaining 2 teaspoons honey, the whole egg, egg white, and oil. Blend to make a firm dough, adding more flour if necessary.

Turn out onto a floured surface and knead until the dough is smooth and elastic, 8 to 10 minutes. Oil a large bowl, add the dough, and turn to coat. Cover and let rise in a warm place until doubled in bulk, about 1 hour 30 minutes. The dough is ready when you push down with 2 fingers and indentations remain. If the dough springs back, let it rise a bit longer.

Punch down the dough and knead for 2 to 3 minutes. Cut the dough into 14 pieces. Roll each piece between floured hands to a rope 7 inches long and 3/4 inch thick. Coil each rope into a ring, moistening the ends so that they stick when turned onto each other. Let stand 10 minutes.

Preheat the oven to 425°F. Lightly oil a baking sheet.

In a large pot, bring 3 quarts of water and the molasses to a boil. Using a slotted spoon, slide each bagel into the boiling water, being careful not to crowd them. When bagels begin to float, boil for 2 minutes on each side. With a slotted spoon transfer the bagels to the baking sheet. (They will be very slippery.)

Mix the egg yolk with 1 teaspoon water. Brush each bagel with the egg yolk mixture and sprinkle with the remaining 1/4 cup oat bran.

Bake for 20 to 25 minutes, until golden brown. Cool on racks.

MAKES 14 BAGELS

SOFT PRETZEL STICKS

Make a variety of pretzel sticks by using a number of different seeds.

- **1 tablespoon active dry yeast**
- **1 1/4 cups warm water (105° to 115°F)**
- **1 tablespoon honey**
- **4 1/2 cups rye flour**
- **1 teaspoon salt**
- **1 large egg beaten with 1/2 teaspoon water**
- **Coarse salt**
- **Caraway, sesame, and/or poppy seeds**

Lightly oil a large baking sheet.

In a large bowl, sprinkle the yeast over the warm water. Add the honey and let stand until the yeast is foamy, about 5 minutes. Stir in 4 cups of the flour and the salt.

Turn out the dough onto a floured surface and knead in the remaining 1/2 cup flour until smooth. Divide the dough into 48 pieces and roll each into a rope about 1/2 inch in diameter and 5 inches long. Place on the baking sheet. Brush with the egg wash and sprinkle with coarse salt and seeds. Let rise in a warm place for 20 to 30 minutes, until light.

Preheat the oven to 425°F. Bake for 15 to 20 minutes, until crisp. Cool on racks.

MAKES 4 DOZEN STICKS

BAKED DOUGHNUTS

This type of doughnut, made with potatoes, is sometimes called a spudnut.

- **1 large potato (about 10 ounces), peeled and thinly sliced**
- **2 teaspoons active dry yeast**
- **1/2 cup milk, scalded**
- **1/2 cup honey**
- **1/3 cup butter**
- **1 large egg**
- **1 1/2 cups whole wheat flour**
- **1 cup unbleached all-purpose flour**
- **1/2 teaspoon salt**
- **Melted butter, for brushing**
- **Confectioners' sugar**

In a small saucepan, cook the potato in enough water to cover until tender. Reserving the cooking water, drain the potato and mash.

Place 2 tablespoons of the potato cooking water in a small bowl. When it has cooled to body temperature, sprinkle the yeast over it. Let stand until the yeast is foamy, about 5 minutes.

In a large bowl, combine the milk, honey, and butter. Stir well and cool to lukewarm.

Stir the yeast mixture into the milk mixture. Add ½ cup of the mashed potato and the egg. Stir in the flours and salt until a dough forms. Oil a large bowl, add the dough, and turn to coat. Cover and let rise in a warm place until light and doubled in bulk, about 1 hour.

Lightly oil a large baking sheet. Turn out the dough onto a floured work surface and knead until smooth, 5 to 8 minutes. With a lightly floured rolling pin, roll the dough out to a ½-inch thickness. Using a 3-inch doughnut cutter, cut out 18 doughnuts. Place the doughnuts on the baking sheet, cover with a dampened towel, and let rise until light, about 45 minutes.

Preheat the oven to 425°F. Bake until lightly browned, about 12 minutes. Remove from oven, brush immediately with butter, and dust with confectioners' sugar.

MAKES 1½ DOZEN DOUGHNUTS

AMARANTH SWEET ROLLS

Look for amaranth flour in your natural foods store.

DOUGH

- **¾ cup milk, scalded**
- **½ cup (1 stick) butter, cut up**
- **⅓ cup honey**
- **1 tablespoon active dry yeast**
- **½ cup warm water (105° to 115°F)**
- **2 large eggs, beaten**
- **Grated zest and juice of 1 lemon**
- **2 cups amaranth flour**
- **2 cups unbleached all-purpose flour**
- **1 cup whole wheat flour**
- **1 teaspoon salt**

FILLING

- **1 cup walnuts, chopped**
- **¼ cup (½ stick) butter, melted**
- **3 tablespoons honey**
- **2 tablespoons molasses**
- **1½ teaspoons cinnamon**

To make the dough: In a large bowl, combine the hot milk, butter, and honey. Let the mixture cool to lukewarm.

In a small bowl, sprinkle the yeast over the warm water. Let stand until the yeast is foamy, about 5 minutes. Add to the milk mixture. Stir in the eggs and lemon zest and juice.

In a bowl, stir together the flours and salt. Add to the milk mixture, 1 cup at a time, until it forms a shaggy dough.

Turn out the dough onto a floured work surface and knead until smooth and elastic, 8 to 10 minutes. Place in an oiled bowl, turning the dough to coat. Cover and let rise in a warm place until doubled in bulk, about 1 hour.

To make the filling: In a small bowl, stir together the nuts, butter, honey, molasses, and cinnamon.

Punch down the dough and turn it out onto a floured work surface. Roll out to an 18 × 12-inch rectangle. Spread half of the filling evenly over the dough. Starting at one long end, roll the dough up. Cut into 24 slices (about ¾ inch thick).

Butter two 12-cup muffin tins and divide the remaining filling among them. Place the rolls cut-side down in the muffin tins. Cover and let rise again until light and doubled in bulk, about 1 hour.

Preheat the oven to 375°F.

Bake until golden brown, about 25 minutes.

MAKES 2 DOZEN ROLLS

HONEY & NUT BUNS

If you don't have mace, just use nutmeg.

DOUGH

- 2 cups whole wheat flour
- 1 tablespoon active dry yeast
- ¼ teaspoon mace
- ½ cup water
- ½ cup milk
- 6 tablespoons butter
- ¼ cup honey
- 2 large eggs
- 1 teaspoon salt
- About 1¼ cups unbleached all-purpose flour

FILLING

- 3 tablespoons honey
- 2½ tablespoons butter, at room temperature
- 2 teaspoons grated orange zest
- ½ teaspoon cinnamon
- ½ cup pecans or walnuts, chopped
- ¼ cup raisins

To make the dough: In a large bowl, combine 1 cup of the whole wheat flour, the yeast, and the mace.

In a small saucepan, heat the water, milk, butter, and honey over low heat until very warm. Gradually add to the flour mixture and, with an electric mixer, beat for 2 minutes on medium speed.

In a small bowl, beat the eggs. Reserve about 2 tablespoons for brushing buns; add the remainder to the dough mixture. Add the remaining 1 cup whole wheat flour to the dough and continue beating for 3 minutes, scraping the bowl often. Stir in the salt and enough of the all-purpose flour to make a fairly stiff dough.

Turn out onto a floured surface and knead until smooth and elastic, 8 to 10 minutes, using only enough flour to keep the dough from sticking. Oil a large bowl, add the dough, and turn to coat. Cover and let rise in a warm place until doubled in bulk, 1 hour to 1 hour 30 minutes.

To make the filling: In a small bowl, gradually beat the honey into the butter. Blend in the orange zest and cinnamon. Fold in the nuts and raisins.

Preheat the oven to 375°F. Lightly oil a large baking sheet.

Punch down the dough. Divide into 16 equal pieces. Flatten each into a 4- to 5-inch round. Place about 1 rounded teaspoon of the filling on the center of each and fold the dough up and around the filling. Pinch together tightly to enclose the filling. Place the buns, pinched-side down, on the baking sheet. Cover with a clean towel and let rise again until doubled in bulk, about 45 minutes.

Brush with the reserved egg. Bake for 20 to 25 minutes, until golden. Cool on a rack.

MAKES 16 BUNS

CORN BREAD

People have differing opinions about whether corn bread should be sweet or not. Ours has just a touch of sugar to bring out the flavor of the cornmeal.

- 1 cup yellow cornmeal, preferably stone-ground
- 1 cup white whole wheat flour*
- ½ cup nonfat dry milk
- 2 tablespoons sugar
- 2 teaspoons baking powder
- ½ teaspoon baking soda
- ½ teaspoon salt
- 1 cup buttermilk
- 2 large eggs
- ¼ cup olive oil

**milled from white wheat grains*

Preheat the oven to 350°F. Oil an 8 × 8-inch baking pan and place in the oven while you prepare the batter.

In a large bowl, stir together the cornmeal, flour, dry milk, sugar, baking powder, baking soda, and salt.

In another bowl, whisk together the buttermilk, eggs, and oil. Make a well in the center of the flour mixture and pour in the buttermilk mixture. Mix just until the ingredients are moistened.

Carefully pour the batter into the hot pan. Bake for 15 to 18 minutes, until browned and a toothpick inserted in the center comes out clean. Cut into 2-inch squares and serve warm or at room temperature.

MAKES 16 SERVINGS

CHILI-CHEESE SKILLET CORN BREAD

Pickled jalapeños are pretty spicy, but here they are tempered by cheese, buttermilk, and cream. If you like things spicy, you can add one or two more. Look for pickled jalapeños in cans or jars.

5 tablespoons vegetable oil
1 medium onion, chopped
1 small red bell pepper, finely chopped
2 pickled jalapeño peppers, seeded and finely chopped
1 cup yellow or white cornmeal
½ cup whole wheat flour
1½ tablespoons baking powder
½ teaspoon baking soda
½ teaspoon oregano
½ teaspoon salt
1 cup frozen corn kernels, thawed
½ cup heavy cream
2 large eggs
1 cup buttermilk
1½ cups grated sharp Cheddar cheese

In a 10-inch cast-iron skillet, heat 2 tablespoons of the oil over medium heat. Add the onion and bell pepper and cook, stirring occasionally until the onion is tender, about 7 minutes. Transfer to a small bowl and stir in the jalapeños. Wipe out the skillet and brush lightly with oil.

Preheat the oven to 400°F and place the skillet in the oven to preheat while you make the batter.

In a large bowl, combine the cornmeal, flour, baking powder, baking soda, oregano, and salt.

In a blender, combine ⅔ cup of the corn and the cream, and blend just until the kernels are coarsely chopped. Blend in the eggs, buttermilk, and remaining 3 tablespoons oil.

Pour the creamed corn mixture over the cornmeal mixture, add the remaining ⅓ cup corn, and stir. Add the onion mixture and 1 cup of the cheese, and stir to combine. Carefully pour the batter into the hot skillet and sprinkle the remaining ½ cup cheese over the top.

Bake for 30 to 35 minutes, until golden brown. Cool in the skillet on a rack for 15 to 20 minutes. Cut into wedges and serve warm.

MAKES 8 TO 10 SERVINGS

NO-KNEAD WHOLE WHEAT BREAD

This mildly sweet yeast bread requires no kneading.

2 tablespoons active dry yeast
About 4 cups warm water (105° to 115°F)
2 tablespoons honey
¼ cup molasses
3½ cups whole wheat flour

3½ cups unbleached all-purpose flour

1½ teaspoons salt

In a large bowl, sprinkle the yeast over 2 cups of the warm water. Stir in the honey and let stand until the yeast is foamy, about 5 minutes. Stir in the molasses.

Add the flours and salt, and stir until well combined. Add enough of the remaining 2 cups warm water to make a sticky dough.

Butter two 9 × 5-inch loaf pans. Divide the batter between the two pans. Cover and let rise in a warm place until doubled in bulk, about 1 hour.

Preheat the oven to 400°F. Bake for 30 to 40 minutes, until the crusts are golden brown.

Cool in the pans for 10 minutes. Remove from the pans and cool on racks.

MAKES 16 SERVINGS

DUTCH PUMPERNICKEL QUICK BREAD

Good with just a little butter spread on top—but even better when topped with smoked salmon and a sprinkling of chopped onion.

1 cup rye flour

½ cup whole wheat flour

½ cup yellow cornmeal

2 teaspoons baking powder

¼ teaspoon baking soda

1½ teaspoons caraway seeds, crushed

1 teaspoon salt

¾ cup milk

2 large eggs

¼ cup molasses

¼ cup vegetable oil

1 small onion, finely chopped

Sesame seeds, for sprinkling

Preheat the oven to 350°F. Butter a 9 × 5-inch loaf pan. Line the bottom of the pan with waxed paper and butter the paper.

In a large bowl, whisk together the flours, cornmeal, baking powder, baking soda, caraway seeds, and salt.

In a small bowl, beat the milk, eggs, molasses, and oil. Pour the egg mixture over the flour mixture and stir to blend well. Stir in the onion. Pour into the loaf pan and sprinkle sesame seeds over the top.

Bake for 50 to 60 minutes, until a toothpick inserted in the center comes out clean. Remove from the pan and cool on a rack.

MAKES 12 SERVINGS

RYE QUICK BREAD

The combination of caraway seeds and rye flour gives this quick bread its decidedly rye flavor.

4 cups whole wheat flour

3½ cups rye flour

2 tablespoons baking powder

1½ teaspoons baking soda

1 teaspoon salt

4 cups buttermilk

½ cup caraway seeds

Preheat the oven to 425°F. Lightly oil and flour a baking sheet.

In a large bowl, mix together the flours, baking powder, baking soda, and salt. Stir in the buttermilk and caraway seeds. The dough will be sticky. Mix with a wooden spoon or with floured hands. If the dough seems too sticky, add a little more flour.

Shape the dough into 3 loaves of any shape and place on the baking sheet, leaving room between them for expansion. With a floured knife, cut several slashes in the tops of the loaves. Lightly sprinkle the tops with flour.

Bake for about 50 minutes, or until the tops have browned and the bottoms sound hollow when tapped. Cool on racks.

MAKES 24 SERVINGS

IRISH SODA BREAD

If you'd like to freeze a loaf, let it cool completely, then wrap in foil, label, date, and freeze. To reheat, place the loaf, still in foil, in a 350°F oven until warmed through.

- **4 cups buttermilk**
- **3 tablespoons honey**
- **2 large eggs**
- **3½ cups whole wheat flour**
- **3½ cups unbleached all-purpose flour**
- **2 tablespoons plus 2 teaspoons baking powder**
- **½ teaspoon baking soda**
- **1½ teaspoons salt**
- **2 cups raisins**
- **½ cup caraway seeds**

Preheat the oven to 375°F. Butter and flour two 9 × 5-inch loaf pans.

In a medium bowl, combine the buttermilk, honey, and eggs. Stir vigorously with a wooden spoon.

In a large bowl, combine the flours, baking powder, baking soda, salt, raisins, and caraway seeds. Pour the buttermilk mixture into the flour mixture and stir well. If you like, flour your hands and then mix with your hands. The dough does not require kneading, however. If the dough seems too damp, add a little more flour.

Divide the dough in half and place in the pans.

Bake for 1 hour 15 minutes, or until well browned and a toothpick inserted in the centers comes out clean.

Let the loaves cool in the pans for 15 minutes, then turn out onto racks to cool completely.

MAKES 16 SERVINGS

DATE-NUT BREAD

Date nut bread and cream cheese make for a delicious sandwich.

- **1 cup plain low-fat yogurt**
- **½ cup honey**
- **2 large eggs**
- **2 tablespoons vegetable oil**
- **1 cup whole wheat flour**
- **1 cup unbleached all-purpose flour**
- **1 teaspoon baking soda**
- **¾ teaspoon salt**
- **1 pound pitted dates, finely chopped**
- **1 cup chopped walnuts**

Preheat the oven to 350°F. Generously butter two 8½ × 4½-inch loaf pans.

In a large bowl, mix together the yogurt, honey, eggs, and oil.

In a small bowl, whisk together the flours, baking soda, and salt. Add to the yogurt mixture, stirring to blend. Stir in the dates and nuts. Pour the batter into the pans.

Bake for 40 minutes, or until a toothpick inserted into the centers comes out clean. Cool in the pans on a rack.

MAKES 12 SERVINGS

RAISIN TEA BREAD

Oats, flax seeds, and wheat bran all add a significant amount of fiber to this raisin-studded quick bread.

1½ cups old-fashioned rolled oats

½ cup flaxseeds

½ cup wheat bran

1 cup unbleached all-purpose flour

½ cup packed turbinado or light brown sugar

2 teaspoons baking powder

¾ teaspoon salt

1½ cups plain low-fat yogurt

⅔ cup honey

1 large egg

1 cup golden raisins

Preheat the oven to 350°F. Lightly oil a 9 × 5-inch loaf pan.

On a jelly-roll pan, toast the oats, flaxseeds, and wheat bran until the oats are golden brown, 7 to 9 minutes. Transfer to a food processor and process until finely ground.

Transfer the ground oat mixture to a large bowl and add the flour, sugar, baking powder, and salt.

In a separate bowl, whisk together the yogurt, honey, and egg. Make a well in the center of the flour mixture and fold in the yogurt mixture until just combined. Fold in the raisins.

Spoon the batter into the loaf pan, smoothing the top. Bake for 1 hour 20 minutes, or until a toothpick inserted in the center comes out clean. Cool for 5 minutes in the pan, then turn out of the pan onto a rack to cool completely.

MAKES 12 SERVINGS

CRANBERRY-NUT BREAD

Not just for Thanksgiving! When cranberries are in the market, pick up a few extra bags and pop them in the freezer to be used throughout the year. No need to thaw before using.

¼ cup (½ stick) butter

½ cup honey

2 large eggs

1 teaspoon grated orange zest

½ cup orange juice

1 cup whole wheat flour

½ cup unbleached all-purpose flour

2 teaspoons baking powder

½ teaspoon salt

¾ cup chopped fresh or frozen cranberries

½ cup chopped walnuts

Preheat the oven to 350°F. Butter and flour a 9 × 5-inch loaf pan.

In a large bowl, beat the butter and honey until light and fluffy. Beat in the eggs, orange zest, and orange juice.

Whisk together the flours, baking powder, and salt. Gradually add portions of the flour mixture to the butter mixture, blending after each addition. Stir in the cranberries and walnuts. Pour into the loaf pan.

Bake for 50 to 60 minutes, until a toothpick inserted in the center of the loaf comes out clean.

Cool 15 minutes in the pan, then remove from the pan and cool completely on a rack.

MAKES 8 SERVINGS

PUMPKIN BREAD

If you have pumpkin pie spice, use 1 tablespoon and omit the nutmeg, cloves, and cinnamon.

- **4 large eggs**
- **1 cup honey**
- **1 can (15 ounces) unsweetened pumpkin puree**
- **1 cup vegetable oil**
- **2 cups whole wheat flour**
- **1¾ cups unbleached all-purpose flour**
- **2 teaspoons baking soda**
- **¾ teaspoon salt**
- **1 teaspoon nutmeg**
- **1 teaspoon ground cloves**
- **1 teaspoon cinnamon**
- **½ cup plain low-fat yogurt or buttermilk**

Preheat the oven to 325°F. Butter two 9 × 5-inch loaf pans.

In a large bowl, whisk together the eggs and honey. Whisk in the pumpkin and oil.

In a medium bowl, whisk together the flours, baking soda, salt, nutmeg, cloves, and cinnamon. Alternately add portions of the flour mixture and the yogurt to the pumpkin mixture, beginning and ending with the flour mixture.

Pour the batter into the loaf pans. Bake for 1 hour 30 minutes, or until a toothpick inserted in the center of a loaf comes out clean. (If the loaves are overbrowning, tent with foil.) Remove from the pans and cool on a rack.

MAKES 12 TO 16 SERVINGS

BANANA BREAD

For the best flavor, use very ripe bananas.

- **1 cup unbleached all-purpose flour**
- **1 cup whole wheat flour**
- **⅔ cup sugar**
- **2 teaspoons baking powder**
- **½ teaspoon salt**
- **1¼ cups mashed bananas (about 3 medium)**
- **2 large eggs, beaten**
- **6 tablespoons butter, melted**
- **2 teaspoons vanilla extract**
- **½ cup chopped walnuts**
- **½ cup dried blueberries**

Preheat the oven to 350°F. Grease a 9 × 5-inch loaf pan.

Whisk together the flours, sugar, baking powder, and salt. Make a well in the center and add the bananas, eggs, butter, and vanilla. Beat with a wooden spoon until well mixed. Fold in the walnuts and blueberries.

Scrape the batter into the loaf pan. Bake for 50 to 60 minutes, until a toothpick inserted in the center of the loaf comes out clean. Let cool in the pan for 15 minutes, then turn out onto a rack to cool completely.

MAKES 12 SERVINGS

CHOCOLATE-CHERRY BANANA BREAD: Use chopped cherries instead of blueberries, and mini chocolate chips instead of walnuts.

ZUCCHINI-RAISIN MUFFINS

This is a perfect place to use up some of that extra zucchini from the garden. You can also make a loaf from the batter (see variation at the end of this recipe).

- **2 large eggs**
- **½ cup vegetable oil**

- ½ cup honey
- 1 teaspoon vanilla extract
- 1 cup whole wheat flour
- ¼ cup toasted wheat germ
- 1 teaspoon cinnamon
- ½ teaspoon baking powder
- ½ teaspoon baking soda
- ½ teaspoon salt
- 1 cup shredded zucchini
- ½ cup raisins

Preheat the oven to 350°F, and butter a 12-cup muffin pan.

In a small bowl, whisk together the eggs, oil, honey, and vanilla.

In a large bowl, combine the flour, wheat germ, cinnamon, baking powder, baking soda, and salt. Make a well in the center, add the egg mixture, and stir just until combined. Fold in the zucchini and raisins.

Pour the batter into the muffin cups. Bake for 25 minutes, or until a toothpick inserted in the center of a muffin comes out clean. Remove from the muffin tin and cool on a rack.

MAKES 12 MUFFINS

ZUCCHINI-RAISIN BREAD: Bake the batter in an 8½ × 4½-inch loaf pan for 45 minutes.

APPLE-HONEY OATMEAL MUFFINS

For an extra nutty flavor, toast the oats: Spread them on a baking sheet and toast in a 375°F oven for 7 to 10 minutes, until lightly browned.

- 1 cup whole wheat flour
- 1 cup old-fashioned rolled oats
- 2 teaspoons baking powder
- ½ teaspoon baking soda
- ½ teaspoon salt
- ½ teaspoon cinnamon
- ⅛ teaspoon freshly grated nutmeg
- 1 large egg
- 1 cup unsweetened applesauce
- ½ cup milk
- ¼ cup honey
- 2 tablespoons butter, melted

Preheat the oven to 375°F. Generously butter a 12-cup muffin tin.

In a large bowl, whisk together the flour, oats, baking powder, baking soda, salt, cinnamon, and nutmeg.

In a small bowl, combine the egg, applesauce, milk, honey, and butter. Make a well in the center of the flour mixture. Add the applesauce mixture and mix with a fork just until moistened. Fill the muffin cups two-thirds full.

Bake for 25 minutes, or until a toothpick inserted into the center of a muffin comes out clean. Remove from the muffin tin and transfer to a rack. Serve warm.

MAKES 12 MUFFINS

BANANA-NUT MUFFINS

For a richer muffin, use whole-milk yogurt.

- 1 large egg
- ¾ cup mashed very ripe bananas (2 medium)
- ⅓ cup vegetable oil
- ¼ cup molasses
- ¼ cup plain low-fat yogurt
- 1 cup whole wheat pastry flour
- 1 cup toasted wheat germ
- ½ teaspoon baking soda

½ teaspoon baking powder

½ teaspoon cinnamon

½ teaspoon salt

½ cup finely chopped walnuts

Preheat the oven to 375°F, and butter a 12-cup muffin pan.

In a large bowl, whisk together the egg, mashed bananas, oil, molasses, and yogurt.

In a small bowl, whisk together the flour, wheat germ, baking soda, baking powder, cinnamon, and salt. Add to the liquid ingredients and stir until combined. Fold in the walnuts.

Spoon the batter into the muffin cups. Bake for 20 minutes, or until golden brown and a toothpick inserted in the center of a muffin comes out clean. Cool on a rack.

MAKES 12 MUFFINS

SPICED BRAN MUFFINS

These have a flavor reminiscent of gingerbread.

1 cup wheat bran

1 cup whole wheat pastry flour

1 teaspoon baking powder

1 teaspoon baking soda

½ teaspoon salt

1 teaspoon cinnamon

1 teaspoon ginger

1 cup buttermilk

3 large eggs, separated

3 tablespoons vegetable oil

3 tablespoons molasses

½ cup raisins

Preheat the oven to 375°F, and butter a 12-cup muffin pan.

In a medium bowl, whisk together the bran, flour, baking powder, baking soda, salt, cinnamon, and ginger. Make a well in the center.

In a small bowl, combine the buttermilk, egg yolks, oil, and molasses. Add to the flour mixture, mixing just to moisten. Do not overmix. Fold in the raisins.

With an electric mixer, beat the egg whites until stiff. Fold them into the batter.

Pour the batter into the muffin cups. Bake for 25 minutes, or until a toothpick inserted in the center of a muffin comes out clean. Cool on a rack.

MAKES 12 MUFFINS

MAPLE CORN MUFFINS

Dense and custardy, these corn muffins are delicious with butter and a drizzle of maple syrup.

¾ cup milk

¼ cup sour cream

⅓ cup maple syrup

2 large eggs

1 cup whole wheat pastry flour

¾ cup yellow cornmeal

½ teaspoon baking soda

½ teaspoon salt

Preheat the oven to 450°F, and butter a 12-cup muffin pan.

In a medium bowl, whisk together the milk, sour cream, maple syrup, and eggs.

In a medium bowl, whisk together the flour, cornmeal, baking soda, and salt, and fold into the liquid ingredients.

Spoon the batter into the muffin cups, filling about two-thirds full. Bake for 15 minutes, or until golden brown and a toothpick inserted in the center of a muffin comes out clean with some moist crumbs attached. Cool on a rack.

MAKES 12 MUFFINS

CHERRY-WALNUT WHOLE WHEAT MUFFINS

Make a batch of these and freeze them individually for a quick weekday breakfast.

1¼ cups whole wheat flour

1 cup unbleached all-purpose flour

2 teaspoons baking powder

½ teaspoon baking soda

½ teaspoon salt

1 cup buttermilk

1 large egg

¼ cup agave nectar

3 tablespoons walnut oil

½ cup dried cherries, coarsely chopped

Preheat the oven to 350°F, and butter a 12-cup muffin pan.

In a medium bowl, combine the flours, baking powder, baking soda, and salt.

In a small bowl, whisk together the buttermilk, buttermilk egg, agave nectar, and oil. Make a well in the center of the flour mixture and add the buttermilk mixture. Stir just until moistened. Fold in the cherries.

Divide the batter among the muffin cups, filling each a little more than halfway full. Bake for 15 to 20 minutes, until a toothpick inserted into the center of a muffin comes out clean. Cool on a rack.

MAKES 12 MUFFINS

WHOLE WHEAT POPOVERS

Popover tins have very deep cups, which help the popovers puff up nice and high. Serve the hot popovers with honey and butter, or make a batch of fruit butter by stirring some pureed fresh fruit into softened butter and then refrigerating to firm up before serving.

1⅓ cups milk

1½ tablespoons vegetable oil

1½ cups whole wheat pastry flour

½ teaspoon salt

3 large eggs

Preheat the oven to 450°F. Generously butter 8 cups of a popover pan or a 12-cup muffin pan.

In a medium bowl, combine the milk, oil, flour, and salt. Beat until smooth. Add the eggs one at a time, beating only until the batter is smooth.

Fill the cups no more than three-quarters full. You'll get 8 popovers from a popover pan, and 12 smaller popovers from a muffin pan.

Bake for 15 minutes. Do not open the oven door during the first 15 minutes of baking. Reduce the oven temperature to 350°F and bake about 20 minutes longer, or until puffed and golden brown.

MAKES 8 OR 12 POPOVERS

CRISPY BACON POPOVERS

The popovers start off at a high temperature to make them rise quickly, then finish at a lower temperature to make sure they are cooked through. The popovers should be crisp, firm, and very light. Serve immediately, before they collapse.

5 slices bacon

1 tablespoon vegetable oil

½ cup unbleached all-purpose flour

½ cup whole wheat pastry flour

1 cup milk

2 large eggs

½ teaspoon salt

¼ teaspoon pepper

¼ cup grated Parmesan cheese

In a medium skillet, cook the bacon over medium-high heat until crisp, 6 to 8 minutes. Drain on paper towels. Crumble the bacon and set aside. Strain the bacon fat, reserving 2 tablespoons. In a small bowl, combine the reserved bacon fat and the vegetable oil.

In a blender, combine 1 tablespoon of the bacon fat mixture, the flours, milk, eggs, salt, and pepper. Blend until smooth. Let the batter rest for 30 minutes at room temperature.

Preheat the oven to 450°F.

Brush a 6-cup popover pan with the remaining 2 tablespoons bacon fat mixture. Divide the batter equally among the popover cups and sprinkle evenly with the reserved crumbled bacon and the Parmesan.

Bake for 15 minutes. Do not open the oven door during the first 15 minutes of baking. Reduce the oven temperature to 350°F and bake the popovers for 15 to 20 minutes longer, until they are puffed and golden brown.

MAKES 6 LARGE POPOVERS

BUTTERMILK-SESAME BISCUITS

Buttermilk gives these biscuits a light, tender crumb.

- **8 tablespoons (1 stick) cold butter**
- **1 cup whole wheat flour**
- **1 cup unbleached all-purpose flour**
- **2¼ teaspoons baking powder**
- **¼ teaspoon baking soda**
- **½ teaspoon salt**
- **¾ cup buttermilk**
- **1½ tablespoons sesame seeds**

Preheat the oven to 450°F. Lightly oil a baking sheet.

In a small saucepan, melt 2 tablespoons of the butter and set aside. Cut the remaining 6 tablespoons butter into small pieces.

In a medium bowl, whisk together the flours, baking powder, baking soda, and salt. With a pastry blender or two knives scissor fashion, cut in the cut-up butter until the mixture resembles coarse crumbs. Add the buttermilk and mix lightly.

Turn out the dough onto a floured surface and knead gently for a few seconds. Roll out to a ½-inch thickness and with a biscuit cutter or the top of a drinking glass, cut into 2-inch rounds.

Place the rounds on the baking sheet and brush with the melted butter. Gently pat the sesame seeds on top. Bake for 12 to 15 minutes, until golden brown. Serve hot.

MAKES 10 BISCUITS

CHEDDAR & PROSCIUTTO BISCUITS WITH ROSEMARY

To keep the prosciutto from sticking to your knife, dust the knife very lightly with a little flour before chopping.

- **4 cups unbleached all-purpose flour**
- **2 cups white whole wheat flour***
- **¼ cup minced fresh rosemary**
- **2 tablespoons baking powder**
- **2 teaspoons coarse salt**
- **1 teaspoon cracked black pepper**
- **1½ cups (3 sticks) cold butter, cut into ¼-inch pieces**
- **2 cups shredded sharp cheddar cheese (8 ounces)**
- **3 ounces prosciutto, finely chopped (¾ cup)**
- **2¼ cups cold buttermilk, plus more for brushing**

**milled from white wheat grains*

Preheat the oven to 400°F with racks in the upper and lower thirds.

In a large bowl, whisk together the flours, rosemary, baking powder, salt, and pepper. With a pastry blender or your fingers, cut in the butter until the mixture resembles coarse meal but with some large pieces of butter remaining. Add the cheese and chopped prosciutto. Stir in the buttermilk just until the mixture forms a dough; it will be crumbly.

Turn out the dough onto a lightly floured work surface and knead quickly to incorporate any loose crumbs. Pat the dough into a 12-inch square. Cut into twelve 3-inch squares and transfer to two ungreased baking sheets. Brush the top of each biscuit with a little buttermilk.

Bake for 30 to 40 minutes, until the biscuits are golden brown and cooked through. Rotate the baking sheets from top to bottom and front to back halfway through. Serve hot.

MAKES 12 BISCUITS

HERBED BUTTERMILK SCONES

You can bake the scones a few days ahead and freeze them. They thaw quickly at room temperature and can be warmed briefly in a hot oven before serving.

2 cups unbleached all-purpose flour

2 teaspoons baking powder

½ teaspoon baking soda

1 tablespoon fresh thyme leaves

½ teaspoon mustard seeds

½ teaspoon salt

¼ teaspoon pepper

½ cup (1 stick) cold butter, cut up

¾ cup buttermilk or plain low-fat yogurt

Preheat the oven to 425°F.

In a food processor, combine the flour, baking powder, baking soda, thyme, mustard seeds, salt, and pepper, and pulse to mix.

Add the butter and pulse just until the mixture forms coarse crumbs. Add the buttermilk and pulse until a soft, crumbly dough forms.

Transfer the dough to a lightly floured work surface and knead 6 to 8 times, until fairly smooth. Pat into an 8-inch round about ½-inch thick. With a floured knife, cut the round into 8 even wedges and place ½-inch apart on a heavy baking sheet.

Bake the scones for 12 to 14 minutes, until lightly browned and crisp. Transfer to a rack and serve warm or at room temperature.

MAKES 8 SCONES

CHOCOLATE CHIP SCONES

Substitute dried currants, minced dried pears, or chopped toasted pecans for the chocolate chips.

1⅔ cups unbleached all-purpose flour

2½ teaspoons baking powder

3 tablespoons sugar

¼ teaspoon salt

6 tablespoons cold butter

2 teaspoons grated orange zest

¼ cup semisweet chocolate chips

1 large egg

¼ cup plus 2 teaspoons heavy cream

Preheat the oven to 425°F.

In a large bowl, whisk together the flour, baking powder, sugar, and salt. With a pastry blender or two knives scissor fashion, cut in the butter until the mixture resembles coarse crumbs. Stir in the orange zest and chocolate chips.

In a small bowl, beat the egg with ¼ cup of the cream. Add the egg mixture to the flour mixture and mix just to combine. Do not overmix.

Turn out the dough onto a floured surface and pat into a round about 1 inch thick. Cut into 8 wedges. Brush with the remaining 2 teaspoons cream.

Place on a baking sheet and bake for 15 minutes, or until golden. Transfer to a rack and serve warm or at room temperature.

MAKES 8 SCONES

Breakfast & Brunch

In most countries, just about anything is fair game for the morning meal. If you look at cultures across the world, you'll find people eating pickled fish, refried beans, and cold meat for breakfast. America, on the other hand, has very specific notions about what belongs on the breakfast table, including our beloved cereal, pancakes, and waffles (not to mention bacon and eggs). In fact we so revere breakfast that we have extended the timeframe for consuming these "morning foods" all the way to 2 o'clock in the afternoon—although it then gets rechristened brunch.

Cereal

Although supermarket aisles abound with boxed cereals, instead of struggling to read the ingredients panel on the side to see if the claims to fiber and whole grains is legitimate, it might just be simpler to make your own. Check out Mixed Grains Hot Cereal (page 584) or Pecan Crunch Granola (page 583).

Pancakes & Waffles

These quintessentially American breakfast foods are often seen as an indulgence these days because people are so used to the idea of serving them dripping with butter and sugary syrups. However, there's no reason to abandon them. It just takes a little attitude adjustment. First, you can make your own pancake mix (try Multi-Grain Pancake Mix on page 587; it has flaxmeal in it); and you can improve the health profile of your waffles by making them with whole grains (Toasted Oat Waffles, page 588). Second, you can wean yourself away from syrup on your pancakes and waffles by topping them with homemade fruit purees (opposite) or other Pancake Toppers (page 586).

French Toast

More American than French, certainly, this is another favorite breakfast food that can benefit from a little attitude adjustment, but it's as simple as using whole-grain bread instead of white bread. You can top French toast with fruit purees, fruit butters, applesauce, or sautéed sliced fruit.

Brunch

Brunch is really just breakfast wearing slightly fancier clothes. Breakfast pancakes, for example, might become crêpes on a brunch menu. Instead of toast and jam to go with coffee, a brunch table might hold an Apple-Maple Coffee Cake or a basket of muffins.

FRUIT PUREES

One of the most healthful toppings you can have on pancakes or waffles is a puree of fresh or dried fruit. Not only will be you getting more nutrients and fiber than you would get from traditional pancake toppings like maple syrup, but you can take advantage of the fruit's natural sweetness and add either no sweetener or just a minimal amount. The same purees can also be used as dessert toppings or as homemade baby food. If you have access to an abundance of fruits, you might consider either freezing or canning them (see "Processing High-Acids Foods," page 639).

The amounts of sweetener (honey or sugar) in the chart below are suggestions. You can start with less, but if you want to add more, add it at the end of the cooking, because sugar interferes with the fruit becoming tender. To puree fruit that's been peeled, use a food processor, blender, or hand blender. For fruits with peel, if you don't want to leave the peel in the puree, push the cooked fruit through a coarse-mesh sieve or a food mill.

KIND OF FRUIT		AMOUNT	WATER (CUPS)	SWEETENER (TBSP)	COOKING TIME (MINUTES)	YIELD (CUPS)
APPLES	Fresh	2 pounds	½	2	8–10	3
	Dried	8 ounces (about 3 cups)	3½	...	10	4
APRICOTS	Fresh	1½ pounds	½	8	5	3
	Dried	8 ounces (about 1¼ cups)	2¼	1	10	2
		11 ounces (about 2 cups)	3	2	10	3
MIXED DRIED FRUIT		8 ounces (about 2 cups)	2¼	...	20	2½
		11 ounces (about 2½ cups)	3	...	20	3½
PEACHES	Fresh*	1½ pounds	¾	6	5	3
	Dried	8 ounces (about 2 cups)	3	3	25	3
		11 ounces (about 3 cups)	4	5	25	4
PEARS	Fresh, firm varieties**	2 pounds	⅔	3	25	3
	Fresh, soft varieties	2 pounds	⅔	3	15	3
	Dried	8 ounces (about 2 cups)	2	...	25	2
		11 ounces (about 3 cups)	3	...	30	3½
PLUMS	Fresh	1 pound	½	4	5	2½
	Dried (unpitted prunes)	1 pound (about 2½ cups)	4	3	25	4

*Fresh peaches need not be peeled before simmering. Their skins will slip off easily after cooking.

**When cooking firm varieties of pears, do not add honey until the final 10 minutes of cooking.

GRANOLA WITH TOASTED ALMONDS & CHERRIES

This is an easy recipe to modify. Just pick your favorite fruit and nut combination.

3 cups quick-cooking oats

½ cup sliced almonds

2 tablespoons flaxseeds

2 tablespoons sesame seeds

¼ teaspoon salt

⅓ cup honey

1 tablespoon turbinado sugar or light brown sugar

1 tablespoon extra-light olive oil

1 teaspoon vanilla extract

1 cup chopped dried cherries

Preheat the oven to 300°F.

In a 9 × 13-inch baking pan, combine the oats, almonds, flaxseeds, sesame seeds, and salt. Bake for 30 minutes, or until the oats and nuts are toasted and fragrant. Increase the oven temperature to 350°F.

Meanwhile, in a small saucepan, combine the honey, brown sugar, and oil. Cook over medium heat until the sugar has melted, about 1 minute. Remove from the heat and stir in the vanilla.

Drizzle the honey mixture over the oats and stir to coat. Bake, stirring occasionally, for 10 minutes, or until the oats are crispy.

With a spoon, break up any clumps. Stir in the cherries. Store in an airtight container.

MAKES 5 CUPS

NANTUCKET GRANOLA

The granola at the Sconset Market on the island of Nantucket has legions of devoted fans who look forward each summer to indulging in their crunchy breakfast treat. The cereal is easy to make at home using the market's original recipe (which we've adapted to household proportions). Stirring the mixture regularly prevents the oats from clumping. Be sure to use a pan with sides to avoid spills.

4 cups old-fashioned rolled oats

1⅓ cups flaked or shredded coconut, preferably unsweetened

1½ cups light brown sugar

1 cup sliced almonds

1 cup sunflower seeds

¾ cup canola oil

¾ cup cold water

1 tablespoon vanilla extract

⅓ cup dried cherries

⅓ cup dried cranberries

½ cup golden raisins

Preheat the oven to 325°F.

In a large bowl, combine the oats, coconut, brown sugar, almonds, and sunflower seeds. Stir well to

---

BREAKFAST IN A GLASS

Batida (page 142)

Date Shake (page 139)

Ginger-Peach Froth (page 137)

Kefir-Banana Froth (page 138)

Mango-Soy Smoothie (page 138)

Sunflower Breakfast Shake (page 138)

combine. In a small bowl, whisk the oil with the water and vanilla, and pour over the dry ingredients. Stir until well coated.

Spread the mixture over the bottom of a large rimmed baking sheet or a roasting pan and bake for 1 hour 20 minutes, stirring every 10 minutes, until golden brown. Remove from the oven and cool.

Transfer the granola to a large bowl and stir in the cherries, cranberries, and raisins. Store in an airtight container.

MAKES 11 CUPS

PECAN CRUNCH GRANOLA

The trick to the crunch in this cereal is the slow baking at a low temperature.

- **3 cups old-fashioned rolled oats**
- **1½ cups shredded coconut**
- **½ cup toasted wheat germ**
- **1 cup hulled pumpkin seeds (pepitas)**
- **¼ cup sesame seeds**
- **½ cup honey, preferably dark**
- **¼ cup vegetable oil**
- **½ cup cold water**
- **1 cup sliced pecans**
- **½ cup raisins (optional)**

Preheat the oven to 225°F. Lightly oil a large shallow baking pan.

In a large mixing bowl, combine the oats, coconut, wheat germ, pumpkin seeds, and sesame seeds. Toss the ingredients together thoroughly.

In a separate bowl, combine the honey and oil. Add to the dry ingredients, stirring until well mixed. Add the water, a little at a time, mixing until crumbly. Pour the mixture into the baking pan and spread evenly to the sides of the pan.

Bake on the middle rack of the oven for 1 hour 30 minutes, stirring every 15 minutes.

Add the pecans and continue to bake for 30 minutes, or until the mixture is thoroughly dry and light brown in color. The cereal should feel crisp to the touch.

Turn the oven off and let the cereal cool in the oven. Add the raisins (if using).

Store in a tightly covered container in a cool dry place.

MAKES 8 CUPS

CINNAMON OATMEAL WITH RAISINS & PEPITAS

Eating this hot breakfast cereal is like eating an oatmeal cookie! Serve it with honey or brown sugar and a little milk.

- **2 cups water**
- **½ cup raisins**
- **1 cup old-fashioned rolled oats**
- **1 teaspoon cinnamon**
- **½ teaspoon vanilla extract**
- **¼ cup hulled pumpkin seeds (pepitas), coarsely chopped**

In a 1-quart saucepan, combine the water and raisins, and bring to a boil. Gradually stir in the oats, cinnamon, and vanilla. Reduce the heat and cook for 10 minutes.

Pour the hot cereal into bowls and top with the pepitas.

MAKES 4 SERVINGS

CRANBERRY-WALNUT OATMEAL: Use dried cranberries instead of raisins and chopped toasted walnuts instead of pepitas.

MIXED GRAINS HOT CEREAL

This is a great use for leftover cooked grains. If you've made too much brown rice or bulgur or millet, just throw it into the freezer in 1-cup containers and then thaw 3 cups' worth when you want to make this hot cereal.

3 cups cooked mixed grains (any combination)

1½ cups milk

½ cup chopped walnuts

¼ cup raisins

¼ cup maple syrup

1 teaspoon vanilla extract

1 teaspoon cinnamon

In a heavy-bottomed 2-quart saucepan, combine the cooked grains, milk, walnuts, raisins, maple syrup, vanilla, and cinnamon. Cook over low heat, stirring occasionally, until warmed through, about 10 minutes.

MAKES 4 TO 6 SERVINGS

SOUTHERN BROWN RICE PANCAKES

Totally wheat-free, these crisp little pancakes need not be limited to breakfast. Try them with maple syrup or fruit as a dessert, a snack, or light lunch.

1½ cups milk

1½ cups cooked short-grain brown rice

6 tablespoons butter

¼ cup honey

2 large eggs, separated

1½ cups brown rice flour

2 teaspoons baking powder

½ teaspoon salt

½ teaspoon cinnamon

⅛ teaspoon nutmeg

In a large saucepan, combine the milk, cooked rice, 3 tablespoons of the butter, and the honey, and heat until the butter melts. Remove from the heat.

BACON THREE WAYS

Take your pick from three different ways to enjoy bacon: sweet, sweet and hot, and sweet and spicy. The method is the same for each, but the toppings get added at different times. These recipes make about 8 servings.

Preheat the oven to 350°F. Set 2 broiler racks or large wire racks over 2 rimmed baking sheets lined with parchment or foil (for easy cleanup). Lay 1 pound of bacon out on the two racks. Bake for 30 to 35 minutes, until the bacon is crisp and cooked through. Drain on paper towels.

Maple Bacon: After the bacon has baked for 20 minutes, brush with ¼ cup maple syrup, preferably Grade B, and bake for 10 to 15 more minutes, until crisp.

Brown Sugar & Pepper Bacon: Sprinkle the bacon with ¼ cup light brown sugar mixed with 2 tablespoons coarsely ground black pepper *before* baking.

Five-Spice Bacon: Sprinkle the bacon with 3 tablespoons sugar mixed with 1 tablespoon five-spice powder or garam masala *before* baking.

Makes 8 servings

In a small bowl, whisk the egg yolks until frothy. Add to the rice mixture.

In another small bowl, mix together the flour, baking powder, salt, cinnamon, and nutmeg, and add to the rice mixture.

With an electric mixer, beat the egg whites until stiff but not dry. Fold into the rice mixture.

In a large heavy skillet, heat 1 tablespoon of the butter over medium heat. Drop the batter by tablespoons onto the skillet and cook on both sides until browned and crisp. Keep warm. Repeat with the remaining batter and butter.

MAKES 2 DOZEN

BARLEY PANCAKES

Yeast makes exceptionally light pancakes, especially important when using a nonwheat flour.

- 1 tablespoon dry yeast
- ½ cup warm water
- 2 tablespoons honey
- 2 large eggs
- 1 cup plain low-fat yogurt
- 1 cup barley flour
- 2 tablespoons vegetable oil, plus more for the griddle
- ½ teaspoon salt

In a medium bowl, sprinkle the yeast over the warm water. Stir in the honey and set aside until bubbly, about 5 minutes.

In a small bowl, blend together the eggs and yogurt. Stir into the yeast mixture. Stir in the flour, oil, and salt. Let the batter sit in a warm place for 20 minutes.

Preheat a griddle and coat lightly with oil.

Drop the batter by ¼ cups onto the griddle, and cook on both sides until golden brown and puffy. Repeat with the remaining batter.

MAKES 10 PANCAKES

BLUEBERRY PANCAKES

Sometimes the blueberries end up sinking to the bottom of the batter bowl. One way to ensure even distribution is to sprinkle some onto the first sides of the pancakes as they cook instead of mixing them into the batter.

- 1½ cups whole wheat pastry flour
- ½ cup wheat germ
- 2 tablespoons baking powder
- ½ teaspoon salt
- 2 large eggs
- 1½ cups milk
- 2 tablespoons vegetable oil, plus more for the griddle
- 2 tablespoons honey
- 1½ cups blueberries

In a large bowl, combine the flour, wheat germ, baking powder, and salt.

In a medium bowl, beat the eggs. Beat in the milk, oil, and honey. Mix gently into the flour mixture, then fold in the blueberries.

Preheat a griddle and brush lightly with oil.

Ladle the batter by ¼ cups onto the griddle and cook on both sides until golden brown. Repeat with the remaining batter

MAKES 16 PANCAKES

BUCKWHEAT PANCAKES

Buckwheat flour makes a very hearty pancake. It would be fitting to serve this with buckwheat honey, which also has a strong flavor.

- ½ cup whole wheat flour
- ½ cup buckwheat flour

1 teaspoon baking powder

½ teaspoon salt

1 large egg

1 cup milk

¼ cup water

2 tablespoons honey

Oil, for the griddle

In a large bowl, combine the whole wheat and buckwheat flours. Whisk in the baking powder and salt.

In a small bowl, beat together the egg, milk, water, and honey. Stir the wet ingredients into the flour mixture until just moistened. Do not overmix. The batter will be thin.

Preheat a griddle and brush lightly with oil.

Ladle the batter by scant ¼ cups onto the griddle and cook on both sides until golden brown. Repeat with the remaining batter.

MAKES 14 PANCAKES

COTTAGE CHEESE & CORNMEAL CAKES

Cottage cheese helps lighten these cakes, which are made with no flour.

¾ cup white cornmeal

1 teaspoon sugar

½ teaspoon salt

¾ cup fat-free milk

⅔ cup low-fat cottage cheese

1 large egg

Oil, for the griddle

In a medium bowl, combine the cornmeal, sugar, and salt.

In a blender or food processor, puree the milk, cottage cheese, and egg. Stir the cottage cheese mixture into the cornmeal mixture.

Preheat a griddle and brush lightly with oil.

Ladle the batter by ¼ cups onto the griddle and

PANCAKE TOPPERS

No need to resort to sweet syrups for your pancakes or waffles. Instead try a fruit topping. Below are a couple of simple recipes.

Applesauce: Cut 1 pound of apples into chunks. Place in a medium saucepan with ⅓ cup unsweetened apple juice and ¼ teaspoon cinnamon. Bring to a boil and reduce to a simmer. Cover and cook until the apples collapse, 5 to 10 minutes. Sweeten if desired.

Apricot-Prune Whip: In a small saucepan, combine 6 pitted prunes and 6 dried apricots with water to just barely cover. Bring to a boil. Remove from the heat, cover, and let sit until cool. Drain the fruit and transfer to a blender or food processor and puree with 5 tablespoons plain low-fat yogurt and 1 teaspoon turbinado sugar.

Mango Cream: Cube 2 large mangoes and place in a food processor. Add 1 tablespoon light agave syrup (or honey) and 1 tablespoon Greek yogurt. Puree.

Spiced Pineapple Sauce: In a small saucepan combine 1 can (8 ounces) crushed pineapple, 1 tablespoon honey, ⅛ teaspoon pepper, and a pinch of allspice. Cook over low heat stirring occasionally, until slightly thickened and syrupy, 12 to 15 minutes.

cook on both sides until golden brown. Repeat with the remaining batter.

MAKES 10 PANCAKES

HIGH-PROTEIN PANCAKES WITH SUNFLOWER SEEDS

Serve with Apricot-Prune Whip (opposite).

- 1½ cups plain low-fat yogurt
- 2 large eggs
- 3 tablespoons vegetable oil, plus more for the griddle
- 1 cup whole wheat flour
- ¼ cup soy flour
- 2 tablespoons oat bran
- 1 teaspoon baking powder
- ½ teaspoon baking soda
- ½ teaspoon salt
- ½ cup sunflower seeds

In a blender or food processor, combine the yogurt, eggs, oil, whole wheat flour, soy flour, oat bran, baking powder, baking soda, and salt. Process to blend.

Preheat a griddle and brush lightly with oil.

Ladle the batter by ¼ cups onto the griddle. Sprinkle each pancake with about 2 teaspoons sunflower seeds. Cook until bubbly, then turn over and cook the reverse side for about 2 minutes. Repeat with the remaining batter and seeds.

MAKES 10 PANCAKES

MULTI-GRAIN PANCAKE MIX

Buttermilk powder is available in the baking section of some supermarkets and from stores (or online sources) that specialize in baking supplies. To make about 8 pancakes: Scoop out 1 cup of pancake mix and place in a large bowl. Make a well in the center of the mix and stir in 1 large egg, ⅔ cup cold water, and 2 teaspoons extra-light olive oil. Add more water if the batter is too thick. For each pancake, use a generous ⅓ cup of batter.

- ½ cup flaxseeds
- 1½ cups whole wheat flour
- 1½ cups brown rice flour
- ½ cup toasted wheat germ
- ½ cup buttermilk powder
- 2 tablespoons maple sugar or light brown sugar
- 4 teaspoons baking powder
- 1 teaspoon baking soda
- 1 teaspoon salt

In a mini food processor or spice grinder, finely grind the flaxseeds.

In large bowl, whisk together the ground flaxseeds, whole wheat flour, brown rice flour, wheat germ, buttermilk powder, maple sugar, baking powder, baking soda, and salt.

Store in the refrigerator.

MAKES 4 CUPS MIX

CORN WAFFLES

Crisp, dense corn waffles would be delicious served with chilled Greek yogurt and a drizzle of honey.

- 4 large eggs, separated
- 2 tablespoons vegetable oil, plus more for the griddle
- 1½ cups milk
- 2 cups yellow cornmeal
- ½ teaspoon salt

In a medium bowl, blend the egg yolks and oil. Stir in the milk. Stirring constantly, gradually add the cornmeal. Stir in the salt.

With an electric mixer, beat the egg whites beyond frothy stage but not until stiff. Mix them into the batter, and beat until the batter is very light and has increased in bulk by about one-third. (The batter will be thin.)

Preheat a waffle iron and brush lightly with oil. Pour in enough batter to just fill. Close and cook until the steaming stops and the waffles are crisp.

MAKES 6 WAFFLES

RICH BUTTERMILK WAFFLES

Serve with apple butter spread on top so that it's captured in the waffle holes.

- 1 cup whole wheat flour
- 1 cup unbleached all-purpose flour
- 2 teaspoons baking powder
- ½ teaspoon baking soda
- ½ teaspoon salt
- 2 large eggs, separated
- 2 cups buttermilk
- ¼ cup (½ stick) butter, melted
- 2 tablespoons honey
- Oil, for the waffle iron

In a medium bowl, whisk together the flours, baking powder, baking soda, and salt.

In a small bowl, combine the egg yolks, buttermilk, butter, and honey. Stir the buttermilk mixture into the flour mixture and blend well.

With an electric mixer, beat the egg whites until stiff but not dry. Fold into the batter.

Preheat a waffle iron and brush lightly with oil. Pour in enough batter to just fill. Close and cook until the steaming stops and the waffles are crisp.

MAKES 4 TO 6 WAFFLES

TOASTED-OAT WAFFLES

Toasting the oats gives these waffles a subtle nutty flavor.

- 1 tablespoon lemon juice
- About 1½ cups milk
- ¼ cup quick-cooking oats
- 1 cup whole wheat flour
- 2 teaspoons baking soda
- ½ teaspoon salt
- 2 tablespoons vegetable oil
- 1 large egg, beaten

Put the lemon juice in a 2-cup measuring cup. Add enough milk to come to 1½ cups. Set aside to curdle.

In a 350°F toaster oven, toast the oats until light brown, about 5 minutes. Transfer to a medium bowl and add the flour, baking soda, and salt.

In a small bowl, combine the soured milk, oil, and egg. Stir the milk mixture into the flour mixture until just moistened. Do not overmix.

Preheat a waffle iron and brush lightly with oil. Pour in enough batter to just fill. Close and cook until the steaming stops and the waffles are crisp.

MAKES 4 WAFFLES

ORANGE BUCKWHEAT CRÊPES

For breakfast, serve 2 crêpes per person, each brushed very lightly with raspberry all-fruit spread or marmalade and folded into quarters. If you're making this for a savory preparation, omit the honey from the batter.

- 5 large eggs
- 1 cup buttermilk
- 1 cup water

1¼ cups buckwheat flour

½ cup whole wheat pastry flour

1 tablespoon honey (optional)

2 tablespoons butter, melted

1 teaspoon grated orange zest

½ teaspoon salt

Oil, for the pan

In a blender, combine the eggs, buttermilk, water, flours, honey (if using), butter, orange zest, and salt. Process until the batter is smooth. Let rest for 2 hours to allow the particles of flour to expand in the liquid, resulting in a tender crêpe. Just before cooking the crêpes, process the batter again briefly to blend the ingredients.

Preheat the oven to low.

Heat a small heavy skillet or crêpe pan to medium-high heat. The pan is ready when a drop of water "dances" on it. Oil the pan well.

Stir the batter and then pour about ¼ cup into the pan. Cook for about 2 minutes, or until golden brown underneath and dry on top. Flip over with your fingers and brown the other side for about 1 minute. Slide onto a heatproof plate and keep warm in the oven. If the first crêpe came out too thick, thin the batter with a little liquid. Continue making crêpes until all the batter is used. The finished crêpes can be stacked on top of each other.

MAKES 16 CRÊPES

WHOLE WHEAT CRÊPES

For breakfast, serve 2 crêpes per person, each brushed very lightly with honey, sprinkled with minced toasted nuts, and folded into quarters. If you're making this for a savory preparation (like Baked Spinach-Stuffed Crêpes, page 318), omit the honey from the batter.

1¾ cups whole wheat pastry flour

1 cup milk

1 cup water

4 large eggs

2 tablespoons butter, melted

1 tablespoon honey (optional)

¼ teaspoon salt

Oil, for the pan

In a blender, combine the flour, milk, water, eggs, butter, honey (if using), and salt. Process until the batter is smooth. Let rest for 2 hours to allow the particles of flour to expand in the liquid, resulting in a tender crêpe. Just before cooking the crêpes, process the batter again briefly to blend the ingredients.

Preheat the oven to low.

Heat a small heavy skillet or crêpe pan to medium-high heat. The pan is ready when a drop of water "dances" on it. Oil the pan well.

Stir the batter and then pour about ¼ cup into the pan. Cook for about 2 minutes, or until golden brown underneath and dry on top. Flip over with your fingers and brown the other side for about 1 minute. Slide onto a heatproof plate and keep warm in the oven. If the first crêpe came out too thick, thin the batter with a little liquid. Continue making crêpes until all the batter is used. The finished crêpes can be stacked on top of each other.

MAKES 16 CRÊPES

BREAKFAST EGGS

Herbed Scrambled Eggs (page 333)

Basic Omelet (page 334)

Fluffy Omelet (page 334)

Garden Omelet (page 335)

Bacon & Avocado Omelets (page 335)

Huevos Rancheros (page 333)

SESAME FRENCH TOAST

Top with sliced bananas and yogurt.

- 1 large egg
- ½ cup milk
- ½ teaspoon vanilla extract
- ¼ teaspoon cinnamon
- 2 tablespoons butter
- 8 slices multi-grain bread
- ¼ cup sesame seeds

In a shallow bowl, beat together the egg, milk, vanilla, and cinnamon.

In a large skillet, melt 1 tablespoon of the butter over medium heat.

Dip 4 bread slices into the egg mixture, turning to coat both sides. Place in the skillet and sprinkle each slice with ½ tablespoon of the sesame seeds. Cook on each side until golden brown. Repeat with the remaining butter, bread, and sesame seeds.

MAKES 4 SERVINGS

FRENCH TOAST WITH BROILED PINEAPPLE

A pineapple ring is just the right size to sit on top of a piece of French toast.

- 1 can (20 ounces) juice-packed pineapple rings
- 3 large eggs
- 2 tablespoons extra-light olive oil
- 8 slices whole-grain bread

Reserving the juice, drain the pineapple.

Preheat the broiler. Broil 8 pineapple slices 4 inches from the heat until lightly browned. Keep warm.

In a shallow bowl, beat the eggs. Beat in ½ cup of the pineapple juice.

In a large skillet, heat 1 tablespoon of the oil over medium heat.

Dip the bread slices into the egg mixture, turning to coat both sides. Place the bread slices in the skillet and cook on each side until golden brown. Repeat with the remaining 1 tablespoon oil and bread.

Serve a pineapple ring on top of the French toast.

MAKES 4 SERVINGS

FRUIT & CHEESE TOAST

Upgrade your morning toast with a savory spread loaded with dried fruit. We use figs, golden raisins, and dates, but dried apricots, cranberries, or cherries are delicious alternatives. If you don't like goat cheese, try crème fraîche, ricotta, queso fresco, or fromage blanc.

- 1 ounce soft goat cheese, at room temperature
- 1 tablespoon butter, at room temperature
- 2 pitted dates, finely chopped
- 1 dried fig, finely chopped
- 1 tablespoon golden raisins, finely chopped
- 2 slices (¼ inch) pumpernickel, dark rye, or raisin bread

In a small bowl, blend the cheese and butter together with a fork. Stir in the chopped fruit.

Toast the bread and transfer to a rack. (This will prevent the toast from steaming and becoming soggy.) Spread equal amounts of the cheese mixture over the toast while it is still warm. Cut into halves before serving.

MAKES 2 SERVINGS

LEEK & BACON BREAKFAST SANDWICHES

Breakfast sandwiches are a nice break from the bagel-and-cream-cheese routine.

3 medium leeks (2 pounds)
½ pound sliced bacon
Salt and pepper
2 tablespoons butter, at room temperature
8 slices seven-grain sandwich bread
1 cup grated Cheddar cheese (4 ounces)

Trim the leeks of all but 1 inch of the dark green tops. Halve lengthwise and thinly slice crosswise. Place the pieces in a bowl of cold water and swish around to rinse. Scoop out and repeat the rinsing if sand is still coming out of the leeks. Drain well.

In a large skillet, cook the bacon over medium-high heat until crisp. Drain on paper towels and pour off all but 1 tablespoon of fat from the skillet.

Add the leeks to the skillet and reduce the heat to medium-low. Cook, stirring often, until the leeks are softened but not browned, 10 to 12 minutes. Season with salt and pepper to taste.

Spread the butter over one side of each slice of bread. Place the bread, buttered-side down, on a work surface covered with waxed paper. Sprinkle the cheddar over 4 slices and top with equal amounts of the cooked leeks. Arrange the bacon over the leeks. Cover with the remaining slices of bread, buttered-side up, and press down gently to compress.

Toast in a toaster oven or under the broiler, watching carefully to avoid burning, until the bread is browned and the cheese is almost melted. Transfer to a cutting board and cut in half. Serve hot.

MAKES 4 SERVINGS

APPLE-MAPLE COFFEE CAKE

Try this with pears and golden raisins instead of apples and currants.

2 cups plus 3 tablespoons whole wheat pastry flour
1 teaspoon baking soda
½ teaspoon salt
¾ cup (1½ sticks) butter
¾ cup buttermilk
1 large egg

BREAKFAST BREADS, MUFFINS & ROLLS

Apple-Honey Oatmeal Muffins (page 575)
Banana Bread (page 574)
Banana-Nut Muffins (page 575)
Cherry-Walnut Whole Wheat Muffins (page 577)
Cranberry-Nut Bread (page 573)
Date-Nut Bread (page 572)
Honey & Nut Buns (page 569)
Maple Corn Muffins (page 576)
Pumpkin Bread (page 574)
Raisin Tea Bread (page 573)
Spiced Bran Muffins (page 576)
Zucchini-Raisin Muffins (page 574)

- ½ cup maple syrup
- 2 apples, peeled and sliced
- 2 tablespoons dried currants
- ½ cup coarsely chopped walnuts
- ½ cup maple sugar
- ½ teaspoon cinnamon
- ¼ teaspoon ground cloves
- ¼ teaspoon nutmeg

Preheat the oven to 375°F. Butter a 9 × 9-inch baking pan.

In a large bowl, whisk together the flour, baking soda, and salt. With your fingers or a pastry blender, cut in ½ cup of the butter until the mixture resembles coarse crumbs.

In a small bowl, combine the buttermilk, egg, and maple syrup. Pour into the flour mixture and beat just until smooth. Pour the batter into the baking pan. Arrange the apple slices on top. Sprinkle the currants and nuts evenly over the apples.

In a small saucepan, melt the remaining ¼ cup butter. In a small bowl, combine the maple sugar, cinnamon, cloves, and nutmeg. Sprinkle the sugar mixture over the fruit and nuts, and drizzle with the melted butter.

Bake for 25 minutes, or until a toothpick inserted in the center of the cake comes out clean. Let cool slightly before cutting and serving.

MAKES 12 SERVINGS

YOGURT COFFEE CAKE

Here is a moist and flavorful breakfast cake with the topping baked right into it!

TOPPING

- ¾ cup chopped nuts
- 2 tablespoons flour
- 2 tablespoons honey, warmed
- 2 teaspoons cinnamon

CAKE

- ½ cup (1 stick) butter
- ½ cup honey, warmed
- 2 large eggs
- 1⅓ cups white whole wheat flour*
- 1 teaspoon baking soda
- ½ teaspoon salt
- 1 cup plain low-fat yogurt
- 1 teaspoon vanilla extract

**milled from white wheat grains*

Preheat the oven to 350°F. Butter and flour a 9 × 9-inch baking pan.

To make the topping: In a small bowl, combine the nuts, flour, honey, and cinnamon.

To make the cake: With an electric mixer, cream the butter. Beat in the honey and eggs.

In a small bowl, whisk together the flour, baking soda, and salt. Beat portions into the butter mixture, alternating with the yogurt. Beat in the vanilla.

Pour half of the cake batter into the baking pan. Cover with half of the topping, then add the remaining batter, and top with the remaining topping. Bake for about 45 minutes, or until a toothpick inserted in the center comes out clean.

Let cool slightly and cut into squares. Serve warm or at room temperature.

MAKES 8 SERVINGS

APPLE UPSIDE-DOWN BREAKFAST CAKE

Most of the "shortening" used to give this breakfast cake a rich flavor is healthful monounsaturated fats from extra-light olive oil.

- ¼ cup apple juice
- 3 Granny Smith apples, peeled and thickly sliced
- 1¼ cups whole wheat flour
- ⅓ cup packed turbinado or light brown sugar
- 1 teaspoon baking powder
- ½ teaspoon baking soda
- 1 teaspoon ginger
- ½ teaspoon cinnamon
- ½ teaspoon salt
- 1 large egg
- 2 large egg whites
- ½ cup buttermilk
- 2 tablespoons extra-light olive oil

Preheat the oven to 350°F. Oil an 8-inch round baking pan.

In a large skillet, heat the apple juice over medium heat. Add the apple slices and cook, tossing occasionally, until the apples are crisp-tender, about 5 minutes. When cool enough to handle, lift the apples from any liquid remaining in the skillet and arrange in the bottom of the baking pan.

Meanwhile, in a medium bowl, stir together the flour, brown sugar, baking powder, baking soda, ginger, cinnamon, and salt.

In a separate bowl, stir together the whole egg, egg whites, buttermilk, and olive oil. Make a well in the center of the flour mixture. Pour the egg white mixture into the well and stir just until the dry ingredients are moistened.

Pour the batter over the apples and smooth the top. Bake for 30 minutes, or until a cake tester inserted in the center comes out clean. Cool in the pan on a rack for 10 minutes. Run a metal spatula around the edge of the cake to loosen it. Turn the cake out onto a serving plate.

MAKES 8 SERVINGS

VEGETARIAN BREAKFAST SAUSAGES

TVP, or texturized vegetable protein, can be bought in bulk in most health food stores.

- ¼ cup dried porcini mushrooms
- ⅔ cup boiling water

BAKED EGGS FOR BRUNCH

Baked eggs make good brunch dishes because they can be served in a buffet setting and do not have to be individually plated. Consider one of these:

Cremini Frittata with Prosciutto & Fontina (page 336)
Cremini Mushroom Quiche (page 340)
Greek-Style Strata (page 342)
Ham & Cheddar Baked Eggs (page 339)
Mexican Strata (page 341)
Pasta Frittata (page 336)
Potato & Greens Frittata (page 338)
Potato Tortilla (page 338)
Scallion Quiche (page 340)
Spinach & Feta Frittata (page 337)
Spinach & Goat Cheese Strata (page 342)
Tomato & White Bean Frittata (page 337)

6 teaspoons olive oil

1 small onion, finely chopped

2 cloves garlic, minced

¼ cup water

1 tablespoon cream of rice

1¼ cups TVP granules

½ cup diced apple

2 large egg whites

¾ teaspoon ground fennel

½ teaspoon salt

¼ teaspoon pepper

In a small heatproof bowl, combine the dried mushrooms and the boiling water, and let stand for 20 minutes, or until softened. Reserving the soaking liquid, scoop out the dried mushrooms and finely chop. Set aside. Strain the soaking liquid through a coffee filter or a paper towel–lined sieve. Set aside.

In a small skillet, heat 2 teaspoons of the oil over medium heat. Add the onion, garlic, and water, and cook, stirring frequently, until the onion is soft and golden, about 10 minutes.

In a small saucepan, combine the cream of rice and 3 tablespoons of the mushroom soaking liquid, and stir over very low heat until tender.

In a large bowl, combine the chopped mushrooms, ¼ cup of the remaining mushroom soaking liquid, the onion mixture, cream of rice mixture, TVP, apple, egg whites, fennel, salt, and pepper. Mix until well combined. Let stand until thoroughly moistened, about 5 minutes.

Shape the mixture into 8 patties. In a large skillet, heat the remaining 4 teaspoons oil over medium-low heat. Add the sausages and cook, turning, until browned and cooked through, about 3 minutes per side.

MAKES 8 SERVINGS

Sauces, Condiments, Salsas & Chutneys

Well-conceived sauces and condiments are those final touches that can elevate a dish from ordinary to memorable. A simple piece of broiled or grilled chicken takes on a whole new meaning when spiked with a spicy tomato salsa, slathered with a sweet-tart barbecue sauce, or drizzled with a decadent French butter sauce.

Sauce Glossary

Although the modern American kitchen doesn't often deal in the classic French sauces, it's not a bad idea for cooks to have a passing acquaintance with some fundamental sauces and techniques. Here's a quick guide:

Béchamel: This basic white sauce is made with a light (unbrowned) roux (see below) and milk.

Beurre manié: A *beurre manié* (kneaded butter) is a classic way to thicken and enrich a sauce all at once. Softened butter is blended into an equal amount of flour. Small pieces are pinched off and stirred into a hot sauce near the end of the cooking. About 2 tablespoons of *beurre manié* will thicken 1 cup of sauce.

Brown sauces: A brown sauce is made by cooking a roux until it turns dark golden to brown. The most common liquid used to make a brown sauce is a beef stock. Meat gravies are also considered a type of brown sauce (see "Gravy for Meat & Poultry," page 596).

Emulsion sauces: Emulsion sauces are made by beating a fat (oil or butter) into eggs or egg yolks so that the fat is held in suspension, or "emulsified." Classic examples of emulsion sauces are Béarnaise, Hollandaise, and mayonnaise.

Glace de viande: A meat glaze, or *glace de viande*, is a meat stock that has been strained and reduced until it is very thick and syrupy. A *glace de volaille* is the same idea, but made from poultry stock. This highly concentrated essence can be used the way you would use a bouillon cube. Just ½ teaspoon can enrich and flavor sauces (as well as soups or stews).

Reduction sauces: Natural cooking juices can be reduced to a sauce consistency by slowly simmering to evaporate the water and concentrate flavors. No thickeners are needed. Sauces thickened by reduction are best seasoned just before being served.

Roux: This flour and butter (or oil) combination, usually of equal parts, is used to thicken sauces. About 1 tablespoon each of flour and butter added to 2 cups of liquid will produce a thin sauce. For a thicker sauce you may double or triple the amount of flour and butter. A roux is cooked to various stages, from white to golden to brown, depending on the type of sauce desired.

Velouté: This classic is a white sauce made from a light roux (not browned) to which poultry, fish, or veal stock is added.

White sauces: A sauce made from a roux cooked just to blend (not browned), to which

TIPS FOR SUCCESSFUL SAUCES

- In general, the amount of sauce to make for a dish should equal about one-third the amount of solid food it dresses. Allow a little more than this for light sauces, and a little less for rich sauces.
- Be especially careful not to boil sauces made with egg yolk or yogurt, or they will curdle.
- Do not overheat a cornstarch-thickened sauce or it may thin out.
- Do not cover a hot sauce, or the steam created may cause thinning out and separation.

---

stock, milk, or cream is added. Classic white sauces include béchamel and velouté.

Gravy for Meat & Poultry

Although most people don't think of gravy as a sauce, of course that's exactly what it is. The pan juices that result from sautéing, roasting, or baking meat or poultry form the foundation. Here's how to make a simple gravy:

Transfer the meat/poultry to a platter. Pour the pan juices into a gravy separator and let sit. Discard the grease and pour the juices into a small saucepan.

Place the original meat cooking pan over a low heat, add some stock, water, or wine to the pan, and stir to scrape up the caramelized meat juices that are stuck to the bottom and sides of the pan. Add this mixture to the juices in the saucepan.

Thicken the gravy in one of three ways:

1. Reduction: Simply cook the degreased pan juices until they are concentrated and flavorful. Taste and season after you've reduced the juices. On French restaurant menus this is often described as au jus (with juice).

2. Flour-thickened: In a small cup, stir some of the degreased pan juices into flour, then add the flour mixture back to the saucepan. Simmer until thickened. For a medium-weight gravy, use about 1 tablespoon flour for every 3⁄4 cup pan juices.

3. Roux-thickened: In the meat-cooking pan, make a roux by cooking an equal amount of butter and flour together and then slowly stirring in the degreased pan juices. Use 1 tablespoon each butter and flour for every 3⁄4 cup pan juices.

You can thin the gravy with water or stock, or you can thin and enrich by adding milk. Let the gravy simmer for about 5 minutes. Taste and adjust the seasoning after the gravy is done.

Marinades

A marinade is a seasoned liquid, cooked or uncooked, in which meat, poultry, or vegetables are steeped. It is sometimes added to a finished sauce for richer flavor. A marinade, aromatic and tenderizing, impregnates the soaking food with its blend of flavors. Vinegar, lemon juice, or wine is usually part of the marinade, along with oil, herbs, garlic, or onion. The acid ingredient helps to tenderize meat and poultry, and to cut down on the cooking time. Marinated vegetables need not be cooked at all.

Size and texture determine how long an ingredient should be marinated. Raw meat and poultry left to marinate longer than 1 hour should be refrigerated. Each pound of food usually requires about ½ to ¾ cup of marinade.

Condiments

Any spice, herb, or aromatic seed is by definition a condiment. But more commonly a condiment refers to any pungent, prepared mixture used in small amounts. A condiment may be anything from simple soy sauce to fancy relishes and pickles. The idea of serving condiments as an accompaniment to foods is usually to accent the taste of the food it dresses—lamb and mint jelly, turkey and cranberry relish, boiled beef and horseradish, for example. Mustard, ketchup, and mayonnaise are among the most commonly used condiments in American cuisine, and can all be made at home.

Most condiments keep well if stored in the refrigerator in tightly sealed jars. Vinegar as an ingredient helps to preserve some condiments, but others are highly perishable, so be sure to refrigerate these and use them quickly. Some condiments do not spoil easily but their flavor may change or deteriorate with time. For example, horseradish turns brown and loses its zip if kept for a long period. It is best to use homemade condiments—which have no preservatives—within a month of making them.

Salsas & Chutneys

The word salsa simply means sauce, and by this definition encompasses a huge range of possibilities. However, the type of salsa that we think of first when we see the word is what Hispanic cooks would call a *salsa cruda*, or raw sauce. The most popular salsas are usually spicy and often tomato-based, but they can be made with any number of fruits, vegetables, and spices. The nice thing about salsas, especially for anyone watching fat intake, is that they have no saturated fat at all, and little to no fat of any kind.

Chutneys, which are spiced mixtures of cut up fruits and vegetables, come in uncooked and cooked forms, though Americans are most familiar with cooked chutneys, such as Major Grey's mango chutney. They are extremely easy to make and, like salsas, have a very low fat profile.

BÉCHAMEL

This is the classic cream sauce used to top vegetables or as a creamy binder in casseroles. It is also the basis for other popular sauces. This yields a medium white sauce. For a thin sauce, use only 1 tablespoon each of butter and flour. For a thick sauce, use 3 tablespoons each of butter and flour.

2 tablespoons butter

2 tablespoons white whole wheat flour*

1½ cups milk

1 teaspoon grated onion (optional)

¼ teaspoon white pepper

⅛ teaspoon nutmeg

Salt

**milled from white wheat grains*

In a heavy-bottomed saucepan, melt the butter over low heat Add the flour and cook, stirring constantly, for 5 minutes.

Whisking constantly, gradually add the milk and cook until thickened, about 10 minutes. Stir in the onion (if using), white pepper, nutmeg, and salt to taste.

MAKES 1¼ CUPS

HOLLANDAISE SAUCE

Hollandaise sauce can be somewhat ticklish to make. If the sauce begins to curdle, transfer it to a blender, add a small amount of water, and blend well. And if you're nervous about eggs that are not completely cooked, seek out pasteurized eggs for this recipe.

3 large egg yolks

2 teaspoons water

½ cup (1 stick) butter, at room temperature

2 tablespoons lemon juice

¼ teaspoon cayenne pepper

Salt

In the top of a double boiler over 2 inches of hot but not boiling water, beat the egg yolks and water together with a wire whisk until slightly thickened. Cut the butter into 3 or 4 pieces and add one piece at a time, beating constantly after each addition, until the sauce is blended, smooth, and thickened. Add the lemon juice, cayenne, and salt to taste. Serve warm.

MAKES ¾ CUP

SAUCE MALTAISE: Add 1 tablespoon orange juice and 1 teaspoon grated orange zest.

SAUCE BÉARNAISE

A flavorful herb sauce especially good served over broiled meat or fish. If you're nervous about eggs that are not completely cooked, seek out pasteurized eggs for this recipe.

6 tablespoons white wine vinegar

2 tablespoons water

2 tablespoons minced scallions

1 tablespoon minced parsley

2 teaspoons minced fresh tarragon or ½ teaspoon dried

¾ cup (1½ sticks) butter

4 large egg yolks

1 tablespoon lemon juice

¼ teaspoon cayenne pepper

Salt

In a small, heavy-bottomed saucepan, combine the vinegar, water, scallions, parsley, and tarragon. Cook slowly until it is almost a glaze. Set aside.

In a small saucepan, melt the butter and keep it hot.

In a blender, combine the egg yolks, lemon juice, and cayenne. With the machine running, slowly add the hot butter and blend until thickened. Add the herb mixture and beat well. Season with salt to taste. Serve warm.

MAKES 1 CUP

HOMEMADE MAYONNAISE

A homemade mayonnaise bears very little resemblance to bottled mayonnaise. If you've never had it, you're in for a treat. Before making this recipe, read "Playing It Safe with Mayonnaise" (below).

- **2 egg yolks, at room temperature, lightly beaten**
- **2 tablespoons lemon juice or vinegar, at room temperature**
- **½ teaspoon dry mustard**
- **½ teaspoon sugar**
- **½ teaspoon salt**
- **1⅓ cups vegetable oil, at room temperature**
- **2 teaspoons boiling water**

Warm a glass or stainless steel bowl and a wire whisk in hot water. Dry thoroughly.

Place the egg yolks in the bowl and add 1 tablespoon of the lemon juice, the mustard, sugar, and salt. Beat well. Continue beating constantly as you add the oil, one drop at a time. Be sure the yolks are absorbing the oil. This may require that you stop adding the oil and just beat the yolks for a few seconds. After about ⅓ cup oil has been incorporated into the yolks, add the remaining oil by the tablespoon. Beat well after each addition.

When the mayonnaise is thick and stiff, beat in the remaining 1 tablespoon lemon juice to thin. Blend in the boiling water (this prevents the mayonnaise from separating).

Store in a covered glass jar in the refrigerator.

MAKES 1¼ CUPS

BLENDER OR FOOD PROCESSOR MAYONNAISE: Warm a blender or food processor container in hot water, then dry thoroughly. If using a food processor, use the plastic blade if you have one. Place the egg yolks, all the lemon juice, the mustard, sugar, and salt in the container. Process at medium speed for about 1 minute.

With the machine running, add the oil a few drops at a time, continuing to process until ⅓ cup oil has been incorporated into the yolks. At this point the remaining oil may be added by the tablespoon, until all the oil has been used.

To ensure against mayonnaise separating, blend in the boiling water.

PLAYING IT SAFE WITH MAYONNAISE

The risk of an egg you use carrying *Salmonella* bacteria is low, about 1 in 20,000 eggs. Nonetheless, it's best to minimize your chances of contracting foodborne illness when you're making a classic recipe like mayonnaise that calls for raw eggs. First and foremost, eggs should be kept well refrigerated. Then if you'd rather not take your changes even though the risk is low, you can use pasteurized eggs. A third option is to follow the National Egg Board guidelines for mayonnaise:

In a small saucepan, whisk together the egg yolks and seasonings and cook over very low heat, stirring constantly, until the mixture bubbles in 1 or 2 places. Remove from the heat and let cool 4 minutes, then transfer to a blender. With the motor running, slowly add the oil and blend until the mayonnaise is thick and smooth. Refrigerate.

AIOLI

Serve this delicious garlic mayonnaise over fish or boiled beef, or use as a dipping sauce for artichokes or other chilled vegetables. Since an aioli is made with raw eggs, you should read "Playing It Safe with Mayonnaise" (page 599) before making this.

3 large cloves garlic, peeled

6 tablespoons lemon juice

2 large eggs

½ teaspoon white pepper

1½ cups olive oil

In a blender, process the garlic and lemon juice. Add the eggs and white pepper, and process again at high speed, stopping frequently to scrape down the sides of the container.

With the machine running, add the oil, a few drops at a time at first, then gradually in a steady stream.

When the mixture has thickened, spoon into a bowl and refrigerate. Stir before serving.

MAKES 2 CUPS

GREEN MAYONNAISE

Serve this delicious herb-y mayonnaise over mixed green salads. It is made with raw eggs, so read "Playing It Safe with Mayonnaise" (page 599) before making it.

1 large egg

2 tablespoons lemon juice

1 cup vegetable oil

3 tablespoons minced parsley or basil

2 tablespoons snipped chives

1 tablespoon minced fresh marjoram, tarragon, thyme, savory, or a mixture

1 clove garlic, minced

Salt and pepper

In a blender, combine the egg and lemon juice. With the machine running, add the oil in a thin, steady stream until a mayonnaise forms and all the oil is incorporated. Add the parsley, chives, fresh herb(s), and garlic. Scrape down the mayonnaise with a rubber spatula, then process at high speed until the herbs are pureed and the mayonnaise turns light green. Store in the refrigerator.

MAKES 1½ CUPS

VEGAN MAYO

Of course you can buy soy mayonnaise, but making it yourself is rewarding, and the flavors are fresher.

10 ounces soft silken tofu, drained (1 cup)

3 tablespoons lemon juice

2 teaspoons Dijon mustard

½ cup vegetable oil

Salt and pepper

In a blender or food processor, combine the tofu, 1 tablespoon of the lemon juice, and the mustard, and process, stopping frequently to scrape down the sides of the container.

With the machine running, add the oil a few drops at a time. Then gradually add about 2 tablespoons of the oil in a steady stream. Slowly add 1 tablespoon of the lemon juice. Dribble in half of the remaining oil and then the remaining 1 tablespoon lemon juice. Slowly add the rest of the oil. Taste and season with salt and pepper. Store in the refrigerator.

MAKES 1½ CUPS

Coconut Cupcakes • *page* 512

Lemon Angel Food Cake ● *page* 502

Rhubarb Crisp • *page 476*

Perfect Plum Pie (far left) • *page 536*
Zucchini Custard Pie (rear) • *page 540*
Pumpkin Chiffon Pie (far right) • *page 542*

Cherry-Pecan Brownies • *page 515*

Green Tea Biscotti (left) ● *page 516*
Fruit-Filled Chocolate Chunks (right) ● *page 619*

Fresh Strawberry Preserves (left) • *page 667*
Sweet Spiced Pumpkin Butter (right) • *page 667*

TOMATO-BASIL BUTTER

Serve with bread to go with a meal, or use to make flavored toasts for an appetizer.

- **1/3 cup butter, at room temperature**
- **1 tablespoon tomato paste**
- **1 teaspoon dried basil**

In a small bowl, combine all the ingredients and beat with a wooden spoon until smooth and creamy. Store in the refrigerator.

MAKES 3/4 CUP

HERBED BUTTER

Slice pieces of this butter, as needed, and place on top of broiled steak, poultry, fish, or steamed vegetables just before serving.

- **1/4 cup (1/2 stick) butter, at room temperature**
- **2 teaspoons chopped parsley**
- **1 teaspoon minced fresh thyme or tarragon**
- **1/2 teaspoon lemon juice**
- **Pinch of cayenne pepper**
- **Pinch of salt**

In a small bowl, blend the butter, parsley, thyme, lemon juice, cayenne, and salt with a fork. Transfer to a sheet of waxed paper and shape into a log. Roll up and refrigerate until firm.

MAKES 1/4 CUP

SCALLION BUTTER

Lemon zest and tarragon add a bright flavor to scallion butter. Use the butter on top of fish, steak, chicken, or vegetables.

- **1/2 cup (1 stick) butter, at room temperature**
- **1 teaspoon grated lemon zest**
- **1/2 teaspoon tarragon**
- **2 scallions, halved lengthwise and thinly sliced**

In a small bowl, blend the butter with the lemon zest and tarragon, stirring until smooth. Stir in the scallions.

Transfer the mixture to a sheet of waxed paper and shape into a log. Roll up and refrigerate until firm.

MAKES 1/2 CUP

PISTOU

Pistou, a basil-garlic sauce from France, is a close relative of Italian pesto, though it has no pine nuts and adds fresh tomato. You can serve it as a pasta sauce, a coating for baked chicken or fish, or as a topping for Soupe au Pistou (page 180).

- **4 large cloves garlic**
- **1/3 cup packed fresh basil leaves**
- **1 medium tomato, peeled, seeded, and chopped**
- **1 cup grated Parmesan cheese**
- **Pinch of cayenne pepper**
- **3/4 cup olive oil**

In a blender or food processor, mince the garlic. Add the basil, tomato, 1/2 cup of the Parmesan, and the cayenne, and puree.

With the machine running, slowly add the oil. Add the remaining 1/2 cup Parmesan and blend until a coarse sauce is formed.

Store in the refrigerator but serve at room temperature.

MAKES 2 1/2 CUPS

CRANBERRY KETCHUP

Serve as topping for hot or cold poultry.

- **1 pound fresh or frozen cranberries**
- **1/2 cup cider vinegar**

½ cup water
¾ cup sugar
2 tablespoons molasses
½ teaspoon cinnamon
½ teaspoon ground cloves
½ teaspoon ginger
Pinch of pepper

In a medium saucepan, combine the cranberries, vinegar, and water. Bring to a boil over medium heat and cook for about 2 minutes. Off the heat, stir in the sugar. Allow to cool slightly. Pour into a food processor or blender and process until smooth.

Add the molasses, cinnamon, cloves, ginger, and pepper and process until the mixture is very smooth.

Pour the puree back into the pot and simmer gently for 5 minutes, stirring once or twice. Let cool. Store in the refrigerator.

MAKES 1 QUART

TARTAR SAUCE

A typical tartar sauce is made with prepared pickle relish. This is a fresher homemade version.

½ cup finely chopped seeded cucumber
¼ cup finely minced onion
2 tablespoons minced green bell pepper
3 tablespoons vinegar
2 tablespoons honey
¼ teaspoon salt
⅛ teaspoon celery seeds
Pinch of allspice
Pinch of turmeric
¾ cup mayonnaise

In a small saucepan, combine the cucumber, onion, bell pepper, vinegar, honey, salt, celery seeds, allspice, and turmeric. Cook until the vegetables are soft and dark yellow from the turmeric, and most of the liquid has evaporated, about 10 minutes . Let cool.

In a small bowl, blend the cooled vegetables with the mayonnaise and let sit for at least 1 hour to meld the flavors. Store in the refrigerator.

MAKES 1 CUP

CILANTRO-LIME TARTAR SAUCE

Green hot pepper sauce is made with fresh jalapeño peppers and has less of a vinegary flavor than red pepper sauce.

½ cup mayonnaise
½ cup chopped cilantro
2 tablespoons lime juice
2 tablespoons chopped sweet onion
2 tablespoons dill pickle relish
1 tablespoon green hot pepper sauce

In a small bowl, combine the mayonnaise, cilantro, lime juice, onion, relish, and hot pepper sauce. Store in the refrigerator.

MAKES 1 CUP

CREAMY SEAFOOD COCKTAIL SAUCE

This makes a great dipping sauce for seafood, but is also an excellent sandwich spread.

⅓ cup mayonnaise
2 tablespoons tarragon vinegar
1 tablespoon drained horseradish
2 teaspoons tomato paste
1 teaspoon Worcestershire sauce
Pinch of cayenne pepper

Pinch of ground allspice

3/4 cup Greek yogurt

In a small bowl, whisk together the mayonnaise, vinegar, horseradish, tomato paste, Worcestershire, cayenne, and allspice.

In a medium bowl, whisk the yogurt to lighten it. Whisk in the mayonnaise mixture and chill well.

MAKES 1 1/4 CUPS

TARRAGON MUSTARD

You can buy tarragon-flavored mustard, but why should you, when you can so easily make it yourself?

1/4 cup dry mustard

1/4 cup hot water

3 tablespoons white wine vinegar

1 small clove garlic, halved

1/4 teaspoon tarragon

1/4 teaspoon sugar

1/8 teaspoon salt

In a small bowl, combine the mustard, water, and 1 tablespoon of the vinegar and let soak for at least 2 hours.

Meanwhile, in a separate bowl, combine the remaining 2 tablespoons vinegar, the garlic, and the tarragon, and let stand for 1 hour. Strain the vinegar (discarding the solids).

Scrape the mustard into the top of a double boiler and stir in the tarragon vinegar, sugar, and salt. Cook over simmering water until thickened, about 15 minutes. (Mustard will thicken a bit more when chilled.)

Remove the mustard from the heat and pour into a jar. Let cool, uncovered. Store in the refrigerator.

MAKES 1/2 CUP

CHINESE-STYLE HOT MUSTARD

This is a real sinus-clearing mustard.

1/4 cup dry mustard

2 teaspoons distilled white vinegar

1/4 cup boiling water

MAYO VARIATIONS

Any of these mayos would perk up a sandwich or a salad. Once made, they'll keep in the fridge for about a week. Start with 1/4 cup commercial mayonnaise and dress it up with one of these combinations:

- 2 tablespoons finely chopped mango chutney, 2 teaspoons Dijon mustard, and 1/4 teaspoon pepper
- 1 tablespoon tomato paste and 1 1/2 teaspoons chipotle or ancho chili powder
- 3 tablespoons finely chopped cilantro, 2 teaspoons lime juice, and 1 teaspoon coriander
- 1 tablespoon snipped chives and 1 tablespoon snipped dill
- 2 mashed anchovy fillets, 1 tablespoon lemon juice, and 1 tablespoon grated Parmesan cheese

In a small heatproof bowl, blend the mustard and vinegar to a paste. Gradually stir in the boiling water. Let stand at room temperature for at least 15 minutes before using. Store in the refrigerator.

MAKES ⅓ CUP

BOURBON MUSTARD SAUCE

Serve this tangy, spicy sauce over bratwurst and burgers for a delicious change. It's also good on grilled steaks and pork kebabs.

- 1¼ cups light molasses
- 1 cup Dijon mustard
- ¼ cup bourbon
- 1 tablespoon Worcestershire sauce
- 2 tablespoons dry mustard
- 2 tablespoons mustard seeds
- ½ teaspoon coarse salt
- ¼ teaspoon ground allspice

In a medium saucepan, whisk together the molasses, Dijon mustard, bourbon, Worcestershire, dry mustard, mustard seeds, salt, and allspice. Bring to a simmer and cook, stirring occasionally, until the sauce begins to thicken, 20 to 30 minutes. Cool to room temperature before serving; it will thicken as it cools. Store in the refrigerator.

MAKES 2 CUPS

STEAK SAUCE

Perfect on steaks, a burger (beef or vegetarian), and even grilled cheese, this sauce rivals many store-bought versions.

- ⅓ cup thinly sliced onion
- 1 clove garlic, slivered
- 2 strips (3 x ½ inch) orange zest
- ⅓ cup orange juice
- ½ cup water
- ½ cup balsamic vinegar
- ⅓ cup raisins or dried currants
- ¼ cup chopped canned tomatoes
- 2 tablespoons molasses
- 1 tablespoon Dijon mustard
- 4 teaspoons soy sauce
- ⅛ teaspoon allspice
- ⅛ teaspoon pepper

In a medium saucepan, combine the onion, garlic, orange zest, orange juice, water, vinegar, raisins, tomatoes, molasses, mustard, soy sauce, allspice, and pepper. Bring to a boil, reduce to a simmer, and cook, stirring frequently, for 30 minutes.

Transfer to a food processor and puree until smooth. Cool to room temperature. Store in the refrigerator.

MAKES 1½ CUPS

HEALTHY BARBECUE SAUCE

This barbecue sauce packs a beta-carotene wallop and relies solely on fruit for its sweetness.

- 1 mango, diced (1 cup)
- ¾ cup red bell pepper
- 1 apple, coarsely chopped
- ½ cup sliced onion
- ¼ cup thinly sliced fresh ginger
- 3 cloves garlic, smashed and peeled
- 1 cup carrot juice
- 1 can (14.5 ounces) whole tomatoes in juice
- 1 cup water
- ¼ cup cider vinegar
- ¾ teaspoon salt

In a medium saucepan, combine the mango, bell pepper, apple, onion, ginger, garlic, carrot juice, tomatoes and juice, water, vinegar, and salt. Bring to a boil and reduce to a simmer. Cover and cook until thebell peppers, apple and onion are soft, about 25 minutes.

Transfer to a food processor and puree until smooth.

MAKES 1 QUART

APPLE-WASABI BARBECUE SAUCE

Wasabi (a fiery Japanese horseradish) is available as a paste, in tubes, at many supermarkets. If you can't find it, substitute 2 tablespoons of drained horseradish. This spicy sauce goes especially well with pork.

- 1 can (12 ounces) frozen apple juice concentrate (no need to thaw)
- 1 teaspoon grated lemon zest
- ½ teaspoon rosemary, crumbled
- ½ teaspoon salt
- 2 tablespoons wasabi paste

In a medium saucepan, combine the apple juice concentrate, lemon zest, rosemary, and salt. Bring to a boil and cook for 15 minutes, or until reduced to 1 cup. Remove from the heat and stir in the wasabi paste.

MAKES 1 CUP

SPICY MANGO BBQ SAUCE

Use this BBQ sauce over pork or chicken.

- 1 cup mango chutney, minced if the pieces are large
- 1 cup ketchup
- ¾ cup honey
- ½ cup apple juice or apple cider
- ½ cup dark rum
- ¼ cup apple cider vinegar
- 3-inch fresh ginger, peeled and grated
- 5 cloves garlic, minced
- 3 tablespoons tomato paste
- 2 tablespoons Worcestershire sauce

HOMEMADE HORSERADISH

Making your own horseradish is incredibly simple. Most people don't do it because they're not aware that the condiment they buy in a bottle actually comes from a fresh vegetable sold in many supermarkets. The horseradish root looks like a very large, forked parsnip. It can weigh well over a pound. Trim and peel before shredding.

In a food processor with the fine shredding blade, shred the horseradish. With the machine running, slowly add distilled white vinegar until you get a wet, coarse, paste. Refrigerate.

You will get between 2 and 4 cups of horseradish, depending on the size of the root. Stored in the refrigerator, it will keep indefinitely.

- **2 tablespoons Dijon mustard**
- **1 tablespoon Asian chili-garlic sauce**
- **1 tablespoon soy sauce**
- **¼ teaspoon pepper**

In a large saucepan, whisk together all the ingredients. Bring to a boil over medium heat, stirring constantly. Reduce the heat to low and simmer, stirring occasionally, until the sauce is thickened and slightly reduced, about 30 minutes.

MAKES 3 CUPS

BALSAMIC GLAZE

Brush this sweet-tart glaze on poultry as it's broiling or baking. Or use it as a dipping sauce for chicken or pork.

- **1½ cups balsamic vinegar**
- **2 tablespoons brown sugar**
- **2½ teaspoons fresh rosemary leaves or 1 teaspoon dried**
- **8 peppercorns**

In a medium saucepan, combine the vinegar, brown sugar, rosemary, and peppercorns. Bring to a boil over high heat. Reduce to medium and cook until thick enough to coat the back of a spoon and reduced to ½ cup, 8 to 10 minutes.

Cool to room temperature, strain, and transfer to a jar with a tight-fitting lid. Store at room temperature for several months.

MAKES ½ CUP

MARINADE FOR VEGETABLES

Pour over raw or lightly steamed vegetables, cover, and marinate in the refrigerator for at least 2 hours, stirring occasionally.

- **½ cup vegetable oil**
- **½ cup cider vinegar**
- **¼ cup minced parsley**
- **2 cloves garlic, minced**
- **1 tablespoon Dijon mustard**
- **1 teaspoon sugar**
- **½ teaspoon oregano**
- **½ teaspoon basil**
- **½ teaspoon tarragon**
- **⅛ teaspoon cayenne pepper**

In a screw-top jar, combine all the ingredients. Cover and shake well.

MAKES 1¼ CUPS

MAPLE-MISO MARINADE

To marinate 2 pounds fish fillets or skinless boneless chicken breasts or thighs, spoon half of the mixture into a shallow pan. Add the fish or chicken and spoon the remaining marinade over (it should generously cover). Cover and marinate in the refrigerator overnight before grilling or broiling. Miso (fermented soybean paste) comes in a number of strengths. Shiro miso is the lightest in flavor as well as in color.

- **1 tablespoon wasabi powder**
- **3 tablespoons water**
- **⅓ cup shiro miso**
- **3 tablespoons maple sugar**
- **1 teaspoon grated lemon zest**
- **3 tablespoons lemon juice**

In a small bowl, moisten the wasabi powder with the water to make a paste.

In a small saucepan set over a larger saucepan of boiling water, stir together the wasabi paste, miso, maple sugar, lemon zest, and lemon juice.

Cook, stirring until smooth, about 10 minutes. Cool to room temperature.

MAKES GENEROUS ½ CUP

ORANGE-CHIPOTLE MARINADE

The deep flavors of this marinade are well suited to strongly flavored meats such as flank steak, duck, and lamb.

- 1 teaspoon grated orange zest
- ⅓ cup fresh orange juice
- 2 tablespoons ketchup
- 3 chipotle peppers in adobo, minced, plus 1 teaspoon adobo sauce
- 1 tablespoon olive oil
- ½ teaspoon allspice
- ½ teaspoon salt

In a medium bowl, stir together all the ingredients. Refridgerate until ready to use.

MAKES ½ CUP

CHIMICHURRI SAUCE

Chimichurri is Argentina's condiment of choice and their answer to ketchup. It is great on grilled chicken, pork, or steak, and also terrific on sandwiches. For the smoothest sauce, use a blender rather than a food processor.

- 2 cloves garlic
- 1 cup parsley leaves
- 1 cup cilantro leaves and tender stalks
- ⅓ cup olive oil
- 2 tablespoons water
- 1 tablespoon lime juice
- ½ teaspoon salt
- ½ teaspoon ground coriander
- ¼ teaspoon ground cumin
- ⅛ teaspoon cayenne pepper

In a small pot of boiling water, cook the garlic for 1 minute (this will take out a little of the bite, but not the flavor). Drain.

In a food processor or blender, combine the blanched garlic, parsley, cilantro, oil, water, lime juice, salt, coriander, cumin, and cayenne, and puree until smooth.

MAKES ¾ CUP

ROASTED TOMATILLO SALSA

Look for tomatillos in the produce department of specialty supermarkets and many larger markets. Before using, remove the outer, papery husk and rinse. This tangy sauce works with vegetables, meat, or fish and as a dip for chips.

- 1¼ pounds fresh tomatillos, husked and rinsed
- ½ small white onion
- 1 fresh jalapeño pepper, halved lengthwise and seeded
- 2 cloves garlic, peeled
- 1 tablespoon vegetable oil
- ½ cup packed coarsely chopped cilantro
- ½ teaspoon salt

Preheat the oven to 400°F.

In a small roasting pan, toss the tomatillos, onion, jalapeño, and garlic with the oil. Roast for 25 minutes, tossing once or twice, until the tomatillos are soft and lightly browned.

Transfer the vegetables and any pan juices to a blender. Add the cilantro and salt, and puree. Serve warm or chilled.

MAKES 2 CUPS

TOMATO & LIME SALSA

This makes enough for a crowd, though salsa can disappear awfully quickly. If you're not partial to the taste of raw garlic, blanch the garlic cloves in boiling water for 1 minute before mincing.

- 2½ pounds tomatoes, seeded and chopped
- ½ cup lime juice (about 4 limes)
- 6 tablespoons chopped scallions
- ½ small red onion, minced
- 2 tablespoons minced cilantro
- 2 small fresh jalapeño peppers, minced
- 2 small cloves garlic, minced
- Salt and pepper

In a medium bowl, combine the tomatoes, lime juice, scallions, onion, cilantro, jalapeños, and garlic. Season to taste with salt and pepper.

MAKES 6 CUPS

FRESH TOMATO-CHIPOTLE SALSA

Serve this fresh salsa with toasted slices of whole-grain Italian bread brushed with a little olive oil and rubbed with cut garlic.

- 3 dried chipotle peppers
- Boiling water
- 1 large yellow bell pepper, cut lengthwise into flat panels
- 3 large beefsteak tomatoes
- ⅓ cup golden raisins
- 2 tablespoons no-salt-added tomato paste
- ½ teaspoon salt
- 4 scallions, thinly sliced
- ½ cup chopped fresh basil

In a small heatproof bowl, cover the chipotles with boiling water. Let stand until softened, about 15 minutes. Drain, then seed and coarsely chop.

Meanwhile, preheat the broiler. Broil the bell pepper pieces skin-side up 6 inches from the heat for 5 minutes. Place the tomatoes, stem-side down, on the broiler rack and broil for about 5 minutes, or until both peppers and tomatoes are charred.

When cool enough to handle, peel the tomatoes, then halve and core them. Gently squeeze out the seeds and juice (and discard). Transfer the tomato pulp to a food processor.

Peel the bell pepper pieces and add to the food processor.

Add the chipotles, raisins, tomato paste, and salt, and process until well combined and slightly chunky. Transfer the salsa to a bowl and stir in the scallions and basil.

MAKES 3½ CUPS

ROASTED VEGETABLE SALSA

Mushrooms are an unexpected ingredient in this earthy salsa. Serve it alongside broiled fish or as an appetizer with thin whole-grain crackers.

- 1 package (10 ounces) frozen corn kernels, thawed
- 1 red bell pepper, diced
- 4 ounces mushrooms, diced
- 1 tablespoon extra-light olive oil
- ¼ teaspoon salt
- ¼ teaspoon black pepper
- ¼ cup chopped cilantro
- 1 small fresh jalapeño pepper, seeded and minced
- ¼ teaspoon grated lime zest
- 2 teaspoons lime juice
- 1 teaspoon white wine vinegar

Preheat the oven to 500°F.

In a medium bowl, toss the corn, bell pepper, and mushrooms with the oil, salt, and black pepper. Spread the vegetable mixture on a nonstick baking sheet. Roast on the top rack of the oven, stirring occasionally, for 15 minutes, or until the bell pepper is tender and the corn has taken on some color.

Transfer the vegetable mixture to a bowl and let cool.

Stir the cilantro, jalapeño, lime zest, lime juice, and vinegar into the roasted vegetables.

MAKES 3 CUPS

AUTUMN PEAR SALSA

This salsa pairs well with grilled pork.

1 large pink grapefruit

2½ pears, peeled and diced

½ cup dried cherries

2 tablespoons minced red onion

1 clove garlic, minced

¼ fresh jalapeño pepper, minced

½ teaspoon grated lime zest

2 tablespoons lime juice

Peel the grapefruit, using a paring knife to cut off all the white pith and membrane. With the paring knife, cut down either side of the membranes separating the segments, and release the sections into a large bowl. Cut the sections into ½-inch chunks.

Add the pears, cherries, onion, garlic, jalapeño, lime zest, and lime juice. Refrigerate for at least 2 hours.

MAKES 4½ CUPS

MANGO-JICAMA SALSA

Jicama is a tuber with a mild, crisp flesh. If you can't find it, use 2 crisp apples (peeled and diced) in its place.

3 large red bell peppers, diced

2 mangoes, diced

1 jicama, peeled and diced

¼ red onion, diced

½ cup chopped cilantro

Juice of 1 lime

1 teaspoon minced fresh ginger

1 teaspoon canola oil

Salt

In a large bowl, combine the bell peppers, mangoes, jicama, onion, cilantro, lime juice, ginger, and oil. Season to taste with salt.

MAKES 6 CUPS

NECTARINE SALSA

Try this salsa with peaches instead of nectarines, but you you'll need to peel them first. Drop them in boiling water for 30 seconds to 1 minute (the longer time for less-ripe peaches), refresh under cold water to stop the cooking, then peel and pit.

4 large nectarines, chopped

1 green bell pepper, diced

2 scallions, chopped

¼ cup minced cilantro

2 cloves garlic, minced

1½ tablespoons lime juice

½ teaspoon red pepper flakes

Salt

In a medium bowl, combine the nectarines, bell pepper, scallions, cilantro, garlic, lime juice, and red pepper flakes. Cover and refrigerate for at least 2 hours. Season to taste with salt.

MAKES 4 CUPS

APRICOT CHUTNEY

Serve this spiced dried apricot chutney with chicken, curry dishes, or any cold meats.

2 cups dried apricots

Boiling water

3 tablespoons honey

1½ tablespoons vinegar

1 teaspoon minced fresh ginger or ½ teaspoon ground ginger

½ teaspoon ground coriander

Pinch of cayenne pepper

½ cup raw cashews, coarsely chopped

½ cup raisins

In a medium, heatproof bowl, combine the apricots and enough boiling water to cover. Let sit until soft, about 30 minutes. Drain and chop the apricots. Return to the bowl.

Add the honey, vinegar, ginger, coriander, and cayenne, and mix well. Add the cashews and raisins and mix well again. Store in the refrigerator.

MAKES 3 CUPS

STONE-FRUIT CHUTNEY

You can make this with 1 pound of any pitted and chopped stone fruit. If your fruit is extremely juicy and soft, reduce the cooking time by 5 to 10 minutes.

2 tablespoons vegetable oil

½ teaspoon coriander seeds

¼ teaspoon cumin seeds

1 cinnamon stick

2 tablespoons chopped fresh ginger

½ fresh jalapeño pepper, seeded and coarsely chopped

3 cloves garlic, chopped

2 teaspoons curry powder

2 firm-ripe plums (8 ounces), coarsely chopped

2 firm-ripe peaches (8 ounces), coarsely chopped

⅓ cup lime juice (about 3 limes)

⅓ cup raisins

¼ cup sugar

In a medium saucepan, heat the oil over medium-high heat. Add the coriander, cumin, and cinnamon, and cook, stirring constantly, until the seeds are fragrant and the cinnamon stick unfurls, about 30 seconds.

Add the ginger, jalapeño, garlic, and curry powder, and cook, stirring, until lightly browned and fragrant, about 4 minutes.

Add the plums, peaches, lime juice, raisins, and sugar, and bring to a boil. Reduce the heat to medium-low and simmer, stirring occasionally, until thick and chunky, about 20 minutes. Store in the refrigerator for up to 2 weeks.

MAKES 2 CUPS

CRANBERRY-CHERRY CHUTNEY

This autumnal relish would be good with any strongly flavored meat or poultry and could even stand in for traditional cranberry relish at Thanksgiving.

1 tablespoon olive oil

1 large red onion, finely chopped

3 cloves garlic, minced

1 package (12 ounces) fresh or frozen cranberries

⅓ cup packed brown sugar

½ cup dried cherries

½ cup pear nectar

2 teaspoons grated orange zest

- ½ teaspoon pepper
- ¼ teaspoon curry powder
- ¼ teaspoon salt

In a large saucepan, heat the oil over medium-low heat. Add the onion and garlic, and cook, stirring frequently, until the onion is tender, about 7 minutes.

Stir in the cranberries, brown sugar, cherries, pear nectar, orange zest, pepper, curry powder, and salt. Cook, stirring occasionally, until the berries have popped, about 10 minutes. Serve at room temperature or chilled.

MAKES 1½ CUPS

FRESH TOMATO-GINGER CHUTNEY

Any tomato will do here, but for really concentrated tomato flavor use either beefsteak tomatoes in season or grape tomatoes.

- 1 cup diced fresh tomato
- ¼ cup minced red onion
- 2 tablespoons minced fresh mint
- 1 tablespoon grated fresh ginger
- 1 tablespoon lime juice
- Salt and pepper

In a bowl, mix together the tomato, onion, mint, ginger, and lime juice. Season with salt and pepper to taste. Store in the refrigerator.

MAKES 1⅓ CUPS

FRESH CRANBERRY RELISH

Cranberries are one of the few fruits that still have an actual season. They are only available fresh for about 4 months out of the year, so take advantage of them while they're around by making this fresh relish.

- 4 cups fresh cranberries
- 2 medium unpeeled red apples, cored
- 1 large or 2 medium navel oranges, peeled and quartered
- ⅔ cup honey

One at a time, coarsely, but evenly, chop the cranberries, apples, and orange quarters in a food processor. Combine all the fruit in a bowl, and blend in the honey. Refrigerate, covered, several hours or overnight.

MAKES 4 CUPS

SPICY CRANBERRY-PINEAPPLE RELISH

The natural sweetness of pineapple contributes to a delicious cranberry relish that is perfect for leftover Thanksgiving turkey sandwiches. When cranberries are in season, throw a couple of bags into the freezer so you can make this relish whenever the spirit moves you.

- 3 cups fresh or frozen cranberries
- ½ cup frozen pineapple juice concentrate
- ¼ cup chopped walnuts
- 2 tablespoons drained horseradish

In a heavy-bottomed medium saucepan, combine the cranberries and pineapple juice concentrate. Cook over low heat, stirring occasionally, until the cranberries begin to pop, 10 to 15 minutes.

Let cool to room temperature. Stir in the walnuts and horseradish. Store in the refrigerator.

MAKES 3 CUPS

CORN RELISH

If it's summer and you can get good, locally grown corn, you'll need 6 ears for this relish.

- 3 cups corn kernels, fresh or frozen
- 1 green bell pepper, diced
- 1 red bell pepper, diced
- 2 medium onions, minced
- ½ cup white wine vinegar
- ⅓ cup sugar
- 4 teaspoons dry mustard
- ½ teaspoon salt
- ¼ teaspoon turmeric

In a medium saucepan, combine the corn, bell peppers, onions, vinegar, sugar, mustard, salt, and turmeric. Bring to a simmer over medium-low heat and cook for 6 to 8 minutes. Serve chilled.

MAKES 6 SERVINGS

CUCUMBER RELISH

The refreshing flavors of cucumber and lime make this a great accompaniment to rich-tasting foods, like lamb.

- 3 tablespoons rice vinegar
- 3 tablespoons lime juice
- 2 teaspoons sugar
- ¼ teaspoon salt
- 1 large cucumber, peeled, halved lengthwise, seeded, and diced
- 1 red bell pepper, finely diced
- ¼ teaspoon red pepper flakes

In a small saucepan, stir together the vinegar, lime juice, and sugar. Bring to a boil over medium heat and cook until the sugar has dissolved, about 1 minute. Stir in the salt and transfer the mixture to a medium bowl. Add the cucumber, bell pepper, and red pepper flakes, and toss to coat. Serve chilled.

MAKES 3 CUPS

SWEET ONION–CAULIFLOWER RELISH

Vidalias are the best known of the sweet onions, but there are plenty of other options like Walla Walla, Maui, Texas 1015, and Oso Sweet. Most domestic sweet onions are available in the spring, but Osos, from Chile, are available in the winter.

- ½ cup distilled white vinegar
- ½ cup white wine vinegar
- ½ cup sugar
- 2 tablespoons mustard seeds
- 1½ teaspoons turmeric
- ½ teaspoon salt
- 1 head of cauliflower, cut into florets
- 2 large Vidalia onions, cut into ½-inch chunks
- 2 yellow bell peppers, diced
- 2 tablespoons yellow mustard

In a large saucepan, combine the vinegars, sugar, mustard seeds, turmeric, and salt. Bring to a boil over medium heat. Add the cauliflower, onions, and bell peppers, and return to a boil. Reduce to a simmer, cover, and cook until the cauliflower is tender, about 12 minutes.

Let cool to room temperature, then stir in the yellow mustard. Serve at room temperature or chilled.

MAKES 8 CUPS

ROASTED ONION RELISH

Allspice and brown sugar underscore the natural sweetness in roasted onions.

- 2½ teaspoons turbinado or light brown sugar
- 1¼ teaspoons oregano

½ teaspoon salt

½ teaspoon pepper

⅛ teaspoon allspice

1½ pounds large red onions, cut into ½-inch cubes

1 tablespoon olive oil

2 plum tomatoes, diced

2 tablespoons red wine vinegar

Preheat the oven to 350°F. In a medium bowl, combine the brown sugar, oregano, salt, pepper, and allspice. Add the onions and oil, tossing well to coat.

Transfer to a 9 × 13-inch baking dish, cover with foil, and bake for 30 minutes, stirring occasionally. Uncover and bake for 10 minutes to lightly brown the onions. Transfer to a bowl and stir in the tomatoes and vinegar. Cool to room temperature. Store in the refrigerator.

MAKES 2 CUPS

Snacks & Sweets

In addition to the importance of eating a balanced diet, eating several snacks a day keeps your metabolism in good working order. The trick, of course, is to find snacks that are good for you, and also to try to keep in the neighborhood of 150 calories. This advice is not just for those trying to lose weight, it's actually an important strategy for healthy eating in general.

The easiest snack of all, of course, is a piece of fruit. But other healthful options include nuts (but watch out with them, because it's very easy to get up to 150 calories), salsa or a low-fat dip with cut-up vegetables, an energy bar, popcorn, and whole-grain crackers.

One of the biggest snack problems for a lot of people is their sweet tooth. It's tempting—and easy—to just buy a candy bar or a bag of jelly beans. So, acknowledging that there a lot of people who love candy, this chapter also includes some sweet snacks that are candies, but with a healthy twist.

SEEDED ALMOND MIX

Unblanched almonds still have their dark-brown skins on them, which contributes flavor to this tasty mix.

4 cups natural (unblanched) almonds
1 cup sunflower seeds
½ cup sesame seeds
2 tablespoons soy sauce
1 teaspoon dark sesame oil

Preheat the oven to 350°F.

In a large bowl, toss together the almonds, sunflower seeds, sesame seeds, soy sauce, and sesame oil. Spread out on a rimmed baking sheet and bake for 10 to 15 minutes, stirring once or twice, until crisp. Store in an airtight container.

MAKES 5½ CUPS

CURRIED CASHEW MIX

The coconut can be sweetened or unsweetened.

3 tablespoons olive oil
2 cups cashews, toasted
½ cup sunflower seeds
1 tablespoon curry powder
Pinch of cayenne pepper
¾ cup golden raisins
1 cup shredded coconut, toasted
½ teaspoon salt

In a large skillet, heat the oil over medium-high heat. Add the cashews and sunflower seeds, and stir for 2 to 3 minutes.

Stir in the curry powder and cayenne. Continue cooking and stirring for 1½ to 2 minutes.

Stir in the raisins and coconut. Remove from heat and sprinkle with the salt. Let cool, stirring often, for 30 minutes. Transfer to paper towels to drain. Store in an airtight container.

MAKES 4 CUPS

PEPPER NUTS

You can make these as spicy as you like, or even add an herb such as rosemary or sage.

- **3 tablespoons sugar**
- **2 teaspoons paprika**
- **1 teaspoon pepper**
- **½ teaspoon ground coriander**
- **½ teaspoon salt**
- **2 teaspoons vegetable oil**
- **2 cups mixed nuts such as almonds, walnuts, pecans, and cashews**

In a small bowl, stir together the sugar, paprika, pepper, coriander, and salt.

In a large skillet, heat the oil over medium heat, swirling to coat the bottom of the pan. Add the nuts and toss until well coated. Gradually sprinkle the sugar mixture over the nuts, stirring to combine. After all the sugar mixture has been added, keep stirring until it has all melted. Immediately pour the nut mixture onto a baking sheet (to stop the cooking). Store in an airtight container.

MAKES 2 CUPS

MEXICAN MIX

Between the pumpkin seeds and the almonds, this snack provides a good amount of potassium.

- **2 cups hulled pumpkin seeds (pepitas)**
- **1 cup slivered almonds**
- **1 teaspoon coarse salt**
- **½ teaspoon ground cumin**
- **¼ teaspoon cayenne pepper**

Preheat the oven to 400°F.

In a bowl, toss together the pumpkin seeds, almonds, salt, cumin, and cayenne. Spread out on a rimmed baking sheet and bake, for 10 to 15 minutes, until crisp. Store in an airtight container.

MAKES 3 CUPS

MAPLE PEPITAS

Pumpkin seeds are a good source of vitamin E and a number of important minerals.

- **2 cups hulled pumpkin seeds (pepitas)**
- **2 tablespoons maple syrup**
- **1½ teaspoons coarse salt**
- **½ teaspoon paprika or cayenne pepper**

Preheat the oven to 425°F. Line a baking sheet with parchment paper.

In a bowl, combine the pumpkin seeds, maple syrup, salt, and paprika, and toss well.

Spread out in a single layer on the baking sheet. Bake for 10 to 15 minutes, until the seeds are golden brown and aromatic. Store in an airtight container.

MAKES 2 CUPS

SPICY ROASTED CHICKPEAS

If you'd rather use home-cooked chickpeas than canned, you'll need about 1¾ cups.

- **1 can (15 ounces) chickpeas, drained, rinsed, and patted dry**
- **1 tablespoon olive oil**
- **1 teaspoon smoked paprika**
- **¼ teaspoon chipotle or ancho chili powder**
- **¼ teaspoon sea salt**

Preheat the oven to 400°F.

On a small rimmed baking sheet, toss the chickpeas with the oil, paprika, chipotle powder, and salt. Roast for 35 minutes, shaking the pan twice during baking, until the chickpeas are crisp and dry. Turn the oven off and leave the chickpeas inside to cool. Store in an airtight container.

MAKES 1¾ CUPS

PAPRIKA CORN WAFERS

Delicate, fragile, and paper thin, here is an inexpensive snack food that can be served as a alternative to potato chips.

- **⅔ cup yellow cornmeal**
- **½ teaspoon coarse salt**
- **⅛ teaspoon chili powder**
- **2 tablespoons butter, cut into small pieces**
- **¾ cup boiling water**
- **Paprika, for dusting**

Preheat the oven to 400°F. Line a large baking sheet with foil and butter the foil generously.

Place the cornmeal, salt, and chili powder in a medium bowl. Put the butter pieces in a small heatproof bowl or jar and pour the boiling water over them, stirring to melt. Add the butter mixture to the cornmeal and stir. Let stand for 5 minutes. The batter will be very thin.

Stirring after each spoonful, drop the batter by the teaspoon onto the baking sheet. Spoon only 3 to a row and no more than 9 on a sheet, because they spread. Bake for 7 to 10 minutes, or until dry and very lightly browned at the edges. Lift off carefully with a wide spatula and place on a wire rack to cool. Repeat with the remaining batter. Dust the wafers with paprika.

MAKES 2 TO 2½ DOZEN WAFERS

TRITICALE PEANUT WAFERS

Paper-thin crackers with the crunchy, nutty taste of freshly roasted peanuts.

- **⅔ cup triticale flour**
- **⅓ cup whole wheat pastry flour**
- **¼ teaspoon salt**
- **Pinch of cayenne pepper**
- **2 tablespoons butter, cut into small pieces, at room temperature**
- **1 tablespoon creamy peanut butter**
- **1 large egg yolk**
- **¼ cup very finely minced dry-roasted peanuts**
- **1 to 2 tablespoons ice water**

Preheat the oven to 350°F. Line 2 baking sheets with foil.

In a food processor, combine the flours, salt, and cayenne, and pulse to blend. Add the butter and peanut butter, and process until crumbly. Lightly stir in the egg yolk, minced peanuts, and just enough ice water to form a stiff dough.

Divide the dough into 18 pieces. Place each piece between sheets of lightly floured waxed paper, and roll into a round until about ¼ inch thick. Place the rounds on the baking sheets, widely spaced, and cover with waxed paper. Continue to roll out as thinly as possible (about ⅛ inch thick) right on the baking sheet. The rounds should not touch after rolling.

Bake for 10 to 15 minutes, or until light golden in color. Carefully transfer the wafers with a wide spatula to a wire rack to cool.

MAKES 1½ DOZEN WAFERS

BARLEY ONION CRACKERS

These large decorative crackers are rimmed with black sesame seeds, which you can find in Asian markets.

- **⅓ cup white sesame seeds**
- **1 cup barley flour**
- **2 tablespoons finely minced onion**

- 1 teaspoon dark sesame oil
- 1 teaspoon soy sauce
- ¼ cup cold water
- 2 tablespoons black sesame seeds
- 1 large egg white, beaten

In a spice mill, coffee mill, or mini food processor, grind the white sesame seeds to a fine meal (be careful not to turn it into a paste). Combine the sesame seed meal and flour in a large bowl.

In a cup, mix the onion, sesame oil, and soy sauce. Add to the flour mixture. Slowly add the water, a bit at a time, working with your hands until the dough holds together. It will be dry. Divide into 4 balls.

In a small skillet, heat 1 tablespoon of the black sesame seeds over medium-low heat until toasted, about 10 minutes. Set aside.

Preheat the oven to 400°F. Lightly oil a baking sheet.

Roll each ball to ¼-inch thickness with a rolling pin. Using a bowl that measures 4½ inches in diameter as a guide, cut out rounds of dough. Gather the scraps and reroll to make a total of 7 large rounds.

With a wide spatula, carefully place the rounds on the baking sheet, and brush with the egg white. Rim the outside of each cracker with the untoasted black sesame seeds and sprinkle the inside with the toasted ones. With a rolling pin, gently press the sesame seeds into the dough.

Bake for 10 to 15 minutes, or until light brown and crisp.

MAKES 7 CRACKERS

FLAX & OAT CRACKERS

Between the oats and flax, there is a sizable amount of heart-healthy soluble fiber in these crackers.

- ¾ cup old-fashioned rolled oats
- 1 cup white whole wheat flour*
- ½ cup oat bran
- ½ teaspoon salt
- ¼ cup plus 2 tablespoons vegetable oil
- 1 tablespoon honey
- ½ cup water
- 2 tablespoons golden flaxseeds

**milled from white wheat grains*

In a spice mill, coffee mill, or mini food processor, grind the oats to a fine meal.

Preheat the oven to 350°F. Lightly oil a large baking sheet.

In a medium bowl, whisk together the oat meal, flour, bran, and salt.

In a large bowl, blend the oil and honey together. Stir in the flour mixture and the water, and mix just until the dough is smooth.

CRACKERS & SPREADS

A homemade spread on a cracker makes a nice mid-afternoon snack. Try one of these spreads:

- Caramelized Onion Dip (page 152)
- Cashew Dip (page 151)
- Creamy Spinach Dip (page 149)
- Edamame Dip (page 150)
- Lemon-Carrot Hummus (page 150)
- Pinto Bean Dip (page 151)
- Roasted-Pepper Hummus (page 150)
- Toasted Walnut-Cheddar Spread (page 153)
- Vegan Onion Dip (page 151)
- Yogurt Cheese with Three Flavors (page 152)

Press or roll the dough to a ⅛-inch thickness right on the baking sheet. Sprinkle with the flaxseeds and press them lightly into the dough so they adhere. With a sharp knife, cut the dough into 2-inch squares.

Bake for 12 to 15 minutes, or until lightly golden. Cool for 5 minutes, then remove from the pan.

MAKES 4 DOZEN CRACKERS

TROPICAL FRUIT BARS

When you drain the canned pineapple, be sure to reserve the juice.

- **1 cup pitted dates, finely chopped**
- **¾ cup well-drained juice-packed crushed pineapple**
- **¼ cup pineapple juice**
- **1½ cups whole wheat flour**
- **1 cup old-fashioned rolled oats**
- **½ cup flaked coconut**
- **¼ cup date sugar**
- **1 teaspoon coarse salt**
- **¼ teaspoon baking soda**
- **½ cup (1 stick) butter, cut into tablespoons**
- **1 large egg, beaten**

In a 1-quart saucepan, combine the dates, pineapple, and pineapple juice. Bring to a boil, reduce to a simmer, and cook, stirring occasionally, until the mixture has thickened, about 5 minutes.

Preheat the oven to 375°F. Butter an 8 × 8-inch baking pan.

In a food processor, combine the flour, oats, coconut, date sugar, salt, and baking soda, and pulse to blend. Add the butter and pulse until the mixture resembles coarse crumbs.

Press half of the crumb mixture firmly onto the bottom of the baking pan. Spread the pineapple-date mixture on top.

Stir the egg into the remaining crumb mixture and spread evenly over the filling.

Bake for 25 to 30 minutes, or until lightly browned. Cool in the pan on a wire rack. Cut into 2-inch squares.

MAKES 16 BARS

ALMOND-FIG TREATS

Figs aren't just tasty and sweet; they also have a good amount of fiber.

- **8 ounces dried figs, chopped**
- **1 cup boiling water**
- **1 cup whole wheat pastry flour**
- **½ cup unbleached all-purpose flour**
- **1 teaspoon baking powder**
- **1 teaspoon baking soda**
- **½ teaspoon salt**
- **½ cup honey, warmed**
- **¼ cup sour cream**
- **¼ cup (½ stick) butter, at room temperature**
- **2 large eggs**
- **1 cup chopped almonds**

Preheat the oven to 375°F. Line 18 muffin cups with nonstick or paper liners.

In a small heatproof bowl, soak the figs in the boiling water for 15 minutes. Drain.

In a medium bowl, whisk together the flours, baking powder, baking soda, and salt.

With an electric mixer on low speed, beat together the honey, sour cream, butter, and eggs for 5 minutes. Gradually beat half of the flour mixture into the sour cream mixture. Beat in half of the figs. Beat in the remaining flour, then the remaining figs. Fold in the almonds.

Spoon the batter into the muffin cups. Bake for

20 minutes, or until a toothpick inserted in the center of a muffin comes out clean.

Cool in the tins on a rack for 5 minutes. Then transfer to racks to cool completely.

MAKES 1½ DOZEN MUFFINS

APRICOT-DATE TREATS: Use 4 ounces chopped dried apricots and 4 ounces pitted dates in place of the figs.

FRUIT-FILLED CHOCOLATE CHUNKS

Tart-sweet cranberries pop in your mouth and contrast beautifully with rich chocolate.

- 2½ cups fresh cranberries
- ⅓ cup packed turbinado or light brown sugar
- 2 teaspoons grated orange zest
- ⅛ teaspoon salt
- ½ cup heavy cream
- 1½ pounds bittersweet or semisweet chocolate, chopped
- 1½ cups coarsely chopped pecans or walnuts
- ⅔ cup dried cherries, chopped if large

Line a 9 × 9-inch baking pan with 2 pieces of parchment paper crisscross fashion, leaving an overhang on two sides.

In a small heavy saucepan, combine the cranberries, brown sugar, orange zest, and salt, and cook over medium-low heat until most of the berries have popped, about 7 minutes.

In a medium bowl set over a saucepan of simmering water, combine the cream and chocolate, and stir until the chocolate has almost melted. Remove from the heat and stir until smooth. Stir in the cranberry mixture, nuts, and dried cherries.

Pour into the pan and cool on a wire rack. Refrigerate until firm, then remove from the pan and break into bite-size pieces.

MAKES ABOUT 2½ POUNDS

DATE BALLS

Dates are not just sweet; they also have significant levels of antioxidants.

- 2 cups chopped dates
- ½ cup (1 stick) butter
- ½ cup honey
- 1 large egg, beaten
- 1 teaspoon vanilla extract
- 2 cups chopped sunflower seeds
- ¼ cup flaked coconut

In a deep, heavy-bottomed pot, combine the dates, butter, honey, egg, and vanilla. Bring to a rolling boil and boil for 1 minute. Cool.

DATE SUGAR

Date sugar is a bit of a misnomer because it's not a sugar that has been extracted from dates (as white cane sugar is extracted from sugar cane). It's actually just very finely ground dates. Date sugar is quite sweet and tends to clump; it can be used in place of dark brown sugar in some recipes, but does not make a good substitute for other sugars in baked goods. Date sugar is sold in natural foods stores, specialty food stores, and many Middle Eastern markets.

Stir in the sunflower seeds. Form the mixture into 1-inch balls and roll in the coconut. Store in the refrigerator.

MAKES 3 DOZEN BALLS

SESAME SQUARES

As an extra health tweak, use a peanut butter that is high in omega-3 fatty acids.

- **⅓ cup honey**
- **⅓ cup peanut butter**
- **¾ cup nonfat dry milk**
- **¾ cup sesame seeds**
- **¼ cup raisins**
- **¼ cup shredded coconut**

In a large bowl, combine the honey, peanut butter, dry milk, sesame seeds, raisins, and coconut.

Spread the mixture into an 8 × 8-inch baking pan and refrigerate for 4 hours. Cut into 1-inch squares.

MAKES 64 PIECES

PRESERVING

Whether you freeze, can, dehydrate, pickle, or make jams and jellies, foods put up at home save money, taste great, and let you enjoy the bounty of summer in the dead of winter. The time it takes to preserve foods at home is time well spent.

Freezing

Freezing is a simple, quick way of preserving most of the goodness—nutrients, taste, texture, color—of fresh foods by slowing the growth of damaging bacteria, molds, and yeasts. And the investment in equipment, other than buying and running the freezer, is minimal.

For top-quality frozen foods, consider the following guidelines for maintaining your freezer and its food supply:

- Use a thermometer to check periodic temperature fluctuations. The freezer should maintain 0°F or less because changes cause deterioration of food quality.
- Freeze foods rapidly because quick freezing helps preserve the texture of foods by keeping ice crystals small. To aid rapid freezing, set the temperature to –10°F or less the night before freezing large quantities of food. Prepare only what can be frozen in 24 hours. As a rule, the maximum amount is 2 to 3 pounds for each cubic foot of freezer space. Place containers near the cold walls of the freezer and leave space between them to allow cold air to circulate.
- Leave an appropriate amount of headspace in the containers to allow for expansion; otherwise, containers or seals will break during freezing. Too much space, on the other hand, allows air (which dries the food) to enter the containers.
- Plan to use food before its quality is diminished by too long a stay in the freezer. The timetables in this and other sections provide guidelines to optimum storage times. Maintaining a current list of foods in the freezer and labeling each package with the freezing date, the type of food, and the quantity will aid in keeping up a steady turnover.

Freezing Equipment

Many materials, both rigid and flexible, are suitable for freezer containers. Select a size that holds the amount you would use for one meal.

Rigid containers—made from metal, plastic, glass, or heavily waxed cardboard—work best for liquid and semi-liquid foods. Choose containers with straight sides instead of those with necks, because foods can slide easily through wide openings while still partially frozen. Also, square containers stack better and use space more efficiently than round ones. Though reusable rigid containers initially cost more than flexible disposable ones, the rigid types are often cheaper in the long run. For dry foods, use flexible containers of heavy foil, heavy plastic, or laminated paper, or use a wrap made of one of these materials.

Either freezer tape or masking tape works well

to seal casserole dishes and packages wrapped in foil, heavy plastic, or laminated paper. Wire twisters covered with paper are useful for closing heavy plastic bags. Carefully press out air before sealing flexible packages, and be certain the seal is secure. If you have an appliance that vacuum-seals foods for freezing, by all means, use it. Exposure to air during freezing will cause freezer burn (dry, tasteless, tough spots).

Gummed labels and colored tape make good labels. Mark them with crayons, ball-point, or indelible markers.

Freezing Fruits

Most fruits freeze fairly successfully. Bananas are an exception; once frozen, they are useful only for pureeing in drinks or for baked goods. Select only choice, blemish-free, ripe fruits for freezing; then wash, dry, peel, and cut as you would for serving fresh.

You can freeze most fruits in any of three different packs: dry, unsweetened, or with syrup. Choose the type of pack that best suits the way you intend to use the fruit. Dry packs and unsweetened packs work well for fruits that are destined for the oven or stovetop, but they have a shorter storage time than the syrup pack. A light syrup benefits fruit to be served uncooked by allowing it to retain good shape and texture. Fruits in syrup also store nicely for a long time.

To pack dry: Sprinkle fruits that tend to darken with an antibrowning solution (see "Pre-

---

DRUGSTORE WRAP

This simple method (also called butcher wrap) of wrapping food makes a neat, airtight package that is very easy to undo when you're ready to use the frozen food. The name of the technique probably dates from the days when many drugstores had lunch counters. It would be more appropriate these days to call it deli wrap.

- Cut wrap (foil, heavy plastic, laminated paper) large enough to go around the food 1½ times. Place food in the center of the wrap.
- Bring together the long edges of the paper over the food (A) and fold over 1 inch (B). Crease the fold, and fold again. Continue folding until the wrap is close to the food. Press the wrap to force out the air.
- Fold the ends to form points (C). Then fold the ends under and toward each other (D). Pull tight and seal all edges with tape.

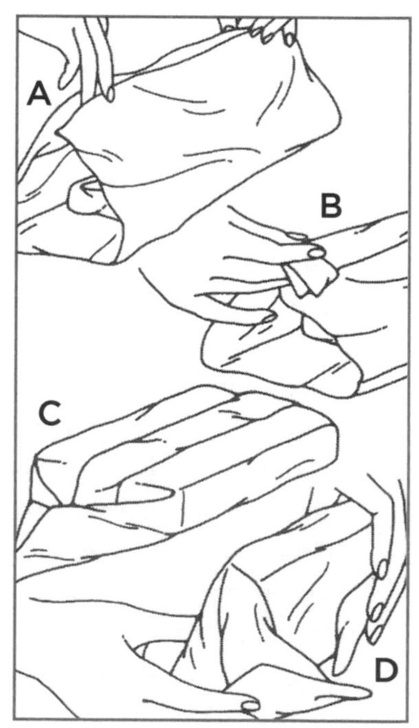

venting discoloration," below), but skip this step for fruits that retain their color well (for example, blueberries). Pack fruits loosely in a container, seal, and freeze. Generally speaking, fruits frozen this way will form a solid block on freezing. If you would like to ensure that frozen fruits will shake freely from the container, spread fruit pieces in a single layer on a tray and freeze. Once they are frozen, pack in a semi-rigid container or freezer bag, seal, and return to the freezer.

To pack unsweetened: Place fruit pieces in a rigid container and shake the container to pack down the fruits without crushing them. Cover the fruits with juice or water containing antibrowning solution if needed (see "Preventing discoloration," below), leaving adequate headspace. Press the fruits under the liquid and hold them in place with crumpled waxed paper, foil, or plastic wrap. Cover and seal.

To pack with syrup: Put fruit pieces in a rigid container and shake to settle; then pour in honey syrup and antibrowning solution (see "Preventing discoloration," below), leaving sufficient headspace. Press fruits under the syrup and hold in place with crumpled waxed paper, foil, or plastic wrap. Cover and seal.

Preventing discoloration: Several kinds of fruit—apples, apricots, cherries, peaches, plums—become dark and brown with exposure to air and during storage and thawing. Slow the browning by dipping pieces cut for dry pack in a solution of ¼ cup lemon juice or 1 to 2 tablespoons rose hip concentrate in 1 gallon water. (Alternatively, ½ teaspoon ascorbic acid powder, crystals, or crushed tablets to make 1,500 milligrams to 4 cups liquid can be used.) For syrup pack add a small amount of acid to the syrup.

HONEY SYRUP FOR FREEZING FRUITS

For a thin syrup: Dissolve 1 cup honey in 3 cups boiling water.

For a medium syrup: Dissolve 2 cups honey in 2 cups boiling water.

Chill before adding to fruits.

Freezing Vegetables

Most vegetables freeze well, retaining good color, fresh flavor, and sufficient body. The exceptions are cabbage, celery, cucumbers, eggplant, potatoes, radishes, salad greens, scallions, and whole tomatoes, which lose characteristic texture during storage. Freeze only fresh, tender vegetables of peak quality. Wash, peel, and cut vegetables the same as you do when serving them fresh. Sort according to size; then blanch most vegetables (below), cool quickly, drain, and pack. (See the table on page 625 for instructions on preparation and packing of vegetables for freezing.) Chill first batches in the refrigerator while processing others; freeze when several batches are ready. (This is best done within 1 hour of blanching.)

Blanching: Blanching destroys the enzymes that mature, or age, vegetables even during freezing; thus it helps to keep the vegetables in prime condition. Blanching can be done either in boiling water or with steam. Several kinds of vegetables—beets, green bell peppers, mushrooms, onions, pumpkins, winter squashes—are not blanched before freezing; instead, they require special handling. For these vegetables, follow the preparation directions in "Freezing Vegetables," page 625.

FREEZING FRUIT

The recommended maximum storage time for all home-frozen fruits is 1 year. For best quality, use within a shorter time.

Headspace: When packing containers, be sure to allow for appropriate headspace. For wide-mouthed containers, leave ½ inch in a pint container and 1 inch in a quart container. For narrow-mouthed containers, leave ¾ inch for a pint, 1½ inches for a quart.

To tray freeze: Spread fruit in a single layer on a tray and freeze. When the fruit is frozen, put it in a semi-rigid container or freezer bag. Seal and return to the freezer.

FRUIT		PREPARATION	TYPE OF PACK
APPLES	Sauce	Cook applesauce. Pack.	Pack with or without honey and lemon juice to taste.
	Slices	Peel, core, and slice. Pack or tray freeze.	Pack dry or sweeten with 2-4 tablespoons honey. To prevent darkening, mix 2 tablespoons lemon juice or 1 teaspoon rose hip concentrate with honey.
BERRIES	Blackberries Blueberries Raspberries	Wash and dry thoroughly. (Or pack unwashed and wash immediately before using.) Pack or tray freeze.	Pack dry.
	Strawberries	Wash and hull. Slice or leave whole. Pack whole berries and slices. Tray freeze whole berries, if desired.	Pack dry if whole. Sweeten with thin honey syrup (see page 623) if sliced.
CANTALOUPE		Cut flesh in slices, cubes, or balls. Pack or tray freeze. (For best texture, eat while partially frozen.)	Pack dry or mix with lemon juice and honey.
CHERRIES	Sour	Wash, stem, and pit. Pack or tray freeze.	Pack dry or mix with a small amount of honey.
	Sweet	Wash, stem, and pit. Pack or tray freeze.	Pack moistened with lemon juice or rose hip concentrate.
CRANBERRIES		Wash and stem. Pack or tray freeze.	Pack dry.
PEACHES		Wash, peel, and pit. leave in halves or slice. Pack.	Pack with thin honey syrup (see page 623) and a small amount of lemon juice or rose hip concentrate.
PINEAPPLES		Pare and remove eyes. Slice, dice, or cut in wedges. Pack.	Pack in own juice or thin honey syrup (see page 623).
PLUMS		Wash and pit. Pack.	Pack with 2 tablespoons lemon juice or 1 teaspoon rose hip concentrate per pint. Sweeten with honey.
RHUBARB		Discard leaves. Wash stalks and cut away woody ends. Slice in 1-inch pieces. Pack or tray freeze.	Pack dry, or cook and pack in thin honey syrup (see page 623).

FREEZING VEGETABLES

The recommended maximum storage time for all home-frozen vegetables is 8 months. For best quality, use within a shorter time.

For vegetables that are blanched, after blanching quickly cool and drain. Pack, leaving ½-inch headspace. Or tray freeze by spreading vegetables in a single layer on a tray and freezing. When the vegetables are frozen, put them in a semi-rigid container or freezer bag. Seal and return to the freezer.

VEGETABLE		PREPARATION	BLANCHING (BOILING) TIME* (MINUTES)
ASPARAGUS		Wash thoroughly; cut off tough part of stalk. Leave in spear lengths to fit container or cut in 1-inch pieces. Blanch.	Thin stalks: 2 Medium stalks: 3 Thick stalks: 4
BEANS	Green and wax	Wash; snap ends. Leave whole, cut in 1-inch lengths, or cut in French style (julienne). Blanch.	3
	Lima	Shell and sort according to size. Blanch.	Small beans: 2 Medium beans: 3 Large beans: 4
BEETS		Wash and sort according to size. Trim tops, leaving ½ inch of stems. Cook in boiling water until tender, 25–50 minutes. Cool in cold water. Remove skins and cut into cubes or slice. Pack with ½-inch headspace, seal, and freeze.	No blanching; beets are completely cooked before freezing.
BROCCOLI		Pare stems if tough and discard woody parts. Slice lengthwise so that heads are no more than 1½ inches across. Blanch. Pack with heads in alternating directions.	3
BRUSSELS SPROUTS		Discard outer leaves. Wash; inspect for insects. Sort according to size. Blanch.	Small heads: 3 Medium heads: 4 Large heads: 5
CARROTS		Remove tops. Wash and peel. Leave small carrots whole. Cut large ones into lengthwise strips, thin "penny" slices, or ¼-inch cubes. Blanch.	Whole: 5 Cubes, slices, or strips: 2
CAULIFLOWER		Discard outer leaves. Trim and separate into florets about 1½ inches across. Blanch.	3
CORN	Kernels	Husk, remove silk, and rinse. Blanch. Cool quickly and drain. Cut kernels from cob with a sharp knife. Pack, leaving ½-inch headspace, seal, and freeze.	4
	On the cob	Husk, remove silk, and rinse. Blanch; cool quickly. Drain and dry. Spread on tray and freeze. Wrap in moisture-resistant material. Seal and freeze.	½–1¾-inch diameter:7 1½–2-inch diameter: 9 Over 2-inch diameter: 11
GREENS		Wash and remove large, tough stems. Blanch in small batches to prevent matting.	Beet, mustard, turnip greens, kale, chard: 2 Spinach: 1½

***Blanching time is for boiling; add 1–2 minutes if blanching in steam.**

FREEZING VEGETABLES—*CONTINUED*

VEGETABLE		PREPARATION	BLANCHING (BOILING) TIME* (MINUTES)
MUSHROOMS		Wash and trim. Divide into stems and caps, leave whole, or slice. Sauté lightly in butter, 3-5 minutes. Cool and package in recipe-size amounts.	No blanching; mushrooms are sautéed before freezing.
ONIONS		Dice, pack, and seal.	No blanching necessary.
PEAS		Shell and sort. Blanch.	1½
PEPPERS, GREEN		Wash; remove seeds and ribs. Halve, slice, or dice. Freeze. (Peppers frozen without blanching may be used in uncooked foods. Blanched peppers are easier to pack.)	Halves: 3 Slices: 2
PUMPKINS		Wash, cut in large sections, and remove seeds. Steam or bake until tender (see "A Guide to Vegetables," page 69). Remove rind and discard. Mash or sieve pulp. Cool and pack with ½-inch headspace. Seal and freeze.	No blanching; pumpkin is cooked before freezing.
SQUASH	Summer	Wash and slice in ½-inch pieces. Blanch.	3
	Winter	See pumpkin.	
TOMATOES	Juice	Wash and cut out stems. Slice or quarter. Simmer 5 minutes. Sieve and cool. Pour into containers, allowing 1½-inch headspace. Seal and freeze.	No blanching; juice is cooked before freezing.
	Stewed	Wash and remove stems. Peel and cut into quarters. Cover and cook until tender, 5–10 minutes. Cool. Pack, leaving 1-inch headspace. Seal and freeze.	No blanching; tomatoes are cooked before freezing.

*Blanching time is for boiling; add 1–2 minutes if blanching in steam.

To blanch in boiling water, fill an 8- to 10-quart pot with at least 1 gallon of water to blanch 1 pound of vegetables. Bring the water to a rapid boil. Place 1 pound or less of vegetables in a wire basket, sieve, or piece of cheesecloth and lower into the boiling water. (The water should return to boiling within a minute. If it takes longer, use a smaller amount of vegetables in the next batch.) Cover the pot and start timing immediately (see page 625 for times); do not overcook. For even heat penetration, shake the basket occasionally. As soon as the time is up, stop the cooking promptly. Remove the vegetables and put them in water chilled with 1 pound of ice, or hold under cold running water. Chill the vegetables until the pieces are cool to the center. Drain and pat dry.

To steam, in a vegetable steamer, steam a single of layer of vegetables at a time. Steam blanching takes 30 seconds to 1 minute longer than blanching in water (see the table on page 625) and fewer vegetables can be blanched at a time. When done, chill as you would for boiling.

Freezing Herbs

Freezing is an excellent way to preserve the delightful flavor and aroma of garden-fresh herbs. Since frozen herbs have the same potency as fresh herbs, use about twice as much as when a recipe calls for dried herbs.

To retain the best color and flavor, blanch the herbs before freezing. Tie 2 or 3 stalks into a bunch, then dip the bunches into boiling water for 1 minute. Next, quickly chill in ice water. Pat dry with clean toweling.

After blanching, remove the leaves from the stalks, and wrap 5 large leaves or 1 tablespoon small leaves in a small piece of plastic wrap. Repeat until all the leaves are packaged. Overwrap each package with foil and spread in a single layer on a tray. Freeze, then bundle the frozen packages in a plastic bag. To use the herbs, mince the leaves while frozen.

Herbs are also handy when frozen in ice cube trays. After blanching, remove the leaves from the stems and mince the leaves. Put 1 tablespoon leaves in each ice cube compartment, fill with water, and freeze. Once frozen, bundle the cubes in a plastic bag. To use the herbs, simply add a cube to a soup, sauce, or stew. If a recipe such as a salad calls for herbs without liquid, thaw the cube in small strainer over a small bowl. Reserve the liquid for a soup, stew, or sauce. It will add a hint of herb flavor and aroma.

Freezing Meat

By removing excess bone and fat from cuts of meat, you can use freezer space wisely. Use the bones to prepare a concentrated stock that can be frozen in ice cube trays (see "Homemade Bouillon Cubes," page 171). Wrap chops and patties in individual portions or in small groups with a piece of waxed paper between each layer for easy separation. For retaining the best quality during freezing, follow recommended storage times (see "Home Storage of Meat table," page 31).

REFREEZING

As a general rule, if a food is safe to eat, it is safe to refreeze. Foods can be refrozen safely if they have been kept cold (40°F or less) and still contain a few ice crystals. Do not refreeze any food that has warmed to room temperature or that has been left for more than 2 hours at room temperature. Of course, raw foods that have been frozen, thawed, and then cooked can be refrozen easily and safely.

Since refreezing results in lowered quality, keep storage time short to prevent further deterioration of flavor and texture. Baked goods such as plain breads, cakes, and cookies are an exception. They can be thawed and refrozen without loss of quality.

Freezing Poultry

Poultry halves, quarters, and disjointed parts take up less freezer space than whole birds. Use plastic freezer bags or other flexible freezer materials to wrap poultry carefully. Pad the bone tips with foil or freezer wrap to prevent them from breaking through the package, and separate pieces with foil or other freezer material so that they may be broken apart for quicker thawing and cooking. When freezing whole birds, never stuff first. For optimum quality use poultry within the recommended storage times (see page 628) and thaw carefully.

FREEZER STORAGE TIME FOR POULTRY

	MAXIMUM STORAGE TIME (MONTHS)
Chicken, cut up	6
Chicken, whole	12
Duck, whole	6
Goose, whole	6
Turkey, cut up	6
Turkey, whole	12

Freezing Fish

Although fish is tastiest when fresh, it can be frozen for a short time. Immediately after catching or buying fish, freeze it in freezer wrap, in a block of ice, or with an ice glaze.

To freeze in freezer wrap: Use the standard "Drugstore Wrap" (see page 622) to cover dressed whole fish, fish fillets, or fish steaks. After wrapping, seal with tape.

To freeze in a block of ice: Fill a loaf pan, wax carton, or coffee tin with cold water. Insert the fish and freeze. If using a pan, you can remove the pan once the water has frozen and wrap the block in freezer packaging material. Seal.

To freeze with an ice glaze: Freeze dressed whole fish unwrapped. Then dip the frozen fish in very cold water and return the fish to the freezer. Repeat until the glaze is $\frac{1}{8}$ to $\frac{1}{4}$ inch thick. Wrap in freezer wrap and seal.

Thaw fish in the refrigerator to prevent excessive loss of juice. Fish that is dry tends to be tough.

Freezing Prepared Foods

Since many baked dishes, braised dishes, soups, and stews freeze very nicely, they are excellent dishes to make in quantity and then put in the freezer in meal-size portions for future use. Frozen cooked dishes will have the most flavor and best texture if you consider the following factors during the initial preparation and cooking:

- Freezing and reheating tends to soften foods, so undercook vegetables, pastas, whole grains, legumes, and meats during the initial cooking. Cool quickly to stop the cooking.
- Seasonings change—some intensify, some diminish—during freezing, so season lightly at first and adjust when reheating.
- Fats blend very poorly when reheated, so use fats sparingly.
- Sauces thickened with flour tend to separate after thawing. Stir while reheating.
- The textures of hard-cooked egg whites, mayonnaise, and potatoes change drastically during storage. Add those foods after thawing the dishes they are to be part of.
- Cold foods freeze more quickly than hot ones. The results are fewer and smaller ice crystals and better texture. To cool hot, cooked casseroles quickly, chill in a pan of ice water.

When packing prepared dishes for freezing, pack food tightly to remove air spaces, and allow sufficient headspace for expansion. Seal casserole lids with tape and overwrap, or line the casserole dish with foil. If lining with foil, cut the liner to extend over the sides of the dish. (There should be enough foil to fold over the contents after the food has frozen.) When the contents have frozen, lift them and foil from the dish and close the foil using the "Drugstore Wrap" (see page 622). The dish is now free for another use. Reheating is simple: Peel off the foil and place the frozen block back in the casserole.

FREEZING PRECOOKED FOODS

FOOD		PREPARATION	APPROXIMATE STORAGE TIME	THAWING AND USING
BREAD, QUICK	Biscuits and muffins	Cool completely; wrap individually in foil or place in plastic bags.	3-6 months	Thaw at room temperature for 1 hour, or heat frozen, in foil, at 300°F for 20 minutes.
	Fruit and nut	Cool completely; wrap in plastic wrap or foil or place in plastic bags.	3-6 months	Thaw in package at room temperature for 45 minutes. Or warm in foil, when thawed, at 400°F for 10 minutes.
	Waffles	Bake to light brown, cool, and wrap individually in foil or place in plastic bags.	1-2 months	Remove from package and heat in toaster.
BREAD, YEAST	Baked	Cool completely; wrap in foil or place in plastic bags.	6-8 months	Thaw at room temperature 45-60 minutes. Reheat in foil at 400°F for 10 minutes.
	Unbaked	Wrap in plastic wrap.	3-4 weeks	Thaw at room temperature before rising and baking.
CAKES	Angel, chiffon, sponge (unfrosted)	Cool completely; place in plastic bags. Store with rigid protective covering to prevent crushing.	2 months	Thaw at room temperature; unwrap and heat at 350°F for 10 minutes.
	Fruit, pound (unfrosted)	Cool completely; wrap in plastic wrap or place in plastic bag.	12 months	Thaw in package at room temperature for about 1 hour.
	Layer (frosted and filled)	It is best to freeze frosting and cake separately. However, if desired, freeze the frosted cake on a flat pan, unwrapped to harden frosting first. Then wrap and freeze in plastic wrap and place in rigid container for protection.	4-6 months	Thaw in refrigerator. Remove wrapping before thawing to prevent it from sticking to frosting.
COOKIES	All (except meringue), baked	Package when completely cool in rigid containers with layers of freezer paper. Crush some paper to fill spaces so cookies do not break.	6-12 months	Thaw in package at room temperature for about 1 hour.
	Refrigerator, unbaked	Shape prepared dough for slicing. Wrap in freezer paper and seal. (Label with baking directions.)	3-6 months	Slice frozen dough using sharp knife or thaw slightly if too hard to slice. Bake in frozen state.

FREEZING PRECOOKED FOODS—*CONTINUED*

FOOD		PREPARATION	APPROXIMATE STORAGE TIME	THAWING AND USING
DESSERTS	Fruit pies and cheesecakes, baked	Cool completely; wrap tightly in foil or place in plastic bags. Store with rigid protective covering to prevent crushing.	3 months	Remove wrapping and thaw at room temperature or in refrigerator.
	Fruit pies, unbaked	Prepare pie as for baking. Do not cut vents in top crust. Freeze before packaging. Wrap in foil. Store in carton, or top with second plate turned upside down. Tape edges and wrap in foil.	4 months	Remove wrapping. Cut vents in upper crust. Bake frozen 15–20 minutes at 450°F, then 375°F for about 30 minutes.
	Mousses and cold soufflés	Prepare recipe in freezer-proof serving dishes. Cover tightly with foil. Use inverted foil pan, or make foil collar, to protect delicate surface.	1 month	Thaw in refrigerator 8 hours.
	Pastry shells, unbaked	Flat sheets: Place on baking sheet or foil-wrapped cardboard. Separate each layer with double wax paper layer; wrap flat in foil (handle carefully—they are very brittle). Piecrusts: Shape the pastry in plates; prick with fork; separate with wax paper. Place empty pie plate inside top shell to eliminate air. Wrap in foil or place in plastic bags.	4–6 months	Flat sheets: Remove each sheet as needed. Place on pie plate and thaw 15 minutes at room temperature before shaping. Shape, prick with fork, and bake unfilled at 425°F for 15 minutes. Piecrusts: Remove wrapping. Bake frozen at 475°F for 8–10 minutes.
MEALS	Casseroles, unbaked	Prepare, except for final baking. Place foil or wrap inside casserole. Fill, seal, and freeze. When frozen, remove contents from casserole or pan, store in freezer, and reuse casserole.	4–6 months	Remove wrapping, return to pan Add any topping at this point, such as cheese or bread crumbs. Cover and bake frozen at 350°F for 1½–2 hours, depending on size.

FREEZING PRECOOKED FOODS—*CONTINUED*

FOOD			PREPARATION	APPROXIMATE STORAGE TIME	THAWING AND USING
MEALS *(continued)*	Cooked meat and poultry	Large pieces	Trim excess fat; wrap snugly.	4–6 months	To serve cold, thaw in package in refrigerator. To reheat, unwrap and bake frozen in 350°F oven for 1 hour.
		Slices	Cook, cover with gravy, then package.	4–6 months	Reheat in 350°F oven for 30 minutes or until gravy bubbles.
	Meat loaf		If baked, cool, remove from pan, and wrap. If unbaked, leave in pan lined with foil. Freeze. Remove pan; store loaf in freezer.	3 months	To serve hot, unwrap unbaked frozen loaf and return it to pan. Bake at 350°F for 1½ hours.
	Cooked shellfish (crab, lobster, shrimp)		Remove meat from shells and pack to top of rigid container. (Slightly tough when cooked and frozen.)	3–6 months	To serve cold, thaw in refrigerator. Or use in cooked dish from frozen state or slightly thawed. Do not overcook.
PIZZA			Prepare as usual, but do not bake. Cool, wrap in plastic wrap or foil on cardboard base.	1 week	Remove wrapping. Bake frozen at 450°F for 20 minutes.
SAUCES, GLAZES, SYRUPS			Pack serving-size portions in plastic containers or jars. Leave ½- to 1-inch headspace.	6 months when using fresh fruit; 1 month when using fruit juices, flavorings, and pudding mixtures	Heat in top of double boiler, or thaw in container in refrigerator.
SOUPS			Whenever possible, freeze soup and stocks to conserve space and add to other ingredients. Package meal-size portions in rigid containers, allowing ½-inch headspace, or freeze stocks in ice cube trays and package in plastic bags for individual soups and sauces.	1-2 months	Heat in frozen state. If concentrated, add liquid.

FREEZING EGGS AND DAIRY

FOOD		PREPARATION	APPROX STORAGE TIME (MONTHS)	THAWING AND USING
EGGS	Whole (1 egg = 3 Tbsp; 5 eggs = 1 cup)	Lightly beat yolks and whites with a fork. Do not incorporate too much air. Add 2 teaspoons sugar or 1 teaspoon honey (for sweet preparations) or ½ teaspoon salt (for savory) for each cup of eggs to stabilize. Freeze in ice cube trays. When frozen, remove cubes and package in plastic bags.	6–9	Thaw in refrigerator or at room temperature. Use promptly in any recipe that calls for whole eggs and honey or salt.
	Whites (1 egg white = 2 Tbsp)	For uniform texture, pass egg whites through a sieve. Freeze in ice cube trays. When frozen, remove cubes and package in plastic bags.	6–12	Thaw in refrigerator or at room temperature. Thawed egg whites will remain fresh in refrigerator for 2–3 days. Egg whites thawed at room temperature produce greater volume when beaten.
	Yolks (1 egg yolk = 1½ Tbsp; 14 yolks = 1 cup)	Strain fork-beaten yolks. Add 2 teaspoons sugar or 1 teaspoon honey (for sweet preparations) or ½ teaspoon salt (for savory) for each cup of yolks to stabilize. Freeze in ice cube trays. When frozen, remove cubes and package in plastic bags.	6–9	Thaw in refrigerator or at room temperature. Use promptly. To make up 1 egg from separately frozen whites and yolks, mix 1 tablespoon yolk and 2 tablespoons egg white.
MILK		All milk can be frozen, but whole milk and 2% tend to separate when thawed. Freeze in the unopened paper carton that the milk comes in if there is room at the top for expansion. If repackaging, allow 2-inch headspace.	1	Thaw in refrigerator.
CREAM	Heavy	Pasteurized cream containing at least 36 percent butterfat can be frozen, but whipping quality will be impaired and cream will tend to separate. Freeze small amounts in rigid containers. Leave ½-inch headspace. Freeze only enough for immediate use after thawing.	3–6	Thaw in refrigerator.
	Heavy, whipped	Whip cream in chilled bowl until stiff enough to hold shape. Drop by spoonfuls (or squeeze through pastry tube to form rosettes) onto baking sheet lined with waxed paper. Place in freezer until solid. Pack in rigid container, separating layers with foil.	3–6	Frozen whipped cream mounds do not need defrosting when used on hot drinks, or warm desserts. Allow a few minutes to soften at room temperature when using on cold desserts.

FREEZING EGGS AND DAIRY—*CONTINUED*

FOOD		PREPARATION	APPROX STORAGE TIME (MONTHS)	THAWING AND USING
CREAM *(continued)*	Light	Light cream can be frozen but tends to separate when thawed. Freeze small amounts in rigid containers. Leave ½-inch headspace. Freeze only enough for immediate use after thawing.	3	Thaw in refrigerator.
	Sour	Sour cream can be frozen but will separate when thawed. It also curdles very easily in cooking. Freeze small amounts in rigid containers. Leave ½-inch headspace. Freeze only enough for immediate use after thawing.	3	Thaw in refrigerator.
YOGURT		Yogurt can be whipped and frozen with fruit and a sweetener much like ice cream. Unwhipped yogurt does not freeze well, although it can be.	3	Allow whipped yogurt to soften slightly at room temperature so that it can be served easily. Thaw unwhipped yogurt in refrigerator.
BUTTER		Salted, unsalted, or home-churned butter must be over-wrapped in plastic wrap or foil.	6	Thaw in refrigerator.
CHEESE	Cream cheese	Overwrap in foil. Becomes crumbly when thawed. Best used in dips or cheesecakes.	4	Thaw in refrigerator.
	Hard or firm cheese (such as Cheddar, Parmesan)	Cut in ¼- or ½-pound pieces; overwrap in foil. On thawing, hard and semihard cheeses become crumbly and lose flavor. Use in cooking or crumbled in salad dressing.	6	Thaw in refrigerator. Bring to room temperature before serving.
	Soft cheese (such as Brie, Camembert)	Overwrap in foil. May crumble slightly when thawed.	4	Thaw in refrigerator. Bring to room temperature before serving.

FOODS THAT DO NOT FREEZE WELL

Not every food freezes well. A few foods are unsuitable for freezing because their texture and flavor change radically during freezing and thawing. The following table lists these foods and the changes that occur when they are frozen.

FOOD	CHANGE THAT OCCURS DURING FREEZING
BREADED AND FRIED FOODS	Both become soggy.
BUTTERMILK, YOGURT, CUSTARD, COTTAGE CHEESE	These dairy products separate into solids and liquids.
CAKE WITH CUSTARD OR PUDDING FILLINGS	Cake becomes soggy as filling separates into solids and liquid.
CREAM CHEESE	Texture becomes dry and crumbly (but okay if blended with other ingredients, as for dips or cheesecake).
EGGS, HARD-COOKED	White becomes tough and rubbery.
EGGS IN SHELL	Shells crack; yolks are unstable.
GELATIN	Surface becomes weepy.
MAYONNAISE	Oil separates from solids.
POTATOES, WHITE, BOILED	Texture becomes mealy.
POULTRY, STUFFED AT HOME	Dressing may not freeze quickly enough to prevent bacteria from multiplying rapidly.
SALAD GREENS, CUCUMBERS, RADISHES	Crisp vegetables become limp.

Freezing Dairy & Eggs

Milk, foods made from milk, and eggs can be frozen, though their textures suffer somewhat. Freeze milk products in their original containers and thaw them slowly in the refrigerator. Remove eggs from their shells before freezing.

Thawing Foods

For the best taste and texture, thaw only the amount of food needed for a single meal and use the food promptly. Also, follow the thawing recommendations discussed in the appropriate chapters and sections of this book to retain nutrients, preserve quality, and ensure safety.

When reheating cooked foods (either frozen or thawed), use the original cooking temperature or the one suggested in the "Freezing Precooked Foods" (page 629). A meat thermometer inserted in the center of the food should register 180°F when the food is ready for serving.

CANNING

Long before effective freezers were available to homeowners, canning was a popular method of preserving food at home. In many areas of the country, canning is still the primary way of storing produce from a bountiful garden.

Canning preserves food by using heat to destroy the enzymes and organisms—molds, yeasts, bacteria—that cause spoilage. The containers are then sealed to prevent new organisms from entering. If you follow the procedures recommended by home economists at the United States Department of Agriculture's National Center for Home Food Preservation(www.uga.edu/nchfp/) and described in this section, your canned foods will be free of bacteria and be very safe to eat.

Clostridium botulism bacteria grow in low-acid foods in airtight containers and produce a deadly toxin. Use a pressure canner to raise the temperature of the food to 240°F and destroy the spores of the bacteria. High-acid foods (tomatoes and most fruits) can safely be canned in boiling water only 212°F.

Canning Equipment

The following equipment helps simplify canning:

Jar tongs: Extremely useful for lifting jars from the water when processing is done

Ladle: Facilitates spooning hot jams and liquids into jars

Long-handled spoon: Permits stirring of large quantities of food

Slotted spoon: Ideal for draining the excess liquid from hot vegetables when spooning them into canning jars

Wide-mouthed funnel: Speeds filling the jars and reduces spills on the rim and outside edges of the jars

Water bath canner: Suitable for processing fruits and vegetables high in acid (such as tomatoes). Select one with a rack and a tight-fitting lid. Be certain the canner is large enough that the jars will not touch and deep enough that the jars will be submerged 1 inch below the surface of the water. Also, the canner should have a flat bottom with no more than 2 inches overhang around the circumference of the burner. Too much overhang will result in poor processing of the jars around the outer edge of the canner.

Pressure (steam) canner: A must for processing all foods that are low in acid—most vegetables, meats, poultry, fish, soups, and stews. Select a pressure canner that has a rack, a lid with a rubber seal, a safety valve, and a petcock (vent). The canner should be designed to maintain 10 pounds of pressure. Check the pressure gauge before starting to can and have it repaired if it is more than 4 pounds off. If less, adjust during processing. (A pressure cooker can be used if you are canning small amounts. Because the cookers heat and cool more quickly, add 20 minutes to all processing times.)

Jars: Containers made of tempered glass and manufactured especially for home canning are best. Never use jars left over from commercially made peanut butter, mayonnaise, or pickles—they may crack during processing and their seals may not be tight. Each year examine your canning jars for cracks or chips before using them, and discard any that are damaged.

Caps: The best caps are two-piece screw band

with flat, metal self-sealing lids. They are preferred because they result in the fewest seal failures. Never reuse metal self-sealing lids because the sealing compound is good for one use only.

Canning Procedures

Prepping Foods for Canning

Select foods at peak quality. Wash all fruits and vegetables thoroughly to remove dirt and surface pesticides. Peel and cut each food according to the recommendations in the tables that begin on page 624. Handle foods quickly and gently to avoid bruising or other damage, and prepare only as much food as you can process at one time.

Prepping Jars & Lids

After checking the jars to be sure there are no chips, cracks, or sharp edges that will prevent an airtight seal or cause breakage, wash the jars and lids in hot, soapy water. Rinse well and leave them in hot, clear water until you are ready to use them. Keeping the jars hot will help prevent cracking from sudden temperature changes when piping hot food is poured into them. Sterilizing, however, is not necessary since processing will sterilize both the jars and the food.

Packing the Jars

There are two safe ways of packing food into jars: hot pack and raw pack (sometimes called cold pack). Hot pack is the preferred method since it removes air from food tissues and results in a slower loss of quality during storage.

Hot pack: Heat foods to the boiling point in water, juice, or syrup; then pack the hot foods loosely in the jars and pour in the boiling liquid to surround the pieces and cover them completely. Most foods with liquid should be packed to ½ inch from the top of the jar, but corn, lima beans, and peas should be packed only to 1 inch from the top since they will expand a bit during processing.

Raw (cold) pack: Put raw, unheated foods directly into the jars. Pack tightly since the pieces of food will shrink during processing; then pour in enough boiling water, juice, or syrup to surround the pieces and cover them. (Meat and poultry are packed raw without liquid.) Use the same headspace that is allowed for the hot pack.

After hot or raw packing of the jars with food and liquid, run a narrow spatula between the food and the sides of the jar to remove air bubbles. Next, wipe the rim and threads of the jar clean. The jars are now ready for capping and processing.

Closing the Jars

Place each lid with the sealing compound next to the glass. Screw the metal band down firmly, but do not use extreme force. After processing, no further tightening is needed. The screw bands can be removed when the jars have cooled for 12 to 24 hours.

Using a Water Bath Canner

A boiling water canner is useful for processing foods high in acid: fruits, tomatoes, pickles, jams, and jellies. For all other foods use a pressure (steam) canner.

Place the rack on the bottom of the canner; then fill the canner half full with hot water. Over high heat bring the water to a boil for hot-packed foods and almost to a boil for raw-packed foods. Next, lower all the jars to the rack, leaving enough room between the jars for the water to circulate. Add boiling water until the jars are covered by 1 to 2 inches of liquid, but do not pour the water directly onto the jars. Cover the canner and return the water to a gentle boil. Start timing the processing when the water begins to boil, and add more boiling water as needed to keep the water 1 to 2 inches above the jars. (See the table on page 639 for processing times.) As soon as the processing is complete, remove the jars.

Using a Pressure Canner

A pressure canner is essential for processing all low-acid foods and combinations of foods: vegetables, meats, poultry, fish, soups, and stews. Follow the manufacturer's directions for using the canner, as well as consulting the general directions given in this section.

Put the rack on the bottom of the canner and fill the canner with 2 to 3 inches of hot water. Place the jars of food on the rack, leaving space for water and steam to circulate between each jar and between the jars and the sides of the canner. Fasten the cover securely; then heat the water to the boiling point and exhaust the canner (allow steam to escape) for 10 minutes. Close the vent or put on the weighted gauge. Begin timing the processing when the gauge reaches 10 pounds of pressure or the weighted gauge jiggles or rocks. (See the table on page 639 for processing times.) Regulate the heat so that the weight moves 2 to 3 times a minute, and process at 10 pounds of pressure for the entire time. When the processing time is up, remove the canner from the heat and let the pressure return to zero. This will take 30 to 60 minutes, depending on the size of the canner. Open the vent slowly (do not open before the pressure drops!), cautiously remove the lid from the canner, and take out the jars.

HONEY SYRUP FOR CANNING

Fruits canned in juice or plain water are delightfully tasty, and they are safe to eat, too, since a sweetener is added primarily for flavor. But for slightly better shape and color, as well as sweeter flavor, pack fruit pieces in a light honey syrup. To make syrup for 6 to 12 pints of fruit, blend 2 cups light honey with 4 cups very hot water; stir well.

Cooling the Jars

As soon as processing is done, remove the hot jars from the canner. Set them upright on a wire rack or folded cloth. (Do not open the jars to add more liquid if it has boiled down.) Leave room between the jars (2 to 3 inches) for air to circulate, yet keep them away from drafts since sudden coolness can crack the jars. After 24 hours, remove the screw bands and store the jars of food.

Testing the Seal

After the jars have cooled for at least 12 hours, check the seal. Press the center of each lid. If the center has a slight dip and will not move, the jar is sealed. An alternate test is to tap the center of the lid with a spoon. The resulting ring should be clear if the seal is good. However, a dull sound may or

SAFE CANNING

Putting up your own food is safe as well as enjoyable if you take a few simple precautions. Avoid spoilage and contamination with botulism toxin by always using recommended procedures and equipment. Never use the open-kettle method of canning foods. (In this method food is cooked in an open pot, then packed into jars with no further processing.) Never process in the oven, slow cooker, or microwave. Do not skimp on processing time, and do not overpack, since it can result in underprocessing. Avoid canning combinations of food. If you must can mixtures, use the processing time for the food that requires the longest time and highest temperature. Do not can overripe foods; their acid content is often very low.

CAUTION: If foods are not correctly processed, deadly botulism spores can grow in airtight jars of low-acid foods. Always process foods at the recommended temperature and for the recommended length of time.

---

may not mean the seal is bad, since food touching the lid can cause dullness.

If any of the jars has a poor seal, the food can be refrigerated and used within two days or reprocessed. To reprocess, empty the jar and, using a clean jar and a new metal lid, repeat all the steps in processing. Reprocessing will lower the quality of the canned food, however.

Storing Home-Canned Foods

As a rule, canned foods stored in a cool (below 70°F), dry, dark place will keep very nicely for up to a year. But foods kept in damp, hot, very cold, or bright areas can deteriorate in 6 months or less. Dampness can corrode the metal lids and cause leakage or allow entry of bacteria; freezing temperatures can change good texture to mushiness and damage seals; sunlight and heat can cause fading and loss of flavor and texture.

Using Home-Canned Foods

Serve fruits that are high in acid straight from the jar or use them to create tasty cooked dishes. But boil low- and non-acid foods—meats, poultry, and most vegetables—for 10 minutes (boil corn and spinach for 20 minutes) before tasting them. If foods foam, produce off-odors, or do not look right during or after boiling, discard them without tasting.

Home-canned foods make delightful soups, stews, and casseroles. Take care, however, not to cook them more than necessary since canned foods are extensively cooked during processing.

Detecting Spoilage

Even with careful preparation, home-canned foods spoil occasionally. Before opening jars, check them for cracks and for loose, bulging, or leaky lids; after opening, check contents for off-colors or odors, mold, sediment, slime, or soft texture. Discard any foods that look suspicious—do not taste them! Reject also any that spurt or fizz when opened.

PROCESSING HIGH-ACID FOODS

High-acid foods (fruits and tomatoes) are processed in a boiling water bath canner (see page 636). The first step in the process is to wash all the fruit very carefully.

High-altitude canning: If you live at 2,000 feet above sea level, add 2 minutes of processing time to all times specified for 20 minutes or less. For more than 20 minutes, add 4 minutes. If you live above 2,000 feet, still more processing time is needed.

FOOD		TYPE OF PACK	PREPARATION	PROCESSING TIME (MINUTES)	
				PINTS	QUARTS
APPLES	Slices	Hot	Peel, core, and slice. To slow darkening, place in 1 gallon water with 2 tablespoons vinegar. Drain and rinse. Boil 5 minutes in water, juice, or light syrup (see page 637). Stir occasionally to prevent burning. Pack in jars, leaving ½-inch headspace. Cover with hot syrup or water to ½ inch of top.	15	20
	Apple-sauce	Hot	Prepare apple slices as above and simmer until tender, about 20 minutes. Stir frequently to prevent burning. For chunky style, pack in jars; for smooth style, press through sieve or food mill and then pack. Leave ½-inch headspace.	15	15
APRICOTS			See peaches. Peeling can be omitted for apricots.		
BERRIES (except strawberries*): blackberries, dewberries, loganberries, raspberries, blueberries, currants, elderberries, gooseberries, huckleberries		Raw	Cap and stem. Pack in jars to ½ inch of top, shaking berries down gently. Cover with boiling juice, light syrup (see page 637), or water, leaving ½-inch headspace.	15	15
		Hot	Drain well after washing. Add ¼ cup honey to each quart currants, elderberries, or huckleberries. Cover and bring to a boil. Blanch blueberries or gooseberries for 15–30 seconds. Cool and drain. For all berries, pack in jars, leaving ½-inch headspace.	15	15
CHERRIES: SOUR AND SWEET		Raw	Stem, remove pits. Sweet cherries can be left unpitted, but sour cherries are best when pitted. For unpitted cherries, prick skin with a sharp knife to prevent splitting during processing. Pack cherries in jars, shaking cherries down gently. Cover with boiling juice or light syrup (see page 637) to ½ inch of top.	20	25
		Hot	Prepare cherries as above. For each quart sweet cherries, add ⅓ cup honey plus ¼ cup water. Bring to a boil. Pack in jars, leaving ½-inch headspace.	15	15

*Strawberries are best when frozen or preserved as jams.

PROCESSING HIGH-ACID FOODS—*CONTINUED*

FOOD	TYPE OF PACK	PREPARATION	PROCESSING TIME (MINUTES)	
			PINTS	QUARTS
FRUIT JUICES	Hot	Prepare juice (see "Making Fruit Juice," page 130). Reheat to simmering, and pack in jars, allowing ¼-inch headspace.	15	15
FRUIT PUREES	Hot	Prepare puree. Press simmered fruit (see page 637) through sieve or food mill. Reheat to simmering and pack in jars, leaving ¼-inch headspace.	15	15
NECTARINES		See peaches.		
PEACHES	Raw	To remove skins, dip in boiling water until skins are loosened, ½–1 minute; then dip in cold water. Slip off skins; remove pits; and cut in halves or slices. To prevent darkening, place in 1 gallon water with 2 tablespoons vinegar. Drain and rinse. Pack in jars (halves with cut-side down) and shake fruit down. Cover with boiling water or light syrup (see page 637), leaving ½-inch headspace.	25	30
	Hot	Prepare as above. Bring to a boil in light syrup (see page 637). Pack in jars and cover with syrup, leaving ½-inch headspace.	20	25
PEARS	Hot	Peel pears, cut in half lengthwise, and core. To prevent darkening, place in 1 gallon water with 2 tablespoons vinegar. Drain and rinse. Boil pears 5 minutes in light syrup (see page 637). Pack in jars. Place cut-side down and fill in layers. Cover with boiling syrup to ½ inch of top.	20	25
PLUMS	Raw	Stem. To can whole, prick skins with table fork to prevent splitting. Or halve and pit freestone varieties. Pack firmly in jars and cover with boiling light syrup (see page 637) to ½ inch of top.	20	25
	Hot	Prepare as above. Heat plums in boiling light syrup (see page 637). Pack in jars and cover with boiling syrup to ½ inch of top.	20	25
RHUBARB	Hot	Cut stalks into ½-inch pieces. Add ¼ cup honey to each quart rhubarb and let stand to draw out juice. Bring to a boil. Pack in jars to ½ inch of top.	15	15

PROCESSING HIGH-ACID FOODS—*CONTINUED*

FOOD		TYPE OF PACK	PREPARATION	PROCESSING TIME (MINUTES)	
				PINTS	QUARTS
TOMATOES**	Whole or pieces	Raw	Dip in boiling water 15–30 seconds to split skins, then dip in cold water. Slip off skins and remove cores. Leave whole, or cut in halves or quarters. Pack in jars, pressing gently to fill spaces, or add hot tomato juice. Do not add water. Leave ½-inch headspace. Add 4 teaspoons lemon juice or ½ teaspoon powdered citric acid per quart to low-acid tomatoes.	35	45
		Hot	Prepare as above. Quarter and bring to a boil, stirring to prevent sticking. Pack boiling hot in jars, leaving ½-inch headspace. Add 4 teaspoons lemon juice or ½ teaspoon powdered citric acid per quart to low-acid tomatoes.	35	45
	Juice	Hot	Remove stems and trim off bruised or discolored spots. Quickly cut about 1 pound tomatoes into quarters and place directly into a large pot. Bring immediately to a boil. Crush pieces and add additional freshly cut pieces slowly to boiling mixture. Crush new pieces once boiling resumes. Keep mixture boiling constantly and vigorously while adding remaining tomato pieces. Simmer 5 minutes after all tomato pieces have been added. Press hot cooked tomatoes through a sieve or food mill to remove skins and seeds. Reheat to a boil. Pour immediately into jars, leaving ¼-inch headspace.	35	35
	Juice blend with vegetables	Hot	To 18 pounds freshly crushed and simmering tomatoes, add no more than 3 cups of any combination of finely chopped celery, onions, carrots, or sweet peppers. Simmer 20 minutes, then press through a sieve or food mill to remove skins and seeds. Bring to a boil. Pour immediately into jars leaving ½-inch headspace.	35	35
	Sauce, plain	Hot	Prepare and press tomato juice as above. Simmer until sauce reaches desired consistency. Reduce volume by one-third for a thin sauce or by half for a thick one. Pour into jars, leaving ¼-inch headspace.	35 (thin) 20 (thick)	35 (thin) 20 (thick)
	Sauce with vegetables	Hot	Prepare the same as juice blend with vegetables (see above). After pressing the juice, simmer it until its volume is reduced by half.	35	35
	Sauce with meat		See "Processing Low-Acid Foods," page 642.		

**Can only high-quality tomatoes. Never can soft, decayed, cracked, moldy, or spotted ones, or those picked from dead vines or vines damaged by frost.

PROCESSING LOW-ACID FOODS

Low-acid foods (vegetables, fish, meat, and poultry) are processed in a pressure canner (see page 637). Unless otherwise noted, the first step in the process is to wash all the vegetables very carefully.

High-altitude canning: If using a canner with a weighted gauge, no adjustment is necessary. If using a canner with a dial gauge, process at 11 pounds pressure for the same amount of time at 2,000 feet above sea level. At higher altitudes, process at still higher pressure.

FOOD		TYPE OF PACK	PREPARATION	PROCESSING TIME WITH 10 POUNDS PRESSURE (MINUTES)	
				PINTS	QUARTS
ASPARAGUS		Raw	Trim off tough scales and stems, wash a second time, and leave whole or cut into 1-inch pieces. Pack tightly in jars, taking care not to crush. Cover with boiling water to 1 inch of top.	25	30
		Hot	Prepare as above. Cover with boiling water and simmer 2–3 minutes. Pack loosely in jars (do not press or shake down) leaving 1-inch headspace. Cover with fresh boiling water to 1 inch of top.	25	30
BEANS	Snap: green, wax	Raw	Trim ends. Cut or snap into 1-inch pieces. Pack tightly in jars, leaving 1-inch headspace. Cover with boiling water to 1 inch of top.	20	25
		Hot	Prepare as above. Cover with boiling water and boil 5 minutes. Pack in jars, leaving 1-inch headspace. Cover with fresh boiling water to 1 inch of top.	20	25
	Lima	Raw	Shell young tender, beans. Pack loosely in jars (do not press or shake down). For small beans, fill pints to 1 inch of top and quarts to $1\frac{1}{2}$ inches; for large beans, fill pints to 1 inch of top and quarts to $1\frac{1}{4}$ inches. Cover with boiling water to 1 inch of top.	40	50
		Hot	Prepare as above. Cover with boiling water and bring to a boil. Pack loosely in jars, leaving 1-inch headspace. Cover with fresh boiling water to 1 inch of top.	40	50

PROCESSING LOW-ACID FOODS—*CONTINUED*

FOOD		TYPE OF PACK	PREPARATION	PROCESSING TIME WITH 10 POUNDS PRESSURE (MINUTES)	
				PINTS	QUARTS
CARROTS		Raw	Peel carrots and slice or dice. Pack tightly in jars, leaving 1-inch headspace. Cover with boiling water to 1 inch of top.	25	30
		Hot	Prepare as above. Cover with boiling water, then bring to a boil. Pack in jars, leaving 1-inch headspace. Cover with cooking liquid to 1 inch of top.	25	30
CORN	Cream-style	Raw	Husk corn and remove silk. Wash. Cut corn from cob at center of the kernel, and scrape cob. Pack in pint jars, leaving 1-inch headspace. Cover with boiling water to 1 inch of top.	95	Not recom-mended
		Hot	Prepare as above. To each quart of corn, add 1 pint boiling water, and heat to boiling. Pack in pint jars, leaving 1-inch headspace.	85	Not recom-mended
	Whole kernel	Raw	Husk corn and remove silk. Wash. Cut corn from cob at two-thirds the depth of the kernel. Pack loosely in jars (do not press or shake down), leaving 1-inch headspace. Cover with boiling water to 1 inch of top.	55	85
		Hot	Prepare as above. Blanch on the cob 3 minutes in boiling water. Cool corn and cut kernels from cob. To each quart of kernels, add ½ pint hot water. Bring to a boil. Pack hot corn mixture in jars, leaving 1-inch headspace.	55	85
MIXED VEGETABLES		Hot	Prepare vegetables in manner described under each vegetable. Mix, cover with boiling water, and boil 3 minutes. Drain; pack in jars, allowing 1 inch headspace. Cover with fresh boiling water to 1 inch of top.	Time according to vegetable requiring longest processing	Time according to vegetable requiring longest processing

PROCESSING LOW-ACID FOODS—*CONTINUED*

FOOD		TYPE OF PACK	PREPARATION	PROCESSING TIME WITH 10 POUNDS PRESSURE (MINUTES)	
				PINTS	QUARTS
PEAS	Sweet green	Raw	Shell and wash peas. Pack loosely in jars (do not press or shake down), leaving 1-inch headspace. Cover with boiling water to 1 inch of top.	40	40
		Hot	Prepare as above. Cover with boiling water; return to a boil. Pack loosely in jars, leaving 1-inch headspace. Cover with fresh boiling water to 1 inch of top.	40	40
	Sugar snap (edible pods)	Raw	Trim ends. Leave whole or cut in 1-inch pieces. Pack in jars, leaving 1-inch headspace. Cover with boiling water to 1 inch of top.	20	35
		Hot	Prepare as above. Cover with boiling water and cook 5 minutes. Pack in jars. Cover with fresh boiling water, leaving 1-inch headspace.	20	25
POTATOES	Cubed	Hot	Peel and cut into 1-inch cubes. Cook immediately in boiling water and drain. Pack in jars, leaving 1-inch headspace. Cover with fresh boiling water to 1 inch of top.	20	35
	Whole (1–2 inches in diameter)	Hot	Peel. Cook in boiling water 10 minutes. Drain and pack in jars, leaving 1-inch headspace. Cover with fresh boiling water to 1 inch of top.	30	40
PUMPKINS		Hot	Seed and peel. Cut into 1-inch cubes and boil 2 minutes. Pack in jars, allowing 1-inch headspace. Cover with cooking liquid (and boiling water if necessary) to 1 inch of top.	55	90
SPINACH AND OTHER GREENS		Hot	Can only top-notch, tender fresh greens. Rinse until greens are free of grit; drain. Remove tough ribs and stems. Steam until well wilted, 3–5 minutes. Pack loosely in jars, leaving 1-inch headspace. Cover with boiling water to 1 inch of top.	70	90
TOMATO SAUCE WITH MEAT		Hot	Prepare sauce according to favorite recipe. Pack in jars, leaving 1-inch headspace.	60	75

PROCESSING LOW-ACID FOODS—*CONTINUED*

FOOD		TYPE OF PACK	PREPARATION	PROCESSING TIME WITH 10 POUNDS PRESSURE (MINUTES)	
				PINTS	QUARTS
TOMATO SAUCE WITH MEAT		Hot	Prepare sauce according to favorite recipe. Pack in jars, leaving 1-inch headspace.	60	75
FISH		Raw	Use only firm, fresh fish. Bleed well. Wash thoroughly. Pack in jars, leaving 1-inch headspace. Cover with boiling water to 1 inch of top.	100	100
MEAT	Ground, chopped	Hot	Choose fresh, high-quality chilled meat. With venison, add 1 part high-quality pork fat to 3 or 4 parts venison before grinding. Shape chopped meat into patties or balls; cut cased sausage in 3- to 4-inch links. Cook until lightly browned. Ground meat may be sautéed without shaping. Remove excess fat. Pack hot in jars, leaving 1-inch headspace. Cover with boiling meat stock, tomato juice, or water to 1 inch of top.	75	90
	Strips, cubes	Raw	Choose high-quality chilled meat. Remove excess fat and large bones. Place meat in jars, leaving 1-inch headspace. Do not add liquid.	75	90
		Hot	Prepare meat as above. Precook meat until rare by roasting, stewing, or browning in small amount of fat. Pack in jars, leaving 1-inch headspace. Cover with boiling stock, meat drippings, water, or tomatoes to 1 inch of top.	75	90
POULTRY		Raw	Choose freshly killed and dressed animals. (Older chickens are more flavorful than fryers.) Dressed poultry should be chilled 6–12 hours before canning. Remove excess fat. Cut chicken into pieces suitable for cooking or canning. Pack loosely in jars (do not press or shake down), leaving 1¼-inch headspace. Do not add liquid.	65 (with bones) 75 (without bones)	75 (with bones) 90 (without bones)
		Hot	Prepare as above. Boil steam, or bake until about two-thirds done. Pack hot pieces in jars, leaving 1¼-inch headspace. Cover with boiling stock to 1 inch of top.	65 (with bones) 75 (without bones)	75 (with bones) 90 (without bones)

Pickling

Often, even after you have put up endless rows of colorful pints and quarts of fruits and vegetables, your garden continues to offer more of the same wonderful foods. When this happens next year, try pickling some foods and treat your family and guests to a delightful change of taste.

Almost any food can be pickled, but cucumbers, sweet peppers, green tomatoes, and corn are among the best and most popular. Though pickled foods are preserved in a salt brine or spiced vinegar solution, remember that they must also always be canned.

Kinds of Pickles

There are four classic types of pickled foods:

Fresh-pack or quick-process pickles: Very easy to prepare at home, these pickles made from whole or sliced vegetables can be processed either with or without salt. In the salt method, the foods (cucumbers are most common, but beets, cauliflower, green beans, and okra are also pickled in this manner) are soaked in a low-salt brine for several hours or overnight, then drained and processed with boiling vinegar, spices, and herbs. In a no-salt method that some cooks use, the foods are initially cooked with a spiced vinegar, then packed and processed immediately. Alternatively, the foods are first packed in the jars, next the spiced vinegar is poured in, and then the processing is done. Pickles made without salt tend to have a soft texture and sharp vinegar flavor.

Fruit pickles: To make these pickles, whole fruits such as peaches, pears, and watermelon rind are simmered in a spicy, sweet-sour syrup, then packed and processed.

Relishes: Mixed fruits and vegetables that have been chopped into small pieces, seasoned, and then cooked, packed, and processed make up this broad category of pickled foods. Hot and spicy, or sweet and spicy, relishes include condiments of all types: ketchup, chili sauce, chowchow, chutney, corn relish, and piccalilli.

Brined pickles: Cabbage (for sauerkraut) and cucumbers are the vegetables usually preserved by curing in a brine. The curing process takes about 3 weeks in either a low-salt or high-salt brine. After curing, the pickles are packed and processed.

Pickling Ingredients

Fruits and vegetables: Although cauliflower, corn, cucumbers, green beans, green tomatoes, onions, peaches, pears, sweet peppers, and watermelon rind are among the fruits and vegetables most commonly pickled, almost any tender one of top quality is a good choice. For the crispest, most flavorful pickled foods, allow no more than 24 hours (preferably less) to elapse between picking and processing; and refrigerate the produce immediately after picking if it will not be processed within an hour.

When possible, select slightly underripe produce; it will result in crisper pickles than if ripe or overripe produce is used. Avoid moldy or badly bruised produce since off-flavor and mushy texture cannot be overcome by seasoning, curing, or processing. And do not use waxed cucumbers or green peppers; the waxed skin will not absorb the brine. To reduce chances of rot, do use cucumbers

PICKLING LOW-ACID VEGETABLES

Although low-acid vegetables—such as corn, cucumbers, green bell peppers, green tomatoes, and zucchini—would ordinarily be canned in a pressure canner, when they are made into pickles they are canned by the water bath process in order to retain crispness. The vinegar and salt added during pickling preserve the vegetables. Just be sure to closely follow the USDA low-temperature pasteurization guidelines for pickles to ensure maximum food safety (see the "Pickle" section at www.uga.edu/nchfp/).

---

with a short piece of the stem left on the fruit.

Rinse fruits and vegetables gently but thoroughly under running water. Drain on towels and tenderly blot dry. Remove any blossoms since they are frequently the source of softening.

Vinegar: Cider vinegar or any other vinegar with a mild flavor makes tasty pickles. But cider vinegar and red wine vinegar discolor light vegetables and fruits such as cauliflower, onions, and pears. Choose white distilled vinegar (it has a somewhat sharp, pungent taste) for those vegetables to preserve the integrity of the color.

Whichever vinegar you choose, be absolutely certain its acidity is 4 to 6 percent. Any less acid can almost guarantee spoilage and dangerous eating. If you find the pickles too sour with the recommended acidity, add sweetener, but never dilute the vinegar.

Sweetener: Granulated sugar or honey can be used in pickling, but note that honey changes color and flavor when boiled. To prevent these changes, instead of boiling the honey, vinegar, and spices together, boil only the vinegar and spices. Then add the honey to the vinegar-spice mixture and bring the syrup to a very brief boil. Add the syrup quickly to the pickles.

Herbs and spices: Fresh herbs and spices lend the most flavor to pickled foods. Tie whole leaves and seeds in a cheesecloth bag or stainless steel spice ball for easy removal before pickles are packed. Spices left in the jar through processing can cause off-flavors and dark pickles. Ground spices, too, tend to darken pickles, so avoid them.

Water: Soft water (either natural or artificially softened) is best for attractive-looking pickles. Iron or sulfur in hard water will darken pickles; calcium and other salts can interfere with the fermentation process and often cause a white scum or precipitate.

Pickling Equipment

Most of the equipment required for pickling is inexpensive and already stocked in the average kitchen. The few essential specialty items that run into more money, such as a canner and jars, can be used repeatedly.

For heating and mixing the vinegar-spice liquid, use a stainless steel, unchipped enameled, or glass saucepan. Avoid aluminum and never use copper, brass, iron, or galvanized pans or utensils. These metals can react with the strong acid of the vinegar and cause unwanted color and taste changes as well as form poisonous compounds.

In the preparation of the fruits and vegetables,

WHAT HAPPENED TO THE PICKLES?

PROBLEM	POSSIBLE CAUSE
Soft or slippery	Vinegar solution too weak; foods not kept submerged in the pickling liquid.
Dark	Water contains iron or sulfur; ground spices were used.
Hollow and float	Cucumbers pickled too long after picking.
Shriveled	Vinegar solution has too much acid or sweetener.
Faded	Pickles kept too long or exposed to bright light during storage.

---

use standard household utensils. Some items you will find helpful are: a cutting board, paring knife, food grinder, ladle, wooden spoon, tray, tongs, and measuring equipment.

For the actual canning process you will need jars and a canner, along with other equipment (see "Canning Equipment," page 635). For pickles, you'll need the boiling water bath type of canner. It is currently considered acceptable for canning pickled foods since these foods have an increased acid content from the added vinegar.

Packing & Processing Pickled Foods

The packing and processing steps for pickled foods are identical to those for plain, high-acid fruits and vegetables, although the liquid used in pickling is a spiced vinegar instead of water, juice, or syrup. Be sure the vinegar mixture surrounds each piece of food.

Process pickled foods for 10 to 15 minutes using the boiling water bath method (see "Using a Water Bath Canner," page 636). Follow the canning instructions for testing the seal and noting signs of spoilage (see page 638).

Storing Pickled Foods

Pickled foods are tastiest when the flavor is allowed to develop for at least 3 weeks before the jars are opened. Store pickled foods, like other canned items, in a cool, dry, dark place.

Jams & Jellies

Jams, jellies, conserves, marmalades, preserves, and fruit butters are easy to make and provide a wonderful way to use up and preserve an overabundance of luscious fruits. Best of all, homemade jams and jellies make lovely gifts for friends and family.

Equipment

Several pieces of equipment simplify the preparation of jams and jellies:

Large pot: This item is essential. Select an 8- to 10-quart pot that will hold four times the volume you will be cooking, since jellies foam when boiled rapidly. The pot should have a heavy, flat bottom.

Jelly bag and stand (or cheesecloth and colander, or fruit press): For crystal-clear jellies, a jelly bag is needed for straining the fruit juices.

Jelly (candy or deep-fat) thermometer: A thermometer takes the guesswork out of making jams and jellies. It is especially important when no commercial pectin is used.

Jellmeter: A graduated glass tube with an opening at each end, a jellmeter is handy for measuring pectin levels in juices.

Jelly glasses (or canning jars): Glasses or straight-sided containers work well for jellies. Old-style jelly glasses were straight-sided jars that were sealed with paraffin (no longer recommended). Modern jelly jars have a similar appearance, but come with a two-piece screwband and lid. Regular canning jars with lids can be used for jams, preserves, conserves, and marmalades.

Other useful kitchen equipment: 1-quart measuring cup, measuring cups and spoons, paring knives, food grinder, food mill, bowls, a wire basket or colander, a long-handled spoon, a ladle, and a household scale.

Ingredients

To jell, all jellies and jams require fruit, acid, pectin, and a sweetener, in proper proportions.

Fruit: The main ingredient, fruit provides the characteristic flavor, color, and aroma for each jam and jelly. It also gives some of the pectin and acid needed to make a gel. Fruits that are firm yet just barely ripe are the richest in pectin and acid. But those low in pectin will still make good jams and jellies if combined with fruits high in pectin or combined with extracted pectin. Fruits high in pectin are: tart blackberries, boysenberries, Concord grapes, crab apples, cranberries, green gooseberries, loganberries, plums, quinces, red currants, sour guavas, and tart apples. Those low in pectin are: apricots, blueberries, cherries, figs, peaches, pears, pineapples, raspberries, and strawberries.

Acid: Both flavor and gel formation benefit from the acid in fruit. If the acid level of the fruit is low, lemon juice is commonly added.

Pectin: A natural component of fruit, pectin is necessary for gel formation. For fruits low in pectin and fully ripe, commercial liquid or powdered pectin can be added to aid jelling. (Directions for use are on the package.) But most commercial pectins require substantial quantities of sugar to set.

If you want to make a less sweet product, alternatives to commercial pectin include low-methoxyl pectin (below) and homemade pectin (see "Make Your Own Pectin," page 652).

Sweetener: Honey makes a pleasant-tasting change from the sugar traditionally used in making homemade jellies but there are some differences between the two. Sugar acts as a preservative and helps to firm the fruit, to produce a clear, bright color, and to heighten sweetness without changing the fruity flavor. Honey, too, is a preservative, but it gives a loose texture, slightly dark color, and mild honey flavor to the gel. In addition, honey tastes sweeter than sugar, so when you're converting a recipe to use honey instead of sugar, the amount of sweetener called for must be reduced. If possible, use a recipe specially developed for honey, since direct replacement usually does not give satisfactory results. Also, recipes for jams, preserves, and conserves made with honey give the most pleasing products; jellies made with honey are often disappointingly loose. When using honey, add it near the end of the cooking period to achieve maximum fruity flavor.

Preserving Procedures

Prepping the Fruit

The preliminary preparation of fruits destined for jams and jellies is the same as for table use. Simply wash the fruit thoroughly but gently, and pat dry. Use a cutting board and a sharp knife, a grinder, or a blender to chop the fruit into small pieces. NOTE: Fruits chopped in a grinder or blender tend to turn dark faster than those chopped by hand.

Extracting Juice

To extract juice, prepare the fruit as directed in the jelly recipe you are using. As a rule, berries are crushed without heating, while other fruits are

---

USING LOW-METHOXYL PECTIN

Low-methoxyl pectin differs from both commercial and natural pectins in that it requires calcium salts instead of sugar to form a gel. So the beauty of using this pectin is that you are free to add as little or as much sweetening as you want. Best of all, using low-methoxyl pectin is simple.

Prepare crushed fruit for jam or juice for jelly as usual, and place in a large saucepan over medium heat. Bring it just to a boil.

Measure 2 tablespoons sugar or honey (or to taste) and ½ teaspoon low-methoxyl pectin for each cup of fruit or juice, and mix them well in a small bowl. Pour the mixture into the boiling fruit; stir until the sweetener and pectin are completely dissolved. Combine ⅛ teaspoon calcium salts with ¼ cup water, then add 1 teaspoon of this solution for each cup of fruit or juice. Stir quickly until well mixed. Remove 1 tablespoon of the jam or jelly to a cold plate, and chill briefly in the freezer to test whether it has jelled. Add juice or calcium salts, if necessary, to adjust consistency. Ladle into jars, adjust seals, and process in a boiling water bath for 15 minutes (see "Using a Water Bath Canner," page 636).

HINTS FOR COOKING JAMS & JELLIES

For best results, carefully follow the directions given in your favorite jelly or jam recipe. And consider these pointers for fine-tuning your skills:

- Do not double or triple the recipe. Best results come from preparing a single batch at a time.
- Cook jams and jellies in a heavy pot over low heat to prevent scorching.
- Start timing the cooking as soon as the mixture comes to a rapid boil that cannot be stirred down.
- Skim off the foam that forms on the surface, as it will detract from the appearance of the finished product.
- Remove whole spices immediately after cooking to prevent darkening of conserves.
- Seal jams, preserves, and marmalades in canning jars with screw bands and metal lids, and process for 15 minutes (see "Using a Water Bath Canner," page 636). Older recipes call for sealing jellies with paraffin, but because the seal can be imprecise and subject to contamination with mold, this method is no longer recommended. Jellies should be processed for 10 minutes in a water bath canner.
- Gently shake jars of jams, preserves, and marmalades several times during cooling to distribute the fruit evenly. Also, use mostly fully ripe fruit, which it is less likely to float to the top.

---

chopped, then heated. Take care not to overcook the fruit; too much heat destroys pectin. Put the prepared fruit in a damp jelly bag or fruit press. The clearest jelly comes from juice that has dripped through a jelly bag without pressing. Though you get more with pressing, pressed juice tends to be cloudy. Re-strain pressed juice through a damp jelly bag or a double thickness of cheesecloth without squeezing.

Checking Pectin Levels

When making jellies without added pectin, use three parts fully ripe fruit to one part underripe fruit. The underripe fruit will have a higher pectin content and help ensure jelling; the fully ripe fruit provides the best flavor. It's best to use fruits that are naturally high in pectin, such as tart apples, cranberries, and quince. But other fruits that are slightly lower in pectin can still be turned into jellies by cooking them longer and thus concentrating the pectin they do have. When making the juice to be turned into jelly, be sure to include the skins, since this is where much of the pectin is found.

The trick is to determine the level of pectin in the fruit juice, since this influences how much sweetener you actually need for proper jelling. Use the following test:

Alcohol test: Mix 1 tablespoon denatured (grain or ethyl) alcohol with 1 tablespoon extracted juice. Stir slightly to mix. Juices rich in

MAKE YOUR OWN PECTIN

Using homemade pectin, often called apple jelly stock, or extract, is one way to boost pectin levels without adding commercial pectin. To make pectin, choose mature apples, which are rich in pectin and acid as well as abundant and inexpensive.

Carefully wash 4 pounds of apples, and cut them into thin slices (include the peel and core since both contain pectin). Put the apples and 2 quarts of water in a large pot. Cover the pot and bring the water to a boil. Simmer rapidly for 20 minutes. Without pressing the solids, strain off the free-running juice through one thickness of cheesecloth or a jelly bag. Reserve the liquid and return it to the pot. Heat the juice, until it is reduced by half. Test the pectin level (see "Checking Pectin Levels," page 651).

Use this pectin immediately for blending with other fruit juices to make jelly or jam, or preserve it by canning or freezing for future use. To can, seal and process for 15 minutes in a boiling water bath (see "Using a Water Bath Canner," page 636). Six to 8 tablespoons of homemade pectin replace approximately 1 tablespoon of commercial liquid or powdered pectin in most recipes.

---

pectin will form one transparent, firm, jelly-like mass. Those with a medium amount of pectin will form two or more jelly-like masses. Those very low in pectin will form little lumps or particles. (Never taste this mixture. It is poisonous!)

High-pectin juices will need about 3/4 cup of sugar for every cup of juice; use a slightly higher ratio if the pectin level is low.

Testing for Jelling Point

A well-made jelly holds its shape when released from a mold, yet it is tender enough to cut with a spoon. Also, good jelly has a fresh fruit flavor, never a caramelized sugar taste. To determine when a jelly has reached the jelling point, use one of these three tests:

Temperature test: This is probably the most accurate test, but to get a reliable reading, it is essential that you know the boiling point for water in your area. Check the temperature of boiling water shortly before making the jelly; then cook the jelly mixture to a temperature 8°F higher than the boiling point of the water. At this point, the mixture should jell nicely when cool.

Sheet test: This test requires a watchful eye. It is very popular but not entirely dependable. With a cool metal spoon scoop up a small amount of the boiling jelly mixture and raise it about a foot above the pot, away from the steam. Quickly tip the spoon and let the jelly run off the edge. If the syrup forms two drops that flow together and fall from the spoon as a sheet (top), the jelly is

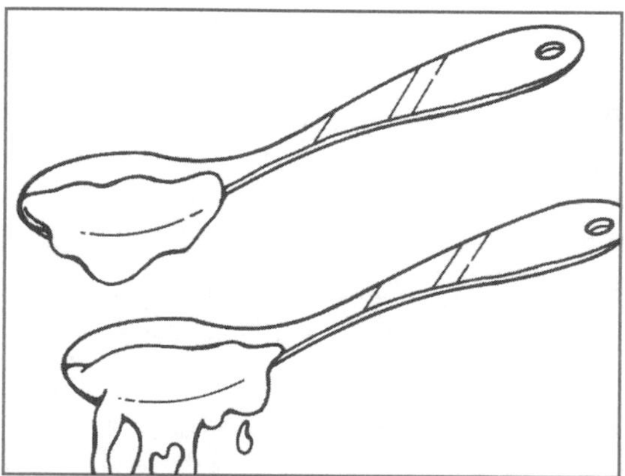

probably done. If it slides from the spoon as separate drops (bottom), cook the mixture a little longer, then test again.

Freezer test: The hot jelly mixture should be removed from the heat during this test. Put a few drops of the jelly on a cold plate; then chill in the freezer for a few minutes. If the mixture jells, it is done.

Storing Jams & Jellies

The brilliant colors of homemade jams and jellies are very sensitive to bright light. To prevent fading of your jams and jellies, store them in a dark place. If you choose a spot that is also cool and dry, the overall quality of the unopened jars will stay high for up to a year. Once opened, jams and jellies should be stored in the refrigerator.

Uncooked jams will keep nicely in the freezer for a year. After thawing and opening an uncooked jam, store it in the refrigerator and use it within 3 weeks.

DRYING

Drying, one of the oldest ways of preserving food, is being rediscovered by people who want a low-cost, energy-efficient method of putting up fresh fruits, vegetables, and herbs. And backpackers, cyclists, and the like also enjoy the benefits of dried foods, which are light in weight, wholesome, and easy to prepare.

Drying preserves food by removing 80 to 90 percent of the water that is required by enzymes and spoilage organisms (molds, yeasts, bacteria) to thrive. Because so much water has been removed, dried foods take up one-sixth to one-third the storage space of whole foods, yet all their goodness remains.

Drying Equipment

To dry foods at home, you will need a solar dryer, an electric dehydrator, or an oven. Drying indoors with controlled heat has several advantages. Drying goes on day and night, unaffected by the weather. Controlled-heat dryers shorten the drying time and extend the drying season to include late-maturing fruits and vegetables. Best of all, foods dried this way have better color and flavor and rehydrate more effectively.

Drying Procedures

PREPARATION FOR DRYING

For full-flavored dried fruits and vegetables, select those that are ripe and of peak quality. Wash the produce thoroughly and peel the varieties with thick skins. To hasten drying, cut the produce into small pieces or slice it very thinly. Keep the size of the pieces uniform so that drying is even. Blanch the produce (see below), then loosely place it on drying trays in single layers. (For specific instructions, see "Drying Fruits & Vegetables," page 657.)

Blanching: Blanching aids the retention of quality in dried foods in three ways. It hastens drying by softening the exterior of the food, making it easier for moisture to escape; it stops the action of enzymes that can cause deterioration during storage; and it facilitates rehydration.

To blanch produce for drying, follow the general steam-blanching directions for freezing (see "Blanching," page 623), but shorten the length of the blanching time slightly since pieces of food cut for drying are exceptionally small and thin. Likewise, the chilling step mentioned for freezing can be skipped because foods are heated somewhat during drying. The chilling step, though not really necessary, prevents the food from overcooking through residual heat.

Preventing Discoloration: Some fruits—apples, apricots, bananas, nectarines, peaches, pears—tend to discolor when sliced. You can preserve the color by soaking the slices in a solution of 1 tablespoon lemon juice to 1 quart water. Soak the fruits for 5 minutes, then drain and spread on trays to dry.

DRYING METHODS

Whether drying in the sun or with controlled heat, try to keep the heat at 140°F for at least two-thirds of the drying time. Build the heat up slowly from 120°F so that the outside of the food will not harden and inhibit the release of moisture from the center. Stir the food often (every 30 to 60 minutes) to keep drying even.

To dry in the oven: Place food directly on oven racks, one piece deep, or, if the slats are too far apart, cover the racks with nylon mesh or cheesecloth and then put the food on top of the cloth. Trays made of wooden slats and mesh, such as those used for drying in the sun, are best if additional surfaces are needed. Separate the trays by placing 3-inch blocks of wood at each corner when stacking in the oven. Leave the door ajar and use a small fan to aid air circulation.

To dry in the sun: Use a well-designed solar collector dryer with good ventilation and covers to protect the food from insects. Start early in the day and dry in full sun on days when the humidity is low. Bring the food in at night to avoid dampness from night dew. Drying should be as quick as possible (about 2 days), to avoid decomposition, but not so rapid that the food scorches.

Testing Dryness

Too much moisture left in dried foods will permit mold to grow during storage, so check foods carefully every day during the drying process. Select a few pieces from the trays, allowing them to cool before testing since hot foods often seem to contain more moisture than they really have. In general, appropriately dried fruits will have no moisture when cut and squeezed. They will feel leathery and be resilient. Well-dried vegetables are brittle and tough and rattle when stirred on the trays. (See "Drying Fruits & Vegetables," page 657, for descriptions of properly dried food.)

Pasteurizing & Conditioning Dried Foods

Once the food is dried, pasteurize it to ensure that no insect eggs will hatch or harmful spoilage organisms will develop. Pasteurizing is necessary since the low heat used in drying is not high enough to kill contaminants. To pasteurize, spread the dried food 1 inch thick on baking sheets or trays, and heat for 10 to 15 minutes in a preheated 175°F oven. Cool the food thoroughly.

After pasteurizing the food, condition it by putting it in an open container in a warm, dry area. Cover the container loosely to keep curious insects and animals out. During the next 4 days, stir the contents several times to bring drier pieces in contact with the more moist ones. In that way, moisture content will be evenly distributed. When conditioning has been done, the food is ready for storage.

NOTE: If the food seems too moist after conditioning, return it to the dryer until the proper consistency is reached.

Drying Herbs

To dry fresh herbs, either hang them in a dry, airy room for several days until they are crumbly, or heat them in a shallow baking pan in a low oven (200°F) until completely dried (about 15 minutes to an hour, depending on the herb). Test the leaves often for crispness. Although they do not possess the same rich quality as fresh herbs, dried herbs may be stored considerably longer. When dried, herbs retain the oils that convey their characteristic aromas and flavors, so they still have a good deal of seasoning power. However, these values will diminish with time and exposure to heat

FREEZER MALFUNCTIONS & POWER FAILURES

If your freezer stops working, slow the thawing of frozen foods with one or more of these measures:

- Do not open the freezer. Even in hot weather, food will stay frozen for about 2 days in a freezer that is full.
- Use dry ice to keep food frozen for longer than 2 days. If the freezer is half full, the ice will keep the food frozen for an additional 2 days; if nearly full, it will keep the food frozen for an extra 3 to 4 days. Allow approximately 2 ½ pounds for each cubic foot of freezer space. Put the ice on cardboard over the food; keep the room well ventilated; and never touch dry ice with your bare hands.
- Transfer food to a commercial locker if dry ice is unavailable.

---

and/or light, so label and date the bottles and store them in a cool dry place away from direct sunlight. If you use a spice rack, hang the rack away from the stove. Do not keep dried herbs for more than a year.

Drying Sea Vegetables

Freshly foraged sea vegetables may be dried to preserve them for future use. Simply rinse them well in fresh water before drying on a clean cloth in the sun. (Setting them to dry on paper, plastic, or rubber may affect their flavor.) Turn the plants over periodically—at least every 45 to 50 minutes, more often if possible—so that they dry evenly. The drying process takes about 12 hours. When the plants are dried, they may be used immediately or stored for future use.

Storing Dried Foods

If stored under the right conditions, dried fruits will retain good quality for up to a year, and vegetables, for up to 4 months. Keep dried foods in tightly closed jars or insect-resistant plastic bags in a cool, dry place. If appropriate shelf space is not available, put dried foods in the freezer. Resist the temptation to store the colorful jars or bags in an area exposed to bright light, because light fades dried foods readily. Instead, protect the foods by placing the containers in brown bags or by wrapping containers in foil.

Using Dried Foods

Dried foods are scrumptious when eaten out of hand or added to cooked dishes. Fairly crisp dried fruits and vegetables can be ground into flour and used as flavorful, nutritious additions to crackers, cookies, quick breads, yeast breads, and pancakes. (For every cup of flour called for in a recipe, you can replace up to ¼ cup with finely ground fruit or vegetable flour.)

For some dishes, dried foods give the nicest texture and flavor when rehydrated before use, but for others, dried foods work well while still

(continued on page 659)

DRYING FRUITS & VEGETABLES

FOOD	PREPARATION	CHARACTERISTICS AFTER DRYING
APPLES	Use firm fruit; peel, core, and slice; blanch 4 minutes.	Soft, pliable, slightly tough
APRICOTS	Use ripe fruit; pit and slice; dip in ascorbic acid solution; blanch 4 minutes.	Soft, pliable
ARTICHOKES	Use only tender hearts; trim leaves, cut in halves; blanch 5 minutes.	Brittle
ASPARAGUS	Trim scales and ends; no slicing; blanch 5 minutes.	Very tough to brittle
BANANAS	Slice; dip in ascorbic acid solution; no blanching.	Pliable to crisp
BEANS, GREEN	Use tender beans; French cut; blanch 6 minutes.	Brittle, crisp
BEANS, LIMA	Shell and wash; blanch 5 minutes	Hard, brittle
BEETS	Remove tops and roots; slice; blanch until tender.	Tough to brittle
BLUEBERRIES	Remove stems; blanch to break skins.	Leathery, pliable, similar to raisins
BROCCOLI	Trim tough stalks; split large stalks; blanch 4 minutes.	Crisp, brittle
CABBAGE	Core and shred; blanch 2–3 minutes.	Brittle
CARROTS	Peel; slice; blanch 4 minutes.	Tough to brittle
CAULIFLOWER	Use only florets; remove from core; split stems; blanch 3 minutes.	Crisp, slightly browned
CELERY	Trim base; cut into ½-inch slices; blanch 1 minute.	Very brittle
CHERRIES	Remove stems; cut in half and pit; blanch 1 minute.	Leathery, pliable, similar to raisins
COCONUTS	Drain milk; remove meat from shell; grate or slice; no blanching.	Leathery to crisp
CORN	Husk ears and remove silk; cut from cob; blanch 5 minutes.	Dry, brittle
CUCUMBERS	Peel; slice; blanch 1 minute.	Crisp
DATES	No pretreatment necessary	Leathery, deep russet color
FIGS	Cut in half to shorten drying; no blanching.	Leathery
GARLIC	Peel; cut into thin pieces; no blanching.	Crisp
GRAPES, SEEDLESS	Blanch long enough to split skins.	Raisins
HORSERADISH	Trim tops; grate or slice; no blanching.	Brittle
LEMON ZEST	Remove from rind with vegetable peeler; no blanching.	Crisp
LIME ZEST	Remove from rind with vegetable peeler; no blanching.	Crisp
MUSHROOMS	Trim woody portion from stem; cut into ½-inch slices; blanch 3 minutes.	Leathery to crisp
NECTARINES	Use mature fruit; pit and slice; blanch 2 minutes.	Leathery, pliable

DRYING FRUITS & VEGETABLES—*CONTINUED*

FOOD	PREPARATION	CHARACTERISTICS AFTER DRYING
OKRA	Cut off tips; slice; blanch 5 minutes.	Tough to brittle
ONIONS	Remove skin and trim bulb ends; dice; no blanching.	Brittle
ORANGE ZEST	Remove from rind with vegetable peeler; no blanching.	Crisp
PAPAYAS	Remove seeds; peel and slice; no blanching.	Leathery to crisp
PARSNIPS	Trim tops; peel and slice; blanch 5 minutes.	Tough to brittle
PEACHES	Use ripe fruit, blanch to remove skins; pit and slice; dip in ascorbic acid solution.	Soft, pliable, leathery
PEARS	Use ripe fruit; peel; blanch 2 minutes.	Soft, pliable, leathery
PEAS	Use fresh peas; shell; blanch 3 minutes.	Wrinkled, brittle
PEPPERS, CHILI	Wear rubber gloves; dice; blanching optional.	Leathery to brittle
PEPPERS, GREEN	Dice; blanching optional.	Leathery to brittle
PINEAPPLES	Use ripe fruit; peel and core; blanch 1 minute.	Leathery, not sticky
PLUMS	Cut in ⅓-inch slices; no blanching.	Leathery, pliable
POTATOES, SWEET	Grate, slice, or dice; blanch 3 minutes.	Tough to brittle
POTATOES, WHITE	Peel; grate, slice, or dice; blanch 6 minutes.	Crisp, brittle
PUMPKIN	Remove stems, seeds, and fibrous tissue; peel outer layer; cut into small, thin strips; blanch 3 minutes.	Very tough to brittle
RHUBARB	Trim and slice diagonally; blanch until tender but not soft.	Tough to crisp
SPINACH	Trim leaves; blanch until slightly wilted.	Crisp, crumbles easily
SQUASH, SUMMER	Cut into thin slices; no peeling; blanch 3 minutes except when making chips.	Leathery to brittle
SQUASH, WINTER	See pumpkin.	Very tough to brittle
STRAWBERRIES	Remove stems; cut into halves or thirds; blanch 1 minute.	Leathery, pliable
TANGERINE ZEST	Remove from rind with vegetable peeler; no blanching.	Crisp
TOMATOES	Slice; blanch 3 minutes.	Leathery
TURNIPS	Remove tops and roots; slice; blanch 5 minutes.	Very tough to brittle

COOKING WITH DRIED FRUITS OR VEGETABLES

There is nothing mysterious or difficult about using dried fruits or vegetables. They must be rehydrated when used in dishes low in liquids. Otherwise, simply add them as they are to soups, stews, sauces, and other dishes high in liquids and increase the cooking liquid accordingly.

To rehydrate: Steeping is the simplest and most reliable method for rehydrating fruits or vegetables other than beans (see "Preparing Dried Beans," page 441). Put the fruits or vegetables in a warm saucepan, and add enough boiling water to just cover (too much water will dilute the flavor). Immediately put a tight-fitting lid on the pan and keep the water hot but not boiling, or rehydrating will be uneven. Stop the process when most of the fruits or vegetables are reconstituted. After removing the newly plumped ingredients, save any unabsorbed liquid—it is flavorful and contains water-soluble nutrients.

When adding dried vegetables to stews, use an extra cup of water for every cup of dried vegetables. For soups, increase the liquid by 2 or more cups for every cup of dried vegetables. The vegetables will absorb the extra water as they rehydrate so that the finished soup or stew will have the consistency called for in the recipe. After combining the vegetables and the liquid, bring everything to a boil, cover the pot, and reduce the heat. Simmer the vegetables for 10 to 20 minutes.

You can also make instant cream soups by grinding dried vegetables to a powder and adding them to hot white sauce.

---

dry. Soups and stews, for example, have so much liquid that rehydration can be skipped. However, casseroles are usually light in liquid so that rehydration before combining ingredients is best. Except for uncooked dishes such as salads, which need fresh ingredients, any dish takes herbs in the dry state beautifully. Baked goods, on the other hand, are enhanced by dried fruit that's been plumped first. For more specifics, see "Cooking with Dried Fruits or Vegetables" (above).

ROASTED RED PEPPERS

If you plan to keep the roasted red peppers for longer than a week, it's best to marinate them (see the variation below).

4 large red bell peppers, cut lengthwise into flat panels

2 cloves garlic, minced

Olive oil

Preheat the broiler. Place the pepper pieces, skin-side up, on a broiler pan and broil 4 inches from the heat for 10 to 12 minutes, or until the skin is charred. Remove from the broiler and turn the pieces skin-side down to cool.

When cool enough to handle, remove the skin and place in a flat dish. Sprinkle with the garlic. Add enough oil to generously coat the peppers. Gently turn to coat. Store in the refrigerator.

MAKES 1 CUP

MARINATED ROASTED RED PEPPERS: Sprinkle on 2 tablespoons red wine vinegar when you sprinkle the garlic.

PICKLED GREEN PEPPERS

Peter Piper would be proud of you for making these. They're great on sandwiches in place of store-bought pickles.

4 large green bell peppers

¼ cup lemon juice

¼ cup olive oil

Black pepper

Preheat the broiler. Place the pepper pieces, skin-side up, on a broiler pan and broil 4 inches from the heat for 10 to 12 minutes, or until the skin is charred. Remove from the broiler and turn the pieces skin-side down to cool.

When cool enough to handle, remove the skin, cut into ½-inch-wide strips and place in a bowl.

In a small bowl, mix together the lemon juice and oil. Pour over the bell peppers. Season lightly with black pepper. Cover and refrigerate for at least 2 hours. Store in the refrigerator.

MAKES 1 CUP

SPICY PICKLED PEPPERS: Omit the oil and black pepper. Mix the lemon juice with ½ teaspoon cayenne pepper.

SWEET-HOT CARROT CHIPS

To cut carrots on the diagonal, hold the knife at about a 45-degree angle to the carrot. A slice created this way will be an elongated oval.

3 carrots

½ cup white or cider vinegar

½ cup water

5 tablespoons honey

1 clove garlic, smashed and peeled

½ teaspoon turmeric

1 dried hot chili pepper, 1 to 2 inches long

Cut the carrots on the diagonal into ¼-inch-thick slices. In a steamer, cook until crisp-tender, 3 to 4 minutes. Rinse under cold running water to stop the cooking. Drain and place in an ovenproof glass or earthenware container.

In a small nonaluminum saucepan, combine the vinegar, water, honey, garlic, turmeric, and chili pepper. Bring to a boil and cook for 5 minutes.

Pour the hot mixture through a sieve over the carrots to cover them completely. Cover and refrigerate several hours or overnight. Store in the refrigerator.

MAKES 2½ CUPS

PICKLED CARROT & MANGO STICKS

You can use other vegetables in this brine: Try cauliflower florets, cucumber spears, or celery sticks.

4 carrots

2 mangoes

6 cloves garlic, smashed and peeled, plus 1 tablespoon chopped garlic

1 cup white wine vinegar

1 cup water

2 tablespoons sugar

1½ teaspoons coarse salt

Cut the carrots into narrow 4-inch-long sticks. In a medium pot of boiling water, blanch the carrots for 2 minutes. Immediately immerse in cold water to stop the cooking. Drain and place in a large heatproof glass bowl.

Cut the mango cheeks off the pits (save trimmings to eat later). Score the mango flesh (still in the peel) into long, thin strips (similar in size to the carrots). With a spoon, scoop the mango slices away from the skin. Add the mangoes to the carrots along with the whole garlic cloves.

In a small nonaluminum saucepan, combine the minced garlic, vinegar, water, sugar, and salt, and bring just to a boil. Pour over the carrots and mango sticks. Cool to room temperature. Refrigerate 1 hour (or longer) before serving. Store in the refrigerator.

MAKES 2 PINTS

RED-PICKLED EGGS

To serve the eggs, cut them into slices or halves and arrange on a bed of lettuce with the beets.

1 cup cider vinegar

2 tablespoons honey

HOMEMADE PICKLING SPICES

3 bay leaves, crumbled

1 tablespoon mustard seeds

1 tablespoon whole allspice berries

1 tablespoon dill seeds (optional)

1 teaspoon fenugreek seeds

1 teaspoon coriander seeds

1 teaspoon peppercorns

1 teaspoon whole cloves

1 teaspoon ginger

½ teaspoon red pepper flakes

Combine all the ingredients and store in an airtight container. To use for pickling, add 2 tablespoons to every quart of pickling liquid.

---

1 teaspoon dry mustard

1 teaspoon allspice

1 teaspoon ginger

2 cups sliced cooked red beets

4 large eggs, hard-cooked and peeled

In a small nonaluminum saucepan, combine the vinegar, honey, mustard, allspice, and ginger, and bring just to a boil.

Place the beets in a medium heatproof bowl. Pour the hot pickling mixture over them and set aside to cool. When cool, add the eggs and refrigerate overnight. Shake the bowl occasionally so the eggs will color evenly. Store in the refrigerator.

MAKES 4 SERVINGS

PICKLED BUTTER BEAN MEDLEY

Butter bean is another name for lima bean, especially in the South. If possible, make this with baby limas or fresh full-grown limas in season. Serve this as part of an antipasto along with thinly sliced meats and cheeses.

- 4 cups cooked lima beans
- 1 carrot, cut into ¼-inch slices
- ½ small head cauliflower, broken into small florets
- 1 red bell pepper, cut into ½-inch strips
- 1 large onion, coarsely chopped
- 5 cloves garlic, smashed and peeled
- 5 bay leaves
- 2½ teaspoons celery seeds
- 3 cups distilled white vinegar
- 1½ cups water
- ¾ cup honey
- 1½ teaspoons dry mustard
- 1 teaspoon coarse salt
- ½ teaspoon turmeric

In a large bowl, combine the lima beans, carrot, cauliflower, bell pepper, and onion. Place 1 clove garlic and 1 bay leaf in each of 5 heatproof pint jars, then fill them to 1 inch from the top with the vegetable mixture. (Try to evenly distribute all vegetables among the jars.) Sprinkle ½ teaspoon celery seeds into each jar.

In a nonaluminum saucepan, combine the vinegar, water, honey, mustard, salt, and turmeric, and bring to a boil. Pour the hot liquid over the vegetables to ½ inch from the top and seal tightly. Cool and refrigerate. Let marinate for at least 1 week before opening, to allow the flavors to develop. Store in the refrigerator.

MAKES 5 PINTS

BREAD & BUTTER PICKLES

These are cinch to make: Simply boil the dressing, toss with the cucumbers, and chill until crisp. You can substitute an equal amount of store-bought pickling spice for the spices.

- 4 kirby cucumbers (1 pound), cut into ¼-inch slices
- ½ small red onion, thinly sliced
- 3 cloves garlic, thinly sliced
- ¼ cup coarse salt
- 3 tablespoons coarsely chopped fresh dill
- 1 cup white wine vinegar
- 1 cup sugar
- 2 teaspoons yellow mustard seeds
- 2 teaspoons celery seeds
- 1 teaspoon ground turmeric

Put the cucumbers, onion, garlic, and salt into a colander set over a large bowl and toss well. Let sit for 15 minutes. Rinse and drain, and transfer to a large heatproof bowl along with the dill.

Meanwhile, in a nonaluminum saucepan, whisk together the vinegar, sugar, mustard seeds, celery seeds, and turmeric, and bring to a boil over high heat. Pour the vinegar mixture over the cucumber mixture, stir, and let cool.

Store in the refrigerator.

MAKES 4 CUPS

PRESERVED LEMONS

Traditionally, preserved lemons take a couple of weeks to make, but here the freezing and thawing help to hasten the process. They have both a sweet and briny taste and can be used the way you would use olives or capers. Try some in chicken salad or lamb stew. A little bit goes a long way, so try a small piece before adding more.

- 3 large organic lemons
- ⅔ cup coarse salt
- 3 bay leaves
- 2 teaspoons coriander seeds
- 2 cinnamon sticks (2 inches)
- ¾ cup lemon juice (3 to 4 lemons)

Cut a small slice from the stem and blossom ends of the lemons. Stand the lemons upright and, starting at the top, but without going through to the bottom, cut each into 8 wedges. Open the lemons like a flower and sprinkle with the salt. Place in a freezer bag or in an airtight freezer container. Add the bay leaves, coriander, cinnamon, and lemon juice. Tightly seal and freeze for 2 days.

Remove from the freezer and thaw at room temperature. Then return to the refrigerator for longer storage.

To use, remove one or more of the wedges and rinse to remove excess salt. Chop as much of the peel with fruit attached as you like.

MAKES 24 WEDGES

TOMATO CONFIT

In the wintertime, use tomatoes that have been ripened for several days in a paper sack.

- **18 plum tomatoes, peeled**
- **¾ cup extra-virgin olive oil**
- **2½ teaspoons minced fresh thyme**
- **¾ teaspoon coarse salt**
- **¾ teaspoon pepper**

Preheat the oven to 250°F. Lightly oil two rimmed baking sheets.

Halve the tomatoes lengthwise and place, cut-side up, on the baking sheets. Drizzle with the oil and sprinkle with the thyme, salt, and pepper. Bake the tomatoes for 5 to 6 hours, until they are dried about halfway through (they should shrink but still be moist). Remove from the oven and let cool on the baking sheet.

Layer the tomatoes in a storage container, such as a jar, and pour the oil from the baking sheets over them. Store in the refrigerator.

MAKES 36 PIECES

SPICY KETCHUP

Making ketchup is a great way to use up extra tomatoes from the garden, and it is also an especially good way to impress your friends.

- **1 small red bell pepper, cut lengthwise into flat panels**
- **3-inch cinnamon stick**
- **1 large clove garlic, chopped**
- **1 teaspoon whole cloves**
- **1 cup cider vinegar**
- **6 pounds tomatoes (15 to 17 medium), peeled and sliced**
- **¾ cup chopped onion**
- **6 tablespoons turbinado or light brown sugar**
- **2 teaspoons salt**
- **1 teaspoon cayenne pepper**

Preheat the broiler. Place the pepper pieces, skin-side up on a broiler pan and broil 4 inches from the heat for 12 minutes, or until the skin is completely charred. Remove from the broiler and turn the pieces skin-side down to cool. Peel the peppers.

Tie the cinnamon, garlic, and cloves in a small square of cheesecloth. Place in a small nonaluminum saucepan along with the vinegar. Simmer for 30 minutes. Discard the spices.

Meanwhile, in a large nonaluminum pot, combine the tomatoes and onion. Bring to a simmer and cook for 30 minutes. Transfer to a food processor. Add the roasted bell pepper and puree. Strain the puree to remove the tomato seeds. Transfer to a large saucepan and stir in the brown sugar.

Bring to a boil over high heat and cook until reduced by one-half. Add the spiced vinegar, salt, and cayenne, and cook, stirring constantly, until slightly thickened, about 10 minutes.

Ladle into clean, hot, sterilized pint jars, leaving a ¼-inch headspace. Adjust the seals and process for 5 minutes in a boiling water bath (see "Using a Water Bath Canner," page 636). When cool, check the seals.

MAKES 2 PINTS

CHILI SAUCE

Tomato-based chili sauce can be a bit hard to find these days, now that there are so many hot sauce options on the market. If you want to be sure of having some on hand, make it yourself.

- 8 pounds tomatoes (about 25 medium), peeled and sliced
- 2 cups chopped red bell peppers
- 2 cups chopped red onions
- 2 cloves garlic, minced
- 2 fresh serrano peppers, chopped
- 1 teaspoon coarse salt
- 1 teaspoon ginger
- ½ teaspoon black pepper
- 2 tablespoons celery seeds
- 1 tablespoon mustard seeds
- 1 bay leaf
- 2 cinnamon sticks (3 inches)
- 3 cups vinegar
- ½ cup honey

In a large nonaluminum pot, combine the tomatoes, bell peppers, onions, garlic, serranos, salt, ginger, and black pepper. Tie the celery seeds, mustard seeds, bay leaf, and cinnamon in a small square of cheesecloth. Add to the tomato mixture and bring to a boil. Cook until reduced by one-half, 2 to 3 hours. Stir frequently to prevent sticking. Discard the spice bag.

Add the vinegar and honey. Bring to a rapid boil, stirring constantly. Reduce to a simmer and cook 5 minutes.

Ladle into clean, hot, sterilized pint jars, leaving a ¼-inch headspace. Adjust the seals and process for 10 minutes in a boiling water bath (see "Using a Water Bath Canner," page 636). When cool, check the seals.

MAKES 8 OR 9 PINTS

PEACH JAM

Tapioca flour, which is available in Asian markets, is a thickener that turns translucent when cooked.

- 4 pounds peaches
- ¼ cup lemon juice
- ½ cup mild honey, or more to taste
- ¼ cup tapioca flour or starch

Bring a large pot of water to a boil. Drop in the peaches a few at a time and boil for 45 seconds (slightly longer if the peaches aren't ripe). Immediately rinse in cold water to stop the cooking. Peel, pit, cut into large chunks, and place in a food processor. Add the lemon juice and pulse on and off to coarsely grind.

Transfer the peach mixture to a 6- to 8-quart saucepan. Bring to a boil over medium heat, stirring constantly, and cook until the peaches are very soft.

Slowly stir in the honey, blending well. Add more honey if desired. Continue stirring and return to a full rolling boil. Add the tapioca flour and cook over medium heat, stirring, until thickened, 10 to 15 minutes.

Ladle into clean, hot, sterilized pint jars, leaving a ½-inch headspace. Adjust the seals and process for 15 minutes in a boiling water bath (see "Using a Water Bath Canner," page 636). When cool, check the seals.

MAKES 3 PINTS

STRAWBERRY JAM

Use locally grown strawberries in season.

4 cups crushed fresh strawberries

½ cup orange blossom honey

¼ cup maple syrup

2 tablespoons tapioca flour or starch

2 tablespoons water

In a large saucepan, bring the berries, honey, and maple syrup to a boil. Reduce the heat to medium and cook until the mixture is reduced by one-third. You should have 3 cups.

Dissolve the tapioca flour in the water. Stir into the berries and cook just until the mixture thickens. Do not overcook.

Ladle into clean, hot, sterilized pint jars, leaving a ½-inch headspace. Adjust the seals and process for 15 minutes in a boiling water bath (see "Using a Water Bath Canner," page 636). When cool, check the seals.

MAKES 1 ½ PINTS

APPLE JELLY

Slightly underripe or tart apples tend to have the most pectin, but use at least 1 pound of sweeter, riper apples for the best flavor to keep the jelly from being too tart. If you want to make this with sugar, the proportions will be the same: ¾ cup for every cup of juice.

4½ pounds apples

Honey

Remove the stems and dark spots from the apples. Quarter but do not peel or core. Place in a 6- to 8-quart pot with just enough water to half cover and cook over low heat until very soft, about 1 hour.

Strain the mixture through a jelly bag. You will get more juice if you squeeze the bag, but it will make a cloudy jelly.

Measure the juice and pour into a large saucepan. Add ¾ cup of honey for every cup of juice. Boil until a good jelly test is obtained (see "Testing for Jelling Point," page 652). Ladle into hot sterilized jelly glasses, adjust the seals and process for 10 minutes in a boiling water bath (see "Using a Water Bath Canner," page 636).

MAKES 1½ CUPS

MINT JELLY: Just before removing the apple jelly from the heat, add a few mint leaves (about ¼ cup mint leaves to 1 quart juice). Stir, remove the leaves, and ladle into jars as directed.

SWEET CHERRY CONSERVE

Domestically grown sweet cherries are available for a fairly short time in the beginning of the summer.

4 oranges, unpeeled, well scrubbed

2 cups water

8 cups pitted sweet cherries

1½ to 2 cups honey, to taste

¾ cup lemon juice

1½ teaspoons cinnamon

2 cups pecan halves

Slice the oranges thinly and remove the seeds.

Place the orange slices in a large nonaluminum saucepan and add the water. Cover and simmer until tender, about 10 minutes.

Add the cherries, honey, lemon juice, and cinnamon. Simmer, covered, for 30 minutes.

Add the nuts. Ladle into clean, hot, sterilized pint jars, leaving a ½-inch headspace. Adjust the seals and process for 15 minutes in a boiling water bath (see "Using a Water Bath Canner," page 636). When cool, check the seals.

MAKES 4 PINTS

GINGER & PEAR CONSERVE

Seckel pears are a small variety with a thick skin, often used for canning.

3 pounds Seckel pears (21 to 24), peeled and sliced

½ orange, unpeeled, sliced and seeded

2 tablespoons chopped fresh ginger

½ cup honey

1 tablespoon lemon juice

Place half the pears in a food processor along with the orange and pulse to coarsely chop. Transfer to a large saucepan.

Tie the ginger in a small square of cheesecloth and add to the saucepan. Add the remaining sliced pears, the honey, and lemon juice. Cover, bring slowly to a simmer, and cook until the pears are tender. Uncover and cook, stirring occasionally, until the desired consistency is reached.

Ladle into clean, hot, sterilized pint jars, leaving a ½-inch headspace. Adjust the seals and process for 15 minutes in a boiling water bath (see "Using a Water Bath Canner," page 636). When cool, check the seals.

MAKES 1½ PINTS

BAKED APPLE BUTTER

There's nothing like homemade apple butter spread on toast, pancakes, waffles, or muffins. It's also delicious mixed into yogurt or on top of cottage cheese. This is a good project if you have access to a pick-your-own apple place.

18 pounds apples

8 cups water

1½ cups honey

Juice and grated zest of 3 lemons

2 teaspoons cinnamon

1 teaspoon ground allspice

½ teaspoon ground cloves

Core and quarter the apples. Place in two 10- to 12-quart pots or 1 canning kettle and add the water. Simmer for 1 hour 30 minutes.

Preheat the oven to 300°F.

Put the apple pulp through a food mill or coarse-mesh strainer and pour back into the original pot (if it is ovenproof) or a roasting pan. Add the honey, lemon juice and zest, cinnamon, allspice, and cloves.

Bake, stirring occasionally, until very thick, several hours or perhaps overnight, depending on how thick you want it.

When thick enough for your taste, ladle into clean, hot, sterilized pint jars, leaving a ½-inch headspace. Adjust the seals and process for 15 minutes in a boiling water bath (see "Using a Water Bath Canner," page 636). When cool, check the seals.

MAKES 4 PINTS

PEACH BUTTER

Blanch the peaches in a large pot of boiling water for 30 to 45 seconds to loosen their skins before peeling.

6 cups sliced peeled peaches

¾ cup water

¼ cup lemon juice

10 whole cloves

2-inch stick of cinnamon

1¼ cups honey

In a large, heavy-bottomed nonaluminum saucepan, combine the peaches, water, and lemon juice. Cover and simmer until the peaches are soft, 10 to 15 minutes.

Transfer to a food processor or blender and puree. Return to the saucepan. Tie the cloves and cinnamon in a small square of cheesecloth and add to the pan. Cook over low heat, uncovered and stirring occasionally, until it reaches the thickness you would like.

Remove the spice bag. Stir in the honey. Ladle into clean, hot, sterilized pint jars, leaving a ½-inch headspace. Adjust the seals and process for 15 minutes in a boiling water bath. When cool, check the seals.

MAKES 1½ PINTS

NECTARINE BUTTER: Use nectarines (no need to peel) instead of the peaches and 4 allspice berries instead of the cloves.

SWEET SPICED PUMPKIN BUTTER

Use pumpkin butter in much the same way as you would use apple butter. This recipe makes a small amount and can be stored in the refridgerator.

- 1 can (15 ounces) unsweetened pumpkin puree
- ½ cup maple syrup
- ⅓ cup packed turbinado or light brown sugar
- ¼ cup orange juice
- 1 teaspoon ginger
- ¾ teaspoon cinnamon

In heavy-bottomed saucepan, combine the pumpkin, maple syrup, brown sugar, orange juice, ginger, and cinnamon. Cook over moderate heat, stirring, until thick enough to spread like jam, 25 minutes. Ladle into sterilized ½-pint jars. Store in the refrigerator.

MAKES 2 CUPS

APRICOT BUTTER

Perfect on a piece of toast, or slathered on bread as part of a cheese, pork, turkey, or chicken sandwich.

- 1 cup dried apricots
- 1 navel orange, peeled, any seeds removed, cut into large chunks
- 1 cup water
- 1 tablespoon dark honey, such as buckwheat
- ½ teaspoon ground cardamom
- ½ teaspoon ginger
- ½ teaspoon cinnamon
- 2 teaspoons lemon juice

In a medium saucepan, combine the apricots, orange, water, honey, cardamom, ginger, and cinnamon. Bring to a simmer over low heat, cover, and cook, stirring occasionally, until the apricots are tender and the water has all been absorbed, about 45 minutes.

Transfer to a food processor, add the lemon juice and puree until smooth. Ladle into sterilized ½-pint jars. Store in the refrigerator.

MAKES 2 CUPS

FRESH STRAWBERRY PRESERVES

In this unusual refrigerator preserve, gelatin is used to firm up the mixture.

- 2 cups water

- 1 envelope unflavored gelatin
- 2 cups sliced strawberries
- 1/3 cup honey
- 1 teaspoon lemon juice

Pour 1 cup of the water into a large saucepan and sprinkle the gelatin over it. Let stand for 5 minutes to soften.

In a blender, puree half the strawberries with the remaining 1 cup water, the honey, and the lemon juice. Stir into the gelatin in the saucepan.

Add the remaining sliced berries. Heat just to a boil, stirring constantly. Ladle into sterilized 1/2-pint jars and refrigerate. Store in the refrigerator or freeze.

MAKES 4 CUPS

SOUR CHERRY PRESERVES

The sour cherry season is fleeting unless you happen to live in an area where they are grown, but the water-packed bottled cherries are a fine substitute.

- 2 cups pitted sour cherries, fresh or jarred (water-packed)
- 1/2 cup sugar
- 1 tablespoon balsamic vinegar
- 1/2 teaspoon pepper
- 1/4 teaspoon allspice
- Pinch of salt

In a medium heavy-bottomed saucepan, combine the cherries, sugar, vinegar, pepper, allspice, and salt. Bring to a boil over high heat, reduce to a simmer, and cook until the cherries are very tender and the mixture has thickened, 15 to 20 minutes. Pack into a sterilized 1/2-pint jar. Store in the refrigerator.

MAKES 1 CUP

CRANBERRY-CHERRY PRESERVES

Since cranberries and sour cherries are available fresh in completely different seasons, one or the other will have to be frozen or jarred—but after it's all cooked down, you won't know the difference.

- 1 bag (12 ounces) cranberries, fresh or frozen
- 2 1/2 cups pitted sour cherries, fresh or jarred (water-packed)
- 1 lime, unpeeled, coarsely chopped and seeded
- 3/4 cup sugar
- 1/4 cup maple syrup
- 1/2 teaspoon cinnamon
- 1/8 teaspoon ground allspice

In a large saucepan, combine the cranberries, cherries, lime, sugar, maple syrup, cinnamon, and allspice. Stir to combine. Bring to a boil over medium heat.

PEELING TOMATOES

Bring a large pot of water to a boil. With a very sharp knife, cut a small X in the skin of each tomato at the blossom end (the bottom). When the water is boiling, drop the tomatoes into the water and boil for 15 seconds for ripe tomatoes, or up to 30 seconds if less ripe. The skin should peel back at the X. Remove with a slotted spoon and refresh in cold water to stop the cooking. Pull off the peel.

Reduce to a simmer and cook, stirring frequently, until the berries pop and the preserves are very thick, 15 to 20 minutes.

Ladle into sterilized ½ pint or pint jars. Store in the refrigerator.

MAKES 4 CUPS

FRUIT LEATHER

Fruit leather is fruit pulp that is dried to form a naturally sweet, confection-like food that will keep in good condition for one year or more. Fruit leather can be made from almost any fruit or any combination of fruits.

- **8 pounds apricots, peaches, or nectarines, pitted**
- **1½ cups pineapple juice**
- **¼ cup honey, or more to taste**
- **2 teaspoons almond extract (optional)**
- **Cornstarch or arrowroot for dusting**

In a large, heavy nonaluminum pot, combine the fruit and pineapple juice. Cover and cook over low heat until soft.

Pour the fruit into a sieve set over a bowl. Drain the fruit well, lifting it from the sides of the sieve to let all the juice run out freely. The more juice strained out, the quicker the process of leather making. (Can or freeze the juice for later use, or drink it fresh.)

Put the drained fruit through a food mill or a coarse-meshed sieve to remove the skins. Sweeten with the honey and add the almond extract (if using). The pulp should be as thick as apple butter or more so. On lightly oiled baking sheets or on baking sheets lined with freezer paper or plastic wrap, spread out the fruit pulp so that it is ¼ inch thick. If it is much thicker than this, it will take very long to dry. Place the baking sheets in an oven or a food dryer. If using an oven, turn the control to warm (120°F) and leave the oven door slightly open to allow moisture to escape. (The pulp should dry in about 12 hours in the oven.)

When the leather is dry enough to be lifted or gently pulled from the baking sheets, place it on wire racks so that it can dry on both sides. When all the stickiness has disappeared, dust lightly with cornstarch. Then stack in layers with freezer paper, waxed paper, or foil between each layer. Cover with freezer paper, waxed paper, or foil and store in a cool dry place.

MAKES 4 PIECES (10 X 15 INCHES)

APPLE LEATHER: Use 8 pounds of apples, and apple cider instead of pineapple juice. Omit the almond extract and add a bit of cinnamon if desired. Before cooking the apples, core them, cut them into large chunks, and coarsely shred them in a food processor. Cover and cook over low heat until soft.

INDEX

Underscored page numbers indicate sidebars and tables. **Boldface** references indicate illustrations. Page numbers followed by * indicate photographs in the color photo insert.